The

INTERNATIONAL CRITICAL
COMMENTARY
on the Holy Scriptures of the Old and
New Testaments

GENERAL EDITORS:

J. A. EMERTON, F.B.A.
Fellow of St. John's College
Regius Professor of Hebrew in the University of Cambridge
Honorary Canon of St. George's Cathedral, Jerusalem

AND

C. E. B. CRANFIELD, F.B.A.
Emeritus Professor of Theology in the University of Durham

FORMERLY UNDER THE EDITORSHIP OF

S. R. DRIVER
A. PLUMMER
C. A. BRIGGS

JEREMIAH

VOLUME I

THE INTERNATIONAL CRITICAL COMMENTARY

A CRITICAL AND EXEGETICAL COMMENTARY

ON

JEREMIAH

BY

WILLIAM McKANE, F.B.A.

Principal of St. Mary's College and
Professor of Hebrew and Oriental Languages in the University of
St. Andrews

IN TWO VOLUMES

VOLUME I

Introduction and Commentary on Jeremiah I–XXV

EDINBURGH
T. & T. CLARK LIMITED, 59 GEORGE STREET

Copyright © T. & T. CLARK LTD, 1986

TYPESET BY C.R. BARBER & PARTNERS (HIGHLANDS) LTD. FORT WILLIAM
PRINTED IN THE U.K. BY PAGE BROS (NORWICH) LTD
BOUND BY HUNTER AND FOULIS LTD. EDINBURGH
FOR

T. & T. CLARK LTD, EDINBURGH

First printed 1986

British Library Cataloguing in Publication Data

McKane, William
    A critical and exegetical commentary on
    Jeremiah.—(The International critical commentary).
    Vol. 1: Introduction and commentary on
    Jeremiah I–XXV.
    1. Bible. O.T. Jeremiah—Commentaries
    I. Title   II. Bible. O.T. Jeremiah. *Hebrew. Liber Jeremiae. 1970*
    III. Series
    244′.206   BS1525.3

ISBN 0-567-05042-4

GENERAL EDITORS' PREFACE

Much scholarly work has been done on the Bible since the publication in 1951 of the latest volume in the International Critical Commentary (that of J. A. Montgomery and H. S. Gehman on the Books of Kings)—and the bulk of the series is, of course, much older. New linguistic, textual, historical, and archaeological evidence has become available, and there have been changes and developments in methods of study. In the last quarter of the twentieth century there will be as great a need as, and perhaps a greater need than, ever for the kind of commentary that the International Critical Commentary seeks to supply. The series has long had a special place among works in English on the Bible, because it has sought to bring together all the relevant aids to exegesis, linguistic and textual no less than archaeological, historical, literary, and theological, to help the reader to understand the meaning of the books of the Old and New Testaments. In the confidence that such a series meets a need, the publishers and the editors have planned both to commission commentaries on those books of the Bible which have never appeared in the series and to replace some of the older volumes. The work of preparing a commentary on such a scale cannot but be slow, and developments in the past quarter of a century have made the commentator's task yet more difficult than before, but it is hoped that the volumes will appear without too great intervals between them. No attempt has been made to secure a uniform theological or critical approach to the problems of the various books, and scholars have been selected for their scholarship and not for their adherence to any school of thought. It is hoped that the new volumes will attain the high standards set in the past, and that they will make a contribution to the understanding of the books of the Bible.

Cambridge and Durham,
January, 1974.

J. A. E.
C. E. B. C.

A MEMORIAL FOR MY PARENTS

Thomas McKane (1877–1964)
Jemima Smith McKane (1878–1957)

PREFACE

I am grateful to the editors, Professor J. A. Emerton and Professor C. E. B. Cranfield, for the help and encouragement they have given me, and to all those who have shared in the production of the book.

The commentary is one which concentrates on fundamentals of biblical scholarship. It aims at exegetical goals, but it is built on the foundation of the Hebrew Bible and the Ancient Versions. The need for such a commentary on the book of Jeremiah in English has long been felt and expressed, and it is my hope that this first volume will supply that need for Jeremiah 1–25.

St. Mary's College
St. Andrews
Whitsunday Term, 1985

CONTENTS OF VOLUME I

INTRODUCTION[1]

A. THE ANCIENT VERSIONS

The interest in the Ancient Versions which is characteristic of this commentary is not only or principally related to their importance for textual criticism. The assumption that the versions are of prime exegetical significance is so fundamental that it would be impossible to separate the treatment which has been given to them from the body of the work and to isolate it in small print as merely technical, textual material. The ancient versions which are used (Septuagint, Aquila, Symmachus, Theodotion, Vulgate, Peshiṭta, Targum) are regarded as indispensable, early witnesses to the exegesis of the Hebrew Bible, and wherever they have a lexicographical contribution to make in connection with difficult Hebrew words, or a grammatical contribution with respect to obscure passages, a conscientious attempt has been made to exploit all the possibilities of help. The non-Semitic versions (Sept., Vulg.) have a value where MT is syntactically obscure, because they may offer an interpretation of the grammar which is worthy of consideration in places where Pesh. simply reproduces the obscurity of the syntax of MT, or Targ. offers a paraphrase which is too general to be helpful. The literalism of the later Greek versions can be turned to lexicographical advantage because of the ease of establishing a one–one correspondence with MT. Thus we can ascertain what meanings were attached to obscure Hebrew words by the later Greek translators, and whether or not we act on this information, we have a duty to be aware of its existence. So far as I am aware there is no modern commentary on the book of Jeremiah which has devoted such attention to the ancient versions, and especially Sept., as interpretations of the Hebrew Bible. The work has been influenced and shaped by this interest.

---

[1] A general review of the literature associated with the study of the book of Jeremiah will appear in the second volume. In the present introduction I have drawn together the main results of my work on chapters 1-25 and have concentrated on what is new in my perception of the character and make-up of this material

1. *Septuagint*: J. Ziegler, *Ieremias, Baruch, Threni, Epistula Ieremias*, 1957; *Beiträge zur Ieremias—Septuaginta*, 1958.

Of the versions Sept. commands most interest and requires most attention, because it represents a shorter text than MT. Vulg., Pesh., and Targ., on the other hand, are mostly in accord with MT. It can be confidently assumed that Targ. always rests on MT, and the deviations of Vulg. and Pesh. from MT are not considerable. There are, however, some interesting agreements of Sept. and Pesh. which will be noted.

(*a*) Deletions made from MT on the foundation of a shorter Greek text:

1.15, משפחות (p. 18); 2.17, בעת מוליכך בדרך (p. 38); 3.1, לאמר
(p. 58); 3.17, לשם יהוה לירושלם (p. 75); 4.30, שדוד (p. 111);
5.13, כה יעשה להם (Sept.ᴬ, pp. 121, 122); 7.24, במעצות (p. 174);
8.3, הנשארים (p. 182); 8.5, ירושלם (p. 183); 8.13, ואתן להם
יעברום (p. 189); 8.17, נאם יהוה (p. 194); 9.2,5, נאם יהוה
(p. 198); 9.14, את העם הזה (p. 207); 9.16, התבוננגו (p. 208);
9.21, דבר (pp. 208, 210); 9.21, נאם יהוה (p. 208); 10.25, ואכלהו
(p. 233); 11.4, אותם (p. 237); 11.13, מזבחות לבשת (p. 240);
11.15, כי (p. 248); 11.16, פרי (p. 249); 11.22, לכן כה אמר יהוה
את הדבר הזה כה אמר יהוה אלהי ישראל צבאות (p. 258); 13.12,
(p. 292); 13.17, ודמע תדמע (p. 300); 17.5, כה אמר יהוה (p. 389);
18.8, אשר דברתי עליו (p. 427); 19.1, זקני (p. 444); 19.11, ובתפת
יקברו מאין מקום לקבור (p. 446); 20.3, מסביב (pp. 461, 463f.);
20.5, מפני רע מעלליהם אתן (p. 465) 21.7, ואת (p. 501); 21.12,
(p. 510); 22.26, אחרת (p. 545); 23.8, אשר העלהו (p. 374);
23.16, הנבאים לכם (p. 578); 23.18, וישמע ואם (p. 581); 23.38,
ולקללה משא יהוה תאמרו (p. 601); 24.9, לרעה (p. 617); 25.18,
ואת כל מלכי ארץ העוץ כיום הזה (pp. 637, 641); 25.20, (pp. 637,
641); 25.24, ואת כל מלכי (ה)ערב (pp. 638f., 641); 25.25, ואת כל
מלכי זמרי הארץ (pp. 639, 641); 25.26, (pp. 640, 641); 25.34,
ותפוצותיכם (pp. 652f.).

(*b*) Other cases of a shorter Greek text:

2.1, ויהי דבר יהוה אלי לאמר הלך וקראת באזני ירושלם; 2.2,
4.8, ותחנף את הארץ; 3.9, אביונים; 2.34, במדבר בארץ לא זרועה
גוי איתן הוא גוי מעולם הוא; 5.15, מאלה; 4.12, שפיים; 4.11, חרון;
5.16, ישוד כשך; 5.26, עזבתם אותי; 5.19, אשפתו כקבר פתוח
5.28, השכם ודבר; 7.13, ויצליחו; 5.28, דברי רע; 5.28, שמנו עשתו
7.26, חרעו; 8.3f., נאם יהוה צבאות ואמרת אליהם (Sept.ᴮˢᴬ); 9.9,
10.16, לקול תתו; 9.12, ולא חלכו בה; 9.16, צבאות; 10.13, עבר
שנית; 13.3, התקם כצאן לטבחה; 12.3, תראני; 12.3, וישראל שבט
13.4, אשר קנית; 13.5, ואלך; 13.7, האזור (second occurrence);
14.4, בשו והכלמו וחפו ראשם; 14.3, החלכים בשרירות לבם; 13.10,

לוא 15.7, בתולת 14.17, גדול 14.17, ויפקד חטאתם 14.10; בארץ
;שבו 15.8, לחם 15.15; תקחני 15.20, נאם יהוה 15.21, והצלתיך
נאם 16.5f., והיתה נבלתם 16.4, (Sept.ˢ, p. 357); ופדיתיך 15.21,
יהוה את החסד ואת הרחמים ומתו גדלים וקטנים בארץ הזאת לא
יקברו (p. 365); 16.17, לא נסתרו מלפני 17.1–4 (p. 384); 17.12,
לאמר 18.11, בחמר 18.11, מרעה 17.24, כה 18.4, מראשון מקום 17.16,
עלות 19.5, ערף ולא פנים 18.17, דרכיכם ו 18.11, כה אמר יהוה
ויחי ממחרת 20.3, ומבקשי נפשם 19.9, ולא דברתי 19.5, לבעל
20.5, תבוא ושם 20.6, ובזזום ולקחום 20.5, ואת כל יקרה 21.2,
אשר בידכם 21.4, אלהי ישראל 21.4, אותנו 21.2, נבוכדראצר
ביד נבוכדראצר 21.7, ואספתי אותם 21.4, את מלך בבל ו 21.4,
ולא יחמל 21.7, וביד (third occurrence); 21.7, מלך בבל ו 21.9,
רבים 22.8, ופקדתי עליכם כפרי מעלליכם נאם יהוה 21.14, ובדבר
וביד נבוכדראצר מלך בבל 22.25, וביד (first occurrence); 22.25,
נפוץ האיש הזה 22.28, העצב 22.28, (לשוב) שם שמה 22.27,
גבר לא 22.30, כה אמר יהוה 22.30, ארץ 22.29, הוא וזרעו 22.28,
יצלח בימיו 23.4, ולא יפקדו 23.8, ומכל הארצות (Sept.ˢ*); 23.10,
מדרכם הרע ו 23.22, על הנבאים 23.15, כי מנאפים מלאה הארץ
היא 25.1, מעל פני 23.39, אתכם נשא 23.39, חלמתי(?); 23.25,
רמיהו הנביא 25.2, השנה הראשנית לנבוכדראצר מלך בבל 25.2,
ולא 25.3, היה דבר יהוה אלי (second occurrence); 25.3, כל
נאם יהוה למען הכעסוני 25.7, לשמע 25.4, כל 25.4, שמעתם
על מלך 25.12, האלה את מלך בבל 25.11, במעשה ידיכם לרע לכם
בבל ו 25.12, נאם יהוה את עונם ועל ארץ כשדים 25.14 (entirely);
25.16, ושתו 25.22, האי 25.26, ומלך ששך ישתה אחריהם
ומפני חרון אפו 25.38, לא יספדו ולא יאספו 25.33, (pp. 640, 641).

The intention is not to assert that the correct explanation of all
these examples is that the Hebrew *Vorlage* of Sept. was a text
shorter than MT, although I have concluded that, in general, this
is the right approach. Nevertheless, every example has to be
considered on its own merits, and the possibilities of abridgement
or accident are not to be excluded in any consideration of the
shorter Greek text. Thus 5.15 may be an abridgement of MT
influenced by Deut 28.49, but if the absence of τῆς γλώσσης
from Sept.ᴬ is an indication that this is a secondary element in
the Greek text, it could be supposed that ἔθνος οὗ οὐκ ἀκούσῃ τῆς
φωνῆς αὐτοῦ represents גוי לא תשמע מה ידבר. A shorter Hebrew
text than MT, consisting of two distichs could then be
reconstructed (below, p. 123). The non-representation of
נאם יהוה ... יקברו (16.5f.) has been explained as an
abridgement of MT and also as a shorter text more original than
MT. Janzen supposes that את החסד ואת הרחמים may be a gloss
on שלומי and לא יקברו may be an addition, but he acknowledges
that v. 6a (MT) is indispensable to what follows and that the
shorter Greek text may be the consequence of an accidental
omission from the Hebrew *Vorlage* of Sept. (below, p. 365). The

non-representation of עֶרֶף וְלֹא פָנִים (18.17b) might be taken as evidence of a Hebrew text shorter than MT (cf. Janzen, pp. 179f.), but Sept. is not a legitimate translation of what remains of MT. Moreover, if we suppose that such a shorter Hebrew text was before the Greek translator, v. 17 is reduced to a tristich. In the case of 21.7 I have argued that MT is a better text than Sept. which does not represent ביד נבוכדראצר מלך בבל וביד איביהם וביד מבקשי נפשם and ולא יחמל. I have deleted which is represented by Sept. The Greek translator had a Hebrew text which required him to assume that והכם should be read וְהִכָּם and this left him with a problem in respect of לא יחום עליהם ולא ירחם. He resolved this difficulty by representing the verbs as first person singular, making Yahweh their grammatical subject (cf. 13.14). Another possibility is that this accommodation may have been already made in his Hebrew *Vorlage* (below, pp. 500f.).

The passages which are the most interesting demonstrations of the thesis that MT arises from expansions of a shorter Hebrew text represented by Sept. have been reserved for special treatment in section (*c*).

(*c*) Tracing the growth of the Hebrew text by a comparison of Sept. and MT:

7.27f. (p. 175): MT is a conflate text: v. 28, for the most part, is not preserved in Pesh. (מוסר . . . ואמרת), and vv. 27 and 28 (as far as מוסר) are variants. Sept. has preserved one variant (v. 28) and Pesh. (v. 27) the other.

8.10–12 (p. 187) and 6.12–15 (pp. 146–148): Only 8.10a is represented by Sept. in chapter 8. The passage is probably original at chapter 6 and secondary at chapter 8 (cf. 16.14f. and 23.7f., pp. 374ff.).

10.1–16 (pp. 217–220, 225): There is a Hebrew text (4QJer[b]) corresponding with Sept., and so we know that Sept. does rest on a Hebrew *Vorlage* shorter than MT. There are reasons for concluding that 10.1–16 was built up by successive additions, each generated by the pre-existing text or part of it. Sept. does not represent vv. 6–8, 10, and v. 9 is located by Sept. after ידברו (MT v. 5). Hence the shorter text recovered is equivalent to MT vv. 1–5, 9, 11, with v. 9 located after ידברו (v. 5).

11.6–8 (p. 238): The Greek translator had a Hebrew text from which vv. 7–8 (MT) were missing (except for ולא עשו), and vv. 7–8* are a historical retrospect deriving from secondary expansion (cf. vv. 4–5).

12.3 (p. 263): תראני and התקם כצאן לטבחה ו are not represented by Sept. which is a better text. The additional

elements in MT are either textual variants or expansions: תראני
is an alternative of ידעתני and התקם כצאן לטבחה (conjoined
with *waw*) of הקדשם ליום הרגה.

16.10–13 (p. 370): Sept. does not represent הגדולה (v. 10) nor
יומם ולילה (v. 13). Of more interest is the shorter text indicated
by Greek minuscules at v. 10 and by Sept.^ and minuscules at
v. 11. One interpretation of this evidence is that a Hebrew text
which began as על מה דבר יהוה עלינו את כל הרעה הזאת was
subsequently supplemented by ומה עוננו and then by ומה
חטאתנו, until v. 10 reached the form of our extant MT with the
further addition of אשר חטאנו ליהוה אלהינו. In v. 11 there is an
indication (the non-representation of וישתחוו להם) of a Hebrew
text at an earlier stage than MT.

16.14f. and 23.7f.: An attempt is made (pp. 374f.) to
reconstruct a shorter Hebrew text with only partial support from
Sept.: אשר העלה ו is not represented by Sept. at 23.8 (p. 375)
and Sept.^S* does not represent ומכל הארצות (p. 375).
אשר נתתי לאבותם and ומכל הארצות אשר הדיחם/הדחתים שמה
(16.15) are secondary additions and the first of these obscures
the sense of the passage. The variants are בית/בני, יאמר/יאמרו,
וישבו/והשבתים and צפונה/צפון.

16.16–18: There is evidence of expansion in v. 17, where לא
נסתרו מלפני is not represented by Sept. ואחרי כן אשלח לרבים
צידים וצדום is not represented by a Greek minuscule (p. 379)
and this may be taken as evidence of a shorter Hebrew text
involving only one figure—that of fishing. ראשונה (v. 18), which
is not represented by Sept., accommodates v. 18 to a promise of
ultimate restoration in vv. 14f. It may be that whoever was
responsible for the insertion of ראשונה understood משנה as a
reference to the events of 597 and 586 (p. 378).

20.12–13: Verse 12 coheres poorly with the context and is
probably an insertion from 11.20 (p. 480). 20.13 is to be
explained as the response of a pious commentator to Jeremiah's
affirmation of confidence (v. 11). Whether v. 13 originally
followed v. 11 and was subsequently separated from it by the
insertion of v. 12 is impossible to determine (p. 481).

21.7, 9 and other passages (p. 505): בחרב וברעב ובדבר. A
comparison of MT and Sept. suggests that the preponderance of
the threefold formula in MT is the consequence of an editorial
process of systematization and expansion which was largely
incomplete when the Septuagint translation of the book of
Jeremiah was made (p. 505). The poetry of Jeremiah (5.12;
15.2) may have generated the twofold and threefold formulae in
the prose passages (pp. 505f.).

22.25: The Greek translator had a Hebrew text which was
shorter than MT, and the latter is the consequence of a process

of supplementation which produced four occurrences of (ו)ביד instead of two occurrences of ביד, and which involved the insertion of וביד נבוכדראצר מלך בבל. In the shorter text ביד מבקשי נפשך (p. 544).

22.28-30: The indications of Sept. are not completely followed by me, but its non-representation of הוא וזרעו (v. 28) and the singular verbs (ידע; השלך; הוטל) are used to construct a shorter text. However, כי לא יצלח ... עוד ביהודה, which is represented by Sept., is identified as an addition with the same tendency as הוא וזרעו (v. 28): it extends the scope of the passage to include Jehoiachin's offspring. On the other hand, גבר לא יצלח בימיו, which is not represented by Sept., is regarded by me as part of the shorter text (pp. 547, 550f.).

23.7-8: The distinctive thought contained in these verses is that a new exodus will replace the old one (p. 376) as the decisive saving event, and this does not have much to do with the ideas of 23.1-6. Moreover, we have a textual indication that vv. 7f. did not have an assured place in chapter 23. In Sept. vv. 7f. appear after v. 40, and the Greek translator could not have made the error of incorporating לנבאים (v. 9, MT) with v. 6, unless לנבאים had followed immediately after צדקנו (p. 566).

23.14-15: According to MT the threat in v. 15 is directed against the prophets (על הנבאים) and for this reason וישביה (v. 14) has been thought inappropriate. The shorter text of Sept. in v. 15 (על הנבאים not represented) eases this difficulty (p. 576).

23.18: The shorter text in Sept. indicates that וירא, which was felt to be difficult, was glossed by וישמע (MT). The non-representation of דברי (K) or דברו (Q) in Sept. is probably a translational rather than a textual point: it was thought unnecessary to represent דברו a second time. Hence the shorter Hebrew text would read: כי מי עמד בסוד יהוה וירא את דברו מי הקשיב דברו וישמע (pp. 580f.).

23.23, 24, 28, 29, 31, 32: נאם יהוה, which is not represented by Sept., is to be regarded as a secondary element in MT.

23.39: The shorter text which I have reconstructed partly accords with Sept. which does not represent אתכם נשא and מעל פני. The original sense of v. 39 was the same as that of v. 33, and it terminated, like v. 33, with ואת העיר אשר נתתי. ונטשתי אתכם לכם ולאבותיכם is an addition which requires a different sense of נטש ('desert'), and מעל פני is a subsequent addition which is appropriate to ונטשתי אתכם but inappropriate to ואת העיר (pp. 601f.).

25.1-7: The elements in 25.1-7 which are not represented by Sept. are set out on pp. 618f. The Hebrew text which underlies Sept. has been expanded and modified in MT. The aim of the process is to represent that 25.1-7 is prophetic reminiscence

rather than prophetic proclamation, and the insertion of היה דבר
יהוה אלי (v. 3) and the change to a reference to Yahweh in the
third person (v. 4) are connected with it. The insertion of ירמיהו
הנביא (v. 2) may be intended to reinforce the same
interpretation, but this is less transparent. On this view even
vv. 5–7 are a recollection by Jeremiah of the content of prophetic
preaching (connecting with v. 4) and not a proclamation which is
now being made in Yahweh's name. Further additions in MT are
of a different kind: the chronological harmonization in v. 1 is a
learned gloss and v. 7b is a textual variant of v. 6b. Verse 3a
('From the thirteenth year of Josiah, son of Amon, king of
Judah, and up to the present time, these twenty three years, I
have addressed you urgently and ceaselessly.') may have
triggered the process by which vv. 1–7 were reshaped as
prophetic reminiscence throughout and which produced MT
(pp. 618–623).

25.8–14: The elements in MT which are not represented by
Sept. are set out on pp. 623–624. The intention of the exegetical
expansions in MT is to identify Judah's enemy with Babylon
and, more particularly, with Nebuchadrezzar, whereas in Sept.
there is no further elucidation of the 'enemy from the north'
(pp. 624–627).

(*d*) Special features of Sept. other than shortness.

1.17: Influences other than textual ones have determined the
form of Sept. μὴ φοβηθῇς ἀπὸ προσώπου αὐτῶν is identical with
the rendering which appears for אל תירא מפניהם at v. 8. The
element of threat in MT has been removed and the aspect of
exhortation and reassurance strengthened: 'For I am with you,
says Yahweh, to keep you safe' (p. 22).

2.2: τοῦ ἐξακολουθῆσαι σε τῷ ἁγίῳ Ισραηλ is a puzzling
feature of Sept. which perhaps arises from the paraphrasing of
לכתך אחרי as 'when you followed after the Holy One of Israel'
(p. 27).

2.20: את צעה has been read as אתצעה (διαχυθήσομαι), 'I shall
be poured out'.

2.24: בחדשה is explained by Kimchi as a reference to the
month when the Jerusalem temple was destroyed, and Sept. ἐν τῇ
ταπεινώσει αὐτῆς is apparently connected with this line of
exegesis.

2.29: Sept. (except Sept.ᴬ) is conflate, with variant renderings
of כלכם פשעו בי, and the argument that Sept.ᴬ is a consequence
of haplography and not a witness to a Hebrew text which agrees
with MT is unnatural (pp. 49f.).

2.30: καὶ οὐκ ἐφοβήθητε has exegetical rather than textual

significance: it is a secondary comment expressive of pious horror, rather than a corruption of הדור אתם into ולא יראתם (pp. 50, 50f.).

2.33: Sept. reads את הרעות as אֶת הָרֵעוֹת and apparently construes למדת as a segholate infinitive with a prefixed *lamedh*: καὶ σὺ ἐπονηρεύσα τοῦ μιᾶναι τὰς ὁδούς σου (p. 53).

3.3: Sept. has associated רבבים with רבב (πολλούς) and has probably inferred that the πολλούς were ποιμένας from v. 1 (רעים, p. 60).

3.8: ὧν κατελήμφθη and ἐν οἷς ἐμοιχᾶτο may be doublets; the latter may be secondary and betray the influence of Jn 8.3f. εἰς τὰς χεῖρας αὐτῆς, which is not represented by MT, corresponds with בידה (Deut 24.1,3) and is evidence of an intention to associate v. 8 more closely with these Deuteronomy passages (p. 65).

3.19: Sept. has apparently interpreted איך as an abbreviation for אמן יהוה כי and has supposed that καὶ ἐγὼ εἶπα γένοιτο Κύριε is a response to the preceding verses.

3.19: צבי is perhaps unrepresented by Sept., and it may have been regarded by the Greek translator as a truncated dittography of צבאות (p. 78).

4.4: Sept.^S*A represents MT, whereas Sept.^B καὶ περιτέμεσθε τὴν σκληροκαρδίαν ὑμῶν) betrays the influence of Deut 10.16 (pp. 88f.).

4.29: Sept. has a longer text than MT and this is not easily explicable as conflate, nor are there compelling reasons for concluding that MT is shorter as a consequence of a scribal mishap (p. 110).

6.11: Sept. καὶ τὸν θυμόν μου (MT, ואת חמת יהוה) is probably a modification made by the Greek translator in the interests of what seemed to him better sense: it changes v. 11 into a word of Yahweh. Alternatively he may have interpreted the *yodh* of חמתי as an abbreviation for יהוה (p. 146).

7.9: The series of questions in MT has the order stealing, murder, adultery and perjury, and the order in Sept. (murder, adultery, stealing and perjury) is perhaps a secondary adjustment designed to produce agreement with Exod 20.13–16 and Deut 5.17–20 (p. 162).

8.2: καὶ πρὸς πάντας τοὺς ἀστέρας and καὶ πρὸς πᾶσαν τὴν στρατίαν are probably doublets, but Ziegler supposes that καὶ πρὸς πάντας τοὺς ἀστέρας is an addition from Deut 4.19, καὶ τοὺς ἀστέρας (p. 181).

8.16: ἵππων is perhaps a gloss on ἱππασίας which normally means 'horse-riding' but here 'horses' (p. 192).

8.21: ὠδῖνες ὡς τικτούσης represents חיל כיולדה additional to MT—an insertion from 6.24 (p. 195).

9.21: Ziegler explains the additional ὑμῶν in Sept. on the assumption that it is an attempt to accommodate doublets (τοῦ πεδίου and τῆς γῆς). The Greek text which Ziegler restores (ἐπὶ προσώπου τῆς γῆς) assumes that על פני האדמה was original at 9.21 as at 8.2 and 16.4, and this has the support of K^{or} and some Hebrew manuscripts. But על פני השדה is probably original at 9.21 and שדה is due to the influence of the simile—the sheaves which are left lying in the field (שדה; p. 211).

10.18: Sept. has periphrastic features; כפעם is not represented, והצרותי להם is apparently paraphrased as ἐν θλίψει and ἡ πληγή σου is supplied as a subject for εὑρεθῇ (ימצאו is read as יִמָּצֵאוּ).

10.24: The differences between Sept. and MT in this verse as in v. 19 (συντρίμματί σου ; πληγή σου) are of exegetical rather than textual significance. Sept. distinguishes more clearly than MT between Jeremiah and those for whom he prays by substituting first person plural suffixes (ἡμᾶς) for the first singular suffixes of MT (תמעטני ;יסרני; pp. 232, 234).

12.13: Sept. reads זרעו, קצרו and ובשו as imperatives (σπείρατε ; θερίσατε ; αἰσχύνθητε) and it derives נחלו from נחל 'inherit'. It departs from MT after ובשו and does not make a decisive contribution to the textual problems of v. 13. MT should be followed apart from מתבואתיכם which cannot follow third person verbs and should be emended to מתבואתיהם. It is tempting to read imperatives throughout, but לא יועלו cannot be preceded by an imperative (pp. 276–277).

13.13: MT לדוד על כסאו is a concentrated expression which is correctly spelled out by Sept. as υἱοὺς Δαυιδ ἐπὶ θρόνου αὐτῶν (p. 292).

13.16: Reliance should not be placed in καὶ τεθήσονται εἰς σκότος in order to reconstruct the Hebrew of this verse (pace Driver). Other features of Sept.'s rendering of v. 16 do not inspire confidence: καὶ ἐκεῖ σκιὰ θανάτου is probably an attempt to circumvent the difficulties of MT (ושמה לצלמות). Sept., Aq., Vulg., and Pesh. all suppose that the constituents of צלמות are צל and מות (p. 299).

13.20: Ἰερουσαλημ is correct exegesis and K (שאי ;וראי) should be preferred to Q (שאו ;וראו). Moreover, MT עיניכם should be emended to עיניך in agreement with Sept. (ὀφθαλμούς σου; p. 306).

13.25: τοῦ ἀπειθεῖν ὑμᾶς indicates מריך over against MT מדיך (p. 311).

14.15: Sept. has ἐν θανάτῳ νοσερῷ for MT בחרב. Apparently בדבר was read and an additional verb (ἀποθανοῦνται) was supplied.

15.1: Sept.^A substitutes Aaron for Samuel and this is probably connected with Ps 99.6 (which is cited by Kimchi): 'Moses and

Aaron among his priests and Samuel among those who call on his name' (p. 334).

15.10: Sept. has read כלה as כָּלָה (ἐξέλιπεν) and ἡ ἰσχύς μου is exegetical expansion rather than the representation of a corruption of כה (כחי) which belongs to the opening of v. 11. Hence the word-division in Sept. is the same as MT and an attempt has been made to get sense out of the impossible form מקללוני by reading it as בִּמְקַלְלָי (ἐν τοῖς καταρωμένοις με): 'My strength is exhausted by reason of those who curse me' (p. 345).

15.16: Sept. can be only imperfectly correlated with MT. It punctuates differently and connects דע שאתי עליך חרפה (v. 15) with v. 16; for נמצאו דבריך it has ὑπὸ τῶν ἀθετούντων τοὺς λόγους σου: 'Know what insults I have received at the hands of those who reject your words.' Thereafter it appears to have read כלם ויהי for MT ואכלם ויהי: συντέλεσον αὐτούς καὶ ἔσται, 'Destroy them and let your word be' etc.

16.7: ἄρτος represents לחם (MT להם) (p. 365).

17.9: βαθεῖα should perhaps be regarded as exegesis of עקב rather than as evidence of a Hebrew text with עמק in place of עקב. The Greek translator has chosen to emphasize the nuance of 'unsearchability' in his rendering. He interprets the deceitfulness of the heart in terms of the recesses which are inaccessible to examination (p. 397).

17.26: Sept. (except Sept.[OL]) has καὶ θυσίαν καὶ θυμιάματα for MT וזבח. The Greek translator of Jeremiah elsewhere uses θυσία to render זבח and so there is reason for urging the originality of καὶ θυσίαν and for regarding καὶ θυμιάματα as a secondary doublet. Since θυμίαμα/θυμιάματα does not appear in Sept. as a rendering of מנחה, the possibility that καὶ θυμιάματα is an alternative to the transcription καὶ μαναα can be dismissed (p. 415).

18.20,22: MT has כרו שוחה in both verses, but the consonantal text indicates שיחה at v. 22. 'ρήματα and λόγον are perhaps renderings of שיחה and, if so, the periphrastic transformations in Sept. are limited to the verb כרו (συνελάλησαν in v. 20 and ἐνεχείρησαν in v. 22). In any case the parallelism in v. 22 (ופחים טמנו לרגלי) suggests that שוחה rather than שיחה is original in that verse (pp. 439f.).

18.23: The curious rendering of Sept. (ἡ ἀσθένεια αὐτῶν) shows that the final mem of מכשלים was taken as a suffix, and this should be compared with Sept.'s rendering of ויכשלום at 18.15 (καὶ ἀσθενήσουσιν). Hence ἡ ἀσθένεια αὐτῶν points to מכשולם (so Rudolph; see below, p. 441).

19.2: The interpretation of גיא as πολυανδρεῖον 'graveyard' is connected with the way that the 'Topheth' theme is used in chapter 7 and here again in chapter 19, although πολυανδρεῖον is not used to render גיא in chapter 7 (φάραγξ, vv. 31, 32). πολυανδρεῖον (cf. 2.23, p. 43) is related to the thought that the valley of Ben Hinnom is the cemetery of children offered in sacrifice and that it will be the graveyard of the nation (p. 444).

19.3: Sept. has a longer text than MT: it represents איש יהודה and והבאים בשערים האלה which may have been taken over from 11.2 (18.11) and 17.20 (22.2) respectively. איש יהודה is not represented by Sept.ᴬ and הבאים בשערים האלה is not represented by Sept.ˢ.

19.15: Sept. has a double rendering of ועל כל עריך: καὶ ἐπὶ πάσας τὰς πόλεις αὐτῆς καὶ ἐπὶ τὰς κώμας αὐτῆς. There is no doubt that καὶ ἐπὶ πάσας τὰς πόλεις αὐτῆς is secondary, perhaps influenced by עיר. καὶ ἐπὶ τὴν πόλιν ταύτην καὶ ἐπὶ τὰς κώμας αὐτῆς (a text supported by the miniscule 106) embodies a correct understanding of the Hebrew, since v. 15 refers to the capital city, Jerusalem, and its dependent villages (p. 447).

22.18: Sept. and MT diverge: Sept. represents additionally הוי על האיש הזה and does not represent והוי אחות and הוי הדה והוי. The contention that a scribe's eye shifted from the closing letters of יהודה to הזה and that he accidentally passed over הוי על האיש הזה does not command assent as an explanation of MT (pp. 532f.).

23.1: Sept. τὰ πρόβατα τῆς νομῆς αὐτῶν (MT, צאן מרעיתי) may be a striving after sense by the Greek translator (a conjectural emendation) rather than an indication of a Hebrew text (מרעיתם) different from MT, but in any case מרעיתם is desiderated (p. 554).

23.6: Sept. renders אשר יקראו as ὃ καλέσει αὐτὸν κύριος and κύριος is probably exegetical expansion with a view to establishing the grammatical subject of יקראו. Alternatively, Ziegler supposes that κύριος may represent a doublet of Ιω (יו), the theophoric element of Ιωσεδεκ (יוצדק). The only person in the Hebrew Bible with this name is the father of Joshua, the High Priest (Ezra 3.2,8). At Zech 6.12 Joshua is designated איש צמח (cf. Zech 3.8). It is difficult to believe that this is a coincidence, that it has no bearing on צמח צדיק (Jer 23.5) and that the Greek translator was uninfluenced by the Zechariah passages in his choice of Ιωσεδεκ. But why did he not represent יהושע rather than his father, since the root ישע is present in v. 6a? There is no satisfactory explanation of this, but it may be observed that יוצדק preserves a link with יהוה צדקנו which would not be achieved by יהושע.

23.10: The view that MT is conflate and that the shorter text of Sept., which does not represent כי מנאפים מלאה הארץ, is superior cannot be sustained, because ἀπὸ προσώπου τούτων hangs in the air in Sept. and is explicable only with reference to

מנאפים. This is seen in Pesh. which, like Sept., reads כי מפני אלה as כי מפני אֵלֶה, but which otherwise, more or less, reproduces MT, so that *mṭl ḥlyn* relates to *gyr' wḥṭwp'* (*wḥṭwp'* = חטאים is additional to MT). Hence v. 10a is needed, and vv. 10a and 10b are not explicable as textual variants (p. 570).

23.17: Sept. has a double rendering of וכל הלך בשררות לבו: (*a*) πᾶσι τοῖς πορευόμενοις τοῖς θελήμασιν αὐτῶν and (*b*) παντὶ τῷ πορευομένῳ πλάνῃ καρδίας αὐτοῦ. The second of these has a better one–one correspondence with MT, but it introduces the thought of 'error' for MT 'stubbornness'. Both variants derive from MT and the significance of πλάνη is exegetical rather than textual: it brings out the sense of 'going astray', as Pesh. and Targ. do with מהבלים (v. 16). Ziegler indicates (*a*) as original and brackets (*b*) in his text. This agrees with Janzen who, however, argues that (*a*) cannot be had from MT (p. 579).

23.20: Sept. misreads מזמות לבו as מְזִמּות לבו (ἀπὸ ἐγχειρήματος καρδίας αὐτοῦ). Aq. has εννοιας 'thoughts' and ενθυμηματα 'stratagems' in agreement with MT (מְזִמּות) and the other versions.

23.27: τοῦ νόμου μου in the main witnesses of Sept. should perhaps be regarded as an inner Greek corruption of τοῦ ὀνόματός μου (which is in Ziegler's text). Apart from this Sept. is representing לשכח את שמי over against MT להשכיח את עמי שמי. Ziegler and Janzen discern textual variants (להשכיח את עמי and לשכח את שמי) and suppose that MT is partly conflate (p. 589).

23.28: τὸ ἐνύπνιον αὐτοῦ represents חלומו and Rudolph supposes that MT חלום may have arisen from a haplography of *waw* (ואשר).

23.29: Ziegler and Janzen detect a conflate text which is fully represented in the main witnesses of Sept. ((*a*) הלא דברי (*b*) כה דברי) and partly present in MT (כה/הלא) and Sept.[OL] (οὐχ οὕτως οἱ λόγοι μου) (p. 591).

24.1: καὶ τοὺς πλουσίους is additional to MT and Ziegler is inclined to equate τοὺς πλουσίους with אולי הארץ (2 Kgs 24.15). Another possibility is גבורי החיל (Hitzig) or אנשי החיל (2 Kgs 24.14,16). The ambivalence of these expressions is illustrated by NEB: גבורי החיל is rendered as 'fighting men' (v. 14) and אנשי החיל as 'men of substance' (v. 16). Either גבורי החיל or אנשי החיל could be rendered as τοὺς πλουσίους, but they are differently translated by Sept. at 2 Kgs 24.14 (τοὺς δυνατοὺς ἰσχύι) and 16 (τοὺς ἄνδρας τῆς δυνάμεως), and at v. 15 אולי הארץ is rendered as τοὺς ἰσχυροὺς τῆς γῆς.

25.9: Sept. represents ולחרבת עולם (MT, ולחרבות עולם). At 25.18 there is a similar word-string (לחרבה לשמה לשרקה ולקללה) and לחרבה is there represented by Sept. This suggests that the

Hebrew text read by the Greek translator at 25.9 was indeed ולחרפה (p. 624).

25.10: Sept. represents ריח מור (MT, קול רחים) and Ziegler supposes that Sept. preserves a better text than MT, since 'the sound of the handmill' does not contribute to the theme of joy and happiness lost in captivity: מור may have fallen out accidentally before ואור, and this, with the corruption of ריח to רחים and the repetition of קול (which occurs four times in the preceding part of the verse), gave rise to MT. The perfume of myrrh, like the joy of wedding festivities and the gleam of the lamp, is a mark of social rejoicing (p. 624).

25.12: καὶ θήσομαι αὐτούς is perhaps a rendering of MT ושמתי אתו rather than an indication that the Greek translator read ושמתי אתם or ושמתים : אתו has been taken as a resumption of הגוי ההוא and so as a collective singular (p. 623).

25.13: אשר נבא ירמיהו על כל הגוים appears in Sept. as a superscription to 25.15f. = MT 49.34ff. (p. 624).

25.26: For reasons which are entirely obscure מלכי הצפון appears in Sept. as Βασιλεῖς ἀπὸ ἀπηλιώτου 'kings of the east' (p. 640).

25.34: On balance the Hebrew represented by Sept. ὥσπερ οἱ κριοὶ οἱ ἐκλεκτοί (כאילי חמדה) should be preferred to MT (כבלי חמדה), although the use of κριοί to render אדירי at vv. 34, 35, 36 has an important bearing on the evaluation of ὥσπερ οἱ κριοὶ οἱ ἐκλεκτοί and raises the question whether it may not be a free rendering of MT inspired by the manner in which אדירי has been translated (pp. 651f.).

25.38: It is difficult to determine whether ἀπὸ προσώπου μαχαίρας τῆς μεγάλης is an indication that the Greek translator read מפני חרב היונה, or whether Sept. is to be explained as a harmonization of 25.38 with 46.16 and 50.16. If the Greek translator had read מפני חרב היונה, we would have expected ἀπὸ προσώπου μαχαίρας τοῦ μεγάλου, 'because of the sword of the powerful (oppressor)'. On the other hand, it should be noticed that at 46.16 and 50.16 Sept. renders מפני חרב היונה as ἀπὸ προσώπου μαχαίρας Ἑλληνικῆς which makes a dent in the hypothesis of harmonization (pp. 654f.).

(e) Special relations of Sept. and Pesh.

2.23: Sept. φωνὴ αὐτῆς ὠλόλυξε and Pesh. 'rymty bqlky are related renderings; both versions have read קלה as קָלָה (p. 43).

2.25: נואש is similarly mistranslated by Sept. (ἀνδριοῦμαι) and Pesh. ('thylt) (p. 44). The entanglement of the versions in 2.23–25 is exceptional and it should be assumed that this arises from the difficulty which the translators found with MT. It is most pronounced in the case of Pesh., and this is all the more remarkable in that Pesh. in Jer 1–25 is marked by its faithfulness to MT. Where there is a difficult Hebrew text, however, interesting agreements of Sept. and Pesh. occur, and these are probably explicable as a dependence of Pesh. on Sept., and as an indication that Sept. was available to the Syriac translator. More generally, the phenomenon of entanglement in the versions can be correlated with instances of an obscure Hebrew text. Pesh. is probably dependent on Sept. for its renderings of בכרה קלה and נואש, and follows Targ. in respect of תאנתה (v. 24, below, p. 44). It would appear that the Syriac translator or a subsequent reviser of Pesh. had Sept. and Targ. open before him (pp. 44f.).

2.30: Sept. μάχαιρα and Pesh. ḥrb' agree over against MT חרבכם (p. 51).

2.34: This is another case where a very obscure piece of Hebrew produces an agreement between Sept. and Pesh.: כי על כל אלה is rendered ἐπὶ πάσῃ δρυί by Sept. and tḥyt kl 'yln by Pesh. (אלה read as אַלָּה) (p. 54).

3.1: Both Sept. (ἐν ποιμέσιν) and Pesh. (br'wt') have vocalized רעים as רֹעִים (p. 59).

3.2: Sept. (ὡσεὶ κορώνη) and Pesh. ('yk n'b') represent ערב 'raven' (MT ערבי 'Bedouin') (p. 59).

3.5: Both Sept. (διαμενεῖ and φυλαχθήσεται) and Pesh. (ntnṭr twice) indicate passivity for ינצר and ישמר, and assume that 'Israel' is the grammatical subject (p. 62).

3.6: Sept. κατοικία and Pesh. 'mwrt' 'settlement' assume a derivation of משובה from ישב not שוב (p. 64).

3.7: τὴν ἀσυνθεσίαν αὐτῆς corresponds with šwqrh and both are additional to MT (p. 65).

3.16: κιβωτὸς διαθήκης (ארון ברית) is transliterated by Pesh. (qbwt' ddytq') (p. 74).

3.18: Sept. and Pesh. represent אבותיהם (MT אבותיכם) (p. 75).

3.22: Ziegler explains ἰδοὺ δοῦλοι as a corruption of ἰδοὺ οἵδε, ἰδού and οἵδε being doublets. The text which Ziegler (Beiträge, pp. 38f.) reconstructs (οἵδε ἡμεῖς ἐσόμεθά σοι) agrees with Pesh. h' ḥnn dylk.

4.8: For MT ממנו Sept. (except Sept.ˢ*) has ἀφ'ὑμῶν, and Pesh., probably in dependence on Sept., mnkwn (p. 92).

4.11: Sept. does not explicitly represent שפיים (Pesh. bšbyl'), but otherwise Sept. and Pesh. agree in their rendering of צח (Sept. πλανήσεως; Pesh. ṭ'yt'). This arises out of the supposition that the community is being compared to a wind in the desert which blows this way and that. This is another case where, confronted by a difficulty, the Syriac translator turns to the Sept. for help (p. 96).

4.20: Sept. has taken רגע as a verb (διεσπάσθησαν), or else has supplied a verb for the second stich and made ἄφνω do service for both פתאם and רגע. The Greek translation is matched by Pesh. which has two verbs (p. 104).

4.21: נס is read as נָס by Sept. and Pesh. (p. 105).

5.10: The thought of 'total disaster' (כלה) has been modified by the insertion of אל in MT (cf. 4.27, p. 109; 5.18, p. 127; 6.11, p. 146). The process of changing the original sense of 5.10 has gone furthest in Sept. and Pesh., where הסירו is replaced by ὑπολίπεσθε and šbwqw respectively, 'leave behind', and 'for they do not belong to Yahweh' has become 'for they belong to the Lord' (cf. 6.11, where נלאיתי הכיל is rendered by Sept. as καὶ ἔπεσχον καὶ οὐ συνετέλεσα αὐτούς, 'I refrained and did not make an end of them'). Pesh. is probably dependent on Sept. at 5.10 (p. 120).

5.22: Sept. (καὶ ταραχθήσεται καὶ οὐ δυνήσεται) and Pesh. (wmtktš wl' mškḥ) represent singular verbs over against MT ויתגעשו ולא יוכלו (p. 129).

5.28: Neither Sept. nor Pesh. represents שמנו and דברי רע (p. 134).

6.26: For עלינו Sept. has ἐφ' ὑμᾶς and Pesh. 'lyky. This has exegetical rather than textual significance: both versions wanted to represent vv. 25f. as word of Yahweh. Ziegler has restored ἐφ' ἡμᾶς conjecturally in his text (p. 151).

6.29: Sept. (ἐξέλιπε), Pesh. (grdy) and Vulg. (defecit) take נחר as 'exhausted' or 'destroyed'. That this sense is derived from חרר 'burn' is clear from Sept.'s rendering: ἐξέλιπε φυστὴρ ἀπὸ πυρός (p. 156).

8.3: Neither Sept. nor Pesh. represents הנשארים (second occurrence). It interrupts a word-string (בכל המקמות אשר הדחתים שם) which, with some variations, is well attested in the book of Jeremiah (p. 182).

8.21: השברתי is not represented by Sept. and Pesh. (p. 195).

9.9: The significance of the deviation of Sept. (λάβετε) and Pesh. (šqwlw) from MT (אשא) is exegetical and formal. It creates a unit consisting of words of Yahweh (vv. 9f.), whereas if אשא is the correct text, Jeremiah must be the speaker (p. 203).

9.11: Both Sept. and Pesh. show a different punctuation from MT (no pause at ויגדה), and Pesh., is probably dependent on Sept. (p. 206).

9.16: התבוננו ו is not represented by Sept. and Pesh. (p. 209).

13.18: Sept. and Pesh. indicate שרים or the like for MT גבירה (δυναστεύουσι(ν) ; rwrbn'). Pesh. renders שרים with the same word at 29.2, where שרי יהודה וירושלם is not represented by

Sept. At 2 Kgs 24.12 שׂריו is rendered as οἱ ἄρχοντες αὐτοῦ, and δυναστεύουσι(ν) is not elsewhere used by Sept. to translate שׂרים. Two hypotheses can be made: (a) The corruption is an inner Septuagintal one, δυναστευούσῃ (Aq.) has been corrupted to δυναστεύουσι(ν). An implication of this is that Pesh. is dependent on Sept. (b) δυναστεύουσι(ν) and rwrbn' are evidences of a Hebrew text which had שׂרים, and, in that case, גבירה might be a secondary accommodation of the Hebrew of 13.18 to Jer 29.2 and 2 Kgs 24.12,15 (pp. 302).

14.16: Sept. has the order 'sword and famine' (MT 'famine and sword') which, on examination, is seen to be normal. Pesh. has the order of Sept. but it also represents דבר (wmwtn').

15.17: ואעלז is perhaps not represented by Sept. (ἀλλὰ εὐλαβούμην ἀπὸ προσώπου χειρός σου) and Pesh. ('l' dḥlt mn qdm 'ydk). There is clearly a special relationship between Sept. and Pesh.: either their renderings are paraphrases of מפני ידך, or else they assume the continuing force of לא (לא ישבתי) with אעלז (p. 353).

17.11: Sept has a double rendering of קרא (πέρδιξ, συνήγαγεν) and Pesh. (ḥgl' dqr') might be similarly explained. On this view of Pesh., however, דגר is not represented, and another possibility is that its paraphrase ('yk ḥgl' dqr' l'ylyn dl' yld) is intended to embrace all of MT. 'Like a partridge which calls to those whose mother she is not' agrees with Rashi's explanation of the stich: he glosses דגר with ציפצוף 'chirping' and comments, 'Thus the קרא draws after it young birds whose eggs it did not lay' (p. 399).

17.17: Sept. has a free rendering of מחסי אתה ביום רעה (φειδόμενος μου ἐν ἡμέρᾳ πονερᾷ) which is closely followed by Pesh. ('l' 'gn 'ly bywm' byš' (p. 413).

18.8: MT is unsatisfactory because רעתו can only mean 'its wrongdoing', whereas the sense required of רעה as the antecedent of אשר דברתי עליו is 'disaster' or 'doom'. Hence the shorter text of Sept. and Pesh. (אשר דברתי עליו is not represented) is superior to MT (p. 427).

23.5: Sept.'s rendering of צמח (ἀνατολή 'rising' or 'arising'), and Kimchi's association of צמח with 'emergence' or 'appearance' raises the question whether Sept.'s rendering has connections with a type of exegesis similar to that which Kimchi has preserved. The matter is further complicated by Pesh. ṣmḥ': the phonemes of צמח are reproduced, but ṣmḥ' means 'brightness' or 'effulgence' in Syriac. If it were supposed that the Syriac translator intended to give this sense to צמח, we would have another point of contact with Sept. ἀνατολή and Kimchi's exegesis, since there is an obvious link between 'arising', 'appearing' and 'brightness'.

23.14: ἀπὸ τῆς ὁδοῦ αὐτοῦ τῆς πονηρᾶς and *mn 'wrḥh byšt'* represent מדרכו הרעה (MT, מרעתו).

23.17: τοῖς ἀπωθουμένοις τὸν λόγον κυρίου and *l'ylyn dmrgzyn bptgmh dmry'* represent למנאצי דְּבַר יהוה (MT, למנאצי דִּבֶּר יהוה) (p. 577).

23.23: Neither Sept. nor Pesh. represents the interrogative particle ה (θεὸς ἐγγίζων ἐγώ εἰμι; *'lh' 'n' dmn qwrb'*). The sense is then that God is effectively near, and that he is not distant, inaccessible and unreal. The antithesis of מקרב and מרחק is supposed to be of the same order as that applied to Yahweh's commandment at Deut 30.11–14 (pp. 584, 586).

25.26: Neither Sept. nor Pesh. represents הארץ and the shorter text is better than MT. It relieves the anomalous grammar noted by Kimchi, and if ממלכות הארץ were to be read, it would add nothing to the sense of the passage (p. 640).

(f) Special relations between Sept. and Vulg.:

3.2: The obscure שפים is rendered similarly by Sept. (εἰς εὐθεῖαν) and Vulg. (*in directum*), and Vulg. is probably dependent on Sept. (p. 59).

3.20: Sept. πλὴν ὡς and Vulg. *sed quomodo si* point to אך כי (MT, אכן). That Vulg. is following Sept. is suggested by a further agreement: both render בגד as 'despise' or 'contemn' (ἀθετεῖ; *contemnar*).

4.21: נס (MT, נס) is read as סם by Sept., Pesh. and Vulg. (p. 105).

4.31: לחרגים (MT, לְהֹרְגִים) is read by Sept., Pesh and Vulg. (*propter interfectos*) as לַהֲרֻגִים (p. 112).

6.15: Sept. καὶ ἐν καιρῷ ἐπισκοπῆς approximates to Vulg. *in tempore visitationis suae*, and indicates בעת פקדתם rather than MT בעת פקדתים. The latter is consistent with a speech by Yahweh, but is inappropriate on the lips of Jeremiah, speaking for his own part. Pesh. (*wbzbn' dmtpqdyn*) has the same rendering at 6.15 as it has for בעת פקדתם at 8.12 (p. 147).

11.16: ἀνήφθη and *exarsit* appear to represent הצת over against MT הצית, and this may also be indicated by Pesh. *šbwqw*: 'They have released fire against it' is the equivalent of 'Fire is kindled against it' (p. 250).

2. Vulgate: *Biblia Sacra iuxta Vulgatam Clementinam*[4] (1965); *Liber Hieremiae et Lamentationes*, Biblia Sacra 14, O.S.B. (Rome, 1972).

Special features of Vulg.:

2.20: Vulg. renders שברתי (*confregisti*) and נתקתי (*rupisti*) correctly as second person feminine singular verbs, but עלך and מוסרתיך appear as *iugum meum* and *vincula mea*, 'You have broken my yoke and snapped my bonds'. This indicates that the discipline thrown off by Israel had been imposed by Yahweh. It is unlikely that the change of suffixes has any textual significance: it is to be understood as an attempt at exegetical clarification rather than as evidence of a Hebrew text different from MT (p. 40).

2.31: There is a curious rendering of מאפליה in Vulg. (*serotina*, 'late-ripening'). This is explicable in terms of אפילת (Exod 9.32) and a use of the Hiphil of אפל in post-biblical Hebrew (*s.v.* אפל in Jastrow): שנים מאפילות means 'years when the crops ripen late' and שהיא מאפלת 'whose crops ripen late'. At Exod 9.32 Vulg. renders כי אפילת הנה as *quia serotina erant* (p. 52).

2.35: Vulg.'s paraphrase of כי נקיתי (*absque peccato et innocens ego sum*), 'I am free from sin and innocent', emphasizes that these are the thoughts which Israel harbours, the assumptions which determine her behaviour. The rendering of אפו as *furor tuus* is perhaps connected with this emphasis: *et propterea avertatur furor tuus a me* ('And so your anger is averted from me') binds together the stichs of v. 35a, whereas they are asyndetic thoughts, the first triggering the second, in MT (p. 54).

3.8: ואַרא, which is a puzzling feature of MT, is not translated by Vulg. which joins the last part of v. 7 (ותראה ... יהודה) to v. 8 (... כי): 'and her sister Judah, the deceiver, saw that because Israel, the apostate, had committed adultery I had sent her away'. It is unlikely that Vulg. arises from a Hebrew text different from MT; rather this is a conjectural response to the difficulty presented by ואַרא (cf. Pesh. *ḥzt* = ותרא).

3.22: Vulg. is the only version which analyses אתנו correctly, discerning that it is equivalent to אתה) אתינו 'come'): *Ecce nos venimus ad te* (p. 80).

4.29: There is a correlation between Vulg. and Targ.: both take the first כל העיר to mean 'citizens' and the second 'cities' or 'towns' (Vulg. *omnis civitas* and *universae urbes*; Targ. כל יתבי קרתא and כל קרויהון) (p. 110).

5.28: Symm. and Theod. (τους λογους μου) have read דברי as דבָרי, and Vulg. represents the same vocalization (*Et praeterierunt sermones meos pessime*, 'They have disregarded my words most wickedly'). But Symm. and Theod. take עבר as 'transgress' (παρεβησαν) not 'overlook' (p. 134).

6.18: את אשר בם is obscure, perhaps unintelligible, and Vulg.

attempts to relieve the problem by what is probably a conjectural insertion (*faciam* = אעשׂה) (p. 150).

15.6–7: Sept. and Vulg. have introduced future tenses wherever an imperfect form occurs with *waw*: ואט (καὶ ἐκτενῶ; *et extendam*); ואשׁחיתך (καὰ διαφθερῶ; *et interficiam*); וזרם (καὶ διασπερῶ; *et dispergam*); even נלאיתי הנחם has been rendered as a future by Sept. (καὶ οὐκέτι ἀνήσω αὐτούς). There is a sufficient degree of correspondence between the two versions to suggest that a relation of dependence exists, and priority should be accorded to Sept. The perplexities which arise with Hebrew verbs in a passage like 15.5–9 are both translational and historical. It does not follow that events which the prophet describes as past actually lie in the past. If they are translated as past tenses, there is no overt indication that they refer to events which lie in the future; if they are translated as future tenses, the exceptional nature of the utterance and perhaps the interior state of the prophet are lost (pp. 342f.).

17.6: The obscure חררים is rendered by Vulg. as *in siccitate*, and this agrees with Symm. ἐν ξηροτησιν.

22.17: The intention of Vulg., Aq. and Symm. is apparently to connect v. 17 with the preceding verses: Jehoiakim failed in the royal responsibilities which Josiah had fulfilled with exemplary diligence. Hence *et ad calumniam* (Aq., Symm. και επι την συκοφαντιαν) is a reference to perjury or defamation in connection with false legal testimony. Again both Vulg. and Aq. (Symm.) derive מרוצה from רוץ 'run' (και επι τον δρομον του ποιειν), and Vulg. improves the sense by inserting *mali*: *Et ad cursum mali operis*, 'and for a course of evil action' is to be understood as epexegesis of *calumniam* (p. 531).

23.39: Targ.'s rendering of (וארחק יתכון) ונטשתי אתכם indicates 'removal into exile'. Vulg. *et derelinquam vos* points to 'abandonment (by Yahweh)', while Sept. (καὶ ῥάσσω ὑμᾶς, 'and I will cast you down') and Pesh. (w'šdykwn, 'and I will cast you out') are less explicit (p. 601).

3. Peshiṭta: S. Lee (ed.) *Vetus Testamentum Syriace* (1823); A. M. Ceriani (ed.), *Translatio Syra Pescitto Veteris Testamenti ex Codice Ambrosianio* (1876–1883); also the Urmia edition of 1852 reprinted by the Trinitarian Bible Society in 1954.

Special features of Pesh.:

2.19: MT has vocalized פחדתי as a noun, 'my fear', but it is correctly identified as second person singular feminine verb by Pesh. which consequently represents אלי (MT, אליך): *wl' dḥlty mny*. Whether this means that the Syriac translator had a different Hebrew text from MT or that he emended it to make sense cannot be determined. The alteration of a postulated, original אלי to אליך may have been caused by a failure to recognize that פחדתי was a verb: with פחדתי 'my fear' אליך rather than אלי was desiderated (p. 39).

2.21: The tendency to change imagery into a flat, didactic paraphrase is a feature of Targ., but the process can be discerned here in both Pesh. and Targ. Pesh. associates סורי with rebellion and paraphrases, 'How your attitude to me has changed! You have rebelled like a vine in its wild state' (cf. Targ., 'How you have changed your relationship to me by your corrupt deeds! You have strayed from my worship and have become like a vine which has no usefulness in it' (p. 42).

2.23–24: There is an interesting interaction of Pesh. and Targ. Pesh. translates משרכת דרכיה as *m'qmt 'wrḥt'*, 'perverting (her) ways', which is close to Targ. מקלקלא אורחתהא, 'corrupting her ways'. מקלקלה is a play on קלילא and may even be an indication that קלה has been rendered as 'vile' (קלילא) rather than 'swift'. Whatever be the correct explanation of the rendering of תאנתה by *'yk yrwr'* in Pesh. and כירורא in Targ., it should be regarded as having originated with Targ. It has been adopted by Pesh., because תאנתה defeated the Syriac translator. This is clear from the circumstance that following *'yk yrwr'* in Pesh. is a rendering of מי ישיבנה (*mn nhpkh*), and so *'yk yrwr'* can certainly be identified with תאנתה. The correct explanation of כירורא or כירודא in Targ. is given by Kimchi, 'It (Targ.) has added כתנים in agreement with שאפו רוח כתנים' (Jer. 14.6), since כתנים in 14.6 is rendered by כירורין or כירודין. Hence תאנתה is unrepresented in Targ. at 2.24 and כירורא betrays the influence of 14.6 (p. 44).

2.31: The perplexity of the Syriac translator in the presence of the unintelligible הדור אתם ראו דבר יהוה is shown by the circumstance that Pesh. follows MT in respect of הדור אתם (*'ntwn dr'*) and Sept. in respect of ἀκούσατε λόγον κυρίου (*šm'w ptgm' dmry'*). Thus Pesh. betrays an acquaintance with both MT and Sept. (p. 51).

3.8: The sense of MT ארא is deficient and Pesh. *wḥzt* supplies what is needed. Whether the Syriac translator read such a Hebrew text or made the adjustment which sense demanded cannot be certainly determined, but the latter is the more probable (p. 65).

5.16: Pesh. has *ggrth* 'their throats' for MT אשפתו 'their quivers'. It is unlikely that the Syriac translator had a text with גרנו. It is more probable that he reacted against the unsatisfactory nature of the imagery which lay before him in the

Hebrew text and took steps to improve the simile by availing himself of the phrase in Ps 5.10. A comparison of the Syriac of Jer 5.16 (*ggrth 'yk qbr' pthyn*) and Ps 5.10 (*w'yk qbr' pth' ggrthwn*) lends support to this view (p. 124).

5.28: Pesh. partly follows Sept. and partly Vulg.: with Sept. it does not represent שמנו עשתו and for גם עברו דברי רע it has *w'brw 'l dyn'* (cf. Sept. καὶ παρέβησαν κρίσιν); with Vulg. it has *l' trsw* for MT ויצליחו (Vulg. *non direxerunt*). Hence it appears that Pesh. made use of both Sept. and Vulg. (p. 134).

6.11: Pesh. reads ואת as וְאַתְּ and the verbs ending in *yodh* (נלאיתי ; מלאתי) are taken as second feminine singular. It would appear that Jerusalem is addressed: the city can no longer contain Yahweh's anger and must pour it out on its inhabitants: 'You are full of the Lord's anger and are weary. Measure (it) and pour (it) out.' (p. 146).

6.11: The proposal that לא should be inserted before מלא ימים claims the support of Pesh. *'m tl' ywmt'*. Could the Syriac translator have read מלא as טלא and in a moment of aberration have forgotten that *tl'* is Syriac but not Hebrew? (p. 146).

6.15: הִכְּלָם (in agreement with 8.12) is superior to הָכְלִים (MT), and is indicated by Pesh. (*wlmttksw*) and Targ. (אתכנעו) (p. 147).

10.9: For MT מאופז both Pesh. (*mn 'wpyr*) and Targ. (מאופיר) represent מאופור which is probably correct in view of the known association between Ophir and gold (p. 223).

10.9: Pesh. relates מעשה חכמים to (כלם) תכלת וארגמן לבושם, and supposes that a skill other than craftsmanship in metal (מעשה חרש וידי צורף) is indicated by the final phrase. This interpretation is also found in Kimchi, 'Clothing it in violet and purple, woven by skilled craftsmen' (p. 223).

10.18: Pesh. follows MT as far as בפעם הזאת, rendering הנני קולע as *h' m'rql 'n'*, 'I will trip up'. The Syriac translator was apparently defeated by והצרותי להם and the only connection of his banal paraphrase with MT is that he reproduces the sense of מצא; *dnb'wnny wdnšbhwnny*, 'that they may seek me and find me'.

10.23: Verse 23b follows MT, but v. 23a ('I know that the Lord's ways are not like man's ways') would seem to have been influenced by Isa 55.8 which is rendered by Pesh. as *w'wrhty l' hwy 'yk 'wrhtkwn 'mr mry*, 'My ways are not like your ways, says the Lord'.

15.11: The obscurity of the Hebrew arises mainly from שרותך (Q שריתך) and הפגעתי בך. Pesh. explains שֵׁרִיתָךְ as a Piel of שרה 'set free', 'forgive' and does not represent the אם of אם לא שריתך, although the second אם לוא, taken as an equivalent of כי אם, is clearly indicated by *'l'*. The resultant sense is, 'I shall not forgive you generously, but I shall waylay you (a menacing sense of פגע) with enemies from the north in a time of tribulation and affliction'. The perfects of MT are rendered as imperfects ('šbqk; 'pg') and the verse assumes the character of a future threat (p. 347).

15.12: Pesh. (see above) has transferred מצפון from v. 12 to v. 11 in order to achieve there a reference to the 'enemy from the north' (b'ldbb' mn grb'). Pesh. then paraphrases arbitrarily the obscure Hebrew of v. 12: The enemy from the north by whom Judah is threatened is qš' 'yk przl' w'yk nḥš', 'as strong as iron and bronze' (p. 348).

17.6: The sense of חררים is uncertain and there is a lexicographical link between Theod. (ἐν χασμασιν) and Pesh. (bḥwln'), both of which give the sense 'holes', 'caverns'.

17.9: There is a puzzling rendering of עקב in Pesh. ('syn) which may have some relation to βαρεῖα 'heavy' (Sept.ᴸ) and תקיף 'powerful' (Targ.). The latter, however, is apparently Targ.'s rendering of אנש. Pesh., by not representing the waw of ואנש and by rendering אנש as 'man', has produced the thought that the לב is too powerful to be amenable to control—man is overruled by the propensities of his לב ('syn lb' mn kl 'nš' hw) (p. 397).

21.9: Pesh. does not represent ונפל and in this respect follows the shorter Hebrew text of 38.2. Moreover, it renders והיוצא על הכשדים at 21.9 as it does ויצא אל הכשדים at 38.2 (wmn dnpq lwt kldy').

22.18: אחות and הדה are represented by Pesh. as 'ḥy and mr' respectively. It is unlikely that these deviations arise from the translation of a Hebrew text different from MT. They are a consequence of the perplexity felt by the Syriac translator in respect of אחות and הדה (p. 532).

22.28: It appears from a comparison of Pesh. and Targ. that Pesh., like Sept., does not represent נפוץ. It could be supposed that בסירא and חלשא (Targ.) represent a double rendering of נבזה and that העצב is unrepresented in Pesh. and Targ. as in Sept. It is, however, certain that Targ. is reading MT and the question which arises is why Pesh. and Targ. translate העצב as 'contemptible' (Targ. בסירא; Pesh. bsyr'). This derives more probably from עצב 'idol' than from עצב 'pot', since we know that בשת 'shame' was a surrogate for בעל (p. 547).

25.26: Pesh. mlk' 'ršky', 'the principal king' ('king of kings') rests on a recognition that ששך is an instance of Athbash. This is clear from the use of the same terminology by Pesh. at 51.41 ('rškyt'), where in view of the parallelism (בבל) the Athbash is unmistakeable (p. 640).

4. Targum: A. Sperber, *The Bible in Aramaic based on old Manuscripts and Printed Texts: iii, The Latter Prophets according to Targum Jonathan*, (1962).

Special features of Targ.:

Nearly all the examples which are treated are illustrations of how the paraphrases of Targ. transform or explain the figurative language of the Hebrew, especially in passages of poetry. The allusiveness and indeterminacy of poetry make it an inappropriate literary medium for pedestrian clarity or didactic explicitness. In Targ. meaning is defined and spelled out by means of longer formulations which narrow the possibilities of interpretation and whose flat prose changes poetry into instruction.

2.2: The marriage imagery disappears (אהבת ; חסד נעורין כלולתיך) and the verse is taken as a general reference to Israel's loyalty and love. She was attached to Yahweh's word and followed his two messengers, Moses and Aaron, for forty years in the wilderness without insubordination.

2.21: Targ. expands and explains the 'vine' imagery: 'I established you before me like a plant, a choice vine. All of you did what was right. How you have changed your relationship to me by your corrupt deeds! You wandered from my worship and have become as a vine which has no usefulness in it' (p. 42).

3.1: Targ. interprets the sexual imagery (ואת זנית רעים רבים) as a reference to idolatry and entanglement with foreign nations: 'You have committed adultery and concluded alliances with many nations' (p. 59).

3.2: Targ. transforms the sexual imagery (איפה לא שגלת) into 'Where have you not allied yourself with others to worship idols?' I have indicated that such sexual imagery in the book of Jeremiah presents a special, exegetical problem. It is probably more than simply metaphor for idolatry and has a special appropriateness to the nature of Israel's unfaithfulness—her involvement in sexual rites connected with the Canaanite cult (p. 63).

3.13: ותפזרי את דרכיך is obscure, but the allusion is almost certainly sexual. It is converted by Targ. into a general charge, 'You have corrupted your ways'. לזרים is paraphrased as 'by associating yourself with nations which worship idols'.

7.20: The metaphor (ובערה ולא תכבה) turns on the heat of Yahweh's anger: it has begun to burn and it will not be extinguished. This figurative element is suppressed in the generalized rendering of Targ., and in the process המקום הזה

rather than חמתי (אפיר ו) becomes the grammatical subject: 'And it will perish without residue'.

8.15,22: Healing (לעת מרפה ; לשלום) is interpreted by Targ. as 'forgiveness of sins' (p. 191). Another medical metaphor in 8.22 is changed by Targ. If there are no medicines or physicians in Gilead to deal effectively with Judah's sickness, her condition is hopeless and there is no cure. Targ. introduces the thought of intercession, Gilead is taken as an allusion to Elijah and 'medicine' to his teaching. Even so powerful an intercessor as Elijah would avail nothing; 'Because they did not repent, healing did not overtake the wound of the community of my people'.

10.8: The sense of the Hebrew text of v. 8b is poor: Targ. gives 'stupidity' (יבערו) the nuance of 'sinfulness', 'The peoples are guilty, one and all' (יחובון). The unintelligible עץ מוסר הבלים is explained as, 'and have worshipped idols which are unreal'. Pesh. ('False teachings concerning a piece of wood will both perish and come to an end') is apparently an attempt to solve the problem of the grammatical subject of יבערו ויכסלו by making מוסר הבלים the subject (p. 224).

10.18: Targ. explains הנני קולע את יושבי הארץ with a full-dress simile and supplies an object for ימצאו : 'Just as one slings stones with a catapult, I will scatter the inhabitants of the land at this time and will oppress them that they may receive retribution for their sins' (p. 230).

13.27: Targ. generalizes the sexual imagery (נאפיך ומצהלותיך זמת זנותך): 'Your follies and mad deeds, your schemes to commit sins of fornication.' זמה has given trouble to the versions and Targ. has taken it as synonymous with מזמה 'plan' (cf. Aq. εννοια 'intention') (p. 312).

14.8b,9a: Kimchi notices that Targ. has avoided the bold anthropomorphisms and anthropopathisms of MT. Targ. has transferred to Israel the similes which were applied to Yahweh. 'Why does your anger alight on us?' has no corresponding elements in MT, but otherwise MT is deliberately changed: 'We are like immigrants in the land and like travellers who turn aside to find lodging for the night. Why does your anger alight on us? We are fickle and apostate, but you are a mighty man able to save. Your Shekinah is in our midst, O Lord, and we are called by your name. Do not desert us.' The boldness of the language of MT and the affront which it offered to Yahweh's majesty were unacceptable to Targ. This stands somewhat apart from the other examples which have been cited, because the operation of theological scruples is more influential in determining the form of Targ. (p. 321).

14.19: Targ. puts a theological interpretation on the imagery of sickness, chastisement and lack of healing: 'We expected well-being, but no good came to us; we expected a time of forgiveness of sins, but retribution for our sins came.'

15.16: The 'eating' of Yahweh's words is explained as the 'implementing' (קיימתינון) of them.

16.16: Targ. simply reproduces the 'hunting' figure, but it interprets the 'fishing' imagery in terms of invasion and military carnage: 'I will send murderous nations and they will slaughter you'.

20.9: This is an unusual case, where Targ. supplies another metaphor for the metaphor of MT. 'Fire imprisoned in the bones' (MT) is replaced by the figure of an overwhelming flood and עצר בעצמתי is rendered as שטפין ית גרמי.

23.15 (9.14): The figure in MT of a meal of poisonous herbs washed down by a poisonous draught is explained, and its reference foreclosed by fully developed similes: 'I am bringing on them distress as bitter as a poisonous herb, and I shall cause them to drink a cup of curse as deadly as a serpent's poison' (also at 9.14).

23.19: Both Pesh. and Targ. offer an interpretation of the metaphor of 'storm' (סערה) rather than preserving it in their renderings. Thus Pesh. interprets it as 'judgement', 'Yahweh's judgement has issued in anger', and חמה is incorporated into the grammar by means of beth (brwgz'). Similarly וסער מתחולל is rendered by wsw'rn' mtgwzl: the whirlwind is interpreted as a judgement which is being kindled. Targ. renders סערה as מזופיתא 'rebuke', and employs the same device as Pesh. with חמה (ברגז), but it retains the figure of 'whirlwind' in its translation of וסער מתחולל (ועלעול משתגש).

There are some further features of Targ. worthy of mention, beginning with a small group which involves comparisons of Targ. and Sept.:

9.7: Sept. has an unusually free and periphrastic rendering at the end of the verse; in the manner of Targ. ובקרבו ישים ארבו is interpreted and generalized rather than translated. The figure of laying an ambush for someone while affecting benevolence is lost and is replaced by a more prosaic statement, καὶ ἐν ἑαυτῷ ἔχει τὴν ἔχθραν, 'and within himself he harbours hostility' (p. 203).

11.19: The rendering of Targ. appears to be related to that of Sept. (ἐμβάλωμεν), and we should accept it as a clue to the sense of Sept. Targ. 'Let us cast lethal poison into his food' suggests that the 'wood' (ξύλον) of Sept. is a poisonous substance, and that what is indicated by Sept. is an attempt to poison the prophet (p. 257).

14.13: Sept. (ἐπὶ τῆς γῆς καὶ ἐν τῷ τόπῳ τούτῳ) expands במקום הזה. This is hardly to be explained as a conflate text with variant renderings of במקום הזה: (a) ἐπι τῆς γῆς (ταύτης) and (*b*) ἐν τῷ τόπῳ τούτῳ. It is rather a 'Targumic' feature in Sept.: it arises from an awareness that מקום could refer to 'land' or 'temple', and by spelling out this ambivalence Sept. preserves a precise equation of במקום הזה with the temple to which ἐν τῷ τόπῳ τούτῳ must refer in its expanded text (p. 325).

17.6: The question should be raised whether there is any relation between Targ.'s exegesis of ארץ מלחה (כארץ סדום 'like the land of Sodom') and Sept.'s rendering of חררים (ἐν ἁλίμοις 'at the seashore'). Sept. may have had the region of the Dead Sea in mind (cf. ארץ מלחה) (p. 390).

The final examples are varied and cannot be grouped under any head:

1.5: Targ. establishes a connection between the גוים of v. 5 (also 1.10) and the oracles against foreign nations. The representation that Jeremiah is to give the nations 'a cup of curse' to drink is the same as that found in 25.15 (Targ.) in connection with the cup of Yahweh's wrath.

1.10: Targ. allocates the constructive part of Jeremiah's ministry to Israel (לבנות ולנטוע) and the destructive part to the גוים : 'I have appointed you over the idolatrous Gentiles to root out and pull down' (p. 10).

3.2 (4.11): Targ. and Pesh. have approximately the same renderings of שפים (נגדין '(mountain) passes'; *šbyl'* 'paths'), and Targ.'s variant (נגרין 'gutters', 'channels') is the foundation of Rash's explanation of שפים : יבלי מים 'channels of water' (p. 59). At 4.11 Targ. has a more complicated paraphrase of שפיים על רישי נגדין דמיין במדבר (במדבר, Sperber). This may represent a double rendering of שפיים (נגדין ; רישי), but in any case דמיין presupposes נגרין (*Miqra'ot Gᵉdolot*) not נגדין. דמיין may be an expansion whose function is to establish the rightness of נגרין over against נגדין (p. 97).

5.3: Targ. changes the sense of the verse fundamentally by supposing that the opening words are indicative of Yahweh's intention to reward the righteous, and it then applies to the wicked the reference to chastisement and unresponsiveness. The figurative ולא חלו, 'but they did not feel pain', is interpreted as 'but they did not repent'.

6.13; 18.18: In both passages נביא is rendered by ספר 'scribe', and this may be connected with the scruple shown by Targ. in reproducing any damaging comments about prophets: pejorative references to prophets are explicitly attributed to 'false prophets'. The different procedure in these two passages may be related to the circumstance that there are indications of friction and conflict between Jeremiah and the סופרים in two passages (2.8 and 8.8f.). The latter refers to falsifications perpetrated by

scribes in the same way as 6.13 speaks of prophets and priests
(p. 436).

16.13 (5.19): Targ. renders ‏ועבדתם שם אלהים אחרים‎ (16.13)
in more or less the same way as it renders ‏תעבדו זרים‎ (5.19):
'And you will be subject there to nations which are worshippers
of idols.' There is little doubt that ‏זרים‎ (5.19) refers to foreign
rulers and that Targ.'s exegesis is on the right lines. The question
is why did Targ. apply this to 16.13, where it was patently
wrong?. The reason for this may have been theological scruple:
an unwillingness to represent that Yahweh had condemned his
people to idolatry. The way of escape taken by Targ. was to lean
on the Hebrew text of 5.19 (‏זרים‎), and its rendering there.

25.38: Targ. has, 'because of the hostile sword which is like
intoxicating wine', over against MT ‏מפני חרון חרון היונה‎. ‏חרב‎
'sword' has the support of some Hebrew manuscripts and of
Sept., but it is unlikely that Targ.'s rendering attests a Hebrew
text other than MT. The explanation is rather that the rendering
of 25.38 has been harmonized with those of 46.16 and 50.16,
where MT reads ‏מפני חרב היונה‎ (p. 655).

B. The Prose of Chapters 1–25: Linguistic Arguments.

These matters have been considered in detail in the body of the
commentary, with particular reference to two approaches
differing in character, one by W. Thiel (*Die deuteronomistische
Redaktion von Jeremia 1–25*, 1973) and the other by H.
Weippert (*Die Prosareden des Jeremiabuches*, BZAW 132,
1973). It would be uneconomical to traverse fully the same
ground again, but an indication of the places where the
contributions of Thiel and Weippert have been discussed will be
followed by a general assessment of the significance of their work
and an appraisal of their methods.

Thiel: 1.10 (p. 13); 1.11–16 (p. 21); 7.1–15 (pp. 164–166);
7.16–20 (p. 171); 7.21–29 (p. 177); 7.30–8.3 (p. 182); 8.19c
(p. 194); 9.11–15 (pp. 205f.); 11.17 (p. 252); 12.14–17 (p. 282);
16.10–13 (p. 369); 18.7–10 (p. 424); 18.11f. (p. 424); 19.2–9
(p. 450); 21.8–10 (pp. 503f.); 22.2–5 (p. 515); 22.17f. (p. 527);
22.24–27 (pp. 542f.); 22.30 (p. 551); 23.3f. (p. 559); 23.7f.
(p. 565); 23.17 (p. 579); 23.32 (p. 595); 24.6f. (pp. 614f.);
25.1–13 (p. 630).

The series of infinitives in 1.10 is found in other passages
(18.7,9; 31.28) which Thiel identifies as D passages (the work of
a Deuteronomistic redactor of Jer 1–25). This will be described
as an 'internal argument' in order to distinguish it from the
logically different procedure of comparing prose in Jer 1–25 with
prose in the book of Deuteronomy and the Deuteronomistic

historical literature. Another example of a largely internal argument is 1.16 which depends on the identification of groups of D passages: for ודברתי משפטי 4.12, 12.1, 39.5, 52.9 (2 Kgs 25.6); for ויקטרו לאלהים אחרים 19.3f., 2 Kgs 22.17, Jer 44.3,7f. I shall endeavour to indicate to what extent Thiel's arguments are internally organized:

Internal Arguments: 1.10; 1.16; 7.17f.; 7.22; 9.11–13; 12.14–17; 18.7–10; 22.2–5; 22.30; 23.7f.; 23.32; 25.1–13.

Largely or partly internal arguments: 7.1–15; 7.23; 7.24–26; 8.19c; 9.15; 16.10–13; 18.11; 19.2–9; 22.24–27; 23.3f.; 24.6f.

Weippert's objective is to establish that the prose of the prose discourses in the book of Jeremiah has special features which set it apart from the prose of the book of Deuteronomy and the Deuteronomistic historical literature. This is pursued in the following ways: (*a*) By demonstrating that prose vocabulary and word-strings peculiar to the book of Jeremiah can be identified. (*b*) By showing that apparent similarities between the prose of the book of Jeremiah and Deuteronomic-Deuteronomistic prose do not stand up to closer examination, because a distinctive function is attributable to the prose vocabulary and word-strings of the book of Jeremiah. (*c*) By establishing that the vocabulary of the poetry of the book of Jeremiah can be discerned in prose passages. I shall argue presently that (*c*) does not necessarily support the conclusion that the same author is responsible for poetry and prose, and I shall maintain that another explanation is to be preferred. Weippert supposes that all these arguments lead to the conclusion that the historical prophet Jeremiah was largely the author of the prose of the discourses. The principal places in the commentary where Weippert's book is considered are as follows:

1.10 (p. 13); 7.1–15 (p. 165, pp. 166–167); 7.3–5,13 (p. 167); 11.1–14 (pp. 241f.); 11.12 (p. 243); 14.11–16 (pp. 326–327); 16.1–4 (pp. 362–363); 16.10–13 (p. 372); 18.1–12 (pp. 423–424); 19 (p. 456); 21.8–10 (pp. 504–505); 22.24–27 (pp. 543f.); 23.25–32 (pp. 596–597); 24.6 (p. 615); 24.9 (p. 615); 24.10 (p. 615); 25.1–14 (pp. 628–629).

In the first place it should be said that a purely lexicographical argument will not enable us to answer the questions which are raised by Thiel and Weippert, and to which they give different answers. An examination of the relations between poetry and prose in the book of Jeremiah may have the form of a general lexicographical enquiry in which an attempt is made to examine the stock of vocabulary which is common to poetry and prose. Such an investigation (cf. W. L. Holladay, *JBL* 79, 1960, pp. 351–367) may be controlled by an assumption different from the one of Weippert noted above, namely that the poetry is a reservoir for the prose. Thus the title of Holladay's article is 'Prototypes and Copies'. This does not commit us to the view that all the poetry is attributable to the prophet Jeremiah and that none of the prose is attributable to him, or that the prose is always later than the poetry. In so far, however, as we assert that the poetry is a reservoir for the prose we are implying that the author(s) of the prose is distinct from the author(s) of the poetry, and we are disagreeing with the interpretation which Weippert places on the appearance of common vocabulary in poetry and prose (see below, p. 167). This is not a disagreement which can be explored and settled by linguistic arguments, because it hinges on the particular view which is taken of the processes of growth and composition which produced the extant book of Jeremiah.

The assertion that narrow, lexicographical arguments will not enable us to decide questions about the prose of the book of Jeremiah or relations between poetry and prose may seem to be contradicted by the pronounced lexicographical orientation of the books of Thiel and Weippert. The attention which they have given to linguistic details is striking and their arguments appear to rest on lexicographical foundations. There is a sense in which this is true, but a more significant and profound sense in which it is untrue. When close attention is devoted to these books, it becomes evident that methods so incompatible are being employed that they must necessarily lead to conflicting conclusions. The clearest and simplest expression of this is given where Thiel is evaluating prose vocabulary which is exclusive to the book of Jeremiah, or which, for the most part, does not appear elsewhere (the 'internal argument') and that is why I have taken the trouble to lay these passages out. Thiel classifies this prose as Deuteronomistic and assigns it to an editor or redactor of Jeremiah 1–25 (D). This involves arguments which are logically different from those which he uses when he is establishing affinities between the prose vocabulary of the book of Jeremiah and the vocabulary of Deuteronomy or the Deuteronomistic historical books. The latter operation may be fairly described as a linguistic one and can be appraised as such: we can examine the alleged parallels and make up our minds about Thiel's account of the resemblances, and the interpretations which he places on them. It is in this area that the critical engagement between Weippert and Thiel is most fruitful, and it is here that her methods and concerns are most unambiguously lexicographical and semantic. This is a comparative activity which principally involves lexicographical skills and a range of linguistic judgements.

So far as Weippert's intention is to impose more refined

evaluations on crude statistics her contribution is valuable. There is a danger of making too much of comparisons of vocabulary in the prose of the book of Jeremiah, on the one hand, and the book of Deuteronomy and the Deuteronomistic historical literature on the other. If these comparisons are too general, they do not possess the significance which is sometimes attached to them, and there is a skill involved in deciding when they are sufficiently particular to enable us to raise the question of direct literary connections. If no more is being done than the cataloguing of isolated items of vocabulary (single words) common to the two areas being compared, there is a danger of assembling statistics which are insignificant or have only a minimal significance, and are not capable of supporting the arguments into which they are pressed. This is so, even if the vocabulary in question occurs only or principally in the prose of Jeremiah, Deuteronomy and the Deuteronomistic historical literature. It is reasonable to regard this as a significant statistic, but to decide what kind or degree of significance is to be attached to it is a matter of the greatest difficulty. It may express affinities which are to be expressed in terms of a cultural and theological consensus and which are sufficiently broad not to be limited to one organized party or movement.

Identical phrases or word-strings in different bodies of literature present similarities with a higher degree of particularity, on the basis of which questions about literary connections can reasonably be asked. Thiel's arguments for the Deuteronomic or Deuteronomistic affiliations of the prose of the book of Jeremiah are often of this kind, and the counter-arguments of Weippert probe for differences in nuance or function, despite a general appearance of resemblance or even identity. The degree of distinctiveness possessed by such word-strings is an important consideration: the extent to which they have striking idiomatic qualities enhances the probability that a special significance should be attached to them, and that they point to direct literary relationships. This is more than terminological identity, because equations involving several items of vocabulary in a string do not, if the vocabulary is ordinary and the manner of grammatical association pedestrian, enable us to conclude that there is a particular literary relationship between the bodies of literature in which they occur. We may find that we have not transcended the generality and relative insignificance of statistics which consist in the cataloguing of individual items of vocabulary common to different bodies of literature.

The most interesting aspect of Weippert's treatment of parallels which are supposed to demonstrate the terminological dependence of the prose of the book of Jeremiah on Deuteronomy and the Deuteronomistic historical literature is the attention she devotes to the semantic functioning of the same vocabulary in different contexts, and the method which she develops for discerning distinctions of nuance and function which disengage terminology in the one body of literature from identical terminology in the other. This is an exegetical interest and is a way of refining and enriching statistics which consist simply of the listing of items of vocabulary common to different bodies of literature. To put the matter simply, the same word may not be used in the same way or have precisely the same sense. It may be that Weippert tries too hard to drive a wedge between the prose of the book of Jeremiah and Deuteronomic-Deuteronomistic prose: the concern becomes all-consuming and there is a tendency to create too fine distinctions. Even where lexicographical nuances are genuine, it does not follow that an absolute semantic distinction between an item of vocabulary in the prose of the book of Jeremiah and the same item in Deuteronomic-Deuteronomistic literature has been established, so that all postulated connections have to be severed.

There are positive and negative judgements which may be attached to Weippert's work. On the negative side it can be said that her methods are not capable of supporting the conclusion which she intends to reach. Her objective is to show that the *Prosareden* are, for the most part, examples of the prose style of the prophet Jeremiah. It would need arguments finely tempered and of striking particularity to achieve this, and it is unlikely that the available evidence, however superbly marshalled, could support such a conclusion. Between a demonstration that there are differences of nuance and function in lexical items common to different bodies of literature and the bold assertion that the distinctiveness of the prose speeches in the book of Jeremiah is nothing less than the prose style of an individual prophet a great gulf is fixed (cf. below, p. 457).

The positive aspect of Weippert's approach is that it woos us away from a too great preoccupation with the Deuteronomic-Deuteronomistic connections of the prose of the book of Jeremiah. Mention was made earlier (above, p. xliii) of the methodological conflict between Thiel and Weippert. The latter might seem to have the better of the engagement, since from her point of view Thiel has a way of arguing which amounts to heads I win and tails you lose. The absence of parallels to prose vocabulary of the book of Jeremiah in Deuteronomy and the Deuteronomistic literature does not deter him from identifying this prose as Deuteronomic or Deuteronomistic. A state of affairs which for her is evidence of distinctive, Jeremianic prose is explained by him as the vocabulary of a Deuteronomistic editor or redactor of the book of Jeremiah. If the prose of the book of Jeremiah has external affiliations, he uses these to demonstrate that it is Deuteronomic or Deuteronomistic and is the work of D. If it does not have these external connections, he still maintains that it derives from this editor, but the argument is internal to the prose of the book of Jeremiah and might be regarded as an argument in a circle. It depends on identifying affinities between different passages of prose, their constitution as a group, and the conclusion that they all have the marks of D. This is a case which is built up gradually by proceeding from one passage to another, and it has cumulative force only if one agrees with every step in the argument. It leans heavily on the identification of the literary habits of D, on a claim to discern his attitudes and objectives which sometimes seems exaggerated, and on the assumption that D's work has a comprehensive and systematic character. I shall return presently to the contention that 'compositions' by D are a feature of the prose passages of the book of Jeremiah and that D is guided by broad overarching principles of composition.

An attempt should be made to overcome the antitheses which arise from the confrontation of the respective methods of Thiel and Weippert. It does not seem reasonable to deny that there are affinities between Jeremianic prose and Deuteronomic-Deuteronomistic prose, but a precise definition of these connections will be difficult to achieve. Where prose vocabulary appears in the book of Jeremiah but not in the Deuteronomic-Deuteronomistic literature, the significance of this state of affairs should not be magnified, and the same holds good for vocabulary common to these bodies of literature but differing in nuance as between one and the other. It is not so surprising that these differences in nuance are discernible, because the prose of the book of Jeremiah is influenced by the *corpus* of which it is part and serves the special characteristics and interests of that *corpus*. Again the interpretation which Weippert places on the prose vocabulary which is special to the book of Jeremiah is not necessarily the right one. Even if one leaves out of the reckoning the supposition that this evidence points to Jeremiah's authorship of the prose, there is still a question whether an emphasis on the 'apartness' of this prose over against Deuteronomic-Deuteronomistic prose is not too much influenced by the apologetic concern of Weippert's work. Instead of driving a wedge between prose vocabulary special to the book of Jeremiah and Deuteronomic-Deuteronomistic prose, it would be entirely reasonable to conclude that the book of

Jeremiah increases and enriches our archive of Deuteronomic-Deuteronomistic prose.

I have insinuated the word *corpus* into the discussion and I must ask that for the time being it should be taken on trust. What is intended by it will not be transparent, until the view of the growth and composition of the book of Jeremiah (1–25) which has arisen from the commentary is explained in a subsequent section of the Introduction. For the time being, in relation to the present discussion, I shall urge that there is a nucleus of the book of Jeremiah which is distinctive, so that the prose which is generated by it, in connection with the processes of growth and aggregation which result in our extant book, is, to a greater or lesser degree, influenced by this distinctiveness. Hence we might expect vocabulary identical with it in the Deuteronomic-Deuteronomistic literature to have different nuances in Jeremiah, because it serves the interests of a *corpus* which has its own particular character and orientation.

The time has come—and this is a departure which Weippert has made—to concentrate more on the internal relations of the constituents of the book of Jeremiah and to be less bothered about comparisons between the prose of the prose discourses of the book of Jeremiah and the prose of other bodies of Old Testament literature. This is not intended as a denial that there are significant resemblances between Jeremianic and Deuteronomic-Deuteronomistic prose, and it is not a statement which arises out of an apologetic concern to demonstrate that the prose of the book of Jeremiah is different from Deuteronomic-Deuteronomistic prose. It gives expression to a view that arguments about which labels are to be attached to the prose of chapters 1–25, while they possess historical and critical importance, may distract us from matters which are more central to the study of the book, namely, the internal relations of its constituent parts. A correct appreciation of how the prose functions in the Jeremianic *corpus* and how it serves the ends of that *corpus* is more important than the attachment of particular labels to it. As matters stand, with continuous cross-references to Deuteronomic-Deuteronomistic prose the fashion of scholarship, one is always in danger of succumbing to a condition of distraction and disorientation.

C. Compositions by D and his comprehensive redaction of 1–25 (Thiel)

I have noted that Hyatt is a forerunner of Thiel, and while Rudolph's interest in Deuteronomic editing has also been noticed in the commentary, his attachment to a source theory (below,

p. lxxxiv) sets his work in a different frame. Thiel's book represents the most detailed and sustained exposition of this kind and it will be advantageous to focus attention on it. How appropriate is Thiel's approach and what degree of explanatory power does it possess to solve the problems which are thrown up by the dispositions of literary material in Jer 1–25? The passages in connection with which Thiel's work has been discussed are set out below. A division is made between shorter and longer postulated Deuteronomistic compositions: this will make clear that D's activity is represented as ranging from the organization of short pieces to an overall concern with the shape of Jer 1–25 and the superimposition of a comprehensive interpretation. It will also make for easier identification of the targets of the criticisms which are attached.

Shorter Passages: 2.20 (p. 41); 4.3f. (pp. 88–89); 6.16–21 (p. 149); 7.16–20 (pp. 171–172); 7.21–29 (p. 177); 12.14–17 (pp. 282–283); 16.10–13, 16–18 (p. 373); 17.19–27 (p. 417); 21.1f. (p. 495); 22.8f. (pp. 521, 522); 22.25–27 (pp. 540, 542–544); 23.1–4 (pp. 555–557); 25.1–7 (pp. 621).

Longer Passages: 7.1–15 (pp. 164, 165); 7.1–8.3 (p. 182); 11.1–14 (pp. 241f.); 13.1–11 (p. 291); 18.1–12* (pp. 424, 425, 426); 19 (p. 446); 19.2–13* (p. 450); 21.1–10 (pp. 493, 494, 495); 21–23.8 (p. 542); 21–24 (pp. 568, 613); 21.11–24 (p. 495); 24 (pp. 612–613); 1.1–25.13 (p. 630).

First it should be said that Thiel is right in representing that the book of Jeremiah has arrived at its extant form as a consequence of long and complicated processes of growth. Hence I have an area of agreement with Thiel which I do not share with Weippert, but, on the other hand, my study of 1–25 has uncovered processes of growth of a different kind from those described by Thiel, and these results will be gathered together in the next section of the Introduction. For the present it will suffice to say that the extra-linguistic concern of Weippert, which influenced the organization and interpretation of her lexicographical material, was to attribute the *Prosareden* to the prophet Jeremiah. The extra-linguistic, higher-critical perception which persuades me of her wrongness is that her conclusions do not engage seriously with the problems raised by the inner relations of the constituent parts of 1–25 which arise out of the processes of growth and composition. We are dealing with a complicated, untidy accumulation of material, extending over a very long period and to which many people have contributed. The supposition that a major part of it, including much of the prose, was already in existence in the lifetime of the prophet Jeremiah is a literary judgement which does not seem to take serious account of the vexatious difficulties and baffling inconcinnities which emerge with a detailed study of the book (see below, p. 240).

In this regard Thiel's handling of the material is more realistic and profound: he gives a prominent place to a Deuteronomistic redaction, and he allows for post-Deuteronomistic accretions of small and large (the oracles against foreign nations) scope. He has a grasp of the long period of time over which the book was in the process of formation. The concept of a Jeremianic *corpus*, which I have adumbrated and will further develop, is incompatible with the cohesiveness and architectonic qualities which Thiel has attributed to 1–25 in view of the editorial operations of D. My particular appeal to *corpus* is not a claim that 1–25 is a well-ordered, literary whole, with a cumulative, teleological significance. Rather it is introduced with the caveat (and in this I confront Thiel) that there is a tendency to underestimate the untidy and desultory nature of the aggregation of material which comprises the book of Jeremiah. One does not have to look far for this: it is not only a lack of large-scale homogeneousness to which I refer, but sharp dissonances of form and content, and examples of erroneous, secondary exegesis, consisting of only a few verses. My recurring criticism of the passages involving Thiel's interpretation which I have laid out above has been that he consistently exaggerates their cohesiveness and coherence. This holds for the small units which he describes as compositions of D no less than the larger editorial complexes which he postulates. He attributes to D comprehensive editorial intentions and policies, and systematic theological principles, which I cannot gather from the text. I am convinced that there is a danger of calling into existence a Deuteronomistic editor, investing him with an editorial policy, determining the contours of his mind, and requiring the prose of 1–25 to be amenable to this hypothesis.

I introduce the idea of *corpus* along with what might seem to be a counter-assertion that the processes which brought about the final product are only partially understood by us, that our explanations have to be tentative, and that we err when we suppose that these processes are always susceptible of rational explanation, or that they must necessarily contribute to a thoughtful, systematic redaction. The objection may be lodged that such an idea of *corpus* is ambiguous, vague and ill-defined, and the only defence which I can offer is that it has helped me to pick my way through the minefield of Jer 1–25. My argument is that there is no comprehensive framework of literary arrangement or theological system within which the parts of 1–25 are fitted together, and that the prose does not supply such a scaffolding. There is more of accident, arbitrariness and fortuitous twists and turns than has been generally allowed for. The processes are dark and in a measure irrecoverable, and we should not readily assume them to possess such rationality that they will yield to a systematic elucidation.

The kinds of impetus which produce growth and enlarge a pre-existing nucleus of Jeremianic material are not necessarily related to a grand, theological scheme and perhaps do not extend beyond narrow contextual limits. The 'trigger' may consist of no more than a single verse or a few verses; the expansion may have no more than a narrow, localized exegetical intention. It may be entirely innocent of the comprehensive, systematic theological objectives which it is customary to seek in the prose of 1–25. We must take more account of expansions of such limited scope in our efforts to understand the processes by which the Jeremianic *corpus* was developed. A type of expansion which consists of commentary on small pieces of text has been neglected. In so far as the growth of the *corpus* has been achieved by accretions of this kind, we should not expect too much coherence or artistic unity from the end product. Nevertheless, even if this amounts to a weak sense of *corpus*, the use of this term is justified in so far as my contention is that the growth of 1–25 is generated and its shape, to a greater or lesser degree, determined by the pre-existing Jeremianic content which triggers it. This idea of a 'rolling *corpus*' can be illustrated in its various aspects by the work done in the body of the commentary, and the next task is to draw all this together.

D. The idea of a rolling *corpus*

1. Information about the nature of expansions gathered from a comparison of a shorter (Sept.) and a longer (MT) text.

This task has been completed in A.1 and especially in A.1(*c*) (pp. xviii–xxi). The advantage of having a foundation in the comparison of *actual* texts cannot be overestimated. The main concern of this enterprise is not to recover an 'original' Hebrew text, but to explore the possibilities of uncovering the history of the Hebrew text. Hence the principal questions which I have asked are these: What do the differences between Sept. and MT tell us about the history of the Hebrew text of Jer 1–25? Is it possible to ascertain which of them represents a more original condition of the Hebrew text? Is Sept. a witness to a different and shorter text than MT, or is there only one Hebrew text to be recovered (MT) from which Sept. is derived by processes of abridgement and modification? I have concluded that Sept. gives us access to a Hebrew text which is shorter than MT, and so enables us to identify expansions of the Hebrew text in the period which lies between the Hebrew *Vorlage* of Sept. and MT. This is a conclusion which is not free from assumptions, but, even so, there is no firmer method than this and none which is so disciplined by objective control, and it is the right point of departure for the examination of the concept of a rolling *corpus*. There is a proximity to the facts which no other method possesses: the examination of extant texts and the observing of differences between them. The intention is not to assert that a higher criticism should never override these indications, or be pursued when it contradicts them, but its procedures are necessarily more speculative and are not controlled by such hard evidence. One should require a particularly sharp argument before assenting to a speculative kind of criticism which contradicts the indications of a more solid, textual evidence.

The expansions considered in detail in A.1(*c*) are often scribal rather than editorial. They have exegetical, interpretative, harmonizing functions, and they do not look beyond the small pieces of text to which they are attached, in some cases individual verses. Other expansions (e.g. 25.1–7; 8–14) can be associated with a broader editorial intention, but not with an overarching editorial plan or a systematic theological tendency. It would be unnatural to interpret the examples of additions to the shorter text of Sept. discussed in A.1(*c*) as evidence of a systematic process of redaction.

2. Similar types of expansions postulated by me for MT without a foundation in textual criticism.

This is necessarily a more chancy procedure. It is an attempt to add to the evidence for a rolling *corpus* by identifying additions similar in kind to those collected in A.1(*c*) which, however, are not indicated as additions in MT by a shorter text in Sept. I am guided by the experience gained from A.1(*c*), and alerted to the possibility that a similar pattern of secondary expansion was already present in the Hebrew *Vorlage* of Sept., so that no process of textual comparison as between MT and Sept. will disclose it. These results rest on nothing more than my judgement and critical acumen; on my nose for secondary processes of expansion which have been superimposed on a shorter, more original, Hebrew text:

5.11: The entire verse should perhaps fall under suspicion. It has been interpolated by someone who wanted a reference in the round to apostasy in both kingdoms. It is a secondary generalizing of an account which concerned the children of mother Jerusalem in particular (p. 118).

6.12b: כי אתה את ידי על ישבי הארץ נאם יהוה should be regarded as a secondary intrusion, and there is nothing corresponding to it in the parallel passage (8.10–12). Verses

12–15 are then a continuation of Jeremiah's speech which consists of vv. 10–15 (p. 144).

8.19c: מדוע הכעיסוני בפסליהם בהבלי נכר creates an impression of formal dissonance in an otherwise cohesive lament. A so-called 'oracular' response interposed between parts of an otherwise continuous lament should be regarded as a secondary disturbing feature (p. 193).

9.25: The intrusive element which produces inconsistency is the entire clause (כי ... ערלי לב) which is therefore secondary and erroneous exegetical development (p. 214).

11.1–5: Verse 2 and the opening words of v. 3 (שמעו ... עליהם) cannot be accommodated to the form of vv. 1–5. They betray a misunderstanding of the nature of vv. 3–5 and are an intrusion. The historical retrospect in vv. 4–5 (אשר צויתי ... כיום הזה), which sets the response at a distance from the curse, may also be secondary (pp. 236–237).

11.10: בית ישראל is exegetical expansion in the interests of comprehensiveness (p. 239).

14.18: כי גם נביא גם כהן סחרו אל ארץ ולא ידעו is prose rather than poetry and does not cohere well with the earlier part of v. 18. It is probably intrusive and is intended to supplement a description of distress, envisaged as parallel to 14.2–6 and leading on to vv. 19–22 (p. 330).

14.22: The verse is not obviously related to the topics of the prayer in 14.20f. It is perhaps an addition with a didactic, theological tendency which betrays the influence of the background of drought in the earlier lament (14.1–10; p. 332).

21.7: The shorter Hebrew text postulated does not follow the indications of Sept. except for ואת העם הנשארים. 'Nebuchadrezzar' is the grammatical subject of the verbs, and וביד איביהם (cf. Jerome) and וביד מבקשי נפשם is secondary expansion, perhaps on the basis of such passages as 19.7, 34.21 and 44.30 (p. 501).

23.17: If v. 17 is to be accommodated to the assumption that vv. 16–22 are direct address, למנאצי is more appropriate than למנאצי דבר יהוה. There is no textual evidence for the deletion of דבר יהוה, but it should be regarded as a secondary, exegetical element whose function is to make explicit that שלום יהיה לכם was spoken in Yahweh's name. In that case למנאצי (MT) preserves the original text and the pointing of MT (דְּבֶר יהוה) correctly indicates the intention of the insertion (p. 577).

23.19: חמה is a gloss showing the same interpretation of סערה as is present in Pesh. and Targ.—an interpretation readily suggested by אף יהוה in v. 20 (p. 582).

24.5,8: Yahweh is disclosing his will to the prophet by means of a vision, and the prophet is giving an account of his experience. The emphasis falls on this disclosure, achieved by dialogue, and not on a responsibility laid on the prophet to communicate God's word to the people. Hence כה אמר יהוה אלהי ישראל is inapposite, because what follows in v. 5 is an explanation of the vision for the benefit of the prophet and not a message which he is required to communicate. כי of כי כה אמר יהוה (v. 8) is not represented by Sept. and כה אמר יהוה is located in corresponding places at v. 5 and v. 8 (before כתאנים at v. 5 and in connection with כתאנים הרעות at v. 8). The intrusive character of כה אמר יהוה אלהי ישראל at v. 5 is more marked because of its redundancy after ויהי דבר יהוה אלי לאמר (v. 4), but כי כה אמר יהוה is probably a related phenomenon and also a secondary intrusion (pp. 608, 609).

3. The 'kernel' idea

This does not make a big contribution to the rolling *corpus* concept and it has no novelty as a critical method. It was associated particularly with an interest in distinguishing between what was 'genuine' and 'ungenuine' in prophetic books (cf. W. McKane, *SVT* 32, 1981, p. 229), and in that case the objective was to recover the *ipsissima verba* of a prophet (the kernel) and to focus attention on them. There was less concern, or even an absence of concern, for the accretions in which the *ipsissima verba* were said to be embedded: the recovery of the 'original' text rather than the shape of the extant text was the consuming critical interest. I have indicated that my preoccupation with the recovery of a shorter, more original Hebrew text is not, for the most part, allied to a policy of making deletions from MT. It is associated rather with a curiosity about the history of the Hebrew text, and with attempts to reconstruct that history in order to enhance our understanding of the extant text. I have made the heading of this section sufficiently general ('kernel' rather than 'Jeremianic kernel') to show that my treatment of 'kernel' is not necessarily connected with the recovery of the *ipsissima verba* of the prophet Jeremiah, but is directed towards the identification of a core, whether or not it is a Jeremianic core. It is an attempt to discern how additional material has been aggregated and organized in relation to that core.

My attitudes to some of material taken from other scholars and set out in this section have been unfavourable, and my reactions have been negative. I have divided the discussions which appear in the commentary into three parts: (*a*) Scholars other than Thiel (*b*) Thiel's contributions (*c*) Applications of the 'kernel' idea which are, for the most part, my own and which contribute to the rolling *corpus* idea.

livCOMMENTARY ON JEREMIAH

(a) References to Jeremianic kernels contained in the commentary, involving scholars other than Thiel:

3.14–18, Peake (p. 75); 7.1–15, Skinner (p. 164); 11.1–14, Skinner (p. 246); 12.14–17, Cornill (pp. 281f.); 16.1–9, Duhm (p. 368); 16.16–18, Rudolph (p. 377); 20.1–6, Holladay (p. 463); 23.33–40, Duhm (p. 602); 24, Erbt (p. 612); 25.15–29, Nicholson (p. 644).

(b) Thiel's identifications and reconstructions of Jeremianic kernels embedded in compositions of D:

7.1–15 (pp. 164f.); 7.16–20 (pp. 171–172); 7.21–29 (p. 177); 11.18–12.6 (p. 254); 13.10f (p. 287); 13.12–14 (p. 297); 15.1–4 (p. 336); 16.1–9 (p. 362); 21.1–10 (pp. 494, 497, 503); 22.28–30 (pp. 548–552); 24: an experiment which Thiel decides is unsuccessful. He opts for a D composition through and through (p. 612).

Thiel's identifications of D kernels in post-Deuteronomistic compositions: 25.1–7 (p. 621); 25.8–13 (p. 626).

The kernel idea is a feature of the rigour of Thiel's investigation of the prose of 1–25 which has received detailed treatment in the commentary. Its distinguishing mark is that a Jeremianic kernel is envisaged as embedded in compositions of D. Admiration for Thiel's thoroughness and critical acumen is mixed with an attitude of scepticism towards the compositions of D which he describes and the Jeremianic kernels which he isolates. Nevertheless, Thiel's critical instinct is right: there is a minimal explanatory power in the assertion that the 'gist' of a passage is Jeremianic, or that it has a Jeremianic core. This is the statement of a problem rather than the formulation of a hypothesis; one must persist in order to improve on such a weak generalization, which explains little or nothing, by effecting a literary-critical separation and identifying the Jeremianic core. Otherwise the generalization is not worth making. From this point of view I do not find Rudolph and Nicholson helpful, where they say that the 'gist' of a passage is attributable to Jeremiah, but make no effort to identify this core (Rudolph: 16.1–9; p. 362; 17.19–27, p. 417; 18.1–6, p. 420; Nicholson: 16.1–9, p. 362; 24, p. 612).

(c) The kernel as a contribution to the rolling *corpus* idea:

7.1–15: The core consists of vv. 4, 9*, 10*, 11*, 12, 14* and it focuses on the temple. It has been expanded and elaborated by the insinuation of a different theme (possession/loss of the land). Only at vv. 1f. and 13 is there support from Sept. for a text shorter than MT, but the identification of a kernel is to be regarded as an attempt to elucidate the character of the extant text and to show how it developed, rather than to recover an 'original' text by making deletions from MT. The core is to be attributed to the prophet Jeremiah, but it is impossible to ascertain whether his own words have been preserved (pp. 164f.).

10.1–16: We know of a Hebrew text which did not have vv. 6–8, 10, and we also know from 4QJer[b] and Sept. that the Aramaic gloss (v. 11) existed before these verses. The point which Wambacq has made about vv. 3–5 is so sharp that we should follow his efforts to trace the history of the text beyond what we are able to do with reference to 4QJer[b] and Sept. Chapter 10.1–16 consists of successive additions, each spurred by the pre-existing text or part of it. Verse 2 may be the kernel (not Jeremianic) to which the passage is reducible, and Wambacq has made an impressive attempt to show how the first stages of growth (vv. 3–5) took place. The circumstance that v. 9 is differently located in MT and Sept. (4QJer[b]) reinforces the view that the passage has a piecemeal character. The attraction of vv. 6f. to vv. 3–5 can be explained with reference to the genre 'Satire on Idols' (cf. Isa 40.14,23,28); the case of v. 8 is more obscure: its second half is corrupt and no satisfactory explanation can be given why it appears where it does. Verses 10, 12, 13 have a general, hymnic form and describe the evidences of Yahweh's creative and ordering activities in nature. Sept. and 4QJer[b] show that vv. 11–13 were part of the text before v. 10. Verses 14–16 deal with the stupidity of men and the emptiness of their idols as compared with the reality of Yahweh (pp. 218–220).

11.18–12.6: I have given careful consideration to a 'kernel' explanation of this passage, although I have come down on the side of another view (see under 'Poetry generates Prose'). The 'kernel' explanation would be that not only 12.1–5 is a Jeremianic core, but that the same assessment should be made of 11.18f. The secondary exegesis attracted to these two kernels would then consist of 11.21–23 and 12.6 (p. 255).

23.33–40: Verse 33 constitutes the kernel. The point of v. 33 is wrongly taken in v. 34 and there are other evidences of unevenness in the passage. Nevertheless, the drawing out of v. 33 in vv. 34–40 possesses a substantial cohesiveness, because it is the elaboration of a satirical use of משׂא which represented a pre-exilic prophet of doom as a pathological pessimist. There is an attempt to recapture the significance of the conflict between שׁלום and doom prophecy in the time of Jeremiah. The prophet has been vindicated by events, and the post-exilic(?) Jewish community must confess that this prophet of doom spoke the word of God and identify themselves with him over against the prophets whose assurances of שׁלום were proved false by destruction, defeat and exile (pp. 597–604).

4. The 'reservoir' idea

I have in mind the approach which was adopted by Holladay in 'Prototypes and Copies' (*JBL*, 79, 1960, pp. 351–367) and which is also a feature of Thiel's treatment of his postulated Deuteronomistic compositions. The fundamental contention is that the vocabulary of Jeremianic poetry is re-used in the prose of the book, so that the poetry is a 'reservoir' for the prose. Some of the examples which are set out below derive from Thiel, but they are not necessarily inseparable from his view of Deuteronomistic compositions. It is not, however, my intention to claim that the 'reservoir' approach makes a decisive contribution to the idea of a rolling *corpus*.

1.9 and 5.14: Thiel's reason for discounting the possibility that 5.14 (הנני נתן דברי לאש) is the reservoir tapped by the prose of 1.9 (הנה נתתי דברי בפיך), namely, that לאש is a distinguishing feature, is not weighty. The circumstance that the poetry of 5.14 refers to the destructive power of the prophet's word rather than to an initial endowment with Yahweh's word does not seriously weaken a hypothesis that Jeremianic poetry is being re-used in the prose of 1.9 (p. 13).

1.17 and 17.18: The latter is a prayer of Jeremiah (יחתו המה ולא אחתה אני) which may be the source of the prose of 1.17 (אל תחת מפניהם פן אחתך לפניהם).

1.18 and 15.20: 1.18 (ואני הנה ... נחשת) is an expanded version of ונתתיך לעם הזה לחומת נחשת בצורה (15.20), and ונלחמו אליך ולא יוכלו לך (15.20) is the model of the same word-string in 1.19. 1.7 may have contributed את כל אשר אצוך (cf. 1.17) and 1.8 כי אתך אני להצילך (cf. 1.19). The latter is also found in 15.20. It is evident that 1.17–19 is a kind of mosaic shaped by phrases quarried from a pre-existing Jeremianic *corpus* (p. 23).

4.4: מפני רע מעלליכם, or the like, occurs in both poetry (4.4; 21.12) and prose (23.2; 25.5; 26.3; 44.2) in the book of Jeremiah. Given the distribution of occurrences (only one occurrence outside the book of Jeremiah at Deut 28.20), it is not (*pace* Thiel) manifestly Deuteronomic/Deuteronomistic vocabulary. The circumstance that it occurs within the book of Jeremiah in both poetry and prose suggests that the prose may have been quarried from the poetry (p. 89).

7.3,5 and 2.33: This is a dubious use by Thiel (pp. 108f.) of the reservoir idea. It is supposed that D has created a new semantic context for יטב (Hiphil) in 7.3 (היטיבו דרכיכם ומעלליכם; cf. 7.5) over against מה תיטבי דרכך (2.33), in order to afford a possibility of amendment which Jeremiah denied.

7.4,8 and 13.25: Holladay (*JBL* 79, 1960, p. 356) supposed

that 13.25 was a poetic prototype. The word-string of 7.4 is אל
תבטחו לכם אל דברי השקר (cf. 7.8), and this is compared with
ותבטחו בשקר (13.25). The difficulty about this is similar to the
one encountered in Thiel's proposal for 7.3: one has to suppose
that a new context is being created for בטח בשקר. In the prose
this phraseology is connected with the conflict between Jeremiah
and the שלום prophets, but שקר in 13.25 is a reference to
idolatry.

7.28 and 2.30: Thiel explains 7.21–29 as a composition of D,
and he suggests that D has appropriated ולא לקחו מוסר (7.28)
from 2.30 (מוסר לא לקחו; cf. 5.3, מאנו קחת מוסר) (p. 177).

7.32 and 23.5: The latter is usually set out as poetry and it
could be argued that the prose occurrences of הנה ימים באים
(p. 179) are modelled on 23.5. There is serious doubt, however,
whether 23.5f. should be assigned to the prophet Jeremiah
(p. 565), and the case for regarding 23.5f. as an item of a
Jeremianic *corpus* in existence before the prose passages which
feature הנה ימים באים is a shaky one.

9.14 and 23.15: The threat formulated in 9.14 is a prose
elaboration of the poetry of 23.15 (cf. 8.14) (pp. 207, 576).

11.11–13 makes use of the vocabulary of 2.27c–28 and 14.8.
In a confession of faith, occurring within a prayer for mercy and
help, Yahweh is described as מקוה ישראל מושיעו בעת צרה
(14.8). The association of 'safety' and 'time of distress' also
appears at 2.27c–28, where another theme, Judah's addiction to
other gods, is also represented (ואיה ... יהודה). These themes
are present in 11.11–13: והושע לא יושיעו להם בעת רעתם (v. 12),
and in v. 13 there is a longer version of 2.28b. The author of the
prose has used 2.28b as a reservoir and has gone one better than
the poet by introducing a second comparison between the
number of streets in Jerusalem and the altars which had been
erected to Baal (pp. 242f.; cf. p. 48).

11.12 and 1.16, 18.15: There are 19 occurrences of קטר (Piel)
in the book of Jeremiah, 2 in poetry (1.16; 18.15) and 17 in
prose, including 11.12. The use of קטר (Piel) in connection with
אלהים אחרים or the like is found in Jeremianic poetry and in the
Deuteronomistic literature, but קטר (Piel) in the prose of the
book of Jeremiah should be regarded more precisely as a feature
of the inner development and growth of that *corpus* rather than
more generally as a case of an external Deuteronomistic
influence. Vocabulary present in the poetry and associated with
the theme of idolatry is re-used in a longer, sermonic expansion
of this theme in the prose (pp. 243–244).

11.22 and 5.12 (14.18; 18.21): 11.22 has the appearance of a
riposte to 5.12, and 14.18 and 18.21 are also poetic passages
which feature חרב and רעב vocabulary. The indication given by

5.12 is especially sharp and we may conclude that it is the reservoir of 11.22.

11.23 and 23.12: Thiel (pp. 159f.) supposes that כי אביא רעה אל אנשי ענתות שנת פקדתם (11.23) is derived from כי אביא אליהם רעה שנת פקדתם (23.12).

14.13 and 4.10 and 5.12: Thiel (pp. 184f.) tentatively suggests that D has been influenced by vocabulary from two sources in his construction of a שלום oracle: לא תראו חרב ורעב לא יהיה לכם is taken from 5.12 (וחרב ורעב לא נראה) and שלום אמת אתן לכם from שלום יהיה לכם (4.10).

14.14 and 23.21: D's reservoir (Thiel, pp. 186f.) in the case of לא דברתי אליהם (14.14) is ולא דברתי אליהם (23.21).

14.19f. and 8.14f.: The correspondence is principally between 8.15 and 14.19, and Kimchi noted the near identity of קוה לשלום ואין טוב לעת מרפה והנה בעתה with 14.19. Duhm interpreted this as a re-use of the vocabulary of 8.15, and he also compared כי חטאנו ליהוה (8.14) with כי חטאנו לך (14.20) (p. 333).

16.20 and 2.11: Since 16.20 is poetry, this is different from most of the examples included in this section: it is a case of Jeremianic poetry being re-used in later and inferior poetry, rather than poetry being re-used in prose. Vocabulary which appears in 16.19 (הבל ; שקר) is found in the poetry of Jeremiah and 16.20 has a word-string (אלהים והמה לא אלהים) identical with one in 2.11. But a different context has been created in 16.20 by the substitution of היעשה לו אדם for החימיר גוי. In 2.11 it is the utter lack of a sense of values among God's own people and in 16.20 the stupidity of the Gentiles (p. 382).

17.13 and 2.13: This is another comparison of poetry with poetry. It involves the inferior and bathetic re-use of a figure which makes a powerful impact at 2.13: אתי עזבו מקור מים חיים (p. 402).

18.12 and 2.25: Thiel (p. 217) supposes that 2.25 has suggested to D the kind of bridge that he might construct between 18.1–11 and 13–17: נואש launches comparable sequences of thought.

19.8 and 18.16: Rudolph and Thiel (pp. 222f.) explain 19.8 as the re-use of the vocabulary and imagery of 18.16 in the context of a Deuteronomic-Deuteronomistic composition. Thiel observes certain modifications which are made: לשמה שרוקת עולם becomes לשמה ולשרקה (also at 25.9,18; 29.18), and ויניד בראשו is replaced by וישרק, thus approximating the verse to the Deuteronomistic 1 Kgs 9.8 (כל עבר עליו ישם ושרק).

20.10 and 20.3: There are differing opinions as to whether מסביב is original in 20.3. Holladay (JBL 91, 1972, 303–320) concludes that Jeremiah's confrontation with Pashhur gave birth to the phrase מגור מסביב, whereas Duhm traces it to a 'Scythian

Song' (6.25). I have argued that מסביב is not original at 20.3 and that it is derived from 20.10 (p. 464).

21.7,9 and 5.12 and 15.2: Against Weippert I have argued that two verses of poetry are the reservoir of the 'triad' (בחרב וברעב ובדבר, or the like) in prose passages. These prose commentators or exegetes who encountered the combination of חרב and רעב in 5.12 and the series מות, חרב, רעב and שבי at 15.2 had an incentive to achieve the systematization which is expressed by בחרב וברעב ובדבר or the like. Moreover, there is textual evidence which indicates that the 'triad' is indeed the product of secondary systematization: there are significantly fewer occurrences of it in Sept. than in MT (p. 505).

22.25 and 4.30: מבקשי נפשך or the like also appears in other prose passages in the book of Jeremiah (11.21; 19.7,9; 21.7; 34.20f.; 44.30; 49.37). There is no evidence that it has been plucked from a Deuteronomic-Deuteronomistic source (Weippert) and 4.30 may be the reservoir (p. 543).

23.1f. and 22.22, 10.21: The vocabulary of 23.1f. (אבד ; רעים ; פוץ) is found in 22.22 (רעים) and 10.21 (פוץ) and there is a reference to exile in all three passages. Thiel concludes that D has re-used the vocabulary of 22.22 and 10.21 in 23.1–4 (p. 555).

23.25,26 (cf. 5.31): Thiel (pp. 249f.) suggests that 23.25 (הנבאים הנבאים בשמי שקר) is the reservoir of similar or identical word-strings in D passages (14.14; 27.10,14,15,16; 29.9,21,23). The right conclusion is rather (p. 596) that 5.31 is the reservoir of all the prose passages including 23.25,26.

23.12c and 11.23: Duhm's view was that 11.23 and 6.15 (emended to בעת פקדתם) were the sources of 23.12c which he regarded as a secondary addition to v. 12. A more probable conclusion is that 23.12c is the source for 11.23 (cf. above, p. lviii).

23.15 and 9.14: I disagree with Duhm's account of the relation between these two verses (see above, p. lvii). Why does he suppose that such striking imagery is original to a verse of prose (9.14) rather than to a poetic passage? Why does he deny such imagery to the prophet Jeremiah, particularly since he attributes וישקנו מי ראש (8.14) to the prophet?

23.17: This is the only piece of poetry where שררות לב appears, and its other occurrences in the book of Jeremiah are in prose contexts (3.17; 7.24; 9.13; 13.10; 16.12; 18.12). Thiel supposes that Deut 29.18 is the ultimate source, but the appearance of שלום יהיה לי in that verse (cf. שלום יהיה לכם in Jer 23.17) is not so significant as might at first sight appear, because the context is different (p. 580). Hence it is a reasonable conclusion that 23.17 is a reservoir for the occurrences of לב שררות in the prose passages noted above (pp. 579f.).

25.5 and 23.22: Thiel holds that 25.5 (שובו נא איש מדרכו
וישבום מדרכם הרע) is plucked from 23.22 (הרע ומרע מעלליכם
ומרע מעלליהם) (p. 583, cf. 629).

23.32 and 23.21: It is tempting to conclude that the
arrangement of the vocabulary in 23.32 is founded on the poetry
of 23.21, but the thesis would be more impressive if דבר rather
than צוה appeared in v. 32. The verbs in v. 32 correspond to
those of 1.7 and only in 14.14 are all the verbs used (צוה ; שלח;
דבר). The poetic form of the call narrative in chapter 1 is
questionable, and I have argued that it reflects the final shape of
the book of the prophet Jeremiah rather than the historical
ministry of Jeremiah. Hence 23.21 is probably the only poetic
passage which should come into the reckoning as a reservoir.
Although, in all probability, 23.25–32 does not derive from the
prophet Jeremiah, there are no decisive internal indications that
it is more appropriate to concerns about true and false prophecy
in the exilic period than it is to the time of the prophet, but 23.21
might be the source of 23.32 (p. 596).

25.32 and 6.22, 10.22: The reservoir of 25.32 is probably a
combination of 6.22 (וגוי גדול יעור מירכתי) and 10.22 (ורעש
גדול מארץ צפון). 25.32 runs:

הנה רעה יצאת מגוי אל גוי

וסער גדול יעור מירכתי ארץ (p. 650).

25.38 and 4.7: There is evidently a relation between these two
verses of poetry. In the latter the figure of a lion (אריה not כפיר)
appears in connection with a threat presented to Judah by the
enemy from the north (4.6). 4.7 runs:

עלה אריה מסבכו ומשחית גוים נסע

יצא ממקמו לשום ארצך לשמה

The intention of 25.38 may be (so Rudolph) to announce that
the destruction of Judah threatened in 4.6f. has been
accomplished. The lion is then Nebuchadrezzar who has ravaged
Judah (עזב ככפיר סכו כי היתה ארצם לשמה). It may be
conjectured that the references to the enemy from the north in
25.8–14 have suggested the re-employment of 4.7 at this point
(p. 653).

It will be noticed that not all the examples which have been set
out command my agreement, but the cases where Thiel discerns
that the poetry of a prior Jeremianic *corpus* is a reservoir of
vocabulary for D do not necessarily stand or fall with the
acceptance or non-acceptance of his account of the operations of
D. They can be disengaged from the contexts of postulated
Deuteronomistic compositions and have the status of
independent observations which await a hypothesis of a different
kind from that of Thiel. One is aware, however, that the
examples discussed, for the most part, have been plucked from

different places in the book of Jeremiah, like flowers picked from
different corners of a garden, that the matching of poetry and
prose is a work of secondary arrangement, that one is leaping
over large areas of text in order to marry a verse of poetry with a
verse of prose, and that there is a chanciness in this procedure
which is a source of logical weakness and cannot be overcome.
The flowers picked from different parts of a garden and arranged
in a vase do not represent the environment and relationships of
each flower, while it lived and grew in the garden. In the same
way the 'reservoir' method is abstract in a damaging sense. It
involves an explanation which is superimposed on verses of
poetry and prose, verses which do not 'live together' in the extant
text, but are brought together to give substance to a hypothesis
that the prose of the book of Jeremiah re-uses and develops
vocabulary and word-strings found in the poetry. There are
different ways of arranging an unsystematic collection of flowers
in a vase, and wherever a process of secondary arrangement or
systematization is involved, it is difficult to prove that one
arrangement is right and the other wrong. Despite this logical
weakness (the danger of arranging the evidence to suit
preconceived ideas or to reach a goal which is descried) which
haunts the 'reservoir' method, it does, in my view, make a
contribution to the idea of a rolling *corpus*.

It does not, however, define problems, awaken perplexities and
demand answers with the same immediacy as textual material
which is scrutinized in actual, extant dispositions and
relationships, and the more stringent arguments for a rolling
corpus must operate in this area. Here we are not matching
far-flung verses in the interests of a preferred hypothesis, but are
trying to find the best explanation of pieces which are associated
in an extant text, characteristically in a relationship of
contiguity, which are not explicable in terms of literary
continuity or highly significant coherence, which force
themselves on our attention and require an elucidation. There is,
at any rate, not the danger of self-deception or indeterminate
generality which attends the construction of a 'system', because
we are engaging with actual arrangements of the text in the book
of Jeremiah and are required to observe exegetical
particularities. It is in these connections that the terms
'generation' and 'triggering' are to be used in the next section,
and this brings us to the central part of the exposition of a rolling
corpus. It will be a demonstration that poetry generates prose,
focusing on poetry and prose in relations of contiguity or virtual
contiguity. It will also be a demonstration that prose generates
prose, and this will involve an examination of longer passages of
prose in 1–25. I shall endeavour to show that to describe these as

'compositions' is to accord them a degree of planning and thoughtfulness which they do not possess. We are encountering aggregations of material with a piecemeal character which are products of generation or triggering; they accumulate from local stimuli which consist of no more than a verse or a few verses of pre-existing text and they have the characteristics of exegetical expansions or commentary. In respect of some prose passages I have operated with the term 'core' or 'kernel', but I have intended something different from the examples of the older 'kernel' idea which I have collected in section D.3. The difference lies in the circumstance that the 'kernel' of D.3 was envisaged as the centre of an organized, coherent body of material—a composition—whereas when I employ a concept of 'core' in the longer prose passages, I describe aggregations to the core which are of a different kind, which are in accord with the 'generation' or 'triggering' process explained above, and which do not produce a cumulative literary unity.

5. The idea of 'generation' or 'triggering'

(*a*) Poetry generates prose:
3.6–11 and 3.1–5,12f.: Verses 6–11 are a secondary exegetical development of vv. 1–5 (especially v. 1) and vv. 12f. It is assumed wrongly by the exegete that vv. 1–5 refer to northern Israel and he interprets 'divorce' as the exile of the northern kingdom. The invitation to return and to repent is also thought to have been addressed to the inhabitants of the former northern kingdom in exile, and the idea that the lesser guilt of Israel as compared with Judah justifies this offer of forgiveness and reconciliation is elaborated. The primary interest shown is the understanding of texts which are available for exegesis. It is a difficult task to recover the historical circumstances and theological tendencies which might have promoted such exegesis, but the similar ideas which appear in Ezek 16.51f. suggest that there was a more general, exilic climate of theological pondering which spurred this particular exegetical activity (pp. 123–126; *SVT* 32, 1980, pp. 229–233).

3.14–17: The evaluation of these verses is fraught with uncertainty and the demonstration that they are secondary exegesis generated by pre-existing parts of the chapter (vv. 1–5, 6–13, 22) cannot be effected in a clear-cut way. The assumption here is not precisely that poetry triggers prose, but that poetry (vv. 1–5, 12f*, 22) and prose (vv. 6–11, 12*) trigger prose. But the metaphor of divorce is not maintained (excepting בעלתי, v. 14), and the saying about the ark, the contrast which it sets up, and the appearance of the 'pilgrimage' tradition, furnish

vv. 14–17 with an intriguing and distinctive content. Moreover, the way in which the return from exile is envisaged has unusual features: exilic communities do not return *en bloc*; it is a community hand-picked by Yahweh which will be reconstituted in Jerusalem (pp. 76–77).

5.18f. and 5.15–17: The imagery used in v. 16 and the fourfold אכל in v. 17 might be taken to indicate annihilation. The 'nevertheless' with which v. 18 opens is indicative of an intention to modify or reinterpret the impression of כלה which is conveyed by the poetry, and there is a firm statement that Judah will not be obliterated (לא אעשה אתכם כלה). The prose passage (vv. 18f.) is also concerned with the need to explain why the exile took place, as the form of v. 19, with its question and answer, makes abundantly clear. It follows from this line of reasoning that אל in the poetry of 5.10 (p. 120) is an insertion with the same function as vv. 18f. and that לא in 4.27 (p. 109) should be emended or deleted (pp. 126–127).

7.29b–34 and 7.29a: A snatch of poetry in v. 29a (גזי נזרך והשליכי ושאי על שפים קינה) has attracted subsequent exegesis or commentary: in v. 29b it has attracted the explanation that Yahweh has rejected his people, and in vv. 30–34 a speech by Yahweh to a third party in which he describes the abominable cultic practices of the Judaeans and threatens them with dire consequences (cf. כי at v. 29b and v. 30). Both v. 29b (את דור עברתו) and vv. 30–34 deal with imminent judgement and are intended to throw light on the proleptic mourning which is commanded in v. 29a. Verses 30–34 are, however, a skilful little composition in their own right. The thought that idolatry is the cause of Judah's death (v. 29a—proleptic mourning) is given precision in terms of the Topheth theme and the valley of Ben Hinnom, a shrine desecrated by Josiah according to 2 Kgs 23.10. Where children were sacrificed, Judaeans will be slaughtered, and the valley will be renamed the Valley of Slaughter. Verse 33 is almost identical with Deut 28.26 (cf. 2 Sam 21.10f.), and v. 34 is to be compared with Jer 16.9 and 25.10. There will be no one to repel the vultures which feed on the unburied corpses and a pall of death will settle on the land. No more marriages will be celebrated and the community will have no hope for the future. Although it has been customary to regard 8.1–3 as a continuation of 7.34, the passage introduces a new train of thought and is not intrinsically related to 7.34 (pp. 176, 182).

9.11–15 and 9.9f.: 9.11–15 is a type of theological reflection generated by the description of desolation and death in vv. 9f. Why is the land destroyed, burned up like a wilderness and abandoned? Verse 9b (כי נצתו מבלי איש עבר) is taken up in v. 11 (נצתה כמדבר מבלי עבר) which alludes to the description of emptiness and desolation in vv. 9f. There is a concern (vv. 12f.) to supply theological reasons for what has happened, and the passage is located between a disaster which has already taken place (an enemy invasion—implied by the question in v. 11), and affliction and exile which are represented as lying in the future and are the subjects of the threats in vv. 14f. The threat in v. 14 is a prose elaboration of the poetry of 23.15 (above, pp. lvii, lix). One might, therefore, see v. 11 as an exegetical development of v. 9, vv. 14f. as taking off from v. 10, and vv. 12f. as a new element of explanation. The passage should be regarded as exilic comment, an attempt to explore and explain the disaster which overtook Jerusalem and Judah (p. 205).

11.17 and 11.15f.: Verse 17 is comment on vv. 15f.: the second person feminine singular suffixes of v. 17 refer to the 'beloved' in vv. 15f.; הנוטע אותך is triggered by the figure of the olive tree and the vocabulary reaches back to the prose in the preceding part of the chapter (רעה, v. 11 and לקטר לבעל, v. 13) (pp. 252f.).

11.18–12.6: 11.18 is generated by 12.1–5, and the difficulty which has been felt with the abruptness of its appearance and its laconic character is to be explained on this assumption. Those whose evil deeds are divulged to the prophet by Yahweh (11.18) are to be equated with those of whom it is said that Yahweh is near to their speech but far from their lives (12.2). Moreover, the interpretation of 12.1–5 which appears in the prose (11.18f., 21–23; 12.6) is wrong. It supposes that the crisis in Jeremiah's faith, which is indicated by 12.1–5, is connected with his persecution at the hands of his kinsmen and fellow-villagers in Anathoth. This interpretation is explicitly given by 12.6 (notice the link established by כי) which is the most obvious representative of the 'Anathoth' exegesis in view of its immediate syntactical connection with 12.1–5. It is a mistake, therefore, to suppose that 12.6 has been displaced, but it is true that it represents the same interpretation of 12.1–5 as is found in 11.18f. and 21–23. 11.20, a verse of poetry surrounded by prose, is perhaps in its original context at 20.12. It is attracted to 11.18–12.6 because of its affinity with 12.3 (pp. 254f.).

12.12,14–17 and 12.7–11: The chaotic state of affairs described in vv. 10f. is explicated in v. 12 as invasion (p. 275). Verses 14f. are generated by the poetry of vv. 7–11 and נחלה serves as a stitch. The 'invader' interpretation of v. 12 is further developed and the invaders are identified as neighbouring nations. A 'prophecy' is composed on the foundation of the notices about the uprooting and resettlement of these neighbours in the oracles on foreign nations (48.47; 49.6), influenced by the vocabulary used in the account of Jeremiah as a prophet to the nations (1.10). Verses 16f. are a subsequent qualifying of the

promise of restoration, and we know from Kimchi that there was
a discussion about the right exegesis of 49.6; that, according to
one interpretation, it was not to be understood as an
unconditional promise, but as one made to those who would
'learn the ways of Israel'. We may assume that vv. 16f. arise out
of this exegetical debate. Verse 15 is one exegesis of
(מואב)עמון שבות ושבתי and vv. 16f. another (p. 284; cf. *VTS*
32, 1980, pp. 233–236). Verse 13 should be regarded as an
independent saying which probably disturbs an original
contiguity of v. 12 and v. 14 (p. 275).

14.11–16 and 14.2–10: 14.11–16 is an independent unit, but it
is probably generated by 14.2–10. Verses 2–10 are related to a
problem which arose when Jeremiah was acknowledged to be a
true prophet, while, at the same time, effective intercession was
regarded as a necessary part of the prophetic office (cf. v. 10).
The difficulty was solved by an assertion that Yahweh had
placed an interdict on Jeremiah's powers as an intercessor, and
this is explicitly stated in v. 11. Hence vv. 11–16 arise intelligibly
as a further elaboration of the concerns of vv. 2–10 (p. 328).
However, vv. 11–16 require a closer scrutiny. The interdict on
intercession stands at the head of this passage as it does in
7.16–20, and the statement that burnt-sacrifices and
grain-offerings will not move Yahweh expresses views similar to
those in 7.21–28 (cf. vv. 21f.). Less significantly, the reference to
lack of burial in the Topheth passage (7.33) is also present in
14.16. Thus two ideas which have triggered passages in chapter 7
(see below under 'Prose generates prose', D.5(c)) are yoked at
the beginning of 14.11–16. The interdict on intercession,
however, is not developed and explained in connection with
idolatry as in 7.16–20, and the negative attitude to sacrifice is
not linked with inveterate disobedience as in 7.21–28. What
follows in 14.13ff. is rather an attempt to elucidate the apparent
harshness of Yahweh's attitude, and, particularly, the interdict
on intercession, and to portray the prophet torn between concern
for his people and his prophetic office. He is perhaps represented
as querying the interdict and exercising his duty to intercede
notwithstanding. He protests that a fatal ambiguity has been
created by the prophets whose credentials as prophets of Yahweh
are, nevertheless, unquestionable, and by whom the people are
inevitably confused and deceived. The continuation of the
prophet's rejoinder is disappointing. Yahweh does not take up
the question which Jeremiah raises, and vv. 14–16, which simply
assert that the שלום prophets are false prophets, that they will be
overtaken by Yahweh's judgement and that the people will be
surrendered to famine and sword, are something of a
non-answer. The right understanding of them is probably that

they reinforce an exilic explanation of why Jeremiah was a true prophet and yet an ineffective prophet: they establish that the שלום prophets were false prophets and so they supplement the explanation of Jeremiah's ineffectiveness conveyed by the representation that he was forbidden by Yahweh to exercise his office as an intercessor. The activity of שלום prophets undermined Jeremiah's prophetic activity and 'jammed' his message to the people (pp. 327f.).

15.1–4 and 14.17–21: 15.1–4 are generated by 14.17–21 (v. 22 is a subsequent insertion, see p. 332). An expression of private anguish and a vision of the end, attributable to the prophet Jeremiah and originally unconnected with a communal lament, has been used to furnish a description of distress (vv. 17f.) which leads on to petition and confession with a corporate reference (Judah; Zion). In relation to 14.17–21, 15.1–4 has the same function as 14.10 and 14.11–16 have in relation to 14.2–9. The change from poetry to prose at 15.1 indicates that the communal lament constructed in 14.17–21 did not originally possess an oracular reply and that this defect has been repaired by 15.1–4. But 15.1–4 is not all of a piece and is the product of more than one process of supplementation. The verses which are a vehicle for the 'interdict on intercession' train of thought do not have the measure of deliberation and coherence which would entitle them to be regarded as a Deuteronomistic 'composition' (Thiel). Rather 15.1 has been variously elaborated in a piecemeal fashion: the question (v. 2) is a transparent device to effect a transition to a threat of sword, famine, pestilence (and exile); v. 3 is spun out of the fourfold threat of v. 2, with another set of ארבע משפחות, so that if ואשר לשבי לשבי (v. 2) is a later addition, v. 3 is later than the insertion of that phrase in v. 2. All this has been capped with a conflation of Deut 28.25 and 2 Kgs 24.3: Judah is an object inspiring horror and terror, and she has been reduced to this condition because she succumbed to the sin of Manasseh (pp. 334, 336).

16.1–9 and 15.17: There is a lack of contiguity between 15.17 and 16.1–9 which weakens the hypothesis that 16.1–9 is triggered by 15.17. Nevertheless, the thought that 16.1–9 is a prose elaboration of the reference to Jeremiah's loneliness at 15.17 (so Rudolph) should be pursued. The main plank of the exposition is Jeremiah's celibacy (16.2–4): it is a sign of a community which has no future and in which children should not be fathered. A further elaboration and widening of this loneliness is the representation that Jeremiah is barred from identifying himself with his people in times of sorrow (vv. 5–7) and joy (vv. 8–9). Here we discern the influence of the theology which has been detected in the communal laments and their

answering oracles (14.2–16; 14.17–15.4). Jeremiah has no
function to discharge as a prophet of comfort and
encouragement (cf. 14.13), and in this connection the theme of
his loneliness is further developed. It is an extraordinary state of
affairs which decrees that a true prophet must proclaim only
doom and which brings about his alienation and isolation. The
statement that Yahweh has removed his שלום from the people
(16.5) is another way of saying that he has debarred Jeremiah
from exercising his office as an intercessor and comforter (cf.
7.16; 11.14; 14.11; 15.1–4), so that he cannot express his
solidarity with his people in bereavement and in marriage, in
ceremonies robbed of their social significance by the hopelessness
of the times (pp. 366–368).

18.18 and 18.19–23: 18.18 is generated by 18.19–23: it is not
intrinsically connected with vv. 19–23 in the sense that vv. 18–23
constitute an original, integrated, literary unity. It is an
exegetical or editorial contribution whose function is to supply a
context and an occasion for Jeremiah's outburst in vv. 19–23.
Whoever supplied it was influenced by the allusions to attempts
on Jeremiah's life in vv. 22f., and, without relying on the more
explicit indications of Sept. and Pesh., we must conclude that לכו
ונחשבה על ירמיהו מחשבות (v. 18) was intended to indicate a
threat to Jeremiah's life: 'Let us build up a case against him, so
that we may indict him effectively'. In the remaining part of
v. 18 a powerful coalition of intellectual and spiritual leadership
is ranged against Jeremiah (so his opponents are urging); he does
not belong to any of these constituencies and should be treated
accordingly (pp. 436f.).

22.1–5 and 21.11f.: Thiel correctly identifies 22.1–5 as a prose
commentary on the 'text' 21.11f. His further conjecture that
22.1–5 were originally contiguous with 21.11f. and that the
immediacy of the connection has been broken by the subsequent
insertion of 21.13f. is attractive (p. 507). What does the author
of 22.1–5 intend to achieve by his extension and modification of
21.12, and, particularly, his treatment of דינו לבקר משפט
והצילו גזול מיד עושק? In 22.3 he refers to specific breaches of
social justice, and it may be thought that these are envisaged as
particularly crucial areas, test cases by means of which the
serious intent and determination of the king to preside over a just
community could be ascertained. It may be that the author of
22.1–5 was operating with a particular exegesis of 21.12 and had
concluded that דינו לבקר משפט והצילו גזול מיד עושק referred to
specific breaches of social justice (robbery and oppressive
behaviour) rather than to a defective functioning of legal
processes (pp. 506–510); that he consequently attached further
concrete demands connected with weak members of the

community who might suffer harsh and arbitrary treatment. The formulation of alternatives in 22.4f. is a device for summing up possibilities similar in kind to 17.24–27 and 21.8–10. There is a place for the Davidic king only if he defends a community which conforms to Yahweh's standards of social justice. This is probably a wider view of royal responsibility than what is intended by 21.12, where the precise point is rather that the king is ultimately responsible for right legal decisions and for the proper functioning of the machinery of justice (pp. 516f.; cf. *VT* 32, 1982, pp. 70f.).

22.11f. and 22.10: There is general agreement that vv. 11f. are a commentary on v. 10 and the renderings of the versions have proceeded on this assumption. They have assumed that vv. 11f. contain a correct exegesis of v. 10, and this view has been widely sustained. But vv. 11f. are not at all concerned with אל תבכו למת ואל תנדו לו and they connect with v. 10 at the point where they identify הלך with שלם. Moreover, v. 10 is presumably addressed to the Judaean or Jerusalem community, whereas vv. 11f. are addressed to Shallum. What the commentator has done is to identify a reference to Shallum in v. 10 and to cast his exegesis in the form of an oracle addressed to Shallum. הלך (v. 10) is correctly taken as a reference to exile and it is attached in vv. 11f. to Shallum who has gone into exile and will never return (pp. 522–524).

23.25–32 and 23.16–22: Verses 25–32 are explicable as a prose commentary on vv. 16–22, and, in particular, they are generated by descriptions of שלום prophets in v. 16 (מהבלים אתכם המה) and v. 17 (וכל הלך בשררות לבו). Hence there is a presumption that vv. 25–32 were originally contiguous with vv. 16–22 and that the connection was broken by the subsequent insertion of vv. 23f. It may have been supposed that these verses had some appositeness as theological comment: whatever ambiguity there might be on the human scene, there was no failure on God's part to distinguish between truth and falsehood. But one has to work hard to explain the intention of this insertion and the person responsible for it may not have been so greatly concerned about its relevance. Verses 23f. have no intrinsic connection with any context in chapter 23 (p. 587).

25.33 and 25.31f.: Verse 33 is constituted by exegetical comment on vv. 31f. (הרשעים נתנם לחרב), and the comment has been constructed by conflating word-strings which appear elsewhere in the book of Jeremiah: לא יאספו ולא יקברו at 8.2 and לא יספדו ולא יקברו at 16.4. It is uncertain whether one should appeal to 12.12 (מקצה ארץ ועד קצה הארץ) as the source of מקצה הארץ ועד קצה הארץ (25.33), since עד קצה הארץ occurs at 25.31

(מירכתי ארץ at v. 32), so that this vocabulary may be more proximately derived (pp. 651, 667).

(b) Poetry generates poetry:

5.23–25 and 5.21f.: Verses 23–25 are formally discontinuous with vv. 20–22 (pp. 128f.) and so vv. 20–25 do not constitute an integrated unit. On the other hand, vv. 23–25 echo the vocabulary of vv. 21f., and reproduce the ideas of that passage so deliberately that they appear to have been generated by vv. 21f. The stubborn and rebellious temper of the people and their *penchant* for apostasy (v. 23) can be related to what is said in v. 21 of their incorrigibility and lack of sense (לב סורר ומורה סרו וילכו and עם סכל ואין לב). Their imperviousness to the majesty and holiness of Yahweh and their incapacity for worship (v. 22a) are resumed with the repetition of ירא in v. 24a. There is also a link between v. 22bc and v. 24b in that both are concerned with Yahweh's management of the created order, although v. 24b makes the different point that Yahweh maintains the seasonal rhythms, provides the rains when they are due and crowns the year with the harvest (p. 130).

8.17 and 8.14: The author of 8.14 was not responsible for 8.17, the latter verse being contributed by someone who misunderstood (v. 14) as the venom of a snake. This is the understanding of מי ראש which appears in Targ. and Rashi and it has triggered the reference to snakes with deadly bites in v. 17. Yahweh threatens to despatch poisonous snakes against his people, snakes which no charmer can pacify and whose bite is lethal (p. 192).

22.23 and 22.20–22: Verse 23 is not moving beyond the point of disaster to which v. 22b refers and threatening a worse disaster in 586 than that of 597. Instead it is an epexegesis of v. 22b and alludes to the same judgement as כי אז תבשי ונכלמת מכל רעתך. But v. 23 is not an original and integral part of a unit consisting of vv. 20–23; it is a secondary elaboration triggered by v. 22. It is generally appreciated that the symbolism of Lebanon in v. 23 is different from that in v. 20; ישבתי בלבנון (v. 23) may have been inspired by ישבת העמק, used of Jerusalem in 21.13, and לבנון and ארזים may have been inspired by 22.6 and 14 respectively. The vocabulary and symbolism of v. 23 disengage it from vv. 20–22 and a factor in its generation may have been the desire to associate vv. 20–23 more clearly with royal sayings (22.6,14), since it is not itself a royal saying (p. 538).

25.38 and 25.34–37: There is no intrinsic connection between 25.27–29 and 25.30–38, and 25.15–38 do not have an original literary integrity. Verse 30 is attached to v. 29 by means of a representation that it and the following verses contain a further message which the prophet has received from Yahweh (cf. נאם

יהוה at the close of v. 31), but vv. 30f., in which Yahweh is referred to in the third person, are not obviously 'word of Yahweh' addressed to a prophet. We may have to reckon with an oscillation between universal judgement and the singling out of Judah and Jerusalem in vv. 30–38. עד קצה הארץ (v. 31) means 'to the ends of the earth' and מירכתי ארץ (v. 32) is also indicative of a world-wide judgement. On the other hand, על נוהו (v. 30) appears to focus on Judah and Jerusalem, and the question whether vv. 34–37 may not refer to the political leaders of Judah (אדירי הצאן ; הרעים) is not an idle one. Rudolph holds that vv. 32, 34–37 allude to the judgement of which Nebuchadrezzar was the instrument and which was visited on the limited number of nations which he retains in his sifted list (vv. 16–26*). The reasons which he gives for disengaging v. 38 from vv. 34–37 are not cogent, but we may agree that if v. 38, which refers to Judah (ארצם) is secondary, it is generated by a particular exegesis of vv. 34–37, namely, that הרעים and אדירי הצאן are to be identified with the political leaders of Judah (pp. 647, 656).

(*c*) Prose generates prose:

7.1–15: This passage has been included under 'kernel' (D.3, p. liv), but the aspect of generation is further developed here. The core of the chapter (vv. 4, 9*, 10*, 11*, 12, 14*) is to be attributed to the prophet Jeremiah, whether or not his *ipsissima verba* are preserved. The theme is the destruction of the Jerusalem temple, and the train of thought reaches its proper climax with the thought that the Jerusalem temple will suffer the same fate as the sanctuary at Shiloh. The manner in which a reference to the land given to the forefathers is introduced at v. 14 is undeniably intrusive, and v. 15 is an exegetical elaboration of the words which have been interpolated at v. 14 (ולמקום אשר נתתי לכם ולאבותיכם). But a juxtaposition of themes is also present in vv. 1–7 and the main generating element is the ambivalence of מקום ('temple'/'city' (Jerusalem) or 'land'). The ambivalence of מקום ('land' in vv. 3, 6, 7) triggers verses which contain a conditional promise of continued possession of the land (vv. 3, 5–7) and this theme is intertwined with the unconditional threat uttered against the Jerusalem temple. Verse 8 is an editorial recapitulation of v. 4 made necessary by the separation of v. 4 from v. 9. This account, it should be admitted, allows a more deliberate editorial superintendence than has elsewhere been envisaged in the exposition of 'generation' or 'triggering', but, on the other hand, the result is much less than a well-rounded composition and the brokenness of the passage cannot be overcome (pp. 164–165).

7.16–20: This passage has a thematic integrity and may

legitimately be described as a little composition. One may,
however, give an account of it involving the idea of generation in
a weaker sense. The statement would be that its core is v. 16 and
that the passage is generated by this verse. The interdict on
intercession (v. 16) recurs at 11.14 and 14.11 (cf. 15.1) and I
have argued (pp. 171f., 245, 328) that it is an exilic apologetic
for the prophet Jeremiah: a reconciliation of his being a true
prophet and yet failing as an intercessor. Verses 17–20 are
intended to explain in a specific way, furnishing examples of
idolatrous behaviour in Judah and Jerusalem, why the interdict
on intercession was imposed on Jeremiah and why the only
possible outcome was a destructive judgement imposed by
Yahweh (military defeat and exile). Hence these verses are
epexegesis triggered by the 'interdict on intercession' idea.

7.21–28: It is not possible to save the structural integrity of
vv. 21–28, nor is the solution that vv. 21–26 constitute one unit
(Yahweh addressing the present generation of Judaeans) and
vv. 27f. another (Yahweh addressing Jeremiah). There is a loss
of coherence already at v. 26, where the 'fathers' cannot be the
grammatical subject of the third person plural verbs in view of
the closing words of the verse (ויקשו את ערפם הרעו מאבותם),
and the brokenness of vv. 21–28 cannot be repaired. Thiel
(p. 122) has identified two Jeremianic elements: עלותיכם ספו על
זבחיכם ואכלו בשר (v. 21) and אבדה האמונה ונכרתה מפיהם
(v. 28). On this basis it could be argued that vv. 22–25 and
vv. 27f. are expansions of Jeremianic kernels, but the argument
in respect of v. 28 is not compelling. On the other hand, it is not
clear that v. 22 is to be disengaged from v. 21 as the work of D,
and the better conclusion is that vv. 23–25 are triggered by the
need which was felt to elucidate further the assertion which is
made in the Jeremianic kernel (vv. 21f.). If Yahweh did not
require burnt-offerings and sacrifices from the forefathers, what
did he require of them? The syntactical unevenness of v. 26
defies all explanation and the connection of vv. 27f. with
vv. 21–25 is loose. Jeremiah is to test the temperature of the
water for himself and he will find that the recalcitrance
described in vv. 24f. is not an exaggeration. He is to draw the
appropriate conclusions and tell the people that they are
incorrigible (pp. 172, 177).

11.1–14: The oscillating character of the passage and the
manner in which it returns on itself lend it a fragmentary
appearance: it has been built up by further explications of
themes which were present but less well-developed in
pre-existing parts of the text. Exegesis of the nature of the
disobedience to the demands of the covenant is thought to be a
necessity, and so disobedience (vv. 3f., 7f.) is spelled out as

idolatry in vv. 9f. The theme of judgement, present in v. 8 as
judgement already executed, is resumed in v. 11, attaching itself
to the preceding allegations of idolatry. It becomes judgement
which is imminent and the 'too late' theme of 2.27f. is elaborated
(vv. 12f.). It is too late to seek help from Yahweh, and when
Judah and Jerusalem call out to him, they will get no response;
when they apply to the gods to whom they have devoted
themselves they will find that these gods are powerless to help.
Nor can the prophet help, for Yahweh has forbidden him to
exercise his function as an intercessor (v. 14) (p. 242; cf.
7.16–20, p. lxx.).

13.1–11: The nucleus of the passage, whether attributable to
the prophet Jeremiah or exilic, is vv. 1–7. Whatever status is
accorded to these verses ('historical' symbolic action; visionary
experience; dramatic parable), their symbolic constituents,
which are not supplied with an explicit interpretation, must refer
to exile. Verses 8–11 are subsequent additions, and their
intention is to offer an interpretation of vv. 1–7, but it is doubtful
whether they can be regarded as constituting a coherent,
secondary interpretation. It is probably that vv. 10f. hang
together, but v. 9 is a separate explanation of vv. 1–7,
remarkable for its generality and its lack of particular reference
to the imagery of the preceding verses. It is triggered by נשחת
(v. 7), but it simply delivers the threat that Yahweh will destroy
(ככה אשחית) the pride of Judah and the overweening pride of
Jerusalem. Verses 10 and 11 are perhaps better explained as a
single exegesis of vv. 1–7 rather than as two separate comments.
The generality of v. 10 is compensated for in v. 11 by an attempt
to come to grips more closely with the imagery of vv. 1–7, and
ידבק (v. 11) is especially related to this intention. Thus vv. 1–11
consist of a nucleus which has generated two separate exegetical
comments (pp. 290f.).

13.12–14:The functioning of the proverbial unit (vv. 12–13),
whether v. 12 is taken as 'Every skin is filled with wine' or 'Every
jar is filled with wine', does not require the idea of 'shattering'
(v. 14). 13.12f. turn on the thought of intoxication: Yahweh will
give his people a cup of wrath to drink, they will be intoxicated
and will behave irrationally and self-destructively. Verse 14 is an
exegetical elaboration which is generated by the assumption that
'jar' is the correct rendering of (v. 12) and that the application of
the proverb turns on the fragility of wine-jars. Hence arguments
for the rightness of 'jar' over against 'skin' which rely on an
original integrity of vv. 12–14 and protest that 'skin' is
incongruous with 'shattering' are invalid (pp. 297f.).

16.10–13 and 16.1–9 (pp. 368f.): There is no intrinsic
connection between vv. 1–9 and vv. 10–13. It is uncertain

whether לעיניכם ובימיכם (v. 9) was inserted in order to provide a
better connection with vv. 10–13 after these verses had been
tagged on, or whether the insertion was associated with an
independent and prior development which transformed v. 9 into
an address to the community, and so supplied a reason
unintentionally for the attaching of vv. 10–13. The
question-answer scheme (cf. 5.19; 9.11–15) like the 'interdict on
intercession' motif is an expression of exilic concern to
understand the judgement which overtook Judah and to explain
the significance of the prophet Jeremiah. 16.1–9 may have
generated 16.10–13 in the sense that the intention vv. 10–13 is to
modify the portrayal of total destruction which is conveyed by
vv. 1–9 (cf. vv. 4, 9), and to substitute גולה (v. 13) for כלה as the
form of Yahweh's judgement. This conforms with a modification
predictable in the exilic period (since there was a residue), and
which I have traced elsewhere (above, p. lxiii).

16.14f. (23.7f.): There is a general agreement that these verses
fit better into the context of 23.1–8, but in chapter 16 they
appear as the final stage of a process of transformation:
unmitigated doom (vv. 1–9) is mitigated to exile (vv. 10–13) and
becomes a hope of return and restoration (vv. 14f.). The original
form of the new oath ('As Yahweh lives who brought the
Israelites out of a northern land'), which envisages only the
return of the Babylonian exiles, has generated a kind of 'rubric'
which indicates how the oath may be standardized and be
applied to dispersed Jews in any quarter ('And out of all the
lands where he had dispersed them'). It thus betrays a concern
for dispersions other than the Babylonian one (pp. 373–376).

16.16–18: This passage has already been considered under
A.1(c), where the evidences of expansion supplied by the shorter
Greek text are treated (p. xix.). One of these is ראשונה (v. 18)
and this is the only aspect of vv. 16–18 which involves
'generation', if vv. 16–18 are an original unit, as I have argued.
Although quantitatively the amount of triggering is minimal, it
deserves consideration, because it betrays the kind of exegetical
interest which I have assumed elsewhere and which is
fundamental to the idea of a rolling *corpus*. ראשונה is an
attempt to mitigate the severity of vv. 16–18, but more precisely
it is the product of a wrong exegesis of v. 16 and of משנה (v. 18).
It is supposed wrongly that in both these places there is a
reference to the events of 597 and 586, and ראשונה makes room
for the entrance of hope and restoration after these judgements.
Moreover it accommodates vv. 16–18 to the note of return and
restoration which is struck in vv. 14f. (pp. 377–379).

17.19–27: There is no answer to the question why this passage
appears where it does and it cannot be explained in terms of a

triggering process. Rudolph's suggestion that it is a resumption of 16.11f. suffers from the disadvantage that the passages are too far apart in the extant text, but even if this were ignored, the case would be weak. There is no overt reference to Sabbath observance in 16.11f., but there is an allusion to idolatry (v. 11) and an indication of a more general recalcitrance (v. 12). One would have to suppose that failure to observe the Sabbath has been identified by an exegete in הנכם הלכים איש אחרי שררות לבו הרע. Thiel suggests that the connection of 17.19–27 is with the sin which is said to be chiselled on the heart of the people, but his final position, which is agnostic, is the right one (p. 417).

18.7–12 and 18.1–6: Verses 1–6 contain a parabolic proclamation of doom, and at least vv. 1–4 are attributable to Jeremiah. The meaning of vv. 1–6 is that Judah has been finally cast off by Yahweh, and the discarding of the pot signifies destruction. Verses 5f. may represent a secondary exegesis (an attempt to interpret the parable), but v. 6 is a non-interpretation in so far as it does nothing to restrict the openness of the imagery in v. 4 or to apply it explicitly. It simply establishes a general analogy between the activity of the potter and the activity of Yahweh. Verses 7–11 are a subsequent exegetical enterprise which qualify and amplify vv. 1–6, and so they are generated by vv. 1–6. The note of unconditional doom sounded for Judah in vv. 1–4(6) is modified and the possibility of repentance is held out for all peoples, with a provision for a revision of Yahweh's intentions to judge and destroy. יוצר (v. 11) is a play on היוצר in vv. 1–6, and the distance between v. 11 and the nearest preceding occurrence of היוצר (v. 6) is a matter which should awaken curiosity. The conclusion which should be drawn is that v. 11 was originally contiguous with v. 6 and has been separated from it by the later insertion of vv. 7–10. Verse 11 explains בית ישראל (v. 6) as 'men of Judah' and 'inhabitants of Jerusalem', and has the form of a word of Yahweh which Jeremiah is instructed to convey to the community. The message is that Yahweh is fashioning (יוצר) doom for his people, but that they may be saved if they repent and amend their way of life. The 'shaping' activity of the potter is correlated with the shaping activity of Yahweh, but the significant, theological modification is the opening up of the possibility of repentance and escape from doom. However indecisive may be the indications gathered from the vocabulary of vv. 7–11, there is little doubt that they embody a view of the prophetic office which agrees with the Deuteronomic typology: there is an emphasis on the intercessory function of the prophet and his concern to appeal for repentance (cf. pp. 324, 338). The conclusion to be drawn is that vv. 7–10 are a second elaboration of vv. 1–6 which disturb the contiguity

of a first exegesis (v. 11) with vv. 1–6. They are a subsequent
theorizing and drawing out of the crucial function of repentance
in the Deuteronomic scheme. They may represent another
attempt to interpret the parable and this would explain why they
have been inserted after v. 6 (so Thiel), but they are not an apt
interpretation of the parable. More probably they attach to v. 11
which they elaborate with a general, theological statement. They
have too abstract an aspect to entitle them to be regarded
seriously as an explication of the parable of the potter and his
clay. Verse 12 is a still later insertion which makes a bridge to
vv. 13–17 (see p. lviii), and it contains a motive clause which is
inappropriate in the mouth of the people (כי . . . נעשה). It is a
patchwork with marks of inferior imitation: the first part echoes
2.25 and the second part makes use of a word-string which
appears elsewhere in the prose of Jeremiah. In all the other
Jeremiah passages except 16.12 (second person), the word-string
is used in third person descriptions, and only here (18.12) and in
Deut 29.18 in association with words put into the mouth of the
people. Verse 12 served as a bridge to vv. 13–17 by establishing
that the invitation to repent had been rejected (pp. 422f., 423,
425f., 426).

19: I am using the idea of 'kernel', but I am not representing
chapter 19 as a composition with a high degree of organization
and cohesiveness. Instead I am describing a kind of growth
which accords with the concept of a rolling *corpus* and which is
achieved by processes of generation or triggering. The nucleus
consists of the account of the shattering of the בקבק and the
explanation of its symbolism (vv. 1, 2 as far as החרסות and
without אשר גיא בן הנם (אל), 10f. without ובתפת יקברו מאין
מקום לקבור). This is probably a historical account of a symbolic
action carried out by Jeremiah and gives us access to the
historical context of his ministry. The next stage is constituted
by a 'sermon' which is an exegetical amplification of the
symbolic action. It was not shaped originally by a 'Topheth'
theme, but was triggered by an intention to elucidate the
symbolic breaking of the בקבק, and there is a play on בקבק
(ובקתי) at v. 7. It consists of the latter part of v. 2
(וקראת . . . אליך), vv. 3f., 7–9, and elaborates further the
primary explanation of the symbolic action which appears in
v. 11 (ככה אשבר את העם הזה ואת העיר הזה). It has nothing to
do with Topheth, but it develops further the threat issued against
Jerusalem. The original explanation of the symbolic action
(v. 11*) is expanded in vv. 12f. and למקום הזה refers to
Jerusalem. Topheth (כתפת) plays an ancillary rather than a
leading role in v. 12 as a paradigm of ruin and devastation, while
כמקום התפת (v. 13) conveys a threat that houses in Jerusalem,

made unclean by idolatry, will be reduced to rubble. Hence תפת
in v. 13 is also used as an exemplar of a place which has suffered
a destructive judgement. If this is a correct explanation of how
the 'Topheth' theme was introduced to 19, the view that its
entrance was connected with the physical adjacency of the 'Gate
of Potsherds' and the valley of Ben Hinnom (cf. v. 2) should be
repudiated.

Verses 5f. were triggered by the presence of תפת in vv. 12f.,
but more immediately by a mistaken exegesis of v. 4. The
references to idolatry in v. 4 were understood as allusions to the
sacrifice of children in the valley of Ben Hinnom and the two
occurrences of מקום were equated with Topheth. In one passage
(Ps 106.38) דם נקי is associated with child sacrifice, and such an
interpretation of the closing words of v. 4 may have encouraged
the exegesis of v. 4 which appears in vv. 5f. The contents of
vv. 5f. are perhaps derived directly from 7.31f., and the
similarity of 7.33 to 19.7 may have encouraged the exegete in his
view that the latter was another item of the Topheth theme in
chapter 19. The final stages of these processes of growth are to
be found in v. 2 (אל) גיא בן הנם אשר), vv. 14f. and ובתפת יקברו
מאין מקום לקבור (v. 11). By means of a patch in v. 2 Jeremiah is
represented as having gone to the valley of Ben Hinnom rather
than to the 'Gate of Potsherds'. This is a consequence of the
transformation effected by vv. 5f. and the supposition that there
is a predominant 'Topheth' theme in the chapter. The function of
vv. 14f. is to effect a link between 19 and 20.1–6. These verses
(14f.) report the return of Jeremiah from Topheth to the temple
and so they presuppose the patch in v. 2. In order that there may
be a confrontation between Jeremiah and Pashhur some reason
must be supplied, and the provocative words spoken by Jeremiah
in the temple (vv. 14f.) fulfil this need. Thus the connection
between 19 and 20.1–6 is entirely artificial. The insertion at the
end of v. 11 is so incoherent that it cannot meaningfully be
incorporated into any account of the growth of chapter 19. It
can, however, be said that it was probably inserted after vv. 5f.,
since whatever impetus there was to insert it was supplied by
these verses. We might have expected it to come after גיא ההרגה
(v. 6), since the words which appear after גיא ההרגה at 7.32 are
very similar to those at the end of 19.11. We may hazard a guess
that ובתפת יקברו מאין מקום לקבור was originally located at the
end of 19.6 (pp. 443–459).

20.4–6 and 20.1–3: מסביב is an insertion in v. 3 (pp. 461, 464)
and vv. 4–6 are generated by an interpretation of מגור (v. 3)
agreeing with that found in Sept., Pesh., Aq., and Symm.: מגור
is derived from גור 'to sojourn' 'to be exiled', is resumed in v. 4
(נתנך למגור) and in an extended exegesis (vv. 4–6) is explicated

as 'exile'. There is good reason for scepticism about the reference to Pashhur as a prophet, but instead of supposing that אשר נבאת להם בשקר (v. 6) is an extraneous element in vv. 4–6, we should understand it as part and parcel of the exegetical intention of vv. 4–6 (pp. 462, 466).

21.1–10: The core is 21.4–6 and בשלח . . . צדקיהו (vv. 1–3*), whatever its relationship to 37.3–5, is probably triggered by a desire to provide a historical occasion for the prophetic words contained in vv. 4–6. The disadvantage of a sudden transition to the final period of the monarchy is tolerated in order to point a contrast in terms of the name 'Pashhur': the prophet who was persecuted by the priest Pashhur ben Immer is consulted by the statesman Pashhur ben Malchiah. If vv. 1–3* are secondary, v. 3 can no longer be regarded as a reliable indication of the destination of the oracle in vv. 4–6, but, in any case, the contents of vv. 4–6 do not agree with the assumption that vv. 1–4 are an original unity. Verses 4–6 are not simply about the fate of Zedekiah, but about his kingdom, capital city and subjects. They are in no sense a private message to Zedekiah, but a public proclamation about the fate of Jerusalem and Judah. It may have been the intention of the final editor of the chapter to represent a sequence of events having a rough correspondence with Jer 52.4–16 (39.1–10: 2 Kgs 25.1–12), but 21.1–10 cannot be accommodated with this scheme. ואחרי כן (v. 7) indicates a continuation, but the sequence which is described does not follow from v. 6, because vv. 5f. portray an all-embracing disaster and with them matters come to an end. Hence the contents of vv. 5f. will not allow the continuation indicated by ואחרי כן (v.7), and the contents of v. 7 will not allow the continuation in vv. 8–10. The insertion of בדבר גדול ימתו (v. 6), which does not contribute to the original sense of v. 6, is triggered by an intention to create a timetable of events, and is part of the same process from which ואחרי כן derives. It associates vv. 4–6 with the description of Jerusalem reduced by famine and decimated by plague in the period of the siege prior to the break-out of Zedekiah and his soldiers (Jer 52.4–6). Verses 8–10 cannot be reconciled with vv. 1–7 and they correspond poorly with Jer 52.12–16. The thought that desertion to the Babylonians is a possible way of escaping death is not present in 52.12–16, where those who had earlier deserted and those in the city at the time of the final assault share the same fate. The choice of life or death fits into the context of chapter 38, where it is offered by Jeremiah to Zedekiah, but it cannot be reconciled with the contents of 21.1–7 (pp. 491–504).

22.8f.: No satisfactory account can be given of why these verses appear where they do in the extant text, and they are only marginally relevant to my concept of triggering. They are an inferior patchwork and the unintelligent portrayal of nations parading past the ruins of Jerusalem is the consequence of the unskilful use of borrowed material. The עֹבֵר עַל feature of 1 Kgs 9.8f. (Jer 19.8; 49.17; 50.13) can be combined neatly enough with the question-answer formulation, provided individual travellers are represented as appalled by what they see (כֹּל עֹבֵר עָל). Jer 22.8f. is a poorly conceived conflation of Deut 29.23–25 (the גּוֹיִם feature) and 1 Kgs 9.8f. or the like (the עֹבֵר עַל feature). The verses have a low order of rationality and their insertion is associated with arbitrariness rather than deliberation (p. 522).

22.24–27: These verses do not have a literary coherence, nor are they explicable on the assumption that vv. 25–27 are exegesis generated by v. 24. Verse 27 (third person plural) does not cohere with vv. 25f. (direct address), nor does v. 26 cohere perfectly with v. 25. Verse 24 is a kernel which has received successive exegetical expansions whose horizons are not wider than v. 24, and we should not suppose that these processes will be wholly amenable to rational explanation. The differences between MT and Sept. in v. 25 deserve attention (above, p. xix), and there is much to be said for Duhm's view that v. 27 is 'an addition to an addition'. It is difficult to believe that the person who cast his contribution in the form of direct address in vv. 25f. is the same as the one whose exegesis is formulated in the third person plural (v. 27). It is clear that v. 27, whatever its relationship to 44.14 (מְנַשְּׂאִים אֶת נַפְשָׁם), does not derive immediately from v. 24, because while v. 24 might have given rise to exegesis in the third person singular in view of יִהְיֶה, it could not have generated exegesis in the third person plural. Hence v. 27 assumes v. 26, because the latter is the verse which introduces the king's mother and makes the plural in v. 27 intelligible (pp. 542, 544f.).

22.28–30: Something has already been said about this (above, p. xx). The saying was concerned originally only with the fate of Coniah, but it has been extended in scope to embrace his children. This exegesis, which is evident in vv. 28 and 30 is triggered by the assumption that עֲרִירִי (v. 30) means 'childless' (p. 551).

23.3–6 and 23.1f.: Verses 1f. cannot be combined with vv. 3f.: v. 1 combines with v. 2 and v. 3 with v. 4, but the two groups do not cohere with each other. The negative and threatening aspect of vv. 1f. cannot be combined with the promises of return from exile and leadership contained in vv. 3f., because such elements have no appropriateness in an address to negligent 'shepherds' whose function is to describe their guilt and predict their

judgement. What then is the relation of vv. 3f. to vv. 1f.? Verses
1f. (see above, p. lix) are exilic prose which serve as a
summing-up of preceding royal oracles and which involve a
re-use of vocabulary and ideas taken from poetic passages
(10.21; 22.22). The contents of vv. 3f. (return from exile and
reconstitution of the community under effective and benevolent
leadership) are generated by an exilic or post-exilic response to a
particular exegesis of vv. 1f., namely, that these verses refer to
dispersion and exile (cf. ואני אקבץ at the beginning of v. 3). If
vv. 3f. are regarded as post-exilic, they are to be explained in the
light of the unfulfilled expectations of a complete and perfect
reintegration of the dispersed of Israel (pp. 556, 558, 559). 21.5f.
are then a further development triggered by v. 4. They envisage
the future in terms of good government and security, but they
are more specific than v. 4, because they affirm that in these
future days leadership will be exercised by a Davidic king
(pp. 560, 565).

23.33–40: The view that v. 33 is the kernel and that vv. 34–40
have been generated by it is correct, but the reason usually given
for dissociating v. 34 from v. 33, that there is no ironical
intention in the question of v. 33 and that v. 34 has wrongly
supposed such an intention, is mistaken. There are other proofs
that v. 33 is separable from vv. 34–40 and that these verses have
been triggered by it: (a) The suggestion that או הנביא או כהן has
been imported into v. 33 from v. 34 (Rudolph, Weiser) should be
supplemented by the observation that the word-order of the three
terms (עם ; נביא ; כהן) differs in the two verses: in v. 33 it is עם,
נביא and כהן ; in v. 34 נביא, כהן and עם. It is not merely that או
הנביא או כהן have been tagged on to העם הזה in v. 33. A more
significant factor is that העם הזה (v. 33) has a different sense
from העם (v. 34): in v. 33 העם הזה means the Judaean
community in an all-inclusive sense, and so או הנביא או כהן is an
unconvincing and superfluous supplementation, whereas העם
(v. 34) means the laymen in the community, those who are
neither prophets nor priests. (b) ופקדתי על האיש ההוא ועל ביתו
(v. 34) does not cohere with v. 33, if, as I have argued, that verse
reflects a conflict of שלום and doom prophecy, for in that case
the matter at stake is not the fate of individuals or households,
but the fate of the nation. Hence is it likely that vv. 34–40
represent the attempts of later, generations, living in historical
circumstances different from those of the late pre-exilic period,
to elucidate the conflict between Jeremiah and the שלום
prophets, in the course of which they identify themselves with
the pre-exilic prophet of doom. Thus the נביא who appears in
association with the כהן in v. 34 is a שלום or establishment
prophet and may be identified with the prophets who opposed

Jeremiah and commanded popular support (pp. 597–604; cf. *BZAW* 150, 1980, pp. 35–54).

24: There is no satisfactory elucidation of this passage and the concept of triggering applies only in marginal respects. Chapter 24 represents that Jews were exiled to Babylon only in 597, and it sets up an antithesis between those who went to Babylon with Jehoiachin and those who stayed behind in Judah with Zedekiah. It is unlikely that the historical prophet Jeremiah ever adopted so negative an attitude to Zedekiah as appears in this passage, and we have evidence from elsewhere in the book that he held out hope to those who remained in Jerusalem after 597 (27.1ff.) and threw in his lot with those who survived after 586 (40). Nor can the account in 24 be shown to fit either in an exilic or a post-exilic situation. The primary contrast is probably between those who went to Babylon in 597 and those who stayed in Judah. The view that the future is reposed in the Babylonian diaspora, thus defined, triggers the secondary, negative reference to the Egyptian diaspora which disturbs the original connection between בארץ הזאת (v. 8) and ונתתים (v. 9). The original contrast between those who went to Babylon in 597 and those who remained in Judah, developed in vv. 9f., is further interrupted and distorted by בכל המקמות אשר אדיחם שם (v. 9). This is another widening of the original theme which is clearly intrusive in vv. 9f. It is probably generated by the negative judgement on the Egyptian diaspora which it extends to all other dispersions. We then have an antithesis set up not only between those exiled to Babylon in 597 and those left behind in Jerusalem, but also between those exiled to Babylon in 597 and all other Jewish dispersions. Further insertions in 24 have been noted above (pp. liif.) and another is לרעה (v. 9) which disturbs a well-established word-string לזועה לכל ממלכות הארץ (pp. 605–617).

25.15–29: Verses 27–29 are not continuous with vv. 15–26. They entertain the possibility of choice, and they are a new and later development in which the imagery of the cup is appropriated and applied in a manner incompatible with vv. 15–17. The possibility that the nations will refuse to drink is countenanced, and the assertion that such a refusal will not be tolerated is connected with a prior judgement which has been inflicted on Jerusalem (p. 642). The judgement of Judah and Jerusalem has no original place in vv. 15–26 and its appearance at vv. 18 and 29, however these verses are related, is an indication of the influence which has been exerted on vv. 15–26 by vv. 1–13(14). In vv. 1–13 the judgement of Judah and Jerusalem comes first and v. 18 is an attempt to establish a correspondence with this in vv. 15–29. If v. 29 were generated

before v. 18, the latter will have been triggered by v. 29 in
particular (p. 637). Other features of vv. 15–29 have been
generated by the concern to make an integrated unity out of
vv. 1–29, and it is probably this impetus which produces the
reference to 'sword' in vv. 16 and 27. The imagery of the
intoxicating or poisonous cup is explained in terms of the bloody
victories of Nebuchadrezzar, but Nebuchadrezzar, who achieves
such a dominant position in the final form of the text of vv. 1–13,
has no place in vv. 15–26, and it is unlikely that the nations
which drink the cup of wrath are to be equated with those
mentioned in vv. 9–11 (p. 636). A final case of triggering,
influenced by the representation of vv. 1–13, is the insertion of
the reference to Babylon (v. 26): Babylon must be the final
recipient of Yahweh's judgement as it is in vv. 12f., in order to
match vv. 15–29 with vv. 1–13(14) and to create the impression
of an integrated whole (pp. 640, 645f.). Other cases of a longer
text in vv. 15–26 (MT) not represented by Sept. are set out on
p. 641. כיום הזה (v. 18) is of special interest, because it locates
the judgement and devastation of Jerusalem and Judah in the
past. It is a modification of the text which accommodates the
passage to an unevenness of fulfilment, by noting that Jerusalem
and Judah have been destroyed, while the judgement of the
nations still lies in the future (p. 637).

Conclusion of section D:

If the assumption is made that the shorter text of Sept. gives us
access to a Hebrew text shorter than MT, the most stringent
demonstration of the rolling *corpus* idea is the examination of
the history of the Hebrew text in the area between the Hebrew
Vorlage on which Sept. rests and the extant Massoretic text. The
nature of these processes of expansion can be gathered from
A.1(*a*) and (*b*) and, especially from A.1(*c*). In the case of A.1(*b*)
there is a recognition that the shorter Greek text is not invariably
to be explained in terms of a Hebrew *Vorlage* shorter than MT;
that there are some cases where an abridgement of the text of
MT is the better explanation of the shorter Greek text.
Nevertheless, the hypothesis that a Hebrew *Vorlage* shorter than
MT is the best explanation of the shorter text of Sept. holds for
the most part and has been developed in detail in A.1(*c*). Here a
comparison of MT and Sept. reveals how the Hebrew text has
developed and shows that we are not encountering a systematic,
comprehensive scheme of editing, but exegetical additions of
small scope, operating within limited areas of text. This
exegetical expansion or commentary is triggered by a verse or a
few verses of pre-existing text, and it is this procedure which is
indicated by the term 'rolling *corpus*'. Such triggering or
generation necessarily has a piecemeal character: the

pre-existing Hebrew text, as represented by Sept., has generated a kind of expansion which does not serve the ends of a thoughtful, all-embracing redaction or a superintending, theological tendency.

Section D.2 is occupied with a similar exercise, except that no support for the hypothesis is available from Sept. The assumption is that the supplementations which are postulated for MT are already present in the Hebrew *Vorlage* of Sept. There is, however, the force of analogy: that the expansions which are identified are of the same kind as those in A.1(c) for which the evidence of Sept. is available. In any case the greater bulk of material is in A.1(c), so that the argument, for the most part, satisfies the stringent condition of a comparison of texts which are actual and extant.

In relation to 'generation' or 'triggering' the kind of demonstration represented by D.3 (Kernel) and D.4 (Reservoir) is subsidiary. Reasons have been given (Section B) why evidences of the re-use of Jeremianic poetry in prose passages should not lead to the conclusion that the prophet Jeremiah is the author of the prose. Rather this is another form of the rolling *corpus*, is associated with the long period over which the *corpus* grew, and is an indication that such growth might involve the redeployment of linguistic capital already in existence. The arguments for generation or triggering which are of a higher-critical rather than textual-critical kind are concentrated in section D.5(a), (b) and (c). In D.5(a) the condition which has to met in order to satisfy rigour is a relation of contiguity or virtual contiguity between poetry and prose. If it is to be shown convincingly that poetry generates prose, the prose must immediately follow the poetry, or, at any rate, be close to the poetry in the arrangement of the material in the extant text. This also holds for the few examples of poetry generating poetry which are collected in D.5(b).

The matter is more complicated in D.5(c), where the contention that prose generates prose in the longer prose compositions sometimes involves the employment of a type of 'kernel' concept as a point of departure: not, however, a kernel around which a coherent composition is organized, but a kernel which triggers piecemeal, exegetical expansions of a near-sighted kind. It can be shown that these have been triggered by small pieces of text and that they can be explained on this basis. As such they will possess differing degrees of relatedness to the kernel, and will achieve a product which is marked by fragmentariness rather than wholeness. The impression of compositeness may also be created by the introduction of a theme or themes which are not present in the kernel and which may have been triggered by a wrong exegesis of pre-existing elements.

It is the interests of exegetes or commentators, concentrated on small pieces of text, which are satisfied by those processes of generation. They may have aspects of arbitrariness, they are not related to a systematic, comprehensive editorial tendency, they may rest on mistaken exegesis, and sometimes they are so dark that no explanation can be offered of them. We are not, for the most part, engaging with highly organized literary compositions informed with all-embracing editorial principles or a theological plan which superintends chapters 1–25 as a whole.

What is meant by a rolling *corpus* is that small pieces of pre-existing text trigger exegesis or commentary. MT is to be understood as a commentary or commentaries built on pre-existing elements of the Jeremianic *corpus*. Where the argument is that poetry generates prose there is an assumption that the poetry which has generated prose comment is attributable, for the most part, to the prophet Jeremiah. Where the thesis is that prose generates prose, the kernel may not be regarded as giving access to the period of the prophet Jeremiah and preserving the sense of words which he spoke. In general, the theory is bound up with the persuasion that the rolling *corpus* 'rolled' over a long period of time and was still rolling in the post-exilic period.

E. Delimitation of units of poetry and source theory

1.(*a*) The arrangement of units of poetry for exegesis: 2.1–3; 2.4–13; 2.14–19; 2.20–28; 2.29–37; 3.1–5; 3.12*–13; 3.19–25; 4.1–4; 4.5–9; 4.11–18; 4.19–22; 4.23–26; 4.27–29; 4.30–31; 5.1–6; 5.7–11; 5.12–14; 5.15–17; 5.20–25; 5.26–29; 5.30–31; 6.1–8; 6.9–15; 6.16–21; 6.22–26; 6.27–30; 8.4–7; 8.8–9; 8.10–12; 8.13; 8.14–17; 8.18–23; 9.1–5; 9.6–8; 9.9–10; 9.16–21; 9.22–23; 10.1–16*; 10.17–25; 11.15–17*; 12.1–5; 12.7–13; 13.15–17; 13.18–19; 13.20–27; 14.1–10; 14.17–15.4* (14.17–21 is poetry); 15.5–9; 15.10–12; 15.13–14; 15.15–18; 15.19–21; 16.19–21; 17.1–4; 17.5–8; 17.9–10; 17.11; 17.12–13; 17.14–18; 18.13–17; 18.18–23*; 20.7–9; 20.10–13; 20.14–18; 21.11–12*; 21.13–14; 22.6–7; 22.10–12* (v. 10 is poetry); 22.13–19; 22.20–23; 23.9–12; 23.13–15; 23.16–22; 23.23–24; 25.30–38.

(*b*) Problems of coherence in units: 5.20–25 (pp. 128f.); 6.1–8 (p. 138); 6.9–15 (pp. 144f.); 6.16–21 (pp. 148f.); 6.22–26 (p. 151); 8.14–17 (pp. 190, 192f.); 9.1–5 (pp. 198f.); 9.6–8 (pp. 198f.); 9.9–10 (p. 203); 9.16–21 (p. 208); 10.1–16 (pp. 218–220); 10.17–25 (pp. 232–235); 12.7–13* (pp. 275, 276f.); 13.12–14 (p. 298); 13.18–19 (p. 302); 13.20–27 (pp. 306–308, 314); 14.17–18 (p. 331); 15.5–9 (pp. 337, 342); 15.10–21 (pp. 344–345); 16.19–21 (pp. 380–381, 382f.); 17.5–10 (pp. 394f., 397); 17.12–13 (pp. 402–404); 20.7–18 (pp. 467–469); 21.11–14 (pp. 506f.); 22.13–19 (p. 527); 22.20–23 (p. 538); 23.9–12 (pp. 569, 573); 23.16–22 (pp. 577f.); 23.23–24 (p. 587); 25.30–38 (pp. 651, 656).

I have nothing new to add to the widely expressed view which is developed with special acuteness by Mowinckel in *Prophecy and Tradition*. My demarcations of units assume that the original units of poetry are short, that exegesis should be concentrated on them as the most significant units of sense, and that connections between them are of a mechanical kind, or else are founded on very general thematic considerations. Such a cluster of sayings in terms of a common theme is a superficial form of association and does not reduce significantly the independence of the individual sayings. The exegetical exploration of supposed, larger, cumulative, literary entities will not repay the labour. A stringing together of units by means of stitch-words or similar devices has been regularly noticed in the body of the commentary, and the clustering of sayings related in theme may be advertised by superscriptions (21.11—royal sayings; 23.9(13)—prophets). It would be wrong, however, to give the impression that these short units of poetry are always seamless, that they have perfect formal proportions and are invariably well-rounded sayings whose parts hang together convincingly and whose compactness is never suspect. They are frequently not free from formal ambiguities and admixtures, from syntactical brokenness and unevenness. Often they will not satisfy the criteria which are employed in form-critical definitions of types of prophetic literature. The 'Laments' or 'Complaints', which are complicated formal structures employing poetry, are treated in another section (G.), and my attitude to the allocation of the poetic units in 1–25 to a source (A) will appear in what immediately follows.

2. The prose in chapters 1–25:

I do not propose to say much about the postulated source B, since this is a hypothesis which exercises a heavier influence on the second part of the book of Jeremiah than on the first. I have noted and rejected Rudolph's view that 19.1,2*,10,11,14f., 20.1–6 constitute the first appearance of a 'Baruch Biography' in the book of Jeremiah (pp. 448–449). A bigger issue is raised by the prose within chapters 1–25 which Mowinckel and Rudolph have allocated to source C (Rudolph: 7.1–8.3; 11.1–14; 16.1–13(18); 17.19–27; 18.1–12; 21.1–10; 22.1–5; 25.1–14), but it will be obvious by now that this theory has exercised no influence on my treatment of the prose. My sharper argument, that poetry generates prose, that the contiguity of poetry and prose in the extant text is a significant relationship, and that such prose cannot be explained as dismembered parts of a once continuous, literary source, does not, for the most part, apply to the material which Rudolph has allocated to source C (only in the case of 7.29–8.3 and 22.1–5/21.11f.). But the view that the source C passages are parts of a once continuous source which has been chopped up and distributed among the poetry (source A), in order to provide a series of frameworks for the poetry, conflicts with my idea of a rolling *corpus*. The passages included in Rudolph's source C are largely those with which I have dealt in D.5(*c*), and there I have supposed that prose already *in situ* in the *corpus* has been enlarged and complicated by the processes of triggering which I have described.

The hypothesis that the prose passages were allocated to the places which they now occupy in 1.–25, fully grown and posssessing the same content as they have in the extant text, as a consequence of the dismemberment of a once continuous literary source, never at any time forced itself on my mind as necessary or valuable in connection with the problems which I was encountering. Source C seems to me an additional, critical superstructure which is not functionally necessary and which ought to be demolished in the interests of economy. Nor does Rudolph pursue the rearticulation of this hypothetical source with great vigour: he does not indicate how the disjointed parts which he has identified should be reconstituted, apart from one suggestion that 22.1–5 is a continuation of 7.1–8.3 (p. 515). The argument that the formula הדבר אשר היה אל ירמיהו מאת יהוה (7.1; 11.1; 18.1; 21.1; 25.1) indicates a common literary source for these passages has some force, and I have no answer to the question why this editorial standardization (which is my understanding of the matter) has been carried out precisely in these passages and not in others. It should be noticed that the argument from the formula is weakened by the circumstance that it does not occur in three passages allocated to source C by Rudolph (16.1; 17.19; 22.1). My conclusion is that the formula is attributable to a superficial kind of editorial superintendence exercised over the *corpus* of the book of Jeremiah and that it is not the signature of a separate, literary source. It is a consequence of editorial tidying-up, and not a mark of passages from a literary source which came with them when they were settled at various places in 1–25. It should also be said that my view of the poetry in 1–25, particularly that which appears in D.5(*a*), where I am representing the poetry as a kind of *proto-corpus*, alienates me from Rudolph's understanding of the relationship between the poetry (source A) and the prose (source C).

The importance which Rudolph attaches to his source hypothesis does, however, reflect an important, critical difference between his work and mine. On the whole, his interest is in establishing that the poetry (source A) and the prose (source C) are alternative records of Jeremiah's prophetic preaching. Although, unlike the poetry, the prose does not preserve the words of the prophet Jeremiah and comes to us in Deuteronomic/Deuteronomistic dress, it does give us access to the historical Jeremiah and, more or less, preserves the sense of his preaching. The view that there are Jeremianic kernels appears from time to time in my account of how prose generates prose, but my insight is rather that the development of this prose by processes of triggering takes places over a long period of time, that it is an aspect of the rolling *corpus* and that it is an activity which removes us from the historical context of Jeremiah's ministry to later times.

3. The original scroll and the enlarged scroll:
I have reviewed different hypotheses about these scrolls in the body of the commentary (pp. 631–633), and I have noticed that there has been considerable speculation about their contents, both about the original scroll (cf. 36.1–8) and the enlarged scroll (cf. 36.27–32). It does not seem to me that there is any way of arbitrating effectively between the various estimates of their respective contents, and at the end of the day one can do little better than take refuge in agnosticism. There is not enough evidence to enable us to pursue the question of the identification of the contents of the original scroll and the enlarged scroll with any chance of arriving at firm conclusions. One reason why there is wide agreement that the search should be concentrated on chapters 1–25 relates to the interpretation which has been placed on 25.1–13, and especially בספר הזה (v. 13). It has been widely held that 25.1–13 are a conclusion for the preceding chapters and that בספר הזה is a reference to the original scroll or to the enlarged scroll. I have argued (pp. 626f.) that vv. 1–13 are an introduction to the oracles against foreign nations and that בספר הזה alludes to this collection of material.

It is, however, necessary, in view of what I have said in E.1, to enquire whether the references to literary compositions in chapter 36 lend first class support to a source theory. They are records of two phases of literary activity which are said to have resulted in two collections of Jeremiah's oracles, both written by Baruch at Jeremiah's direction, and the second larger collection replacing the one destroyed by Jehoiakim. If one supposes that these were constituted by the poetry or some of the poetry in chapters 1–25, there are excellent reasons (so it might be argued) for accepting the hypothesis of a source A. It should be said, however, to avoid a misleading over-simplification that some prose is included in Rudolph's definition of the contents of the original scroll and the enlarged scroll, and that these extend beyond chapters 1–25, notably to include oracles against foreign nations in the original scroll (25.15–38; 46–49.33) and the enlarged scroll (49.34ff.), and chapter 27 in the enlarged scroll.

Nevertheless, if we concentrate on the poetry of 1–25 (the oracles of doom against Judah and Jerusalem) and its connection with speculations about the contents of the scrolls, we have to ask whether the notices in 36 lend important reinforcement to the postulated source A of Mowinckel and Rudolph. I would urge that this expectation is defeated by the evidence which comes to light when the poetry of 1–25 is subjected to close scrutiny. I have already stated that the short piece of poetry is the centre of exegetical interest, so that the significance of any literary ordering of these units should not be over-estimated, even if it were supervised by Jeremiah himself. A more powerful consideration is that the condition of the Hebrew text in these poetic units, the formal and syntactical brokenness to which I have called attention (E.1.(*b*)), make it impossible for me to believe that the extant text is to be identified with collections of poetry which (*ex hypothesi*) were conceived by the prophet Jeremiah and written down by Baruch.

If the contention is rather that it is to source C that we should look for the contents of the scrolls, the difficulties encountered are no less formidable. The argument is (O. Eissfeldt, *The Old Testament: An Introduction*, 1966, pp. 350–53) that the prose passages of source C were written by Jeremiah as a deliberate, thoughtful review or summing-up of twenty three years of prophetic activity; they are a considered retrospect in prose of the sense and implications of the individual oracles which were proclaimed; they are a potted version of a long period of prophetic preaching, and the date given in 25.1 (the fourth year of Jehoiakim = 605) agrees with that of 36.1, where the writing of the original scroll is described. The highest significance that can be attached to the coincidence of dates is that they express an editorial view that chapters 25.1–13 and 36.1ff. should be correlated. This may rest on an assumption that בספר הזה (25.13) is a reference to the scroll. In any case I have argued that 25.1–13 are not correctly understood as a conclusion of what precedes them, and, in particular, that בספר הזה refers to the collection of oracles against foreign nations. Moreover, the prose of 1–25 does not have the characteristics which are required of it by Eissfeldt. It does not combine to form a concerted narrative which draws together all the threads of Jeremiah's activity and presents a luminous, well-rounded conspectus of the individual constituents of years of prophetic preaching. The account which I have given of the functioning of this prose (D.5(c)) is incompatible with the characteristics which Eissfeldt attributes to it. Hence my conclusion is that although the references in chapter 36 might initially be regarded as important evidences for a source theory, there is opposing evidence arising from a detailed scrutiny of the poetry and prose in chapters 1–25 to which a greater weight should be attached.

F. Historical problems

1.(*a*) Dubious attachments of pieces of text, especially poetry, to external historical events:
1–6 (p. 5); 1.11–16 (p. 16); 1.13–16 (pp. 19–21); 2.14–15 (p. 36; cf. pp. 55, 57); 3.10 (p. 66); 3.15 (p. 73); 5.1–6 (p. 117); 5.15–17 (p. 124); 5.21–29 (p. 135); 7.16–20 (p. 171); 9.24–25 (p. 214); 12.1–6 (p. 265); 12.7–13 (pp. 277–278); 12.14–17 (pp. 283f.); 13.1–11 (pp. 289f.); 13.12–14 (p. 297); 13.15–17 (pp. 300f.); 13.20–27 (pp. 306f.); 16.10–13 (p. 369); 17.1–4 (p. 387); 17.9–11 (p. 398); 20.1–6 (p. 467); 20.7b (p. 471); 22.1–5 (p. 515); 22.20–23 (p. 540); 23.9–12 (p. 573); 25.11,12 (pp. 627f.); 25.15–26 (pp. 641–643); 25.30–38 (p. 656).
(*b*) Intense anticipations of disaster cast in form of disaster which is taking place or has taken place:
4.6b–8 (p. 93); 4.15–17 (pp. 99, 100); 4.19–21 (pp. 103f.); 4.23–26 (pp. 106f.); 4.28 (p. 109); 4.5ff. (p. 113); 5.6 (p. 115); 8.16 (p. 192); 8.19 (pp. 193, 195); 8.23 (p. 196); 9.9–10 (p. 204); 9.16–21 (pp. 209, 210); 10.17 (p. 229); 10.20 (p. 231); 10.22 (pp. 232, 234); 12.7–13 (pp. 277–278); 13.15–17 (pp. 300f.); 14.17–18 (pp. 329f.); 15.5–9 (pp. 338, 342f.).

I am throwing doubt on a procedure which has been pursued by generations of critical scholars. The assumption has been that exegesis is incomplete or insufficiently sharp, unless a passage is explained in connection with a particular set of historical circumstances. I am not objecting to this as an ideal requirement, but I am saying that pieces of poetry in Jer 1–25 cannot usually be so correlated and that the correlations which are offered are sometimes a kind of guesswork. They are instantaneous intuitions which function by making a stab at what is supposed to be an appropriate historical setting for pieces of text which themselves give no firm indication how they are historically anchored. There are exceptions to this statement, notably sayings with royal connections which can be satisfactorily located (13.18f.; 22.10–12; 22.13–19; 22.24–27;

22.28–30), and also a passage like 6.1–8 (pp. 139f.), where one can bring detailed historical considerations into play, but the correlations which are made by scholars in 1–25 are frequently of the 'instant' variety and are logically extremely weak. Even the 'Scythian' discussions, in which external evidence has been used in a detailed manner, seem to me to run into the sand (1.13–16, pp. 19–21; 5.15, p. 124).

The conclusion presses that here is an area where the compulsion of a historical-critical orthodoxy, which describes how the exegesis of texts must be carried out, has exercised a heavy influence and has produced an unusual intellectual torpor and docility. These attempts to relate passages of poetry in 1–25 to external history and to precise historical situations are much more shaky and speculative than has been generally recognized. My experience has been that often a passage contains nothing that will enable us to establish with a sufficient degree of probability that it relates to a particular set of historical circumstances. This stepping out from the inner world of the *corpus* of the book of Jeremiah into the particulars of external history has appeared to me as the most problematic aspect of my entire investigation. I am profoundly sceptical of some of the historical correlations which have been found for pieces of poetry and to which their exegesis has been bound. These impressionistic attachments of pieces of text to external historical events have an uncommon resemblance to the process of selecting from a range of possibilities by sticking a pin in one of them. No more can be said about the result than it might be right but it might equally be wrong.

Nor do the chronological notices attached to passages necessarily alleviate the situation, although in saying this I have passed to a problem which is distinct from the one that has just been occupying me, where I was dealing with short pieces of poetry to which no overt, chronological indications are attached. To rely on chronological notices in prose passages may be a form of begging the question: since the passage is part of the Jeremianic *corpus* it must be set in the times of the historical Jeremiah. The chronological notice, where it occurs, will always locate a passage in a pre-exilic setting, since it can do no other. Passages will inevitably come to us with some items of pre-exilic dress, but this does not show that their background is pre-exilic or that they give us access to the historical Jeremiah and his concerns. I have, however, in this paragraph digressed to touch on evidence which is internal to the *corpus*, and the impact of this on historical problems is considered more fully in section F.2.

I return to the main business of F.1 by focusing attention on the passages which I have collected in 1.(*b*). These pieces, which seem to be firmly associated with experiences of invasion, siege, terror, hunger, carnage and military defeat, and so with the historical conditions of 597 or 586, are, in my judgement, intense premonitions of disaster which cannot be pressed into such precise historical associations. They form a special group and they present us with distinct exegetical problems. Those who interpret them differently from me, and who conclude that all or some of them describe events which are taking place or have taken place, will suppose that they supply firm indications of particular historical backgrounds. We are encountering the problems associated with the so-called 'prophetic perfect', and also the puzzling mixture of 'perfects' and 'imperfects' which sometimes appears (cf. 15.5–9, pp. 342f.). There is no entirely satisfactory translational procedure for dealing with these matters. If we assume that these pieces are premonitions, so branded on the prophet's soul that he describes the events as having already taken place, do we render a 'prophetic perfect' as past or future? There are disadvantages attaching to either procedure. If 'prophetic perfects' are rendered as past tenses, there is no overt indication that (*ex hypothesi*) they refer to events which still lie in the future. If they are translated as future tenses, the exceptional character of the prophetic utterance, and perhaps of the interior state of the prophet, are lost. Neither pastness nor futurity *simpliciter* does justice to the sense. The oddness which should be preserved is precisely that the prophet speaks of future events as if they were past events or present events, because he is overwhelmed by a sense of the inevitability of their unfolding. If, however, these passages are so interpreted as premonitions or anticipations, they are not directly connected with particular, external historical events or experiences of disaster, and so they do not cause me to modify what I have said about the dubious attachments of pieces of text, especially poetry, to particular sets of historical circumstances.

2. Dating founded on internal criteria:

(*a*) Exilic passages: 3.6–11 (pp. 67–69); 5.18, cf. 5.10, 4.27 (pp. 109, 127); 7.1–15 (pp. 164f.); 7.16–20 (pp. 171f.); 11.1–14 (pp. 245f.); 13.1–11 (pp. 290–292); 14.2–10 (p. 323); 14.11–16 (p. 328); 14.17–15.4 (p. 333); 16.1–9 (pp. 367f.); 16.10–13 (pp. 371f.); 16.16–18 (pp. 377–379); 18.7–12 (pp. 424, 426).

(*b*) Exilic or post-exilic passages: chapter 1* (pp. 24f.); 3.14–17 (p. 76); 10.1–16 (pp. 219f.); 16.19–21 (pp. 382–383); 23.1–4 (pp. 558–559); 23.5–6 (p. 565); 23.34–40 (pp. 603); 25.15–26 (pp. 645–647).

(*c*) Post-exilic passages: 12.14–17 (pp. 283f.); 16.14–15 (p. 374); 23.7–8 (see 16.14–15); 17.19–27 (pp. 418f.).

No part of my work is so incomplete or is touched with such

uncertainty and couched in so tentative terms as this attempt to assign pieces of text in 1–25 to historical periods. Arguments about the internal relations of the constituents of the *corpus* (see especially section D), to which I have devoted much attention, are complicated and controversial, but they belong to a genuine area of debate, where detail is available for appraisal and the attempt to establish temporal relationships—an order of growth—within the *corpus* is a strenuous, intellectual activity. In the course of the commentary I have repeatedly expressed my awareness of facing problems which I could not effectively grapple with or solve, whenever I attempted to go beyond the boundary of the *corpus* and attach pieces of text to periods of external history. Some of these efforts involve an extension of a chain of reasoning which was operative within the *corpus*, but they are always, so it has seemed to me, the most fragile links in the chain. In these cases I could discern no other way of reaching historical conclusions, except by extending an argument, the last part of which was conspicuously the weakest.

In this area there are evidences of hesitation in my work, of self-criticism (cf. 13.1–7; 25.30–38), and of a tendency to set up an argument with myself. Thus although I have consented to the view that 7.1–15 and 7.16–20 are exilic passages, I have been impressed by the extent to which the concerns expressed in chapter 7 and the attitudes struck can be identified with those of the historical prophet Jeremiah (p. 182), and a similar tension is discernible in my treatment of 23.25–32 (pp. 595–597). The circumstance that I have not been able to achieve a sharper, historical definition than 'exilic or post-exilic' for some passages is an indication of my hesitancy and tentativeness. The assigning of pieces of text to particular, historical periods is founded on decisions sufficiently subjective to make it inevitable that they will be opposed reasonably by contrary judgements. These are decisions which set out from evidence internal to the book of Jeremiah, but they unavoidably lack certainty or even a high degree of probability.

Among them is the conclusion that the contents of certain passages are best explained as subsequent reflections on Jeremiah's career as a pre-exilic prophet and its relationship to the crushing experience of exile. These passages are then thought to belong to the exilic period and to represent a search after understanding or the satisfaction of pressing theological concerns on the part of the exilic community. In the case of a special group of passages, those dealing with the interdict on intercession (7.16–20; 11.1–14; 14.2–10; 14.11–16; 14.17–15.4; 16.1–9; 18.7–12), I have concluded that we are encountering a view of the prophetic office which accords primacy to the intercessory function and which may, therefore, be described as Deuteronomic (cf. 15.1–4). These passages, on my view on them, ventilate a theological problem and concern which exercised the exilic community. The affirmation of that community that Jeremiah *qua* prophet of doom was a true prophet had to be reconciled with its conviction that effective intercession was a mark of the true prophet, and the reconciliation was achieved by representing that Yahweh had placed an interdict on intercession. I have acknowledged elsewhere that my decisions cannot be set free from theological assumptions (16.19–21; 18.7–12; 23.1–4; 23.5–6; 23.7–8), and, in particular, that my conclusions concerning chapters 1 and 25.15–26 are bound up with my assumption that the historical Jeremiah was not a prophet to foreign nations. The historical period assigned to 10.1–16 depends on the lateness of the theological ideas which I have discerned in these verses, and the passages which I have deemed post-exilic are supposed to reflect the historical and social conditions of that period. A consideration of the historical period appropriate for chapter 24 had no positive outcome: I could find no set of historical circumstances which would answer the requirements of this puzzling chapter (pp. 610–614, 616f.).

G. Lament interpretation

(a) 8.18–23 (pp. 193f., 196f.); 10.19–25 (pp. 233f.,235); 12.1–5(6) (pp. 265–267); 14.2–10 (pp. 322f., 324); 14.11–16 (p. 327); 14.17–15.4 (pp. 332f.); 15.10–21 (pp. 344f., 345f., 350,358f.,360f.); 17.9–18 (pp. 394,408,413–414); 18.19–23 (p. 437); 20.7–9 (p. 469).

(b) Interdict on intercession theme: 7.16–20 (p. 171); 11.14 (p. 245); 14.2–10 (pp. 320,324); 14.11–16 (p. 328); 14.17–15.4 (p. 333).

I have not been greatly exercised with terminological niceties, but 'Lament' has served my purpose better than 'Complaint', because I have discussed work which assumed that the liturgical structure of individual and communal laments in the book of Psalms has influenced these passages in the book of Jeremiah; also because I needed a term which would embrace both passages with an individual reference (Jeremiah's 'Complaints' about his hard lot as a prophet) and those with a corporate reference, where he is represented as interceding for Yahweh's community.

In my interpretation of the laments I have disagreed with Baumgartner at one pole and Reventlow at the other, but I have more in common with Baumgartner than with Reventlow. There are communal laments in Jer 1–25 (14.2–10; 14.17–15.4), but I have steadily disagreed with Reventlow's contention that there is nothing but communal laments, that we have no access to the privacy of Jeremiah's inner struggles, and that he always speaks the language and expresses the concerns of a public, cultic intercessor (pp. 196f., 233,266, 322,345, 350,358, 408,413). The relentlessness with which Reventlow pursues his thesis and the disproportion which ensues is nowhere better seen than in his treatment of 17.14–18 which he identifies as an individual lament, but, nevertheless, interprets as a communal lament on the ground that it has been so redeployed (pp. 408,413). In the case of 10.19f., 22–24 I have argued that even though we may allow that there is a total identification of Jeremiah with his community, this does not lead to the distinction between Jeremiah as a private individual and Jeremiah as a representative, communal intercessor which Reventlow seeks to enforce. Whether we say that 10.19f, 22–24 are attributable to a personified community, or whether we say that they are attributable to Jeremiah, the reference of our words is the same, if Jeremiah is the poet. In a deeper appreciation of the passage any attempt to make a distinction between Jeremiah and the community with which he identifies himself is wooden and unreal. It has significance only if we suppose, as Reventlow does, that the words uttered are public property, rather than being a creation of Jeremiah and an expression of his solidarity with his people. In the latter case one does not reach Reventlow's destination: the prophet's individuality and singularity are not destroyed by the circumstance that his concern for his people is so total. On the contrary, this is a testimony to the exceptional nature of his individuality and the fineness of his spiritual texture: only an individual who had made the community's brokenness his own could have spoken like this. At this level of appreciation a distinction between the voice of Jeremiah and the voice of the community disappears. Reventlow's mistake is in supposing that the community with which Jeremiah identified himself, one broken and near to death, would have been recognized by the empirical community as none other than itself. He does not do justice to the profundity and rarity of the prophet's insight, and in this connection there are words of Calvin on v. 19 which will bear repetition: 'We must then bear in mind that the prophet speaks here not according to the feeling which the people had, for they were so stupified that they felt nothing, but that he speaks of what they ought to have felt' (cf. pp. 234f.).

Baumgartner holds that the models of the laments are to be found in the book of Psalms, but in describing the use which is made of them and the modifications imposed on them he exaggerates the originality of the prophet Jeremiah. I have accepted his view that there is an oracular conclusion, the reverse of what was expected, at 12.5, and, in other respects, his contention that Jeremiah is filling with a prophetic content models which he takes from the book of Psalms and driving them towards conclusions which are at odds with their cultic function has exercised some influence on me (pp. 196,265–266,321f., 345f., 358f., 394,413,469). I have urged that 15.10–11(12) and 15.15–21 are expressions of vexation and anguish which may be regarded as private to Jeremiah, arising as they do out of his prophetic vocation, that they are comparable with 12.1–5 and are not to be denied to the prophet Jeremiah (p. 361). I have noticed, however, that there are laments which have no oracular conclusions (8.18–23; 17.12–18; 18.19–23; 20.7–9), and that at 15.11(?) and 15.19–21 there are concluding oracles which are not refusals. Moreover, I have dissociated the prophet Jeremiah from the content of the communal laments (14.2–10; 14.17–15.4), and also from a recurring type of oracular statement, the interdict on intercession, which appears in connection with the communal laments as a negative answer (14.10; cf. 14.11–16, 15.1–4) and in other contexts (7.16; 11.14).

The arguments used for 14.2–10 apply also to 14.17–15.4 and it will be enough to rehearse them for the former passage. Baumgartner has pointed to the imagery in vv. 8b and 9a as evidence of prophetic originality and this deserves some consideration. Otherwise, his case depends mainly on the reversing of the expected *Heilsorakel* at 14.10 and 15.1–4 in which he discerns a radical reinterpretation of a cultic *Gattung*, attributable to the prophet Jeremiah (see, p. 322). Is this indeed evidence of a prophetic contribution to what is otherwise a complex of cultic stereotypes? The figures in vv. 8b and 9a, however striking, do not modify in any way the theology of the communal lament: by charging Yahweh with negligence or indifference these laments seek to elicit a reassuring response. It is difficult to believe that Jeremiah would have identified himself with a theology whose climax was a שלום oracle, or would have offered a prayer which he knew to rest on a foundation of שקר. The appropriation of the apparatus of the communal lament as a mere device or trick, for no other reason than to lead his audience to a moment of truth in v. 10, might be a testimony to his 'originality', but it is incompatible with the high seriousness and personal integrity of the prophet (cf. pp. 323f.). The 'interdict on intercession' theme has already been noticed in section F.2 (cf. 14.10; 14.11–16; 15.1–4). Instead of enlisting this as evidence of Jeremiah's originality over against the cultic models which he employed, we should see it as an attempt by the exilic community to throw light on pressing theological problems which were made the more urgent by the high priority which they accorded to the intercessory aspect of the prophetic office. It was a formula which enabled them to affirm their theology of prophecy, while, at the same time, to account for the disaster of exile and to assert that Jeremiah was a true prophet. The true prophet is indeed the effective intercessor; Jeremiah was a true prophet, but because Yahweh placed an interdict on intercession he could not exercise his powers to avert the exile. Thus 14.2–10 and 14.17–15.4 are to be seen as exilic constructions, communal laments culminating in oracles which publish Yahweh's interdict on intercession and which are a device for projecting exilic, theological concerns and supplying an answer to them.

Two books have appeared since I finished my work in the body of the commentary. The first (N. Ittmann, *WMANT*, 54, 1981) draws a distinction between 'laments' and 'confessions'. I have understood 'confession' as a constitutive part of the 'lament' *Gattung*, but Ittmann uses it of passages which involve a confrontation between Jeremiah and Yahweh (11.18–23; 12.1–6; 15.10–21; 17.12–18; 18.18–23; 20.7–13), whereas complaints, in which no challenge to Yahweh is issued, are called laments (4.19a; 4.21; 8.22; 13.17). The reason for Ittmann's exclusion of the communal laments (14.2–15.4) is presumably that he intends to deal only with what he regards as expressions of personal anguish and rebelliousness by the prophet Jeremiah.

Ittmann distinguishes by means of literary analysis between kernels of confessions (11.18–20;22–23a; 12.1–3,4b–6; 15.10–11,15–20; 17.14–18; 18.18–22; 20.7–11,13) and pre-Deuteronomic 'actualizations', and a form-critical analysis leads him to conclude that individual laments in the book of Psalms (which featured largely in Baumgartner's pioneer work) are a model for earlier confessions (11.18–20,22–23a; 12.1–3,4b–6; 18.18–22) only to a limited degree and are not at all influential in respect of later confessions (15.10–11,15–20; 17.14–18; 20.7–11,13). Here he is going beyond Baumgartner in the emphasis which he lays on the 'originality' of Jeremiah, although it is not an originality constituted by a radical reinterpretation of a cultic *Gattung*. The newness of the theme in the later confessions (so Ittmann) is so striking that new forms are created by Jeremiah to convey the revolutionary content. The new departure consists of an awareness that no distinction can be made between Jeremiah's anguish and what is essential in his prophetic proclamation. The truth which God would convey through him is manifested in his sufferings: the form of God's revelation to him is his anguish. His suffering as a human being and his prophetic function cannot be separated.

The feature of Ittmann's book which is most remarkable is
that the cultic interpretation of the laments (or confessions or
complaints), of which Reventlow is the most advanced exponent,
exercises no influence on him, and the wheel has turned full
circle, so that interest is focused again on Jeremiah as a human
being. Ittmann has reversed a movement of thought, to which
Baumgartner supplied the first major impetus, by minimizing
the extent to which the laments can be regarded even as free
imitations of a cultic *Gattung*. I have no particular quarrel with
his elucidation of the theological significance of the laments, and
what I have said in the commentary is in general accord with it.

The second book (F. Ahuis, *Der klagende Gerichtsprophet:
Studien zur Klage in der Überlieferung von den
alttestamentlichen Gerichtspropheten*, 1982) has a narrow
form-critical foundation but extends in all directions. It has a
different aim from the form-critical research which Reventlow
focused on the laments in the book of Jeremiah: it has no interest
in establishing that the prophet who speaks in these passages is a
public, cultic intercessor. It presses form-critical judgements to
achieve far-reaching conclusions and to include passages which
have usually been regarded as outside the sphere of 'lament'
interpretation. The fundamental premiss that the lament is
closely related to doom prophecy does not awaken surprise or
provoke controversy. Two modes are discerned: (a) A lament
which arises from the sorrow and contradiction endured by
Jeremiah in fulfilling his duty as a messenger of doom, in
connection with which he lays accusations against Yahweh (e.g.
20.7–9). (b) A lament which is a transformed oracle of doom
and whose elements are similar to those of the individual lament
in the book of Psalms. The prophet's resentment is directed to his
enemies rather than to Yahweh; he affirms his benevolence and
faithfulness as a prophet and calls down Yahweh's vengeance on
those who persecute him (e.g. 18.18–23).

The ambitiousness of the book consists in the attempt to
employ these and other form-critical criteria in order to recover
the original text of units of lament and to elucidate their extant
text as the consequence of a D redaction. In so far as this
enterprise assumes an intimate understanding of an alleged
far-reaching redaction by D, my attitude to it is the same as that
expressed in relation to Thiel (section C). I agree with Ahuis
that the view of the prophetic office which appears along with the
theme 'interdict on intercession' is Deuteronomic (*Der klagende
Gerichtsprophet*, pp. 76f.), but, for the most part, he is
committed to a speculative kind of scholarship which I cannot
follow. He has a faith in form-critical criteria and a discernment
of the operations of D which leads him to create a new Hebrew

text rather than to wrestle with the extant text. Not only does he claim to recover the original text of units of lament; he also supposes that the dispositions of these units in the extant text, severed as they are from each other, are the outcome of disturbances of an original order caused by a D redaction. Thus he undertakes the reconstruction of a literary complex which not only involves changes of text and order within individual units, but also changes of order and a disregard of discontinuities in the extant text in the relations postulated between units (cf. p. 123: 13.1–10a*b; 12.*1–4,5: 16.*5,7; 15.10,17,18,19b,20a: 17.14–18: 18.19,20a*b,22b,23: 18.1–6a; 19.1–2a*,10–11a; 20.7–9: 20.14–18. The colons mark the delimitations of units). The furthest outreach of this kind of speculation is yet another attempt to recover the contents of the *Urrolle* on the assumption that its contents were laments and passages related to laments. The following document is postulated (cf. p. 185): 1.11–14: 4.5a–7b,11a–12a,13,15,16,19–21: 5.1* (8.6f.), 4f.; 6.9–11a: 13.1–9,*10; 1.1–3,*4b,5: 16.*5,7; 15.10,17,18,20a: 17.14–18; 18.19,20,22b,23: 18.1–6a; 19.1,2a*, 10–11a; 20.7–9: 20.14–15,16b–18.

H. Exegesis and theology

1.4–10 (pp. 9f.); 12.1–5 (p. 266); 15.15–21 (pp. 358f.); 16.1–9 (p. 364); 18.1–12 (p. 427f.); 20.9 (pp. 473–475); 20.14–18 (p. 490); 23.25–32 (pp. 592f.).

There is a concern strongly expressed in Weiser's commentary (12.1–5; 15.15–21; 16.1–9; 18.1–7; 23.25–32) to establish that 'God' is not a device for objectifying inner convictions of whose truth the prophet is powerfully impressed; that the words attributed to Yahweh conflict with the prophet's own objectives and set him on a path which he would rather have avoided. The theological problems raised by this way of speaking are considerable and are not solved by a literalism which affirms that the prophet did in fact, in vision or in trance (below, p. 17) hear Yahweh speaking Hebrew, or see his hand, or feel his touch, because the possession of abnormal psychological experiences is not a guarantee that God has been encountered, that is, that truth has been appropriated. It may be rather an indication of derangement and delusion. When we affirm that the prophet Jeremiah was not deluded, we are influenced by the quality of truth in what he represents as 'word of Yahweh'.

The reason why this problem cannot be explored thoroughly in a commentary is not simply that the commentator already has enough to do. The deeper reason is that such theological problems do not arise immediately out of the activity of exegesis.

It is unwise for exegesis in a commentary to attempt too much in this area, because it is a mistake to suppose that the ineffability of a prophet's meeting with God can be contained and expressed in any linguistic account of it; that it can be reproduced in a straightforward way, with a simple correspondence between the mysterious event and its reduction to language, as if both were on the same linguistic plane and the Hebrew text 'recorded' a time of revelation. What we have rather are utterances in a language which only human beings speak, and it is this linguistic deposit which is the business of a commentary. In assuming a linguistic form the ineffable has necessarily become human, and there is a significant sense in which the exegete of a Hebrew text is dealing only with the grammar of a human document, and not immediately with 'God' or with a hinterland of truth claims. He is grappling with the utterances of a prophet who claims to have been apprehended by God and his exegesis must make this clear, but the highest reaches of a theology of prophecy, an examination of the truth claims made by Hebrew prophets in terms of 'inspiration' and 'revelation' is not a major preoccupation of this commentary. These are ultimate theological questions which, because they are meta-linguistic in important respects, are beyond the limits of a plain exegesis of the Hebrew text.

Those who disagree with this limitation will do so because they understand 'word of God' more literally than I do, and because they do not accept that 'speech of God' is analogical language. We cannot be content with a pedestrian, simplistic analysis of language when we are trying to understand an encounter between man and God. Language can achieve no more than an approximate account of the mystery, and, because the linguistic mode of expression belongs to man and not to God, the interiorizing and humanising of the ineffable is an inescapable theological task. Verbalization is a 'translation' or 'transmutation' of a prophet's meeting with God, and we must not follow Weiser in his satisfaction with an external, 'talking' God as the terminus of our understanding of 'revelation' and 'word of God'. The prophet absorbs the mysterious experience into his humanity, filtering it through human modes of apprehension and evaluation and causing it to issue in a linguistic form which is human and not divine. In so far as a commentary on a prophetic book is concerned with this linguistic outcome, it is engaged with a human product, and the methods employed (lexicographical, philological, grammatical, textual-critical, higher-critical and historical) do not transcend the limits of a humanist scholarship.

This is not intended as a statement about my lack of belief in the truth claims which the prophets make, or my lack of interest in the hinterland of theological problems. I take the truth claims of Jeremiah seriously, but I do not believe that a commentary is the right genre for a thorough exploration of matters which in important respects are meta-linguistic. It follows from my premiss ('All language is human language and God does not speak') that I regard as unreal the kind of dichotomies between psychological and transcendental, speech of Jeremiah and speech of Yahweh, the man Jeremiah and the prophet Jeremiah, which Weiser sets up on linguistic foundations in his disagreements with Rudolph (see on 18.21–23; 20.14–18). I regard them as unreal not because I favour psychologizing exegesis, but because I reject the 'talking' external God of Weiser and affirm that all language is human.

In these connections the effects of form-criticism have been baneful, in so far as it has been supposed that a form-critical category ('word of God'—a prophetic oracle) can be converted simply into a theological category and taken as a demonstration that the 'speaking' God has a serious contribution to make to the theology of prophecy. The further drawing-out of form-critical methods noticed in Reventlow (below, pp. 12f.) dissolves the question of the truth claims of a Hebrew prophet by urging that there is no need to explore the significance of a lonely encounter between prophet and God: the matter can be reduced simply to the authority which derives from a cultic office. According to Reventlow, my questions are unreal and the answer is a simple and pedestrian one. But then it all depends on whether the reduction of a question about prophetic truth or 'word of God' in a profound theological sense to installation into a cultic office, in which truth hangs on our willingness to accept that the cultic institution is a repository of truth, is to be regarded as a satisfactory outcome of the intellectual quest.

ABBREVIATIONS

AASOR	Annual of the American Schools of Oriental Research
ABR	Australian Biblical Review
AJSL	American Journal of Semitic Languages and Literatures
ANVAO	Avhandlinger utgitt av det norske Videnskaps-Akademi i Oslo
AOAT	Alter Orient und Altes Testament
Aq.	Aquila
ATANT	Abhandlungen zur Theologie des alten und neuen Testaments
BDB	Brown-Driver-Briggs
BETL	Bibliotheca Ephemeridum Theologicarum Lovaniensium
BHK	Biblia Hebraica Kittel
BHS	Biblia Hebraica Stuttgartensia
BHTh	Beiträge zur historischen Theologie
BJRL	Bulletin of the John Rylands Library
BL	Bauer-Leander
BSOAS	Bulletin of the School of Oriental and African Studies
BWANT	Beiträge zur Wissenschaft vom alten und neuen Testament
BZ	Biblische Zeitschrift
BZAW	Beihefte zur Zeitschrift für die alttestamentliche Wissenschaft
CAD	Chicago Assyrian Dictionary
CBQ	Catholic Biblical Quarterly
CML	Canaanite Myths and Legends
CSEL	Corpus Scriptorum Ecclesiasticorum Latinorum
ET	Expository Times
FRLANT	Forschungen zur Religion und Literatur des alten und neuen Testaments
GK	Gesenius-Kautzsch
HTR	Harvard Theological Review
HUCA	Hebrew Union College Annual
IB	Interpreter's Bible
IEJ	Israel Exploration Journal
JAOS	Journal of the American Oriental Society
JBL	Journal of Biblical Literature
JEA	Journal of Egyptian Archaeology
JJS	Journal of Jewish Studies
JNES	Journal of Near Eastern Studies
JQR	Jewish Quarterly Review

JSOT	Journal for the Study of the Old Testament
JSS	Journal of Semitic Studies
JTS	Journal of Theological Studies
K	K°tîb
K^{Or}	Oriental K°tîb
KB	Köhler-Baumgartner
KJV	King James Version
KS	Kleine Schriften
MGWJ	Monatsschrift für Geschichte und Wissenschaft des Judentums
MT	Massoretic Text
NEB	New English Bible
OTS	Oudtestamentische Studiën
PEQ	Palestine Exploration Quarterly
Pesh.	Peshiṭta
PG	Patrologia Graeca
PWM	Prophets and Wise Men
Q	Q°rê
Q^{Or}	Oriental Q°rê
RB	Revue Biblique
RHR	Revue de l'Histoire des Religions
ROS	Religion of the Semites
RQ	Revue de Qumrân
RSO	Rivista degli Studi Orientali
RSR	Recherches de Science Religieuse
RSV	Revised Standard Version
RV	Revised Version
SBT	Studies in Biblical Theology
SEÅ	Svensk Exegetisk Årsbok
Sept.	Septuagint
SNVAO	Skrifter utgitt av det norske Videnskaps-Akademi i Oslo
StTh	Studia Theologica
SVT	Supplements to Vetus Testamentum
Symm.	Symmachus
Targ.	Targum
TGUOS	Transactions of the Glasgow University Oriental Society
Theod.	Theodotion
ThLZ	Theologische Literaturzeitung
ThR	Theologische Rundschau
ThStK	Theologische Studien und Kritiken
ThZ	Theologische Zeitschrift
UUÅ	Uppsala Universitets Årsskrift
VT	Vetus Testamentum
Vulg.	Vulgate

WMANT Wissenschaftliche Monographien zum alten und neuen Testament
ZAW Zeitschrift für die alttestamentliche Wissenschaft
ZDMG Zeitschrift der deutschen morgenländischen Gesellschaft
ZPVP Zeitschrift des deutschen Palästina-Vereins
ZNW Zeitschrift für die neutestamentliche Wissenschaft
ZTK Zeitschrift für Theologie und Kirche

COMMENTARIES CITED

Blayney, B., *Jeremiah and Lamentations: a new Translation with Notes, critical, philological and explanatory* (Oxford, 1784).

Bright, J., *Jeremiah: Introduction, Translation and Notes.* Anchor Bible 21 (Garden City, New York, 1965).

Calvin, J., *Praelectiones in Librum Jeremia et Lamentationes*[3] (Geneva, 1589).

Cappellus, L., *Commentarii et notae criticae in Vetus Testamentum,* (Amsterdam, 1689).

Condamin, A., *Le Livre de Jérémie: Traduction et Commentaire*[3] (Paris, 1936).

Cornill, C. H., *Das Buch Jeremia* (Leipzig, 1905).

Dathe, I. A., *Prophetae Majores ex recensione Textus Hebraei et versionum antiquarum Latine versi notisque philologicis et criticis*[3] (Halle, 1831).

Duhm, B., *Das Buch Jeremia.* Kurzer Hand-Commentar zum AT, 9 (Tübingen and Leipzig, 1901).

Elliger, K., *Leviticus.* Handbuch zum AT 4 (Tübingen, 1966).

Elliott Binns, L., *The Book of the Prophet Jeremiah.* Westminster Commentaries (London, 1919).

Ewald, H., *Die Propheten des Alten Bundes ii: Jeremja und Hezeqiel mit ihren Zeitgenossen*[2] (Göttingen, 1868).

Freehof, S. B., *Book of Jeremiah*: The Jewish Commentary for Bible Readers (New York, 1977).

Giesebrecht, F., *Das Buch Jeremia.* Handkommentar zum AT, iii, 2 (Göttingen, 1897, 1907[2]).

Graf, K. H., *Der Prophet Jeremia* (Leipzig, 1862).

Habel, N. C., *Jeremiah, Lamentations.* Concordia Commentary (Saint Louis and London, 1968).

Hitzig, F., *Der Prophet Jeremia*[2]. Kurzgefasstes exegetisches Handbuch zum AT, 3 (Leipzig, 1866).

Houbigant, C. F., *Biblia Hebraica cum notis criticis, iv: Prophetae Posteriores* (Paris, 1753).

Hyatt, J. P., *The Book of Jeremiah.* IB 5 (New York and Nashville, 1956).

Kimchi, D., Cited from *Miqrā'ôt Gᵉdôlôt.*

Kraus, H. J., *Psalmen*[2]. Biblischer Kommentar Altes Testament 15 (Neukirchen, 1961).

Lowth, W., *A Commentary upon the Prophecy and Lamentations of Jeremiah* (London, 1718).

Luzzatto, S. D., *Commentary on Jeremiah* (Hebrew), Lemburg, 1870.

Naegelsbach, C. W. E., *The Book of the Prophet Jeremiah* (Edinburgh, 1871).

Nicholson, E. W., *The Book of the Prophet Jeremiah 1–25*. The Cambridge Bible Commentary on the New English Bible (Cambridge, 1973).

Nötscher, F., *Das Buch Jeremias*. Die Heilige Schrift des AT vii, 2 (Bonn, 1934).

Peake, A. S., *Jeremiah and Lamentations* i. Century Bible (London, 1910).

Rashi, Cited from *Miqrā'ôt Gᵉdôlôt*.

Reiter, S. (ed.), Hieronymi Sancti Eusebii, *In Hieremiam Prophetam* (Vienna, 1913).

Rosenmüller, E. F. C., *Jeremiae Vaticinia et Threni, Latine vertit et annotatione perpetua*, i–ii. Scholia in Vetus Testamentum 8 (Leipzig, 1826–1827).

Rothstein, J. W., *Das Buch Jeremia*. Die Heilige Schrift des AT i (Tübingen, 1922⁴).

Rudolph, W., *Jeremia³*. Handbuch zum AT 12 (Tübingen, 1968).

Rudolph, W., *Das Buch Ruth, Das Hohe Lied, Die Klagelieder*. Kommentar zum AT, xvii (Gütersloh, 1962).

Schmidt, H., *Die grossen Propheten übersetzt und erklärt*. Die Schriften des AT, II 2 (Göttingen, 1923).

Schreiner, J., *Jeremia 1–25.14*. Die Neue Echter Bibel (Würzburg, 1981).

van Selms, A., *Jeremia i–ii*. Die Prediking van het Oude Testament (Nijkerk, 1972, 1974).

Venema, H., *Commentarius ad Librum Prophetiarum Jeremiae* (Leeuwarden, 1765).

Volz, P., *Der Prophet Jeremiah²*. Kommentar zum AT 10 (Leipzig, 1928).

Weiser, A., *Das Buch Jeremia⁶* Das Alte Testament Deutsch 20/21 (Göttingen, 1969).

Wildberger, H., *Jesaja i–iii*. Biblischer Kommentar Altes Testament 10 (Neukirchen, 1972, 1978, 1982).

OTHER WORKS CITED

Ackroyd, P. R., 'Jeremiah x.1-16', *JTS,* NS 14 (1963), pp. 385-390).

Aharoni, Y., *The Land of the Bible* (London, 1966).

Aharoni, Y., 'Beth-haccherem', *Archaeology and Old Testament Study.* ed. by D. Winton Thomas (Oxford, 1967), pp. 171-184.

Ahiṭuv, S., 'Pashhur', *IEJ* 20 (1970), pp. 95f.

Ahuis, F., *Der klagende Gerichtsprophet. Studien zur Klage in der Überlieferung von den alttestamentlichen Gerichtspropheten.* Calwer Theologische Monographien 12 (Stuttgart, 1982).

Albright, W. F., 'The Babylonian Matter in the Predeuteronomic Primeval History (JE) in Gen 1-11', *JBL* 58 (1939), pp. 91-103).

Albright, W. F., 'The Oracles of Balaam', *JBL* 63 (1944), pp. 207-233.

Albright, W. F., 'A Catalogue of Early Hebrew Lyric Poems', *HUCA* 28 (1950/51), pp. 1-39.

Albright, W. F., 'Dedan', *Geschichte und Altes Testament.* Alt Festschrift, BHTh 16 (1953), pp. 1-12.

Albright, W. F., 'Northwest-Semitic Names in a List of Egyptian Slaves from the Eighteenth Century B.C.', *JAOS* 74 (1954), pp. 222-233).

Alonso Schökel, L., *The Inspired Word. Scripture in the Light of Language and Literature* (London, 1967). An English translation by Martin F. of *La Palabra Inspirado* (Barcelona, 1966).

Alt, A., 'Hic murus aheneus esto', *ZDMG* 86 (1933), pp. 33-48.

Alt, A., 'Sihor und Epha', *ZAW* 57 (1939), pp. 147f.

Augustin, F., 'Baruch und das Buch Jeremia', *ZAW* 67 (1955), pp. 50-56.

Bach, R., 'Bauen und Pflanzen', *Studien zur Theologie der alttestamentlichen Überlieferungen.* Von Rad Festschrift (Neukirchen, 1961), pp. 7-32.

Bach, R., *Die Aufforderung zur Flucht und zum Kampf im Alttestamentlichen Prophetenspruch,* WMANT 9 (1962).

Bailey, K. E. and Holladay, W. L., 'The "young camel" and "wild ass" in Jeremiah ii 23-25', *VT* 18 (1968), pp. 256-260.

Baltzer, K., 'Considerations regarding the Office and Calling of the Prophet', *HTR* 61 (1938), pp. 567-581.

Bardtke, H., 'Jeremia der Fremdvölkerprophet', *ZAW* 53 (1935), pp. 209-239; *ZAW* 54 (1936), pp. 240-262.

Bauer, H.—Leander, P., *Historische Grammatik der hebräischen Sprache des Alten Testamentes* (Halle, 1922, Hildesheim, 1965).

Baumann, E., 'Der linnene Schurz. Jer 13.1–11', *ZAW* 65 (1953), pp. 77–81.

Baumgartner, W., *Die Klagegedichte des Jeremia*, BZAW 32 (1917).

Baumgartner, W., 'Das Aramäische im Buche Daniel', *ZAW* 45 (1927), pp. 81–133.

Baumgartner, W., *Hebräisches und Aramäisches Lexikon zum Alten Testament* (= KB³), unter Mitarbeit von Hartmann B, und Kutscher E. Y. (Leiden, 1967, 1974, 1983).

Bea, A., 'König Jojachin in Keilschrifttexten', *Biblica* 23 (1942), pp. 78–82.

Bentzen, A., 'The Ritual Background of Amos i 2–ii 16', *OTS* 8 (1950), pp. 85–99.

Berridge, J. M., *Prophet, People and Word of Yahweh. An Examination of Form and Content in the Proclamation of the Prophet Jeremiah.* Basel Studies of Theology 4 (Zürich, 1970).

Birkeland, H., *Zum hebräischen Traditionswesen. Die Komposition der prophetischen Bücher des Alten Testaments.* ANVAO II, 1938/1 (Oslo, 1938).

Blau, J., 'Über Homonyme und angeblich homonyme Wurzeln', *VT* 6 (1956), pp. 242–248.

Blau, J., 'Über die *t* Form des Hif'il im Bibelhebräisch', *VT* 7 (1957), pp. 385–388.

Bochart, S., *Geographia Sacra . . . cui accedunt variae dissertationes* (Leiden and Utrecht, 1707).

Bochart, S., *Hierozoicon sive De Animalibus S. Scripturae*, ed. Rosenmüller E. F. C. (Leipzig, 1793–1796).

Bodenheimer, F. S., *Animal Life in Palestine: an introduction to the problems of animal ecology and zoo geography* (Jerusalem, 1935).

Boehmer, J., 'Jeremia und der "Euphrat" ', *ThStK* 82 (1909), pp. 448–458.

De Boer, P. A. H., 'La racine *qwh*', *OTS* 10 (1954), pp. 225–246.

De Boer, P. A. H., 'The Counsellor', *SVT* 3 (1955), pp. 42–71.

De Boer, P. A. H., *Gedenken und Gedächtnis in der Welt des Alten Testaments*, Franz Delitzsch-Vorlesungen 1960 (Stuttgart, 1962).

Bright, J., 'The Date of the Prose Sermons of Jeremiah', *JBL* 70 (1951), pp. 15–35.

Bright, J., *A History of Israel³* (London, 1981).

Brockington, L. H., *The Hebrew Text of the Old Testament. The Readings adopted by the Translators of the New English Bible* (Oxford and Cambridge, 1973).

Brongers, H. A., 'Der Zornesbecher', *OTS* 15 (1969), pp. 177–192.

Broughton, P. E., 'The Call of Jeremiah', *ABR* 6 (1958), pp. 40–46.

Brown, F.-Driver, S. R.,—Briggs, C. A., *A Hebrew and English Lexicon of the Old Testament* (Oxford, 1907, reprinted with corrections, 1966).

Bruston, C., 'Jérémie fut-il prophète pour les nations?', *ZAW* 27 (1907), pp. 75–78.

Buber, M., *The Prophetic Faith* (New York, 1949).

Burkitt, F. C., 'Yahweh or Yahoh: additional note', *JTS* 28 (1927), pp. 407–409.

Burkitt, F. C., 'Justin Martyr and Jeremiah xi 19', *JTS* 33 (1932), pp. 371–373.

Cadoux, C. J., 'The Religious Value of Sacrifice', *ET* 58 (1946/7), pp. 43–46.

Carmignac, J., 'Précisions apportées au vocabulaire de l'hébreu biblique par la guerre des fils de lumière contre les fils de ténèbres', *VT* 5 (1955), pp. 345–365.

Carmignac, J., 'Le texte de Jérémie 10,13 (ou 51,16) et celui de II Sam 23,7 améliorés par Qumran', *RQ* 7 (1969), pp. 287–290.

Carroll, R. P., 'A non-cogent Argument in Jeremiah's Oracles against the Prophets', *StTh* 30 (1976), pp. 43–51.

Cazelles, H., 'Sophonie, Jérémie et les Scythes en Palestine', *RB* 74 (1967), pp. 24–44.

Cazelles, H., 'Israel du Nord et l'arche d'alliance', *VT* 18 (1968), pp. 147–158.

Ceriani, A. M. (ed.), *Translatio Syra Pescitto Veteris Testamenti ex Codice Ambrosiano sec fere vi, photolithographice edita curante et adnotante*, i–ii (Milan, 1876–1883).

Childs, B. S., *Introduction to the Old Testament as Scripture* (London, 1979).

Christensen, D. L., ' "Terror on every Side" in Jeremiah', *JBL* 92 (1973), pp. 498–502.

Clements, R. E., *God and Temple. The Idea of the Divine Presence in Ancient Israel* (Oxford, 1965).

Clines, D. J. and Gunn, D. M., 'Form, Occasion and Redaction in Jeremiah 20', *ZAW* 88 (1976), pp. 390–409.

Cocceius, J., *Lexicon et commentarius sermonis Hebraici et Chaldaici Veteris Testamenti* (Amsterdam, 1669).

Cocceius, J., *Opera omnia theologica, exegetica, didactica, polemica, philologica* i–viii (Amsterdam, 1675).

Cogan, M., 'A Note on Disinterment in Jeremiah', Gratz College Anniversary Volume (1971), pp. 29–34.

Colunga, A. and Turrado L. (ed.), *Biblia Sacra iuxta Vulgatam Clementinam*[4] (Madrid, 1965).

Condamin, A., 'La "colère de la colombe" ', *Biblica* 12 (1931), pp. 242f.

Cooke, G. A., *A Text-Book of North-Semitic Inscriptions* (Oxford, 1903).

Cowley, A. E. (ed.), *Gesenius' Hebrew Grammar as edited and enlarged by the late E. Kautzsch*[2] (Oxford, 1910).

Cowley, A. E., *Aramaic Papyri of the Fifth Century B. C.* (Oxford, 1923).

Coxon, P. W., 'The Problem of Consonantal Mutations in Biblical Aramaic' *ZDMG* 129 (1979), pp. 8–22.

Cross, F. M. and Freedman, D. N., 'The Song of Miriam', *JNES* 14 (1955), pp. 237–250.

Cross, F. M., *The Ancient Library of Qumrân*[2] (New York, 1961).

Dahood, M. J., 'The Value of Ugaritic for Textual Criticism', *Biblica* 40 (1959), pp. 160–170.

Dahood, M. J., 'Two Textual Notes on Jeremia', *CBQ* 23 (1961), pp. 462–464.

Dahood, M. J., 'Philological Notes on Jer 18:14–15', *ZAW* 74 (1962), pp. 207–209.

Dahood, M. J., 'Ugaritic Studies and the Bible', *Gregorianum* 43 (1962), pp. 55–79.

Dahood, M. J., 'Denominative *riḥḥam* "to conceive, enwomb" ', *Biblica* 44 (1963), pp. 204f.

Dahood, M. J., 'Hebrew-Ugaritic Lexicography I', *Biblica* 44 (1963), pp. 289–303.

Dahood, M. J., 'Emphatic Lamedh in Jer 14:21 and Ezek 34:29', *CBQ* 37 (1975), pp. 341f.

Dahood, M. J., 'The Emphatic Double Negative *m'yn* in Jer 10:6–7', *CBQ* 37 (1975), pp. 458f.

Dahood, M. J., 'Ebla, Ugarit and the Old Testament', *SVT* 29 (1978), pp. 81–112.

Dalman, G. H., *Arbeit und Sitte in Palästina*, i–vii (Gütersloh, 1928–42).

Dalman, G. H., *Aramäisch-Neuhebräisches Handwörterbuch zu Targum, Talmud und Midrasch*[2] (Göttingen, 1938).

Davies, G. I., *The Way of the Wilderness. A Geographical Study of the Wilderness Itineraries in the Old Testament*. The Society for Old Testament Study Monograph Series 5 (Cambridge, 1979).

Deist, F., 'Zu כתמר מקשה in Jer 10.5', *ZAW* 85 (1973), pp. 225f.

Delekat, L., *Asylie und Schutzorakel am Zionheiligtum: eine Untersuchung zu den privaten Fiendpsalmen* (Leiden, 1967).

Doniach, N. S., 'Studies in Hebrew Philology', *AJSL* 50 (1933/4), pp. 177–179.

Donner, H. and Röllig, W., *Kanaanäische und aramäische Inschriften* i–iii, (Wiesbaden, 1962–1964).

Dozy, R., *Supplément aux Dictionnaires Arabes*[3] i–ii (Leiden and Paris, 1967).

Driver, G. R., 'Some Hebrew Words', *JTS* 29 (1928), pp. 390–396.

Driver, G. R., 'Studies in the Vocabulary of the Old Testament I', *JTS* 31 (1930), pp. 275–284.

Driver, G. R., 'Hebrew Notes on the "Wisdom of Jesus ben Sirach" ' *JBL* 53 (1934), pp. 273–290.

Driver, G. R., 'Studies in the Vocabulary of the Old Testament VIII', *JTS* 36 (1935), pp. 293–301.

Driver, G. R., 'Linguistic and Textual Problems: Jeremiah', *JQR, NS* 28 (1937/8), pp. 97–129.

Driver, G. R., 'Hebrew Notes', *VT* 1 (1950), pp. 241–250.

Driver, G. R., 'Difficult Words in the Hebrew Prophets', *Studies in Old Testament Prophecy*. T. H. Robinson Festschrift (Edinburgh, 1950), pp. 52–72.

Driver, G. R., 'Jeremiah xii 6', *JJS* 5 (1954), pp. 177f.

Driver, G. R., 'Problems in the Hebrew Text of Job', SVT 3 (1955), pp. 72–93.

Driver, G. R., 'Birds in the Old Testament. II Birds in Life', *PEQ* (1955), pp. 129–140.

Driver, G. R., 'Two Misunderstood Passages of the Old Testament', *JTS* 6, NS (1955), pp. 82–87.

Driver, G. R., *Canaanite Myths and Legends*. Old Testament Studies iii (Edinburgh, 1956). 2nd ed. by J. C. L. Gibson (Edinburgh, 1978).

Ehrlich, A. B., *Randglossen zur Hebräischen Bibel. Textkritisches, Sprachliches und Sachliches*, iv Jesaia, Jeremia (Leipzig, 1912).

Ehrman, A., 'A Note on בוטח in Jer 12.5', *JSS* 5 (1960), p. 153.

Eissfeldt, O., 'Jahwe Zebaoth', Miscellanea Academica Berolinensia II 2 1950, pp. 128–150; *KS* iii (Tübingen, 1966), pp. 103–123.

Eissfeldt, O., 'Das Alte Testament im Lichte der safatenischen Inschriften', *ZDMG* 104 (1954) pp. 88–118; *KS* iii, pp. 289–317.

Eissfeldt, O., 'Silo und Jerusalem', *SVT* 4 (1957), pp. 138–147; *KS* iii, pp. 415–425.

Eissfeldt, O., *Einleitung in das Alte Testament*[3], Tübingen, 1964; translated by P. R. Ackroyd, *The Old Testament*: an *Introduction* (Oxford, 1965).

Elliger, K., 'Der Sinn des hebräischen Wortes שׂפי. Zugleich ein

Beitrag zum Verständnis der alten Versionen', *ZAW* 83 (1971), pp. 21–29.

Emerton, J. A. 'Notes on Jeremiah 12.9 and on some suggestions of J. D. Michaelis about the Hebrew words *naḥā, 'aebrā* and *jadä*', *ZAW* 81(1969), pp. 182–191.

Emerton, J. A., 'A Problem in the Hebrew Text of Jeremiah vi.23 and l.42, *JTS*, NS 23 (1972), pp. 106–113.

Emerton, J. A., 'Notes on some problems in Jeremiah v 26', Festschrift Cazelles, *AOAT* 212 (1981), pp. 125–133.

Engnell, I., *The Call of Isaiah: an exegetical and comparative Study*. UUA 1949: 4 (Uppsala and Leipzig, 1949).

Epstein, V., 'The Day of Yahweh in Jeremiah 4.23–28', *JBL* 87 (1968), pp. 93–97.

Erbt, W., *Jeremia und seine Zeit. Die Geschichte der letzten fünfzig Jahre des vorexilischen Juda* (Göttingen, 1902).

Esh, S., 'Note on אצי', *VT* 4 (1954), pp. 305–307.

Fenz, A. K., *Auf Jahwes Stimme hören: Eine biblische Begriffsuntersuchung*. Wiener Beiträge zur Theologie 6 (Vienna, 1964).

Fishbane, M., 'Jeremiah iv 23–26 and Job iii 3–13: a recovered use of the creation pattern', *VT* 21 (1971), pp. 151–167.

Fohrer, G., 'Jeremias Tempelwort (Jeremia 7.1–15)', *ThZ* 5 (1949), pp. 401–417; *BZAW* 99 (1967), pp. 190–203.

Fohrer, G., 'Neuere Literatur zur alttestamentlichen Prophetie', *ThR* 20 (1952), pp. 295–361.

Fohrer, G., 'Remarks on Modern Interpretation of the Prophets', *JBL* 80 (1961), pp. 309–319.

Fohrer, G., *Die symbolischen Handlungen der Propheten*[2]. ATANT 54 (1968).

Fox, M. V., 'Jeremiah 2.2 and the "Desert Ideal" ', *CBQ* 35 (1973), pp. 441–450.

Gaster, T. G., 'Jeremiah v.28', *ET* 56 (1944/5), p. 54.

Gelb, I. J.-Jacobsen T.-Landsberger B.-Oppenheim A. L., *The Assyrian Dictionary ... of the University of Chicago* (Chicago, 1956ff.).

Gelston, A., 'Some Notes on Second Isaiah', *VT* 21 (1971), pp. 517–527.

Gerard L. Saint Paul, 'La colère de la colombe', *RB* 40 (1931), pp. 92f.

Gerstenberger, E., 'Jeremiah's Complaints. Observations on Jer 15.10–21', *JBL* 82 (1963), pp. 393–408.

Gesenius, W., *Thesaurus Philologicus Criticus Linguae Hebraeae et Chaldaeae Veteris Testamenti*, i–iii (Leipzig, 1835–1858).

Gevirtz, S., 'The Ugaritic Parallel to Jeremiah 8:23', *JNES* 20 (1961), pp. 41–46.

Gibson, J. C. L. *Text Book of Syrian Inscriptions: i Hebrew and Moabite Inscriptions* (Oxford, 1971).

Gibson, J. C. L., *Canaanite Myths and Legends*[2] (Edinburgh, 1978). See G. R. Driver.

Goldmann, M. D., 'Was Jeremiah married?', *ABR* 2 (1952), pp. 42–47.

Gordon, T. C., 'A New Date for Jeremiah', *ET* 44 (1932/3), pp. 562–565.

Graetz, H., *Emendationes in plerosque Sacrae Scripturae Veteris Testamenti libros* (Breslau, 1892–1894).

Granild, S., 'Jeremia und das Deuteronomium', *StTh* 16 (1962), pp. 135–154.

Gray, J., *The Biblical Doctrine of the Reign of God* (Edinburgh, 1979).

Gressmann, H., 'Ἡ κοινωνία τῶν δαιμονίων' *ZNW* 20 (1921), pp. 227–229.

Gressmann, H., 'Ursprung und Entwicklung der Joseph Sage', EUCHARISTERION, Gunkel Festschrift, FRLANT 19, I (Göttingen, 1923).

Gunneweg, A. H. J., *Mündliche und schriftliche Tradition der vorexilischen Prophetenbücher als Problem der neueren Prophetenforschung*, FRLANT 55 (1959).

Gunneweg, A. H. J., 'Konfession oder Interpretation im Jeremiabuch', *ZTK* 67 (1970), pp. 395–416.

Gunneweg, A. H. J., 'Ordinationsformular oder Berufungsbericht in Jeremia 1', *Glaube, Geist, Geschichte*. Festschrift für E. Benz (Leiden, 1967), pp.91–98.

Habel, N., 'The Form and Significance of the Call Narratives', *ZAW* 77 (1965), pp. 297–323.

Hammershaimb, E., *Some aspects of Old Testament Prophecy from Isaiah to Malachi*. Teologiske Skrifter: Série de Théologie 4 (Copenhagen, 1966).

Haran, M., 'The Ark and the Cherubim: their symbolic significance in Biblical ritual', *IEJ* 9 (1959), pp. 30–38, 80–94.

Haran, M., 'The Disappearance of the Ark', *IEJ* 13 (1963), pp. 46–58.

Haran, M., *Temples and Temple-Service in Ancient Israel. An Inquiry into the Character of Cult Phenomena and the Historical Setting of the Priestly School* (Oxford, 1978).

Hentschke, R., *Die Stellung der vorexilischen Schriftpropheten zum Kultus*. BZAW 75 (1957).

Herdner, A., *Corpus des tablettes en cunéiformes alphabétiques découvertes à Ras Shamra-Ugarit de 1929 à 1939*. Mission de Ras Shamra 10.1 (Paris, 1963).

Herrmann, J., 'Zu Jer 22.29; 7.4', *ZAW* 62 (1950), pp. 321f.

Herrmann, S., *Die prophetischen Heilserwartungen im Alten Testament. Ursprung und Gestaltwandel.* BWANT 5.5 (1965).

Hertzberg, H. W., 'Jeremia und das Nordreich Israel', *ThLZ* 77 (1952), 595–602.

Heschel, A., *Die Prophetie.* Akademie ja Umiljetności. Mémoires de la Commission Orientaliste 22 (Krakow, 1936).

Hobbs, T. R., 'Jeremiah 3.1–5 and Deuteronomy 24.1–4', *ZAW* 86 (1974), pp. 23–29.

Hölscher, G., *Die Propheten. Untersuchungen zur Religionsgeschichte Israels* (Leipzig, 1914).

Holladay, W., *The Root Šûbh in the Old Testament with particular reference to its Usages in Covenantal Contexts* (Leiden, 1958).

Holladay, W., 'Prototypes and Copies. A new approach to the Poetry-Prose Problem in the book of Jeremiah', *JBL* 79 (1960), pp. 351–367.

Holladay, W., ' "On every high hill" and "under every green tree" ', *VT* 11 (1961), pp. 170–176.

Holladay, W., 'The so-called "Deuteronomic Gloss" in Jer. viii 19b', *VT* 12 (1962), pp. 494–498.

Holladay, W., 'Style, Irony and Authenticity in Jeremiah', *JBL* 81 (1962), pp. 44–54.

Holladay, W., 'The Background of Jeremiah's Self-Understanding: Moses, Samuel and Psalm 22', *JBL* 83 (1964), pp. 154–164.

Holladay, W., 'Jeremiah and Moses: Further Observations', *JBL* 85 (1966), pp. 17–27.

Holladay, W., 'The Recovery of Poetic Passages of Jeremiah', *JBL* 85 (1966), pp. 401–435.

Holladay, W., 'The Covenant with the Patriarchs overturned. Jeremiah's intention in "Terror on every side" ', *JBL* 91 (1972), pp. 305–320.

Holladay, W., 'Jeremiah ii 34b—a fresh Proposal', *VT* 25 (1975), pp. 221–225.

Holladay, W., 'Structure, Syntax and Meaning in Jeremiah iv 11–12a', *VT* 26 (1976), pp. 28–37.

Honeyman, A. M., 'The Pottery Vessels of the Old Testament', *PEQ* (1939), pp. 76–90.

Honeyman, A. M., 'Observations on a Phoenician Inscription of Ptolemaic Date', *JEA* 26 (1940), pp. 57–67.

Honeyman, A. M., 'The Evidence for Regnal Names among the Hebrews', *JBL* 67 (1948), pp. 13–25.

Honeyman, A. M., '*Māgôr mis-sābîb* and Jeremiah's Pun', *VT* 4 (1954), pp. 424–426.

Hooke, S. H. (ed.), *Myth and Ritual: Essays on the Myth and*

Ritual of the Hebrews in Relation to the Cultic Pattern of the Ancient Near East (Oxford, 1933).

Hooke, S. H. (ed.), *The Labyrinth: Further Studies in the Relation between Myth and Ritual in the Ancient World* (Oxford, 1935).

Hooke, S. H. (ed.), *Myth, Ritual and Kingship: Essays on the Theory and Practice of Kingship in the Ancient Near East and in Israel* (Oxford, 1958).

Horst, F., 'Die Anfängen des Propheten Jeremia', *ZAW* 41 (1923), pp. 94–153.

Hossfeld, F. L. and Meyer, I., *Prophet gegen Prophet. Einer Analyse der alttestamentlichen Texte zum Thema wahre und falsche Propheten.* Biblische Beiträge 9 (Fribourg, 1973).

Hvidberg, F. F., *Weeping and Laughter in the Old Testament* (Leiden and Copenhagen, 1962). An English translation by Løkkegaard F, of *Graad og Latter i det gamle Testamente. En Studie i kanaanaeisk-israelitisk Religion* (Copenhagen, 1938).

Hyatt, J. P., 'The Peril from the North in Jeremiah', *JBL* 59 (1940), pp. 499–513.

Hyatt, J. P., 'The Original Text of Jeremiah 11.15–16', *JBL* 60 (1941), pp. 57–60.

Hyatt, J. P., 'Jeremiah and Deuteronomy', *JNES* 1 (1942), pp. 156–173.

Hyatt, J. P., 'The Deuteronomic Edition of Jeremiah', *Vanderbilt Studies in the Humanities* i (1951), pp. 77–95.

Ittmann, N., *Die Konfessionen Jeremias. Ihre Bedeutung für die Verkündigung des Propheten*, WMANT 54 (1981).

Jahnow, H., *Das Hebräische Leichenlied im Rahmen der Völkerdichtung BZAW* 36 (1923).

Janssen, E., *Juda in der Exilszeit. Beitrag zur Frage der Entstehung des Judentums.* FRLANT 51 (1956).

Janzen, J. G., *Studies in the Text of Jeremiah.* Harvard Semitic Monographs 6 (Cambridge, Mass., 1973).

Jastrow, M., *A Dictionary of the Targumim, the Talmud Babli and Yerushalmi, and the Midrashic Literature* i–ii (New York and London, 1903).

Jean, C. F. and Hoftijzer, J., *Dictionnaire des Inscriptions sémitiques de l'ouest* (Leiden, 1960–65).

Jenni, E., *Die politischen Voraussagen der Propheten*, ATANT 29 (1956).

Johnson, A. R., *The Cultic Prophet in Ancient Israel*[2] (Cardiff, 1962).

Johnson, A. R., *Sacral Kingship in Ancient Israel*[2] (Cardiff, 1967).

Joüon, P., 'Le sens du mot hébreu *špy*', *Journal Asiatique*, Ser 10, 7 (1906), pp. 137–142.

Joüon, P., 'Divers emplois métaphoriques du mot "yad" en hébreu', *Biblica* 14 (1933), pp. 452–459.

Jüngling, H. W., 'Ich mache dich zu einer ehernen Mauer: Literarkritische Überlegungen zum Verhältnis von Jer 1,18–19 zu Jer 15,20–21', *Biblica* 54 (1973), pp. 1–24.

Kapelrud, A. S., *Joel Studies*. UUÅ, 1948: 4 (Uppsala and Leipzig, 1948).

Kelso, J. L., *The Ceramic Vocabulary of the Old Testament*. *BASOR* Supplementary Studies 5/6 (New Haven, 1948).

Kennicott, B., *Vetus Testamentum cum variis Lectionibus* i–ii (Oxford, 1776–1780).

Klausner, J., *The Messianic Ideal in Israel* (London and New York, 1955).

Köberle, J., *Der Prophet Jeremia; sein Leben und Wirken*[2]. Erläuterungen zum Alten Testament 2 (Stuttgart, 1925).

Köhler, L., 'Beobachtungen am hebräischen und griechischen Text von Jeremia Kap. 1–9', *ZAW* 29 (1909), pp. 1–39.

Köhler, L., 'Hebräische Vocabeln I', *ZAW*, 54 (1936), pp. 287–293.

Köhler, L. and Baumgartner, W., *Lexicon in Veteris Testamenti Libros*[2] (Leiden, 1958) = KB[2].

Koestler, A., *The Act of Creation* (London, 1964).

Kraus, H. J., *Worship in Israel. A Cultic History of the Old Testament*. (Oxford, 1966). An English translation of *Gottesdienst in Israel. Grundriss einer Geschichte des alttestamentlichen Gottesdienstes* (Munich, 1962).

Kruse, H., 'Die "dialektische Negation" als semitisches Idiom', *VT* 4 (1954), pp. 385–400.

Kuhl, C., 'Die "Wiederaufnahme"—ein literarkritisches Prinzip', *ZAW* 64 (1953), pp. 1–11.

Kutsch, E., 'Gideons Berufung und Altarbau, Jdc 6,11–14', *ThLZ* 81 (1956), 75–84.

Lee, S. (ed.), *Vetus Testamentum Syriace* (London, 1823).

Lemke, W. E., 'Nebuchadrezzar, my servant', *CBQ* 28 (1966), pp. 45–50.

Lewy, J., *Forschungen zur alten Geschichte Vorderasiens*. Mitteilungen der Vorderasiatisch-Aegyptischen Gesellschaft 29 (Leipzig, 1925).

Liddell, H. G. and Scott, R., *A Greek-English Lexicon*[9] (Oxford, 1940).

Long, B. O., 'Prophetic Call Traditions and Reports of Visions', *ZAW* 84 (1972), pp. 494–500.

Long, B. O., 'The Stylistic Components of Jeremiah 3, 1–5', *ZAW* 88 (1976), pp. 386–390.

McKane, W., *Prophets and Wise Men*, SBT 44 (London, 1965).

McKane, W., 'The Earlier History of the Ark', *TGUOS* 21 (1967), pp. 68–76.

McKane, W., *Proverbs: a new Approach*, Old Testament Library (London, 1970).

McKane, W., 'Jeremiah ii 23–25. Observations on the Versions and History of Exegesis', *OTS* 17 (1972), pp. 73–88).

McKane, W., 'Observations on the *tiḵḵûnê sōpᵉrîm*'. *On Language, Culture and Religion*; in Honor of E. A. Nida (The Hague, 1974), pp. 53–77.

McKane, W., 'Jeremiah 13:12–14: A Problematic Proverb', *Israelite Wisdom: Theological and Literary Essays*, in Honor of Samuel Terrien (Missoula, 1978), pp. 107–120.

McKane, W., 'Prophecy and the Prophetic Literature'. *Tradition and Interpretation*, ed. G. W. Anderson (Oxford, 1979), pp. 163–187.

McKane, W., 'Functions of Language and Objectives of Discourse in Proverbs 10–30', *La Sagesse de l'Ancien Testament*, BETL 51 (1979), pp. 166–185.

McKane, W., 'משא in Jeremiah 23,33–40', Fohrer Festschrift, *BZAW* 150 (1980), pp. 35–54.

McKane, W., 'Poison, Trial by Ordeal and the Cup of Wrath', *VT* 30 (1980), pp. 474–492.

McKane, W., 'The Construction of Jeremiah Chapter xxi', *VT* 32 (1982), pp. 59–73.

Malamat, A., 'Jeremiah and the last two kings of Judah', *PEQ* (1951), pp. 81–87.

Marcus, R. (ed.), *Josephus VI*. Loeb Classical Library (London and Cambridge Mass., 1937).

Martin, J. D., 'The Forensic Background to Jeremiah iii 1', *VT* 19 (1969), pp. 82–92.

May, H. G., 'Towards an objective Approach to the book of Jeremiah: The Biographer', *JBL* 61 (1942), pp. 139–155.

May, H. G., 'The Chronology of Jeremiah's Oracles', *JNES* 4 (1945), pp. 217–227.

Meek, T. J., 'Was Jeremiah a Priest?', *The Expositor* 25 (1923), pp. 215–222.

Mettinger, T. N. D., 'The Veto on Images and the aniconic God in Ancient Israel'. *Religious Symbols and their Functions*. Scripta Instituti Donneriani Aboensis 10 (Stockholm, 1978), pp. 15–29.

Meier, G. (ed.), *Die assyrische Beschwörungssammlung Maqlû* (Berlin, 1937).

Meyer, I., *Jeremia und die falschen Propheten*. Orbis Biblicus et Orientalis 13 (Freiburg and Göttingen, 1977).

Michaelis, J. D. (ed. Tychsen T. C.), *Supplementa ad Lexica Hebraica* (Göttingen, 1792).

Migne, J. P. (ed.), *Patrologia Graeca* 48 (Paris, 1862).

Milgrom, J., 'The Date of Jeremiah Chapter 2', *JNES* 14 (1955), pp. 65–69.

Miller, J. W., *Das Verhältnis Jeremias und Hesekiels sprachlich und theologisch untersucht mit besonderer Berücksichtigung der Prosareden Jeremias* (Assen, Neukirchen, 1955).

Molin, G., 'What is a Kidon?', *JSS* i (1956), pp. 334–337.

Mowinckel, S., *Zur Komposition des Buches Jeremia.* Videnskapsselskapets Skrifter iv, Hist.—Filos. Klasse, 1913 No. 5 (Oslo, 1914).

Mowinckel, S., *Psalmenstudien iii. Kultprophetie und prophetische Psalmen.* Videnskapsselskapets Skrifter ii, Hist.—Filos. Klasse, 1923 (Oslo, 1923).

Mowinckel, S., *Le Décalogue.* Études d'histoire et de philosophie religieuses (Paris, 1927).

Mowinckel, S., *Prophecy and Tradition: The Prophetic Books in the Light of the Study of the Growth and History of the Tradition,* ANVAO II, Hist.—Filos. Klasse, 1946 No. 3 (Oslo, 1946).

Mowinckel, S., *The Psalms in Israel's Worship* i–ii (Oxford, 1962). An English translation by D. R. Ap-Thomas of a revision of *Offersang og Sangoffer* (Oslo, 1951).

Mowinckel, S., 'Drive and/or ride in OT', *VT* 12 (1962), pp. 278–299.

Müller, H. P., ' "Der bunte Vogel" von Jer 12.9', *ZAW* 79 (1967), pp. 225–228).

Nestle, E., 'Ein aramäisch-hebräisches Wortspiel des Jeremia', *ZDMG* 61 (1907), pp. 196f.

Neubauer, A. (ed), Abu'l Walîd Marwân ibn Janâh, *The Book of Hebrew Roots* (Oxford, 1875).

Nicholson, E. W., *Preaching to the Exiles. A Study of the Prose Tradition in the Book of Jeremiah* (Oxford, 1970).

Nielsen, E., *Oral Tradition: a modern Problem in Old Testament* SBT 11 (London, 1954).

Noth, M., *Die israelitischen Personennamen im Rahmen der gemeinsemitischen Namengebung* BWANT III 10 (Stuttgart, 1928).

Noth, M., *Überlieferungsgeschichtliche Studien. Die Sammelnden und Bearbeitenden Geschichtswerke im alten Testament*[2] (Tübingen, 1957).

Noth, M., *Exodus.* Old Testament Library (London, 1962). An English translation by J. S. Bowden of *Das zweite Buch Mose, Exodus,* Das Alte Testament Deutsch 5 (Göttingen, 1959).

Overholt, T. W., 'The Falsehood of Idolatry: an interpretation of Jer x.1–16', *JTS,* NS 16 (1965), pp. 1–12.

Overholt, T. W., *The Threat of Falsehood. A Study in the Theology of the Book of Jeremiah*, SBT 2nd Series, 16 (London, 1970).

Paul, S. M., 'Cuneiform Light on Jer 9,20', *Biblica* 49 (1968), pp. 373–376.

Perles, F., *Analekten zur Textkritik des Alten Testaments* (Leipzig, 1922).

Pines, S. (ed.), Maimonides M., *The Guide of the Perplexed*, i–ii (Chicago and London, 1963).

Van der Ploeg, J. P. M., 'Le Rôle de la Tradition Orale dans la Transmission du Texte de L'Ancien Testament', *RB* 54 (1947), pp. 5–41.

Plöger, O., 'Siebzig Jahre', Baumgärtel Festschrift, Erlanger Forschungen, A:10 (Erlangen, 1959), pp. 125–130.

Press, R., 'Das Ordal im Alten Israel I', *ZAW* 51 (1933), pp. 121–140.

Press, R., 'Das Ordal im Alten Israel II', *ZAW* 51 (1933), pp. 227–255.

Prijs, L., 'Jeremia xx 14ff.: Versuch einer neuen Deutung', *VT* 14 (1964), pp. 104–108.

Quell, G., *Wahre und Falsche Propheten: Versuch einer Interpretation*. Beiträge zur Förderung christlicher Theologie 46:1 (Gütersloh, 1952).

Rabin, C., 'Noṣerim', *Textus* 5 (1966), pp. 44–52.

Rackham, H. (ed.), *Pliny, Naturalis Historia*. Books viii–xi. Loeb Classical Library (London and Cambridge Mass., 1940).

Von Rad, G., *Studies in Deuteronomy*. SBT 9 (London, 1953). An English translation by D.M.G. Stalker of *Deuteronomium-Studien* (Göttingen, 1948).

Von Rad, G., *Old Testament Theology* i–ii (Edinburgh, 1962, 1965). An English translation by D. M. G. Stalker of *Theologie des Alten Testaments* i–ii (Munich, 1957, 1960).

Von Rad, G., *Der heilige Krieg im alten Israel*[4] (Göttingen, 1965).

Reider, J., 'Etymological Studies in Ancient Hebrew', *VT* 2 (1952), pp. 113–130.

Reider, J., 'Contributions to the Scriptural Text', *HUCA* 24 (1952/3), pp. 85–106.

Reventlow, H. G., *Liturgie und prophetisches Ich bei Jeremia* (Gütersloh, 1963).

Reventlow, H. G., 'Gattung und Überlieferung in der "Tempelrede Jeremias"', *ZAW* 81 (1969), pp. 315–352.

Richter, W., *Die sogenannten vorprophetischen Berufungsberichte. Eine literatur-wissenschaftliche Studie zu 1 Sam 9.1–10,16, Ex 3f. und Ri 6.11b–17.* FRLANT 101 (Göttingen, 1970).

Rietzschel, C., *Das Problem der Urrolle. Ein Beitrag zur Redaktionsgeschichte des Jeremiabuches* (Gütersloh, 1966).

Ringgren, H., 'Vredens kalk', SEÅ 17 (1952), pp. 19–30.

Robinson, T. H., 'Baruch's Roll', *ZAW* 42 (1924), pp. 209–221.

de Roche, M., 'Is Jeremiah 25:15–29 a Piece of reworked Jeremianic Poetry?', *JSOT* 10 (1978), pp. 58–70.

de Rossi, J. B., *Variae Lectiones Veteris Testamenti*, i–iv (Parma, 1784–1788).

Rowley, H. H., 'The Text and Interpretation of Jer 11:18–12:6', *AJSL* 42 (1926), pp. 217–227.

Rowley, H. H., 'The Religious Value of Sacrifice', *ET* 58 (1946/7), pp. 69–71.

Rowley, H. H., 'The Prophets and Sacrifice', *ET* 58 (1946/7), pp. 305–307.

Rowley, H. H., 'Ritual and the Hebrew Prophets', *JSS* i (1956), pp. 338–360.

Rowley, H. H., 'The Early Prophecies of Jeremiah in their Setting', *BJRL* 45 (1962/3), pp. 198–234.

Rudolph, W., 'Zum Text des Jeremia: I Zum Griechischen Text', *ZAW* 48 (1930), pp. 272–286.

Sanders, J. A., *The Dead Sea Psalms Scroll* (New York, 1967).

Sauer, G., 'Mandelzweig und Kessel in Jer 1.11f.', *ZAW* 78 (1966), pp. 56–61.

Sawyer, J. F. A., 'A Note on the brooding Partridge in Jeremiah xvii 11', *VT* 28 (1978), pp. 324–329.

Schmökel, H., *Heilige Hochzeit und Hohes Lied*. Abhandlungen für die Kunde des Morgenlandes, 32/1 (1956).

Schottroff, W., 'Jeremia 2,1–3. Erwägungen zur Methode der Prophetenexegese', *ZTK* 67 (1970), pp. 263–294.

Schmuttermayer, G., 'Beobachtungen zu Jer 5,13', *BZ*, N.F. 9 (1965), pp. 215–232.

Schwally, F., 'Die Reden des Buches Jeremia gegen die Heiden', *ZAW* 8 (1888), pp. 177–217.

Seierstad, I. P., *Die Offenbarungserlebnisse der Propheten Amos, Jesaja und Jeremia*. SNVAO II, 1946/2 (Oslo, 1946).

Sekine, M., 'Davidsbund und Sinaibund bei Jeremia', *VT* 9 (1959), pp. 47–57.

Skinner, J., *Prophecy and Religion: Studies in the Life of Jeremiah*[2] (Cambridge, 1926).

Skoss, S. L., 'The Root בוטה in Jeremiah 12.5, Psalms 22.10, Proverbs 14.16 and Job 40.23'. *Jewish Studies in Memory of G. A. Kohut* (New York, 1935), pp. 549–553.

Skoss, S. L., *The Hebrew-Arabic Dictionary of the Bible known as Kitāb al-Jāmi' al-'alfāẓ (Agrōn) of David ben Abraham al-Fāsī, the Karaite*, i–ii (New York and London, 1936–1945).

Smith, J. A. and Ross, W. D., (ed.), *The Works of Aristotle translated into English*, vi *Historia Animalium*, translated by D'Arcy Wentworth Thompson (Oxford, 1910).

Smith, W. Robertson, *Lectures on the Religion of the Semites. The Fundamental Institutions*³ (Edinburgh, 1927).

Snaith, N. H., 'The Prophets and Sacrifice and Salvation', *ET* 58 (1946/7), pp. 152f.

Snijders, L. A., 'The Meaning of זר in the Old Testament', *OTS* 10 (1954), pp. 1–154.

Von Soden, W., *Akkadisches Handwörterbuch* (Wiesbaden, 1959–81).

Soggin, J., 'Jeremias xii 10a: eine Parallelstelle zu Deut. xxxii 8/LXX?', *VT* 8 (1958), pp. 304f.

Soggin, J., 'Einige Bemerkungen über Jeremias ii 34', *VT* 8 (1958), pp. 433–435.

Soggin, J., 'Der prophetische Gedanke über den heiligen Krieg als Gericht gegen Israel', *VT* 10 (1960), pp. 79–83.

Soggin, J., ' "La tua condotta nella valle". Nota a Geremia 2,23a', *RSO* 36 (1961), pp. 207–211.

Soggin, J., 'La negazione in Geremia 4,27 e 5,10a, cfr. 5,18b', *Biblica* 46 (1965), pp. 56–59.

Speiser E. A. and Pfeiffer, R. H., *One Hundred New Selected Nuzi Texts*, AASOR 16 (1935/6).

Sperber, A., *The Bible in Aramaic based on Old Manuscripts and Printed Texts: iii The Latter Prophets according to Targum Jonathan* (Leiden, 1962).

Spohn, M. G. L., *Ieremias Vates e versione Iudaeorum Alexandrinorum ac reliquorum interpretum graecorum emendatus notisque criticis illustratus*, i–ii (Leipzig, 1824).

Spiegelberg, W., 'Eine Vermutung über den Ursprung des Namens יהוה', *ZDMG* 53 (1899), pp. 633–643.

Stade, B., 'Miscellen', *ZAW* 4 (1884), pp. 149–159.

Stade, B., 'Emendationen', *ZAW* 22 (1902), p. 328.

Stade, B., 'Der "Völkerprophet" Jeremia und derjetzige Text von Jer Kap 1', *ZAW* 26 (1906), pp. 97–123.

Stoebe, H. J., 'Jeremia, Prophet und Seelsorger', *ThZ* 20 (1964), pp. 385–409.

Stolz, F., *Strukturen und Figuren im Kult von Jerusalem. Studien zur altorientalischen, vor und frühisraelitischen Religion*, BZAW 118 (1970).

Streane, A. W., *The Double Text of Jeremiah (Massoretic and Alexandrian) compared together, with an Appendix on the Old Latin Evidence* (Cambridge, 1896).

Sutcliffe, E. F., 'A Gloss on Jeremiah vii 4', *VT* 5 (1955), pp. 315f.

Sutcliffe, E. F., 'A Note on Jeremiah v 3', *JSS* 5 (1960), pp. 348f.

Sutcliffe, E. F., 'A Note on לא הוא, Jer 5,12', *Biblica* 41 (1960), pp. 287–290.

Swete, H. B., *The Old Testament in Greek according to the Septuagint*[4], iii (Cambridge, 1912).

Swetnam, J., 'Some Observations on the Background of צדיק in Jeremias 23,5a', *Biblica* 46 (1965), pp. 29–40.

Thiel, W., *Die deuteronomistische Redaktion von Jeremia 1–25*, WMANT 41 (1973).

Thomas, D. Winton, 'Jeremiah v 28', *ET* 57 (1945/6), pp. 54f.

Thomas, D. Winton, 'A Note on מועדים in Jeremiah 24,1', *JTS*, N.S., 3 (1952), p. 55.

Thomas, D. Winton, 'מלאו in Jeremiah iv. 5: A Military Term', *JJS* 3 (1952), pp. 47–52.

Thomas, D. Winton, 'Some Observations on the Hebrew word רענן', *SVT* 16 (1967), pp. 387–397.

Torczyner, H., 'Nachträge und Berichtigungen zu meinen Proverbiastudien ZDMG 71, 99–118', *ZDMG* 72 (1918), pp. 154–156.

Torczyner, H., 'Dunkle Bibelstellen', Marti Festschrift. *BZAW* 41 (1925), pp. 274–280.

Torczyner, H., 'Biblische Kleinprobleme II', *MGWJ* 75 (1931), pp. 15–19.

Torczyner, H., 'משא יהוה'. *MGWJ* 76 (1932), pp. 273–284.

Tristram, H. B., *The Natural History of the Bible, being a review of the physical geography, geology and meteorology of the Holy Land, with a description of every animal and plant mentioned in Holy Scripture*[6] (London, 1880).

Tristram, H. B., *The Fauna and Flora of Palestine* (London, 1884).

Tsevat, M., 'Alalakhiana', *HUCA* 29 (1958), pp. 109–134.

Ullendorff, E., 'The bawdy Bible', *BASOS* 42 (1979), pp. 425–456.

United Bible Societies *Fauna and Flora of the Bible*. Helps for Translators II (London, 1972).

Vischer, W., 'The Vocation of the Prophet to the Nations: an Exegesis of Jeremiah 1:4–10', *Interpretation* 9 (1955), pp. 310–317.

Vogt, E., 'Die neubabylonische Chronik über die Schlacht bei Karkemisch und die Einnahme von Jerusalem', *SVT* 4 (1957), pp. 67–96.

Wächter, L., 'Überlegungen zur Umnennung von Pašḥur in *māgôr missābîb* in Jeremia 20.3', *ZAW* 74 (1962), pp. 57–62.

Wallenstein, M., 'Some Aspects of the Vocabulary and Morphology of the Hymns of the Judean Scrolls', *VT* 7 (1957), pp. 209–213.

Wambacq, B. M., 'Jérémie x 1–16', *RB* 81 (1974), pp. 57–62.

Weil, H. M., 'Exégèse de Jérémie 23,23–40 et de Job 34,28–33; (Jérémie 44,9)', *RHR* 118 (1938), pp. 201–208.

Weinfeld, M., 'Jeremiah and the Spiritual Metamorphosis of Israel', *ZAW* 88 (1976), pp. 17–56.

Weippert, H., 'Jahwekrieg und Bundesfluch' in Jer 21.1–7', *ZAW* 82 (1970), pp. 396–409.

Weippert, H., *Die Prosareden des Jeremiabuches*, BZAW 132 (1973).

Welch, A. C., 'The Call and Commission of Jeremiah', *Expositor* 21 (1921), pp. 129–147.

Werblowsky, R. J. Zwi, 'Stealing the Word', *VT* 6 (1956), pp. 105f.

Wernberg-Møller P., 'The Pronoun אתמה and Jeremiah's Pun', *VT* 6 (1956), pp. 315f.

Whitley, C. F., 'The Term Seventy Years Captivity', *VT* 4 (1954), pp. 60–72.

Whitley, C. F., 'A Note on Jeremiah 7.4', *JTS, NS* 5 (1954), pp. 57–59.

Whitley, C. F., 'The Seventy Years Desolation—a Rejoinder', *VT* 7 (1957), pp. 416–418.

Whitley, C. F., 'The Date of Jeremiah's Call', *VT* 14 (1964), pp. 467–483.

Whitley, C. F., 'Carchemish and Jeremiah', *ZAW* 80 (1968), pp. 38–49.

Whybray, R. N., *The Intellectual Tradition in the Old Testament*, BZAW 135 (1974).

Widengren, G., *The King and the Tree of Life in Ancient Near Eastern Religion*, UUÅ 1951: 4 (Uppsala, 1951).

Widengren, C., *Literary and Psychological Aspects of the Hebrew Prophets*, UUÅ 1948: 10 (Uppsala and Leipzig, 1948).

Wiéner, C., 'Jérémie ii 2 "Fiançailles" ou "Épousailles"?', *RSR* 44 (1956), pp. 403–407.

Wildberger, H., *Jahwewort und prophetische Rede bei Jeremia* (Zürich, 1942).

Wilke, F., 'Das Skythenproblem im Jeremiabuch', *Alttestamentliche Studien für Rudolf Kittel*, BWANT 13 (Leipzig, 1913), pp. 222–254.

Wiseman, D. J., *Chronicles of Chaldaean Kings (626–556 B. C.) in the British Museum* (London, 1956).

Wiseman, D. J., 'The Vassal Treaties of Esarhaddon', *Iraq* 20 (1958), pp. 1–99, plates 1–53.

Wolff, H. W., 'Das Thema "Umkehr" in der alttestamentlichen Prophetie', *ZTK* (1951), pp. 129–148.

Wood, P. S., 'Jeremiah's Figure of the Almond Rod', *JBL* 61 (1942), pp. 99–103.

Würthwein, E., *Der 'amm ha'arez im Alten Testament*, BWANT 69 (Stuttgart, 1936).

Wright, W., *A Grammar of the Arabic Language*[2] (Cambridge, 1875).

Yadin, Y. (ed.), *The Scroll of the War of the Sons of Light against the Sons of Darkness* (London, 1962).

Ziegler, J. (ed.), *Ieremias, Baruch, Threni, Epistula Ieremias.* Septuaginta Vetus Testamentum Graecum Auctoritate Societatis Gottingensis editum 15 (Göttingen, 1957).

Ziegler, J., *Beiträge zur Ieremias—Septuaginta.* Nachrichten der Akademie der Wissenschaften in Göttingen I Phil.—Hist. Klasse 1958: 2 (Göttingen, 1958).

CHAPTER I

THE SUPERSCRIPTION (1.1–3)

¹This is a record of the words spoken by Jeremiah, son of Hilkiah, who belonged to a priestly family settled at Anathoth in the district of Benjamin. ²The word of Yahweh came to him in the thirteenth year of the reign of Josiah, son of Amon, king of Judah. ³He also prophesied in the reign of Jehoiakim, son of Josiah, king of Judah, and until the end of the eleventh year of Zedekiah, son of Josiah, king of Judah—until the deportation of the inhabitants of Jerusalem in the fifth month.

The verb in ירמיהו is either רמה (BDB) or רום (M. Noth, *Die israelitischen Personennamen*, 1928, p. 201 n. 2) which latter the Greek transcription Ἰερεμίας may indicate. Hence the possibilities are 'Yahweh loosens (the womb)', 'Yahweh exalts', 'May Yahweh exalt'. מן הכהנים certainly refers to Hilkiah and v. 1 tells us nothing about whether or not Jeremiah was a priest or had any official standing in the Jerusalem temple. Since Abiathar was banished to Anathoth (1 Kgs 2.26) it has been suggested (Rudolph[1]) that Jeremiah's family may have been descendants of his. The information that Jeremiah came from Anathoth has been called in question (T. J. Meek, *Expositor*, 1923, pp. 215–222). It is also given at 11.21f., 29.27 and 32.7 and it may have been extracted by the compiler of the superscription from these passages.

There are no severe problems about the coherence of vv. 1–3. It is generally agreed that the verses are editorial and that they appear to refer to 1–39 (Rudolph, Weiser). Verse 1 states that what follows is a record of Jeremiah's prophetic utterances and gives details about his family connections. In vv. 2 and 3 different phases of his prophetic activity are specified: it began in Josiah's reign and continued through the reigns of Jehoiakim and Zedekiah until the exile in 587. He received his call five years before the reform of Josiah in 626 and was active through five reigns of which two very short ones (Jehoahaz and Jehoiachin) are not mentioned. Most of the witnesses of Sept. do not indicate תם and where it is attested this probably represents a secondary harmonization with MT (see J. Ziegler, *Ieremias*, 1957 *in loc.*). According to 2 Kgs 25.3ff. and Jer 52.6ff. Zedekiah was taken prisoner in the fourth month and the exile of the people followed in the fifth month (2 Kgs 25.11/Jer 52.15). 'Until the deportation of the inhabitants of Jerusalem in the fifth

---

[1] Commentators are referred to only by name, unless there is a possibility of ambiguity. Full bibliographical information is supplied at the end of the commentary.

month' has the appearance of an adjustment produced by second thoughts in the interests of a more complete accuracy, whether by the original editor or by a later one: the end of the story is not the capture of Zedekiah but the going into exile of the inhabitants of Jerusalem.

According to Kimchi דברי ירמיהו (v. 1) refers to what Jeremiah spoke and what happened to him as a consequence of his speaking, so that it embraces the experiences of the prophet as well as his utterances. This interpretation has been adopted by Rudolph and if the superscription relates to the contents of 1–39 or the extant book of Jeremiah (Nicholson), such an exegesis of דברי ירמיהו arguably provides a more adequate description of them. If it is held that the superscription does not cover 1–39, there are special reasons for dissenting from Rudolph's view that דברי ירמיהו should be translated *Die Geschichte Jeremias*, but even on his own account of the scope of the superscription the correct rendering is almost certainly 'The words of Jeremiah' (cf. Weiser who shares Rudolph's opinion about the scope of the superscription and who translates *Worte Jeremias*).

Instead of דברי ירמיהו Sept. has τὸ ῥῆμα τοῦ θεοῦ ὃ ἐγένετο ἐπὶ Ἰερεμίαν and this corresponds to the type of superscription which appears in Hos 1.1, Mic 1.1, Zeph 1.1 and Joel 1.1, except that אלהים is indicated instead of יהוה. MT דברי ירמיהו, on the other hand, is the same as the superscription of the book of Amos (דברי עמוס). The right conclusion is that Sept. has accommodated Jer 1.1 to a more common type of superscription (so Rudolph and W. Thiel, *Die deuteronomistische Redaktion von Jeremia 1–25*, 1973, pp. 50f.), but the recognition that דברי ירמיהו is a type of superscription and that דברי עמוס certainly means 'The words of Amos' is a further argument against Rudolph's view that *Die Geschichte Jeremias* is a correct translation (cf. Thiel, p. 49, n. 2). If this appreciation of Τὸ ῥῆμα τοῦ θεοῦ ὃ ἐγένετο ἐπὶ Ἰερεμίαν is just, Sept. does not furnish evidence that v. 2 is secondary and disturbs an original connection between v. 1 (following Sept.) and v. 3 (so F. Horst, *ZAW* 41, 1923, pp. 98f.). Thiel's efforts to recover what is original in vv. 1–3 lead him in a direction opposite to that of Horst: he supposes that the kernel of the superscription is דברי ירמיהו בן חלקיהו which originally stood at the head of a collection of sayings of Jeremiah, perhaps, the scroll which was dictated to Baruch in 605 (36.4; Thiel, pp. 49f.).

Thiel's account is that the original superscription, perhaps of the scroll written in 605, was דברי ירמיהו בן חלקיהו and that the remainder of it (vv. 1b–3) is the work of D. The effect of this addition is to make vv. 1–3 a superscription for 1–25 (pp. 55ff.). The appropriateness of 'The words of Jeremiah' as a description of the contents of 1-25 had already been emphasized by Duhm. He contrasted 1-25 in this respect with 26ff., but his explanation of the limitation of the superscription in vv. 1-3 to 1-25 is a different one. For Duhm there is no question of postulating stages of construction for 1.1-3: it had no existence prior to its extant form which was fashioned in connection with a late introduction to 1-25.

Attention must now be focused on the date given for Jeremiah's call in v. 2—the thirteenth year of Josiah—and, in the first place, on how this date was derived by the compiler of vv. 1-3. The same date is given in 25.3 and there can be little doubt that it is intended as the year of Jeremiah's call and that the difference between מן שלש עשרה שנה and בשלש אשרה שנה (indicated by Sept.) is not significant. No assured conclusion can be drawn about the literary relationship between the two passages, although Thiel holds that 1.2 is attributable to D, whereas 25.3 is post-Deuteronomistic, in which case 25.3 is derived from 1.2 and has no corroborative significance. Even so, the double occurrence of the thirteenth year of Josiah creates difficulties for the view that שלש עשרה שנה is an accidental corruption of שלש עשרים שנה and that the call of Jeremiah took place in 616 (so T. C. Gordon, *ET* 44, 1932/33, pp. 562-565; H. Bardtke, *ZAW* 53, 1935, pp. 218-220). The hypothesis of accidental corruption cannot be maintained if the two occurrences of the thirteenth year are independent of each other, but even if one is dependent on the other it has to be supposed that the prior one was corrupted before it became the source of the dependent one.

In terms of literary-critical analysis the other dates which are proposed in place of 626 do not fare any better. The dates on which Hyatt and Whitley found their conclusions are not in fact presented as dates of Jeremiah's call, but they are treated by these scholars as if they were. There can be no doubt that they are intended as dates of particular utterances of the prophet Jeremiah and the circumstances that Hyatt founds on one (26.1) and Whitley on another (25.1) is in effect a demonstration that neither is a date of Jeremiah's call. Both cannot be and one is not distinguishable in form and function from the other (J. P. Hyatt, *IB*, p. 798; *ZAW* 78, 1966, pp. 205-208; C. F. Whitley, *VT* 14, 1964, p. 483; *ZAW* 80, 1968, pp. 38-42). Hyatt is followed by Holladay not only in respect of the date of Jeremiah's call (609), but also in respect of the strange proposal (cf. Rudolph's criticism) that 626 is the year of Jeremiah's birth (W. L. Holladay, *JBL* 83, 1964, p. 161). Not only does Whitley misinterpret the nature of the chronological notice in 25.1, by holding that it indicates the year of Jeremiah's call, but he places

an impossible construction on בראשית ממלכות יהויקים (cf.
Hyatt's criticism, *ZAW*, 1966, p. 205) by supposing that it could
be an expression for the fourth year of Jehoiakim (605) and so
establish that Jeremiah's call came after the battle of
Carchemish. The best of the literary-critical arguments
employed against the 626 date are those of Horst (above, p. 2).
According to Horst v. 2 is intrusive and the date which it
supplies has no value as a historical datum since it is the product
of a Deuteronomistic interpretation of the prophet Jeremiah
whose tendency was to connect his activity with the reign of
Josiah and the Josian reform. Hence v. 3 should be regarded as
continuous with v. 1 and in that case the beginning of Jeremiah's
prophetic activity is indicated by ויהי בימי יהויקים, 'He was
active in the reign of Jehoiakim'. The date of his call should then
be placed in 609 (the same date as that favoured by Hyatt).

Other passages (3.6; 36.2) which connect Jeremiah's activity
with the reign of Josiah do not, according to Hyatt (*JNES* 1,
1942, pp. 165f.) provide any independent attestation, since they
too derive from editorial activity whose object is to represent that
Jeremiah began his public career in the reign of Josiah. Thiel
(pp. 59f.) accepts this judgement for 3.6 but not for 36.2 which
he therefore claims as a general corroboration of the 626 date in
1.2. In the case of 36.2, which Thiel (pp. 59f.) attributes to
Baruch, a different view from that of Hyatt is set out. That there
is Deuteronomistic or post-Deuteronomistic interference in the
verse is allowed by Thiel, but he finds it in מיום דברתי אליך and
not in מימי יאשיהו: מיום דברתי אליך is a secondary exegesis
which explains מימי יאשיהו as precisely a reference to
Jeremiah's call. Hence Thiel holds that 36.2 is a witness to the
prophetic activity of Jeremiah in the reign of Josiah which is
independent of the more particular indication in 1.2.

Another literary-critical move whose indirect consequence is a
justification of the reliability of the date 626 is the proposal that
v. 2 (Hitzig and others) or the notice containing the date in v. 2
(Rudolph, Bright, Rietzschel, p. 135; N. Habel, *ZAW* 77, 1965,
pp. 307f.) should be attached to the beginning of the call
narrative in v. 4. The original function of מימי יאשיהו בן אמון
מלך יהודה בשלש עשרה שנה למלכו was to supply a date for the
call narrative and it was quarried from this source by the editor
who compiled the superscription. Either he deleted it from v. 4
because it no longer seemed necessary to have it there once it
was present in the superscription or else these considerations led
to its subsequent deletion. Since these scholars hold that the call
narrative is attributable to the prophet Jeremiah and was part of
the scroll written down in 605 (Rudolph, Rietzschel, pp. 130f.),
they are advancing an argument for the reliability of the date

626. This method of finding a reliable source for the 626 date must, however, be regarded as unsatisfactory. The hypothesis is one over which no control can be exercised and for which no test can be devised. The conclusion to be drawn is that there is no way of demonstrating the historical reliability of the date 626, but that, on the other hand, 1.2 is the only notice about the date of Jeremiah's call which we possess. It is not the case that there are contending dates between which a choice can be made and the literary-critical efforts to show that there are alternatives to be considered should be dismissed.

There are more general reasons for a dissatisfaction with the date 626 and the literary-critical activity to find another date may be regarded as largely a consequence of this prior dissatisfaction. It is argued that the evidence supplied by the contents of the book of Jeremiah locate the activity of the prophet mainly in the reign of Jehoiakim and that those who hold that he received his call in 626 have to posit a long period of inactivity between 621 and 609. Moreover, it is urged that evidences of prophetic activity before the reform of Josiah, which have been detected in 1–6, are not so firm as has been supposed (see, however, Rietzschel, p. 131 and Thiel, p. 58) and that the lack of any mention of Jeremiah in connection with the events of 2 Kgs 22 casts doubt on the assumption that he was already a prophet in 621. References to cultic abuses and malpractices may indicate that the reform was not so thoroughgoing and successful as has been supposed or that by the beginning of Jehoiakim's reign its effectiveness had worn off and there was a regression to pre-reform practices. The references which connect Jeremiah with the reform of Josiah and the book of Deuteronomy (notably chapter 11) are not to be regarded as historical sources: they do not show that the historical prophet Jeremiah participated in the reform and its programme, but only that the book has been edited or redacted by Deuteronomists whose concern was to present the prophet Jeremiah in this light. In view of all these considerations and, particularly, of the silence between 621 and 609, which those who hold to the 626 date posit, there is a clear case (so it is argued) for the application of Occam's razor and the conclusion that Jeremiah did not begin his ministry until the reign of Jehoiakim (F. Horst, *ZAW*, 1923, pp. 94f., 132f.; J. P. Hyatt, *JNES*, 1942, pp. 158–161, 173; H. G. May, *JNES* 4, 1945, pp. 227f.).

THE CALL NARRATIVE (1.4–10)

⁴The word of Yahweh came to me: ⁵Before I formed you in the womb, I singled you out, and before you came out of the womb, I set you apart; I appointed you a prophet to the nations. ⁶I replied, Alas!, Lord Yahweh, I am only a young man and have no skill of utterance. ⁷Do not say 'I am only a young man' said Yahweh to me; you are to go on whatever mission I send you and to speak whatever I command you. ⁸Do not be afraid because of them, for I shall be with you to keep you safe. You have my word. ⁹Yahweh stretched out his hand and touched my mouth and said to me, I have now put my words in your mouth. ¹⁰As from now I have made you responsible for nations and kingdoms, to root out and to pull down, to destroy and to demolish, to build and to plant.

The passage has been set out as prose, although it is customary to hold that the words spoken by Yahweh in vv. 5, 7, 8, 9, 10 are metrically formed (cf. BHS). Thiel (pp. 63f.) has remarked that this view is not without its difficulties; he has emended v. 7 to make it better poetry (see below) and has described vv. 9–10 as rhetorical prose.

K vocalized as אֶצֻּורְךָ can be derived from צור 'to fashion' (Exod 32.4; 1 Kgs 7.15) and Q אֶצָּרְךָ is from יצר with the same meaning. Sept.ᴮˢ (the sigla are those of Ziegler) indicates πρὸς αὐτόν (MT אלי) and the effect of this is to make ויהי דבר יהוה אלי לאמר into an editorial introduction to vv. 5ff. rather than words spoken by Jeremiah himself. This is, probably (so Rudolph), a deliberate adjustment rather than an accidental assimilation to the 3rd person account of the superscription. ידע is synonymous with בחר 'choose' as in Amos 3.2: Jeremiah's vocation was settled by Yahweh before his foetus was formed in the womb. Before his life had begun, its direction was determined and its end foreknown by God.

The statement in v. 5, 'I appointed you a prophet to the nations' (cf. v. 10) is, on any reckoning, a crux and must have a profound effect on the interpretation of vv. 4–10. Since גוי is used of Israel (e.g. Ps 106.5), it can be argued that גוים includes Israel as well as the Gentile world, but it is odd that a prophet whose concern was focused so intensely on Judah should receive his call in such terms that Judah is subsumed under גוים . B. Stade (*ZAW* 26, 1906, pp. 102f.) was dissatisfied with Giesebrecht's statement that a ministry to Judah involved one to the nations, and Duhm remarked that a passage like 27.1ff., even if it shows that Jeremiah advised non-resistance to Nebuchadrezzar not only to Judah but to small, surrounding nations, does not adequately account for נביא לגוים נתתיך . The observation that Judah lived in a world that was dominated by greater powers, that she was their tributary and that her own destiny could not be considered apart from them (Rudolph,

Weiser) leaves the same nagging dissatisfaction that worried Stade and Duhm. This is not repaired by the different twist given to the argument by Vischer who sees the fate of the nations as hanging on that of Judah (W. Vischer, *Interpretation* 9, 1955. p. 314).

It may be this perplexity which is reflected in the reading εἰς ἔθνος in some manuscripts of Sept. (see Ziegler) in v. 5. This is a deliberate, exegetical modification rather than evidence that a Hebrew text with לגוי was read. It represents the restriction of Jeremiah's ministry to Judah and is paralleled by Rashi's exegesis of לגוים : the reference is to Israel, since they were conducting themselves like Gentiles (idolaters). The intention of Stade's emendation (לגוים to לגויי 'to my nation', *ZAW* 22, 1902, 328) is also to limit Jeremiah's ministry to Judah. Although Bruston's proposal (*ZAW* 27, 1907, pp. 75–78) that גוים is an unusual spelling of גאוים does not command assent, there is virtue in its appreciation that גוים in vv. 5 and 10 have to be considered together. He disposes of the reference to foreign nations and holds that גאוים 'grandees' goes well with 'kings' in v. 10 (on the analogy of Phoenician ממלכה 'prince' or 'king', see Jean-Hoftijzer, s.v. ממלכה) and is suitable in v. 5, since it was with powerful and influential men in his own community that Jeremiah had to contend. Bardtke (*ZAW* 53, 219f.), on the other hand, maintains that Jeremiah, called to be a prophet in 616, prophesied doom to foreign nations and salvation to Judah until 615/614, and that it is this circumstance which is reflected by the references to גוי in vv. 5 and 10. Bardtke is not to be followed, but it should be noted that לבנות ולנטוע (v. 10) is not represented in the text of Sept.^, so that Jeremiah's authority over the nations is defined in entirely destructive terms.

The elucidation of גוים on which Duhm alighted was that it pointed to an apocalyptic theology which linked the destiny of the Jews to that of the whole world and that chapter 1 was thereby marked as a very late composition originating in a time far removed from the historical prophet Jeremiah.

Moses protests his lack of fitness on the ground of inarticulateness and Jeremiah on the ground of inexperience and lack of rhetorical expertise (cf. Rashi). He is young and without a commanding presence and authority, and he has had no practice in the skills of public speaking. His response has also been contrasted to that of Isaiah (Rudolph) whose reaction to a vision of Yahweh's majesty and purity is that he is an unclean man in an unclean community. His strong conviction that the unclean community must be warned overcomes any personal misgivings or sense of inadequacy (Isa 6). The age which is indicated by נער can only be conjectured (e.g., H. G. May,

JNES, 4, 1925, p. 225—perhaps 20; J. P. Hyatt, *IB*—17 or 18; Weiser—25), but from the range which נער covers 'young man' rather than 'child' is appropriate.

Rudolph's view that על (v. 7) = אל is in agreement with the indication of Sept. (πρὸς πάντας) and follows Kimchi. The problem of finding an antecedent for מפניהם (v. 8) is not so sharp as Rudolph represents, and even if על כל אשר אשלחך is translated 'on whatever mission I send you', it is clear that מפניהם refers to those whom he encounters in the process of discharging his mission.

Thiel's objection to the originality of ואת אשר אצוך תדבר is too fastidious, but he is right (p. 66 n. 15) to the extent that he departs from Rudolph's view (following Giesebrecht and A. B. Ehrlich, *Randglossen zur Hebräischen Bibel*, 4, 1912(1968), p. 233) that the first כי is adversative (= 'but').

The most interesting aspect of the comments of Rashi and Kimchi is that they do not envisage Jeremiah's work as hinging altogether on the definition of his prophetic task which is given in v. 5 (נביא לגוים נתתיך). Rashi supposes that כי על כל אשר אשלחך תלך refers to the Gentiles, and ואת כל אשר אצוך תדבר to Israel, whereas Kimchi, who takes על כל אשר אשלחך as equivalent to אל כל אשר אשלחך, follows Targ. (לכל אתר) and supposes that the place which is alluded to is Jerusalem, where Jeremiah's work will be centred and his task will be to reprove king and people. The important point, which will have to be considered further, is whether the terms of the call narrative, as it develops subsequent to v. 5, do not envisage Jeremiah as a prophet to Judah rather than a prophet to the nations. Rashi and Kimchi are already moving towards this position in their comments on v. 7, although Rashi's solution is to include both Israel and the Gentiles within Jeremiah's remit.

The right to decline the vocation to which he is called is not allowed to Jeremiah. No notice is taken of his feelings of inadequacy or his conviction that the task is not for him. His own inclination is to decline the office modestly, to disengage himself from a task so public and crushingly responsible. But it is not to be. Those who feel most wretched and inadequate in the presence of the divine call are, nevertheless, those who have been singled out as God's servants and for them there is no release.

He must expect resistance and hostility (v. 8), just as Isaiah (6.9f.) and Ezekiel (2.6f.) were warned of unresponsiveness and Ezekiel of hostility (2.6f.) and obduracy (3.8f.). But these words are the beginning of a message of comfort to the prophet. It is a hard destiny and he will attract to himself hatred and violence, but Yahweh will be with him to keep him safe. He stands before a life of unknown dangers and undefined demands, a daunting prospect which mocks his human weakness, but there is a limit to this abyss of uncertainty and foreboding.

The comparisons which have just been made between Jeremiah and other prophets lead on to a consideration of form-critical studies of prophetic call narratives. There is a large literature and many issues are raised, but the general contention is that the formulations of the call narratives of the canonical prophets have the formal elements of a pre-existing *Gattung* or genre (E. Kutsch, *ThLZ* 81, 1956, cols. 75–84; N. Habel, *ZAW* 77, 1965, pp. 297–323; K. Baltzer, *HTR* 61, 1968, pp. 567–581). There is a considerable agreement about the identification of these formal elements, although W. Richter (*Die sogenannten vorprophetischen Berufungsberichte*, 1970) does not find Divine Confrontation or Theophany in the earlier call narratives which he studies (cf. B. O. Long, *ZAW* 84, 1972, pp. 494–500). The items which are identified in the Jeremiah call narrative are Revelation (v. 4), Commission (v. 5), Objection (v. 6), Rebuttal and Reassurance (vv. 7–8) and the Sign (vv. 9–10).

In v. 8 Kimchi supposes that the reference is to the persecution suffered by Jeremiah and Baruch at the hands of Jehoiakim and the concealment which was necessary in order to save their skins (36.19). The paradoxical aspect of all this is that form-critical considerations which are supposed to demonstrate that the call narrative of Jeremiah is a whole, with a strict, formal composition, direct attention to its incoherence and lack of integration. Jeremiah is described in v. 5 and again in v. 10 as a prophet to foreign nations, and this has to be given a plain interpretation, but the experiences which he must expect as a prophet, as these are indicated by v. 8 (and vv. 17–19—see below), almost certainly have in view opposition in his own community (Judah) and not among foreign nations.

The new element in vv. 9–10 is tactual experience and it has been customary to say (Cornhill, Volz, Rudolph) that only here do we become aware that Jeremiah receives his call in the context of a vision, in which he hears Jahweh's word, sees his outstretched hand and feels its touch on his mouth. But efforts to deal with the reality of the divine encounter in exegetical terms face the same difficulties, whether it is the hearing of God's voice or the seeing of his hand or the feeling of his touch. There is a concern in Rudolph's theological appreciation of the call narrative—one which is strong throughout Weiser's commentary—to establish that 'God' is not a device for objectifying inner convictions of whose truth the prophet is powerfully impressed. The problems here are enormous and they are not solved by a literalism which affirms that the prophets did in fact, in vision or trance, hear Yahweh speaking Hebrew or see his hand or feel his touch, because the possession of abnormal psychological experiences is not a guarantee that God has been encountered—in the sense that truth has been appropriated. It may be rather an indication of derangement and delusion.

It is unwise for exegesis in a commentary to attempt much more than this, because it is a mistake to suppose that the ineffability of the prophet's encounter with God can be simply reproduced, that what we have in the Hebrew text are 'recordings' of times of revelation. What we have rather are human statements in a language which only humans speak, and in order to become human the ineffable has necessarily been transmuted. There is therefore a significant sense in which the exegete of a Hebrew text is dealing only with human documents and does not deal directly with God. He is dealing with men who claim to have experiences of God and his exegesis must make this clear, but the truth claims involved in these experiences are beyond the limits of plain exegesis.

The touching of Jeremiah's mouth by Yahweh indicates that Yahweh is the source of the prophetic utterance. It is a striking figure to communicate the sense that the prophet speaks authoritatively for Yahweh (Kimchi). The written scroll in Ezekiel's call narrative functions similarly (2.8ff.) and it is unsafe to make theological deductions from the different imagery in the two books, that in one prophecy is still the dynamic and plastic spoken word, whereas in the other it pre-exists as a written scroll. We are dealing in both with a prophet's credentials and authorization: Yahweh puts his words in Jeremiah's mouth and Ezekiel digests a scroll which makes him an authentic prophet of doom.

One item of the series of infinitives ולהרוס in v. 10, where Jeremiah is again depicted as a prophet to the nations, is not indicated by the principal manuscripts of Sept. (see Ziegler). J. G. Janzen (*Studies in the Text of Jeremiah*, 1973, p. 35) supposes that ולהרוס has come into v. 10 from such passages as 24.6, 42.10, 45.4, and that ולהאביד is probably secondary and derived from 12.17 and 18.7. Thus the original text which he posits has two negative terms and two positive and this coincides with Volz's emendation which produces a chiastic arrangement, since נטע/נתש and בנה/נתין are pairs. In 24.6, 42.10 and 45.4 constructive and destructive terms are arranged as antithetic pairs, but this design may not be held up in order to draw conclusions about the series which appears in 1.10, 18.7,9, 31.28, where an accumulation of destructive terms (3 or 4) is followed by the two constructive terms which are consistently used (cf. H. Weippert, *BZAW* 132, 1973, p. 194).

Targ. has allocated the destructive part of Jeremiah's ministry

to the nations, and the constructive part ('building and planting')
to Israel. Bardtke's explanation (*ZAW*, 1935, 212–220) is in
accord with his view that at the outset Jeremiah was a prophet of
weal to Judah and of woe to the nations and so he allocates the
destructive and constructive terms in the same way as Targ.
(also Rashi). Different conclusions about the significance of the
alternation of doom and salvation are drawn by R. Bach
(*Studien zur Theologie der alttestamentlichen Überlieferungen*,
1961, pp. 7–33). He supposes that the 'building and planting'
elements, which appear in all the passages, supply a clue to the
original *Sitz*: we have to envisage that these terms were once
used in an agricultural community as an expression of 'best
wishes' in connection with the birth of a son (p. 22). 1.10,
because of the alternation of doom and salvation, is not to be
connected with the scroll which contained only proclamations of
doom (36.3). Hence 1.10 must have originated at a time when
the book of Jeremiah contained proclamations of both doom and
salvation (pp. 31f.). This kind of literary-critical elucidation,
with its implication that chapter 1 is a type of introduction which
throws light on the composition of the book of Jeremiah,
corresponds with the comments which were made above (pp. 6f.)
on גוים.

Although Rudolph's interpretation of the series in v. 10 is
attractive, it is, probably, too tidy to be true. According to it
there is a temporal order of doom and then salvation: the prophet
is instructed that first he must destroy false ideas and corrupt
institutions; lies must be exposed and wrongs rooted out. It is a
time for demolition, or a time for drastic action to kill the weeds
and clean the ground. Rebuilding can only be done from the
foundations, or a time of barrenness must be endured before
there can be a return to fruitfulness. But if the verse is to be
regarded as proleptic in relation to a prophetic activity which is
about to commence, there is something to be said for Weiser's
concept that what is indicated is less a temporal order of
operations than a perception that the true prophet will never
secure release from a tension between warning and promise,
demolition and construction. It is a balance which he will have to
maintain, a tug of war which he will have to endure.

There are important differences in the appreciation of the call
narrative which are connected with divergent, critical
estimations of it and a convenient division of opinions can be
made, even if the resultant classification is not watertight.

(*a*) There are those who are confident that the narrative
should be attributed to the historical prophet Jeremiah and that
it is what it purports to be, the record of an experience. It is then
in essence a biographical notice, throwing some light on what is

inward, mysterious, personal and crucial for a particular prophet, and indicating how, given the texture of his individuality and temperament, he reacted to the pressure of a call. It is supposed by some that he set it down in writing first for his own clarification and private use, and that only subsequently was it published in connection with the first scroll or the enlarged scroll, eventually becoming an introduction to 1–25, matching the conclusion in 25.1–13a (Bright). In its public existence its primary function is that of validation: it constitutes a claim on the part of the prophet, in the face of bitter opposition, that he has the authority of Yahweh for all that he says. It is the record of an initial, decisive encounter, even if it did not become a public record until an interval of some twenty years had elapsed (Rudolph, Weiser, Bright; H. W. Jüngling, *Biblica* 54, 1973, pp. 21–24; also, from a different point of view, Bardtke, see above p. 7).

(*b*) The position of the form critics, whose work on the call narrative has been noted (above, p. 9), is differently proportioned, because there is less emphasis on the psychological particularities of an individual prophet, although there is no resiling from the view that the call narrative enables us to make contact with the historical prophet, Jeremiah. The modification as compared with (*a*) is achieved by holding that a call narrative, even if it has a particular, historical uniqueness and has features which derive from a prophet's individuality, nevertheless, has a public character, because a prophet does not create it *ex nihilo*, but makes use of a scaffolding and regular scheme of construction given to him by earlier call narratives.

(*c*) Although H. G. Reventlow's account of the call narrative (*Liturgie und prophetisches Ich bei Jeremia*, 1963, pp. 24–77) has strong form-critical connections, he takes a further, decisive step which distinguishes him from those whose views are gathered under (*b*). He urges that the call narrative is an ordination formula and that as such it is a special kind of cultic transaction which can be subsumed under liturgical dialogues of a more general kind, involving a worshipper and a cultic official who speaks in the name of Yahweh (e.g., the priestly oracle of salvation, pp. 70–77). Thus there is a sense in which Reventlow, if he does not solve the difficult, theological problems of prophecy which have been alluded to (above, pp. 9f.), does appear to dissolve them. A. H. J. Gunneweg's riposte to Reventlow (*Glaube, Geist, Geschichte*, 1967, pp. 91–98) more or less places him in the ranks of those gathered under (*b*). He is interested in Reventlow's account of the ancestry of the prophetic, call narrative, but he insists that whether or not it has evolved out of cultic transactions of the kind which Reventlow describes, it is now no longer a liturgy of ordination but a call narrative.

(*d*) This represents a development and modification of the positions which were defined under (*a*). The call narrative is attributable to the prophet Jeremiah, but it has been subjected to Deuteronomistic editing (Thiel, pp. 62–72; E. W. Nicholson, *Preaching to The Exiles*, pp. 113–115). Nicholson singles out the same elements as Thiel in vv. 7 and 9 and states that they are dependent on Deuteronomy (pp. 114f.), but the correspondence between the Jeremiah passages and the Deuteronomy passages is not sufficiently exact to establish literary dependence (so Rudolph). Again the reason given by Thiel for discounting the possibility of a relationship between הנה נתתי דברי בפיך and הנני נתן דברי בפיך לאש (5.14), namely, that לאש is a distinguishing feature, is not impressive. If we are searching for a prototype for הנה נתתי דברי בפיך, the poetry of 5.14 is a likely candidate, and the circumstance that the latter refers to the destructive power of the prophet's word rather than to an initial endowment with Yahweh's word does not detract much from a hypothesis that Jeremianic poetry is being re-used as prose in 1.9. Thiel's argument about the infinitives in v. 10 is turned on its head by Weippert (*Die Prosareden*, pp. 193–202). It is unlikely that progress will be made with the problems of the prose of the book of Jeremiah by either of these types of argument. Weippert is right in so far as she is saying that Thiel cannot have it both ways: if comparisons between prose passages in the book of Jeremiah, on the one hand, and passages in Deuteronomy and the Deuteronomistic literature, on the other, are to be the basis for establishing the Deuteronomic-Deuteronomistic connections of the prose in the book of Jeremiah, the absence of any correspondences should indicate the lack of any such connections. The series of infinitives in v. 10 is not paralleled in Deuteronomy or Deuteronomistic literature and so Weippert claims that it furnishes an example of prose which is peculiar to the book of Jeremiah.

There is a difference between the positions which have just been sketched and the kind of relationship between Moses and Jeremiah which is posited by Broughton and Holladay (P. E. Broughton, *ABR* 6, 1958, pp. 41–46; W. L. Holladay, *JBL* 83, 1964, pp. 153–164; 85, 1966, pp. 17–27). The implication of what Thiel and Nicholson are saying is that there is a loss of contact with the historical Jeremiah as a consequence of the use of a Deuteronomic model with which he is made to conform. The approach of Broughton and Holladay, on the other hand, assumes an intimate knowledge of the self-consciousness of the emerging prophet Jeremiah.

(e) Duhm's insight that גוים in vv. 5 and 10 constitute a crux is unerring (see above, p. 7), and subsequent discussion has taken off in different directions from this recognition. Whether or not there are early elements in the call narrative which derive from the historical prophet Jeremiah is a question which is not capable of an answer, but the most probable explanation of the characterization of Jeremiah as a prophet to the nations in vv. 5 and 10 is that it alludes to the oracles against foreign nations (MT 46–51) and presupposes a book of Jeremiah which contained these oracles (cf. Nicholson on 1.5). Thiel (p. 69) has taken some account of this, but he interprets the relationship between גוים in vv. 5 and 10 and the oracles against foreign nations in a different way: he supposes that the priority lies with the occurrences of גוים in the call narrative and that these were a *point d'appui* for attaching the oracles against foreign nations to the book of Jeremiah.

The call narrative is part of an introduction (chapter 1) to the book of Jeremiah and the introduction is constructed from the evidence supplied by the extant book. In that case the call narrative is retrospective rather than proleptic: it does not come from the historical prophet Jeremiah, but it is an estimate of him after he has run his course. It affirms that notwithstanding the opposition which he aroused, the hostility which he awakened, and the rejection which he suffered, he was indeed a prophet called by Yahweh. The lack of inner consistency is caused simply by the concern to include all the contents of the book and the attempt to do justice to them.

THE ALMOND BRANCH (1.11–12)

[11]This word of Yahweh came to me, What is it that you see, Jeremiah? I am looking at an almond branch, I answered. [12]You have observed well, said Yahweh to me, for I am keeping watch over my word to fulfil it.

Vulg. renders שָׁקֵד as *virgam vigilantem*, 'watchful branch' and, according to Jerome, this was also the rendering of Aq. and Symm. In v. 12 both Targ. (מוחי) and Pesh. (*msrhb*) render שָׁקֵד as 'hastening' rather than 'watching' and this emphasis on imminence of fulfilment appears in Rashi and Kimchi. The opinion that the almond tree is called שָׁקֵד because it is 'wakeful' is found in BDB and KB[2] and is supported by G. Dalman's observation that the tree is so called because it blossoms so early that it appears not to take the sleep of winter (*Arbeit und Sitte in Palästina*, 1, 1928, pp. 255f.). Other explanations have been offered by P. S. Wood (*JBL*, 61, 1942, pp. 99–103) and G. Sauer (*ZAW*, 78, 1966, pp. 56–61).

It is unlikely that the effect which is sought in vv. 11–12 depends on a semantic content which is to be postulated for 'almond tree', as Vulg. has supposed and as the rendering of NEB indicates, 'An almond in early bloom'. The thought of a tree which blossoms swiftly or awakens early from the sleep of winter is not part of the machinery of vv. 11f. The effect rather depends on the virtual homonymy of שָׁקֵד and שֹׁקֵד, as Jerome observed (so Rudolph and Reventlow, op. cit., p. 78). The effect of the Hebrew depends simply on the association of almost identical sounds, whereby a transition is made from 'almond branch' to the thought of Yahweh's surveillance and vigilance (שֹׁקֵד אֲנִי).

If the form of the literary presentation of vv. 11f. were thought to be a decisive consideration, we might conclude that the experience which is described, involving a dialogue between the prophet and Yahweh, is a prophetic vision with auditory elements (Kimchi). Rudolph (Weiser and Bright) explains the sighting of the almond branch as an everyday observation and as an example of how the extraordinary sensitivity and perceptiveness of the prophet could be released by an unexceptional occurrence. The process of transition is so involuntary and the effect so powerful and irresistible that the experience is recorded by the prophet as a word from Yahweh rather than a thought of his own. A different kind of explanation in terms of vision, where vision is metamorphosed into a cultic transaction, is offered by Reventlow (p. 85). It follows the lines of his account of the call narrative. But how can כי הראני אדני יהוה (Amos 7.1 and 8.2) be contained in a regular, predictable ritual?

It is generally agreed that vv. 11–12 are not continuous with vv. 4–10 and that they constitute a separate literary unit, but differences emerge when the relation of these verses to the call narrative is more closely defined. Both Rudolph and Bright suppose that the experiences which are recorded in vv. 11–16 are to be located early in Jeremiah's ministry, before the strong impression made by his call had lost anything of its impact. Proposals to link literary units with historical occasions should be looked at very hard and in this case there is hardly anything to go on, unless more general assumptions are made about the way in which chapter 1 was edited. There are no compelling reasons for disengaging the units vv. 11–12 and 13–16 from the historical prophet Jeremiah, but vv. 11–12 do not provide us with an historical anchorage to which they may be attached (cf. Reventlow, pp. 86f.).

Rudolph and Bright are influenced by their view that chapter 1, consisting as it does of independent literary units, has been put together by the prophet Jeremiah. Although vv. 11–12 are not continuous with vv. 4–10, the principle of arrangement adopted by Jeremiah is an indication that the experiences recorded in vv. 11–16 were temporally adjacent to the call narrative and so are to be located near the beginning of his ministry. This also involves an assumption about the call narrative: that it records an experience which launched Jeremiah on his prophetic career and that it is his composition (see above, p. 14).

The other aspect of this matter is that Rudolph has two points of reference for his exegesis of vv. 11–16, parallel to the two stages which are postulated for the call narrative. The experiences which are recorded in vv. 11–16 are first to be understood as sources of consolation and encouragement to the young prophet and, as such, have a private, rather than a public significance. Later, in connection with the writing down of the first scroll in 605 (36.4), they become a constituent part of chapter 1, and they assume a public significance and have a threatening aspect for those to whom they are addressed. Jüngling's account is similar (op. cit., p. 24).

A COOKING POT ON THE BOIL (1.13–16)

[13]Yahweh's word came to me a second time, What is it that you see? I am looking at a pot fanned by flames and tilted to the south, I said. [14]Yahweh said to me, Evil will be unleashed from the north against all the inhabitants of the land. [15]I am summoning all the kingdoms[1] of the north and each king will come and set up his throne at the entrance to the gates of Jerusalem. They will encircle its walls and besiege all the towns of Judah. This is my word. [16]I shall establish their guilt in respect of all their evil doing: they have forsaken me by burning sacrifices to alien gods and have bowed down to gods made with their own hands.

It is doubtful whether either vv. 14–16 or 17–19 qualify as Hebrew poetry (Rudolph; BHS), or whether they are sufficiently distinct from the verses which precede them to merit a different treatment. The occurrence of שנית (v. 13), as already observed by Kimchi, is an indication that vv. 11–12 and vv. 13–16 are bound together, but it cannot be determined whether this is simply an editorial connection which creates a composite unit or whether it shows that the two experiences had an original, historical connection and occurred one after the other. What שנית does show (so J. Bright, *JBL*, 1951, p. 28 n. 43; Thiel p. 72) is that one of the independent units of which chapter 1 is

---

[1] Deleting משפחות, see below, p. 18.

composed is vv. 11–16 (or 11–14, see below) and that this was
formed before these verses were placed after vv. 4–10 with which
they have no original connection.

Sept. renders נפוח by ὑποκαιόμενον in v. 13 and תפתח by
ἐκκαυθήσεται in v. 14. A סיר נפוח is a cooking pot which is being
heated fiercely and which is on the boil or coming to the boil (so
Rashi and Kimchi). The interest of ἐκκαυθήσεται is that it
continues the metaphor of v. 13 and suggests that the Hebrew
may have been תֻּפַּח or תִּנָּפַח (cf. Ehrlich, op. cit., p. 233). If this
emendation were adopted, the sense would be, 'Evil will be
fanned from the north' instead of 'Evil will be unleashed from
the north' (MT is confirmed by Pesh. ttptḥ). Evil or disaster is
envisaged as the spilling over of the contents of a cooking pot
which will scald Judah severely.

Rashi supposes that פניו (v. 13) refers to the scum on the
surface of the boiling contents of the pot and a somewhat similar
view is adopted by Rudolph. פניו then refers to the surface level
of the liquid in the pot. It is tilted towards the south and when
the contents boil over, Judah will be scalded. G. R. Driver's
emendation (JQR, 28, 1937/38, p. 97), ופנוי מפני צפונה, 'and it
is turned (tilted) away from the north', yields the same sense and
disposes of the difficult פניו. Rothstein proposes ופיו, with
reference to Zech 5.8, where פיה is used of the mouth of a vessel
(איפה), and Kimchi, in his comment on סיר נפוח, speaks of
steam issuing from its mouth (מפיו). סיר is described by A. M.
Honeyman (PEQ, 1939, p. 85) as probably a large, two-handled,
round based, open-mouthed cooking pot.

Rudolph again rejects the view that the boiling pot involves
visionary experience, the matter is left more open by Bright, and
Reventlow regards it as a vision in the special sense which has
been explained in connection with vv. 11–12 (above, p. 15) I. P.
Seierstad (SNVAO, 1946, pp. 68–70, 110–115) takes a view
about vv. 11–12 and 13–16 which is complicated and unclear:
they constitute visionary experience and their foundation is a
deep, sub-conscious conceptuality which is symbolized by the
almond branch and the cooking pot. Skinner's view (J. Skinner,
Prophecy and Religion, 1922, p. 31) makes vv. 13–16 a
combination of sense experience and visionary experience: the
pot boiling on the domestic hearth is transformed into a magic
cauldron 'brewing in the mysterious north and sending forth
deadly fumes which will carry ruin and desolation over the
world'.

Rudolph's approach is the one which should be adopted. The
prophet has a premonition of impending judgement which arises
out of an ordinary experience. He had been looking at a pot
resting on a fire and had noticed that it was tilted, that the

contents were threatening to lap over one side and that there
would be a spillage in that direction when the pot boiled. This
ordinary observation took on the character of revelatory
experience for one who was absorbed in his prophetic calling and
devoured by a concern to discharge his responsibility. The pot
perched unevenly on the fire has its message and the utter
transparency and inevitability of the parable stamp it as a word
of Yahweh. The almond branch by an association with another
sound and its meaning is mysteriously transmuted into a word of
Yahweh, and the boiling pot placed unevenly on the fire can
elicit a question from Yahweh and be transformed into the
certainty that he has declared a word of judgement, so that the
prophet knows what he must now do and say. It is on Judah that
the judgement will fall, for there is no doubt that עֹל כֹּל יֹשְׁבֵי
הָאָרֶץ (v. 14) means 'inhabitants of Judah' and not 'inhabitants
of the earth' (see further below).

W. F. Albright (*JBL*, 63, 1944, p. 218 n. 70; *HUCA* 23,
1950–51, p. 34) has explained the difficult Hebrew text in v. 15
by assuming that מַמְלְכוֹת, on the analogy of Phoenician מַמְלַכֹת
'king' (see above, p. 7), means 'kings'. Bright adopts this
proposal, but supposes that מִשְׁפָּחוֹת and מַמְלְכוֹת are variant
readings and omits מִשְׁפָּחוֹת from his translation. Janzen (op.
cit., p. 10) notes that Sept. does not represent מִשְׁפָּחוֹת and,
following Rudolph, supposes that it is a secondary insertion from
25.9 (אֵת כֹּל מִשְׁפְּחוֹת צָפוֹן). πάσας τὰς βασιλείας may be no
more, than an attempt by the Greek translator to simplify כֹּל
מִשְׁפְּחוֹת מַמְלְכוֹת but it may, on the other hand, be an indication
that מִשְׁפָּחוֹת was missing from his Hebrew *Vorlage*, in which
case Sept. represents a shorter text than MT.

There are perplexing features in the portrayal of v. 15. Those
who refuse to interpret וּבָאוּ וְנָתְנוּ אִישׁ כִּסְאוֹ פֶּתַח שַׁעֲרֵי יְרוּשָׁלַ͏ִם as
a judgement scene (A. C. Welch, *Expositor*, 21, 1921, p. 139;
Rudolph) are right, because a judgement scene is not compatible
with the continuation of the verse whose vocabulary is that of
siege. What is apparently intended by the odd representation
that the invading kings will set up their thrones at the gates of
Jerusalem is that the capital will be under siege. This is the only
sense which וְעַל כֹּל חוֹמֹתֶיהָ סָבִיב will bear and the translation of
the Hebrew has to be filled out to make it clear. The meaning of
v. 15 is that Jerusalem and all the towns of Judah will be
encircled and under siege.

For Duhm v. 15 was an indication that we have to reckon not
with historical events but with an apocalyptic theology, and so it
was another mark of the lateness of chapter 1. Welch (op. cit.,
p. 139) was also of the opinion that v. 15 had apocalyptic traits
and that it was a mistake to pursue specific, historical

identifications, but he supposed that this interpretation was compatible with the ascription of the passage to the prophet Jeremiah. Something of this tendency is also present in Reventlow (op. cit., p. 110) who refers to the 'North' as the incorporation of the world which threatens Israel, but whose interpretation is particularly oriented towards a reverse concept of 'Holy War' (pp. 94–121).

Verse 16 emphasizes Yahweh's participation in the judgement which falls on his people. In person he leads for the prosecution and establishes their guilt (דברתי משפטי אותם is legal terminology). Wherein does their guilt consist? In apostasy and idolatry. Hence v. 16 offers an interpretation of military defeat and disaster. What does it mean? It means that Yahweh has found his people guilty and has exacted an appropriate punishment.

Duhm, who described certain passages in the book of Jeremiah as 'Scythian Songs' (4.5–8, 11–17*, 19–21, 23–26, 29–31; 6.1–5, 22–26; 8.14–17; 10.19–22*) does not apply his theory to the references to an enemy from the north in 1.13–15. Venema, who is usually reckoned to have been the first to introduce the hypothesis to the book of Jeremiah, does not in fact make any connection between the Scythians and the enemy from the north and does not mention the Scythians in any of the passages described by Duhm as 'Scythian Songs'. One may very easily be misled, therefore, when he is named as the pioneer of the Scythian hypothesis, as it affects the book of Jeremiah (cf. J. P. Hyatt, *JBL* 59, 1940, p. 500; H. H. Rowley, *BJRL*, 45, 1962–63, p. 199 n. 8). In 1.13–15 he identifies the enemy from the north with Nebuchadrezzar and the Babylonians and wherever the enemy from the north appears in Duhm's 'Scythian Songs' he identifies it with the Babylonians. Hence his Scythian theory has nothing to do with the problem of the enemy from the north and has a much narrower basis in 5.15–17, the only passage where he introduces it.

Duhm's view of 1.13–16, as we have seen, is that it is a product of late apocalyptic theology, and so the enemy from the north in these verses is unrelated to the enemy whom he identifies as the Scythians in the passages which he locates in the reign of Josiah—his 'Scythian Songs'. Rudolph contents himself with a wide statement of the possibilities: the Babylonians and their allies or the Assyrians or the Scythians or peoples from Asia Minor. Weiser, from a somewhat similar critical position, argues that in the early period of Jeremiah's ministry it is vain to ask what nation or nations Jeremiah had in mind, because the threat to which the prophet gave expression did not have the clarity or concreteness to make that kind of identification

possible. In his commentary (1965) Bright's position is not very
different from that of Rudolph, but in an earlier work (*JBL*, 70,
1951, p. 28 n. 43) he dissociates himself from the Scythian
theory and also from the view that 1.13–16 are not far removed
from the date of Jeremiah's call in 626. On the strength of other
passages involving the enemy from the north, which he locates in
the reign of Jehoiakim, he dates 1.11–16 c. 612. Rietzschel's
position (op. cit., pp. 133–135) is similar, but he advances an
additional literary-critical argument, that בימי יהויקים בן
יאשיהו מלך יהודה (v. 3) was originally attached to vv. 11–16 and
was moved to its present position by the editor of the
superscription.

The evidence which the passages featuring the enemy from the
north in chapters 2–6 (Duhm's 'Scythian Songs') were thought
to supply concerning an activity of Jeremiah in the reign of
Josiah has been questioned, the assessment of 1.13–16
correspondingly revised, and it is held that the only ministry of
Jeremiah for which there is any evidence lies in the reign of
Jehoiakim (T. C. Gordon, op. cit., p. 564; J. P. Hyatt, *JBL*,
1940, p. 509; H. G. May, *JNES*, 1945, 225–227; C. F. Whitley,
ZAW, 80, 1968, pp. 42–49). A possible reply to Duhm's point
about 1.15 (it has late apocalyptic features) is that a
literary-critical separation should be made between vv. 13–14
and 15–16, so that the later elaboration of צפון in v. 15 is not an
embarrassment to those who would connect 1.13–14 with the
other passages involving the enemy from the north (see further
below). Hyatt, on the other hand, identifies כל משפחות ממלכות
צפונה (1.15) with the Neo-Babylonians, and their allies, the
Medes. The arguments of F. Wilke (*BWAT*, 13, 1913,
pp. 222–254) against the credibility of connecting passages in
the book of Jeremiah with a threat constituted by Scythian
incursions exercised a powerful influence on the movement of
thought which has just been described. Wilke was particularly
concerned to point out historical improbabilities in the account
of Herodotus (I, 105) concerning a Scythian invasion of Syria
and Palestine. On the one hand, he argued that the supposition
of a hostile presence of Scythians in Syria-Palestine when
Jeremiah's prophetic activity was beginning (626) cannot be
reconciled with what is otherwise known of the external history
of that period. On the other, he held that the passages in the
book of Jeremiah, which were alleged to refer to the Scythians,
contained descriptions which fitted the Chaldaeans and were
inappropriate for the Scythians (cf. S. Mowinckel, *VT* 12, 1962,
p. 287). The Scythian theory still has its defenders: H. H.
Rowley (*BJRL*, 1962–63, p. 217) has argued that the 626 date
for Jeremiah's call should be maintained, and that the 'enemy

from the North' in chapters 2–6 is to be identified with the Scythians. H. Cazelles (*RB*, 74, 1967, pp. 24–44) has urged that a period of Scythian domination of Syria-Palestine began in 639/8 and lasted until 611/10; that it was the Scythians who held up the Egyptians at Ashdod for 29 years (640–611); that the argument (advanced by Wilke) that the Scythians would not have penetrated an area which was subject to Assyria is to be met by the statement that they were agents of Assyria and representatives of her power.

When Targ. paraphrases סיר נפוח (v. 13) as 'a king boiling like a pot' we are left in no doubt that Nebuchadrezzar has been identified as the enemy from the north, and both Rashi and Kimchi identify that enemy with Babylon. Even if there was an earlier enemy from the north, the only enemy from the north now on view in the book of Jeremiah is Babylon, and, according to Rudolph, this was already true when the passages which have been associated with the Scythians appeared in the context of the first scroll in 605. This provokes the thought that if there were original allusions to the Scythians, they were so short-lived and were transformed into allusions to Babylon so soon, that their existence, if they ever existed, is reduced to exegetical insignificance (cf. Nicholson).

According to Rudolph (Weiser, Bright) v. 16 is an indication of the extent to which the early prophet Jeremiah was influenced by Hosea and shared his concern about apostasy and idolatry. Hence Rudolph rejects the view of Welch (op. cit., p. 139) and Hyatt (*IB*, 1956, pp. 808f.) that vv. 15–16 are redactional. Thiel (op. cit., pp. 74–76) detects D at work in vv. 11–16: it was D who located vv. 11–16 in this position in chapter 1 which is his composition. A somewhat different approach to that of Thiel is, perhaps, required: vv. 15–16 are a secondary exegetical, elaboration of a Jeremianic core (vv. 13–14). They have a style which marks them off from the compressed laconic character of vv. 11–14; they have an interest in the communication of more detail. The nature of the threat from the north and how it will materialize are spelled out, as are the sins of which Judah has been guilty, and the disaster which looms is explicitly interpreted as the verdict which Yahweh has passed and the punishment which he will exact. The connective כי (v. 15) is then indicative of a subsequent (exilic?) concern to convert the terse record of Jeremiah's experience into more deliberate teaching.

RECAPITULATION: DO NOT WEAKEN OR YOU WILL BE LOST
(1.17–19)

[17]But you are to gird your loins and stand up and speak to them all that I command you. Do not be unnerved because of them, lest I break your nerve in their presence. [18]I am making you now into a fortified city, a pillar of iron, a wall of bronze,[1] that you may withstand the whole land, the kings of Judah, its statesmen, its priests and its people. [19]They will make war on you, but will not defeat you, for I shall be with you to keep you safe. You have my word.

Ziegler (*Beiträge*, pp. 88f.) supposes that at v. 17 Sept. represents a better Hebrew text than MT (cf. Janzen, pp. 30, 96), with superior parallelism (אל תירא מפניהם ואל תחת לפניהם). The argument from parallelism has force only if it is supposed that vv. 17–19 are poetry (see above, p. 25). Sept. is less impressive than MT and should not be adopted. It has been influenced by v. 8 from which μὴ φοβηθῇς ἀπὸ προσώπου αὐτῶν, probably, and ὅτι μετὰ σοῦ ἐγώ εἰμι τοῦ ἐξαιρεῖσθαί σε certainly, derive (cf. v. 19). Hence influences other than textual ones have perhaps operated to determine the form of v. 17 in Sept.: the element of threat in MT constituted by פן אחתך לפניהם has been removed and the aspect of exhortation and reassurance reinforced.

Both Rashi and Kimchi associate the girding of the loins with speedy and decisive action. The prophet must raise himself to the highest pitch of preparedness like a soldier on the eve of battle (Rashi) or like Elijah who girded his loins to run before Ahab (1 Kgs 18.46; so Kimchi, cf. Rudolph and Weiser). No inner weakness or failure is to obstruct him at the time of testing, when he becomes aware of determined opposition and hostility. Pesh. ('*tbrk*) and Targ. (אתברינך) appropriately indicate the sense 'shatter' for אחתך. If the prophet is weak and fearful, Yahweh will surrender him in his brokenness to his enemies. The prophet is called to wage war against determined enemies and in his isolation is like a city under siege (Weiser; Thiel, p. 77). On the other hand, he has a strong position and is well equipped for his warfare: the piling up of figures—a fortified city, an iron pillar, a wall of bronze—is indicative of the massiveness of his strength, if only he will realize it in obedience to his vocation. A. Alt (*ZDMG*, 86, 1933, pp. 31–48) has remarked that when the figure 'a bronze wall' is used in Egyptian texts with reference to the Pharaoh and the gods, it is a symbol of the protection which they afford to others—they are an encircling, defensive wall. In the case of Jer 1.18 (Alt, pp. 46–48) the bronze wall is related to the self-defence of the individual who is beleaguered and isolated and who has to be persuaded that his position is defensible. The

[1] Reading ולחמת (MT, ולחמות), with Sept., Vulg. and Targ.

portrayal recalls Ezek 3.8f., where conflict is viewed as inseparable from the prophetic office. The prophet must match and outreach his enemies in strength and determination.

The opposition is universal—עַל כָּל הָאָרֶץ (v. 18). These words are not represented by Sept. and are paraphrased by Targ., 'to give a cup of curse to drink to all the inhabitants of the land (or 'earth')'. Targ. uses the same image in v. 5 in connection with גוים but there is no doubt that הָאָרֶץ in v. 18 means 'the land of Judah' and not 'the earth', for the list which follows establishes this. But in v. 18 there is a more particular designation of the prophet's opponents: they are located among the political and ecclesiastical leaders of the community, kings, statesmen and priests. Both Rudolph and Bright suppose that עַם הָאָרֶץ is a designation of a class and not a reference to the general population. Following E. Würthwein (*BWANT*, 4, 1936, p. 17) and G. von Rad (*Deuteronomium-Studien*, 1948; E. Tr. by D. Stalker, *Studies in Deuteronomy*, 1953, pp. 60–66) they hold that עַם הָאָרֶץ means 'full citizens' or 'landed gentry' (Bright). Sept. indicates 'populace' (καὶ τῷ λαῷ τῆς γῆς) for עַם הָאָרֶץ rather than a particular class for which עַם הָאָרֶץ is a title. The view that עַם הָאָרֶץ is an allusion to a class should be rejected. The opposition to Jeremiah is to extend to the common people. Hated in the palace and the temple, he will not find support in the streets or the market place. He will be the antithesis of a popular prophet.

Three different critical points of view attaching to vv. 17–19 may be considered. That of Rudolph who regards vv. 17–19 as the work of Jeremiah and chapter 1 as his introduction to the scroll which was written in 605. The closing verses constitute an effective concentration and finalization of what the prophet intended to communicate. Thiel is saying the same about vv. 17–19, but from a different, critical point of view: the strong, unifying conclusion which these verses furnish for chapter 1 is to be attributed to his Deuteronomistic editor. It is D who has put this coping-stone on the chapter, carrying forward the editing by which he has already impressed his stamp on the other literary units and binding them together by means of a summary in which all the themes are concentrated.

A third, critical view, of which Duhm may be regarded as a representative, is that vv. 17–19 are a kind of pastiche and that this is a mark of lateness. Verses or parts of verses from elsewhere in the book are re-used in order to supply a conclusion for chapter 1. The intention is to encapsulate in vv. 17–19 the essential prophet Jeremiah and to capture with a few strokes the key features of his ministry. This understanding of vv. 17–19 deserves serious consideration.

The supposition that vv. 17–19 were originally continuous with the call narrative and have been separated from it by the subsequent insertion of vv. 11–16 is not compatible with the view that Jeremiah himself edited the chapter and arranged the constituent units in 605. Those who share Rudolph's critical position ought not to advance such an argument and there is an inconcinnity when Bright says, on the one hand, that chapter 1 may have been put together by the prophet Jeremiah and, on the other hand, that vv. 17–19 may have been originally continuous with vv. 4–10. Jüngling's argument (op. cit., pp. 22–24) is that vv. 11–16 were introduced in connection with the enlargement of the scroll as a consequence of Jehoiakim's response to the first scroll. This is intelligible only if the editing of chapter 1 on that occasion was undertaken by someone other than the prophet Jeremiah. It cannot be supposed that Jeremiah did not know the facts about the provenance of the units which are attributed to him (vv. 4–10 and vv. 17–19) and that he edited them in such a way as to break a connection which was original. Only those who ascribe the editing of the chapter to someone other than Jeremiah can sensibly make the assumption that an editor has inserted a unit consisting of vv. 11–16 between vv. 4–10 and 17–19 (cf. Nicholson).

It would be unwise to attempt to say too much about the principles which have guided the editing of chapter 1. The description of Jeremiah's commission and the scope of his responsibilities in the call narrative show that the oracles against foreign nations were part of the book when that narrative was composed. The concern to do justice to the contents of the book of Jeremiah produces an unevenness in the call narrative. The dichotomy between the description of him as a prophet to the nations and the subsequent concentration on a bitter opposition, which has to be understood in terms of a mission to Judah, is the consequence of an inability to effect a perfect reconciliation between two different objectives. The need to take account of all the contents of the book has been met, but this is not altogether compatible with a recognition that he is essentially a prophet to Judah. There are no reasons for disengaging vv. 13–14 from the prophet Jeremiah, but vv. 15–16 are a secondary, exegetical elaboration of vv. 13–14. Whether they were added to vv. 13–14 after the editing of chapter 1 or were already part of that unit when it was made a constituent part of the chapter cannot be determined. The editor of chapter 1 supposed that vv. 11–16 (or vv. 11–14) enhanced the view of Jeremiah and his ministry which he was attempting to capture in chapter 1. The prophet who had no success was, nevertheless, assured that the words which he spoke would not fall to the ground, and that these words portended doom for Judah is the burden of vv. 13–16. If vv. 17–19 are a pastiche of the kind supposed by Duhm, this is another indication that chapter 1 is built out of a book of Jeremiah already in existence. It is a gathering up of the themes of the chapter: the prophet will be subjected to enormous pressures, but his position is strong and it is essential that he should not capitulate.

The chapter was not put together by Jeremiah and not very much in it is attributable to him. It does not have the coherence Thiel claims for it as a consequence of the work of D, but it is an interesting and moving effort to capture in an introductory chapter the significance of a prophet whose activity lay in the past, on the basis of a record of it contained in a book bearing that prophet's name which was extant. If this is a correct critical evaluation, and, in particular, if the book which chapter 1 presupposes contained the oracles against foreign nations, the chapter is exilic, at the earliest, and, more probably, post-exilic.

CHAPTER II

RECOLLECTION OF A LOST LOVE AND LOYALTY (2.1–3)

¹This word came to me from Yahweh: ²Go and proclaim in Jerusalem: These
are Yahweh's words:
> I remember the loyalty of your youth,
> your love for me as a bride,
> when you followed me in the wilderness,
> in a land unsown.
> ³Israel was devoted to Yahweh,
> the firstfruits of his harvest.
> Any who ate her incurred guilt,
> evil overtook them.
>   This is Yahweh's word.

The principal manuscripts of Sept. have a shorter text than MT,
and Janzen (pp. 111–114) supposes that the transition from 1.19
to זכרתי לך (2.2) may have been effected by כה אמר יהוה. καὶ
εἶπε represents ויאמר, and MT and Sept. display 'variant,
secondary, transitional glosses'. The correct reading of Sept. is
that it does not represent ויהי דבר יהוה אלי לאמר הלך נקראת
באזני ירושלם and that it renders לאמר כה אמר יהוה as καὶ εἶπε
Τάδε λέγει κύριος. The difficulty of a specific mention of
Jerusalem over against more general references to Israel which
follow (v. 3) was felt by earlier scholars (Cornill, H. Schmidt,
Rothstein), and Duhm was inclined to remove all of vv. 1–2a,
although he thought that כה אמר יהוה might be retained 'at a
pinch'. His view of הלך וקראת באזני ירושלם is that its intention
was to represent chapters 2–6 as a great sermon which was
delivered in the Jerusalem temple or at the gates of the city. The
contents of 2–6 did not originate as speeches and we are not to
think of them as oral communications which were subsequently
reduced to writing. Rather they originated with Jeremiah as
written compositions and were thereafter 'published' in order to
be read. Hence the superscription (so Duhm) must be declared
entirely inappropriate in respect of the material which it
purports to introduce.

Another explanation of the appearance of 'Jerusalem' and a
more positive estimate of its function associates it with the
reading of the scroll by Baruch in the Jerusalem temple in 605
(Rudolph, Weiser). What is indicated by it is that there was a
decisive moment in 605 when Jeremiah concentrated the sum of
his prophetic witness in a public reading by Baruch in the
Jerusalem temple and required an audience of Judaeans to
reconsider it in the light of the historical realities which they now
had to confront. On this view the significance of the

superscription is as a witness to a reapplication and intensification of Jeremiah's witness.

Janzen (p. 26; cf. Ziegler, *Beiträge*, p. 93) explains the non-representation of במדבר בארץ לא זרועה in Sept. on the assumption that these words were missing from the Hebrew text which was before the Greek translator. A more intriguing feature of the Greek text is τοῦ ἐξακολουθῆσαί σε τῷ ἁγίῳ Ἰσραηλ. But the original text of Sept. conjectured by Ziegler has a strange appearance and the transition from λέγει κύριος to ἀρχὴ γενημάτων αὐτοῦ is so harsh as to be unacceptable. ἅγιος Ἰσραηλ τῷ κυρίῳ, which is deleted as a doublet, is indispensable to the sense and Ziegler has no manuscript evidence to support its deletion. The obscurity lies in τοῦ ἐξακολουθῆσαί σε τῷ ἁγίῳ Ἰσραηλ and any account of it must be conjectural. A possibility which should be entertained is that Sept. had a Hebrew text without במדבר בארץ לא זרועה and paraphrased אחרי 'after me' as 'after the Holy One of Israel'.

The argument which Schottroff (op. cit., pp. 270ff.) conducts with a view to showing that זכרתי לך חסד נעוריך is not compatible with a reference to Israel's loyalty and must be indicative of Yahweh's loyalty is unsuccessful. Schottroff goes against the testimony of Sept. and Targ., for these versions understood זכרתי לך חסד נעוריך אהבת כלולתיך as a reference to Israel's loyalty and love. The contention that the verse refers to Yahweh's loyalty and love (Schottroff and M. V. Fox, *CBQ* 35, 1973, pp. 443ff.) is not new and is found in two eighteenth century English commentaries, those of Lowth (1718) and Blayney (1784). P. A. H. de Boer (*Gedenken und Gedächtnis in der Welt des Alten Testaments*, 1962, p. 59) holds that the sense of זכרתי לך is 'I make you aware of' and that v. 2 is not simply recollection of a lost love and loyalty, but that a call to repentance is implied in it. This is as old as Rashi who comments, 'If you would return to me, my desire would be to have compassion on you, for I remember the loyalty of your youth'. Fox (pp. 443ff.) has a particular interest in showing that v. 2 refers only to Yahweh's grace. Jerome's authority can be invoked for this, *totumque hoc non ad meritum eius refert, sed ad suam misericordiam*.

BDB and KB³ indicate 'betrothal' for כלולה, which occurs only once, and this rendering is found in Rudolph and Weiser. C. Wiéner (*RSR*, 44, 1956, pp. 403–407) has argued that 'marriage' is the right sense for כלולתיך, that Vulg. *charitatem desponsationis tuae* may refer to the ceremony of marriage and that it is so understood by Jerome (*instar sponsaliorum*). There is no use of כלה in Biblical Hebrew which requires the sense 'betrothed' and a narrower sense of the word is 'a young girl on her wedding day', 'a bride'. That כלולתיך refers to 'honeymoon' or the first days of a marriage rather than to 'betrothal' is a correct conclusion and is represented by Bright and NEB ('the love of your bridal days'). It agrees with Rashi's view that the entrance of the bride into the bridal chamber and the consummation of the marriage are indicated by אהבת כלולתיך, and both Sept. and Pesh. should, probably, be interpreted in this way: Pesh. (*rḥmt' dmsybrnwtky*) 'love of your continence' means the chaste love of a bride and Sept. (καὶ ἀγάπης τελειώσεώς σου) does not really represent a misunderstanding of כלולה (its being connected with כלה rather than כלל) as Schottroff maintains (p. 265). הכליל in post-biblical Hebrew means 'complete', 'perfect', and *kll* occurs in Ugaritic with the sense 'complete' (J. C. L. Gibson, *CML*, 4, 5, 72, p. 61, *ykllnh*; A. Herdner, *Mission de Ras Shamra*, 10 (1963), p. 26). Hence τελείωσις, 'perfection', 'fulfilment' is a reference to the consummation of marriage.

The versions translate v. 3 with present tenses and this understanding of the verse is also indicated by Rashi and Kimchi. The verbs (יאשמו and תבא) lend themselves to this rendering, but the sense is easier if past tenses are assumed (cf. Lowth). Among modern commentators Bright translates the verbs in v. 3 as present tenses and Rudolph and Weiser as past tenses (so also NEB). Targ. explains the phrase 'firstfruits of his harvest' at some length: just as those who eat the fruits of the harvest before they have satisfied the priests' entitlement are guilty of a capital crime, so all who despoil Israel are guilty and shame will come upon them (cf. Kimchi). Past tenses are required to make good sense of v. 3; there is then an implied contrast between Israel's past state and her present faithlessness and fickleness; between the protection which she then enjoyed and her present weakness and defencelessness in the face of her enemies. Hence v. 3 completes Yahweh's recollection of what Israel once was.

The wilderness is opposed to the arable land as the place where Israel responded to Yahweh's love with the rapture of a pure bride. We may not conclude that wilderness conditions are right for pure Yahwism and that life in Canaan brought inevitably in its train apostasy and corruption. The wilderness was the place of Israel's first, joyful surrender to Yahweh, and, associated with the occupation of Canaan, there was a continuous deterioration in the relationship between Yahweh and Israel. It is therefore a matter of history rather than of culture; the more essential contrast is not that of wilderness and arable land, but of a perfect beginning and a failure to maintain a relationship characterized by simplicity and wholeness (see below on v. 7). It is understandable, however, that, in recollection or retrospect, Canaan should be a figure of complication, distraction and plurality, the land where Israel is responsive to many lovers, and the wilderness the figure of absolute fidelity and all-consuming love, where Yahweh is all in all.

Yet the figure which is selected in v. 3 to describe the special relationship of Israel to Yahweh is agricultural: Israel is the firstfruits of Yahweh's harvest. According to Deut 32.8f. Yahweh delegated responsibility for the government of the nations to divine beings, but himself exercised direct rule over Israel. He has a closer link with Israel than he has with the nations, for Jacob is חבל נחלתו 'his allotted portion' (NEB). Present tenses in v. 3 might be taken as indications of the continuing reality of Israel's special bond with Yahweh. More probably, v. 3 is part of Yahweh's recollection of what once was and is no more. Then Israel's condition of wholeness and safety corresponded to the quality of her devotion to Yahweh; now her condition of disintegration and weakness in the face of insult and attack indicates the loss of her first estate.

Schottroff's account of vv. 2–3 appears to assume that homogeneous complexes are easily identifiable in the book of Jeremiah, that there will be no difficulty in agreeing on the principles of composition and theological tendency which inform them, and that the achievement of a common point of departure in these terms will not be contentious. It assumes that the extant form of the book has been determined by processes and considerations which are everywhere deliberate and thoughtful and that these are so luminous that they will be generally admitted. The case to be made against this is that the short units in the poetic parts of the book of Jeremiah are, on the whole, less problematic than their principles of association and that the order of priorities which he proposes is not sensible: to begin at a place where the difficulties are multiplied and the uncertainties have deepened is a wrong beginning.

The most fundamental aspect of the matter is that exegesis is made to hinge entirely on the theological function alleged to have been discharged by a complex of units in a given situation. There is a shift of emphasis from the 'words of Jeremiah' to the theological tendency of an exilic traditionist. Hence vv. 1–3 may not be interpreted as 'Recollection of a lost love and loyalty', because as such they would have had no relevance for an exilic traditionist and would not have been 'transmitted'. There is an assumption that the concern to preserve a literary record of Jeremiah's words is not a factor in transmission: that it is not an adequate account of the preservation of vv. 1–3 to say that they were believed to be words of Jeremiah, and that it is essential always to demonstrate that units have a high degree of coherence, that they are related as components of a composition which has a master plan and is informed by systematic theological considerations.

A HISTORY OF APOSTASY: THE CASE AGAINST ISRAEL (2.4–13)

⁴Hear the word of Yahweh, house of Jacob, all families of the house of Israel.
⁵These are Yahweh's words:
> What evil did your fathers find in me,
> that they removed themselves from me,
> going after idols and committing idolatry?
> ⁶Never did they ask, Where is Yahweh,
> who brought us up from Egypt,
> who guided us in the wilderness,
> through a barren and pitted land,
> through parched and gloomy country,
> where no travellers pass,
> and no settlers make their home?
> ⁷I brought you into a fertile land,
> to eat its fruits and enjoy its bounty;
> but you defiled my land when you came to it,
> and changed my heritage into a loathsome thing.
> ⁸Never did the priests ask, Where is Yahweh?
> Those who interpreted the law did not know me,
> the shepherds rebelled against me,
> and the prophets prophesied by Baal;
> they followed gods powerless to help them.
> ⁹Therefore this is Yahweh's word:
> I press my charge against you,
> and against your descendants I press my charge.
> ¹⁰Cross to the islands of Kittim and observe,
> send to Kedar and examine well;
> see whether anything like this has happened.
> ¹¹Has a nation ever bartered its gods,
> although they are non-gods?
> But my people has given away its glory,
> and got nothing in exchange.
> ¹²Be appalled at this, O Heavens,
> be horrified and utterly desolated.
> This is Yahweh's word.
> ¹³My people have done two wrongs,
> they have forsaken me,
> a spring of running water,
> to dig cisterns for themselves,
> broken cisterns which do not hold water

AN ACCUSING QUESTION (2.4–5)

וילכו אחרי ההבל ויהבלו is certainly a reference to idolatry, although this is not to be gathered from Sept., Vulg. and Pesh. which offer literal translations of MT: Israel has pursued non-existent objectives and gained nothing (Pesh.). Targ.'s rendering of הבל by טעותא is correct exegesis, and idolatry is the principal preoccupation of the chapter (cf. Kimchi). Thiel (p. 81) concludes that וילכו אחרי ההבל ויהבלו is an insertion by D and that it disturbs an original continuity of כי רחקו מעלי and ולא אמרו איה יהוה. It is metrically unsatisfactory, since it has to be analysed (so Cornill and Rudolph) as a stich (וילכו אחרי ההבל) and half a stich (ויהבלו). D's intention is to spell out כי רחקו מעלי as idolatry and to indicate the punishment which will be exacted for it (ויהבלו). It is unlikely that this is a correct understanding of ויהבלו: what it indicates is not a penalty which will be inflicted, but a disillusionment which will be suffered (so Volz and Rudolph). וילכו אחרי ההבל ויהבלו should, perhaps, be regarded as a third stich in v. 5 rather than a short line, but the presence of an odd number of stichs should not be regarded as an indication that one of them is secondary. There is no textual evidence to support the view that וילכו אחרי ההבל ויהבלו is secondary.

Those addressed are described as 'House of Jacob, all families of the house of Israel' (v. 4) and this is deliberately archaic (Jacob is the 'father' of the twelve tribes) and comprehensive, envisaging the old entity 'Israel'. The reason for this may be found in the historical retrospect undertaken by the chapter. The prophet speaks to Judah and Jerusalem, but there is a continuity in the concept 'Israel', despite the consequences of political brokenness. The matter is more complex than this, for the prophet appears to address all generations of Israel and not just his own generation. There is an indivisibility of responsibility and the hearers have to answer not only, 'Why did you remove yourselves from me?', but also, 'Why did your fathers remove themselves from me?'. The interrogation with which Yahweh opens his case against his people relates to the beginnings of a history of apostasy, to the point when Israel first settled in Canaan. It was then that the first, fatal tendencies towards disloyalty and folly began to manifest themselves. It is the emptiness of these pursuits on which the prophet dwells: it is a following after non-existent gods, an activity without substance.

THE FIRST COUNT OF THE INDICTMENT (2.6–8)

G. R. Driver (*JQR*, 1937–38, p. 98) holds that שׁוחה (v. 6) has the sense 'soft sand' rather than 'pit(s)', on the analogy of Arabic *sāha* 'sink'. It is, however, perhaps not a desert of sand which is indicated, but a wilderness with an irregular, difficult surface over which progress is slow and painful. צלמות is explained as 'shadow of death' by Pesh. and Targ. (cf. Vulg. *imaginem mortis*). Rashi glosses צלמות with חשך 'darkness' and this sense can be related to a different morphology, צְלָמוּת or the like from צלם (cf. Arabic, *ẓulmatu(n)*).

A more contentious matter is the precise sense of תפשי התורה. תפשי is translated literally by Sept. (οἱ ἀντεχόμενοι), Vulg. (*tenentes*) and Pesh. ('*ḥdy*), and תורה is rendered as 'law' (Sept. νόμος; Vulg. *legem*; Pesh. *nmws'*). Targ. paraphrases, 'Those who teach the law'. There is a question whether תורה may mean something less than Law in the definitive sense of later Judaism. In that case תורה is, perhaps, the authoritative ruling or decision, to deliver which a knowledge of previous rulings given in comparable circumstances is necessary (cf. Rudolph, 'written and oral instruction'). The question about the meaning of תורה cannot be dissociated from a decision about the significance of תפשי התורה. Modern commentators (Rudolph, Bright) suppose that they are priests with a specialized function, that of preserving the תורה, and Rudolph explains the double reference to priests on the ground that they bear a primary responsibility for the religion of the people. We have noted that according to Targ. תפשי התורה are teachers of the תורה and Kimchi identifies them with חכמים. This is in general accord with views about תפשי התורה which I have expressed elsewhere (*PWM*, 1965, pp. 102ff., 111f.).

The question of v. 5, although it is accusing, is yet evidence of concern and pained bewilderment. Yahweh's people are occupied with other concerns and loyalties, but it is an illusory fulness which they possess. The priests serve Yahweh's cult, but they have forgotten Yahweh (v. 8). It is impossible to discover what particular dereliction of duty is envisaged here. It may be the story of Israel's deliverance summarized in vv. 6–7 (cf. Deut 26.5–9) that they have forgotten. The cult of Yahweh is no longer distinguishable from the cult of Baal (so Rudolph). There is the more general consideration that a life full of cultic punctiliousness may be devoid of serious, religious concern. Similarly, the scholars of the law know everything about it and yet know nothing. The indictment of the prophets is a quite general one; it was limited by Targ. to 'false prophets', and it has been suggested (Rudolph and Weiser) that we are to suppose a particular reference to degenerate ecstatics, unworthy successors of Elijah, who have succumbed to the enticements of Baal. The final part of v. 8 ('They followed gods powerless to help them') is understood by Rudolph (also by Weiser) as a general, concluding summary about the behaviour of the people as a whole. More probably, ואחרי לא יועלו הלכו is a development of נבאו בבעל which emphasizes the emptiness and uselessness of the prophets' devotion to Baal (so Duhm, Bright, NEB).

There are two aspects to the loss of historical memory (vv. 5–6). The people have forgotten how Yahweh guided them on a dangerous journey and they have abused the good land to which Yahweh brought them. There is no glorification of the wilderness and no deprecation of the land of Canaan, but this is not necessarily at odds with vv. 2–3 which need not be interpreted as signifying that only by remaining in wilderness conditions could Israel have maintained her pure relationship with Yahweh. They defiled the promised land and made Yahweh's heritage into an object of loathing. But Israel's apostasy is more complex than the open idolatry of Baal worship. The superficiality of תפשי התורה is compatible with Yahwistic orthodoxy and the rebellion of the rulers is the elevation of what is regarded as political realism and expertise over the claims of Yahweh's word (*PWM*, pp. 48ff.). There was no reason why Israel should not have enjoyed the bounties of Canaan and yet remained faithful to Yahweh. The fault lay with Israel and not with Canaan.

YAHWEH PRESSES HIS CHARGE AGAINST ISRAEL (2.9–13)

Rashi understands עד (v. 9) to mean that this is a last attempt to reprove and persuade: ריב then has the sense of 'argument' and is an effort to convince Israel and bring about a change (similarly Kimchi). There are, however, no elements of pleading in the section: it is not an argument aimed at inducing repentance, but is the unfolding of a charge against Israel. The thought that vv. 9–13 move from the past into the present (Kimchi) has been taken up by Rudolph and בניכם has been associated with Baruch's public reading of the scroll in 605. An earlier speech of Jeremiah has been modified by the addition of בניכם (emending MT with Vulg. and 3 manuscripts) on account of the composition of Baruch's audience in 605. MT בני בניכם (indicated by Sept., Pesh. and Targ.) does not suit this exegesis because it means 'descendants' and not 'the next generation'. It is, perhaps, still the whole history of apostasy which is being recorded and so it is still early Israel and later Israel that is being addressed ('you and your descendants').

In v. 10 either הן is to be explained as an Aramaism = אם, or the consonants are to be disposed as הנחיתה (so H. Grätz, *Emendationes in plerosque Sacrae Scripturae Vetus Testamenti Libros*, 1892–94). The Targum's line of exegesis is followed by

Rashi, according to whom the Kittim and the Kedarites were nomadic tent dwellers and shepherds. This is not really the point of the juxtaposition of Kittim and Kedar. Rather they are paradigms of communities which are culturally far apart: כתיים is precisely Cyprus, but is used here more generally of the islands and coastlands of the Mediterranean Sea; Kedar is an Arabian tribe, but is used as an omnibus term for nomadic communities. Hence whether one examines the habits of more sophisticated peoples or those of communities which live on the fringes of the desert nothing comparable to Israel's behaviour will be found.

כבודו is a type of תקון ספרים to be classed with Ps 106.20 and Hos 4.7 (W. McKane, *On Language, Culture and Religion*, 1974, pp. 60f.). If כבודי were a circumlocution for 'me'=Yahweh and if כבודו were an attempt to remove this, the intention must have been to refer the suffix of כבודו to Israel and to understand כבוד as the true religion which was Israel's 'glory'. It is thus uncertain whether much is to be gained by postulating that an original כבודי has been altered to כבודו, but the latter may be a circumlocution for יהוה as NEB supposes.

The indictment in vv. 10–11 is touched with satire. Israel has no religious discrimination and is like those who have no business sense and who exchange a valuable product for a useless one. Israel has bartered Yahweh (NEB) for non-gods and has suffered a great loss. She is invited to travel abroad to the Mediterranean and to the fringes of the desert, to observe and investigate and ponder over the religious habits of other communities. Israel's behaviour is doubly incomprehensible: it is unnatural in that it conflicts with the religious habits of men in general who do not exchange their gods as one would a product in the market place, but who revere them and cling to them, even though they have no reality. It is also an apostasy from a true religion and the embracing of a false one.

The function of the heavens in v. 12 is not strictly that of a witness (cf. Bright). They are addressed and are personified, but they are asked only to react emotionally to what they see of Israel's incredible behaviour. MT שׂערו and Sept. ἔφριξεν both indicate the bristling of the hair as a reaction to terror. Pesh. renders שׂערו *zw'w* 'be agitated' and both Rashi and Kimchi explain it as סערה 'agitation'. חרבו (MT) is obscure and Sept. ἐπὶ πλεῖον apparently indicates: שׂערו הרבה מאד, 'Be exceedingly greatly horrified'. Pesh. renders חרבו by *dḥlw* 'be afraid' and the emendation which Rudolph (BHS) adopts (חרדו) gives this sense. חרב is used of 'desolation' in relation to the world of nature, but this would be the only example of its application to 'desolation' in an emotive sense.

In v. 13 the contrast between spring and cistern is sufficient to bear the main weight of the exegesis (so Kimchi) and the defective construction of the latter is at the periphery of the metaphor. Rashi explains how the action of the water on the edges and walls of a cistern destroys its watertight properties. Kimchi supposes that the 'broken cisterns' are an allusion to misguided political alliances (cf. vv. 16–18) as well as to idolatry. The two evils are the neglect of true religion and zeal for false religion (cf. Targ.). Israel refuses the true religion of which Yahweh is the only source; she refuses Yahweh's living water and busies herself with the construction of her own water supply. This is idolatry, for it is an attempt by men to make their own religion and to fashion gods in their own image. It is what happens when dependence on God and acceptance of the living water which is in his gift has become an offence. The end of ingenuity and industry when these are applied to the construction of a religion is emptiness.

WHY HAS ISRAEL BEEN HUMILIATED? (2.14–19)

[14]Is Israel a slave? Was he born into slavery?
Why has he become a prey?
[15]Why do lions growl and snarl at him?
His land has been devastated,
his towns are destroyed and abandoned.
[16]Men of Noph and Tahpanhes will crush your skulls.
[17]Does not your forsaking of Yahweh, your God,
bring this on you?[1]
And now, why do you go to Egypt
to drink the water of the Nile?
[18]Why do you go to Assyria
to drink the water of the Euphrates?
[19]Your evil-doing will discipline you,
your apostasy correct you.
You will have to learn how evil and bitter it is
to forsake Yahweh, your God
and to have no respect for me.[2]
This is the word of the Lord, Yahweh Sabaoth.

ילִיד בִּית is rendered correctly by Sept. (οἰκογενής) and Vulg. (*vernaculus*), that is, a slave born in the house—a slave from birth. Kimchi, however, does not understand ילִיד בִּית as an intensification of עֶבֶד (not only a slave but a slave from birth). His exegesis turns rather on the rights of ילִיד בִּית : the master of the house has consorted with a שִׁפְחָה in order to secure an heir (cf. Gen 16.1ff.) and the child (ילִיד בִּית) has the status of a son (so also Blayney). The juxtaposition of יִשְׁאֲגוּ and נָתְנוּ is difficult

---

[1] Deleting בְּעֵת מוֹלִיכֵךְ בַּדֶּרֶךְ (see further below, p. 38.).
[2] Emending MT אֵלָיִךְ to אֵלַי, with Pesh. (see further below, p. 39.).

to understand: both verbs appear to have the same function and it is not obvious why the forms should be different. יִשָּׁאֲגוּ can be explained as a frequentative (Rudolph), but in that case נָתְנוּ would also have to be frequentative.

נִצְּתָה (v. 15) is given by K and נִצְּתוּ by Q. נִצְּתָה can be elucidated as a 3rd feminine sing., in which case there is a lack of congruence between verb and subject, which may be allowable, or as a 3rd feminine plur. (GK 44m). נִצְּתָה can be derived from נצה 'destroy' or יצת 'burn', but נִצְּתוּ can be derived only from יצת. The expression תְּצִינָה מֵאֵין יוֹשֵׁב (4.7) is similar to נִצְּתָה מִבְּלִי יֹשֵׁב and lends some support to a derivation from נצה and the adoption of K in 2.15. A few Hebrew manuscripts read נִתְּצוּ and a few others נִתְּצָה , giving the sense 'demolish'. Vulg. (exustae sunt) certainly represents Q נִצְּתוּ as does Rashi (נִצְּתוּ בָאֵשׁ, 'burnt down'). Kimchi mentions both possibilities, 'destroy' and 'burn'.

The questions in v. 14 have the musing, reflective character of the recollection in vv. 2–3. They are the prophet's questions (or Yahweh's questions); they draw attention to Israel's present humiliation and there is an implied indictment of Israel for having brought itself to such a pass. The further question in v. 17 is rhetorical and demands the answer 'Yes', and the questions in v. 18 are a device for asserting that diplomatic manoeuvres will serve no useful end. Verse 14 is a condemnation of the servility and weakness of Israel, v. 17 of her faithlessness and v. 18 of her wrong-headed reliance on foreign pacts. It is doubtful whether the attempt to relate vv. 14–15 to particular, historical events can be other than speculative. Duhm supposes that it is the Assyrian hegemony and Judah's condition of subjection which is indicated. Rudolph views the verses against a longer history of weakness, defeat and servility: the overthrow of Samaria by the Assyrians and the overrunning of Judah by the armies of Sennacherib. J. Milgrom (*JNES* 14, 1955, pp. 65–69) has argued that chapter 2 reflects a historical situation which did not obtain after 616, when Assyria and Egypt ceased to be rivals and became allies (cf. 2.18, 36). He urges that 2.8 is a clear reference to a corrupt cult before the reform of Josiah in 622. On these historical assumptions the references to oppression and harassment cannot refer to the final ordeal of Judah in the reign of Nebuchadrezzar.

The difficulty of fitting v. 16 into the context has been noticed by Rudolph. The different conclusions which have been reached about the tense of יִרְעוּךְ are not unconnected with these difficulties. Lowth rendered it as a past tense ('have broken the crown of thy head'; cf. Bright) and did not differentiate it in this respect from the verbs of v. 15a, but a distinction is maintained by those (Rudolph, Weiser, NEB) who refer v. 15a to the past and v. 16 to the future (NEB, 'will break your heads'). The recognition that v. 16 is a later insertion (Bright) is also allowed by Rudolph who connects the verse with the reading of the scroll by Baruch in 605. Whatever be the particular historical reason for the insertion of v. 16, there is no doubt that it is intrusive and another indication of this is that it probably interrupts a connection between v. 15 and v. 17.

Noph is identified with Memphis by all the versions and תחפנס is transliterated. The name is written elsewhere in the Hebrew bible as תחפנחס (Jer 43.7,8,9; 44.1; 46.14; Ezek 30.18). BDB and Bright identify תחפנחם with Greek Δάφναι, modern Tell Defneh (see G. I. Davies, *The Way of the Wilderness*, 1979, p. xi), while Rudolph, following A. Alt (*ZDPV*, 1943, pp. 66ff.), distinguishes it from Greek Δάφναι (the Δάφναι of Herodotus) and identifies it with a border fortress east of the delta beside Pelusium. Memphis was the capital of lower Egypt, situated south of modern Cairo.

MT ירעוך 'will pasture you' makes poor sense; some Hebrew manuscripts read ירעך and the Hebrew *Vorlage* of Sept. (ἔγνωσάν σε) was apparently one of them, but no improvement in the sense results. Sept. has a different text from MT: ἔγνωσάν σε καὶ κατέπαιξόν σου, 'have known you and made fun of you'. ירעוך should be read, pointed differently from MT: יְרֹעוּךְ from רעע, rather than יִרְעוּךְ from רעה. רעע is the Aramaic form of רצץ 'break', 'crush' and is found elsewhere in the Hebrew bible (Jer 15.12; cf. 11.16). Rashi and Kimchi assume רעע = רצץ and Kimchi glosses ירעוך with ישברוך. This sense appears in the translations of Lowth and Blayney and is adopted by Ehrlich (p. 237). Rudolph and Weiser (following Duhm) emend ירעוך to יְעָרוּךְ 'will shave your head', indicative of military defeat and prisoner-of-war status.

The names Memphis and Tahpanhes are, as Rashi and Kimchi note, paradigmatic. They are a device for expressing in a vivid way the outcome of a mistaken policy of cultivating the friendship of Egypt and entering into political arrangements with her. Those whose favours were sued and who were regarded as influential friends will turn out to be brutal assailants. This secondary comment on the subject of foreign alliances is probably occasioned by the circumstance that the subject is raised in vv. 18–19. It may be that the event which the commentator had in mind was the defeat at Megiddo and Josiah's death (Blayney, Bright), but it is a larger assumption that Jeremiah himself made the insertion in connection with Baruch's reading of the scroll in 605 (Rudolph).

Vulg., Pesh. and Targ. smooth the grammatical difficulty

away in v. 17 by inserting 'because', 'Has not this happened to you because you have forsaken Yahweh, your God?' Rashi is explicit that זאת refers to Israel's punishment and that עזבך את יהוה אלהיך is the subject: 'Will not the guilt and iniquity with which you have forsaken Yahweh, your God, bring on you this evil and punishment?' According to Duhm this grammar (which is also accepted by Kimchi) necessitates the emendation of תעשה to יעשה (also Giesebrecht, Rudolph).

Another topic for discussion in v. 17 is בעת מוליכך בדרך which is not represented by Sept. These words were explained by Duhm as a corrupt dittography of the opening words of v. 18 (ועתה מה לך לדרך) and he held that the force of this argument was more evident when the *matres lectionis* were removed (בעת מלכך ועת מלך לדרך: בדרך). Rudolph and Bright take this view of בעת מוליכך בדרך and Janzen (p. 10) supposes that MT has a conflate reading.

The preceding part of the chapter (vv. 4–13) recounts a history of apostasy and it is this which has brought Israel into weakness and contempt (vv. 14–15). This is the background of v. 17 and the connection has been broken by the secondary insertion of v. 16. The question, 'Is it not your forsaking of Yahweh, your God that brings this on you?' (v. 17) arises out of a prior, wide-ranging historical appraisal, and the closing words of the verse restrict it in a way which does not seem right. The statement that Israel forsook Yahweh in the wilderness, if this were thought to be the sense, would conflict with the representation of vv. 2–3 that the wilderness period was marked by loyalty and undivided love, and with the representation of v. 7 that the rot set in with Israel's arrival in Canaan.

Sept.'s translation of שחור (Γηών) may rest on an identification of גיחון in Gen 2.13 with the Nile. Vulg. *turbidam* reads שחור as שחור 'blackness' (Lam 4.8) and Targ. renders שחור by נהרא 'Nile' and נהר by פרת 'Euphrates'; Rashi equates שיחור with נילוס. שחור (Š-Ḥr 'pool of Horus') is one of the most easterly arms of the Nile or one of the lakes east of the delta (A. Alt, *ZAW*, 57, 1939, pp. 147f.). Targ. correctly understands v. 18 as a reference to foreign pacts and diplomatic moves, but interprets 'to drink water' as a reference to drowning in the Nile and crossing the Euphrates into exile. Rashi and Kimchi also explain the verse in terms of a false reliance placed on foreign alliances and Rashi has the same explanation of 'drinking water' as Targ. But 'to drink water' is indicative of a quest after satisfaction and well-being, and the question implies that the quest is mistaken and doomed to failure. This attitude may be taken as an indication of Jeremiah's *a priori* conviction that such policies will not achieve the ends at which they aim; that they will increase Judah's insecurity and hasten her final collapse.

MT וְלֹא פַחְדְתִּי אֵלַיִךְ (v. 19) makes poor sense ('My fear is not to you') and assumes a noun פחדה of which this would be the only occurrence in Biblical Hebrew. פחדתי should be pointed as פָחַדְתְּ, a 2nd person fem. sing. verb of the same type as שברתי and נתקתּי in v. 20 (GK 44h): 'You will have to learn how evil and bitter it is to forsake Yahweh, your God, and to have no respect for me' (for the construction cf. GK 114r). This requires the emendation of MT אֵלַיִךְ to אֵלַי, but וְלֹא פַחְדְתְּ אֵלַי is supported by Pesh. (*wl' dḥlty mny*). Whether this means that the Syriac translator had a different Hebrew text from MT or that he emended it to make sense cannot be determined. The alteration of a postulated original אֵלַי to אֵלַיִךְ in MT may have been caused by the unusual form of the 2nd person fem. sing. verb which, being erroneously identified as a noun, seemed to demand אֵלַיִךְ rather than אֵלַי. The use פחד (verb) + אֶל is established by Hos 3.5 (וּפַחֲדוּ אֶל יהוה וְאֶל טוּבוֹ בְּאַחֲרִית הַיָּמִים). O. Eissfeldt holds that צבאות in יהוה צבאות is an attributive meaning 'mightiness'—a reference to Yahweh's lordship over all other powers (*K.S.* 3, 1966, pp. 119ff.). The assumption that the relationship is a construct one is probably wrong.

The meaning of v. 19 is that Israel has for long ignored the address to her reason and conscience and that the process of discipline and correction must be effected by disastrous events which are to be regarded as arising directly out of her apostasy. There are traces of vocabulary common in the book of Proverbs (יסר and יכח). Israel is like the incorrigible son or pupil who is incapable of submitting to parental or scholastic discipline, or of deferring to wisdom and experience.

ISRAEL IS DEGENERATE AND HELPLESS (2.20–28)

[20]Long ago you broke your yoke
and burst your ropes.
I will not be subject to you, you said;
on every high hill
and under every leafy tree
you lay down and fornicated.
[21]I planted you as a Sorek vine,
a strain tested for purity
How is it that you have become a rogue vine, a vine of unknown strain?[1]
[22]Though you scour yourself with soda
and lather yourself with soap,
the stain of your sin will be seen by me.
This is the word of Yahweh, the Lord.

[1] Reading לְסוֹרִיָּה, see below, p. 42.

²³How can you say, I am not defiled,
I have not gone after the Baalim?
Look at your track in the valley,
consider what you have done.
You have been like a fleet she-camel
dashing this way and that;
²⁴you have been like a wild ass
whose home is the wilderness,
which snuffs the air in her lust.
When she is excited who can hold her back?
A mate need not tire himself chasing her,
when she is in heat he will find her.
²⁵Stop before your sandals are worn out,
and your throat parched with thirst.
But you said, No, there is no hope,
I love strangers and must go after them.
²⁶As a thief who is found out is disgraced,
so Israel is in disgrace;[1]
²⁷to a tree they say, You are my father,
to a stone, You are my mother.
They have turned their backs on me
and will not look towards me;
but when disaster comes they say,
Do something to save us.
²⁸Where are the gods you made for yourselves?
Let them do something to save you when disaster comes.
You have as many gods as you have towns, O Judah.

ISRAEL'S INSUBORDINATION HAS FRUSTRATED YAHWEH'S DESIGN (2.20–22)

The versions disagree as to whether שברתי and נתקתי are 1st person sing. or 2nd person sing. fem. Sept. translates them as 2nd person sing. fem. (συνέτριψας; διέσπασας). Vulg. also renders שברתי (*confregisti*) and נתקתי (*rupisti*) in the 2nd person, but עלך and מוסרתיך appear as *iugum meum* and *vincula mea*, 'You have broken my yoke and snapped my bonds'. Both Pesh. and Targ. render שברתי and נתקתי as 1st person sing. and the reference is then to the emancipation of Israel by Yahweh's action. Pesh. follows K and Targ. Q (לא אעבר), but both take כי as 'but', because Pesh. interprets לא אעבד (K) not as a refusal to be obedient to Yahweh but as a promise by Israel not to worship other gods.

שברתי and נתקתי should be taken as 2nd person fem. sing. (see above p. 39), the speech of Israel should end at לא אעבד, and אעבד (K) should be preferred to אעבר (Q). לא אעבד is then not a promise of amendment by Israel (Pesh., Kimchi), but a rebellious utterance (Sept. οὐ δουλεύσω ; Vulg. *Non serviam*). The figure is that of an ox with a wooden yoke and ropes or

---

[1] Deleting v. 26b, see below, pp. 47f.

leather thongs (Rashi) to hold the yoke in place. Such an ox has a master who exercises control over it and directs it to do his work. Israel is like the ox which is not amenable to discipline, which refuses to accept the yoke and cannot be made to contribute to the growing of food or other gainful activities. Israel mistakes licence for freedom and does not understand that impulsive and chaotic waywardness is inimical with ordered liberty.

צעה (v. 20) indicates that, like a prostitute, Israel is lying down and stretched out, ready to receive her lovers (so Rashi). It is a matter of great difficulty to determine whether imagery of this kind is merely metaphorical, so that harlotry is to be transposed into apostasy and this makes the interpretation complete (cf. Kimchi); or whether there is over and above this an allusion to the sexual immorality which is involved in the apostasy (cf. Hos 4.13f.). There is also the more general consideration that the prostitute symbolizes a rootless, feverish and restless life (cf. אשה זרה in Prov 5.6; 7.11). The thought of 'indiscipline', consequently, attaches to the second figure (the prostitute) as well as the first (the stubborn ox).

Different views about the provenance of the vocabulary in כי על כל גבעה גבהה ותחת כל עץ רענן את צעה זנה are expressed by W. L. Holladay (*VT* 11, 1961, pp. 171–176) and Thiel (pp. 80–82). Holladay holds that the phraseology derives from Hos 4.13 through Deut 12.2 and is attributable to the prophet Jeremiah. It should be said that the resemblance in vocabulary between Hos 4.13 and Jer 2.20 is slight (ועל הגבעות). For Thiel the vocabulary in 2.20 (כי על כל גבעה ... רענן) is evidence of the activity of D and has been supplied by him. Hosea derived it from Deuteronomy and D takes it from Deuteronomistic sources, the correspondence between Jer 2.20 and 1 Kgs 14.23 (2 Kgs 17.10) being precise. We do not have the intimate knowledge of Jeremiah's literary habits or of the genealogy of the vocabulary which Holladay affects. Thiel, for his part, says of ותאמרי לא אעבד that it must be part of the 'original', because it arises out of the metaphor of the stubborn ox, and he then supposes that the 'original' fourth stich, containing צעה זנה was remodelled by D in order to accommodate it to his insertion. But the 'prostitute' metaphor is inseparable from the vocabulary which is alleged by Thiel to be D's insertion and Thiel has made for himself difficulties much greater than the metrical deficiencies of כי על כל גבעה גבהה ותחת כל עץ רענן which launched him on his train of thought. The alleged insertion of D cannot be disengaged from v. 20 in the manner attempted by Thiel and the verse should be left as a structure of six stichs.

That שרק (v. 21) is the name of a particular strain (cf. נחל

שׂרק, Judg 16.4) is borne out by the phrase כלה זרע אמת which emphasizes its purity and choiceness. Rashi and Kimchi (cf. Sept. καρποφόρον) define שׂרק in terms of the fruit which it produces and Kimchi distinguishes between edible (ענבים) and inedible (באושׁים) grapes. On the assumption that נכריה is an attributive of גפן it has been suggested that הגפן הנכריה should be read (GK126z) and a redivision of the consonants producing לסוריה גפן נכריה (Duhm) has found wide favour (cf. Sept. πῶς ἐστράφης εἰς πικρίαν ἡ ἄμπελος ἡ ἀλλοτρία, 'How is it that you have turned into bitterness, a foreign vine?'). סוריה, 'stinker', 'rogue vine', is a hypothetical form for which there is no attestation, and if it is adopted, the sense of the Hebrew becomes, 'How is it that you have turned into a rogue vine, a vine of unknown strain?' Sept. has rendered הגפן נכריה as ἡ ἄμπελος ἡ ἀλλοτρία and Vulg. similarly ignores the difficulty (vinea aliena). It represents סורי as pravum 'degenerate'.

Targ. follows its customary practice of expanding and explaining the metaphorical language: 'All of you did what was right. How you have changed your relationship to me by your corrupt deeds! You have wandered from my worship and have become as a vine which has no usefulness in it.' Pesh. similarly associates סורי with rebellion. One has to suppose that the first stich ends at סורי (סוריה) and that גפן is part of the second stich. This means that a construct relationship between סורי and הגפן cannot be maintained. The best that can be done is to rearrange סורי גפן הגפן as סוריה גפן. This produces two stichs: ואיך נהפכת לסוריה and גפן נכריה. The emendation of לי to ל is supported by Sept.

The metaphor is illustrative of Israel's degeneration and apostasy. Israel should have produced good fruit; instead she has yielded the bitter and inedible fruit of an uncultivated vine. The fault is not in her endowment, which was good at the beginning and would have remained good, if she had not chosen to induce a process of degeneration. There is here something of the mystery of Israel's disobedience, the irrationality of the manner in which she has exercised her freedom.

Both Rashi and Kimchi explain that נתר is washing powder and they gloss ברית with French savon 'soap'. Kimchi reports another opinion that ברית is a kind of grass (עשב) with cleansing properties and this is in agreement with Sept. (πόαν) and Vulg. (herbam borith). According to KB[3] ברית is an alkaline salt extracted from a plant mesambrianthemum crystallinum. נכתם is interpreted by Targ. as רושם כתמא 'bloodstain' and this is reproduced by Rashi, 'Like a bloodstain which resists cleaning, so is the greatness of your guilt in my eyes'.

The three verses (20–22) agree in their estimate of the deep-seated character of Israel's sinfulness and express a scepticism about the possibility of reformation. The prophet switches from metaphor to metaphor, but all of them in different ways contribute to this impression. Deeply ingrained habits have brought about an inner perversion so fundamental that repentance, a change of heart and new patterns of behaviour, would seem to be ruled out. The momentum of her slide towards disintegration is not to be arrested. What Israel does accords with the degenerate nature which she has assumed. Can she reverse such a deterioration and recover the characteristics of a Sorek vine? There is no way of cleansing Israel from her sin; nothing will remove the stain; it is indelible and resists the most strenuous efforts to remove it (cf. Rudolph).

PURSUIT OF THE BAALIM IS COMPULSIVE BEHAVIOUR (2.23–25)

The rendering of בגיא (v. 23) by ἐν τῷ πολυανδρίῳ 'in the graveyard' (Sept.) may, as Rudolph suggests, be the consequence of the equation of גיא with the valley of Hinnom, where children were offered as sacrifices (7.31; 19.5), Sept. renders בכרה קלה משרכת דרכיה by ὀψὲ φωνὴ αὐτῆς ὠλόλυξε, τὰς ὁδοὺς αὐτῆς ἐπλάτυνεν: קלה has been read as קֹלָהּ and בכרה has been understood as a verb with the sense 'raised aloud' or 'raised in wailing'. So far as can be seen this is nothing more than a guess; it appears in Pesh. and the question of dependence is settled by the circumstance that Pesh. has less right to be regarded as a translation of MT than Sept. בכרה does, at least, have the form of a 3rd fem. sing. verb and Sept. has so rendered it, but Pesh. ('rymty bqlky) makes no attempt to translate בכרה קלה.

The closing words of v. 23 (משרכת דרכיה) appear in Sept. at the beginning of v. 24 as τὰς ὁδοὺς αὐτῆς ἐπλάτυνεν (משרכת is rendered as ἐπλάτυνεν 'extended'). If it is assumed that פרה is a variant spelling of פרא 'wild ass', problems arise concerning grammatical agreement in v. 24. פרה למד indicates that פרה is masc., as does נפשו (K), but the remaining verbs and suffixes referred to פרה are fem. Q נפשה is a response to this difficulty, but even then the incongruence of למד remains. The suggestion that פרה = פרא is epicoena, that is, 'having both genders' (GK122d) does not solve the problem, since, even it were epicoena, one would not expect it to be both masc. and fem. gender in the compass of a single verse.

In v. 25 מנעי רגלך מיחף is translated ἀπόστρεψον τὸν πόδα σου ἀπὸ ὁδοῦ τραχείας 'Keep your foot from a rough road'.

ἀνδριοῦμαι in the same verse is a mistranslation of נואש and is another link between Sept. and Pesh. (*'thylt*). Both are indicative of a wilful resolve on the part of Israel to continue in her own way: ἀνδριοῦμαι means 'I summon my manly resources' and *'thylt* 'I strengthen myself (to resist)'.

תאנתה (v. 24), which has given difficulty to all the versions, is apparently rendered as כירורא (*'yk yrwr'*) in Pesh. and Targ. The significance of כירורא is discoverable in connection with Jer 14.6 (ופראים עמדו על שפים שאפו רוח כתנים). These words ('Wild asses stand on the summits, they snuff the air like jackals') are cited by Rashi and Kimchi in the course of their treatment of 2.24. Both Rashi and Kimchi give the reading of Targ. as כירורא (see A. Sperber, *The Bible in Aramaic*, 3, 1962) and Kimchi remarks, 'It (Targ.) has added כתנים in argreement with שאפו רוח כתנים (Jer 14.6). This is certainly the correct explanation of כירורא or כירודא in 2.24, since כתנים in 14.6 is rendered as כירורין or כירודין by Targ. Hence, on the analogy of 14.6, 'like a jackal' and not 'like a wild ass' (Jastrow) is what Targ. intends in 2.24 by כירירא or כירידא.

כירורא should be regarded as having originated with Targ. It has been adopted by Pesh. from Targ. as a rendering of תאנתה, a word which apparently defeated the Syriac translator. This is clear from the circumstance that following *yrwr'* in Pesh. is a rendering of מי ישיבנה (*mn nhpkh*), and so כירורא can be equated certainly with תאנתה. The impression is that Targ. knew what it was about in the use of כירורא, whereas the Syriac translator did no more than lift it from Targ. in order to solve a translation problem which he had with תאנתה.

ראי דרכך בגיא (v. 23) is paraphrased by Targ. as, 'Lift up your eyes on your ways (that is, review your past behaviour) and note what you did when you were in the valley opposite Beth Peor' (Num 25—where Israel fornicated with Moabite women). The wild ass (v. 24) is a parable of Israel. 'So the congregation of Israel has rebelled and wandered from the law and is not willing to repent.' The closing words of v. 24 (כל מבקשיה לא ייעפו בחדשה ימצאונה) are applied to the law: 'All who seek it will not be abandoned: in its time they will find it.' מיחף is explained as מלאתתברא לעממיא, 'from making foreign alliances' and וגורנך מצמאה as 'and your mouth from the worship of idols'.

The entanglement of the versions which has emerged from this study is exceptional. It must be assumed that the difficulties which the translators found with MT caused the deviations which the versions show, and also the phenomenon of entanglement. This is most pronounced in the case of Pesh. which is all the more remarkable in that Pesh. in the book of Jeremiah is marked by its faithfulness to MT. Pesh. is dependent

on Sept. for its rendering of בכרה קלה and, perhaps, for its
rendering of נואש; it follows Targ. in respect of תאנתה. It would
appear that the Syriac translator or a subsequent reviser had
Sept. and Targ. open before him.

In the later history of the exegesis of vv. 23–25 there is a
general recognition that the imagery is sexual although this
impression is not conveyed by Sept., Targ. and Pesh. (cf W. L.
Holladay, *VT* 18, 1968, pp. 257f.). The view that Israel is
portrayed in this passage as a promiscuous woman should be
accepted and the more modern and conjectural phase of the
criticism of Jer 2.23–25 traversed from this point of departure
(for details on all aspects of the interpretation of this passage see
W. McKane, OTS 17, 1972, pp. 73–88). אחרי הבעלים לא הלכתי
is deleted by Ehrlich (p. 239) as a gloss on לא נטמאתי, and לא
הלכתי by Duhm, on the ground that such an assertion is
incredible in the mouth of Israel. They are not denying that they
are devotees of the Baalim, but they are insisting that they are
not thereby defiled or disloyal to Yahweh. One should not
however expect reasonable utterances from Israel: she is like a
woman abandoned to impulsive behaviour, subject to a
determinism which makes her a slave, and it would be strange if
her speech were represented as a model of consistency.

The rendering of גיא by πολυανδρεῖον in Jer 19.6, where there
is an explicit reference to the Valley of Ben Hinnom, shows that
this valley must be intended by Sept. in 2.23 (ἐν τῷ
πολυανδρείῳ), and this is an exegesis which was adopted by
Jerome and which has won the approval of a long line of
subsequent commentators. It has been argued for in some detail
by J. A. Soggin (*RSO* 36, 1961, pp. 207–211). It is difficult to
choose between 'track' and 'behaviour' for דרך (Kimchi opted for
'track' and Targ. for 'behaviour' and NEB follows the latter,
'Look how you conducted yourself in the valley'), but, in any
case, if v. 23 is about a woman pursuing her lovers and deceiving
her husband, a reference to the gruesome cult practised in the
valley of Ben Hinnom does not seem to be appropriate and a
more general pattern of idolatry is indicated (so Duhm).

MT indicates that פרה = פרא (v. 24) and many Hebrew
manuscripts witness to פרא. It is indicated by Vulg. (*onager*),
Pesh. ('*rd*') and Targ. (ערודא), but it is not represented by Sept.
L. Köhler (*ZAW* 29, 1909, pp. 35f.) noted that in Gen 28.14
ופרצת is rendered by Sept. as καὶ πλατυνθήσεται and he held
that ἐπλάτυνεν in Jer 2.24 was an indication that some form of
פרץ was the original of the Hebrew text; ἐφ'ὕδατα arises from
the correction or corruption of למד to למי and למד מדבר from a
dittography of מד. By inserting a צ between the ר and ה of פרה
he obtains פרצה למדבר; the second animal disappears and it is

the בכרה קלה which 'breaks out into the desert'. There are flaws in Köhler's procedure: τὰς ὁδοὺς αὐτῆς ἐπλάτυνεν represents משרכת דרכיה and, if so, ἐπλάτυνεν is a rendering of משרכת and cannot be equated with a restored פרצה. H. Torczyner (*MGWJ* 75, 1931, pp. 18f.) connects משרכת with שרוך 'shoe-lace' (Rashi and Kimchi make the same association and cite Gen 14.23) and postulates a meaning 'join'. 'A fleet she-camel which joins her ways with a wild ass' refers to the unnatural lust of a female camel for a male of another kind. G. R. Driver (*JQR*, 1937–38, 98f.) emends פרה למד מדבר to מפרדה למדבר, 'fleeing alone to the desert', and supposes that the picture is one of a she-camel leaving the herd or encampment and bolting alone into the desert, from where she hears the call of the bulls in the rutting season. Driver's statement that his emendation is achieved by 'a mere transposition of consonants' is disarming. פרה should be retained, not because this is an entirely satisfactory solution, but because all other solutions seem less satisfactory.

תאנתה is a ἅπαξ λεγόμενον with which only Vulg. (*amoris sui*) among the versions had any success. Rashi glosses it with יללה 'wailing'; Kimchi connects it with III אנה (BDB and KB³), 'be opportune'. תאנתה מי ישיבנה would then mean 'Who can resist the sovereignty of her desire?'. Kimchi (also Calvin) assumes that חדש refers to the pregnancy of the wild ass. The sense is rather that when the wild ass is in heat there is no need for males to run after her. She is already running towards them in order to satisfy her sexual appetite. Hence חדש, as has been generally recognized (S. Bochart, *Hierozoicon sive De Animalibus S. Scripturae*, 2, 1794, p. 230) has the same sense as תאנה.

If יחף in v. 25 is an adjective, there is a grammatical disagreement between it and רגל. Calvin suggested that יחף was a noun and this is how it is taken by BDB. E. Zolli appeals to Arabic (*Seferad*, 14, 1954, pp. 363–366) and connects יחף with *whf* 'to hasten': it is not bare feet which are to be avoided but haste. The thought of wearing the shoes from the feet is in accord with the picture of the frantic, feverish activity of the woman abandoned to passion (v. 23) and this is clear from the closing words of v. 25 כי אהבתי זרים ואחריהם אלך.

ואחריהם אלך is to be translated 'and after them I must go'. The verse describes the restlessness of a promiscuous woman, not cultic rites performed barefooted nor an incessant crying to a god which produces thirst and hoarseness (Hitzig). Nor should it be thought that there is a veiled sexual reference in מנעי רגלך מיחף, that רגל means 'private parts'. This interpretation is found in Lowth, coupled with the thought that thirst is an allusion to drunkenness.

Israel in her frenzied devotion to the Baalim is like a woman
driven by passion in search of lovers (v. 23). She is like a fretful,
restive animal incapable of resisting elemental, sexual drives
(v. 24). In her pursuit of strange gods Israel is like the woman
who can do no other than pursue strange men (v. 25). Israel's
answer to the appeal in v. 25 is not a denial, but an admission
that she is impelled by an uncontrollable desire towards the rites
of Baal worship. The irrationality of her assertion of innocence
in v. 23 is followed by a moment of rationality which is, however,
a cry of despair and hopelessness. The verses contain elements of
dialogue, but Israel's contribution is either irrational denial or
hopeless acquiescence in her slavery. The summons in v. 25 is not
so much an authentic call to penitence as a device for
underlining Israel's total inability to respond, and so a way of
summing up the finality of her despair.

ISRAEL'S DISGRACE (2.26–28)

'Let them act if they will save you when you are in trouble'
(v. 28) is tantamount to a question which expects a negative
answer, 'Will they act to save you when you are in trouble?'
That such sceptical overtones are present is clear from the
circumstance that Israel has already appealed to Yahweh for
help (קומה והושיענו). Sept. 'Will they act to save you when you
are in trouble?' catches the nuance of MT. Sept.'s longer text in
v. 28 corresponds with 11.13 (MT). Cornill's view that the
longer text is the better one finds favour with Rudolph and
Janzen (p. 121). The argument is that 2.28 (Sept.) has been
expanded from 11.13, but that 11.13 was derived in the first
place from 2.28 and has preserved the original form of 2.28. A
better conclusion is that secondary processes of explication have
affected 11.13. In that case the entire second part of the verse
may be a subsequent expansion of the shorter text of 2.28 (MT)
by which 2.28 (Sept.) has been influenced. MT should be read at
2.28.
    The charge is made that the house of Israel ('sons of Israel' in
Sept. and Pesh.) is disgraced by its idolatrous habits (v. 26). It
might be supposed that the comprehensive term בית ישראל is
enough and that a listing of the leaders of the community tacked
on by המה does not serve much purpose. We can suppose that its
function is to indicate that these political and ecclesiastical
leaders (kings, statesmen, priests and prophets) bear a primary
responsibility for what has happened. This is, more or less, how
Thiel (p. 83) describes the intentions of D to whom he attributes
v. 26b. Duhm had detected secondary editing in v. 26b and had

deleted it, and Rudolph (cf. Thiel) holds that it disturbs an
original connection between בית ישראל and אמרים. This is the
sharpest argument for the deletion of v. 26b, because it is hard to
believe that the words of v. 27 are envisaged as spoken by the
house of Israel, kings, statesmen, priests and prophets. There
does not appear to be a particular connection between the
subject matter of vv. 26–28 and the specific causes of conflict
between Jeremiah and his political and ecclesiastical adversaries.
The conflict with king and statesman was about political policies
(*PWM*, pp. 65f.) and his clash with prophets and priests was not
about idolatry. It was about the Jerusalem temple, the principal
embodiment of Yahwism whose orthodoxy the prophet
threatened.

It is arguable that בשת does not refer so much to the thief's
shame (his feelings; cf. Kimchi) as it does to his loss of
reputation (his disgrace), although the opposite is indicated by
Vulg. which supposes that the thief's feelings and Israel's
feelings are described (*Quomodo confunditur fur quando
deprehenditur, sic confusi sunt domus Israel*). A more
important consideration is whether the verse is a threat of future
judgement ('will be disgraced') or a description of Israel's
present conditon ('are in disgrace'). The former is indicated by
Sept. and the latter by Vulg. There is merit in the view that a
threat of future judgement is intended, since this interpretation
establishes the unity of vv. 26–28 by locating in vv. 27 and 28 the
development of the simile of v. 26. Israel's disgrace will be that
of a thief caught in the act, in that when disaster overtakes her
she will have to admit the impotence of the idols on whom she
lavished her devotion and seek help from Yahweh whom she
deserted. But it is doubtful whether vv. 26–28 possess this kind
of unity and the simile in v. 26 is not very apposite, if this is how
it is to be expounded.

The point of the simile is that Israel's guilt is as
incontrovertible and self-evident as that of a thief who is caught
in the act. Verses 26–28 are not then a threat of a coming
judgement which will bring her into open disgrace, but are a
description of her present condition. Israel says to a tree 'You
are my father' and to a stone 'You are my mother'. She is bound
to the gods of Canaan in as compulsive and inescapable a way as
children are bound to their parents.

When disaster comes, the gods to whom access was
guaranteed and whose help seemed to be assured are found to be
non-gods, and in her extremity Israel cries to Yahweh for help.
This is not to be seen merely as an exposure of her irrationality,
for it is a deeply grounded tendency in all men. Yet here again
the compulsiveness of Israel's behaviour is revealed. She cannot

avoid these extravagances of idolatry, but she is not amenable to reasonable appeal. In a moment of danger she sees clearly, but soon her judgement is clouded and she is overruled and overrun by dark, destructive, irrational drives (see on vv. 22–25).

ISRAEL'S DISOBEDIENCE AND FOLLY ARE INEXPLICABLE (2.29–37)

[29]Why do you try to put me in the wrong?
You have all rebelled against me.
    This is Yahweh's word.
[30]I chastised your sons with no effect;
they did not respond to correction.
Your sword devoured your prophets
like a man-eating lion.[1]
[31]Was I like a wilderness to Israel,
or a land of deep gloom?
Why did my people say, we have set ourselves free,
we shall never again return to you?
[32]Can a virgin forget her finery,
or a bride her ribbons?
Yet long, long ago my people forgot me.
[33]With what careful preparations you seek out love!
So you have become expert at evil behaviour.
[34]There is blood on your skirts,
the blood of the innocent poor.
You did not catch them in the act of housebreaking.[2]
[35]You said, I swear I am innocent.
No doubt, his anger has passed me by!
I am about to pass sentence on you
because you say, I have done no wrong.
[36]What a trifling matter you make it
to alter your course!
You will be let down by Egypt,
just as you were by Assyria.
[37]You will go out from here into exile,
with your hands on your heads.
Yahweh has rejected your security pacts,
and they will avail you nothing.

ISRAEL IS GUILTY AND HAS NO DEFENCE (2.29–30)

תריבו in למה תריבו אלי is legal vocabulary and this is indicated by Vulg., Pesh., Targ. and Rashi. πάντες ὑμεῖς ἠσεβήσατε εἰς ἐμέ and πάντες ὑμεῖς ἠνομήσατε εἰς ἐμέ look like variants of כלכם פשעתם בי and Sept.[A] (see Ziegler) reads πάντες ὑμεῖς ἠνομήσατε εἰς ἐμέ. Ziegler (Beiträge, pp. 89f.) supposes that the shorter text in Sept.[A] is caused by haplography (a jump from the

[1] Deleting הדור אתם ראו דבר יהוה (see below, pp. 51f.).
[2] כי על כל אלה is unintelligible (see below, p. 54).

first to the second occurrence of πάντες ὑμεῖς) and is undecided whether or not there was a Hebrew *Vorlage* for the longer text of Sept. (cf. Janzen, p. 30). The conclusion that Sept. is a conflate text is the more probable one and the argument that Sept.^ is the consequence of haplography and not a witness to a shorter text is unnatural.

For מוסר לא לקחו (v. 30) Sept. has παιδείαν οὐκ ἐδέξασθε, 'you did not accept discipline' and for חרבכם it has μάχαιρα (so also Pesh. ḥrb'). καὶ οὐκ ἐφοβήθητε is thought by Janzen (p. 85) to arise from a corruption of הדור אתם (MT v. 31) into ולא יראתם. The complexity of the meaning of מוסר is indicated by the renderings of the versions in which the ideas of instruction, discipline and punishment are combined (Sept. παιδείαν; Pesh. *mrdwt'*; Vulg. *disciplinam*; Targ. אולפן). Israel supposes that she has grounds for engaging in legal controversy with Yahweh or, perhaps, even (Pesh. and Targ.) for sitting in judgement on him. According to Rashi her confidence that she can win a legal action against Yahweh rests on her assumption that she is innocent (ולומר לא חטאנו). In fact she is in the wrong and she has no case to argue, no right of redress.

Difficulty has been felt with בניכם (v. 30) and the emendation to אבותיכם (Giesebrecht) has been associated with the acceptance of Sept. ἐδέξασθε (לקחתם or תקחו). The prophet is saying that the punishment inflicted on earlier generations has had no deterrent effect on their descendants. Similarly Rudolph will not allow that there is any emphasis on a long history of apostasy, but he emends בניכם to אבות ובנים—an older and younger generation of listeners comprising the present audience of the prophet. MT should be retained and should be explained in connection with the indivisibility of Israel's apostasy which began during the earliest period in Canaan (see on vv. 1–3). Israel is addressed and the reference to 'sons' is a device for spanning the generations and indicating that the tendency to apostasy which began early has been maintained throughout the subsequent history. Israel's 'sons' are like the incorrigible and unteachable 'sons' encountered by the wisdom teacher (Prov 17.10; 20.30).

The words אכלה חרבכם נביאיכם כאריה משחית introduce a new element of allegation into the chapter. Hitherto Israel has been described as compulsively idolatrous, as insubordinate and as incapable of offering to Yahweh a steady allegiance. It is a portrait of addiction, irrationality and decay, but there is no hint of a persecuting tendency. This is the charge which is now preferred against her. Prophets have been butchered—treated with a savagery which they might have feared from man-eating lions. καὶ οὐκ ἐφοβήθητε (Sept.) is, perhaps, a secondary

comment evoked by such impiety rather than a corruption of
הדור אתם, as Janzen supposes (above, p. 50). It is an expression
of horror that there should be such a lack of reverence for the
prophetic office.

Rudolph supposes that Jeremiah had in mind particularly the
'shedding of innocent blood' in the reign of Manasseh (2 Kgs
21.16) and Rashi identifies the slain prophets as Isaiah and
Zechariah. The legend of Isaiah's martyrdom in the reign of
Manasseh appears in a pseudepigraphical work, the Martyrdom
of Isaiah, and there is a reference to the death of Zechariah in
the gospels (Mt 23.35; Lk 11.51).

A different interpretation of נביאיכם, associated with the
adoption of החרב (Sept. μάχαιρα; Pesh. ḥrb') instead of MT
חרבכם, is found in Duhm. The contention that נביאיכם, 'your
prophets', is an indication that they are false prophets and that
Yahweh would have described true prophets as 'my prophets',
which is made by Duhm, is as old as Jerome and is favoured by
Kimchi. That Jerome intends the interpretation 'false prophets'
is clear from his exegesis of Sept. The meaning is that false
prophets (= נביאיכם) will be consumed by the sword of an enemy
who is Yahweh's agent. MT should be retained and the
argument founded on 'your prophets' should be rejected (Targ.
נביאיכון without 'false' is a significant exegetical pointer). We
should suppose that the second person plural suffix emphasizes
Israel's responsibility for the treatment meted out to these
prophets—'my prophets sent to you'.

Above all others Jeremiah was the prophet who evoked the
violent response. That he did so is a mark of the relevance of his
message and his nearness to the great issues which faced his
generation. His words seemed to threaten the very existence of
those who dissented from them, to be the first stage in the
demolition of the temple or the first breach in the fabric of the
state.

ISRAEL'S REBELLION IS UNNATURAL AND UNINTELLIGIBLE
(2.31–32)

הדור אתם ראו דבר יהוה is probably not original and is, perhaps,
to be explained as marginal comment which has worked its way
into the text (so Duhm, Janzen, p. 133). Vulg. preserves MT
entirely (*generatio vestra videte verbum domini*) and Pesh. and
Targ. represent it in part: Pesh. partly follows MT (*'ntwn dr'*)
and partly Sept. (*šm'w ptgm' dmry'*).   Thus Pesh. betrays an
acquaintance with both MT and Sept. Kimchi explains that
there is a seeing with the mind and it is this insight or

discernment which is indicated by ראו. Hence he glosses it with הבינו. הדור אתם ראו דבר יהוה then constitutes an appeal to the contemporaries (הדור אתם) of the man who made the addition in which he urges that thoughtful consideration should be given to Yahweh's word. It is likely that ἀκούσατε λόγον κυρίου represents a normalizing of an unusual expression by Sept. rather than a Hebrew text (שמעו דבר יהוה) different from MT.

In v. 31 the desert is a paradigm of danger, barrenness and inhospitality. ארץ מאפליה is rendered as γῆ κεχερσωμένη 'wasteland' or 'parched land' by Sept. (similarly Pesh. 'r" ḥrbt' and Targ. ארע חרבא). Kimchi compares the morphology of מאפליה with that of שלהבתיה (Ct. 8.6): in both cases יה is a shorter form of יהיה functioning as a superlative. Hence מאפליה = 'intense darkness' and שלהבתיה = 'bright flame'. Another explanation is that מאפליה is adjectival, as indicated by the yodh, and that it is then fem. sing. in agreement with ארץ. If מאפליה is correctly analysed as מַאְפֵּלְיָה, with יה functioning as a superlative, there is some reason to suppose that צלמות is correctly analysed as 'shadow of death', with מות having the same superlative function as יה in מאפליה (see on v. 6 where another explanation of צלמות has been offered). There is an interesting rendering of מאפליה in Vulg.—serotina 'late-ripening'. This is explicable in terms of אפילת (Exod 9.32) and a use of the Hiphil participle of אפל in post-biblical Hebrew attested by Jastrow (s.v. אפל).

Yahweh asks whether he has been a wilderness to Israel: a land where men dwell in deprivation and fear. Has he been a blight on their prospects, a withering influence on their lives? If his hand on Israel had been oppressive, her declaration of independence would have been understandable. In the circumstances, however, her resolve to break free of Yahweh and disavow her allegiance is mystifying and inexplicable.

Sept. and Kimchi (רדנו is an assertion of ממשלה, 'sovereignty') indicate that רוד has been taken in the sense of רדה. Pesh. (nḥtn) associates רדנו with ירד 'descend', also Rashi, in the sense of 'withdraw (from Yahweh's control)'. Vulg. recessimus is, probably, also founded on an equation of רוד with ירד (cf. Rudolph). The circumstance that Aq. (ἀπεστημεν) and Symm. (ανεχωρησαμεν) also produce the idea of 'withdrawal' in their renderings strengthens this conclusion.

There is a clear indication from Sept. (στηθοδεσμίδα) and Vulg. (fasciae pectoralis) that קשרים (v. 32) is taken as a reference to a band or bandage which supports the breasts. One would expect in view of עדיה that something less functional and more decorative is intended and that קשרים are finery—ribbons or sashes. עדי and קשרים are items of dress and adornment

beloved of a young girl. That she should ever forget to deck
herself out with them when she is dressing up is inconceivable.
The picture of the girl who is consistently devoted to her finery
and ribbons focuses attention on the incredible forgetfulness of
Israel, on the puzzle of her ingratitude and insubordination.

The sense of ימים אין מספר (v. 32) is difficult to ascertain. Is it
'times without number' or 'these many years'? The latter is
probably indicated by Kimchi (זה כמה ימים ושנים) and is the
translation adopted by Rudolph (*seit zahllosen Tagen*) and
Bright ('days beyond count'). This is, perhaps, correct and in
that case the thought is not that Israel has forgotten Yahweh
again and again, but that there has been a long history of
apostasy (cf. vv. 4–13): long ago, in the remote past, Israel
defected from Yahweh.

ALLEGATIONS AND THREATS (2.33–37)

For מה תיטבי דרכך the idea of fastidious preparation (cf. Sept.
καλόν) is indicated by Rashi who correctly explains the verse
(also Duhm and others) as a reference to Israel's infatuation
with the Canaanite fertility cult, while Kimchi connects it with
'love of the nations', following Targ. לאתחברא לעממיא —
foreign alliances (so Volz). The grammar of לכן גם את הרעות
למדתי את דרכיך is difficult. Vulg. indicates that both הרעות and
דרכיך are objects of למדתי. Sept. reads את as אַתְּ, הרעות as
הָרָעוֹת and apparently construes למדתי as a segholate infinitive
with a prefixed *lamedh* which is rendered τοῦ μιᾶναι. The Greek
translator would appear to have disregarded the final *yodh* (as Q
does) and to have guessed the sense 'to corrupt' for a postulated
לָמֶדֶת, 'But you have done evil to corrupt your ways'. למדתי (K)
is a form of the 2nd person fem. sing. which is indicated by all
the versions (see on 2.20). Lowth interprets 'evil ones' (רעות) as
'evil nations' and his exegesis is similar to Kimchi's
understanding of Q: 'Thou hast by this means, not only
confirmed those nations in their idolatrous practices, but hast
also taught them to practise new idolatries which they were not
accustomed to.' The Hebrew is obscure, but למדתי should be
understood as 2nd person fem. and רעות as 'evil things' rather
than 'evil women' (RSV and NEB). The sense is then something
like, 'You have even made yourself into an expert at evil doing'
(so Duhm, Rudolph, Weiser, Bright).

In v. 34 Sept. reads καὶ ἐν ταῖς χερσί σου εὑρέθησαν αἵματα
ψυχῶν ἀθώων. This indicates a Hebrew text with בכפיך for
בכנפיך and without אביונים. בכפיך is also represented by Pesh.
(*b'ydyky*) which, however, follows MT in respect of אביונים

(*mskn'*). Janzen (p. 11) concludes that either MT is a conflate text with אביונים and נקיים variants or אביונים is a secondary insertion from a similar context featuring נפש אביון (Jer 20.13; Ps 62.13; Job 31.35). J. A. Soggin (*VT* 8, 1958, pp. 433–435) prefers Sept., but whether it is blood on the garments or blood on the hands the exegesis is not greatly affected, nor is the inclusion or exclusion of אביונים a matter of great consequence.

Sept. (εὕρον), Vulg. (*inveni*) and Pesh. ('*škḥt*) all indicate that מצאתי is 1st person. Both Rashi and Kimchi correctly identify מצאתים as 2nd person fem. sing. with suffix. במחתרת is elucidated by Exod 22.1 (אם במחתרת ימצא הגנב והכה ומת אין לו דמים) which is cited by Kimchi. Soggin (following Duhm and others) supposes that לא . . . מצאתים means 'I (Yahweh) did not find them' and the other aspects of his exegesis are strongly influenced by Duhm: מחתרת is *abstractum pro concreto*, 'housebreaker', and the blood on the hands is that of human sacrifices. In respect of כי על כל אלה Soggin follows Sept. and Skinner (op. cit., p. 62 n. 1), but it is doubtful whether there is any solution to these baffling, final words of v. 34 and W. L. Holladay's suggestion that כי עֻלֵּךְ לְאָלָה, 'indeed your yoke has become execrable', should be read, is unlikely to find much support (*VT* 25, 1975, pp. 221–225). אלה is rendered as 'tree' by Sept. (ἐπὶ πάσῃ δρυΐ) and Pesh. (*tḥyt kl 'yln*). So translated ('beside every tree', 'under every tree'), it appears to be a fragment which was part of a description or condemnation of Israel's devotion to the fertility rites. NEB, 'You did not get it by housebreaking but by your sacrifices under every oak' (אלה = אֵלָה, Brockington, p. 199) is following Sept. and Pesh. and is adopting an interpretation similar to that of Duhm but different in its understanding of מצאתים.

Rashi explains ותאמרי (v. 35) as ותאמרי בלבך. These are the thoughts which Israel harbours, the assumptions which determine her behaviour. This is emphasized in Vulg.'s paraphrase of כי נקיתי: *absque peccato et innocens ego sum*, 'I am free from sin and innocent'. For שב Pesh. Targ. and Vulg. indicate a perfect rather than a participle and this is probably correct. The meaning is not that Yahweh's anger now rests on Israel, and that he will relent in view of her innocence ('His anger will retreat from me'). It is rather that Israel supposes herself to enjoy immunity from Yahweh's anger ('It is certain that his anger has passed me by').

According to MT (תֵּזְלִי) תזלי (v. 36) is to be derived from אזל 'go' and this is how it is interpreted by Kimchi, 'Why do you go here and there to seek help?' The versions all derive תזלי from זלל 'make light of' and the Hebrew should be pointed תָּזֵלִּי (Hiphil). Rashi (זלזול) agrees with the versions. Our

understanding of the picture which is drawn by v. 37a depends
on the sense which is attached to גם מאת זה תצאי. The view that
מאת זה means 'from Egypt' is found in Jerome. This is also
Lowth's exegesis ('The ambassadors thou sendest to Egypt shall
return with disappointment and confusion') and it is a generally
held interpretation of the verse (Duhm, Rudolph, Weiser,
Bright). The envoys become aware of the bankruptcy of their
policies and set out for home crestfallen and humiliated. We
expect, however, a reference not merely to the discomfiture of
negotiators, but to a final disaster in which the policy of seeking
security through foreign alliances will culminate—defeat and
exile (so Kimchi). This is the understanding of the verse
indicated by NEB, 'You shall go out from here (=Jerusalem),
each of you with his hands above his head'. This is probably
correct and what is then indicated is the posture of a file of
captives leaving Jerusalem to go into exile after defeat and
capitulation. The 2nd person fem. sing. verb (תצאי), which must
refer either to Judah or Jerusalem, is better suited to this
exegesis than to the other one.

With what fastidious care Israel organizes her search after the
Baalim! (v. 33) She has become a specialist in evil behaviour or
she has made evil doing a fixed habit (Rashi הנהגת = למדתי; so
Rudolph). What a trifling matter it is for her to change her
course! This is the sense of v. 36a rather than Vulg. 'How cheap
you have become!' (*Quam vilis facta es nimis*) or Targ. 'What a
great fool you have made of yourself!' (מא את מסתכלא לחדא).
She regards as of small importance decisions which should only
be made after great agonizing and with an awareness that they
are fraught with momentous consequences. The exclamation in
v. 36 leads on to threat introduced by גם. Judah's dalliance with
foreign powers will prove no more successful in the present
(Egypt) than it did in the past (Assyria). All her diplomatic
suppleness will bring nothing but disillusionment. Rashi and
Kimchi cite 2 Chr 28.20 (ויצר לו ולא חזקו) to illustrate the
disastrous consequences of Ahaz's Assyrian policy and Kimchi
also refers to Hezekiah's treating with Sennacherib (2 Kgs
18.13ff.). The reference to Egypt is related by Kimchi to the
events following the death of Josiah at Megiddo (609), when
tribute was paid to Pharaoh Necho (2 Kgs 23.31ff.). This is in
line with Rudolph's interpretation, since he concludes that
vv. 36–37 (also v. 16) came from a later period than the
remainder of the chapter and are subsequent additions by
Jeremiah (see above, p. 37). On the other hand, Volz, Weiser
and Milgrom (*JNES* 14, 1955, pp. 66f.) argue that the decline of
Assyria would be evident in the earliest period of Jeremiah's

ministry, and that the fall of Nineveh (612) cannot be assumed from v. 36b.

Accusation and threat also feature in vv. 34, 35 and 37. Israel has innocent blood on her hands, not the blood of those who were caught in the act of housebreaking, for then there would be no case for her to answer at law (cf. Exod 22.1). The poor are murdered in their innocence, which is all the more despicable for the circumstance that the poor are those who can be murdered with impunity—without legal consequences. Israel affects innocence (v. 35), her speech or, perhaps, her attitude (Rashi) declares that she has no crimes for which to answer. Faced by this grotesque misunderstanding (לא חטאתי) Yahweh declares that he will bring legal proceedings against her; he will arraign her (Sept., Vulg., Pesh.), condemn her and pass sentence on her (Targ.). The threat of v. 36b is gathered up into the specific and ultimate threat of exile (also introduced by גם). The Judaeans will be miserably deported with their hands on their heads—a humiliating symbol of their prisoner status. Yahweh has rejected Judah's security arrangements and she will derive no benefit from them.

The relation of vv. 34–35 to v. 33 is not so close as to require us to assume that the shedding of innocent blood must have some connection with fertility rites or human sacrifice, although this connection may be indicated by Sept.'s rendering of כי על כל אלה and we have noted that it is assumed in modern exegesis of v. 34 (above, p. 54). In the case of vv. 36–37 it is clear that a period in the history of Judah and not the entire history of Israel's apostasy in being described.

The chapter opens on a note of recollection. There was a time before her fatal infatuation with the gods of Canaan when Israel was wholly devoted to Yahweh (vv. 2–3). There follows a section (vv. 4–13) in which Israel is indicted for having transferred her affections from Yahweh to the Baalim as soon as she arrived in Canaan, and in which the puzzling and irrational nature of this preference is indicated. In vv. 14–19 (whether or not v. 16 is a subsequent addition) Israel's humiliation at the hands of the nations is attributed to causes other than idolatry. Although it should not be argued that vv. 1–13 constitute an integrated whole, there is more continuity of theme between v. 3 and vv. 4–13 than there is between v. 3 and vv. 14–19 (*pace* Bright).

In vv. 20–28 the subject matter is kindred to that of vv. 4–13. The nature and consequences of Israel's history of apostasy are further explored and she is characterized as a hardened and inveterate rebel, a compulsive devotee of the Baalim who has no rational control over her behaviour. She is addicted to idolatry, stained beyond cleansing and guilty without a shadow of doubt.

Verses 29–37 are not a unity: vv. 29–30 stress Israel's manifest guilt, vv. 31–32 the unnatural and unintelligible character of her insubordination, and vv. 33–37 contain allegations and threats. The former are directed not only at her idolatry (v. 33), but also at her bloodthirsty oppression of the innocent and defenceless (vv. 34–35) and her diplomatic shifts (vv. 36–37). Even if v. 16 and vv. 36–37 are regarded as later additions to the chapter, there is a reference to foreign alliances in vv. 17–19 (which, however, Nicholson assigns to the reign of Jehoiakim; cf. Milgrom, above, p. 60). Hence, while the chapter is monopolized by the theme of idolatry, it also arraigns Israel for social oppression and for what is another form of apostasy—her trust in powerful allies rather than in Yahweh.

The device of asking a question is used in this chapter in order to secure different effects. There are accusing questions in vv. 5, 6 and 29 which put Israel in the wrong. These are to be compared with the reproachful and accusing exclamations in vv. 33 and 36. In verses 11, 21, 31 and 32 the question is a device for pointing to Israel's incredible behaviour; in v. 14 it draws attention to Israel's humiliation, in v. 17 to the causes of that humiliation, and in v. 18 to the futility of Israel's policies. In v. 28 the question is ironic, taunting and challenging.

The chapter is rich in metaphorical language, especially in vv. 20–28. There are references to a honeymoon period (v. 2), to Israel as Yahweh's firstfruit (v. 3), to an unbelievably bad bargain (v. 11), to spring and cistern (v. 13), to Israel, the slave (v. 14), threatened by lions (v. 15); Israel is a recalcitrant ox (v. 20), a harlot (v. 20), a choice vine which has reverted to the wild (v. 21), a restive she-camel, a wild ass in heat (vv. 23–24), a thief caught in the act (v. 26). She drinks the water of the Nile and the Euphrates (v. 18); she is like a parched traveller whose shoes are disintegrating (v. 25). Soda and soap will not cleanse her (v. 22), she is like a man-eating lion (v. 30). Has Yahweh been like a wilderness? (v. 31). Can a bride forget her finery? (v. 32).

The aspect of legal debate is prominent: in vv. 4–13 Yahweh indicts Israel, in vv. 29–30 Israel is said to have no defence against Yahweh's charges, and in vv. 33–37 there are three allegations and two threats of punishment. Yahweh will take Israel to court and prove her guilt in the face of her professed innocence (v. 35). Along with this instance of legal vocabulary (הנני נשפט אותך), the occurrences of ריב in vv. 9 and 29 are to be noticed.

CHAPTER III

CAN ISRAEL, THE HARLOT, BE REINSTATED AS YAHWEH'S WIFE? (3.1–5)

¹If a man divorces his wife[1]
and she leaves him
and goes to live with another man,
can he take up with her again?
Is not that woman defiled for ever?[2]
You have played the harlot with many lovers
and do you think that you can come back to me?
    This is Yahweh's word.
²Look up to the hill-tops!
Is there any place where you have not fornicated?
You waited for them at the roadside
like Bedouin in the desert;
you have defiled the land
with the evil of your harlotry.
³The showers were withheld
and the spring rains never came,
but you had the hard face of a harlot;
you refused to give way to shame.
⁴Just then you called to me, My father,
you are the teacher of my youth.
⁵Will his wrath last for ever?
Will it go on raging?
These were your words,
but your aptitude was for evil deeds.

There is no trace of לאמר in Sept. and Pesh. Targ. (למימר) reproduces MT and Vulg. has *vulgo dicitur*, 'it is a common saying'. Rashi explains לאמר as 'It is open to me to say that you no longer suit me as is the way with a man who divorces his wife'. Kimchi connects לאמר with כי מאס יהוה במבטחיך (2.37). לאמר is a fragment of which nothing can be made and it should be deleted.

For MT הישוב אליה עוד Sept. has μὴ ἀνακάμπτουσα ἀνάκαμψει πρὸς αὐτὸν ἔτι and Rudolph emends to השוב אליו. He argues that MT has been adjusted to agree with Deut 24.4 (לא יוכל ... לשוב לקחתה, 'Her first husband who divorced her may not take her back again as wife').

MT הארץ ההיא should be emended to האשה ההיא in agreement with Sept. (ἡ γυνὴ ἐκείνη) and Vulg. (*mulier illa*), and Rudolph's supposition that γῆ is original in Sept. and that γυνή is a correction conflicts with Ziegler's view (*Beiträge*,

---

[1] Deleting לאמר (see below).
[2] Emending הארץ ההיא to האשה ההיא (see below).

p. 38). The pollution of the land is a consequence of the pollution of the woman and a reference to it ought not to appear until v. 2.

Sept. (ἐν ποιμέσιν πολλοῖς) has vocalized רעים as רֹעִים, 'with many shepherds' (also Pesh. br'wt' sgy''). Vulg. *cum amatoribus multis* rests on MT רֵעִים and agrees with Rashi (אוהבים). Targ. (cf. Kimchi) interprets the sexual imagery as a reference to idolatry and entanglement with foreign nations: 'You have committed idolatry and concluded alliances with many nations.'

MT ושוב אלי is to be explained as a question without the interrogative particle: an indignant question according to GK 113ee ('And thinkest thou to return again to me?'), but, perhaps, rather a rhetorical question which requires a negative answer. It is a question which issues in a premiss ('Israel cannot be reconciled to Yahweh'—so T. R. Hobbs, *ZAW* 86, 1974, pp. 25f.) or which prepares the ground for an indictment (B. O. Long, *ZAW* 88, 1976, p. 387). Sept. (καὶ ἀνέκαμπτες πρὸς με;) has understood the Hebrew in this way, but שוב is taken as an imperative by Vulg. (*Tamen revertere ad me, dicit Dominus, et ego suspiciam te*), Pesh. (*twbw lwty*) and Targ. (ותוב מבען לפלחני). The *waw* is then adversative as is evident in Vulg. *tamen*; the exegetical addition *et ego suspiciam te* brings out the sense clearly, 'Nevertheless, return to me and I will reinstate you' (similarly Rashi). Kimchi, on the other hand, correctly takes ושוב אלי to be a question which requires a negative answer. Israel cannot repent until her guilt has been purged by exile and she has been finally cured of her idolatrous tendencies.

על שפים (v. 2) was found difficult by the early translators. Targ. על נגדין, 'upon (mountain) passes'? and Pesh. šbyl' 'paths' contrast with Sept. εἰς εὐθεῖαν and Vulg. *in directum*, 'straight ahead'. The variant נגרין (Targ.), 'gutters', 'channels (for water)', is the foundation of Rashi's explanation of שפים as יבלי מים, 'channels of water'. Kimchi gives the meaning which is now generally attributed to שפים: they are the high places which are centres of idolatrous worship. (See further W. McKane, *Festschrift Cazelles*, AOAT 212, 1981, pp. 319–35; cf. A. Gelston, *VT* 21, 1971, pp. 518–21; K. Elliger, *ZAW* 83, 1971, pp. 21–29.)

What is indicated by על דרכים ישבת להם? Is the figure that of a prostitute who loiters for trade, or is it rather that of the prostitute who lays an ambush? The simile in Vulg. (*quasi latro in solitudine*) points unambiguously to an ambush. Sept. ὡσεὶ κορώνη ἐρημουμένη and Pesh. 'yk n'b' bmdbr, 'like a solitary raven', indicate עֹרֵב. There is clearly a special relationship between Sept. and Pesh. and almost certainly Pesh. is dependent on Sept. Kimchi, explains the point of the simile exactly: desert dwellers sit by the side of the road awaiting the caravans which pass by in order to buy and sell. Israel is a prostitute who sits at the roadside touting for custom and she is likened to the Bedouin who sit at the edge of the road soliciting trade.

The first reference to the pollution of the land comes in v. 2c (see above, pp. 59f.). הארץ in v. 1 has arisen through an erroneous anticipation of the interpretation of the legal model. The thought that the entire sphere of natural goodness and fruitfulness can be infected by human evil, so that drought, barrenness and desolation ensue, is found elsewhere in the book of Jeremiah (12.4; 14.1ff.). According to BL (p. 606, 76k) זנותיך is an anomalous singular form (cf. Kimchi) and זנותך is attested by 4 Hebrew manuscripts and Pesh. (znwtky). בזנותיך וברעתך is a hendiadys, 'the evil of your harlotry'.

At the beginning of v. 3 Sept. (καὶ ἔσχες ποιμένας πολλοὺς εἰς πρόσκομμα σεαυτῇ) diverges from MT. πολλούς apparently indicates that רבבים has been associated with רבב 'to be many' (cf. Kimchi who explains רבבים in terms of the weight of rain which falls). That the πολλούς were ποιμένας has probably been inferred from רעים רבים (v. 1), read by Sept. as ἐν ποιμέσι πολλοῖς (רֹעִים רַבִּים). πρόσκομμα indicates a corruption of MT מלקוש into מוקש 'snare'. Vulg. renders, 'therefore the showers are inhibited and the late-ripening (serotinus) rain does not fall.' Vulg. serotinus (see above, p. 52) belongs to the same tradition of interpretation as is found in Rashi and Kimchi. The rain is a factor in the final process of ripening and swelling the grain.

For MT ומצח אשה זונה Sept. has ὄψις πόρνης, but this may indicate that the Greek translator was striving for economy of expression rather than that he had a Hebrew text which read ומצח זונה. אשה and זונה cannot be regarded as variants, since they are not interchangeable and ומצח אשה אשה היה לך would not give the necessary sense. Nor can אשה, if it is secondary, be regarded as a gloss on זונה, and we are brought to the conclusion that there is no obvious way of explaining how אשה came to be inserted into the text. MT should be retained. It is indicated by Vulg., Targ. and Pesh.

Targ. renders הכלם by לאתכנעא, 'to be under authority' or, perhaps, 'to submit in penitence', and Pesh. by lmttksw, 'to be deterred'. The Syriac translator may have been influenced by וימנעו (although he renders it by 'tklyw) and may have intended to associate the inhibition of the rain with the prostitute's lack of inhibitions.

קראתי (v. 4) is a 2nd person sing. fem. (see above on 2.20, 33, pp. 39, 53). Kimchi, as at 2.33, assumes that the K–Q differentiation is significant. K means, 'Whenever I called out to you through my prophet, "My son", your practice was to say to me, "My father, you were the teacher of my youth". But your

deeds did not match your professions.' Q means, 'Was it not your
practice at the moment when you saw that I had withheld the
rain to return to me and call out to me, "My father, you were my
teacher in my youth"?' Hence מעתה is explained by Kimchi as
'at the moment when you saw that I had withheld the rain'.
Rashi comments on מעתה, 'Will you not desist from your evil
and call out to me, "My Father", and if you do, will your Lord
hold against you for ever the sin which you committed against
him?' Hence, according to Rashi (cf. Vulg.), הלוא מעתה means
'Will you not abandon your evil as from now?' The question of
v. 5a then requires the answer 'No'. Israel's sin will not be
remembered if she has truly repented, but her actions do not
match her words (v. 5b). The exegesis of Lowth has a striking
resemblance to this.

But v. 4 is an indictment of Israel's effrontery rather than an
invitation to her to turn to Yahweh and seek mercy. She makes
an appeal to Yahweh for old time's sake and she expects his
anger to relent, but she has no intention of changing her ways or
abating her wickedness (v. 5). Even so מעתה remains a problem:
the sense 'as of now', which is indicated by Targ. (מכען; cf. Pesh.
mkyl) is less apposite than 'just then' (cf. Ehrlich 'thereupon' or
'in such circumstances'). The uncertainty about מעתה is
reflected in the variety of modern translations. Rudolph emends
to גם עתה, 'nevertheless'. The rendering 'nevertheless' underlines
the impudence and shamelessness of Israel's appeal to Yahweh
and this is generally correct.

אלוף means 'teacher' and not 'friend' (*pace* Rudolph and
others) and this has been argued elsewhere (W. McKane,
Proverbs, on 2.17). אב, probably, also has the sense 'teacher',
since in the setting of the school the pupil is addressed as בני (see
Proverbs, especially on chapters 1–9; cf. P. A. H. de Boer, *SVT*
3, 57f., אב = 'counsellor'). Sept. puts v. 4 into indirect speech and
renders אלוף as ἀρχηγόν, 'leader' (cf. II אלף, KB³). Both Sept.
and Vulg. (*dux virginitatis meae tu es*) connect נערי with
virginity, no doubt influenced by the foregoing figure of Israel,
the harlot. She harks back to the time of her youth and this is
interpreted as a recall of the days when she was pure and
unsullied. נערי, however, has nothing to do with virginity and
refers rather to the time of youth in connection with education
(cf. Targ. עלמא; Pesh. *ṭlywt'*).

Rudolph is right in saying that אב (v. 4) cannot mean
'husband', but wrong in supposing that it betrays the influence of
the different figure which is used in v. 19, where the Israelites are
described as Yahweh's children (following Duhm). We have to
ask whether the husband-wife figure is giving place to a
teacher-pupil figure or whether we are still to think of Yahweh

qua husband as the teacher (so Volz and Hyatt, *IB*). The reference is then to the husband in his capacity as instructor of the young wife. נֹעַרִי is connected by Kimchi with the נְעוּרַיִךְ of 2.2 and so the metaphor is interpreted as a reference to a time when the nation was young, and gladly submitted to the authority of her teacher.

Sept. φυλαχθήσεται (v. 5) is an indication that 'Israel' and not 'Yahweh' has been taken as the grammatical subject. Pesh. agrees with Sept., 'Will it (Israel) be kept for ever? Will it be preserved in perpetuity?' Targ. also uses passive verbs, but like Vulg. gives the sentence the form of a question addressed directly to Yahweh, 'Is it possible that sins will be remembered by you for ever, or that you will punish unrelentingly for ever?'

Rashi's understanding of הַיִנְטֹר לְעוֹלָם אִם יִשְׁמֹר לָנֶצַח is the correct one, 'Will he (Yahweh) keep up (his anger)? Will he maintain (it) for ever?' If G. R. Driver's philology is adopted for נטר and שמר (*JTS* 32, 1931, pp. 361f.), Yahweh remains the subject of these verbs and the sense is not altered, although it is no longer necessary to supply objects. Following Driver's philology, NEB renders Jer 3.5, 'Will he be angry for ever? Will he rage eternally?' There is, however, difficulty in the supposition that Hebrew נטר is an equivalent of Accadian *nadāru*, since according to the regular scheme of phonemic correspondence Accadian *nadāru* should appear in Hebrew as נדר. Ziegler (*Beiträge*, p. 18) notes that μηνιῶ, 'be angry with', renders אטור at Jer 3.12, but he rightly rejects the conjecture μηνιεῖ at 3.5, where Sept. διαμενεῖ is bound up with the supposition that 'Israel' is the subject. μηνιῶ at 3.12 does not show that the Greek translator knew Driver's philology, but that he assumed the object 'anger' and rendered לֹא אטור as οὐ μηνιῶ.

דֵּבַּרְתְּ (Q) is unnecessary, since דֵּבַּרְתִּי (K) is to be read as 2nd person fem. sing. (see above, p. 60). הִנֵּה דִבַּרְתִּי is a reference to the fine words which Israel has just spoken, and there is a contrast between these words and her actions (וַתַּעֲשִׂי הָרָעוֹת וַתּוּכָל), with the *waw* of וַתַּעֲשִׂי, perhaps, an adversative 'but'. 'Behold, you have spoken!', can, perhaps, bear the sense 'These were your words!', but Volz points הִנֵּה as הֵנָּה in order to get this meaning. Sept. apparently represents וְלֹא תוּכָל. This gives a different twist to the sense of v. 5b which then means, 'Because of your incapacity you were incapable of acting in accordance with your words'. MT and Vulg. (*et potuisti*) indicate, 'But you did evil and became expert at it' (cf. Rashi וַתּוּכַל לִמְרוֹת, 'and you became an adept at rebellion'). Pesh. (*w'thylty*) indicates the stiffening of Israel's resolve to do evil. Bright ('But you did evil to your utmost') inclines to Targ. (וְאַסְגֵית), while Rudolph's rendering (*und tatest das Böse mit Meisterschaft*) emphasizes Israel's expertise as an evil-doer.

The intention of the legal premiss in v. 1 (cf. J. D. Martin, *VT* 19, 1969, pp. 82–92) is to establish *a fortiori* that Israel who has become a common prostitute cannot be reinstated as Yahweh's wife. The sexual imagery seems to be more than a metaphor for idolatry (Targ., Kimchi) and to have a special appropriateness to the nature of Israel's unfaithfulness. Her involvement in sexual rites associated with the Canaanite cult lends such a particular appositeness to the sexual imagery that it is more than a metaphor for idolatry which could be replaced without loss by another metaphor not involving sexual imagery.

The main issue, however, is that, if the legal model is binding, Yahweh is precluded from accepting Israel's repentance. This cannot take place, any more than a man can reinstate a former wife who has lived with a second husband. The question in v. 1 (Will he take her back?) has to be answered negatively. It is a possibility which is to be dismissed. Israel like the woman described in the legal clause is permanently defiled.

Israel is a prostitute who has lain with lovers wherever they chose to take their pleasure with her. She is like the Bedouin who haggle with passing caravans (Kimchi) or, perhaps, like the Bedouin who lie in wait to ambush passing caravans (Bright). The thought that the prostitute lays an ambush for her victims is present in the book of Proverbs (see W. McKane, *Proverbs*, on 7.10ff. and 9.18). The pollution of the land consequent on Israel's harlotry is evidenced by drought (v. 3) with its effects of barrenness, famine and death by starvation. Israel is a hard-faced prostitute whose trade is sexual intercourse (see *Proverbs*, on 7.13 and 30.20) and who knows no shame.

There is something incongruous and incredible about the way in which Israel addresses Yahweh in v. 4. She hopes that Yahweh's anger will pass away, but all the while she becomes a more expert evil-doer. She makes an appeal to her old teacher, but she blatantly continues to disregard his teaching. As in 2.23ff. the gulf between Israel's better resolves and the compulsiveness of her behaviour is brought to light, and the negative answer which flows from the legal model in 3.1 is to be compared with the conclusion of 2.22 that there is no way in which Israel can be cleansed from her defilement. Will Yahweh's anger ever relent? Is the possibility of repentance open to her? Is the legal model decisive? If so, she is separated from Yahweh for ever and has no hope of reconciliation. The question (v. 5a) is not addressed to Yahweh; it is, perhaps, an unspoken question, one which Israel hardly dare formulate, but which is there, nevertheless, in the depths as a silent concern, the great question of her existence.

It is not that the legal model is necessarily decisive. More to the point is the circumstance that Israel cannot translate this great, sorrowing question into a consistent response. She is dedicated to evil-doing: her great question is an empty one, because her behaviour is inconsequential and there is nothing which she can do about this inconsequentiality. Her tragedy is the dichotomy between these glimpses of self-understanding and the vice-like grip of a compulsive behaviour which makes her expert only at evil-doing, and which nullifies her brief moments of illumination. These transient gleams enable her to grasp what her relationship with Yahweh demands of her, and it is at these moments of self-understanding that she asks herself if Yahweh will take her back. But she has no power to make her way back.

ISRAEL'S GUILT IS LESS THAN THAT OF JUDAH (3.6–11)

[6]Yahweh said to me in the reign of King Josiah, Do you see what fickle Israel has done? She has played the harlot on every high hill and under every leafy tree. [7]I thought that after she had done all these things she would return to me, but she did not return. Her faithless sister, Judah, saw[1] it all. [8]She saw[2] that because of all the acts of adultery committed by fickle Israel I had sent her away and issued a bill of divorce to her. Yet her faithless sister, Judah, was undeterred and she in turn played the harlot. [9]Because she thought harlotry was a trifling matter, she defiled the land and committed adultery with stone and tree. [10]In spite of all this her faithless sister, Judah, did not return to me with all her heart, but only made a pretence of repentance. This is Yahweh's word. [11]Yahweh said to me, Fickle Israel is less guilty than faithless Judah.

מְשֻׁבָה has given difficulty to the versions: the renderings of Sept. (κατοικία) and Pesh. ('mwrt'), 'settlement', assume a derivation from יָשַׁב. Targ.'s paraphrase of מְשׁוּבָה, 'who have made a resolve to return to my worship', indicates good intentions which never became effective and which did not prevent Israel from being despatched into exile. Vulg. is nearer the mark with *aversatrix* 'cheat' and both Rashi and Kimchi indicate the sense 'apostate'. Rashi notes that the *yodh* in וַתִּזְנִי is redundant and Kimchi says that the form should be וַתִּזְנֶה (cf. וַתֵּרֶא which is given by K in v. 7).

In v. 7 Sept., Vulg. and Pesh. render שׁוּב as an imperative. The translation would then be, 'And I said after she had done all these things, "Return to me".' Rashi also supposes that אֵלַי תָּשׁוּב is an invitation to repent—the same invitation as was

---

[1] K וַתֵּרֶא?; Q וַתֵּרֶא.
[2] Reading וַתֵּרֶא (MT וָאֵרֶא). See below, p. 65.

issued by all the prophets. MT is rather to be translated, 'And I
thought that after she had done with all this she would return to
me.' Pesh. does not translate בגודה and Sept. does not translate
אחותה, but šwqrh corresponds to the additional τὴν ἀσυνθεσίαν
αὐτῆς in Sept. This is another indication of a special relationship
between Sept. and Pesh. (cf. their agreement in rendering
משובה).

What could משובה translated 'settlement' have meant to the
Greek and Syriac translators? Is it a reference to Israel
(= northern kingdom) in exile? Israel, banished from her own
land and settled in foreign parts, is משובה. At any rate for Sept.
and Pesh., with this interpretation of משובה in vv. 6 and 12, the
main weight of accusation falls on Judah, and this is
understandable in so far as vv. 6–11 function as a prelude to a
call to 'return' issued to Israel in v. 12.

The versions were puzzled by וארא (v. 8). Pesh. (ḥzt)
represents ותרא and this is what is desiderated and should be
adopted (on (ε)ιδε(ν) attested by Sept. Q^c and L, see Ziegler). It
is not clear how ὧν κατελήμφθη (v. 8) should be evaluated,
although it may be a doublet of ἐν οἷς ἐμοιχᾶτο and this is what
Ziegler has indicated by bracketing the latter in his text. The
sense of καταλαμβάνω is the one found in Jn 8.3, 4, where it is
used of a woman taken in the act of adultery. Is it possible that
we have a Christian gloss influenced by this passage? It was
Spohn's view that ὧν κατελήμφθη was the gloss, but Ziegler by
bracketing ἐν οἷς ἐμοιχᾶτο in his text indicates the reverse (cf.
Beiträge, p. 93). εἰς τὰς χεῖρας αὐτῆς (v. 8) is an addition in
Sept. over against MT and it corresponds to בידה in Deut 24.1,
3. Hence it is evidence of an intention to associate v. 8 more
closely with the Deuteronomy passages. It is deleted by Ziegler
from his text, although it is attested by the principal manuscripts
of Sept.

Yahweh's divorce from Israel is legally attested. He has issued
her with a written document which apparently makes the divorce
between him and her final. The long exile of the northern tribes,
the apparent finality of their expulsion from their own land, is an
expression of the finality of their divorce from Yahweh. But the
intention of vv. 6–11 in connection with vv. 12–13 is to establish
that the divorce is, nevertheless, not final (so Kimchi).

In v. 9 ותחנף את הארץ is not represented in Sept. MT should
be retained, but the other versions indicate that ותחנף is
transitive (Vulg., Pesh. and Targ.) and it should be pointed as
וַתַּחֲנֵף (cf. וַתְּחַנִּפִי in v. 2). מקל is rendered εἰς οὐθέν by Sept.
('Her harlotry was as nothing') and facilitate by Vulg. ('by her
adeptness at fornication') and this is probably an indication that
קל has been derived from קלל. This is certainly how מקל was

taken by Pesh. (*wmṭl dzlyl'*), Targ. (מדקלילא בעינחא), Rashi, Kimchi, BDB, Rudolph and Bright, whereas KB[2] notes another possibility: קל = 'noise' in a pejorative sense, 'rabble' or 'orgy'.

The attempt to connect the reference to Judah's defective repentance (v. 10) with a particular, historical occasion is already found in Rashi and Kimchi. Kimchi contrasts Josiah's wholehearted repentance (2 Kgs 23.3) with a repentance which is בשקר. The view that there is an allusion to measures of reform in either Hezekiah's or Josiah's reign has been widely held: Hezekiah's reform according to Rudolph; Hezekiah's or Josiah's reform according to Bright and H. W. Wolff (*ZTK* 48, 1951, p. 139); Josiah's reform according to Giesebrecht, Duhm, Cornill, Welch (*The Expositor*, 1921, pp. 469–472) and Skinner (*Prophecy and Religion*, p. 82). Thus Rudolph supposes that there is also a reference to Hezekiah's reform in v. 9 and he achieves this by emending ותנאף את האבן ואת חעץ to ותנאץ את האבן ואת העץ, 'And cast off (the worship) of stone and tree'. Hezekiah, according to 2 Kgs 18.4, broke the pillars (= האבן) and cut down the Asherah (= העץ). Rudolph's contention that v. 10 must refer to a historical moment of reform and that what he has supplied in v. 9 is essential begs the question. His other point that the allusion to adultery with stone and tree is too late, coming as it does after the mention of the pollution of the land, is not impressive and MT should be retained in v. 9. There is much to be said for Weiser's scepticism about the value of searching for a particular historical anchorage in connection with the reference to defective repentance in v. 10 (p. 28 n. 3).

A greater degree of guilt attaches to Judah than to Israel (v. 11) and that this is forensically conceived is correctly indicated by Rashi's comment, 'She is acquitted and is freed from judgement'. The centre of interest and concern in vv. 6–11 is Israel, and the establishing of Judah's greater sinfulness leads on to an invitation to Israel to return to Yahweh. Israel is not severed from her land forever. Although Yahweh in exiling her issued her with a bill of divorce, he is not bound by legal protocol as are husbands who divorce their wives. The way is open for Israel to return to her land and to Yahweh, and she is invited to do so (v. 12). Yahweh can take Israel back; he is unfettered by legalities and he wills in mercy to recover his lost people and to be reconciled to them.

There are reasons why the unit has been defined as vv. 6–11 (so also Nicholson) rather than vv. 6–13, although the latter is normally regarded as the correct delimitation. That v. 1 is seminal in relation to vv. 6–11 is indisputable, since 'divorce', interpreted as the exile of the northern kingdom supplies the author of vv. 6–11 with the theme. The treatment of that theme is certainly influenced by the supposition that vv. 12–13 are addressed to the inhabitants of the former northern kingdom, but vv. 6–11 are not more intrinsically related to vv. 12–13 than they are to vv. 1–5, although they have been editorially connected to vv. 12–13 with greater deliberation. It is unlikely that the interpretation of vv. 1–5 which is assumed by vv. 6–11 is the right one, since there is no reason to suppose that vv. 1–5 relate so particularly to the former northern kingdom. If vv. 1–5 are from Jeremiah, it would be more natural to conclude that they were spoken to Judah. Nor should it be assumed that the interpretation which has been put on the poetry of vv. 12–13 by the connecting piece in v. 12 is necessarily correct. The expression משובה ישראל is common to v. 12 and vv. 6–11, but it does not follow from this that there is an original literary continuity between vv. 6–11 and vv. 12–13, in the sense that they are both from the same hand. Another possible explanation is that משובה ישראל was appropriated by the author of vv. 6–11 from v. 12 in the same way as he took the idea of divorce from v. 1 and developed it.

The logic of what has just been said is that if vv. 1–13 are all attributable to the prophet Jeremiah (Graf, Giesebrecht, Cornill, Volz, Rudolph, Weiser), there are as good reasons for making a unit of vv. 1–13 as there are for making a unit of vv. 6–13, because the connection between vv. 6–11 and vv. 12–13 is no more intrinsic than the connection between vv. 1–5 and vv. 6–11. Hence, given his assumptions, H. W. Hertzberg (*ThLZ* 77, 1952, pp. 598f.) is entirely logical in making a unit out of vv. 1–13 by embracing vv. 1–5 and supposing that these verses too were addressed by Jeremiah to the inhabitants of the former northern kingdom. It might be objected that v. 5 connects impressively with v. 19 and this has often been said, but it will not stand up to close scrutiny (see further below). If, however, we go along with the view that vv. 6–13 constitute a unit, we have to suppose that the historical notice in v. 6 is to be taken seriously, and that what we have is an indication of Jeremiah's concern for the inhabitants of the former northern kingdom, whether before or after Josiah's reform in 621, perhaps, related to the political interest shown by the king in the former northern kingdom. It is then a matter of dispute whether in vv. 12–13 we have an address to exiles, as most suppose, or whether שובה excludes the nuance of 'Return' and is to be understood as a call to repentance issued to those who were not deported to Assyria and were still resident in Palestine (A. C. Welch, *The Expositor*, 1921, p. 467; Thiel p. 91).

Another view disengages vv. 6–11 from the prophet Jeremiah, while maintaining that vv. 6–13 constitute a significant unit. In the case of W. L. Holladay (*The Root Šûbh in the Old Testament*, 1958, pp. 132–134) and Thiel (pp. 85–91) this goes with the assertion that vv. 6–13 are the composition of a Deuteronomistic editor. Hyatt (*IB*), who also holds that vv. 6–11 are a Deuteronomistic composition, takes a different view of vv. 12–13, since he doubts whether vv. 12–13 originally referred to the inhabitants of the former northern kingdom. This is a position which is close to that of Duhm (see further below). Against the contention that vv. 6–11 are Deuteronomistic Rudolph notes that Hyatt himself has conceded that the passage 'has little D diction', and Thiel, for his part, acknowledges that there is little Deuteronomistic vocabulary in vv. 6–12aα (p. 89).

There is an important respect in which Thiel's view of vv. 6–11 (p. 88) is the right one. Whoever composed vv. 6–11 borrowed his ideas and quarried his vocabularly from surrounding passages. Thiel is right to suppose that משובה ישראל has been derived from v. 12, that the 'divorce' idea has been developed in v. 8 (ואתן את ספר כריתתיה אליה), in dependence on Deut 24.3 and that the epithet בגודה or בגדה (vv. 7, 8, 10) has been suggested by 3.20 The content of vv. 6–11 is determined by a particular interpretation which has been put on vv. 1–5 and 12–13.

Whether one can go any further than this and establish the particular historical circumstances and theological concerns which prompted such exegesis is doubtful. The argument that the polemical situation which had developed between Jews and Samaritans rules out the post-exilic period (Thiel, p. 90) is one which depends for its effectiveness on the assumption that this kind of exegetical activity has to be related significantly to a historical moment and a theological climate. It would be dogmatic to assert that the interest which is reflected here is 'purely' exegetical and that vv. 6–11, being no more than an attempt to deal with problems which were thought to inhere in existing texts (What did the 'divorce' of Israel signify? Why did Jeremiah address an offer of reconciliation to Israel?), do not require an explanation in terms of appropriate historical circumstances. But it may not be so easy as is sometimes supposed to demonstrate the appropriateness of the exilic period and the inappropriateness of the post-exilic period. The secondary character of vv. 6–11 and the circumstance that their interpretation of the texts out of which they arise is, almost certainly, wrong (see below, on vv. 12–13) establishes that they are not the work of the prophet Jeremiah and that they are at least as late as the exilic period. A 'purely' exegetical account of them is inadequate, because the correspondence between vv. 6–11 and Ezek 16.51–52 is (so Cornill; *pace* Thiel, p. 90) close and impressive. It appears that these were ideas which were abroad among Jews in Babylon consequent on the fall of Jerusalem (according to Zimmerli 16.51f. are exilic) and it is a reasonable conclusion that behind the particular exegetical operations of the author of vv. 6–11 there is this general current of speculation and questioning.

The understanding of vv. 6–11 which is being advanced is that they represent a secondary exegetical development which arises from vv. 1–5 (especially v. 1) and vv. 12–13. It is assumed wrongly by the exegete that vv. 1–5 refer to northern Israel and the idea of 'divorce' is interpreted by him as the exile of the northern kingdom. The invitation to return and repent in vv. 12–13 is thought also to have been addressed to the inhabitants of the former northern kindom in exile, and the exegete develops the idea that the lesser guilt of Israel over against Judah justifies this offer of forgiveness and reconciliation. His primary interest is in understanding texts which are available for exegesis. It is a difficult task to recover the historical circumstances and theological tendencies which might have promoted such exegesis, but the similar ideas which appear in Ezek 16.51–52 suggest that there was a more general climate of theological pondering which spurred the particular, exegetical activity.

REPENT OF YOUR SINS AND RETURN TO ME (3.12–13)

[12]Go and proclaim these words towards the north:
Return fickle Israel. This is Yahweh's word.
I shall not keep up my wrath against you.
I am constant in my love. This is Yahweh's word.
My anger will not rage for ever.
[13]But you must realize how sinful you are;
you have rebelled against Yahweh, your God;
you have spread your legs[1] for strangers
under every leafy tree;
you have not obeyed my voice.
This is the word of Yahweh.

צפונה is equated by Kimchi with the former territory of the ten tribes, rather than with the place of their exile. The significance of speaking such a message does not lie in the circumstance that the former inhabitants of the northern kingdom, whether still resident in their own territory or in exile, can hear it, but only in its being a public disclosure of Yahweh's gracious intentions to the prophet's audience (the elders of Judah, according to Kimchi). The renderings for משבה adopted by Sept. and Pesh.

[1] Reading ירכיך (MT דרכיך). See below, pp. 70f.

(see above, p. 64) probably indicate that these versions understood vv. 12–13 as an address to Israel (the ten tribes) in exile. שׁוּבָה rather than the more correct שׁוּבִי is, perhaps, connected with the desire to achieve a play on vowel sounds—שׁוּבָה מְשֻׁבָה (Rudolph).

Thiel has supposed (p. 91) that the distinction between 'Return (from exile)' and 'Repent' as translations of שׁוּבָה is highly significant, but this is true only if שׁוּבָה מְשֻׁבָה is so interpreted as to exclude the possibility that both senses are involved—the procedure of Welch and Thiel (above, p. 68). The making of a sharp distinction between 'Return (from exile)' and 'Repent' is meaningful only where there is an exegetical concern to exclude the nuance 'Return from exile'. 'Return' has a geographical significance ('Come back to the land which I have given you, for your exile is over'), but it contains a prior reference to forgiveness and reconciliation ('You have become a confirmed apostate, but I am ready to forgive you and reinstate you'). The sense of חֶסֶד (Yahweh's unchanging and constant love) is brought out by Sept. (ἐλεήμων), Pesh. (ṭb) and Targ. (ארי מסגי למעבד טבון אנא, 'for my acts of kindness are great'). Similarly Kimchi explains חֶסֶד as a superfluity of kindness which transcends what is deserved (יותר על הראוי).

G. R. Driver (SVT 3, 1955, p. 88) explains לוא אפיל פני בכם as 'I shall not darken my face against you' rather than 'I shall not cause my face to fall on you' (cf. NEB, 'I will no longer frown on you'). אפיל is derived from אפל and the form אפיל develops from אאפיל through an elision of the aleph. The metaphor which results from a derivation from נפל 'fall' is entirely satisfactory (so Rudolph). 'Causing the face to fall' is indicative of inflexible anger and displeasure' (Targ., Rashi, Kimchi) and לוא אפיל פני בכם then provides an apt parallel to לא אטור לעולם (on נטר see above, p. 62).

ותפזרי את דרכיך (v. 13) is obscure and Sept., Vulg. and Pesh. all offer literal translations. Both Targ. and Kimchi are content to indicate a general reference to idolatry without paying attention to a possible sexual allusion (cf. NEB which renders זרים as 'foreign gods', but which indicates the sexual reference by translating דרכיך as 'promiscuous traffic'). The sexual allusion is recovered more explicitly by Cornill's emendation of דרכיך to דודיך which would yield some such translation as, 'You have distributed your favours to strangers under every leafy tree'. Israel is likened to a cult prostitute, welcoming all who make advances to her. This is in accord with Rashi's supposition that דרכיך is a euphemism, a polite evasion of רגליך ('You opened your legs'). דרכיך may be a deliberate alteration of ירכיך in the interests of decorum and the original text may have been

ותפזרי את ירכיך. Duhm's emendation ותפשקי את ברכיך yields
the same sense ('And you opened wide your knees'). Duhm
assumes that פזר (usually 'scatter') cannot give the sense 'open
wide', but Arabic *bzr* means 'separate', 'divide'. Rudolph adopts
Cornill's דודיך and follows Cornill in deleting תחת כל עץ רענן,
as also does Thiel (p. 88). His argument in brief is that the
word-string שמע בקול יהוה is also predominantly
Deuteronomistic, but it may be doubted whether so ordinary a
combination of words can be used to make the critical
distinctions which Thiel is striving after (cf. A. K. Fenz, *Auf
Jahwes Stimme hören*, 1964, pp. 47, 69, who holds that the
expression is not a mark of Deuteronomic or Deuteronomistic
vocabulary; also H. Weippert, Die *Prosareden*, p. 36, n. 43).

The way back to Yahweh is not painless and undemanding.
Israel must acknowledge that she has broken trust and defied
authority; everything that she could have done to destroy her
relationship with Yahweh she has in fact done. That there is a
way back for her is a testimony only to the constancy of
Yahweh's love.

Verses 6–11 have been joined to the address to משבה ישראל in
vv. 12–13 by הלך וקראת את הדברים האלה צפונה ואמרת. The
effect of this is to identify משבה ישראל (v. 12) with the 'Israel'
which is opposed to Judah in vv. 6–11. If it is held that the editor
of vv. 6–13 is not the author of the saying in vv. 12–13, the
question can be raised whether or not the editor has understood
the meaning of vv. 12–13 correctly. There is (*pace* Thiel, p. 91)
at least one modification to the original sense of vv. 12–13 which
has been made by the editor. It can be argued that the prophet
Jeremiah in the reign of Josiah addressed a call to repentance to
those who had not been exiled and were still resident in the
former northern kingdom. It cannot be argued that this was the
sense of שובה משבה ישראל intended by the editor of vv. 6–13,
because in vv. 6–11 he interprets 'divorce' as the exile of the
northern kingdom and there is no doubt that, in connection with
vv. 6–11, שובה משבו ישראל is an address to Israel in exile,
although the nuance 'Repent' is also present in שובה.

'Israel' in chapter 2 (vv. 3, 4, 14, 26, 31), which can also be
addressed as 'Judah' (v. 28), is not to be equated with the ten
tribes, and Skinner has shown (*Prophecy and Religion*, p. 83
n. 1) that the overall use of 'Israel' in the book of Jeremiah
would not lead us to suppose that the Jeremianic saying in
vv. 12–13 is addressed to northern Israel. Jerome assumed that
'Israel' was used inclusively in v. 12. With this should be
compared Duhm's view that Jeremiah had in mind the Israel
consisting of Judah, Benjamin and a possible remnant of
northern Israel.

Those who regard the saying in vv. 12–13 as having been addressed originally by Jeremiah to Judah (Duhm, Skinner, pp. 84f., Nicholson) should be followed, but the continuity is between vv. 1–5 and 12–13 (so Duhm) rather than between vv. 12–13 and 21ff. (Skinner—he supposes that vv. 19f. are secondary). The connection between vv. 1–5 and vv. 12–13 has been disturbed by the secondary vv. 6–11 and the link at the beginning of v. 12. Judah, the harlot, whose divorce appears to be irrevocable, is, nevertheless, invited to repent and return to her husband. When Yahweh describes himself as חסיד it is probable that the husband-wife metaphor is being maintained and that what is intended is the constancy of his love as husband for his wayward wife. If vv. 12–13 are so continuous with vv. 1–5, it is likely that the epithet משובה refers originally to Israel's (Judah's) wantonness and harlotry, just as בגדה or בגדה is probably derived from a verse in which בגד is used of a wife's unfaithfulness to her husband (3.20). A final point (noted by Duhm) is that the question הינטר לעולם (v. 5) is answered in v. 12 by לא אטור לעולם. Hence there is enough evidence to support the conclusion that an original continuity between v. 1–5 and 12–13 has been disturbed.

RETURN AND I SHALL RESTORE YOU (3.14–18)

[14]Return, wayward sons, for I have taken you back under my care. This is Yahweh's word. I shall pick one of you from a town and two out of a community and bring you to Zion. [15]I shall set over you shepherds of my choice and they will guide you with knowledge and understanding. [16]In the future when there are large numbers of you in the land, no one will ever say, The Ark of the Covenant of Yahweh. This is Yahweh's word. No one will think about it, it will not be remembered or missed and another one will not be made. [17]At that time Jerusalem will be called Yahweh's throne; all nations will gather to it[1] and will give up the evil of their wilfulness. [18]In those days Judah and Israel will walk side by side and together will come from a northern land to the land which I gave to their fathers.[2]

If v. 14 is addressed to Judaeans, as the reference to Zion would suggest, what is indicated is a return from exile, but the thought of repentance (בנים שובבים) is also present (*pace* Rudolph). This was the opinion of Jerome who thought that v. 14 alluded to the return of Jews to Jerusalem with the permission of Cyrus and under the leadership of Zerubbabel, and who noted the partial character of that return. Kimchi notes that his father equated בעל with קוץ 'loathe', because of the connection of בעלתי בם with apostasy in Jer 31.32 (cf. Rudolph who remarks that some

[1] Deleting לשם יהוה לירושלם (see below, p. 75)

[2] Reading אבותיהם (MT אבותיכם). See below, p. 75

modern scholars hold this view, but who does not appear to be aware of its age). Kimchi glosses בעלתי בכם with 'I sent you away (divorced you), but I shall resume conjugal relations with you' (so Sept., Vulg.) and this view should be followed. The metaphor of marriage and divorce is still effective and Yahweh's resumption of relations with his people is conceived on the analogy of the resumption of conjugal relations after a period of separation. Since, however, the sexual imagery cannot be disengaged from its references to apostasy, it may be that there is an allusion to past dalliance with the Baalim (Peake and others).

Targ. interprets 'shepherds' (v. 15) as 'governors' (פרנסין). As good shepherds are careful of their sheep, this new breed of rulers, hand picked by Yahweh (כלבי), will feed the community with knowledge and good sense. The view that the רעים of v. 15 are Davidic kings, envisaged as guardians of the Torah, is found in Duhm in connection with an assumption that the passage is very late. The 'Davidic' interpretation is also present in H. Cazelles, associated with very different critical and historical assumptions (VT 18, 1968, pp. 147–158). The broader interpretation of רעים favoured by Kimchi should be adopted. Davidic kings of a new stamp are, perhaps, comprehended by the term רעים, but we have to think also of שרים, 'statesmen' who raise the level of government to new heights of wisdom and benevolence. The vocabulary (דעה והשכיל cf. Targ. במדע ובחכמה) suggests that the רעים are envisaged as a new race of חכמים who have a sure touch in directing the destiny of Yahweh's community.

Carefully nursed by wise rulers the land will prosper and its population will be built up. At that time the saying 'The Ark of the Covenant of Yahweh' (perhaps, to be thought of as an impressive cultic formula like the threefold היכל יהוה in 7.4) will pass into disuse (v. 16). Instead of the ark being Yahweh's throne, Jerusalem will be Yahweh's throne. Sept., Vulg. and Pesh. all suppose that the obscure יפקדו means 'search for' or 'seek out'. NEB 'resort to it' is in line with the indications of these versions and this or 'miss' (Bright) would seem to be the right sense. There is a distinctive Jewish exegesis of ולא יפקדו ולא יעשה עוד. Targ. translates, 'They will not tremble (יזועון) and will wage no more wars with it.' If 'tremble' is the right rendering of יזועון, there is, perhaps, a reference to the lethal character of the ark (cf. 1 Sam 4–6; 2 Sam 6). Rashi (also Kimchi) follows Targ. with respect to לא יעשה עוד : in new circumstances of permanent peace the ark will all but be forgotten. The dependence of Pesh. on Sept. is illustrated in an unusual way in v. 16: Sept.'s rendering of ארון ברית (Κιβωτὸς διαθήκης) is transliterated by Pesh. (qbwt' ddytq').

If לא יעשה עוד means 'and it will not be remade', the loss of the ark would appear to be implied, and M. Haran (*IEJ*, 13, 1963, pp. 46–58; *Temples and Temple Service in Ancient Israel*, 1978, pp. 281f.) has argued that it was removed by Manasseh. In any case whether or not there is an implication that the ark had disappeared, there is agreement that it had become obsolescent, but there are different ways of accounting for its being redundant. Peake associated v. 16 (emended) with the kind of thinking which is found in 7.4: he saw in it the same transcending of a limited, cultic religion as is evidenced by Jeremiah's blast against the Jerusalem temple. More recently M. Weinfeld (*ZAW*, 88, 1976, pp. 17–56) has made a connection between 3.16 and 7.4 and has set the matter in a similar framework of interpretation.

If the loss of the ark is implied (Rudolph), the sense is that sorrow for the lost ark will no longer exercise anyone. In what sense will Jerusalem be Yahweh's throne? Jerome's answer is that he will be enthroned in the hearts of his people who trust in him. A community adorned with righteousness and wisdom, which depends wholly on Yahweh, is a more glorious throne for Yahweh than the cherubim and the ark.

O. Eissfeldt has argued (*KS* 3, pp. 119f.; pp. 421f.) that יושב הכרובים was an epithet acquired by Yahweh in connection with the union of the ark and the cherubim throne, which took place at the Shiloh temple, and that Solomon reproduced the conjunction of ark and throne with modifications in the Jerusalem temple (cf. W. McKane, *TGUOS* 21, 1967, p. 74). M. Haran (*IEJ*, 9, 1959, pp. 30–38, 89–94) maintains that the cover of the ark (כפרת) is also part of Yahweh's throne and that the ark itself was his footstool (cf. T. Mettinger, *Religious Symbols and Their Functions*, 1978, p. 21). The Deuteronomic interpretation of the ark as the container of the tablets of the law had the effect of obscuring the older understanding of it, but here we have a text which is still in touch with the older ideology. It is doubtful, however, whether such an argument can establish the earliness of vv. 14–18 or even of v. 16, all the more so since the title which is given to the ark (ארון ברית יהוה) is the Deuteronomic one and the ברית element in it derives from the view that it is a container of the law (so M. Noth, *Überlieferungsgeschichtliche Studien*, 1957, p. 101; cf. W. McKane, *TGUOS*, 1967, p. 73).

Verse 17 continues with the thought that Jerusalem is to be the spiritual guide and mentor of the Gentile world and these are ideas which are found in Isa 2.1–4 (Mic 4.1–3). לשם יהוה

לירושלם has the appearance of secondary epexegesis of אליה; it is not represented by Sept. and the Greek translator apparently read a Hebrew text from which it was absent (cf. Janzen, p. 97). It should be deleted. The emendation of כל הגוים to מכל הגוים (cf. Rudolph) would make the verse refer to the Jews of the dispersion coming up to Jerusalem as pilgrims for the festivals of the temple. The phrase שררות לבם הרע is used elsewhere in the book of Jeremiah of Jews and not Gentiles and the emendation would make שררות לבם הרע conform to its standard use.

Israel and Judah are represented (v. 18) as returning together from the places of their exile in order to reoccupy the areas of the promised land allocated (הנחלתי) by Yahweh to the several tribes (so Rudolph). Both Sept. (τοὺς πατέρας αὐτῶν) and Pesh. (l'bhyhwn) indicate אבותיהם (MT אבותיכם) and this is a necessary adjustment, although it is unlikely that Sept. and Pesh. read a text other than MT. This may be another example of the dependence of Pesh. on Sept. Whether or not the preceding verses refer to a return from exile, whether they allude to Judah or the ten tribes, it is certain that they do not depict a joint return from exile of Israel and Judah in the manner of v. 18, so that the final verse introduces an entirely new conception.

If it is thought that vv. 12–13 are correctly understood as an address to the inhabitants of the former northern kingdom, it is understandable that the same constituency should be assumed for vv. 14ff. and this view has been widely held (Cornill, Peake, Volz, Weiser). On the other hand, other logics can operate (cf. Duhm and Rudolph). The difficulty in the assumption that vv. 14ff. are addressed to northern tribes is not removed by the deletion of the reference to Zion (Volz), because, apart from this particular item, there is a strong impression that the passage is focused on Jerusalem. Those who hold that the passage is not about exile, or that it goes on to consider what is to happen after a return (Duhm), are aiming to meet this objection. The nub of Cazelles' exegesis (op. cit., pp. 149–158) is that in vv. 14–17 Jeremiah, in the reign of Josiah, is addressing those who live in northern Palestine and is inviting them to return to their religious allegiance, to the Davidic dynasty and to the ark.

Rudolph holds that vv. 14–17aα (up to כסא יהוה) are to be attributed to the prophet Jeremiah and, in that case, he is already looking beyond the exile of Judah, which has not yet taken place, and is predicting that, after it has been endured, there will be a return of Jews to Zion. אחד מעיר ושנים ממשפחה is indicative of the partial and selective character of that return and this modest expectation is for Rudolph a mark of earliness, since he contrasts it with the grander, eschatological portrayals of restoration which came later. One of the factors which influences Rudolph's judgement has already been noticed (above, p. 75). Another is his conviction that the thought of the nations streaming to Jerusalem for enlightenment, whether or not it was born before the exile, was not entertained by the prophet Jeremiah (hence the deletion at v. 17). Nor does the emendation of כל הגוים to מכל הגוים entirely satisfy him, because he holds that Jeremiah would not have regarded the undertaking of pilgrimages to festivals in Jerusalem by Jews of the dispersion as evidence of a change of heart.

Thiel concludes that vv. 14–17 are post-deuteronomistic and provides a long list of considerations to support his view (pp. 91f.). Some of these depend on a distinction between the linguistic habits of his postulated deuteronomistic editor (D) and the vocabulary of vv. 14–17. The point which he raises about שררות לבם הרע has already been dealt with, and all that need be said is that its use in relation to Gentiles is taken by him as evidence of a development later than the normal usage of the phrase in the prose of the book of Jeremiah. He supposes that the 'pilgrimage tradition' presupposes the exile and that it arises from the transformation of an earlier tradition about an attack by the nations on Jerusalem. This should be compared with Weinfeld who associates the pilgrimage tradition or the streaming of the nations to Jerusalem with a change in the religious climate of Yahwism effected by the pre-exilic prophets (*ZAW*, 1976, p. 22).

We may begin our summing up with v. 18 of which Thiel has given a correct account. If v. 18 is a harmonizing device which presupposes the existence of vv. 6–17, there is an implication that whoever was responsible for it interpreted vv. 14–17 as a reference to Judah. In other words the attempt at harmonization is generated by the assumption that vv. 6–13 refer to the northern tribes and vv. 14–17 refer to Judah (so Thiel).

The evaluation of vv. 14–17 is full of uncertainty, but, on balance, it seems best to make the same kind of assessment of these verses as was made of vv. 6–11, although the demonstration that they are secondary exegesis generated by pre-existing parts of the chapter (vv. 1–5, 6–13, 22) cannot be made in so clear-cut a way. This is because the metaphor of marriage and divorce is not maintained (excepting בעלתי, v. 14) and because the saying about the ark, the contrast which it introduces, and the appearance of the pilgrimage tradition furnish vv. 14–17 with an intriguing and distinctive content. Moreover, the way in which the return from exile is envisaged has unusual and striking features. It is not a matter of exilic communities returning *en bloc*; it is a community which has been hand-picked by Yahweh which will be reconstituted in Jerusalem. The individuals who return to Zion are those who have made the decision to go back *qua* individuals and who have left their communities behind.

On the other hand, the pervasiveness of formations from שוב and the exploitation of their semantic polarity (שובה/משובה in vv. 6–13 and שובבים/שובו in vv. 14–17) is maintained. On the view which is being presented שובו בנים שובבים (v. 14) has been appropriated from v. 22 and the intention of the author of vv. 14–17 is to portray a return from Babylon to Jerusalem of exiled Judaeans. The thought that vv. 14–17 balance vv. 6–13 should perhaps not be stressed too much and another possibility is that vv. 14–17 is an exegetical elaboration which hangs only on v. 22. The reconstituted community will have small beginnings (אחד מעיר ושנים ממשפחה), but it will be built up into a nation (v. 16) which will no longer need the ark as a throne for Yahweh, because he will be enthroned in its common life and nations will stream to it for healing and enlightenment.

If vv. 14–17 depend to any degree on vv. 6–13, they are later than these verses which are, probably, exilic. Again, since v. 18 certainly presupposes vv. 6–13 and 14–17 it is later than these verses. Anything more than this that is said about vv. 14–17 is little better than a hunch, but the best indicator is, perhaps, אחד מעיר ושנים ממשפחה, and a possible interpretation of this is that it reflects the size and the experience of the post-exilic Jerusalem community: there had not been a general return of Jews from Babylon to Jerusalem. If the verses are post-exilic, they show up the post-exilic Jewish community in a very good light.

I SHALL HEAL YOUR APOSTASY (3.19–25)

[19]I thought, How gladly will I make you my sons!
I will give you a pleasant land,
the fairest possession in the world.
You will call me, Father, I thought,
and will never forsake me.
[20]As a woman deceives her husband for her lover's sake,[1]
you have deceived me, House of Israel.
    This is Yahweh's word.
[21]A sound is heard on the heights,
Israelites are wailing as they pray;
they have corrupted their way of life,
they have forgotten Yahweh, their God.
[22]Return, wayward sons,
I will heal your apostasy.
We are coming to you,
for you are Yahweh, our God.

[1] See below, pp. 79f.

[23]The hills are a fraud
and the mountains a rabble;[2]
in Yahweh, our God,
lies Israel's safety.
[24]From our youth Shame has consumed
what our fathers worked hard for:
their sheep and cattle,
their sons and daughters.
[25]Let us lie down in our shame
and let our disgrace cover us;
we have sinned against Yahweh, our God,
both we and our fathers,
from our youth up till now;
we have not obeyed Yahweh, our God.

The reading εἰς ἔθνη (Sept.[B]; v. 19) has, perhaps, been influenced by the subsequent occurrence of גוים in v. 19 (Ziegler, *Beiträge*, p. 38). καὶ δώσω σοι γῆν ἐκλεκτὴν κληρονομίαν θεοῦ παντοκράτορος ἐθνῶν appears to indicate that צבי has been rendered by θεοῦ and צבאות by παντοκράτορος, 'I shall give you a choice land, the inheritance of the Almighty God of the nations'. Another possibility is that θεοῦ and παντοκράτορος are both derived from צבאות (cf. Sept. 38.36=MT 31.35, where κύριος παντοκράτωρ renders יהוה צבאות), and in that case צבי is untranslated (cf. Pesh. 'the army of the armies of the nations'). Vulg. follows MT closely, connects צבי with the sense 'splendour' and assumes that צבאות is to be derived from צבא, 'army' (The rendering of Symm., κληρουχιαν <θρησκειαν> των συρατιων των εθνων, is similar, see Ziegler). צבי צבאות is rendered חדות תשבחת by Targ. and צבאות is clearly not derived from צבא, 'army'; but חדות is not an accurate rendering of צבי and תשבחת does not demonstrate that צבאות has been identified as a plural of צבי.

Rashi comments correctly that what is indicated by ואנכי אמרתי is an intention or purpose rather than an overt declaration. He explains צבי צבאות גוים as 'desire of all the hosts of the nations' (similarly Kimchi; following Vulg. and Symm.). צבאות is to be explained as a plural of צבי and the construct relationship functions as a superlative (BDB, KB[2], GK 93x): 'beauty of beauties' = most beautiful.

The general elucidation of the verse is best achieved in terms of the representation of Deut 32.8–9, according to which עליון allotted to the nations of the world their respective territories (בהנחיל עליון גוים) and fixed their boundaries, making the number of nations coincide with the membership of his heavenly court (reading בני אלהים for MT בני ישראל with Sept. ἀγγέλων θεοῦ and a Qumran fragment. See, W. McKane, *On Language*,

---

[2]See below, pp. 81.

Culture and Religion, 1974, pp. 64f.). Within this framework we can interpret his resolve to make Israel his 'sons' and to give them the fairest land in the world. There is here as in vv. 12–13 an oscillation between the corporate entity and the individuals who make it up. The representation of the personified land as a female is normal (cf. Rudolph who would make the suffixes of אשיתך and לך masc.), but it does not bear particularly on the exegesis of the verse, and the masculine aspect of בנים is not significant in the way supposed by Duhm. The meaning is not, 'I shall treat you as males and so give you full legal entitlement'. It is rather, 'I shall give you a favoured position over against the other nations of the world.' Yahweh permits an insight into the hopes which he cherished. Israel will call him 'Father' and will never waver in her attachment to him. Yahweh is recalling his intentions, in order to draw attention to the frustration of his designs by the settled apostasy of Israel. The 'Israel' which stands before us in this passage (cf. vv. 20–21, 23) is a favoured community which, nevertheless, from the beginning of its association with Yahweh ('from our youth', vv. 24, 25) has been unfaithful and disloyal (v. 20).

The difficulty of אכן בגדה אשה (v. 20) is reflected in the versions. There is the possibility that Vulg. may be dependent on Sept. The latter may have read a Hebrew text which was different from MT or the translator may have decided that better sense could be had out of the Hebrew if *nun* were changed to *kaph* and the consonants divided as אך כבגד האשה מרעה (האשה = 'a wife' rendered by γυνή).

Sept. (εἰς τὸν συνόντα αὐτῇ), Pesh. (*bḥbrh*) and Targ. (כבעלה) appear to indicate ברעה, but these renderings arise from the consonants of MT through the assumption that the *mem* of מרעה is the preposition מן rather than the *mem* of a noun מרעה. But neither רעה nor מרעה can mean 'husband' (cf. Ehrlich, *Randglossen*, 4, p. 247) and the two possibilities which remain are 'But like a woman who is unfaithful to her lover' (NEB, similarly Bright) and 'But like a woman who deceives (her husband) on account of her lover' (Ehrlich, p. 247, Rudolph). Sept., Vulg. and Pesh. go with the first of these renderings, except that Sept. and Vulg. have understood בגד to mean 'despise' or 'contemn' (Sept. ἀθετεῖ; Vulg. *contemnar*). The right interpretation of this is almost certainly that Vulg. has followed Sept. and this reinforces the opinion that there is a similar dependence at the beginning of the verse (see above). 'Like a woman who breaks faith for the sake of her lover' gives a different sense to the verse. In the one case the lover who is deceived is Yahweh; in the other, Israel, who breaks faith with Yahweh, is likened to a woman who deceives her husband for the

sake of a lover with whom she has a clandestine affair. That רֵעַ is
'lover' rather than 'husband' (*pace* BDB) is shown by 3.1 (וְאַתְּ
זָנִית רֵעִים רַבִּים). The conclusion is that Ehrlich is to be followed
and that מֵרֵעָהּ should be translated 'for the sake of her lover'.
Israel has played Yahweh false, just as a woman plays her
husband false for the sake of a clandestine affair (reading אַךְ
כְּבֹגֵד הָאִשָּׁה for MT אָכֵן בָּגְדָה אִשָּׁה).

Both Duhm and Rudolph recognize that the שְׁפָיִם (v. 21) are
the hill-tops where the rites of Baal religion are consummated.
Rudolph supposes that there is an allusion in v. 21 to v. 2, where
the connection between the שְׁפָיִם and cultic prostitution is
explicitly made. Another verse which has to be drawn into the
discussion is 7.29, where lamentation on שְׁפָיִם is held to involve
the renunciation of Nazirite vows and where a clause introduced
by כִּי (cf. 3.21b) declares that 'Yahweh has rejected and
forsaken the generation on which his wrath is poured out'. This
parallel suggests that the wailing rites in 3.21 are marks of
apostasy, and not signs of penitence (the usual view). In that
case the כִּי clause is explanatory: Israelites have corrupted their
way of life and are no longer exercised by the demands which
Yahweh makes on them. Rudolph supposes that 3.21ff. describe
a prophetic vision or insight which penetrates to the sadness and
sorrow, to the deepest longings of those who take part in the
fertility rites (following Duhm). But the invitation issued by
Yahweh to his people and the promise of healing (vv. 22ff.) can
follow a description of their apostasy without reading into v. 21
die Sehnsucht nach etwas Besserem, nach dem wahren Gott
(Rudolph).

Kimchi explains the medical metaphor in v. 22: just as a
wound caused by a blow is healed by the medical care which it
receives, so is it with a wound of the soul; the remedy for sin is a
forgiveness which responds to repentance (cf. Targ.'s
interpretation, 'I shall forgive you when you repent', a rendering
of אַרְפֵּא מְשׁוּבֹתֵיכֶם (= אַרְפָּא), apparently taking מְשׁוּבֹתֵיכֶם in
the sense, 'your acts of repentance').

In vv. 22b–25 we have a confession from the lips of a
personified community, and, first of all in v. 22b, an expression of
penitence and of a will to return to Yahweh. ἰδού, according to
Ziegler (*Beiträge*, pp. 38f.) arises in Sept. because οἶδε is an
unusual form; δοῦλοι is then a corruption of ιδου + οιδε. Pesh. (*h'
ḥnn dylk*) probably arises from an inability to elucidate אָתָנוּ
which would more normally be written as אָתִינוּ (from אתה).
The Massoretes have pointed אָתָנוּ (אָתְנוּ) in a way that is
appropriate for a *lamedh aleph* verb. Vulg. has accurately
translated MT as *Ecce nos venimus ad te*.

There is an interesting difference between Sept.'s rendering of

שׁובבים in v. 22 (ἐπιστρέφοντες) and the rendering in v. 14 (ἀφεστηκότες): those addressed in v. 14 are 'apostate' and those in v. 22 'repenting'. The other versions attach a positive connotation to שׁובבים in both passages, although since Syriac *tyb'* can mean both 'apostate' and 'penitent', one cannot be certain about Pesh. It is likely, however that its intentions are the same as those of Vulg. (*revertentes*) and Targ. (דמתחסנין למתב). The positive sense attributed to שׁובבים can hardly be the right one; it is pejorative, indicative of fickleness and waywardness.

In v. 23 (23a is obscure) the community would seem to acknowledge the emptiness and futility of the noisy and crowded acts of Baal worship conducted on the hill-tops and to affirm that Israel's safety is in Yahweh alone. The rendering of v. 23a in Sept., Vulg. and Pesh. does not deal faithfully with מגבעות, and presupposes הָמוֹן (MT הָמוֹן). Kimchi glosses לשׁקר מגבעות as 'The safety for which we hoped from the hills is vain' and makes a point that הָמוֹן is not in a construct relationship (cf. Targ. whose paraphrase apparently presupposes that הָמוֹן הרים is a nominal sentence). Both Bright and NEB (Brockington, p. 199) redivide the consonants of לשׁקר מגבעות and read לשׁקרם גבעות: Bright supposes that the *mem* is an enclitic and NEB (which is to be followed) that it is the *mem* of a defectively written plural. The translation which has been offered by me assumes הָמוֹן, but הָמוֹן הרים, 'the din on the mountains' (cf. Bright, 'the hubbub on the heights') is also a possibility. The sense of v. 23a is, in any case, ill assured. In general, it continues the declaration of intent which began with v. 22b: Israel acknowledges the emptiness of the religious rites with which she has been so obsessed and admits that her only hope of safety and well being is in Yahweh.

Rudolph's suggestion that והבשׁת אכלה (v. 24) may represent a deliberate modification of והבעל אכלה labours from the disadvantage that the versions all indicate בשׁת (Targ., 'the shame of our sins') and, more particularly, from the circumstance that the reference to 'shame' recurs in v. 25. Nevertheless, both Rashi and Kimchi equate בשׁת with Baal worship or with idolatry and this is correct. מנעורינו in vv. 24 and 25 indicates that the corporate entity Israel is confessing to attitudes which have characterized her from the earliest period of her existence up to the present time (so Bright; *pace* Rudolph). The hard toil with which family and possessions were built up in generation after generation has been made of none effect by an incurable tendency to idolatry and apostasy (cf. Kimchi, 'We did evil as we saw it done by our fathers'). Thus even if v. 24b is a secondary gloss (Rudolph), it is not a misleading gloss, because it develops a sense which is already given by v. 24a.

It is not clear that the language of v. 25 constitutes an exhortation to repent. There is a suggestion of a sleep induced by the unbearable shame of being awake, a deliberate cultivation of amnesia, a desire for forgetfulness under a blanket of disgrace. It is as if Israel, having begun the journey back to Yahweh (v. 22b), is paralysed by shame and remorse and has no energy or decisive resolve to be reconciled to the One she has so greatly wronged. A different and more positive view of v. 25 generally appears and is represented by Duhm's interesting suggestion that the verse contains a reference to rituals of penitence and fasting, when the normal comforts of life are surrendered, when the ground becomes one's bed and remorse and penitence the bed-clothes (cf. David's behaviour when Bathsheba's child was ill, 2 Sam 12.15ff.).

There is some ambiguity or tension in vv. 19–25 and it should be recognized that this is a measure of the profundity of the prophet's vision of the future and of the inner tug of war which he has to endure. Formally, the verses are made up of speech of Yahweh (vv. 19–20, 22a), speech of the prophet (v. 21) and speech of the people (vv. 22b–25), but we have to resolve this into an inner, complex prophetic prognostication (so Rudolph). It is perhaps less a ringing affirmation of hope in Yahweh's mercy than an oscillation between hope and despair. At any rate it is clear that the differences and even polarity in Jeremiah's utterances are not to be accounted for by applying a time scale to them and attributing them to different stages of his ministry.

The thread on which the different parts of the chapter are strung is constituted by שוב and its derivatives. The legal model in v. 1 establishes that a divorced wife cannot 'come back' to her husband. Yahweh's will to forgive is not limited by the letter of a law and he waits for his wife, Israel, to 'come back' to him. Only when she refuses does he divorce her. Judah, having imitated her sister, Israel, pretends to 'come back' to Yahweh, Yahweh invites his people to 'come back' to him (v. 12) and vv. 14–18 open with a similar invitation which also appears in v. 22.

The view that vv. 19–25 are a continuation of vv. 1–5 was expressed by B. Stade in 1884 (ZAW 4, pp. 151–154), it has been repeated by many scholars (for example, Rudolph and Bright) and it is still being said (M. Weinfeld, ZAW 88, 1976, p. 21). It has been argued (above p. 72) that vv. 12–13 resume vv. 1–5 and the task remains to show why the connection of vv. 19–25 with vv. 1–5 is not so impressive as has been widely maintained. It is true that the metaphor of adultery is implied in v. 20 and this is the most important piece of evidence for those

who are concerned to establish the continuity of vv. 19–25 with
vv. 1–5. It is not certain, however, that it is precisely a
marriage-divorce analogy which is functioning in v. 20. It is a
more general type of simile which compares Israel's
unfaithfulness to Yahweh with the deceit practised by a married
woman who is having a clandestine love affair. However, even if
this evidence were allowed its full weight, it has to be set against
the circumstance that the passage (vv. 19–25) opens with a
figure which is incompatible with the marriage-divorce model in
vv. 1–5. To jump from husband-wife to father-sons is a transition
so harsh that it makes the hypothesis of an original, intrinsic
connection between vv. 1–5 and vv.19–25 very difficult to believe.

The view of chapter 3 which has been presented is that
vv. 1–5, 12–13 and 19–25 are words of Jeremiah, that there is an
intrinsic connection between vv. 1–5 and 12–13, but that
vv. 19–25 constitute an independent unit. All of these are
addressed to Judah in so far as Judah is the Israel of the present
with whom the prophet is concerned. Since, however, he sees the
present as arising out of the past he has in his view an Israel
which transcends these limitations and which is coextensive with
the old totality. Verses 6–11 and 14–17 are secondary, exegetical
material which is generated by these pre-existing texts, although
this demonstration can be carried out more convincingly for
vv. 6–11 than for vv. 14–17: vv. 6–11 are triggered by vv. 1–5
and vv. 12–13 and vv. 14–17 have a residual trace of the
marriage-divorce metaphor (בְּעַלְתִּי בָכֶם, v. 14); שׁוּבוּ בָנִים
שׁוֹבָבִים (v. 14) may have been appropriated from v. 22.
Otherwise the content of vv. 14–17 is distinctive and the verses
are set apart from the remainder of the chapter. Verses 6–11
refer to the northern tribes and vv. 14–17 to Judah. Verse 18 is
later than vv. 6–11 and 14–17 and is an effort at harmonization
which embraces both Israel (the northern tribes) and Judah (cf.
W. McKane, *SVT* 32, 1980, pp. 229–233).

CHAPTER IV

REPENT OR THE FIRE OF JUDGEMENT WILL CONSUME YOU
(4.1–4)

¹If you repent, O Israel,
you may return to me. This is Yahweh's word.
If you put away your idols
and worship me alone without wavering;
²if when you say, As Yahweh lives,
your oath is truthful, just and honest,
the name 'Israel' will signify blessing
and symbolize renown for the nations.
³This is the word of Yahweh to the men of Judah and Jerusalem.
Plough for a good tilth,
do not sow seed among thorns.
⁴Be circumcised to Yahweh's service,
remove the foreskins of your hearts,
men of Judah and inhabitants of Jerusalem;
else my anger will burst into flames
and no one will extinguish the blaze.
This is how I will punish your evil-doing.

RETURN IF YOU WILL REPENT (4.1–2)

In vv. 1–2 Sept. is far removed from MT and the matters which
are raised by Ziegler (*Beiträge*, p. 90) and Janzen (p. 30) do not
indicate the extent of the problem. The 3rd person reference in
ἐκ στόματος αὐτοῦ cannot be dissociated from the circumstance
that all the verbs in vv. 1–2 are rendered in the 3rd person. The
difficulty which has produced this type of translation in Sept. is
caused by the two occurrences of וב in v. 2; in order to
accommodate them, the verbs in v. 1 and 2a are taken as 3rd
fem. sing. instead of 2nd masc. sing., and שקוציך is rendered as if
it were שקוציו (τὰ βδελύγματα αὐτοῦ). In the case of תשוב
(ἐπιστραφῇ; ἐπιστραφήσεται), תסיר (περιέλῃ) and תנוד
(εὐλαβηθῇ) grammatical form allows this, but ונשבעת cannot
possibly be regarded as 3rd person and is illegitimately rendered
as ὁμόσῃ. The intention of the translator is to identify the וב of
v. 2 with Israel and this is why he has used masc. suffixes with
βδελύγματα and στόματος. This, however, creates a further
confusion of 3rd person sing. masc. and 3rd person sing. fem.:
the first 4 verbs in v. 1 are explicable only as fem. (if they are 3rd
person) and so he ends up with 'Israel' oscillating between fem.
and masc. gender. The full rendering of ובו יתהללו (καὶ ἐν αὐτῷ
αἰνέσουσι τῷ θεῷ ἐν Ιερουσαλημ) confirms that the two
occurrences of וב refer to Israel. Since ἐκ στόματος αὐτοῦ cannot

be disengaged from the overall tendency of Sept.'s rendering of the Hebrew, it probably derives from the same kind of shift to 3rd person as is evidenced by τὰ βδελύγματα αὐτοῦ. In that case we have to suppose that מפני has been read as מפיו, perhaps, under the influence of Zech 9.7 and that what we have in Sept. is a double representation of מפני.

The paraphrase of Targ. ('for as long as your decree has not been sealed') may be interpreted generally as a reference to a final sealing of doom after which no possibility of repentance exists, or the decree (גזירתך) may connect with ספר כריתתיה (3.8) and this would be an indication that the translator is still thinking in terms of the legal model: for as long as Israel's divorce from Yahweh is not final and irrevocable, the way is open for her to return to him.

There are differences of opinion about the syntax of vv. 1–2. The versions all indicate that v. 1a is to be constructed as protasis and apodosis, but they disagree as to whether v. 1b consists of protasis and apodosis (Vulg. and Pesh.) or of two protases (Sept. and Targ., following MT). The syntax of Vulg. and Pesh. arises from the circumstance that their renderings represent לא תנוד (MT ולא תנוד), and v. 2 is then an elaboration of the apodosis לא תנוד, with ונשבעת tending to have the force of an imperative (Vulg. *Et iurabis*; Pesh. *wt'm'*). Rudolph, who deletes the *waw* of ולא תנוד, follows Vulg. and Pesh., except that he takes ונשבעת as the begining of another protasis-apodosis construction (*und schwörst du ... so werden Völker*). Weiser, on the other hand, follows MT and constructs vv. 1b–2 as a series of three protases culminating in an apodosis. A still different syntax is found in NEB which represents a series of five protases followed by a final apodosis.

מפני ולא תנוד is to be regarded as a converse of ואם תסיר שקוציך, a second protasis which expresses positively (remain constant to Yahweh) what has already been formulated negatively (put away idols; abstain from idolatry). Hence both these stichs have to be considered in connection with such a demand as לא יהוה לך אלהים אחרים על פני (Exod 20.3), where על פני may have a cultic reference: Yahweh's cult is exclusive and other gods may not participate in it (see M. Noth, *Exodus, in loc.*). 'To seek Yahweh's face' (Ps 24.6; 27.8) is to worship him at his sanctuary.

It has been noticed that בו is referred by Sept. to 'Israel' (above, p. 84) and this is explicitly done by Targ. (בישראל וביה). Vulg. renders והתברכו as active and transitive (*Et benedicent eum gentes, ipsumque laudabunt*) and *eum* and *ipsum* must be identified with Yahweh: nations will bless and praise Yahweh. Rashi follows Targ. and identifies the 3rd person suffixes with

Israel, but Kimchi's preferred interpretation is that the contrast is between Yahweh and אלילים: the nations will praise Yahweh and not idols. Calvin remarked 'Some refer this (ובו ... בו) to the Israelites, but not correctly', and the view that the suffixes refer to Yahweh is found in Venema and Lowth, and in a recent commentary by Freehof, Duhm states that this part of v. 2 has been lifted out of Gen 22.18 or 26.4 without any attempt having been made to change בו into בך . But the passages do not support this contention, for בזרעך is not the same as בו and is as readily convertible into בך as it is into בו. The only Genesis passage which supports the idea that an unadjusted 3rd person sing. suffix appears in v. 2 is Gen 18.18, where ונברכו בו is used in connection with Abraham, but the verb is Niphal and not Hithpael.

The emendation which Rudolph adopts restores grammatical congruence (בך ... ובך), but the sense of v. 2b is still a matter of some difficulty—the same difficulty as is encountered in the Genesis passages. Is it a reference to blessings which will be mediated to the world through Israel or is it that other nations will regard Israel as a paradigm of blessedness? The second is almost certainly correct (so Duhm and Rudolph) and the point of v. 2 then is that if Israel satisfies the conditions which are laid down in the protases, her prosperity will be proverbial. If Israelites abstain from idolatry, are constant in their allegiance to Yahweh and employ the oath 'As Yahweh lives' with complete integrity, such will be their well-being that nations will use the formulae, 'May you be blessed like Israel' or 'May you be renowned like Israel'.

An influential factor in Duhm's thinking is his interpretation of the oath in v. 2a. He notes the expression ובשמו תשבע in Deut 6.13 and 10.20 and he supposes that the oath in v. 2a is associated with confessional affirmation: it is a promise and pledge to cleave to Yahweh and to subscribe to the demands of the Deuteronomic law. Duhm follows Vulg. and Pesh. in v. 1b (see above, p. 85), and so מפני לא תנוד is an apodosis and a reference to security from exile. It could be urged (*pace* Duhm) that v. 2a does not hinge on the taking of an oath or the making of a confession. It hinges rather on complete truthfulness and the absence of deceit and hypocrisy. Yahweh's name is not to be used as a cloak for evil; when the solemn words of the oath, 'As Yahweh lives' are invoked, special vigilance has to be exercised in order to maintain complete probity. The third protasis (v. 2) has to be considered in conjunction with the two which precede it and might be regarded as offering an illustration (but no more than an illustration) of what is intended by the demand for constancy in the second protasis. Rudolph supposes that it is a question of using Yahweh's name but giving allegiance to Baal and this would also have the effect of linking the third protasis to the two which precede it. The demand would then be that the solemn taking of Yahweh's name should not be divorced as it had been in the past from a total allegiance to him. But the vocabulary suggests that the demand is rather for a moral integrity which matches high religious language.

Verses 1–2 should be separated from vv. 3–4 to which they are linked in MT by an editorial כי. Their independence of vv. 1–2 is suggested not principally by כה אמר יהוה, with which they are introduced, but by the circumstance that the sayings which are strung on the thread of שוב and its derivatives come to an end at v. 2 (3.1–4.2). Although vv. 3–4 have the same theme as vv. 1–2, new metaphors are employed to develop it (agreeing with Thiel, p. 93).

SUPERFICIAL CHANGE IS NOT ENOUGH (4.3–4)

The connection between the two figures of speech, ploughing up a good tilth (v. 3) and circumcising the heart (v. 4) is that both set out a demand for deep as opposed to superficial repentance. Sept. Θεώσατε ἑαυτοῖς νεώματα (Vulg. *Novate vobis novale*) gives the sense 'fallow ground' for ניר and this is found in the dictionaries (BDB, KB²) and NEB, 'Break up your fallow ground'. The interpretation of Targ. moves away from the thought of a deep repentance to that of producing fruits of repentance, 'Perform good deeds and do not seek salvation through sins'. Kimchi explains ניר as the ploughing of the land before sowing: the thorns and other bad weeds are removed by the ploughing (=Rashi) and the field is then fit for sowing. The interpretation of the משל is that the people should amend their hearts so as to discern Yahweh's words and receive them with a right disposition. This is like ploughing the soil to make it ready for the seed, whereas pretending to repent (he cites 3.10) is like sowing on thorns to no effect.

The view that Hos 10.12f. is an exact parallel (cf. Rudolph, Bright, Thiel, p. 96) is not well founded, since the intention of the imagery in that passage is different. If the seed is צדקה, the crop will be חסד; if it is רשע, the crop will be עולה. In Jer 4.3, on the other hand, there is no antithesis of good and bad seed, but only of well-prepared and ill-prepared soil: the seed which is sown on thorns produces nothing, but the fault is not in the seed. Hence Rashi and Kimchi are right in their interpretation which they elaborate further by connecting the killing of the weeds with the ploughing process. The imagery is indicative of depth of

repentance and a cleansing of the heart, and these are conditions
of the renewal of a fruitful relationship with Yahweh. Pesh.
renders נירו לכם ניר as *'nhrw lkwn šrg'*, 'Light for yourselves
lamps'. It is clear that נירו and ניר have been associated with נור
(נר, 'lamp'), but the sense which is intended is not so obvious.

Circumcision is the figure which indicates depth of repentance
in v. 4. Like v. 3 this has the form of word of Yahweh and one
would expect לי (so Rudolph; cf. Thiel, p. 96 n. 59) rather than
ליהוה. It is unclear whether v. 4 is spoken by Yahweh, or
Jeremiah, for his own part. Sept. clearly presupposes (τῷ θεῷ
ὑμῶν and ὁ θυμὸς αὐτοῦ) that Jeremiah is the speaker. Vulg.
(*Domino* and *indignatio mea*) and Pesh. (*lmry'* and *ḥmty*) retain
the ambiguity of MT, as also does the paraphrase of Targ. The
latter has interpreted the metaphor of circumcision, whereas
Sept.[B] partially retains it (περιτμήθητε τῷ θεῷ ὑμῶν) and
partially interprets it (rendering והסרו ערלות לבבכם by καὶ
περιτέμεσθε τὴν σκληροκαρδίαν ὑμῶν). We have, however, to
reckon with inner-Septuagintal differences and the text which
Ziegler prefers (Sept.[S*A]; *Beiträge*, p. 39) matches MT καὶ
περιέλεσθε τὴν ἀκροβυστίαν τῆς καρδίας ὑμῶν).

המלו ליהוה is explicated by והסירו ערלות לבבכם: המלו ליהוה is
a demand for a dedication to Yahweh which is inward and
profound and is not exhausted by an external rite. The carrying
out of the rite of circumcision is one thing; the removal of the
foreskin of the heart is another matter. This is not necessarily a
denigration of the rite of circumcision; it may be seen rather as
an affirmation about its range and profundity. The requirement
of such a thoroughgoing inward amendment is laid on Judah,
and this commitment to deep, inward change is part of the
significance of circumcision. To the requirement there is added a
threat that the smouldering anger of Yahweh may at any time
burst into flames and burn until destruction is complete.
Yahweh's people should not suppose that they will be given time
to repent at leisure; let them repent now, before Yahweh reacts
to their wrongdoing with a fire of judgement which no man can
extinguish.

Both Duhm and Thiel (pp. 95–97) agree that לאיש יהודה
ולירושלם (v. 3) and איש יהודה וישבי ירושלם (v. 4) are to be
denied to the prophet Jeremiah, but for different reasons: Duhm,
because he holds that Jeremiah addresses 'Israel' and not the
inhabitants of Judah and Jerusalem; Thiel, because he considers
that איש יהודה וישבי ירושלם (v. 4) is Deuteronomistic
vocabulary. Duhm supposes that vv. 3–4* are the conclusion of a
collection of poems (p. xiii) and that the appearance of כה אמר
יהוה may represent an attempt to make the conclusion
impressive. Thiel, as already remarked (p. 87), detaches vv. 3–4

from vv. 1–2 and treats them as an independent unit. On the question whether there is anything deriving from the prophet Jeremiah in v. 3 the difference between the two scholars is less marked, but Thiel holds more firmly than Duhm that there is a Jeremianic core (נירו לכם ניר ואל תזרעו אל קוצים). Duhm, with his metrical assumptions, considers that two stichs are wanting and concludes: *Doch est es möglich dass v. 3 dem Jer nicht angehört*. The circumstance that נירו לכם ניר appears in Hos 10.12 does not influence either scholar greatly: Duhm suggests that נירו לכם ניר may be a popular proverb, and in that case we are not to suppose that a relationship of direct dependence obtains between the two passages. Duhm, on the other hand, attributes v. 4, for the most part, to Jeremiah: only איש יהודה and וישבי ירושלם and מפני רע מעלליכם are ascribed to the *Ergänzer*. Jeremiah has used Deut 10.16 or 30.6.

D (so Thiel) has modified Deut 10.16 (ומלתם את ערלת לבבכם) by inserting ליהוה והסרו and has quarried פן תצא כאש חמתי ובערה ואין מכבה from Jer 21.12, where it is original. מפני רע מעלליכם, which appears at 21.12, is also the work of D. It is not represented by Sept. at 21.12 and has been attracted to that verse through a secondary harmonization with 4.4. Hence there is nothing Jeremianic in 4.4 (*pace* Duhm, Rudolph), except the stichs which have been appropriated by D from 21.12.

All that can be said is that the reasons advanced for the deletion of both indications of who is addressed (Duhm and Thiel) or one of them (v. 4, Rudolph, involving a dubious metrical argument) are not firm enough and that MT should be retained. Again, there are not sufficient grounds for denying נירו לכם ניר ואל תזרעו אל קוצים (v. 3) to Jeremiah. If the verse is thought to be dependent on Hos 10.16, this does not constitute a reason; if both occurrences are independent appropriations of a proverb, that is not a reason either. Further, if it is assumed that המלו ליהנה . . . לבבכם (v. 4) is dependent on Deut 10.16, this is not a reliable indication that Jeremiah is not the author: Duhm makes this assumption and yet ascribes the words to Jeremiah. If פן תצא כאש חמתי ובערה ואין מכבה (21.12) is to be attributed to Jeremiah, there can be no certainty about the argument that the same words in v. 4 are to be denied to him.

Finally, the argument about the secondary character of מפני רע מעלליכם in 4.4 cannot be pressed to an assured conclusion (Thiel, p. 95). It is admitted that רע מעלליכם or the like occurs in 'old texts' (Isa 1.16; Hos 9.15; Ps 28.4), and the attempt by Thiel to distinguish within the books of Jeremiah between a Deuteronomistic (מפני רע) and a Jeremianic usage (מן רע) is not impressive. Given the distribution of use, and the fact that מפני רע מעלליכם or the like occurs in both poetry and prose in the book of Jeremiah, the vocabulary can hardly be described as 'Deuteronomistic'. Rather the answer should be sought within the book of Jeremiah itself, and the prose uses should be regarded as having been quarried from the poetry. Hence the best conclusion is that MT should be retained in vv. 3–4. Whether מפני רע מעלליכם (Q) is original in 21.12 is another matter whose consideration may be postponed. The difference in this case is that there is textual evidence to support deletion.

PREPARE FOR INVASION (4.5–9)

⁵Make this announcement in Judah,
proclaim it in Jerusalem;
sound¹ the trumpet throughout the land,
give this message the fullest publicity:
⁶Go to the fortified towns and assemble there,
put up a signal—To Zion!
Make for safety without delay,
for I am bringing disaster from the north,
a great disaster which will crush you.
⁷A lion has come out of its lair,
a destroyer of nations is on the move;
he has come out of his camp
to lay waste your land;
your towns will be destroyed² and deserted.
⁸Clothe yourselves then in sackcloth,
mourn and wail,
for there has been no abating
of the heat of Yahweh's anger.
⁹On that day—This is Yahweh's word—
kings and statesmen will lose their nerve,
priests will be at a loss
and prophets reduced to silence.

The form of vv. 5–8 is perplexing in two respects: it is not entirely clear who the speaker is, and the two occurrences of ואמרו in v. 5 create uncertainty about where the message which is to be proclaimed begins. Surgery less drastic than that of Duhm takes away the first ואמרו and emends the second to מהרו (Rudolph; following Volz), giving a different structure to vv. 5–8. The opening words of v. 5 are capable of only one explanation, that the prophet is being addressed by Yahweh, and, with ואמרו deleted, these instructions directed to the prophet may be supposed to run as far as קראו מלאו. The message itself, introduced by ואמרו, begins with האספו (or, with Rudolph's emendation, it begins with מהרו). Although MT has the support of the versions, the first ואמרו should be deleted and

¹ Deleting ואמרו (see below, pp. 90f.).
² Reading תנצינה (see below, p. 92).

the view of vv. 5–8, which has just been set out, should be adopted. In that case Yahweh is the speaker throughout; in v. 5 he requires the prophet to make every effort to secure the maximum publicity for the message, and the message itself opens with האספו. The only difficulty in the way of this elucidation is the circumstance that Yahweh refers to himself in the 3rd person in v. 8b (Duhm), but we cannot be certain that a reference to Yahweh in the 3rd person in a speech made by Yahweh is to be ruled out as inadmissible.

On תקעו (Q; K ותקעו) Rashi remarks that the trumpet is used to sound a retreat and that a warning to the inhabitants of the land is intended (similarly Kimchi). The trumpet in this context is, perhaps, the instrument of the herald or public crier. If this is so, v. 5b is an elaboration of v. 5a and קראו מלאו is a further demand that maximum publicity should be given to the message. This is how it was understood by the versions (Sept. κεκράξατε μέγα; Vulg. *clamate fortiter*; Pesh. *grw bql' rm'*; Targ. אכלו אסגו). The fact that מלא apparently means 'company' in Isa 31.4 (מלא רעים; NEB, 'muster of shepherds') or that התמלא means 'band together' (Job 16.10) does not necessarily commend the translation 'Sound the muster' (NEB) for קראו מלאו (cf. D. W. Thomas, *JJS*, 1952, pp. 47ff. who argues that מלא is military terminology, 'to call up', 'to mobilize', and that מלאו (מלוא) means 'Declare mobilization'). Rather קראו מלאו is a hendiadys, 'Give (sc. the message) the fullest publicity'. The rendering 'Declare mobilization' makes קראו מלאו part of the message which would then begin with תקעו שופר and these words would also have a martial connotation: they would signify a trumpet-call to arms. If this interpretation were followed, the second occurrence of ואמרו rather than the first would have to be deleted.

The announcement is to the effect that the populace should make for the fortified cities and that organized resistance to the impending attack should be concentrated there. There is no time to waste and nothing less than swift obedience to the call will suffice (v. 6). It is not a moment for inaction (העיזו אל תעמדו), for danger is in the air and deliberation or debate makes no sense. Vulg. (*levate signum in Sion*) and Targ. (זקופו אתא על ציון) understand MT שאו נס ציונה as 'Raise a signal on Zion' (so Kimchi). Sept. (ἀναλαβόντες φεύγετε εἰς Σιων) has apparently read נס as נַס = נֻסוּ, 'Get up and flee to Zion'. According to NEB ('Raise the signal—To Zion!') the Hebrew refers not to the place where the signal is to be hoisted (so Duhm, Rudolph), but to the content of the signal which is to be sent: 'Send this signal, "Make for Zion" '. Rashi's comment on ציונה, 'to flee to Zion', is in general accord with NEB's interpretation. If this interpretation is correct, we have to suppose that שאו נס is a variant of שאו משאת (6.1) which is generally explained as a smoke signal or beacon (NEB, 'Fire the beacon'). שאו נס could then mean 'Send this signal', but if נס is a flag or standard, the sense of שאו נס must be 'Hoist a flag (on the flag pole)'. The best conclusion, in all the circumstances is, perhaps, that שאו נס and שאו משאת are synonymous expressions and that NEB's view of שאו נס ציונה should be adopted (see further on 6.1). We then have a signal 'Make for Zion and find safety there' which is parallel to the earlier instruction, 'Proceed to the fortified towns and assemble there': Zion gets a special mention as the principal place of assembly and centre of resistance (so Duhm).

Verse 6b explains why action is a matter of such great urgency, but it gives a fatalistic twist to the message and this tone is maintained to the end of v. 8. It is not the conclusion that vv. 5c and 6a would have led us to expect: from the thought of organizing effective resistance to the invasion in Jerusalem and the other fortified towns we pass to a defeatist description of inevitable disaster and doom. Kimchi was aware of this element of discord in the passage. With v. 6b there is a transition from military advice to threat—the threat of a crushing disaster inflicted by an invading army from the north, but which is ultimately caused by Yahweh himself (אנכי מביא).

The *waw* of ומשחית (v. 7) has the same formal function as *waw* in Prov 26.3, 7, 9, 14, 20, 21 (*Proverbs*, p. 594)—it is an indication of a simile. Just as a lion rouses itself from its lair in order to wreak havoc among its prey, so this king (Pesh., Targ.; equated with Nebuchadrezzar by Rashi and Kimchi) has emerged from his base camp, and his destination is Judah. The consequences of his depredations will be wholesale destruction, derelict and abandoned towns. If MT נצתה (9.11; 46.19) is derived from נצה, the form is Niphal (cf. K נצתה in 2.15), and in that case תצינה should be emended to תִּנָּצֶינָה in 4.7 (so Ehrlich, p. 248).

In v. 8 חרון is not represented by Sept. and Janzen (p. 36) supposes that it is secondary in MT. Doom is certain and disaster unavoidable, because the heat of Yahweh's anger has not abated and will not now abate. Hence a message which began with a demand to organize effective resistance ends with the anticipation of defeat. The mourning rites which should follow the defeat (death) of Judah can begin now: the sackcloth should be worn and the public lamentations commence before the battle has been joined, so certain is the outcome. Sept. (ἀφ' ὑμῶν) and Pesh. (*mnkwn*) point to מכם (Ziegler has ἀφ' ἡμῶν in his text, following Sept.⁵*). מכם dissociates the prophet from his community, whereas ממנו stresses his solidarity and identification with it. The agreement between Sept. and Pesh. should be explained as a dependence of Pesh. on Sept.

Duhm disengaged vv. 9–11a from his 'Scythian songs': the first consisted of vv. 5–8* and the second began at v. 11b. Duhm is giving expression to a genuine difficulty, but it is arguable (cf. Rudolph) that ביום ההוא (v. 9) does not necessarily imply a projection into a distant future (as Duhm supposes) and that it refers here rather to the historical moment which the prophet has just been describing. It is unlikely that there is an original, intrinsic connection between vv. 5–8 and v. 9, but there is a community of theme, and והיה ביום ההוא is, perhaps, a stitching device whose intention is to associate v. 9bc with the time of disaster to which vv. 6b–8 refer. There is also a question of whether vv. 6b–8 contain a description of events which are actually taking place, or whether the prophet's premonition of imminent disaster is so intense that he represents these events as already taking place. On the day when disaster strikes, all the leaders of the community will suffer a loss of nerve. The thought of a crumbling of morale and a failure of nerve is well indicated by Targ., 'The nerve (lit., "heart") of the king and his statesmen will be broken'. The king, according to Kimchi, is Zedekiah and the priests are those who officiate at the high places and who will be demoralized because their worship will be seen to be null and void. The prophets are false prophets (so also Targ.) who will be at a loss when their assurance of שלום to the people is seen to be unfounded. The disintegration of political leadership will be matched by the phrenetic and disorganized response of the religious leaders (cf. Sept. καὶ ἐκστήσονται for ונשמו).

YOU ARE A DECEIVER, YAHWEH! (4.10)

[10]I said, You cannot deny, Lord Yahweh, that you have deceived the people of Jerusalem with your words, You will be safe and prosperous, for the sword is pointed at their throats[1]

The prose form (so NEB, *pace* Rudolph) is an indication of the independence of v. 10 but its location at this point in chapter 4 is understandable. The cruelty of the deception which has been practised on Judah and Jerusalem becomes apparent when they are on the point of being overwhelmed by an invading army and it is this onset of disaster which is described in vv. 5–9 and in the part of the chapter which follows v. 10. The observation that the

[1]Or, 'our throats' (NEB). Hebrew, עד הנפש; the 3rd person possessive adjective has been supplied in agreement with Sept. (ἕως τῆς ψυχῆς αὐτῶν).

rightness of ואמרו in v. 10 precludes the possibility that Jeremiah is the speaker in vv. 11–12 (Rudolph) would be relevant only if vv. 11f were a continuation of v. 10. The merit of the suggestion that ואמר should be emended to ואמרו has therefore only to be considered for v. 10 itself, and the difficulty is then that of reconciling ואמר with the characterization of the שלום prophets as men who speak lies, whose words derive from their own invention and not from Yahweh (cf. 23.16f., 25). Too much labour should not be expended in establishing a theological consistency for Jeremiah (cf. Rudolph, p. 30, n. 1), nor is it the case that there is a serious issue of consistency. Jeremiah is not necessarily saying that he believes that these prophets are commissioned by Yahweh to proclaim שלום, but he is attributing responsibility to Yahweh in so far as they have been permitted to appear before the people and to speak with the full weight of Yahweh's authority (cf. Kimchi). All the versions except Sept.^A (καὶ εἶπαν = ואמרו) support ואמר. Rudolph (following Cornill) would also emend לעם חזה ולירושלם to לנו, assuming that the former is derived from v. 11. It is then the people who speak in v. 10 and who charge Yahweh with misrepresentation: he has deceived them through the words of the שלום prophets.

The words שלום יחיה לכם appear in 23.17 and are attributed to prophets who wrongfully claim Yahweh's authority for their words and who are not to be listened to. In 6.14 there is a reference to prophets and priests who say שלום שלום when there is no שלום and who are likened to medical quacks. Here and also at 8.11 and 15 שלום is the 'wholeness' or 'health' or safety of the community which cannot be achieved by the mere proclamation of שולם (cf. 12.12; 14.13).

According to 14.13 the prophets assert that שלום will be enjoyed במקום חזה, and the terminology suggests that the assurance of שלום has a special connection with the city of Jerusalem and its temple. The meaning of ירושלם is obscure (cf. BDB and KB³). It has been explained as ירוש שלם, 'possession of peace', or ירו שלם, 'foundation of peace' (or, 'foundation of (the god) Shalem'). ירו = 'foundation' is based on the use of ירה in Gen 31.51 (המצבה אשר יריתי) and Job 38.6 (מי ירה אבן פנתה). The probability that the second element of ירושלם is to be associated with שלום is increased by the evidence from certain psalms, where juxtapositions of ירושלם and שלום suggest that there is a deliberate play on the שלם element of Jerusalem (29.10f.; 85.9; 72.7; 37.11; 122.6; 147.12ff.). The two psalms in which שלום and ירושלם are most strikingly juxtaposed are 122 and 147. In Ps 122.6, which is written in praise of Jerusalem as Yahweh's sanctuary, his worshippers are bidden שאלו שלום ירושלם: this may mean 'Seek the שלום of which Jerusalem is the source' rather than 'Pray for the peace of Jerusalem' (NEB), but in either case there would appear to be deliberate word play between ירושלם and שלום. This impression is reinforced by the appearance of שלום in v. 7 ('May שלום be within your ramparts') and v. 9 ('May שלום be within you'). Finally, in Ps 147.12ff. Jerusalem (Zion) is bidden to praise Yahweh for the benefits which he has bestowed on her, included among which is שלום (v. 14, השם גבולך שלום). Hence the view of S. Granild (*St. Th.*, 16, 1962, p. 149) that at 4.10 Jeremiah is referring to Deuteronomy which comes from God and yet is an instrument of deceit, is not to be followed.

The conclusion to be drawn from this is that the proclamation of שלום belongs to the Jerusalem cult and that it is made to those who trust in Yahweh. Jeremiah's contention is that Yahweh has permitted this ambiguity whose only outcome can be the deception of the people and in שלום יהיה לכם he reproduces *verbatim* the message of these prophets, represented as Yahweh's word. Hence in relation to the people his complaint to Yahweh in v. 10 may be regarded as a plea in mitigation. There is no conflict between this and his fundamental conviction that the proclamation of שלום has degenerated into an assertion about the inviolability of Jerusalem which does not leave room for an authentic faith in Yahweh.

When prophets proclaim שלום in a community which has made its religion into a lie, they are crying שלום שלום where there is no שלום. The truth of the matter is that Judah is confronted with stark threat and mortal danger—the sword is pointed at her throat. Whether נפש is understood as 'throat' or 'life' (Sept. ἕως τῆς ψυχῆς; Vulg. *ad. animam*) makes little difference exegetically, but the metaphor of the sword pricking the throat is an attractive one, and the sense 'throat' is established for *npš* in Accadian and Ugaritic; also in Ps 69.2 ('For the waters have risen up to my neck', NEB) and Jonah 2.6 ('The waters about me rose up to my neck', NEB). There are also further examples of נפש = 'throat' in biblical Hebrew (see *Proverbs*, pp. 269f.; 384f.).

THE ENEMY IS CLOSING IN AND THE END IS NEAR (4.11–18)

[11]At that time it will be said to this people and to Jerusalem:
A scorching wind is sweeping over the desert heights,
blowing towards my people;
it is not a wind for separating grain from chaff.
[12]A wind too tempestuous for winnowing comes at my bidding,
now it is I who will pass sentence on them.
[13]He rises like the clouds,

> his chariots are like a whirlwind,
> his horses are swifter than eagles;
> our lot is hopeless and our destruction certain
> [14]Wash your heart clean of evil, O Jerusalem,
> so that you may be saved.
> How much longer will your evil designs lodge within you?
> [15]A messenger has just come from Dan,
> another brings bad news from Mount Ephraim.
> [16]Make the nations aware of these things,[1]
> announce them to Jerusalem.
> Besiegers are coming from a distant land
> and threaten the towns of Judah;
> [17]they have encircled her borders as men encircle a field,
> for it is against me that she has rebelled.
>   This is Yahweh's word.
> [18]Your way of life and your evil deeds
> have brought this on you.
> Your evil will have bitter consequences,
> even your heart is infected by it.

בעת ההיא integrates vv. 11–17 with the theme of vv. 5–8 and indicates that what follows is spoken against a background of invasion. Verse 11a is then a secondary, editorial link and its vagueness (יאמר לעם חזה ולירושלם) may reflect an uncertainty about who the speaker is and a deliberate leaving open of both possibilities (Yahweh or Jeremiah). According to the versions רוח צח שפיים במדבר דרך בת עמי is to be understood as a metaphor or a simile. The simile is explicit in Pesh. ('Like a wayward wind on desert tracks, so is the behaviour of the daughter of my people') and Targ. Among modern commentators who follow the versions are Hitzig, Graf and Giesebrecht. Rashi and Kimchi take דרך as an accusative of direction and this understanding of the grammar, which is correct, appears in KJV and NEB, and, among commentators, in Duhm, Rudolph, Bright and others ('blowing towards my people'). The רוח צח or רוח מלא is entirely unsuitable for the process of separating the grain from the chaff: it is a destructive wind.

The understanding of צח as 'wayward' or 'misleading', which is a special feature of Sept. (πνεῦμα πλανήσεως) and Pesh. (rwḥ' ṭ'yt') has been encouraged by the supposition that the community is being compared to a wind in the desert which blows this way and then that, and Pesh. is probably dependent on Sept. for its interpretation of צח. The wind is then a figure of the fickleness and inconstancy of Judah; she too like the wind is always changing direction and is without steadiness in her religious and political allegiances. Rudolph supposes that צח is a noun in the construct state rather than an adjective (BDB, KB²).

---

[1]Reading הנה as הֵנָּה (see below, p. 100).

If צח is an adjective, שפיים, like דרך , must be accusative of direction, 'from heights in the desert'. שפיים is apparently not represented by Sept., and Vulg. and Pesh. follow their normal practice of translating it as 'ways', 'paths' (as in 3.2 and 21). Targ. has a more complicated paraphrase of שפיים במדבר (על רישי נגדין דמיין במדברא). This may represent a double translation of שפיים (רישי and נגדין), but even so the reference to watercourses in the desert is not explained. דמיין presupposes נגרין (Miqra'oth G'doloth.) not נגדין (Sperber, see on 3.2, p. 59). דמיין may be an expansion whose function is to establish the rightness of נגריך over against נגדין (cf. Rashi). Targ. טיחרין for צח is, perhaps, 'midday' and so 'hot' (Dalman) rather than 'sweeping' (cf. Jastrow). Vulg. *urens*, 'scorching' is the sense which is indicated for צח by כחם צח (Isa 18.4), צחה צמא, 'parched with thirst' (Isa 5.13), צחצחה (Isa 58.11) and צחיחה (Ps 68.7), 'scorched land'.

The scorching wind which blows in from the desert has no beneficent aspect or social usefulness. It is not a wind which can be put to constructive tasks; it cannot be harnessed to the processes of agriculture. The wind is not the friend of man and society, but a hostile, destructive force.

Yet it is the strength rather than the heat of this wind which makes it unsuitable for winnowing, and what is indicated is an extraordinary gale rather than a regular desert wind (so Duhm). If MT רוח מלא מאלה (v. 12) is retained, מאלה has to be referred back to לוא לזרות ולוא להבר. There are temperate winds suitable for winnowing, but this is a wind of gale force, too tempestuous to fulfil a constructive function. מאלה is not represented by Sept. (πνεῦμα πληρώσεως), רוח מלא is interpreted by Targ. as רוח דשקר 'spirit of falsehood', and מאלה יבוא לי is paraphrased as 'because of these things the armies of the nations will come against them'. The second part of v. 12 (עתה גם אני אדבר משפטים אותם) is more naturally attributable to Yahweh than to Jeremiah and there is little doubt that both Targ. and Rashi regard Yahweh as the speaker in v. 12. Rashi's understanding of יבוא לי ('From these (מאלה) punishment will come at my bidding') is the one found in Lowth ('at my commandment'), Rudolph, and NEB ('will come at my bidding'). The best conclusion is that vv. 11–12 are speech of Yahweh rather than a speech of Jeremiah, for his own part (*pace* Kimchi; also Duhm who deletes v. 12b).

Whatever conclusion is reached about this, it is impossible to discover a formal unity in vv. 11–17. Since Yahweh is not the speaker in v. 13 (אוי לנו כי שדדנו) and since vv. 14–15 are, probably, spoken by Jeremiah rather than by Yahweh, it would then be possible to maintain that vv. 11–15 (or, perhaps,

vv. 11–16) are words of Jeremiah and not of Yahweh. The
scheme, however, breaks down in the second stich of v. 17 (כי
אתי מרתה נאם יהוה) which cannot be other than words of
Yahweh. Moreover, it is probable that v. 16 should also be taken
as speech of Yahweh (see below). There is, therefore, no way of
achieving a formal congruence.

A final consideration of v. 12 should concentrate on מלא מאלה.
מאלה is not represented by Sept. and Janzen (p. 21) supposes
that it may be a corruption of מלאה, a doublet of מלא —fem. in
agreement with רוח (so Duhm; Rudolph; cf. Ziegler, Beiträge,
p. 87). KJV renders 'from those places' and refers אלה to שפיים.
This is how מלא מאלה was understood by Vulg. (plenus ex his),
but Calvin prefers the sense 'stronger than these', and, if מאלה is
to be retained, this is the more probable construction. אלה then
refers to winds of a strength suitable for the process of
winnowing (so Ehrlich, p. 249). W. L. Holladay (VT 26, 1976,
pp. 28–37) has offered a speculative reconstruction of vv. 11–12a
which assumes that שפיים means 'caravan tracks' (following P.
Joüon, Journal Asiatique, 1906, pp. 137–142), that דרך should
be pointed דֶּרֶךְ, that במדבר belongs to the 4th stich of v. 11 and
that אלה should be pointed אָלָה 'curse'. The last of these
suggestions goes back to L. Cappellus (1689) who renders מאלה
as ex maledictione. This interpretation is noted by Venema
(1765) and is adopted in a modified form by Blayney (1784).
MT should be retained (so NEB, 'a wind too strong for these').

In v. 13 the progress of an invader who is about to swoop on
Judah (cf. משחית גוים, v. 7) is described in three similes. His
movement is like that of clouds racing across the sky; his chariots
have the speed of a wind of extraordinary velocity, and his horses
cover the ground swifter than eagles soar through the heavens.
The similes all point to the breathtaking speed with which the
invader approaches. Against this lightning approach no effective
defence can be organized and no escape devised.

According to Sept., Vulg., and Pesh. מחשבות אונך is the
subject of v. 14b in which case there is a lack of congruence
between תלין (fem. sing.) and מחשבות (fem. plur.). This,
however, may be explained in terms of GK 145k. Kimchi, on the
other hand, supposes that מחשבות אונך is object rather than
subject and that the lack of grammatical agreement is between
תלין and ירושלם (since if תלין refers to ירושלם, the form ought
to be תליני, 2nd person fem. sing.). Kimchi's grammar (cf.
NEB) requires a Hiphil usage of תלין which, according to BDB,
is given by 2 Sam 17.8 and, according to KB³, by Lev 19.13.
Since, however, 3rd fem. sing. for 3rd fem. plur. is the more
tolerable type of incongruence and since the Hiphil of לין is rare,
מחשבות אונך should be regarded as the subject. That מחשבות

אונך means something like 'evil designs' is indicated by Vulg. *cogitationes noxiae* and Pesh. *mḥšbtky byšt'*. Jerusalem is giving hospitality to evil designs, harbouring them in her heart, treating them as honoured guests.

There is an inconsequentiality in the summons to repentance in v. 14a, associated with the keeping alive of the hope of safety, after the doom-laden conclusion of v. 13 (אוי לנו כי שדדנו). The figure of speech is similar to that of 2.22. In this awkward transition we should find a reflection of the intense, personal pressure to which the prophet is subject in this time of high crisis. He knows that his people are doomed and yet he knows that he must urge repentance on them and keep the hope of safety alive until the very moment when they are engulfed by destruction.

The כי at the beginning of v. 15 adds to the urgency of the appeal in v. 14, or it may take no account of that moment of appeal and flicker of hope, and connect rather with אוי לנו כי שדדנו (v. 13), as if v. 14 had never been spoken. The latter alternative is the more probable and then v. 14 occupies a position of sad isolation in a passage which is laden with doom and has nothing to say about repentance and safety. There is a temptation to suggest that since v. 14 disturbs the connection between v. 13 and v. 15 it should be regarded as an intrusion, and this was the view of Duhm.

The prophet envisages how the end will come about (vv. 15–17), for this is surely an imaginative construction of events or a vision of the end rather than a description of an invasion which is already in progress. The inevitability of disaster and the imminence of attack are felt so intensely that they are translated into a graphic account of the progress of the enemy advance. The first bad news comes from Dan (v. 15), the northern border of Israel (Kimchi, גבול ארץ ישראל), and then another messenger arrives to say that the invader has penetrated south as far as the Samarian hill country.

The opening words of v. 16 make poor sense in MT (הזכירו לגוים הנה, 'Tell to the nations, behold!'). NEB, 'Tell all this to the nations' presupposes הַגֵּד (Brockington, p. 199). Sept. makes sense by inserting ἥκασιν after ἰδού ('Behold! they have come') and Vulg. by connecting *ecce* with *auditum est in Jerusalem*. But the problem is not limited to הנה; it extends to לגוים. News has been brought that the invading army has reached Mount Ephraim and in view of this information a *communiqué* is released which begins at נצרים באים (v. 16b) and ends at עליה מסביב (v. 17a). It is not obvious why this should be broadcast to the world at large (NEB, 'Tell all this to the nations'), since its contents (ויתנו על ערי יהודה קולם) indicate that it is a warning

to Judah that an invading army is swiftly approaching her
borders and is poised for a final assault. Rudolph's emendation is
הזהירו לבנימין, 'Give a warning to Benjamin'. The enemy is
pushing deeper to the south (Dan, Ephraim and Benjamin are
stages of his advance) and soon Jerusalem will be overwhelmed.
השמיעו על ירושלם is equally troublesome. Does על mean
'concerning' (Calvin, Blayney, Weiser) or is על = אל? Sept.
(ἀναγγείλατε ἐν Ιερουσαλημ) and Vulg. (*auditum est in
Jerusalem*) indicate the latter. If גוים is removed by emendation
(Rudolph), the way is open to render השמיעו על ירושלם as
'Proclaim to Jerusalem' (cf. Rudolph, *schickt Botschaft an
Jerusalem*). The best that can be done, if the consonants of MT
are to be retained, is to read הנה as הֵנָּה and to suppose that
there are two constituencies; that the nations are to be told about
the invasion which has engulfed Judah and that a proclamation
is to be made in Jerusalem (אל = על) giving news of impending
invasion.

Who issues the order that the message is to be proclaimed? Is
it Yahweh or Jeremiah, for his own part, who says הזכירו לגוים
הנה השמיעו על ירושלם? Since Jeremiah is certainly the speaker
in v. 13 (אוי לנו כי שדדנו) and, probably, also in vv. 14–15, one
might suppose that it is he who issues this fateful *communiqué* in
connection with his intense anticipation of the invasion. This
would suggest that the message originally ended with מסביב and
that כי אתי מרתה נאם יהוה is secondary and arises from the
mistaken assumption that Yahweh and not Jeremiah issues the
message. Doubts about the wisdom of attempting a critical
resolution of the formal incongruence have already been
expressed (above, pp. 97f.) and the best that can be done is to
regard   הזכירו לגוים הנה השמיעו על ירושלם   (v. 16) and the
following message as word of Yahweh.

The message itself is that נצרים are coming from a distant
land and threaten the towns of Judah. נצרים is given its usual
sense by Vulg. (*custodes*), but the other versions have adopted
different renderings (Sept. συστροφαί. 'crowds'; Pesh. *knš* '*mm*',
'crowds of peoples'; Targ. (cf. Kimchi) משרית עממין, 'armies of
peoples'). חטופון כקטופין ('robbers like grape-gatherers')
appears in Jer 49.9 and Obad 5 as Targ.'s rendering of בצרים
and it is likely that it has come into the verse from these passages
(cf. C. Rabin, *Textus* 5, 1966, pp. 45f.).

Rudolph adopts Volz's emendation (צרים, 'enemies', cf.
Rashi), and NEB נצרים (Brockington, p. 199) is a variant of
this. It has the advantage of not requiring any change in the
consonantal text and the disadvantage of postulating a Niphal of
צור not otherwise attested. Rabin (pp. 45ff.) urges that the
versions were not simply guessing what seemed an appropriate

sense when they rendered נצרים as 'crowds', and he urges that
נצרים should be derived from Syriac and Jewish Aramaic *nṣr*,
'chirp', 'murmur', Ugaritic *nṣr*, 'shriek' or 'sob' (Gibson, *CML*
16 6.5, p. 101; A Herdner, p. 76). Kimchi's view of the grammar
is that the towns of Judah have already been besieged (ויתנו)
and that the enemy is about to deploy his army against
Jerusalem. That נצרים and כשמרי are related in some way (cf.
Bright) is a suggestion which deserves consideration. The
invaders are 'keepers' of a sinister kind and this is brought out by
the simile in v. 17. We may then have to reckon with an ironic
sense of נצרים which is eludicated by the following simile (so
Lowth).

This encirclement of Judah, a ring of steel around her, is
likened to a ring of watchmen around the perimeter of a field
(שדי = שדה, so Rashi, BDB, KB²). Kimchi explains that such
watchmen ring the field in order to prevent animals from gaining
access to it and eating the crops. The figure is applied in reverse,
for the circle of steel around Judah will prevent anyone from
getting out and effecting an escape.

It is doubtful whether v. 18 has an original and intrinsic
connection with v. 17 and נאם יהוה might be supposed to mark
the end of the unit constituted by vv. 11–17. Verse 18 stands
between this and vv. 19–21, a sharply differentiated unit in
which the tempestuous emotions of the prophet find expression.
Verse 18 could be spoken either by Jeremiah or by Yahweh and
it is connected with the theme of the preceding verses, especially
with the closing words of v. 17. Disaster is the consequence of
rebellion against Yahweh. If כי אתי מרתה נאם יהוה were
regarded as intrusive (Duhm), v. 18 could be attached to
vv. 11–17 as the conclusion of the message which begins with
נצרים (v. 16). In that case v. 18 would be word of Yahweh and
vv. 16b–18 a message which Jeremiah is required to proclaim.

עשו has been read as a 3rd person plur. by the versions (Sept.
ἐποίησαν; Vulg. *fecerunt*; Pesh. *'bdw*; Targ. גמרו) rather than as
an infinitive absolute (MT עשׂו). The grammar of v. 18b is
difficult: זאת רעתך, perhaps, resumes דרכך ומעלליך, in which
case the two motives clauses (introduced by כי) link up with
v. 18a. This is how v. 18b is construed by Sept., Vulg. and Pesh.
Targ. introduces the idea of remedial punishment and looks
forward to a time when it will have salutary consequences (so
Kimchi). But כי נגע עד לבך means (*pace* Targ. and Kimchi) that
the vital centres of personality and motivation have been invaded
by a corruption which cannot be eradicated. The deadly trend of
the disease is now irreversible and will work out its bitter
consequences. The disintegration imposed by historical forces is
matched by an inward demoralization and sickness unto death.

This interpretation of v. 18b can be founded on an adjectival מר (BDB) or on the assumption that)מר is a pausal form of a verb (Giesebrecht, Duhm, Cornill, Volz, KB³). The emendation of מר כי to מריך (BHK, NEB, Brockington, p. 199) does not have a profound effect on the exegesis, although if it were adopted רעתך could be taken as 'your disaster' or 'your punishment': 'This is the punishment you must bear, for your rebelliousness has penetrated to your heart'.

SORROWFUL PREMONITIONS OF DOOM (4.19–22)

> [19]Oh, the writing of my bowels!
> Oh, the pounding of my heart!
> Feelings overwhelm me,
> I cannot keep silent.
> I hear[1] the blast of the trumpet,
> the battle-cries which are raised.
> [20]News comes in of one disaster after another,
> the whole land is in ruins;
> in a trice my tents are in shreds,
> my tent-coverings in tatters.
> [21]How much longer shall I see the signal
> and hear the blast of the trumpet?
> [22]My people are fools;
> they do not know me.
> They are foolish not discerning children;
> they are expert at evil-doing,
> but ignorant of how to do good.

The cohortative form of אחולה (K) is explained by GK 108g as indicative of compulsive action (cf. Rudolph, *ich muss mich winden*, the pain makes me writhe—my writhing is involuntary). Rashi glosses אחולה (Q אחילה, 'I hope'?) with חיל ורתת, indicating that it is a severe pain which induces writhing, and Kimchi explains אחולה as חיל כיולדה, 'pain like that of a woman in child-birth'. On מעי מעי Kimchi observes that the repetition is in the style of those who utter laments (הנוחים). Kimchi's comments are valuable in so far as they call attention to the storm of intense feeling which breaks with the exclamation מעי מעי and to the circumstance that the language (אחולה) is metaphorical and that the prophet is not complaining about severe pains in his bowels (cf. Sept. and Vulg.). The significance of the appearance of מעי is that the pit of the stomach is believed to be the seat of the most intense emotions, and there may be an empirical foundation for this, namely, that this is where there are physical repercussions when one is subject to severe emotional stress. Mental and spiritual anguish resembles the

---

[1] Deleting נפשי (see below, p. 104).

pains of a woman in labour in so far as it stretches human
powers of endurance to breaking point.

The volcanic character of Jeremiah's language—the erupting
of pent up feelings into staccato bursts of speech—continues
with קירות לבי: The קירות (so Kimchi) are partitions which
divide the heart into sections, and here is another physical
concomitant of severe emotional pressure—palpitation, an
alarming and involuntary pounding of the heart (so Rudolph,
Bright). המה לי לבי לא אחריש marks a transition from a
convulsive, sobbing utterance, from short, sharp cries of anguish,
to more coherent and composed speech. It is a transition from
exclamation to syntax, from the immediacy of bursts of feeling
to a coherent sentence construction and a rational discourse. The
second מעי is not represented by Sept.[B,S*], but Sept. has what
appears to be a double rendering of המה לי לבי. Ziegler
(*Beiträge*, p. 90) and Janzen (pp. 30f.) are inclined to conclude
that נפשי, which appears in v. 19c in both MT and Sept., belongs
originally to v. 19b and that המה לי נפשי preserves the correct
form of the Hebrew text (Sept. μαιμάσσει ἡ ψυχή μου). In this
connection it is pointed out that לבי has already occurred in
v. 19a. This consideration influences Rudolph who (following
Duhm and Volz) adopts המה לי נפשי.

המה לי לבי refers to severe, emotional disturbance, to a storm
of feelings which destroy composure and induce chaos and
madness. לא אחריש may be indicative of a loss of inner quietness
and stability, or the prophet may be saying that he has to find
release from the intolerable tensions which rend him by issuing
great cries of anguish. The latter explantion is the one which the
versions point to (Sept. οὐ σιωπήσομαι; Vulg. *non tacebo*; Pesh.
wl' štq; Targ. לא שתיק). נפשי in the phrase שמעתי נפשי, is
related by Rashi and Kimchi to the visionary experience of the
prophet: 'From behind the curtain there has come to me news of
the clamour of war' (Rashi). 'There has come to me' (באתני) is
apparently a paraphrase of 'my נפש has heard' (so Sept. ἤκουσεν
and Vulg. *audivit*), but Rashi does not explain how he reconciles
this with either שמעתי (K) or שָׁמַעַתְּ (Q, 2nd person fem. sing.).
Kimchi's comment, 'For the hearing is the hearing of the נפש'
implies the translation, 'You have heard, O my soul' (= Q).
Kimchi notes that K has a final *yodh* and remarks ואחד הוא עם
הקרי. This is correct, for שמעתי can be explained as a 2nd
person fem. sing. form of the same type as the two examples in
2.20a (see above, pp. 40f.). This intense, agonizing premonition
of the end (so Rashi and Kimchi—correctly) is worse than
experiencing the terrible events themselves. It lacks nothing of
realism and terror; it is a full entering into the sorrow and panic
of the final invasion and it is a solitary anguish endured by a

prophet who is destined to bear a double burden alone, for he has been through it all and he must suffer it again when these events come to pass (so also Duhm). Bright agrees with this, in general, although he supposes that some verses, especially vv. 19–21, 'were probably wrung from Jeremiah as invasion struck' (p. 34).

Rudolph raises the question whether we have to reckon with prophetic vision or exalted poetry, although he acknowledges that the line of demarcation between powerful, imaginative projections of profound insights and visionary experience is not easily drawn (cf. J. Skinner, *Prophecy and Religion*, pp. 49–51). He thinks that vv. 19–21 and vv. 23–26 could be assigned to the latter category, but his main point is that the outward, literary form of some of the units in chapter 4 will mislead us, if we interpret them in a literal way. Those which appear to be addressed to Judah and Jerusalem had no public function, until they were incorporated in the scroll which was written in 605. Up till then they had the character of a poetic materialization of Jeremiah's deepest thoughts and convictions and they served the ends of his own inner clarification. These are creations by means of which his inchoate thoughts are given form and concrete content, and they are also an unpublished, literary deposit which nourishes his public utterances.

The decision which has to be made is whether שמעתי נפשי (v. 19) is to be read, in which case the translation must be, 'You have heard, O my soul', or whether נפשי is to be deleted and שמעתי taken as 1st person (Duhm, Rudolph). 'You have heard, O my soul' has a ring of improbability and נפשי should be deleted. The argument that נפשי is original in v. 19b, to which it should be transposed, is not entirely convincing (see above, p. 103). The prophet's tragic foreknowledge transports him into the time of mobilization against attack (v. 19b). He hears the trumpet summoning the people to the defence of their country. That נקרא is to be derived from קרא and not קרה is indicated by Sept. (ἐπικαλεῖται) and Vulg. (*vocata est*), while Targ. (אתערע) and Pesh. (*n't*) point to נקרה = נקרא. Kimchi equates נקרא with נקרה, and this is preferred by Duhm, Bright and NEB ('Crash upon crash'='Crash follows on crash'). Rudolph notes both possibilities, but prefers the idea of 'proclamation'.

Sept. has taken רגע as a verb which it has rendered by διεσπάσθησαν. This, at any rate, is the interpretation placed on Sept. by the NEB translators (Brockington, p. 200) who point רגע as רֻגַּע. The assumption presumably is that I רגע (BDB), 'disturb' can yield the sense 'tear'. The Greek translation is matched by Pesh. which also has two verbs (*mn šly 'tbzz mškny wnpl yry'ty*) and which is, probably dependent on Sept.

All the *communiqués* which are issued (נקרא) record a

succession of disastrous and crushing defeats (שבר על שבר),
accompanied by a scale of physical destruction which reduces
the land to a vast ruin (כי שדדה כל הארץ). All this happens with
unnerving and uncanny speed, as the consequence of lightning
attacks against which defence is ineffective and unavailing. אהלי
and יריעתי are deliberately archaic and יריעתי ('tent curtains'
or 'tent furnishings') is, probably, a synecdoche for 'tent'. אהלי
and יריעתי are the homes of the people, the material expressions
of family and community life (cf. Targ., 'Suddenly my land is
laid waste, all my cities in an instant').

Sept. renders עד מתי אראה נם (v. 21) as ἕως πότε ὄψομαι
φεύγοντας, that is, נם has been read as נָם (cf. 4.6) and rendered
as a plural. The same understanding of נם appears in Vulg.
fugientem (sing.) and Pesh. *ld'rq* ('the one who flees').
According to this reading of the Hebrew text there is a reference
to refugees, to those whose homes became a front line. Almost
certainly, however, נם should be pointed נֵם, as in 4.5 and this is
what is indicated by Targ. (סימון = σημεῖον), Rashi and Kimchi.
We are faced again with the question of the character of the
signal (see above, pp. 91f.) and Rashi supposes that it is a flag or
standard; Kimchi adds the suggestion of a trumpet-call. What is
expressed in v. 21 is a total weariness with the sounds of war.
The raising of standards or the sending of signals, the blowing of
trumpets, the techniques of mobilization or of systems of early
warning—all the evidences of military organization and
flurry—are empty gestures and noises and an aggravation of the
prophet's agony, for he knows that it is all in vain.

Despite the conjunctive כי which indicates that v. 22 depends
on the preceding verses, there is no intrinsic or original
connection between it and the cry of anguish uttered by
Jeremiah in vv. 19–21 (*pace* Bright (following Kimchi) who
supposes that vv. 19–22 are a unit and that v. 22 is 'Yahweh's
complaint'). Kimchi relates the verse to the theme of Deut 4.6
that the תורה is Israel's wisdom in the face of the world (כי
הוא חכמתכם ובינתכם לעיני העמים). Yahweh's people are אויל,
not in the sense that they are stupid or of low intelligence, but
rather because they are not amenable to the discipline imposed
by a teacher and are incapable of learning. They have ability and
expertise (חכמים המה להרע), a kind of destructive cleverness,
but they are, nevertheless, fools, lacking wisdom and
discernment (cf. *Proverbs*, pp. 413ff.).

This is Yahweh's verdict on his people, but when he says אותי
לא ידעו we have to reckon with the comprehensive sense of דעת
יהוה which is found in the prophetic literature (Hos 4.6; Isa
28.9; Jer 9.22f.) and whose scope is clearly indicated in Jer
22.15f., 'Did not your father eat and drink and do justice and

righteousness? Then it was well with him. He dealt out justice to the poor and needy. Is not this to know me?' This knowledge of Yahweh presupposes instruction (תורה), but it is more than knowledge which derives from instruction or education. When Yahweh says of his people, 'They do not know me', it is their rejection of him at the deepest levels of decision of which he speaks, their rebellion, their unbelief and withholding of commitment (cf. *PWM*, pp. 88–90).

A VISION OF DESOLATION (4.23–26)

[23]I saw the earth and it was utter chaos,[1]
I saw the heavens and all their lights were out.
[24]I saw the mountains and they were shaking,
all the hills were trembling.
[25]I looked and saw no human life,
and all the birds had taken wing.
[26]I looked and saw that farmlands had become desert,
and all their townships were in ruins.
This is what Yahweh's hot anger has done.

This unit is sharply differentiated formally from the verses which surround it by the device of beginning vv. 23 and 24 with ראיתי and vv. 25 and 26 with ראיתי והנה. These lines contain the elements of a vision of desolation, and the unit is rounded off by the theological interpretation—all this devastation has been wrought by the heat of Yahweh's anger. This interpretation and vv. 27–28 are thought by Duhm to be late expansions, the authenticity of vv. 23–26 has been disputed (Giesebrecht, Volz), and V. Epstein (*JBL* 87, 1968, p. 97) describes v. 23 as 'either proto-apocalyptic or a gloss by an apocalyptist'.

Kimchi emphasizes that ראיתי is not used of sensory perception but of a prophetic vision, in which a time of national disaster takes on terrifying, extra dimensions and assumes the character of ultimate, cosmic disturbance (cf. Bright). What is envisaged is an *eschaton*: a return to the chaos which prevailed before the world was ordered by Yahweh's creative acts (cf. Kimchi כמו בתחילת בריאתה, 'as at the beginning of his creation'). Rudolph holds that there are metrical reasons for the deletion of תהו which has been added on the analogy of Gen 1.2. It is not clear that Sept. οὐθέν is an indication that the Greek translator had a Hebrew text from which תהו was absent, but κενὴ καὶ οὐθέν shows that Aq., Symm. and Theod. equated οὐθέν with בהו and supplied κενὴ καί as an equivalent of תהו. Rather than a demonstration that Sept. had a Hebrew text without תהו

---

[1] Deleting תהו (see below pp. 106f).

ז, οὐθέν might be a compact rendering of תהו ובהו (so
Giesebrecht), although the conclusion which was drawn by Aq.,
Symm. and Theod. about the Hebrew text behind Sept. is,
perhaps, the right one. The rendering of תהו ובהו at Gen 1.2 is
so different (ἀόρατος καὶ ἀκατασκεύαστος) that it does not help
the process of elucidation very much.

According to v. 23 there has been a collapse of cosmic order
and an invasion by the powers of chaos. The luminaries, which,
according to Gen 1.14, establish the contrast between light and
darkness, between night and day, and which also measure the
passage of months and years, no longer shine from the sky (so
Targ.). With the extinction of the sun there is also a
fundamental disturbance of the established rhythms of nature.
Light, which is also a principle of contrast, definition and
structure, is overcome by the darkness which it overcame when
the world was being made (cf. Rudolph).

The mountains which are symbols of stability and immoveable
strength (הררי אל) are shaken and dissolve. According to
Kimchi, all this has the character of משל: it is a kind of
hyperbole which is indicative of a situation of extreme distress.
This may be too neat a way of limiting the imagery. The
anguished foreseeing of disaster requires a factor of
magnification: only the defeat of order by chaos, only a
mythology which multiplies the dimensions of the catastrophe is
an adequate form of expression. From a myth and ritual point of
view this is a New Year festival situation in reverse, with no
happy outcome to the struggle between creative, salutary forces
and the powers of chaos (cf. S. H. Hooke Myth and Ritual,
1933; The Labyrinth, 1935; Myth, Ritual and Kingship, 1958).

There is more indication of a particular, historical situation in
v. 25 which portrays a land abandoned by its population,
perhaps, in the wake of a military disaster. Yet even here there
are intimations of a collapse which is more total, and the birds
have all been banished (the birds which God made). It is an
empty and dark world; chaos has returned. Targ. (also Kimchi)
correctly understands הכרמל as 'arable land'; it has been taken
as a locality by Sept., Vulg., and Pesh. Some Hebrew
manuscripts read נצתו 'burned' and this was the Hebrew text
translated by Sept. (ἐμπεπυρισμέναι), whereas Vulg. (destructae
sunt) and Pesh. ('t'rq) represent נתצו (MT). Conversely in 2.15
a few Hebrew manuscripts read נתצו (Q נצתו). The arable land
which has been brought to a peak of fertility by years of
sustained and careful husbandry will revert to desert almost in a
moment. The townships lie in ruins and this is not simply the
blind cruelty of natural or historical disaster. It is the deliberate
action of Yahweh.

Giesebrecht and Volz deny vv. 23–26 to Jeremiah, because they hold that Jeremiah only envisages judgements which are historically caused. He does not speak the language of apocalyptic and this passage, because it contains such vocabulary, betrays its lateness. But this may be a misjudgement of the intention of the portrayal in vv. 23–26. The antithesis between particular and universal, or historical and cosmic may be an over-simplification, since a prophet who is also a poet, and who is stretching his powers of expression to the limit, may find that the universalizing of a moment of historical disaster which he anticipates is the ultimate power which he possesses to convey the totality of the coming catastrophe. We may not, therefore certainly conclude that a prophet who mythologizes a historical disaster has ceased to be a prophet and has become an apocalyptist.

It is arguable that we have a reverse creation narrative, an antitype which presupposes the existence of its type. תהו ובהו (v. 23; cf. Gen 1.2), however, should not be used to bolster this argument (see above, pp. 106f.). Thoughts about the uncertainty of the cosmic order and its vulnerability to the inroads of chaos have been located in a very wide context of ancient Near Eastern thought, and we may not suppose, therefore, that a cosmos-chaos opposition has to be derived from Gen 1 in particular. M. Fishbane (*VT* 21, 1971, pp. 151-167) contrasts the two passages in a way which is hardly legitimate. It is not evident that the destructive power of the 'Word', as opposed to its creative power in Gen 1, is an idea which is operative in vv. 23–26. W. L. Holladay (*JBL*, 85, 1966, p. 406) supposes that תהו ובהו is an allusion to the P creation narrative and yet he holds that Jeremiah is the author of vv. 23–26, perhaps a combination of incompatible premisses.

DEVASTATION AND FLIGHT (4.27–29)

[27]This is the word of Yahweh:
    The whole land will be desolate,
    and I will make its destruction complete.[1]
[28]   The earth will be in mourning for this,
    and the heavens above wear black.
    I have spoken and will not relent,
    I have made a plan and will not change it.[2]
[29]   At the sound of horsemen and archers,
    all the land[3] is in flight;
    they go to ground in thickets,

[1]Reading וכלה לה אעשה (see below, p. 109).
[2]Reading כי דברתי ולא נחמתי זמתי ולא אשוב ממנה (see below, pp. 109f.).
[3]Reading כל הארץ (see below, pp. 110f.).

they climb up into the rocks.
Every town¹ is deserted,
No one lives in them.

The difficulty of the negative in וכלה לא אעשה (v. 27) is one
which recurs at 5.10 and 18. The setting of a limit on the extent
of the destruction is out of keeping with what is otherwise
indicated in chapter 4, in which every effect which would convey
the impression of total disaster is utilized (cf. Rudolph, 'excluded
by v. 28b'). There is no textual evidence for the deletion of לא.
Duhm's view is that the clause should be deleted from 4.27 and
5.10 and that the source is 5.18, where it represents a
modification which was necessary in the light of exilic experience
(cf. Rashi on 4.27). More limited critical operations focus on לא
in 4.27 and אל in 5.10: Rudolph emends לא to לה and J. Soggin
(*Biblica* 46, 1965, pp. 56–59) considers proposals that לא =
lamed emphaticum with *scriptio plena* and that אל is to be
equated with the emphatic particle *'l* in Ugaritic. His own
suggestion for 4.27 is that the *aleph* of לא (לא אעשה) is a
dittograph. The text which is postulated for 4.27 is then וכלה
לאעשה 'I will certainly make the destruction complete'. A better
approach is the assumption that לא is a secondary, negative
element which has been imported into 4.27 for the reasons
indicated above, and Rudolph's supposition that לה has been
modified to לא is more in accord with this view of the matter.

The mourning of the earth and the heavens is proleptic: it is
for a desolation which is decreed, but which has not yet come to
pass. Or is it, rather, that when the devastation is complete and
Judah is reduced to waste and emptiness heaven and earth will
put on mourning clothes and fulfil the rites of mourning? Is it
'Let them now mourn in view of the impending end' or 'They will
mourn' (NEB) when the desolation has become an accomplished
fact'? It is, probably, proleptic mourning—a poetic expression of
the certainty that death is coming to Judah: Yahweh will not
change his mind or be deflected from his purpose. That v. 28b
has this sense is clear, despite the uncertainty which attaches to
matters of detail. על כי is difficult, and Duhm supposes that διότι
represents כי. A related problem is constituted by זמתי which
MT has read as a verb and which is so taken by Sept., Vulg.,
Pesh. and Targ. The different order of words indicated by Sept.
(διότι ἐλάλησα καὶ οὐ μετανοήσω, ὥρμησα καὶ οὐκ ἀποστρέψω
ἀπ'αὐτῆς) is adopted by Duhm and Rudolph (כי דברתי ולא
נחמתי זמתי ולא אשוב ממנה), and both these scholars solve the
problem of על כי by supposing that על is a dittography of the על
of ממעל. It is clear that זמתי or a replacement of it (ולא נחמתי

¹Reading כל עיר (see below, pp. 110f.).

— see above) must belong to the first stich (*pace* Vulg.). NEB's rendering, 'For I have made known my purpose; I will not relent or change my mind' appears to rest on the pointing זִמָּתִי, and this is a tempting solution whose weakness is that זמה means 'lewdness' rather than 'plan' (normally מזמה) and that the only attestation of the sense 'plan' is the obscure verse, Job 17.11 (where זמתי נתקו, 'my plans? are broken?', is in parallelism with ימי עברו, 'my days have passed'). עַל כִּי should be emended to כִּי and the word order of Sept. should be followed. Kimchi attaches significance to the change from perfect (ולא נחמתי) to imperfect (ולא אשוב): 'I have not changed my mind up to the present and I shall never depart from it, for as I have purposed and spoken, so it will come to pass. Hence it is inevitable that the land should mourn.' This is in accord with the thought of mourning for what has not yet come to pass but whose advent is inevitable.

The supposition that εἰσέδυσαν εἰς τὰ σπήλαια and εἰς τὰ ἄλση ἐκρύβησαν were variants in v. 29 was made by Giesebrecht and Cornill, whereas Volz and Rudolph reconstruct the Hebrew on the model of Sept. (cf. Rudolph, באו במערות ויחבאו בעבים). Ziegler (*Beiträge*, p. 91; cf. Janzen, p. 31) does not come to a firm conclusion, but is inclined to the view that Sept. derives from a longer Hebrew text than MT. There are difficulties about a doublet hypothesis. If MT preserves one of the doublets (באו בעבים), we have the problem that this would be the only place where בוא is rendered by εἰσδῦναι, and we have to suppose that עבים is translated by σπήλαια, 'caves'. If the assumption is made that Sept. derives from a Hebrew text which is superior to MT, the shorter text is explained as a consequence of scribal mishap: the omission of במערות ויחבאו is due to *homoioteleuton* (Volz, Rudolph); the scribe confused באו with the ending of ויחבאו which consists of the same consonants and so במערות ויחבאו was omitted. A decisive metrical reason is needed to support the adoption of the longer text. If MT is followed, the second line becomes 2+2 instead of 2+2+2, and who is to say that 2+2 is not to be tolerated in a verse which, on Rudolph's own reckoning, displays metrical variety?

The double occurrence of כל העיר in v. 29 is troublesome. Sept. translates the first by πᾶσα χώρα and the second by πᾶσα πόλις. The other versions differentiate between the two occurrences, but in different ways (Vulg. *omnis civitas* and *universae urbes*; Pesh. *klh qryt'* and *klhyn qwry'*; Targ. כל יתבי קרתא and כל קרויהון). There is an interesting correlation between Vulg. and Targ.: both take the first כל העיר to mean 'citizens' and the second 'cities' or 'towns' (similarly Kimchi). Sept. πᾶσα χώρα is, probably, a device for dealing with the awkward double occurrence of כל העיר. All the versions are

forced into a plural rendering of the second כל העיר by the
presence of בהן, and πᾶσα πόλις is Sept.'s device for dealing
with this difficulty. Rudolph emends the first כל העיר to כל הארץ
(following Sept.) and assumes that the second כל העיר can mean
'every town'. Sept. should be followed in respect of כל הארץ and
כל עיר, even if these have no more than the status of conjectural
emendations.

Verse 29 contains a description of the civil population fleeing
for their lives before the advancing cavalry and archers, taking
cover wherever they can and making themselves as inaccessible
to the invading armies as they can contrive to be. The towns,
which were the centres of civilization, are abandoned, and the
citizens are reduced to a regimen of bare survival. Their habitats
become those of animals rather than of men; they go to ground
in thick undergrowth or they perch on lofty fastnesses, making
the eyries of eagles their homes (so Rudolph and Bright).

JERUSALEM ARRAYED FOR LOVE BUT NEAR TO DEATH (4.30–31)

> [30]What do you think you are doing,[1]
> wearing scarlet and decked with gold jewellery,
> your eyes painted with stibium?
> You beautify yourself to no purpose;
> your lovers spurn you
> and are out to kill you.
> [31]I hear cries of anguish as of a woman in labour,
> a woman bearing her first child.
> It is the daughter of Zion, gasping in agony,
> crying with her hands outstretched:
> A sorrowful lot is mine,
> for I am at the mercy of murderers.

אתי (K) is an older form of the 2nd sing. fem. pronoun than אַתְּ
(Q), preserving the ending found in Arabic, 'antī. Sept. does not
represent שדוד (v. 30). Kimchi observes on שדוד that sometimes
the masculine, sometimes the feminine is used with כנסת ישראל
(cf. GK 145t). שדוד should be deleted, for it lacks grammatical
congruence and has the appearance of an interpolation into an
original ואת מה תעשי. It may have been a laconic, marginal
comment on the fate of Jerusalem which has been incorporated
in the text. There is no textual evidence to support the view that
עדי is a dittography of the immediately preceding consonants
(Rudolph). Dittography is not normally invoked unless the
extant text is unintelligible or makes poor sense: it would be a
coincidence if a copying error produced a text which made sense.

ואתי מה תעשי points to the incongruous and senseless

---

[1] Deleting שדוד (see below).

behaviour of the citizens of Jerusalem: they are oblivious of the fate which hangs over them. The versions explain תקרעי as a smearing or painting of the eyes. It is explained by Rashi as מחריב קרע העין, 'widening the opening? of the eye'; presumably, a kind of eye-shadow which enhances the brilliance of the eyes and makes them appear larger than they are. Jerusalem is like a prostitute keeping up appearances to the end, with her fine clothes, jewellery and cosmetic aids, but she is unaware that death is round the corner and that those who have made love to her now have murder in their hearts. The עגבים, who are her customers, are, according to Rashi, notorious womanizers, experts at different kinds of sexual play.

Jerusalem is unaware that she is wearing her finery for a final assignation with death, and this is an indication that she is divorced from reality. It is also a mark of her deterioration, of a process of hardening and coarsening which has opened up a great gulf between herself and God: 'How can you be saved, for you are dressed up in scarlet and are resigned to punishment and indifferent to the evil which is about to come on you and do not show penitence?' (Kimchi). There is, however, in this exegesis also the suggestion that beneath the frivolity and cultivation of illusion there is some distant awareness on Jerusalem's part that she is engaging in a masquerade.

The death throes of Jerusalem are likened to the pangs of a woman bearing a child (v. 31): צרה כמכבירה is an intensification of the משל, for it is assumed that a woman bearing her first child has to suffer more severe birth pangs than other women. This interpretation assumes that חָלָה = חולה; this is an assumption which is made by Kimchi and is in accord with the versions, except Pesh. ('yk kryht', 'like one who is sick'). Kimchi explains צרה as a compressed expression for 'cry of distress' (so Sept.) and this should be followed. צְרָה* 'cry of anguish' from צרח 'roar' has been adopted by Rudolph and Bright. The near homonomy of תתיפי and תתיפה is a deliberate artistic effect (Rudolph). תתיפה is a *hapax legomenon* whose lexicography is obscure and the sense 'gasping' (Bright), 'gasping for breath' (NEB) assumes that יפח is related to נפח. The versions took the sense to be 'worn out', 'exhausted'. That בת ציון is the speaker in v. 31c is made explicit by Pesh. (*w'mr'*), Targ. (אמרא) and Rashi (כך אומרת). Jerusalem laments that her spirit has failed, her vitality has ebbed away, and that, in her weakness and weariness, she is at the mercy of her killers. Sept. (τοῖς ἀνῃρημένοις, 'Those who are being removed for burial'), Vulg. (*interfectos*, 'Those who have been killed') and Pesh. (*qṭyly* = Vulg.) are representing לַהֲרֻגִים (MT לְהֹרְגִים). If this is preferred, the meaning is that a great weariness of spirit has settled on Jerusalem, her heart is sick at the sight of so many corpses—the evidence of slaughter in Jerusalem (cf. NEB, 'weary of slaughter'). It is not clear how פרש can mean 'clench' (NEB), and 'with her hands stretched out' should be understood as a gesture appropriate to a cry of death rather than as a reaction to agony: Jerusalem resigns herself to death and beckons it. Nevertheless, birth pangs and death throes are related as type and anti-type: the mother suffers to give birth and produce a living child, but Jerusalem's pain is a final ordeal before death and oblivion.

Both Duhm and Rudolph locate these references to war and invasion (4.5ff.) in the early part of Jeremiah's ministry; hence they have the character of premonitions and anticipations of events which lie in the future, and this is a fundamental agreement with Rashi and Kimchi. The enemy from the north (v. 6) who will spill into Judah is, according to Duhm, the Scythians (similarly Skinner (*Prophecy and Religion*, pp. 44f.)). Rudolph's opinion is that the enemy from the north may have had an earlier, historical reference than Babylon, but that the threat is one which eventually materializes in Nebuchadrezzar and the Babylonians (see above, pp. 19–21).

CHAPTER V

JERUSALEM IS TOTALLY APOSTATE (5.1–6)

[1]Go around the streets of Jerusalem
and pay close attention;
search its thoroughfares
for a just man,
for anyone who does what is right,
who seeks after truth,
so that I may forgive the city.
[2]If they use the oath, As Yahweh lives,
they do it only to commit perjury.
[3]Is it not truth that you fix your eyes on, O Yahweh?
You chastised them but they felt no pain,
you restrained them[1] but they would not be disciplined;
they made their faces harder than rock,
they refused to repent.
[4]I said, But these are poor, unlearned people,
they do not know the way prescribed by Yahweh,
what their God has declared to be right.
[5]I shall go to the great
and converse with them,
for they know the way prescribed by Yahweh,
what their God has declared to be right.
But they to a man have broken their yoke,
they have burst their ropes.
[6]Therefore a lion from the forest will maul them,
a wolf from the plains savage them;
a leopard will prowl around their towns,
anyone who comes out will be torn apart;
for many are their transgressions,
countless their apostasies.

Rudolph supposes that the unit is to be explained as a dialogue
between Yahweh and Jeremiah: Yahweh speaks in v. 1,
Jeremiah replies in vv. 2–5 and Yahweh's final rejoinder comes
in v. 6. Bright, who takes the unit as vv. 1–9, also postulates a
dialogue to which Jeremiah's contribution is vv. 2–5 or 3–5 or
3–6. His reasons for extending the limits of the unit beyond v. 6
are not clearly stated. The supposition that there is a dialogue is
an attempt to deal with structural difficulties, but it is a solution
of dubious value. If Jeremiah is being addressed by Yahweh in
v. 1, why are the verbs 2nd person plural? (noted by
Giesebrecht). Then, again, עַל כֵּן (v. 6) is more intelligible in
connection with a previous word of Yahweh in which he has laid
an accusation against Jerusalem, than it is as a rejoinder to
words spoken to him by Jeremiah in conversation. We do not
know who is being addressed by Yahweh in v. 1: formally, it is

---

[1]Reading כְּלִיתָם = כִּלֵּאתָם (below, p. 116).

the same kind of situation as is found in Isa. 40.1, where it has been suggested that Yahweh is giving instructions to members of his heavenly court. The possibility that Jeremiah is the speaker in v. 1 (and throughout vv. 1–6; Duhm; Ehrlich, p. 252) is ruled out by ואסלח לה (v. 1), and Sept. has explicitly attributed the verse to Yahweh (λέγει Κύριος).

If Yahweh is speaking to the people of Jerusalem in v. 1, we have to assume that those who live in Jerusalem are capable of observing and acknowledging the truth about themselves and their city. It would be more natural to suppose that the observers and examiners are from the outside and that Yahweh's words are spoken because they have been urging him to have mercy on Jerusalem in the manner of Gen 18.23–33. He advises them to go into the city and see things at first hand. If they can point to a single person who does what is right by Yahweh's definition and who is steadfast in his adherence to Yahweh, the city will be spared. The lack of integrity and obedience is to be seen in the circumstance that even an oath sworn in Yahweh's name has no substance or honesty in it. This may be regarded as final evidence of apostasy. לכן (v. 2) 'therefore' is not entirely suitable in the context and Pesh. has rendered it as if it were אכן (šryr'yt) 'surely'. G. R. Driver (JQR 28, pp. 100f.) notes that Arabic lkn = 'but' and suggests 'yet' here and at Job 34.25 and 42.3: 'Though they swear, "As the Lord lives", yet they swear only to deceive.'

It would seem best to take v. 6 as continuous with v. 2 and this implies that vv. 1–6 are now being sub-divided into two units. One (vv. 1, 2, 6) is a word of Yahweh and the other (vv. 3–5) consists of words spoken by Jeremiah. The attaching of vv. 3–5 to vv. 1–2 may be explicable in terms of the picking up of אמונה (v. 1) in v. 3. In vv. 1–2 Yahweh has concluded that there are no possible grounds for sparing Jerusalem and the threatening word follows in v. 6. It is, however, uncertain whether v. 6 contains a threat of future judgement or a reference to a judgement which has been carried out and the indications of the verbs might be regarded as conflicting (הכם and ישדדם). If the form of the second verb is Poel, one would expect it to be pointed יְשָׁדְדֵם; if it is Qal, the form should be יְשֻׁדֵּם. The testimony of the versions, in respect of the tenses in v. 6a, is uneven, but there is little doubt (despite the awkwardness of הכם) that על כן should be taken as introducing a threat of future judgement.

ערבות has been connected with ערב 'evening' by Aq., Vulg., Pesh., Targ. and Kimchi. Rashi, on the other hand, interprets זאב ערבות correctly as זאב מדבר (also noted by Kimchi). The reason for the rendering 'wolves of the evening' is the phrase זאבי ערב (Hab 1.8; Zeph 3.3). Hence we have a poetic description of the disaster which will overtake Jerusalem when the city is invaded by ruthless foes: it will be as if its inhabitants were mauled by lions, savaged by wolves, ambushed by leopards, and the reason for this punishment is given in a final כי clause. It is the consequence of their many sins and apostasies.

What Yahweh looks for from his people is אמונה (v. 3): he expects a constancy of regard and commitment which matches the constancy of his loving purposes for his people. With this thought the prophet's train of reflection is initiated. Yahweh has inflicted blows on his people, but they have felt no pain; he has checked them, but they have rejected corrective punishment (v. 3). They are unbending in their resistance to his discipline—with faces harder than rock they refuse to return to him. According to the Massoretic pointing חָלוּ is to be derived from חול 'to writhe in pain'. Sept. (ἐπόνεσαν), Vulg. (doluerunt), Pesh. ('tkrhw) and Kimchi (כאבו), probably, derive חלו from חלה, in which case the form should be written חָלוּ. The thought that the people do not feel pain, despite the punishment which is inflicted on them can be matched by examples from the book of Proverbs, where it constitutes an allusion to the ineffectiveness of corporal punishment when administered to a fool (Prov 17.10; 29.1) or the unawareness of a drunk man that he is doing himself injury (23.35). The last mentioned verse is particularly significant, because its vocabulary coincides with that of v. 3: הכוני בל חליתי (Prov 23.35) and הכיתה אתם ולא חלו (v. 3). Hence there is no need for Driver's solution (JQR 28, p. 101; cf. JTS 29, p. 392), founded on the derivation of חלו from חלה =Ethiopic ḥalaya, 'take thought for', 'consider': 'You inflicted blows on them, but they gave no thought'. This philology has been adopted by NEB both at Jer 3.3 and Prov 23.35.

On the other hand, there is a genuine difficulty with כליתם ('you destroyed them') which does not hang together with 'but they refused corrective punishment', and Kimchi has eased the problem with his interpretation of כליתם ('bringing them to the point of death'). The same tendency is discernible in Vulg. (attrivisti eos.). E. F. Sutcliffe (JSS 5, 1960, pp. 348f.) has noted that כליתם is regarded as hyperbolic by Vulg. and Kimchi, by Rosenmüller (1826), and Giesebrecht (1897). The best of the conjectural emendations which he records is כלאתם = כליתם, 'you held them in check' (G. R. Driver, JQR 28, 1937, p. 101). This involves a change of pointing (כְּלִיתָם instead of MT כִּלִּיתָם, but otherwise כליתם may be regarded as an alternative spelling of כלאתם.

At first, Jeremiah was inclined to conclude that the obtuseness and insensitivity of which he was aware must be characteristic of only one section of the population; that he should not form a judgement on the whole, on the basis of what he had seen of the poor and unlettered people who did not know any better. This crumb of comfort was to be taken away from him, for when he extended his observations to the more influential reaches of the community, to those who wielded power and held office, he discovered that they were no less ignorant and unresponsive. His closing remark ('They too, one and all, have broken the yoke and burst the ropes'), confirms the rightness of the interpretation offered at 2.20. The imagery is indicative of indiscipline and incorrigibility.

It is not certain that the portrayal furnishes us with so specific, chronological indications as Duhm supposes; that it records a shock felt by a young rural prophet in Jerusalem, one which he would soon absorb. It is true that the mode of presentation is dramatic, but caution is required in any attempt to convert such an artistic foreshortening into historical conclusions. We may be in the presence of positions which were not reached without considerable experience of life in Jerusalem and sustained reflection on it.

THE END OF UNFAITHFULNESS WILL BE DESTRUCTION (5.7–11)

[7]How can I forgive you for this?
Your children have forsaken me
and have sworn allegiance to non-gods.
I made them swear allegiance to me,[1] but they have committed adultery
and have gashed themselves in a harlot's house.
[8]They are well-fed, lusty stallions,[2]
each neighing after his neighbour's wife.
[9]Ought I not to punish them for this?
Should I not take my revenge on a nation such as this?
    This is Yahweh's word.
[10]Go along her rows of vines and create havoc;
destroy them totally;[3]
remove her branches,
for they do not belong to Yahweh.
[11]Israel and Judah have been utterly disloyal to me.
    This is Yahweh's word.

In vv. 7–9 Jerusalem (or Judah) is addressed by Yahweh as a mother and the apostasy of her children is described. There is a correspondence between אי לזאת אסלוח לך (v. 7) and העל זאת לא אפקד . . . ואם בגוי אשר כזה לא תתנקם נפשי (v. 9). The first can be translated either 'How can I forgive you for this?' or 'In view of this how can I forgive you?'—referring to the preceding

[1] Reading ואשביע (see below pp. 118f.).
[2] See below p. 119.
[3] Deleting אל (see below p. 120).

indictment. In either case a negative answer is required. The impossibility of forgiveness implies the inevitability of a destructive judgement and this is the thought which finds expression in v. 9, 'Ought I not to punish (them) for all these things? Ought I not to take vengeance on a nation such as this?'—where the answer required is 'Yes'. 'Them' (בם) is indicated by some Hebrew manuscripts here and at v. 29. In v. 10, on the other hand, Yahweh is apparently inciting those who are to attack Jerusalem (and Judah) to begin their work of destruction. We have then to assume that Yahweh refers to himself in the 3rd person, even although he is the speaker (כי לא ליהיה המה). Verse 11, with its reference to בית ישראל ובית יהודה, is especially puzzling. It has been interpolated by someone who wanted to refer to the apostasy of both kingdoms in the round and to make a transition from the particular to the general. Hence כי בגוד בגדו בי latches on to the description of Jerusalem's apostasy in v. 7. Different views are represented by Rudolph and Weiser. Rudolph holds that ובית יהודה should be deleted and that its insertion is related to the circumstance that Judah has the epithet בגודה in 3.7ff. This has the effect of making 'House of Israel' into a general designation of Yahweh's community and disengaging it from the northern kingdom. Weiser (p. 47 n. 1) urges that MT should be retained and that the point which is being made is that Judah is heading for the kind of judgement which destroyed the northern kingdom.

The versions (Sept., Vulg., Pesh., Targ.) all support the reading ואשביע over against ואשביע. The argument can go either way: it may be urged that the reference to swearing oaths by non-gods, which immediately precedes, points to the rightness of ואשביע. The faithless children of mother Jerusalem (or Judah) have deserted Yahweh and have sworn oaths by idols which are empty of reality. This interpretation would suggest that 'adultery' is a figure for apostasy (the breaking of the oath concluded with Yahweh) and that the self-infliction of wounds in a harlot's house is a reference to idolatrous rites. On the other hand, the words in v. 8 ('Each man neighs after his neighbour's wife') suggest that 'adultery' in v. 7 should be construed in its ordinary sense, and in this case there are, probably, no cultic implications in the mention of בית זונה.

Rashi explains יתגדדו as a denominative of גדוד 'band', and this is apparently how it has been taken by Vulg., Pesh. and Targ. whose renderings are related to the thought of 'banding together' (Vulg. *luxuriabantur* 'behaved licentiously'; Pesh. *'tkīšw* 'behaved riotously'; Targ. מסתיעין 'assembled'). This is the sense which is found in Calvin and it has been maintained in the English versions (KJV, RV, RSV) until NEB. It is found in

Gesenius (*Thesaurus* 1, 1835, p. 264) and in BDB. Gesenius and
BDB are influenced by Mic 4.14 (עַתָּה תִתְגֹּדְדִי בַת גְּדוּד) which
suggests that הִתְגֹּדַד can be a denominative of גְּדוּד, and they
conclude that this is the most likely sense at Jer 5.7. It has been
supposed that Sept. κατέλυον points to יִתְגֹּרָרוּ and Gesenius had
noted that two of De Rossi's manuscripts had this reading. If
וְאַשְׁבִּיעַ (MT) is kept and יִתְגֹּרָרוּ is read (Duhm, Rudolph,
NEB—Brockington, p. 200, KB³), we have a picture of base
ingratitude associated with licentious behaviour. Despite the
indications of v. 8 (adultery in a plain sense), it is, probably, best
to make 'idolatry' the key to the interpretation of v. 7, to read
וְאַשְׁבִּיעַ and to take יִתְגֹּדָדוּ in the well-attested sense of 'gash
themselves'. The children of Jerusalem were unfaithful to
Yahweh and gave their allegiance to empty idols. Yahweh put
them on oath, but, although they had sworn allegiance to him,
they gashed themselves at heathen shrines in connection with
acts of idolatrous worship.

The two ἅπαξ λεγόμενα in v. 8 (מֵיזָנִים ; מַשְׁכִּים) cannot be
elucidated with any confidence, but the general meaning of the
verse is not in doubt. The children of mother Jerusalem are
well-fed (K^Occ מוּזָנִים) and their sexual behaviour is like that of
lusty stallions (each neighs for his neighbour's wife). If מְיֻזָּנִים is
read instead of מוּזָנִים the meaning will be 'weighted', and, in
association with the conjecture מְאֻשְׁכִּים 'with big testicles', this
is taken as a reference to heavy genitals. מַאֻשְׁכִּים which is
postulated as a denominative of אֶשֶׁךְ 'testicle' (Lev 21.20) is
noted by Gesenius (*Thesaurus*, 3, 1853, p. 1403) and is
attributed to Fuerst (cf. J. Fuerst, *Hebräisches und
Chaldäisches Handwörterbuch*, 1, 1857, p. 798). Sept. renders
מֵיזָמִים מַשְׁכִּים as θηλυμανεῖς 'mad about women' (=Old Lat.
furentes circa femina). Similar indications are given by Vulg.
amatores et emissarii (cf. Jerome) and Pesh. 'ἕλκοντες (Aq. and
Theod.) represents מַשְׁכִּים and this is also understood by Jerome
as a reference to large genitals (*ut ostenditur magnitudo
genitalium*).

שׁוּרָה (for MT שָׂרָה) is supposed by BDB and KB² to mean 'a
row of vines or olive trees', but its only other occurrence is at Job
24.11 and there the meaning 'wall' seems appropriate (cf. NEB,
בֵּין שׁוּרֹתָם 'where two walls meet'). 'Walls' is the translation of
Vulg. (*muros*) and Pesh. (*šwryh*); Sept. has προμαχῶνας
'battlements'. Kimchi observes that the reference is to the walls
of Jerusalem and this is evidently what the versions represent
throughout v. 10.

Rashi has put his finger on the weakness of this line of
interpretation by observing that נְטִישׁוֹת are 'roots of a vineyard'
and that the vineyard imagery does not correspond particularly

with the assault on a city and the reduction of its defensive walls. If שרות means 'row of vines' (Rudolph, Bright, NEB), nothing is left of the 'wall' imagery. There is no doubt that Rashi is right in general about נטישות whose two other occurrences refer to branches of the vine (Isa 18.5; Jer 48.32). The first of these texts is particularly instructive, since it is clearly part of a description of the total destruction of a vineyard (cf. 18.6), and the verb which is combined with הנטישות (הסיר) is the one which appears in Jer 5.10.

It can be asserted with some confidence that v. 10 describes the total destruction of a vineyard, and, in view of the 3rd person fem. sing. suffixes attached to שרות and נטישות, we should suppose this to represent the total destruction of Jerusalem (and Judah). In that case the אל which appears before תעשו is not original (see above on 4.27, p. 109), although there is no textual support for its deletion. The process of changing the original sense of Jeremiah's words has gone furthest in Sept. and Pesh., where הסירו is replaced by ὑπολίπεσθε and šbwqw 'leave behind', and 'for they do not belong to Yahweh' becomes 'for they belong to the Lord'. It should be noted, however, that the presence of an intention to portray a complete destruction is not admitted by all scholars (cf. Duhm, who deletes וכלה אל תעשו, and Bright who finds no difficulty with the clause).

YAHWEH'S POWER IS DENIED BUT HIS JUDGEMENTS WILL ENSUE (5.12–14)

> [12]They have denied Yahweh,
> He is powerless, they say,
> Disaster will not overtake us,
> we shall not see sword and famine.
> [13]But these prophets are windbags,
> they do not have the word[1] (of Yahweh).[2]
> [14]Therefore, this is the word of Yahweh, God of Sabaoth (to me):
> Because they speak[3] this word,
> I shall make my words like fire in your mouth;
> this people will be the fuel
> and the fire will consume them.

An integrated unit is made out of vv. 12–14 by supposing that the words in v. 13 are part of a speech which begins with לא הוא (v. 12) and ends with אין בהם (v. 13). According to this view the prophets referred to in v. 13 are doom prophets like Jeremiah and those who deny Yahweh's power (v. 12) are saying that the

---

[1] Reading וְהַדָּבָר (MT וְהַדִּבֵּר).
[2] Deleting כה יעשה להם (see below, pp. 121f.).
[3] Emending דברם to דברכם (see below, p. 121).

predictions of judgement which these prophets make are empty and will not be fulfilled. This is Jerome's view, it is found in Calvin and Lowth and it is represented by such modern scholars as Duhm, Rudolph and Weiser. The residual difficulties are overcome (Duhm, Rudolph, Weiser) by transposing כה יעשה להם (v. 13) to v. 14 (after צבאות) and by emending דברכם (v. 14) to דברם . If v. 14 is a word of Yahweh addressed to Jeremiah, the emendation of דברכם to דברם is necessary, and the versions (Sept., Vulg., Pesh., Targ.), which all indicate דברכם, do not succeed in making sense of v. 14.

Targ.'s view that v. 13 refers to prophets who are opponents of Jeremiah is correct and לרוח (ללמא) is indicative of emptiness (it is glossed by Rashi with יהפכו לחבל, 'be turned to emptiness'). Kimchi, like Rashi, follows Targ.'s interpretation of v. 13: he elucidates לרוח as כמוץ לפני הרוח, 'as chaff before the wind', and identifies the prophets of v. 13 with the שלום prophets (cf. Jer 6.14; 8.11). Broadly, G. Schmuttermayr (*BZ* 9, 1965, pp. 215–232) is following Targ. by identifying הנביאים (v. 13) with Jeremiah's opponents and by noticing (p. 223) that the words which constitute the speech in v. 12 have a marked similarity with those elsewhere attributed to שלום prophets (Jer 14.13, 15; 23.17). Bright, who also follows Targ. and correctly explains v. 13, transposes כה יעשה להם to v. 14 (after יען דברם את הדבר הזה)

Rudolph and Bright are right in regarding Jeremiah and not Yahweh as the speaker in v. 12 and NEB has underlined the circumstance that Jeremiah is still the speaker in v. 14: he is reporting a word which he received from Yahweh. Hence, on the assumption that Jeremiah is the speaker throughout vv. 12–14, it might appear that there is no problem in regarding vv. 12–14 as a unity. All the more so if v. 11 is a secondary insertion (as has been argued above, p. 118) and an original connection between v. 11 and 12 is not to be assumed. The words which Jeremiah reproduces are those of the שלום prophets (v. 12) and he proceeds to make a parenthetical observation about these prophets (v. 13). The other possibility is that v. 13 breaks the original continuity of vv. 12 and 14; that it is an isolated remark by Jeremiah about his prophetic opponents which has been inserted here, or that it has been inserted as a comment by someone who identified the words in v. 12 as characteristic of the message of the שלום prophets. The character of v. 12 would account for the insertion of v. 13, whether we suppose the latter to be attributable to Jeremiah or to a commentator.

According to the interpretation of Targ., which is followed by Rashi and Kimchi, by Calvin, Lowth ('denying his Government over Human Affairs'), Blayney, Rudolph and Bright, it is

Yahweh's power of retribution and not his existence which is being denied. E. F. Sutcliffe (*Biblica* 41, 1960, pp. 287–290), who reviews the history of the interpretation of לא הוא (v. 12), notes that Jerome's interpretation is similar: it is a denial that there is a moral design maintained by Yahweh. Hence what is threatened by the doom prophets will not come to pass. The view that לא הוא means 'He does not exist' is found in E. F. C. Rosenmüller (1826) and has been adopted by NEB. Yahweh's reaction, as indicated by v. 14, would seem to be more precisely a rejoinder to an allegation that he lacked the power to enforce his judgements than to a denial of his existence, although both could be involved and there is no incompatibility between them. It is unlikely, however, that we have to reckon here with a theoretical atheism.

Yahweh will put into Jeremiah's mouth words with the destructive potential of fire, and the Jerusalem or Judaean community will be the fuel fed to the flames. Hence vv. 12, 14 indicate how Yahweh counters the charge that the prophet's threats are innocuous by solemnly asserting that he is investing these words with a power of destruction like that of fire.

Older commentators like Calvin and Lowth, who supposed that v. 13 was part of the speech beginning with לא הוא, and that הנביאים (v. 13) were consequently prophets of doom, interpreted כה יעשה להם in connection with the opprobrium heaped on prophets of doom: it means that the disasters with which they threatened others will fall on their own heads. There is no satisfactory solution of כה יעשה להם, but it may well be a secondary, minatory comment. Its non-representation in Sept.^ is slender evidence to support its deletion, but it is seized on by NEB (Brockington, p. 200). If it is regarded as a secondary comment, it has to be understood as founded on the assumption that v. 13 is part of the speech which begins with כה לא הוא. יעשה להם is then directed at those who pour such contempt on the prophets of doom.

What we have otherwise in v. 13 is not altogether Mowinckel's antithesis of 'spirit' and 'word' (*JBL* 53, 1934, pp. 199–227). It is unlikely that Jeremiah is asserting that his prophetic opponents are ecstatics (cf. A. H. J. Gunneweg, *FRLANT*, 55, 1959, pp. 88f.), and this is the connotation of רוח in Mowinckel's opposition of רוח and דבר. The conflict between Jeremiah and the שלום prophets is not a matter of the style of their prophecy. It hinges on the content of their message and this is the criticism which is contained in the assertion that they do not possess the word of Yahweh. לרוח is better elucidated by a comparison with Mic 2.11 (לו איש הלך רוח ושקר כזב), where רוח is indicative of emptiness and falsehood, than by a comparison with Hos 9.7, where it has connections with wild ecstasy.

DESTRUCTION AT THE HANDS OF INVADERS (5.15–17)

[15]I am bringing against you, O Israel, a remote nation,
a nation long established,
an ancient nation;
a nation whose tongue will be unfamiliar to you
and whose speech you will not understand;
[16]whose quivers are an open grave,
all of whom are picked soldiers.
[17]They will consume your grain and your bread,
your sons and your daughters,
your flocks and your herds,
your vines and your fig-trees.
They will reduce by force[1] your fortified cities,
in which you thought that you were secure.

Verses 15–17 have the form of direct address by Yahweh to the 'House of Israel' (= Jerusalem and Judah, see above, p. 119) and are not continuous with v. 14 which consists of words of Yahweh spoken to Jeremiah. The end of the unit vv. 15–17 is marked by a transition from poetry to prose and by the words וגם בימים החמה (v. 18). Stylistic features of vv. 15–17 are the fourfold repetition of גוי in v. 15, matched by the four occurrences of אכל in v. 17. The attachment of vv. 15–17 to what precedes is explicable in terms of a general community of topic (the doom prophecy of Jeremiah will be fulfilled in a military disaster) and, more particularly, in terms of אכל (vv. 14, 17): Jeremiah's word consumes like fire and the invader will consume both lives and wealth.

Sept. represents a shorter text in v. 15 and of MT v. 16 only כלם גבורים (πάντες ἰσχυροί) is indicated. Janzen (pp. 97, 117) explains both aspects of the shorter text of Sept. in v. 15 as a consequence of haplography: the first caused by a confusion between the second and fourth occurrences of גוי and the second by a confusion between the first and second occurrences of לא. Janzen (like Ziegler) regards τῆς φωνῆς as a secondary element in the extant text of Sept. and supposes that the original text was ἔθνος οὗ οὐ γνώσῃ ἃ λαλεῖ καὶ οὐκ ἀκούσῃ τῆς γλώσσης αὐτοῦ. Rather Sept. is an abridgement of MT, and Deut 28.49 has exercised some influence on the abridgement. תשמע has been adopted as the verb and תרע has been dropped; τῆς φωνῆς αὐτοῦ, which in Deut 28.49 is a rendering of לשנו, is utilized in order to represent מה ידבר and לשנו is represented as τῆς γλώσσης αὐτοῦ.

---

[1] See below, p. 125.

It has already been observed (above, p. 19) that Venema identifies the enemy of vv. 15–17 with the Scythians, that his reasoning has a particular attachment to these verses and this chapter, and that he does not assume references to the Scythians in Duhm's 'Scythian Songs'. The distant nation with whom Yahweh threatens the people is identified by Jerome, Rashi and Kimchi with Babylon. It was founded in deep antiquity (מֵעוֹלָם הוּא) and it has maintained a continuous existence since its foundation (אֵיתָן). That it has so maintained its existence is an indication of strength and it is this derivative aspect of אֵיתָן which is expressed by the versions (Vulg. *robustam*; Pesh. *'syn'*; Targ. תקיף) and in Rashi (תקיף) and Kimchi ('A strong people against whom you will not be able to fight'). The unintelligibility of the language which the invaders speak increases the terror of their aspect and invests them with an appearance of inhumanity. In a situation where no communication is possible and no accommodation or understanding can be reached with a conqueror, a new dimension of anxiety and misery is created, and it is this utter ignorance and uncertainty about his intentions and the springs of his actions which gives him a fiendish rather than a human aspect. It is just possible that Rashi's reference to the Tower of Babel may have some connection with this condition of incommunicability between invader and invaded.

In v. 16 אשפתו כקבר פתוח (a difficult simile) is not represented by Sept. Janzen (p. 97) offers alternative assessments: (*a*) The phrase is a gloss (also, Duhm) generated by the theme of voraciousness in v. 17 and partly dependent on Ps 5.10 (קבר פתוח גרנם). (*b*) The phrase has an original connection with v. 17 from which it was accidentally omitted. There has been a tendency to make the phrase easier by replacing אשפתו with אשר פיהו (Volz) or שפתו (Ehrlich, p. 253). אשפתו is indicated by Vulg. (*pharetra*) and Targ. (בית אזיניה), but Pesh. *ggrth* 'their throats' represents גרנו. The Syriac translator probably reacted against the unsatisfactory character of the figure which lay before him in the Hebrew and took steps to improve it by availing himself of the phrase in Ps 5.10. A comparison of the Syriac in v. 16 (*ggrth 'yk qbr' ptyḥyn*) and Ps 5.10 (*w'yk qbr' ptyḥ' ggrthwn*) lends support to this view. At any rate the reading of Pesh. anticipates the kind of emendation which is proposed by Volz and Rudolph and produces a simile which is explicable as a mythological allusion (see *Proverbs*, pp. 269f.). It is probable, however, that אשפתו כקבר פתוח is original and that we simply have to reckon with an infelicitous metaphor: the arrows fired by enemy deal out death and so their container is described as an open grave.

The invaders are not just ordinary soldiers, but picked troops, professionally competent and battle-hardened (כלם גבורים). The emendation which is favoured by Rudolph (כלו מגזבים, 'They are more destructive than locusts') is intended to link v. 16 with the uses of אכל in v. 17 which indicate destruction of crops and fruit. MT yields satisfactory sense and is represented by the versions (Sept., Vulg., Pesh., Targ.).

What is described in v. 17 is the damage to the cultivation of the land caused by military operations or by looting, and the loss of children who will be casualties of war, despatched by a ruthless invader. The renderings of ירשש in Sept., Vulg. and Targ. indicate a derivation from רשש, in which case ירשש is a Poel form (cf. Mal 1.4, רששנו, Pual, 'We are beaten down', NEB). Those whom Yahweh addresses have absolute confidence in their fortified cities (a Maginot line mentality), but the invader will demolish them. Pesh. (nmskn), Rashi (ימסכן) and Kimchi (who explains ירשש in connection with רש 'poor' and רישות 'poverty') all derive ירשש from רוש 'to be poor' and so take it as a Polel form. The thought of impoverishing fortified cities is not so immediate as that of demolishing them. Another problem is constituted by בחרב which goes ill with ירשש. Rashi argues that בחרב connects immediately with ירשש and that the position of בחרב at the end of the verse is an example of an unnatural word order (מקרא מסורם). Rudolph (also NEB, Brockington, p. 200) deletes בחרב, but if one were to accept Rashi's view that the phrase is ירשש בחרב, it could, perhaps, be accommodated with the sense 'reduce by force'.

The relation of vv. 15–17 to Deut 28.49–53 is considered by Thiel (p. 97) who notices that there are significant differences of vocabulary in the two passages and who inclines to the view of Giesebrecht, Hyatt (JNES, 1942, pp. 172f.) and Rudolph that the Jeremiah passage is prior and has influenced Deut 28.49–53. The most striking points of agreement in the two portrayals are the representations that the enemy comes from a remote part of the world and that he speaks a language which is unintelligible. Thiel is inclined to dismiss the idea that these may have been stock items in descriptions of invasions and that this rather than any direct literary relationship may explain their presence in both passages. In any case, distance, remoteness, utter foreignness, a language which is unintelligible—these are all ingredients of dire presentiments and are outriders of terror.

SERVITUDE IN A FOREIGN LAND (5.18–19)

[18]But at that time I will not completely destroy you. This is Yahweh's word. [19]And when they say[1] (to you), For what reason did Yahweh, our God, bring all these things on us?, you must say to them, Just as you forsook me[2] and served foreign gods in your own land, so you will be subject to foreigners in a land which is not your own.

The imagery used in v. 16 and the fourfold אכל in v. 17 might be supposed to indicate annihilation. Hence the 'nevertheless' (גם) with which the prose of v. 18 begins and the assertion that the destruction of the community will not be total. Verses 18–19 have the character of a prophecy after the event: it is represented as a prophecy from the time of Jeremiah and so בימים ההמה is a reference to judgement and exile located in the future. In fact לא אעשה אתכם כלה is a reflection of how events have turned out rather than a reassuring message directed to the future. Similarly what appears to be a threat of future servitude (v. 19) is a comment on the experience of exile (cf. Thiel, pp. 97f.). The passage hinges on the need to explain why the exile took place and the form of v. 19, with its question and answer, makes this abundantly clear. Kimchi does not intend to describe vv. 18–19 as a prophecy after the event, but his recognition that it is appropriate to exilic conditions is significant. Thiel (pp. 97f.), whose account is in broad agreement with the one which has just been given, urges that the concern which finds expression in the question and answer of v. 19 was one which featured in the community instruction carried out by the Deuteronomists in the exilic period.

In v. 19 תאמרו should, probably be emended to יאמרו, although there is no textual support for the change and in either case there is an unevenness as between v. 18 and v. 19. NEB preserves a continuity with אתכם (v. 18) by retaining תאמרו and gets out of the difficulty which is encountered later on in v. 19 by assuming that ואמרת is an unusual spelling of ואמרתי (Brockington, p. 200) and by not translating אליהם —an item which is incompatible with the interpretation of v. 19 which is offered. Verse 19 makes better sense on the assumption that it is the prophet who is being addressed by Yahweh, but this requires the emendation of תאמרו to יאמרו : Yahweh instructs him how to answer the people when they demand an explanation of their condition of exile. Janzen (p. 36) argues, following Volz, that עזבתם אותי, which is not represented by Sept., overloads the verse and spoils the sharpness of the correspondence between כן תעבדו and כאשר תעבדו. There is no doubt that this

[1] Reading יאמרו (MT תאמרו).

[2] 'Me'=Yahweh (cf. Pesh. which inserts hkn' 'mr mry' after אליהם).

interpretation of זרים ('foreigners') is correct and that Jerome is mistaken in equating זרים with 'alien gods'.

This is a convenient place to consider the three passages (4.27; 5.10, 18), where עשה כלה occurs with a negative (לא in 4.27 and 5.18, and אל in 5.10). The general view of the meaning of the phrase is that a limit is set to the extent of Yahweh's judgement of his people: they will be severely punished but not annihilated. This is the exegesis which is found in Jerome at 5.10. That this is also Kimchi's view is clear from his comment on לא אעשה אתכם כלה, 'I shall put into the mind of the enemy to leave you a remnant'. Another line of interpretation is to be found in Calvin, Lowth and Blayney. According to Calvin the meaning of לא אעשה אתכם כלה, or the like, is that Yahweh will not put any check on his retributive zeal, until he has completely destroyed them. Lowth, for reasons which are not obvious, adopts this interpretation at 5.10 and 18, but not at 4.27, where he prefers the other exegesis. A refinement of Calvin's exegesis would be the supposition that כלה is an unusual spelling of כלא 'restraint'. The Achilles' heel of this exegesis is, however, 5.18, and it will be obvious from what has been already said about that verse that לא אעשה אתכם כלה can only mean 'I shall not annihilate you; I shall leave you a remnant'. The position is different in the two other passages, where Calvin and those who followed him were striving to understand the phrase in a way which was agreeable with the context. The latter pointed to total destruction and וכלה לא אעשה or וכלה אל תעשו was brought into line with these indications. When all these considerations are weighed, the most probable conclusion is that 5.18 has influenced 4.27 and 5.10, whether or not we suppose that it was the (Deuteronomistic) author of chapter 5.18 who modified the text at 4.27 and 5.10 in view of the circumstance that there were survivors of the fall of Jerusalem (cf. Thiel, p. 98). Alternative solutions of the problem of 4.27 and 5.10 have been discussed (above, p. 109).

SIN UNDOES YAHWEH'S BENEVOLENT ORDER (5.20–25)

[20]Declare this to the house of Jacob,
proclaim it in Judah:
[21]Listen to this you foolish and senseless people,
who have eyes with no sight
and ears with no hearing.
[22]Have you no fear of me?
Do you not tremble before me?
This is Yahweh's word.
I made the sand the sea's limit,
an ancient boundary which it cannot pass;

it will rage to no effect,[1]
its waves will roar but they will not pass it.
[23]The heart of this people is rebellious and undisciplined;
they have turned aside and gone their own way.
[24]They have no mind to say,
Let us fear Yahweh, our God,
who gives the rain[2] in season,
who maintains for us the weeks[3] of harvest.
[25]Your iniquities have disordered these things,
your sins have cut off nature's bounty from you.

Rudolph has noticed that vv. 20–25 do not fit into the general context of chapter 5 which is occupied with enemy invasion and its disastrous consequences. It is true that the content of these verses does set them apart from the preceding part of the chapter. The same judgement, however, would have to be made about vv. 26–31 which also break new ground: vv. 26–29 concentrating on a description of wicked men in the Judaean community and vv. 30–31 on the betrayal of the prophetic and priestly offices. This is Duhm's logic, since he denies vv. 20–31 to Jeremiah. In v. 12 the threat which is dismissed is that of famine which is the consequence of war, whereas in vv. 20–25 the disturbance of the rhythm of nature is attributed directly to sin. The form of address in v. 20 is new, but בית יעקב almost certainly functions as a synonym of יהודה and is not a reference to the northern kingdom (cf. Jerome, *Israhel enim multo iam tempore in Assyriis exsulabat*; see Duhm on 2.4). The plural imperatives in v. 20 raise the same kind of structural difficulty as that discussed in connection with v. 1 (above, pp. 114f.). Whether or not v. 20 is original (cf. Rudolph), vv. 20–25 do not constitute an integrated unit. Verses 21–22 are directly addressed to Judah, but in vv. 23–24 Yahweh is speaking *about* his people to a third party, and v. 25 reverts to direct address. We do not know to whom Yahweh is represented as speaking in vv. 23–24, but we could assume that he is describing the characteristics of the people to Jeremiah. The book of Jeremiah betrays this tendency towards the representation of conversation between Yahweh and his prophet: a message conveyed by Yahweh to his prophet for communication to the people is replaced by conversation between Yahweh and his prophet about the people. One must, therefore, say that there are two units, vv. 20–22 or 21–22 and vv. 23–25. It may be asked whether a question (v. 22) can rank as a message and whether this is another indication of the disintegration of the form of the prophetic oracle. A further factor is that the message, which

[1] Reading ויתגעש ולא יוכל (see below, p. 129).
[2] Deleting וירה ומלקוש (see below, pp. 130, 131).
[3] Deleting חקות (see below, p. 131).

should be the dominant element, is almost swamped by description in v. 21 (עינים ... ישמעו) and v. 22 (... אשר יעברנהו).

YAHWEH'S QUESTION TO THE PEOPLE (5.20–22)

The vocabulary used to describe the people's lack of sense has affiliations with Proverbs and Ecclesiastes. The remaining occurrences of סכל, apart from the two in the book of Jeremiah (4.22; 5.21) are found in Ecclesiastes (2.19; 7.17; 10.3, 14). In the phrase ואין לב (v. 21), לב has the cerebral sense ('mind', 'wits') which is common in Proverbs (חסר לב in Prov 6.32; 7.7; 9.4, 16; 10.13; 11.12; 12.11; 15.21; קנה לב in 15.32 and 19.8; cf. *PWM*, pp. 15f.). Yahweh's question, which constitutes the message, is an accusing one; so hardened are they that they are incapable of awe and no longer feel the impact of Yahweh's majesty.

Vulg. *dolebitis* 'feel pain or anguish' agrees with Kimchi's view that תחיל (v. 22) is a reference to labour pains (חיל כיולדה). The parallelism (תיראו) points to an anguish caused by fear (so probably Pesh. and Targ.) rather than by pain ('shaking with terror'), and NEB has attempted to preserve the word-play (חול — תחילו) by rendering, 'Will you not shiver before me, who made the shivering sand to bound the sea?' Following the accusing question comes a description of Yahweh's power over the sea which invites comparison with the P creation story, according to which the waters which covered the whole earth were gathered into a limited area by Yahweh and assigned boundaries which they might not transgress (cf. Gen 1.9—the comparison is made by Kimchi).

Sept. indicates singular verbs for ויתגעשו ולא יוכלו and their subject in that case is ים. It is unlikely that the Greek translator had a different Hebrew text from MT; it is more probable that he decided to solve a grammatical and exegetical difficulty by this device. Pesh., which also has singular verbs, has, probably followed the lead of Sept. Rashi and Kimchi suppose that the subject of the plural verbs is גליו. This grammar is tolerated by NEB, but it is difficult to believe that גליו can be the subject of the two verbs which precede והמו, especially since ויתגעשו ולא יוכלו is a sense unit and a new stich begins with והמו. One might conjecture that the subject of the verbs of the first stich (מימיו or the like) has been lost, but the best that can be done is to follow Sept. and Pesh.

Sept., Vulg., Pesh., Targ., Rashi and Kimchi, all suppose that חוק means 'law' or 'statute' rather than 'boundary' or 'limit' (cf.

Bright 'eternal decree'). This law is the most impressive of all the testimonies of Yahweh's authority, for it is infallibly observed (cf. Kimchi). This is a characteristic to which the תורה cannot lay claim, for it can be infringed by the free will of Yahweh's human creatures (רצון). Despite this interesting exegesis of Kimchi, the rendering 'limit' or 'boundary' should be adopted for חוק: גבול and חק are synonyms. The functioning of the sand as a boundary for the sea is as old as the created order itself, and any infringement would cause a relapse into a watery chaos. Hence Yahweh is represented as the one who preserves the very foundations of the created order.

IMPIETY AND REBELLIOUSNESS HAVE DISTURBED THE RHYTHMS OF NATURE (5.23–25)

Verses 23–25 are not continuous with vv. 20–22 (above, pp. 128f.) but they echo the vocabulary of these verses and reproduce their ideas so deliberately that they appear to have been generated by vv. 21–22. The stubborn and rebellious temper of the people (v. 23) can be related to what is said of them in v. 21, while their imperviousness to the majesty and holiness of Yahweh (v. 22a) are reiterated with the repetition of ירא in v. 24a. There is also a link between v. 22bc and v. 24b in that both are concerned with Yahweh's management of the created order.

Rudolph is attracted by Ehrlich's emendation (p. 254) which matches ויתגעשו ולא יוכלו (v. 22c—referring to the sea) with סרו וַיֵּלָכוּ (v. 23), and so produces an echo of v. 22c: they are apostate and have become expert at it. The idea is good, but the emendation is unnecessary, since סרו וילכו, where וילכו is indicative of wilfulness, makes entirely satisfactory sense. The words or reflections desiderated of these rebels are reproduced *verbatim*, beginning with נירא and ending with לנו. What is then indicated is that they do not have the right attitude of respect and gratitude. It is likely that ירח ומלקוש (Q ירה ומלקוש) is a gloss on גשם (Rothstein, Rudolph). Rudolph also supposes that שבעות is a dittography—the five, preceding consonants are שבעתו, so that one has to assume a metathesis of ת and ו. חקות קציר ישמר לנו then means 'keeps for us the fixed period of harvest'='assures to us the season of harvest'. This is more or less the same rendering as that of Bright ('and the weeks appointed for harvest secures for us') and NEB ('who brings us unfailingly fixed seasons of harvest'), both attempting to render MT unaltered.

Of the versions Sept., Vulg. and Pesh. have all read שבעות as

שׁבעות or the like (also Blayney), while חקות is indicated as a singular, with the sense 'ordinance' (προστάγματος) in Sept. and 'season' (*annuae*) in Vulg. Jerome notes that Aq. (*prima editio*) and Symm. have understood שׁבעות as 'weeks'. Targ. is the most interesting of the versions, because its rendering assumes the reversal of the order of שׁבעות and חקות. Otherwise, it reads שׁבעות as שׁבעות 'weeks' in agreement with MT. It is certain that Targ. was reading MT and that the positions of שׁבעות and חקות were reversed in order to improve the sense. 'Who preserves for us seasonably the ordinance of the weeks of harvest' refers to the period of seven weeks (cf. Jerome on Aq. and Symm.) which is stipulated in Deut 16.9–12 and Lev 23.10–17, and both Rashi and Kimchi rest their exegesis on this foundation. In Deut 16.9–12 the opening and closing rites of this festival period are described and the concluding words are ועשׁית את החקים האלה (v. 12). In Lev 23.14 and 21 each of these rites is described in turn as חקת עולם (cf. חק עולם, Jer 5.22). חק in the Deuteronomy and Leviticus passages has the sense of 'ritual duty' and Rashi's explanation of חקות (Jer 5.24) is influenced by this.

The conclusion to be drawn is that חקות and not שׁבעות is the secondary element in Jer 5.24, and this for the following reasons: (*a*) Good sense cannot be had out of MT with the word order שׁבעות חקות. (*b*) The insertion of חקות was caused by the interpretation of שׁבעות as the festal period of seven weeks under the influence of the Deuteronomy and Leviticus passages. (*c*) חקות 'statutes' or 'ritual duties' does not suit v. 24 which refers to the unfailing order of the seasons (so Kimchi). חקות so elucidated adds to the evidence of glossing from the book of Deuteronomy in Jer 5.23–25. The phrase סורר ומורה occurs at Deut 21.18, 20; Rudolph held that this was the source of ומורה in Jer 5.23 and that the metre had been spoiled by the insertion. וירה ומלקושׁ (Jer 5.24), which looks like a gloss, is, probably, derived from Deut 11.14 (ונתתי מטר ארצכם בעתו יורה ומלקושׁ).

Yahweh tells his people that their sins have disturbed the regularity of the seasons (v. 25; הטו אלה), and the implication is that this has led to famine conditions (so Rashi). Famine is here related to a natural disorder which is the direct consequence of sin, whereas in v. 12 it is envisaged as an aftermath of war and invasion (וחרב ורעב). The view that vegetation and animals languish and suffer because of the sins of men finds expression in 12.4 and 14.1–10.

THE OPPRESSORS AND THEIR DEVICES (5.26–29)

[26]There are evil-doers among my people;
  they are waiting their chance,[1] crouching like fowlers;
  they have set a deadly snare
  and it is men that they hunt.
[27]As a cage is full of birds,
  their houses are full of loot;
  so they have become powerful and wealthy,
[28]they are fat and well-fed
  and shut their eyes to evil deeds.
  They do not uphold justice:
  they do not maintain the rights of orphans,
  nor do they defend the poor at law.
[29]Ought I not to punish them for this?
  Should I not take my revenge on a nation such as this?
    This is Yahweh's word.

The speaker in v. 29 can only be Yahweh and the unit vv. 26–29 should, therefore, be regarded as speech of Yahweh. The unit closes with the same threatening questions as appear in v. 9. Once again we have to assume that Jeremiah is the person to whom Yahweh relates this tale of violence, greed, and injustice, and from whom he expects an affirmative answer to the questions put in v. 29. Although v. 26 links vv. 26–29 with what precedes, the transition from an address to the community in v. 25 to comment about the community (vv. 26–29) indicates a lack of structural integrity. There are grounds for regarding vv. 26–29 as a further spelling out of v. 25.

There are both lexicographical and grammatical problems in v. 26: שכך occurs elsewhere in the Qal with the sense 'abate' (Gen 8.1) and in the Hiphil with the sense 'allay' (Num 17.20). The same form as is posited in Jer 5.26 (infinitive construct Qal) appears as שׁךּ not שׁךּ in Esth 2.1 with the sense 'abate' (abatement of anger as opposed to abatement of waters in Gen 8.1). The sense 'crouch', for which support is claimed from Arabic *skk* (BDB) is, therefore, dubious. The problem with ישׁור is one more of grammar than of lexicography. From a meaning 'to look' or 'to gaze' a development to 'keep a look out' or 'lie in wait' is understandable and ישׁור is glossed by Rashi as יארב (cf. Hos 13.7) and by Kimchi as יביט. If, however, the subject is רשׁעים, the singular form is difficult to account for, especially in view of the plurals which follow (הצּיבו; ילכדו). Rudolph's elaborate emendation (כיוקשׁים (ה)שׁבכו ישׂרכו, 'They lay a net like fowlers') creates new lexicographical obscurities, because שׂרך occurs only at Jer 2.23, and שׂבכה 'net' is attested only at Job 18.8, but the form שׂבך, which Rudolph needs for the credibility of his emendation, is not attested. Driver's

[1]Reading ישׁורו (MT ישׁור). See below, p. 133.

rearrangement of the text (*JQR* 28, pp. 101f.) involves what he calls 'a mere transposition of consonants' (p. 102). It yields the following text:

כי נמצאו בעמי רשים עשרו וכשו
כיקושים הציבו משחית אנשים ילכדו

שׁ(א)ר has the sense 'tyrant' at Prov 13.23, 28.3 (see Driver, *JTS* 31, p. 278 and my *Proverbs*). כשה 'gorged' is attested at Deut 32.15. Driver translates:

For there are found among my people tyrants,
   they grow rich and are gorged;
like fowlers they set engine(s) of destruction
   (that) they may catch men.

The difficulty of the verse is reflected in the versions. Sept. represents יקושים הציבו לשחת אנשים וילכדו and ישׁור כשׁך is not indicated. Vulg. represents ישׁור כשׁך by *insidiantes quasi aucupes*, 'lying in wait like fowlers', renders יקושים as *laqueos* 'snares' and משחית as *pedicas* 'traps'. Kimchi explains יקושים as a synonym of מוקשים, and this was probably the assumption made by Sept. and Vulg. Pesh. also has a shorter text than MT and does not represent ישׁור and משחית. The latter is a term for a bird-trap, according to Kimchi.

An attempt to make sense of MT as it stands is found in Rashi: ישׁור is explained as יארב and כשׁך יקושים is elucidated as the crouching position of those who catch gazelles by the legs (יקושים = 'hunters'). ישׁורו should be read for ישׁור (an inescapable change) and an attempt should be made to wring sense out of כשׁך יקושים, even if the result is less than convincing. ישׁורו כשׁך יקושים will then be understood as 'They keep watch, crouching like fowlers'. J. A. Emerton (*Festschrift Cazelles*, 1981, pp. 125–133) suggests כּשׁךּ (cf. Lam 2.6, שׂכּוֹ 'booth'): 'They watch as in a fowler's hide'. It is possible that the difference of form as between הציבו and ילכדו is significant. They have laid their trap and they await developments; what they expect to catch is not birds but men. This is in line with the punctuation of MT and the metre should be indicated (*pace* Rudolph, 3+2, 3+2) as 3+3, 2+2.

The thought of plunder or loot is involved in the simile of v. 27. The bird-cage, according to Targ. (בית פטמא), Rashi and Kimchi, is the place where birds are fattened, and along these lines Kimchi elucidates the simile. The birds do not have to fend for themselves, but are supplied with food and drink to fatten them; similarly the houses of the רשעים are full of loot (מרמה = ממון). This is a correct understanding of the verse and so מרמה is 'wealth gained by fraud', a sense which is not brought out by the versions (Sept. δόλου; Vulg. *dolo*; Pesh. *nkl'*; Targ. נכלין), all of which indicate 'deceit'.

The sense of עשתו (v. 28) is obscure: the meaning is derived from עשת 'plate' (Ct. 5.14) and עשות 'smooth'? (Ezek 27.19) by postulating a semantic development from 'shiny' to 'smooth' to 'sleek'. NEB does not make the deletion (שפטו ... דין) which Driver proposes (*JQR* 28, p. 102), but its rendering, 'They grow rich and grand, bloated and rancorous; their thoughts are all of evil', depends on the switching of עשתו and עברו ('rancorous') and the sense 'think' for עשת (cf. Jon 1.6).

Sept. does not represent דברי רע nor שמנו עשתו nor ויצליחו. Thus גם עברו דין is rendered as καὶ παρέβησαν κρίσιν and לא דנו דין יתום as οὐκ ἔκριναν κρίσιν ὀρφανοῦ; χήρας represents אלמנה (MT אביונים). Symm. and Theod. (παρέβησαν τους λογους μου εις πονηρον) have read עברו דברי as עברו דברי רע עברו and Vulg. represents the same vocalization (*praeterierunt sermones meos pessime*, 'They have disregarded my words most wickedly'). ויצליחו (*non direxerunt*) is supplied with a negative and its ambiguity is resolved: the reference is not to the ill-gotten prosperity of oppressive judges (as Driver supposed), but to their failure in respect of the legal rights of orphans. Pesh. partly follows Sept. and partly Vulg.: it does not indicate שמנו עשתו and for גם עברו דברי רע it has *w'brw 'l dyn'*, 'and they transgressed (or 'violated') justice' (cf. καὶ παρέβησαν κρίσιν). ויצליחו is rendered as *l' trṣw*, 'they did not set right' (=Vulg.). It looks as if Pesh. is dependent on both Sept. and Vulg.

Bright's view that עברו דברי רע means 'They overlooked (turned a blind eye to) evil behaviour or lawlessness' has some support from Vulg. (*praeterierunt*, 'disregard'). The use of עבר with על in Biblical Hebrew in the sense of overlooking or forgiving (Mic 7.18; Prov 19.11; cf. Amos 7.8 and 8.2) is close to the one which is desiderated here and doubt is created only by the absence of על in this instance. Bright should be followed in this particular. Another matter concerns the absence of any equivalent of שמנו עשתו in Sept. and Pesh.: שמנו עשתו may be a secondary elaboration of גדלו ויעשירו (cf. Targ. which renders שמנו עשתו as 'They are rich, more they acquire wealth'), but if שמנו עשתו is deleted, we are left with an odd number of stichs in vv. 27–28. Finally there is the problem of ויצליחו. The reading of Vulg. and Pesh. is to be explained as an attempt to offer a firm exegesis of the obscure Hebrew of MT. Gaster's conjecture (*ET* 56, p. 54) that צלח should be associated with Ethiopic *ṣalḥawa* 'deceive' or 'defraud' makes 'the wicked' the subject of ויצליחו and this agrees with the grammar (but not the sense) indicated by Driver. It has support from Targ. and Kimchi (ואף על כן ויצליחו, 'And, nevertheless they prosper') whose lexicography, however, is that of Driver (*JQR* 28, p. 102) and not of Gaster. The other view, which should be adopted is represented by

Rudolph and is found in Bright and D. W. Thomas (*ET* 57, 54f.): יתום is the subject of ויצליחו, 'so that they (the orphans) might enjoy their rights'. NEB has a rendering of exactly the same type as Vulg. and Pesh. ('The claims of the orphan they do not put right').

The oppressors in v. 28 fail to ensure that the weak members of the community have proper access to judicial processes and enjoy a real equality before the law over against more powerful contestants. They connive at injustice and do not take a stand on behalf of justice. Because of this Yahweh addresses to the prophet (v. 29) the same questions as appeared in v. 9. These are questions which admit of only one answer and this is full of the threat of judgement.

There are differences between vv. 21–29 and the preceding part of chapter 5. There is no doubt that one has an impression of moving into a different literary atmosphere with new characteristics which can be stated. The topics are more recondite and theological and there is less of an involvement in urgent, historical events; there is a preoccupation with creation doctrine and a connection is made between sin and natural disorders. The leap which Duhm takes in assigning vv. 21–29 to the post-exilic period is, perhaps, a leap into the darkness. To be so critically bold as he is on the basis of the kind of evidence which is available is unwise. There is nothing in vv. 21–29 which could make us sure or even generate a probability that the ideas expressed are post-exilic rather than those of the late pre-exilic period.

It has been noted that only in vv. 21–22 do we have 'proclamation' and that even in these verses there is a predominance of description. There is also the evidence of an unfolding of ideas, of a development of a train of thought—a picking up of vv. 21–22 in vv. 23–24 and a filling out of v. 25 in vv. 26–29. This is an interconnection of ideas which marches with structural discontinuity. It might be regarded as a literary process and it could be explained as 'second thoughts', so that only one author is involved, or as a 'second' and, perhaps, 'third' hand. Here again a sharp, critical solution cannot be achieved, but our minds are now focused on the question of the relation between a prophet's preaching and the literary deposit which is available to us. We have tended to assume too easily that the relationship between what the prophet said and what was subsequently written down is a simple one. Our discussion is, however, not always simply about recall or preservation; there may be more subtle considerations, more intrinsic processes of transformation effected in the transition from oral delivery to literature. These are factors which should make us hesitate to

conclude that whenever we encounter more reflective or
theological pieces in the book of Jeremiah, this of itself is an
indication that we have been transported from his age into a
later age of Judaism.

A SHOCKING AND HORRIBLE PERVERSION (5.30–31)

[30]A shocking and horrible thing is present in the land:
[31]the prophets prophesy falsehoods,
the priests are in league with them,
and this is how my people like it.
But how will you fare when the sequel comes?

There is disagreement about בשקר: Does it mean 'falsely' or is
שקר a surrogate for בעל? Rudolph believes that the latter is true
and that נבאו בשקר is elucidated by נבאו בבעל (2.8) and הנבאו
בבעל (23.13—referring to prophets of Samaria). Milgrom
(*JNES*, 1967, p. 67) argues that שקר in 5.31 has to be
interpreted against the catalogue of charges in vv. 26–28 and this
is Rashi's view, since he explains שקר in terms of a gulf between
preaching and behaviour—the prophets steal and exact money
(vv. 26–28). This assumes the continuity of vv. 26–31, but it is
unlikely that vv. 30–31 are continuous with vv. 26–28. Even if
the questions in v. 29 do not certainly mark the end of a unit (cf.
v. 9), the subject matter of vv. 30–31 has a greater affinity with
vv. 12–13 than it has with vv. 26–28. The view that נבאו בשקר in
v. 31 means נבאו בבעל should be ruled out (see below on 23.14);
nothing of the kind is indicated by Sept. (ἄδικα), Vulg.
(*mendacium*), Pesh. (*šwqr'*) and Targ. (שקר), and the most
probable conclusion is that we have a reference to the false
assurances of שלום which are touched on in vv. 12–13.

The sense of ירדו על ידיהם is obscure. A. R. Johnson (*The
Cultic Prophet in Ancient Israel*, 2nd ed., 1962, p. 64) connects
ירדו with I רדה 'rule' and renders 'rule under their
direction'—the priests are dominated by the prophets. Duhm
associates ירדו על ידיהם with וירדהו אל כפיו (Judg 14.9) and
with II רדה (BDB and KB²), and this is the lexicography of KB².
The sense, according to Duhm, is that the priests line their own
pockets with bribes. This goes back to Kimchi who observes that
רדה may have the sense 'rule', but who cites Judg 14.9 and
remarks that the priests accepted bribes to pervert justice
(harking back to v. 28). Driver (*JTS* 36, 1935, pp. 297f.) has
grouped Judg 14.9, 1 Kgs 5.4,30, 9.23, Isa 14.6, Jer 5.31 and
Lam 1.13 in connection with Accadian *ridū* and Syriac *rd'*
'drive', 'follow', 'journey' and has rendered Jer 5.31, 'And the
priests ran beside them' (imitated them). The exegesis is not

new, for Rashi suggested that the sense of the passage might be
that the priests imitated the behaviour of the prophets. More
recently Holladay (*VT* 15, 1965, pp. 111–113) has reviewed the
efforts which have been made to deal with the difficulty of ירדו
על ידיהם. He notices that Cornill's emendation of ירדו to יורו
has been adopted by Rudolph—the priests teach off their own
bat, or according to their own norms. Holladay's solution, which
involves Judg 14.9, is an improbable one: 'filling the hands' is the
terminology of priestly consecration and 'scraping out' is
indicative of deconsecration.

The ancient versions do not provide a great deal of help: Sept.
and Vulg., 'applaud with their hands', indicate that the priests
wholeheartedly approve of the prophets' behaviour; Pesh., 'grasp
their hands', and Targ., 'support them', perhaps, indicate that
there is a conspiracy, and this is coming close to NEB 'go hand
in hand with them'. Prophets and priests conspire to fill the
people with a false religious confidence by saying on Yahweh's
authority that the future is rosy. This is what constitutes שקר,
for these are empty prophecies with no substance in them. The
shocking and horrible thing which is present in the land—the
unholy alliance of prophets and priests—will draw judgement on
Judah. Verses 30–31 are Jeremiah's words, spoken on his own
account and not as Yahweh's word. In ועמי אהבו כן indictment
is mixed with feelings of solidarity and concern (עמי), and the
final question which descries inevitable doom is that of a man
defeated by folly and hardly able to contemplate its
consequences: 'But how will you fare when the sequel comes?'

CHAPTER VI

JERUSALEM AND THE IMPENDING ATTACK (6.1–8)

[1]Make for safety, men of Benjamin,
get out of Jerusalem,
blow the trumpet in Tekoa,
kindle a beacon on Beth-hakkerem;
for disaster peers out from the north
—a shattering defeat.
[2]The daughter of Zion, beautiful and pampered,
is near her end;[1]
[3]shepherds are approaching her,
bringing their flocks,
they encircle her with their tents,
each grazing his allotted pasture.
[4]Prepare for battle against her;
let us make our attack at noon.
Impossible! it is too late for that,
the shadows of evening are lengthening.
[5]Let us make our attack at night
and destroy her fortifications.
[6]These are the words of Yahweh Sabaoth:
Cut down trees,
raise ramps against Jerusalem;
she is the city on which judgement will fall,
oppression is everywhere within her.
[7]As a well keeps its waters cold,
she keeps her evil fresh;
sounds of violence and murder are heard in her,
disease and wounds are always before my eyes.
[8]Mend your ways, Jerusalem,
or I will tear myself apart from you;
I will make you desolate,
a land without inhabitants.

If vv. 1–8 are indeed a whole, we have to suppose that they are a complex unity within which now Jeremiah speaks (vv. 1–3), now the enemy investing Jerusalem (vv. 4–5), now Yahweh, addressing the enemy and describing the corruption of the city (vv. 6–7), and finally issuing to Jerusalem a last call to repentance (v. 8). First of all we encounter Jeremiah as he warns Benjamites who are resident in the doomed city to get out while there is time. He describes Jerusalem, personified in v. 2 as a beautiful and pampered woman, at the moment when hostile armies are about to lay siege to her. In vv. 4–5 we have access to a council of war and to speeches which set out the strategy for attack. There follows Yahweh's direct encouragement to the enemy to get on with the siege, his account of Jerusalem's

---

[1] Reading דמתה (MT דמיתי). See below, p. 141.

decadence and his last-minute call to repentance whose finality is explicit (vv. 6–8).

Vulg. (*Confortamini filii Beniamin in medio Ierusalem*) supposes that Benjamites are being advised to prepare fortified positions within the city. Sept. like Rashi ('Get out to your fortified cities and guard them') envisages that a stand is to be made outside and not inside Jerusalem (Vulg. takes מקרב as *in medio*). The idea of 'flight' is the one which is taken up by Targ. (גלו) and Kimchi (הנסו). The background to the warning is that Jerusalem is doomed and that those from the countryside to the north who have sought shelter there must get out with all speed. The view that the mention of בני בנימן indicates that Jeremiah was especially concerned for his own kinsmen is as old as Kimchi. Rudolph sees it rather as a poetic concreteness—a particularizing of the message which lends it urgency. The concern for artistry is evidenced by the assonances in v. 1—בני בנימן and ובתקוע תקעו (the latter noted by Kimchi who cites Zeph 2.4, ועקרון תעקר).

It has been generally supposed that the enemy is advancing from the north (נשקפה מצפון) and that places further south than Jerusalem are to be warned that they will soon be overrun. The blowing of the trumpet and the lighting of a beacon can be interpreted as general alarm signals which give notice to those who live in these areas that they should flee for their lives (Kimchi), or they may be thought of in narrower, military terms: the beacon as a method of signalling and the trumpet as a call to arms. The function of the beacon in a military context is illustrated by one of the Lachish letters (4 reverse, 10–13) in which we read: 'Let him also know that we are watching for the beacons [vocalized as מַשְׂאֹת by Gibson] of Lachish (interpreting them) in accordance with all the code signals which my lord has given. But we do not see Azekah' (J. C. L. Gibson, *Hebrew and Moabite Inscriptions*, 1971, p. 42; cf. H. Donner—W. Röllig, *Kanaanäische und aramäische Inschriften*, i, 1962, p. 35; ii, 1964, pp. 194f.). This letter is sent by an officer called Hoshaiah to his superior officer Jaush. Hoshaiah is in command of an outpost in the south of Judah and Jaush is stationed at Lachish. It has been suggested that the laconic ending ('But we do not see Azekah') may indicate that this place had fallen to the Babylonians (J. Bright, *A History of Israel²*, 1972, p. 329; Y. Aharoni, *The Land of the Bible*, 1966, p. 353; cf. Gibson, op. cit., p. 43 n. 12).

This has relevance for our verse in view of Aharoni's supposition ('Beth-haccherem', *Archaeology and Old Testament Study*, ed. D. Winton Thomas, 1967, p. 182) that it deals with the advance 'of an enemy approaching Jerusalem from the south', and that the military situation which it reflects is the one indicated by 2 Kgs 25.1, Jer 34.6f., 52.4 and by the Lachish letters (cf. J. Bright, *History*², p. 329). Before the final onslaught on Jerusalem in 587 the Babylonian army mopped up all the strong points of resistance in the southern part of Judah and this phase is reflected in the Lachish letters. It is because he assumes that this is the military background to Jer 6.1 that Aharoni (cf. *The Land of the Bible* p. 353) speaks of a movement on Jerusalem from the south rather than from the north: hence the order Tekoa, Beth-hakkerem (identified with Ramat Raḥel—between Jerusalem and Bethlehem) and then Jerusalem itself. The references to sounding the trumpet in Tekoa and lighting a beacon on the height of Beth-hakkerem (cf. Aharoni, 'Beth-haccherem', p. 171) will then be understood simply as general alarm signals, warning the population of these areas to flee to the north from the approaching enemy. The thought of military intelligence and a call to arms connects, on the other hand, with the organization of resistance against an army which was pressing into Judah from the north, and we have noticed that העזו in v. 1 lends some encouragement to this idea (cf. Sept., Vulg. and Rashi).

The decision hinges on whether נשקפה מצפון (v. 1) can mean anything other than 'from the north' and there are two passages which are germane, Gen 11.2 and 13.11. According to BDB (p. 578) ויהי בנסעם מקדם (11.2) means 'as they journeyed eastwards'; ויסע לוט מקדם (13.11) means 'and Lot took the road eastwards'. The decisive consideration, however, is that שקף is not a verb of motion and that other uses (Ps 85.12; 102.20; Deut 26.15) of שקף with מן (Niphal and Hiphil) indicate that נשקפה מצפון must mean 'peers out from the north' or 'looms from the north'. The disaster looming out of the north (Babylon, or the Scythians, according to Duhm) will break Judah in pieces; the blow which is struck will be fatal and Judah will disintegrate.

It is difficult to make sense of v. 2 (MT): דמיתי could be 2nd per. sing. fem., since forms of this type (with a final *yodh*) are found elsewhere in the book of Jeremiah (e.g. 2.20). The translation would then be, 'You are like a beautiful and pampered woman, O daughter of Zion'. Vulg. has read דמיתי as דְּמִיתִי and has assumed that the *yodh* is indicative of 1st per.: 'I liken the daughter of Zion to a beautiful and pampered woman' (also Kimchi). It is in connection with this translation of v. 2 that Jerome raises the question whether רעים (v. 3) might not be vocalized רֵעִים 'lovers'. Sept. is perhaps, a summarizing paraphrase of Hebrew which was ill understood. הנוה והמענגה is not represented and דמה may have been taken as 'be at an end' (ἀφαιρεθήσεται). The paraphrase of Targ. ('Therefore the

congregation of Zion suffers disgrace') also appears to rest on
the assumption that דמה means 'to be at an end' (also Rashi).
The object of Rudolph's emendation (הלנוה מענג דמתה בת ציון)
is to establish a connection with the figure of v. 3 (shepherds and
their flocks): 'Is the daughter of Zion like luxuriant pasture?'
Arguably the sense which is sought requires הלא לנוה, and מענג,
'luxuriant' is lexicographically dubious. A smaller emendation is
the substitution of דמתה = רמת or דמתה for דמיתי (Brockington,
p. 200), 'The beautiful and pampered daughter of Zion is near
her end'. The 3rd per. suffixes in v. 3 are not consistent with a
direct address to בת ציון in v. 2. We have, therefore, to settle for
the emendation of דמיתי to דמתה, and the sense 'to be at an end'
is better in the context than 'to be like'. The daughter of Zion is
portrayed as a woman who is doomed—disaster and shattering
ruin are peering out of the north. (v. 1).

The peaceful, pastoral sketch of shepherds with their tents and
flocks takes on a threatening aspect (v. 3). The dispositions with
a view to allocation of pastures project the menace of
encirclement—the grazing of the pastures is the stripping bare of
the country by invaders (so Targ. and Kimchi). The final stich of
v. 3 is obscure (רעו איש את ידו). Ziegler (*Beiträge*, p. 41) has
observed that the special sense of יד has not been recognized by
Sept., and 'each man pastures with his hand' (cf. Pesh.) does not
help with the elucidation of MT. Vulg.'s paraphrase, 'Each man
pastures those (sheep) which are under his control' makes sense:
it can be transposed into military terms and understood as
divisional commands. A similar exegesis is achieved by Rashi
and Kimchi who gloss ידו with מקומו. Reider (*HUCA* 24,
1952–53, p. 89) has a different lexicography for יד which,
nevertheless, has the same exegetical implications as Vulg. The
idea of each shepherd looking after his own strip of pasture is
adopted in the renderings of Rudolph, Bright and NEB ('each
grazing his own strip of pasture'), but the expression is an
obscure one which P. Joüon (*Biblica* 14, 1933, p. 453) has
attempted to elucidate with a suggestion that יד means 'bord' or
'bordure' which, translated into military terminology, is 'secteur'.

There is no doubt that vv. 4–5 are a transcript of a council of
war in the enemy camp. קדשו, probably, has the weakened sense
of 'begin' (Rudolph) or 'prepare' (Sept. παρασκευάσασθε; Pesh.
ṭybw; Rashi and Kimchi זמנו). In קדשו עליה מלחמה, קדשו may,
however, indicate that there is a background of religious ritual in
connection with such final dispositions for battle. The
proceedings of the council of war are reported in a quaint way. It
is as if the strategists are not aware what the time of day is until
they suddenly realize that it is too late for a noon attack. The
intention may be to indicate that they were not willing to let

another day pass and resolved to launch their attack that night (cf. Jerome, 'Let us attack by night that our adversaries may know that victory does not depend on timing but on men'). The plan is to destroy Jerusalem's fortifications in a night attack and so render the city defenceless.

Authorities, ancient and modern, associate עצה with 'tree'; Qᵒʳ and the ancient versions have read it as עצה 'its tree' or 'its trees'. עץ is understood as a collective form by Sept. (τὰ ξύλα αὐτῆς) and Pesh. (qysyh); Vulg. renders it with a singular noun (lignum eius). Rashi and Kimchi note the absence of the mappîq in the final ה and explain the form עצה as 'many trees'. Rudolph, Bright and NEB all read עצה as עצה. It is, however, worth considering whether כרתו עצה might not be an idiom of the same type as כרת ברית, in which case the sense would be 'Finalize the plans'. The time for strategic discussions is over and the attack must be launched: 'Build a ramp from which to attack Jerusalem'. If כרתו עצה refers to the felling of trees (Rashi, Calvin, Venema, Lowth, Blayney and Duhm, among others), this is preparatory to the building of a ramp. סללה is glossed by Kimchi as תל גבוה (cf. Targ. מליתא) and the sense indicated by Vulg. is similar: Fundite circa Jerusalem aggerem, 'Build a rampart around Jerusalem'. The sense of שפך סללה על , misunderstood by Sept. and Pesh., is sufficiently well established in Biblical Hebrew (2 Kgs 19.32; Isa 37.33; Ezek 4.2; 26.8).

Yahweh, having addressed the attackers and encouraged them to proceed with the reduction of the city, describes the condition of Jerusalem. היא העיר הפקד poses a problem of grammatical incongruence (עיר is fem., הפקד masc.), but, otherwise, it can be translated, 'This is the city on which judgement is about to fall' (הפקד is a relative clause without אשר). This is the grammar which is indicated by Pesh. and Targ. Vulg. appears to take הפקד as a noun in construct relation with עיר, while Sept. ὦ πόλις ψευδής (= הוי עיר שקר?) bears little resemblance to MT. Driver (JQR, 28, p. 102) notes that Volz (following a De Rossi variant) reads הוי עיר הפקד (cf. Sept.), and he suggests as a variation of this אהה עיר הפקד, 'Alas city of licence!' (metathesis of ה and א, deletion of yodh). MT should be retained and rendered, 'She is a city on which judgement is about to fall'.

Jerusalem is full of an oppressive injustice: she keeps her wickedness fresh as a well or cistern keeps its waters fresh. The cries of those robbed with violence are to be heard in the city. Yahweh sees nothing but disease and wounds. The form הקיר indicates a derivation from קור, whereas הקרה points to קרר. It is unlikely that the one is to be derived differently from the other; we have to conclude either that הקיר is double ayin with the form of ayin waw (GK 67w) or that הקרה is ayin waw with the form of double *ayin*. Both forms should be derived from קרר as they are in Sept. ($\psi\acute{v}\chi\epsilon\iota$, twice) and Vulg. (*frigidam fecit*, twice). In place of the thought of 'refrigerated evil' or 'evil on ice', that is, evil in tip-top condition, Rashi and Kimchi substitute the thought of the ampleness or copiousness of evil: it flows without cessation like the waters of a perennial spring. Rudolph follows Rashi and Kimchi, deriving הקיר and הקרה from קור.

Sept. and Pesh. connect חלי ומכה with הוסרי (v. 8) and not with על פני תמיד. What would then be indicated is that the enemy invasion is a severe corrective discipline rather than a totally destructive judgement. Something of this is, however, indicated, even with the punctuation of MT. The events which are engulfing Jerusalem may stop short at severe correction if she is corrigible, but otherwise she will be laid waste and become an abandoned city. 'Accept correction, O Jerusalem, else I shall tear myself away from you.' Bright renders פן תקע נפשי ממך as 'lest I turn from you in disgust' (similarly NEB), but the thought is perhaps that of a violent and indescribably painful wrench (cf. Gen 32.26, ותקע כף ירך יעקב בהאבקו עמו). Rashi glosses תקע with תנתק 'wrenched' and Kimchi with תפרד 'severed' (cf. Rudolph, *losreissen* 'tear off'). Yahweh will not evade the issue and will act decisively against his people, but the severing of ties with them will inflict on him the deepest hurt.

NOTHING BUT CORRUPTION IN JERUSALEM (6.9–15)

⁹These are the words of Yahweh Sabaoth:
Glean[1] as you would a vine,
save[1] whatever you can of the remnant of Israel;
go over the branches again
as a vintager would.
¹⁰To whom can I speak?
Who will listen if I testify?
Their ears are uncircumcised,
they are incapable of listening;
the word of Yahweh gives offence to them,
they are not well disposed to it.
¹¹I am full of Yahweh's wrath,
I am exhausted trying to contain it.
I shall pour it out[2] on children in the streets,
on youths who band together;
a man shall be taken with his wife,
an old man with his contemporaries.
¹²Their houses will pass to strangers,
along with their fields and their wives.[3]
¹³All of them, small and great,

¹ Reading עולל עולל (see below, p. 145).
² Reading שָׁפוֹךְ (see below, pp. 144, 146).
³ Deleting v. 12b (see below, pp. 144f., 146).

are greedy for gain;
there is no prophet or priest
but practises falsehood.
[14]They treat my people's wounds on the surface,
saying, You are cured, when there is no cure.
[15]Their abominations should make them ashamed,
but they have no sense of shame,
nor do they feel disgrace.[1]
Therefore, they will be among the victims,
when judgement falls on them[2]they will stumble.[3]

A structural integrity can be claimed for this unit if it is supposed (cf. Rudolph) that the gleaning imagery in v. 9 relates to the possibility of saving a remnant and not a threat of total destruction. In that case Yahweh addresses Jeremiah in v. 9 and the prophet replies that he is powerless because his words fall on deaf ears (v. 10). If Sept. is followed in v. 11 (καὶ τὸν θυμόν μου and ἐκχεῶ), this marks the beginning of a speech of Yahweh to his prophet which runs on to the end of v. 15. There are, however, difficulties in this, for if Yahweh is saying to Jeremiah in v. 9, 'Try to save a few', it is strange that he should speak in v. 11 of an anger which he cannot contain and which he must pour out on Jerusalem. One must rather say that the readings of Sept. in v. 11 are related to the view that Yahweh addresses the enemy and not Jeremiah in v. 9 (καλαμᾶσθε καλαμᾶσθε—the interpretation of v. 9 maintained by Rashi and Kimchi). If this were so, Jeremiah's words in v. 10 would have to be understood as a cry of anguish—he hears the terrible command but there is nothing he can do, for no one will listen to him. Rudolph combines his view of v. 9 ('Try to save a few') with the assumption that Yahweh begins to speak (שְׁפֹךְ) at v. 11b (also Bright). NEB assumes that Jeremiah's contribution to the dialogue runs from v. 10 to v. 12a and that Yahweh begins to speak at כִּי אֶטֶּה אֶת יָדִי. This overcomes a decisive objection to the scheme of Rudolph and Bright, namely, that in view of the relatedness of the imagery there cannot be a change of speaker between v. 11a and v. 11b: being full of anger and the pouring out of that anger must be parts of the same speech. NEB (Brockington, p. 200) points שָׁפַך as שָׁפֹךְ and (following Sept.) renders 'I must pour it out'. Rudolph observes that with this change (cf. BHS), the deletion of v. 12b, the emendation of פְּקַדְתָּם to פְּקַדְתִּים and the deletion of אמר יהוה (v. 15), vv. 10–15 can be construed as a reflective utterance of Jeremiah in which he presages disaster and explains why it will happen, in a general indictment of the community. In this connection it should be

[1]Reading הִכְלָם for MT הַכְלִים (see below, p. 147).
[2]Reading פְּקַדְתָּם (see below, pp. 144, 147f)
[3]Deleting אמר יהוה (see below, pp. 144, 147f.).

noted that Jer 8.10–12, which is substantially similar to 6.12–15, has nothing corresponding to כי אטה את ידי על ישבי הארץ נאם יהוה and supports the emendation of פקדתם to פקדתים.

It will be seen that this passage bristles with difficulties. It illustrates the tendency for 'word of Yahweh' to become dialogue between Yahweh and the prophet in the book of Jeremiah, if one follows Rudolph, Bright and NEB. If one adopts the more radical solution through deletion and emendation, the extant text illustrates the tendency to convert reflections of Jeremiah into word of Yahweh. It is only this bold reconstruction which deals faithfully with the problems of structural coherence. We then have a word of Yahweh to Jeremiah in v. 9 ('Try to save a few') and the reflective lament of the prophet in vv. 10–15—no one will listen to him; all he can do is to let his destructive word of doom flow over the community, and this is what they deserve. If Jeremiah is the speaker in vv. 10–12a, as NEB holds, the transition to word of Yahweh in v. 12b is very harsh. Why the connective כי, since *ex hypothesi* v. 12b does not connect with the words of Jeremiah in vv. 10–12a? It introduces another speaker.

If MT (עולל יעוללו) is retained, the subject must be the enemies of Jerusalem and the gleaming imagery is threatening: what is left of Israel (שארית ישראל) will be destroyed. The difficulty then consists in the transition from plural indicative or jussive to singular imperative (השב ידך) in the last line of v. 9. The Greek translator (Sept.) may have read three singular imperatives which he rendered as plurals (καλαμᾶσθε, twice, and ἐπιστρέψατε), because he supposed them to refer to the enemy (cf. chapter 5.10). If this were so, we should read עולל for יעוללו, whether the first עולל is also taken as imperative (Volz) or as infinitive absolute (Rudolph, Weiser, Bright). סלסלות is connected by Sept. and Vulg. with סל 'basket' (cf. Kimchi). The image is then that of the swift transference of what is gleaned from vine to basket—the gleaner's hand moves like a shuttle. The image, according to Rashi, is that of gleaning the fruit on the higher (cf. Prov 4.8) and less accessible parts of the vine which have been missed at the first picking (cf. Rudolph, Bright and NEB).

In v. 10 Jeremiah, having heard Yahweh's instruction to the enemy to destroy Jerusalem without remainder (*pace* Rudolph), expresses his sense of powerlessness. There is a hard unwillingness to believe that a threat of judgement can be a word of Yahweh, and when Jeremiah speaks he gives deep offence (חרפה). The image of uncircumcised ears does not indicate total deafness but selective deafness—receptivity to illusions and an incapacity to hear the truth. Jeremiah is full of Yahweh's anger:

the message of judgement which he preaches and which no one
will embrace fills his being. He feels and knows the truth of it so
intensely that he demands its instant consummation. In this
sense he can no longer contain Yahweh's wrath. Let the enemy
come then and wreak havoc in Jerusalem, on children and youths
in the streets, on a husband and wife at home, and on the old
men who have gathered to share their memories of the past.

Sept. (τὸν θυμόν μου) has changed v. 11 into a word of
Yahweh. This is, perhaps, a modification of חמת יהוה made by
the Greek translator in the interests of what seemed to him
better sense. נלאיתי הכיל (v. 11) is rendered by Sept. as καὶ
ἔπεσχον καὶ οὐ συνετέλεσα αὐτούς. Apparently הכיל from כול has
been given the sense of כלה. This looks like a type of deliberate,
mitigating alteration similar to 4.27 and 5.10 ('I refrained and
did not make an end of them'). Targ.'s paraphrase significantly
changes the sense of MT. The message is so terrible that the
prophet is inhibited from uttering it. Pesh. has read ואת as וְאַתְּ,
and the verbal forms ending in *yodh* have been taken as 2nd sing.
fem. and not as 1st per. It would appear that Jerusalem is
addressed: the city can no longer contain Yahweh's anger and
must pour it out on its inhabitants. שפך should be pointed as שְׁפָךְ
(Sept. ἐκχέω). When Jeremiah says, 'I will pour it out', he is
expressing his conviction that judgement is about to fall on
Judah and Jerusalem (cf. Rashi, 'My heart is full of the
prophecy that Yahweh's anger will come upon them'). Jerome's
comment is along the same lines: *propheta praecipit in spiritu
venienti Chaldaeo*. Rudolph's proposal that לא should be
inserted before מלא ימים (haplography) should not be adopted,
although it has the support of Pesh. ('*m ṭl' ywmt'*): the point is
missed by introducing a contrast of young and old. What is
intended is rather natural groupings—children playing in the
streets, young men in company, a husband and wife at home and
a 'club' of old men.

Verses 12–15, with v. 12b deleted (above, pp. 144f.), are a
continuation of Jeremiah's speech. What remains of v. 12 deals
with the passing of property into the hands of foreigners שדות
ונשים יחדו is a curious combination and in the parallel passage
(8.10) שדותיהם ליורשים provides better parallelism with ונסבו
בתיהם לאחרים: 'Their houses will pass into the hands of
strangers and their fields to new owners.' But 6.12 (MT) should
stand, all the more so since 8.10 has אתן את נשיהם לאחרים
where 6.12 reads ונסבו בתיהם לאחרים. Verse 13, which begins
with כי, explains why the community is exposed to such a
judgement. Everywhere, among high and low, there is a grasping
avarice; priests and prophets alike are masters of the lie and
practise falsehood. בוצע בצע, 'are greedy for gain', is

generalized by Sept. (συνετελέσαντο ἄνομα) and Pesh. (*nklyn nkl'*, 'act deceitfully').

The appearance of עמי in v. 14 might be thought more appropriate to Yahweh than to Jeremiah, but it should be taken as a mark of the intensity of the prophet's identification with his people and compared with 8.23 (את חללי בת עמי), where Jeremiah is the speaker. Prophet and priest lack integrity and their words and deeds have the hollowness of falsehood: 'They have prescribed a superficial cure for the wounds of my people, saying, "Health, health", where there is no health.' One feels the need to sustain the medical imagery in the translation of שלום ('wholeness' or 'health'), rather than to interpret the imagery and render שלום as 'well-being' or 'prosperity'. The medical metaphor is already being interpreted at על נקלה by the versions (also Rashi and Kimchi) rather than sustained; hence it is explained not as a superficial treatment of wounds but as superficial talk—שלום prophecy which has no substance in it.

The view that v. 15 opens with a question is already found in Jerome (also Calvin, Lowth, Blayney), and Driver (*JQR* 28, p. 102) emends הבישו to הֲבוֹשׁוּ (also Bright and NEB, Brockington, p. 200): 'Are they ashamed when they practise their abominations? Ashamed? Not they!' (NEB). As an alternative Bright suggests 'They ought to be ashamed' (similarly Rudolph) and this is what is indicated by Targ. (עליהון למבחת) and Rashi (עליהון למיבחת) and should be adopted. It leads on more naturally to גם בוש לא יבושו גם הכלים לא ידעו than does the assumed question. With הכלים read as הֵכָּלֵם in agreement with 8.12 (supported by Pesh. *wlmttksw* and Targ. אתכנעו at 6.15) we can render: 'They ought to be ashamed because they have done abominable things; yet they have no sense of shame, nor do they feel disgrace.' Those in positions of religious and moral leadership (prophets and priests) have spoken words of false assurance to the people and yet they have no awareness that they have betrayed a trust and are stained with dishonour. They are incapable of knowing the truth that they are ripe for Yahweh's judgement, because the lie that they speak in Yahweh's name has taken complete possession of them. The threat of whose presence they are unaware is introduced in the final line of v. 15 by לכן. These prophets and priests will be numbered among Yahweh's victims; when his judgement falls on them, they will stumble fatally. Vulg. represents בעת פקדתם at 6.15 (*in tempore visitationis suae*), as does Pesh., with the same rendering as it has at 8.12 (*wbzbn' dmtpqdyn*). There is no support from the versions for the deletion of אמר יהוה. The main point is that פקדתים (MT, 6.15) is consistent with a speech by Yahweh, but is inappropriate on the lips of Jeremiah, speaking for his own part. פקדתם, on the other hand, while it does not preclude Yahweh from being the speaker, is consistent with the interpretation which has been followed and which requires the deletion of אמר יהוה.

A REFUSAL TO BE GUIDED OR WARNED (6.16–21)

[16]These are the words of Yahweh:
Stand at the crossroads and take thought,
enquire about the ancient paths;
ask which is the good way and take it;
then you will be free from trouble.
But they said, We will not take it.
[17]I appointed watchmen to warn you;
(I said) Give heed to the sound of the trumpet.
But they said, We will not give heed.
[18]Therefore, listen O nations
and take careful note[1]
what I will do[2] to them.
[19]Listen, O earth:
I will bring evil on this people,
the fruit of their own schemes.
They give no heed to my words
and they reject my instruction.
[20]Frankincense from Sheba means nothing to me,
nor do fragrant reeds from a distant land.
Your burnt-offerings are not acceptable
and your sacrifices do not placate me.
[21]Therefore these are the words of Yahweh:
I will place stumbling-blocks before this people
and they will be tripped up by them;
fathers and sons will perish,
friends and neighbours will perish.

This section is dominated by words of Yahweh: first he directly addresses his people in vv. 16–17, although the observations on their unresponsiveness at the end of each verse (יואמרו לא נלך and ויאמרו לא נקשיב) do not have the form of direct address. Either they have to be regarded as comment by the prophet himself or comment by Yahweh to a third party (cf. Thiel, p. 99). As a consequence of this total lack of response Yahweh calls up the 'nations' and the 'earth' as witnesses and issues a threat of retribution. This is reported to the witnesses and not directly communicated to those who are being threatened. In v. 20 Yahweh turns again to his people and addresses them: all their fastidiousness in cultic preparations are pointless, because their sacrifices are unacceptable to him. It is uncertain whether v. 21 is part of the unit or whether it stands by itself. It

[1] Reading ודעו דעה (see below, p. 150).
[2] Inserting אעשה, with Vulg. (see below, p. 150).

introduces a specific threat—Yahweh will trip his people up and they will stumble fatally—and there is a case for regarding vv. 16–20 as prose and v. 21 as poetry (so NEB).

Thiel (pp. 99–102), who supposes that vv. 16–21 is a composition by a Deuteronomistic author, suggests that a connection between vv. 16f. (the old and well-tried paths) and v. 21 may have been interrupted by vv. 18–20. He urges that the latter passage takes an unexpected turn at v. 20 (polemic against sacrifice), that its gist is in v. 19, and that in this verse there are evidences of Deuteronomistic vocabulary, although the linguistic indications are not entirely conclusive. His conclusion is that vv. 16–21 have been put together by D: to vv. 18f. (regarded as an insertion by Duhm and Cornill) was added an isolated verse containing a polemic against sacrifice (v. 20), and, as a consequence of these additions, vv. 16f. were separated from the word of judgement in v. 21 to which they were originally joined. The argument is a curious one, because the so-called Deuteronomistic 'composition' (vv. 16–21) is acknowledged to lack organic unity and its effect (*ex hypothesi*) is to disturb an original continuity between vv. 16f. and v. 21 which existed prior to the moment of Deuteronomistic interference.

A choice has to be made (v. 16) and Yahweh urges his people to make the right choice as they stand at the crossing of ways; they should do it on the foundation of such guidance as is given by the past experience of the community. There are old paths established by Yahweh and along these the people may safely walk. Let them ask which is the right road (Targ. אורחא דתקנא) or the road that leads to well-being and let them walk in it; so they will win a quietness of mind which will arm them for all the demands and difficulties of life's journey. But they refuse the guidance of tradition and תורה. Rudolph argues that על דרכים is too vague to bear the translation 'at the crossroads' and accepts Driver's emendation (*JQR* 28, p. 103) עמדו על דרכי מראש, 'Stand by the old paths'. This produces parallelism between 'old ways' and 'ancient paths' (נתבות עולם), but וראו is not obviously a corruption of מראש. Moreover, וראו makes perfectly good sense and is not manifestly a corruption.

והקמתי is taken by the versions as a past tense. The *waw* consecutive perfect may be explained as a frequentative, 'Time and again I have appointed watchmen to warn you' (Rudolph). The past tense is assumed in the exegesis of Rashi (העמדתי לחם כבר) and Kimchi. The latter likens the צפים to נביאי אמת, associates the שופר with flight from an enemy and observes that lack of response is due to the conviction that those who reside in Jerusalem have a guarantee of safety (שלום). This is almost certainly the correct interpretation: v. 17 refers to a deafness to the special witness of the prophets of judgement who interpret Yahweh's will for his people by delivering urgent messages against a background of crisis and emergency.

At v. 18 Giesebrecht's emendation (ודעי דעה for ודעי עדה) is adopted by Ehrlich (p. 258) and Rudolph who also inserts אעשה after אשר (the latter expedient is the one which was adopted by Vulg.: *Quanta ego faciam eis*). The effect of this is to dispose of the second subject (עדה) and the verse then reads: 'Therefore hear, O nations, and note well what I shall do to them.' When the 'earth' has been similarly summoned, Yahweh issues his threat (v. 19). Sept. has καὶ οἱ ποιμαίνοντες τὰ ποίμνια αὐτῶν (= והרעים את עדריהם?) which bears little resemblance to MT. Aq. has καὶ γνῶτε μαρτυρίαν and Jerome reproduces Symm. as *et cognoscite testimonium* (= ודעו עדה, with עדה derived from עוד and not יעד). This does not entirely dispose of the difficulty, although it is more acceptable than עדה 'congregation'. 'All you who witness it' (NEB's rendering of עדה —*abstractum pro concreto*) leaves us with a specific reference to witnesses, followed by a general one, followed by another specific one. The other difficulty (את אשר בם) is insoluble. Rashi's elucidation scores more points than that of NEB: את הרעה = את אשר בם אשר בידם, 'the guilt which on their hands' (cf. NEB, 'the plight of this people').

In v. 19 Targ. erroneously interprets הארץ as ארעא דישראל, whereas Kimchi associates הארץ with passages in which heaven and earth are combined. Wildberger (*Jesaja, BKAT* 10) commenting on שמעו שמים והאזינו ארץ (Isa 1.2), where heaven and earth are invoked by Yahweh as witnesses, suggests that 'earth' means 'the inhabitants of the earth'.

מחשבות is used pejoratively as in Job 21.27, where the parallel expression is מזמות. It is this pejorative understanding of מחשבותם and not a different Hebrew text (משובתם, cf. BHS) which is reflected in Sept. τὸν καρπὸν ἀποστροφῆς αὐτῶν (similarly the paraphrase of Targ., תשלמת עובדיהון, 'recompense of their deeds'). Yahweh will 'implement' their plans by bringing disaster on them ('fruit of their plans'). The unusual construction (ותורתי וימאסו בה) is connected with the emphatic position accorded to תורתי, since תורתי מאסו בה could mean 'my תורה which they have rejected' (cf. Rashi).

To bring frankincense from South Arabia or fragrant reeds from a distant land is pointless, because such ritual care and scrupulousness will not serve to make burnt-offerings and sacrifices acceptable to Yahweh. לרצון is a technical term which von Rad describes as a 'declaratory formula' (cf. Lev 23.11; Isa 56.7). The priest delivers an authoritative ruling whether or not a sacrifice is acceptable to Yahweh; לרצון is a positive judgement

(G. von Rad, *Old Testament Theology*, 1, p. 261). The point
here (so Kimchi) is that the sacrifices are not acceptable to
Yahweh, even when the most stringent endeavours have been
made to ensure ritual purity. Yahweh is laying down a criterion
of acceptability which transcends cultic punctiliousness and
since his community, deaf to his תורה and the דבר of his
prophets, cannot satisfy it, their sacrificial conscientiousness is
insignificant. If הטוב is pointed as הַטּוֹב, the construct relation
can stand. The threat in v. 21 that Yahweh will trip his people up
and that they will stumble fatally is understood by Sept.
(ἀσθένειαν) as a threat of disease (perhaps with v. 14 in view).
Judgement is envisaged as a fall which has fatal consequences
(reading יֹאבֵדוּ with K; Q וְאָבְדוּ); 'fathers and sons' and 'a man
with his neighbour' emphasize inclusiveness rather than
indicating particular sections of the community.

JERUSALEM MUST PREPARE FOR DEATH (6.22–26)

[22]These are the words of Yahweh:
A people are on their way from a northern land,
a great nation is roused at the ends of the earth.
[23]Bow and sword are in their grasp,
they are ruthless and pitiless;
their roar is like the roar of the sea,
they are mounted on horses,
every soldier[1] deployed for battle
against you, daughter of Zion.
[24]We have had news of them, our hands hang limp,
distress like a woman's birth pangs has seized us.
[25]Do not venture into the open country,
do not embark on a journey,
for the enemy's sword is unsheathed—terror is on every side.
[26]Daughter of my people, wrap yourself in sackcloth,
Sprinkle yourself with ashes;
mourn as for an only son,
make bitter lamentations,
for suddenly the attacker will swoop on us.

The tone of vv. 22–23 is an important consideration and raises a
query about the rightness of the introductory formula (כה אמר
יהוה) which indicates that Yahweh is the speaker in vv. 22–23.
At any rate עלינו (v. 26) shows that Jeremiah and not Yahweh is
the speaker in vv. 25–26, and the appearance of ἐφ' ὑμᾶς in Sept.
and 'lyky in Pesh. has exegetical rather than textual significance.
In other words Sept. (on which Pesh. is probably dependent)
wanted to represent vv. 25–26 as speech of Yahweh (Ziegler has
restored ἐφ' ἡμᾶς conjecturally in his text). Verses 22–23 should

---

[1] Reading איש (MT כאיש). See below, p. 152.

be regarded as description by Jeremiah rather than threat by Yahweh, a description which is, perhaps, founded on an inner certainty that the end is near rather than on precise information about the movements of the enemy. It is an account which elicits a cry of despair and anguish from the inhabitants of Jerusalem (v. 24), after which Jeremiah tells them that they are trapped in a circle of terror and urges them to engage in proleptic mourning for the death of their city. Hence v. 26 picks up רפו ידינו (v. 24).

The enemy is armed with קשת וכידון (v. 23). It has been urged in the light of descriptions of weapons in the Qumran War Scroll (J. Carmignac, *VT* 5, 1955, pp. 357f.; G. Molin, *JSS* 1, 1956, pp. 334–337; Y. Yadin, *The Scroll of the War of the Sons of Light against the Sons of Darkness*, 1962, pp. 129–131) that a כידון is a scimitar or sword and not a javelin or lance or spear, and Yadin has compared the כידון with the Roman *gladius*. The evidence which is produced from the War Scroll is not decisive, because it can only establish what כידון meant among Jewish sectarians in the Roman period. When the invading soldiers utter their war cries and the lust for victory and spoil is expressed in terrible unison (cf. 5.15–17), it is as if one were listening to the roaring of the sea. The invaders are mounted on horses—they have chariots also, according to Sept. (καὶ ἅρμασι). They deploy for battle and the object of their attack is Jerusalem. Sept. παρατάξεται ὡς πῦρ εἰς πόλεμον πρὸς σέ ('They are deploying like fire for war against you') has read אש (MT איש). Emerton (*JTS*, 23, 1972, pp. 106–113) has discussed the precise significance of the phrase ערוך כאיש למלחמה, whether the reference is to the deployment of an army or the dispositions of individual soldiers. His preference is for the deletion of כ as a dittography of the כ of ערוך. The precise reference of the phrase is then to the dispositions of the individual soldiers who make up the attacking force.

The inhabitants of Jerusalem await the Babylonian threat with an abject passivity (their hands hanging slackly at their sides). The image of the woman in childbirth is used in order to represent the extremity of anguish which enters into this moment of helplessness. When they say שמענו את שמעו (v. 24), they are not indicating that the enemy is within earshot and they can hear the thunder of horses' hooves. They are rather, as the versions indicate, taking up the words of v. 23 and saying, 'Yes, we too have heard news of the enemy'.

The 2nd per. sing. fem. (K תצאי; תלכי) in v. 25 is understandable: the prophet is addressing Jerusalem and city and inhabitants are regarded as inseparable. The roads and countryside around Jerusalem are in control of the enemy and there is no way out of the city. If any of its inhabitants try to

escape, they will meet certain death. The final clause of v. 25 is
obscure. The versions have rendered לאיב as a genitive (Sept.
ῥομφαία τῶν ἐχθρῶν; Vulg. *gladius inimici*; Pesh. *ḥrb' db'ldbb'*;
Targ. חרבא דסנאה) and have dealt variously with מגור. Sept.
renders it by παροικεῖ which indicates a derivation from גור 'to
dwell'; Vulg. offers a literal translation of MT, *pavor in circuitu*;
Pesh. *dkryk' mn ḥdryky*, 'taking up position round about',
perhaps, derives מגור in the same way as Sept. and the rendering
of Targ. is similar. Rashi glosses מגור with יראה and Kimchi
comments, 'In all your environs there is terror (פחד)'.
Honeyman (*VT* 4, 1954, pp. 424–426) supposes that מקטלא
לדמתכנשין (Targ.) is a double rendering of מגור, and he
observes that this combination of 'destruction' and 'assembly' (so
Ibn Janâh, ed. Neubauer, p. 129) occurs in Targ. in the other
Jeremianic occurrences of מגור (20.3,10; 46.5; 49.29). The
explanation which he offers of this is that 'destruction' is
indicative of a derivation from מגר and 'assembly' of a derivation
from גור. It is not obvious that the sense of 'destruction all
around' is superior, and Honeyman's interpretation of Targ.'s
paraphrase is not certainly correct: מקטלא may be an elaboration
which arises out of חרב ('sword' becomes 'death-dealing sword')
rather than a rendering of מגור which assumes a derivation from
מגר. The sense 'fear' (Vulg.) is found in Calvin, KJV, Venema
and Blayney.

Jerusalem herself (בת עמי) must wear the dress of a mourner
and, paradoxically, fulfil her own mourning ceremonies (v. 26).
פלש has the sense 'dig', 'break through' in Akkadian, Syriac and
post-Biblical Hebrew, but its sense in Biblical Hebrew is not
well-established (Mic 1.10; Jer 6.26; 25.34; Ezek 27.30). Here
'sprinkle' (so NEB) is indicated by Sept. (κατάσπασαι), Vulg.
(*conspergere*) and Pesh. (*w'ttpyly*). Sept. has apparently read
יריד (πένθος ἀγαπητοῦ) instead of MT יחיד (noted by Jerome).
It will be a time of bitter weeping and insupportable sorrow, as if
the death of an only son were being mourned. It is anticipatory
mourning which signifies imminent destruction, even if the day
or the hour is not known: 'For suddenly the attacker will swoop
on us'.

JEREMIAH AN ASSAYER (6.27–30)

²⁷I have made you an assayer of my people,¹
you are to search and test their way of life.

¹ Deleting מבצר (see below, pp. 154f.).

[28]They are all arch-rebels[1] and malicious tale-bearers;[2]
all of them pursue destructive ends.
[29]The bellows are scorched,
the lead is consumed by the fire,
the smith refines to no purpose:
evil-doers are not removed.
[30]Call them[3] reject silver,
for Yahweh has rejected them.

Jeremiah is addressed by Yahweh and told that he must assay
Judah in the way that a metal is assayed for purity. Already in
v. 28 it is indicated that the process of assaying will have
negative results and that, indeed, it is a waste of time. The
smelting imagery in vv. 29–30 has, however, different
presuppositions: it is not asserted that there is no silver, but only
that the separation of the silver from the base elements cannot be
achieved and that the verdict passed by the assayer on Judah will
be 'Reject Silver'—silver incapable of refinement.

מבצר (v. 27) is deleted by Rudolph and Bright and is
explained either as a correct gloss on בחון 'assayer' (Sept.,
Vulg., Pesh.) or as an incorrect gloss which assumes the sense
'watch-tower' (cf. Isa 23.13; 32.14—בְּחָן). If it is an incorrect
gloss, it should be pointed מִבְצָר and its insertion may be due to
the influence of 1.18 (Cornill, Giesebrecht). If it is a correct
gloss, it should be pointed מְבַצֵּר 'examiner' (cf. Duhm). Sept. is
connecting מבצר with testing or assaying and Aq. (Theod) with
fortification. This indicates that the latter has understood בחון
as 'watch-tower', as Symm. has apparently also done, taking
מְבְצָר to mean 'besieged'. Targ., 'I have made you like a strong
fort among my people', clearly connects מבצר with 'fortification'
not 'testing'. Rashi and Kimchi (following Targ.) have both
understood בחון as 'watch-tower'. The latter explains בחון and
בחנת as a deliberate artistic use of words with different
meanings which are similar in sound.

Driver's solution (*JQR* 28, 103; *JTS* 6, 1955, pp. 84–87) is
reflected in the rendering of NEB, 'I have appointed you an
assayer of my people; you will know how to test them and will
assay their conduct.' This rests on a redivision of מבצר ותדע into
מבצרו תדע: מבצרו is explained as an Aramaizing infinitive of
the same kind as מגרש (Ezek 36.5). The circumstance that (*ex
hypothesi*) בעמי is resumed by a singular suffix at מבצרו and a
plural suffix at דרכם is a bigger difficulty than Driver allows.
מבצר should be deleted and explained as a gloss on בחון,
wrongly understood as 'watch-tower'. Its presence betrays the

[1]Reading שרי סוררים (see below, p. 155).
[2]Deleting נחשת וברזל (see below, pp. 155f.).
[3]Reading קְראו (see below, p. 157).

influence of 1.18 (cf. Janzen, p. 133). Jeremiah has been appointed an assayer by Yahweh and his task is to test Judah's way of life (דרכם). His examination must be searching (ותדע ובחנת), and its object is to see whether a separation can be made between righteous and wicked, between pure and impure.

Driver (*JTS*, 1955, p. 85) elucidates סרי סוררים (v. 28) as two homonyms from different roots (סור and סרר) which combine to exercise a superlative function, סוררים being a type of abstract noun with a masculine plural ending, 'persons turning aside in disobedience'. Alternatively (cf. Rudolph and Bright) the superlative function may be thought to arise from the construct relationship of two concrete terms, similar in meaning, 'Apostates of rebels', that is, past-masters at rebellion. In BHS Rudolph notes the manuscript support for שרי סוררים which would more easily yield the meaning 'arch-rebels' (NEB). Vulg., Pesh. and Targ. all represent שרי or the like.

The tortuous attempts of Pesh., Targ., Rashi and Kimchi to make sense of נחשת וברזל only serve to confirm that the phrase is out of place in v. 28. Bright suggests tentatively that נחשת וברזל might be incorporated into v. 27 and then מבצר נחשת וברזל, 'a tester of bronze and iron' would be a parallel expression to 'assayer'. Driver (see below) employs נחשת וברזל as part of his solution of the difficulties in v. 29. These expedients are further indications that נחשת וברזל is intrusive in v. 28. The conclusion to be drawn (cf. Janzen, p. 133) is that נחשת וברזל are not original to the passage. They may betray further influence of 1.18, or their insertion may have been encouraged by the list of metals in Ezek 22.18 (copper, tin, iron, lead) or 22.20 (copper, iron, lead, tin). The people of Judah are arch-rebels against Yahweh (שרי סוררים); they have perfected the skills of insubordination and are dedicated to destructive (כלם משחיתים המה), anti-social behaviour. By engaging assiduously in malicious gossip they contribute only to the disintegration of the community.

Modern commentators tend to favour a derivation of נָחַר (v. 29) from נחר 'snort', 'roar' (Akkadian *nahāru*; Arabic *nahara*; Syriac *nḥar*). Driver (*JQR*, 28, p. 103; *JTS* 6, p. 85) supposes that a second instance of נחר is found in Biblical Hebrew at Ct 1.6 (נחרו בי, 'they snort at me'). This view of נחר is adopted by Rudolph, Bright and NEB ('puff and blow'). נָחַר, according to Driver, describes the noise made by bellows working at full blast. A further proposal by Driver is that by a redivision of consonants מפח מאשתם should be read as מפחם אש תם : מפחם is then a contracted form of the dual (= מַפְּחַיִם) and this agrees with Dahood (*Biblica* 44, 1963, p. 298). נחר מפחם אש תם is associated with the improbable sense of 'is prepared' for תמם, and the new elements of textual explanation do not affect the translation which Driver offered earlier (*JQR* 28, p. 104) and which runs as follows:

The bellows roar, the fire is prepared,
lead, copper and iron,
the refiner hath refined in vain—
and the wicked have not been separated;
refuse silver shall men call them,
for the Lord hath rejected them.

It will be observed that נחשת וברזל have been incorporated from v. 28 and located after עפרת. The only modifications which are subsequently made by Driver (*JTS* 6, pp. 86f.) concern רעים and נתקו. The former is explained as a singular with reference to Arabic *ru'âm* 'dust' and the latter is consequentially emended to נתק. Prov 12.12 (מצוד רעים, 'a fortress of crumbling clay') is cited in support, but even if the sense 'dust' is allowed for רעים, the transition to 'metal' is a considerable one (cf. Rudolph). The influence of Driver on NEB is evident (Brockington, p. 201).

Dahood supposes that אשתם (pointed אֶשְׁתָּם) like מפחם is a dual form and he translates, 'The lead is heated by bellows, a double fire'. It is not clear what the cogency of this is. His other suggestion is that לא נתקו should be emended to לא אנתקו (haplography of א) and that אנתקו should be explained as a form with an infixed ת from נקה ('The wicked are never purified'). Dahood is right in one respect—in deriving נחר from חרר. The versions give no support to this derivation: Sept. ἐξέλιπε φυστὴρ ἀπὸ πυρός, ἐξέλιπε μόλιβος indicates a different punctuation from MT, since it connects מאש with מפח, but otherwise it represents MT (Q מאש תם). An odd feature is that both נחר and תם have been rendered as 'exhausted' or 'spent'. נחר is taken in the same way by Vulg. and Pesh., whereas Pesh. *mn nwrhwn* 'from their fire' is probably what is intended by K. Targ. paraphrases: 'Like the smith's bellows, which are scorched in the fire, so the voice of the prophets who urged them to return to the Law, is silenced. Like lead which is melted away in a furnace, so the words of the prophets who prophesied to them were annulled in their eyes. To no purpose their teachers taught them; they did not leave off their evil deeds.' The lead is used in the smelting process as a flux in order to effect the separation of the base elements from the pure and to achieve a refined product (so Jerome).

Similarly Rashi observes that when silver is being refined lead is fed into the furnace in order to effect the refining process. He continues his comment, 'But as for you, when I come to refine you, the bellows are over-heated and scorched because of the strength of the fire and the lead is entirely consumed.' Kimchi remarks, 'He (Yahweh) also likens them (the inhabitants of Judah) to the work of a refiner who, when he refines silver, puts lead in with the silver, so that the flames may not consume the silver, and the smith fans the flames with bellows to refine the silver.' Kimchi continues, 'He (Yahweh) says that the bellows are burnt because of the protracted use made of them by the smith.' Among the later representatives of this exegesis are Calvin, Lowth, Blayney and Duhm. If עפרת is fem. there is a grammatical incongruity between עפרת and תם. Graf's supposition that there has been a haplography of ת and that תתם should be read is intended to relieve this.

The correct understanding of vv. 29–30 is something like this. The refining process has not been going well; the bellows have been used excessively and have been scorched and damaged by the heat; the lead which is in the furnace as a flux, and which is essential to the refining process, has been consumed by the flames, because the operation has been abnormally protracted. In the end it is a failure and pure silver is not extracted. Hence when the assayer examines it, he announces that it does not have the requisite standard of purity and must be rejected. This is the verdict which Jeremiah must pass in Yahweh's name as the assayer of his people, for Yahweh has rejected them. The assayer's verdict is best communicated by the imperative קְרָא which is supported by Sept. and Vulg. 'They shall be called (קְרָאוּ) reject silver' does not relate so appositely to the circumstance that Jeremiah has been appointed an assayer and that it is he who should pronounce on the final product. Yahweh informs him what this pronouncement must be, 'Call them reject silver'. One would then have expected 'for I have rejected them', instead of which Yahweh refers to himself in the third person. The difficulties involved in the assumption that רעים means 'ore' have already been noted (above, p. 156). It is better to allow that a mixture of imagery and interpretation is original, that we have an interpretation of the smelting imagery in v. 29 (רעים = 'wicked') and that the imagery reasserts itself in v. 30. There is no test which can be applied to separate the righteous in the community from the wicked and so all must be rejected by Yahweh.

CHAPTER VII

A FALSE SENSE OF SECURITY (7.1–15)

[1]Jeremiah received this word from Yahweh: [2]Stand at the gate of Yahweh's house and proclaim there this word: Hear the word of Yahweh all you men of Judah who come through these gates to worship Yahweh. [3]These are the words of Yahweh Sabaoth, God of Israel: Amend your ways and your deeds and I will give you secure tenure of this place. [4]Do not put your trust in these false words: This place[1] is the temple of Yahweh, the temple of Yahweh, the temple of Yahweh. [5]If you truly amend your ways and your deeds, if you act justly in your dealings with others; [6]if you do not oppress aliens, orphans and widows, if you desist from shedding[2] innocent blood in this place and do not follow other gods to your own hurt, [7]I will give you secure tenure of this place, the land which I gave to your forefathers for all time coming. [8]You are putting your trust in false words which are valueless. [9]Will you thieve, murder, commit adultery, perjure yourselves, sacrifice to Baal and follow other gods of whom you have no knowledge, [10]and then come and stand before me in this house which bears my name and say: We are safe? Are you indeed kept safe to enable you to commit all these abominations? [11]Do you think that this house which bears my name is a robbers' cave? I see what is going on—This is Yahweh's word. [12]Go to my sanctuary at Shiloh where I established my name long ago and see what I did to it because of the wickedness of my people Israel. [13]And now, because you have done all these things (This is Yahweh's word), because you did not listen when I addressed you urgently and ignored me when I summoned you, [14]I will do to the house which bears my name, in which you put your trust, and to the place which I gave to you and to your forefathers, what I did to Shiloh. [15]I will cast you out from my presence, just as I cast out all your brethren, the whole race of Ephraim.

The view that the shorter Greek text at the beginning of the chapter is the more original is represented by Duhm, Cornill and Janzen (pp. 36f), whereas Volz, Rudolph and Thiel (p. 107 n. 17) suppose that Sept. is an abridgement of MT. It is probable that the longer text of MT is the result of secondary additions. On this view MT gives an indication of the way in which the Hebrew text was supplemented and elaborated subsequent to its translation into Greek. The motive would be to compensate for the lack of information in the bald introduction (שמעו דבר יהוה כל יהודה, so Sept.) and to give a detailed and specific indication of the place and occasion of Jeremiah's speech. It is clear that the formula הדבר אשר היה אל ירמיהו מאת יהוה לאמר or the like has to be considered on a broader basis than Janzen provides (cf. Thiel, pp. 106f): the belief that 26.2 furnishes more reliable information about where the speech was delivered than 7.2 is, presumably, bound up with a critical assumption about the relation between the two passages. The unsatisfactory character

---

[1]Reading המה as הם ה" (see below, p. 160).

[2]Reading לא (MT אל) See below, p. 161.

of this type of argument may be judged from the circumstance
that Reventlow (*ZAW* 81, 1969, p. 333) has turned it on its head
by arguing that 7.2 preserves precise information where
Jeremiah delivered his speech and that the significance of this is
lost in the paraphrase of 26.2

The difference between MT and Sept. at the beginning of
chapter 7, at least, raises a question in our minds whether the
circumstances with which the proclamation of Yahweh's word is
associated in MT should exert too great an influence on the
interpretation of the passage (cf. Reventlow, p. 333). That the
Septuagint preserves the original text is probably the right
conclusion, but this is a case where a text-critical logicality
produces results which lack proportion. The differences between
Hebrew (MT) and Greek texts are considerable and in a
commentary on MT it is more judicious to treat MT as a
different, longer text rather than to reconstruct an original
Hebrew text on the foundation of Sept. and make the
appropriate deletions from MT.

If we attend to MT in v. 2, the thought of an 'Entry Torah'
(Reventlow) is an attractive one. Its function, as exemplified in
Ps 15 and 24, was to remind the intending worshipper at the gate
of the temple that, unless he satisfied certain conditions relating
to his spiritual state and moral conduct, he was not fit to take
part in temple worship (cf. G. von · Rad, *Old Testament
Theology*, 1, pp. 377f.; H. J. Kraus, *Worship in Israel*, 211f.). It
is suggested that the nomenclature שַׁעֲרֵי צֶדֶק (Ps 118.19) is
connected with this test. What Jeremiah is represented as saying
conforms to the pattern of Entry Torot in so far as he is laying
down a standard of fitness, although he does not simply state (cf.
Reventlow, p. 335) what these standards are: instead of
participles, which serve the ends of statement and definition,
there is direct address and admonitions (vv. 3ff.). Entry Torot,
however, do not call in question that those who are adjudged fit
to enter the temple enter Yahweh's presence. On the contrary,
the assumption underlying their function is that the temple is
Yahweh's house and that only those who satisfy the prescribed
conditions should enter it. The word which Jeremiah speaks calls
in question whether the congregation worshipping in the temple
is any longer in the presence of Yahweh, and this constitutes a
deeper questioning than that represented by the Entry Torot in
their normal use.

The 'Entry Torot' hypothesis, promising though it may be,
runs into further difficulties at v. 3, where, if MT is followed, the
sense of הַמָּקוֹם הַזֶּה can hardly be 'this temple'. It is not simply a
matter of observing that the expression for temple in v. 2 is בֵּית
יהוה and not מָקוֹם, since there would be no great difficulty in

assuming that an alternative term for temple is introduced at
v. 3. The problem is deeper, because וְאִשְׁכְּנָה אֶתְכֶם בְּמָקוֹם הַזֶּה
can only mean 'and I will make your possession of this place
secure' or 'so that I may make your possession of this place
secure', and the reference must be to possession of the land
(Judah) or of Jerusalem, its capital city. שׁכן (Piel) occurs with
מקום 'temple' in a formula of quite a different kind in the book of
Deuteronomy (12.11; 14.23; 16.2, 6, 11; 26.2). The statement
that Yahweh chooses to establish his name in the Jerusalem
temple is not approximated to Jer 7.3, even if וְאִשְׁכְּנָה אתכם
במקום הזה is read as וְאִשְׁכְּנָה אֶתְכֶם בְּמָקוֹם הַזֶּה (Vulg., Calvin,
Blayney, Ehrlich, pp. 259f.; Volz, Rudolph; Reventlow, p. 329
n. 76), 'And I will dwell with you in this place', or 'So that I may
dwell with you in this place'. Moreover, an attempt to save a
reference to the temple in v. 3 will necessitate further rescue
attempts at vv. 6 and 7. In other words, another quite distinct
theme cannot be excluded from vv. 1–15—that of 'possession of
the land'. Verse 3 makes possession of the land conditional on a
way of life which accords with Yahweh's demands, and this is a
theme which is common in the book of Deuteronomy (6.18f.;
7.12f.; 8.1; 11.8f.; 16.20; 19.8f.), where מקום is principally used
of temple or sanctuary, although it does refer to the Promised
Land in a number of places (1.31; 9.7; 11.5; 26.9).

Verse 4, in which another word (היכל 'palace'or 'temple')
denotes the Jerusalem temple, and in which there is a threefold
occurrence of היכל יהוה, is generally regarded as the citation of
a formula. One may compare this with the threefold ארץ in Jer
22.29 or with the trisagion in Isa 6.3 (Reventlow, p. 329),
although Herrmann (ZAW 62, 1950, pp. 321f.) urges that Isa
6.3 is a liturgical formula of a different kind from Jer 7.4, 22.29
and Ezek 21.32. He notes examples of words thrice repeated in a
Babylonian collection of incantations (Maqlû, edited by G.
Meier, 1937), and, in particular, a threefold 'earth' (cf. Jer
22.29) at Maqlu i, 37 (irṣitum irṣitum irṣitum). The addition in
Sept. at v. 4 may derive from v. 8, where לבלתי הועיל is rendered
ὅθεν οὐκ ὠφεληθήσεσθε, following דברי השקר (cf. Janzen, p. 63).
According to Targ. the threefold formula is part of the armoury
of the שלום prophets (cf. Reventlow, p. 329) and the source of
their confidence that all will be well (similarly, Kimchi).
Torczyner's suggestion that המה is a corruption of an
abbreviation of המקום הזה (BZAW 41, 1925, p. 276), has been
adopted by NEB (Brockington, p. 201). Other solutions have
been offered by Sutcliffe (VT 5, 1955, pp. 313f.) and Whitley
(JTS 5, 1954, pp. 57–59). According to Sutcliffe היכל יהוה המה
was originally a marginal note on דברי השקר and so the twofold

היכל יהוה of Sept. preserves the original Hebrew text. The puzzle of המה is unsolved.

Yahweh urges his people not to rely on false or empty words, solemnly intoned and affirming that the temple, because it is Yahweh's dwelling place, gives them an unconditional guarantee of security. These are solemn and powerful words; they have a spell-like character (cf. Herrmann, above, p. 298) and they rivet themselves in the minds of those who recite them or hear them recited. The false doctrine is reinforced by a liturgy.

The point of departure in vv. 5–6 is a repetition of the general demand of v. 3 and from this flow more specific demands: fair dealing in relations with other members of the community is required and so too is a special tenderness and concern for those who are weak and vulnerable (the orphan and the widow) or those who are at a social and legal disadvantage (resident aliens). The grammatical construction of vv. 5–7 is a series of protases culminating in an apodosis (cf. v. 3). Hence one has to read the אם of אם עשו תעשו with all the following verbs in vv. 5–6, and it follows that the אל of אל תשפכו is grammatically unacceptable. Hence a minimum emendation is the substitution of לא for אל, and if one is content with this, מקום, in the context of the demands laid down in vv. 5–6, must mean 'land' or 'city' and not 'temple'. Another way of dealing with the difficulty of אל תשפכו is to suppose (Rudolph; cf. Bright) that ודם נקי אל תשפכו במקום הזה has been inserted secondarily from Jer 22.3. This will (ex hypothesi) have been encouraged by the circumstance that there is a superficial similarity between 22.2 (הבאים בשערים האלה) and 7.2 (הבאים בשערים האלה). It is clear, however, from 22.1 that Jeremiah's stance is at the gates of the palace (בית המלך) and not the gates of the temple. ודם נקי אל תשפכו במקום הזה makes sense in 22.3 as a demand issued to royal officials who are entering the palace precincts. To the ethical requirements set out in v. 6 is attached a warning against apostasy (ואחרי אלהים אחרים לא תלכו) and this combination of ethical and theological demands is also a feature of v. 9.

Verse 7 is a recapitulation of the last clause of v. 3 and again מקום, in conjunction with a reference to the land which Yahweh gave to Israel's forefathers in perpetuity, must mean 'land' and not 'temple'. Hence the proposal that ושכנתי אתכם should be read as וְשָׁכַנְתִּי אִתְּכֶם is to be resisted here for the same reasons as obtained at v. 3 in respect of ואשכנה אתכם (above, p. 160).

The most fundamental thing to be said about vv. 8–14 is that the theme 'possession of the land' is absent from them and that they hinge on a false sense of security encouraged by a belief in the inviolability of the Jerusalem temple. The second, principal observation is that a framework of interpretation constituted by an appeal to Entry Torot is spared the difficulties which arose in the earlier part of the chapter through the intrusion of the theme 'possession of the land'. There is a marked verbal similarity between the opening of v. 4 and the opening of v. 8, although admonition (v. 4) gives place in v. 8 to accusation, 'You are relying on lies which will do you no good'. Further, the moral earnestness of the dissuasives in vv. 5–6 gives place to a more biting, ironical technique of using interrogatives in order to underline the absurdity and impudence of the assumptions to which those addressed are addicted. In Ps 15 and 24 one can detect the strong social emphasis of the morality which is prescribed: the person who would worship Yahweh must be candid (15.2); he must abstain from malicious gossip and do nothing that would injure a friend (15.3). The prohibition of perjury which is implied by Jer 7.9 (וְהִשָּׁבֵעַ לַשֶּׁקֶר) is present in Ps 24.4, and an associated prohibition—taking a bribe as the price of securing the condemnation of an innocent person—appears in Ps 15.5. The degree of correspondence between Jer 7.9 and the clauses of the Decalogue should not be missed: the charges which are implied by the series of questions are stealing, murder, adultery and perjury. The order in Sept. is murder, adultery, stealing and perjury; this is, perhaps, a secondary adjustment designed to produce agreement with the order in Exod 20.13–16 and Deut chapter 5.17–20. Mowinckel's contention that the Decalogue was derived from Entry Torot (*Le Décalogue*, 1927, pp. 141–156) is discounted by Kraus (*Worship in Israel*, p. 212 n. 74). The actual form of vv. 9–10 is more consonant with indictment than with the imposition of a test. Those who are addressed have a crass misunderstanding of Yahweh and his temple and attention is focused on this.

What were once items of a test are presented as counts of an indictment: the outrage that is being committed against Yahweh and true religion is thereby set out in strong terms. Those who break the laws which are the cement of family and society are represented as saying in the temple, 'We can safely continue to perpetrate our so-called abominable deeds'. Or more attention should, perhaps, be paid to the *athnach* at נִצַּלְנוּ, in which case לְמַעַן עֲשׂוֹת אֵת כָּל הַתּוֹעֵבוֹת הָאֵלֶּה, if it is original (see further below), should be regarded as a riposte to נִצַּלְנוּ (so NEB, 'Safe, you think, to indulge in all these abominations'). Either way, there is an ironical intention in the representation. These are stupid, arrogant and benighted men. The indictment has the objective of shocking them into an appreciation of the truth. The language of worship is preserved in the temple, but the language of the heart is, 'We enjoy immunity and we can behave in the future as we have done in the past'. Sept. rendered נִצַּלְנוּ as

ἀπεσχήμεθα and inserted a negative before עֲשׂוֹת: ἀπεσχήμεθα
τοῦ μὴ ποιεῖν πάντα τὰ βδελύγματα ταῦτα, 'We have abstained
from doing all these abominable deeds'. This changes the sense
of MT drastically and we have a denial of wrong-doing and an
affirmation of innocence.

In the light of the foregoing exposition doubt may be
expressed about the originality of וקטר לבעל והלך אחרי אלהים
אחרים אשר לא ידעתם in v. 9. The issue is whether this introduces
a kind of idolatry different from that with which the prophet
grapples in this passage. This other idolatry is associated with
the infiltration of Yahwism by elements of Baal religion, and
Josiah's law of the single sanctuary was an attempt to put an end
to it. Jeremiah, on the other hand, deals with a different kind of
idolatry or superstition which has received an impetus and has
waxed strong as a consequence of the reform of Josiah and the
enhanced prestige of the Jerusalem temple. This is not caused by
a confusion between Yahweh and Baal, or by loyalties which are
divided between Yahweh and Baal, but by a divorce between cult
and community, between worship and way of life. One may not,
however, be too dogmatic about all this and we shall see
presently that another way of appreciating v. 9 is to assume that
וקטר לבעל is original and that והלך אחרי אלהים אחרים אשר לא
ידעתם is secondary (so Skinner, below, p. 164).

The attack is resumed in v. 11 with another ironical question:
Do you suppose that this temple is a cave where thieves can find
asylum? L. Delekat (*Asylie und Schutzorakel am
Zionheiligtum*, 1967, p. 167 n. 1) has suggested that 'den of
robbers' was a pejorative name for places of asylum—an allusion
to a feeling among respectable members of the community that
rights of asylum were frequently abused by knaves and
scoundrels. This is what temple worship has come to: the temple
is a place where thieves, murderers, adulterers and perjurers
assemble to assure themselves that they can continue their
activities with perfect safety and from which they go out to
resume them. Amid the extraordinary confusion which is created
by this blending of superstition, base motives and destructive
behaviour with solemn rites of worship and high, liturgical
language, Yahweh himself is not deceived. Historical precedent
is not on the side of those who suppose that the Jerusalem
temple, as Yahweh's dwelling-place, is an absolute guarantee of
safety to the community (v. 12). Shiloh, an earlier Yahwistic
sanctuary, was destroyed by the Philistines, because of the
corruptness of the Israelite community. (On the representation
that Yahweh establishes his name at a sanctuary or causes his
name to dwell there, see von Rad, *Studies in Deuteronomy*,
1953, pp. 37–44.)

The speech concludes with a threat which culminates in v. 14 (the Jerusalem temple will be destroyed as the temple at Shiloh was), but the other theme of 'possession of the land' intrudes in this verse, for it is evident that מקום in conjuction with אשר נתתי לכם ולאבותיכם must mean 'land' or 'city' and not 'temple'. Further, it is this intrusive element in v. 14 which is developed in v. 15 and Rudolph is probably correct in his assumption that v. 15 is secondary. It deals with loss of the land: Judah will go into exile just as the northern kingdom was banished to Assyria. It is difficult to resist the conclusion that the train of thought which is set in motion by v. 8 (or, perhaps, v. 4—see below) has reached its proper conclusion with the threat that the Jerusalem temple will suffer the same fate as the sanctuary at Shiloh and that v. 15 is something of an afterthought. These are matters for nice appreciation which do not only affect vv. 8–15, but also touch on the appraisal of the interaction of 'temple' and 'possession of the land' themes in vv. 1–7.

The impression that v. 4 is surrounded by verses dealing with another theme has given rise to the hypothesis that v. 4 belongs with vv. 8–14 and that v. 8 itself is an editorial variation on the first part of v. 4, necessitated by the separation of v. 4 from its original connection with v. 9. This was how Skinner (*Prophecy and Religion*, pp. 170f.) approached the problems of vv. 1–15. He held that vv. 3, 5–7 formulate a conditional promise of continued possession of the land and that they are not at all concerned with a belief attached to the temple. He urged that the original, absolute prophetic threat is preserved in vv. 4, 9–15 and that the conditional character of the admonitions in vv. 3, 5–7 is an indication that they are not to be attributed to the prophet Jeremiah. He believed that the *ipsissima verba* were best preserved in vv. 4, 9–15 and he tried to get nearer to these by detecting and excising editorial elaborations.

Thiel (pp. 105–119) follows Skinner's scheme quite closely, but disagrees with him in respect of v. 15 (see above) and finds additional evidences of editorial intervention.

Only at vv. 1–2 and at v. 13 is there any support from the versions for a text shorter than MT. At vv. 1–2 Thiel discounts the textual value of Sept. (above, p. 158). At v. 13 השכם ודבר is not represented by Sept. and Janzen (p. 37) argues that MT represents the confusion of two distinct word-strings. The one, which is represented by 7.13 does not have השכם ודבר or the like as a constituent (cf. Jer 35.17; Isa 65.12; 66.4), while the other does (cf. Jer 7.25; 26.5; 29.19; 35.14).

The view that 7.1–15 has a core (vv. 4, 9*, 10*, 11*, 12, 14*), focusing on the temple, which has been expanded and elaborated by the application of a different theme (possession/loss of the land) should be accepted (cf. Nicholson, *Preaching to the Exiles*, p. 69), provided this does not imply an attempt to reconstruct an 'original' text. It is to be regarded as an explanation of how MT has come to assume its present shape, but it is not to be carried to a textual-critical conclusion (see above, p. 159). The emphasis is not on creating a new text but on furnishing some understanding of the nature of the extant text. The core is to be attributed to the prophet Jeremiah, although it is impossible to say whether his own words are preserved. Skinner supposed that there was a dependence on Jeremiah's memoirs (p. 170) and Thiel has proposed that v. 14 has a metrical structure. Thiel's other suggestion (p. 115) that an original indictment in v. 4 may have been changed to an admonition under the influence of the editor raises the question whether the opening words of v. 8, which have the form of allegation, do not preserve the original. In that case v. 4 of the core should be read as, 'You are trusting in false words, "The temple of Yahweh, the temple of Yahweh, the temple of Yahweh, is this place" '.

Thiel argues (p. 116) that the editor has changed Jeremiah's temple saying into a sermon whose principal characteristic is the formulation of alternatives (salvation or doom). The structure of this type of sermon is, he holds, best preserved in 17.19–27 and 22.1–5, and is deficient in 7.1–15, where the second alternative is not formulated. Even on Thiel's own account it is difficult to see how the passage could possibly possess the degree of literary shapeliness and theological deliberation which he finds in it. However, it is clear that the intention of these editorial interventions is to establish that the land is held conditionally and that possession of it is lost when these conditions are not fulfilled. Thiel makes the reasonable assumption (pp. 117–119) that this way of developing the core of the chapter is connected with an attempt to explain why the exile took place, and is to be associated with an exilic setting, where the need for such an explanation was urgent (cf. Nicholson, *Preaching to the Exiles*, pp. 69f.). H. Weippert's contention (*BZAW* 132, 1973, p. 41) that the style of the passage fixes its date for us, and demonstrates that it is not later than the events with which it purports to deal, is impressionistic and unconvincing. Her intention is to claim the actual words of vv. 1–15 for the prophet Jeremiah and to explain the passage as a speech set in the historical context of his ministry.

Thiel's detailed examination of vocabulary in vv. 1–15 (pp. 107–114) is connected with his attempt to demonstrate that the editorial additions have a Deuteronomic or Deuteronomistic vocabulary and that the editor may therefore be identified as

Deuteronomistic. He is right (also Nicholson, *Preaching to the Exiles*, p. 70) to repel a general objection lodged against this view, namely, that the attitude to the temple in the (*ex hypothesi*) core of vv. 1–15 is one diametrically opposed to the paramountcy accorded to the Jerusalem temple in the book of Deuteronomy (Weiser; Bright, *JBL* 70, 1951, p. 28). Thiel (p. 104 n. 106) points to 2 Kgs 23.27, a Deuteronomistic text in which Yahweh is represented as saying that he has rejected Jerusalem which he chose and the House of which he said that his name would be there. One has to reckon with the effect of the fall of Jerusalem and the destruction of the temple on Deuteronomistic thinking in an exilic context, and the view that a Deuteronomistic editor constructed a homily on a foundation that traced Judah's undoing to a false temple theology cannot be demolished with the kind of sledgehammer blow which Bright endeavours to deliver.

Despite the heaviness of the detail Thiel's method is essentially simple. He looks for confirmation that the editor of Jer 7.1–15 is Deuteronomistic, in the book of Deuteronomy and the Deuteronomistic literature. If there is nothing in these sources, he focuses attention on other prose passages in the book of Jeremiah and is satisfied that these can be classified as Deuteronomistic in view of the elements of vocabulary which are common to them. The first of these operations appears reasonable, although the question may be raised whether the resemblances are sufficiently distinctive to establish particular literary connections between the prose of the book of Jeremiah and the book of Deuteronomy or the Deuteronomistic literature. There is an argument that we are encountering a style of prose which was characteristic of a historical period (the age of Jeremiah) rather than of a particular literary and theological school (Bright, *JBL* 70, 1951, pp. 27–29). The other objection (H. Weippert) is that when the apparent similarities of vocabulary are examined more carefully, it will emerge that there are significant differences of nuance as between items of vocabulary in the prose of the book of Jeremiah and the same items in the book of Deuteronomy or the Deuteronomistic literature.

It is, however, with the second of Thiel's operations that difficulties are bound to arise, because there is a suspicion that he is arguing in a circle. It is inevitable that he and H. Weippert are entirely at cross-purposes in this area, because the absence of any parallels to the prose of the book of Jeremiah in the book of Deuteronomy and the Deuteronomistic literature is seized upon by Weippert as evidence of an independent prose tradition in the book of Jeremiah: that is, prose which is neither Deuteronomic nor Deuteronomistic.

Given the style of the argument it is predictable that Weippert will reach conclusions contrary to those of Thiel in respect of היטיבו דרכיכם ומעלליכם (vv. 3, 5; pp. 144–148) and השכם ודבר (v. 13; pp. 123–127). In the case of the former she gathers together the passages of prose from the book of Jeremiah in which this word-string appears (7.3, 5; 18.11; 26.13), and other passages, some poetry (4.8; 17.10; 23.22) and some prose (25.5; 26.3; 32.19; 35.15), where verbs other than יטב are associated with דרכים and מעללים (שוב) in 23.22; 25.5; 26.3; 35.15). The most that can be demonstrated by this procedure is that this combination of words is virtually absent from the book of Deuteronomy and from the Deuteronomistic literature (cf. Judg 2.19). It is not an assured conclusion that the prose passages in the book of Jeremiah are directly associated with or derived from occurrences of דרך (דרכים) and מעללים in the poetic passages. In any case, this would not prove that if Jeremiah is the author of these poetic passages, he must also be the author of the prose passages. The correct interpretation may rather be that items of vocabulary have been quarried from the poetry of Jeremiah in connection with the subsequent growth of the Jeremianic corpus through prose additions. Weippert's conclusion outreaches the the limitations of her method. Her conclusions about השכם ודבר (v. 13) have the same tendency: it is a characteristic feature of the prose of the book of Jeremiah and it has no connections with Deuteronomy or the Deuteronomistic literature (p. 126).

Weippert (pp. 26ff.) makes acute observations about the considerable difficulties which are encountered when 26 is allocated to a different source (B) from 7 (C), as they are in Rudolph's analysis. If a source hypothesis is to be formulated, the resemblances of vocabulary and phraseology in the two passages would suggest that they belong to the same source. Nor does there appear to be any justification of the view that 26 preserves the actual words of the prophet Jeremiah better than 7. On the contrary, there is more scope for disengaging a Jeremianic core in 7.1–15 than there is in 26.1–6. If the logic which is normally applied in the comparison of Sources B and C were to prevail in a comparison of chapters 7 and 26, the results would contradict those to which this logic is elsewhere held to lead: Source C (7) would emerge as prior and Source B (26) as dependent on Source C (so Weippert, pp. 35–37). This is a type of questioning which has raised doubts in the minds of scholars about the so-called Source B and its relation to Baruch. Thus Nicholson (*Preaching to the Exiles*, pp. 52–55) has argued that 26 is not primarily concerned with an incident in the life of the prophet Jeremiah, but rather with the rejection of the word of Yahweh spoken by his servants the prophets and the sad consequences of this for Judah. It therefore has an exilic setting as an edifying narrative, just as 7.1–15 has (Nicholson, pp. 69f.). Hence both Thiel and Nicholson conclude that 26 no less than 7 is a Deuteronomistic composition, although in the case of 26 Thiel maintains that a Source B text (vv. 1f., 6*, 7–9) has undergone a Deuteronomistic redaction (p. 106; cf. p. 133). The conclusions which Weippert is inclined to draw are of a different kind and follow from the tendency of her investigation. She discerns a prospect of reclaiming the prose of the book of Jeremiah for the historical prophet, Jeremiah, and this is what she aims to achieve for 7.1–15 (pp. 37ff.).

Finally something should be said about Fohrer's argument (Th.Z. 5, 1949, pp. 401–417=*BZAW* 99, 1967, pp. 190–203) that 7.1–15 has a metrical structure and consists of *Kurzversen*. These, according to Fohrer, are lines of poetry, constituted by a stich of 2 or 3 beats and falling into a strophic arrangement. This is Hebrew poetry without *parallelismus membrorum* (*Langvers*) which has usually been regarded as one of its primary identification marks. Other passages in the postulated sources C (7.16–20, 21–23; 11.1–14; 16.1–9; 18.1–11; 22.1–5; 25.1–14; 34.8–22; 35) and A (1.4–10, 11–12; 3.1, 6–13) are analysed as *Kurzvers* (p. 195).

7.1–15 may be regarded as a test case of Fohrer's hypothesis of *Kurzvers* and Rudolph (p. 47 n. 1) has observed that the demonstration which he offers is unsatisfactory. The following objections may be raised against Fohrer's procedures:

(*a*) It is arguable that all he has done is to divide and sub-divide a piece of Hebrew prose so as to achieve 60 lines and 12 strophes each of 5 lines (p. 195).

(*b*) Poetry is not created by the simple expedient of breaking up a text into a particular arrangement of pieces. The process does not inspire any conviction that it has a *rationale*, nor does it create any impression of inevitability. When Fohrer's final product is inspected, there is no strong impression that this is how it must be and no other structure is possible or probable.

(*c*) The concept of *Kurzvers* is itself formally too vague. Hebrew poetry without *parallelismus membrorum* is a difficult doctrine and the onus of proof is on Fohrer. Can a new kind of Hebrew poetry be established by a statement which is so vague that it hardly serves as a definition? As a formal definition the statement that *Kurzvers* consists of a stich of 2 or 3 beats is seriously deficient.

(*d*) Even so, Fohrer only arrives at his final result by meting out unequal treatment to the material before him. One has a strong

impression that he has made up his mind to get five lines for each
of his 12 strophes and that he is determined not to be thwarted
however recalcitrant the material may be.

DO NOT PRAY FOR THIS PEOPLE (7.16–20)

[16]You are not to intercede for this people; do not make prayers and petitions
for them; do not remonstrate with me, for I will pay no heed to you. [17]Are you
aware of what they are doing in the towns of Judah and the streets of
Jerusalem? [18]Children are collecting wood, fathers are kindling fires and
wives are kneading dough to make cakes for the Queen of Heaven; libations
are poured to alien gods so as to provoke me. [19]Are they really provoking me?
This is Yahweh's word. Are they not rather provoking their own humiliation?
[20]Therefore these are the words of Lord Yahweh, My hot anger will pour
down on this place, on man and beast, on trees and crops, and the fire will not
be extinguished.

Verses 16–20 have the form of address by Yahweh to the
prophet Jeremiah, forbidding him to intercede for the people
(v. 16) and calling attention to open acts of idolatry in Judah and
Jerusalem (vv. 17–19). The passage concludes with a threat,
introduced by לכן and concerning Judah, but intimated to
Jeremiah and not addressed directly to Judah (v. 20).

It is probable that Sept. τοῦ ἐλεηθῆναι αὐτούς is a rendering of
בעדם and that καὶ μὴ εὔχου is a rendering of רנה ותפלה. καὶ μὴ
προσέλθῃς μοι περὶ αὐτῶν for ואל תפגע בי introduces the
appropriate thought of 'lobbying' and this is also indicated by
Vulg. et non obsistas mihi, 'Do not plant yourself in my path'
(pace Ziegler, Beiträge, p. 20, who conjecturally emends τοῦ
ἐλεηθῆναι αὐτούς to τοῦ δεηθῆναι περὶ αὐτῶν.) That intercession
was as much a part of the prophetic office as the transmission of
Yahweh's word has been emphasized in studies on the cultic
connections of prophecy (S. Mowinckel, Psalmenstudien 3,
Kultprophetie und prophetische Psalmen, 1922; A. R. Johnson,
The Cultic Prophet in Ancient Israel[2], 1962) and this is related
to Jeremiah in particular by Reventlow (Liturgie und
prophetisches Ich bei Jeremia, 1963). The function of messenger
and spokesman of Yahweh is the one which the prophet is seen to
discharge, but here and elsewhere in the book of Jeremiah
(11.14; 14.11f.; 15.1f.) the prophet is represented as one who
identifies himself with his community and intercedes for it. Thus
it is an extraordinary proscription when Yahweh forbids him to
discharge this office. ואל תפגע בי is spoken in the context of
Jeremiah's persistence: he plants himself in Yahweh's path
(Vulg.) and insists on pleading for his people.

Is the prophet aware of what is going on openly in the towns of
Judah and the streets of Jerusalem? (v. 17) It is difficult to

believe that he would persist with his pleas for the people, if he were fully apprised of the enormities of their idolatry—this is the implication of the question. There may also be an ironical intention in the representation that idolatry is a co-operative enterprise by which families are unified (v. 18): the children gather the fuel, the fathers tend the fire and the wives bake cakes.

Von Soden (*Akkadisches Handwörterbuch*, 1963, p. 430a) associates כון with *kamānu* 'cake' (cf. KB³), and the much older view (Kimchi) that it is a formation from כון 'prepare' is found in BDB. The thought that כונים are representations of a star (cf. NEB 'crescent-cakes') appears in Rashi (דפוס כוכב = 'star-shaped') and Amos 5.26 (כיון צלמיכם כוכב אלהיכם) should be considered in this connection. כיון is equated with Akkadian *kayyamānu* (von Soden, 420a), Arabic *kaywān* and Syriac *k'wn* by BDB and KB³, 'Saturn'. There are two points to be gathered from Amos 5.26: (*a*) if כיון means 'Saturn' consideration should be given to the possibility that כון (Jer 7.18) is variant form of כיון . (*b*) כוכב אלהיכם is perhaps an epexegesis of כיון צלמיכם and this has a bearing on למלכת השמים (Jer 7.18; cf. 44.19) which is rendered by Targ. as לכוכבת שמיא, 'to the star of heaven' and is explained by Rashi as לכוכב הגדול, 'to the great star' (cf. Kimchi, לכוכב גדול, 'to a great star'). Both Rashi and Kimchi gloss מְלֶכֶת (MT) with מלוכה, indicating a heavenly power or a heavenly body, but the sense is not very different from that obtained by reading לְמַלְכַּת הַשָּׁמַיִם (cf. Vulg. *reginae caeli*). The pointing לְמְלֶכֶת appears in four other prose passages in Jeremiah (44.17, 18, 19, 25) as part of the phrase למלכת השמים. Rudolph suggests that מְלֶכֶת = מלאכת (so many Hebrew manuscripts and noted by Kimchi) arose from the circumstance that מלאכה is associated with צבא (referring to heavenly bodies) in Gen 2.1f. Pesh. *lplḥn šmy'* probably represents למלאכת השמים, with מלאכה understood as 'worship', while Sept. τῇ στρατιᾷ τοῦ οὐρανοῦ represents צבא, probably under the influence of 8.2, where צבא השמים is rendered as τὴν στρατιὰν τοῦ οὐρανοῦ. Aq., Symm. and Theod. have τη βασιλισση του ουρανου at 7.18 and this is Sept.'s rendering in the four other passages noted above ('to the Queen of Heaven'). The Judaeans suppose that they are vexing Yahweh by offering cakes to the Queen of Heaven (Astarte) and pouring out libations (the participle לשות is resumed by the infinitive absolute והסך, GK 113z) to other gods, but it is themselves that they are spiting. They do not cause vexation or hurt to Yahweh, but they do themselves injury and are reduced to hopeless confusion.

On the appropriateness of the metaphor in v. 20 (ובערה ולא תכבה) Kimchi notes that the sense 'heat' is associated with חמה (חום). נתכת, according to Kimchi, refers to the great speed with which the judgement will fall (לרוב מרוצתה): Yahweh's anger will descend on his people and the judgement will be a kind of conflagration which no one will be able to extinguish. The thought that the judgement, when it falls, will involve the animal world and will destroy natural fertility reappears in Jer 12.4, where famine conditions and the disappearance of birds and beasts are said to be the consequence of human wickedness.

Thiel argues (pp. 119–120) that, like vv. 1–15, vv. 16–20 are a composition of D and that the 'core' is a Jeremianic saying which is preserved or partially preserved in v. 18a and which has a metrical structure:

הבנים מלקטים עצים
והאבות מבערים את האש
והנשים לשות בצק

This view that v. 18a preserves a saying of the prophet Jeremiah has to take account of the circumstance that the evidence of the popularity of the cult of the Queen of Heaven is principally contained in chapter 44 which purports to deal with the period at the end of Jeremiah's ministry. Duhm maintained that 7.16–20 was entirely dependent on 44, that the cult was one which achieved popularity, especially among women, after the fall of Jerusalem, that it had a rural setting among the lower classes, and that the reference to 'the cities of Judah and the streets of Jerusalem' is entirely inappropriate in connection with the gathering of wood and the tending of fires. Thiel disagrees with Duhm and holds that the worship of Ishtar (Duhm did not offer an identification of the Queen of Heaven) has to be correlated with the political subservience of Israel and Judah to Assyria. It was revived after Josiah's death and chapter 44 is an indication that there were those who attributed the disaster of 587 to the neglect of the cult. Hence he concludes that his postulated Jeremianic core can be assigned to the reign of Jehoiakim.

The most important critical issue raised by this passage is connected with the interdict on intercession (v. 16). Thiel, who notes that the theme recurs in 11.14, and 14.11, supposes that 14.11–16 has the best claim to be regarded as the original context of the interdict. On 7.16–20 he observes that the Queen of Heaven cult is seized on by D as an example of the gross idolatry which prevailed in Judah in the reign of Jehoiakim and which justified the interdict on intercession. Only a thoroughgoing return to Yahweh would justify a change of heart on his part, and since there were no signs of such deep stirrings, it was pointless for a prophet to engage with Yahweh in pleading for the people.

It is not certain, however, that the interdict on intercession, and the circumstances which elucidate it, are connected with the community towards the end of the pre-exilic period. It will be sufficient to say for the time being that Thiel's general view of D, that he was active in the exilic period and was addressing his words primarily to the needs of that community, does not influence his treatment of vv. 16–20 to the extent that we might have anticipated. The question arises whether the representation that Jeremiah was forbidden to intercede is connected with a problem which made itself felt in the context of exile. There is a tradition that the true prophet is a powerful intercessor (cf. 15.1ff.). Why then were the pre-exilic prophets (if they were true prophets) unable to prevent the disintegration of the community by their intercession? On the other hand, the onset of the exile had vindicated these prophets, since what they predicted had come to pass. How could these polarities be reconciled? They had proclaimed doom powerfully and unerringly, but they had had no effect as intercessors with a view to preventing the onset of the disaster. The answer which was given to this problem was that an interdict had been placed by Yahweh on their function as intercessors.

CHRONIC APOSTASY (7.21–29)

[21]These are the words of Yahweh Sabaoth, God of Israel: Add your burnt-offerings to your sacrifices and eat flesh. [22]I made no demands on your forefathers concerning matters of burnt-offering and sacrifice, when I brought them out of Egypt. [23]But I did make this demand on them, Obey me, so that I may be your God and you may be my people. Walk in all the ways that I enjoin on you, so that it may be well with you. [24]They did not listen, nor pay heed; they followed their own stubborn and evil inclinations[1] and turned away from me. [25]From the time that your forefathers came out of Egypt up to this present day, I sent to you all my servants, the prophets, urgently and ceaselessly. [26]But they did not listen to me; they paid no heed; they stiffened their obstinacy and were worse than their forefathers. [27]You are to speak these words to them, but they will not listen to you; you are to preach to them, but they will make no response to you. [28]Say to them, This is the nation which does not obey the voice of Yahweh, its God, and which will not be instructed. Integrity has perished; it is severed from their speech.
    [29]Cut off your tresses and cast them away,
      raise a lament in the open places.
Yahweh has rejected and cast off the generation on whom his wrath will fall.

It is not possible to save the structural integrity of this section, not even by supposing that vv. 21–26 constitute one unit and vv. 27–28 another. There is a loss of coherence at v. 26, where one cannot suppose that the 'fathers' are the subject of the 3rd per. plur. verbs in view of the closing words of v. 26. (הרעו מאבותם) and Rudolph's insertion of עמי does not effectively

---

[1]Deleting במעצות (see below, p. 174).

relieve the difficulty. We have to suppose that in v. 26 Yahweh is speaking to the prophet or to some other third party about the present generation of Judaeans who are said to be more evil than their forefathers. The section opens with an address by Yahweh to Jeremiah's contemporaries advising them that sacrifices were not enjoined by him on their forefathers and that they have no significance for him at the present time (vv. 21–22). The content of what Yahweh required of the fathers is given in v. 23 and vv. 24–25 record a history of apostasy from the earliest period up to the present. So far the form of direct address by Yahweh to the present generation of Judaeans is preserved, although אליכם in v. 25 is a crack in the structure which is not repaired by emending אליכם to אליהם (so Pesh.). According to NEB the transition from past to present is effected in v. 25, and from ואשלח אליהם to the end of v. 26 there is a reference to the present generation. This can only be so, however, if we assume that the present generation is no longer directly addressed after היום הזה (v. 25) and that what follows to the end of v. 26 is spoken to Jeremiah about his contemporaries. The structural problem arises in connection with the shift from past to present and a single phrase, whether it be אליכם or אליהם (v. 25), cannot do service to both past and present: the entire history of apostasy, including the most recent history, is covered by אליהם, but the present time in which Yahweh still addresses his people through prophets and meets a total lack of response requires אליכם.

The scholarly discussion which vv. 21–22 have attracted (cf. Amos 5.25) has been noted by Rudolph. He is right to be suspicious of the efforts which have made by Rowley (*JSS* 1, 1956, pp. 338ff.) and many others (cf. the debate between Cadoux, Rowley and Snaith in *ET* 58, 1946/7, pp. 43ff., 69ff., 152f., 305ff.; G. Fohrer, *ThR*, 1952, pp. 330ff., 350ff.) to make a passage like Jer 7.21f. turn on the establishment of an order of priorities. This has been justified grammatically by H. Kruse (*VT* 4, 1954, pp. 393f.) and is in line with Rowley's interpretation of Hos 6.6: it says no more than that *ḥesed* takes precedence over sacrifice (cf. Thiel, p. 127). To say that Jeremiah's ignorance of the fact that sacrifice had been a part of Yahwistic practice in the past is incredible, is not so deadly a rejoinder as has been commonly supposed. The reply which this invites is that the nature of the denial contained in these verses requires a more careful consideration. It is not a denial that sacrifices have been a feature of empirical or institutional Yahwism (Exod 20.24; 23.18; Deut 12.6ff.), but it is a denial that they are of the essence of Yahwism. It is somewhat more than this according to Rudolph and Hentschke (*BZAW* 75,

1957, pp. 114–116): it is an assertion that the developed sacrificial system has arisen in the context of Canaanite temple worship and that it is not an aspect of the distinctiveness of Yahwism.

That apologetic instincts were early aroused by this passage can be seen in Rashi's contention that v. 21, far from being anti-cultic, is concerned with the failure to observe cultic regulations. Kimchi's interpretation partly resembles the one noted above (Rowley). עולות and זבחים are not acceptable to Yahweh, 'because there are no acceptable deeds preceding them'. The תמידים which are commanded are for 'the glory of the House' (לכבוד הבית), but otherwise Yahweh does not require sacrifices unconditionally, as he does משפט and מצוה. There are some similarities between Kimchi's exegesis and that of Rudolph. The latter also notices that there is no requirement of sacrifice in the Ten Words and he develops further Kimchi's observation that ספו (v. 21) is not a straightforward imperative. The intention is ironical: Yahweh, in effect, tells the Judaeans that nice cultic distinctions mean nothing to him and that it is a matter of supreme indifference to him whether or not they are punctilious in maintaining right practice in relation to different kinds of sacrifices (the contrary of Rashi's exegesis). What Yahweh lays down as an indispensable requirement is obedience (שמעו בקולי) and it is this response and commitment which cements the relation between God and people. A community of Yahweh and his people is called into existence only in so far as this essential response is forthcoming: Conduct your lives as my words require (והלכתם בכל הדרך אשר אצוה אתכם) and then I shall be your God and you will be my people. Herein lies the possibility of true prosperity and abiding enrichment (v. 23).

But the history of apostasy, beginning from the time that Yahweh rescued the fathers of the nation from Egypt (v. 25), is constituted by the circumstance that all the generations consistently refused to meet this demand. The fatal flaw is described as a stubborn tendency towards evil (v. 24). Since Sept. represents וילכו בשררות לבם הרע Cornill and Rudolph suppose that במעצות is an insertion from Ps. 81.13, where both שרירות and מועצות appear. Bright suggests that מעצות is a doublet of שררות and this is a view which is favoured by Janzen (p. 11). The pejorative sense of מעצות (Hos 11.6; Mic 6.16; Ps 5.11; 81.13; Prov 1.31) is appropriate at Jer 7.24 ('schemes', 'intrigues'). In view, however, of the pattern established by other passages in the book of Jeremiah (3.17; 9.13; 11.8; 13.10; 16.12; 18.12; 23.17) במעצות should be deleted.

ויהיו לאחור ולא לפנים indicates a stubborn and perverse wilfulness which thwarts Yahweh's purposes. The meaning of the sentence is, perhaps, that they turned away from Yahweh rather than towards him—they turned their backs on him. Their stance is symbolic of their refusal to hear him or to be led by him (cf. Calvin). Both Lowth and Blayney suppose that the figure is that of refractory oxen which will not submit to the yoke (cf. Jer 2.20; 5.5). The thought that there is a reference to backsliding in לאחור ולא לפנים (7.24) appears in Lowth's and Bright's exegesis. If למן היום . . . היום הזה is taken with לאחור ולא לפנים (as Rudolph, Thiel, p. 122, and NEB do against the Massoretic punctuation), what is being said is that the tendency has always been to apostasy and never to obedience from the time of the Exodus onwards. In that case the remainder of v. 25 and v. 26 (with אליכם emended to אליהם, so NEB) can only be construed as a word addressed to Jeremiah by Yahweh concerning the present generation (הרעו מאבותם). If the punctuation of MT is maintained, the meaning is that there has been a continuous and insistent (השכם ושלח) prophetic witness from the earliest period to the present which has been met with an unyielding and perverse obstinacy whose dimensions have grown with the passing of time, so that it can be said of the present generation ויקשו את ערפם הרעו מאבותם (v. 26).

יום (v. 25), which is grammatically difficult, has been taken by Vulg. (*per diem*), Pesh. (*bklywm*) and Targ. (בכל יום) as equivalent to יום יום and this is how it is explained by Kimchi. Ehrlich (p. 261) conjectures that יום is a dittography of the penultimate and final letters of הנביאים. The other possibility is that יום has been lost through haplography and that יום יום was the original text. However, the support of Vulg., Pesh. and Targ. should not be claimed for יום יום : it is likely that they read יום and gave it the same force as יום יום and this is, perhaps, the best decision that can be made. It is doubtful Hebrew, but it should be tolerated.

There is a shorter Sept. text in vv. 27–28 (supposed by Thiel, p. 124 n. 52 to be an abridgement of MT) and a shorter Pesh. text in v. 28. The shorter Greek text can be described in different ways: one might suppose (cf. BHS) that ודברת אליהם (v. 27) is represented by καὶ ἐρεῖς αὐτοῖς, that τὸν λόγον τοῦτον is an approximation of את כל הדברים האלה and that there is nothing in Sept. corresponding to ולא ישמעו אליך וקראת אליהם ולא יענוכה. The main difficulty with this explanation is that καὶ ἐρεῖς αὐτοῖς is more probably a rendering of ואמרת אליהם (MT, v. 28) than of ודברת אליהם (MT, v. 27) and for this reason Janzen (pp. 37f., 204 n. 8) approaches the matter differently. One of his suggestions is that the original text is preserved in v. 28 (Sept.), that most of v. 27 (MT) is a paraphrase of v. 13 and an insertion, and that ודברת אליהם את כל הדברים האלה

(v. 27, MT) corresponds to καὶ ἐρεῖς αὐτοῖς τὸν λόγον τοῦτον, ואמרת having been changed to ודברת under the influence of ואדבר (v. 13). Janzen's final thoughts (p. 204 n. 8) are, perhaps, the most valuable. Since most of v. 28 is not represented by Pesh. (ואמרת . . . מוסר), there is a case for arguing that v. 27 and v. 28 (as far as מוסר) are variants, that MT has a conflate text, that Sept. has preserved one variant (v. 28) and Pesh. the other (v. 27). There is a slight discrepancy in this account in so far as the (ex hypothesi) conflate text of MT lacks anything corresponding to τὸν λόγον τοῦτον in v. 28.

Jeremiah is advised by Yahweh that when he delivers his message, as he must, he will find that communication is blocked by a wall of unresponsiveness (cf. Isa 6.9f.; Jer 1.16–19; Ezek 3.7–11). He is to remind the people that they have a history of addiction to apostasy, that it has become second nature for them to turn away from Yahweh rather than to turn towards him. אמונה ('faithfulness', 'steadfastness', 'integrity') has died, because the community does not have roots which will nourish it. If the quality of life in the community and relations between its members do not derive from אמונה, there is no foundation for honest religious language and the most solemn liturgical affirmations are empty. The absence of integrity in speech is bound up with a total loss of social integrity (אבדה האמונה ונכרתה מפיהם).

There is a similarity between v. 29 and 6.26, where Jerusalem, personified as a woman, is enjoined to anticipate the imminent destruction of the city and to engage in mourning rites for her own demise. There is a question whether the snatch of poetry in v. 29 includes כי מאס יהוה ויטש את דור עברתו (so Rudolph, Bright, NEB). The poetry of v. 29a is addressed directly to בת ירושלם (?), whereas what follows is a reference in the 3rd person to Yahweh's people. Hence the two parts of v. 29 do not cohere properly. Another consideration is that כי of v. 29 should perhaps be related to כי in v. 30. In other words the snatch of poetry has invited secondary exegetical elaboration: in v. 29b it has attracted an observation that Yahweh has rejected his people and in vv. 30–34 a speech by Yahweh to a third party in which he describes the abominable cultic practices of the Judaeans and threatens them with dire consequences. Both v. 29b (את דור עברתו) and vv. 30–34 deal with imminent judgement and throw light on the proleptic mourning which is commanded in v. 29a. Although it has been common to regard 8.1–3 as a continuation of 7.34, this passage introduces a new train of thought and is not intrinsically related to 7.30–34 (see further below).

Symm. has connected נזרך with the long hair required by the Nazirite vow, but Rudolph has indicated the difficulty of

assuming a direct reference to Nazirites in view of the fem.
gender of the imperatives. There can be little doubt that it is a
woman (Jerusalem) who is told to cut off her tresses (Sept.,
Vulg. and Pesh.) as a sign of mourning and sorrow. Kimchi
correctly explains נזר as a great head of hair, especially
therefore the hair of a woman, and as a usage which is derived
from the long hair of the נזיר (Nazirite). Jerusalem must cut off
her flowing tresses and cast them away—she is to be shorn for
her own mourning rites. As at 3.2, 21 and 4.11 the versions have
difficulty with שפים. Sept. ἀνάλαβε ἐπὶ χειλέων θρῆνον, 'Take up
a lament on your lips', connects שפים with שפה 'lip'. שפים does
not certainly mean 'bare heights' and such philological
indications as there are indicate 'open country' or the like (see
below at 14.6). It is, however, associated with Canaanite rites at
3.2 and 21 and the assumption that these took place at במות has
encouraged the inference that שפים means 'bare heights'. There
is then a possibility that שפים has associations with Canaanite
rites in 7.29, and, if so, a different interpretation of the verse is
suggested: it does not represent proleptic mourning rites, but
mourning rites in the context of a Canaanite shrine—the
shearing of the hair and wailing for the dead god. On this view
v. 29b (כי מאס ... עברתו) refers particularly to the ineluctable
decree of Yahweh to bring judgement on his people: the time for
repentance and amendment is past, so carry on with your
idolatry.

According to Thiel (p. 122) vv. 21–29 are a Deuteronomistic
composition within which sayings of the prophet Jeremiah are
embedded, including עלותיכם ספו על זבחיכם ואכלו בשר (v. 21).
In so far as he is showing that the vocabulary and word-strings of
his postulated editor D have no parallels in the book of
Deuteronomy or the Deuteronomistic literature, it could be
argued (as it is by Weippert) that this is evidence of the
independence of the prose of the book of Jeremiah over against
Deuteronomy and the Deuteronomistic literature (see above,
p. 166f.). His suggestion that ולא לקחו מוסר (v. 28) is derived
from poetry attributable to the prophet Jeremiah (2.30; cf. 5.3)
represents another way of looking for the sources of the prose
within the Jeremianic corpus rather than outside it.

Thiel exaggerates the coherence of vv. 21–29, particularly,
v. 29. He is right to argue against the view of Rudolph and
Weiser that v. 29 is related to vv. 30ff. (p. 125 n. 57), but wrong
in supposing that it integrates with the verses which precede it.
אבדה האמונה ונכרתה מפיהם (v. 28) also has a detached
appearance and does not resume the preceding part of the verse
in a convincing way. Whether or not Thiel is correct in his
supposition that vv. 28b (ולא לקחו ... מפיהם) and 29 are sayings

attributable to the prophet Jeremiah, there is no doubt that they have an isolated appearance and do not cohere with the context. This is underlined by the circumstance that v. 29 is poetry.

The other saying of Jeremiah which Thiel identifies in the Deuteronomistic composition which he postulates is located in v. 21 and he observes (pp. 126f.) that Jeremiah has the same attitude to temple worship and the sacrificial system as the other major prophets. He urges that the Deuteronomistic attitude to these matters was similarly negative (cf. above, pp. 165f) and, in particular, that vv. 21–29 have to be interpreted in connection with the exilic situation which called forth D's words. In offering an interpretation of Israel's history D is seeking to explain why the exile took place: it was the consequence of a history of disobedience and failure from the Exodus on. Yahweh's revealed law (Deuteronomy) was ignored and his prophetic messengers were rejected. The negative view of the wilderness period contradicts Hosea and the early Jeremiah (2.2). The negative attitude to sacrifice may represent an adverse judgement on the provisional cult which, according to Jer 41.4ff., was set up on the site of the ruined temple.

DARK RITES IN THE VALLEY OF BEN HINNOM (7.30–34)

[30]The Judaeans have done what is evil in my eyes. This is Yahweh's word. They have installed idols in the house which bears my name and have desecrated it. [31]They have built a Topheth altar[1] in the valley of Ben Hinnom to burn as offerings their sons and daughters. This I never required nor did it cross my mind that I should. [32]Therefore, the time is coming (This is Yahweh's word) when the altar will no longer be called Topheth nor the valley Ben Hinnom; it will be called the Valley of Slaughter and there will be burials in Topheth until no room is left. [33]The corpses of this people will be food for the vultures and the wild beasts, and there will be no one to scare them off. [34]I will banish from the towns of Judah and the streets of Jerusalem sounds of joy and gladness, the voice of the bridegroom and the bride; for the land will be laid waste.

Verses 30–34 contain a description of gross idolatry within the Jerusalem temple (v. 30) and of dark rites in the valley of Ben Hinnom, followed by a threat of punishment introduced by לכן (vv. 32–34). Kimchi associates the שׁקּוּצִים of v. 30 with the syncretistic practices of Ahaz and Manasseh and this accords with Thiel's view (p. 129) of the historical reference of this verse and of v. 18 (above, p. 171). The other possibility is that there is an allusion to the post-Josian relapse into idolatry of which we hear elsewhere in the book of Jeremiah (44) and in Ezekiel. A particularly gruesome rite was associated with the shrine of

---

[1] Reading בָּמָת (see below, p. 179).

Topheth in the valley of Ben Hinnom. The plural form במות
(v. 31) is difficult to account for and ובנו is an unusual way of
indicating a past tense in Hebrew. Sept. (βωμόν) and Targ.
(במת) indicate a singular form and this emendation should be
made. Rudolph suggests that תֹּפֶת is a disparaging pointing on
the model of בֹּשֶׁת, perhaps influenced by the homonym תֹּפֶת
'spitting'—also a gesture of contempt (cf. Job 17.6). Rudolph
supposes that the correct pointing is תֵּפֶת and that the meaning is
'hearth' or 'fire-altar'. There is a picturesque description of תפת
in Rashi who comments on במות התפת: 'That is, it is made of
bronze and they heat it from below and its hands are stretched
out and are red-hot. They put the child in its hands and it is
burnt and cries out; the priests beat on drums, so that the father
will not hear the cries of the child, and so they stifle his
compassion.' The reference to the beating on drums (תופים) is
an etymology of תפת.

The offering of children as sacrifices was something which
Yahweh did not command and which he could never have
contemplated. The formula with which v. 32 opens (לכן הנה
ימים באים) is common in the prose sections of the book of
Jeremiah, in association with both oracles of salvation (16.14;
23.5, 7; 30.3; 31.27, 31; 33.14) and oracles of doom (7.32; 9.24;
19.6; 48.12; 49.2; 51.47, 52). The threat in v. 32 is that the valley
of Ben Hinnom, in which the shrine Topheth is located, will be
renamed the Valley of Slaughter. The combination בן הנם
suggests that הנם is a personal name (so Rudolph). According to
Jerome there may be a play on חן 'graciousness', 'favour' and so
an antithesis of הנם and ההרגה. The threat is presumably that
there will be a massacre of the civilian population consequent on
military defeat, and that there will be mass burials in the valley
of Ben Hinnom מאין מקום. This is rendered by Sept. as διὰ τὸ μὴ
ὑπάρχειν τόπον ('because no other place exists') and by Vulg. as
eo quod non sit locus ('because there is no room elsewhere').
Rudolph and NEB agree with Sept. and Vulg., whereas Bright
renders 'till there is no room left'. The latter is the more
probable, if v. 33 is envisaged as a consequence of the state of
affairs described in v. 32. It is, however, arguable that v. 33
describes a further aggravation (so Thiel, p. 130; cf. Kimchi) of
the problem—not even in the Valley of Ben Hinnom is there any
space left.

At any rate the corpses, heaped up in the Valley of Ben
Hinnom, are denied the dignity of burial and become carrion for
vultures and wild beasts (cf. Rashi's comment on ואין מחרית —
את העופות מן הפגרים, 'the vultures from the corpses'). This is
well illustrated by the story of Rizpah (2 Sam 21.10f.) who
played the part of a מחרידה and beat off the vultures from the

corpses of her children (cf. Deut 28.26). There are two ways of understanding the final verse of this section. It may be supposed that a general reference to the banishment of laughter and gaiety from the towns of Judah and the streets of Jerusalem (קוֹל שָׂשׂוֹן וקול שמחה) is followed by a particular reference to the cessation of all wedding festivities. The other possibility is that קול ששון וקול שמחה as well as קול חתן וקול כלה refers to the cessation of wedding festivities. This gives a sharper point to the verse: weddings are not only occasions of joy, but are signs that the life of the community is always being renewed. They are acts of faith in its future and a promise that there will be new families and new generations to carry on its life. But this is a land which will be totally devastated, and a community which has no future continuous with the old conditions of its existence.

In his account of 7.30–34 Thiel (pp. 128f.) makes out a good case for a direct literary relationship between v. 33 and Deut 28.26. The vocabulary is strikingly similar and ואין מחריד only occurs in these two passages. He takes 16.9 as a word of the prophet Jeremiah and suggests that some influence may have been exerted by Hos 2.13. He urges, however, that a distinction can be made between 16.9 and the two other passages in the book of Jeremiah which contain references to the silencing of notes of joy and the absence of wedding festivities (7.34 and 25.10): in the latter passages evidences of the vocabulary of D missing from 16.9 can be detected.

The erecting of idolatrous images in the temple is (so Thiel) associated with Manasseh in the Deuteronomistic literature (2 Kgs 21.2–8), and the cult of sacrificing children with Ahaz and Manasseh (2 Kgs 16.3; 21.6). It was suppressed by Josiah (2 Kgs 23.10), but there was a recrudescence after his death (see above, p. 171, on v. 18) and a polemic was directed against it in the exilic period (Lev 18.21; 20.2–5; Ezek 16.21; 23.37). It will be noticed that Thiel's exegesis of this passage is not greatly influenced by his assumption that it is the work of an exilic editor with the needs of the exilic community in the forefront of his mind. What he says, however, does fit into his general view that reasons are being given for the exile and that its onset is being justified. Judah's idolatry was dark and fiendish and the blow which shattered the community was Yahweh's response to rites from which he dissociated himself totally and which he abhorred.

CHAPTER VIII

THE DEAD DISHONOURED AND THE LIVING IN DESPAIR (8.1–3)

¹At that time (This is Yahweh's word) the bones of the kings of Judah, the bones of its statesmen, priests and prophets and of those who lived in Jerusalem, will be unearthed from their graves. ²They will be exposed to sun, moon and all the host of heaven: objects which they loved and served, which they followed and consulted and worshipped. They will not be gathered and reburied; they will become dung on the surface of the ground. ³Death will be desired more than life by all the survivors of this wicked people in all the places[1] where I have scattered them. This is the word of Yahweh Sabaoth.

The unit is introduced by a formula (בעת ההיא) which elsewhere introduces prose units in the book of Jeremiah, as a variant of בימים ההמה (3.17) or in combination with it (33.15). It has been attached to the preceding verses because there is some similarity of content: the portrayal of unburied corpses in 7.30–34 attracts the thought that the graves of Judaean kings, political and religious leaders, and the general citizenry of Jerusalem, will be desecrated and that their bodies will be exhumed. The violation and dishonouring of graves is, however, quite a separate matter, and if it is connected with enemy action, it would come in the aftermath of defeat and subjection. It was connected by earlier commentators with the excesses of the victorious Chaldaean army on the rampage (Calvin, Venema) or, more particularly, with a search for treasure concealed in graves (Lowth, Venema, Blayney). Cogan (Gratz College Anniversary Volume, 1971, pp. 29–34) has suggested that it is to be understood as the penalty exacted by an overlord for the violation of treaty oaths. There is evidence that such conditions and threats were attached to Assyrian vassal treaties (D. Wiseman, *Iraq* 20, 1958, 476f., 483f.).

The representation envisages a kind of *lex talionis*: the corpses will be exposed to the effects of the elements, to the heavens and the heavenly bodies which living men worshipped as gods, with which they were infatuated and from which they sought guidance. This will be a final dishonouring and disintegration of their bodies which will not be redeemed by any process of reburial. They will become humus which will serve to fertilize the land. The longer Greek text in v. 2 might be regarded as conflate (καὶ πρὸς πάντας τοὺς ἀστέρας and καὶ πρὸς πᾶσαν τὴν στρατίαν being doublets), but Ziegler (*Beiträge*, p. 91) supposes that καὶ πρὸς πάντας τοὺς ἀστέρας is an addition from

---

[1] Deleting הנשארים (see below, p. 182).

Deut 4.19 (καὶ τοὺς ἀστέρας) and that the motive was to produce a triad of sun, moon and stars (cf. Janzen, p. 31).

In v. 3 הנשארים (second occurrence) is not indicated by Sept. and Pesh. and should be deleted (cf. Janzen, p. 38). It breaks into a word-string (בכל המקמות אשר הדחתים שם) which, with some variations, is well-attested in the prose of the book of Jeremiah (16.15; 23.3, 8; 24.9; 29.14,18; 30.11; 32.37; 40.12; 43.5; 46.28). Those who survive defeat and dispersal reckon themselves to be in a worse state than those who died before the event. To live in exile in a condition of despair is worse than having one's corpse defiled.

The disengaging of 8.1–3 from 7.1–30 is an expression of disagreement with Thiel's conclusion (pp. 133f.) that 7.1–8.3 is a great sermon constructed by D. It is also associated with a conviction that Thiel exaggerates the literary unity of chapter 7 by representing that D used material deriving from the prophet Jeremiah (vv. 4, 9a*, 10a*, 11*, 12?, 14, 18a, 21*, 28b, 29) to construct a succinct account of the leading themes of the prophet's ministry. When so much has been conceded to authentic Jeremianic contents in chapter 7, an exilic situation is not transparently the only one or the right one. The interdict on intercession (v. 16; see above, p. 172) is, perhaps, best accounted for as an exilic apologetic for Jeremiah, but, in many respects, the interests and emphasis of chapter 7 satisfy what we have reason to believe were paramount concerns of the historical prophet Jeremiah.

INVETERATE REBELS (8.4–7)

⁴'Say to them, These are the words of Yahweh:
If men fall, do they not get up again?
If someone goes away, does he not come back?
⁵Why is this people¹ so fickle?
Why is its apostasy so rampant?
They have taken hold of deceit;
they have refused to come back.
⁶I strained to listen;
their words were twisted;
no one repents of his wickedness.
What have I done wrong?, they say;
each goes off on his own course,
like a war-horse careering into battle.
⁷The stork in the sky
knows when to migrate;
dove, swift² and swallow³(?)

¹ Deleting ירושלם (see below, p. 183).
² Reading סים (Q). See below, pp. 184f.
³ See below, pp. 184f.

observe the right time to depart;
but my people do not know
what Yahweh's order is.

The words נאם יהוה צבאות ואמרת אליהם (vv. 3–4) are not indicated by Sept.[BSA] and both Rudolph and Bright regard ואמרת אליהם כה אמר יהוה as a redactional link. Nevertheless, the speaker in vv. 4–7 would appear to be Yahweh, and the only impediment to this assumption is את משפט יהוה (v. 7), since את משפטי would be more natural, but it is safer to grant the existence of a convention that Yahweh may refer to himself in the third person than to deny that he could be the speaker. The rendering of Targ. in v. 6, where a circumlocution designed to mitigate an anthropomorphism appears (וגלי קדמי for ואשמע), indicates clearly the view of this translator, but Kimchi, on the other hand, asserts that Jeremiah is the speaker in v. 6. It is probable that the shorter Greek text in vv. 3–4 is the more original.

The question which is asked in v. 4 is rhetorical and demands a negative answer. It would be extraordinary if someone who had fallen and was uninjured chose to remain supine. The second question must have a similar tendency, but the repetition of ישוב is a new factor over against the unambiguous antithesis of יפלו and יקומו. The second antithesis is conveyed through homonymy and the two senses employed are 'going away' and 'coming back', that is, apostasy and repentance. It makes no difference to the sense whether we suppose that a single root שוב conveys opposite meanings, or whether we postulate another root for 'going astray' whose distinctness is not preserved by Hebrew phonology (so G. R. Driver, *JQR* 28, p. 105).

Why is it that Yahweh's people are so unrelenting in their apostasy? The lack of congruence between שובבה and העם can be removed by assuming a dittography of ה (BHS) and it is likely that ירושלם represents an intrusion into the text. It is not indicated by Sept.[BSA] and perhaps originated as an exegetical gloss on העם הזה. The straying of the people amounts to rampant apostasy (משבה נצחת): שובב is another formation from שוב (cf. v. 4) and משבה נצחת is further explicated as a clinging to treachery or deceit and a refusal to repent.

In v. 6 הקשבתי ואשמע is a hendiadys, 'I strained my ears to listen', and what Yahweh heard was conversation which lacked integrity (כן). This interpretation of כן is supported by Vulg., Pesh., Targ., Rashi and Kimchi, but not by Sept. (οὐχ οὕτως λαλήσουσιν) which is followed by Bright, 'No such word did they say', that is, no word indicative of any resolve to repent. But it is later in v. 6 that מה עשיתי, 'What is this that I have done?', is offered as proof that the apostates have no inclination to change their evil ways. They are like a war-horse which has the scent of conflict, which is committed to the battle beyond recall and which will not be checked in the charge on which it has launched itself. כלה (ה is an earlier orthographical representation of the 3rd masc. sing. suffix than ו, see J. C. L. Gibson, *Syrian Semitic Inscriptions* i, 1971, p. 29 n. 2) is not significantly better matched by מרצתם (Q) than by the plural מרצותם (K). במרצתם is interpreted in Pesh. (*bṣbynhwn*) and Targ. (ברעות נפשהון) as a reference to wilful behaviour.

The behaviour of birds, which conform to Yahweh's משפט (v. 7; cf. Isa 1.3, noted by Jerome and Kimchi), shows up human conduct in an unfavourable light. The nuance of 'order' in משפט is sufficiently comprehensive to bridge the gap between the world of birds and the world of men (cf. Jer 5.22, where the sea's respect for the limits prescribed by Yahweh is contrasted with the failure of men to keep his תורה; above, pp. 129–130). The instincts of the birds work unerringly to indicate times for migration (the sing. מועדה appears in a few Hebrew manuscripts and is represented by the versions) and return, but Yahweh's people do not possess the moral discernment or the commitment to righteousness needed to uphold Yahweh's order. They are free human beings, but they do not have the moral capacity to discharge their responsibility. Yahweh's people, unlike the birds, are endowed with שכל (so Kimchi), but exercise their endowment in such a way that they are in conflict with Yahweh's order. In this sense 'they do not know Yahweh's משפט'.

Ziegler (cf. Janzen, p. 26) supposes that ἀγροῦ (ἀγουρ; so Aq. and Symm.) and στρουθία are doublets, but the possibility that στρουθία is an insertion consequent on the corruption of ἀγουρ to ἀγροῦ should be considered. If ἀγροῦ was identified as a genitive sing. of ἀγρός, something had to be done to overcome the deficiency of sense, and it is clear that this was how Jerome took ἀγροῦ στρουθία (*agri passeres*, 'sparrows of the field'; cf. 'hedge-sparrows').

The point of the figure requires that the birds should be migrants and it has been argued that this enables us to choose between 'swallow' (Sept. and Vulg.) and 'swift' for סום (סים; cf. Aq. σεις). It is not altogether clear how sharply this can be put. The statement that the swallow is resident in Palestine (G. R. Driver, *PEQ*, 1955, p. 131; cf. H. B. Tristram, *The Fauna and Flora of Palestine*, 1884, p. 82) may not take sufficient account of the different kinds of swallows (cf. F. S. Bodenheimer, *Animal Life in Palestine*, p. 164). Tristram (op. cit., pp. 82f.) observed that the piercing cry of the swift is a more appropriate simile for a cry of pain (Isa 38.14) than the twittering of a swallow, and

Bodenheimer's remark that the note emitted by the swift is *si-si* enables us to identify סיס as onomatopoeic (also Tristram). סוס was identified by Targ. and Pesh. with the crane (also Rashi and Kimchi) and this, along with the equation עגור = 'swallow', is taken up by KJV and is found in Lowth, Venema and Blayney. Calvin, who has 'dove, swallow and crane' is influenced by Sept. and Vulg. in respect of סוס (סיס) and follows Saadya's identification of עגור with 'crane' (cf. W. Gesenius, *Thesaurus* ii, 1840, p. 990; Tristram op. cit., pp. 126f.).

עגור is not represented by Sept. at Isa 38.14 and the conclusion to be drawn from its absence is that it is a gloss on סוס and that whoever provided the gloss believed that סוס and עגור referred to the same bird. Hence there is little doubt that עגור in Jer 8.7 refers to a bird, but it cannot be certainly identified. It was transliterated by Sept., identified with 'stork' (*ciconia*) by Vulg., with 'swallow' by Pesh., Targ., Rashi (whose French gloss makes this intention certain) and Kimchi, with 'crane' by Saadya. Köhler's suggestion (*ZAW* 54, 1936, pp. 288f.) that it is a type of thrush (the yellow-vented Bulbul) does not find favour with Driver (*PEQ*, 1955, p. 132) who maintains that the Bulbul is 'a permanent resident in Palestine'. Driver's own preference is for the 'wryneck' (Arabic *'ajara*, 'to bend the neck') and this appears in NEB at Jer 8.7. There is no satisfactory solution to this. סוס (סיס) should be identified with the swift, and עגור in Isa 38.14 is an attempt to provide another name for the same bird. In that case we might suppose that the gloss represents a confusion of 'swift' and 'swallow' and that Pesh., Targ., Rashi and Kimchi are right in identifying עגור with 'swallow'. This tentative and shaky conclusion is the best that can be achieved. The assertion that the swallow was not a migrant bird is not so certain as to preclude it (cf. Bodenheimer, p. 164).

AGAINST WISE MEN AND SCHOLARS (8.8–9)

[8]How can you say, We are wise men
and Yahweh's law is in our custody?
Undoubtedly it has been changed[1] to falsehood
by the falsifying pens of scribes!
[9]The wise are in disarray,
they will be broken and ensnared.
They have rejected Yahweh's word
and what wisdom is left to them?

Verses 8–9 are directed against the claim of the חכמים or ספרים

[1] Reading עָשָׂה, see below, p. 186.

to be official interpreters of the תורה. They constitute evidence of the existence of a learned class with this kind of status in the late pre-exilic period (cf. W. McKane, *PWM*, 1965, pp. 102–112), and of a conflict between the interpretation and development of תורה associated with this class and the דבר spoken by a prophet in the name of Yahweh. The speaker could be either Yahweh or the prophet Jeremiah, for his own part, but if the former, we have to assume that Yahweh refers to himself in the 3rd person as in v. 7. The reference to the false pen of the scribes (reading עָשָׂה) suggests that we have to reckon with a process of editorial elaboration and development of written law, or even the drafting of new laws, but too exclusive reliance ought not to be placed on the allusion to the 'pen' of the scribes. We do not necessarily for example, have an indication of the unfavourable attitude of the prophet to the 'second law'—the code of Deuteronomy. A more general interpretation of the allusion should also be allowed, namely, that the prophet is concerned with what he regards as false rulings in connection with contemporary issues which he believes to be crucial. The learning and expertise of those who make these rulings do not save them from error or triviality.

The wise men will be disconcerted and demoralized and their reputations as intellectual and spiritual leaders will be destroyed. The precise sense of חתו וילכדו is not clear. That חתו has the sense 'terrified' is the view of Sept. (ἐπτοήθησαν) and Vulg. (*perterriti*). The versions understand וילכדו as a threat that the wise men will be carried off as prisoners (cf. Sept. ἑάλωσαν), perhaps as a consequence of a military defeat (Vulg. *capti sunt*). Both Pesh. (*w'ttbrw*) and Targ. (איתברו) have taken חתו in the more literal sense of 'shattered'. Even if the sense 'shattered' were retained for חתו, we should envisage a shattering of morale rather than a shattering defeat, and וילכדו may simply indicate the onset of Yahweh's judgement rather than a reference to particular, external events by which they will be overtaken: they will be caught in a trap from which there is no escape. It is improbable that וילכדו means 'and have lost their wits' (NEB).

NO SENSE OF SHAME (8.10–12)

[10]Therefore I will give their wives to strangers
and their fields to new owners.
All of them, small and great,
are greedy for gain;
there is no prophet or priest
but practises falsehood.
[11]They treat my people's wounds on the surface,

saying, You are cured, when there is no cure.
¹²Their abominations should make them ashamed,
but they have no sense of shame,
nor do they feel disgrace.
Therefore they will be among the victims,
when judgement falls on them they will stumble.
This is Yahweh's word.

Verses 8–9 is a self-contained unit, consisting of indictment in
v. 8 and a mixture of threat and indictment in v. 9. The terms of
allegation and threat in vv. 10–12 are much wider and embrace
all sections of Jerusalem society (מקטן ועד גדול). There is
nothing in the general character of the threat in v. 13 to connect
it with the wise men or scribes, and a comparison of vv. 10–12
with 6.12–15 suggests that this unit is complete at v. 12. Hence
v. 13 cannot be related to what precedes it, and since it does not
appear to be connected with what follows, it must be taken as an
isolated verse. It is likely that vv. 10–12 are secondary in the
context of chapter 8 and have, for the most part, been imported
from chapter 6 (Rudolph; Janzen, pp. 11, 95f.). The passage,
with the exception of v. 10a, is not represented by Sept. If we
conclude that 8.10–12 is secondary and that the original context
of the passage is chapter 6, the circumstance that Sept.
represents v. 10a, and has rendered v. 13 (אסף אסיפם appears as
καὶ συνάξουσιν τὰ γενήματα αὐτῶν) in a manner which
establishes a connection with v. 10a, is not a sufficient reason for
excluding v. 10a from the overall judgement that vv. 10–12 are
secondary in chapter 8. There is, however, no proposal to delete
vv. 10–12 because (a) MT is not a text which makes poor sense
or is unintelligible, and so it is not a case where emendation is a
matter of urgency or is unavoidable. (b) The quantitative factor
is of over-riding importance. It is one thing to be prepared to
delete a word or a phrase which appears to be secondary and
intrusive (a gloss or the like); it is quite another matter to
acquiesce in removing 3 verses from MT in order to implement
textual-critical indications supplied by Sept.

The exegesis of vv. 10–12 does not differ significantly from
that of 6.12–15 (see above, pp. 146–148), but the following
additional textual differences should be noted: (a) 6.12a differs
in some respects from 8.10a, and of the two 8.10a reads better:
the association of 'fields and wives' is an odd feature in 6.12a
(above, p. 146). One might conjecture that 'fields' is a variant of
'houses' and belongs to the first stich of 6.12a, and that the
threat in its original form (retained in 8.10a) is directed against
wives and property. (b) Janzen supposes (pp. 95f.) that
פקדתים/פרקתם and גם הכלים/והכלם (8.12 and 6.15) are no more
than orthographical variants, but there are weighty reasons for

questioning this: they were not regarded as orthographical variants by the Massoretes whose pointing imposes morphological distinctions, and הִכָּלֵם would be an unusual spelling of the Niphal infinitive construct in Biblical Hebrew as would פְּקַדְתָּם of a 1st person sing. verb + suffix. (c) בַּת עַמִּי (8.11) is to be compared with עַמִּי (6.14). Janzen (p. 38) supposes that בַּת is an insertion in 8.11 from 8.21 (שֶׁבֶר בַּת עַמִּי; cf. 8.19, 22, 23).

It has been argued that 6.10–15 should be regarded as speech of Jeremiah, for his own part, rather than word of Yahweh and אָמַר יהוה has been deleted at 6.15 (see above, pp. 144, 148). The difference between לָכֵן אֶתֵּן (8.10) and וְנָסַבּוּ (6.12) is such that the same solution cannot be adopted for 8.10–12. The prophet for his own part, would not say, 'I will give their wives to strangers and their fields to new owners'. This might be regarded as an indication that a wrong decision had been made at chapter 6, but if the passage is original there, its formal problems should be worked out in that context. It has to be acknowledged, however, that the indications of 8.10–12 throw doubt on the rightness of deleting אָמַר יהוה (6.15). On balance, however, it seems better to let two different formal evaluations of these verses stand rather than forcing agreement between 6.12–15 and 8.10–12. Consequently אָמַר יהוה is being deleted at 6.15 and allowed to stand at 8.12.

A HARVEST OF TOTAL JUDGEMENT (8.13)

> [13]I will gather them for final destruction.
>> This is Yahweh's word.
> There will be no grapes on the vine,
> no figs on the fig-tree,
> and the leaves will be withered.[1]

'I would gather their harvest' (NEB) assumes that אָסֹף (v. 13) should be vocalized as אֶאֱסֹף = אֹסֵף (cf. GK 68b) and that אֲסִיפָם should be vocalized as אֲסִיפָם. The latter is indicated by Sept. τὰ γενήματα αὐτῶν, whereas the rendering of אָסֹף by a 3rd plur. would seem to indicate that it has been taken as an infinitive absolute (אָסֹף = συνάξουσιν). Vulg. congregans congregabo eos represents אָסֹף אֶסְפֵּם (?). NEB, 'I would gather their harvest but' is not the sense which is desiderated. Harvest is rather a figure of judgement and the thoroughness of the process of harvesting constitutes a threat of total judgement: there will be no grapes (left) on the vine, no figs on the fig-tree and the leaves will be withered.

[1] Deleting וָאֶתֵּן לָהֶם יַעַבְרוּם (see below, p. 189).

There is good reason for retaining MT (אֹסֵף אֲסִיפֵם).
Moreover, 'gather' can be accommodated to the threatening
sense of אסיפם ('I will make an end of them') and has a semantic
appropriateness in association with it (so Calvin). The sense of
אסף אסיפם is thus 'I will destroy them totally' and the aspect of a
fateful 'gathering' or harvest is spelled out in what follows:
'There will be no grapes left on the vine' and so on. Such an
interpretation of אסף אסיפם is supported by Aq., Pesh., Targ.,
and by Rashi and Kimchi. Kimchi notes that two roots are
involved in אסף אסיפם and holds that both have the sense כליון
'final end' (also Venema and Blayney).

Only in Sept.[OL] (see Ziegler) is ואתן להם יעברום represented
and there is nothing corresponding to it in the other manuscripts
of Sept. παρῆλθον (παρῆλθεν—Aq. and Theod.) supports MT
over against יעברום which appears in many Hebrew
manuscripts. Targ. expands and paraphrases in order to make
sense, 'because I have given them my law from Sinai and they
have transgressed it'. This is adopted by Rashi and is noted by
Kimchi. The adoption of יעברום does not help much, although
one might suppose that ואתן להם יעברום means, 'I have given
(them) over to them (their enemies) and they (Judah) will serve
them'. Rudolph's massive emendation produces ואתן להם
מבערים ובערום, 'I have assigned fire-raisers to them who will set
them alight'. Driver (*JQR* 28, p. 105) suggests tentatively
ואתנם למבערה, 'And I will give them to be burned' — מִבְעֵרָה a
verbal noun on the analogy of מַכְפֵּכָה. Driver says that this can
be achieved by 'merely transposing certain letters'. In fact it
requires a complicated reshuffling of consonants. It would appear
that the Hebrew text rendered by Sept. did not have the words
ואתן להם יעברום and that their representation in Sept.[OL] is a
harmonization with MT. Since their sense is so suspect, they
should be deleted (so NEB, Brockington, p. 201).

THE VOICE OF DESPAIR (8.14–17)

[14]Why are we sitting in idleness?
Let us mobilize ourselves and go to the fortified towns;
there let us suffer our doom,
since Yahweh, our God, has decreed doom for us:
he has given us poison to drink,
for we have sinned against Yahweh.
[15]We expected prosperity, but it did not come;
we expected a cure, but terror confronts us.
[16]The snorting of their horses is heard from Dan;
while their stallions neigh, all the land shakes.
They come and devour the land and all it contains,
towns and their inhabitants.

> [17]I am sending among you deadly snakes,
> against which no charm will avail,
> and they will bite you lethally.[1]

We are to envisage that vv. 14–16 are spoken by the prophet as the people's representative (Kimchi, בלשׁון ישׁראל) or by the people themselves at a point when the inevitability of disaster has been impressed on them. נשׁמע (v. 16) could be either a 3rd person Niphal or a 1st person Qal: Vulg. (*auditus est*) and Pesh. ('*štm'*) indicate the former, Sept. (ἀκουσόμεθα) the latter. Aq. (ἠκουσθη) and Symm. (ἀκουσθησεται) both read נשׁמע as a Niphal, the latter as a prophetic perfect. Verse 17, in which Yahweh is the speaker (whether or not נאם יהוה is original), cannot be combined with vv. 14–16, despite the particle כי.

The turn which 8.14 takes at ונדמה שׁם is entirely unexpected, but it is evident that the shock has been deliberately administered. We have to reckon with a literary device and not simply a lack of coherence. We have no reason to doubt that the advice given in the first part of v. 14 is seriously intended. The plain sense of it is that an invasion is about to be launched against Judah and that it is not a time for dithering and indecision. The defence of the country must be organized with speed and resolution. What we might expect to follow this is something like, 'And there we shall do all in our power to withstand the invader'. It is a shock when, instead of this, we encounter an expression of immutable doom (*pace* Duhm and Weiser). It does not matter very much whether דמם means 'silence' in an ominous sense (so Aq., Symm., Pesh. and Targ.), or whether it is shown as III דמם 'to be destroyed' (KB³). In any case the semantic polarity of ונדמה ('be secure') and הדמנו, proposed by Calvin, is unacceptable.

The prophet is dealing seriously with two different levels of reality, the one political and the other theological. To rally to the defence of their land is what the Judaeans must do and they would be fools and cowards if they acted otherwise. Yet there is an impending theological event which will nullify their courage and military competence: Yahweh's judgement on his people.

Being given מי ראשׁ to drink is brought into an immediate connection with the guilt of those who suffer, and this is done by means of a כי clause, 'For we have sinned against Yahweh'. The poison which is consumed is associated with a condition of guilt. It is not enough to say that the imagery probably derives from a *Trankordal* (Rudolph) or to state that the people are given poison to drink (Duhm and Rudolph). If we say simply that the people are given poison to drink, this might mean no more than

---

[1] Deleting נאם יהוה and attaching מבלי גהת (see below, p. 194).

death by poisoning, or poisoning as a method of capital punishment. Targ.'s paraphrase of מי ראש at 8.14 ('A cup of curse as toxic as a snake's venom') indicates that a connection is being established between מי ראש and המים המאררים in Num 5.18, 19, 22, 24, 27 (Targ. מיא מלטטיא). According to Targ. (Jer 8.14) the reason why the cup contains a poison is because it incorporates a curse, and it incorporates a curse (cf. Num chapter 5) because those who drink it are guilty. If they were innocent, their innocence would be established by the circumstance that the cup did them no harm (like the woman suspected of adultery in Num chapter 5). Judah is at a juncture where her guilt in relation to Yahweh will be demonstrated by defeat and disintegration. It is as impossible to escape from this as it is to evade the outcome of trial by ordeal.

The drinking of poison is both a legal verdict and the exaction of a penalty. No more is being attempted than the elucidation of a metaphor, the finding of a particular reference for the striking expression וישקנו מי ראש. The metaphorical use is far removed from the limited area of trial by ordeal indicated by the Numbers passage and the clauses in the Code of Hammurabi (G. R. Driver and J. C. Miles, *The Babylonian Laws*, 1955, pp. 52f.), and Press (*ZAW*, 51, 1933, p. 127) has supposed that the connections of 8.14 are with Exod 32.20. The link is then 'apostasy', but the reference to the powdered residue of the golden calf is obscure and the supposition that ויגף (Exod 32.35) connects with v. 24, and is a reference to the effects of the ordeal is dubious. An emphasis on 'Fate' rather than trial by ordeal in connection with 8.14 will be found in H. Ringgren (*SEÅ* 17, 1952, pp. 19–30) and H. A. Brongers (*OTS* 15, 1969, pp. 177–192) and a fuller consideration of this point of view has been undertaken elsewhere (W. McKane, *VT* 30, 1980, pp. 474–492).

NEB makes v. 15 a question which demands a negative answer: 'Can we hope to prosper when nothing goes well? Can we hope for respite when the terror falls suddenly?' NEB's formulation is not the most natural one. Even if a continuation of the 1st person plur. of v. 14 is assumed, v. 15 is compatible with a condition of hopelessness (*pace* Rudolph who urges that it is secondarily imported from 14.19b). Verse 15 does not indicate that hope is still entertained, but that hope which was entertained in the past has been disappointed and that nothing is left but despair. The people hoped that the wounds of the community would be healed ('healing' is interpreted by Targ. as סליחות חובין, 'forgiveness of sins'), but what they experienced was terror (Kimchi צרות גדולות, 'great afflictions'), the enervating effects of a fear that the worst was about to happen to them. The versions support the view that v. 15 describes the dashed hopes of the community and they interpret קוה as 1st person plur.

Sept. renders נשמע as ἀκουσόμεθα, 'we shall hear' and Symm. renders it as ἀκουσθήσεται, 'will be heard'. The sense 'is already heard' is represented by Vulg. (auditus est) and Pesh. ('štm'). It seems better to take v. 16 as descriptive of the approaching sounds of war already within earshot of the populace, although allowances have to be made for poetic licence or for an anticipation of disaster so intense that it is expressed as an eventuation. The snorting of the enemy's horses is heard from Dan and the ground shakes at the din of the neighing of his stallions. The invader has arrived and the land suffers the ravages of invasion: crops are destroyed, towns devastated and the population exposed to death and dispersal. For מקול מצהלות אביריו. Sept. has ἀπὸ φωνῆς χρεμετισμοῦ ἱππασίας ἵππων αὐτοῦ. Ziegler deletes ἵππων from his text (cf. Beiträge, p. 99; Janzen, p. 26) on the ground that ἱππασίας and ἵππων are doublets and that the more common word ἵππων is a gloss on the rarer ἱππασίας ('horse-riding' but here 'horses'). The other versions have taken אביריו in the sense of 'warriors' and have understood 'neighing' (מצהלות) as poetic language alluding to the blood-curdling cries of the invading army. Rashi and Kimchi (סוסיו = אביריו) agree with Sept.

Reventlow (Liturgie und prophetisches Ich bei Jeremia, p. 192) explains v. 17 as Yahweh's response to a communal lament contained in vv. 14–16. Verse 16 describes an invasion which will envelop the entire land of Judah, and we might suppose that the poisonous snakes which cannot be charmed and which will bite lethally (v. 17) are the invaders against whom no resistance is possible. Or we may suppose, as R. Press does (ZAW, 51. 1933, p. 127), that the figure of the poisonous snake is to be elucidated as an allusion to Num 21.6, where snakes were sent against the rebellious Israelites. This idea is also found in Reventlow (p. 192): in Numbers the snakes were counteracted by the bronze serpent, but on this occasion there will be no effective charms or antidote.

The probability is that the figure in v. 17 is generated by an interpretation of מי ראש (v. 14) of the same kind as appears in Targ. and Rashi, namely, 'the venom of a snake'. What then remains to be determined is whether this is a correct understanding of מי ראש and a negative answer should be given for the following reasons: (a) ראש refers to a plant or herb in Deut 29.17, Hos 10.4 and Amos 6.12, and in two of these passages (Deut and Amos) ראש is associated with לענה which thereby is also shown to be a herb. (b) In that case the likelihood

is that a combination of מי ראש and לענה (Jer 9.14; 23.15) is
one of poisonous herbs and not of a poisonous herb and snakes'
venom, מי ראש being a potion made from the herb ראש. (c) In
the passage where מי ראש occurs without לענה (Jer 8.14) it is
improbable that it has a different sense from the one which it
bears in Jer 9.14 and 23.15 (see further, W. McKane, *VT* 30
(1980), pp. 478–487). The implication of this line of reasoning is
that the author of Jer 8.14 was not responsible for 8.17, the
latter verse being contributed by someone who wrongly
understood מי ראש in v. 14 as snakes' venom. In v. 17 Yahweh
threatens to despatch poisonous snakes against his people, snakes
which no charmer can pacify and whose bite is lethal (צפענים is
in apposition to נחשים —a generic word for 'snake' is qualified
by an indication that a particularly lethal variety is intended;
NEB ('viper').

A CRY FROM THE HEART (8.18–23)

¹⁸Sorrow overwhelms me,
I am sick at heart.
¹⁹I hear the voice of my people
coming from a distant land:
Is Yahweh not in Zion?
Is her king no longer there?[1]
²⁰The harvest is past, autumn is over,
but we have not been saved.
²¹The wounds of my people have wounded me,
I am in deep mourning, desolation has seized me.
²²Is there no balm in Gilead?
Is no physician to be found there?
Why do my people's wounds not close and heal?
²³O that my head were a cistern
and my eyes[2] a well of tears,
that I might weep day and night
for those of my people who will perish!

These verses consist of a lament by Jeremiah into which is
incorporated a prophetic anticipation of Judah's dispersion in
exile (v. 19a), and in which the words of the despairing exiles are
reproduced (vv. 19b, 20). The third distich of v. 19 ('Why have
they provoked me with their images and foreign gods?') is more
naturally attributed to Yahweh than to Jeremiah and disturbs
the continuity of the prophet's *cri de coeur*. It is represented by
all the versions (Sept., Vulg., Pesh., Targ.) and is thought by
Baumgartner (*BZAW* 32, 1917, p. 73) and Reventlow (p. 195)
to fit into the formal structure of the lament as Yahweh's

---

[1] Deleting מדוע . . . נכר (see below, pp. 193f.).
[2] Reading עיני with the versions (MT עיני 'my eye').

answer. Rather it creates a formal dissonance in an otherwise
cohesive lament (vv. 18–23), and Thiel is right to regard it as
intrusive (p. 135). Thiel's criticism of a differently directed
attempt by Holladay (*VT* 12, 1962, pp. 494–498) to establish the
originality of the distich is also just (p. 135 n. 2). He is correct in
challenging the notion of a threefold question: אם ... ה is a
complete structure and מדוע falls outside it. Thiel holds that
v. 19c has been contributed by D and he compares its vocabulary
with that in other passages which he has assigned to the same
editor. D's intention, according to Thiel (p. 136), is to show that
the question asked by the people in v. 19b is unjustified. There is
an implication that Yahweh has failed them and D wishes in an
exilic situation to correct this by asserting that their misfortunes
flow from their idolatry.

There is a serious textual problem in v. 18, where מבליגיתי
(MT), 'my source of brightness'? gives poor sense. Another
difficulty is created by עֲלֵי יגון עָלָי (MT), 'upon sorrow upon
me'?, but it is likely that Driver is right in his view (*JQR*, 28,
p. 105) that the first עלי (pointed עָלָי) is an alternative spelling
of עָלָה (3rd person sing. Qal) and that the emendation of עלי to
עלה or יעלה (Rudolph) is unnecessary (cf. גלוי, passive Qal
participle of גלה).

Aq. understands מבליגיתי as 'my mirth' and otherwise
reproduces MT literally. The case is the same with Vulg., except
that מבליגיתי is taken as *dolor meus* 'my sorrow'. Pesh. achieves
better sense with a dubious paraphrase: 'I am worn out with my
distress and my heart is sick within me'. Symm. has χλευαζεις
με, 'you scoff at me', for מבליגיתי עלי. The same type of
rendering of מבליגיתי (the reason for which is not obvious) is
found in Targ.: 'because they were scoffing at the prophets who
prophesied to them'. מבליגיתי is written by some Hebrew
manuscripts as מבלי גיתי and Sept. ἀνίατα 'incurable' indicates
מבְּלִי גֵהָת or the like (Jerome, *insanabiliter*). There is a case for
following Sept. and for reading מבלי גהת. The attachment of
מבלי גהת to the end of v. 17, with נאם יהוה (not represented by
Sept.) deleted (so Rudolph), is supported by Sept., according to
Swete's punctuation, but not according to the punctuation of
Ziegler's text. מבלי גהת , attached to v. 17 (so Ehrlich, p. 265),
corresponds precisely to אשר אין להם לחש: there is no cure or
antidote for the bites which are inflicted. It should be noticed,
however, that the adoption of מבלי גהת is not necessarily
associated with the conjoining of these words to v. 17, since we
can read מבלי גהת עלי יגון עלי לבי דוי, 'Incurable sorrow has
overwhelmed me, my heart is sick'. A sickness which strikes at
the heart (cf. Prov. 14.30; 15.13,15; see W. McKane, *Proverbs*)
is the most fundamental kind of ailment (cf. Prov 6.15; 29.1).

Isaiah 33.17 shows that 'far and wide throughout the land' (Rudolph and Bright) is a possible rendering of מארץ מרחקים, but 'from a distant land' (so NEB) is supported by the versions (Sept., Vulg., Pesh., Targ.) and is the sense which is needed. The circumstance that the exile has not yet taken place is not inconsistent with this prophetic envisaging of the ultimate consequences for the Judaean community of the carrying out of Yahweh's judgement. So Blayney (cf. Lowth), 'The prophet anticipates in his imagination the captivity of his countrymen in Babylon, "a far country".' Part of the intense prophetic suffering of which Jeremiah speaks is just this capacity to descry the dismemberment of Judah and the misery and despair which flow from it. The cry of the broken and scattered community is the form which the prophet gives to his own compassion and anguish as well as to his incontrovertible insight into the final outcome of a tragic predestination by which he is burdened.

The cry of the exiles is about Yahweh's kingship, with which is associated Zion and the season of harvest (vv. 19–20). It is hard to resist the conclusion that this alludes to hopes which had been connected with the Autumn New Year Festival of which the kingship of Yahweh was a theme and in connection with which שלום and ישועה had been assured to the community and experienced by it (cf. S. Mowinckel, *The Psalms in Israel's Worship*, i, 1962, pp. 106–192; J. Gray, *The Biblical Doctrine of the Reign of God*, 1979, p. 151). The prophet puts these words into the mouths of Judaeans whom he envisages as scattered in exile. The season of the great autumn festival has approached and passed, but Yahweh's kingship has not been made manifest and there has been no change in their condition. They had their eyes on Jerusalem and their smouldering expectations had been kindled. Nothing had happened, their doubts grow and a cold despair afflicts them: Is Yahweh still present in Zion? Does he still exercise his kingship there? 'Harvest is past, autumn is finished, but we have not been saved.' Have the presuppositions of the Jerusalem cult been finally falsified? The prophet has no doubt that they are false, but he mirrors the condition of those who after exile will nurse ailing hopes that they may still be proved true.

The brokenness of Judah is not a condition of which he has a spectator's view; it is a suffering and sickness in which he is immersed. His heart is sick and his spirit dissolves; he is shattered, enveloped in darkness and seized with desolation. Or, perhaps, קדרתי is rather an indication that he is afflicted by the sadness of a mourner and wears a mourner's garb (so NEB, 'I go like a mourner'). השברתי (v. 21) is not represented by Sept. and Pesh. and חיל כיולדה is represented by Sept. (ὠδῖνες ὡς τικτούσης). Both Ziegler (*Beiträge*, pp. 91f.) and Janzen (pp. 31, 63) suppose that חיל כיולדה is an insertion from 6.24.

If there are no medicines or physicians in Gilead (v. 22)—apparently renowned for its *materia medica* and its doctors—who can deal effectively with Judah's sickness, then her condition is hopeless and there is no cure (cf. v. 17). No new skin will grow over the wounds to close them and give proof of an effective process of healing.

All that remains for Jeremiah is to weep inconsolably and he summons himself to such interminable weeping (v. 23). Gevirtz (*JNES* 20, 1961, pp. 41–46) has noticed resemblances of vocabulary between v. 23 and the Ugaritic text KRT (A. Herdner, *Mission de Ras Shamra*, x, 1963, p. 72: 16 1.27–30; cf. J. C. L. Gibson, *Canaanite Myths and Legends²*, 1978, p. 95). Both Herdner and Gibson indicate *mḥ rìšk*, 'marrow of your head', and Gevirtz's conjecture *my rìšk*, which produces a more exact correspondence with ראשי מים (v. 23) should be discounted. Otherwise *qr 'nk* corresponds with ועיני מקור, *mḥ rìšk* with ראשי מים and *ủdm't* with דמעה. The Ugaritic lines run, 'Do not exhaust, my son, the well of your eyes, the marrow of your head with tears.' There is no doubt that hyperbolic imagery is employed in v. 23. Would that the prophet's head were a reservoir and his eyes unfailing wells of tears, that he might weep proleptically and ceaselessly on account of the ultimate human toll of this coming disaster. Here again the prophet feels his way to the end of the process; he descries the victims of war and carnage and he knows how terrible will be the outcome.

The general line of interpretation which has been taken in vv. 18–23 is in agreement with Baumgartner (*BZAW* 32, p. 73), but conflicts with Reventlow. Baumgartner seeks proofs that Jeremiah's composition is formed on the model of Laments in the book of Psalms, but he, nevertheless, considers that it has a distinctive, prophetic character. It is true that Baumgartner retains the 3rd distich in v. 19, but his emphasis is on the prophetic character of the passage and the original way in which Jeremiah utilizes his models. What we have is an imaginative projection of the prophet's deepest insights and of his harrowing premonitions of doom.

Reventlow (pp. 195f.) supposes (cf. Volz) that איה יהוה (cf. Jer 2.6) has an original connection with pilgrims making their way to Jerusalem, and that היהוה אין בציון represents a twist given to this question: it becomes an indictment of Yahweh and discharges the function of a regular component (indictment) of the lament. This kind of reversal he also detects in v. 22, where the theme of 'Yahweh the Healer' (Exod 15.26) has been changed into an assertion that there is no healer or medicine which will avail to cure the wounds of the people. 'I' may indicate a particularly lively identification of the prophet *qua* person with his people in this passage, but it is not personal in the sense that it is associated with a surge of private feeling. Jeremiah, in a cultic context, is discharging a representative function as an intercessor.

CHAPTER IX

A LONGING TO ESCAPE FROM THE UGLINESS OF THE HUMAN SCENE (9.1–5)

[1]Oh that I might go to a traveller's lodging in the wilderness
and make a final break with my people!
They are all adulterers, a crowd of traitors.
[2]They use their tongues like bows,
falsehood not truth[1] prevails[2] in the land;
they go from one evil deed to the next
and do not know Yahweh[3,4]
[3]Let a man beware of his friend,
let there be no trust between brothers:
for every brother is a deceiver
and every friend a slanderer.
[4]Each man holds his friend in contempt
and does not speak the truth;
they have all become experts at telling lies.
[5]They behave deviously, they have no will to repent;
oppression is heaped on oppression,[5] deceit on deceit.
They refuse to know Yahweh.[3,4]

Chapter 9.1 has been joined to 8.23 because of the almost identical beginnings of both verses (מי יתן and מי יתנני), but 9.1ff. is not intrinsically connected with what precedes it (so Duhm). מי יתנני (9.1) introduces a new mood of revulsion: Jeremiah is sickened by the behaviour of his community which he paints in the blackest colours, and he seeks a remote place and the purifying efficacy of solitude. Verses 1–5 and 6–8 are word of Yahweh according to MT and this structure is preserved by Duhm and NEB. Rudolph holds that vv. 1–7 constitute a unit and are spoken by Jeremiah; that v. 8 is intrusive and belongs to chapter 5, where it occurs as a refrain at vv. 9 and 29.

It follows from this view of the matter that other indications in vv. 1–7 that Yahweh and not Jeremiah is the speaker should be regarded as the consequence of a mistaken editorial evaluation of the unit. These are (*a*) א(ו)תי and נאם יהוה (not represented by Sept.) in vv. 2 and 5, and (*b*) the formula which introduces v. 6 (לכן כה אמר יהוה צבאות). It may be supposed (Rudolph) that אתי is a corruption of את י" = את יהוה and that the insertion of נאם יהוה is a consequence of this corruption. The formula which introduces v. 6 is deleted by Volz and Rudolph

[1] Reading אמונה (see below, p. 200).
[2] Reading גברה (see below, p. 200).
[3] Reading את יהוה (see below, p. 198)
[4] Deleting נאם יהוה (see below, p. 198).
[5] See below, p. 201.

because Jeremiah has already been portrayed as an assayer in
6.27, and it is argued that there is no difficulty in the assumption
that he speaks for his own part in 9.6

The most important consideration is whether vv. 1–7 are a
unit of the kind supposed by Rudolph. Apart from the
circumstance that all the versions introduce vv. 6–8 as word of
Yahweh, the principal stumbling-block is that the assaying
imagery (v. 6) does not fit convincingly into a unit (vv. 1–7) in
which Jeremiah is assumed to be the speaker throughout. This
difficulty is not met by recalling that Jeremiah has already been
portrayed as an assayer (6.27), because there is no place here for
an assaying function in connection with the sentiments of the
prophet as expressed (*ex hypothesi*) in vv. 1–5. The reference to
assaying makes better sense here if vv. 6–8 are regarded as word
of Yahweh (so Bright) and in that case 'assaying' is a reference
to the judgement and the process of refinement through suffering
which Yahweh is to implement. This is how the figure is
interpreted by v. 8, whether or not that verse is original. It is a
verse which only Yahweh could utter and it clearly has no place
if vv. 1–7 are regarded as an expression of Jeremiah's sentiments
(Rudolph). If, however, vv. 6–8 are word of Yahweh, v. 8
correctly interprets the assaying imagery and the question
whether it is primary or secondary in this chapter is not one on
which important exegetical decisions hang.

What is then proposed is that vv. 1–5 (suitably emended) are
an expression of Jeremiah's sentiments, in which he longs for the
utmost solitude and describes his revulsion at the ugly social
behaviour of his people. Verses 6–8 also describe a community,
poisoned by slander and engaging in a kind of internecine
warfare, against which Yahweh issues a threat of judgement.

The other side of Jeremiah's concern for his people and his
solidarity with them in the face of impending judgement (8.21)
is a feeling of revulsion at their behaviour by which he is
overwhelmed. The aspect is so unattractive and hideous that he
longs to escape from it. It is unlikely that the reference to
adultery (כלם מנאפים) is to be taken literally: it is a figure for a
failure to keep faith with Yahweh, the 'husband' of Judah (so
Lowth), as in 2.20ff. and 3.1–5. Instead of being Yahweh's
community, they are a crowd of traitors and their treacherous
tendencies are displayed in the ways that they behave towards
each other. Their speech (v. 2) is barbed and vicious and is
designed to inflict injury. The punctuation of MT indicates that
שקר goes with קשתם, and although this is grammatically
difficult, it is followed by Targ., 'They are like a deceptive bow',
and is expounded by Kimchi: 'Their arrows are the false and
bitter words which they speak'. All the versions interpret לשונם

קשׁתם as a simile. The different punctuation of Sept. and Pesh. (connecting שׁקר with ולא לאמונה גברו בארץ) should be followed. The corruption of אמונה to לאמונה and of גברה to גברו may have come about by wrong punctuation: MT was construed as, 'They bend their tongue like a deceptive bow; it is not through truth that they prevail in the land.' Thus Kimchi comments on ולא לאמונה גברו בארץ, 'They do not rule equitably, they do not see that justice is done and they do not hold oppressors in check'. Sept. (καὶ ἐνέτειναν τὴν γλῶσσαν αὐτῶν ὡς τόξον. Ψεῦδος καὶ οὐ πίστις ἐνίσχυσεν ἐπὶ τῆς γῆς) represents אמונה and גברה, and should be followed (so Rudolph, Bright and NEB).

The situation described by Jeremiah is one where evil is on the increase as men become more and more bold in their socially destructive enterprises. The general summing-up is that they do not know Yahweh: they have no commitment to him, no faithful adherence to his demands. The absence of this will is indicated particularly by habits of destructive speech, and the dominant figure, which appears also in v. 7, is that of the tongue as a murderous weapon. Men use it in a deliberately injurious way and the very foundations of common life are threatened (For a discussion of this in the context of the book of Proverbs see W. McKane, *BETL* 51, 1979, pp. 166–185). Speech is not a cement or a therapy: it does not promote understanding, tolerance and social health.

Verse 3 describes the worst kind of civil war, where mistrust has become part of the ordinary life of the community and where every social encounter has to be regarded as a possible trap. It is arguable that the meaning is not so much that you cannot trust a member of your own family as that you cannot trust anyone in the community. In that case a precise differentiation between אח ('brother' or 'kinsman') and רע ('neighbour' or 'friend') is not to be made. However, עקוב יעקב does indicate that there is an allusion to Jacob who deceived his brother (Rudolph, Bright, NEB footnote).

In Jer 9.3 Sept. renders עקוב יעקב as πτέρνῃ πτερνιεῖ. In Gen 27.36, where the allusion to Jacob is explicit, it renders ויעקבני as ἐπτέρνικεν γάρ. In Hos 12.4, where there is another explicit reference to Jacob, it renders עקב by ἐπτέρνισεν. The circumstance that Sept., Vulg. and Pesh. use the same word to translate עקב in Jer 9.3 as they do in the explicit Jacob passages is less than a demonstration that they detected an allusion to Jacob in Jer 12.3, but it does suggest this conclusion. We should therefore discern a reference to social disintegration in the narrow circle of the family as well as in wider communal relationships (so Calvin).

A suicidal individualism makes life intolerable, since it creates a demand for constant, unremitting suspicion. The imperatives in v. 3 are a device for pointing to an intolerable state of affairs which now exists. This is what things have come to: all the supports of social solidarity—benevolence, sympathy, freedom of intercourse—are casualties, when human transactions are dominated by a calculated malice. The deceit and treachery of which v. 3 complains is again specified (cf. v. 2) as anti-social verbal habits. Speech is the mode by which deception is practised: it is no longer a method of communication but a smoke-screen behind which motives and objectives are concealed. The demise of plain, honest speaking destroys the value of language for constructive ends and makes it into a corrosive agent (v. 4). This examination of the destructive potential of speech is also a feature of v. 7: men's tongues are arrows which inflict deadly wounds. The debased character of their verbal behaviour is all the more apparent in that they affect friendship and sympathetic concern and cover their evil designs with a veneer of affability.

The textual problems in vv. 4–5 reside in the final words of MT v. 4 (הֵעוֹה נֶלְאוּ) and in the opening words of v. 5 (שִׁבְתְּךָ בְּתוֹךְ מִרְמָה בְּמִרְמָה). MT, which gives poor sense, has been read by Symm., Vulg. and Pesh.: בְּמִרְמָה is joined to מֵאֲנוּ דַעַת אוֹתִי ('In deceit they refuse to know me'), but 'Your dwelling is in the midst of deceit' is then a residue deficient in sense. The rendering of Sept. (ἠδίκησαν καὶ οὐ διέλιπον τοῦ ἐπιστρέψαι) indicates that the difficulty is caused by a wrong division of consonants and a false *plene* spelling. שִׁבְתְּךָ should be written as שָׁב תָּךְ and בְּתוֹךְ as בְּתָךְ (Ewald). Sept. is rendered by Jerome as 'They act unjustly and they will not desist in order to repent'. It is not obvious, however, why תָּךְ has been translated by Sept. as τόκος 'usury' (Jerome, *usura super usuram*). It is unlikely that τόκος originated as a transliteration of תָּךְ, but, on the other hand, the word-play between תָּךְ and τόκος must be deliberate: oppressiveness is explained as money-lending on harsh terms. The text should be reconstructed as follows:

הֵעוֹה נֶלְאוּ שָׁב

תָּךְ בְּתָךְ מִרְמָה בְּמִדְמָה

'They behave deviously (infinitive absolute=3rd per. plur.), they do not have the will to repent. Oppression is heaped on oppression, deceit on deceit.' The people are addicted to injustice; they do not have the spiritual resolve nor the moral energy to repent; they refuse to 'know' Yahweh—in the sense of 'know' indicated above (p. 200).

NOTHING BUT DECEIT AND MALICE (9.6–8)

⁶Therefore these are the words of Yahweh Sabaoth:
I will refine and assay them,
for how else can I deal with my people?
⁷Their tongues are lethal arrows,
their speech nothing but deceit.
Their conversation affects friendship,
while they are setting traps for each other.
⁸Ought I not to punish them for this?
Should I not take my revenge on a nation such as this?
This is Yahweh's word.

The assaying metaphor (v. 6) is explained by Targ. as 'I shall bring distress upon them' (see above, p. 199) and the same interpretation is found in Rashi. The obscure part of v. 6 (כי איך עמי בת מפני אעשה) is connected by Kimchi with this process of testing, 'For how could I do otherwise and not refine them?'. Volz's emendation (רעתם מפני for עמי בת מפני) is adopted by Rudolph and Bright and produces a sense agreeable to the interpretation of Targ. ('in view of the sins of the congregation of my people').

There is little to be said in favour of Driver's way (*JQR* 28, pp. 105f.) of dealing with this passage. In one respect he has misinterpreted the evidence of Sept.: he says that כי is not represented by Sept. and this encourages him to assume that כי איך is a corruption of איככה. His assumption that Sept. ὅτι renders איך or איככה rather than כי is mistaken. The element of MT which lacks representation in Sept. is not כי but איך and this was certainly the view of Aq. and Symm. who added πῶς (= איך) in order to represent MT fully. There are two main exegetical alternatives:

(*a*) We can follow Targ. and Kimchi and explain אעשה איך כי עמי בת מפני as 'What course is there open to me but to test and refine this people in view of the deep roots which evil has in them?'

(*b*) We can suppose that the expression is simply one of perplexity and exasperation, 'What is there that I can possibly do with a people like this?'

In v. 7 (see above, p. 200) there is a question of punctuation (דבר), a K-Q (שחוט — שוחט) and an awkward change from plural to singular (בפיו and לשונם). שוחט is supported by Sept. and Vulg., while Pesh. and Targ. indicate שָׁחוט חץ 'a sharpened arrow'. שוחט חץ should be adopted, with the sense 'lethal arrow'. The MT punctuation of v. 7 is followed by Vulg. and Pesh. who both attach בפיו to what follows it. Sept. (δόλια τὰ ῥήματα τοῦ στόματος αὐτῶν) makes בפיו part of the second stich and this is what the metre requires. דבר has been read as דְּבֶּר; Rudolph supposes a different Hebrew text from MT (מרמה דברי פיו). At the end of v. 7 the figure of laying an ambush for someone while affecting benevolence is lost and is replaced by a more prosaic statement, καὶ ἐν ἑαυτῷ ἔχει τὴν ἔχθραν, 'and within himself he harbours hostility'. According to v. 7 a state of affairs has been reached where confidence in language has been destroyed by the circumstance that words never mean what they appear to mean. Moreover, they are used with intent to wound and destroy, and so have a murderous aspect like lethal arrows; civilized and apparently friendly conversation is carried on, but there is no foundation of benevolence, and language has been debased into a means of cloaking intentions and objectives, of lulling others into a sense of false security, while the trap is set or the ambush laid (on v. 8 see p. 118, p. 198).

DESOLATION AND DEATH (9.9–10)

⁹I weep and lament for the hill-pastures
and for the rough grazing lands.
They have been burned and are abandoned,
the sounds of flocks are no longer heard,
birds and animals have vanished.
¹⁰I will make Jerusalem a heap of rubble;
it will become the home of jackals.
I will devastate the towns of Judah
and make them into deserted places.

The core of this section is the summons to lamentation and the expressions of lament in vv. 16–21. The prose passage (vv. 11–15) is secondary expansion (so Rudolph). The introductory formulae (vv. 16, 21) which indicate words of Yahweh are the consequence of mistaken editorial interpretation, and alterations of MT in Sept. (vv. 17, 20) are also dictated by the conviction that Yahweh rather than Jeremiah is the speaker.

If MT אשא is original in v. 9 Jeremiah must be the speaker (so Kimchi), whereas the reading of Sept. (λάβετε) and Pesh. (šqwlw) is compatible with a unit (vv. 9–10) consisting of words of Yahweh. The emendation of אשא to שאו appears to be an attractive solution, but there are reasons why it should not be too readily accepted. The effect of it is that Yahweh issues a summons to lamentation in v. 9, whereas it is evident from the first person plurals in vv. 16–21 that the summons to lamentation appearing there is not issued by Yahweh. There is a suspicion that the only Hebrew text which ever existed is the one extant in MT and that Sept. λάβετε arises out of an attempt to repair the formal discrepancy between v. 9 and v. 10 (where Yahweh is the speaker) and to make a unit of vv. 9–10. If the independence of Sept. and Pesh. were allowed, this would be a weighty argument for a Hebrew text with שָׂא, but it is probable that the Syriac translator, aware of the difficulty, is adopting the solution which he finds in Sept.

That the disaster has not fallen is indicated by the future tense of the threat in v. 10, but the prophet has such an intense premonition of devastation that he speaks of it as if it had already taken place. The parallelism (וְעַל נְאוֹת מִדְבָּר) indicates that עַל הֶהָרִים must mean 'on behalf of the הרים' and not 'on the הרים'. This devastation is the consequence of a scorched earth policy (נצתו) carried out by the invading enemy. The precise sense 'burn' is indicated by Vulg. (*incensa sunt*); the other versions have more general renderings. There are indications in Aq., Vulg. and Sept. that נאות troubled the translators, but Pesh. (*dyr') and Targ. (דירות*), 'camps for shepherds', are more specific, and Rashi and Kimchi offer similar explanations: Rashi's 'dwellings of shepherds among the pastures' agrees with Kimchi's אהלי המדבר, and the latter's further comment מקומות מרעה 'places of pasture' is correct. The absence of any representation of עבר in Sept. is noted by Janzen (p. 38) and he supposes that it has been imported into MT v. 9 from v. 11 (מבלי עבר).

Kimchi relates מבלי איש עבר (v. 9) not simply to a general portrayal of abandonment and cessation of human traffic, but specifically to the disappearance of flocks from the pastures and the consequent withdrawal of those who tended them ('There is not even anyone in these parts to shepherd the flocks'). This is, probably, a correct understanding of the matter: v. 9 describes an eerie emptiness. The proper order of nature and of creaturely activity has been superseded by a chaos-like void: there are no flocks, no shepherds, no birds or animals, and with the skies empty and the land desolate, there is a fateful foretaste of total cessation and death.

It may be that v. 9 was understood not as premonition, but as a description of a disaster which had actually taken place, but even so the elucidation of the relation between v. 9 and v. 10 is not much advanced. One might suppose that there is an intention to juxtapose Jeremiah's premonition of the end (or description of the end—if this is the preferred interpretation of v. 9) with a word of Yahweh predicting the destruction of Jerusalem and Judah. There is a transition from rural scenes to centres of urban life. Jerusalem will suffer a final, crushing blow which will make the victory of the invader irreversible and defeat for Judah inevitable. Jerusalem, reduced to a heap of ruins, will become the haunt of תנים. This word has given the versions trouble: it was confused with תנין 'snake', 'sea-monster' by Sept. (δρακόντων) and Vulg. (*draconum*); Targ. has the readings ירודין 'wild asses' and ירורין (Sperber) which also appears in Pesh. (*lyrwr'*) and which perhaps means 'jackals'. There is, however, still a division of opinion about the identification of the animals named תנים and NEB prefers 'wolves'.

Since Sept. renders לגלים as εἰς μετοικίαν (Jerome, *in transmigrationem*), it evidently connected לגלים with גלה and saw in לגלים a reference to exile. It is correctly explained by Kimchi as a reference to the rubble accumulated from demolished buildings. In what was once a religious metropolis and a capital city, where there was a vigorous and busy urban life, human voices will no longer be heard, but the ruined buildings will echo to the cries of prowling jackals. The towns of Judah will likewise be reduced to the silence of desolation and abandonment.

WHY HAS JUDAH BEEN DESTROYED? (9.11–15)

[11]Who is wise enough to know this or to whom has Yahweh spoken that he might divulge the answer? Why is the land destroyed, burned up like a wilderness and abandoned? [12]Yahweh said: Because they forsook my law which I set before them; they did not obey me nor observe it. [13]They followed their own wilful inclinations: they followed the Baalim, as their forefathers had taught them. [14]Therefore these are the words of Yahweh Sabaoth, God of Israel: I will give them a poisonous herb to eat[1] and a poisonous potion to drink. [15]I will scatter them among nations as unknown to them as they were to their forefathers, and I will pursue them with the sword until I destroy them totally.

The circumstance that vv. 11–15 are prose creates a general presumption that they represent exegetical amplification and this is reinforced by more particular indications: v. 9b (כי נצתו מבלי איש עבר) is taken up again in v. 11 (נצתה כמדבר מבלי עבר) and על מה אבדו הארץ (v. 11) alludes to the description of desolation, emptiness and dereliction in vv. 9–10. There is also a concern (vv. 12–13) to supply theological reasons for what has happened and the ostensible point in time to which the passage belongs is located between a disaster which has already taken place (an enemy invasion—implied by the question in v. 11) and affliction and exile which lie in the future and are the subjects of a threat in vv. 14–15. One might, therefore, see v. 11 as a development of v. 9, vv. 14–15 as taking off from v. 10 and vv. 12–13 as a new element of explanation.

A much more detailed analysis of vv. 11–15 is offered by Thiel

[1] Deleting את העם הזה (see below, p. 207).

(pp. 136–138) who attributes the passage to his Deuteronomistic editor (D), who finds in it literary procedures characteristic of other prose passages in the book of Jeremiah which he also assigns to D, and who reinforces his arguments by an examination of vocabulary. The situation in 9.11–13 is different (*pace*, Thiel) from the one, where the prophet is addressed by Yahweh and told: 'If the people ask such and such a question, this is the answer which you are to give to them.' The implication of the first question in v. 11 is that neither wise man nor prophet has been able to give a satisfactory answer to the second question. The consequent puzzlement and perplexity in the face of a disaster which appears inexplicable is put to an end by Yahweh's revelation of why it has come about (vv. 12–13). Thiel's conclusion is that 9.11–15 is a composition by D with a Question-Answer form which seeks to establish that the cause of the catastrophe which has overtaken Judah is the negative attitude to Yahweh's will as revealed in Deuteronomy (תורה) and an addiction to Baal worship. D has made use of Jeremianic expressions: in v. 11 there are borrowings from v. 9; הלך אחרי הבעלים may be influenced by 2.23 and the figure involving מי ראש and לענה is derived from 23.15.

Swete is correct over against Ziegler in concluding that Sept. assumes a different punctuation from MT at v. 11 and that the *athnach* at ויגדה is not observed. דבר is read as דְּבַר and the verse consists of a question ('Who is the wise man that understands this?'), and a challenge in connection with which there is an implication that no one will be able to take it up. Pesh. arranges the verse in the same way as Sept. and is almost certainly dependent on Sept. Vulg. also reads דבר as דְּבַר, but maintains the punctuation of MT and so preserves על מה אבדה הארץ נצתה כמדבר מבלי עבר as an independent question. Since the second question, so constructed, has a quasi-metrical structure (cf. BHS, where it is set out as poetry), this would seem to be a correct reading of the syntax of v. 11.

NEB's translation ('What man is wise enough to understand this, to understand what the Lord has said and to proclaim it?') lumps two different issues together and so obscures the second one. The first reference is to the wise man and the second to the prophet who receives a דְּבָר from Yahweh. Is there any חכם who in virtue of his intellectual grasp and rational power is able to explain why Judah is devastated and at the point of death? Has Yahweh disclosed to any prophet in a revelatory דְּבָר the reasons for these catastrophic events? The זאת of v. 11a anticipates the question in v. 11b, and it is the answer to this question (על מה אבדה הארץ נצתה כמדבר מבלי עבר) which neither wise man nor prophet can supply.

Janzen (p. 38) notes that ולא הלכו בה (v. 12) is not
represented by Sept. and suggests that these words may be a
gloss on על עזבם את תורתי, the form of which is influenced by
passages like 26.4 and 44.10. He holds that τῆς κακῆς (v. 13) is
an addition to the Greek text (cf. Pesh. *byš'*), influenced by 3.17
and 7.24 (p. 63). In v. 12 the shorter Greek text is probably the
more original. It is arguable that forsaking the תורה and
disobeying Yahweh exhausts the indictment and that ולא הלכו
בה has been tagged on, but these words are not obviously
extraneous to the syntax of v. 12.

The crucial area of Judah's disobedience and rebelliousness,
where she neglected the salutary demands of תורה and wilfully
chose evil and disaster, was her addiction to the בעלים. In this
she continued the pattern of apostasy set by earlier generations
and enacted the final, fateful stages of a long history of apostasy.
The essential task of the prophet is to call for repentance and
amendment on the foundation of the criteria supplied by the
תורה given at Sinai, and this is a Deuteronomic view (cf. Thiel,
pp. 136–138). That the disaster which overtook Judah was the
consequence of a failure to meet the demands of the תורה is
presented as a new revelation—an answer to a hitherto
unanswered question—and this should probably be correlated
with the exilic setting of vv. 11–15. The implication of vv. 11–13
is not only that there is no reasonable, human answer to
questions about the disaster which overwhelmed Judah, but also
that hitherto there has been no prophetic answer.

את העם הזה (v. 14) is probably a secondary expansion of the
suffix of מאכילם and should be deleted. It is not represented by
Sept. (cf. Janzen, p. 11). The threat which is formulated in v. 14
should be regarded as a prose elaboration of the poetry of 23.15.
The details of the vocabulary and imagery have already been
discussed in connection with 8.14, where מי ראש appears without
לענה (see above, pp. 190f., 192f.). There will be no mitigation of
Yahweh's judgement and the circumstance that it will inflict
death on Judah will be a demonstration of her guilt. Verse 15,
which is a continuation of Yahweh's threat, describes a
scattering of his community among nations unknown to either
the present or past generations. Some influence may have been
exercised by the poetry of 5.15–17, where לא תדע occurs (גוי לא
תדע לשונו ולא תשמע מה ידבר) and where the terror of conquest
and disintegration is enhanced by the utter strangeness of those
who bring it to pass.

A SUMMONS TO LAMENTATION (9.16–21)

[16-17]Summon[1] the keening women,[2]
send for the women expert at lamentation.
Let them come without delay,[3]
let them raise laments over us;
that our eyes may flow with tears
and our eye-lids be soaked with weeping.
[18]Sounds of lamentation are heard from Zion:
We have been despoiled,
our humiliation is complete;
we have abandoned our land,
we have been evicted from[4] our homes.
[19]Listen, O women, to Yahweh's word,
have regard to what he utters.
Teach your daughters the art of lamentation,
let every woman instruct her friend.
[20]Death has come through our windows,
it has gained access to our strongholds,
cutting off children from the streets,
young men from the street-corners.
[21]Corpses[5] fall to the ground,[6]
like[7] sheaves behind the reapers
and there is no one to gather them.

In vv. 16–21 Jeremiah is speaking for his own part and is
identifying himself with his community. The formula which
introduces the passage is erroneous. Sept. has gone further in
representing these verses as words of Yahweh by substituting
2nd person plurals for 1st person plurals in vv. 17 and 20, Sept.
διὰ τῶν θυρίδων ὑμῶν and εἰς τὴν γῆν ὑμῶν. In view of this it is
odd that Ziegler (*Beiträge*, pp. 14, 94) is volunteering to
reconstruct an original Hebrew text from Sept. which,
nevertheless, as he acknowledges, has, in view of the changes in
vv. 17 and 20, shown less appreciation of the texture of the *ex
hypothesi* original text than MT. The alterations in Sept. at
vv. 17 and 20 have to be seen as an attempt to reduce the
discrepancy between the formula (v. 16) and the contents of
vv. 16ff. The same problem is encountered again at v. 21, where
דבר כה נאם יהוה (not represented by Sept.) is entirely
inappropriate in relation to v. 22 and breaks the connection
between vv. 21 and 22. דבר pointed as דַּבֵּר in MT ('Speak, these

---

[1] Deleting כה אמר יהוה צבאות (see below, pp. 208f.) and התבוננו ו (see below, pp. 208f.).

[2] Deleting ותבואינה (see below, p. 209).

[3] See below, p. 209.

[4] Reading הֻשְׁלַכְנוּ (see below, pp. 209f.).

[5] Deleting כה נאם יהוה (see below, pp. 208f.) and דבר (see below, p. 210).

[6] Deleting כדמן (see below, p. 212).

[7] Deleting ו (see below, p. 212).

are the words of Yahweh') has been read as דֶּבֶר by Sept.[OL] and Theod. (θανατω) and this is almost certainly a reliable clue as to how it originated: it was a marginal comment on v. 20 and is an indication that מות was interpreted as plague or pestilence. כה אמר יהוה צבאות (v. 16) and דבר כה נאם יהוה (v. 21) should be deleted.

One cannot be certain whether vv. 16–21 are to be understood as a description of events which have already taken place or whether they represent a premonition of what is about to happen. On the whole, it seems better to assume that they are a prophetic projection and so an expression of Jeremiah's absolute conviction that nothing can now save Jerusalem and Judah. Hence, even before the blow has fallen, there is nothing left for the prophet but to call for a public act of lamentation.

The women who are summoned are experts in the art of קינה and נהי. They are professionals whose special skills are indicated by the titles מקוננות and חכמות. It is תבואינה rather than תבואנה which is suspect (so Duhm, Rudolph; *pace* Ehrlich, p. 267). תשנה (v. 17) is an unusual orthography of תשאנה (GK. 74k). התבוננו ו (v. 16), which is not represented by Sept. and Pesh., should be deleted (so NEB, Brockington, p. 202; cf. Ehrlich, p. 267). Verses 16–17 should then be rearranged as follows:

קראו למקוננות ואל החכמות שלחו
ותבואנה ותמהרנה ותשנה עלינו נהי

This achieves a chiasmus in v. 16 and a hendiadys in what becomes the first stich of v. 17 ('Let them come quickly'). The skills of the מקוננות are to be employed in order to create a climate of sorrowfulness and to induce an unrestrained, public grief.

קול נהי (v. 18) which is heard from Zion ('in Zion', according to a few Hebrew manuscripts and Sept.) relates to the prophet's incontrovertible premonition of what is about to happen. There is a question whether the whole is a lament controlled by the introductory איך, or whether the second line consists of two motive clauses. The latter is the view of the versions (Sept. ότι; Vulg. *Quia*; Pesh. *mṭl d*; Targ. ארי) and also of Rudolph and Bright. The other possibility is that both occurrences of כי in v. 18 are asseverative ('surely') and that v. 18bc constitutes a unit of lamentation. This is indicated by NEB's translation:

How fearful is our ruin! How great our shame!
We have left our lands, our houses have been pulled down.

The other difficulty in v. 18 (השליכו) is already evident in the renderings of the versions. There is serious doubt whether השליך can mean 'demolish' (Vulg., Pesh., Targ.) and another proposal is that there has been a haplography of מ, but that otherwise the consonants indicated by Sept. ἀπερρίψαμεν should be read: השלכנו ממשכנותינו, 'We have been evicted from our homes', gives the required sense and should be adopted (so Bright; cf. Rudolph).

Verse 19 is addressed particularly to women, and this reinforces the impression gained from vv. 16–17 that they have the responsibility of creating and inducing a universal outpouring of grief. It might be supposed that the word of Yahweh to which v. 19a alludes, but which is not reproduced *verbatim*, is contained in v. 19b (ולמדנה ... קינה), but the suffixes in v. 20 establish that Jeremiah and not Yahweh is the speaker in that verse, and it should therefore be concluded that Jeremiah is also the speaker in v. 19b. Hence the word of Yahweh to which reference is made in v. 19a is the threat of impending judgement on the basis of which Jeremiah issues a call for lamentation and the verbs in v. 20 have to be taken as 'prophetic perfects' with a future reference. On this assumption vv. 19–20 have the same time scale as the preceding verses: they are set in the context of an overpowering conviction that desolation and death hover and the מקוננות are urged to transmit their skills to their daughters and friends. Sept.[OL] and Theod. (above, pp. 208f.) have indicated that מות in v. 20 (Sept. θάνατος) is a reference to death by plague and have connected דבר (θανατω) with v. 20. דבר should rather be regarded as a marginal gloss which embodies an exegetical opinion on v. 20, namely that there are no safe places when pestilence is abroad and no defence against it (cf. Ehrlich, p. 268).

The parallelism of בחלונינו and בארמנותינו (v. 20) is troublesome and matters are not improved by emending בארמנותינו to באדמתנו on the foundation of Sept. εἰς τὴν γῆν ὑμῶν (assuming an original εἰς τὴν γῆν ἡμῶν, so Ziegler). The confusion of ר and ד is readily understandable, but 'in our land' is a poor match for 'through (or "in") our windows'. Even those who have translated בארמנותינו 'in our palaces', have not intended to set up a contrast between ordinary houses and royal residences and to explain the text as an assertion that those who live in royal houses (cf. Vulg. *domos nostras*; Theod. εις τας οικησεις) will not be exempt. Thus 'palaces' are understood as a symbol of strength and security (Calvin and Lowth). In order to emphasize that ארמנות is symbolic of thick walls and barred gates Ehrlich (p. 268) urges that the rendering 'fortified places' or 'castles' is the right one (so Aq., Symm., Pesh. and Targ.). The meaning is that there is no security against plague, not even for those who reside behind walls and bars: neither ordinary houses nor fortified places like castles afford safety. Another possibility which might be considered is that עולל is related particularly to בחלונינו and בחורים to באַרמנותינו: children in their homes are not safe, nor are soldiers in their barracks. The decisive objection to this is the way in which the parallelism of עולל and בחורים functions in v. 20b, since this demonstrates that באַרמנותינו does not have any such specialized sense and that what is intended is children in the streets and youths at street corners (cf. Blayney).

The parallelism of *ḥln* and *ùrbt* in Ugaritic has encouraged the thought that באַרמנותינו may be a corruption of בארבותינו, 'in our lattices'. There are a number of occurrences of אר(ו)בות in Biblical Hebrew, principally in the phrase 'windows of heaven' (Gen 7.11; 8.2; 2 Kgs 7.2, 19; Isa 24.18; Mal 3.10). Baal declines an offer made by Kothar and Khasis to put windows in his palace (J. C. L. Gibson, *CML*, 4.5.123f., 125ff., p. 62; A Herdner, op. cit., p. 27). It has been urged that Baal was motivated by a fear of the god Mot ('Death'), that Mot was supposed to gain access to houses through windows. As far as one can gather from a fragmentary text Baal fears *ym* ('Sea') and not Mot (4.6.12ff., Gibson, p. 62). It is not clear why Baal relents (4.7.17f., Gibson, p. 64; 24ff., Gibson, p. 65) and eventually takes up the offer of Kothar and Khasis. It is evident, however that Mot is Baal's ally who will deal effectively with his enemies. Hence the text cannot be used in order to establish an equation between מות in Jer 9.20 and the Canaanite god Mot (agreeing with S. M. Paul, *Biblica* 49, pp. 373–376). It could still be urged that *ḥln* and *ùrbt* are established as a traditional pair in ancient Canaanite poetry and that this of itself is a sufficient reason for raising the question whether באַרמנותינו is a corruption of בארבותינו. In view of the difficulties associated with the elucidation of באַרמנותינו this is an attractive idea and if the graphic resemblance of בארבותינו to באַרמנותינו were more complete, it would deserve serious consideration. Paul (p. 376) discovers a Mesopotamian mythological allusion in Jer 9.20: Death is personified as a demon comparable to the Lamaštu demon in that both attack human beings by entering through windows and climbing over walls (cf. *CAD* 3, p. 190).

Sept. ἐπὶ προσώπου τοῦ πεδίου τῆς γῆς ὑμῶν (v. 21) is explained by Ziegler (*Beiträge*, pp. 98f.; cf. Janzen, p. 27) as a conflate reading: ὑμῶν arises out of the attempt to make a credible combination of τοῦ πεδίου and τῆς γῆς and the 'original' Greek, which Ziegler restores in his text, was ἐπὶ προσώπου τῆς γῆς. This implies that the Hebrew text which was translated was different from MT, and that it was the same as at 8.2 and 16.4 (על פני האדמה). At 9.21 על פני האדמה has the support of K^Or. and of some Hebrew manuscripts. על פני השדה is probably original in 9.21 and שדה is due to the influence of the simile—the sheaves which are left lying in the field (שדה). More important exegetically is the question whether כדמן may not be secondary in v. 21, having been imported from 8.2. It is not clear that the two similes can be combined credibly and כעמיר, as Kimchi's exposition shows, is capable of conveying the complete sense. ו has been added to עמיר in order to accommodate the insertion of כדמן.

So severe will be the toll exacted by the accumulated ravages of war and plague that corpses will lie unburied, just as sheaves are sometimes missed at harvest and lie in the fields ungathered and neglected. Here, as in 7.32–8.3, the picture of the corpses functions as a symbol of the furthest outreach of calamity and ruin. When corpses lie unburied, all the assumptions of religion and civilization have been falsified and the supports of life have crumbled.

KNOWLEDGE OF YAHWEH IS MAN'S ONLY BOAST (9.22–23)

> [22]These are the words of Yahweh:
>> Let not the wise man boast of his wisdom,
>> nor the powerful man of his power,
>> nor the wealthy man of his wealth.
> [23] If there is to be boasting let it be in this:
>> in knowing and understanding me;
>> for I, Yahweh, maintain integrity,
>> perform justice and righteousness in the world.
>> It is in willing these that I take pleasure.
>>> This is Yahweh's word.

There is a sharp contrast between the antithesis of חכמה and גבורה in some wisdom sentences, or the representation in others that חכמה and עשר are complementary, and the condemnatory lumping together of wisdom, power and wealth in vv. 22–23 (cf. Prov 16.32; 21.22; Eccles 9.16ff.). A pejorative attitude to wealth is not normal in the book of Proverbs, although it is attested in 11.28 and 28.11. In 28.11 we have a correlation of impiety and wealth, and of piety and poverty which is more characteristic of certain Psalms than of the book of Proverbs. The impression which is to be had elsewhere in Proverbs is a different one. Wisdom has length of days in her right hand, wealth and honour (עשר וכבוד) in her left hand (3.16; cf. 8.18). Wealth is the crown of wise men (14.24).

The attitude which is expressed in Jer 9.22–23 may be described as a prophetic one and the positive element which is emphasized is דעת יהוה. The meaning of this effective knowledge of Yahweh (השכל וידע אותי) is indicated by the account which is given of Yahweh's activity in relation to his world. His aim is to create a community in which there is mutual trust and solidarity and where justice is effectively expressed. This is what he wills for the world and those who 'know' him are committed with him to this great enterprise. Thus Kimchi observes that 'knowledge of God' is to walk in his ways and do משפט חסד, and צדקה. He appositely cites Jer 22.15f., 'Think of your father: he ate and drank, dealt justly and fairly; all went well with him. He dispensed justice to the lowly and poor; did this not show he knew me?, says the Lord' (NEB). Hence if there is any reason for pride and complacency, it is a paradoxical one. It does not reside in the possession of human wisdom or worldly power or wealth, but in the possession of an insight for the lack of which nothing can compensate. It consists of an awareness of the ethical texture of Yahweh's world and a commitment to his morality. This is the only valid reason for human self-satisfaction.

The lack of connection between vv. 22–23 and what precedes it or follows it is striking, and the same can be said of vv. 24–25. The appearance of גוים in 10.2 (cf. כל הגוים in 9.25) does not significantly relieve the isolation of vv. 24–25. Too painfully contrived attempts to establish connections serve as a confirmation that there is no obvious affinity between vv. 22–25 and the remainder of chapter 9, and Duhm supposes that 9.22–10.16 consists of late and inferior material.

JUDGEMENT ON THOSE THAT ARE CIRCUMCISED (9.24–25)

[24] The time is coming—this is Yahweh's word—when I will punish all those who are circumcised: [25] Egypt, Judah, Edom, Ammon, Moab and the desert dwellers who crop the hair on their temples. All the nations are uncircumcised and Israel's heart is uncircumcised.

The difficulty of MT is that the concluding כי clause establishes an antithesis between Israel and the nations which is not consistent with Judah's inclusion among the nations. This could be overcome if Duhm's view that ערלים and ערלי לב have the same meaning were accepted (so, apparently, NEB). But ערלים and ערלי לב, far from being identical, have been deliberately distinguished from each other, and this plain, lexicographical distinction, which is indicated by Sept., Vulg., Pesh. and Targ., may not be ignored. Rudolph's explanation is that post-exilic Jews, for whom circumcision was a mark of exclusiveness and separation from all Gentiles, could not accommodate the representation of vv. 24–25 that circumcision created a bond between Judah and certain other nations. On this view the

substitution of עֲרֵלִים for a postulated original הָאֵלֶּה in v. 25 is
due to the theological significance of circumcision in these times.
The passage (so Rudolph) was originally associated with the
formation of a coalition of circumcised nations against the
uncircumcised Babylonians.

There is a phrase of uncertain sense in v. 24 (מוּל בְּעׇרְלָה) of
which Targ. and Kimchi take a different view from the
remaining versions. The latter are agreed that the sense of מוּל
בְּעׇרְלָה is 'cut on the foreskin', that is, circumcised. The
rendering of Targ. rests on the assumption that מוּל בְּעׇרְלָה,
means 'circumcised and uncircumcised alike': although the
house of Israel is circumcised in a physical sense, it is
uncircumcised in so far as its way of life is indistinguishable
from the uncircumcised nations. Kimchi's exegesis is the same as
that of Targ. With the exegesis of Targ. and Kimchi vv. 24–25
can be explained as a consistent unit. Yahweh threatens
circumcised and uncircumcised alike with a punitive judgement;
the nations mentioned in v. 25 other than Judah are the
'uncircumcised' and Judah alone is 'circumcised'. There follows
that statement that all the nations are uncircumcised and that
the house of Israel, despite its having the physical mark of
circumcision, is uncircumcised in heart.

KJV 'All them which are circumcised with the uncircumcised'
is following Targ. and Kimchi, and Calvin, who is similarly
influenced, takes the meaning to be that Yahweh will not
recognize any distinction between circumcised and
uncircumcised in executing his judgement. Lowth's exegesis is
similar, 'God tells them, when he sends his judgements abroad in
the world, they shall find no more favour than those who are not
circumcised.' The influence of Sept., Vulg. and Pesh. has, on the
other hand, prevailed with Duhm, Rudolph, Bright and NEB
('all the circumcised'). The renderings of Sept., Pesh. and Vulg.
constitute an impressive testimony to the meaning 'cut on the
foreskin', that is, circumcised. Another consideration is that the
position of Judah in the list does not suggest that any
differentiation between Judah as circumcised and the others as
uncircumcised is intended: Judah comes second—not first nor
last. The change of terminology from 'Judah' in the first part of
v. 25 to 'house of Israel' in the כִּי clause is a suspicious feature.
Instead of emending עֲרֵלִים to הָאֵלֶּה (Rudolph) we should
recognize that the secondary intrusive element which produces
inconsistency is the entire כִּי clause. It rests on the assumption
that circumcision is the badge of exclusiveness which marks
Israel off from the nations, while maintaining that physical
circumcision is not enough. With the כִּי clause deleted vv. 24–25
amount to a threat issued by Yahweh against a group of

circumcised nations, including Judah. This, however, is a type of passage where one should be content to explain how MT has arrived at its present form without deleting in the interests of an 'original' text.

The versions take קצוצי פאה as a reference to a particular type of hair-cut, and the rendering of Targ. at 9.25 and the other two Jeremiah passages (25.23; 49.32) establishes a connection between קצוצי פאה and Lev 19.27, where this way of cutting the hair is forbidden (cf. W. R. Smith, *Religion of the Semites*[3], 1927, p. 325 n. 2). Rashi and Kimchi suppose that קצוצי פאה are those who live in the deep desert, at the furthest edges of civilization (קצה = קצץ). The phrase *pàt mdbr* (*mlbr*) occurs in Ugaritic with the sense 'fringe of the desert' (J. C. L. Gibson, *CML*[2], 1978, 12.1.35, p. 134; 14, 193, p. 87; 23, 68, p. 127). Hence the interpretation of Rashi and Kimchi deserves some consideration. It was taken over by KJV ('All that are in the utmost corners'), it is found in Blayney and has reappeared in NEB. Lowth, on the other hand, who has a learned note on קצוצי פאה, prefers a KJV marginal reading, 'They that have the corners of their hair polled'. This understanding of קצוצי פאה is the one which is generally adopted by modern commentators (Duhm, Rudolph, Weiser, Bright, Freehof).

There is no doubt that קצוצי פאה occurs in the context of desert communities in all three Jeremiah passages, but this does not establish that its meaning is 'those who live in the deep desert'. It shows that קצוצי פאה live in the desert, but it does not disprove that the phrase refers to a peculiarity of their hair style. Further הישבים במדבר follows immediately after קצוצי פאה in 9.25 and it is probable that השכנים במדבר similarly originally followed קצוצי פאה in 25.23f. If the order were reversed, we could say that קצוצי פאה is a more precise designation (those in the deep desert) than הישבים במדבר. As it is we have (*ex hypothesi*) a precise term followed by a weaker, general one which does not have any function.

CHAPTER X

IDOLS ARE VACUOUS BUT YAHWEH IS THE CREATOR (10.1-16)

[1]Hear the word which Yahweh has spoken to you,[1] O Israel. These are the words of Yahweh:
[2]Do not acquire the habits of the nations:
do not be terrified by signs in the heavens,
such as terrify the nations;
[3]for the rites of foreign peoples have no foundation.
Idols are no more than trees felled in a forest,
shaped by a craftsman with his chisel,
[4]adorned with silver and gold,
fixed with hammers and nails,
so that they will not topple.
[5]Like scarecrows in a cucumber field they cannot speak;
they have to be carried because they cannot walk.
Do not be afraid of them for they cannot injure you,
no more are they capable of doing you good.
[6]Where is there anyone like you,[2] O Yahweh?
You are great and your greatness is in your power.
[7]Who does not fear you, king of the nations?
Fear is fitting tribute for you.
Where among wise men and kings the world over
is there anyone like you?[2]
[8]To a man they are undiscerning and foolish.
. . . . [3]

[9]Beaten silver is brought from Tarshish,
gold is brought from Ophir:[4]
idols are the handiwork of craftsmen and smiths;
they are clothed in violet and purple,
all the products of skilled men.
[10]But Yahweh is God in truth,
he is a living God, an everlasting king.
When he is angry the earth quakes,
nations cannot withstand his fury.
[11]This is what you are to say to them: The gods who did not create heaven and earth will perish from the earth and from beneath these heavens.
[12](Yahweh) made the earth by his power,
set the world in order by his wisdom,
unfolded the heavens by his understanding.
[13]At his thunderous command[5] the heavenly waters are massed
and clouds rise from the ends of the earth;
he makes lightning to produce rain
and brings out the wind from his storehouses.
[14]All men are without discernment and knowledge,
every smith will be let down by his idol.

---

[1] אליכם = עליכם.
[2] Reading מאין (MT מִאַיִן) as מֵאַיִן (see below, pp. 223f.).
[3] The text is unintelligible (see below, p. 224).
[4] Emending מאופז (MT) to מאופיר (see below, p. 223).
[5] Emending לקול תתו (MT) to לתתו קול (see below, p. 225).

The images which he has cast[1] are a falsehood
and lack the breath of life.
[15]They are nonentities, objects of contempt;
they will perish on their day of reckoning.
[16]The God allotted to Jacob is not like these,
for he is Creator of all things
and Israel is his special care:
Yahweh Sabaoth is his name.

Verses 6–8 and 10 (MT) are not represented by Sept. and v. 9
(MT) is located by Sept. after ידברו (MT, v. 5). A fragment of
Hebrew text from Cave 4 at Qumran (4QJer.ᵇ) enables us to
make further progress with the evaluation of these different texts:

MT v. 4 ב ייפהו במקבות

v. 9 תכלת וארגמן

v. 11 יאבדו מן ארעה

We are dependent on the transcriptions and interpretations
which are supplied by F. M. Cross (The Ancient Library of
Qumran², 1961, p. 187, n. 38) and Janzen (pp. 121f., 181f.). On
this basis a calculation can be made which shows that the
available space would have been filled by a Hebrew text
corresponding in length to Sept. There is room for כתמר מקשה
המה ולא ידברו (MT, v. 5) before v. 9, for the remainder of v. 5
(MT) after v. 9, but there is no room for MT vv. 6–8, 10 between
וגם היטיב אין אותם and v. 11.

We have the remains of a Hebrew text more or less the same
as the one which was before the Greek translator, and a
particular feature which strengthens this view is the order
'mallets and nails' (v. 4) indicated by the fragment (ייפהו
במקבות), since this agrees with Sept. (ἐν σφύραις καὶ ἥλοις)
over against MT (במסמרות ובמקבות). In the face of this it can
no longer be supposed that the text of Sept. is the consequence of
an abridgement of MT, as Ackroyd was inclined to maintain
(JTS 14, 1963, p. 385 n. 3). Moreover, it is very doubtful
whether attempts to improve the coherence of MT by alterations
in the order of the verses (Rudolph, Weiser) can survive this new
evidence, because they are founded on an understanding of MT
which has been falsified.

By the same logic attempts to demonstrate the coherence of
10.1–16 on the basis of the extant order of the verses, and to
claim an impressive literary structure for it, are doomed to
failure. There can be no doubt that in Sept. we encounter the
Hebrew text at an earlier point in its history than we do in MT,
that MT has been reached by a process of piecemeal aggregation
and that we do not touch the beginning of this process in Sept.
The last of these matters is clear from the circumstance that

[1] See below, p. 227.

MT, Sept. and 4QJer[b] all have the Aramaic gloss (v. 11), since
this cannot be regarded as an integral part of a Hebrew text,
whatever its date. T. W. Overholt's assertion (*JTS* 16, 1965,
pp. 4f.) that the Aramaic does not 'interrupt' the Hebrew text is
strange, but it is, nevertheless, clear that he regards v. 11 as a
'liturgical' insertion.

Because of the different orthographies of the same word in
v. 11 (ארקא and ארעא) W. Baumgartner (*ZAW* 45, 1927,
p. 101; cf. P. W. Coxon, *ZDMG* 129, 1979, p. 17) supposed that
it derived from a period when the spelling ארקא was giving way
to ארעא, and so the fifth century B.C. This is not the only
interpretation which could be put on the facts, but it is a
reasonable one. The Aramaic gloss, which is common to MT,
4QJer[b] and which is represented by Sept., belongs to an earlier
stage of the history of the text than does vv. 6–8, 10 which are
not represented by Sept. and 4QJer[b]. Hence, if the Aramaic gloss
is to be dated in the fifth century, these additions to the Hebrew
text, present in MT, were made not earlier than the fifth century.

A passage which has been built up by piecemeal contributions
is not necessarily one which is entirely devoid of unity: one might
expect a general, thematic affinity of the parts, in so far as later
supplements are generated by the existing text. This, however, is
not the kind of unity which Weiser, Ackroyd (*JTS* 14, 1963,
pp. 385–390) and Overholt are seeking. In the case of Weiser
and Ackroyd it is a unity which is said to reside in a cluster of
important, cultic traditions relating to idolatry: in Weiser, as one
would expect, the 'Covenant cult' looms large. For Overholt the
unity arises out of Jeremiah's untiring engagement with and
struggle against falsehood.

B. M. Wambacq (*RB* 81, 1974, pp. 56–62), whose approach is
the right one, observes that vv. 3–4 connect poorly with v. 2 and
that the awkwardness of the transition from דרך הגוים to חקות
העמים is not simply a stylistic incongruence. Thus Wambacq
attributes v. 3a (כי ... הוא) to a first redactor: it is a comment
on v. 2 and the intention of the commentator was to declare that
the astrological rites referred to in that verse had no foundation
of truth in them: that they were illusory and empty (הבל). A
second commentator fastened on to הבל and misunderstood it as
a reference to idolatry (cf. Jer 2.5; 8.19; 10.8; 14.22) and so
made a comment on the manufacture of idols with a view to
illustrating the futility of idol worship (vv. 3b–4; כי עץ ... יפיק).
This line of thinking has been developed by further contributors
(vv. 5, 8, 9) and others have introduced doxologies in praise of
Yahweh's sovereignty over the world (vv. 6, 7, 10). Verse 11 is
liturgical acclamation and vv. 12–16 consists of a hymn in praise
of Yahweh, the creator. Wambacq reaches the conclusion that

v. 2 is the kernel: its subject matter is different from the remainder of the passage and does not feature in the passages with which 10.1–16 is usually compared. These comparisons are effected by concentrating on 10.3–9. The astrological reference is present only in Ep Jer 66 which, however, probably depends on Jer 10.1–16. Wambacq holds that the character of 10.2 is compatible with Jeremianic provenance and he supposes that it was directed particularly to the inhabitants of the northern kingdom who had not suffered deportation in 722.

Wambacq's attempt to disengage v. 2 from an exilic context by associating מְעוֹנֵן with עָנָן 'cloud', and so with pre-exilic, astrological rites, is unsatisfactory lexicographically (cf. BDB). He has, perhaps, been too ambitious in his efforts to uncover the history of the text and one should be guided as far as possible by the harder evidence which is available (see above, p. 217). The point which Wambacq has made about vv. 3–5 is so sharp that in this regard we should follow his efforts to trace the history of the text beyond what we are able to do with reference to 4QJer[b] and Sept. If his explanation of v. 3a is accepted, that element relates to v. 2. If it is argued that חֻקּוֹת means something other than 'rites' or is to be emended in order to make vv. 3–5 all of a piece, the difficulty remains that vv. 3–5, presented as supporting argument for v. 2 (כִּי ... כִּי), are a *non sequitur*, because the satire on the manufacture of idols and the demonstration that they can never be more than the material from which they are made has no particular relevance to the heavenly signs of v. 2.

Overholt is more strongly attached to Jeremianic authorshihp than Weiser and Ackroyd, but he is surely wrong in insisting that Jeremiah's concern with falsehood takes precisely this form at any other place in the book. We can certainly show that the verb עָשָׂה is used in connected with a proscription of idolatry in the second clause of the Decalogue (Exod 20.3)—a point which Weiser regarded as important—and that עָשָׂה is similarly used in condemnations of Israel's idolatry in the book of Jeremiah (1.16; 2.28; 16.20). But two different matters are being confused: the one is a bare prohibition of making gods with one's own hands and the other is a new genre in which a polemic against idols and their manufacture is developed in quite an elaborate way and in which room is found for satire and ridicule. Where else in the book of Jeremiah is such an interest shown in the manufacture of idols? We are here in the presence of a genre with which we are principally acquainted from its appearances in Deutero-Isaiah (40.18–20; 41.6f.; 44.9–20) and this is why Jer 10.1–16 has been widely regarded as exilic or post-exilic (so Janzen, p. 132; cf. Thiel, p. 43, n. 45—post-deuteronomic) in provenance.

The right way to use such knowledge of the history of the text as we possess is to make it enhance our understanding of the final product (MT). There is textual evidence that a Hebrew text shorter than MT and corresponding to Sept. did actually exist and there are reasons for concluding that 10.1–16 consists of successive additions, each generated by the pre-existing text or part of it. Verse 2 may be the core to which the passage is reducible and Wambacq has made an impressive attempt to show how the first stages of growth (vv. 3–5) took place. The circumstance that v. 9 is differently located in MT and Sept. (4QJer^b) is further support for the view that the passage has a piecemeal character. Verses 6–7 deal with Yahweh's superiority to the חכמים and their attraction to vv. 3–5 can be explained with reference to the genre 'Satire on idols and their makers' as it appears in Deutero-Isaiah (40.14, 23, 28). The verbs are more appropriate to those who worship idols or make them than they are to the idols themselves (cf. נבער in v. 14 and נבערו in v. 21). The second half of v. 8 is corrupt and nothing very satisfactory can be said to explain why the verse appears where it does. Verses 10, 12, 13 are hymnic in form and describe Yahweh's power and majesty as these are displayed in his creative and ordering activities in nature. Sept. and 4QJer^b show that vv. 11–13 were part of the text before v. 10 (for the fragment of v. 13 in 4QJer^b, see Janzen, p. 182). Verses 14–16 are concerned with the stupidity of men, and the emptiness of their idols as compared with the reality of Yahweh: it is none other than the creator of the earth who has taken Israel into his special care (cf. vv. 6–7).

In v. 2 the construction of תלמדו with אל is unusual (cf. Kimchi who cites Judg 7.25 and Ps 2.7 to support his view that אל = את) and its awkwardness is reflected in the different renderings of אל in the versions. Duhm's emendation (את for אל; cf. Kimchi) is adopted by Rudolph, and Driver (*JQR* 28, p. 106) suggests on the basis of Syriac *lmd b*, *'tlmd 'l* and *'tlmd l* that למד אל means 'to be addicted to'. The sense of the Hebrew is probably that indicated by the versions through various expedients, namely, learning from foreign nations or imitating their behaviour (cf. NEB, 'Do not fall into the ways of the nations'). דרך הגוים may simply convey general advice not to ape the customs and style of life of other nations, or the subsequent part of v. 2 may be intended as an epexegesis of דרך הגוים. Those addressed are reminded that true religion is an emancipation from habits and beliefs which promote fear and impose a sense of fate. The reference is to the dread which arises from predictions founded on astrological observations, when it is believed that what is predicted must inexorably follow.

Alternatively, there is the possibility that the allusion is
particularly to abnormal and frightening heavenly phenomena,
but even so the terror is not created only by the phenomena
themselves but by their fatefulness and the disasters which they
are thought to portend.

חקות (v. 3) is not normally associated with idols, but the verse
from the second כי onwards is clearly about the making of idols.
Since הבל is used elsewhere in the book of Jeremiah of idols, it
may be concluded that v. 3 is entirely concerned with idols, but
in that case there is a defective connection between v. 2 and v. 3
(see above, p. 219). Nevertheless, this is the view of v. 3 which
has generally been pursued and so it is thought that חקות refers
to images of gods (NEB). Bright's suggestion that חקות may
have the sense 'religious customs' accords with Wambacq's
elucidation of הבל, whereas the emendation of חקות to חתת or
חתת 'objects of fear' (Giesebrecht, followed by Rudolph) is
intended to produce an allusion to idolatry. Giesebrecht's
conjecture is supported by Pesh. dḥlt', but it is more likely that
this is an attempt by the Syriac translator to interpret חקות than
that he read a Hebrew text with חתת. In view of the
characterization of חקות as הבל and the manner in which v. 3
continues it is understandable that an allusion to idols has been
detected in חקות. This is the conclusion of Kimchi who glosses
חקות with צלמים 'images'.

On this view v. 3 opens with an assertion that idols are
vacuous and insubstantial and goes on to describe the various
stages of their manufacture. First a suitable tree is felled and is
shaped by a craftsman with his axe or chisel. Then comes the
stage of adornment with silver and gold, and, finally, the idol is
safely anchored. In the final part of the description a satirical
tendency can be detected: the object, after all the care and
expense which have been lavished on it, cannot maintain itself in
an upright position. Since both the idol and the craftsman are
singular in v. 3 (חרש ; כרתו) and in the first stich of v. 4 (ייפהו),
יחזקום must be regarded as an aberration: the consequence of
forgetfulness that the theme has been previously developed with
reference to a craftsman, not to craftsmen.

The gist of v. 5 can easily be stated: the idols have no power of
speech or locomotion; they are dumb and they have to be carried
about. The statement that they can do neither evil nor good may
be taken in the more restricted and literal sense that they are
neither beneficent nor threatening and lack the power either to
bless or punish; or it may be an idiomatic way of saying that they
are incapable of achieving effects of any kind. If the latter
interpretation is followed 'evil and good' exhausts all the
possibilities of effective action and the idols are said to be

ineffective over the whole range. The problems of grammatical congruence encountered in v. 4 persist in v. 5 and Sept. and Pesh. have perhaps rendered יפיק as plural in v. 4 in order to achieve consistency with three successive plural references to idols. The second one appears in MT (ידברו) and the third has the support of some Hebrew manuscripts (ינשאו).

The only substantial difficulty in v. 5 is the obscure simile with which it opens (כתמר מקשה המה). 'They can no more speak than a scarecrow in a plot of cucumbers' (NEB) is founded on Ep Jer 69 (ὥσπερ γὰρ ἐν σικυηράτῳ προβασκάνιον). This is the favoured modern interpretation of the passage (Rudolph, Bright), although προβασκάνιον is taken by Duhm (cf. Freehof) as 'pole' rather than 'scarecrow' and is explained as an object which offers magical protection to a field from any kind of depredation. תֹּמֶר occurs only here and at Judg 4.5 and in the latter passage it means 'palm-tree'. The sense 'cucumber-plot' suggested for מקשה is attested only at Isa 1.8 (BDB and KB[2] derive מקשה from קשא in both passages). Sept. understood מקשה as 'hammered work' or the like, since מקשה is rendered by τορευτόν in other passages where it has this sense (Exod 25.18, 31, 36). Both Aq. and Theod. (ὡς φοινιξ) translate כתמר 'like a palm tree', while Symm. renders (כ)תמר מקשה המה as ρινητα και τορευτα εστιν, 'They are objects shaped by the file and hammer'. The other versions (Vulg., Pesh. and Targ.) have all taken תמר as 'palm tree' and have, with differing degrees of explicitness, associated מקשה with the sense 'hammered iron-work'. Targ. describes it explicitly as עובד נגיד, 'an artifact of beaten iron'. Rashi and Kimchi offer an explanation which sets out from the erectness of the palm tree, that is, they fasten on to זקיפין of Pesh. and Targ. The emphasis on erectness appears in Calvin and KJV ('They are upright as the palm tree'). Lowth renders תמר as 'pillar', the sense attached to it in KJV at Ct. 3.6 and Joel 2.30. Venema and Blayney, who opt for 'palm tree', suppose that the point of the comparison is the smoothness and solidity of the idol. F. Deist (ZAW 85, 1973, 225f.) in a more recent attempt to advance our understanding of כתמר מקשה supposes that the reference is to sculpted palm trees with which the gates and other parts of the temple structure were decorated (cf. 1 Kgs 6.32–35; Ezek 41.18, 25f.). This is an attempt to associate מקשה with artistic work and so bring it nearer to the sense attached to it elsewhere.

In the light of Sept. οὐ πορεύσονται BHS queries whether we should not assume the Syriac sense of *dbr* ('walk') in ולא ידברו (so, NEB, 'for they cannot walk'). The other versions, including Pesh. (*wl' mmllyn*), indicate the normal sense of דבר. Another possible explanation of οὐ πορεύσονται (Sept.) is that it is a misplaced doublet of οὐκ ἐπιβήσονται (MT לא יצעדו), and that there is nothing in Sept. corresponding to MT ולא ידברו. In all the circumstances the best that can be done is to adopt the dubious 'like a scarecrow in a cucumber field' for כתמר מקשה and to follow the normal sense of דבר in Hebrew. This has the advantage of preserving a double characterization of idols: they are incapable of speech ('dumb idols') and they have no power of movement.

The locating of v. 9 after v. 4a (ייפהו; Rudolph and Bright) is dictated by the desire to place it in its proper context. The circumstance that במקבות follows immediately after ייפהו shows conclusively that 4QJerᵇ does not support Rudolph's order. We have two Hebrew texts with the verses differently ordered, but a third conjectural order, with no textual support, should not be entertained. In view of its affinity with vv. 3–5 it will be convenient to deal with v. 9 at this point.

BHS deletes מעשה חרש (v. 9) and transposes מעשה חכמים כלם to replace it. Both Pesh. (*mn 'wpyr*) and Targ. (מאופיר) indicate מאופיר which may be correct in view of a known association between gold and Ophir (Isa 13.12; Ps 45.10; Job 28.16; 1 Chr 29.4). A further exegetical contribution by Pesh. is the connection which it makes between תכלת וארגמן לבושם and מעשה חכמים (כלם). Thus מעשה חכמים is rendered as *zqwr' dhkym'*, 'woven garments of skilled craftsmen'. This means that a skill other than craftsmanship in metal is indicated by the final phrase (so also Kimchi). Verse 9 describes the places from which precious metals used in the adorning of idols are imported: beaten silver is brought from Tarshish (Targ. מאפרקא, 'from Africa'=Carthage(?); for the various conjectures about the location of Tarshish see Rudolph) and gold from Ophir, and these are worked by craftsmen in metal. The splendid garments in which the idols are clothed are the products of expert weavers (*pace* BHS, see above).

The versions, for the most part, have interpreted מאין (vv. 6, 7) in accordance with the pointing of MT (מֵאֵין) and have treated it as synonymous with אין, but Theod.'s rendering (πόθεν ὥσπερ σύ) assumes מֵאַיִן. BDB (p. 35) urges that מֵאַיִן should be read ('Whence is there any like you?'), while KB³ (p. 41), following Duhm, takes the contrary course of emending MT מֵאַיִן (Jer 30.7) to מֵאֵין (double negation—privative מִן). Another account of the 'double negative' מאין has been given by M. Dahood (*CBQ* 37, 1975, pp. 458f.) who renders 'There is absolutely no one like you'. According to Dahood the elements of מאין are מָ(ה) + אֵין, and he claims that he has found such a use of *ma* at Ebla (*SVT* 29, 1978, p. 97). There is very little at stake exegetically between 'Where is there a god like you?', which implies 'There is no god like you', and the explicit negative particle. NEB adopts מֵאֵין in all three Jeremiah passages (10.6, 7; 30.7) and should be followed. Yahweh is incomparable, a great God who manifests his power and has a claim on the reverence of all nations as their king. Homage paid to such a God is fitting (Pesh. *dlk hw y'y' mlkwt'*, 'For sovereignty befits you'). Vulg. (*Et in universis regnis eorum*) and Theod. (καὶ ἐν πασι τοις βασιλευσιν αυτων) treat מלכותם as a case of *abstractum pro concreto*.

The sense of v. 8b (MT) is poor, but this is the text which has been read by Vulg. (*Doctrina vanitatis eorum lignum est*) and by Symm. (και παιδεια ματαιοτητων εν αυτοις ξυλον εστιν). Pesh. renders, 'False teachings concerning the worship of a piece of wood will both perish and come to an end' (*w'khd' n'bdwn wnswpwn ywlpn' sryq' ddhlt' dqys'*). This is an attempt to solve the problem of the grammatical subject of יבערו ויכסלו by making מוסר הבלים the subject. The same problem is felt by Kimchi who argues that the subject of these verbs is חכמי הגוים (v. 7). In so far as Kimchi is dissenting from the view that the idols are the grammatical subject of יבערו ויכסלו (so Rudolph) he is to be followed (see above, p. 220). NEB (cf. Targ.) correctly attributes v. 8a to worshippers of idols ('They are fools and blockheads one and all') and manfully attempts to make sense of מוסר הבלים עץ הוא, 'learning their nonsense from a log of wood'. מוסר הבלים עץ הוא perhaps owes its present position to the circumstance that the idols were thought to be the grammatical subject of יבערו and יכסלו. Even so עץ הוא is not easily reconciled with the plural verbs in v. 8a nor with a grammatical entity consisting of v. 8b and we may have to reckon with two independent glosses in v. 8b (מוסר הבלים and עץ הוא) as Duhm supposed. In any case there is apparently a play on הבל (v. 3) in מוסר הבלים: 'instruction given by idols' and 'empty instruction' (cf. NEB). The position of v. 9 in MT (as opposed to its position in Sept.) is perhaps connected with the circumstance that v. 8a is thought to refer to the stupidity of the idols themselves, but more certainly with the appearance of עץ in v. 8b which takes us back to a stage which had been reached at כי עץ מיער כרתו (v. 3) and provides a peg on which to hang an account of the materials used in the adornment of the tree trunk and the artistic skills which are involved (v. 9).

The earth, which Yahweh created (v. 10) and over which he rules, shakes when he is angry and the inhabitants of the world cannot withstand his rage. The גוים have a symbolic function: they are the most impressive manifestations of political power in his world, yet they are subject to him and cannot withstand his anger (cf. v. 7). When Yahweh is characterized as אמת, an

attribute which contrasts with the הבל of the idols is brought to
the fore: Yahweh has a massive substantiality; he is truth and
effectiveness.

Targ. has a long paraphrase of the Aramaic gloss (v. 11), the
opening sentence of which is intended as an explanation of why
v. 11 is written in Aramaic, and the same type of explanation
appears in Rashi who says that the letter in question was sent by
Jeremiah to Jehoiachin and the exiles. Kimchi, following Targ.,
states that this was the answer which the Jewish exiles in
Babylon were required to give to the Chaldaeans when they were
commanded to worship their gods. Only the beginning of the
letter (so Kimchi) has been preserved in the language in which
Jeremiah wrote it. There is value in these remarks in so far as
they establish a relationship between v. 11 and vv. 12–16, for it is
not difficult to discern that v. 11 has the character of an Aramaic
summary of vv. 12–16. It should be noted particularly that the
reference to the perishing of the idols which did not make the
heavens and the earth (v. 11) is matched by what is said of them
(described as הבל and מעשה תעתעים) in v. 15, namely, בעת
פקדתם יאבדו.

In v. 12 Yahweh's creation and control of the universe
(heavens and earth) is seen as the supreme manifestation of his
power and wisdom and architectural grasp. This theme is
renewed in v. 13 which opens with the obscure לקול תתו המון
מים בשמים. Sept. (καὶ πλῆθος ὕδατος ἐν οὐρανῷ) has apparently
not read לקול תתו. Duhm, with a reference to 2 Sam 21.10 (עד
נתך מים עליהם מן השמים), emends לקול תתו to לקולו נתך and
this is adopted by Rudolph. לקולו נתך המון מים בשמים gives the
sense, 'At his command the volume (multitude) of waters in the
heavens is poured out'. Driver (JQR 28, p. 106) notes
Houbigant's proposal that המון should be emended to המיון and
himself suggests יהמיון. The emendation which appears in
Brockington assumes that the verb of the original text is תמה
and it endeavours to find a place for most of the consonants of
MT which it reshuffles (לקול תתו המון is emended to לקולו
יתמהון). לקולו יתמהון מים בשמים is rendered as 'At the thunder
of his voice the waters in heaven are amazed' (NEB). Rashi is
apparently accepting לקול תתו as a variant expression for לתתו
קול (cf. Duhm). The best and simplest emendation is to alter לקול
קול to לתתו קול; the emendation on which NEB is founded is
too elaborate and the change from המה to תמה is for the worse.
With לתתו קול, המון can stand in a nominal sentence: 'When he
issues his word of command (or perhaps rather, 'When he speaks
through the thunder'), the waters in heaven are massed'
(literally, 'there is a multitude of waters in heaven'). The
thunder is envisaged as setting in motion a train of events which

will produce rain, and v. 13 is taken up with dispositions which lead to a rain storm. When Yahweh thunders, the waters in heaven are massed or perhaps set in commotion; he brings up rain-bearing clouds from the ends of the earth, he creates lightning and summons the wind—all with a view to the production of rain. Sept. φῶς = אור instead of MT רוח is inferior, even if it is, as Ziegler argues (*Beiträge*, p. 42), more original in Sept. than ἄνεμους.

NEB's rendering 'He opens rifts for the rain' rests on the emendation of ברקים to ברקים (Brockington, p. 202) and makes good sense. It would be a reference to the 'windows of heaven' through which the heavenly waters escape to make rain. A corruption of ד to ר is easily accounted for, but MT should be retained for the following reasons: (*a*) As argued above, thunder and lightning, and rain-bearing clouds driven by the wind form a composite picture. (*b*) ברקים למטר עשה occurs at 51.16 and Ps 135.7 and this circumstance is enough to establish its correctness.

It would be interesting to know why J. Carmignac (*RQ* 7, 1969, pp. 287–290) is persuaded that the manuscript from Cave 11 at Qumran, which he describes as a 'Psalm Scroll', is citing Jer 10.13/51.16 rather than Ps 135.7. Presumably it is because there is agreement with the Jeremiah passages where they deviate from the passage in Ps 135.7 (Jer ויעל/ויעלה and ויוצא; Ps 135.7 מעלה and מוצא). The order in the Qumran manuscript is different from that of the three occurrences in the Hebrew Bible: the order of the latter is clouds, lightning, wind, and the Qumran order is wind, lightning, clouds. Carmignac uses parts of both to reconstruct what he believes to be the right order: wind, then clouds and finally a rain-storm. If there is a problem in the order, it consists more in the circumstance that the lightning has been separated from the thunder than in the circumstance that ברקים למטר עשה is not the final item.

The grammatical difficulty in v. 14 is constituted by the two different grammatical functions of מן in the phrases מדעת and מפסל. In view of the metrical form and the parallelism one would expect that מן would be privative with מפסל as it is with מדעת: נבער כל אדם מדעת הביש כל צורף מפסל. In order to make sense, however, the second מן has to be translated 'because of'. This is nicely illustrated by the non-Semitic versions which use different prepositions for מן (1) and מן (2): Sept. ἀπὸ γνώσεως and ἐπὶ τοῖς γλυπτοῖς αὐτοῦ; Vulg. *a scientia* and *in sculptili*. Targ., on the other hand, appears to indicate the same grammatical function for מן in both places (מלמעבד צלים and מלמידע חכמא) and its sense is, 'All nations are foolish and without knowledge; every smith will be put to shame and will make no more idols.' This point can be reinforced by comparing Targ. with Pesh., since *mn glyp' d'bdw* can only mean 'because of the idols which they have made'. Calvin does not recognize the privative מִן of מִדַּעַת nor does KJV ('Every man is brutish in his knowledge: every founder is confounded by the graven image'). Lowth, whose commentary is founded on KJV, is more perceptive: 'The former part of the verse may be thus rendered, Every man is brutish for want of knowledge' (so Rudolph, Bright, NEB). The differing senses of מִן (1) and מִן (2) have to be allowed, the first privative and the second causative, but it is an odd feature of the verse.

The first stich of v. 14 is a general observation on men who are devoted to idols: they are no better than animals, for they lack a truly human discrimination. The second and third stichs are a more particular polemic against those who lavish their skills on idols: they will be utterly discredited, because they have made a nonentity which lacks the breath of life. Not only are the idols devoid of the vitality of the one, true God, but also of the derivative vitality possessed by those who make them or worship them (cf. Gen 2.7, in virtue of נִשְׁמַת חַיִּים breathed into him by Yahweh, man is נֶפֶשׁ חַיָּה). The choice between נִסְכּוֹ (MT) and נָסְכוּ (Targ.) is not crucial, for the sense is much the same in either case, but one has to render either 'His molten images are a falsehood' or 'The images which he has cast are a falsehood', for the sake of an even translation (in view of בָּם; cf. Rudolph, נְסָכָיו 'his molten images'). Idols are totally unreal, objects deserving contempt (v. 15) and in Yahweh's good time they will be exposed for what they are and will perish; but Yahweh is the creator of all things and this is a primary distinction between him and the idols (v. 16). There is a point of contact here with the Yahwist creation narrative, where יצר (Gen 2.7) and עשׂה (Gen 2.4; cf. Jer 10.12) are used as compared with ברא in the priestly account.

The two principal difficulties in v. 16 are the phrases חֵלֶק יַעֲקֹב and שֵׁבֶט נַחֲלָתוֹ. Sept. does not represent וְיִשְׂרָאֵל שֵׁבֶט and Janzen (p. 39) supposes that this is an addition to the Hebrew text inspired by such passages as Deut 32.9, Isa 63.17, Pss 74.2 and 78.71. The sense, however, is damaged rather than improved by deleting וְיִשְׂרָאֵל שֵׁבֶט. The variants of שֵׁבֶט נַחֲלָתוֹ which occur at Isa 63.17 (שִׁבְטֵי נַחֲלָתֶךָ, 'tribes allotted to you'), where שֵׁבֶט נַחֲלָתֶךָ is parallel to עֲבָדֶיךָ, 'your servants', and at Ps 74.2, where שֵׁבֶט נַחֲלָתֶךָ is parallel to עֲדָתֶךָ, 'your congregation', establish that שֵׁבֶט נַחֲלָתוֹ in Jer 10.16 must mean 'the tribe which has been allotted to his special care'. The passage which best elucidates חֵלֶק יַעֲקֹב is Deut 32.8f., according to which עֶלְיוֹן allotted גּוֹיִם to the gods (emending MT בְּנֵי יִשְׂרָאֵל to בְּנֵי אֱלֹהִים with a Qumran fragment and Sept. ἀγγέλων θεοῦ; for the details see W. McKane, *On Language, Culture and Religion*, pp. 64f.),

Israel being allotted to Yahweh (cf. Deut 32.9). The problem in Jer 10.16 is that Yahweh is said to be allotted to Jacob. It is no doubt against this background that NEB reads חלק as חֹלֵק (Brockington, p. 202) and renders, 'Jacob's Creator is not like these'. 'Creator', however, obscures the sense of 'allot' or 'apportion'. Against the עֶליון background of Deut 32.8f. חֵלק יהוה עַמוֹ (Deut 32.9) means 'Yahweh has been apportioned to his people (Jacob)', while חֵלֶק יעקב (Jer 10.16) means 'The God who has assumed special responsibility for Jacob'. What follows in 10.16 shows that the עֶליון background has been lost ('for he is the Creator of all things'). This is in accord with Kimchi who comments on חֵלֶק יעקב, 'Not as the idols who are the portions of the nations is the Creator God who is Jacob's portion'.

JUDAH BROKEN AND ABOUT TO BE DESTROYED (10.17–25)

[17]Collect your chattels and get out of the land,
you who have been living[1] under siege.
[18]These are the words of Yahweh:
Now I will eject the inhabitants of the land,
I will press them until they are squeezed dry.[2]
[19]How agonizing are my wounds!
—injuries which cannot be cured;
a sickness which I know must be endured.
[20]My tent is in ruins, all my tent ropes are severed,
my sons have left me and are lost to me;
there is no one to pitch my tent again,
no one to erect the curtains.
[21]The shepherds are undiscerning,
they do not seek guidance from Yahweh;
so they are incompetent
and all their flock is scattered.
[22]News reports are coming in:
a great commotion, an army from the north
to lay waste the towns of Judah,
to make them the homes of jackals.
[23]I know, O Yahweh, that man does not dispose his way;
it is not a man's part to make his footsteps firm.
[24]Chastise me, O Lord, but as justice requires,
do not act in anger lest you annihilate me.
[25]Pour out your anger on the nations who do not know you
and on the peoples who do not worship you;
for they have devoured Jacob[3] and consumed him,
and have laid waste his homeland.

Kimchi observes on v. 17 that there is no difference of meaning as between יֹשַׁבְתִּי (?) and Q יֹשֶׁבֶת, and he follows Targ. (דיתבא)

---

[1] Reading Q יֹשֶׁבֶת (see below, p. 229).
[2] Reading יִמָּצֵאוּ (see below, p. 230).
[3] Deleting וַאֲכָלֻהוּ (see below, p. 233).

in his assumption that both forms are participial. This is also the
view of Sept. (κατοικοῦσα) and Pesh. (ytbt), but not of Vulg.
(quae habitas) which apparently reads יֹשַׁבְתִּי (K) as יָשַׁבְתְּ (a
form of the 2nd sing. fem. perf. with a yodh ending). GK 90n
supposes that יֹשַׁבְתִּי and שֹׁכַנְתְּי (Jer 51.13) are cases of formae
mixtae: the form is suspended between יֹשֶׁבֶת (participle) and
יָשַׁבְתְּי (2nd fem. sing. perf.).

BDB shows only I כנע whose normal sense in Biblical Hebrew
is 'humiliation' or 'abasement'; it arrives at the sense 'bundle' for
כנעה by appealing to Arabic kn' 'fold'. KB³ connects כנעתך with
kinaḫḫu which, according to Speiser (AASOR 16, pp. 21ff.),
means originally Phoenicia (a mercantile community) in the
phrase (māt) kinaḫḫu, and is more generally used of Canaan.
Sept. has understood כנעתך as 'your property' and Jerome takes
this as a reference to crops and livestock. Vulg., on the other
hand, connects כנעתך with the normal sense of כנע in Biblical
Hebrew and renders confusionem tuam—'confusion' in the sense
of 'being confounded' (similarly Pesh. ṣ'rky 'your shame'). The
sense 'trade' is found in Symm. (τὴν ἐμπορειαν σου) and Targ.
(סחורתיך). Rashi cites Targ. and quotes Hos 12.8, כנען בידו
מאזני מרמה, 'a merchant in whose hands are falsified scales'.
'Baggage' would seem to be the right sense and there may be a
connection between this and כנעני, the merchant or 'packman'
who carries his wares around (cf. KJV, 'Gather up thy wares').

The meaning of ישבתי במצור is not seriously in doubt. Sept.
(ἐν ἐκλεκτοῖς) is puzzling, but the sense 'siege' for מצור is
indicated by Symm. (εν πολιορκια) and Vulg. (in obsidione).
אספי מארץ כנעתך is terse Hebrew. The meaning is probably,
'Collect your baggage and prepare to evacuate your homeland'
(cf. BDB, 'and take it (the baggage) out of the land'). ישבתי
במצור is then not 'you who will have to withstand a siege in the
immediate future', but 'you who have been living under siege and
have capitulated'. This is probably not a plain, historical
indication that the defences of Judah have been breached and
that deportations are under way. It is rather, as in v. 22 (see
below, p. 232), an expression of prophetic certainty that this is
about to happen. The 2nd person sing. fem. verb (אספי) and
suffix (כנעתך) indicate that a personified Judah or Jerusalem is
addressed and that the deportations are envisaged under this
figure.

Yahweh will dislodge (v. 18) or eject his people from their
own land: he will exert strong pressure on them and will squeeze
them as one might sqeeze the last drop of moisture from a cloth.
(Driver, JQR 28, p. 107). The assumptions of this exegesis are
these: (a) ימצאו = ימצו ימצה (מצה spelt as מצא). (b) ימצאו, so
understood, should be read as יִמָּצְאוּ not as יִמְצָאוּ (MT). Driver

elucidates קוֹלֵעַ with reference to Arabic *ql'* 'uproot' and has been followed by NEB ('I will uproot'), but violent ejection is a more striking and original figure than uprooting and קוֹלֵעַ should be explained as a denominative of קֶלַע.

The rendering by Sept. of קוֹלֵעַ as σκελίζω 'overthrow' (Jerome, *supplantabo et cadere faciam*) lends some support to Driver's view that קוֹלֵעַ is 'uproot' rather than 'eject', but Aq. and Symm. (σφενδονήσω) confirm 'eject'. Aq. has read יִמְצָאוּ as יְמֻצְּאוּ and has understood it as 'found out', 'exposed', 'condemned' (ἐλεγχθῶσιν). Vulg. *longe proiiciam* supports 'eject' and *ut inveniantur* points to לְמַעַן יִמְצָאוּ. קוֹלֵעַ has the sense 'sling' in Targ.: 'Just as one slings stones with a catapult, I will scatter the inhabitants of the land at this time, and I will oppress them that they may receive retribution for their sins.' The other fact which emerges from this paraphrase is that Targ. has read יִמְצָאוּ with MT and has supplied an object for יִמְצָאוּ. In both these respects Rashi and Kimchi follow Targ.: Rashi supplies שְׂכַר פְּעוּלָתָם ('the wages which they deserve').

There are two figures in v. 18: one is indicative of a violent dislodgement of the Judaeans from their land and links up with אֹסְפִי מֵאֶרֶץ כְּנַעְתֵּךְ in v. 17; the other suggests severe and sustained pressure. Yahweh will squeeze the life out of his people, using the kind of pressure with which one extracts every drop of moisture from a cloth.

Jerusalem and Judah are broken beyond recovery and sick beyond cure; or we may say rather that the prophet Jeremiah takes to himself the shattered body politic and experiences the reality of it as his own pain and incurable sickness (v. 19). Rudolph holds that v. 19b is indicative of a misjudgement by the community about the nature of the sickness and a dismissing of it as something which will pass: 'It is no more than a sickness which I can bear'. On this view the voice of the prophet is not heard until v. 21. A similar interpretation is found in Kimchi who relates v. 19 to v. 20 in such a way that v. 20 serves to belie the hope that the sickness is one from which Judah will recuperate: 'I thought that I could endure the sickness but it has turned out otherwise, (for) my tents are knocked down...'. Calvin considered a similar though not identical view and dismissed it. The correct sense of v. 19b is rather that indicated by KJV ('I must bear it'), Lowth ('But then I endeavoured to compose myself, and patiently submit to God's afflicting hand'), Duhm (*Und ich muss ihn tragen*) and NEB ('But this is my plight, I said, and I must endure it'). Driver (*JQR* 28, p. 108) is suspicious of the text and suggests אֵי כָזֶה for אַךְ זֶה, 'But I said, "Where is sickness such as this that I should bear it?"' In other words, 'Could I have been required to endure a more grievous

sickness than this?' The sense is rather that there is no escape
from this time of suffering and despair (incurable sickness), and
what is then indicated is a tragic acceptance of the inevitable.
The sickness of the community is unto death and the prophet
feels it as his sickness. There is nothing to be done except to
endure it.

In the first stich of v. 20 (cf. below, p. 233, on v. 19) Sept.^{BS}
reads ἡ σκηνή σου ἐταλαιπώρησεν ὤλετο, καὶ πᾶσαι αἱ δέρρεις
σου διεσπάσθησαν, and this has to be taken with the text of
Sept.^{BS} in v. 19, where the speaker (Jeremiah) is differentiated
from 2nd person sing. objects (the community). The remainder
of v. 20 in Sept.^{BS} has 1st person sing. suffixes, and for the first
stich Ziegler (*Beiträge*, p. 94) departs from Sept.^{BS}, as he did in
v. 19. שדד is rendered by both ἐταλαιπώρησεν and ὤλετο (cf.
Janzen, p. 26). Further, Sept. οἱ υἱοί μου καὶ τὰ πρόβατά μου οὐκ
εἰσίν represents בני וצאני אינם over against MT בני יצאני ואינם.
The Greek appears to be derived from בְּנֵי וצֹאני אינם and it
might be supposed that this is a corruption of בְּנֵי צוֹני אינם, 'The
sheep of my flock are no more'. The strength of the suggestion
lies in the circumstance that there is a figurative use of shepherds
(='rulers') in v. 21. יצאני is explained by Rashi as יצאו ממני and
Kimchi similarly elucidates the grammar by citing two
examples: the normal כי חזק ממני (2 Kgs 3.26) and a case where
the מן is suppressed, חזקתני ותוכל (Jer 20.7). The function of מן
in these examples is, however, comparative, and different from
its function in 'have departed (from) me'.

The ruined tent and severed tent ropes are indicative of a
disaster proleptically experienced, to which there will be no
quick reaction, and no possibility of speedy reconstruction and
rehabilitation will emerge. The prophet makes the community
speak these words not because it is aware of such a hard destiny
but because he knows and feels that this is the future which will
eventuate. 'Sons' will go away—disappear into the oblivion of
exile.

Those who rule the country ('shepherds'='kings', according to
Targ.) are totally lacking in discernment (v. 21) and make their
decisions without reference to Yahweh: ואת יהוה לא דרשו means
that they take no steps to avail themselves of Yahweh's
guidance. They assume that in the area of statesmanship they
are the experts and that a prophet has nothing to say about
critical, political decisions or issues of national leadership. For
this reason they have no success in government (Rashi, לא
הצליחו במלכותם; cf. Kimchi who cites 1 Sam 18.14, ויהי דוד
לכל דרכו משכיל) and fail to safeguard the integrity and
well-being of the community (see, W. McKane, *PWM*,
pp. 65ff.). The flock has not been cared for by the shepherds and

as a consequence is scattered: the community has not been well guided and educated by its leaders and will suffer the fate (or, has suffered the fate—if v. 21 is comment after the event) of dispersion and exile (see below, p. 234).

Verse 22 is an anticipation of invasion so intense that it is felt to be already in progress. שמועה is 'report', 'news', rather than 'noise', 'din' (so Sept. φωνὴ ἀκοῆς and Vulg. *vox auditionis*). Hence קול שמועה is not synonymous with רעש גדול: the sense is not 'There is the sound of approaching noise, the thunder of a great army advancing from the north', but 'News is coming through, the thunder of a great army is drawing nearer from the north'. The end is near; hostile forces are converging on the towns of Judah which will be devastated, and abandoned by their human inhabitants to become the homes of jackals (for תנים see 9.10, above p. 205). σειρηνων 'singing birds' (Aq. and Symm. cf. Theod. δρακοντων) has to be classed with Sept. στρουθῶν.

Verse 23 is a reflection on human incapacity which issues in the confession of v. 24. The 'I' of v. 23 is not to be differentiated from the 'I' of vv. 19–20 and v. 24 (see below, p. 234) Man may plan the course of his life, but he does not have the power to command circumstances to bend to his purpose (cf. Prov 16.9). Only if Yahweh assists him will his intentions be confirmed and the way opened up for him. והכין should be construed as an infinitive absolute (GK 72z) co-ordinated with a participle (*pace* Rudolph), and the sense is then as indicated above. Rashi correctly interprets MT, 'There is not in any man's grasp the power to establish his way successfully'. Similarly Kimchi: a man does not have the power to establish his steps, for he does not know what he will meet and does not have the capacity to prepare himself for it.

Rudolph, Bright and NEB (Brockington, p. 202) prefer the 1st person plur. suffixes in v. 24 which are indicated by Sept. (ἡμᾶς), but MT should be retained (see below, p. 234). Verse 24 is an implicit confession of sin and an acknowledgement of the need for correction. It is a plea for equity rather than for mercy and clemency (cf. Rashi who glosses במשפט with ביסורין). Yahweh's reaction should be a controlled one; if it goes beyond the bounds of what justice requires, it may not stop short of the destruction of the people. Rashi observes that the danger of over-reaction is כלייה 'annihilation' and Kimchi similarly supplements פן תמעטני with מחיות גוי.

Rudolph and Bright suppose that 10.17 was once stitched to 9.21 (אספי — מאסף) and that the stitch has been broken by the insertion of 9.22–10.16. Even if this were so it would amount to something less than a demonstration that there was a significant or necessary continuity between 9.21 and 10.17ff. Hence the unit on which attention has now to be focused is 10.17–24. Verse 25, which approximates to Ps 79.6f., is an insensitive addition which seems to presuppose that both Israel and Judah (יעקב a comprehensive term) have been dispersed and dismembered (כי אכלו את יעקב). It is a call for divine retribution against nations which do not worship Yahweh (אשר בשמך לא קראו) and whose lives are not shaped by a commitment to him (אשר לא ידעוך). There is an implied opposition of Jewish piety and the impiety of the גוים, and there is a demand for vindication. ואכלהו is not represented by Sept., is absent from the Hebrew text of Ps 79.7 and should be deleted (cf. Janzen, pp. 11, 190 n. 3).

In v. 17 the prophet tells the besieged inhabitants of Jerusalem to gather their luggage into a bundle and prepare themselves for deportation. He then transmits to them a message from Yahweh that they will be forcibly ejected from their own land and will suffer consequent privations (הצרותי in v. 18 echoes מצור in v. 17). There is doubt about the identity of the speaker in vv. 19–24. According to Rudolph vv. 19–20 constitute a communal lament, with the community personified as an 'I' vv. 21–22 are spoken by Jeremiah and vv. 23–24 are a prayer of Jeremiah. Bright follows Kimchi's view that Jeremiah is the speaker throughout and describes vv. 19–20 as 'a soliloquy by Jeremiah'. Nicholson supposes that the communal lament runs from v. 19 to v. 22. The only factor common to these three accounts is that they all take vv. 23–24 as a prayer of Jeremiah.

According to Sept.[BS], also the text which Ziegler prefers, Jeremiah distinguishes himself clearly from the community in v. 19, but in Ziegler's text he does proceed to identify himself with his people, saying that their wounds are his wounds. This is a bridge to v. 20, where (in Ziegler's text) a distinction between prophet and community is obliterated. Jerome cites Sept. v. 19a as *vae super contritione tua, pessima plaga tua* and remarks: 'According to the Hebrew Jerusalem herself speaks as one who is greatly afflicted and suffers incurable wounds; according to LXX it is the prophet who speaks to Jerusalem and commiserates with her over her injuries and wounds.'

Verse 22 is a key to the proper understanding of vv. 19–25 according to Reventlow (pp. 196–199). It contains a reference to the enemy from the north, but this has a mythological-liturgical character and is not a reference to a specific, historical threat. The vocabulary of v. 19 is medical (מכתי ; נחלה ; שברי) and is associated with the individual lament, but v. 20 shows that the subject matter is communal stresses and not the personal problems of the prophet Jeremiah. Verse 23 again has the appearance of an individual lament, but תמעטני (v. 24) must refer to the diminishment of the community and v. 25 has a

collective reference. The function discharged by Jeremiah in
vv. 19–25 (so Reventlow, pp. 200–205) is that of an intercessor.
The prophet represents the people and is inseparable from them
when he confronts Yahweh as their representative. Only in this
sense is the 'I' who appears in these verses an individual 'I': we
are told about Jeremiah's condition only in so far as his
solidarity with his people is complete and he is inseparable from
them. Reventlow rejects Condamin's view that there is a
dialogue between prophet and people and he makes Jeremiah do
all the speaking. It is then a dialogue only because we are asked
to believe that Jeremiah wears one cap (that of intercessor)
while he speaks vv. 19–20, changes his cap to become Yahweh's
spokesman before he utters v. 21, and puts on the first cap again
before he utters vv. 22–25.

We must attribute vv. 19–24 either to Jeremiah, or to a first
person singular personification of the community, although such
a distinction is perhaps more apparent than real. On any
reckoning v. 21 follows badly from the preceding verses. There is
an aesthetic conflict between emotionally charged utterance and
the motive clause of v. 21a which introduces a more deliberate
kind of rationalizing and indictment. It raises the question
whether v. 21 is not a secondary contribution. It is dubious
whether there is a good case for following Sept. (so Rudolph,
Bright, NEB) in v. 24 and substituting 1st per. plur. suffixes for
the 1st per. sing. suffixes of MT. The difference betwen MT and
Sept. (as in v. 19) is probably exegetical rather than textual in
significance. Sept. distinguishes more clearly between Jeremiah
and those for whom he prays. MT leaves us with a more
mysterious relation between prophet and community, an
identification of prophet and community so complete that no
distinction can be enforced. In all the circumstances it seems
best to conclude that vv. 23–24 should be interpreted in the same
way as vv. 19–20 and that the 1st person sing. form is indicative
of the completeness of the prophet's identification with his
community. It follows that Cornill's suggestion (followed by
Ehrlich, p. 272, and Rudolph) that יָדַעְתִּי (v. 23) should be
emended to יָדַעְתָּ is mistaken.

The passage is charged with the impressions of a mind
stretched by great tensions and thronged with invading images.
There is no response and no assured literary continuity here; only
the assault on the mind of a series of impressions: a cry of
anguish in vv. 19–20, an imagining of the beginning of an
invasion in v. 22, reflection in v. 23 and a prayer in v. 24. Is
Jeremiah speaking in sober, pedestrian terms about the
beginning of an invasion, or does he (as the description of v. 22
already given suggests) pre-empt the event, as one who was both

a prophet and a poet might well do? Does he pre-empt it in the
sense that he translates the premonition of its certainty into a
description of its launching?

The model to which the elements in vv. 19–24 best relate is
perhaps that of the individual lament (cf. S. Mowinckel, *The
Psalms in Israel's Worship*, 2, pp. 1–25). But it should be made
clear that the argument which is being conducted is not one
which reaches Reventlow's destination: the prophet's
individuality and singularity are not destroyed by the
circumstance that his concern for his people is so total. On the
contrary this is a testimony to the exceptional nature of his
individuality, the fineness of his spiritual texture. We may not
describe the structure of this passage too nicely, but we can say
that only an individual who had made the community's
brokenness his own could have spoken like this, and that at this
level of appreciation the distinction between the voice of
Jeremiah and the voice of the community must disappear.
Reventlow's mistake is in supposing that the community with
which Jeremiah identified himself, one broken and near to death,
would have been acknowledged by the empirical community as
none other than itself. He does not do justice to the profundity
and rarity of the prophet's insight. Calvin touches on this in his
comment on v. 19, 'We must then bear in mind that the prophet
speaks here not according to the feeling which the people had,
for they were so stupefied that they felt nothing, but that he
speaks of what they ought to have felt.'

CHAPTER XI

COVENANT DISOBEDIENCE BRINGS JUDGEMENT (11.1–14)

¹Jeremiah received this word from Yahweh.¹ ³These are the words of Yahweh, God of Israel: Cursed be the man who does not obey the terms of this covenant ⁴which I laid on your forefathers, when I brought them out of Egypt, out of the smelting-furnace. I said: Obey me and do² all that I bid you, that you may be my people and I may be your God; ⁵that the oath which I swore to your forefathers to give them a land flowing with milk and honey may be fulfilled. This is how matters stand to-day. I answered: So be it Yahweh. ⁶Yahweh said to me: Proclaim all these words in the towns of Judah and the streets of Jerusalem: Hear the terms of this covenant and fulfil them. ⁷I solemnly and urgently warned your forefathers to obey me from the day I brought them out of Egypt up to the present time, ⁸but they were heedless and regardless, following their own stubborn and evil inclinations, and so I brought on their heads all the terms of this covenant to which I required obedience and which they did not fulfil. ⁹Yahweh said to me: A conspiracy has been disclosed among the men of Judah and the inhabitants of Jerusalem. ¹⁰They have returned to the sins of their earliest forefathers; they have refused to attend to my words and have gone after alien gods and worshipped them; Israel and Judah have broken my covenant which I made with their forefathers. ¹¹Therefore, these are the words of Yahweh: I am about to bring on them a disaster which they will not be able to escape; they will cry out to me, but I will give no heed to them. ¹²Then the towns of Judah and the inhabitants of Jerusalem will cry out to the gods to whom they have made sacrifices, but they will be powerless to save them in their time of disaster. ¹³You have as many gods as you have towns, O Judah, and the altars which you have set up to sacrifice to Baal³ are as numerous as the streets of Jerusalem. ¹⁴But you are not to pray for this people; you are not to call out in prayer on their behalf, for I will give no heed when you cry out⁴ to me because of the disaster which has overtaken them.

Verses 1–5 and 6–8 have a similar theme and the second could be described as a variation on the theme of the first. They are constituted by a call to obey את דברי הברית הזאת and are associated with an account of the nature and function of this in relation to the entire sweep of the history of Yahweh's people. There are, however, formal differences between vv. 1–5 and 6–8: the first is spoken by Yahweh to Jeremiah and the prophet is asked to give his assent to the curse which is laid on those who do not keep the terms of the covenant. The second is a word received by Jeremiah from Yahweh for transmission to the people.

According to v. 2 Jeremiah is addressed by Yahweh in the plural (שמעו) and MT is no doubt seeking to reduce the area of

---

¹ Deleting שמעו ... אליהם (see below, p. 237).

² Deleting אותם (see below, pp. 237f.).

³ Deleting מזבחות לבשת (see below, p. 240).

⁴ Reading קראך (see below, p. 240).

this difficulty by pointing וֹדברתם as וֹדִבַּרְתֶּם. וֹדִבַּרְתֶּם is indicated by Vulg. (*loquimini*) and Targ. (וֹתמללוןֹ). Sept. renders the Hebrew as καὶ λαλήσεις and Pesh. as *w'mr* (sing. imperative), apparently representing וֹדִבַּרְתָּ. Hence Sept. and Pesh. (Codex Ambrosianus) reproduce the mixture of plural and singular which is indicated by the Massoretes, but in the Peshitta edition of Urmia (1852), both verbs are shown as singular. These adjustments of the Hebrew text, of which only the last-mentioned produces a verse altogether consistent with an address to Jeremiah, are indications of the difficulty which was felt with v. 2 (cf. Ehrlich, p. 272). Even so, the coherence of vv. 1–5 is not achieved, unless it is supposed (Volz) that אמן יהוה (v. 5) means 'I will carry out your command and transmit this message'. This is an incorrect construction to put on אמן יהוה which, in view of Deut 27.15–26, must be regarded simply as Jeremiah's assent to the curse uttered by Yahweh in v. 3.

The nucleus of these verses is a curse uttered by Yahweh (v. 3) to which Jeremiah responds with אמן יהוה (v. 5); the historical retrospect contained in vv. 4–5 has the effect of setting the response at a distance from the pronouncing of the curse. This suggests that the parenthesis may have the character of secondary elaboration (cf. Skinner, pp. 98, 101), but there is no textual support for this conjecture. Hence v. 2 and the opening words of v. 3 (ואמרת אליהם) are an addition which betrays a misunderstanding of the nature of vv. 3–5 and should be deleted (so Rudolph). Verse 4 is a word of admonition and exhortation spoken by Yahweh to the fathers in the past. On the assumption that Jeremiah is being addressed and that Yahweh has launched into a historical retrospect at the beginning of v. 4, the only inconcinnity is אבותיכם which ought to be אבותיך (*pace* Thiel, p. 148). It is likely, however, as already indicated, that we have to reckon here with an insertion which has broken an immediate connection between את דברי הברית הזאת and ואמר אמן יהוה. The best that can be done is tolerate אבותיכם and to attempt to accommodate vv. 4–5 (up to כיום הזה) with the interpretation of vv. 1, 3–5 indicated above: only Jeremiah is addressed and so it is Jeremiah who responds.

The reminiscence in vv. 4–5 is linked to את דברי הברית הזאת (v. 3) and establishes that the forefathers of the nation were bound in terms of this covenant at the time of their deliverance from Egypt. What then follows is the actual words which were used when this obligation was laid on them (שמעו . . . וֹדבש).

אותם (v. 4) is not represented by Sept. and Vulg. (cf. Janzen, p. 39); Pesh. ('*ntwn*) represents אַתֶּם. It should be deleted. Israel's acceptance of Yahweh's demands will effectively establish a covenant relationship between the two parties and the

objective is the implementation of the solemn promise made to
the patriarchs. Hence the 'fathers' (אבותיכם) of v. 4, who are
the generation delivered from Egypt, are not identical with the
'fathers' of v. 5, who are the patriarchs. Addressing the
generation of the Exodus Yahweh indicates that the objective of
the ברית which he is concluding with them is the
implementation of the solemn promise which he made to the
patriarchs. This association of Israel's possession of Canaan with
the promise to the patriarchs is found in J (Exod 13.5; 33.3), in
Deuteronomy (11.9; 26.15; 31.20), Josh 5.6 and Jer 32.22
(another prose passage). The words כיום הזה are not part of the
reproduction of Yahweh's address to the generation of the
Exodus: their function is to relate Yahweh's statement to those
who had been delivered from Egypt with the subsequent
unfolding of Israel's history. The shape of Israel's future was
wholly determined by the circumstance that Yahweh's promise
to the Exodus generation was made good.

In v. 6 Jeremiah receives a message for his contemporaries
from Yahweh. He has to proclaim the terms of the covenant in
the towns of Judah and the streets of Jerusalem and to require
obedience to them. If the historical reminiscence (vv. 7–8*),
which is not represented by Sept., is ignored (cf. Janzen,
pp. 39f.), all that follows is the simple statement by Jeremiah
(v. 8) that his preaching had no effect (ולא עשו). The transition
from ועשיתם אותם (v. 6) to ולא עשו (v. 9) is not so harsh as has
been represented (Cornill). The circumstance that we have to
assume that the grammatical subject of עשו is those addressed
by the prophet, on whose response he reports, is not unduly
difficult. Where it is supposed that the shorter Greek text is the
consequence not of accident but of deliberate abridgement of
MT, the discussion becomes speculative and Thiel (pp. 149f.)
offers one suggestion after another to explain the shorter Greek
text. The explanation which is nearest to hand is, perhaps, the
best one, namely, that the translator had a Hebrew text in which
vv. 7–8 (except for ולא עשו) were not represented (so Streane,
Duhm). The residual doubt is whether אשר צויתי לעשות ולא
עשו is not all of a piece. At any rate the function of vv. 7–8 is to
establish that from the time of the Exodus up to the present
Yahweh, through his (prophetic) spokesmen, has unremittingly
and urgently laid on his people the necessity of obedience to the
terms of the covenant. Despite these solemn representations they
have a record of unrelieved apostasy.

A further reason why vv. 7–8 might be suspected is that they
represent Yahweh's judgement as already complete (וָאָבִיא
עֲלֵיהֶם) and in this respect contrast with v. 11 (הנני מביא עליהם).
The weight attaching to this observation depends on the kind of

unity and cumulative wholeness which is claimed for vv. 1–14.
The expressions used in vv. 8 and 11 represent doom or
judgement as the operation of the curse which follows
non-fulfilment of the terms of the ברית. Thus Rashi comments
on v. 8, 'The curses (אלות) which are laid down in the ברית with
respect to the words which I commanded them to do and they
refused to do' (also Kimchi). If this is a correct understanding of
v. 8, it is impossible to make a convincing unit out of vv. 6–8.
Despite כי (v. 7) vv. 7–8 do not supply reasons for obedience to
Yahweh's word. Instead they portray a long history of apostasy
extending to the present which has finally made the curses of the
covenant operative against Yahweh's people. The indication
which this gives is that the concern which is expressed in these
verses is not that a judgement still in the future should be
avoided but that a judgement which lies in the past should be
further elucidated. To this extent Thiel (pp. 139ff.) should be
followed.

The context of קשר (v. 9) in other Old Testament passages (2
Sam 15.12; 1 Kgs 16.20; 2 Kgs 11.14; 12.21; 14.19; 15.15, 30) is
political: it is associated with the overthrow of government, and
in Jer 11.9 the political model of 'conspiracy' is used to elucidate
the nature of Judah's insubordination in relation to Yahweh. In
v. 10 קשר is defined as a relapse to sins of earlier generations
(אבותם הראשנים) and this suggests a reformation which
effected an improvement for a time but which did not last. Since
11.7ff. envisages a longer history of apostasy, it is likely that
Kimchi's exegesis of אבותם הראשנים (the generations of Amon,
Manasseh and Ahaz) is too restrictive. The phrase alludes rather
to the entire history of apostasy from which the community was
rescued by the reform of Josiah. Once again they have resumed
their idolatrous worship of אלהים אחרים and have broken the
ברית which Yahweh concluded with their fathers (v. 10).

The deletion of ובית ישראל (a reference to the Northern
Kingdom) would improve the cohesiveness of vv. 9–10, but there
is no textual evidence to support it. The קשר of v. 9 is found
specifically באיש יהודה ובישבי ירושלם. Without ובית ישראל we
could conclude that ברית (v. 10), as in the earlier verses of the
chapter, refers to the law code on which Josiah's reformation
was based (Deuteronomy), although this is not to be envisaged
as a ברית wholly distinguishable from the Sinai covenant. With
the extant form of MT there appears a more general reference to
a history of apostasy involving both Northern and Southern
Kingdoms and את ברית אשר כרתי את אבותם would then refer
more naturally to the Sinai covenant.

Yahweh's threat issued against his people follows the
indictment in vv. 9–10. They will not be able to avoid the disaster

which is about to fall on them and their prayers for deliverance will have no effect. The inhabitants of Judah and Jerusalem will appeal to the gods to whom they offer their idolatrous worship, but they will find that these gods can afford them no effective help when disaster looms over them (vv. 11–12). Judah has as many altars on which she offers sacrifices to Baal as there are towns in her territory or as there are streets in Jerusalem (v. 13). Sept. does not represent מזבחות לבשת and Janzen (p. 12) suggests that MT is conflate, the variants being (a) מזבחות לבשת and (b) מזבחות לקטר לבעל. This is the right kind of conclusion: it is clear that בשת is a theologically motivated modification of בעל and מזבחות לקטר לבעל is an expansion (so Janzen) of an original מזבחות לבעל.

Yahweh turns to his prophet (v. 14) and forbids him to exercise his function as an intercessor. Just as the prayers of the people to Yahweh will effect nothing, so he must not suppose that he can change the course of events. This exegesis assumes that קראם should be emended to קראך (cf. Jer 7.16, כי אינני אל תתפלל בעד קראם אלי :שמע אתך): בעת קראם אלי is inconsequential after העם הזה. בעת רעתם, which is the reading of many Hebrew manuscripts over against MT בעד רעתם, is represented by Sept., Vulg., Pesh. and Targ. Good sense can be had either way: the versions may have been influenced by the commonness of בעת רעתם.

The arguments which are connected with the assertion that the prose of the book of Jeremiah is sixth century prose reach out to more particular conclusions, namely, that, for the most part, this prose is attributable to the prophet Jeremiah (H. Weippert, *BZAW* 132, 1973). But her success in establishing that prose in the book of Jeremiah does not have Deuteronomic or Deuteronomistic affiliations can never amount to a demonstration that the prophet Jeremiah is the author of that prose (see above, p. 165). The contents of the book cannot be squeezed into the period of the ministry of the historical prophet Jeremiah and attributed to him for the most part. The composition of the book has to be understood as a much longer process of untidy accumulation which eventually produced the book of Jeremiah as we have it. This was not a process subject to rational control or dictated by a master-plan; it was too haphazard to be recoverable in all its details.

The nature of the conflict between Thiel and Weippert in their different approaches to the prose of the book of Deuteronomy has been indicated in connection with chapter 7 (above, pp. 165f.). Thiel can win his argument by adducing parallels in Deuteronomy and the Deuteronomistic literature, but he does not concede defeat, as Weippert thinks he ought, in the absence

of these, because he can fall back on prose passages in the book
of Jeremiah with common features of vocabulary and style
which are held by him to be marks of D (pp. 142–155).

The following examples from Weippert will show the different
tendency of her observations:

(a) Jer 11.4 (31.32; 34.13) is distinguished from Deut 29.24
and 1 Kgs 8.21 by the additional element ביום and by the use of
את instead of עם. In the case of 11.4 את is the accusative particle
not the preposition, and is associated with צויתי not כרתי
(pp. 98f.; cf. Thiel, pp. 142f.).

(b) All the occurrences of השכם (v. 7) are in the prose of the
book of Jeremiah, except for 2 Chr 26.15, and this lexical
element cannot be used as evidence of Deuteronomistic
influence. Its absence from Deuteronomistic contexts is more
significant than its absence from the poetry of the book of
Jeremiah, because it belongs to a word-string more appropriate
to prose than to poetry (pp. 123–126).

(c) There are (v. 8) 8 occurrences of לא שמע + לא הטה in the
prose of the book of Jeremiah. Something similar is found in 2
Kgs 19.16 (=Isa 37.17) and Ps 17.6, but the verbs in these
passages are positive, the order is different (הטה + שמע) and the
mode is imperative (pp. 127–129).

(d) אלהים אחרים (v. 10) has Deuteronomic-Deuteronomistic
connections and is not distinctive Jeremianic vocabulary, but, in
comparing the Deuteronomic-Deuteronomistic occurrences, on
the one hand, and Judg 2.12, 19, 1 Kgs 11.10 and the 7
occurrences in the book of Jeremiah on the other, it should not
simply be assumed that the Deuteronomic-Deuteronomistic
occurrences are prior. Weippert shows that אחרי + הלך + a
substitution for אלהים אחרים (בעלים or הבל or the like) occurs
in the poetry of the book of Jeremiah (2.5, 8, 23, 25). Since
Jeremiah and the Deuteronomists made common cause in their
battle against the אלהים אחרים, it is not surprising that they
shared the same vocabulary (pp. 215–222).

Aspects of Thiel's rigour are admirable, but it is important not
to allow one's judgement to be smothered by the weight of his
detail. He has not established convincingly that vv. 1–14 have a
degree of coherence which entitles them to be regarded as a
planned composition. The circumstance that ברית appears at
different places (vv. 2, 3, 7, 8,10) is insufficient to achieve this
demonstration (cf. Thiel, p. 152), and if it is described as a
'stitch-word', this rather suggests that the stitches are made by a
succession of different people. There are, however, more
important and decisive considerations. Even with the deletion
which he makes in v. 2, he has not shown vv. 1–5 to be a coherent
unit, nor can they be on his terms, unless אמן has a different

sense from the one which he holds to be correct (p. 142; see
above, p. 237). Again, with this understanding of אמן vv. 1–5,
the integration of vv. 1–5 with vv. 6–8, in which Jeremiah is
given a message to proclaim, is less impressive than Thiel would
have us believe. At v. 8, as Thiel observes, judgement is a past
event, but a backward jump is taken in v. 11 and judgement is
viewed in the imminent future. His account of D's operation in
vv. 11–13 (pp. 153–155) is particularly perverse, because he
invites us to believe that this editor modified Judg 10.13f. to suit
his purposes, but did not modify Jer 2.28 and so produced an
uneven passage. But if he was capable of modifying one passage
why did he not modify the other and get his syntax right? Hence
the observation that vv. 11–13 have a conflate character is a
lame explanation of their unevenness in view of the freedom
which D is said to have exercised with one member of the
conflation. Moreover, the case for Judg 10.13f. as a source for
vv. 11–12 is far from decisive: there is a resemblance, but it is
not so close as to create a probability that it was a source.

Verses 1–14 are more fragmentary than Thiel allows. The
oscillating character of the passage and the manner in which it
returns on itself invites the assumption that it has been built up
by supplementations of themes which were present but less
developed in the pre-existing part of the text. Thus exegesis of
the nature of the disobedience to the demands of the covenant
(vv. 3–4, 7–8) seems called for and this is spelled out as idolatry
in vv. 9–10. The theme of judgement, present in v. 8 as
judgement already executed, is resumed in v. 11, attaching itself
to the foregoing allegations of idolatry. It becomes judgement
which is about to fall and the 'too late' motif of Jer 2.27f. is
elaborated. It is too late to seek help from Yahweh, and when
Judah and Jerusalem call out to him, they will get no response;
when they apply to the gods to whom they have devoted
themselves, they will find that these gods are powerless to help.
Nor can the prophet help, for Yahweh has forbidden him to
exercise his function as an intercessor.

Thiel has suggested in connection with נמצא (v. 9), מאן
(v. 10) and מספר עריך היו אלהיך יהודה (v. 13) that the poetry of
the book of Jeremiah may be a reservoir for the vocabulary of
the prose. This is a matter which has been treated by Holladay
(*JBL* 79, 1960, pp. 351–367), and there are two items in
vv. 1–14 which deserve fuller consideration:
(*a*) 11.11–13 makes use of the ideas and vocabulary of 2.27c–28
and 14.8. In a confession of faith, occurring within a prayer for
mercy and help, Jahweh is described as מקוה ישראל מושיעו בעת
צרה (14.8). The association of 'safety' and 'time of distress' also
occurs in 2.27c–28, where another element, Judah's addiction to

other gods, is also present. In their time of distress (בעת רעתם)
Yahweh's people appeal to him for help (קומו והושיענו). There
follows in v. 13 a longer version of 2.28b, 'For you have as many
gods as you have towns, O Judah, and the altars which you have
set up to make offerings to Baal are as numerous as the streets of
Jerusalem.' The author of the prose has excerpted from 2.28b
and has gone one better than the poet by introducing a second
comparison between the number of streets in Jerusalem and the
altars which had been erected to Baal (see above, p. 47).

(b) In connection with מקטרים להם (v. 12) M. Weippert has
argued (p. 25, pp. 218–22) that the contexts of the Piel of קטר in
the Deuteronomistic literature are clearly distinguishable from
those in the prose of the book of Jeremiah. The argument is that
the Deuteronomistic uses are all related to the doctrine of the
single, legitimate sanctuary, and that the במות to which
reference is made are Yahwistic sanctuaries which, in terms of
this doctrine, are illegitimate. As such they are to be
differentiated from במות which are centres of idolatrous
worship—shrines of אלהים אחרים. The neatness of this
distinction hangs on the assumption that 4 occurrences of קטר in
the book of Kings are pre-Deuteronomistic (2 Kgs 18.4; 22.17;
23.5, 8). There are two further occurrences of קטר in the book of
Kings which cast doubt on the distinction which Weippert seeks
to make. According to 2 Kgs 16.1ff. the behaviour of Ahaz did
not meet with Yahweh's approval and in this regard he did not
follow David, his forefather. He followed the practices of the
kings of Israel (the northern kingdom) and engaged in the
abominable Canaanite ritual of passing his son through the fire.
He offered sacrifice (ויקטר) on the במות and under every green
tree. Even if we accept that v. 2 has a meaning not essentially
different from 2 Kgs 14.4 and refers to a failure to enforce the
law of the single sanctuary, there can be no doubt that vv. 3–4
point to idolatrous worship and not just to the illegitimate
worship of Yahweh. 2 Kgs 17.9–11 deals with the inhabitants of
the northern kingdom. Their deeds were not acceptable to
Yahweh: they built במות in all their towns; they set up מצבות
and אשרים on every high hill and under every green tree. They
offered sacrifice at all the במות (ויקטרו שם בכל במות) after the
manner of the peoples whom Yahweh drove out of Canaan for
their benefit. Here again it is certain that קטר is used in a
context of idolatrous worship.

In addition to the precise indications in 1.16 (ויקטרו לאלהים
אחרים) and 18.15 (לשוא יקטרו) that this vocabulary is used in
Jeremianic poetry, there is plentiful evidence in the poetry that
the theme of harlotry (that is, idolatry and apostasy) exercised
Jeremiah strenuously. The use of קטר in connection with אלהים

אחרים or the like is found in the poetry of Jeremiah and in the Deuteronomistic literature, but the occurrences of קמר in the prose of the book of Jeremiah should perhaps be regarded more precisely as a feature of the inner development and growth of that corpus which is now the book of Jeremiah rather than more generally as a case of Deuteronomistic influence. In other words vocabulary which is already present in the poetry generates a fuller treatment in the prose.

Rudolph's contention (also Weiser) that the ברית which is in view in chapter 11 is the Sinai covenant rather than Deuteronomy is founded on the circumstance that את דברי הברית הזאת is further defined as אשר צויתי את אבותיכם ביום הוציאי אותם מארץ מצרים (v. 4). We have seen (above, p. 239) that Kimchi associated the ברית of this chapter with Josiah's reform, and so with Deuteronomy, and Duhm has no doubt that the intention is to represent that Jeremiah played a leading part in the Deuteronomic movement. The latter assumption is denied by Thiel (pp. 146–148) who, nevertheless, is convinced that the ברית of chapter 11 is Deuteronomy. The antithesis of Sinai covenant and Deuteronomy on which Rudolph's case rests is, according to Thiel, a false one. Thiel holds that the tendency of the portrayal in 11.1–14 is abstract and theological and that it does not have the concreteness assumed by those who find in it an intention to represent the prophet Jeremiah as a Deuteronomic preacher. Its concern is rather with the alternatives of blessing and curse which attach to different responses to the ברית — in Deuteronomistic thinking the equivalent of תורה.

Nicholson (*Preaching to the Exiles*, p. 67) similarly argues that the covenant made in Moab should be regarded as a filling out or enriching of the Sinai covenant. Apart from one passage in the book of Exodus (ספר הברית, 14.7; כל הדברים האלה, 14.8; cf. Kimchi) the terminology is concentrated in the book of Deuteronomy and the Deuteronomistic literature:

(a) דברי הברית (הזאת) in Deut 28.69, 29.8 and 2 Kgs 23.3.

(b) הברית (לחות) לוחת in Deut 9.9, 11, 15.

(c) כבל אלות הברית in Deut 29.20. Rashi has this in mind when he takes ואביא עליהם את כל דברי הברית הזאת (Jer 11.8) as a reference to the curses (אלות) associated with the ברית.

(d) את כל דברי ספר הברית (2 Kgs 23.2) and ספר הברית הזה (2 Kgs 23.21; cf. Exod 24.7).

A further exact indication of the connection of Jer 11.1–14 with Deuteronomist and Deuteronomistic vocabulary is the metaphor כור הברזל. This is unusual and striking and it is found elsewhere only in Deut 4.20 and 1 Kgs 8.51. It functions similarly in all three passages:

(a) ‏ביום הוציאי אותם מארץ מצרים מכור הברזל‏ (Jer 11.4)
(b) ‏ויוצא אתכם מכור הברזל ממצרים‏ (Deut 4.20)
(c) ‏אשר הוצאת ממצרים מתוך כור הברזל‏ (1 Kgs 8.51)

It is correctly explained by Kimchi: just as gold and silver are
refined in a furnace, the hardships endured by the Israelites in
Egypt were a testing and refining process. The metaphor is an
important   clue   to   the   Deuteronomic-Deuteronomistic
connections of ‏ברית‏ in Jer 11.1–14

Also decisive is the more general circumstance that Jeremiah
qua prophet of doom is portrayed according to a
Deteronomic-Deuteronomistic theology of prophecy. The
prophet's task is to represent urgently to the people the demands
which are laid on them in virtue of the Mosaic covenant: the
blessing which flows from obedience and the curse which flows
from disobedience. Hence Yahweh's curse (v. 3) to which the
prophet replies ‏אמן יהוה‏ (v. 5; cf. Deut 27.15–26), and in v. 8 the
onset of judgement, is interpreted as the operation of the curses
associated with the ‏דברי הברית‏. Why did Jeremiah's prophetic
ministry issue in doom rather than ‏שלום‏? The answer which is
given to this question is that the final disaster was the
culmination of a long history of apostasy; that Jeremiah, as
essentially a spokesman for the Mosaic covenant, confronted the
people with the alternatives of weal and woe, life and death; that
they refused to listen to his urgent appeals and by so doing
forfeited blessing and exposed themselves to curse.

There is a feeling here that only an exceptional and irrational
obduracy could put a prophet in a position where he was
unavoidably a prophet of doom. According to this view a prophet
is an intercessor between Yahweh and his people whose proper
function is to effect reconciliation and bring ‏שלום‏. This is what is
indicated by v. 14 (cf. 7.16; 14.11f.; 15.1). So the question which
is being asked by the Deuteronomistic theologians is: Why was
the community not saved by the effective intercession of
Jeremiah? The answer which is given is that Yahweh placed an
interdict on his function as an intercessor, and so he was denied
the prophetic power to plead for the life of the people (see above,
pp. 171f.).

We should conclude (*pace* Thiel) that there is an intention to
represent Jeremiah as active on behalf of the Deuteronomic
reform. Those who hold that the language of vv. 1–14 is
attributable to the prophet Jeremiah are relieved of all further
critical anguish, for in that case the interpretation which has to
be followed is one similar to that favoured by Kimchi, namely,
that vv. 1–14 deal with preaching activity of the prophet
Jeremiah in the reign of Jehoiakim, a period when there had
been a falling away from the objectives of Josiah's reform. A

modification of this view is represented by Bright (cf. Rudolph) who holds that the passage has come down to us in Deuteronomistic dress but that it, nevertheless, reflects accurately the activity and attitudes of the prophet Jeremiah in the reign of Jehoiakim.

A further modification is represented by Skinner (*Prophecy and Religion*, p. 101): there is a kernel attributable to the prophet Jeremiah (vv. 1, 3b, 5b, 6) and this accurately preserves 'a vivid, momentary experience of the prophet in which he stands revealed as wholly in sympathy with the aims of the Deuteronomic movement' (for the many variations of the 'kernel' see Thiel, p. 139 n. 4). But for the remainder of vv. 1–14, which has to be elucidated in terms of historical circumstances different from those of the prophet Jeremiah, an interpretation which assumes Deuteronomistic activity is appropriate. It is the possibility of disengaging such a Jeremianic kernel which Bright denies and in this he is followed by Nicholson (*Preaching to the Exiles*, p. 67). The latter, however, differs from Bright and resembles Skinner in so far as he finds more than one exegetical level in the passage. He is like Bright in urging that the text supplies information about the activities and attitudes of the historical prophet Jeremiah, but he postulates another level of exegesis whose significance lies in its disclosure of the attitudes and objectives of exilic traditionists, particularly, their concern to commend the Law to their own generation.

Thiel resembles Nicholson to the extent that his exegesis has an exilic background, but he differs from Nicholson in disengaging the passage entirely from the prophet Jeremiah. This disengagement is correct, but it is the most difficult matter of all to assign a passage of this kind to a particular date. How can we determine whether Duhm (post-exilic) or Thiel (exilic) is right? To sum up, the intention of vv. 1–14 is to represent that the prophet Jeremiah was actively engaged on behalf of the Deuteronomic measures of Josiah's reform and that he subscribed to a theology of prophecy which coincided with the Deuteronomic-Deuteronomistic one. The problem is then to explain why he was a prophet of doom. The reconciliation is achieved by representing that he was forbidden by Yahweh to intercede. But the passage has probably been built up in a quite unsystematic way by successive supplementations over an unknown period of time. Thus by its very nature it will defeat all attempts to date it or to explain its conceptual texture in terms of a particular period. It is not earlier than the exile (cf. v. 8), but otherwise its literary history cannot be recovered in detail.

UNWORTHY OF LOVE AND FIT FOR THE FIRE OF JUDGEMENT
(11.15–17)

[15]What right has my beloved[1] in my House?
She has been busy[2] with intrigues.
Can fattened animals[3] offered for sacrifice
enable you to escape[4] your impending doom?[5]
Then you would have reason for self-congratulation!
[16]'A luxuriant olive tree beautiful[6] to behold',
that was the name which Yahweh gave you.
When he kindles the flame,
it will ignite with a great roar
and its branches will be wrecked.
[17]Yahweh Sabaoth, who planted you, has threatened you with disaster
because of the wrong done by Israel and Judah: the offering of sacrifices to
Baal which they made to give me provocation.

Since it is the practice of Aq. and Symm. to translate literally
the Hebrew text which is before them, we can conclude that the
text which they had was more or less identical with our
problematic MT. We may begin with לידידי and ask whether
'beloved', used by Yahweh of his people, does not involve a
bridgegroom-bride or husband-wife figure, as in chapters 2 and
3. Driver (*JQR* 28, p. 111) argues that ידידי refers to עמי (cf.
v. 14) and he notes the rendering of Targ. (also Rashi), 'What is
the matter with my people who are beloved by me?' But the text
indicates clearly that the 'beloved' is envisaged as a woman and
the impression which is gained from Driver's reconstruction
(*JQR* 28, pp. 108–111) is that he made an initial, wrong decision
(defending ידידי) and then had to accept the consequences of it
by a wholesale alteration of feminine forms to masculine forms.

לידידי has to be accepted as anomalous or has to be emended
to לידידתי. The latter is indicated by Sept. (ἡ ἠγαπημένη) and
Pesh. (ḥbybty), and is adopted by Giesebrecht and Bright. It
should be said, however, that Aq. was following a Hebrew text
which had לידידי and that the Greek (Sept.) and Syriac
translators probably did not have a Hebrew text which differed
from MT. Rudolph emends מה לידידי to מה לי דודיך and
supposes a reference to baskets of first fruits which matches the
following mention of animal offerings. He urges that the figure
(Judah is Yahweh's Beloved) is incongruous in the context of a
threat.

[1] Reading לידידתי (see below, pp. 247f.).
[2] Reading עשתה (see below, p. 248).
[3] Reading הבריים (see below, p. 248).
[4] Reading יעברו as יַעֲבְרוּ (see below, pp. 248f.).
[5] Deleting כי (see below, pp. 248f.).
[6] Deleting פרי (see below, p. 249).

By asking the question מֶה לִידִידִי בְּבֵיתִי Yahweh is inferring that his people have forfeited their right to come into his presence and offer worship to him. The attitude which is expressed is a characteristically prophetic one, namely, that sacral or ritual zeal combined with a general disregard of Yahweh's moral demands is unacceptable. But there are grammatical (עֲשׂוֹתָהּ) and morphological (הַמְזִמָּתָה; cf. GK 90 g) obscurities. עֲשׂתָהּ (agreeing with a feminine 'beloved') is attested by many Hebrew manuscripts and is indicated by Sept. (ἐποίησεν) in association with ἡ ἠγαπημένη. Pesh. ('bdty) also matches a feminine 'beloved', 'You (fem.) have done'. Driver and Rudolph propose עָשִׂיתָ, 'You (masc.) have done'. A corruption of עֲשׂוֹתָהּ to עָשִׂיתָ is more easily explicable than a corruption of עֲשׂוֹתָהּ to עָשְׂתָהּ, but if עָשִׂיתָ is read, consequential changes from fem. to masc. forms have to be made and for this reason עָשְׂתָהּ should be adopted. Aq. Vulg. and Pesh. have attempted to construe הָרַבִּים with הַמְזִמָּתָה (taken as a plural form) and this is the grammar of Kimchi's comment. It is dubious whether מְזִמָּתָה, as opposed to זִמָּה, can have the sense 'abominable thing' (Sept.) or 'abominable things' (Vulg. and Pesh.), or that it can refer to idolatry, as supposed by Targ. Hence Aq. (τοὺς διαλογισμοὺς) offers a more accurate rendering of הַמְזִמָּתָה and the translation of the first line of v. 15 should run, 'What right has my beloved to be in my House? She has been busy with intrigue'.

It might be assumed that the Greek translator (Sept. μὴ εὐχαί) had a Hebrew text with הַנְּדָרִים (Rudolph and Bright), or that he so emended הָרַבִּים in the interests of intelligibility (cf. Duhm). It would be an advantage to explain הָרַבִּים as a corruption in a more convincing way, and the adjacency of וּבְשַׂר קֹדֶשׁ might be thought to indicate that it contains a reference to sacrificial victims. The latter factor influenced Giesebrecht (חֲלָבִים), modified by Duhm and Ehrlich (p. 273) to הַחֲלָבִים, and Hyatt's הַבְּרִיִּים is an attempt to do justice to both factors (JBL, 1941, p. 58). Irenaeus adipes points to חֲלָבִים or בְּרִיִּים and the advantage of the latter is that הָרַבִּים can be explained as a corruption arising from a metathesis of ב and ר (הַבְּרִיִּים = הָרַבִּים = הַבְּרִיאִים; cf. Driver, JQR 28, p. 109). Reider's proposal (VT 2, 1952, p. 119) that הָרַבִּים should be connected with Arabic ribāb 'tenth' is less probable. The remainder of the line can be read if יַעַבְרוּ is pointed as a Hiphil (Giesebrecht) and כִּי is deleted, 'Can fat animals offered for sacrifice save you from the consequences of your wrongdoing?' Or, perhaps, רָעָתֵכִי should be taken to mean 'the doom which you deserve' (so Hyatt, Rudolph, Bright and NEB). Kimchi takes עָבַר in the sense 'neglect' and comments: 'You are neglecting to offer these sacrifices: that is to say, as if it brought you no profit to fulfil them.' Hence, according to Kimchi, the verse deals with cultic negligence rather than misplaced ritual zeal.

Both Hyatt and Rudolph explain כי (which is not represented by Sept. and Vulg.) as arising from a dittography of the כ of מעליך. Driver supposes that the intention of the expression כי אז תעלזי (with כי so transposed) is ironical: 'Surely thou wouldst then exult!': that is, you would chuckle with satisfaction if you could atone for your misdeeds by cultic zeal, but be sure that it will avail you nothing. כי is not indispensable to the conveying of satirical intentions (cf. Vulg. *In quibus gloriata es?*, 'What do you have to exult about?'). Sept. (ἢ τούτοις διαφεύξῃ, 'Do you think that you will escape (punishment) by these devices?') is probably an exegesis of אז תעלזי rather than an indication of a Hebrew text different from MT, as supposed by Hyatt and Bright. Both Hyatt and Rudolph are dissatisfied with אז תעלזי: Hyatt deletes it as a marginal gloss which has found its way into the text (Did the Syriac translator, who does not represent אז תעלזי, have a Hebrew text from which these words were absent?). Rudolph emends to (הַ)אֲזַכֶּה עַל זאת (*ZAW*, 1930, p. 282), 'Shall I acquit (you) on this account?', and J. Coppens to הֲתִזְכִּי עַל זאת, 'Will you be acquitted on this account?' (*Le Muséon*, 1931, p. 80). Neither of these emendations can be related very convincingly to the extant text: if it is assumed that there was no interrogative particle, the first two consonants of אזכי can be identified with אז; כה is unaccounted for and על זאת can be related to תעלזי with only partial success.

The 'beloved' is likened to a luxuriant olive tree described as יפה פרי תאר (v. 16). פרי is not represented by Sept., while Pesh. supposes that יפה פרי תאר is a condensed expression equivalent to יפה פרי ויפה תאר, and this is how the matter is understood by Targ. and Kimchi. Ehrlich (p. 274) deleted פרי following Sept., and both Driver and Bright suppose that פרי and תאר are doublets. Driver (*JQR*, NS 28, pp. 109f.) thinks that because יפה פרי is a less common expression than יפה תאר it is perhaps original in this context, but יפה פרי is an odd association of 'beauty' and 'fruitfulness'. יפה תאר (Brockington, p. 203) should be read.

Driver urges that קרא should be pointed קֹרָא (Pual—following Michaelis) and that יהוה should be deleted because it overloads the metre (p. 110). This rests on a view, which also influences Hyatt's reconstruction (*JBL*, 1941, p. 58), that vv. 15–16 have a 3 : 2 metre. Hyatt deletes יהוה, אז תעלזי, and לקול המולה גדולה and achieves a strophe of 4 lines with a 3 : 2 metre, whereas Driver, with תאר and יהוה deleted, postulates 2 strophes each of 2½ lines. Rudolph (cf. Brockington, pp. 202f.) transposes לקול

(ח)אזכה על זאת לקול המולה and makes a line of המולה גדולה
גדולה, 'Shall I acquit you on account of this, when the great
uproar erupts?'. Verse 15 has then 3 lines and v. 16 has 2 lines.
All the versions indicate יהוה and there are no compelling
reasons for deleting it.

המו(ו)לה occurs only here and at Ezek 1.24 and its sense is not
well established. The noise (קול) of the moving wings seen by
Ezekiel is said to be קול המלה כקול מחנה, and 'like the sound of
an army' is the only clue which we possess. Apparently המלה is a
noise of some magnitude which can be compared to the hubbub
of a military camp or to the thundering feet of an army on the
march. The versions made little of it: it was read as הַמּוּלָה
'circumcision' by Sept. which makes nonsense; גדלה would
appear to have been transposed to follow עליה, a fact which is
not taken into account by Janzen (p. 27) and Ziegler who
suppose that ἀνήφθη πῦρ ἐπ' αὐτήν and μεγάλη ἡ θλίψις ἐπὶ σε
are doublets. Ziegler deletes ἀνήφθη πῦρ ἐπ' αὐτήν from his text,
although it is attested by all the witnesses. There is a question
whether μεγάλη ἡ θλίψις ἐπὶ σε is really a doublet or whether it
is a free expansion of MT גדלה. The Latin and Syriac translators
have read המו(ו)לה (cf. the form at Ezek 1.24) as הַמִּלָּה 'the
word'. Hence the sense of Vulg. and Pesh. is that when Yahweh
gave the word for the destructive judgement to fall, flames
devoured the olive tree, and this is paraphrased by Targ. as,
'Nations which are as powerful as fire will come against you'
(also Rashi and Kimchi). לקול המולה גדלה probably refers to the
roar which marks the outbreak of a conflagration, but it could
possibly refer to a clap of thunder (Bright) and then the idea is
that the fire is started by lightning.

　The problems of the last line of v. 16 are these: (a) There is a
grammatical disagreement between זית (masc.) and עליה (fem.).
(b) The meaning of ורעו is obscure. (c) Sept. (ἀνήφθη πῦρ ἐπ'
αὐτήν) and Vulg. (grandis exarsit ignis in ea) appear to indicate
הצת and Pesh. (šbwqw nwr' 'lyh) could also be derived from
such a pointing, that is, 'They have released' is a way of
indicating the passive. Hence Driver and Hyatt both read הצּת:
Driver argues that the change to הצית was consequent on the
insertion of יהוה, and he further holds that אש is the subject of
ורעו which he explains as equivalent to ורעה (an archaic form
retaining the final waw of a Lamedh Waw verb, unrecognized by
the Massoretes and pointed as a plural). The following
observations may be made on Driver's proposals: (a) אש is
feminine gender almost uniformly. It might be fair to conclude
that in Jer 48.45 the Hebrew manuscripts which disagree with
MT are reinstating the normal gender of אש, but in Jer 20.9 and
Job 20.6 the agreements are such that אש is indicated as both

masc. and fem. However, in a text which is parallel to Jer 48.45 (Num 21.28) MT has אֵשׁ יָצְאָה מֵחֶשְׁבּוֹן, and in the remaining passage where אש is treated as masc. (Ps 104.4—אֵשׁ לֹהֵט) a Qumran fragment attests אֵשׁ לֹהֶטֶת (J. A. Sanders, *The Dead Sea Psalm Scroll*, 1967, p. 160). Hence the masc. gender of אש is a precarious foundation on which to build, and if אש were the subject of הצת and ורעו (= ורעה), the forms ought to be הצתה and ורעתה. (*b*) There is no attested sense of רעה in Biblical Hebrew which matches precisely the one postulated here by Driver: '(but) a fire was kindled against it and consumed its shoots'. רעה meaning 'to shepherd' or 'to graze' in a sinister sense is present in Mic 5.5, Jer 6.3, Pss 49.15 and 80.14, but רעה is never used of the devouring power of fire and the meaning attributed to it here by Driver and NEB ('Fire sets its leaves alight and consumes its branches') is dubious. Hence to achieve this sense Rudolph, following Volz, emends to בערו. Rashi glosses ורעו דליותיו with רצצו את עֶנְפָיו and Kimchi similarly glosses רעו with ישברו. The derivation of ורעו from רצץ = רעע 'crush' is the best of the solutions on offer.

The only item remaining for discussion is עָלֶיהָ, and Kimchi's view that the feminine suffix is due to a wavering between the image (the olive tree) and its application to the 'beloved' (fem. gender) is attractive. The prophet insinuated into his figure an indication of how it was to be interpreted, and this has resulted in grammatical incongruence. Both Driver and Hyatt emend עָלֶיהָ to עָלָיו, whereas Rudolph (following Ricciotti) reads בְּעָלֵהוּ, 'Yahweh sets its leaves alight'. This interpretation (without an emendation) is noted by Kimchi and is attributed to his father: 'My father (may his memory be blessed) interpreted עָלֶיהָ as עֲלֵה זַיִת, that is, הִצִּית אֵשׁ בְּעָלֶיהָ. The conclusion is that the suffix of עָלֶיהָ refers to זַיִת, but that the incongruence of the fem. suffix should be tolerated for the reasons given above: an element of interpretation has crept into the figure and the equation of זַיִת with יְדִידָתִי obtrudes. This cannot be indicated in translation and הִצִּית אֵשׁ עָלֶיהָ has to be rendered as, 'He (Yahweh) will set it alight'.

The 'beloved' has become a harlot (chapter 2) or the wife is divorced from her husband (chapter 3): the people who are the objects of Yahweh's love expose themselves to the impact of a destructive judgement which is no less an expression of his nature than his love. It is this that explains the strange juxtaposition of love and threat. The intensity of the relationship indicated by describing Yahweh's people as his 'beloved'—his bride or his wife—makes the threat of impending judgement all the more tantalizing and tragic.

The people are busied with מְזִמָּה : with their own schemes dictated by self-preservation and self-interest, perhaps socially injurious, perhaps diplomatic manoeuvres with other nations, but certainly constituting a practical denial of Yahweh's will for his people. If indeed ritual punctiliousness were a substitute for obedience in the areas of life where obedience is costly, then those devoted to it might rejoice. But what a vain hope this is! There is no such 'sanctuary' against impending doom.

The name bestowed by Yahweh on his 'beloved' is 'luxuriant olive tree beautiful to behold': a symbol of health, well-being and fruitfulness. The passages to which Hyatt (*JBL*, 41, p. 59) appeals in order to elucidate זית רענן are inapposite, since all of them refer to trees set in a context of idolatry (Jer 2.20; 3.6, 13; 17.2), where the allusion to Baal shrines is unmistakeable. But there is nothing pejorative about the identification of Yahweh's Beloved with זית רענן יפה תאר. On the contrary, the threat is constituted precisely by the circumstance that this fine tree is to be destroyed, and it is here that there are overtones of waste and frustration. There are also elements of contradiction—that this splendid tree is to be destroyed by a conflagration kindled by Yahweh. The Beloved, although she is in truth beloved, will suffer the ravages of a strange work of retribution.

Verse 17 is connected in respect of topic and vocabulary with the preceding section of chapter 11: according to v. 11 Yahweh will bring רעה on his people and in v. 17 he threatens them with רעה; the statement in v. 13 that they build altars לקטר לבעל should be compared with v. 17, where the nature and intention of their behaviour are summed up in the words להכעסני לקטר לבעל. The thought that Yahweh has planted his people (which Kimchi correctly connects with the זית רענן representation of v. 16) should be compared particularly with 2.21. The idea of 'planting' by Yahweh as the antithesis of 'uprooting' occurs in 24.6 and 42.10, and these and other passages (31.28; 32.41) where Yahweh is portrayed as a 'planter' are oriented towards the reconstitution of Jerusalem or of Israel and Judah. 11.17, like 2.21, is directed to the original institution of Israel and to Yahweh's gracious initiative which has been thwarted in a senseless way by apostasy, and which is to issue in the destruction of the 'plant' (cf. 5.10) rather than in growth and fruitfulness.

Thiel's view (p. 156) that v. 17 is secondary commentary on vv. 15–16 is correct: the 2nd person fem. sing. suffixes of v. 17 refer to the 'beloved' in vv. 15–16, הנוטע אותך is triggered by the figure of the olive tree, and the vocabulary reaches back to the preceding prose. Thiel views the verse not only as a conclusion in relation to what precedes but also as a bridge to what follows.

In conclusion, we may say that 11.17 attaches itself to the

thought of a long history of apostasy (cf. chapter 2), in so far as a distinction is made between those immediately addressed and בית ישראל ובית יהודה. The objectives envisaged in the act of election have not been achieved and Israel has become a wild vine (cf. 2.21). The process of reversion has been under way for a long time and its final consequences are about to be disclosed. There is little doubt that עשו להם is to be understood as an ethic dative (so Sept. ἐποίησαν ἑαυτοῖς).

JEREMIAH—A LAMB LED TO THE SLAUGHTER (11.18–23)

[18]Yahweh informed me and so I knew; you showed me, (O Yahweh), how they were acting. [19]I was being led like a pet lamb to the slaughter; I was unaware that they were hatching plots against me: Let us destroy the tree while the sap runs in it;[1] let us cut him off from the land of the living, that his name be remembered no more.

[20]But you, Yahweh Sabaoth, judge with equity,
you test men's deepest thoughts.
Let me see you wreak vengeance on them,
for I have confided my case to you.

[21]Therefore these are the words of Yahweh concerning the men of Anathoth who seek your life and who threaten you: If you do not desist from prophesying in the name of Yahweh, you will die at our hands.[2] [22]I am about to punish them: their young men will die by the sword and their younger children will die of starvation. [23]None of them will be spared, for I will bring disaster on the men of Anathoth, when my punishment falls on them.

There is a tendency to assume in discussing the connection of 11.18–23 with 12.1–6 that a tidy logical progression is to be expected and can be required, and that a rearrangement of verses which achieves it will probably correspond to the original order. One may, for example, inspect Rowley's involved arguments (*AJSL* 42, 1926, pp. 217–227), which are designed to expose the disorderly arrangement of ideas and the lack of literary evenness in 11.18–12.6, and the question which rises in the mind is whether the criteria which Rowley is applying have any validity in relation to the book of Jeremiah and the processes by which it has reached its extant shape. This applies to all attempts to rearrange the order of 11.18–12.6 in order to produce a more coherent literary unity. We may set out one or two of these reconstructions:

Cornill: 12.1–2, 4–6; 11.18–23; delete 12.3 (cf. Bright.)

Rowley: 11.18; 12.6; 11.19–20; 12.1–3; 11.21–23; (12.4–5).

Rudolph: 11.18; 12.6; 11.19–20a; 12.3; 11.20b–23; 12.1–2; 12.4*–5.

Thiel: 11.18; 12.6; 11.19–23; 12.1–4*; 12.5.

[1]Pointing בלחמו as בְּלֵחְמוֹ (below, p. 257)

[2]Deleting לכן כה אמר יהוה צבאות (see below, p. 258).

The point from which these reconstructions set out is the observation that there is no adequate preparation for the appearance of 11.18 which, so to speak, comes out of the blue, and that, in particular, there is no prior indication of the reference of the suffix of מעלליהם. Cornill endeavours to put this right by advancing 12.1–2, 4–6, so that they lead on to 11.18ff. The method of Rowley, Rudolph and Thiel (p. 158) is to locate 12.6 immediately after 11.18, so that the suffix of מעלליהם is seen to refer to Jeremiah's relatives.

One aspect of the matter which seems to have been somewhat neglected (cf., however, Thiel, p. 159) is that 11.18–19, 21–23 and 12.6 is prose, whereas 11.20 and 12.1–5 is poetry. The difficulties associated with the relation of 11.18–19, 21–23, 12.6 to 11.20, 12.1–5 should perhaps be considered as a particular instance of the general problem of the relation of poetry to prose in the book of Jeremiah. In that case it might be assumed that the poetry is primary and that the prose is derived from the poetry, either in the sense that there are echoes of the vocabulary of the poetry or that a particular, exegetical elaboration of the poetry is discernible. 12.1–5 should be treated as a unit, and the question of the relation of 11.20 to 12.3 should be raised.

If we envisage that the prose arose out of the poetry, the suggestion that 11.20 and 12.3 should be associated (Rudolph) is no longer controlled by the objective of achieving a linear continuity from 11.18 to 12.6. The question may then be asked whether 11.20, which is a fragment of poetry in the prose section 11.18–23, is not out of context, and this thought is strengthened by the circumstance that 11.20 is reproduced, with small variations, at 20.12: there are stronger reasons (*pace* Rudolph) for doubting the originality of 11.20 in a prose context than for doubting the originality of 20.12 in a context of poetry. The affinity of 11.20 with 12.3, in respect of vocabulary and ideas, may explain the intrusion of 11.20 into the context 11.18–12.6. Thiel's view (p. 159) is that the unit 11.18, 12.6, 11.19, 20(?) has a Jeremianic core, but owes its present form to a Deuteronomistic editor. It was D who removed 12.6 from its original place to its present one in pursuit of the composition of 11.1–12.6 which is attributable to him (cf. Nicholson who urges that 11.18–19 'must be regarded as Jeremiah's own words').

11.20 is out of place in the prose unit 11.18–23 as the following considerations show. If 11.18 is generated by the poetry of 12.1–5, the difficulty which has been felt with the abruptness of its appearance and its laconic quality is capable of explanation. If 12.1–5 is assumed, those whose evil deeds are divulged to the prophet by Yahweh (11.18) are to be equated with those of whom it is said that Yahweh is near to their speech but far from their lives (12.2). There is, moreover, the circumstance that the particular interpretation of 12.1–5 which appears in the prose (11.18–19; 21–23; 12.6) is wrong. The prose wrongly assumes that the crisis of Jeremiah's faith which is indicated by 12.1–5 is connected with his persecution at the hands of his kinsmen and fellow-villagers in Anathoth (cf. Skinner, *Prophecy and Religion*, p. 113). This interpretation is clearly indicated by v. 6 (notice the connective כי) which is offered as an explanation of Jeremiah's predicament and which relates this to the hostility of his kinsmen. 12.6 represents the same interpretation of 12.1–5 as is found in 11.18–19 and 21–23. It is the most explicit element of this interpretation, since it has a direct syntactical connection with 12.1–5. With 11.20 removed we can see that the principal intention of the prose is to foster this interpretation and the following aspects should be noted:

(*a*) The figure of sheep being led to the slaughter occurs in 11.19 and 12.3, but instead of the vengeful Jeremiah (so 12.3), we have in 11.19 a portrait of the prophet as an innocent, unaware of the murderous intrigues directed against him, and so being led like a lamb to the slaughter.

(*b*) Traces of the vocabulary of 12.3 and 4 appear in 11.18–19; ידע (Qal and Hiphil) and ראה (Hiphil) in 11.18; ידע (Qal) in 11.19; ידע and ראה (both Qal) in 12.3 and ראה (Qal) in 12.4. In 12.3 and 4 these verbs give expression to the transparency of Jeremiah's sincerity. The function of ידע and ראה in 11.18 and 19 is quite different: Jeremiah is portrayed as the innocent victim who did not know (v. 19) the machinations of his enemies against his life, but who was made aware and forewarned by means of a revelation from Yahweh (v. 18).

The correct explanation might turn out to be more complicated than what has been supposed in the argument conducted above. 11.18–19 would be assessed as a fragment attributable to the prophet Jeremiah and 11.21–23 as a secondary commentary on this fragment (cf. Nicholson). In this connection it should be noted that there is no mention of Anathoth in vv. 18–19. There are those who are plotting murderously against the prophet, but no clue as to their identity is offered (Skinner, op. cit, p. 110, assumes that they are inhabitants of Anathoth). It is precisely the function of the exegesis in vv. 21–23 to identify Jeremiah's assailants with the inhabitants of Anathoth. The position would then be that we have two Jeremianic passages (11.18–19 and 12.1–5), both of which have received a secondary 'Anathoth' exegesis (12.21–23 and 12.6) and this is an alternative approach to 11.18–12.6 which should not be neglected (cf. Thiel, pp. 159f.).

We come to a more detailed consideration of the contents of

11.18–19, 21–23 and the fragment of poetry in v. 20. The form הודיעני (v. 18) could be vocalized either as a perfect or an imperative. The former is indicated by MT and Targ. and the latter by Sept. (γνωρισόν μοι) and Pesh. (ḥwny). Neither overcomes the awkwardness created by הראיתני later in the verse. Whether we read, 'Yahweh informed me and so I knew; then you showed me their evil deeds', or 'Inform me, O Yahweh, that I may know (וְאֵדְעָה; MT וָאֵדָעָה); then you showed me their evil deeds', there is a manifest unevenness. Sept. (εἶδον) represents ראיתי, but this should be regarded as an adjustment to deal with the roughness of MT rather than as an indication of a different Hebrew text available to the Greek translator. Duhm suggests that a *yodh* (an abbreviation for יהוה) has been omitted by haplography after הראיתני and this is adopted by Rudolph. It should not be leaned on as a precise textual solution, but the assumption of a vocative 'Yahweh' in conjunction with הראיתני is the best that can be done for the text, 'Yahweh informed me and so I knew; it was then, O Yahweh, that you showed me their evil deeds'.

Prior to this illumination the prophet was unaware of the plots which his enemies were hatching and of the danger in which he stood. He was like a pet lamb being led to the slaughter (v. 19). Sept. is the only version which goes against the Massoretic punctuation and connects ולא ידעתי with what precedes: 'led to the slaughter all unawares'. We find a description of what is intended by כבש אלוף in the כבשה אחת קטנה of 2 Sam 12.3. The lamb of Nathan's parable had been adopted by the poor man's household and had attained the status of a family pet (cf. Vulg *mansuetus*; similarly Aq. and Symm.). The point of כבש אלוף in Jer 11.19 is that a pet lamb is less able to take care of itself than a lamb reared in the ordinary way, and so the figure magnifies the degree of Jeremiah's innocence and defencelessness in the face of his enemies (cf. Skinner's translation, 'tame, pet lamb', *Prophecy and Religion*, p. 110). His instincts of self-preservation are undeveloped and he is unable to envisage the moves which are being made against him, far less to take steps to ensure his safety in a dangerous world. Calvin, KJV and Lowth follow Rashi and Kimchi (אלוף = אלף 'ox'), but Blayney and Venema have the sense 'tame lamb' and it is represented by Rudolph (*zutrauliches Lamm*). Bright ('innocent lamb') follows Sept. (ἄκακον).

The difficulty in the second part of v. 19 is concentrated in the words נשחיתה עץ בלחמו, 'Let us destroy the tree with its bread (or food)'. Sept. renders ἐμβάλωμεν ξύλον εἰς τὸ ἄρτον αὐτοῦ, 'Let us cast wood into his bread'—the suffix of בלחמו has been referred to Jeremiah and not to עץ (also Vulg. and Targ.), and

ἐμβάλωμεν is apparently translating נשליכה (MT נשחיתה).
Targ., 'Let us cast lethal poison into his food', suggests that the
'wood' of Sept. is a poisonous substance and that what is
indicated is an attempt to poison the prophet. This is in
agreement with Kimchi's exegesis: he glosses עץ with עץ שהוא
סם המות, 'wood which is deadly poison'. Burkitt's guess (JTS
xxxiii, 1932, pp. 371–373) that Aq. did not differ from Sept. at
11.19 is partly disproved by the material available in Ziegler
(Aq. ξυλον εν αρτω αυτου), although we do not know whether
Aq. had ἐμβάλωμεν with Sept. or διαφθειρωμεν with Symm.

It is unlikely that MT can mean, 'Let us destroy the tree with
the fruit thereof' (KJV), although this would be an apposite
metaphor of threat spelled out by, 'Let us cut him off from
among living men and let his name be remembered no more'. A
desire to preserve the tree metaphor and at the same time to deal
with the difficulty of בלחמו is reflected in Hitzig's emendation of
בלחמו to בְּלֵחוֹ, 'Let us destroy the tree with its sap', and this is
adopted by Duhm and Rudolph. An attempt to achieve this
result with the consonants of MT is found in Bright and NEB
(Brockington, p. 203—בְּלֵחֻמוֹ). Bright attributes the suggestion
that בלחמו should be retained and מו understood as a suffix to
Dahood (Gregorianum, 43, 1962, p. 66), but the suggestion that
בלחמו might be analyzed into the elements לח and מה is at least
as old as Venema (1765): Quae si nondum satisfaciant, בלחמו
verti poterit, in virore vel succositate ejus, e לח et מו. The only
new item in Dahood's analysis is the description of the mem of
בלחמו as 'enclitic'. Another way of proceeding is to follow Sept.,
and Ehrlich (p. 274) emends נשחיתה to נשיתה (Sept.
ἐμβάλωμεν) and understands עץ as a poisonous substance (so
Targ.).

Burkitt reconstructed the text as לכו ונשיתה עצב לחמו,
'Come, let us make trouble his food'. He gets לכו ו from Sept.
Δεῦτε καὶ and he notes that both Sept. and Targ. (λέγοντες;
אמרין) have inserted 'saying' to indicate the entrance of direct
speech. Burkitt remarks that שית appears with a double
accusative in Ps 88.9 and 110.1 and maintains that the idiom of
Jer 11.19 is represented in לחם העצבים ('bread of worry', Ps
127.2). This should be compared with לחם עצלות 'bread of
idleness' (Prov 31.27). It is clear, however, that 'bread of
idleness' means 'bread which has not been earned' and לחם
העצבים would appear to refer to the grinding toil which is
necessary to eke out a livelihood (cf. NEB, 'toiling for the bread
you eat').

The major weakness of Burkitt's account lies in the
circumstance that nowhere else does Sept. render שית by
ἐμβάλλω or Targ. render שית by רמי. This suggests that Sept.

and Targ. are not derived independently and directly from the same Hebrew text. One of them may be derived from a Hebrew text, but if we were to think along these lines נשליכה (Hitzig) would offer a better explanation than נשיתה. It is probable that either Sept. is dependent on Targ. נרמי for ἐμβάλωμεν or *vice versa*. If one were thinking in terms of accidental corruption and assuming that MT נשחיתה is original (an entirely different approach from that of Burkitt). נשיתה would have more explanatory power than נשליכה, since נשחיתה becomes נשיתה through the omission of one consonant (ח). What is then left unexplained is why the postulated נשיתה was rendered as ἐμβάλωμεν by Sept. and נרמו by Targ. The best that can be done is to retain MT and to read בלחמו as בְּלֵחָמוֹ (NEB, 'Let us cut down the tree while the sap is in it').

The threat uttered by Yahweh in v. 21 follows naturally on the revelation (v. 19) that Jeremiah's enemies have designs on his life and are set on his destruction. It identifies the conspirators as the men of Anathoth and it reproduces an ultimatum which they have delivered to the prophet. 'Do not prophesy in the name of Yahweh and you will not die by our hands' is in the English idiom more naturally expressed as, 'If you do not refrain from prophesying in the name of Yahweh, you will die at our hands' (cf. Sept. and Pesh). It is evident from vv. 22–23 that Yahweh is not communicating a threat in the form in which Jeremiah is to convey it to the men of Anathoth who seek his life. Rather, Yahweh is speaking directly to the prophet and informing him about the judgement which is to fall on his adversaries. In these circumstances נפשך is appropriate (so Bright) and נפשי inappropriate (*pace* Rudolph, Brockington, p. 203). There are no serious difficulties in vv. 21–23, but לבן כה אמר יהוה צבאות is otiose at the beginning of v. 22 and the shorter text of Sept. is superior (Janzen, p. 85). What is intended by הבחורים (*pace* Rudolph) is that the young men who answer the call to arms will die on the battlefield, whereas the younger children who remain at home will die of hunger as a consequence of siege conditions.

The fragment of poetry in v. 20 has, as already indicated (above, p. 254) affinities with 12.3. Yahweh's scrutiny of the hidden, interior world of men's motives and intentions is so exhaustive and all-embracing that nothing can be hidden from him. The 'test' which he imposes is definitive and final (בחן כליות ולב) and the decisions which he reaches when he 'judges' men are altogether what justice demands. The forensic character of the entire representation is clear from certain elements of the vocabulary (ריב; צדק; שפט). Jeremiah believes that he has a good 'case' for vindication and reparation and he expects that

Yahweh's verdict will be in his favour and that the wicked will be discomfited.

The only linguistic problem in the verse is constituted by גליתי את ריבי, 'I have revealed my case to you' or 'I have confided the details of my case to you'. This is the sense which is indicated by Sept., Vulg., Pesh. and Targ. It is entirely appropriate, but Rudolph, Bright and NEB (Brockington, p. 203) adopt Duhm's emendation (גלותי) and appeal to Ps 22.9 and 37.5. Rudolph reproduces Duhm's fussy logic and urges that 'I have confided my case to you' contradicts the representation of v. 20a, according to which Yahweh does not need to be informed. The objection to גלותי is that the two occurrences cited are difficult to elucidate and that their significance can only be estimated from the contexts in which they appear: 'Roll towards Yahweh', presumably means something like 'Rely on Yahweh'. MT should be retained at Jer 11.20.

CHAPTER XII

NO RESPITE FOR THE PROPHET (12.1–6)

¹I admit that you are just, O Yahweh, though I contend with you;
yes—engage in legal arguments with you.
Why do the wicked enjoy prosperous lives?
Why do all those who lie habitually live at ease?
²You planted them and they have taken root,
they grow and bear fruit.
They are always using your name,
but you are far away from their affections.
³O Yahweh, you know me, you see what I am;
you have tested my commitment to you.
Drag them off like sheep to the slaughter-house,
set them apart for a day of slaughter.
⁴How long will the land suffer from drought
and the green countryside be parched?
Beasts and birds have perished, because those who inhabit it are evil,
for they say, He does not foresee what our end will be.
⁵If you have raced against men and they have worn you out,
how will you contend with horses?
If you fall down when the going is easy,
how will you fare in the thickets of the Jordan?
⁶Even your brothers and your father's family have practised treachery on you;
even they are calling loudly for your blood. Do not trust them if they should
speak fair words to you.

The ambiguity of כי in 12.1 is illustrated by the differences of
translation in the ancient versions. Sept. ὅτι ἀπολογήσομαι πρὸς
σέ does not make particularly good sense after Δίκαιος εἶ κύριε,
but the following πλὴν suggests that what is intended is
something like, 'Your will for justice is so assured that I cannot
call it in question; nevertheless (πλὴν) I am going to raise legal
questions with you.' This is also the sense of Symm., Pesh. and
Targ.; different nuances are achieved by Vulg. and Aq. through
the rendering of כי as *si* 'even if' and οταν 'whenever', combined
(in the case of Vulg.) with *verumtamen* 'nevertheless'. The sense
of Aq. is, 'Whenever I engage in legal argument with you, you
are seen to be in the right, O Lord'. Vulg. introduces a note of
apology or deference: 'Even if I argue with you' suggests that
there is something exceptional and, on the face of it, outrageous
in the procedure. The prophet intends to persist (*verumtamen*)
and yet he wishes to establish that Yahweh's justice is above
question. Kimchi's exegesis reinforces this nuance.

These differing emphases are reflected in modern translations.
The removing of the irreconcilable elements from the address to
Yahweh and the replacing of them by a calm, assured statement
of confidence (so NEB) does not do justice to צדיק אתה יהוה כי

אריב אליך. Nor does Bright's rendering, 'Just art thou, O Yahweh; I cannot dispute with thee', entirely communicate the divided state of the prophet's mind. This is more adequately indicated by Rudolph, 'You remain in the right, O Yahweh, even if I argue with you. Nevertheless, I shall raise legal points with you.'

The vocabulary of the verse is legal (צדיק; אריב אליך; אך משפטים אדבר אותך) and Jeremiah addresses Yahweh as a judge. Baumgartner (*BZAW* 32, p. 54) notes that the expression משפטים דבר את refers elsewhere in the book of Jeremiah to the activities of Yahweh as judge (1.16; 4.12) and that the prophet uses it in relation to his own activity and against Yahweh in 12.1. Baumgartner underlines the rebellious attitude of the prophet—he stands on the brink of contumacy. If Yahweh is a righteous judge, why should the believer not enjoy the same degree of demonstration as is granted in a normal judicial context? Why should the evidence not be sifted by a process of legal argument and the verdict be seen to be just? Over against the unthinkable thought that Yahweh's righteousness can be impugned, there is dissatisfaction with a faith which seems to be merely obscurantist, and there is an unwillingness to make lack of comprehension into a theological virtue: 'If we are to use this kind of language, why can we not press its implications and have a debate about its validity?'

The contradiction which threatens the integrity of his belief is felt as an intensely personal problem, but it is a bigger issue than the vindictiveness of his fellow-villagers or kinsmen (above, pp. 253–256). It is a matter of general experience and not simply reflection on a peculiarly painful private offence. The question which is asked in the second part of v. 1 envisages the problem as a comprehensive one about the tenability of the doctrine of theodicy. Is it not contradicted on every side? The wicked go from strength to strength and prosperity is founded on a lie. Hence the question, as Kimchi indicates, is this: How can the prosperity of the wicked be reconciled with Yahweh's righteousness?

The charge made by Jeremiah in 5.2 is not that this state of affairs has come about because Yahweh has lost his grip and is no longer able to maintain his theodicy. Instead, as Kimchi observes, Yahweh is said to cause the prosperity of the wicked. Yahweh himself has made them well-rooted, vigorous and fruitful plants. Although they speak the language of piety, they have no commitment to Yahweh and their lives are divorced from his control. The drives which impel them to action have nothing to do with their religious vocabulary, and so their words are a thoroughly debased currency which will be dishonoured when put to the test. ילכו may perhaps have the sense 'grow' as in Hos 14.7 (NEB, 'grow up'), and Ehrlich (p. 275), who thinks along these lines, suggests 'develop'. Rudolph follows Volz and reads ילחו 'full of sap'. Sept. interprets the metaphor and supposes that 'fruitfulness' means enjoying the blessing of children, whereas Targ. inteprets the imagery of growth and fruitfulness in terms of wealth rather than children.

The men who prosper are apparently hoodwinking Yahweh (v. 3). Jeremiah's own life is all of a piece without any discrepancy between its surfaces and its depths. Surely Yahweh can see that he has this transparency and consistency! But what if Yahweh does not have this order of perceptiveness? Let him then chase away these doubts by reinforcing Jeremiah's belief in the effectiveness of a theodicy. The language used in v. 3b is strong, throbs with impatience and conveys an undercurrent of powerful emotion, perhaps even a trace of vindictiveness: Let me see whether what I affirm is an empty doctrine or whether it has substance. The picture is apparently that of sacrificial victims being prepared for the altar, although this is explicit only in the second stich of v. 3b. The language which is employed is violent: Put them in the position of sheep which are dragged off to be slaughtered in circumstances where their wishes are a matter of no consequence—sheep which have a kind of absolute violence done to them and are defenceless in the face of it.

Verse 4 does not connect in an obvious way with what precedes: it describes a condition of drought in which vegetation languishes and animals and birds are expiring and it attributes this state of affairs to the wickedness of the human inhabitants of the land. But this is hardly the same kind of problem as the one which exercised the prophet in the preceding verses. A breakdown in theodicy which is seen in the prosperity of the wicked and a failure on Yahweh's part to vindicate the righteous is clearly different from a general condition of drought and desolation attributable to the wickedness of the community at large.

Reventlow (*Liturgie und prophetisches Ich bei Jeremia*, p. 244) points to Jer 14.1–15 and argues that the drought motif is better accommodated to a communal than an individual lament, since it is the kind of situation which precipitates a general crisis and requires representations on behalf of the whole community. From this consideration he advances to the conclusion (pp. 244–251) that elsewhere in vv. 1–5, where Jeremiah might seem to be speaking as an individual, his function is really a representative one. The final part of v. 4, 'For they say, "He does not foresee what our end will be" ' (or, if Sept. is followed, 'He does not see how we behave'), does not arise naturally out of what precedes. Rather, it marks a contrast with Jeremiah's awareness and belief that his deepest thoughts and intentions are open to Yahweh's scrutiny (v. 3) (cf. Rudolph who retains only this final part of v. 4 and locates it after v. 2). There is no textual evidence to support the deletion of the whole or part of v. 4, and it represents a kind of unevenness which should be tolerated. If v. 4 were grammatically unintelligible something would have to be done, but the situation is rather that it is intelligible in itself but not in its context. The matter is somewhat different in v. 3, where Sept. attests a shorter text; it is probably a superior text, but this judgement should not be pressed to the extent of deleting the additional elements in MT (as Rudolph does). Sept. is probably a better text, because the elements of MT which it does not represent look like either textual variants or expansions: תראני is an alternative of ידעתני, and התקם כצאן לטבחה (conjoined with *waw*) of הקדשם ליום הרגה.

Verse 5 undoubtedly connects with the main complaint of the preceding verses to which it serves as a divine answer. If Jeremiah has not been able to stand the pace of a race on foot, how will he ever compete (תתחרה, Tiphel of חרה?; cf. GK 55h; J. Blau, *VT* 7, 1957, pp. 385–388) against horses? If he feels secure in a safe land, how will he fare in the גאון of the Jordan? Jeremiah earns no sympathy from Yahweh and is advised that the apparent unevenness of Yahweh's justice, of which he has complained, is no more than a pin-prick in comparison with the strains and pressures which he will have to withstand in the future. But 'If you feel secure in a safe land' does not seem to be right and it is likely that the οὐ πέποιθας of Sept. rests on this perception rather than on a Hebrew text which was different from MT (Sept. is followed by Erbt, Baumgartner, Volz). Rudolph holds that the original reading of Sept. is συ of Sept.ᴬ and Ziegler has σὺ πέποιθας in his text. The insertion of 'only' at Jer 12.5 cannot be justified by means of Ps 118.20b (Rudolph), because 'only' is not implied at 12.5 as it is in the statement 'The righteous will pass through it'. Hitzig's conjecture (בורח) has been adopted by others (Duhm, Cornill): 'If you feel a fugitive in a safe land'. Vulg. and Symm. sought another way out of the difficulty by supposing בוטח to refer to a false sense of security or lack of vigilance: 'If you are off your guard in a safe country'. G. R. Driver's elucidation of בוטח, 'fall flat on the face' (*JQR*, 28, pp. 111f.), which is rejected by Rudolph, has been adopted by a number of scholars (E. Zolli, *Biblica* 34, 1953, pp. 564f.; J. Blau, *VT* 6, 1956, p. 244; A. Ehrman, *JSS* 5, 1960, p. 153). Driver (cf. *JQR* 28, pp. 111f.) subsequently became aware that the philology was mediaeval (T. H. Robinson Festschrift:

Studies in Old Testament Prophecy, 1950, pp. 59–61; cf. S. L. Skoss, *Jewish Studies in Memory of G. A. Kohut*, 1935, pp. 549–553) and that it had been adopted by I. A. Dathe in the eighteenth century (*Prophetae Majores*, 3rd. ed., 1831, p. 222b). It is found in Al-Fasi, who glossed אתה בוטח (Jer 12.5) with *inbaṭaḥta*, 'you have fallen flat on your belly' (*Kitāb Jāmiʻ*, ed. S. A. Skoss, i, p. 215), and in Rashi (on Prov 14.16): 'Slipping (מחליק) and falling on the ground as in בארץ שלום אתה בוטח'. There is a question whether the Targ. of Jer. 12.5 (את מתבטח ונפיל) does intend to indicate the sense 'fall down' for בוטח (as Rashi supposed in his comment on Prov 14.16). Another possibility is that נפיל is simply an additional element and is not a clue that Targ. was equating בוטח with נפיל. The intention of the paraphrase is rather that the negligence arising from a false sense of security leads to a fall. If this were a correct account, Targ.'s exegesis would have to be seen as a spelling-out of the type of rendering of בוטח which is represented by Vulg. and Symm. (see above, p. 263). NEB's rendering ('fall headlong') rests on the philology noted above: it offers a way out of the difficulty at Jer 12.5 and should be accepted.

The other philological crux is constituted by גאון. This is translated by most of the versions as 'pride'. Jerome interprets Vulg. *superbia* as a reference to the 'swell' of the Jordan and comments 'How will you fare when you cross Jordan and encounter that spate?' The circumstance that Pesh. renders גאון with *'wšn'* shows that it too supposes a reference to the 'swell' of the Jordan. Pesh. is rendered by Theodoret (see Ziegler), 'How will you cross the Jordan when it is in spate?' Kimchi's interpretation agrees with this: גאון is the place where the waves of the Jordan rear their head and the expression is a משל for the שרים of Judah and Jerusalem with whom Jeremiah will have to contend. The other ancient interpretation, which is present in Targ., is maintained by Rashi. He founds on Jer 49.19, 50.44 and Zech 11.3 which establish that גאון הירדן is a kind of jungle where wild beasts have their *habitat*, and he observes on Jer 12.5 that גאון הירדן is the place of lions and leopards. Targ. is an interesting case because it has a rendering which represents the 'jungle' interpretation, while in an attaching comment it assumes the 'swell' interpretation. The children of righteous fathers will receive blessings and consolations from Yahweh and these are likened to the flood-waters of the Jordan.

To decide between these alternatives is not easy. What tells against the 'swell' interpretation, probably decisively, is the circumstance that גאון הירדן cannot mean 'swelling current of the Jordan' in the other places where it occurs (Jer 49.19; 50.44; Zech 11.3). 'Dense thickets' agrees with Rudolph and Bright and rests on a tradition of exegesis which goes back to Targ. and Rashi. KJV 'swelling of the Jordan' has the other interpretation and is followed by Lowth and Blayney. KJV has the same translation at Jer 49.19 and 50.44, and the reconciliation is effected (cf. Lowth, Venema, Blayney) by assuming that in all three passages 'swelling of the Jordan' refers to an overflowing of its banks which drives lions and other wild beasts from their usual dens and makes them a danger to residents and travellers. גאון הירדן is not susceptible of this interesting but improbable explanation in Zech 11.3 and it is significant that KJV renders it there as 'pride of the Jordan'.

The exegesis of Rashi and Kimchi is dominated by the presupposition that the situation of which Jeremiah complains is directly associated with his experiences at the hands of relatives and fellow-villagers in Anathoth. Kimchi associates v. 5 with Jeremiah's arrival on the Jerusalem scene, but he also supposes that there may be an allusion to Nebuchadrezzar 'who was about to mass his armies on the other side of the Jordan' (cf. Blayney). The characteristic antithesis which comes out of this approach (cf. Lowth and Blayney) is that the vindictiveness and hostility offered to Jeremiah in Anathoth (the safe country) will be nothing compared to the powerful opposition which he will awaken in the circles of the great in Jerusalem ('the swelling of the Jordan').

'Jeremiah asks a question about the prosperity of the wicked and God does not answer him' (Kimchi). This is an aspect of the matter which deserves attention. Rudolph remarks that it is a strange answer which Yahweh gives to his prophet; stripped of the metaphor it is: If you complain about a light task, how will you ever endure heavy burdens? This is somewhat pedestrian—a crisis of faith must not be reduced to a grumble that life is too hard—but Rudolph and Weiser are right to disengage v. 6 from vv. 1–5 and to decline to treat Jeremiah's complaint as one which arises directly out of his Anathoth experiences. This assumption prevails with Baumgartner, who regards vv. 1–6 as the unit, but who, nevertheless, breaks new ground. His distinctive contribution consists in his association of vv. 1–6 with the individual lament (pp. 52–60) and he is impressed with the originality of the divine answer in v. 5 over against the model which he posits in the book of Psalms. It is the reverse of the reassuring, oracular answer which he regards as characteristic in the liturgical setting of the individual lament: 'The acerbity of the answer alone would establish its genuineness' (p. 59). Hence there is no intention to urge that there is a correspondence between a *Gattung* and a cultic function. The argument is rather that the *Gattung* has been redirected in so striking a way that evidence of prophetic originality is provided. There is thus a decisive difference between Baumgartner and Reventlow in this regard. The latter's exegesis of v. 5 (*Liturgie und prophetisches Ich bei Jeremia*, pp. 249–251) assumes that his treatment of vv. 1–4 (pp. 242–249) has shown that vv. 1–5 constitute a communal lament. In Jer 49.19 a lion coming up from גאון הירדן against a sheepfold is a figure for the savaging of Edom by her enemies and a similar figure is applied in 4.7 to the expedition of a destroyer of nations, advancing on Judah from the north. Reventlow holds that 'horses' are stock imagery in connection with the theme 'enemy from the north' (4.13; 6.23) and that the context with which they are traditionally associated is public not private, corporate not individual. Hence the reference to horses in 12.5 and the allusion to גאון הירדן persuades him that the verse is addressed to the nation and not to the prophet.

S. Mowinckel (*The Psalms in Israel's Worship*, i, 1962, pp. 217f.; ii, pp. 58–61) has maintained that an answering oracle is part of a psalm of lamentation, although it is not normally preserved in the extant text (see, however, Pss 12.6; 60.8–10; 108.8–10). Mowinckel has urged that the 'certainty of a hearing' element in these psalms (an expression of such resounding confidence and thanksgiving that deliverance appears to be already accomplished) presupposes the preceding intervention of a priest or cultic prophet with an oracle promising salvation. The only oracle compatible with the liturgical forms of psalms of lamentation is then a *Heilsorakel*. On this view the interpretation of 12.1–5 does not hinge on whether it is related to the individual or communal psalm of lamentation, but on the absence of the *Heilsorakel*, which is common to both, and the substitution of an *Unheilsorakel* (op. cit. ii, p. 65). Elsewhere (14.1–10) Jeremiah makes use of the structure of the communal lament, but the concluding oracle in that case also is a threat and not a promise. It is surprising that Reventlow has nothing to say about the paradoxical character of the oracle in 12.5: Jeremiah's use of the forms of the lament, instead of establishing that he exercised cultic functions, is an expression of dissent (so Mowinckel).

Weiser's view of Jeremiah is that he is too pugnacious and demanding in his approach to Yahweh and that he is required to retreat from his path of enquiry. But is this an adequate understanding of vv. 1–5? Do we not rather have there a transmutation of a process of inner debate and elucidation by means of which a prophet resolves contradictions which arise out of his religious beliefs and clarifies his presuppositions? We may assert that the conclusion has been accorded the status of

revelation, but we may not sever it from the struggles of the soul
out of which it has come. The prophet is not compelled to
become an unthinking and docile pietist.

It has already been argued that the function of 12.6 is to
provide a secondary 'Anathoth' interpretation for v. 5 (above,
pp. 255f.) and it remains to consider the text in a more detailed
way. The main point of difficulty is מלא, but the ground has been
partly covered in connection with קראו מלאו (4.5, above, p. 91),
since the two passages (12.6—קראו אחריך מלא) hang together.
Rudolph urges that sense cannot be had out of קראו אחריך מלא
on any reckoning, because v. 6b indicates that Jeremiah's
opponents use deceit as a tactic. The sense of v. 6 may rather be
that they threaten and wheedle by turn, but, at any rate,
Rudolph's emendation of קראו אחריך מלא to קשרו אחריך כלם
(following Volz) should not be adopted. The sense of קראו
אחריך מלא, according to Winton Thomas (cf. 4.5), is, 'They have
raised a hue and cry after you (קראו?); they have massed
together to hunt you down' (*JJS* 3, 1952, p. 49). Driver's
contribution (*JJS* 5, 1954, pp. 177f.) is along the same lines: he
observes that Arabic *tamalla'a* means 'was massed' and that
mala'u(n) means 'full number', 'massed body'. How this relates
to the syntax of v. 6 is not entirely clear. Is the sense (*ex
hypothesi*), 'They shout after you, rousing the mob against you'?
Something akin to this is to be found in Lowth on the foundation
of KJV, but Lowth prefers the other elucidation of מלא: 'The
words may be more properly translated, "They pursue thee with
a great cry as a common malefactor"' (cf. Duhm, קול = מלא
מלא). Venema is aware of both exegeses and he has a variant of
the 'assembly' interpretation. The sense is not simply that a mob
is to be whipped up, but that powerful adversaries are to be
persuaded to act in concert in order to harass Jeremiah.

Winton Thomas notes that מלא is represented by
ἐπισυνήχθησαν in Sept.: the Greek translator has connected
אחריך with מלא and not with קראו. It is not obvious how the
passive ἐπισυνήχθησαν 'they were assembled' comes out of מלא,
but, in any case there is a contrast between the rendering of קראו
מלאו (κεκράξατε μέγα) at 4.5 and קראו אחריך מלא (ἐβόησαν, ἐκ
τῶν ὀπίσω σου ἐπισυνήχθησαν) at 12.6. Rashi and Kimchi have
the 'assembling' sense in both places. Rashi glosses מלא with
קבוצת אנשים, 'a gathering of men' and Kimchi comments, 'They
massed themselves against you', citing מלא רעים (Isa 31.4)
which he explains as קבוץ רעים. Winton Thomas disagrees with
Streane (*The Double Text of Jeremiah*, 1896, p. 136) who had
held that Sept. was right about מלאו at 4.5 and wrong at 12.6.
Calvin should perhaps have the last word: 'Either sense may be
admitted. I will not therefore dwell on the point, for it makes but

little difference whether we say that they followed the prophet with a loud clamour, or that they in a troop conspired against him.'

Verse 6, supplying an 'Anathoth' exegesis for 12.1–5, represents that the prophet's perplexity and anguish arise from the hostility of members of his own family who have plotted against him with malice and treachery. They have bayed at him, have made loud, angry and threatening verbal gestures. When the mood of Jeremiah's enemies changes and they are apparently conciliatory, they are not to be trusted. The benevolence of their language is no guide to their intentions; they are ruthless and their enmity is implacable.

JUDAH IS DOOMED (12.7–13)

[7]I have forsaken my house,
I have abandoned my people;
I have given my beloved into the power of her enemies.
[8]My people act towards me like a lion in the wild,
they raise their voices against me and I have come to hate them.
[9]Do my people treat me as a hyena[1] would?
Vultures are circling to attack them.
Come, gather[2] all you wild beasts,
come[3] to the feast.
[10]Many shepherds have ruined my vineyard;
they have trampled my chosen land.
They have made my desirable land into a desolate wilderness.
[11]They have laid it waste;[4]
its desolation makes me mourn.
All the land is desolate,
for there is no one to tend it.
[12]Across the open tracts of the wilderness raiders have come (There is a devouring sword in Yahweh's hand). From one end of the land to the other no person is left unscathed.
[13]They have sown wheat and reaped thorns,
they have sifted[5] and got no product.
They have suffered disappointment at their yield.[6]
Yahweh's hot anger is the cause of it.

Rudolph has made two suggestions to account for the location of vv. 7–13: the passage is cited as an example of how Yahweh's people have conspired against him; alternatively, and more probably, vv. 7f. were wrongly understood as spoken by

---

[1] Deleting עִיט and reading הַצָּבוּעַ (below, p. 273).
[2] Reading אִסְפוּ (below, p. 273).
[3] Reading אָתָיוּ (below, p. 273).
[4] Reading שָׁמֵם (below, p. 275).
[5] Reading נָחֵלוּ (below, pp. 276f.).
[6] Reading מתבואתיהם (below, p. 277).

Jeremiah, constituting his response to what was revealed to him about the attitude of his relatives in v. 6. Weiser supposes that there may be a conceptual link between vv. 1–5 and vv. 7–13: a lament by Yahweh is attached to a lament by Jeremiah and the problem of reconciling Yahweh's actions with justice is thereby further explored. The verses disclose tensions in God's inner life, conflicts of love and hate, justice and mercy, election and judgement.

The sense of נחלה (above, p. 227) coheres well with the view that ביתי refers here (v. 7) to Israel as Yahweh's family and chosen people. The explanation of בית as temple (Targ., Kimchi) is found in Lowth who comments, 'The words are spoken of the desolation of the temple by the Chaldaeans, as if it were already brought to pass, a way of speaking usual in the prophets'. Duhm concludes that בית 'land' is a better parallel for נחלה than 'temple' and is followed by Rudolph and Weiser. The third term in v. 7 (ידדות נפשי) again turns on the special attachment of Yahweh to Israel (the bond of love between him and them), and when the three terms are held together 'people' rather than 'temple' is seen to be the more appropriate rendering of בית. Moreover, the way in which נחלתי is used in v. 8 establishes that it is Yahweh's people rather than simply Yahweh's land on which interest focuses: they are like a roaring lion, they make threatening noises and turn a relationship of love into one of hate. Hence vv. 7–8 are concerned to assert that Yahweh has abandoned his people, has surrendered the objects of his special affection to the power of their enemies.

Sept. renders both occurrences of עיט (v. 9) as σπήλαιον and assumes that ה is the interrogative particle in both instances (as does MT). It supports MT אספו (συναγάγετε) and takes כל חית השדה as an object. The opening of the verse then runs, 'Has my possession become a hyena's cave to me', but this is followed by ἢ σπήλαιον κύκλῳ αὐτῆς which makes poor sense. The hyena (so Jerome, referring to Sept.) has disgusting eating habits, digs up corpses from graves and will feed on dead bodies of any kind. The point in comparing Yahweh's people to a hyena's cave is to underline the grievous offence given to Yahweh by their uncleanness: they have utterly polluted his land. The obscure Hebrew (העיט סביב עליה) is rendered by Vulg. as *Numquid avis tincta per totum*?, so that Vulg. supposes that nothing new is contributed by העיט סביב עליה: the words are simply a reiteration that the bird עיט has variegated feathers (צבוע). But עליה must refer to נחלה (vv. 7, 8) and Vulg.'s rendering of the Hebrew, which is dubious in any case, is put out of court by this circumstance.

Pesh. has apparently read both occurrences of העיט as הָעַיִט

and it adheres to the view that צבוע denotes speckled feathers. In the latter part of the verse Pesh., like Sept., assumes that Yahweh is addressing a third party, 'Go, assemble all the wild beasts; bring (them) to the feast'. On the other hand, Vulg. renders אספו with a reflexive nuance (*congregamini*) and represents that Yahweh issues an invitation to the wild beasts to come to the feast. Kimchi also attaches a reflexive nuance to אספן but supposes (following his father's exegesis) that the vultures issue the invitation to the wild beasts. Rashi has alternative explanations of עיט צבוע: (*a*) They are birds contaminated with the blood (of victims) which attract other birds to them. (*b*) They are speckled birds which arouse the hostility of other birds. In either case העיט סביב עליה is a reference to the swift-moving armies which are encircling Judah (following Targ.). Calvin follows Vulg. closely: Yahweh is the speaker and he invites the wild beasts to the feast. Calvin rejects the idea that the point of the figure is that the speckled bird awakens the hostility of other birds (Rashi) and he makes the image hinge on the 'wildness' of birds and beasts, connecting this with Judah's behaviour as described in v. 8—snarling at Yahweh like a lion: You acted against me like a wild creature. Very well! you will be set upon by birds of prey and wild beasts. Hence for Calvin צבוע is not an important component of the imagery.

The rendering of עיט צבוע as 'speckled bird' is found in KJV: this version is perhaps influenced by the thought that a speckled bird attracts the enmity of other birds. Yahweh is represented as addressing third parties and requiring them to issue an invitation to the wild beasts (Sept. and Pesh.). Lowth, commenting on KJV, has an exegesis similar to that of Calvin, with the emphasis falling on the 'wildness' of the עיט and with a reference to the lion of v. 8. Lowth remarks, 'The word צבוע ... is of an uncertain signification ... The Septuagint understand it of the *hyaena*, which sense is followed by Bochart. But if we take it in either signification, the sense is much the same.' S. Bochart (*Hierozoicon sive De Animalibus S. Scripturae*, ed. F. C. Rosenmüller, ii, 1794, pp. 176f.) explains צבוע as 'speckled' and עיט צבוע as a circumlocution for 'hyena'. Venema is influenced by Bochart, but his exegesis is similar to that of Calvin, with 'hyena' substituted for 'vulture' (cf. Lowth's remark). Judah has acquired the characteristics of a hyena, but she herself will be encircled by rapacious beasts (העיט סביב עליה). כל חית השדה which, according to Venema's rendering, are to be summoned by third parties, are the Chaldaeans.

Blayney accepts Bochart's view that צבוע means 'speckled' and that it may be used of birds, animals or reptiles, but he parts company with him over עיט which, he holds, must be a bird. עיט

is a generic for 'bird of prey' and צָבוּעַ 'speckled' specifies the
bird of prey as an eagle or a falcon. Blayney holds that the
second occurrence of עַיִט (הַעַיִט — vocative) also refers to birds,
since there is an intention to combine birds of prey and wild
beasts. The exegetical outcome of Blayney's lexicography does
not set him apart conspicuously from Calvin and Lowth: the
ravenous bird (Judah) is to be attacked by other ravenous birds
(the Babylonians).

The identification of עַיִט with 'bird of prey' has largely
prevailed and it is capable of different exegetical applications.
The supposition that the speckled bird draws the hostility of
other birds (Rashi, KJV, Lowth) was developed by Hitzig; it is
found in its plain form in Rudolph, with modified versions in
Duhm and Weiser. It is supposed that the 'decoy-bird' idea can
be subsumed under the general notion that the speckled bird
excites the hatred of other birds (cf. Duhm, Weiser). It is
because this is so, so it is urged, that the tactic of the decoy-bird
is a successful one: the other birds which are to be trapped are
drawn to attack it by feelings of hostility. As Emerton has
pointed out (*ZAW* 81, 1969, p. 184) a figure with this kind of
function is not what is desiderated. We expect a reference to
Judah's hostility to Yahweh which will match the description of
her behaviour in v. 8, where she is said to snarl at Yahweh like a
lion. The 'wildness' of the עַיִט plays no part in Duhm's exegesis.
A more fundamental objection is that the function of a
decoy-bird is to lead other birds into a trap, but the birds coming
to Judah are predators, not the potential victims of hunters.
They are a figure for the invaders who will execute Yahweh's
judgement. Weiser deletes עַיִט¹ (an emendation proposed by
N. H. Tur Sinai, according to Freehof) and takes הַצָּבוּעַ to refer
to a small, speckled bird which is beset by birds of prey (הַעַיִט
סָבִיב עָלֶיהָ). He emends לִי to כִּי (as Rudolph does) and the whole
becomes an expression of Yahweh's pity for his people, a
compassion which cannot be completely suppressed, even if the
demands of justice must prevail. Weiser supposes like Rudolph
(following Kimchi) that the invitation to the wild beasts is
extended by the vultures. He reads הֵאָסְפוּ and אֵתָיוּ with
Rudolph and renders, 'Come, assemble all you wild beasts, come
to the feast'.

The supposition that עַיִט¹ and עַיִט² are homonyms is found in
Ehrlich (pp. 275f.): עַיִט² is a bird of prey (to be pointed הַעַיִט),
but עַיִט¹ is to be associated with Arabic *ġayẓun* 'rabidness'. עַיִט
צָבוּעַ means 'rabidness of a hyena' (?) = 'a rabid hyena'.
Emerton (p. 185) has noted that Ehrlich's proposal assumes an
irregular exchange of consonants between Arabic and Hebrew,
since Arabic *ġayẓun* ought to appear in Hebrew as עַיִץ. G. R.

Driver (*PEQ*, 1955, p. 139) assumes that there is a deliberate play on homonyms and that עִיט [1] is to be explained in connection with Arabic *ġawṭun* 'hollow', 'cavity', 'pit' or the like. This explanation of Sept. σπήλαιον is in Bochart (op. cit., ii, p. 176). The second עִיט, which was wrongly elucidated by Sept., is onomatopoeic, indicates 'screaming' and refers to a bird of prey. צבוע should be pointed צָבוּעַ 'hyena' (so Brockington, p. 203) and is cognate with Arabic *ḍabu'un* (Sept., Ehrlich). If we follow Driver, we achieve a sense similar to what is adumbrated by Jerome on the foundation of ὑαίνης in Sept. Judah has the disgusting habits of a hyena, and its cave, littered with partially devoured corpses, will attract vultures. The vultures (הָעַיִט) are the destructive agents, figures of the invaders who will execute Yahweh's judgement on Judah. It is Yahweh who invites the wild beasts to the feast, and, if so, אספו should be pointed as הֶאָסְפוּ (cf. Cornill הֵאָסְפוּ; Driver *JQR* 28, p. 112) and התיו emended to אתיו.

Emerton (*ZAW*, 1969, pp. 182–191) has dealt decisively with H. P. Müller's attempt (*ZAW* 79, 1967, pp. 225–228) to find another solution for v. 9 and has in turn declared his support for Driver. Müller urges that עִיט [1] is the consequence of an error of hearing and that the original was עַד 'spoil', 'prey' (Gen 49.27; Isa 33.23). His translation indicates that he is reading הֹעַיִט [2] and he supposes that the wild beasts (vocative) are being addressed by Yahweh. His reconstruction falls to the ground, because the account which he gives of Sept. is incredible. If הֹעַיִט [2] represents the original Hebrew text, and this he grants with his rendering 'vultures', the second σπήλαιον of Sept. is a rendering of עִיט. If σπήλαιον[2] is a rendering of עִיט [2], the economical hypothesis is that σπήλαιον[1] derives from MT עִיט [1].

One expects on the analogy of היתה לי נחלתי כאריה ביער (v. 8) that נחלתי לי in v. 9 will also be associated with some expression of hostility towards Yahweh on the part of Judah. In relation to this test of what is apposite in the first stich of v. 9a, all those explanations which make Judah into a victim rather than an aggressor appear to be defective. This would take care of the view that Judah is the speckled vulture which draws the hostility of other vultures (Rashi, Hitzig, Rudolph), or that she is a decoy-bird (Duhm), or that she is a little speckled bird which awakens Yahweh's compassion because it is at the mercy of vultures (Weiser). On the other hand, the explanations which hinge on the 'wildness' of Judah's attitude clearly meet this test better, since they are influenced by v. 8 and are endeavouring to prolong a portrayal of Judah's attitude to Yahweh which appears in that verse. The weakness of an exegesis which hinges on the 'wildness' of Judah (Calvin, Lowth, Blayney) is that it makes no particular use of צבוע and, indeed, has no need of it.

It is a merit of Ehrlich's proposal ('madness of a hyena'='a rabid hyena') that he incorporates all the Hebrew text in his exegesis. Judah has behaved like a rabid hyena, but vultures are encircling her and will tear her to pieces. Again it is fundamentally the same thought as Calvin's: Judah has been savage and will herself be dismembered. Driver's solution may be, as Emerton has argued, the best that has emerged, but there are aspects of it which awaken reservations: (a) We expect on the model of v. 8 that the first stich of v. 9 will compare Judah to an animal or bird of prey, not to the cave of an animal. If העיט צבוע נחלתי לי means 'Has my possession taken on the appearance of a hyena's cave for me?', the emphasis can no longer fall on the violence of Judah's behaviour to Yahweh, and a switch has to be made to the thought of disgusting behaviour and the defilement of Yahweh's land. (b) If Driver is right, נחלה in v. 9 means 'land', whereas נחלה in v. 8 means 'people', and this is shown up clearly in NEB's translation which is founded on Driver's philology (v. 8, 'my own people'; v. 9, 'this land of mine'). There is no textual evidence to support the deletion of עיט [1], but it may be conjectured that this has arisen through reading צבוע as צָבוּעַ and interpolating עיט in view of its appearance later in the verse. Driver assumes that there has been a deliberate play on homonyms, but it is, as Blayney observed, a disadvantage to be dependent on such an assumption. In view of these considerations resort should be had to a conjectural emendation, עיט [1] should be deleted and הֲצָבוּעַ נחלתי לי should be read, 'Do my people treat me as a hyena would?'

The hypothesis that the wild beasts themselves are being addressed rather than that Yahweh is commanding third parties to address them is the more economical, but this result cannot be had from MT because of התיו (Hiphil imperative: הֵאָתִיו > הֵתִיו) 'bring'. However, in Isa 56.9, where there is similar vocabulary, the Qal imperative of אתה rather than the Hiphil appears, and Brockington (p. 203) has noted that 3 Hebrew manuscripts read אתיו at Jer 12.9. התיו should be emended to אתיו and אספו should be read as אֶסְפוּ (see above, p. 272). Verse 9b should be rendered, 'Assemble all you wild beasts, come to the feast'. The precise connection of this with the earlier part of the verse is not altogether clear, and it was perhaps to establish a firmer connection that the vultures were represented as inviting the wild beasts after they themselves were sated.

J. A. Soggin (VT 8, 1958, pp. 304f.) notes that 20 Hebrew manuscripts read נחלתי (v. 10) and that τὴν κληρονομίαν μου appears in the margin of Syh. (see Ziegler). He concludes that

חלקתי is the *lectio difficilior* and should be retained (*pace* Volz, Rudolph, Weiser). Rashi (cf. Targ., 'great kings') equates the רעים with the commanders of the divisions of Nebuchadrezzar's army (citing Jer 6.3), just as Kimchi observed that the birds and beasts of v. 9 were a משל for nations which would come under Nebuchadrezzar's command to destroy Jerusalem. There is little doubt that v. 10 refers to the destruction of Judah's agricultural prosperity by a military invasion, and Duhm has suggested that the foundation of the metaphor is the conflict of interests which obtains between settled farmers and itinerant shepherds. The grass in the vineyard is regarded as legitimate pasture for the sheep, and the flock will be driven through it irrespective of the damage which is done to the vines. One must also, however, take account of a stylized use of כרמי, and the explanation of why Canaan is described precisely as Yahweh's vineyard is not unconnected with the paradigmatic status of כרם as a symbol of Yahweh's land and people which can be gathered from Isa 5 (cf. Jer 6.9). Vineyards and arable fields are ruined by military operations which are naturally accompanied by destruction. Soldiers ruin vineyards and trample down crops, and the carefully tended agricultural scene is changed to one of desolation.

Verse 11 contains two items which have given rise to different interpretations: the first is אבלה עלי שממה and the second כי אין איש שם על לב. Sept. and Vulg. depart from the punctuation of *MT* in different respects, but *MT* is followed by Aq., Symm., Pesh. and Targ., and its punctuation should be retained. Nevertheless, the sense of אבלה עלי שממה is obscure and the obscurity is not entirely relieved by explaining עלי as קדמי, 'before me' (Targ.; cf. Rashi לפני). The meaning could be either that the land is personified as a mourner ('It laments before me in its desolate state') or that its desolation has a mournful effect on Yahweh ('Its desolation makes me mournful'). The sense, according to Kimchi, is, 'In its desolate condition the land is calling out to me like a mourner'. This is how it is taken by KJV ('*and being* desolate it mourneth unto me') on which Lowth comments, 'It lies in a neglected and doleful condition ... and makes a sort of silent complaint, and begs to be restored to its former prosperity.' Blayney inclines to the other sense: 'Through me it mourneth being desolate' indicates that the clause refers to the effect which the sad state of the land has on Yahweh. Duhm (*zu ihm trauert das Land*) follows Kimchi, KJV and Lowth, whereas NEB makes Yahweh the mourner ('waste and waterless to my sorrow'). Rudolph attaches אבלה to שָׁמֵם לְשְׁמָמָה either as a relative clause (אֲבֵלָה) or as an adjective (אֲבֵלָה), 'They make it into a mournful waste' (also Weiser). The pointing שָׁמֵּה is grammatically necessary and should be adopted (MT שְׁמָּה).

The other matter concerns כי אין איש שם על לב (v. 11), where Duhm (followed by Cornill, Rudolph and Weiser) proposed that כי אין should be emended to ואין. The argument is that the destruction is represented as a judgement, a consequence of invasion not of neglect, and that כי would be apposite only if it were the latter. It may be allowed that there is no intention to administer a rebuke, but כי does not necessarily do this. It merely registers that in the chaotic situation which exists the cultivation of the land and its proper conservation are bound to suffer. The sense is that a country which has been thrown into turmoil by invasion is not one which will be able to persevere with normal tasks of tending and cultivating the land, and כי can stand.

Verses 12–13 contain references to Yahweh in the 3rd person (cf. Weiser) which go awkwardly with the assumption that he is the speaker. Duhm removes this difficulty from v. 12 by deleting כי חרב ליהוה אכלה and he supposes that v. 13 is an addition. Rudolph identifies כי חרב לחוה אכלה as an eschatological gloss brought about by a misinterpretation of מקצה ארץ ועד קצה הארץ — ארץ taken wrongly as 'earth' instead of 'land'. Weiser supposes that with כי חרב ליהוה אכלה deleted v. 12 can be set out as poetry (4 stichs), but it is dubious poetry and NEB is probably correct to arrange it as prose. There is a convention that Yahweh refers to himself in the 3rd person and we are not, therefore, precluded from regarding Yahweh as the speaker in v. 12, even if MT is retained. But v. 12 is almost certainly prose and it should be regarded as secondary supplementation rather than as an original component of a unit consisting of vv. 7–12. It develops the thought that the country is in a chaotic state. אין שלות לכל בשר explains why the inhabitants of the land, for their part, are unable to proceed with normal tasks: they are exposed to extreme insecurity and danger and the order within which the pattern of their lives was fulfilled has disappeared. Verse 13 can be related quite well to the contents of vv. 7–11, but it should be regarded as an independent saying with a proverbial flavour and a theological component (מחרון אף יהוה) which gives it a reference to a judgement executed by Yahweh.

The lexicographical difficulty of שפים (v. 12) has already been noted (above, p. 177). It is uncertain that 'high places' or 'dunes' is the right sense, and Blayney ('plains') envisages, probably correctly, the open spaces of the desert which afford opportunities for the swift movement of armies. The view that שפים are elevated places is found in Kimchi and 'high bare places' (NEB) is a widespread rendering whose philology, however, is shaky. More interesting, in view of Rudolph's observations on כי חרב ליהוה אכלה (above, p. 275), is Kimchi's equation of ארץ with 'world' and with Nebuchadrezzar's world-wide conquest. There is no doubt (whether or not כי חרב ליהרה אכלה is an intrusion) that מקצה ארץ ועד קצה הארץ means 'from one end of Judah to the other'. The intention is to describe the over-running of the entire land by those who pour into it from the desert. Not even the remotest corners will be spared and no one will be immune from the blast of war. If we assume כי חרב ליהוה אכלה to be an original part of the verse, its function is to offer an interpretation of the disaster which has engulfed Judah. The invaders are fulfilling Yahweh's plan and they wreak destruction with his sword.

The philology of נחלו has caused uncertainties and there is a grammatical incongruence in מתבואתיכם, unless בשו is rendered as an imperative, and this was, presumably, MT's intention. Sept. takes בשו as an imperative and departs from the text of MT at that point. Ziegler (Beiträge, p. 21) supposes that the Hebrew text translated by Sept. was בשו מחרפת יהוה, and that the rendering ἔναντι κυρίου rather than simply κυρίου is a matter of theological refinement. At any rate, Sept. does not deal with the awkward מתבואתיכם, but the transition from imperatives (σπείρατε ... θερίσατε) to a 3rd person plural (ὠφελήσουσιν) and back again to an imperative (αἰσχύνθητε) is harsh. Vulg. accommodates מתבואתיכם by taking בשו as an imperative (Confundemini), and this has the same degree of unevenness as MT. Pesh. uses imperatives to render all the verbs and achieves consistency (zrw'w; ḥṣwdw; l'w; bhtw). That l'w is imperative is clear from l' mwtryn 'ntwn. It would appear that Pesh. has associated נחלו with חלה 'be sick' (so MT; Sept. and Vulg., נחל 'inherit'), but the translator has taken liberties in so far as נחלו is not a possible imperative form of חלה. He has taken 'sickness' in the sense of 'exhaustion' or 'fatigue'. The association of נחלו with חלה is found in Rashi, who glosses נחלו with חולי (חֲלִי) 'disease', and in Kimchi who refers to unsuccessful labour. Kimchi's interpretation of the imagery in v. 13 does not establish a particular connection with vv. 7–12. He supposes that the verse deals with the fruitless labour of Yahweh's prophets, but he also reproduces his father's exegesis which connects the verse with the futility of foreign alliances and diplomatic manoeuvres.

An interpretation of the proverbial language of v. 13 in terms of foreign alliances removes it from the context of vv. 7–12—invasion and devastation of the land. This exegetical trend is continued in Calvin and Lowth. Lowth observes that a proverbial expression capable of a wide range of application has been particularly applied: 'It is here applied to the Jews' fruitless endeavours to save themselves from the evils that threatened them, by courting the assistance and alliance of idolators'. Duhm renders all the verbs as perfects (נחלו, 'they agonized') and emends מתבואתיכם to מתבואתיהם. This is the kind of textual adjustment which is made by Rudolph, Weiser and NEB (Brockington, p. 203). The assumption of this emendation, which should be adopted, is that the change from an original מתבואתיהם to מתבואתיכם (MT) has arisen through the wrong identification of בשׁו as an imperative (the 3rd person plural perfect and the 2nd person plural masc. imperative forms are the same). Duhm, Rudolph, Weiser and Bright all derive נחלו from חלה (Rudolph, 'They have gained nothing from the trouble which they have taken'), but NEB has a new philology for נחלו which connects it with Arabic naḥala, Syriac, nḥal, Akkadian naḥālu, 'sift'. 'Sift' is apposite in combination with 'sowing' and 'reaping', and the proposal should be adopted (G. R. Driver, *JQR* 28, p. 112). It is tempting to represent imperatives throughout, but we then fall foul of לא יועלו which cannot be preceded by an imperative. The crop will be so poor that there will be virtually no product after the sifting operation has been completed.

Rudolph holds that the unit consists of vv. 7–13, and so he offers an interpretation of the 'proverb' which connects v. 13 with the theme of vv. 7–12. Sowing wheat, reaping thorns and sifting with no result (or, being exhausted to no effect) are related to an invasion which has frustrated the proper unfolding of the agricultural year and which brings bitter disappointment at the time of harvest: 'They have suffered disillusionment with their yield.' The state of the fields and the loss of the harvest are attributable to Yahweh's anger. Judah has been overtaken by a divine judgement not by an accidental disaster (cf. v. 12 כי חרב ליהוה אכלה).

Kimchi explains vv. 7–13 as an anticipation of impending events of so intense a kind that they are described as past events. The same assessment is found in Calvin: 'He indeed speaks of future things; but he uses the past tense, which is commonly done by the prophets.' Rudolph raises the question whether we are to think in terms of such a prophetic premonition, or whether we have a description of an incursion and devastation which have already taken place. He tends towards the second alternative, because he holds that it accords better with the sharpness of the portrayal and the detail which is supplied. It is not obvious that this part of his argument carries very much weight. There are aspects of the description which are cryptic (v. 9) and others which are metaphorical and cannot be pinned down to particular historical circumstances (vv. 8, 10). There is nothing in what remains of such striking particularity that only one historical situation will satisfy the details. The picture of devastation is somewhat unspecific and repetitive, and the older commentators who searched for a historical anchorage tended to think in terms of the incursion of Nebuchadrezzar and his armies (Rashi, Kimchi, Blayney). Duhm gave some consideration to the identity of the רעים רבים and concluded that the allusion was probably to the Scythians, although the direction from which they are said to come (He held this part of v. 12 to be genuine) makes this identification questionable.

There is a need to look very hard at all such correlations. In this particular instance there is nothing in the passage to enable us to establish with a sufficient degree of probability that it relates to a particular, historical situation which can be identified. However, Rudolph and Weiser hold that the events referred to in the passage are those of 601/600, B.C. when Chaldaean, Aramaean, Moabite and Ammonite forces invaded Judah and ravaged it (2 Kgs 24.2). Rudolph's extra-biblical source is a chronicle of Chaldaean kings (D. J. Wiseman, *Chronicles of Chaldaean Kings, 626-556 B.C.*, 1956). He correlates Jehoiakim's submission to Nebuchadrezzar with 'All the kings of the Hatti-land came before him and he received their heavy tribute' (604 B.C.; Wiseman, pp. 68f.). He correlates Jehoiakim's rebellion with 'The king of Akkad and his troops turned back and returned to Babylon' (601/600 B.C.; Wiseman, pp. 70f.). Jehoiakim was loyal to Nebuchadrezzar for three years (2 Kgs 24.2) and his rebellion coincided with the period when Nebuchadrezzar suffered losses in a battle against Egypt (Wiseman, pp. 70f.) and returned to Babylon. He did not come back to Syria-Palestine until 599 B.C., but he had left Babylonian contingents behind and they, along with countries neighbouring Judah which were his vassals, were given the task of dealing with Jehoiakim's rebellion. This fills in the historical background needed to understand the reference to Chaldaeans, Aramaeans, Moabites and Ammonites in 2 Kgs 24.2.

The passage is probably premonition rather than a description of what has taken place and it will defeat attempts to locate it in a particular set of historical events. We may say that the verbs are 'prophetic perfects', but the awareness that they refer to the future should not be implemented by translating them as future tenses, because this would not convey the intensity of premonition and anticipation which is in them. In order to indicate the conviction that their eventuation is a matter of certainty and is inescapable, they must be rendered as past tenses.

EXILE AND RESTORATION (12.14–17)

¹⁴These are the words of Yahweh: Concerning my evil neighbours who encroach on the land which I allotted to my people, Israel: I will uproot them from their lands and I will tear Judah apart from them. ¹⁵After I have uprooted them, I will have compassion on them again and restore each to its land and territory. ¹⁶If they strive to learn the ways of my people and swear in my name the oath, 'As Yahweh lives', as they once taught my people to swear by Baal, they will be established in the community of my people. ¹⁷But if they are unheeding, I will uproot and utterly destroy these nations. This is Yahweh's word.

Rudolph has supposed that דרך (Sept.) accords better than דרכי (MT) with the proselytisation of Judah's neighbours which he takes to be the sense of v. 16. He cites 10.16, where he explains דרך הגוים as a commitment to an alien religion and way of life. Sept., Vulg., Pesh. and Targ. all assume that אשוב ורחמתים means something like, 'I will return (relent) and show them mercy'. The view that אשוב has an adverbial force, which is probably correct, is represented by Lowth: 'I will again have compassion on them' (departing from KJV). It is unlikely that Sept. ἐπιστρέψωσι (v. 17) is indicative of a different Hebrew text from MT: Targ. has explained ישמעו as יקבלון אלפן 'receive instruction', and it is probable that ἐπιστρέψωσι is a similar attempt to elucidate ישמעו as 'repent', rather than an indication that a Hebrew text with ישובו was translated.

Ehrlich (pp. 276f.) has argued that הנגעים ב means no more than 'whose borders are contiguous with those of Judah', and it could be argued that this is the indication which is given by Sept., Vulg. and Pesh., but is more probable that all these are literal renderings of נגע ב 'touch' (cf. KJV) and that there is no intention in them to indicate 'adjoin' rather than 'encroach on'. The latter sense is certainly represented by Targ. (דמנזקין באחסנתא) and is found in Rashi (ומנזיקין אותם) and Kimchi (להרע). Lowth, commenting on KJV, took 'touch' in the sense of 'breach Israel's territorial integrity'. The evil neighbours have been identified from Jerome on with the small nations which border on Judah: Edomites, Philistines, Moabites and Ammonites, according to Jerome; Rashi and Kimchi omit Edom and add Tyre and Sidon.

The exegesis of this verse has, for the most part, been guided by the understanding of הנגעים בנחלה which is found in Targ., Rashi and Kimchi. According to Ehrlich the point is that the adjacency of these neighbours has exerted an evil influence on Judah which has been infected with idolatry and immorality. These nations are, therefore, to be uprooted from the areas which they presently occupy and this will remove the source of

corruption from which Judah suffers. If they are expelled, Judah
will be effectively separated from them, and it is this separation
which is intended by ואת בית יהודה אתוש מתוכם. The
association of these nations with Judah in the future will be
conditional on their willingness to embrace Yahwism. The
thought that the neighbouring nations will be removed to enable
Judah to 'recuperate' is strange and is unlikely to represent a
correct understanding of v. 14. Moreover, it is not clear that we
have a unit consisting of vv. 14–17, which is all of a piece, so that
one can interpret v. 15 on the assumption that the restoration to
which it refers is conditional. The conditions which are
formulated in vv. 16–17 have the marks of a subsequent
modification of v. 15.

According to Duhm the evil neighbours are settled in what
they regard as their own countries, but the point of view of the
passage is that the entire area within which their territories are
enclosed belongs to Israel. The neighbouring nations are to be
expelled, so that Israel can possess her נחלה, but before they are
deported those Israelites resident in these communities are to be
removed and repatriated to Judah. He remarks disarmingly that
all this would be clearer if the text had אדמתי instead of אדמתם.
Duhm holds that the passage is very late and he illustrates his
exegesis by referring to the practice of the Maccabaeans who
repatriated Jews from Galilee and trans-Jordan. If the entire
area is Israel's נחלה (Duhm), there should be no question of the
return of her former neighbours. One cannot escape from this by
urging that the return is conditional on conversion to Judaism,
because vv. 16–17, as Duhm recognises, is a secondary
circumscribing of the statement in v. 15.

Other explanations of את בית יהודה אתוש מתוכם have this in
common with Ehrlich and Duhm, that they regard the final
clause in v. 14 as an allusion to deliverance and not to exile. Thus
Kimchi comments on אתוש מתוכם : 'Those (of my people) who
went into exile in their midst, I will root out from them, when I
restore the fortunes of my people.' It is not certain what Kimchi
means by this. It could be urged that he envisages Jews exiled in
these neighbouring lands who are to be repatriated to Judah
(Duhm and Volz), but it is more probable that he refers to Jews
in exile in Babylonia who are mixed up with Ammonites,
Edomites, Moabites etc. What he is then saying is that after the
exile Jews will be effectively separated from their neighbours,
and so he has the post-exilic Jerusalem community in mind. In
connection with v. 15 he cites passages in the oracles on foreign
nations which refer to the restoration of Moab (48.47) and
Ammon (49.6). When Judah and Benjamin return from their
exile in Babylon, their former neighbours will also be restored.

The conditions, however, are those set out in v. 16. On v. 17 he refers to an exegesis of 49.6 according to which the promise of restoration is confined to those Ammonites who 'learn the ways of Israel'. Kimchi's perception of the historical setting in which sense can be made of the passage is one to which we should attend carefully, and, in particular, his interpretation of the enigmatic clause ואת בית יהודה אתוש מתוכם could be the right one. The obvious criticism to be applied to the latter is that נתש is used in vv. 14 and 15 of 'uprooting' (exiling) Judah's neighbours, and that a different sense of נתש ('separating') is difficult to maintain in ואת בית יהודה אתוש מתוכם, but there may be a play on the preceding occurrences to convey the stringency of Jewish separation from neighbouring nations—the 'uprooting' of all associations. The understanding of אתוש מתוכם in terms of deliverance is also found in Calvin and Lowth, but in the different context of 'the restoration of the Jews from their several dispersions' (Lowth).

In more recent times אתוש מתוכם has generally been taken to refer to the exile of the Judaeans. Hitzig elucidated it in connection with Jer 25.29, according to which the series of Yahweh's judgements against foreign nations would be preceded by his action against Jerusalem—העיר אשר נקרא שמי עליה. Hence Hitzig supposed that v. 14 indicated the exile of Judah before her evil neighbours (מתוכם) and this would seem to be what Rudolph also intends when he says that the Jews are to be removed from the midst of neighbouring nations whose exile is imminent. Both Rudolph and Weiser assume that there is an intrinsic connection between vv. 7–13 and v. 14, that the latter is attributable to the prophet Jeremiah, and that כל שכני הרעים can be equated with רעים רבים (v. 10) and שדדים (v. 12). Those neighbouring states which invaded Judah to put down Jehoiakim's rebellion against Nebuchadrezzar in 601/600 will themselves suffer the fate of exile. But his message takes an unexpected turn and he shocks his hearers by proclaiming that Judah too will suffer exile (cf. Amos 1.1–2.16). Rudolph's Jeremianic core consists only of v. 14. He remarks that v. 15 is consistent with Jeremiah's responsibility as a prophet to the nations (1.10), but he holds that the connection between v. 14 and v. 15 is defective and that vv. 15–17 are later additions. His exegesis of those verses is similar to Duhm's: Judah's neighbours will be restored, provided they embrace Judaism.

An earlier and different attempt to find a Jeremianic core in vv. 14–17 is that of Cornill. The omission of any reference to the exile of Judah was felt to be a serious deficiency and ואת בית יהודה אתוש מתוכם was inserted (also Giesebrecht) to make the record complete. Cornill assumes that the original Jeremianic nucleus had a metrical structure, that it had no reference to the exile of Judah and that v. 17 is a later addition. In order to achieve poetry Cornill makes extensive deletions in v. 14 and deletes את דרכי עמי and חי יהוה in v. 16. He obtains 3 verses each of 4 stichs and regards ונבנו בתוך עמי as a remnant of another stanza. Judah's neighbours are to be exiled, but Yahweh will graciously restore them, and provided they swear allegiance to Yahweh, they will have the closest relations with Judah. The alterations to MT are so extensive that Cornill's treatment of the passage will not recommend itself to many.

NEB's attempt to make vv. 14–17 cohere better by postulating an order of verses (14*, 16, 17, 14*, 15) different from MT is misguided and has a semblance of credibility only if 'their land' is emended to 'that land' (v. 14). We do not know what Hebrew is intended by 'that land', since Brockington (p. 203) does not record any emendation of אדמתם. The intention of NEB's emendation of 'their land' to 'that land' is apparently to remove any reference to the exile of neighbouring nations. The sense is then simply that they will be removed from Judah's territory on which they have encroached, but will be allowed subsequently to become part of Yahweh's community, provided they embrace Judaism (vv. 16–17). The second part of the passage then deals with Judah which will be exiled and then restored to its own land. Verse 15 does not mean that each Jew (איש) will recover his family allotment of land, as NEB supposes, but that each of the neighbouring nations will recover its נחלה.

Thiel (pp. 162–168) attributes vv. 14–17 to D and concludes that the passage is exilic in date. He argues against the post-exilic date assumed by Duhm and Volz for vv. 14–17 and by Rudolph for vv. 15–17. He holds that the texts which are cited to show the lateness of vv. 14–17 (Isa 2.2–4; 19.19–22; Zech 14.16–21) are dominated by a different idea—the pilgrimage of the nations to Zion. The exile and restoration of the גוים are not the concerns of these texts, and the affiliations of vv. 14–17 are rather with the oracles on foreign nations. This is a correct insight and Thiel's appreciation that the author of vv. 14–15 has latched on to נחלה in vv. 7, 8, 9 is likewise a significant observation. The oracles against foreign nations are according to Thiel (p. 273) post-Deuteronomistic, and if that is so, he ought not to claim 12.14–17 or the call narrative for his Deuteronomistic editor (see above p. 13). The presence of vocabulary from 1.10 in vv. 14–17 (אבד; בנה; נתש) reinforces the view that these verses have far-reaching literary connections, and that they are composed at a date later than that of the call narrative and the oracles on foreign nations.

The circumstance that נחלה means 'people' in vv. 7, 8, 9 and

'land' in vv. 14, 15, and that נחלה has this latter nuance in
Deuteronomic and Deuteronomistic use, is not a powerful
linguistic argument for the Deuteronomistic provenance of
vv. 14–15. There is nothing special about such a use: it is the
ordinary sense of נחלה and it is the poetry of vv. 7, 8, 9 which
uses נחלה in a somewhat special way. Again one should not
expect that an argument for Deuteronomistic authorship
founded on the presence of השיב (v. 15) would carry much
weight. Thiel's contention that vv. 14–17 have the coherence of a
deliberate composition should be challenged. The formulation of
alternatives, said to be a characteristic of D, would be an
account only of vv. 16–17, but these verses have to be seen as a
secondary qualifying of a statement about the restoration of
Judah's neighbours which was unconditional. In so far as
vv. 16–17 are not a formal feature in an integrated composition
consisting of vv. 14–17, Thiel's argument has no force.

The 'evil neighbours' of D's *ex eventu* prophecy (so Thiel) are
the רעים רבים (v. 10) and the שדדים (v. 12) and its foundation is
the events of 582 B.C. (cf. Nicholson), when, according to
Josephus (*Ant.* x 181f.) Nebuchadrezzar marched against
Coele-Syria, occupied it, subdued Moab and Ammon and
carried off Jewish captives to Babylon. The last notice can be
correlated with the reference in Jer 52.28–30, according to
which seven hundred and forty-five Judaeans were deported by
Nebuzaradan in Nebuchadrezzar's twenty-third year (582—this
agrees with the date given by Josephus). Thiel brushes aside the
questions which R. Marcus raises (*Josephus* VI, Loeb Classical
Library, 1937, pp. 258f.) about the sources available to
Josephus. He may have used Jer 52.28–30 for the latter part of
his statement, although he does not mention Nebuzaradan.
What sources did he have for his references to Moab and
Ammon? Marcus says that these are loosely founded on the
notices in the foreign oracles about the uprooting of these
nations. Since Josephus was writing centuries after 582 B.C., we
need to know more about his sources before we can found on his
statements a conclusion that an exilic editor was alluding to a
punitive Babylonian expedition against Moab and Ammon in
582 B.C.

A historical anchorage of this kind should not be sought for
vv. 14–17. It is a late, artificial prophetic composition
(vv. 14–15) to which qualifications have subsequently been
added (vv. 16–17). It is a 'composition' in the sense that it is
composed from pre-existing passages of scripture, especially the
definition of Jeremiah's prophetic office in the call narrative (a
prophet to the nations who is to uproot and to build) and the
notices about the exile and restoration of Judah's neighbours in

the foreign oracles of the book of Jeremiah. This awareness of the connection of vv. 14–15 with other Old Testament passages is already present in Kimchi and can be seen also in Lowth. The expression used in Jer 48.47 and 49.6 is ושבתי שבות, 'And I will restore the fortunes of …'. This is recorded as a decision by Yahweh without reference to the 'repentance' or 'conversion' of those who are restored (Moab and Ammon), and in that regard it is comparable with אשוב ורחמתים והשבתים (v. 15).

Verses 14 and 15 are generated by the poetry in vv. 7–11 and נחלה serves as a stich. The invaders who execute Yahweh's judgement on Judah are identified as neighbouring nations and a prophecy is composed on the foundation of the notices about the uprooting and resettlement of these neighbours in the oracles on foreign nations (48.47; 49.6). The vocabulary is influenced by the account given of Jeremiah as a prophet to the nations in 1.10. Verses 16–17 are a subsequent qualifying of the promise of restoration and it is interesting that we know from Kimchi that there was discussion about the right exegesis of 49.6; that, according to one interpretation, it was not to be understood as an unconditional promise, but as one made to those who would 'learn the ways of Israel'. We may conclude that vv. 16–17 arise out of this kind of interest and concern: v. 15 is one exegesis of ושבתי שבות עמון (מואב) and vv. 16–17 is another. ואת בית יהודה אתוש מתוכם, on the interpretation which has been adopted, is indicative of the effective separation of the Jews from surrounding Gentiles. Such a state of affairs could be said to exist in a Jewish community in Babylon enforcing its separation and apartness from the Gentile world by a stringent interpretation of Yahwism, but the geographical area which is envisaged in vv. 14–15 is Judah and its environs. Hence we should think in terms of the post-exilic Jerusalem community: vv. 14–15 are post-exilic and vv. 16–17 are post-exilic *a fortiori*. This is a judgement which differs from Kimchi only in so far as it assumes that vv. 14–17 are *ex eventu* prophecy. The neighbours who gloated over Judah's misfortunes and took advantage of her weakness when she suffered dismemberment and exile (Obad 10ff.; Zeph 2.8), themselves suffered in turn, as the prophet Jeremiah had predicted. The post-exilic Jerusalem community, effectively separated from the corrupting influences of her neighbours has nothing to fear, even when these neighbours are restored to their former territories, as scripture predicts. But, according to vv. 16–17, their restoration is to be entertained only in so far as they swear allegiance to Yahweh and are integrated in his community.

CHAPTER XIII

EXILE AND DISINTEGRATION (13.1–11)

¹These were the words of Yahweh to me: Go and buy yourself a linen loin-cloth and wear it on your loins, and keep it away from water. ²So I bought the loin-cloth, as Yahweh had instructed me, and wore it on my loins. ³Yahweh's word came to me a second time: ⁴Take the loin-cloth which you bought and are wearing and go to the Euphrates, and conceal it there in a cleft in the rock. ⁵So I went and concealed it at the Euphrates, as Yahweh had required me. ⁶After a long period of time Yahweh said to me: Go to the Euphrates and recover the loin-cloth which I required you to conceal there. ⁷So I went to the Euphrates and dug up the loin-cloth from the place where I had concealed it, but it had rotted and was entirely useless. ⁸Yahweh's word came to me: ⁹These are the words of Yahweh: Likewise I will destroy the pride of Judah and the overweening pride of Jerusalem. ¹⁰This evil nation which refuses to listen to my words, which stubbornly follows its own bent and goes after alien gods to worship them and bow down to them, will be like this loin-cloth which is entirely useless. ¹¹As a loin-cloth is bound to a man's loins, so I have bound all Israel and Judah to myself, that they might be my people, a source of fame, praise and glory for me. But they have refused to listen. This is Yahweh's word.

The evidence of the versions has exegetical significance in relation to פרתה (vv. 4, 6, 7) and בפרת (v. 5). There is no doubt that Sept. and Vulg. take all these as references to the Euphrates, but the evidence of Pesh. and Targ. is also significant in view of the appeal made by Bright to the form פרתה in his tentative equation of these references with *ēn fārā* = Khirbet el-Farah, 4 miles north-east of Anathoth. Bright's argument (which does not account for בפרת in v. 5) is that פרתה, a form with ה *locale*, can be derived from פרה (cf. הפרה, Josh 18.23). It has also been observed that where פרת is used of the Euphrates, it is nearly always preceded by נהר (the exceptions are Jer 51.63; 2 Chr 35.20). There is also the circumstance that Aq. does not indicate the Euphrates (so Rudolph), but his εἰς φαραν ('to Paran') is quite obscure. It is clear that neither Pesh. nor Targ. understands פרתה as פרה with ה *locale*, since they render it throughout as *lprt*, and there can be little doubt that they intend the Euphrates.

The exegetical issue which is raised by פרת is the status of the narrative in vv. 1–11. The problem was known to Kimchi who opposes the opinion of Maimonides that the entire action took place within the framework of a prophetic dream or vision. This sets the stage for the modern debate in which three main opinions are represented: (*a*) The narrative is about actual, symbolic actions which the prophet carries out as Yahweh instructs him. (*b*) The narrative is a container for a prophetic, dream experience and everything which is transacted is contained within the duration of this dream or vision. (c) The form of the portrayal has a purely literary significance; representations of oracular communications and symbolic actions subserve the ends of communication in the context of a parable or allegory. The first view has a natural correlation with the assumption that the autobiographical form of the account is to be taken seriously and the same is true of the second view: these are events of waking life or visionary experiences in which the historical prophet Jeremiah was involved. In respect of the third view, the scope for critical differences is larger, since the evaluation of the passage as parable is not necessarily an assertion that it is late or that it has no foundation in prophetic experience, but its alleged disregard of the canons of credibility and its laboriously contrived allegory have persuaded Duhm that it is very late.

The suggestion that פרתה is to be equated with ēn fārā, a watercourse in the vicinity of Anathoth, is as old as al-Fāsī (S. L. Skoss, op. cit., ii, 1945, p. 486), was revived by B. C. Schick in 1867 (cf. K. Marti, ZPVP, 3, 1880, p. 11) and has subsequently been adopted, among others, by H. Schmidt, Bright, Thiel, p. 174, Nicholson, NEB (Perath). It may be refined by the additional idea that there is an intentional allusion to the Euphrates conveyed by the near homonymy of the names of the two watercourses. This may be regarded as an attempt to overcome an objection which was powerfully stated by Duhm (cf. Rudolph, Hyatt) that it is not enough to find an obscure watercourse in the vicinity of Anathoth with which פרתה may be equated: the allusion must be to a place which was celebrated and was capable of employment as a symbol. We need no longer envisage long journeys by Jeremiah (cf. Ezra 7.9), but can think instead (so the argument runs) of symbolic actions carried out in the vicinity of Anathoth which would be meaningful, because they would be witnessed by those to whom they were addressed. Thiel (pp. 174f.) notices that no public consequences are attributed to the actions described in vv. 1–11 and that there is no express mention of eye-witnesses. He is convinced, however, that the event must have been public, that Jeremiah's actions were witnessed by others and that פרתה must be identified with ēn fārā. Somewhat similar considerations influenced an earlier scholar, J. Boehmer (ThStK 82, 1909, pp. 448–458) who supposed that vv. 1–11 had the residents of Anathoth particularly in mind and that a place in the vicinity of Anathoth is therefore understandable. For separate reasons, and at different times, פרה was changed into פרת in MT and Sept. An earlier attempt to avoid the identification of פרת with the

Euphrates appears in S. Bochart (*Geographia sacra*, 1707, p. 956) and is found in Venema (1765): פרת is equated with אפרת and it is assumed that there is an allusion to the territory of Bethlehem.

The argument that פרת must mean 'Euphrates', since its symbolic associations are necessary to make the passage intelligible (Duhm, Cornill, Rudolph, Hyatt) is questioned by Thiel (pp. 170ff.). He finds evidence of the activity of D in vv. 10–11. It is D who has allegorized the passage, but a Jeremianic core can be disengaged in v. 10: ויהי העם הזה הרע כאזור הזה אשר לא יצלח לכל 'This evil people will become like this loin-cloth which is entirely useless.' While it may be thought that Cornill's strictures on the bathetic character of v. 9 are excessive, it must be said that the ending which Thiel has produced for the alleged original form of Jeremiah's symbolic action is weak and pedestrian. Another attempt to explain vv. 1–9 as actual symbolic action in connection with ēn fārā, on the assumption that vv. 10–11 are Deuteronomic expansion, is found in Nicholson. The loin-cloth is buried and recovered at ēn fārā, but there is a play on פרת and an allusion to the Euphrates. Just as the loin-cloth has rotted, so Judah will rot in exile beyond the Euphrates. The attempt to combine ēn fārā and 'Euphrates' looks rather like an attempt to have the best of both worlds. The symbolism will not embrace both the corruption which leads to exile and the exile which is the consequence of corruption.

We have noticed that the second view of the passage, that it deals with visionary experience, was already held by Maimonides (*The Guide of the Perplexed*, translated by S. Pines, ii, 1963, pp. 405f.; cf. Freehof). This view is represented by Calvin and in the eighteenth century by Lowth and Blayney. Lowth observes that most commentators hold that the actions described were performed by the prophet only in a vision, 'It not being probable that God should send him on two such long journeys as are mentioned here (v. 4) and ver. 6 meerly upon this errand' (similarly Blayney). That Jeremiah in fact did not make two round journeys to the Euphrates is something which, according to Giesebrecht, hardly needs to be asserted. According to I. P. Seierstad (op. cit., pp. 167 n. 4, 182) the action described is a purely inward, spiritual experience. The introductory formula affords no clue that we have to do with a vision (cf. Thiel, p. 173), nor is the appeal to the vague sense of time characteristic of dream experience (with reference to מקץ ימים רבים) a decisive pointer. Jeremiah carries out Yahweh's directive (vv. 1–2), and after an interval (שנית) he is instructed by a second divine communication (vv. 3–5). When a long period of time has elapsed (מקץ ימים רבים) he is required by a further revealed word to retrieve the loin-cloth which he had concealed (vv. 6–7). In a final disclosure Yahweh gives him a detailed explanation of the symbolic actions which he had undertaken (vv. 8–11). On the face of it, there is no reason to suppose that the time-span of the narrative is other than the time of normal experience, that is, public chronology. The problem is that unless we relinquish this 'natural' way of interpreting the narrative, we are landed in insuperable difficulties. We should be aware, however, that we are making a special effort to win a framework of interpretation for the narrative, when we enclose it in dream experience. In effect a new dimension of interpretation is being added to the narrative: it is not really made up of oracles and symbolic actions, but is a dream about oracles and symbolic actions.

The third opinion which was picked out above (p. 286) does not necessarily imply that the passage is to be disengaged from the prophet Jeremiah or that it has no foundation in prophetic experience, although it may have this implication (Duhm). It is vulgar invention (so Duhm) and superficial edification, without a sense for real life or for spirituality of intrinsic worth, intended for a public which had no discernment. The author could have jettisoned all his representations of symbolic action and allegorical equipment and have achieved his end in one sentence: 'As a loin-cloth rots in water, so Judah will rot'. Hence the passage is made up of vulgar legend and superfluous allegory.

According to Volz we do not have a record of public events, nor yet a simple transcript of visionary experience, but a *Gleichnisgeschichte* which is a transmutation of experience into a form of literature and is not merely literary device and furnishing. Hence it is 'revelation', it is a form of the prophetic word, but the primary experience has been given a literary dress, that of a dramatic parable. A distinctive feature of his interpretation of the parable or allegory is his view that the אזור is a decorative or ceremonial item of dress, worn with a sense of pride, and in this way he correlates the rotting of the אזור with the threat that the pride of Judah and Jerusalem will be destroyed (v. 9). According to his exegesis the parable has nothing to say about corrupting, Mesopotamian influences (idolatry; foreign alliances) prior to the exile: it deals with the exile itself and the humiliation and depression of the Jews as a consequence of this event. Thus Volz takes the allegorical correspondences of the passage seriously and extracts from them a prophetic word concerning exile and shame.

For Cornill, on the other hand, the genuine word of Jeremiah is contained in vv. 1–7, a dramatic parable which is not supplied with an interpretation. The allegorical correspondences which are attached in vv. 9–11 are secondary and misguided efforts to explain the imagery of vv. 1–7. The parable itself is not concerned with the exile and its consequences, but with corrupting Assyrian influences which Jeremiah discerned in Judah at the beginning of his ministry.

There are some problems which are common whatever view is taken of the status of vv. 1–11. A fundamental decision which has to be made is whether allegorical correspondences are to be pressed, or whether the interpretation of the passage is rather to be made to hinge on a single point of illumination after the manner of a parable. Rudolph, whose presuppositions are different from those of Cornill, nevertheless, also finds the meaning of the passage summed up in 2.18—Judah has drunk the water of the Euphrates. She has so succumbed to the influences of the Fertile Crescent that she is totally corrupted. In order to establish that the passage is entirely concerned with the present condition of Judah (= Cornill) and contains no threat for the future Rudolph has to emend MT at v. 9 (אשחית to נשחת) and v. 10 (וְיהִי to וַיְהִי).

Another account which finds no reference to exile in the passage and which disregards allegorical correspondences is that of E. Baumann (*ZAW* 65, 1953, pp. 77–81). The concealing of the loin-cloth בנקיק הצלע is thought to point to the reliance of Judah on the might of Babylon, and we are then to suppose that the decayed state of the cloth when Jeremiah retrieved it was counter to all expectations: what was taken as a guarantee of Judah's safety (the shelter afforded by the power of Babylon) turns out to be the cause of her disintegration. In essence Baumann is following Cornill, but he attaches a particular symbolism to בנקיק הצלע, thus reinforcing the symbolism of the 'Euphrates'.

Rudolph's criticisms of Volz and Weiser are only partially justified. He urges that if the hiding of the cloth by Jeremiah is indicative of the banishing of Judah to Babylon by Yahweh, its retrieval must be indicative of Judah's restoration by Yahweh to her own land. But then (so Rudolph) we are faced with the absurdity that the nation which is destroyed and good for nothing is to be restored to its own land. It is true that this is how the matter is seen by Jerome (*post longum autem tempus ipse propheta in typum dei populum liberat de captivitate*), but the discovery on retrieval is that the cloth has rotted and there is nothing in the account which indicates a return (so Bright). Rudolph's stance is related to his view that 13.1–11 is to be dated perhaps before the reform of Josiah but certainly before 597, whereas Weiser supposes that the passage is connected with questions raised in Jeremiah's mind as a consequence of the deportation in 597—either it represents second thoughts over against chapter 24, or it is indicative of an oscillation of moods and of conflicting thoughts concerning the fate of the exilic community. It will not be able to withstand the exposure to alien influences in Babylon; it will be subject to destructive pressures and will disintegrate.

On 'Do not bring it into contact with water' (v. 1) Rashi comments: 'To wash it; so that it might be full of sweat in order to hasten the rotting of the fabric' (cf. Kimchi). Rudolph is correct in holding that the loin-cloth concealed בנקיק הצלע is destroyed by humidity (*pace* Baumann, p. 178), but incorrect in assuming that there is a connection between this and the command in v. 1, ובמים לא תבאהו (cf. p. 86 n. 2). Weiser offers two explanations of v. 1: (*a*) The constant wearing of the loin-cloth is an indication of Yahweh's continuous care for his people and the indissolubility of their relationship. Hence the cloth must never be taken off. (*b*) The cloth, unwashed and soiled with sweat, is an indication of Yahweh's forbearance with his people. The second point should be dismissed, but the first interpretation is the one which has been worked out in v. 11. According to this verse ובמים לא תבאהו is a way of saying, 'On no account and in no circumstances are you to take off this loin-cloth, not even for what might seem the most elementary and necessary reason—to wash it,' The point which v. 11 makes is that the constant contact of the loin-cloth with Jeremiah's body is indicative of the indissolubility of the bond between Yahweh and his people. This is elucidated in terms of Israel's election and the dignity which she derives from Yahweh's choice of her.

The final assault on this difficult passage may be begun with the assertion that the symbolism in vv. 1–7 must be taken to refer to the exile. It is the exile which breaks the bond between Yahweh and his people and Kimchi is right when he connects the taking off of the loin-cloth and its concealment בנקיק הצלע with the exile. An aspect of the interpretation of vv. 1–7 which has perhaps been somewhat neglected is the indispensability of Israel's occupation of her own land to the maintenance of the bond between herself and Yahweh. Whatever status is accorded to vv. 1–7, the symbolic constituents, which are not supplied with an explicit interpretation, must refer to exile. Hence vv. 8–11 are subsequent additions and their intention is to interpret vv. 1–7, but it is doubtful whether they can be regarded as constituting one coherent interpretation. It is probable that vv. 10–11 hang together, but v. 9 is a separate explanation of vv. 1–7, remarkable for its generality and its lack of particular reference to the imagery of the preceding verses. It is triggered by נשחת

(v. 7), but it simply delivers the threat that Yahweh will destroy (ככה אשחית) the pride of Judah and the overwhelming pride of Jerusalem, and takes no account otherwise of the particular imagery in these verses.

The view that vv. 10–11 hang together as a Deuteronomic explanation of the preceding symbolism has been expressed by Nicholson, and this agrees largely with Thiel's view of these verses, although he has attempted to extract a Jeremianic core from v. 10 (above, p. 287). Verse 10 offers an interpretation which must also (cf. v. 9) be regarded as very general, but which achieves some particularity by picking up כאזור הזה אשר לא יצלח לכל (cf. v. 7). It explains vv. 1–7 in terms of a refusal to obey Yahweh's law or the message of his prophets (דברי) and an addiction to the worship of אלהים אחרים. It is because of this that a rot has set in and the community will disintegrate like the loin-cloth. Sept. does not represent ההלכים בשררות לבם (v. 10) and Janzen (p. 40) supposes that MT has been secondarily supplemented from such passages as 7.24, 11.8 and 23.17. The Deuteronomic or Deuteronomistic affinities of the vocabulary are evident in v. 10 and in v. 11. דבק in v. 11, however, arises immediately out of the attempt to give an account of the imagery in vv. 1–7 and there is no case for dragging in Deuteronomic or Deuteronomistic uses of דבק (*pace* Thiel, p. 171). It is likely that vv. 10–11 constitute a single interpretation of vv. 1–7 rather than two separate interpretations. The generality of v. 10 is compensated for in v. 11 by an attempt to come to grips more particularly with the symbolism of vv. 1–7. The Deuteronomic affinities of v. 11 are seen in את כל בית ישראל ואת כל בית יהודה and in ולשם ולתהלה ולתפארת which could be a citation of Deut. 26.19, although the positions of תהלה and שם have been reversed.

The proposal that there is a play which enables us to reckon with both *ēn fārā* and the Euphrates should be discounted: it is not an economical hypothesis and it is a shift to which resort is had in order to save the character of vv. 1–7 as public action and, at the same time, secure a satisfactory symbolic reference for פרת. If vv. 1–7 do not describe public, symbolic acts in which the prophet Jeremiah engaged, are they attributable to the prophet as visionary experience, or as parable which casts prophetic experience in a literary mould? There are no features on the surface of the passage to encourage the view that it is a transcript of visionary experience (cf. Thiel, p. 173). If it is a dramatic parable or allegory, this is a form of communication not normally associated with the prophet Jeremiah, but the subject (judgement and disintegration) is one with which he was deeply concerned. If it is a kind of parable, we have to consider whether the historical Jeremiah would have expressed a דבר

יהוה in such an extravagant literary form. Verses 1–7 may themselves be exilic, and representative of a view of the exile as a severance from Yahweh which poses the threat of a total disintegration, rather than a parabolic expression of a prophetic insight of the historical Jeremiah.

INTOXICATION AND DISINTEGRATION (13.12–14)

> [12]You are to say to this people:[1,2] Every jar (skin) is filled with wine. They will say to you: Do you suppose we do not know that every jar (skin) is filled with wine? [13]You are to say to them: These are the words of Yahweh: I will make all the inhabitants of this land drunk, the kings who sit on David's throne, the priests, the prophets and all the inhabitants of Jerusalem. [14]I will smash them against each other, fathers against sons. I will not spare them; I will not pity them nor show mercy, so as to stop short of destroying them. This is Yahweh's word.

The text of MT v. 12 (אליהם) has perhaps been influenced by an attempt to bind vv. 12–14 to the preceding section of the chapter: v. 11, which ends with ולא שמעו, is thought to require a further threat of punishment and this is uttered in vv. 12–14. The attachment of vv. 12–14 may also have been encouraged by the circumstance that מהשחיתם appears in v. 14 (cf. נשחת, v. 7; אשחית, v. 9). If vv. 12–14 constitute an independent unit in prose (Rudolph, Weiser, Bright, Nicholson), Sept. (πρὸς τὸν λαὸν τοῦτον) may represent a more original Hebrew text than MT and one more appropriate to the opening of a new unit (ואמרת אל העם הזה). Further, Yahweh's speech does not come until v. 13 and has its own introductory formula, so that את הדבר הזה כה אמר יהוה אלהי ישראל (v. 12) appears to be superfluous. These words are not represented by Sept. and should be deleted (so Rudolph): כל נבל ימלא יין is a proverbial saying and its introduction by a formula indicative of a 'revealed' word of God is inappropriate. The spelling out of MT in Sept., rather than the translation of a Hebrew text different from MT, can be seen in the following cases: (a) ואמרו אליך (v. 12); καὶ ἔσται ἐὰν εἴπωσι πρὸς σέ (pace Rudolph) (b) ואת המלכים (v. 13); καὶ τοὺς βασιλεῖς αὐτῶν (c) לדוד על כסאו (v. 13) is a concentrated expression which is correctly elucidated by Sept. as υἱοὺς Δαυιδ ἐπὶ θρόνου αὐτῶν, that is, the kings of the Davidic dynasty (similarly Vulg.).

The classification of the occurrences of נבל (v. 12) in W. Gesenius (*Thesaurus*, ii, 1840, p. 844) is the same as that of BDB and is maintained by A. M. Honeyman (*PEQ*, 1939,

---

[1] Reading אל העם הזה with Sept. (see below)

[2] Reading את הדבר הזה כה אמר יהוה אלהי ישראל (see below).

p. 85). Gesenius reproduces a comment of Kimchi on נבל in Jer
13.12 (נאד העור או כד היוצר) which Honeyman considers and
on which he comments (p. 85, n. 1), 'That an earthen vessel is
here intended, is more than a possibility, as Gesenius (*s.v.*)
states. The verb refers not to the deflating of a skin, but to the
smashing of pottery as in Judges 7.19.' When all the uses of נבל
are reviewed it appears that the meaning 'jar' can be gathered
with certainty from some of the contexts, but that the meaning
'skin' is not well-founded. This is conceded by Gesenius: he
divided the uses into two classes, class 1 'skin' and class 2
'jar'—the same classification as BDB—but he observed of the
uses which he gathered under class 1, *quanquam haec exempla
etiam ad no. 2 referri possunt*. Gesenius's view of the semantic
development of נבל is as follows: 'Since, however, ancient men,
for the most part, were accustomed to use skins for containing
and carrying water, milk and wine, this name was then
transferred to any kind of water-vessel.' The same view is
maintained by Honeyman (p. 85). The conclusion that נבל can
mean 'skin' would seem to have been reached not on the evidence
supplied by the actual uses but in terms of a postulated semantic
development.

The following are the occurrences where the sense
'earthenware pot' or the like appears to be well-established for
נבל:

(*a*) כלי הנבלים, 'earthenware vessels' (Isa 22.24).

(*b*) כשבר נבל יוצרים, 'like the shattering of a vessel made by a
potter' (Isa 30.14).

(*c*) ונבליהם ינפצו, 'and they will shatter their pots' (Jer 48.12).

(*d*) נבלי חרש, 'earthenware vessels' (Lam 4.2).

(*e*) נבל with נפץ 'shatter', if Jer 13.12–14 is a unity.

The sense 'skin' is not well-founded for נבל, although it is
given by Gesenius and BDB in respect of 1 Sam 1.24, 10.3,
25.18, 2 Sam 16.1 and Job 38.37. Only in the case of Job 38.37
is there any contextual help: the parallelism of נבלי שמים and
שחקים might be thought to point to 'skins'. KB², however,
associates נבל in נבלי שמים with מבול 'flood' and this becomes
more probable if מבול means strictly the ocean above the
firmament as W. F. Albright (*JBL* 58, 1939, p. 98) and F. Stolz
(*BZAW* 118, 1970, p. 165) suppose. It is then understandable
that נבלי שמים should be an expression for 'rain-waters', that is,
waters released from the upper ocean through the 'windows' of
heaven. The evidence of the versions is conflicting and has been
examined by me in detail elsewhere (*Terrien Festschrift*,
pp. 109f.). The most interesting renderings of Job 38.37 are
those of Aq. and Targ. Aq.'s απορρεοντα ουρανου, 'overflowing
waters of heaven' suggests that he connected נבלי with מבול (see

above, p. 293), so that this understanding of נבלי שמים is supported by an early witness. Targ., on the other hand, gives explicit support to the view that נבלי שמים means 'skins of heaven'.

When we turn to Jer 13.12, in particular, we find that 'skin' is represented by Sept. (ἀσκός) and 'jar' or the like by Vulg. (*laguncula*). Pesh. (*grb'*) and Targ. (גרב) probably indicate 'jar'. The variations in the later Greek versions are noted by Jerome: *verbum Hebraicum nebel Aquilae prima editio lagunculam, secundum ipsum nebel, Symmachus craterem, LXX utrem, Theodotio vas interpretati sunt.* Hence Aq., having hazarded 'jar' or 'pitcher' (ὑδρια) as a translation would seem to have retreated to a transliteration (cf. Ziegler). Symm. (κρατηρ) supposes that נבל is the bowl in which wine was mixed with water preparatory to serving it, and Theod. (αγγειον) clearly indicates a pottery vessel and not a skin.

The lexicographical enquiry has shown that there is no use of נבל in biblical Hebrew for which the sense 'skin' is certainly established. The possibility that נבל has the sense 'skin' in כל נבל ימלא יין (Jer 13.12) should be left open, although all the versions except Sept. indicate a pottery vessel rather than a skin and the commentators are almost unanimously in favour of 'jar' or the like (Calvin, Lowth, Venema, Graf, Hitzig, Giesebrecht, Duhm, Peake, Volz, Rudolph, Weiser, Bright, van Selms, Nicholson). The clash between נבל rendered as ἀσκός 'skin' and ונפצתים (v. 14) 'smash' does not arise for Sept. because ונפצתים is rendered as καὶ διασκορπιῶ αὐτούς, 'and I will scatter them'. Vulg. has 'jar' in v. 12, but it too renders ונפצתים as 'disperse' (*dispergam*), as also does Pesh. (*'bdr*). There are two ways in which these translations might be accounted for:

(*a*) נפץ has been taken as a variant root of פוץ 'scatter'.

(*b*) The renderings of Sept., Vulg. and Pesh. contain an element of interpretation and 'smashing' is explained as dispersion and exile.

The general view of both Rashi and Kimchi is that נבל means 'earthenware vessel' (כלי חרש) and that ונפצתים means 'smash'. The unity of vv. 12–14 and the functioning of the משל are thought to require this correlation of 'earthenware vessel' and 'smash'. Kimchi attaches two proverbial nuances to נבל:

(*a*) Just as the entire capacity of a jar is taken up with the wine that fills it, so Judah will be entirely filled with שכרון (explained as great distress and tribulation); and just as a drunk man is no longer fully aware of what he is doing, so they, under the pressure of privations and sufferings, will become bewildered and confused.

(*b*) The Judaeans are likened to a נבל, because when one jar is struck against another, both are reduced to fragments. Civil discord between families and between older and younger generations will lead to a total disintegration. The community will be so weakened that external enemies will easily finish it off.

The thought that the judgement on Judah will finally be executed by external enemies, whose task will be made easy by the inner disintegration of the community, is implied in the references to dispersion and exile in Sept., Vulg. and Pesh., is explicit in Kimchi's exegesis, and is represented by Venema. Commentators are divided as to whether or not there is a reference to civil war in v. 14 (Yes: Calvin, Elliott Binns, Volz; No: Graf, Hitzig, Giesebrecht, van Selms). The cup of wine is seen by some as the cup of wrath which Yahweh requires his people to drink (Lowth, Venema, Blayney, Graf, Hitzig, Giesebrecht, Duhm, Peake, Volz).

At least three explanations of the proverb 'Every jar (skin) is filled with wine' are offered and these are arranged here in an ascending order of probability: (a) The proverb is expressive of a false sense of security and of a belief that prosperity will be enjoyed without interruption. The prophet handles it in such a way that he reverses a tenacious, popular attitude (Elliott Binns, Habel). Just as wine bottles are liable to be filled with wine in the normal course of events, so Judah in due course will be rewarded by Yahweh (Elliott Binns). (b) 'Every jar is filled with wine' is a משל adopted or coined by the prophet and is indicative of God's cup of wrath and of the imminent 'shattering' of the community. Where the saying is envisaged as a popular proverb which Jeremiah has taken up (Bright, van Selms, Nicholson), it is thought to mean something like, 'Every vessel receives the contents for which it is intended', or 'Everything has its right use'. It is appropriated in this sense by those who hear it and this is explained by the commentators mentioned above as either an accidental or wilful misconstruction of the prophet's words (Lowth, Blayney, Bright). Bright supposes that a popular proverb which means 'Everything has its right use' is twisted into a toper's jest and then developed by the prophet as a threat of judgement in terms of a cup of wrath and a shattering of wine jars. Blayney's view of the matter is that Jer 13.12–14 can be compared with Nathan's parable in 2 Sam 12. The first attempt to communicate parabolically is thwarted by a failure to grasp the point of the parable and it becomes necessary for the prophet to spell the matter out. Hence Blayney continues, 'But the prophet is directed to deal more plainly with them, and to tell them that the wine he meant was not such as would exhilarate, but such as would intoxicate; being no other than what would be poured out of the wine cup of God's fury to the subversion of all ranks and orders of men among them.' (c) The commentators who are assembled under (c) make particular use of the thought that the opening saying, 'Every jar is filled with wine', is commonplace or banal, that this banality is deliberate and that it triggers the process of communication (Calvin, Giesebrecht, Duhm, Peake, Volz, Rudolph, Weiser). 'Every jar is filled with wine' is in the first instance not to be understood as a serious attempt to communicate proverbially, but as a saying of such ordinariness that those who hear it are struck by its incongruity on a prophet's lips and are jolted into attention. A graphic representation of the manner in which the banality of the opening saying may be supposed to have awakened the attention of the audience is given by Calvin. A more specialized application of this mode of interpretation is associated with the assumption that the proverb, 'Every jar is filled with wine', is a toper's witticism (Giesebrecht, Duhm, Rudolph) and that the occasion is a drinking-bout, perhaps an abuse associated with a cultic occasion (Peake, Volz, Rudolph, Weiser).

How do the ideas of 'intoxication' and 'shattering' combine or interact in vv. 12–14? Different answers to this question give rise to different views about the functioning of the proverb in vv. 12–14. There are those who have not been greatly exercised to demonstrate that the passage has a complex unity and who have been content to assume that there are two images of judgement ('intoxication' and 'shattering') which are loosely connected, in so far as the vessels which are shattered are wine jars, but which otherwise function more or less independently, the second reinforcing the first (Lowth, Hitzig). The dissociation of the two images of 'intoxication' and 'shattering' is most pronounced in van Selms who introduces the thought of an earthquake as the background to the 'shattering' image: the tremor causes jars which are stacked in rows to break against each other.

There are those who have explained vv. 12–14 on the assumption that 'intoxication' and 'shattering' are inter-connected images which contribute to a complex parabolic unity (Graf, Giesebrecht, Peake, Volz). But if the thought of drunk men (who are full wine jars) is present in v. 14, ונפצתים does not seem to be appropriate, because the shattering ought to be a consequence of collisions of drunkards (full wine jars) and ought not to be described as a further act of Yahweh (cf. Peake). In order to find a place for ונפצתים Volz has to suppose that v. 14 contains both an image of 'shattering' which hangs together with the intoxication of v. 13 and an interpretation of that image ('so Yahweh will shatter etc.').

Some remarks have been made on the text of vv. 12–14 and on

the view that the passage constitutes an independent unit (above, p. 292). Thiel regards אליהם (v. 12) as a redactional device for linking vv. 12–14 to vv. 1–11 (pp. 176f.). Otherwise he describes vv. 12–14 as a composition by D built up from a fragmentary, Jeremianic core in order to enlarge on the theme of judgement which appears in vv. 9f. The opening part of v. 12 (MT), which is redactional and establishes a connection with what precedes, may or may not be attributable to D and the same holds for the inapposite messenger formula in v. 12. The list of classes inserted in v. 13 is the work of D (deleted by Erbt, Cornill, Giesebrecht, Volz), as is the final part of v. 14 (deleted by Cornill), by means of which D emphasizes Yahweh's implacability. With regard to this particular, Thiel appeals to Jer 21.7, which he regards as another D passage, whereas Weippert (pp. 28f.) associates the threefold affirmations of 13.14 and 21.7 as examples of the prose of the prophet Jeremiah. Rudolph explains vv. 12–14 on the assumption that the historical background is the reign of Zedekiah, while Weiser maintains that since the threat is a future one which was fulfilled in the civil strife of Zedekiah's reign it must have been issued at an earlier period. Rudolph understands the passage not only as the issuing of a threat of civil strife and disintegration which is to eventuate in the future, but also as a description of existing conditions and a search for self-understanding on the part of the prophet. Jeremiah saw the beginnings of the end in the reign of Zedekiah and was concerned to understand the source of the madness (the intoxication) which was bearing the community to destruction, as well as to issue a threat of fragmentation.

More reserve is needed (*pace* Rudolph) in the postulation of such particular relations between pieces of text and historical moments. So far as the text itself is concerned, there is a further doubt whether the images of 'intoxication' and 'shattering' can be combined so as to create a credible unity out of vv. 12–14 (cf. Duhm). Verses 12–13 (the list of classes in v. 13 may be secondary) constitute a proverbial unit, but v. 14, which introduces the idea of 'shattering', does not integrate satisfactorily with this unit. That v. 14 should have been attached secondarily to vv. 12–13 is understandable, for if the proverb in v. 12 is taken to mean 'Every jar is filled with wine', the fragility of these jars provides a *point d'appui* for the thought of 'shattering'. Nevertheless, if we were not distracted by the introduction of the idea of 'shattering', we would see that what really follows from 'Every jar (skin) is filled with wine' is the threat of 'intoxication'. Hence the area of thought in which vv. 12–13 are located is that of the 'cup of wrath' (Jer 25.15–29; 48.26; 49.12; 51.57; Isa 51.17; Hab 2.16; Lam 4.21; Rev 14.10;

16.19). The banqueting-cup is changed to a cup of poison, or, perhaps, the chalice brings curse instead of blessing and induces suicidal behaviour (cf. W. McKane, *VT* 30 (1980), pp. 474–492).

If vv. 12–13 contain an allusion to the distended belly of the toper (so Rudolph), there is something to be said for rendering the proverb, 'Every skin is filled with wine', since the correspondence of the full wine skin and the full belly of the toper has more proverbial finesse than the correspondence between the full wine jar and the full belly of the toper. If vv. 12–14 are not an original unit, the argument that there is an incongruity between 'skin' and 'shatter' no longer applies. The argument that vv. 12–13 are the original proverbial unit, with which v. 14 imperfectly coheres, does not, however, depend on the assumption that נבל in v. 12 means 'skin' and is compatible with the assumption that נבל means 'jar'. The argument in relation to v. 14 would then be that whoever was responsible for this exegetical development of vv. 12–13 correctly understood נבל in v. 12 as 'jar' and redirected it towards 'shattering' rather than 'intoxication' in terms of the fragility of wine jars.

DARKNESS IS CLOSING IN (13.15–17)

> [15]Listen and pay heed, do not be arrogant,
> for it is Yahweh who speaks.
> [16]Give glory to Yahweh, your God,
> before darkness sets in,
> before your feet stumble
> on darkening hill-sides.
> You expected light but he turned it to darkness;
> he made it[1] into gloom.
> [17]If you refuse to listen,
> I will weep secretly in anguish;[2]
> my eyes will flow with tears,
> for Yahweh's flock must go into exile.

Driver's explanation of ישמה (*JQR* 28, p. 112) that ה here and elsewhere represents the masculine suffix (וְשָׂמֹה) is the correct one (ה is an earlier orthography than ו, cf. J. C. L. Gibson, *Syrian Semitic Inscriptions*, i, 1971, p. 29 n. 2). Driver's other proposal is linked to an appeal to Sept. (καὶ τεθήσονται εἰς σκότος) which he explains as a misreading of וְשָׁתוּ (taken as וְשָׁתוּ). The telescoped texts of Vulg. and Pesh. (ישית or ושית is not represented) represent an interpretation of MT which accords with that of Kimchi, namely that ישית לערפל is another way of expressing ושמה לצלמות (cf. Volz who supposes that the

---

[1] Reading יָשִׁית.

[2] Deleting ודמע תדמע (see below, p. 300).

second is a gloss on the first). Hesitation in placing Driver's construction on καὶ τεθήσονται is reinforced by other features of Sept.'s rendering of v. 16: καὶ ἐκεῖ σκιὰ θανάτου is probably an attempt to circumvent the difficulties of MT (ושמה לצלמות read as וְשָׂמָה לצלמות). Sept., Aq., Vulg. and Pesh. all suppose that the elements of צלמות are צל and מות. צלמות is perhaps rather a form with an *ût* ending from *ṣlm*, to be compared with Arabic *ẓalamat* 'darkness' (the phonemic correspondences are exact). The difficulty of drawing metrical considerations into the argument is illustrated by the differing analyses of Rudolph and Driver:

Rudolph: v. 15   3+2   v. 16 4+2   3+2   4+2
Driver: v. 15   3+2   v. 16 3+3   3+2   3+3

In v. 17 both Rudolph and NEB ('If in those depths of gloom you will not listen') contradict the punctuation of MT and attach במסתרים to what precedes. NEB assumes that במסתרים can mean 'depths of gloom' and so follows the indication of Aq. (ἐν σκοτεινοῖς), while Rudolph concludes that all the attempts to make sense of במסתרים have been unsuccessful. He rejects Duhm's suggestion (followed by Cornill and Weiser) that there is an allusion to the persecution of the prophet and Baruch by Jehoiakim which necessitated their going into hiding (36.26). Hence he emends במסתרים to either במסררים or במסרבים and connects this with what precedes, 'If in your rebelliousness, you will not listen'. The suggestion that במסתרים should be connected with the preceding part of the verse is already found in Blayney who supposes that מסתרים are 'secure places': Calvin and Lowth, on the other hand, both observe the punctuation of MT and conclude that Jeremiah is intimating that he can no longer effectively discharge his public, prophetic office.

Sept. differs from MT only in respect of ἡ ψυχὴ ὑμῶν (MT נפשי): instead of the prophet weeping in secret as a consequence of the failure of the people to respond to his pleas, Sept. represents the issue of a threat—you will have ample time to mourn privately over your failure to listen and obey (when you are in exile). Vulg, Pesh. and Targ. render במסתרים as 'in secret' and Kimchi explains it by drawing a distinction between secret and open grief, between the pain in the prophet's heart and the tears which stream from his eyes: 'I shall weep in secret, for I can see your bitter end'. The weeping of the soul in secret is ראגה —a sorrow and care which eats the heart away. Kimchi's exegesis merits consideration: the outer manifestation of grief does not consist of crocodile tears, but is a rising to the surface of a well of sorrow in the depths of the prophet's soul.

If גוה is a shortened form of גאוה 'pride' (BDB), it picks up אל
תגבהו (v. 15). The rendering of Targ. (מן קדם יערי מנכון יקרכון,
'because he will take away your glory from you') is the source of
the first of Rashi's explanations ('because of their pride which
would become null and void'), and Pesh. ('because of distresses')
is similarly founded on the view that 'because of pride' means
'because of pride which will be removed'. It is not obvious that
satisfactory sense can be had from תבכה נפשי מפני גוה, if גוה =
גאוה 'pride' (cf. Ehrlich, p. 279 who emends גוה to יגון 'sorrow').
Pesh., Targ. and Rashi were clearly influenced by the subsequent
reference to exile in the verse and supposed that there was a
parallelism between this and מפני גוה : the prophet's grief is
caused by the prospect that the dignity and status of the
community will be destroyed. Alternatively one might conclude
that the source of his grief is the stiff, disastrous pride of the
people which makes them totally unresponsive to his prophetic
word. N. S. Doniach's proposal (*AJSL* 50, 1933–34, pp. 177f.)
that גוה should be associated with Syriac *gw'* 'inward part',
Arabic *jwy* 'violent emotion', either of joy or grief, is attractive.
גוה is then a reference to an inner anguish which is the source of
Jeremiah's tears (cf. NEB, 'then for very anguish'). It is dubious,
however, whether the other occurrence of גוה (Job 33.17) can be
used to reinforce this lexicography, as Doniach contends, but
'inner anguish' gives superior sense at Jer 13.17 and Doniach's
lexicography should be adopted for that verse.

ודמע תדמע (v. 17) is not represented by Sept. and Rudolph
(following Duhm) deletes it as superfluous and metrically
disturbing. There is no doubt that ודמע תדמע complicates the
metre of the verse and produces an uneven number of stichs,
unless one supposes that ודמע תדמע ותרד עיני דמעה is a single
stich, but this can hardly be right. The shorter text of Sept.
should be adopted.

Rudolph supposes that נשבה (v. 17) is a prophetic perfect, so
that it refers to a future captivity and not to one which has
already taken place. This hinges on the date which is assigned to
the piece, and Rudolph suggests that it belongs to a period just
before 597 (similarly Weiser). Bright and Nicholson, on the
other hand, suppose that a deportation has already taken place.
Nicholson locates the piece between 597 and 586, correlating
these dates with 'twilight' and 'darkness' respectively. Both Sept.
(συνετρίβη, 'broken in pieces') and Vulg. (*quia captus est*)
indicate a past rather than a future event. But a precise answer
cannot be given to such historical questions on the foundation of
vv. 15–17, nor is it possible to achieve the historical correlations
after which it has been customary for scholars to strive. It is
impossible to decide with any assurance whether the passage is

wholly proleptic or whether it is partly retrospective and partly proleptic.

For Nicholson עֵדֶר is the clue to the imagery in vv. 15–16: 'The image is one of shepherds who have guarded their flocks (cf. v. 17) on the hill-sides during the night and now await the dawn and the coming of day.' For Weiser, on the other hand, עֵדֶר is an element of a complex of liturgical vocabulary and concepts which he discerns at the base of the passage. Thus Weiser connects the reference to 'light' in v. 16 with the brilliance associated with Yahweh's appearance (theophany), and also with the light of salvation guaranteed to Yahweh's faithful people in and through the cult. Targ. does not regard עֵדֶר as an important constituent of the imagery: עֵדֶר is paraphrased as עַמָּא, but the principal elucidation is offered in connection with an extensive paraphrase of v. 16: darkness is equated with distress and disaster, and light with prosperity and safety. The Judaeans are likened to those who are in danger of losing their footing in difficult and dangerous conditions on mountain tracks. Struggling in poor light, they hope that daylight will come and that they will then be able to make safe progress. But what if the daylight does not come? In that case they will perish. Similarly the ill-founded hopes of the Judaean community will prove to be illusory: there are no better times round the corner and they will perish.

Kimchi relates 'pride' to political attitudes and this is confirmed by his comment on אוֹר which he connects with reliance on foreign allies: 'hoping for light' means hoping for safety through a pact with Egypt. Thus הָרֵי נָשֶׁף is explained by Rashi as בְּלֶכְתָם בַּגּוֹלָה (cf. Volz's conjecture that גוה should be emended to גּוֹלָה which Rudolph thinks should be seriously considered). It is dubious whether the light for which they look and which never appears can be interpreted as the light of a homestead (so Rudolph). It is rather the light which should follow darkness and which would enable those who await it to extricate themselves from their danger on precarious mountain tracks. The 'darkness' of judgement is comparable in respect of the terror which it awakens and the shock which it administers to the preternatural darkness created by the non-arrival of daybreak. There is something to be said for the view that עֵדֶר (v. 17) should be read back into v. 16: the people are like a flock of sheep marooned on precipitous sheep-tracks and deserted by their shepherds (cf. 13.13, 20). If they escape the worst during the hours of darkness, they should manage to extricate themselves safely when daylight returns. But what if there should be a long, unbroken, unnatural darkness? Must they not then surely perish? This is the condition of Judah. The people

suppose that deliverance is round the corner; in truth what
beckons them is not the light of salvation, but the darkness of
judgement and exile, and this will be like a long, unending night.
Darkness is falling and there is time for only one more appeal by
Jeremiah; thereafter he must retire from his public, prophetic
responsibility and suffer the private sorrow of awaiting an exile
which must ensue. It is not clear whether the prophet speaks
throughout for his own part, or whether there is an element of
'word of Yahweh' in vv. 15–17. The presence of ליהוה אלהיכם
instead of לי in v. 16 does not preclude the possibility that
vv. 15–16 are word of Yahweh. In that case v. 17 is a personal
postscript by Jeremiah, touched with anguish, in which he makes
his last appeal: if you refuse to listen to Yahweh's word, sorrow
will cut me to the quick.

THE CRUMBLING OF KINGSHIP (13.18–19)

> [18]Say to the king and queen mother:
> Take a lowly seat,
> for your splendid crowns have fallen from your heads.[1]
> [19]The towns of the Negeb are under siege
> and there is no force to relieve them.
> All Judah has been carried off into exile,
> has been entirely[2] removed.

The difference between MT (אָמֹר) and Sept. (εἴπατε) and Pesh.
('mrw) reflects a divergence of view on the form of the passage.
Sept. and Pesh. apparently suppose vv. 18–19 to be an
instruction conveyed to an unspecified group by the prophet
Jeremiah: 'Go and say this to the king and the queen mother'.
This understanding of the passage may prevail (as it does with
Kimchi), even when MT is followed. The issue is raised by
Weiser who holds that vv. 18–19 were attached to vv. 15–17
because they were thought to refer to the same situation,
connecting as they do with the mention of captivity in v. 17 and
the warning against pride in v. 15. Weiser correctly understands
vv. 18–19 as a word of Yahweh to Jeremiah. His further
suggestion that v. 18 was wrongly taken as a continuation of
Yahweh's address in v. 16 (p. 116 n. 42) goes ill with the
circumstance that v. 17 is certainly not a word of Yahweh (see
above, p. 302).

The sense of גבירה is determined by contextual support rather
than by strict linguistic considerations, since it can mean both
'queen' (1 Kgs 11.19) and 'queen-mother' (1 Kgs 15.13). It is

---

[1] Reading מַרְאֲשׁוֹתֵיכֶם (see below, p. 304).
[2] On abstract nouns with masc. plur endings (שׁלומים) see GK 124d.

likely that the address to the king and גבירה in vv. 18–19 is to be
related to the event recorded in Jer 29.2 (cf. 22.26) and 2 Kgs
24.12,15, and that the גבירה is Nehusta (2 Kgs 24.8), the
mother of the eighteen year old Jehoiachin (cf. Jerome, *ut
loquatur regi Iechoniae et matri eius*). The versions, however,
give no clear indication of this identification. The most
interesting and puzzling readings are those of Sept.
(δυναστεύουσι(ν)) and Pesh. (*rwrbn'*) at 13.18. Since Pesh.
renders שרים with the same word at 29.2, it is reasonable to
conclude that the Hebrew behind Sept. and Pesh. at 13.18 is
שרים. It should be said, however, that שרי יהודה וירושלם is not
represented by Sept. at 29.2 and that δυναστεύουσι(ν) is not
elsewhere used by Sept. to render שרים. Hence BHS suggests
that Sept. and Pesh. are representing גבורים at 13.18 (cf. Jerome
'geburoth'), and, in that case, גבורים is a corruption of an
original גבירה or *vice versa*. There are two hypotheses which can
be made:

(*a*) The corruption is an inner Septuagintal one: δυναστευούση
(Aq.) has been corrupted to δυναστεύουσι(ν). An implication of
this would be that Pesh. is dependent on Sept. at 13.18.

(*b*) δυναστεύουσι(ν) and *rwrbn'* are evidences of a Hebrew text
other than MT which read שרים. In this case גבירה might
represent a secondary accommodation of the Hebrew of 13.18 to
Jer 29.2 and 2 Kgs 24.12, 15.

It has been urged that we may gather from this and other
passages that the queen mother had an official status at court (cf.
Duhm, Rudolph, Weiser, Nicholson; see 1 Kgs 2.19; 15.13). But
1 Kgs 2.19 does not show that the queen mother had a throne
sited permanently at the right of the king's throne (*pace*
Nicholson; cf. Weiser). וישם כסא לאם המלך ('throne' may be an
over-translation of כסא) in fact contradicts the view that the
queen mother had a throne permanently located in a place of
precedence. We should not suppose that it was the unmarried
status of the youthful Jehoiachin (cf. 2 Kgs 24.15) which
accounts for the close association between him and his mother
(Jer 22.26; 29.2; 2 Kgs 24.12, 15), but his extreme youth, and
the extraordinary difficulties and dangers attending the
circumstances of his accession make it understandable that the
queen mother should have been a power behind the throne. It
would be better simply to recognize that the mother of a king has
a great potential for exerting political influence and that the
extent to which she exercises it depends on her own personality
and that of her son, as well as on the internal and external
political situation in which she is operating. ויסרה מגבירה (1 Kgs
15.13) does not contradict this, because it need mean no more

than that a גבירה was removed from the sphere of influence which she would normally occupy.

השפילו שבו (v. 18) is a hendiadys: two ideas ('abasement' and 'sitting') are to be combined in order to give the sense, 'Sit in humiliation' (cf. G.K 120g). Kimchi glosses it with שבו בשפל, 'sit in lowliness'. The most interesting of the versions is Pesh. which has read שבו as שבו and has produced the sense, 'Abase yourselves and repent' ('tmkkw wtwbw). This, however, does not make much sense, not even in connection with Weiser's contention that the disaster alluded to has not yet befallen the king and the queen mother (p. 117 n. 1) and that the verbs in v. 19 may have a future reference. The motivation in v. 18b, introduced by כי, is only compatible with the utterance of hard words in v. 18a and not with an appeal for repentance.

The incongruence of ירד and עטרת (v. 18b) was noted by Kimchi (Duhm emends to ירדה). מֵרָאשֵׁיכֶם (Duhm, Rudolph) has support from the versions (Sept. ἀπὸ κεφαλῆς ὑμῶν; Vulg. de capite vestro; Pesh. mn rškwn), although it should be noted that they indicate the singular form (מראשכם) which is proposed by Ehrlich (p. 278). Targ.'s paraphrase shows that מראשותיכם has been assigned the sense 'glory': 'Because your glory has gone into exile and is cut off from you'. Kimchi is following this line of interpretation when he glosses מראשותיכם with רשות 'political power' and ממלכה 'sovereignty'. The king and his mother are stripped of the reality of regal power; the exile will be a great leveller and Jehoiachin will find himself a prisoner along with his people (cf. Rudolph). M. J. Dahood (*CBQ* 23, 1961, p. 462) explains מראשותיכם as 'from your heads' and defends the feminine form (מֵרָאשׁוֹתֵיכֶם) with reference to Ugaritic riš which has both masculine (rašm) and feminine (rašt) plural forms. This explanation may be the correct one.

Rudolph says of v. 19 that it constitutes the only biblical evidence about the course which the Babylonian invasion took, indicating that the towns in the south of Judah were invested by the enemy and cut off from Jerusalem. This is probably a correct construction of v. 19a, but earlier commentators explained the reference to ערי הנגב differently. Blayney observes that 'the cities of the south' may mean the cities of Judah in general (so Rashi, Lowth), but, as an alternative explanation, he suggests that what is indicated is the total subjugation of Judah: if the towns which were furthest away from Nebuchadrezzar's point of departure were invested, those to the north of them had already been taken. There is some resemblance between this and Duhm's view that ערי הנגב are the 'last Judaean towns'.

Weiser holds that there are particular, historical circumstances to which v. 19a should be attached, but he opposes

the view of Volz, Rudolph and Bright that vv. 18–19 are related
to the capitulation and deportation of Jehoiachin. According to
Weiser the occasion of the saying is the occupation of a large
part of the land by the enemy (v. 19a). Jeremiah is saying to the
king and queen mother: 'Do not affect royal splendour, for the
reality of the situation does not allow it. You are in a position of
extreme weakness, so do not make an empty show of kingship.'
On the other hand, the verbs in v. 19b are prophetic perfects,
according to Weiser (p. 117 n. 1): the radical pessimism of
Jeremiah in v. 19b stems from the conviction that the occupation
of the fortified towns of the south is the beginning of an
irreversible trend of events which must, sooner or later, lead to a
general disaster. Rudolph interprets v. 19b as a miscalculation
by Jeremiah of the significance of Nebuchadrezzar's invasion of
Judah in 597: his measures were not so draconian as the prophet
had anticipated.

There has been a tendency to emend the difficult הגלת שלומים
(v. 19b) to גלות שלמה with reference to Amos 1.6 (BDB, Duhm,
Ehrlich, KB³, GK 118q) and Sept. (ἀποικίαν τελείαν). הגלת
שלומים is retained by Rudolph, who explains שלומים as an
accusative of manner ('completely'), by Bright ('wholly
deported') and NEB ('swept clean away'). The phrase gave
trouble to the versions: Sept. συνετέλεσεν ἀποικίαν τελείαν read
כלה as כֻּלָּה and connected it with the final part of the verse. If
the Greek translator is reading MT, הגלת has been taken as a
noun ('exile'), and the same holds good for Vulg.
(*transmigratione perfecta*) and Pesh. (*šbyt' šlmt'*). The main
question is whether we should conclude that the versions (Sept.,
Vulg., Pesh.) had a Hebrew text with גלות שלמה instead of MT
הגלת שלומים. The answer should be in the negative: there is
evidence that Pesh., Targ. and Vulg. were influenced by their
renderings at Amos 1.6, 9, but we should not suppose that they
had a Hebrew text other than הגלת שלומים at Jer 13.19. What is
indicated rather is that all the versions were perplexed by הגלת
and that they have all taken הגלת שלומים as more or less an
equivalent of גלות שלמה. Targ. has a second rendering of הגלת
שלומים, 'They have received the retribution which their deeds
merited'. This accords with the rendering of שלומים in Aq. and
Theod. (ανταποδοσεων) and with a reading of Sept. reported by
Jerome, but not otherwise attested (see Ziegler). On הגלת
instead of הגלתה, the common form in Biblical Hebrew, see
Duhm and GK.75 i, m (הגלתה > הגלת > הגלית).

The metre (*qînāh*) does not make this piece a dirge, for it does
not have the character of a dirge. It is a harsh reminder to the
king and his mother that they must swiftly come to terms with
the events which have overtaken them. Jehoiachin's royalty has

been demeaned by defeat and deportation; he must accept a verdict which, in any case, cannot be gainsayed, and not continue to pose as a paper king with a hollow royalty. The hard message is reinforced and developed in v. 19. The country is largely under enemy control and any hopes of a quick change for the better should be banished. Rather it should be accepted that sooner or later the Babylonians will inflict on Judah a total defeat which will lead to national disintegration and exile.

STAINED AND DESERVING PUNISHMENT (13.20–27)

[20]Lift up[1] your eyes[2]
and see[1] those coming from the north.
Where is the flock given into your care,
the sheep in which you took such pride?
[21]What can you say when your enemies afflict you?
It was you who accustomed them
to exercise authority over you.
Will not birth-pangs seize you,
as they seize a woman in labour?
[22]If you ask yourself,
Why have these things happened[3] to me?
For your many sins your skirts are lifted,
your modesty[4] is violated.
[23]Can a Nubian change the colour of his skin?
Can a leopard remove its spots?
No more are you able to do good
who are practised in evil-doing.
[24]I will scatter you[5] like chaff
dispersed by a desert wind.
[25]This is your lot,
the portion meted out to you by me, says Yahweh,
for you have neglected me
and trusted in false gods.
[26]I myself will raise your skirts over your face
that your shame may be disclosed.
[27]Your adulterous acts and cries of passion,
the lewdness of your harlotry!
On hill-top shrines throughout the countryside
I have seen your detestable deeds.
Woe to you, Jerusalem, you are unclean!
How much longer will it be so?

The Massoretes, who read the imperatives as plurals in v. 20, were influenced by the plural suffix of עיניכם and perhaps also

[1] Reading שׂאי and וראי.

[2] Emending עיניכם to עיניך (see below, p. 307).

[3] (קרה) קרוני = קראני.

[4] Literally 'your heels'; perhaps the rendering should be 'Your nakedness is uncovered' (see below, p. 311).

[5] Emending ואפיצם to ואפיצכם (see below, pp. 307, 314).

by the belief that there was a continuity between vv. 18–19 and
v. 20. The choice of K (שׂאי ; ראי) involves the emendation of
עיניכם to עיניך (cf. Sept. ὀφθαλμούς σου). The singular
imperatives are explicitly referred to Jerusalem in Sept.
('Ανάλαβε ὀφθαλμούς σου 'Ιερουσαλήμ) and this is probably a
correct explanation. שׂאי עיניך וראי (Duhm, Ehrlich, p. 278)
should be read. The effect of Sept.'s text is to remove the
incoherence between v. 20a and v. 20b and to make of vv. 20–22
a unit in which Jerusalem or Zion is addressed throughout.

There is no intrinsic connection between vv. 20–22 and the
preceding verses (so Rudolph, Weiser, Bright, Nicholson).
Jerusalem has failed to take care of the flock which was once her
pride. Exposed and unprotected, it will be scattered (or, is
scattered) by an enemy from the north—identified by Kimchi
with the Babylonians. Rudolph urges that there is no explicit
reference to exile except in v. 24 (ואפיצם), but איה העדר נתן לך
(v. 20) implies the imminent or actual scattering of the flock by
an enemy from the north. He favours the early period of
Jeremiah's activity as the setting of vv. 20–22 (so Volz) rather
than the reign of Jehoiakim, when Josiah's reform had lost its
effectiveness (so Cornill), and his conclusions about the date of
vv. 20–22 are linked to his conviction that the exile is hardly ever
explicitly mentioned (only in 6.19) in oracles deriving from the
early period of Jeremiah's activity. Hence Rudolph holds that
vv. 23–24 are a separate unit and that v. 22 is resumed by v. 25.
The plural verb in v. 23 (תוכלו) and the plural suffix in v. 24
(ואפיצם) constitute the main grounds for such a view. The case
for regarding vv. 20–27 as a unity (Weiser) is not very strong. It
could be argued that זה גורלך (v. 25) picks up the threat of exile
in v. 24, but the force of this is weakened when it is seen that it
could equally well pick up the threat in v. 22b and that there is
congruence between the verbs and suffixes of v. 22 and those of
v. 25. In any case ואפיצם (v. 24) disagrees with תוכלו (v. 23b),
so that an emendation (ואפיצכם) is unavoidable, although there
is no versional support. The difficulty of relating vv. 23–24
precisely to v. 27, and of taking the latter as an expression of the
utter improbability of repentance, lies in the deep obscurity of
אחרי מתי עד. Of vv. 25–27 it can be said that they take up the
figure of the woman in disgrace and resume the imagery which
appears in v. 22. This, together with the considerations of
grammatical congruence touched on above, suggests that
vv. 20–22 and vv. 25–27 constitute a unity. This agrees with
Rudolph's conclusions but does not rest on his arguments.

Jerusalem has failed to safeguard her flock (vv. 20–22), now
threatened by an enemy from the north, and is portrayed as a
woman suffering deep anguish and bitter disgrace. Her lot or

portion (vv. 25–27) has been determined by Yahweh himself and he personally superintends the punishment inflicted on her for her idolatry: he carries out the ceremony which brands her as an adulterous woman and exposes her to shame. There are two factors which may help to explain why vv. 23–24 were located where they appear: (a) The reference to 'scattering' in v. 24 links with the thought of the scattered flock in v. 20b. (b) The indelible stains of the inhabitants of Judah and Jerusalem connect with v. 27c, if this is taken to mean that Jerusalem's impurity is an irreversible condition.

The versions do not contribute much to the elucidation of v. 21. Sept., for the most part, is a literal translation of MT with a result less intelligible than MT itself. Symm. attempts to get better sense out of the Hebrew, but he does it by rendering עָלַיִךְ אֲלָפִים illegitimately as κατα σεαυτης συνηθεις, 'according to your own teachings'. The other feature of his translation which deserves mention is ἐπιζητηθη which indicates that he read יפקד as יִפָּקֵד, in which case NEB's reading (יְפָּקְדוּ, Brockington, p. 203), but not the sense attached to it, was, more or less, anticipated by Symm. Pesh. reproduces MT יפקד (npqd), takes אֲלָפִים as 'teachings' (ywlpn'= Sept.) and renders 'You taught them teachings that they should be as head'. That is, you instructed and equipped them for the exercise of sovereignty over you and contributed to your own subjection. In view of this it is likely that Pesh. supposes the enemy from the north to be the grammatical subject of יפקד (so Sept. and Kimchi): 'What will you say when they (the sing. verb is collective) exercise control over you?' Targ. makes Yahweh the subject of יפקד, and paraphrases כי יפקד עליך as ארי יסער עלך חובך, 'when he punishes you for your sin' (also Vulg. and Rashi). Kimchi like Targ. takes אלוף to mean 'chief' and this is the sense indicated by Ibn Janâh who associates אלוף תימן (Gen 36.15) and אלופים לראש (A. Neubauer, The Book of Hebrew Roots, p. 51). Kimchi alludes to the occasion when Ahaz applied for help to Assyria in the face of a hostile Syro-Ephraimite coalition (Isa 7): Judah has brought disaster on her own head, for she has encouraged a distant power to come to her country as a saviour and has showed it the road by which it could subsequently come as a hostile invader (cf. Pesh.).

Calvin follows Kimchi in taking the enemy from the north as the subject of יפקד and in understanding אלפים as 'leaders'. He makes an indirect reference to Isa 7 and 39.2 and remarks: 'They had called them (the Chaldaeans) in as auxiliaries; they had accustomed them to rule, and, as it were, had set them over themselves.' Lowth and Blayney both follow KJV in supposing that Yahweh is the subject of יפקד, but they too attach the sense 'chiefs' to אלפים. Lowth detects a reference to the plea for help which Ahaz made to Tiglath-Pileser (Kimchi). The sense 'friends' or 'lovers' for אלפים appears in Venema, but it does not result in an exegesis noticeably different from those which we have been considering. It is interpreted in connection with Judah's pacts and diplomatic entanglements—her dalliance now with Egypt, now with Babylonia. The other interesting feature of Venema's exegesis is his supposition that ואת למדת אתם עליך אלפים is parenthetic and that לראש connects with יפקד עליך. This has been revived by Weiser. According to Venema, Yahweh is the subject of יפקד and the sense is: 'What will you say when he sets in authority over you (כי יפקד עליך לראש) those whom you taught to be your colleagues (or, lovers)?'.

Both Rudolph and Weiser adopt the view that אלפים means 'friends' or 'lovers'. Weiser follows Venema, but the translation is dubious, and this criticism also applies to Rudolph's rendering, 'Those whom you have grown accustomed to regard as close friends'. Otherwise, Rudolph appeals to Sept. (ἐπισκέπτωνται), as Duhm had done, to justify יפקדו, which he points as יִפָּקְדוּ and to which he attaches the sense 'punish': the invaders will inflict punishment on Judah. He further assumes that לראש is a corruption of ירושלם = ירוש which he transposes to follow the first occurrence of עליך. Weiser associates the thought of the passage with 4.30, but otherwise his interpretation follows familiar lines: there is an allusion to the foreign political and diplomatic entanglements of Judah, in particular, to the attitude of Ahaz in the face of the Syro-Ephraimite threat.

NEB reads יִפָּקְדוּ and renders אלפים as 'leaders', transposing it to the position proposed by Duhm (after the first occurrence of עליך): 'What will you say when you suffer because your leaders cannot be found?' Hence the sense 'be absent', 'be missing' is postulated for פקד. ואת למדת אתם עליך לראש is then rendered as, 'Though it was you who trained them to be your head'. This links v. 21 to the thought of remiss and negligent 'shepherds' in v. 20. Since NEB does not indicate any emendation of עיניכם to עיניך in v. 20 (cf. Brockington, p. 203), it must be concluded that שאו and וראו are being read. The position then is that v. 20a is addressed to the 'shepherds', the political leaders, and v. 20b to Jerusalem, personified as a woman. Both are responsible for the disaster which is overtaking the country, for the 'flock' belongs to Lady Jerusalem (נתן לך), and the 'shepherds', who are charged with the care of the flock, have a primary responsibility. There is much obscurity, but, on balance, 'leaders' is better than 'lovers'; it should be justified as a nuance of אלפים 'teachers' (cf. Sept. and Vulg.; see above, p. 61 and *Proverbs*, p. 286).

We should suppose that the grammatical subject of יפקד is the enemy from the north and this sense can be achieved without emending יִפְקֹד to יִפְקְדוּ (Rudolph). Jerusalem has brought disaster on her own head by encouraging those who will eventually subdue her to exert authority over her and to assume that they are arbiters of her destiny (taking v. 21b in the sense, 'You have accustomed them to the idea that they are your authoritative teachers (leaders)'). She has betrayed the trust that was confided in her: 'Where is the flock that was given to you, the flock in which you took such pride?' (v. 20).

The figure of the woman suffering birth pangs (v. 21c) is elsewhere employed by Jeremiah (4.31; 6.24; 22.23) and the striking aspect of this is its entirely negative implication: birth pangs are viewed as a particularly sharp suffering, not as an agony which leads to the joy of a birth. Paradoxically it is the death throes of Lady Jerusalem which are referred to as labour pains (on לדה instead of the usual לדת see GK 128t).

The nuance of v. 22 is: 'You may ask yourself why this has happened to *you*. If so, I shall tell you the reason.' Jerusalem will find it hard to accept that she has brought her suffering and woe on her own head. But if she should utter a querulous 'Why?', she will receive a devastating answer. As a punishment for her sins, or because of the magnitude of her sins (ב *pretii*), she has been publicly exposed and disgraced.

The suggestion that שׁוּקַיִךְ should be read for שׁוּלַיִךְ (Cornill) is understandable, since 'your legs have been exposed' is a more normal expression than 'your skirts have been exposed'. Sept. paraphrases שׁוּלַיִךְ as τὰ ὀπίσθιά σου, 'your posterior', and Vulg. similarly understands שׁוּלַיִךְ as *verecundiora tua*, 'your private parts'. Pesh. renders נֶחְמְסוּ עֲקֵבָיִךְ by *w'tgly 'qbyky*, 'and your heels are uncovered'. With this should be compared Ehrlich (p. 279) who emends נֶחְמְסוּ to נֶחְשְׂפוּ. An attractive proposal is that נֶחְמְסוּ is in synonymous parallelism with נִגְלוּ (cf. NEB), and Prov 26.6 emended to שָׁתֹם חֵמֶם, 'his buttocks bare', may be thought to support this (H. Torczyner, *ZDMG* 72, 1918, p. 156; *Proverbs*, p. 597; E. Ullendorff, *BASOS* 42, 1979, p. 426). None of the versions offers a normal translation of נֶחְמְסוּ, but it is unlikely that the right explanation of this is that they had a different Hebrew text from MT or that they were perplexed by a unique occurrence of the Niphal of חמם (cf. Ehrlich, p. 279). Rashi glosses שׁוּלַיִךְ as שִׁיפּוּלֵי הַבְּגָדִים, 'underskirts' (cf. Pesh. *špwlyky*) and comments, 'As when they strip off the clothes of a woman in disgrace, raising her skirt over her head'. This probably indicates that the revealing of the underskirts is a preliminary to the pulling of her skirts over her head in order to show her nakedness, and that this is to be envisaged as a public degradation consequent on some serious moral failure—perhaps adultery (cf. Nicholson). The phrase in v. 26 will then have to be taken as a reference to the carrying out of this public humiliation by Yahweh himself: 'I have pulled your skirts over your face.' If v. 22 is connected with v. 26 in this way, an allusion to rape in v. 22 is inappropriate, and this may explain the unwillingness to offer a normal translation of נחמסו.

The thought that punishment fit for a harlot is described in v. 22 appears in Lowth, and a similar interpretation of נגלו שוליך is found in Venema, namely, that the punishment fits the crime: *sicut tu scortando fecisti, ita ego in poenam tibi infligam*. On the other hand, Venema supposes that נחמסו עקביך is an allusion to Jerusalem's obduracy and insensitivity: she is incorrigible and incapable of responding to any appeal. The view that עקביך is a euphemism of the same order as רגלים (Duhm) is adopted by Rudolph, Weiser and Bright in combination with the supposition that there is an allusion to rape in נחמסו עקביך. Jerusalem will be violated by those to whom she made love: they will tear off her skirts and rape her. This has to be interpreted in terms of the disastrous consequences of her attempts to win security by flirting with foreign powers (Weiser). It is doubtful, however, whether there is such a decided political colouring in vv. 20–22 and whether the sense of v. 22b can be so different from that of v. 26. In other words, unless one argues that v. 26 is secondary and should be deleted (Cornill, cf. Nah 3.5), it militates against the conclusion that there is an allusion to rape in v. 22 and suggests rather the thought of a judicial punishment (Lowth, Venema).

This disgrace is Jerusalem's lot and it has been meted out by Yahweh (מנת מדיך מאתי). Here, for the first time (v. 25), there is an explicit indication that Yahweh is the speaker (נאם יהוה), and if vv. 25–27 are continuous with vv. 20–22, it can be assumed that he is also the speaker in these earlier verses. Sept. (καὶ μερὶς τοῦ ἀπειθεῖν ὑμᾶς ἐμοί) represents ומנת מֶרְיֵךְ מאתי. The confusion of ד and ר is easily understandable, but it is not evident that the sense of Sept. is superior to that of MT, although it is preferred by Rudolph, KB³ and NEB (Brockington, p. 204). מד elsewhere means 'cloth' or 'garment' and Ehrlich (p. 279) urges that it does not yield the sense 'measure' for which the form מדה is required. Kimchi supposes that מדה is capable of forming its plural with *îm* or *ôt* endings and that consequently מדיך can be derived from מדה. Kimchi comments on מנת מדיך זה גורלך : 'According to what you have meted out to me, I will mete out to you. You have forgotten me and I will forget you.' Similarly מנת מדיך is glossed by Rashi as חלק מדותיך. The unusual character of the form מדיך does, however, lend some weight to the proposal that Sept. represents a better Hebrew text.

The 'forgetting' of Yahweh is further specified (v. 25) as a trusting in שקר, and v. 27 suggests that שקר, here as elsewhere (e.g. Jer 10.14) does not mean 'falsehood' in the abstract, but refers particularly to involvement in idolatrous worship. Jerusalem is an adulterous woman and her 'adultery' consists of her faithlessness to Yahweh and her shameless flirtation with Canaanite fertility cults (cf. Kimchi—adultery is a משל for עבודת אלילים. The hill-tops are specifically the places where Jerusalem 'commits adultery', and the selection of this metaphor for idolatry is no doubt influenced by the sexual aspects of the Canaanite fertility cults.

There is a question whether וגם אני חשפתי שוליך על פניך can have the sense, 'I, in person, have pulled your skirts over your face' (v. 26). This is how it is taken by Rashi, Kimchi, Rudolph, Weiser and Bright. NEB, without any versional support, emends פניך to פני and locates it after זנותך (Brockington, p. 204). A better balance is given to the metre in vv. 26–27 (v. 26: 3+2; v. 27; 2+2, 2+2), and על פני, 'are an offence to me' is perhaps a little easier than the combination of חשפתי שוליך with על פניך. Vulg. *femora* might be thought to point to שוקיך, but it is a rendering of שוליך of the same type as *verecundiora* in v. 22 (cf. Sept. τὰ ὀπίσθιά σου and τὰ ὀπίσω σου). The tenses of Pesh. are future (in agreement with Sept. and against Vulg.), and Pesh. introduces a second verb (*w'rm'*) in order to relieve the obscurity of MT: 'and will throw (them) over your face'. Rashi's interpretation is unambiguous and is the same as that of Pesh.: 'I have uncovered your underskirts in order to throw them over your face' (להפכם על פניך). Sept., Pesh. and Targ. take v. 26 as a threat for the future, whereas Vulg. understands it as a reference to a penalty which Yahweh has already inflicted (so Rudolph, Weiser, Bright, NEB).

In the heat of her passion Jerusalem's (Judah's) cries are like those of copulating horses (v. 27), 'like the neighings of randy horses' (Kimchi). זמה has given trouble to the versions and Targ. has taken it as a synonym of מזמה 'plan' (cf. Aq. εννοια 'intention'). Vulg. *scelus fornicationis tuae*, 'the lewdness of your fornication', has captured the right sense (cf. Symm. μυσος 'abomination', 'defilement'), while Sept. has the interesting but problematic rendering ἀπαλλοτρίωσις, given by Jerome as *alienato* 'alienation'. At Neh 13.30 ἀλλοτρίωσις is used to render נכר, and elsewhere נכר is associated with foreign gods or foreign things. This is its meaning at Neh 13.30: 'Thus I purified them from everything foreign' (וטהרתים מכל נכר). Hence Sept.

ἀπαλλοτρίωσις at Jer 13.27 probably indicates an addiction to foreign gods (apostasy) and so is an exegesis of זמה.

Does אוי לך ירושלם לא תטהרי אחרי מתי עד (v. 27) give expression to the conviction that no process of cleansing and purification is conceivable? This is how the matter is understood by Weiser and Rudolph. There may be a faint glimmer of hope (Rudolph), but what appears is a cry of woe rather than a convincing appeal for a new beginning and a recovery of purity. Jerusalem's uncleanness has been likened to that of an adulterous woman and according to 3.1ff. she may not be taken back by her husband. The marks of apostasy are indelible. There is little doubt that תטהרי (whether pointed as a Qal or a Hithpael תִּטַּהֲרִי, cf. Rudolph) is a statement rather than a question and this is what the versions indicate. An interrogative form is assumed by Calvin and KJV ('Wilt thou not be made clean?') and repudiated by Venema (non enim interrogative sed affirmative capienda sunt). Sept. and Vulg. have read אחרי as אַחֲרַי. 'You are not pure after me' or (if the Hithpael is read) 'You have not purified yourself after me' makes poor sense, and the punctuation of MT should be retained, although אחרי מתי עד presents severe difficulties. Pesh. renders the Hebrew by 'dm' l'mty twby, and 'dm' l'mty is the rendering of עד מתי at Jer 4.14, 21, so that the Hebrew indicated by the last part of 5.27 is apparently עד מתי שובי, but it is improbable that a Hebrew text different from MT is represented. Nor is it likely that Driver's elucidation of Pesh. (JQR 28, pp. 112f.), on the assumption that it renders MT with a different philology of עוד (עָד 'went round', 'repented') is the right one. The sense 'How much longer will you delay in repenting?', which is indicated by the paraphrase of Pesh., has had a wide currency (Rashi, Calvin, Venema, Blayney). The view that 'delay' is the central idea has encouraged the emendation of אחרי to תְּאַחֲרִי. Volz's emendation (עד מה תאחרי לשב, 'How long will you delay in repenting?') does not correspond closely with MT, not even if אשר at the beginning of chapter 14 is thought to be part of the corruption. Driver (JQR, p. 112) supposes that אחרי מתי is a corruption of מַתְאַחֲרִי = מה תאחרי, 'Why dost thou tarry still (to repent)?'. NEB's emendation (Brockington, p. 204) juggles with אחרי מתי עד, putting עד (= עָד) first and אחרי (emended to תאחרי) last, 'How long, how long will you delay?' (cf. Pesh. which indicates עד מתי).

The other main line of interpretation stems from Kimchi. The closing words of v. 27 are not principally concerned to raise the question whether or not repentance is a possibility, nor are they asking how much longer Jerusalem or Judah will delay the act of repentance. The sense is rather: 'You are unclean. How much

longer can this state of affairs continue?' In other words אחרי
מתי עד is a veiled threat of judgement and exile. This is not so
very far removed from Duhm's exegesis of אחרי מתי עד, 'It will
be a very long time before you are clean'. Duhm supposes that
the 'cleansing' of the land will be effected by the invader who
will destroy Judah's institutions and sweep its inhabitants into
exile; but, according to Duhm, there is an ultimate expectation
of repentance. Only if vv. 20–27 were regarded as a unit and
vv. 23–24 were accepted as a guide to the sense of v. 27, would
the entire exclusion of the thought of repentance seem a
necessity.

In vv. 23–24 all the versions support the 3rd person suffix of
ואפיצם, but Sept. represents the verb as aorist ($\kappa\alpha\grave{\iota}$ $\delta\iota\acute{\epsilon}\sigma\pi\epsilon\iota\rho\alpha$
$\alpha\grave{\upsilon}\tau\upsilon\acute{\upsilon}\varsigma$). Thus, according to Sept., the exile and dispersion is an
accomplished fact. The nuance of v. 23 (cf. Pesh.) is as follows:
'If the Nubian can change the colour of his skin or the leopard
cause its spots to disappear, you can change your ways.' In other
words, the condition which is laid down is one which is
manifestly incapable of fulfilment, and by this device the
bondage of Jerusalem to her evil ways and the impossibility of
relieving her slavery are expressed. This aspect of habituation
leading to a slavery which is irredeemable (cf. Rudolph and
Weiser) is suggested by למדי הרע. The inhabitants of Judah will
be scattered (ואפיצם), just as chaff is carried away by the wind
at winnowing-time and disappears without a trace (cf. 4.11;
18.17). If vv. 23–24 are originally independent of vv. 20–22,
25–27, we can explain their contiguity with vv. 20–22 in
connection with איה העדר נתן לך (v. 20) which may be fairly
taken as an allusion to a flock which is dispersed or is in the
process of being dispersed (cf. v. 24). Again, it may be that
vv. 23–24 were located in their present position because לא
תטהרי (v. 27) was taken to mean 'You will never again be pure'.
You cannot effect the change from impurity to purity any more
than a Nubian can change the colour of his skin or the leopard
its spots. The tone of vv. 20–22 and vv. 25–27 was perceived as in
accord with the thought that Jerusalem was indelibly stained
and that her evil habits held her fast like bands of steel.

CHAPTER XIV

A PLEA REFUSED (14.1–10)

¹The word of Yahweh which came to Jeremiah concerning the drought:
²Judah mourns and its towns are despondent;
they sit on the ground like mourners,
Jerusalem's cry of distress rises up.
³Nobles send out their servants to find water;
when they reach the cisterns, there is no water in them.
They come back with their vessels empty,
they cover their heads in shame and disappointment.
⁴Because the ground is cracked
—no rain has fallen on the land—
the farmers cover their heads in chagrin.
⁵Even the hind abandons her young in the open at birth,
for there is not a blade of grass anywhere.
⁶The wild asses stand on high ground(?),¹
snuffing the wind like jackals;
there is no grass and their eyesight fails.
⁷Though our sins testify against us,
act, O Yahweh, for the sake of your name;
our apostasies are many,
we have sinned against you.
⁸Hope of Israel, its saviour when disaster threatens!
Why do you behave like an alien, resident in the land,
like a traveller who interrupts his journey only to find a lodging?
⁹Why do you behave like a man reduced to a stupor,
like a hero who cannot bring help?
Yet you are in our midst, O Yahweh,
and we are the objects of your care.
Do not forsake us.
¹⁰These are the words of Yahweh to this people:
They love to go astray as their words show;
they do not keep their feet on the path.
Yahweh does not show them favour;
now he will take account of their guilt
and punish their sins.

In v. 1 the initial אֲשֶׁר (which also occurs at 46.1; 47.1; 49.34) is difficult to understand and both Sept. (καὶ ἐγένετο) and Pesh. (whw') represent יְהִי. There is general agreement that the verse is editorial, but whereas Rudolph and Bright comment on its inappositeness on the ground that what follows is not a word of Yahweh, Weiser appeals to it to support his view that we need a wider definition of 'word of Yahweh' than the one commonly employed. It is uncertain what scope is intended for the superscription: it could be regarded as an editorial indication of the occasion of Jeremiah's utterance(?) in vv. 2–10, since the references to drought are, for the most part, or, perhaps, entirely,

¹ See below, p. 319.

confined to this section. 14.22 contains what might be regarded as an allusion to drought ('or do the heavens send showers of themselves'), but the famine which is mentioned in association with 'sword' (14.15, 18) is not to be thought of as a consequence of drought. It results rather from a 'scorched earth' policy by an invader, or from destruction and exappropriation of crops, coupled with siege conditions. Blayney is impressed by this consideration and he attaches על דברי הבצרת to אבלה יהודה, 'Because of the drought Judah mourneth'. The superscription is then rendered as 'The word of Jehovah which came to Jeremiah'. Sept., Vulg. and Pesh. all read בצרות as a singular (cf. Rudolph, plural of extension, or singular בצרות). Thiel's considered conclusion (pp. 180f., 193) is that the superscription is probably the final item of the redaction of 14.1–15.4 and is post-Deuteronomistic. The circumstance that it describes only 14.2–10 should be taken as evidence of lack of editorial skill and a failure to devise an adequate general heading, rather than as an indication that the superscription was originally devised for 14.2–10.

The description of distress, which is a regular, formal element of the communal lament, runs from vv. 2–6, and the parallelism of אבלה and אמללה raises some interesting and difficult problems. There are passages relating to vegetation and crops, where 'wither' and 'wilt' would seem to be appropriate renderings for אבל and אמלל (Isa 24.4, 7; 33.9; Joel 1.10), and there are others where these verbs are used of human feelings (Isa 19.8; Jer 14.2, Lam 2.8). In Hos 4.3 אבל is used of הארץ and אמלל of כל יושב בה, so that 'wither' is appropriate for the first and 'mourn' for the second (although 'mourn' is also a possibility for the first). KB³ postulates two roots: Jer 14.2 is assigned to I אבל 'mourn', and Jer 12.4 and 23.10, where אבל is associated with הארץ, is assigned to II אבל 'wither'. The justification for the creation of a second root is sought in Akkadian *abâlu*, where the sense 'dessicated', 'withered', predominates. The versions support the sense 'mourn' for אבל at 14.2 (Sept. ἐπένθησαν; Vulg. *luxit*). אמללו is rendered by Sept. as ἐκενώθησαν, 'abandoned' or, perhaps, 'exhausted' and by Vulg. as *corruerunt* 'collapsed'; by Pesh. as ṣdw 'desolate' and by Targ. as חרובא 'laid waste'. The mourning aspect of the verse is confirmed by קדרו לארץ which Duhm correctly explains as a condensed expression requiring a second verb before ל to fill it out, 'They are in mourning, lying (or 'sitting') on the ground' (cf. 2 Sam 12.15ff.). Only Aq. and Symm. of the versions certainly indicate that the behaviour of mourners is envisaged (εσκυθρωπασαν, 'are sad of countenance'). The state to which the land and its communities have been reduced by drought is

the primary aspect of the description. Hence the view that
שעריה is the grammatical subject of קדרו is almost certainly the
right one (BDB, Duhm), and that this was the view of the
versions is shown by the co-ordination of אמללו and קדרו (Sept.,
Vulg., Pesh.). According to Rashi שעריה is a synecdoche
(= עריה; cf. Weiser, p. 121 n. 3, *pars pro toto*), but the thought
may be that the 'gates' are the focus of the public life of the
community which has been drained of its vitality by drought.
The latter idea appears in Kimchi who cites Lam 5.14 ('Elders
have left off their sessions in the gate', NEB).

Another view is that there is a change of grammatical subject
at קדרו, and this is represented by Lowth, Blayney and NEB
('Her men sink to the ground'). Blayney supposes that 'gates' is a
metonymy for 'people' and that קדרו לארץ refers to persons who
appear in public with the dress and mien of mourners. There is a
danger of attempting to impose too fine distinctions, but,
nevertheless, we have to say that there is a personification of
שעריה, יהודה and ירושלם in v. 2, and that something is lost if
these are simply translated into 'people of Judah', 'persons in
public places' and 'inhabitants of Jerusalem'. צוחת ירושלם is a
description of distress rather than a cry for deliverance: vv. 2–6
constitute the foundation of an appeal, are intended to influence
Yahweh, and prepare the way for petition (vv. 7–9).

H. G. Reventlow (*Liturgie und prophetisches Ich bei Jeremia*,
pp. 156ff.) has suggested that there is a mythological
background to the allusion to mourning rites (v. 2) and,
following A. S. Kapelrud (*Joel Studies*, 1948, pp. 17f.), he
supposes that the lament over drought, in the context of the cult
of Baal, was principally connected with the failure of the vine
harvest. He also refers to F. F. Hvidberg's monograph (1938;
English translation, *Weeping and Laughter in the Old
Testament*, 1962), where a view is expressed that cultic weeping
originates in the context of ancestor worship and that it became
part of a lament for a dead god in the setting of vegetation cults.
According to this view the link between the senses 'wither' and
'mourn' in respect of אבל and אמלל is mythological: the two
nuances arise out of a situation where the seasonal diminution of
growth is equated with rites of mourning for a dead god.

The masters or nobles who send out their servants to fetch
water are identified by NEB as 'flock-masters' (following
Ehrlich, p. 279), under the influence of אדירי הצאן (25.34). It is
not clear that NEB is correct in connecting this with the
watering of flocks. It is more likely that the shortage of water is
envisaged as having reached such serious proportions that it has
become a necessity to find it in order to stay alive. In these
circumstances the heads of great families have sent their

servants to scour the countryside in search of it. When they reach the places where water normally collects (Rashi בורות שמים מתכנסים) and find that the pools have dried up, they come back from their mission unsuccessful, with the water-pots empty. The words at the end of v. 3 (בשו הכלמו וחפו ראשם) are not represented by Sept., and Janzen (p. 12) postulates a doublet in MT (cf. v. 4, בשו אכרים חפו ראשם). The words are deleted by Hitzig, Duhm (a variant of v. 4b), Rudolph, Weiser and NEB (Brockington, p. 204). NEB attaches the sense 'uncover' to חפה here and elsewhere (2 Sam 15.30; Esth 6.12), and Arabic *hafay* can mean both 'reveal' and 'conceal'. In 2 Sam 15.30 and Esth 6.12 there are references to mourning rites and the assumption of NEB is apparently that a reference to the uncovering rather than the covering of the head is desiderated in connection with mourning, failure and disappointment.

The opening of v. 4 is awkward and Kimchi raises the question whether בעבור האדמה חתה attaches to what precedes or to what follows it. If the former is supposed, the grammar would be: they cover their heads, because the earth is cracked with drought. On the latter assumption the grammar would be: because the earth is cracked with drought, the farmers have lost heart and cover their heads (as a sign of despair). The rendering of חתה by 'cracked' follows Kimchi (נשברה) and KJV ('chapt'): cracks or fissures have appeared in the ground because of the exceptional drought. בארץ is not represented by Sept. and Pesh., and Janzen (p. 40) supposes that it has been imported secondarily from 1 Kgs 17.7 (it is deleted by NEB, cf. Brockington, p. 204). It is possible to accommodate חתה only if it is construed as a relative clause without the particle אשר (so BDB). This solution is satisfactory and should be adopted, but the versions have not discerned this grammar and Rudolph is dissatisfied with it. Sept. (τὰ ἔργα) and Pesh. ('bdyh) have read עבודת or the like, and Bright's 'Tilling the soil has stopped' (עבודת האדמה חדלה) follows Sept. The emendation adopted by Duhm and Ehrlich (p. 280), ועבדי האדמה חתו, 'Those who cultivate the land are dismayed', also shows the influence of Sept. and Pesh. NEB conjectures עבור 'produce' (Brockington, p. 204) and renders, 'The produce of the land has failed'. Targ. אתברו and Kimchi should be followed rather than Sept. (ἐξέλιπεν), Symm. (ηττηθησαν 'discomfited') and NEB: חתה refers to the cracks which appear in the ground as a consequence of severe drought and the other sense of חתה 'terrified', 'exhausted', should not be invoked. The lack of rain has rendered the ground incapable of cultivation and the farmers are thoroughly dismayed and dejected.

The hind (v. 5) is not mentioned at random, but because it has some value as a paradigm. An animal which in normal circumstances is devoted to its young is forced into the unnatural course of abandoning its calf, under a pressure to which it has to yield. There is no grass to be found, and the mother has no choice but to desert her calf and make a desperate and slender bid to survive. In both 2.24 and 14.6 there is a reference to an animal 'snuffing the wind' (2.24, שאפה רוח; 14.6, שאפו רוח). However, in 2.24 the snuffing of the wind is a symptom of lust or sexual heat (באות נפשו), while in 14.6 it is apparently an attempt to take in draughts of fresh air after climbing to high ground (Kimchi), in an atmosphere of suffocating heat and drought (so Lowth, 'They gaped after the cool air upon the Tops of the Mountains, and drew it in greedily with their mouths'). The versions have the same difficulty with שפים here as they had at the other verses which have already been considered (3.2, 21; 4.11; 7.29; 12.12). 14.4 is a verse which might be thought to lend contextual support to 'high places', (see the exegesis above), although the reference may simply be to the wide, open spaces of the desert which are the *habitat* of the פרא (cf. 2.24, פרה למד מדבר), and Blayney renders 'on the plains' (see above, pp. 177, 275). כלו עיניהם כי אין עשב is almost certainly a reference to a condition of hunger and physical debilitation which leads to the darkening of sight—perhaps an intimation of the onset of the darkness of death. כתנים, which appears in the Targ. of 2.24, gave the versions trouble here, as it did at 9.10 and 10.22. It is not represented by Sept., and it is confused with תנין 'serpent' or 'dragon' by Vulg. (*quasi dracones*), Aq. and Theod. (ὡς δρακων). Pesh. (*yrwr'*) and Targ. (ירורין) represent 'jackals'. NEB renders תנים here and elsewhere as 'wolves'.

Verse 7 marks the transition from description of distress to petition. The first person plural suffixes and the plural imperatives are to be explained on the assumption that Jeremiah is exercising a representative, intercessory role. He identifies himself with his community and the prayer is an expression of deep personal concern (Kimchi). The other opinion (Baumgartner, pp. 77–79) would disengage Jeremiah's own insights and concerns from vv. 7–9 (especially, p. 79). The tendency is then to urge that the intercessory element is present only because it is part of the liturgical structure which Jeremiah appropriated and that its significance is limited. We are to suppose only a replica of the prayer uttered by a cultic intercessor in the context of the communal lament. The strength and intensity of the prophetic conviction are reserved for v. 10 which expresses Jeremiah's conviction that what awaits Judah is not an assurance of שלום but an implementation of judgement (see above, pp. 265–267). This resting of the entire weight of the interpretation on v. 10 should, however, not go unquestioned. Verse 10, which like vv. 11–16 is prose, may be part of an exilic elucidation of Jeremiah's ineffective intercession rather than a disclosure of the prophet's own mind (cf. above, pp. 171f.; see further below).

The community, through its intercessor, confesses its sin and apostasy, but it, nevertheless, turns to Yahweh hopefully (מקוה ישראל ; cf. P. A. H. de Boer, *OTS* 10, 1954, p. 242— מקוה 'assurance' rather than 'hope') and expects deliverance from its present distress. The form of the appeal to Yahweh is that he should act for the sake of his name (Sept. *ἕνεκεν σοῦ*). In view of v. 9 (ואתה בקרבנו יהוה ושמך עלינו נקרא) this could be connected with the thought that Yahweh has 'elected' Zion as his dwelling-place or as the place where he causes his name to dwell. How then can he finally desert them? It is, however, unlikely that למען שמך (v. 7) belongs to such a pattern of thought and something simpler and more naïve is perhaps implied. Yahweh's land is devastated by drought and Israel has been brought to a desperate condition of want and distress. She has nothing to say in her own defence, and yet because she is the community for whom Yahweh is held particularly responsible and from whom he cannot be dissociated, she asks him to act for the sake of his own (world-wide) reputation.

The למה which appears in vv. 8a and 9a is a regular formal element of the communal lament and gives expression to perplexity and complaint. Why does Yahweh behave as if he were a foreigner temporarily settled in the land? Why does he act as if he were simply passing through it, making a digression in order to get a night's lodging *en route*? The land is Yahweh's possession (נחלה) and its well-being is a primary responsibility of his. Why then does he behave as if it were a peripheral matter to him? The sense of נטה ללון in Jer 14.8 is that of leaving a road along which one is travelling in order to find a bed for the night (so Rudolph; *pace* NEB). This is what the ארח does; Kimchi's comment (נטה בעיר ללון) supports this interpretation. Sept. (ὡς αὐτόχθων) apparently reads כאזרח 'like a native', but the sense which this yields is poor.

NEB renders גבור (v. 9) as 'man' (Sept. and Pesh.) without indicating any emendation (Brockington, p. 204) and reads להושיע as a Niphal (לְהִוָּשֵׁע). The point, however, is not that Yahweh *qua* גבור cannot save himself, but that he belies the title גבור by his powerlessness to help his people—he is a paper tiger. Kimchi glosses נדהם with מבוהל 'terrified' and remarks that his father explained it from Arabic *dhm*, used of a person whose mind has been clouded or impaired by sickness. Hence it is to be connected with דהום 'stupor'. Similarly Gesenius (*Thesaurus* i,

1835, p. 323), with a reference to Kimchi, explains כאיש נדהם as
vir stupefactus. Why is God so overwhelmed by circumstances
and reduced to a kind of inaction characteristic of a weak man
who loses his nerve in a tight corner? Kimchi notices that in v. 8b
and v. 9a Targ. has avoided the bold anthropomorphisms and
anthropopathisms of MT. He remarks that, as a rule, both
Onqelos and Jonathan avoid such representations and that in
these verses Targ. has transferred to Israel the similes which
were applied to Yahweh. The boldness of the language of MT
and the affront which it appeared to offer to Yahweh's majesty
were unacceptable to Targ.

ויפקד חטאתם (v. 10) is not represented by Sept. and Janzen
(p. 40) concludes that it has been added secondarily from Hos
8.13. The relationship between the two passages led Duhm and
Cornill to delete v. 10b, on the ground that the reference to
Yahweh in the 3rd person (ויהוה לא רצם ... ויפקד חטאתם) does
not accord well with the circumstance that Yahweh is the
speaker. The implication is that the words are original in the
Hosea passage and secondary in the Jeremiah passage. This
argument, however, can be differently ordered and it can be
urged that the awkwardness of the style is caused by the fact
that the prophet Jeremiah is citing Hos 8.13 (Volz). The
rejection of Israel's plea (v. 8, מקוה ישראל) by Yahweh and the
reference to judgement is taken by Targ. as a threat of exile, and
Rashi supposes that כן אהבו לנוע is an allusion to exile rather
than to a waywardness and fickleness which brings on exile as a
punishment. Kimchi connects כן אהבו לנוע רגליהם לא חשכו with
the journeys of Judaean statesmen seeking help from Egypt and
Assyria. But כן אהבו לנוע רגליהם לא חשכו does not refer to love
of exile (Rashi) or to ambassadors making journeys to Egypt and
Assyria. It describes rather the apostasy of Israel in Canaan
(Targ.) and her infatuation with אלהים אחרים —her going after
alien gods (cf. Jer 2.19ff.).

There is a general recognition that the formal elements
identifiable in vv. 2–10 are those of the communal lament (W.
Baumgartner, op. cit., pp. 77–79; S. Mowinckel, The Psalms in
Israel's Worship, i, 1962, p. 197; H. G. Reventlow, op. cit.,
pp. 149ff.). It is accepted that the occasion with which this piece
is associated—a community crisis caused by drought—would
call forth a public lament in the setting of a special day set apart
for prayer and fasting (cf. Rudolph). If this is so, Weiser's
attempt to relate the passage to leading concerns of the
'Covenant cult' is not altogether well directed (cf. Reventlow,
p. 158, who says of this passage that the impetus is a particular
catastrophe nicht ein Glied des regelmässigen Jahreszyklus).
Apart from this, divergence of opinion is more significantly

related to the degree of originality or idiosyncrasy which is attributed to Jeremiah in his use of a cultic form, the *Sitz* (cultic or non-cultic) which should be supposed, and the nature of Jeremiah's role.

The relation of the formal elements of 14.2–10 to the psalm of public lamentation is adequately set out by Baumgartner who is influenced (p. 81) by Gunkel's presuppositions about the character of extant psalms in the psalter. They are 'spiritual compositions', derived from cultic prototypes, and so he has no doubt that the communal lament in Jer 14.2–10 is a non-cultic phenomenon. The principal question which he asks is whether the genre is earlier than Jeremiah or whether the prophet is to be regarded as its creator. His answer is that Jeremiah is utilizing a pre-existing genre, and he is confirmed in this view by the circumstance that there are places where he discerns the substitution of a provocative, prophetic content for conventional themes. Thus he holds that the stereotyped content is preserved at vv. 2–7, 8a and 9b, whereas there are striking prophetic contributions at vv. 8b and 9a, and, most of all, in the reversing of the standard *Heilsorakel* in v. 10 (p. 90).

Mowinckel (op. cit. pp. 193ff.) has no doubt that the genre of the communal lament, as it is attested in the book of Psalms, relates to a cultic situation and that these laments are liturgical texts. That the oracle was an integral part of the liturgical complex was deduced by Mowinckel from the dramatic change of mood which is discernible within these laments. Mowinckel was able to show that in one or two cases the oracular reply is preserved in national and individual psalms of lamentation (12.6; 60.8–10; 108.8–10; 91.14–16) and that other psalms have a direct or indirect reference to such oracles (20.7; 21.9; 35.3; 62.12; 27.8, 14; Lam 3.57), so that the fact and the form of this oracle are attested (cf. *Psalms in Israel's Worship*, ii, 1962, p. 58 n. 30; cf. *Psalmenstudien* iii, 1923, pp. 64ff.; Reventlow, pp. 129ff., 149ff.). Mowinckel's view (also that of A. R. Johnson, *The Cultic Prophet in Ancient Israel*[2], 1962, p. 49 n. 2) is that this is necessarily a *Heilsorakel*. If the unit is indeed vv. 1–10, the most radical aspect of Jeremiah's use of the genre (assuming that he is the author) is his reversal of the *Heilsorakel*, and this is ground which Baumgartner and Mowinckel, despite their different assumptions, share, and which is also a feature of Weiser's interpretation of Jer 14.1–10. But Weiser has a cultic setting and occasion in mind: a public plea by Jeremiah on behalf of the community in the context of the 'Covenant cult'.

This thought that Jeremiah fulfils a public, cultic function is taken further by Reventlow (pp. 129ff., 149ff.). Jeremiah as a public intercessor is discharging a recognized cultic office. The circumstance that v. 10 contains a refusal by Yahweh to save his people should not be taken as evidence of an idiosyncratic and provocatively original use of the oracle by Jeremiah, and the view that within the liturgical structure only a positive answer can be envisaged should be resisted. Reventlow leans heavily on Jer 4.10 and 11f.: he describes 4.10 as a verse which has verbal affinities with the *Heilsorakel* (שלום), but he also regards it as a kernel of a communal lament to which vv. 11f. are the answering oracle. It is not clear that vv. 11f. are a response to a prayer in v. 10, and it is much less clear that v. 10 is the petitionary element of a communal lament in which vv. 11f. function as an oracle. Hence Reventlow's claim that he has found in 4.11f. an oracle other than a *Heilsorakel* in a communal lament is not substantiated.

14.10 (see above, p. 321) does not have the form of an address by Yahweh to the community and Yahweh (the speaker) refers to himself in the 3rd person. Rudolph supposes that an adequate explanation of this is simply to posit that the content was lifted from Hos 8.13. Mowinckel has pointed to two oracles (Pss 12.6; 91.14–16) where, instead of a direct address, there is a reference to the worshipper in the 3rd person (*Psalms in Israel's Worship*, ii, p. 60). The technical use of רצה in 'declaratory formulae' (Lev 1.4; 7.18; 19.7; 22.25, 27) has been noted by G. von Rad (*Old Testament Theology*, i, 1962, p. 261; cf. Reventlow, p. 164). These formulae are used to convey authoritative priestly rulings on whether sacrifices are acceptable or unacceptable, whether a leper is cured or still leprous and so on (For the use of רצה in connection with moral judgements in the book of Proverbs see W. McKane, *Proverbs*, p. 448). Hence לא רצם is indicative of an authoritative refusal of the plea of the community, and it is followed by a statement about the consequences of this refusal.

The view that Jeremiah is the author of vv. 2–10, but that vv. 2–9 exist only for the sake of v. 10 (see above, pp. 319f.) still does not recommend itself (cf. J. Skinner, op. cit., pp. 130f.), although Baumgartner's point about the striking character of the imagery in vv. 8b and 9a deserves some consideration. Is this evidence of a prophetic contribution to what is otherwise a complex of cultic stereotypes? This is unlikely, because, however striking, these figures do not modify in any way the theology of the communal lament: by charging Yahweh with negligence or indifference they seek to elicit a reassuring response. It is difficult to believe that Jeremiah would have identified himself with a theology whose climax was a שלום oracle. Bright has set out v. 10 as poetry and it is doubtful whether the alleged prose character of v. 10 is a weighty argument for its separation from

vv. 2–9. If v. 9b can be shown as poetry with a metre 3+3+1 (Rudolph), there is no reason why v. 10b should not be so regarded with a metre of 3+3+2. If Sept. were supposed (see above, p. 321) to represent a better Hebrew text than MT, v. 10 (with ויפקד חטאתם deleted) could be arranged as four stichs (3+3; 3+3—excluding the introductory formula).

The conclusion to be drawn is that vv. 2–10 are a unit, but that they are not attributable to the prophet Jeremiah. They are connected with later, perhaps exilic, reflections on the failure of Jeremiah, acknowledged to be a true prophet, to prevail with Yahweh as an intercessor. The concern was to explain why the Judaean community had suffered disaster and exile. Jeremiah receives from Yahweh a message of doom rather than a *Heilsorakel*. The clearest expression of this pattern of reflection, which seeks to vindicate Jeremiah and yet to preserve the view that powerful and effective intercession is normally an aspect of the prophetic office, is the statement (7.16; 11.14; 14.11; 15.1–4) that Yahweh placed an interdict on Jeremiah's exercise of his powers as an intercessor. The same considerations apply to vv. 11–16.

YAHWEH'S WORD IS NOT SALVATION BUT DOOM (14.11–16)

[11]Yahweh said to me, Do not pray for the prosperity of this people. [12]Though they fast, I will not hear their cry; though they present burnt-sacrifices and grain-offerings, I will not accept them; by sword, famine and pestilence I will make an end of them. [13]But I said, Alas! Lord Yahweh, the prophets are saying to them, You will not see the sword nor suffer famine, for I will give you lasting security in this place. [14]Yahweh said to me, The prophets use my name to utter falsehoods; I did not send them nor give them instructions nor communicate with them. False visions, empty divinations and their own self-deceptions are what they prophesy to them.[1] [15]Therefore these are the words of Yahweh concerning the prophets who prophesy in my name, though I did not send them; who say, There will be no sword and famine in this land. The end of those prophets will be death by sword and famine. [16]The people to whom they prophesied will be cast out into the streets of Jerusalem, victims of famine and the sword: they, their wives, their sons and their daughters, and there will be no one to bury them. I will pour out their doom upon them.

The references to חרב, רעב and דבר (v. 12) and to חרב and רעב (vv. 13, 15, 16) raise the question of the precise relationship of vv. 11–16 to vv. 1–9, where the threatened disaster is envisaged solely in terms of drought (cf. Thiel, pp. 178–180). Sept., Pesh. and Targ. understand דבר as 'deadly pestilence', and this should be noted in connection with Weippert's contention (p. 165 n. 256) that מות is a variant of דבר in 15.2, 18.21 and 43.11. The false prophets give an assurance that there will be no enemy

[1] Emending לכם (MT) to להם (see below, p. 325).

invasion and that its concomitants will not be suffered. The derivation of תִרְאוּ (v. 13) from ראה is confirmed by נִרְאָה (5.12) and this is how 14.13 was understood by the versions, but 42.16 (הַחֶרֶב אֲשֶׁר אַתֶּם יְרֵאִים) gives a different indication and 'see' and 'fear' may be variants in this type of expression. תִרְאוּ (14.13) but not נִרְאָה (5.12) could be derived from ירא, but 'You will not see the sword nor experience famine' hangs together better than 'You are not to fear the sword and you will not experience famine'. Weiser's contention that מָקוֹם means 'temple' (*pace* Duhm, 'Jerusalem') is supported by Sept. which expands MT so as to make explicit the equation of מָקוֹם with 'temple' (ἐπὶ τῆς γῆς καὶ ἐν τῷ τόπῳ τούτῳ). On this view there is a particular reference to the inviolability of the temple and also a more general assurance that territorial integrity will be maintained.

The שָׁלוֹם prophets claim an authority (נִבְּאִים בִּשְׁמִי) which they do not truly possess (v. 14), for they are not sent by Yahweh and are not recipients of his word (cf. 1.7, where these appear as the marks of the prophet who is called by Yahweh). The sources of their predictions are variously described: false visions, worthless divinations, and projections of their own inner confusion and self-deceit. The emendation of וֶאֱלוּל (or וֶאֱלִיל) to אֱלִיל is proposed by Duhm, Ehrlich (p. 280) and Brockington (p. 204). וְקֶסֶם וֶאֱלוּל is explicable as a hendiadys ('false divination'). Sept. (καὶ οἰωνίσματα) and Pesh. (wnḥš') suppose that there is a reference to a special type of divination, obtained from observing birds or from attending to their cries. Kimchi cites an opinion of Rashbam that there are genuine diviners whose endowment is of a different nature from that of the true prophet, but there is no intention here of allowing a science of קֶסֶם. The implication is rather that all aspects of divination have the character of illusion and falsehood.

Rudolph supposes that vv. 11–16 take us back to a point in Jeremiah's ministry when he had only just emancipated himself from the theology of the *Heilsorakel* and that this is indicated by לָכֶם which includes Jeremiah with those who hear the words of assurance and salvation (similarly Weiser). This is a lame explanation of לָכֶם and לָהֶם is needed. It is represented by many Hebrew manuscripts and by Sperber's text of Targ. (לְהוֹן), and has been adopted by NEB (Brockington, p. 204). Even if this is a secondary correction of לָכֶם (supported by Sept., Vulg. and Pesh.) in the Hebrew manuscripts where it appears, it is a correction which is demanded by the sense. Further, Rudolph and Weiser see evidences in vv. 11–16 of a conflict between the involvement of the prophet with his people and the word of doom which Yahweh requires him to proclaim, so that v. 13 is an indication of his refusal to accept Yahweh's verdict (vv. 11–12), and is an attempt by Jeremiah to exonerate the people, or at least, to mitigate their guilt by placing the blame on the false prophets.

The שלום prophets will themselves die either by the sword or of hunger, and those who relied on their assurances will be the victims of war and famine. Their corpses will be heaped up in the streets of Jerusalem and they will suffer the last and supreme indignity—lack of burial (v. 16). ושפכתי עליהם את רעתם can mean either (a) 'I shall requite the evil which they have done', or (b) 'I shall bring disaster on them'. The first sense of רעה is the one which is indicated by the versions, by KJV, Lowth and Blayney. Calvin is aware of the other possibility, and 'doom' is preferred by Weiser and Bright and is noted as an alternative by Rudolph. NEB conflates both ideas: 'I will pour down on them the evil (= disaster) they deserve'.

Weippert (p. 79 n. 230) notes that Thiel (pp. 178ff.) attributes vv. 11–16 to a Deuteronomistic redaction and she maintains that they derive from Jeremiah. The following comments relate to her treatment of 14.11–16 (pp. 148–191):

(a) The circumstance that the prose writers in the book of Jeremiah (however they are to be labelled) utilize Jeremianic vocabulary from pre-existing parts of the corpus should not be misread as a demonstration that the prophet Jeremiah is the author of this prose.

(b) All the passages cited in connection with the compact series רעב חרב, and דבר, excluding 15.2, are prose. If Jeremiah could have created the compressed tripartite formula on the basis of earlier use, there can be no objection in principle to the assumption that prose writers subsequent to Jeremiah made the innovation on the basis of earlier use. Moreover, as commentators on Jeremiah's words who found the combination of חרב and רעב in 5.12 and the series מות (= דבר), חרב, רעב and שבי in 15.2, they had the motive of achieving the systematization which is expressed in בחרב וברעב ובדבר. The conclusion which Weippert draws is not inescapable, nor is it the most reasonable or probable conclusion.

(c) It is clear from chapter 5.12 and 14.13, 15 that the combination of חרב and רעב originates in the proclamation of the opponents of Jeremiah and that he takes them up in the course of his rejoinder. The argument that 14.11–16 are not attributable to Jeremiah is not inconsistent with the view that they preserve an authentic recollection of his polemical encounter with the שלום prophets and correctly represent that the vocabulary under discussion originated in the oracular pronouncements of these prophets. The polemic against the שלום prophets, which is found in passages attributable to Jeremiah

(5.12f.; 23.15–24), was also a Deuteronomic concern (Deut 18.20–22) and was a continuing concern in the exilic period (Jer 14.11–16; 23.25–40; 27; 28; 29.15–23).

(d) The view that בחרב וברעב ובדבר is a stylized literary resource which has been shaped as a convenient form of expression for total destruction (Weippert, p. 178 n. 323) is not at all incompatible with the use of it in relation to particular, political circumstances. It is difficult to resist the conclusion that the intention of vv. 11–16 is to describe defeat at the hands of Nebuchadrezzar and his army, and the carnage, famine and epidemic which are caused by war and siege conditions.

Thiel (pp. 182–188) considers that vv. 11–16 are a composition of D and have been largely formulated by D who attached them to vv. 2–10 in which he had no part. Verse 12a or part of it (cf. Hitzig, Skinner, p. 131 n. 1) and a fragment of v. 16 may be Jeremianic material appropriated by D (p. 188). Verse 11 is stitched to vv. 7–9 on the assumption that the prayer in these latter verses was offered by Jeremiah (cf. Skinner, p. 131, n. 1) and v. 12 is stitched to v. 10 by רצה. The appearance in vv. 13, 15 and 16 of the first two members of the 'triad' in v. 12 (חרב and רעב) effects a connection between vv. 11–12 and vv. 13–16. Hence vv. 11–12 function as a bridge by means of which D passes from vv. 2–10, where the prayer (vv. 7–9) and Yahweh's refusal to grant it (v. 10) arise out of distress caused by drought, to the new subject of שלום prophecy, its use by Jeremiah to mitigate Judah's guilt, and the threats issued by Yahweh against שלום prophets and those who attend to their reassurances.

The disparateness of v. 11–16 over against vv. 2–10, suggested by the reference to military disaster rather than drought, or by the new subject of שלום prophecy, should not be over-estimated. This is Thiel's tendency, but he is right in holding that vv. 11–16 form an independent unit. It has been argued that vv. 2–10 are related to a problem which arose when Jeremiah was acknowledged to be a true prophet, while, at the same time, effective intercession was regarded as a necessary part of the prophetic office. The transition from drought to military disaster is awkward and creates an impression of discontinuity, but military defeat leading to disintegration and exile are the circumstances on which we would expect the problem to focus rather than on drought. Nor should it be supposed that the confusion caused by שלום prophecy is disengaged from this complex of considerations, because these are precisely the prophets who claimed that they were able to intercede effectively for the people and to bring them a reassuring oracle from Yahweh. The assertion that Jeremiah was a true prophet whose powers as an intercessor were interdicted is complemented by the assertion that the prophets who claimed to bring a message of שלום from Yahweh were false prophets. Hence vv. 11–16 arise intelligibly as an elaboration of vv. 2–10, and, for their own part, they hang together better than is suggested by the statement (Thiel) that vv. 11–12 are a bridge between vv. 2–10 and vv. 13–16.

It has been argued that the view of the prophetic office which appears in 7.16, 11.14, 14.11 and 15.1–4 is a Deuteronomic-Deuteronomistic one (see above, p. 245). Jeremiah is embraced by these circles as a true prophet, but since their models (Moses and Samuel) lead them to believe that such a prophet was a powerful intercessor and an effective preacher of repentance, Jeremiah's failure in these regards was perplexing to them and called for an explanation. Two principal reasons are given for his lack of success. In the first place it is said (14.11; cf. 7.16; 11.14) that Yahweh had placed an interdict on intercession, and the unfavourable answer to the communal lament (v. 10) as well as the statement that fasting and sacrifices will not stave off military disaster (v. 12) have to be related to this circumstance. The second part of the explanation is connected with the activities of the שלום prophets. The people were beguiled by prophets whose credentials they had no reason to question and who promised them immunity from danger and lasting peace in Yahweh's name. What therefore the exilic interpreters postulate (and in this they represent Jeremiah's situation correctly) is the most confusing and dangerous condition which can be imagined, where falsehood assumes the guise of a word of Yahweh. Those who listened were conquered by an inner spiritual darkness and were so utterly deceived that Jeremiah's words could have no impact on them.

A SECOND REFUSAL (14.17–15.4)

[17]You shall speak these words to them:
Let my eyes stream with tears,
day and night without ceasing;
the virgin daughter of my people is mortally wounded,
felled by a lethal blow.
[18]If I go into the country,
there are those slain by the sword;
if I go into the town,
there are those ravaged by famine.
Both prophets and priests wander about the land and are at a loss.
[19]Have you finally rejected Judah
or taken a loathing to Zion?
Why have you afflicted us with incurable ills?

Why does evil come to us when we expect relief,
terror when we look for healing?
²⁰We confess our wickedness, O Yahweh,
the sins of our forefathers and our sins against you.
²¹Do not despise (us) for the sake of your name;
do not bring into contempt the throne where your glory dwells.
Remember your covenant with us and do not annul it.
²²Are there among the gods of the nations those who give rain? Or do the
heavens themselves produce showers? Are you not, O Yahweh, God alone,
our God to whom we look? It is you that have made all these things.
¹Yahweh said to me: If Moses and Samuel were to stand before me, I would
show no favour to this people. Dismiss (them) from my presence and let them
go away. ²If they ask you, Where shall we go?, you shall say to them: These
are the words of Yahweh: Those destined for plague will die of plague, those
for the sword will die by the sword, those for famine will die of famine, and
those for exile will go into exile. ³I will visit on them four kinds of doom (This
is Yahweh's word): the sword to slay, dogs to tear, birds and wild beasts to
devour and mutilate. ⁴I will make them an object of horror to all the
kingdoms of the earth, because of the sins committed by Manasseh, son of
Jehoiakim, king of Judah, in Jerusalem.

The introductory formula at 14.17 is as inappropriate as the one
which introduces vv. 2–9, although it is defended by Weiser on
the same grounds as those adduced for 14.1 (see above, p. 315).
We cannot gather from vv. 17–18 that there is any intention on
the part of Jeremiah to address the people or to exert pressure on
them to change their attitudes. Rather we have a summons to
weeping which the prophet addresses to himself in view of the
sad condition of his community. גדול and בתולת are not
represented by Sept., but if they are deleted on the ground that
the line is overloaded (Rudolph, Janzen, p. 40), the sense is not
greatly altered, although Calvin and Lowth suppose that בתולת,
applied to the personified Jerusalem, is intended to convey that
hitherto she has not been violated.

Is the prophet describing events which have taken place or are
already taking place? Or is this a prophetic premonition of a
community suffering from mortal wounds? In support of the
view that this is a vision of imminent disaster (Rudolph) there is
the precedent of Kimchi's exegesis. Weiser and Bright, on the
other hand, suppose that these are not simply gruesome allusions
to wounds about to be inflicted, but that the nation is already
bleeding from its wounds. The right understanding of v. 17 is
perhaps that the prophetic anguish is induced by the
excruciating certainty that the events which are foreseen must
inevitably unfold and that nothing can stay their onset. It is a
situation in which Jeremiah's foresight is a recipe for a double
agony: the agony of not being taken seriously by those on whom
the disaster is to fall, and the agony of knowing that they are
about to be engulfed.

When it takes place, there will be a scene of suffering and

death. Corpses will lie on the battlefield and the emaciated bodies of those ravaged by famine will be seen in the towns. It is a picture of a land overrun by an invading army, where hunger is the consequence of chaos, the destruction and commandeering of food stocks, and siege conditions. שבר is used of broken health or of wounds and injuries for which there is no cure, and the medical metaphor is noticed by Lowth: 'The dissolution of a government or a body politic is called a *breach* (שבר) by way of allusion to the breaking or disjointing the limbs of a human body.'

Whatever construction is put on the last line of v. 18, it is not brought into a particularly convincing connection with the earlier part of the verse. There are two considerations which conspire to throw doubt on the final כי clause: it is prose rather than poetry and it does not hang together particularly well with the stichs to which it is joined. The different interpretations offered are connected principally with the sense which is attached to סחרו and the construction which is put on ולא ידעו or לא ידעו (the latter is represented by Sept. and Vulg. and is found in Hebrew manuscripts). לא ידעו can be taken as a relative clause. Kimchi's exegesis accords with the indications of Sept. and Vulg. and he explains סחרו by observing that the Judaeans had perforce to go into exile by a circuitous route (סבבו ללכת לגלות). The view that there is a reference to exile is the one adopted by KJV ('go about into a land that they know not') and Lowth, and it is assumed in Condamin's emendation of סחרו to נסחבו ('be dragged'). Blayney translates 'go trafficking about the city and take no knowledge', and this should be compared with 'ply their trade through the land and have no knowledge' (RSV) and with Hyatt's comment that venal prophets and priests carry on with their usual business of bolstering false expectations, even in a time of distress. The view that the 'trading' sense of סחרו (סוחר 'merchant') is not to be pressed is found in Calvin (*circumeunt*) and Venema (*vagantur*), and Calvin offers three interpretations of ולא ידעו, coming down in favour of the third: (*a*) It refers to the ignorance and bewilderment of prophets and priests—they do not understand why they have been overtaken by disaster. (*b*) It is an allusion to exile in a strange land. (*c*) It indicates that prophets and priests have been deprived of the power of reason, or else that God will confound all their efforts to exercise these powers in order to effect their escape. This is also the interpretation which is favoured by Venema who comments: *Ultima verba, et nihil, sciunt ... significat eos nihil scire, quo sibi aut aliis opem ferant, esse itaque consilii inopes. Quod est facillimum et huc apte quadrat, nec tamen, nisi a Calvino, observatum.*

Pesh. *ḥdrw l'r'' wl' yd'w*, 'They go around the land in circles and are at a loss', produces a sense which is near to that favoured by Rudolph and Weiser and which is more easily obtainable if אל is emended to את (Duhm, Rudolph). The spiritual leaders of Judah will be overwhelmed by the catastrophe and will be unable to offer effective advice or initiate decisive action. NEB attaches the sense 'beg' to סחרו on the basis of Syriac usage and appropriates Winton Thomas's derivation of ידע from Arabic *wada'a* (cf. *Proverbs*, p. 367). Prophets and priests are reduced to the status of itinerant beggars and as such are continually on the move. The picture is rather that of prophets and priests, unable to command and control the situation which has engulfed them, wandering about the land distraught and demoralized (so Rudolph and Weiser).

Verses 17–18 will not pass for a constituent part of a communal lament. They may have been pressed into service in order to provide a description of distress which triggers the appeal to Yahweh in vv. 19ff., but this is not their original function. They describe the grief awakened in the prophet because of the incurable disease which has afflicted his people and the pain caused by a vision of carnage, famine and pestilence, but this fully discharges their function. They deal with private sorrow and encapsulate an unshared vision, but they do not lead on naturally to a prayer in which 1st person plural suffixes and verbs appear. It is likely, however, that the intention of the editorial arrangement is to put them to such a use: the prophet who agonizes and foresees becomes the prophet who pleads on behalf of his people, hence a private expression of sorrow and prescience is transformed into a description of distress in the context of a communal lament, and a composition with a structure (14.17–15.4) similar to that of vv. 2–10 is attempted.

Verse 19 opens with questions which are indicative of bewilderment and are touched with complaint (cf. ה ... אם and מדוע with למה in vv. 8 and 9). A confession of sin uttered on behalf of the people appears in v. 20, a plea to Yahweh for them in v. 21, and an affirmation of faith in Yahweh, the Creator, in v. 22. Why has chastisement not had remedial effects? Why must they suffer one blow after another and become sick at heart and disorganized by terror, without any hope of returning to conditions of safety, social health and prosperity? Over against the first lament (vv. 2–10) Rudolph and Weiser find in the second the somewhat paradoxical confluence of greater deference and greater intensity of feeling. The questions are not so bold nor so contumaciously phrased, but the tone is more profound and there is a greater throb of anguish. There has been no resurgence of vitality, only the chill of growing terror. This exegesis is controlled by the assumption that vv. 19–22 are attributable to the prophet Jeremiah and that the historical circumstances of his ministry provide a key to their interpretation.

The supposition that 14.17–15.4 traverses again the ground covered in 14.2–10 influences Kimchi's treatment of the second passage, but the conclusion that 14.19–15.4 assumes a background of drought is also found in Duhm and Hyatt. Duhm (cf. Kimchi) holds that v. 19 refers to distress caused by drought and supposes that v. 21 has in mind the reduction of the Jews to a laughing-stock in the eyes of the world, because of Yahweh's failure to give rain. Both he and Hyatt appeal particularly to v. 22. Rudolph, Weiser and Bright also maintain that there is a specific reference to drought in v. 22, and that some connection between the conditions giving rise to the first and second laments has to be allowed. Rudolph conjectures that Jeremiah confines his plea in vv. 19–22 to the matter which is of most immediate urgency (drought) and makes no representations about the impending disasters of war and famine which he foresees. Bright founds a far-reaching reconstruction on the supposition that there is a reference to drought in v. 22. There are general as well as more particular considerations which cast doubt on the view that vv. 19–22 assume a background of drought and we begin with a general argument against it. If the intention of the editor was to make vv. 17–18 a description of distress leading into a communal lament, we must conclude that vv. 19–22 refer not to drought but to the consequences of invasion, siege and military defeat which are the subjects of vv. 17–18. Moreover, the transition to sword and famine has already been made in vv. 11–16. More particularly, the assertion that there is a reference to drought in v. 22 should be questioned. The verse could be taken rather as a concrete expression of faith in Yahweh's control over the order of nature, and this is more in accord with its deliberate theological tone than the supposition that it alludes to an emergency situation caused by drought. The idols cannot produce rain and the heavens themselves are not to be envisaged as rain-making deities. It is Yahweh who presides over the orderly and fertilizing processes of nature. The final clause, which asserts that Yahweh is the creator of all things (so Duhm, Rudolph) sums up the intention of the verse. There can be little doubt that this is how כי אתה עשית את כל אלה is to be taken and that NEB's footnote 'madest all these things' is better than its text, 'doest all these things'. Verse 22 is not obviously related to the topics of the prayer in vv. 20–21, and the manner in which the theme of Yahweh versus the idols has been

illustrated may have been influenced by the background of
drought in the first lament (cf. Thiel, p. 193). Even if v. 22 is
original in the context of vv. 17–22, it does not demonstrate that
these verses turn on a threat to the life of the community caused
by drought, and the nature of Yahweh's reply confirms the view
that what Jeremiah has sought to ward off is military defeat and
its consequences (15.2f.).

An expression of private anguish and a vision of the end,
attributable to the prophet Jeremiah and originally unconnected
with a communal lament (vv. 17–18*), has been used to furnish
a description of distress, but otherwise 14.17–15.4 corresponds
closely with 14.2–10. Jeremiah is portrayed as one who seeks to
prevail with Yahweh on behalf of the people, but his plea is
refused and a threat of carnage, famine, pestilence and exile is
issued. For those who ponder these matters, probably in the
exilic period, there are exceptional factors which influence the
outcome of Jeremiah's ministry and make him both a true
prophet and an ineffective intercessor. It was a time, so they
represent, when not even Moses and Samuel could have deflected
Yahweh from his purposes of retribution. A more specific reason
for denying vv. 19–21 to the prophet Jeremiah is that these
verses contain an appeal to Jerusalem or to the temple as
Yahweh's dwelling-place, and we have reason to believe that
Jeremiah regarded this as a doctrine which blinded the people to
the truth of their condition (see above, p. 328. Thiel (pp. 192f.)
finds that the vocabulary of vv. 19–21 has exilic connections and
that the topics are not the normal ones of the communal lament
as represented in the book of Psalms. He supposes that we may
have to reckon with a lament which was in use in public rituals
of lamentation in the exilic period. Kimchi noted the near
identity of קַוֵּה לְשָׁלוֹם וְאֵין טוֹב וּלְעֵת מַרְפֵּא וְהִנֵּה בְעָתָה with 8.15
and Duhm interpreted this as the re-use of the vocabulary of
8.14f., especially v. 15, in 14.19–20.

The main points of exegetical interest are לְמַעַן שִׁמְךָ and כִּסֵּא
כְבוֹדֶךָ (v. 21). The versions do not give a clear lead. If Vulg. is
followed the sense of MT is 'Do not despise (us) for the sake of
your name', where the appeal is to Yahweh's honour or
reputation: 'Do not make us despicable else you will make
yourself despicable' (cf. 14.7). NEB (Brockington, p. 204) reads
לְמַעַן שְׁמֶךָ as לְמַעַן שִׁמְךָ (cf. M. J. Dahood, CBQ 37, 1975,
pp. 341f.) and achieves a parallelism of מַעַן שִׁמְךָ and כִּסֵּא כְבוֹדֶךָ.
שֵׁם is then not Yahweh's reputation, but is the Name of
Deuteronomic theology—the Name which Yahweh has caused
to dwell in the Jerusalem temple. It is not evident what the
grammatical function of לְ is on this interpretation (an emphatic
particle—Dahood). Another dissuasive factor is the occurrence

of לְמַעַן שְׁמֶךָ at 14.7. כִּסֵּא כְבוֹדֶךָ is identified by Weiser with the ark and cherubim throne and by Kimchi, Duhm and Rudolph with Jerusalem. It is probably unnecessary to disjoin these possibilities (cf. Lowth), but there may be a special relationship with the view of 3.17 that the ark has become superfluous since Jerusalem is now Yahweh's throne (see above, pp. 74–75), and in that case כִּסֵּא כְבוֹדֶךָ is to be equated with Jerusalem.

The main issue in the final stich of v. 21 is whether we are to envisage Yahweh's covenant with David and his dynasty (Ps 89.4, 29, 34; 132.12; Jer 33.21) or the covenant which was concluded with Yahweh by Josiah on the basis of a book of the law (דִּבְרֵי הַבְּרִית הַזֹּאת) found in the temple (2 Kgs 23.2f.) and commonly identified with the book of Deuteronomy or part of it. On general, contextual grounds we would expect the allusion to be to the Davidic covenant. There are more particular pointers to this conclusion. Attention is concentrated on an appeal to Yahweh not to abrogate his covenant, whereas in 2 Kgs 23.2f. the emphasis is rather on the duty of human response: only if this response is adequate will the covenant be effective and operational. A more weighty consideration is the occurrence of פרר in Ps 89.34 and Jer 33.21 in connection with the stability and permanence of the Davidic covenant.

No doubt the substitution of Aaron for Samuel in Sept.^ at 15.1 has some relationship to Ps 99.6 where all three are mentioned (cf. Kimchi). Pesh. and Targ. explain אֵין נַפְשִׁי אֶל הָעָם הַזֶּה as Yahweh's refusal to accept Jeremiah's plea on behalf of the people and this agrees with Rashi and Kimchi who gloss נַפְשִׁי with רְצוֹנִי (see above, p. 323). Janzen (pp. 73f.) has noticed the differences between Sept. and MT in 15.1 He supposes that אֲלֵיהֶם (πρὸς αὐτούς) may have been the text of the Hebrew *Vorlage* of Sept. and that a marginal correction (τὸν λαὸν τοῦτον), related to MT הָעָם הַזֶּה may have been subsequently inserted into the text at the wrong place (after ἐξαπόστειλον). The meaning would then be that Moses and Samuel would suffer peremptory dismissal were they to attempt to intercede for the people at this juncture, but MT gives better sense. Rudolph (following Pesh. and Vulg.) reads שַׁלַּח and assumes a haplography of מ. He explains מֵעַל פְּנֵי in terms of suppliants who have sent in their advocate to plead with a great man and who wait in the outer hall to hear the outcome of his representations. The advocate is unsuccessful and is told to send his clients away. Weiser, on the other hand, connects מֵעַל פָּנַי with the meeting of Yahweh and his people in a cultic context, with Jeremiah as the intercessor. Yahweh's refusal is spelled out to them when they ask 'Where shall we go?' The artificial and highly contrived character of this question was, however, pointed out by Duhm (cf. Thiel, p. 190): it exists only to serve the interests of a harsh transition from v. 1 to vv. 2–4. An inference which might be made from this observation is that Yahweh's answer consisted of 15.1 only (cf. 14.10) and that 15.2–4 are a piecemeal elaboration of 15.1.

The only item common to 15.2 and 15.3 is חרב and the remaining items in 15.3 may be regarded as specifications of חיה רעה in Ezek 14.21. 15.2 and Ezek 14.21 have three items in common (מות = דבר), but in place of שבי the Ezekiel passage has חיה רעה. One interpretation of 15.3 would be that death comes by the sword and that corpses are mutilated by dogs, vultures or wild beasts, but another possibility is that these are to be envisaged as four different ways of encountering death (ארבע משפחות). The former is perhaps the more probable, and לאכל ולהשחית will then refer to the mutilation of corpses which become carrion. At any rate the reference to exile in 15.2 is strangely out of place, since the other allusions are either to death by sword, famine and pestilence, or to the defiling of corpses (cf. Rizpah's vigil and her defence of corpses from birds of prey in 2 Sam 21.10–14). This suggests that ואשר לשבי לשבי is the same kind of exilic or post-exilic modification as occurs in those places where a negative particle appears to have been inserted before כלה (4.27; 5.10). The indication of complete destruction had to be modified, since it had been proved wrong by events. Verse 2 is an exilic or post-exilic composition and the impulse to produce another set of ארבע משפחות triggers v. 3. The idea that death as described in v. 2 has an ascending order of terror (מות = death in general) is found in Rashi and Kimchi (cf. Rudolph), but the view that מות is a synonym of דבר is certainly correct.

Despite Weiser's dissuasive (see below, p. 336) it is hard to resist the conclusion that there is something Deuteronomistic in the concentration of blame on Manasseh (cf. Thiel, p. 191). Since the purity of the cult at Jerusalem is of supreme importance, nothing can be more damning than the introduction of idolatrous practices there (cf. 2 Kgs 21.11–17; 23.26; 24.3). The meaning of v. 4 is apparently that the punishment which is to fall on Yahweh's people will be so terrible that they will be a paradigm to the rest of the world. All men will point at them as a community which is an object of horror, which has been through the fires of tribulation and has experienced the ultimate in suffering. Thus Rashi glosses זועה with מגורה and comments, 'All those who hear of the disaster which has come on them will shiver with fear'. Sept. καὶ παραδώσω αὐτοὺς εἰς ἀνάγκας refers to subjugation and dispersion, and Sept. renders לזועה at 24.9, in an identical context, as εἰς διασκορπισμόν, 'I shall cause them to be dispersed through all the nations of the earth'. The nuance of 'movement' in זוע is interpreted as 'dispersion' (cf. Kimchi who glosses זועה with תנועה).

This estimate of 15.1–4 as, in all probability, an exilic production, is not shared by Rudolph, Weiser and Bright. Rudolph and Bright dissociate only v. 4 from Jeremiah: Rudolph (cf. Thiel, p. 189) holds that v. 4 is a modified conflation of Deut 28.25 (וחיית לזעוה לכל ממלכות הארץ) and 2 Kgs 24.3 (בחטאת מנשה ככל אשר עשה). Weiser, who assigns vv. 1–4 to Jeremiah, urges that the reference to Manasseh is not evidence of a Deuteronomistic standpoint: it does not indicate that the entire blame is to fall on Manasseh, but only that he was a particularly notorious offender (p. 128 n. 3).

Thiel (pp. 189–191) regards 15.1–4 as a Deuteronomistic composition in which a Jeremianic core (אשר למות ... לשבי) has been encapsulated (cf. Nicholson). The case for Deuteronomistic traits in 15.1–4 has been adequately made by Thiel, but it is not so clear that the postulated Deuteronomistic editor made use of a Jeremianic fragment. The assumption that אשר למות ... לשבי is poetry (cf. Nicholson) and the remainder of 15.1–4 prose exercises an influence on this conclusion. In his commentary Rudolph sets out the passage in prose and deletes ואשר לשבי לשבי (see above, p. 335), whereas in BHS he shows it as poetry with four stichs. The view that v. 2 is prose should be adopted; ואשר לשבי לשבי is not to be deleted, but is evidence of the exilic or post-exilic provenance of v. 2. It is not established, therefore, that there is a need to dissociate v. 2 (Thiel, Nicholson) from the editor assumed to be responsible for vv. 1–4.

Another way of viewing vv. 1–4 has been canvassed (above, p. 335) and this would raise a question-mark against its description as a composition and would suggest that it does not have this degree of deliberation and coherence. The suggestion is that 15.1 has been further elaborated in a piecemeal fashion, that the question (v. 2) is a transparent device to effect a transition to a threat of sword, famine, pestilence and exile and that v. 3 develops from the fourfold threat of v. 2, with another set of ארבע משפחות. All this has been capped with a conflation of Deut 28.25 and 2 Kgs 24.3: Judah is an object inspiring horror and terror in the rest of the world, and she has been reduced to this condition because she succumbed to the sin of Manasseh.

CHAPTER XV

DOOMED AND UNLAMENTED (15.5–9)

⁵Who will take pity on you, Jerusalem?
Who will console you?
Who will make the effort to offer you condolences?
⁶You forsook me, says Yahweh,
you turned away from me;
so I stretched out my hand to strike you
and I destroyed you.
I had grown weary of relenting.
⁷I scattered them as with a winnowing-fork
in every town of the land;
I caused people to perish
and bereft them of their children.
They had not turned from their (evil) ways.
⁸I made widows of more women
than the grains of sand on the seashore;
I brought against them invading soldiers[1]
to despoil them at noonday.
I made anguish and terror alight on them suddenly.
⁹The mother of seven wilted and swooned away;
her sun had set while it was still day;
she was put to shame and suffered disgrace.
What is left of them I will give up to the sword
when they confront their enemies.
        This is Yahweh's word.

כי, which is not represented by Sept. and Pesh., is a redactional link (Duhm, Rudolph, Weiser; cf. Janzen, pp. 25, 119). It is generally agreed that vv. 5–9 constitute an independent piece, and Weiser makes the further suggestion that it may have been placed in its present context in view of the element of lament in v. 5. J. M. Berridge (*Prophet, People, and the Word of Yahweh*, 1970, pp. 176–179) has noted the *qînāh* metre in v. 5 and he and Weiser have compared the vocabulary of v. 5 (ינוד) with other groups of passages: with the association of נוד and נחם as synonyms in Isa 51.19, Nah 3.7, Ps 69.21, Job 2.11 and 42.11; with the use of אין מנחם or the like as a description of the condition of Jerusalem in Lam 1.2, 16, 17, 21. Berridge rejects Reventlow's view (op. cit., pp. 181ff.) that vv. 5–9 is a continuation of the drought liturgy of 14.2ff. and urges that this is not demonstrated by such items of vocabulary as בושה, אמללה and חפרה. He assumes that v. 5 is spoken by Jeremiah and that vv. 6–9 contain Yahweh's reply, but vv. 5–9 should rather be explained as a mixture of address and soliloquy attributable to Yahweh.

[1] Reading הבאתי עליהם לאם בחור (see below, p. 340).

Rudolph, Weiser and Berridge are all agreed that the passage reflects the historical circumstances of 597 (Nicholson 597 or 601), and other supporters of this date are Hyatt and Bright. Duhm urges that the prophet descries the future and that vv. 8f., which indicate sudden catastrophe, cannot be reconciled with the protracted character of the event which produced a climax of defeat and retribution in 597 and 586. Rudolph argues that if the date had been 586, the fate of the capital city would have been more in the foreground, and that if it had been 601 (so Volz who connects the passage with Jer 12.7ff. and the events described in 2 Kgs 24.2), the disaster would not have been described in such drastic terms. Thus Rudolph settles for 597, before the fate of Jerusalem was sealed, but when Judah was overrun by Babylonian armies. Weiser supposes that 15.5–9 arise out of the same extraordinary, public act of lamentation as provides the setting for 14.2–15.4, and that this was a reaction to the crisis of 597 at a point when capitulation was near. The entire discussion illustrates how difficult it is to establish a precise historical reference for a piece of prophetic literature.

We must suppose that the wagging of the head or other bodily movements (ינוד) belong to the rituals of mourning and are indicative of commiseration, and this sense of sharing sorrow is conveyed by Vulg., Pesh. and Targ. Rashi glosses ינוד with יקונן 'lament' and Kimchi with 'commiseration' (נחמת האבל). The support of human understanding and compassion, normally offered to the distressed, will be utterly denied to Jerusalem. No one will take the trouble to turn aside from his normal pursuits and preoccupations (cf. Rashi לנטות מדרכו אליך) ; no one will make the journey to the stricken 'house' in order to fulfil a mission of consolation. Berridge cites Ps 122.6 (שאלו שלום ירושלם) and remarks, 'Very possibly we have here a reflection of Jeremiah's fear that Jerusalem may lose for ever her old exalted position' (pp. 178f.). Rather there is an implied indictment of Jerusalem, that she suffers the consequences of her own folly and has brought herself to this pass.

In v. 6 Yahweh describes what his people have done to bring down his wrath on them, and Weiser notes (p. 129 n. 1) that the expression 'stretching out the hand', used of Yahweh, can signify both salvation and doom (cf. Exod 6.6; 24.11; Isa 5.25; 30.30; 31.3; Deut 4.34; 5.15). They have rejected him and become apostate, and he has initiated a destructive judgement on them. He is firmly committed to this course and nothing will make him change his mind or relent. His forbearance is at an end and no appeal for mercy will avail; he is tired of showing clemency and there can be no more of it (נלאיתי הנחם).

The winnowing process—the separation of the wheat from the

chaff—serves as a figure of judgement in v. 7. It is used in a way
which recalls the imagery of 4.11f. The wind is too strong to
effect the winnowing successfully and is an entirely destructive
agency. Rudolph supposes that v. 7 is no longer particularly
concerned with Jerusalem (עמי) and that the effects of enemy
action which are described in this and the following verses are
not to be thought of as involving the capital city itself. Judah has
been ravaged by invaders, but the fall of Jerusalem has not yet
taken place. Rudolph's concern to exclude Jerusalem is clearly a
consequence of his conviction that the historical background is
the events of 597. בשערי הארץ has been taken by Pesh. (*bqwryh
d'r"*) and Targ. (בקרוי ארעא) as synecdoche or *pars pro toto* (so
Duhm, Weiser, Bright and NEB). Kimchi comments, 'He
mentions gates instead of towns, because they go in and out of
the town by way of the gate' (cf. Weiser). There is a possibility
that the expression בשערי הארץ is connected with the
winnowing imagery: it is a winnowing of men and not of grain
and so the process is effected at the recognized place of public
concourse and not at the threshing-floor. The winnowing
imagery is understood by Rashi as an indication that those who
have been overrun by the enemy will be scattered far and wide
and will not all go into exile in one place (cf. Kimchi, 'I shall
scatter them in exile in all the cities of the world'). Kimchi takes
הארץ to mean 'world' rather than 'land' and the obscure
rendering of Sept. καὶ διασπερῶ αὐτοὺς ἐν διασπορᾷ ἐν πύλαις
λαοῦ μου (עמי over against MT הארץ) may have exegetical
rather than textual significance and may also indicate exile.

Rudolph makes the point that מדרכיהם לא שבו (v. 7) should
not be contrued as a principal clause ('They did not turn from
their (evil) ways'), but as a subordinate clause. He suggests
either 'since they did not repent of their ways' (cf. NEB, 'for
they would not abandon their ways') or 'because of their ways
from which they did not turn' (לא שבו a relative clause—so
Volz). There is no versional support for the view that מדרכיהם
לא שבו is a subordinate clause, but Sept. does not represent לא
שבו and so מדרכיהם (διὰ τὰς κακίας αὐτῶν) connects with what
precedes. Vulg. and Pesh. represent ומדרכיהם לא שבו and
Blayney knows of 2 Hebrew manuscripts which have this text.
The asyndetic association (Vulg. and Pesh. supply 'and') of a
word for a particular kind of bereavement with a general word
for death (שכלתי אבדתי), and the circumstance that the
particular word comes first, are odd stylistic features, unless
אבדתי is an auxiliary of שכלתי and both together constitute a
kind of hendiadys. שכלתי אבדתי would then indicate the hard lot
of mothers whose sons have perished in battle: 'I have destroyed
the flower of the nation's youth (and have thereby robbed many

mothers of their sons).' This has to be considered in relation to
עַל אִם בָּחוּר (v. 8) and יֹלֶדֶת חִשְׁבְּעָה (v. 9).

The versions give no help with the nuance of עָצְמוּ לִי (v. 8).
This is to be compared with יָבוֹא לִי, 'comes at my bidding'
(4.12) and is correctly understood by Ehrlich (p. 249) and NEB,
'I made widows among them more in number than the sands of
the sea'. Rudolph reads אַלְמְנֹתָם with Sept., Pesh. and Targ., but
the 3rd person plural suffix of the versions should be regarded as
a secondary harmonizing with מִדְרְכֵיהֶם (v. 7) and לָהֶם (v. 8). Q
אַלְמְנֹתָיו should be read in connection with עַמִּי (v. 7), and the
unevenness of מִדְרְכֵיהֶם and אַלְמְנֹתָיו has to be tolerated. There is
little to be gained by tampering with the order of v. 8 (*pace*
Rudolph), but, in any case, there are more serious textual
problems associated with it. לָהֶם, which is not represented by
Sept., is taken by Pesh. (*'lyhwn*) and Targ. (עֲלֵיהוֹן) as
equivalent to עֲלֵיהֶם, and Rudolph adopts עֲלֵהֶם with 2 Hebrew
manuscripts. If an attempt is made to read MT, it has to be
supposed that לָהֶם or עֲלֵיהֶם anticipates עַל אִם בָּחוּר, 'on the
mothers of young men' (אִם and בָּחוּר collectives; cf. Kimchi who
cites Exod 14.7, שֵׁשׁ מֵאוֹת רֶכֶב בָּחוּר). This is possible, but even if
the text of Sept. is followed (so Bright), and לָהֶם is deleted, the
effect is that mothers are the target of the invader, whereas the
sense which is needed is that mothers are bereft of their sons (cf.
v. 9). It has been suggested that the reference to noon is intended
as an indication that this is no furtive night raid (so Kimchi), but
an attack backed by such overwhelming force that it can be
advantageously executed by day (Volz). The point is perhaps
rather that in weighing up the best time to attack an army would
reckon with noon and night as serious alternatives (cf. 6.4f. and
especially קוּמוּ וְנַעֲלֶה בַצָּהֳרָיִם).

There has been a general tendency to relieve the
unsatisfactory sense of MT by emending עַל אִם בָּחוּר. Ehrlich
(p. 282) supposes that עַל אִם is a corruption of עֲלֵיהֶם which
arose as a correction of לָהֶם. Hence his text is הֵבֵאתִי לָהֶם בָּחוּר
שֹׁדֵד בַּצָּהֳרָיִם, 'I brought against them warriors, despoilers at
noonday'. Rudolph proposes לְאֵם מַחֲרִיב (*ZAW*, 1930, p. 283),
and he achieves a sense similar to that produced by NEB with a
different text (הֵבֵאתִי עֲלֵיהֶם לְאֵם בָּחוּר), 'I have brought upon
them a horde of raiders to plunder at high noon'). This is
perhaps the best than can be done with a dubious test (see
Brockington p. 204).

One of the difficulties in the last line of v. 8 is constituted by
עָלֶיהָ which is apparently a reference to Jerusalem and may be
indicative of the centre of the prophet's concern to which he
tends to return. Vulg. regards עָלֶיהָ as an anticipation of עִיר =
'towns' (collective) and translates *Misi super civitates repente*

terrorem (cf. Aq. πολιν και σπουδας). עיר occurs with the meaning 'agitation', 'trembling' only here and perhaps at Hos 11.9. It is so understood by Sept. (τρόμον) and Pesh. (*dlwḥy'*). It will have been noted that Aq. associates בהלות with haste (σπουδας) rather than terror. The former is represented by Sept. (σπουδήν) and the latter by Vulg. (*terrorem*) and Pesh. (*rtyt'*). Kimchi states that עיר was taken as 'adversary' by his father on the strength of 1 Sam 28.16. Blayney translates 'an enemy and terrors' and comments, 'עיר ובהלות may by an *Hendiadys* stand for "a terrible enemy".' The sense 'town' (= Jerusalem) is maintained by Ehrlich (p. 282) who reads עליהם and deletes ובהלות. The meaning of the line, according to Ehrlich, is that Yahweh will bring down the city (in ruins) on the heads of its inhabitants. Driver (*JQR* 28, p. 113) connects עיר with Arabic *ĝârat* 'raid'. MT makes satisfactory sense on the assumption that עיר means 'agitation' or 'anguish' and בהלות 'terror' rather than 'haste' (Duhm, Rudolph, Weiser, Bright). NEB is apparently based on Driver's philology of עיר, 'I have made the terror of invasion fall upon them all in a moment'.

Because of the obscurity of the language (אמללה and נפחה נפשה) it is not clear whether the death of a mother of 'seven' is described in v. 9, or whether she falls into a faint when she hears the terrible news of the death of her sons. Thus Lowth comments, 'fainting away and ready to die with grief for the loss of her children'. Rudolph, Bright and Nicholson suppose that it is a case of a mother swooning when she learns that her own sons have fallen in battle, whereas Weiser concludes that she dies of a broken heart. Duhm also supposes that the mother expires (נפחה נפשה), but Ehrlich (p. 282) observes that if she is exposed to shame and disgrace, we must assume that she is still alive. Sept. and Vulg. support Bright's view that נפשה is the grammatical subject ('her throat gasps'—not a particularly apposite expression for fainting). Rashi explains נפחה as דאבה and notes that in the Targ. of Deut 28.65 ודאבון נפש is rendered as ומפחן נפש 'exhaustion' or 'despair' (similarly Kimchi). Kimchi correctly interprets 'seven sons' as 'many sons' and observes that שבעה is an expression for a large number (ענין רבוי; cf. 1 Sam 2.5; Prov 24.15; Ruth 4.15). The unnatural darkening of the sun is explained by Kimchi as a משל, indicative of an extraordinary intensity of distress. He notes that שמש can be either feminine or masculine gender, but it remains unclear why the Massoretes indicate a 3rd masculine verb (Q בא) over against the consonantal text (באה).

The 'mother of seven' is a typical figure: one whose motherhood has been richly fulfilled and who in the normal course of things might expect to reap the reputation and esteem which is her due. But at what should have been the high noon of her life the light is vanquished by darkness, and this will be her environment for the rest of her days. The course of her life has been wrecked and her hope is lost. In view of בושה וחפרה (so Ehrlich) we should envisage that the terror of the news that her sons have fallen in battle causes her to swoon and that henceforth she is a broken woman living in a dark world with only death to look forward to.

There is in vv. 5–9 the untidiness of the mixture of address (vv. 5–6) and soliloquy (vv. 7–9), and of feminine singular and masculine plural suffixes, all of which hinder a firm interpretation of the passage. It is not at all clear that these verses reflect a historical situation when Judah had been overrun by an invader and Jerusalem was still intact. When Yahweh addresses Jerusalem in v. 6, he appears (if we take the verbs at their face value) to refer to a work of destruction which is already accomplished (וָאַט; וָאַשְׁחִיתֵך). There is consequently no reason to conclude that those referred to in vv. 7–8, again with verbs which apparently relate to past events, exclude the inhabitants of Jerusalem. The harshness of the transition from address to soliloquy should be noted.

The difficulties associated with the tenses of the verbs can be seen clearly in Sept. and Vulg. There is only one place in vv. 5–9 where we can be confident that there is a reference to a future event (אתן v. 9) and both Sept. (δώσω) and Vulg. (dabo) render אתן as a future. Otherwise, on a straightforward view of MT, all the other verbs ought to be rendered as past tenses, and the natural conclusion would be that they refer to events lying in the past. Sept. and Vulg. have introduced future tenses wherever the grammatical possibility seemed to exist, that is, wherever an imperfect form occurs with waw they have assumed that it should be pointed יִ (rather than יַ of MT): וְאַט (Sept. καὶ ἐκτενῶ; Vulg. et extendam); וָאַשְׁחִיתֵך (Sept. καὶ διαφθερῶ; Vulg. et interficiam); וָאֶזְרֵם (Sept. καὶ διασπερῶ; Vulg. et dispergam). Even נִלְאֵיתִי הִנָּחֵם has been rendered as a future by Sept. (καὶ οὐκέτι ἀνήσω αὐτούς). The perplexities which are encountered, both historical and translational, with Hebrew verbs in a passage like this have a more general application. Even if the correct translational procedure is to render verbs in the past tense, it does not follow that the events which a prophet describes as past actually lie in the past. The question arises whether when a judgement is made that verbs are 'prophetic perfects', it is right to render them as future tenses or as past tenses, and there are clearly disadvantages in both procedures. If they are translated as past tenses, there is no overt indication that they refer to events which still lie in the future. If they are translated as future tenses, the exceptional nature of the prophetic utterance and perhaps of the interior state of the prophet are lost. The oddness which should be preserved is precisely that he speaks of future events as if they were past events. Thus we may be misrepresenting his intention, if we suppose that he is 'predicting' future events. We should consider whether he speaks of future events as if they were past because their unfolding is so inevitable for him.

So far as vv. 5–9 are concerned, there is no doubt that, for the most part, the prophet describes events as if they lay in the past, but we may have to reckon with a prophetic premonition so intense that it can only be expressed by creating a grammatical paradox and locating future events in the past. Hence we should not suppose that it is a straightforward matter to pinpoint historically a passage of this kind, and it would be difficult to achieve a better balance than that of Skinner (*Prophecy and Religion*, p. 270): the passage refers to the final downfall of Jerusalem and Judah and this is viewed as already accomplished even if the language of the passage 'be only the language of prophetic anticipation'.

WHY WAS I EVER BORN? (15.10–14)

(15.10–12)

[10]Woe is me!, O my mother, that you bore me,
a man in strife and contention with all the world.
I have neither borrowed nor lent,
(but) everyone reviles me.[1]
[11]Yahweh answered:
There shall be a better future for those who survive,[2]
(but) I will expose you to enemy attack
in a time of disaster and affliction.
[12]Can iron crush iron from the north and bronze?

15.13–14 (see 17.3–4)

[13]Your wealth and treasures I will give for spoil
as the price[3] of all your sins[4]
in every part of your land.[5]
[14]I will make you subject[6] to your enemies
in a land which is strange to you;
for my anger has kindled a flame

[1] Reading כלהם קללוני (see below, pp. 345f.).
[2] Reading שאריתך (see below, pp. 347, 349).
[3] Reading במחיר (see below, pp. 385, 387).
[4] Reading כל חטאותיך (see below, p. 387).
[5] Reading בכל גבוליך (see below, p. 387).
[6] Reading והעבדתיך (see below, p. 385).

(and) it will burn for ever.[7]

The main critical problem is the determining of the degree of unity in vv. 10–21, and this task is complicated by textual uncertainties. It is tempting to isolate vv. 11–14 as a pocket of textual obscurity, and to explain vv. 10, 15–18 as a complaint by Jeremiah which is followed by an oracle containing Yahweh's reply (vv. 19–21). This was the analysis of Ewald and Giesebrecht. Weiser thinks of a cultic setting, although he wishes to retain the flavour of individual anguish, and will not have Jeremiah as a typical intercessor using public, liturgical forms (p. 131 n. 2; cf. Reventlow, pp. 210ff.). Baumgartner (pp. 33–40) supposes a conscious imitation by Jeremiah of the form of the individual lament.

The more elaborate textual proposals of Rudolph and Weiser have this in common that they suppose v. 11 to be a continuation of Jeremiah's complaint which begins with v. 10, and Weiser's emendation of v. 12 transforms this also into a continuation of Jeremiah's complaint. Hence the effect of their dispositions is that Jeremiah speaks continuously up to the end of v. 18 and that the break in this continuity caused by v. 11 in MT, which has the form of a reply by Yahweh to Jeremiah's words in v. 10, is removed. Alternatively, it may be supposed that there are two units, both conforming to the structure of the individual lament and consisting of a complaint by Jeremiah followed by an oracle from Yahweh (Baumgartner and NEB). The first and much briefer of the two then consists of Jeremiah's complaint in v. 10 and Yahweh's reply in vv. 11–12 (Baumgartner, pp. 60–63). NEB differs structurally (there are also textual and exegetical differences) from Baumgartner in so far as it tacks אתה ידעת (v. 15) to the end of v. 12. If the first unit is taken as 15.10–12, the second will consist of a complaint in vv. 15–18 and a reply in vv. 19–21. (NEB deletes vv. 13–14, Brockington, p. 204).

The dissuasive against the first solution consists of the textual obscurities in v. 11 and v. 12, and the emendations which are necessary to make these into utterances of Jeremiah. Sept. makes poor sense and the wisdom of appealing to it in respect of אמן (γένοιτο), רעתו (κακῶν αὐτῶν), צרתי (θλίψεως αὐτῶν) and אל האיב (πρὸς τὸν ἐχθρόν) is very questionable. With these and other emendations, Jeremiah is envisaged as defending his record as a prophet. The degree of his magnanimity towards his enemies and his concern for them are expressed in the discharge of his intercessory office. Why should he find himself so isolated and detested? 'Truly (אמן), O Lord, I have given of my best in serving you (שרתיך לטוב); I have interceded for my enemies (אל

= עַל) when they were in trouble and distress. You must know this' (similarly Bright). Weiser takes v. 12 into this scheme: 'I have shattered iron and bronze' (הרעותי Volz) is a type of proverbial expression, and Jeremiah's intention is to say that he has done everything in his power and has strained every nerve to carry out Yahweh's commission.

Reventlow's defence of the originality of vv. 13–14 (pp. 210ff.) is tied up with his view that vv. 10–12 are expressive of communal distress, and not of the private anguish of the prophet Jeremiah. Reventlow turns the argument round in relation to vv. 13–14 by urging that they are clearly words of Yahweh addressed to the nation and are therefore a confirmation that his total view of vv. 10–14 is correct. He makes the point that if vv. 13–14 are held to be intrusive, some explanation should be given of why they have intruded. Weiser does attempt such an explanation by suggesting that the insertion of vv. 13–14 was encouraged by the corruption of v. 12 into what was understood as a threat by Yahweh concerning the enemy from the north. Rudolph has raised the question whether, in view of the substantial identity of vv. 13–14 and 17.3–4, v. 12 may not be a corrupt form of 17.1.

Given all these factors, a decision about the structure of 15.10–21 cannot be taken with any confidence. Verses 13–14 can be eliminated from the discussion, but the question is then whether we are left with two units, each consisting of a lament and oracle, or only one unit with this structure. A decision has to be made in order to allow the exegesis to proceed and Baumgartner will be followed rather than Rudolph, Weiser and Reventlow. It will be assumed that vv. 10–12 are a unit, consisting of Jeremiah's complaint in v. 10 and Yahweh's answer in vv. 11–12. Verse 12, however, is included with hesitation and reserve in view of its unconvincing sense and the possibility that it may have been squeezed out of a mutilated form of 17.1.

On the assumption that the consonants of the last two words in v. 10 are to be redivided to give כלהם קללוני (Michaelis, Duhm, Rudolph, Weiser, Bright, Reventlow), it is argued that an adversative particle is needed and that כי ('yet', 'nevertheless') has been omitted by haplography in view of its proximity to the כ of כלה (כלהם). Giesebrecht's proposal, of which Baumgartner and Reventlow approve, that Sept. ἡ ἰσχύς μου (כחי) represents a corruption of an original כה, which appeared before אמר at the beginning of v. 11, should not be adopted. The Greek translator has read כלה as כָּלָה and ἐξέλιπεν is a rendering of this. ἡ ἰσχύς μου should be understood as an exegetical expansion—the supplying of a subject for ἐξέλιπεν in the interests of intelligibility. It follows from this that the word division reflected in the Greek translation at the end of v. 10 is the same as that of MT. What appears to have happened in Pesh. and Targ. is that כלה = כֻּלֹּה has been taken as collective and has been rendered with a plural suffix (*wklhwn* ; כולהון), but the מ has clearly been read as a component of מקללוני (*pace* Baumgartner who cites Pesh. in particular). Vulg. (*omnes maledicunt mihi*) appears to support כלהם קללוני, although this should be understood as a tidying-up process and not as a demonstration that a Hebrew text different from MT was read. Nevertheless, the emendation of Michaelis is economical and acute and should be adopted.

Cursing the day of one's birth (v. 10) has the appearance of a singular rather than a collective, representative activity, and Reventlow is aware of the parallel in Job 3.3ff. Nevertheless, he holds that it belongs to the liturgical structure of the communal lament as an opening gambit by means of which the representative pleader assumes an aspect of utter wretchedness, so that he may move Yahweh to a favourable response. He is disposed to accept the view that v. 10 with ריב and מדון refers in the first place to a forensic situation, where an individual faces charges in a court of law. It then becomes a fixed element in the liturgy of an individual lament, and the present passage illustrates how a feature which belonged to the individual lament has been reinterpreted in the context of a communal lament. The reference to borrowing and lending is thus explained in the first place as an avowal of innocence made by a man who has been brought to court on a charge of usury or in connection with other dubious financial transactions within his own community. Verse 10 is representative only in so far as it represents the conflict and anguish which belong to the prophetic vocation (cf. Jer 1.17–19; Ezek 2.7–9; Amos 7.10ff.). Rather than following Reventlow's cultic interpretation we should envisage a prophet bowing beneath the burden of his vocation, unable to bear the injustice that he should be caught up in an insoluble conflict with his own people. Well might he curse the mother who bore him and wish that he had never been born.

Rashi takes the 'borrowing and lending' reference to mean that Jeremiah had none of the financial involvements with other men which are a potential and ready source of friction. Kimchi's exposition is a simple literal one and Lowth and Blayney also suppose a narrow reference to abstention from usury. Other commentators envisage differing degrees of literalness: Duhm thinks that it is probably a proverbial expression and Calvin sums it up with *Je n'ay point traffiqué*. Hence Calvin, like Rashi, takes the sense to be that business dealings are most productive of strife and that the prophet has had no part in these. Hence his

experience of strife and rejection was all the more inexplicable
and difficult to endure (similarly Rudolph and Weiser).

The obscurity of v. 11 arises mainly from שרותך (Q שריתך)
and הפגעתי בך. Gunkel's conjecture (אשרתיך, 'lead you'), which
is adopted by Baumgartner, depends in a loose way on Sept.
κατευθυνόντων αὐτῶν, and παρέστην σοι points to a reassuring
rather than to a threatening sense of הפגעתי בך. The uncertainty
of Hebrew manuscripts about שרותך goes beyond the K-Q
differentiation (see BHS) and allows the possibility of שאריתך
which is represented by Aq. and Vulg. Both suppose that
Yahweh speaks words of consolation and reassurance: הפגעתי is
taken in the sense of 'alight' rather than 'intercede', and Vulg.
adversus inimicum represents אל האיב (על) over against MT
את האיב. Pesh. gives a dark and menacing interpretation to the
verse. The translator reads שריתך (Q) which he takes as a Piel of
שרה ('set free', 'forgive') and Rashi also notes this possibility.
The Syriac rendering rests, in all probability, on a decision of the
translator to read לא שריתך instead of אם לא שריתך. Thus the
second אם לא is clearly indicated by *'l'*. The resultant sense is as
follows: 'I shall not forgive you generously, but I shall waylay
you (a menacing sense of פגע) with enemies from the north in a
time of tribulation and affliction.' The perfects of MT have been
rendered as imperfects, and the verse assumes the character of
future threat. Another point is that the reference to the enemy
from the north has been advanced from v. 12 to v. 11, so that
v. 11 contains an explicit mention of this enemy.

If we sum all this up before passing to a more modern phase of
exegesis, we find that שאריתך is presupposed by Aq., Vulg.,
Targ. and Kimchi and is noted as a possibility by Rashi, whereas
שרה (שרית(י)ך) 'set free') is noted by Rashi and is present with a
negative particle in Pesh. Both שריתיך and שרותיך (from שרר
'strengthen; so NEB, Brockington, p. 204) are verbs more
common in Aramaic than Biblical Hebrew, but Reventlow
(p. 211), who does not decide between the two, is willing to
entertain the use of such Aramaisms by Jeremiah. As for
הפגעתי, nowhere in the versions (except perhaps in Targ.) is the
thought of intercession to be detected, but the idea of 'being
present with' in a reassuring sense is found in Sept., Aq., Symm.
(αντεστην) and Vulg., while a more neutral sense is indicated by
Kimchi.

Baumgartner's interpretation rests on the emendation of
שרותך to אשרתיך (already noted) and on the sense of הפגעתי בך
present in Sept,. Aq., Symm. and Vulg.: 'Assuredly I will give
you the best guidance, I will stand by you in the time of disaster
and distress.' The difficulty of relating הפגעתי to את האיב is
resolved by emending the latter to אתה אהבי, 'you are my

friend'. A reassuring message is also achieved by the rendering of NEB, although in this case an attempt is made to make sense of שרותך (K, see above, p. 347), and את האיב (identified with the 'enemy from the north' of v. 12) is construed as an object of הפגעתי בך, 'I will bring the enemy to your feet' (the translation is dubious). The details of the exegesis of v. 11 offered by Rudolph, Weiser and Bright have already been indicated (above, p. 344). Jeremiah has served Yahweh to the best of his ability and has been alive to his responsibilities as an intercessor, even to the extent of praying for his personal enemies when they were caught up in distress and affliction. 'You know this, Yahweh (so Rudolph and Bright, attaching אתה ידעת to the end of v. 11), why then am I so isolated and so destitute of esteem?'

Reventlow's view (pp. 210ff.) is that vv. 11–14 constitute Yahweh's answer to Jeremiah's complaint in v. 10 and that the manifestly public character of the threat in vv. 13–14, with the allusions to looting by an invading army and to exile (reading העבדתיך as in 17.4), should be taken as a clue that vv. 11–12 are also spoken to the community and do not relate to Jeremiah's inner conflicts. There is (so Reventlow) an opposition or antithesis between v. 11a and 11b. The first refers to earlier experiences of a *Heilsgeschichte* (cf. 2.3) and the second to a future judgement, when Yahweh will punish his people for their sustained apostasy. One obvious difficulty which attends this exegesis is that both verbs are perfects, but one is rendered as a past (שרותך or שריתך) and the other (הפגעתי) as a future. Hence Reventlow concludes that הפגעתי בך is being used in a threatening sense, and in this regard he follows Pesh.

Is we assume that v. 12 is a continuation of Yahweh's reply it is natural to take מצפון as a reference to the enemy from the north, whatever obscurity attaches to the verse as a whole. The same interpretation of הירע is found in Aq. (αρμοσει), Vulg. (*foederabitur*) and Targ. The last-mentioned, however, differs from Aq. and Vulg., since it does not issue a dissuasive against foreign alliances, but envisages a hostile coalition of kings mobilizing in the north for an attack on Jerusalem. Pesh. has transferred מצפון to v. 11 (above, p. 347), and it then offers a paraphrase of v. 12. The enemy from the north by whom Judah is threatened is qš' 'yk przl' w'yk nḥš', 'as strong as iron and bronze'. Rashi connects הירע with רעע (an Aramaizing form) = רצץ 'crush', and so he glosses הירע with הירוצץ. This elucidation of הירע is also present in Kimchi (הירע = הישבר) who explains that the allusion to the north is connected with the threat posed by Babylon (also Rashi), and that a mixture of iron and bronze is stronger than iron by itself.

This account of הירע is followed by Baumgartner (who points

הירע as הֵירַע, Niphal, rather than הֵירֵעַ, Qal) and by NEB, 'Can iron break steel from the north?' According to Baumgartner, מצפון is not a reference to the enemy from the north, but to the quality of Pontus iron. On this view the question asked in v. 12 ('Does iron break, iron from the north and bronze?') fulfils a similar function to that of 12.5. Jeremiah is given no guarantee of release from conflict, but is required to 'steel' himself in order to withstand formidable opposition. He has complained of the personal cost of discharging his vocation, of his isolation and the hostility which he has incurred. He is told that it will always be like this, only more so in the future, and that he will need an iron will in order to endure the great pressures which will be exerted on him and which otherwise would crush him into ineffectiveness. It is an attractive interpretation, but it is improbable that מצפון can be disengaged from 'the enemy from the north' in this obscure verse.

Since Jeremiah does not receive much of an answer (vv. 11–12) to his intensely felt private anguish, there is some justification for Reventlow's contention that the whole must be interpreted as having a public rather than a private and personal significance; as dealing with a crisis in the life of the community rather than a tumult in the prophet's soul. Reventlow's way should not be followed, but it should be recognized that there are difficulties in whatever direction one seeks a solution. The first stich of v. 11 can hardly be a word of assurance to the prophet, if what follows is a threat issued against the prophet or even against his community. No more can we grant that the first stich is continued by a further guarantee of well-being to Jeremiah. The parallels which are cited (Jer 36.25; Isa 53.12) do not in fact help us to attach the sense 'intercede' to the Hiphil, of פגע in v. 11. The grammar will not allow such a sense and can hardly be reconciled with 'cause to intercede'. Again, 'I shall be at your side to counter the enemy' (emending את to אל = עַל) presupposes a reassuring sense of פגע which is unlikely. The best of the variants attested in Hebrew manuscripts is שאריתך (Aq., Vulg., Targ., Rashi, Kimchi), although Ehrlich (p. 283) argues that אם לא must be followed by a verb and not a noun. With this text vv. 11–12 constitute a credible answer to Jeremiah's complaint in v. 10, because the distinction between private and public cannot be pressed too rigorously.

It is not inapposite that Yahweh's answer to Jeremiah's outburst should have a public orientation, since the relief of his inner, insupportable disarray will come from some mitigation of his hard destiny as a prophet of doom. This does, however, involve the admission that a remnant is contemplated, over against those passages where nothing less than total dissolution seems to be envisaged in Jeremiah's utterances. The comfort which Jeremiah receives, is a word of qualified hope for the future of his people. A remnant will survive to embrace a better future, but first of all the land will be ravaged by an invading army with all the sufferings and excesses which attend such a catastrophe. Yet the collapse of the old, with all its destructive aspects and the choking dust of demolition, is not simply a violent end, but a levelling of the ground and an uncovering of new foundations for the renewal of a common life in company with Yahweh.

IS THERE NO END TO INSULT AND SUFFERING? (15.15–18)

¹⁵You know (the truth) O Yahweh,
remember me and come to my help,
let me have my revenge on those who harry me.
Withhold your anger and do not remove me,
be mindful of the insults which I have borne for you.
¹⁶Your words came to me and I ate them;
your words were a delight to me
and rejoiced my heart;
for I am called by your name,
Yahweh, God of Sabaoth.
¹⁷I did not sit jesting in merry company;
I sat alone because I felt your hand on me.
You have filled me with (your) anger.
¹⁸Why is my pain unending,
my wound incurable, unyielding to treatment?
You have been false to me,
a spring whose water has failed.

It is possible that וּפָקְדֵנִי (v. 15) is part of the cry for vengeance or vindication, although its connections may rather be with זָכְרֵנִי (cf. Pss 8.5; 106.4). Targ., by means of a double translation, has attached to it both a positive and negative aspect: 'Visit me to do good to me and bring retribution on my enemies.' According to a number of scholars (Baumgartner, Weiser, Bright, Reventlow, Berridge, p. 118) there are circumstances which make וְהִנָּקֶם לִי (cf. Jer 11.20; 12.3; 20.12) less reprehensible than the expression of a simple spirit of revenge. Weiser, Bright and Berridge hold that Jeremiah is motivated by a tender regard for Yahweh's honour more than by a thirst for personal revenge, and Baumgartner, with the same intention, refers to the 'enemies' of individual laments in the book of Psalms (7.2; 25.3; 119.157). It is for Yahweh that the prophet suffers so much (Ps 69.8, 10) at the hands of those who despise Yahweh's word (Pss 10.3, 13; 74.10, 18). The separation of vindication from personal revenge is even more marked in Reventlow (p. 219) for whom the 'I' of

vv. 15–18 is representative throughout. Hence there is no question of being able to detect in these words a spirit of revenge in Jeremiah's soul.

The view which will prevail in what follows is different from the one which has emerged in the preceding paragraph. It will be urged (*pace* Reventlow) that vv. 15–18 do reflect a personal and private anguish of the prophet Jeremiah, and (*pace* Baumgartner, Weiser, Bright, Berridge) that there should be less anxiety to make Jeremiah's deep, human cry for vengeance into a pious regard for the honour of Yahweh. It is better (so Rudolph) to pay attention to this testimony of stress, agony and fallibility in the prophet than to offer a pious mitigation.

אל לארך אפך תקחני (v. 15) is difficult and is unacceptable to Baumgartner who reads אל תארך אפך ונקני, 'Do not prolong your anger, but establish my innocence'. Baumgartner appropriates אל תארך from Duhm and conjectures ונקני, where Duhm had followed Sept. and deleted תקחני. Targ., like Sept., does not represent תקחני and could be appealed to in support of אל תארך, although it is unlikely that the rendering has this textual significance: 'Do not prolong my humiliation' (ולא תתן ארכא לעלבני). It is likely that what is indicated by תקחני is a point at which the prophet will crack under the pressures which he has to endure. This is Kimchi's interpretation (אל תמיתני, 'Do not kill me'; cf. Bright who associates אל תקחני with Jeremiah's death at the hands of his persecutors). Jeremiah calls for a realistic recognition on Yahweh's part of how much he has had to suffer in the discharge of his office. There is a limit to what any man can bear and his breaking-point has just about been reached. Both Rudolph and Weiser discern a transition from a sense of bitterness against men to the launching of an accusation against God. Jeremiah also requires, according to Rudolph and Weiser, that Yahweh should make good the promise which he issued to the prophet at his call (1.18f.)

Duhm's proposal that Sept. ὑπὸ τῶν ἀθετούντων τοὺς λόγους σου (v. 16) represents מנאצי דבריך over against MT נמצאו דבריך (cf. Ehrlich, p. 283) is adopted by Baumgartner and Driver (*JQR* 28, p. 114). These scholars have presumably been influenced by the circumstance that ἀθετέω is used once in Sept. (1 Sam 2.17) to render נאץ and that MT can be explained as a corruption arising from the metathesis of מ and נ and the mistaking of י for ו. Driver vocalizes ואכלם as וָאֶכָּלֵם, follows the punctuation of Sept. and renders: 'Know that for thy sake I have suffered reproach from them that despise thy words, and have endured them.' NEB (Brockington, p. 204) is similar, but it vocalizes ואכלם as וָאֶכְלָם and translates freely, 'I have to suffer those who despise thy words.'

The eating of Yahweh's words (v. 16) has been explained as an obedient response to them. Kimchi comments, 'When your words of prophecy were revealed to me, I received them with approval.' Kimchi's contention that v. 16 refers to the prophetic word leads us into an area of modern exegetical debate concerning v. 16. Sept., Aq., Symm. and Vulg. render the first and second occurrences of דבריך (K) differently: the first according to K and the second according to Q (דברך). Baumgartner notes Hölscher's view that 'words' ('word') in v. 16 should be related to the *Gebot* or Law of Yahweh, which figures prominently in Ps 119, rather than to the דְּבָר which the prophet himself received, that is, the oracles disclosed to him. Baumgartner concludes that the reference is to oracles which Jeremiah had received, and so he supports Kimchi's view of the matter. Scholars have continued to be exercised with the question whether v. 16 refers to Jeremiah's own reception *qua* prophet of Yahweh's word, or whether the allusion is to the words of earlier prophets, or to the Law of Yahweh which features in certain psalms (e.g., נר לרגלי דברך, 119.105). Berridge (p. 119) urges that v. 16 does not allude to earlier oracles delivered to the prophet Jeremiah, but to 'such literary works as Judah possessed at this time, including, in particular, earlier prophetic words'. Berridge makes too much of the difficulty of נמצאו as a reference to Jeremiah's own words and similarly of את אשר תמצא (Ezek 3.1) as a reference to Ezekiel's own words.

The argument in favour of equating 'words' ('word') in v. 16 with the Law of Yahweh in the psalms is developed by Reventlow who is impressed by the contribution of H. Stoebe (*Jahrb. der Theol. Schule* Bethel, 4, 1955, pp. 135f.). The choice of דבריך (K) rather than דברך (Q) is significant in connection with this view, and it is urged that Jeremiah's prophecies of doom could not have been described as a source of delight to him. Verse 16 is then to be taken as an indication of Jeremiah's readiness to listen to or to read words of God which came to him from others. Reventlow explains נמצאו ... לבבי as a standardized declaration of innocence made by a prophet who speaks for all pious individuals in the community: for those who find their delight in the Law of Yahweh which they make part of themselves. The final part of v. 16 (כי נקרא שמך עלי) is thought by Reventlow to be a confirmation of his view that the person who speaks is an official, cultic mediator, employing liturgical formulae (pp. 220f.). He thus rejects Rudolph's interpretation of נקרא שמך עלי in terms of a prophet indwelt by Yahweh, possessing an inner, irrefragible certainty that Yahweh is with him, notwithstanding all appearances in an outside world of contradiction and suffering. Weiser (p. 133 n. 1) comes nearer to what Reventlow is after in holding that Yahweh's שם is a claim or title to ownership and that the phrase has a legal nuance and a corporate reference.

In connection with וַיְהִי, which has been seen as a difficulty, we have to consider the bitter-sweet quality of Jeremiah's experience in relation to his appropriation of a message of doom. The passage which throws most light on our verse (v. 16) is the call narrative of Ezekiel, where the prophet eats a scroll containing words of lamentation and woe which, nevertheless, taste as sweet as honey. To suppose that this is an indication that Jeremiah and Ezekiel had different temperaments or psychological constitutions is a mistake. It is not that Ezekiel is a cold fish and Jeremiah a warm-hearted compatriot who cannot bear the tensions which arise from the proclamation of doom over his community, and would be incapable of bitter-sweet experience. Both passages are rather indicative of a mysterious dialectic, a strange tension of suffering and joy, of pain and satisfaction. There is a joy which even a prophet of doom finds when he stands in the path of duty and says what he must.

Rudolph explains the grammar of v. 17 by assuming that the לא of לא ישבתי is still operative with אעלז, and this would seem to be implied in NEB's rendering, 'I have never kept company with any gang of roisterers, or made merry with them'. Another possibility is that ואעלז should be read as וָאֶעְלֹז and taken as a final clause, 'that I might rejoice (with them)'. The negative (ולא חדיתי) is explicit in Targ., but it should be noticed that Targ. connects ולא אעלז with what follows, and that Sept. and Pesh. do the same if ולא אעלז is part of their identical paraphrase. Pesh. is almost certainly dependent on Sept. Vulg.'s punctuation also differs from that of MT, but the sense of Vulg. is different from that of the other versions: according to Sept., Pesh. and Targ. Jeremiah cuts himself off from social pleasures for the sake of his vocation; according to Vulg., Aq. and Symm. Jeremiah takes pride in or finds joy in his prophetic task, even in the solitariness which it imposes on him (no negative is assumed with ואעלז). Vulg. (also Aq. and Symm.) do not seem to have attached any element of sinfulness or impiety to סוד משחקים, since the contrast is between good company, on the one hand, and the peculiar joy of the prophetic way of life on the other. This view of the matter blunts the impression of lament or complaint which must be preserved in any exegesis which is to be taken seriously.

Even if we adopt the punctuation of MT, as seems best, there remains the question whether any impious behaviour is imputed to those who sit בסוד משחקים. It is likely that Sept. (ἀλλὰ εὐλαβούμην), Pesh. (*'l' dḥlt*) and Targ. (ולא חדיתי) put a pejorative construction on בסוד משחקים. The rendering of this phrase in Sept. (ἐν συνεδρίῳ αὐτῶν παιζόντων) and Vulg. (*in concilio ludentium*) could have innocent connections, but Pesh. (*bknwšt' dmbzḥn'*) has the nuance of impious scoffers. However, with the punctuation of MT it is doubtful whether there is a case for relating סוד משחקים with the kind of impiety which is indicated by מושב לצים (Ps 1.1). The sense of the verse is rather that the prophetic vocation requires of Jeremiah an unnatural way of life and that he is set apart in loneliness from normal social pleasantries.

Targ. clearly connects כי זעם מלאתני (v. 17) with the message of doom which the prophet has been given to proclaim: Jeremiah has been filled with a 'prophecy of curse'. Rashi follows Targ. on זעם and introduces the thought that, cut off from normal social intercourse because of his dedication to his vocation, Jeremiah lives the life of a perpetual mourner. Kimchi's comments are similar in some respects, but he connects זעם with מכה and כאב (v. 18) rather than with the contents of a prophecy of doom. These words allude to the way in which Jeremiah was despised and cursed up to the point where physical violence was used against him.

The line of exegesis indicated for כי זעם מלאתני by Targ., and Rashi is probably the right one, and with this provisional estimate we may turn to modern commentators. Baumgartner, wedded to ויהי (v. 16), thinks of Jeremiah as an unsuccessful escapist: Jeremiah grasps after a way of escape from the darkness which envelopes him, but after a moment of escape he is brought back sharply to the realities of the present (v. 17)—his loneliness and isolation (p. 36). Hence there is a note of complaint in Jeremiah's voice: the awful clarity of his vision of doom (כי זעם מלאתני ; cf. 10.19ff.; 14.18) disqualifies him as a merry companion. Baumgartner equates the weight of Yahweh's hand which the prophet feels with the burden of the prophetic vocation and the element of compulsion to which the prophet is subject (= Rashi, Kimchi).

Rudolph's treatment of v. 17 agrees broadly with this: מפני ידך refers to the compulsion exercised by Yahweh, and Jeremiah's complaint arises from the wedge driven between him and his own kin and compatriots in virtue of his acceptance of a prophetic vocation. The זעם with which Jeremiah is filled is to be equated with the message of doom which he is commissioned to proclaim. His awareness that men avoided him and that he was not accepted as a normal human being, was hard for him to endure. His pent-up emotions had to find an outlet and they

found it in a railing against God who had called him to be a
prophet and had brought him to this pass.

Weiser also thinks in terms of an alienation from normal,
social life demanded by the prophetic vocation, but, following
Kimchi and Hölscher, interprets כי זעם מלאתני as an allusion to
prophetic suffering, and so he associates it with the afflictions
and sufferings of v. 18. This difference of opinion over כי זעם
מלאתני assumes its full significance in the exegesis of Reventlow
who dissociates himself from the commentators previously
mentioned (Rashi, Baumgartner, Rudolph) not only in respect of
זעם, but also in the construction which he puts on the preceding
part of v. 17. He argues that the reference is not to innocent
pleasures but to impious arrogance (cf. Pesh., above, p. 354).
Reventlow's review of the uses of שחק and עלז in Biblical
Hebrew can only show that they are capable of conveying both
innocent pleasure or delight and impious arrogance and scorn,
and so the result is inconclusive. He is, however, persuaded that
בסוד משחקים has the same nuance as מושב לצים (Ps 1.1). Nor is
the second part of v. 17 connected with the prophetic vocation
(so Reventlow), and מפני ידך (in the sense of Pss 32.4 and 38.3)
and כי זעם מלאתני refer to the sorrow and pain of the solitary
invalid (cf. Lev 13.46). The 'I', as a corporate personality,
incorporates the godly in the community whose innocence he
confesses and of whose unmerited sickness and suffering he
complains (pp. 221–224).

Rashi, Duhm, Baumgartner and Rudolph have grasped the
essentials of the verse. The content of the message (כי זעם
מלאתני) is what, in the last analysis, alienates Jeremiah from his
community, and it is the point at which this becomes unbearable
which is marked by v. 18. It would be difficult to better Lowth's
summing up of the matter: 'Jeremy quickly found the joy which
he had conceived from the honour of being a prophet was turned
to heaviness; all his prophecies contained nothing but terrible
denunciations of God's indignation against a sinful people. This
makes me, saith he, sit alone, renounce all cheerful conversation,
and give myself to solitariness and pensive thoughts.'

BHS suggests that the Aramaic sense of נצח 'overpower'
(v. 18) may be reflected in Sept. κατισχύουσι (cf. Pesh. which
renders נצח by 'šyn 'strong'). Sept. πόθεν ἰαθήσομαι for MT
מאנה הרפא indicates that מאין rather than מאנה has been read
by the Greek translator. The sense of 'chronic', 'not yielding to
treatment' which apparently attaches to אנושה is represented by
Sept. στερεά 'unrelenting' (similarly Pesh. ḥsyn'; Targ. תקיפה;
Kimchi חזקה and כברה). אכזב, according to Rashi and Kimchi,
is not simply an adjective meaning 'false', but is a specific term
for an unreliable spring (Rashi, מקור פוסק; Kimchi מקור אכזב),

and so furnishes a precise parallel to מים לא נאמנו (cf. NEB). On למה היה כאבי נצח Kimchi comments, 'I have no respite from strife from one day to another'. It is clear from this that Kimchi (*pace* Reventlow) does not take literally the references to physical pain and incurable wounds.

On the other hand, Kimchi's supposition that Jeremiah's anguish is associated with a condition of innocence (Why do I suffer thus? What sin is there in me?) leans towards Reventlow's pattern of interpretation: Jeremiah (like Job), assured of his innocence and assuming a connection between sin and suffering, asks why he should be made to suffer. But Jeremiah's individuality (so Reventlow, p. 225) retreats entirely behind his office. It is, therefore, not a question of the innocence of Jeremiah *qua* prophetic individual (as Kimchi supposed), but it is a case of a representative mediator asserting the claims of the righteous among the people for the *Heil* which Yahweh has promised them.

According to Weiser Jeremiah charges God unjustly (v. 18) for he had not been assured that he would enjoy normal social experience (cf. 1.19). Jeremiah falls under the judgement of his own words (2.13—the leaking cisterns constructed by men as opposed to the living water which only God can supply) with his reference to a spring of water which fails when it is most needed. This was the *impasse* which Jeremiah had to reach before he could take up Yahweh's word again as the only way of escape. This is a too complacent and pietistic view of the matter. Jeremiah's anguish arises from the unendurable tension between his prophetic message and the sentiments of compassion and solidarity which draw him to identify himself with his fellows. The medical vocabulary in v. 18 is metaphorical, but profoundly metaphorical; the two complexes of imagery are used to describe the intense, spiritual anguish of Jeremiah: pain from which there is no relief and wounds for which no treatment will avail, on the one hand, the failure of the spring of water through whose constant and ample supply he had hoped to endure on the other. His loneliness, his tortured and irreconcilable loyalties, the nadir of his hope and the brokenness of his spirit are gathered up in the language of v. 18. Why should he have been brought to such a point of contradiction, where the wholeness of his life was destroyed and where he could not both fulfil his prophetic calling and be a man among his people?

RETURN TO ME AND I WILL SUPPORT YOU (15.19–21)

[19]These are the words of Yahweh:

If you turn (to me) I will restore you;
you shall stand in my presence.
If you separate what is precious from the trash,
you shall be my spokesman;
they will turn to you
rather than that you should turn to them.
²⁰Over against this people I will make you
a wall of bronze which is fortified;
they will fight against you,
but will not prevail over you,
for I am with you to keep you safe and to deliver you.
    This is Yahweh's word
²¹I will deliver you from the power of evil men
and redeem you from the grasp of the ruthless.

There are some differences between MT and Sept.: ἄξιον (Ziegler, ἀναξίου, following Hippolytus) is inexplicable as a rendering of זולל (v. 19), and Sept. has a shorter text than MT in vv. 20–21, where נאם יהוה והצלתיך is not represented. Further ופדתיך (v. 21) is not represented by Sept.ˢ, and it is this text which Ziegler adopts. Janzen (p. 117) explains the shorter Greek text as a consequence of haplography, whether in the Hebrew *Vorlage* or in the Greek transmission of the text. Targ's erroneous paraphrase of ואם תוציא יקר מזולל ('If you turn wicked men into righteous men') is followed by Rashi and Kimchi. That the מן is privative is indicated by the translations of Calvin (*et si separaveris pretiosum a vili*) and Blayney ('And if thou wilt separate the precious from the vile'). According to Baumgartner זולל refers to human complaints (v. 18; also Duhm) which must be distinguished from the word which Yahweh communicates to Jeremiah and whose exclusion is essential, if he is to discharge his prophetic office (agreeing with the renderings of Bright and NEB). Hence ואם תוציא יקר מזולל shares the same concern as the remainder of v. 19: it is not connected with the prophet's duty to convert others (Targ., Rashi and Kimchi), but with a more immediate need to purge his word of all worthless and trivial elements, so that it bears the hallmark of word of Yahweh.

Kimchi elucidates לפני תעמד (v. 19) with special reference to the prophetic office and notes that it is used of Moses and Samuel (15.1). According to Kimchi, v. 19 requires Jeremiah to return to a proper, prophetic stance and to utter only words which are agreeable with it. He is not to give up any ground to those who contend with him; his task is to bring them to his standpoint: 'Take care lest you are led astray by their arguments when you contend with them. You must bring them to your point of view'.

In general, later commentators have followed this line of

exegesis. Baumgartner recalls 12.5 and remarks that 15.19–21 is no more a word of consolation for Jeremiah than 12.5 was. He supposes (cf. Bright) that the word-play in v. 19 contributes to the enigmatic quality of the divine answer which gradually sheds its opaqueness and becomes more luminous as it proceeds. Like Kimchi, Baumgartner considers that there is an allusion in v. 19 to the sharpness of Jeremiah's indictment of Yahweh (v. 18): the אם תשוב of v. 19 implies that Jeremiah has defected from Yahweh and has run away from his prophetic duty. Baumgartner cites 1 Kgs 17.1 (cf. Duhm), 18.15, 2 Kgs 3.14 and 5.16 to show that עמד לפני is used particularly of the prophetic office, and, in view of כפי תהיה, he is in no doubt that it has this special reference in Jer 15.19. It is doubtful whether the grammar of v. 19 allows ואשיבך to be construed as an auxiliary of תעמד ('I shall make you stand before me again' = אשוב אעמידך), as Rudolph supposes, but apart from this he is concerned, as Duhm and Baumgartner were, to formulate a psychological or interior elucidation of vv. 19–21. Jeremiah recovers his senses like a man who is restored from the delirium of a fever, and this recovery of proportion and self-possession constitute the voice of Yahweh. He comes to understand that for him a life of suffering is a mark of authenticity.

Against the psychologizing conclusion Weiser says that vv. 19–21 are 'genuine revelation' and that the divine answer conflicts with the interior attitudes of Jeremiah: the crisis is overcome not because Jeremiah has achieved a better insight into his vocation, but because he has submitted to Yahweh's revelation. This is similar to his treatment of 12.1–5 (above, pp. 266f.), and it appears to preclude any attempt to relate the answer in vv. 19–21 to the prophet's experience, to a process of intellectual striving and spiritual growth. Weiser appears to relish the thought that Jeremiah's search for self-understanding in relation to his religious faith and vocation has to be checked and finally crushed before he can recover an assurance of 'salvation' and be steadfast in his prophetic task.

Reventlow argues against Duhm, Baumgartner and Rudolph that vv. 19–21 do not represent the 'voice of Jeremiah's conscience' but are a liturgically announced divine answer: 'The prophet and his psychology are entirely out of view' (p. 228). On the level of form-critical description there is no difficulty in granting that 15.15–21 belong to a dialogue constituted by the prophet's petition and complaint, on the one hand, and Yahweh's reply on the other, and this aspect of the matter is clearly indicated by Baumgartner who discusses in some detail the structure of vv. 15–21. The difference between Baumgartner and Reventlow in form-critical respects arises from their differing evaluations of this structure. Baumgartner holds that it is an imitation of a cultic *Gattung* (cf. E. Gerstenberger, *JBL* 82, 1963, p. 407) and that a prophetic reshaping is evident: 'The prophetic standpoint betrays itself explicitly in the contents of vv. 16, 17, 19, 20, and also in the passionate reproach of v. 18b which would hardly be thinkable in the psalms' (p. 40). Reventlow insists on the ultimate public character of complaint and answer and this corresponds with his view that the literary structure has a cultic *Sitz* and that the prophet employs the *Gattung* in order to discharge a cultic function.

Reventlow argues that these verses are directed to the community, even if the divine reply at first glance may seem to contradict this conclusion, in so far as it refers particularly to the prophetic office. Like Rudolph, he makes out that vv. 19–21 are expressive of a renewal of Jeremiah's vocation, but he supposes that such renewals were regularly repeated cultic acts (pp. 226f.). The answer in vv. 19–21 (so Reventlow) rebuts the prophet's plea of innocence and denies that he is a paradigm of piety. Rather, a thoroughgoing repentance is required of him and this he cannot effect without Yahweh's help. Further the charge of unreliability levelled against Yahweh (v. 18) is dismissed as frivolous, and here too a change of heart is needed on the part of the prophet before he can experience Yahweh's support. So far this is not much different from what Kimchi, Duhm, Baumgartner and others have said about the passage. Kimchi relates the threats to Jeremiah's safety not to Jehoiakim and his שׂרים (Duhm, Baumgartner, Rudolph, Nicholson; cf. Jer 36f.), but to his ecclesiastical opponents. When they purposed to kill him, he was shielded by the שׂרים who said, 'This man does not deserve death, for he has spoken to us in the name of Yahweh, our God' (26.16).

The rebuke uttered by Yahweh in vv. 19–21 is not only for Jeremiah, but also for the community whose attitudes Jeremiah has represented (Reventlow, p. 228). He must correct his one-sided espousing of the cause of the people. When he exercises his office properly, they will turn to him and thereby turn to God, and עָמֹד לְפָנַי refers to the faithful performance of this cultic function as mediator and not principally to the fulfilling of a private, individual prophetic destiny. This makes Jeremiah, in his corporate role, into an Exemplar and Guide, and this is a different view of the prophet's function in relation to the communal lament from the one which Reventlow otherwise employs, where the prophet's utter solidarity with the people makes the two indistinguishable and inseparable. Reventlow is now saying that the proper exercise of the prophetic office introduces an element of conflict and a lack of solidarity between the prophet and his community, and this is a measure of the difficulty which he has in reconciling his corporate interpretation of the laments in the book of Jeremiah with 15.15–21.

Reventlow's point that dialogue cannot be reduced to introspection is connected with a too facile transformation of form-critical categories into theological statements. 'Revelation' has to be made as intelligible as possible and if so, has to be related to inner processes of mental and spiritual suffering and the clarification which is distilled from them. That is not to say that 'word of Yahweh' is to be reduced to 'voice of conscience' or to introspective activity, nor is it to admit that interior analysis is incompatible with a dialogical view of vv. 15–21. 'Dialogical' (in this more sophisticated theological sense) is the insistence that there is an encounter between Yahweh and Jeremiah, that the issue has the status of a 'word of Yahweh' and is not exhaustively explained as the outcome of psychological processes of conflict and resolution. In other words, one cannot be content, as Weiser and Reventlow apparently are, with an absolute divorce between the psychological or human and the transcendental.

Gerstenberger (p. 406) identifies in vv. 19–21 a Deuteronomistic view that the fate of Israel was determined by her hostile attitude to the prophets, but he acknowledges that Jeremiah, as he is presented in v. 15–18, does not match this understanding of the prophetic office, because he belongs in some measure with the apostate people and is required to repent (v. 19). The argument is unsatisfactory: if 15.15–21 was composed by a Deuteronomistic editor in late exilic times (p. 407), why is Jeremiah not portrayed as one who was entirely on the side of Yahweh and who fits perfectly the postulated Deuteronomistic view of the prophetic office? Gerstenberger has not successfully demonstrated the exilic character of 15.15–21, and the absence of any specific allusions to Jeremiah's complaints in the divine answer has been reasonably explained by those who have understood vv. 19–21 as a deliberate non-answer. His grievances are not taken up because they are dismissed, and he is reminded that he has never been promised immunity from strife and suffering, from alienation and hostility, but only the strength to endure (cf. 12.5).

Nevertheless, a view has been taken of the structure of Jer 14.1–15.21 which is broadly in accord with that recommended by Gerstenberger (op. cit., pp. 393–408), namely, that it contains four laments (14.1–9; 17–22; 15.10; 15–18) and four divine answers (14.10–16; 15.1–4; 11–12 (13–14); 19–21). With some help from emendations another view of the structure can be arrived at (see above, p. 344): 15.10–18 is to be construed as

lament and 14.1–15.21 then consists of three laments and three
divine answers. 15.5–9, which fall out of this structure, have
been defined as a mixture of address and soliloquy and the
change from direct address to third person in v. 7 has been noted.
Gerstenberger's view has some affinity with this: he describes
vv. 7–9 as an expansion of thoughts contained in v. 6 and
concludes that the passage is set in a context of devastation with
the final catastrophe still to come. He suggests a date after 597
and supposes that the Deuteronomistic editor of 14.1–15.21 used
old material to drive home the futility of Israel's complaints.

Gerstenberger holds that the Deuteronomistic editors portray
the prophet as a decisive mediator and that 14.11–16 and 15.1–4
illustrate this view of the prophetic office (pp. 399ff.), but his
description of the exilic concerns which inform 14.2–15.4 are not
precisely those which have been set out the preceding pages. It
has been urged there that having espoused Jeremiah as a true
prophet the exiles were left with the problem of explaining why
he did not save Judah from disaster. Why was he not an effective
intercessor, since a true prophet is by definition an effective
intercessor? One answer (14.13–16) is that the people were
confused by assurances of שלום which they had every reason to
expect from true prophets (effective intercessors), but which in
fact were uttered by false prophets and wrongly attributed to
Yahweh. The principal answer is that it was Jeremiah, the
prophet of doom, who spoke for Yahweh and that this has to be
correlated with the circumstance that Yahweh had placed an
interdict on his powers as an intercessor (14.10–12; 15.1–4).
Another way of expressing the difference between Gerstenberger
and the views expressed in the preceding pages is to observe that
he has not maintained a distinction between communal laments
and expressions of vexation and anguish which may be regarded
as private to Jeremiah and as arising out of his prophetic
vocation. It is to this personal dilemma that 15.10–11(12) and
15–21 should be related (*pace* Gerstenberger, p. 407) and these
passages are comparable with 12.1–5. It is not obvious why they
should be denied to Jeremiah or why they should be regarded as
the product of Deuteronomistic activity. These verses are denied
to the historical Jeremiah on different grounds by A. H. J.
Gunneweg (*ZTK*, 67, 1970, pp. 399, 403–406, 412–416) who
substitutes a kerygmatic for a psychological interpretation, so
that they do not give us access to the texture of Jeremiah's soul,
to the inner struggles and doubts with which he was beset. We
are to think of these verses, according to Gunneweg, as a
subsequent generalizing interpretation of the significance of
Jeremiah's life in connection with which he has become a model
or exemplar of every righteous person who suffers.

CHAPTER XVI

SIGNS OF DISSOLUTION (16.1–9)

[1]The word of Yahweh came to me: [2]You are not to marry or have sons and daughters in this place. [3]These are the words of Yahweh concerning sons and daughters who are born in this place, concerning the mothers who bear them and the fathers who beget them in this land. [4]They will die in agony; they will not be mourned or buried; they will become dung on the surface of the land; they will meet their end through sword or famine and their corpses will be food for birds of prey and wild beasts. [5]These are the words of Yahweh: Do not enter a house to share in a funeral-meal; do not go in to mourn or to console, for I have removed my peace from this people, my constancy and mercy. This is Yahweh's word. [6]The great and the humble will die in this land; they will not be buried or mourned, no one will gash himself or shave his head for them. [7]No one will give a piece of bread[1] to a mourner[1] to comfort him for the dead; no one will offer him[1] a cup of consolation for the loss of father or mother. [8]Do not enter a house to share in a banquet, to sit down with those who eat and drink. [9]These are the words of Yahweh Sabaoth, God of Israel: I will bring to an end in this place, before your eyes and in your days, sounds of joy and gladness, the voice of the bridegroom and the bride.

The view that there is a Jeremianic core in 16.1–9 is represented by Rudolph, Thiel (pp. 195–198) and Nicholson. According to Rudolph, who compares v. 4 with 7.33 and 8.2, and v. 9 with 7.34, vv. 1–9 are extant in the language of Source C, but their gist is attributable to the prophet Jeremiah. Thiel endeavours to ascertain the precise contributions of his Deuteronomistic editor and concludes that these are not very considerable. Hence vv. 1–3a, 4a, 5–8, 9* is an autobiographical account attributable to the prophet Jeremiah which D has transmitted. It has been located by D at this point in the book in order to enlarge on the loneliness of Jeremiah (15.17) and to relate this loneliness to his message. Bright explains the position of 16.1–9 in terms of the themes of Jeremiah's loneliness, and famine and sword: the first is taken up from 15.10–18 and the second appears at 14.11–18 and 15.1–4.

H. Weippert (pp. 166f.) describes vv. 1–4 as *Kunstprosa* and notes devices of repetition and parallelism which create affinities with poetry and have led scholars (Condamin; W. L. Holladay, *JBL* 85, 1966, p. 414–417) to urge that the passage is metrical. Weippert's appraisal of 16.1–4 is related to her argument that the juxtaposition of חרב, רעב and דָּבָר is a feature of Jeremiah's prose style and to her general concern to differentiate between Jeremianic prose and Deuteronomic/Deuteronomistic prose. Her particular interest in 16.1–4 is to explain why the 'triad' has been dismembered in this passage. Her answer is that the

---

[1] Reading לחם, אָבֵל and אותו (see below, pp. 365f.).

conventions of *Kunstprosa* have brought this about: ממותי
תחלאים (v. 4) has been substituted for דבר and the references to
חרב and רעב appear unnaturally late in that verse. The
conventions of style take precedence over the normal unfolding
of sense, since the mention of חרב and רעב would otherwise
precede the references to death, mourning and lack of burial.
Weippert assigns the prose of vv. 1–4 entirely to Jeremiah (cf.
Bright) and reinforces her arguments by a consideration of the
closing part of v. 4 (והיתה ... הארץ) which she describes as
belonging to the immediate context of the 'triad' (pp. 183–186;
cf. 185, where the relevant word-strings in the book of Jeremiah
and elsewhere in the Old Testament are set out in a table: Jer
7.33; 15.3; 16.4; 19.7; 34.20; Deut 28.26; Ps 79.2; 1 Sam
17.44,46; 1 Kgs 14.11; 16.4; 21.24; Ezek 29.5; 39.4). She
develops a detailed argument in connection with Deut 28.20–27
(pp. 151–153; cf. the table on p. 188). Her case is that Deut
28.20–25a is a paraphrase of the 'triad' (vv. 21, 22a = דבר;
vv. 22b–24 = רעב; v. 25a = חרב) and that vv. 25b–26 have been
added by someone who detected this paraphrase and
supplemented it with a motif belonging to the immediate context
of the 'triad' (והיתה ... מחריד). She argues that היתה נבלתם
הארץ ... or the like which occurs five times in Jeremiah (7.33;
15.3; 16.4; 19.7; 39.20) and only once in Deuteronomy (28.26)
has more right to be regarded as Jeremianic prose than as
Deuteronomic prose, and similarly with ונתתים לזועה or the like
which occurs four times in Jeremiah (15.4; 24.9; 29.18; 34.17)
and only once in Deuteronomy (28.25).

From another point of view the book of Jeremiah might be
regarded as a quarry for prose having similarities in vocabulary
and style with Deuteronomic/Deuteronomistic prose—as an
archive which enlarges our sample of this type of prose. The
counting of occurrences as between word-strings in the book of
Jeremiah, on the one hand, and Deuteronomic/Deuteronomistic
literature, on the other, would then become pointless. The fact
that there are five occurrences of the word-string in question in
the book of Jeremiah and only one in the Deuteronomistic
literature could be seen as a random factor. Weippert's appeal to
1 Kgs 16.4 and 21.24 (pre-Deuteronomic—so Noth) does not
deter her from claiming the word-string as a feature of
Jeremiah's prose. But if so, it could equally well have become a
Deuteronomic/Deuteronomistic stereotype. In any case, if we
are not confident about the use of the 'triad' as a norm of
Jeremianic prose, all the arguments which derive from it are
unsatisfactory.

The question has been raised whether or not Jeremiah's
celibacy, his abstention from mourning rites and from joyful

celebrations, is represented in vv. 1–9 as a kind of symbolic action. This was the view of G. Fohrer (*ATANT* 25, 1953, pp. 64f.) and it is found in Rudolph, Weiser, Berridge (op. cit., pp. 125–127) and Thiel (pp. 196, 201). Weiser compares the passage with Hosea's experience of marriage and with Isaiah 7 and 8 (the names of the prophet's children) and supposes that celibacy *qua* symbolic action is to be located in the early years of Jeremiah's ministry, since it was the custom in the ancient orient to marry at an early age. Rudolph, on the other hand, doubts whether celibacy was regarded by the historical Jeremiah as symbolic action, although he agrees that this is how it is developed in vv. 3–4 and cites the case of Hosea, Isa 8.18 and Ezek 24.15ff. Weiser sees Jeremiah's celibacy, his absence from social occasions, whether funerals or marriages, as forms of prophetic proclamation and rejects explanations founded on interior attitudes of the prophet in relation to the background of his times and vocation, whether (*a*) That the onerousness of the prophetic vocation was incompatible with a proper concern for wife and family, or (*b*) That the hopelessness of the times inhibited joy in wife and family. What Rudolph says is that, constrained by his prophetic vision and the burden which his calling laid on him, Jeremiah found it impossible to contemplate marriage and this inner obstacle was interpreted by him as a divine interdict. Whether or not this is the right approach depends on the validity of Rudolph's distinction between a Jeremianic core in vv. 1–9 (from which he derives his interior analysis) and a Deuteronomistic elaboration (which makes the prophet's stance into a symbolic action). The interpretation of this passage will come out differently depending on whether it is judged to be entirely Jeremianic (Weiser, Bright, Weippert), or partly Jeremianic and partly Deuteronomistic (Rudolph, Thiel, Nicholson) or entirely divorced from the historical prophet Jeremiah (a possibility still to be considered).

ממותי תחלאים (v. 4) is represented by Sept. as ἐν θανάτῳ νοσερῷ, 'death by epidemic' (cf. Pesh. *mwt' dmṭrpy kpn'* and Targ. ממתי ממרעי כפן, 'the death(s) of those struck down by famine'). These are unnatural terminations of lives, whether by sword, famine or pestilence, involving suffering on a great scale and in a setting of national catastrophe as at 8.2 and 9.21. והיתה נבלתם (v. 4) is not represented by Sept., and the order of the remaining part of MT is not preserved. Rudolph supposes that the Greek translator has attempted to ameliorate the 'illogical and pleonastic' style which is characteristic of Source C.

The sense of בית מרזח (v. 5) is uncertain and the only other occurrence is at Amos 6.7 (מרזח סרוחים, 'sprawling and revelry', according to NEB; cf. BDB, 'revelry of sprawlers'). Rudolph

notices that מרזח has the sense 'funeral rites' in post-biblical
Hebrew and Aramaic and suggests this sense here. The reference
is to a social occasion associated with bereavement—a meal in
which the mourners take part (cf. Sept. εἰς θίασον αὐτῶν, 'to
their feasting'; Vulg. *domum convivii*, 'house of banqueting').
Pesh., on the other hand, renders בית מרזח as *byt mrqwdt'*
'house of mourning'. Vulg. makes no distinction between בית
מרזח (v. 5) and בית משתה (v. 8) which it also renders as *domum
convivii* and this accords with Rashi's glossing of מרזח with
משתה (also Aq. and Symm. render בית מרזח as εἰς οἰκον
εστιασεως and εἰς οικον εταιριας respectively). Kimchi explains
מרזח as 'the sorrow of mourning'. Rudolph's view that a
distinction has to be drawn between מרזח and משתה is correct.
This is indicated by distinct renderings for בית משתה in Sept.
(εἰς οἰκίαν πότου), Pesh. (*byt mšty*) and Targ. (בית אסחרותא,
'banqueting-house'). The social occasion of v. 5 is associated
with a time of sadness and that of v. 8 with a time of joy. The
usage of מרזח in Amos 6.7, however, shows that it is a
ceremonial meal whether associated with joy or with sorrow (cf.
KB[3] and especially Ugaritic *mrzḥ* 'banquet', banqueting-hall').
Duhm supposes that the point of the use of מרזח at Jer. 16.5 is
that a noisy and drunken funeral meal is indicated and that the
use is therefore not different from that of Amos 6.7.

In vv. 5–6 Sept. does not represent נאם ... יקברו, and Janzen
(p. 98) notes that this has been explained as an abridgement of
MT (Giesebrecht, Volz, Rudolph), and as a shorter text more
original than MT (Duhm, Cornill). Janzen suggests that את
החסד ואת הרחמים may be a gloss on שלומי and supposes (p. 45)
that MT has added לא יקברו (v. 6) before ולא יספדו. He urges,
however, that otherwise v. 6a (MT) is indispensable to what
follows and assumes that the shorter Greek text may be the
consequence of an accidental omission from the Hebrew *Vorlage*
of Sept.

In v. 7 Sept. has read לחם (ἄρτος) instead of MT להם and this
has been generally followed by modern commentators
(Giesebrecht, Duhm, Ehrlich, p. 284, Rudolph, Weiser, Bright,
NEB—Brockington, p. 205). Only Vulg. (*Et non frangent inter
eos lugenti panem*) supports the pointing of אבל as אָבֵל, but this
too has been adopted by the commentators mentioned above.
Kimchi remarks that his father preferred אָבֵל to אֵבֶל and that
the sense 'breaking bread for the mourner' provides a better link
with לנחמו על מת (cf. Ehrlich, p. 208, who prefers 'divide' to
'break' for פרם).

There are elements of grammatical incongruence in vv. 6–7
which Rudolph has explained on the assumption that 'one' can
be expressed in Hebrew by the third person singular or the third

person plural. The unevenness which is present has been handled by the versions in different ways. Pesh. achieves congruence in vv. 6–7 by representing plurals throughout and similarly with Targ. The only difference between Pesh. and Targ. is that the latter retains the singular suffixes of MT at the end of v. 7, but indicates a distributive usage by means of גבר, whereas Pesh. has plural suffixes. Kimchi notes גבר of Targ. and accepts its view of the matter which can also be applied to לנחמו על מת. This, however, does not explain why the distributive usage has not been maintained throughout the verse—why אותם occurs instead of אותו.

The fact that פרס is construed with ל (cf. Isa 58.7, פרס לרעב; Lam 4.4, פרש אין להם; לחמך) and the appearance of להם (twice) in v. 6 may have contributed to the corruption of יפרסו להם (Sept., a few Hebrew manuscripts) into יפרסו להם. It is clear that the versions read על and understood it in the sense 'concerning' or 'on behalf of', but instead of emending על to אל (Giesebrecht) we may appeal to the measure of interchangeability between על and אל. Either על = 'in respect of' (cf. ל in Isa 58.7 and Lam 4.4) or על = אל gives the necessary sense (cf. NEB, 'No one shall give the mourner a portion of bread'). It is possible to make sense of MT ('No one is to give them a piece of bread in connection with mourning (rites)', but the repointed text (אֵבֶל) coheres better with לנחמו על מת, and אותם should be emended to אותו (agreeing with Brockington, p. 205).

The awareness that vv. 1–9 may be an elaboration of the reference to Jeremiah's loneliness (15.17—Rudolph), and Weiser's observation that the passage is related to the 'confessions of Jeremiah' in chapters 14 and 15 are insights which should be pursued. The first one offers a way of viewing the prose of the book of Jeremiah as a kind of commentary which has its point of departure in a theme which was touched on more briefly in a piece of pre-existing poetry (see above, pp. 68–69, 283–284). The second one raises the question whether the theological framework which has been detected in the communal laments and the answering oracles (14.1–16; 14.17–15.4) may not help with the interpretation of 16.1–9. Here again the thought is that Jeremiah has no mediatorial function to discharge as a שלום prophet and it is in this connection that the theme of his loneliness is developed. Yahweh has removed his שלום from the Judaean communuty (v. 5) and in these circumstances Jeremiah cannot both be faithful to Yahweh and effectively express his solidarity with his people as an effective intercessor.

Hence it is doubtful whether the right way of approaching

16.1–9 is to distinguish between a Jeremianic core and a Deuteronomistic elaboration of that core (Rudolph, Thiel, Nicholson), or to suppose that these verses are entirely Jeremianic (Weiser, Weippert) and give us direct access to a stance of the historical prophet Jeremiah. They give expression to a communal concern, but it is not clear that they represent symbolic action in any precise sense. It is arguable that there is no original, private psychological constituent in this passage and no autobiographical core, and that in this account of Jeremiah's loneliness we have an exilic interpretation which establishes a parallel between the style of the prophet's life and the fate of the community from which Yahweh has withdrawn his שלום. The prophet may not marry because he knows that those who are born will soon die; he cannot mourn the dead or comfort the bereaved; he cannot take part in a memorial meal for the departed, nor bring the comfort of fellowship and solidarity in sorrow to those who are left. All this he cannot do because he has a foreknowledge of a disaster so massive that the socially valuable customs of mourning lose their meaning. When corpses are left for wild beasts and birds of prey or when they return to the soil as a kind of manure, a measured and civilized response to the experience of loss and death will have disappeared.

It has been noticed that the mourning rites which are mentioned in v. 6 (cutting oneself and shaving the head) are proscribed in Lev 19.28, 21.5 and Deut 14.1. One can only say that they are referred to here as normal rites and that there is no hint of disapproval. The mention of food and drink in v. 7 is explained either on the assumption that the house containing a corpse was unclean and food and drink had to be brought by the mourners to sustain those who were bereaved (Rudolph and Weiser), or in connection with the food and drink which was offered to the mourner when he broke his fast (Weiser and Nicholson; cf. 2 Sam 12.16ff.). Both Blayney and Duhm connect the verse with mourning customs. According to Blayney (who cites Jerome) the friends of the mourner brought along food and drink to sustain him.

Just as vv. 4–7 have a special reference to funerals, there can be little doubt that vv. 8–9 are particularly connected with marriages, and this is a widening or generalizing of the theme with which the chapter opens. Jeremiah, knowing that the nation is close to death, may not himself marry, and no more may he participate in marriage celebrations. When the sounds of wedding festivities are no longer heard, death is overtaking life, for a community with a future is one in which new homes are always being made and children continue to be born (cf 7.34). Jeremiah cannot exercise his vocation as a giver of שלום, when he is no longer able to weep with those who weep and to rejoice with those who rejoice. In the light of impending dissolution, the mediatorial office of a prophet has assumed an appearance of unreality and pointlessness. Hence he is frozen into loneliness and isolation. This is an exilic view of Jeremiah: Yahweh has forbidden him to mediate—has withdrawn his שלום.

A final note may be appended to this account of vv. 1–9. Duhm held that vv. 5–7 might be a Jeremianic nucleus and noted that the attitude taken to the funeral rites mentioned in v. 6 (cutting oneself and shaving the head) agrees with that of Amos (8.10) and Mic (1.16). It could be argued that the disagreement between v. 6 and Deut 14.1 (Lev 19.28; 21.5) is an indication that Jeremiah's attitude to these rites rather than an exilic attitude is represented in v. 6. This is a factor which should be weighed, but it is not necessarily an indication that the verse does not have an exilic provenance.

Another consideration is the transition from כלה (16.4) to גולה (16.13)—from obliteration to exile. It might be urged that the representation of כלה in 16.4 (as opposed to גולה in 16.13) is an indication that we have access to a pre-exilic situation and to a threat in the form in which the historical Jeremiah uttered it (see above on 4.27, p. 109; 5.10, p. 120; 5.18, p. 126.). Thus some substance can be given to arguments for a Jeremianic core in vv. 1–9, but the considerations which have just been raised do not necessitate a revision of the view of vv. 1–9 as exilic elucidation which has been presented. The weight of the second point (the transition from כלה to גולה) should not be exaggerated. The issues which are addressed in vv. 1–9 and 10–13 are different, and this circumstance affects the modes of representation which are adopted. The object of vv. 1–9 is to represent the magnitude of the disaster which overtook Judah and to ask how this can be reconciled with the circumstance that Jeremiah was a true prophet. The point of departure of vv. 10–13 is the fact of exile and the concern is to explain how it comes about that the Jews have been ejected (והשלתי אתכם) from their own country.

QUESTION AND ANSWER: EXPLANATION AND THREAT (16.10–13)

[10]When you inform this people of all these matters, they will say to you: Why does Yahweh threaten us with such a great disaster as this? What sins and transgressions have we committed against Yahweh, our God? [11]You are to answer them: It is because your forefathers forsook me, says Yahweh, and went after alien gods and served them and did obeisance to them; they forsook me and did not keep my law. [12]And you, for your part, have exceeded

your forefathers' wickedness; even now each of you follows his own wilful and
evil inclinations and disobeys me. [13]I will cast you out of this land into a land
unknown to you and to your forefathers. There you will serve alien gods day
and night and I will not extend mercy to you.

Both Rudolph and Weiser suppose that there is a significant
continuity between vv. 1–9 and vv. 10–13. The latter passage
anticipates that the prophet may be asked by the people to
supply reasons why a destructive judgement is to fall on them.
Duhm, on the other hand, is convinced that the manner of
connecting vv. 10ff. with what precedes (the postulating of a
question and the supplying of an answer) is a transparently
artificial literary device, and Thiel (pp. 198, 201) considers that
vv. 10–13 are a composition of D which adopt the same
question-answer scheme as found at 5.19 and 9.11–15, whose
function is to supply reasons for the judgement which is to be
consummated. The circumstance that לעיניכם ובימיכם are
absent from 7.34, which has verbal similarities with v. 9, is not a
decisive consideration, but it does at least raise the suspicion that
these words may be secondary in v. 9. The switch from an
address to the prophet to one to the community comes out of the
blue and is hard to tolerate. Thiel (p. 197) has explained לעיניכם
ובימיכם as an insertion by D whose function was to establish a
link between vv. 1–9 and vv. 10ff. It is probable that לעיניכם
ובימיכם is not original in v. 9 which is not an address to the
community, but an explanation to Jeremiah of why he should not
become involved in marriage festivities (see above, pp. 367f.).
    Even if this is the right conclusion and there is no original
connection between vv. 1–9 and 10–13, an attempt has been
made to create such a link, and in order to represent this final
intention of MT לעיניכם ובימיכם has been retained. Whether
these words were inserted in order to provide a better connection
after vv. 10–13 were tagged on, or were associated with an
independent and prior development which transformed v. 9 into
an address to the community and supplied a reason for attaching
vv. 10–13, or were devised as a connecting link in association
with an overall editorial management of chapter 16 (Thiel) are
matters for speculation.
    The question and answer scheme in vv. 10–13, which for Thiel
is a mark of his exilic editor, is supposed by Weiser to be a
pre-exilic cultic feature, associated with the 'covenant tradition'
and located in the 'covenant cult'. But the circumstance that a
similar use of question and answer is found in the poetry of
Jeremiah (13.22) does not show that vv. 10–13 are pre-exilic and
Jeremianic, any more than a similar use in Deut 29.23–27 and
1 Kgs 9.8–9 shows that vv. 10–13 are Deuteronomic/

Deuteronomistic. An argument may be developed that the question-answer procedure can be identified as a technique of the Deuteronomistic editor of the book of Jeremiah (Thiel), but, in general, we are confronting a feature of style which does not conduct us to particular, historical conclusions. Apart from this there is a flaw in Weiser's logic, for there is no necessity that what is written in any period must correspond with or reflect the religious conditions and usages of the time when it is written. It may be, for example, the intention of an exilic writer to represent a pre-exilic situation, and he may be more or less successful in doing this.

Sept. is interesting principally because of the indications in it of a Hebrew text shorter than MT. ἡμερας και νυκτος (v. 13) is Hexaplaric supplementation and is a secondary harmonizing of Sept. with MT, and Janzen (p. 40) supposes the הגדולה (v. 10), is an intrusion into the Hebrew text from 32.42. Of more interest is the shorter text indicated by 106 and 410 in v. 10 and by Sept.^A, 106 and other miniscules in v. 11 (see Ziegler). It is doubtful whether Ziegler's elucidation of this is the correct one. It is hard to believe that the scribe of 106 was so accident-prone that he made mistakes of the same kind in two successive verses, or that there are three examples of errors caused by *homoioteleuton* within the compass of two verses, two by 106 and one by 410. It should be asked whether 106 and 410 do not mark some of the stages by which a Hebrew text which began as על מה דבר יהוה עלינו את כל הרעה הזאת was supplemented by ומה עוננו (106) and then by ומה חטאתנו (410), until v. 10 finally reached the form of our extant MT with the further addition of אשר חטאנו ליהוה אלהינו. Further, the lack of any representation of וישתחוו להם (v. 11) in Sept.^A, 106 and other Greek manuscripts may be an indication of a stage of the Hebrew text earlier than MT (και εδούλευσαν αυτοῖς και εμε εγκατέλιπον = ויעבדום ואתי עזבו).

Another matter of some interest is the way in which the versions render the awkward Hebrew at the end of v. 13 (אשר לא אתן לכם חנינה). In the first place this should perhaps be seen as an attempt to resolve a grammatical difficulty: if אשר is a relative pronoun what is its antecedent? According to Sept. and Vulg. its antecedent is אלהים אחרים, but this can only be maintained with a 3rd person plural in place of a 1st person singular verb (Sept. δώσουσιν; Vulg. *dabunt*). Pesh. simplifies the Hebrew by substituting 'and' for אשר (*wl' 'tlkwn lrḥm'*). חנינה should perhaps be associated with תחנה and תחנונים 'prayer for mercy' rather than with חן, and אשר לא יתנו לכם חנינה (Sept. and Vulg.) could mean '(alien gods) who will not answer your prayers' (cf. 2.27ff.). Sept. with ἔλεος for חנינה has inclined to the nuance 'will show you no mercy', while Vulg. with *requiem* indicates 'will grant you no respite' (nearer to חן 'favour'). Pesh. (*rḥm'*) and Targ. (רחמין) render חנינה as 'mercy', and Kimchi who glosses חנינה with רחמים comments, 'The enemies (= Targ.) will not show mercy to you, but will deal oppressively with you'. Thus MT can be taken as either 'I will show no mercy to you' (I will reject your supplications) or 'for I will show you no favour' (NEB — אשר = 'for').

The topics which are not present in 5.19 but which feature in 16.11–13 are the apostasy of earlier generations of Israelites and the utter strangeness of the land of exile. With regard to the first of these it is striking that all the detail of the description of apostasy occurs in connection with it. The fathers forsook Yahweh, went after אלהים אחרים, served and worshipped them, forsook Yahweh (repeated) and did not keep his תורה ; the present generation has committed greater evils than those of the fathers. These are defined in a general way as a total disregard for Yahweh's will and as unbridled wilfulness and rebellion. The thought of a history of apostasy which reaches its climax in the prophet's generation, on which judgement will fall, is found in the poetry of Jeremiah (cf. 2.7ff.) and may be derived from it. The other theme (16.13) is the terror of the unknown and this also appears elsewhere in the book of Jeremiah, although with reference to strange people rather than the strangeness of the land of exile (5.15–17; 9.15). 16.13 develops the thought of the terror of the unknown with reference to a strange land of exile. The terrible novelty of the experience, for which the nation is totally unprepared by its earlier history, is indicated by the reference to the fathers. There is a significant difference between the thought of an unknown land of exile evoking terror, and the terror evoked by peoples so far removed from acquaintance that they take on the aspect of sub-human creatures. Another passage (Deut 28.64) has a view of dispersal closer to 9.15 than to 16.13 (והפיצך יהוה בכל עמים מקצה הארץ ועד קצה הארץ), but the idea of 'novelty' is applied here to the idolatry which will be enforced on Israel. There is a significant agreement between Deut 28.64 and Jer 16.13 only in respect of the idea that Israel will be coerced into idolatry. Janzen (p. 40) supposes that לילה ויומם (Deut 28.66) is the source of יומם ולילה — a secondary element in 16.13 (see above, p. 370). It could be supposed that the resemblance between Jer 16.13 and Deut 28.64 was noted and that this encouraged the appropriation of לילה ויומם. The cogency of this, in any case dubious, is destroyed by lack of verbal identity between יומם ולילה and לילה ויומם.

The setting of vv. 10–13 is not earlier than the exilic period: the exile has taken place and the author's task is to explain why it eventuated. The circumstance that themes (inveterate apostasy; the terror of the unknown) may be connected with the poetry of the pre-exilic prophet Jeremiah need not be construed as an indication of the pre-exilic and Jeremianic character of this prose. It may be regarded as a further illustration of the thesis that the poetry is one of the sources of the prose in the book of Jeremiah. These Jeremianic features of vv. 10–13, which have been discussed above, are wrongly elucidated when they are thought to point to the pre-exilic prophet Jeremiah as the source of the prose (Weiser, Bright, Weippert). That there are Deuteronomistic features in the prose of vv. 10–13 is maintained by Thiel (pp. 198f.), largely in connection with his identification of the lexicographical habits of D, and so by grouping passages of prose within the book of Jeremiah, but also with reference to the book of Deuteronomy.

Weippert (pp. 215–217) describes the string וילכו אחרי אלהים אחרים (16.11) as Deuteronomic, but assumes that the historical Jeremiah appropriated the vocabulary from this milieu. The circumstance that אחרי שררות לב + הלך is found only in the prose of the book of Jeremiah (3.17; 9.13; 16.12) leads her to conclude that it is a coinage of the prophet Jeremiah (p. 218, n. 506). It is obvious that Thiel and Weippert are at cross-purposes in this kind of situation: Thiel forms a group of prose passages within the book of Jeremiah and identifies them as the work of D, whereas the circumstance that these word-strings are found only in the book of Jeremiah persuades Weippert that they are to be assigned to the prophet Jeremiah. The view that the prose of vv. 10–13 has Deuteronomic/Deuteronomistic affinities, but is influenced by the vocabulary of Jeremianic poetry and is tailored to the function which it discharges within a distinctive *corpus*—the *corpus* constituted by the book of Jeremiah—can accommodate all the other matters raised by Weippert. Her comparison of הלך + אחרי in the poetry of Hosea and Jeremiah with אחרי + הלך in prose such as 16.10–13 is not a comparison of like with like. Even if Jeremiah inherited אחרי + הלך from Hosea and used it in his poetry to express the same nuance of harlotry/idolatry, this does not demonstrate that prose in the book of Jeremiah in which these items of vocabulary are embedded and which in its totality is a different literary kind from prophetic poetry, was composed by the prophet Jeremiah.

A NEW EXODUS AND A RETURN OF THE DISPERSED OF ISRAEL
(16.14–15)

[14]Therefore the time is coming, says Yahweh, when men will no longer say, As Yahweh lives who brought the Israelites out of Egypt. [15]Instead they will say, As Yahweh lives who brought the Israelites out of a northern land (and out of all the lands where he had dispersed them),[1] and I will restore them to their own land, the land which I gave to their forefathers.

There is general agreement that these verses (14–15) fit better into the context of 23.1–8, where they also appear (Giesebrecht, Duhm, Rudolph, Weiser, Bright, Nicholson, Thiel, p. 201). Some reservations, however, are expressed about the supposed inappropriateness of 16.14–15 in the context of 16.10–18 and about the appropriateness of 23.7–8 in the context of 23.1–8. Weiser attempts to explain the nature of the continuity between 16.14–15 and what precedes by means of a double exegesis of לכן : it points to the severity of the exilic experiences through which Israel must pass as well as the momentous character of the reintegration which will be effected by Yahweh. But if לכן were to be meaningful in relation to vv. 10–13, it would have to be followed by further threats and there is no way of wriggling out of this. It already exercised Rashi who commented, 'Although you dealt treacherously with me, I am under oath to redeem you'. This has some similarities with Weiser's exegesis in so far as it seeks to preserve an element of threat in לכן.

Rudolph supposes that the insertion of vv. 14–15 is connected with the dilution of the aspect of threat which was demanded in view of the use of the passage in the synagogue, and that the presence of לכן reflects a later eschatological dogma—the greater present woes, the nearer the time of final salvation. This has the merit that it attempts to explain why vv. 14–15 have been inserted after vv. 10–13, but a more limited and less speculative statement is perhaps all that can be achieved. It would seem that vv. 16–18 have a kind of continuity with vv. 10–13, since they resume the note of threat, and that we may posit an earlier form of the text from which vv. 14–15 was absent. This is the view of Thiel (pp. 199, 201) who urges that vv. 14–15 disturb the connection between vv. 10–13 and vv. 16–18, both of which he regards as compositions of D. Verses 14–15 neutralize the intimation of judgement by opening up a perspective of return beyond the threat of exile. Along with vv. 19–21 they represent the contribution of the final post-Deuteronomistic editor of chapter 16. In general Janzen does not disagree with this view of vv. 14–15 (pp. 92f.), and yet he develops arguments which are designed to throw doubt on

[1] See below, p. 376.

23.1–8 as a good context for 23.7–8, and like Weiser he endeavours to overcome the inconsequentiality of לכן.

The form of 16.14–15 presupposes the exile (Nicholson): one must locate it either in the exilic period or in the post-exilic period. Its point of departure is perhaps a partial return and restoration and the anticipation of a complete gathering in of Jews from all the lands in which they are exiled. צפון (v. 15) and צפונה occur in the poetry of the book of Jeremiah in references to the direction from which Judah is threatened by an enemy (1.13; 6.1,22) and צפונה is used in prose (3.12) as an indication of the direction of exile. It is likely that the use of צפון in prose derives from an established exegesis of צפון in poetry: if the enemy from the north is identified with Babylon, the place of exile can be described as ארץ צפון (16.15). We are reminded by vv. 14–15 of the insistence that 'former things' should no longer command attention or be a focus of hope (Isa 42.9; 43.18f.). It is true that a reference to the exodus from Egypt has to be read into these texts, so that a contrast between it and a new exodus is not entirely explicit. It is hard to resist the conclusion that this is what is intended by Isa 51.9–11, where vv. 9–10 allude to the victory of Yahweh over the Egyptian taskmaster (Rahab) and the dividing of the waters of the Red Sea. This is the background of a new and glorious return to Zion.

To what extent will a comparison of the texts of 16.14f. and 23.7f. help us to trace the history of the Hebrew text in this passage? There are some divergences which can be described as variants, and in assessing these we can take account of the evidence of the versions. These can be set out as follows:
(a) יאמרו/ואמר (b) בית/בני (c) הביא/העלה (d) ישבו/השבתים (g) צפונה/צפון (f) שם/שמה (e) הדחתים/הדיחם.
No comment is needed on (a), (e) and (f), but the others need further elucidation and may be taken in turn:

(b) It is unlikely where there is such a deliberate juxtaposing of two oaths that the differences of vocabulary between the one and the other are original. Hence בני (16.14) followed by בני (16.15) is better than בני followed by בית (Sept.). We may suppose, however, that there was a variant text in 16.14f. and 23.7f. which is preserved by Pesh., namely בית followed by בית, and in that case MT זרע (23.8) will be a gloss on an original בית. The indication given by Sept. is, however, that זרע is original at 23.8 and בית secondary. We have reached a point where further speculation is vain, but if the Syriac of 16.14f. and 23.7f. derives directly from a Hebrew text, it supports the hypothesis that בני and בית are textual variants.

(c) On general grounds a text with אשר העלה in both oaths (16.14f.) might be supposed more probable than one with העלה

in the first and הביא in the second (23.7f.). One might therefore conclude that ואשר הביא (23.8) is a secondary expansion of אשר העלה. Since Sept. renders העלה by ἀναγαγών (16.14) or ἀνήγαγε (16.15; 23.7), συνήγαγεν (23.8) points to הביא rather than העלה. A secondary equalization with MT is found in manuscripts of the Lucianic recension (ἀνήγαγεν καὶ εἰσήγαγεν, see Ziegler). Thus the Greek evidence indicates that the Hebrew text translated was אשר הביא and that the secondary element in MT of 23.8 is אשר העלה ו. This could be explained as a conflate reading constructed by incorporating אשר העלה from 16.15 and using ו as a link. Again, as with (b), there are conflicting considerations. Sept. points to an original אשר הביא in 23.8 and in that case the reading of MT is a conflate (see above). On the other hand, if אשר העלה is read at 23.8, this gives us uniform vocabulary throughout, and, moreover, ואשר הביא is readily explicable as secondary expansion in 23.8.

(d) We can discern in the versions an equalizing tendency which produced הדחתים (Vulg.) or הדיחם (Sept.) in both 16.15 and 23.8, but otherwise the versional evidence is not very helpful, and the most that can be done is to elucidate the exegetical implications of choosing one (הדיחם) or the other (הדחתים). This is bound up with a decision about the extent of the new oath in 16.14 and 23.8. Are the words of the oath, 'As the Lord lives who brought Israel up from a northern land', or does the oath run as far as שמה (or שם)? The shorter form affords a better parallel to the old oath, 'As the Lord lives who brought Israel up from the land of Egypt'. This difficulty is somewhat relieved if we suppose that the shorter Hebrew text indicated by the first hand of Sept.[s] (ומכל הארצות is not represented) at 23.8 is better than MT. The oath would then run, 'As the Lord lives who brought Israel up from a northern land, where he had dispersed them' (reading הדיחם). Whatever may be thought of this, the point should be made that הדיחם is a possible reading only if the words of the oath are assumed to extend to שמה (שם). This is improbable and so הדחתים should be regarded as a better reading than הדיחם. The assumption that the oath ran as far as שמה (שם) was what produced הדיחם at 16.15. What Yahweh is represented as saying at 16.15 and 23.8 (reading הדחתים) is that the terms of the new oath may be varied according to the nature of the deliverance which has been experienced: 'Egypt' may be replaced in the oath by another place of exile (ומכל הארצות אשר הדחתים שמה). A view which has only partial support from the first hand of Sept.[s], but which is plausible, is that ומכל הארצות אשר הדחתים שמה is secondary elaboration (an 'umbrella' device which indicates that the oath can be used comprehensively), that the oath ended at צפון (צפונה) and was followed by והשבתים or וישבו.

(g) Sept. indicates והשבתים at 16.15 (καὶ ἀποκαταστήσω αὐτούς) and וַיְשִׁיבֵם at 23.8 (καὶ ἀπεκατέστησεν). This modification at 23.8 is connected with the circumstance that Sept. represents הדיחם rather than MT הדחתים, and so, according to the Greek of 23.8, the oath runs to the end of the verse, 'As the Lord lives who brought all the seed of Israel from a northern land and from all the lands where he had dispersed them and restored them to their own land'. It is clear, however, that 16.14f. (23.7f.) has a future reference (ימים באים) and that the new oath is one which will be used in changed conditions when the promise of restoration has been realized. The dispersed of Israel will be brought home, and when they are resettled in their own land this is the oath which they will employ. The shorter text of 23.8 (represented by the miniscule 490 at 16.15, see Ziegler) is probably more original and אשר נתתי לאבותם (16.15) is secondary expansion. It is impossible to discriminate textually between והשבתים and וישבו, and to establish that one is better than the other.

A new oath will be used to replace the old one which referred to the deliverance from Egypt. This will follow from the transcending of the old act of Yahweh by a new exodus and the repossession of the promised land. The oath of the future reflecting this new foundation of Israel will be, 'As Yahweh lives who brought the Israelites from a northern land' (= Babylon). The only important exegetical addition to the text is

ומכל הארצות אשר הדחתים שמה

and its effect is to widen the concept of exile and return: not only the exiles in Babylon, but all the dispersed of Israel will be gathered and restored. The passage in its postulated earlier form implies that the exile to Babylon has taken place, and in its extant form is perhaps best explained as early post-exilic longing arising out of an experience of partial and mediocre restoration. The object of the foregoing discussion was to gain some insight into the history of the text, but not to emend MT. However, אשר העלה and אשר הביא at 23.8 are manifestly doublets which have been combined by the use of *waw*, and one or other should be deleted, perhaps אשר העלה which occurs at 16.15 (see above, pp. 374f.). Moreover זרע and בית (23.8) may be doublets (see above, p. 374), although it is possible to translate MT, 'who brought the descendants of Israel back from a northern land' (NEB).

HUNTED AND PUNISHED (16.16–18)

[16]I will send many fishermen, says Yahweh, and they shall catch them; afterwards I will send many hunters and they shall hunt them out from every mountain and hill, from the crevices in the rocks. [17]I see what they are doing; they are not hidden from me, and their wrong-doing is not concealed from my view. [18]I will first repay twofold their wrong-doing and sin, because they have defiled my country with the corpses of their disgusting idols and have filled my own land with their abominable images.

Rudolph (similarly Weiser) supposes that v. 18 is secondary and erroneous exegesis of v. 16. The two figures of v. 16 (fishing and hunting) have been interpreted as a double punishment (מִשְׁנֶה), and this is understood as an allusion to the experiences of invasion and deportation in 597 and 586. With this is associated Rudolph's view (shared by Thiel, p. 200) that vv. 16–17 are words of the prophet Jeremiah, and so he does not accept Cornill's judgement that vv. 16–18 in their entirety constitute prophecy after the event. מִשְׁנֶה apparently explains the reference to fishermen and hunters in a manner contrary to the original sense: what was intended was a concentration on the totality and inescapability of judgement, not an allusion to successive judgements (so Thiel; cf. Rudolph and Weiser).

Rudolph (Weiser, Thiel) and Cornill, explain מִשְׁנֶה (v. 18) in the same way: whether as a correct or an erroneous interpretation of the figures of v. 16, it indicates simply that Judah was punished on two separate occasions. It is not therefore comparable (so Rudolph) to the thought of a weight or quantity of sufferings which is double what is demanded by Israel's sins, and so is distinguishable from כִּפְלַיִם בְּכָל חַטֹּאתֶיהָ (Isa 40.2). Bright, on the other hand, supposes that the same idea is expressed by both passages, namely that of a double dose of punishment. Another interpretation of מִשְׁנֶה, which has interest in view of the emphasis on the sins of the fathers in vv. 10–13, and the representation of a history of apostasy elsewhere in the book of Jeremiah (for example, in chapter 2), is the one found in Rashi and Kimchi—'their own sin and the sins of their fathers'. This introduces the thought of an accumulated debt of retribution which has to be paid off by the generation on which Yahweh's judgement finally falls. Other uses of מִשְׁנֶה (Isa 61.7; Zech 9.12; Job 42.10) indicate that Jer 16.18 could express the same idea as כִּפְלַיִם בְּכָל חַטֹּאתֶיהָ (Isa 40.2).

The explanation of מִשְׁנֶה as 'equivalent payment' (cf. Ehrlich, pp. 218f., 285) was advanced by M. Tsevat (*HUCA* 29, 1958, pp. 125f.) on the foundation of a usage of *mištannu* in the Alalakh texts. Tsevat held that *mištannu*, given by the owner of a fugitive slave to the person who returned him, was to be elucidated as 'equivalence' and that משנה had this sense at Deut 15.18 and Jer 16.18. This has exerted an influence on NEB in both passages. *Mištannu* is explained as 'payment' by W. von Soden (*Akkadisches Handwörterbuch*, p. 661; cf. G. von Rad, *ZAW* 79, 1967, pp. 80–82; KB³, s.v. משנה). Von Rad's premiss is that משנה in Deut 15.18 and Jer 16.18 means 'equivalence' and this is the basis of his argument that 'equivalent retribution' rather than 'double retribution' is the sense of כפלים בכל חטאתיה (Isa 40.2).

It is clear that ראשונה (v. 18), which is not represented by Sept., is part of a later process of adjustment (post-Deuteronomist according to Thiel, pp. 200f.) which is represented also by vv. 14f. and vv. 19–21. In particular, ראשונה accommodates v. 18 to the promise of ultimate restoration in vv. 14f. (Rudolph, Bright, Nicholson). This accords with Jerome's (pre-critical) view of the function of ראשונה. He notes that it is not indicated by Sept. and comments on *primum* of Vulg., *post quam receperint mala, recepturi sint et bona*. The conclusion of the matter is that v. 18 (without ראשונה) is not correctly understood as a later and erroneous interpretation of v. 16 and that משנה is not a reference to the events of 597 and 586. Verses 16–18 (without ראשונה) are all of a piece and משנה means either 'double punishment for their wrongdoing' or 'punishment equivalent to their wrongdoing' (cf. Isa 40.2). It is possible that whoever was responsible for inserting ראשונה understood משנה differently and intended to say that only after the disastrous and painful experiences of 597 and 586 had been endured would the prospects of a future restoration open up for the Jews.

The fishing metaphor (v. 16) is used of Babylon in Hab 1.14ff. and it is no doubt the invasion of Judah by the Babylonians which is indicated by the language of v. 16 (cf. Targ., Rashi, Kimchi). Verse 16 has a figurative character, v. 17 is parenthetical (Yahweh misses nothing of his people's wrongdoing and his retribution will flow from a full cognizance of their guilt), and then v. 18 speaks more plainly of retribution and of the idolatry which is regarded as the principal manifestation of Israel's apostasy. The figurative character of v. 16 is noteworthy, but is not a sufficient ground for detaching vv. 16f. from the remainder of the prose in chapter 16 and attributing them to the pre-exilic prophet Jeremiah (*pace* Rudolph and Thiel). It is arguable that vv. 16–18 have an exilic (cf. Bright) rather than a post-exilic provenance and that they represent a mode of thought which is present in Isa 40.2: the sufferings of dispersion and exile are a double (or an exact) punishment for all Israel's sins against Yahweh.

There is evidence of expansion in v. 17, where לא נסתרו מלפני
is not represented by Sept. Janzen (p. 117) explains this as
haplography of לא (לא before נסתרו has been confused with לא
before נצפן). More interesting is the case of v. 16, where
Ziegler's view that the omission of καὶ μετὰ ταῦτα ἀποστέλω
τοὺς πολλοὺς θηρευτάς, καὶ θηρεύσουσιν αὐτούς by the miniscule
490 is due to haplography may not be correct (αὐτούς after
ἁλιεύσουσιν confused with αὐτούς after θηρεύσουσιν). This might
be rather evidence of a shorter Hebrew text: an indication that
originally only one figure was employed—that of fishing—and
that it was subsequently elaborated with a hunting figure. The
form ודיגום (v. 16) is explained (GK 73b) as a denominative Piel
of דג 'fish'. If it were Qal, one would expect וְדָגוּם (cf. וצדום).
The odd word-order of לרבים צידים (v. 16) is observed by Duhm
who makes two suggestions: either רבים is a gloss on צידים
('hunters' elucidated as 'archers') or לרבים צידים is a scribal
error for לצידים רבים.

According to MT, which has the *athnach* at ארצי, בנבלת
שקוציהם is to be connected with what follows, and the ב of נבלת
also governs תועבותיהם. The words following ארצי are then an
explication of 'defiling my country'. The renderings of Vulg.,
Pesh. and Targ. indicate the *athnach* at שקוציהם (so Rudolph,
Weiser, Bright, NEB) in which case בנבלת שקוציהם connects
with what precedes and ותועבותיהם with what follows. Still
another syntax is represented by Sept. which takes מלאו את ארצי
as a relative clause (without אשר): ἐν αἷς ἐπλημμέλησαν. On this
view both בנבלת שקוציהם and ותועבותיהם connect with על
חללם את ארצי. The interpretation of the verse is not greatly
affected by these changes of syntax, and no decisive advantage is
obtained by transferring the *athnach* from ארצי (MT) to
שקוציהם.

Ehrlich's view of נבלת (p. 285) is that it must be associated
with נְבָלָה and not נְבֵלָה. But נְבָלָה is used predominantly with
עשה and nearly always (the exception is Job 42.8) with
reference to sexual sins and perversions. Hence בנבלת שקוציהם
should be understood as 'their lifeless idols' rather than 'their
senseless idolatry'. The phrase is then similar to פגרי גלוליכם
(Lev 26.30) and the thought is that the idols are so many corpses
which defile the land and make it unclean (cf. Lev 5.2 and
11.1ff.). Not only are the idols insubstantial (cf. 16.19, הבל
ואין בם מועיל), but they also transmit defilement like cadavers.
To the thought of the vacuity of idols is added the other idea that
in virtue of their deadness they may be likened to corpses which
pollute the land.

THE NATIONS EMBRACE TRUE RELIGION (16.19–21)

> [19]O Yahweh, my strength and my stronghold,
> my refuge in the day of trouble;
> to you the nations will come,
> from the ends of the earth they will come and say,
> Our forefathers inherited false gods,
> empty idols which were useless.
> [20]Can men make a God for themselves?
> What they make are non-gods!
> [21]Therefore, now I will enlighten them,
> now I will show them my power and might,
> and so they will know that my name is Yahweh.

The difficulty of envisaging vv. 19–21 as a unit is constituted not
only by the change of speaker at v. 21, where a word of Yahweh
is introduced by לכן, but is already present within vv. 19–20 in
the form of a harsh transition between v. 19a and 19bc,20. It is
not evident why a reference to Yahweh as a stronghold and
refuge in time of distress, which would naturally be related to
personal experiences of the speaker (represented as the prophet
Jeremiah), should lead on to an affirmation (or petition?—see
below) that nations will come from the ends of the earth to
Yahweh and confess the futility of their idol worship (cf. Thiel,
p. 201).

This awkwardness was felt by Targ. and Kimchi (who follows
the lead of Targ.). Targ. renders ידי as פורענותי 'my retribution'
and גבורתי as מחת גבורתי 'my destructive power' (v. 21): 'I
shall disclose myself to them; on this occasion I shall show them
my retribution and destructive power.' On this interpretation
v. 21 is a threat uttered by Yahweh against those among the
nations (cf. Duhm) who do not submit to him and acknowledge
him as the true God. In connection with this view of v. 21
Kimchi endeavours to display vv. 19–21 as a unit: Verse 19a is
address rather than affirmation, 'O Lord you are my strength
and fortress' (agreeing with Sept. and Vulg. against Aq., Symm.
and Theod.). The thread runs from a sorrowful reflection by
Jeremiah that he has suffered in the course of his unsuccessful
attempts to wean his own people from idolatry to the prospect
that the nations will come to Yahweh, acknowledge him, and
confess the emptiness of their idols, in the Messianic Age.

Kimchi's ingenuity is taxed in his efforts to establish the unity
of vv. 19–21 and some modern scholars have argued differently.
Verse 21 is the conclusion of the threat of retribution uttered
against Judah in vv. 16–18 and has been separated from v. 18 by
the later insertion of vv. 19–20 (Duhm; cf. Ehrlich, p. 285). In
that case בפעם הזאת (v. 21) refers back to the twofold
retribution of v. 18. Yahweh has shown great forbearance in

tolerating his people's idolatry, but he will show mercy no longer and they will suffer under a demonstration of his massive retributive power (v. 18). They will then understand what neither offers of mercy nor warnings of punishment have impressed on them and 'know' the kind of God with whom they have to reckon (v. 21).

Both Rudolph and Weiser (despite their differences) are at one in disagreeing with this view of v. 21 and in their conviction that vv. 19–21 constitute a unit. They explain v. 21 as an answer to the prayer uttered in vv. 19–20: vv. 19–20 are invocation (see above, p. 380), followed by petition or confident affirmation (so NEB). According to Rudolph בפעם הזאת (v. 21) is an indication of a disappointed hope that Yahweh would be acknowledged by all nations. Hence he infers from 'on this occasion' (meaning 'at last', 'after many disappointments') a connection with the preaching of Deutero-Isaiah who had associated a polemic against idolatry and a demand that the nations should embrace the only true religion with his proclamation of Israel's homecoming. The verbal resemblances between Jer 16.19–21 and Isa 45.20ff., cited by Rudolph, are not particularly close, apart from כל אפסי ארץ (Isa 45.22) and מאפסי ארץ (Jer 16.19). The other important element in Rudolph's exegesis is his effort to explain the nature of the connection between v. 19a and vv. 19bc,20. The same act as achieves security and asylum for Israel will convert the world to true religion, and this is the thread which connects v. 19a with vv. 19bc–21. This assumes that the prophet speaks in a representative capacity in v. 19a whose vocabulary then refers to the safety and refuge which the nation Israel has found in the midst of tribulation. Weiser, here as elsewhere in his commentary, tends to force a 'covenant' framework of interpretation on the text, but apart from this his view of the passage is similar to that of Rudolph.

There is little doubt that שקר and הבל (v. 19) are surrogates for 'idols' (on the analogy of בעל = בשת): this view is supported by 10.14 (כי שקר נסכו, where שקר = פסל or the like) and 13.25 ('They have forgotten Yahweh and rely on השקר'). The way in which הבל is used in 2.5 shows that וילכו אחרי ההבל can be equated with וילכו אחרי אלהים אחרים or the like, and הבל meaning 'idols' is found at 10.3 and 15. The striking expression 'our forefathers inherited idols' is altered by Targ. to the more conventional 'our forefathers worshipped idols' (נחלו paraphrased as פלחו). According to Kimchi's exegesis the thought is that of idolatry as a way of life transmitted from time immemorial and regarded as the inalienable property of a society. It is this weight of tradition and badge of identity whose discarding has in a flash of illumination suddenly become possible and necessary.

The associations of the vocabulary of vv. 19–21 with the poetry of Jeremiah have already been indicated for שֶׁקֶר and הֶבֶל. The almost verbal identity of 16.20 with 2.11 should be noted, but, more particularly, the different context which is created for the sentence by the substitution of הֲיַעֲשֶׂה לּוֹ אָדָם for הֶחֵמִיר גּוֹי. In 2.11 it is the abysmal lack of a sense of values among Yahweh's own people who barter the true God for worthless idols. In 16.20 it is the stupidity of the Gentiles who suppose that men can construct a God and are not aware of the vacuity of idols. One should not be content with a statement that the passage 'swarms with Jeremianic expressions' (Bright; cf. Weiser). Such Jeremianic vocabulary as can be detected in vv. 19–21 has been transported to a new setting: שֶׁקֶר, הֶבֶל and אֱלֹהִים וְהֵמָּה לֹא אֱלֹהִים, are not being used of Israel's insensate idolatry but of the idolatrous Gentile world. Moreover, one has to cast the net wider than the poetry of Jeremiah in order to deal with the vocabulary of v. 19a (for the description of Yahweh as a fortress and refuge (in time of trouble) compare Pss 37.39; 46.2; 59.17; 61.4; Nah 1.7). What Weiser has missed is the metamorphosis which is associated with the Jeremianic vocabulary in vv. 19–21, and the right conclusion is probably that the verses are a late and inferior imitation of Jeremianic poetry. They presuppose a situation, perhaps post-exilic, when the Jews believed that they were no longer vulnerable to the charge of idolatry once levelled against them by the pre-exilic prophet Jeremiah, and when the vocabulary with which he had once constructed his indictment could be redeployed against the Gentiles.

The patchwork or atomistic character of these verses is the fact on which attention should be finally focused. In this connection Thiel's view (pp. 200f.) that vv. 14–15, רִאשׁוֹנָה in v. 18 and vv. 19–21 are all elements of a post-Deuteronomistic modification of chapter 16, which sought to mitigate the aspect of threat and doom by opening up the prospect of future restoration, does not answer all the questions which are raised by vv. 19–21. Their untidiness may be the result of the aping of Jeremianic poetry by an inferior mind, but it may originate in quite different and undiscoverable circumstances. At any rate the attempts to establish the unity of vv. 19–21 are unconvincing. The natural interpretation of v. 19a is that it has a reference to the painful experiences of the prophet Jeremiah and the refuge which he found in Yahweh. The transition from this to affirmation or petition concerning the Gentiles and their conversion to Yahwism is harsh. On Rudolph's view vv. 19–21

are linked to vv. 14–15 which deal with the end of Israel's exile
and the return to the homeland. One has then to posit that they
once followed vv. 14–15 and were separated from v. 15 by the
subsequent insertion of vv. 16–18, or else that they were added
subsequent to the secondary insertion of ראשונה in v. 18.

It is not, however, simply a case of having to account for the
present place of vv. 19–20 (Rudolph), but rather of not being
able to show that they have an internal coherence. In these
circumstances it is perhaps best to salvage v. 21 by assuming that
it is the conclusion of the threat developed in vv. 16–18 (Duhm,
Ehrlich), and this would have some support from the
circumstance that בפעם הזאת has a threatening nuance at 10.18.
In that case the 'illumination' to which v. 21 refers (מודיעם ;
וידעו ; אודיעם) and the manifestation of Yahweh's power (ידי ;
גבורתי) will come to the Judaeans at the time when judgement
falls on them. Its association with vv. 19–20, however, may
betray an intention to make the verse an allusion to the
enlightenment of the Gentiles. All that we can say of vv. 19–20 is
that it is a barely intelligible fragment whose connection with the
preceding part of the chapter cannot be explained, except in so
far as 'idolatry' is a stitch: the idolatry of Judah in v. 18 and the
idolatry of the Gentiles in v. 20 (cf. Nicholson).

CHAPTER XVII

AN INDELIBLE RECORD OF JUDAH'S SIN (17.1–4)

¹Judah's sin is inscribed with an iron tool,
engraved with a diamond point on the tablet of the heart,
incised on the horns of their altars;¹ ²when their sons
recall their altars and sacred poles beside leafy trees
and on high hills—on solitary(?) mountains.²
³Your wealth (and) all your treasures I will give for spoil,
as the price of your sins³
in every part of your land.
⁴You will let go your hold⁴ of the land I gave you,
and I will make you subject to your enemies
in a land which is strange to you;
for my anger has kindled⁵ a flame
(and) it will burn for ever.

15.13–14 (see above, p. 343) is to be regarded as a fragment of
17.1–4 which does not fit into the context of chapter 15 but
which has a contribution to make to the textual criticism of
17.1–4. The variants as noted by Kimchi are: והעברתי :
והעבדתיך ; קדחה : קדחתם ; עליכם : עד עולם. Modern scholars
also suppose that במתיך (17.3) is a corruption of מחיר (Duhm)
or במחיר (Rudolph, Weiser, Bright) or לא במחיר
(NEB = 15.13). לא is assumed to be a secondary insertion by
Duhm, Rudolph, Weiser and Bright. 17.1–4 is missing from the
principal manuscripts of Sept., and the view that this is caused
by a haplography of יהוה יהוה (יהוה at the end of 16.21 confused with
יהוה at the beginning of 17.5), proposed by Cornill, is followed
by Rudolph and Janzen (p. 117). The interaction between the
texts of 15.14 and 17.4 is discernible in Sept.^{OL}, in Aq., Symm.
and Theod., and also in Pesh.

Duhm takes over מחיר, בחטאותיך (15.13, ובכל חטאותיך), and
קדחה from 15.13–14, 'Your wealth and treasures I give up to
plunder as a payment for your sins in all your territories'.
Rudolph, Weiser and Bright take במחיר בכל חטאותיך and קדחה,
while NEB (Brockington, p. 205) takes בחטאותיך, לא במחיר and
קדחה. The deletion of אשר before לא ידעת (17.4; cf. 15.14) by
Rudolph (following Duhm) is of significance in relation to his
view that 17.1–4 are poetry. These verses are set out as prose by
NEB, and v. 2 (including הררי בשדה) is shown as prose by

¹Reading מזבחותיהם (see below, p. 385).
²Reading הָרֲרִי (see below, p. 385).
³Reading במחיר חטאותיך (see below, p. 386)
⁴Reading ידך (see below. pp. 386f.).
⁵Reading קדחה (see above).

Bright. Rudolph assumes that 17.2 (excluding כזכר בניהם which
he emends to לזכרון בהם and connects with what precedes) is a
late gloss which details 'further forbidden cult symbols in their
customary order'. He argues that 15.12 is a corrupt remnant of
17.1 and his intention is to develop a comparison of 15.12–14
and 17.1–4 which will show that 17.2 is a secondary gloss. On
another view, namely, that not only 17.2 but also 17.1 and the
first line of 17.4 are unrepresented in 15.12–14, Rudolph's
argument does not look so good.

בלבם, indicated by Pesh. for MT בניהם (v. 2), has perhaps
exegetical rather than textual significance. The transition from
יהודה (v. 1) to בניהם (v. 2) is harsh and by resuming לבם (v. 1)
with בלבם (v. 2) a better continuity is achieved. מזבחותיהם (MT
מזבחותיכם), which is represented by Pesh., Vulg. (*et in cornibus
ararum eorum*) and Sept.[L] (και εν τοις κερασιν των
θυσιαστηριων αυτων) should be adopted. Weiser's conversion of
all the suffixes into 2nd. person plurals takes no account of the
textual evidence. There is a single incongruence caused by
מזבחותיכם and he deals with this by changing לבם to לבכם,
אשריכם to אשריהם and מזבחותיכם to מזבחותם.

The sense of MT כזכר בניהם is elucidated by Rashi and
Kimchi (followed by Weiser) on the assumption that בניהם is
the object and not the subject (so Sept.[o], Theod., Vulg.) of כזכר.
The meaning is then (so Weiser) that they love their idolatry
with the same compulsive and uncontrollable affection that they
have for their children. This, however, is asking a great deal of
the Hebrew text and would need something like כזכר בניהם כן
יזכרו. The difficulty caused by הררי בשדה to the versions is
evident from the different periphrastic devices to which they
have resorted in order to deal with it. Pesh. has resolved the
problem by connecting הררי בשדה with v. 2: *wbṭwr' wbdbr'*, 'and
in the mountains and the open country' (cf. Vulg.). Rashi
explains הררי בשדה as a reference to Jerusalem, and so, as
Kimchi observes, it is vocative. Jerusalem is set on a mountain
with a מישור around it—a מישור שדה. With this should be
compared Lowth who equates הררי בשדה with the temple. The
form הֲרָרִי is explained on the analogy of עַרְבִי (Isa 13.20; Jer
3.2): עַרְבִי is one who dwells in the עֲרבה and הררי one who
dwells in the mountains. Duhm appeals to Theod. (ορεων), Pesh.
and Targ. in support of הֲרָרֵי and he explains הררי בשדה,
'mountains in the שׁדה' as 'isolated mountains', the sites where
the cult of Baal was practised. On this view הררי בשדה connects
with the references to Baal worship which precede it in v. 2 (cf.
Vulg. and Pesh.).

There is little doubt that what is indicated by חילך כל
חילך וכל אוצרותיך or אוצרותיך (Sept.[OL], Theod., Vulg., Pesh.,

Targ. and many Hebrew manuscripts) is 'your wealth and all your treasures', and that חילך is better rendered by Pesh. and Targ. ('your possessions') than it is by the Greek versions and Vulg. ('your strength'). Hence חילך is correctly glossed as ממונך by Rashi and Kimchi. Targ., 'Because of the sin of your worship of idols throughout all your territory', has paraphrased במתיך בחטאת במתיך בכל גבוליך as if the word-order were כל בחטאת במתיך בכל גבוליך. This is in line with Kimchi who argues that במתיך בחטאת is a reversal of normal word-order, and who supposes that Targ.'s paraphrase rests on the awareness of such a reversal. Targ., Rashi and Kimchi are all deriving more or less the same sense from these words. They are a reference to the sins of idolatry perpetrated at shrines throughout the land 'on every high hill and under every green tree'.

במתיך is explicable as a gloss on בכל גבוליך. It is a correct gloss, since בכל גבוליך must be an allusion to shrines scattered up and down the country which were centres of idolatrous worship. Verse 2 might then be accounted for as a more extensive gloss on this last part of v. 3 which, with the help of 15.13, should be reconstructed as במחיר כל חטאותיך בכל גבוליך. The corruption of במחיר into לא במחיר (15.13) arose from the desire to connect במחיר with the words that precede it (לבז אתן) and to represent that Judah's treasures would be looted and no price paid for them. This led to the insertion of a *beth pretii* before כל חטאותיך which is redundant if במחיר connects with כל חטאותיך or חטאותיך. The meaning is that Judah will be sacked as the price of the sins of idolatry which she has committed at shrines throughout her territory.

The textual problem in 17.4 is constituted by ובך, and the attractive emendation ידך (cf. Deut 15.3, תשמט ידך), which is adopted by Duhm, Rudolph, Weiser and Bright, is as old as J. D. Michaelis. The sense of the opening words of v. 4 is then, 'You will have to let go your hold on your own land which I gave you'. The 'alone' ($\mu o \nu \eta$) element of the renderings of Sept.[OL] and Aq. appears in Vulg. (*et relinqueris sola*). It may be that $\mu o \nu \eta$ and *sola* and especially $\mu o \nu \eta$ $\sigma \nu$ (Aq.) derive from לבדך (BHS), but the sense which is then achieved is unsatisfactory. There is nothing in Pesh. corresponding to ובך and ושמטתה מנחלתך is explained as w''brk mn yrtwt', 'And I will deport you from your own land'. The most interesting aspect of Targ.'s extended paraphrase of 17.4 is the connection which is established between ושמטתה and the Sabbatical year and this is further developed in Rashi: ובך is explained as ובך אנקם, 'And I will take vengeance on behalf of your inheritance which I gave to you, because you did not perform my will and let it lie fallow (in the Sabbatical years)' (similarly Kimchi). The influence of this exegesis can be seen in Lowth.

The meaning of 17.1–4, according to Rudolph (with מזבחותם בשדה . . . deleted), is that Judah's sin is deep-seated—written on the 'tablet' of the heart with a diamond point. It is also recorded on the horns of their altars, and Rudolph connects this reference with the critique of the cult of Yahweh elsewhere associated with the prophet Jeremiah (6.20; 7.4ff.,21ff.; 11.15; 14.12). The ritual which is indicated is the smearing of the horns of the altar with blood in connection with sacrifices which atone for sin. (The passages which are cited by Rudolph, Weiser and Nicholson are Lev 4.7,30,34; 8.15; 16.18; Exod. 29.12). The traces of the blood smeared on the horns of altars are a memorial against them (Rudolph—לזכרון בהם), because they testify to their belief that the blood of animals can atone for sin. 'Sin which you have committed throughout your land' (17.3) is an allusion to the revival of idolatrous worship in shrines throughout the land after a falling away from the reform of Josiah in the reign of Jehoiakim. Hence Rudolph's view is that the passage should be assigned to the prophet Jeremiah. Weiser similarly says that Jeremiah is criticizing a superficial interpretation of the cult of Yahweh with his allusion to blood smeared on the horns of altars: he is reinterpreting the ritual of the Day of Atonement (cf. Volz) by urging that the blood smeared on the altar is a symbol of the seriousness of sin rather than a facile mechanism for disposing of it.

It is unlikely that ולקרנות מזבחותיהם (v. 1) is a reference to altars in the context of Yahweh's cult. Nor is it likely that there is an allusion in v. 1 to pricks of conscience (Duhm). It is probable that the indelible, interior record of Judah's sin, on which the passage turns, relates to idolatry, just as the other figures which depict the ineradicability and compulsiveness of Judah's sinful tendencies relate to her idolatry (2.22; 13.23). That v. 1 through its imagery indicates the permanency of the record which indicts Judah is indicated by Rashi, and Kimchi comments, 'What a man writes with an iron tool and inscribes on a stone is a record which lasts for ever'. On Job 19.24, which Kimchi invokes, the comment is, 'He mentions עפרת because the chiselled letters are filled with lead, so that the edges of what is incised may not break and the shape of the writing be lost.'

The monumental record of Judah's idolatry chiselled on the 'tablet' of her heart is a figure of a corruption which is deep-seated and ineffaceable (cf. 2.22; 13.23). The view that v. 1 (as far as לבם) refers to a fatal, inner predisposition to idolatrous behaviour can be related to the sins which Judah has committed בכל גבוליך (v. 3). There is no doubt that this is a reference to idolatrous worship 'beside every leafy tree and on every high hill', and the possibility should be considered that everything from ולקרנות (v. 1) to בשדה (v. 3) originates as exegesis of במחיר חטאותיך בכל גבוליך and is not part of a more original form of the passage.

Judah is compulsively attached to idolatry and for this she will be punished by the shock and terror of enemy invasion, by sacking and looting. The hot and unrelenting flame of Yahweh's anger burns against her and she will suffer deportation and enslavement (והעבדתיך) at the hands of her enemies. עד עולם conveys the sense of an awful finality. The passage is about Judah's infatuation with idols, not about a superficial appropriation of Yahweh's cult. Even if the explanation of ולקרנות מזבחותיהם offered by Rudolph and Weiser were thought to be correct, a criticism of a mechanistic view of the ritual of atonement does not cohere with the figure of chiselling Judah's sins on the 'tablet' of the heart, and the introduction of this thought would have to be regarded as a redirection of the earlier sense of the passage. In any case it is not obvious why מזבחותיכם (מזבחותיהם) should be thought to refer to the worship of Yahweh when מזבחותם (v. 2) is so unmistakably associated with Baal worship. What has been said about the more original form of the passage accords well with the view that it is to be assigned to the prophet Jeremiah, since we know that Judah's compulsive attachment to idolatry was one of his themes.

THE RESILIENCE OF THE MAN WHO TRUSTS IN YAHWEH (17.5–8)

[5]'Cursed[1] is the man who trusts in men,
who leans for support on material power,
whose mind is alienated from Yahweh.
[6]He is like one living destitute in a wilderness:
he is unaware when good comes,
he lives in parched places of the desert,
in an uninhabited salt waste.
[7]Blessed is the man who trusts in Yahweh,
who makes Yahweh his source of safety.
[8]He is like a tree planted beside waters,
stretching out its roots along a stream.
It has no fear[2] when heat comes,
its leaves remain green;
in a year of drought it has no anxiety
and does not cease to bear fruit.

Rudolph comments on the lack of continuity between 17.1–4 and

[1] Deleting כה אמר יהוה (see below, p. 389).
[2] Reading ירא (K).

5–11 and notes the suggestion of Cornill that v. 5ff. come after
the threat of exile because an editor supposed that they alluded
to the actions and fate of Zedekiah, an interpretation which was
perhaps influenced by the use of comparable imagery in a
passage which does refer to Zedekiah (Ezek. 17.5–10). The same
question had already exercised Rashi who ventured the opinion
that the theme of the Sabbatical year was the link between
vv. 1–4 and 5ff. and who commented on יבטח באדם (v. 5): 'In his
ploughing and reaping, saying, "I shall sow in the Sabbatical
year and I shall eat" '. But chapter 17 is an aggregate of pieces
which are not intrinsically connected (cf. Bright, p. 119,
Nicholson) and vv. 5–8 constitute an independent and
artistically well-rounded unit. The introductory formula (v. 5,
כה אמר יהוה), which is not represented by Sept., is inappropriate
in relation to vv. 5–8 which are not cast in the form of words of
Yahweh (Duhm, Rudolph, Weiser, Bright).

ערער or ערוער is a rare word in Biblical Hebrew and the
pattern of use (Jer 17.5, ערער במדבר; 48.6, ערוער במדבר) does
not enable one to choose between the senses 'destitute' and
'juniper bush' or the like with any degree of confidence. W.
Gesenius (*Thesaurus* ii, pp. 1073f.) has indicated a preference
for the sense 'ruined buildings' in Jer 17.5 and 48.6, and also in
Isa 17.2 (ערי ערער = 'ruined towns'). The more modern
lexicographers (BDB, KB[2]) suppose that there is a reference to a
tree or a bush in Jer 17.5 and 48.6. On the other hand, ערירי
(ערירים) means 'stripped', 'childless' (Gen 15.2; Lev 20, 20–21,
Jer 22.30) and תפלת הערער (Ps 102.18) is 'the prayer of the
destitute'. Hence the case for 'juniper bush', or for a bush of any
kind, at Jer 17.5 and 48.6 is not well-made, and the argument of
Duhm and others that since a tree appears in the second image
(vv. 7–8), a bush or tree must feature in the first (vv. 5–6), is not
one on which heavy reliance should be placed. Nevertheless, all
the versions understood ערער as a type of plant. They are
followed in this by Jerome (who reproduces Symm.), by Kimchi
who notes Targ. and by most modern commentators. Although
Rashi connects ערער with ערירי (Gen 15.2), he explains it as
עץ יחידי, 'a solitary tree'.

It should be noted (although too much should not be made of
it) that in Ps 1 the figure of the well-watered tree is used only of
the man whose delight is in the Law (v. 3), whereas a different
image (chaff scattered by the wind) is used of the wicked man
(v. 4). If ערער is 'juniper' or the like, it is natural to conclude (as
the versions and modern commentators have done) that the
grammatical subject of יראה and ושכן is the same as the subject
of יהיה, and that the verse from ולא יראה to the end is about the
man who ekes out his existence in a barren, inhospitable and

uninhabited desert (Rudolph, Weiser, Bright, NEB). Kimchi, on the other hand, supposes that עַרְעָר is the grammatical subject of the verbs which follow it and that the simile continues to the end of v. 6. The right conclusion is rather that there is no tree imagery in v. 6 and that its simile has a different character from that of v. 8: the man who trusts in human power is likened to a destitute person who knows nothing of the good life and suffers a solitary existence in a wasteland.

Another word (חררים), which occurs only once in Biblical Hebrew, has been a source of perplexity (v. 6), and was variously rendered by the versions. Sept. ἐν ἁλίμοις, 'at the seashore', is of special interest in connection with Targ.'s paraphrase of ארץ מלחה (כארץ סדום): the desert (מדבר) is identified by Targ. with the 'land of Sodom', and Sept. may have had the region of the Dead Sea in mind (cf. ארץ מלחה) when it rendered בחררים by ἐν ἁλίμοις. O. Eissfeldt (*ZDMG* 104, 1954, pp. 100f.) raises the question whether ערבה and חררים are references to particular areas rather than simply general indications of barren tracts. The sense 'lava fields' is the one given in KB[3] (cf. NEB, 'among the rocks in the wilderness') over against the earlier lexicography, 'parched places' (חרר 'burn', Kimchi, BDB). It is dubious whether the intention of the description in v. 6 is to represent that the person who is in these inhospitable surroundings is one who is wandering alone and helpless in the desert and who faces the prospect of certain death (Rudolph and Weiser). The one portrayed is rather condemned to know only a straitened and solitary existence in a parched or stony wasteland, lacking vigour and drained of vitality.

When the imagery of vv. 7–8 is compared with that of Ps 1.3 a partial identity appears, though the ordering of the images does not coincide in such a way as to suggest that one is copied from the other:

Jer 17.8

1 והיה כעץ שתול על מים
2 ועל יובל ישלח שרשיו
3 ולא ירא כי יבא חם
4 והיה עלהו רענן
5 ובשנת בצרת לא ידאג
6 ולא ימיש מעשות פרי

Ps 1.3

1 היה כעץ שתול על פלגי מים
3 ועלהו לא יבול
2 אשר פריו יתן בעתו

וכל אשר יעשה יצליח is an application of the imagery which signifies the prosperity of the righteous man, to which nothing corresponds in Jer 17.8. Otherwise, it is clear from the comparison that there is a richer development of the image of the tree fed by underground water in Jer 17.8, and that the three elements which are common to the two passages do not appear in the same order in the two accounts. What might be regarded as a more logical order (healthy foliage followed by fruitfulness) is reversed in Ps 1.3. In Jer 17.8 the vitality of the tree is related to the location of its roots (2), and its healthiness and 'sense of security' are shown to arise from its being independent of external, climatic conditions (4, 5). ועל יובל is taken by Sept., Vulg., Targ. and Kimchi as an indication that the roots are always moist. Along with Targ. (יחזי) and Rashi, Kimchi follows Q (יראה) in v. 8 and remarks that both יראה and ידאג are anthropopathisms. The other versions follow K (ירא): Sept. οὐ φοβηθήσεται; Vulg. et non timebit; Pesh. wl' ndḥl.

An argument can be made for Q יראה in terms of a structural correspondence between יראה of v. 6 and יראה of v. 8, both taken as anthropopathisms. Thus, if the simile in v. 6 has the same scope as the simile in v. 8, and if ערער means 'bush', the stunted bush has no awareness or enjoyment of the generosity of nature, and the tree fed by underground springs (Targ. renders מים by מבוע דמין) is not aware when external climatic conditions are such as might produce wilting and barrenness. Kimchi, who assumes this order of correspondence, was no doubt impressed by the near identity of ולא יראה כי יבוא טוב (v. 6) and ולא ירא כי יבא חם (v. 8), and so was predisposed to accept Q in v. 8 and to achieve complete identity. Hence he concluded that just as חם indicated 'drought', so טוב indicated 'rain'. The case for this is less strong when the opinion that ערער 'bush' is the grammatical subject of יראה (v. 6) has been given up. If, as has been argued, there is an absence of tree imagery in v. 6, the case is even less impressive (see above, p. 390). The parallelism of ירא and ידאג (v. 8) is more impressive than the counter-consideration that יראה (v. 6) should be balanced by יראה (Q) in v. 8. Hence the anthropopathisms in v. 8 should be regarded as self-contained, and their function is to emphasize the 'sense of security' felt by the tree which has a hidden, interior source of vitality and is not at the mercy of harsh climatic conditions. It will continue to thrive and produce fruit, even when lack of rain has brought on drought conditions and all around it are signs of drooping and barrenness.

Whether or not Rudolph is right in his view that Ps 1 is dependent on Jer 17.5–8, in the sense that the imagery is transferred from a setting of trust in God to one which is agreeable with the ideal of Pharisaic piety ('freedom from sin, and study of the Law'), there is no doubt that he puts his finger on an important difference between the thought of the two passages. It should also be noticed that there is no formal antithesis of blessing and curse in Ps 1: ברוך or אשרי and ארור are not juxtaposed as they are in Jer 17.5–8. Ps 1 is about one type of man (אשרי האיש, v. 1), and the contrast with another type of man is incidental rather than the product of a deliberate, formal scheme—לא כן הרשעים (v. 4). Certainly an antithesis of צדיקים and רשעים appears, but the theodicy is affirmed with special reference to the Law. There is no problem of theodicy for the man who fills his mind with the Law and orders his life by its precepts. The way of death (v. 6) is taken by those who ignore the study of the Law and whose lives run counter to its guidance. The main issue is that Jer 17.5–8 is not manifestly about righteousness and unrighteousness and has nothing explicit in it of the belief that the righteous are rewarded and the wicked are punished (*pace* Nicholson). The antithesis which it formulates is between trust in man and trust in God. One cannot therefore deny this passage to the prophet Jeremiah on the ground that its theology contradicts what we know of him and his deepest convictions from other passages.

Rudolph aptly cites Isa 31.3 in order to elucidate בשר (v. 5), and this brings us into an area elsewhere described as one of conflict between prophets and wise men (*PWM*, pp. 72f.). Isa 31.1–3 dwells on the futility of making a political pact with Egypt and relying on Egyptian military equipment for safety. It is this manifestation of power which is described as בשר, and it is contrasted with power of a different order, less tangible, more refined, existing in the realm of the spirit and accessible to those who stake their survival and well-being entirely on Yahweh. Such power is רוח and not בשר. Another terminological link between this debate and our passage is the motive clause attached to the threat of exile in Jer. 2.37: כי מאס יהוה במבטחיך ולא תצליחי להם, 'For Yahweh has rejected your security arrangements and you will derive no benefit from them'. This is to be compared with the use of בטח in Jer 17.5 and 7, and, particularly, with the use of מבטח in v. 7.

There is, however, a decisive difference between Jer 17.5–8 and these other passages. The latter relate to matters which are crucial for the corporate life of Judah; Jer 17.5–8, on the other hand, focuses on the individual (ברוך הגבר ; ארור הגבר) and on the security which is sought in a context where the ultimate privacy of the individual has to be granted. It would be artificial to urge that הגבר (v. 5) is to be envisaged as a man wielding public authority on whose concept of political responsibility the well-being of Judah depends. Ahaz was such an individual according to the account of Isa 7: one who opted for בשר rather than for רוח, for the power of the Assyrians rather than the power of Yahweh. It is improbable that the individual *qua* king or statesman is the concern of Jer 17.5–8. Either it is about Everyman, in which case, although it deals with the individual in his loneliness, it has a universal potential, or it has a biographical character as a reflection on Jeremiah's prophetic experience and what he had learned about 'security' from it.

The latter alternative is perhaps the less probable and the wisdom-sentence form of Jer 17.5–8 may be thought to tell against it. If Jeremiah is speaking about himself in vv. 5–8, about his spiritual Odyssey and his mature appreciation of trust in Yahweh, the passage which invites comparison is Jer. 12.1–5. We may suppose that the form of this latter passage (vv. 1–4, complaint and petition; v. 5, divine answer) is a kind of transcription or translation of a process of interior debate and clarification—that it gives us an insight into the struggles of a prophetic soul. Trust which makes demands or calls for guarantees is no longer trust, but is a form of enslavement, and liberation is achieved by a deeper understanding of security as an interior vitality which is independent of external support. The correspondence on which Jeremiah had built so much was after all an unholy alliance of trust in Yahweh and trust in בשר, but the deeper understanding which comes to expression in v. 5 is a turning from בשר to רוח. It is a recognition that more severe tests await him than those which he has hitherto endured, and that if he is to survive them it will be in virtue of inner resources not external support or acceptance. Similarly we might suppose that in 17.5–8 Jeremiah, in a more oblique way, declares that his security is independent of external conditions and experiences: independent of hardship, rejection and contempt, of persecution and death. All can be borne if his trust is in רוח and not בשר; all can be endured if the inner fortress is inviolate.

If 17.5–8 is a word for Everyman, no particular arguments can be advanced to associate these verses with the prophet Jeremiah. The individual has to decide on what foundation he is to build his life, whether he will place reliance on God or on man, whether he will seek security in בשר or in רוח. It is true that 17.5–8 must not be dissociated absolutely from those passages in which Isaiah and Jeremiah confront the statesmen of Judah with the demand that they trust in Yahweh. Trust in Yahweh is, in the last analysis, indivisible, whether it is envisaged in the area of great public decisions or in the private decisions by which an individual nourishes his spirit and shapes his destiny, but the distinction between public and private is, nevertheless, necessary and significant. Lack of trust in Yahweh which takes the form of reliance on בשר is fully comprehended without any consideration of the absence or presence of idolatry (*pace* Weiser). It is compatible with a kind of orthodoxy and it raises much more subtle issues than the presence of public, idolatrous rites.

If Jer 17.5–8 makes trust in Yahweh the foundation of the well-being of Everyman, there is no reason why it should be thought uncharacteristic of Jeremiah. If an individual's understanding of power is a materialistic one and he builds his life on the assumption that solidarity with the big battalions is the way of prosperity, he will find himself one day in a desert—alone in an arid environment. The emphasis, however, falls rather on the kind of vitality possessed by the man who trusts in Yahweh: even when the external world has become a desert and everything around him is wilting, he draws on unfailing resources of vitality, because his trust in Yahweh does not demand or depend on easy and spacious conditions of life. There is no sense in which the passage supports the expectation of prosperity as a reward for faith. On the contrary it describes a man who survives because he is like a tree which is fed by ample and unfailing underground waters, waters which nourish its vitality and fruitfulness. His trust in Yahweh gives him access to spiritual resources which do not fail him. He endures and thrives because he has an energy which emancipates him even from the bleakest of external worlds and he is never pulled down to the level of paralysis and despair.

YAHWEH SEARCHES THE HEART AND GIVES EACH MAN HIS DUE (17.9–10)

⁹More deceitful than anything else is the heart;
it is incurably sick and who can fathom it?
¹⁰I, Yahweh, search the heart
and test man's inmost parts,
giving to each according to his ways,
according to the fruit of his deeds.

Baumgartner (pp. 43f.) makes the tentative proposal that vv. 9–10 are the concluding oracle of vv. 12–18 (cf. Cornill and Duhm); that they constitute a rejection of Jeremiah's prayer coupled with the assurance that Yahweh sees into the depths of the heart beyond the cry for vengeance and will not judge the prophet too harshly. His final conclusion, however, is that vv. 9f. are an independent piece or a fragment of a bigger passage which is otherwise lost. Its stylistic resemblance to the psalms is unmistakeable, it contains nothing distinctively prophetic, and in view of its small compass no judgement can be made whether or not it is to be assigned to the prophet Jeremiah.

Kimchi saw a connection between the description of the לב as עָקֹב (v. 9) and the withdrawal of the לב from Yahweh which was a characteristic of the individual who put his trust in men (v. 5). Rudolph envisages vv. 9f. as a reply to an objection which might readily be raised against the affirmation contained in vv. 5–8. Does not everyday experience contradict the view that reliance on men brings misfortune and trust in God prosperity? Yahweh himself replies that the doctrine of deserts cannot be undermined; where it appears to be inoperative this is explicable in terms of the recesses of the לב which only Yahweh can explore. But vv. 5–8 (*pace* Rudolph) are not at all concerned with an equilibrium of righteousness and reward or unrighteousness and retribution. Rudolph's correct appreciation of vv. 9f. heightens the theological discrepancy between vv. 5–8 and vv. 9f. and emphasizes the degree of intrinsic discontinuity. The theodicy of vv. 9f. is more complacent and superficial; it is less sorrowful, questioning and profound. The man who survives because his inner spiritual resources are nourished by unfailing springs when the world around him has become a desert, is not the man who asserts a precise allocation of rewards and punishments on the basis of Yahweh's infallible scrutiny of the לב of every individual.

Duhm is perhaps right in supposing that v. 10a refers to the deficiency of our self-understanding rather than our inability to appreciate the springs of motivation in others, but it is doubtful whether the lack of coherence between v. 10a and v. 10b is so fundamental as he represents. He is perhaps the victim of a too fussy logic, since the function of the reference to Yahweh's scrutinizing and testing of the לב is to lay the foundations for a doctrine of theodicy and v. 10b is simply a way of developing this more explicitly. The two aspects find neat expression in Ps 7.10, where צדיק, as an attribute of God, is an expression of his judicial infallibility in the allocating of deserts to individuals (וּבֹחֵן לִבּוֹת וּכְלָיוֹת אֱלֹהִים צַדִּיק). The combination of לבות and כליות cannot be elucidated more precisely than as a reference to the labyrinthine interior of man, and the disposition and conflicts of elemental drives, emotions and motives which are not necessarily faithfully reflected in external patterns of speech and behaviour. Hence the intention of v. 10 is to assert that God sees actions for what they truly are and that he is not deceived by appearances; he traces them to the interior dispositions from which they derive.

The connections of the vocabulary of vv. 9f. may be

investigated in the following ways: (a) with reference to חקר (b) with reference to חקר and בחן (c) with reference to בחן (d) with reference to כפרי מעלליו. (a) Ps 139.1; (b) Jer 17.10; Ps 139.23; (c) Jer 11.20 (20.12); 12.3; Ps 7.10; 17.3; 26.2; 66.10; Prov 17.3; 1 Chr 29.17; (d) Isa 3.10; Mic 7.13; Jer 6.19; 17.10 (32.19); 21.14.

Jer 17.10 stands apart from all the passages cited under (a), (b) and (c) in that it is the only place where Yahweh himself declares that he searches the heart and tests the inner recesses of men's motives. In other passages Yahweh is invited to subject the individual to the most exacting scrutiny (note the additional figure of testing by a process of smelting in Pss 17.3, 26.2, and Prov 17.3), as in Pss 139.23, 26.2, or an affirmation of integrity is made on the basis that the individual has already been thoroughly tested by Yahweh (Ps 139.1; 17.3; 66.10; Jer 12.3), or Yahweh is described as the one who tests לבות and כליות, and this is linked to the thought of theodicy (Ps 7.10; Jer 11.20 = 20.12).

Berridge (p. 118; cf. J Bright, *JBL* 70, p. 30) deals with some passages not included under (d), and focuses attention on the conjunction or parallelism of דרך or דרכים and מעללים. Nine occurrences of דרך or דרכים coupled with מעללים in the book of Jeremiah are produced by Berridge, seven prose and two poetry. One of the poetic passages (4.18; דרכך ומעלליך עשו אלה לך) is an assertion that Judah has brought her corporate doom on her own head by her inveterate apostasy. This is a kind of 'theodicy', but it is set in the context of a prophetic proclamation of judgement and doom for Judah. Even if it were held that an individualized theodicy is developed from the threat of corporate doom, these are, nevertheless, two clearly distinguishable theological areas. The other poetic passage (23.22) and all the prose passages (7.3,5; 18.11; 25.5; 26.13; 35.15) are associated with calls for repentance and amendment of life, and this again is a context demonstrably different from 17.9f.

A more useful exercise is to take into consideration the passages gathered under (d), since they have a more precise connection with one of the figures used in 17.10—פרי מעלליו. Isa 3.10 is especially relevant, but the others are significant in so far as they show that the expression פרי מעלליו or the like (cf. Jer 6.19, פרי מחשבותם) is used by Micah and Jeremiah in formulating their prophecies of doom (cf. Jer 4.18). Isa 3.10 is more closely comparable with Jer 17.9f., because the focus of interest is the individual. It is described by Wildberger (pp. 119, 126) as a wisdom formulation and he denies it to the prophet Isaiah, although he ascribes it to a circle of disciples who were close to the prophet and does not therefore suppose that the

content was alien to his way of thinking. There is no doubt that
Isa 3 consists of threats directed against Judah and Jerusalem,
and that vv. 10f. fit ill into it.

Verses 9f. may represent a stage in Jeremiah's spiritual
pilgrimage, such a stage as is indicated by 12.1–4, 11.20
(20.11f.). Or it may have been an attitude which tended to
dominate him, and a demand for vindication which he could not
stifle, in times of intense stress, when the injustice of his situation
seemed too cruel to bear. However this may be, there is a
theological distance between 17.5–8 and 9–10 which cannot be
bridged in the way suggested by Rudolph. We have to recognize
that this is a particular case of the general brokenness and
discontinuity which attaches to chapter 17.

Rudolph may be right in holding that Sept. βαθεῖα is to be
regarded as an exegesis of עקב rather than evidence of a Hebrew
text with עמק in place of עקב. The Greek translator (and this is
also what Duhm does) has chosen to emphasize the aspect of
unsearchability in his rendering. He interprets the deceitfulness
of the heart in terms of those profound, labyrinthine recesses
which are inaccessible to examination, so that overt speech or
action cannot be related to this cavernous area of motivation
with any assurance. This exegetical trend is extended by Ehrlich
(pp. 286f.) who emends עקב חלב מכל ואנש to עמק חלב מכל אנוש.
The plainest translation of עקב as 'crooked' or 'deceitful' appears
in Aq., Symm., Vulg. and Targ. Rashi explains עקב as 'full of
pretext and deviousness', and Kimchi glosses it with מרמה
'deceit': deceitful words and actions proceed from the evil
propensity (כונה) of the heart.

Pesh. by omitting any representation of the ו of ואנש and by
rendering אנש as 'man' (cf. Ehrlich), has produced the thought
that the heart is too powerful for any man to control—man is
overruled and dominated by the propensities of his לב ('šyn lb'
mn kl 'nš' hw). Thus we can observe different exegetical
orientations in the handling of עקב: (a) It refers to the
deceitfulness of the inmost centre of motivation and the
discrepancy between the springs of speech or action and their
overt forms of expression. (b) It refers to the labyrinthine and
inscrutable processes of human motivation. (c) It refers to the
oppressive power of the לב, to the pressure of an inner force
against which man is too weak to contend, and which dictates
the pattern of his life.

Jerome produces a range of meanings for אנש ('man',
'inscrutable' and 'incurable') and shows that Vulg. et
inscrutabile is intended as a rendering of ואנש. The text which is
given by Joannes Chrysostomus (Migne, *Patrologia Graeca*, 64,
p. 917) may contain a double rendering of אנש, 'hidden' and

'man'. The text reads καρδία βαθεῖα κεκρυμμένη ἄνθρωπός ἐστι καὶ τις γνώσεται αὐτόν 'Man is deep and hidden and who can know him?' Apparently מכל is unrepresented and אנש is rendered twice, first as אֱנָש and then as אָנָש. NEB's alternative rendering, 'The heart is too powerful for any man' (מכל אנש instead of MT מכל ואנש) has affinities with Pesh., and Ehrlich. Jerome's *desperabile* is the sense which is indicated by Rashi and Kimchi and which has become firmly established in modern times (NEB, 'desperately sick'; so Rudolph, Weiser, Bright). The foundation for it was laid by the Massoretes in so far as their vocalization excludes the sense 'man' and points to the sense 'sick'. The combination of עקב and אָנָש ('incurably sick') is significant (cf. Kimchi), and it shows that v. 9 does not turn on the unfathomability of the heart but on the incurable sickness of perversity and deceit with which it is afflicted. Hence 'Who can know it?' is not so much a reference to unexplored depths (to the unknowability of the heart), as it is to its immeasurable capacity for wickedness and the deep-seated disease which grips it.

NO LASTING BENEFIT FROM ILL-GOTTEN GAINS (17.11)

A partridge hatching eggs which it does not lay
is like a man making wealth by unjust means:
in his middle age it will desert him
and at the end of his life he will be seen as a fool.

Weiser attempts to establish a particular connection between vv. 9f. and v. 11 in terms of Jehoiakim. This, however, rests on an unacceptable exegesis of vv. 9f. which he relates to the aftermath of Jehoiakim's submission to the Babylonians in 603/2. It appeared to be a successful policy, since it was followed by a period of quiet which caused men to doubt the truth of prophetic threats founded on the premiss that righteousness brings reward and unrighteousness punishment. Verse 11 is then a conclusive answer to these questionings, alluding as it does to Jehoiakim's premature death at the age of 36 ('half his days') and to the ill-gotten gain which he had to leave behind (Jer 22.13; 2 Kgs 23.36ff.).

Verses 9f. and v. 11b do, however, have a shared topic which makes their continuity understandable, and there is a common mode of doubt and perplexity which gives rise to both: Why is God's justice not seen to be done in the lives of individuals? Why do wicked men prosper? In vv. 9f. the answer is that men are never sufficiently well-informed to make a sound judgement on these matters: the recesses of the human heart are explored

adequately only by God and human perplexity is the product of a
too superficial scrutiny. The answer in v. 11 allows for a
postponement in the operation of theodicy and introduces the
thought of a final outcome (אחרית) as a corrective to the
temporary imbalances of God's moral order. The wicked man
may prosper for a time, but his prosperity is ephemeral and his
final state will be that of a fool.

The partridge (קרא) serves as a model of the man who gains
his wealth by unjust means. Sept. has a double rendering of קרא
in a text which makes poor sense and from which Ziegler deletes
ἐφώνησεν (ἐφώνησεν πέρδιξ, συνήγαγεν ἃ οὐκ ἔτεκεν). Pesh.,
which also apparently renders קרא twice, makes better sense
than Sept. with a paraphrase: 'yk ḥgl' dqr' l'ylyn dl' yld, 'like a
partridge which calls to those whose mother she is not'. It is clear
from Rashi's French gloss (קוק "ו) that he takes קרא to mean
'cuckoo'; he glosses דגר with ציפצוף 'chirping' or 'whistling' and
comments, 'Those to whom the קרא chirps will not follow it
when they grow up, for they are not of its kind. So is he who
makes wealth by unjust means'. In this view that דגר has the
sense 'chirp' Rashi stands alone and his version of the partridge
story is different from that which derives from the assumption
that דגר means 'collect' or 'incubate'.

Both these meanings appear in the paraphrase of Targ.: 'Like
a partridge which collects (דמכניש) eggs which are not its own
and incubates (ומשחין) chicks which will not go with it.' The
sense 'keep warm', 'incubate' appears in Aq. (ἐθάλψεν) and
Vulg. (fovit), and Kimchi also has Targ.'s version of the
partridge story, giving דגר the sense 'incubate' or 'hatch'. In
Biblical Hebrew דגר is used only at Jer 17.11 and (again in
connection with 'hatching') at Isa 34.15 (ובקעה ודגרה). NEB
gives דגר the sense 'hatch' in the Isaiah passage and the sense
'gather' (Sept. συνήγαγεν) in the Jeremiah passage.

G. R. Driver (PEQ, 1955, pp. 132f.) mentions two types of
partridge both of which are termed קרא in the Old Testament:
the sand-partridge (caccabis sinaica) at 1 Sam 26.20 (also קפוז
at Isa 34.15, according to NEB) and the commoner grey
partridge (caccabis chukar) at Jer 17.11. According to Driver
קרא like chukar is onomatopoeic. On the partridge story in Jer
17.11 Driver remarks, 'The second passage alludes to the curious
belief recorded also by the Arab historian al Damîr (Bochart and
Rosenmüller, Hierozoicon, II, p. 85) that the mother partridge
visits a neighbour's nest and taking the eggs incubates them, but
that the chicks when they come to fly return to the mothers who
have laid them. The story may have arisen from the fact that the
chukar (caccabis chukar) lays two clutches of eggs, one for
herself and one for the cock.' In Fauna and Flora of the Bible

(United Bible Societies, 1972, p. 64) notice is taken of the allusion in Jer 17.11 to the 'ancient belief that the partridge steals eggs from other nests, but that the hatched fledglings return to their own mother'. Driver's explanation is given along with another, that the hen lays an unusually large number of eggs. The source of the statement that 26 eggs were found in one nest (which is not acknowledged) is H. B. Tristram (*The Natural History of the Bible*, 6th ed., 1880, p. 225): 'I once took a nest of 26 in the wilderness of Judah.'

We have seen that there is an allusion to the stealing of eggs of other birds in Targ. and Kimchi and that a variant version (the stealings of chicks) appears in Rashi. There is a reference in Jerome (on Jer 17.11) which appears to give valuable information, but which disappoints when it is followed up (cf. J. F. A. Sawyer, *VT*, 28, 1978, pp. 327ff.). S. Reiter (the editor of Jerome's commentary) notes (p. 212) that no story of the kind indicated by Jerome is preserved in the extant works of Aristotle, Theophrastus and Pliny, although Jerome cites these sources. He asks whether Jerome may not have confused the partridge with the cuckoo which 'admittedly does not incubate eggs not its own, but, on the contrary, puts its own eggs in strange nests'. Reiter's suggestion that Jerome may have confused the partridge with the cuckoo is weak in so far as the behaviour attributed to the cuckoo (putting its eggs in strange nests) is not closely related to Jerome's partridge story which is the same as the one in Targ. and Kimchi. Aristotle (*The Works of Aristotle*, iv, *Historia Animalium*, Oxford, 1910) makes two observations about the partridge which are interesting in relation to the accounts already considered: (*a*) The partridge lays a large number of eggs (613b, 22–23). (*b*) It lays two clutches and the cock sits on one of them (564a, 20–24). Both Pliny Secundus (*Naturalis Historia*) and Aristotle comment on the sexual proclivities of partridges, and how this leads to the capture of males and females when fowlers use decoy birds (Aristotle, 614a, 26–30; Pliny X, li,100–103). It might be supposed that Aristotle's two observations are the data which have given rise to an aetiological tale. They are, however, inadequate data for this purpose, because they do not account for the part of the partridge story which is crucial for its parabolic functioning in Jer 17.11, namely, that the birds which come from eggs not laid by the partridge fly away whenever they are able.

Sawyer (pp. 324–29) goes back to an exegesis which is compatible with KJV and which is the same as that offered by Tristram (p. 225). The קֹרֵא is robbed of the eggs on which it sits by human and other marauders and so is unable to hatch all of them. Those who acquire wealth by unjust means will have it

taken away from them and will not be permitted to enjoy it to
the full. Although Sawyer supposes that his preference for דגר
'incubate' over דגר 'gather' is highly significant, it can be shown
that the crucial choice is between ילד 'lay (eggs)' and ילד 'hatch
(eggs)'. For example, Vulg. has *fovit* which agrees with Sawyer's
view of דגר, but it combines this with *quae non peperit* which
certainly refers to the laying of eggs and not the hatching of
eggs. Similarly Venema combines *incubat* and *et non peperit*,
whereas Calvin who renders דגר by *quae congregat*,
nevertheless, interprets *et non parit* as a reference to the
hatching of eggs. This demonstrates that either 'gather' or
'incubate' is compatible with the two divergent interpretations
and that it is the sense of ילד on which attention should be
focused. The principal argument against KJV, Tristram and
Sawyer is that the simile which emerges from their account of
the functioning of the imagery is a lame one. The קרא loses the
eggs to which it is justly entitled because it suffers depredations,
but this does not furnish a good basis for a statement about the
removal of wealth which has been acquired by injustice. It is
likely that these considerations influenced Lowth who was
commenting on KJV, but who observed of 17.11: 'The sentence
may best be rendered thus. As the bird Kore hatcheth eggs
which she did not lay, so he that getteth riches etc.' (followed by
Blayney). Hence Lowth's exegesis is the same as that of Targ.
and Kimchi. We reach the conclusion that the figure is that of a
partridge(?) sitting on or hatching eggs which it has not itself
laid, since this enables the simile to function in the way that is
desiderated: the   partridge   acquires   chicks   by   the
misappropriation of eggs and the unjust man acquires ill-gotten
wealth.

The similitude is applied to the man who acquires wealth by
unjust means. The ambivalence of יעזבנו (either, 'He will leave
the wealth behind' or 'Wealth will leave him') is reflected in the
different renderings of the versions. Sept. (also Bright and NEB)
clearly   indicates,   'They   (riches)   will   leave   him'
(ἐγκαταλείψουσιν αὐτόν), while Vulg. (*derelinquet eas*) and
Targ. (שביק להון) indicate 'He will leave wealth behind'. The
two exegetical evaluations of יעזבנו, rest on different grammar
and both cannot be right:

(*a*) The man who gained his wealth by unjust means loses it
before his life is half over, and the circumstances that his end is
marked by poverty, emptiness and lack of fulfilment is evidence
of the false foundations on which he has laid his life and rested
his hopes.

(*b*) The man who has gained his wealth by unjust means will
die prematurely and will have to leave it behind. The futility of

his feverish grabbing of wealth will be underlined by his premature death without reputation or memorial.

Kimchi and Rudolph incorporate both alternatives in their exegesis, but the latter allows the emphasis to fall on the ephemeral character of wealth which is accumulated by unjust means. Weiser, on the other hand, since he ties his exegesis to the person of Jehoiakim, lays all the weight on the thought of premature death.

There are two principal reasons why 'They (riches) leave him' should be regarded as the correct interpretation:

(a) If the partridge story, as it is developed in Targ., Jerome and Kimchi is a correct interpretation of קרא דגר ולא ילד, it suits the thought of ephemeral or dissolving wealth rather than premature death: the young birds fly away from the partridge, and wealth gained unjustly takes wings and flies away.

(b) The contrast between ill-gotten and ephemeral wealth, on the one hand, and wealth which is solidly based on the other, can be traced in Egyptian wisdom literature (see, *Proverbs: A New Approach*, pp. 60f.) and is well-established in the book of Proverbs. There are passages which presuppose the appropriateness of a combination of עשר and כבוד (3.16, ibid., pp. 295f.), or of צדקה כבוד, and solid wealth (הון עתק). This solid wealth, accumulated over a long period, is contrasted with the wealth gained by speculative means which is soon won and soon lost (13.11, *ibid.*, pp. 458f.). With all of this taken into account Jer 17.11 should be interpreted to mean that ill-gotten wealth is ephemeral and that a spectacular but unprincipled material prosperity will peter out in emptiness and misery. That a man should reach his אחרית — his final destination in life—with reputation and material prosperity and an undiminished regard for justice, is a mark of true wisdom. We have no strong reason for supposing that the prophet Jeremiah would be concerned to coin such proverbial wisdom.

INVOCATION AND AFFIRMATION (17.12–13)

[12]O throne of glory exalted from the first,
the place of our sanctuary.
[13]O Yahweh, on whom Israel's hope is set,
all who forsake you will suffer shame.Those who turn aside from you[1] will be written in the dust, for they have forsaken the fountain of living water (even Yahweh).[2]

Rudolph supposes that an original continuity of vv. 12–13 with

[1] Reading וסורַיך (see below, p. 407).

[2] את יהוה is a gloss.

vv. 1–4 has been broken by the intervening vv. 5–11, but this
rests on the assumption that an antithesis can be established
between the heathen altars (v. 2) and the Jerusalem temple
(v. 12), and the analysis of the textual history of vv. 1–4 which
has been undertaken above (pp. 384–388) makes it improbable
that this was an original feature of the literary structure of
vv. 1–4, 12–13. Another part of Rudolph's argument is that
vv. 12–13 are not to be assigned to Jeremiah, whereas vv. 14–18
are the prophet's work, and that, therefore, vv. 12–18 are not a
unity. His objection to the vocative in v. 12 is not well-founded: it
focuses on מקום מקדשנו which need not be construed as a
vocative, but rather as appositional to the vocative כסא כבוד: 'O
Throne of Glory exalted from the beginning, the place of our
sanctuary'. Baumgartner's view (pp. 40–44) is that vv. 12–13
constitute a hymnic introduction to an individual lament which
is contained in vv. 14–18. He notes that there is only one
example of such a hymnic introduction to an individual lament
in the book of Psalms (80.2f.), but he cites late examples of this
pattern and observes that the hymnic introduction in
Babylonian-Assyrian laments demonstrates the antiquity of the
feature.

In taking v. 12 as indicative rather than vocative Reventlow
(pp. 229ff.) is influenced by Ps 48.2 (בעיר אלהינו הר קדשו),
since he holds that both passages contain a 'Zion liturgy'. His
exegesis of Jer 17.12f. is too complicated to be credible: v. 13a is
the response of a second choir to the affirmation in v. 12, sung by
a first choir. The structure is liturgical as in Ps 48 and
Jeremiah's prayer is public not private. Reventlow is not
deterred by the circumstance that there is no lament or prayer in
vv. 12, 13a which requires a divine answer, and he persuades
himself that hymnic invocation or confident affirmation can be
converted into petition or complaint.

Volz's view that vv. 12f. are a patchwork in which expressions
found elsewhere in the book of Jeremiah are associated in a
somewhat wooden way is rejected by Baumgartner, Weiser and
Reventlow, but it merits serious consideration. Volz's aesthetic
judgement ought to carry more weight, certainly in respect of
v. 13, than the not particularly formidable form-critical
argument of Baumgartner or the cult-functional argument of
Weiser for the cohesiveness of vv. 12f. and the unity of
vv. 12–18. The aspect of bad imitation and unconvincing
juxtaposition of expressions lifted from other contexts can be
more confidently detected in v. 13 than in v. 12 which may have
an ideological coherence. This is a matter of aesthetic judgement
and is necessarily subjective, but when I read v. 13, I have a
strong impression that it is a patchwork: כל עזביך יבשו is lame

after מקוה ישראל יהוה and, in particular, כי עזבו מקור מים חיים, coming after the obscure יסורי בארץ יכתבו, is an inferior and bathetic re-use of a figure which makes a powerful impact on its first appearance at 2.13. The conclusion which is suggested by all this is that vv. 12f. have no connection with anything that precedes or follows them in chapter 17 and that they are not intrinsically related to each other. The former is the less problematic, while the latter is disjointed, obscure and inconsequential.

Two issues are intertwined in the arguments of Baumgartner, Rudolph, Weiser and Reventlow. These are, (a) Whether vv. 12f. cohere with each other and with what precedes and follows them in chapter 17 and (b) Whether vv. 12 and 13 (especially v. 12) are attributable to the prophet Jeremiah. On v. 12 Rudolph holds that the celebration of Yahweh as God of the temple can hardly be reconciled with Jeremiah's stance, in spite of 14.21 and 3.16. The second of these passages may be dismissed from the discussion, because a special point of view is represented in it. The first passage, occurring as it does in the context of a communal lament, should be dissociated from Jeremiah's personal view of temple religion (see above, p. 333) and should not be assigned to the prophet. Baumgartner, with some agonizing, concludes that 17.12 may be assigned to the prophet, although he observes that the verse appears to conflict with passages (7;26) where Jeremiah criticizes the temple (p. 42). The considerations which Baumgartner himself has brought into play ought to have led him to a contrary conclusion. The problem of overcoming the antithesis between prophet and cult is much more easily resolved by Weiser and Reventlow, since the first envisages a cultic setting for vv. 12–18 and the second maintains that Jeremiah is acting as a public, cultic intercessor and not as an individual giving vent to his private distress.

The defence of the Jeremianic authorship of 17.12 which is offered by Weiser, Reventlow and Nicholson, namely, a simple differentiation between temple worship and its abuses, or between a proper understanding of the temple and a magical view of it (7.4), is too facile and superficial. It is clear (cf. chapters 7 and 26) that the conflict between Jeremiah and temple worship goes deep and that it is not enough to say that he would have approved of institutional religion if only it had been purged of its abuses. It is a matter of how momentous was the 'doom' which Jeremiah envisaged, and we shall not do justice to the dimensions of the conflict or the tragic depth of the prophet's anguish, if we suppose that at the end of the day he still entertained the hope that the Jerusalem cult purged from 'abuses' could serve the ends of truth as he saw it, or that his message of doom would have exhausted itself had the Jerusalem cult been 'reformed'.

THE TEMPLE IS THE THRONE OF GLORY (17.12)

BHS supposes that Sept. ὑψωμένος may represent מוּרָם (cf. Pesh. *'ttrym*; Brockington, p. 205), but the most important deviation of Sept. from MT in v. 12 is the absence of any representation of מראשון מקום. Janzen (p. 117) supposes that the shorter Greek text is caused by haplography which was probably already present in the Hebrew *Vorlage*. What he means by this is apparently that the scribe having written מרום was under the impression that he had written מקום and so passed from מרום to מקדשנו. In the rendering of Vulg. מקום מקדשנו is set in apposition to כסא כבוד and so is regarded as its equivalence, and this equivalence is also indicated by the shorter Greek text. Kimchi offers three interpretations of v. 12, the second of which supposes that the verse is to be explained as, בית המקדש מכוון כנגד כסא הכבוד, 'The sanctuary founded to correspond with the throne of glory'. Kimchi's first interpretation agrees with Sept. and Vulg. (Pesh.), the second with Targ. and Rashi, while the third draws a sharper distinction than the second between the throne in the highest heaven and the Jerusalem sanctuary. The second apparently envisages the Jerusalem sanctuary *qua* throne of Yahweh as a copy of a heavenly prototype.

Duhm urges that כסא כבוד is a reference to Yahweh's heavenly throne and that it is related to מקום מקדשנו, because the latter is a representation and manifestation of Yahweh's majesty and rule. מראשון, however, is given a historical elucidation by Duhm: he connects it with the hill in the 'land of Moriah' (Gen 22.2ff.), where God appeared to Abraham and supposes that this is envisaged as a prototype of the hill of Zion. If one accepts the cultic interpretation of Isaiah's inaugural vision offered by I. Engnell (*The Call of Isaiah*, UUÅ, 1949), all that is required to explain Isa 6.1 is the cultic throne (the ark in the Holy of Holies). It is true that Yahweh is described as רם ונשא, but if the cultic hypothesis is adopted, this has to be understood as a visionary metamorphosis of an item of cultic ritual. Hence if the exegesis of 17.12 is to take this direction (as it does in Weiser), it should set out from the first of Kimchi's positions, namely, that all the expressions in the verse refer to the Jerusalem temple. We then have to reckon with a synthesis of cosmological (or mythological) and historical elements in the description of the Jerusalem temple, along the lines indicated by R. E. Clements (*God and Temple*, 1965, pp. 45ff.).

On the historical plane Zion became a sanctuary of Yahweh after David captured Jerusalem and Solomon built the temple, although the historical genesis (cf. Duhm) is set in a deeper antiquity by the account of Abraham's meeting with Melchizedek, a priest-king of Jerusalem (Gen 14.18–22) whose God, El Elyon, 'Creator of heaven and earth', is equated with Yahweh (14.22). Hence Clements' view that Yahwism was enriched by elements of a creation theology inherited from the Jebusite deity, El Elyon, and that the cosmological or transcendental Zion ideology also comes from this source is probably correct. מראשון is even more ultimate than the historical genesis indicated by Gen 14.18–24 which establishes a connection between the founding father of Israel and the Jerusalem sanctuary. The character of this narrative which points beyond Abraham to the mysterious priest of El Elyon encourages a meta-historical interpretation of Yahweh's relation to Jerusalem.

Light is thrown on מרום and כסא by the Ugaritic texts. Thus *mrym ṣpn* is an expression for the mountain where Baal has his seat (Gibson, *CML*, 3 D 45 (p. 50); 3 D 82 (p. 52); 4 4.19 (p. 59)), and it is probable that מרום (Jer 17.12) is elucidated by this use (cf. G. R. Driver, *CML*, p. 161 n. 27): Mount Zion is similarly envisaged as a transcendental or mythological mountain where Yahweh dwells. The aspect of Baal's kingship, which is prominent in the Ugaritic texts, will also explain כסא כבוד, particularly the passage which refers to Baal's expulsion 'from the heights of the north' (*bmrym ṣpn*),'from the throne of his kingship' (*lkse' mlkh*), 'from the resting-place, the seat of his dominion' (*lnḥt lkḥt drkth*; Gibson, 3 D 45–47, p. 50). *kse' mlkh*, 'seat of his sovereignty' or 'throne of his sovereignty' is acceptable as an equivalence of כסא כבוד, and so, on the Canaanite analogy, all the expressions in v. 12 can be elucidated as references to the Jerusalem temple on Mount Zion *qua* residence and throne of Yahweh. Into this scheme fits the view already expressed that מראשון does not refer to a historical beginning, but to a transcendental origin which temporalities cannot contain.

APOSTATES WILL SUFFER DISGRACE AND OBLIVION (17.13)

It has already been argued that v. 13 is a patchwork, that it is disjointed and obscure. Attention is now focused particularly on יסורי בארץ יכתבו. The sense which Kimchi derives from יסורי

'those who defect from you', is indicated explicitly by Vulg. (*Recedentes a te*), and the emendation וסוריך (Ewald, Giesebrecht, Baumgartner, Rudolph, Weiser and Bright) is supported by this version. Duhm prefers either וסוּרֵי or וְסוּרֵי, 'the apostates in the land'. The first person suffix (וסוּרַי, 'those who defect from me') is tolerable only if one supposes, as Reventlow does, that Yahweh is the spokesman in v. 13b. The second of Kimchi's explanations of Q (וסורי = וסורים) accords with the renderings of Sept., Symm., Pesh. and Targ. NEB's emendation (וסורי בארץ ; Brockington, p. 205) follows Duhm, but it is doubtful whether 'all in this land who forsake thee' can be had from וסורי בארץ, or that it can claim the support of Sept.

The troublesome יכתבו is emended by Ewald, Cornill and Duhm to יכלמו, and NEB proposes יכבתו (metathesis of ב and ת ; Brockington, p. 205). This has no versional support, nor does כבת appear in Biblical Hebrew or Aramaic. It has to be justified by a reference to Arabic *kabata* 'humbled', while Targ. is cited in support. It is, however, difficult to assess the textual significance of the paraphrase of MT in Targ. G. R. Driver (*JQR* 28, p. 114) and NEB (Brockington, p. 205) assume that Targ. read a Hebrew text with יכבתו 'shall be humbled', and that 'are about to fall into Gehenna' is a paraphrase of 'shall be humbled'. The most interesting feature of Targ.'s rendering is the supposition that בארץ refers to the underworld (בגיהנם), a sense which is adopted by Baumgartner. A similar line of exegesis can be detected in Rashi and Kimchi, somewhat cryptic in the former and more explicit in the latter. The complement to Kimchi's reference to a book of life written in heaven by the angels is the addition *in libro mortis* in the Old Latin (see Ziegler). This type of exegesis has been revived and supplemented by F. M. Cross and D. N. Freedman (*JNES*, 14, 1955, p. 247 n. 39) and by M. J. Dahood (*Biblica* 40, 1959, pp. 164–166), with an appeal to Ugaritic evidence. It is improbable, because, with its assumption of an antithesis between heaven and hell, a book of life and a book of death, it attaches a penal significance to 'underworld'. Such a far-reaching departure from the Old Testament view of Sheol—a place to which all men must descend and accept an attenuated existence at the end of their earthly lives—ought not to be assumed. Nevertheless, this understanding of the passage is ancient and is firmly established in Jewish exegesis from Targ. onwards, even if it were concluded that *in libro mortis* is Christian supplementation.

The main alternative is the supposition that בארץ יכתבו refers to writing on the ground or in the dust—writing which is easily blurred or effaced. Rudolph and Weiser construct a cultic framework and assume that the writing on the ground is a kind of symbolic action: the writing and its erasure in an execration ritual, according to Weiser. Rudolph (see above, pp. 402f.), finds a contrast between ineffaceable and effaceable writing. The sins of Israelites are incised on their hearts with a diamond point (v. 1), but the record which might preserve a memorial of them and save them from oblivion is written with a finger on rootless dust. Over against those who leave behind a 'name' and a memorial, apostates disappear into nothingness and are lost in oblivion.

HEAL MY BROKENNESS AND TAKE VENGEANCE ON MY ENEMIES
(17.14–18)

> [14]"Heal me, O Yahweh, and I shall be healed;
> save me and I shall be safe;
> you are the object of my praise.
> [15]Men are saying to me,
> Where is the word of Yahweh?
> Let it come if it will!
> [16]I have not been hasty in casting off your guidance,
> I did not desire a day of anguish;
> you know what issued from my lips,
> it was fully revealed to you.
> [17]Do not bring about my ruin,
> you are my refuge when disaster comes.
> [18]Let those who pursue me suffer shame, not I,
> let them be shattered, not I;
> bring on them a day of disaster,
> break them in small pieces.

The pain and suffering which are indicated by the prayer for healing (רפא) refer, according to Kimchi, to contempt and contumely. Jeremiah's soul is scarred by rejection and scorn, by hostility and misrepresentation, and he asks for healing and 'salvation'. He uses language appropriate to a sick man in the style of the individual lament (Pss 6.3; 41.5; 60.4), but his sickness is of the spirit rather than the body (Baumgartner, Weiser). Reventlow (pp. 235ff.) has noticed that an analogous metaphorical use of רפא is found at Jer 8.22 and 14.19, where the 'health' or 'wholeness' of the body politic is the antithesis of its condition of brokenness and 'disease'. However, the circumstance that רפא (14.19) and ישע (14.8) are found in corporate laments in connection with the brokenness of the body politic is not a demonstration that they would be inappropriate in an individual lament in connection with the brokenness of an individual. The combination of רפא and ישע in v. 14 does indicate that the verse refers to a condition of bitterness, despair and spiritual defeat rather than to physical disease.

Jeremiah's opponents keep reminding him (v. 15) that the terrible words of doom which he utters are, so far as the evidence goes, empty words (cf. Baumgartner, p. 42). He has thundered his denunciations and made dire threats in the name of Yahweh, but nothing has happened, nor will anything ever happen—this is what is implied (Targ., 'Where are the words which you have prophesied in the name of the Lord? Let them be established now'). Similarly Rashi comments on איה דבר יהוה יבוא נא, 'The retribution which you were prophesying', and Kimchi remarks, 'Let it come if it will, for we do not believe that the Lord has threatened to lay waste his city'.

Reventlow (p. 237) stands out against this understanding of דבר with his view that there is no particular reference in v. 15 to the דבר which a prophet speaks (see above, p. 352). איה דבר יהוה יבוא נא has its particular connection with the cry for help in v. 14 to which it is a mocking rejoinder: it is an expression of scepticism over against the claim that there is a theodicy. These exegetical observations have to be viewed within the general framework of Reventlow's interpretation. They form a sharp contrast to Baumgartner's treatment of v. 15 which turns on the special prophetic content of דבר over against the more general concern with *Weltregiment* in examples of the individual lament in the book of Psalms (p. 42).

It may be accepted that the attitude which comes to the surface in v. 15 has occasioned Jeremiah's cry for help (Reventlow), and that in such an outpouring of the spirit as is contained in vv. 14–18 too nice a connection between v. 15 and v. 16 need not be required: the continuity is one of mood rather than of firm logical connection. Duhm's conjecture that v. 15 has been inspired by Isa 5.19 and that its insertion disturbs a connection between v. 14 and v. 16 perhaps arises out of too high logical expectations. Moreover Duhm's contention that v. 18 is secondary hangs on the interpretation of the obscure ואני לא אצתי מרעה אחריך (v. 16). He urges that Jeremiah is saying that he has not harried Yahweh with pleas for retribution (reading מֵרָעָה) after the manner of Jonah, and on this premiss he concludes that the vengeful sentiments of v. 18 are out of place. απο κακιας (Aq., Symm.) lends support to the vocalization of J. D. Michaelis (מֵרָעָה) and to the elucidation (Giesebrecht and Duhm) which follows from this: 'I have not importuned you to bring disaster'. Pesh. understands ואני לם אצתי אחריך in the same way as Sept. ('I have not relinquished following after you'—Sept. ἐκοπίασα has the sense 'became weary', 'desisted'). Sept. does not represent מרעה and Pesh. renders מרעה as if it were בְּרָעָה and locates it after וַאֲנִי: w'n' bbyšt' l' pšt mnk, 'And I did not give up following you in evil times'. Targ., like Pesh., indicates that Jeremiah is defending his record as a prophet, but its paraphrase cannot be correlated with the Hebrew text beyond וַאֲנִי לֹא אַצְתִּי which it renders as 'And I did not resist'. רֹעֶה is explicit in the rendering of Vulg.: *non sum turbatus te pastorem sequens*, 'I have not been agitated (unsteady) in following you as a shepherd'. It is unlikely that the figure of 'shepherd' in this translation is a reference to Jeremiah's prophetic office. Rather, it is Yahweh who is the shepherd and Jeremiah is asserting that he has never faltered in following him. The view that 'shepherd' is a reference to the prophetic office is found in Rashi and Kimchi. Similarly Berridge (op. cit., p. 140) glosses רֹעֶה with נביא.

Three lines of exegesis arise from differences of opinion about the sense of וַאֲנִי לֹא אַצְתִּי מֵרֹעֶה אַחֲרֶיךָ.

1. 'I did not importune you to send disaster' (מֵרָעָה ; cf. NEB, Brockington, p. 205). A modification of this (לְרָעָה) is adopted by Baumgartner, Rudolph and Bright; Rudolph renders לְרָעָה as 'with evil intent', whereas Baumgartner and Bright discern a reference to a day of disaster. Jeremiah was not given to badgering Yahweh that he should execute judgement on his community.

2. 'I did not withdraw myself from the office of shepherd (prophet) in your service' (Weiser; Berridge, p. 140), or, 'I did not become impatient for results (Rashi) and fail in my obedience to you in exercising the office of prophet' (Rashi and Kimchi). Jeremiah affirms that he has not succumbed to impatience and that he has persevered in his efforts to effect a reconciliation between Yahweh and his people. The difficulty is that elsewhere in the book of Jeremiah (6.3; 10.21; 12.10) רֹעֶה is a figure for a political leader and that this would be the only instance of its use in connection with the prophetic office (*pace* Berridge who wrongly supposes that רֹעִים in Jer 2.8 means 'prophets').

3. 'I did not waver in following you as a shepherd'. This is probably the sense indicated by the Massoretic vocalization and it is the rendering of Vulg. Jeremiah is affirming that his faith in Yahweh as his leader and guide has not wavered and that he has been constant in his allegiance.

Targ. is the only version to support the view that יוֹם אָנוּשׁ refers to the day when Yahweh's judgement will fall on his community, but there is an unevenness between Targ.'s understanding of וַאֲנִי לֹא אַצְתִּי מֵרֹעֶה אַחֲרֶיךָ, on the one hand, and וְיוֹם אָנוּשׁ לֹא הִתְאַוֵּיתִי on the other. The first stich means, 'I spoke the hard words which you delivered to me in order that I might bring your people to repentance'. The second stich means, 'I had no desire to see a day of judgement—of sickness unto death—fall on your community to which I also belong'. A similar unevenness can be detected in Rashi who comments, 'I did not desire the חלי of retribution'. Kimchi, with a different emphasis, connects the second stich of v. 16a with v. 17 and with Jeremiah's prayer that he may not become a מחתה. He relates this to the words in the call narrative, אל תחת מפניהם פן אחתך לפניהם (1.17). On this view יום אנוש is not a day of judgement for Judah, but a painful crisis for Jeremiah associated with the prophetic office.

There is considerable uncertainty about the meaning of יום אנוש. Sept., Vulg. and Pesh. (who read אנוש as אֱנוֹשׁ 'man') perhaps had 17.5 in mind—the reference to הגבר אשר יבטח באדם. Jeremiah is then saying that he has not expected or desired any relief or victory deriving from worldly power. Targ. and Rashi suppose that יום אנוש refers to a day of judgement for Judah, and Kimchi relates it to the sharp pain of the prophetic vocation. But there is a fundamental obscurity in v. 16a which is compounded rather than simplified by all the efforts to relieve it. Although there are minor problems in v. 16b, it is clearly an affirmation of innocence on which a confident appeal to Yahweh is founded. The major problem is that of relating v. 16a to v. 16b.

Modern commentators suppose (Duhm, Baumgartner, Rudolph, Weiser, Bright) that v. 16a refers to the day of doom for Judah. Jeremiah is saying, 'I did not importune you to hasten the disaster, nor did I desire a day of doom for Judah', or, according to Weiser, 'I did not withdraw myself from the office of prophet in your service, nor did I desire a day of doom for Judah'. Ehrlich (pp. 287ff.), on the other hand, follows the line of Kimchi and relates יום אנוש to Jeremiah's suffering as a prophet (cf. Calvin, Blayney and, especially, Lowth). Weiser, Berridge (pp. 139ff.) and Reventlow (pp. 237ff.) assume that there is an allusion here and in v. 17 (יום רעה) to the concept of the 'Day of Yahweh' (Amos 5.18; Isa 2.11f.) which is being depicted as a day of judgement and not of salvation. According to Weiser, it is a day of the 'Covenant Festival' when Yahweh executes judgement on his enemies. These interpretations of v. 16a do not cohere well with the opening of the lament (vv. 14–15) or with its conclusion (vv. 17f.), or, more immediately, with the affirmation of innocence in v. 16b. In view of v. 16b something about the private anguish of the prophet—the contradictions and sorrows which perplex him—is desiderated in v. 16a. A defence against the charge that he has neglected his duty, or that he has been urging Yahweh to hasten the day of doom for Judah, lacks cogency in the context.

All the versions except Vulg. suppose that it is Yahweh's knowledge of Jeremiah's words which is indicated by אתה ידעת מוצא שפתי נכח פניך היה; he is fully apprised of their content (so Baumgartner, Rudolph, Weiser and Bright). Vulg's rendering (*rectum in conspectu tuo fuit*) indicates that the point is Yahweh's approval of Jeremiah's utterances rather than his full awareness of them. The meaning 'approval' for נכח פניך or the like is given by BDB for Jer 17.16, Ezek 14.3 and Lam 2.19, and is adopted by NEB at Jer 17.16. The transfer of the *athnach* to שפתי (Baumgartner, Rudolph, Bright and NEB) improves the balance of the two stichs, but whatever punctuation is adopted נכח פניך היה should be explained as epexegetical of אתה ידעת and so as a reference to Yahweh's complete knowledge rather than his approval.

The best that can be done with ואני לא אצתי מרעה אחריך is to retain the vocalization of MT (מֵרֹעֶה) and to follow the lead of Vulg.: 'I have not impetuously given up following you and relying on you to guide me like a shepherd.' Despite all his perplexities and sorrows Jeremiah has not taken refuge in pique or resorted to rebellion, and the brokenness of his spirit is not a condition which he secretly enjoys. Yahweh knows all that he has said and all that is in his heart. He pleads for vindication without a shred of doubt that he is innocent. There is nothing about a day of retribution for Judah. What we have is an affirmation of innocence and constancy by Jeremiah; a protest that the scars on his soul are deep and are not being exaggerated by him, and a plea for the vindication which he merits (cf. 12.3).

This disposes of two types of exegesis of vv. 17f.:

(*a*) That of Baumgartner and Rudolph, where a reference to doom for Judah is seen in v. 16, but where יום רעה (v. 17) is explained in connection with Jeremiah and his enemies. It is no longer necessary to say with Baumgartner that vv. 17f. betray a different mood from v. 16—a consideration which moved Cornill and Duhm to delete v. 18. Rudolph introduces the thought of a loss of patience by Jeremiah, but he also makes a distinction between Jeremiah's attitude towards the people as a whole (v. 16) and his attitude towards his enemies (v. 18). Verses 16–18 deal only with Jeremiah's personal distress (v. 16), his prayer for Yahweh's support in the midst of it (v. 17) and his call for revenge against his enemies (v. 18).

(*b*) The second type of exegesis assumes that יום אנוש and the two occurrences of יום רעה (vv.17, 18) refer to days of corporate punishment (Weiser, Berridge, Reventlow, p. 238), and this is associated with an apologetic tendency which theologizes the aspect of revenge in order to make it more respectable. It is said that Jeremiah's prayer in v. 17 is made in anticipation of a 'Day

of Judgement' and reflects his sense of insecurity and
apprehension at the prospect of an apportioning of *Heil* and
Unheil by Yahweh (Weiser, Berridge, p. 148). Against this it has
to be asserted that vv. 16–18 take place between the prophet and
his opponents and comprise only the prophet's own anguish, his
plea for help that his nerve may not break, and his prayer for
revenge. Thus Rashi connects the 'persecutors' of v. 18 with the
men of Anathoth (12.6).

The sense of 'shatter' for חתת is indicated by Pesh., Targ. and
Kimchi. The last-mentioned connects 17.17 with 1.17, where the
prophet is charged not to lose his nerve in the face of opposition.
If his nerve breaks Yahweh will break him in full view of his
enemies. Not very much hangs on the choice between 'shatter'
and 'terrorize', since both can point to this collapse of morale,
and the latter is represented by Aq. and Symm. ($\epsilon\iota\varsigma$ $\pi\tau o\eta\sigma\iota\nu$)
and Vulg. (*formidini*). The free rendering of Sept. ($\mu\grave{\eta}$ $\gamma\epsilon\nu\eta\theta\widehat{\eta}\varsigma$
$\mu o\iota$ $\epsilon\grave{\iota}\varsigma$ $\grave{\alpha}\lambda\lambda o\tau\rho\acute{\iota}\omega\sigma\iota\nu$) focuses attention on the prophet's
alienation—his prayer is that he may not suffer alienation from
Yahweh (cf. Jerome's translation of Sept., *non fias mihi
alienus*). Sept.'s rendering of מחסי אתה ביום רעה is also free
($\phi\epsilon\iota\delta\acute{o}\mu\epsilon\nu\acute{o}\varsigma$ $\mu o\upsilon$ $\grave{\epsilon}\nu$ $\grave{\eta}\mu\acute{\epsilon}\rho\alpha$ $\pi o\nu\eta\rho\widehat{\alpha}$), and Pesh. agrees so closely
that it should perhaps be regarded as dependent on Sept. for this
detail (*'l' 'gn 'ly bywm' byš'*), 'But protect me in the evil day'.
Rudolph (cf. Duhm who cites משנה עונם, 16.18) supposes that
the concept of *jus talionis* underlies משנה שברון: Jeremiah's
enemies are to suffer twice as much as the prophet has done.
Kimchi's understanding of משנה שברון is different: שברון אחר
שברון כמה פעמים, 'one blow after another without respite'. Out
of his own suffering Jeremiah prays that their suffering may be
even more intense and unrelieved.

Baumgartner (pp. 43f.) analyses vv. 14–18 as an individual
lament (v. 14, Petition; v. 15 Lament; v. 16, Theme of innocence;
v. 17, Petition and trust; v. 18, Petition and curse). He notes that
vv. 14–18 have no oracle attached to them and he raises the
question whether 17.9f. should not be positioned after v. 18 as
Yahweh's answer to Jeremiah's pleas: a refusal tempered with a
word of consolation that Yahweh sees beyond the desire for
revenge into nobler thoughts lodged in the prophet's soul.
Baumgartner, having toyed with this thought and described
vv. 9f. as less 'original' than 12.5 and 15.19ff., comes to the
conclusion that vv. 9f. are better taken in isolation as a fragment
surviving from a larger whole. Reventlow (pp. 235–240), setting
out from the premiss that 17.14–18 has the form and vocabulary
of an individual lament, proceeds by a laboured process of
exegesis to explain it as a communal lament. But does it in fact
make sense as a paradigmatic or representative individual

lament? It does not, because there is a particular, prophetic reference in v. 15 and because the medical vocabulary (vv. 14,16a) is being used metaphorically to describe a special kind of sickness. The person who prays is not a pious man stricken with bodily disease, but a prophet trembling with anguish and near to physical collapse in the face of the sorrows and contradictions of his vocation.

In 17.14–18 the prophet in a condition of bitterness and brokenness calls out for healing and for the strength to endure (vv. 14,17), however hard and cruel the circumstances of his life and vocation. His anguish is related to the scorn with which his prophecies of doom have been received (v. 15). He has not been precipitate in throwing off his allegiance to Yahweh, nor has he ceased to rely on him for guidance. He does not find a perverse kind of pleasure in being reduced to isolation and tasting rejection (v. 16a). With the renewed plea that his nerve may not break in the face of intense opposition and hostility is coupled a cry for revenge (v. 18). It is a mistake to dress this up as something theologically respectable or profound. It is to be compared with the cry for revenge in 12.3b, and if it is a mark of Jeremiah's fallibility, it also demonstrates the authenticity of his humanity. He cries that enough is enough and demands vindication. We may say without any exegetical strain, and with v. 15 in mind, that there is more involved than *amour propre* or self-gratification (cf. Kimchi, 'Bring on them the word whose fulfilment they doubted'), and that it is the calling in question of his prophetic vocation which is at the heart of his anguish; it is a confirmation of this which he principally seeks, but it is a mistake to attempt to expunge or apologize for a cry for revenge which throbs with so great suffering.

SABBATH OBSERVANCE: THE KEY TO THE FUTURE (17.19–27)

[19]These were the words of Yahweh to me: Go and stand at the People's (?) Gate[1] through which the kings of Judah go in and out, and at all the gates of Jerusalem. [20]Say unto them, Hear the words of Yahweh, kings of Judah, all you men of Judah, and all you inhabitants of Jerusalem who pass through these gates. [21]These are the words of Yahweh: You are putting your lives in danger when you carry a load on the Sabbath day and bring it through the gates of Jerusalem. [22]Do not bring any load out of your houses on the Sabbath day, nor do any work; keep the Sabbath day holy as I commanded your forefathers. [23]But they did not listen nor pay heed, and they stiffened their resolve to disobey me and refuse instruction. [24]If you will truly obey me, says Yahweh, and not bring any load through the gates of this city on the Sabbath day, keeping the Sabbath day holy and doing no work on it, [25]kings who sit on the throne of David with their courtiers will pass through the gates of this

[1] See below, pp. 415f.

city, riding in chariots or on horses, they, their courtiers, the men of Judah and the inhabitants of Jerusalem, and this city will be inhabited for ever. ²⁶People will come from the towns of Judah and from the environs of Jerusalem, from the region of Benjamin, the Shephelah, the hill-country and the Negeb, bringing whole-offerings and sacrifices, grain-offerings and frankincense, bringing thank-offerings to the House of Yahweh. ²⁷But if you refuse to listen to my demand that you keep the Sabbath day holy and refrain from carrying any load and coming through the gates of Jerusalem on the Sabbath day, I will set your gates alight, and fire not to be extinguished will devour the palaces of Jerusalem.

It appears that the Greek translators have taken שבת (v. 24) as feminine (ἐν αὐτῇ; cf. Exod 31.14), whereas the Massoretes (Q) at Jer 17.24 have indicated בו, in all probability because they regarded שבת as masculine (cf. Ehrlich, p. 288). There is, however, no need for a Q reading at v. 24, since בה = *bô* is an early orthography. Rudolph (cf. Graf and Duhm) considers that שרים (v. 25) is a corrupt dittography of ישבים (cf. Janzen, p. 133). Its deletion is also proposed by Weiser and NEB (Brockington, p. 205), but there is no versional support for it. Rudolph's objection to MT is that שרים do not sit on the throne of David, but this can be circumvented by supposing that what is intended is kings with their retinue of שרים. In v. 26 the main codices of Sept. read καὶ θυσίαν καὶ θυμιάματα, apparently a double rendering of וזבח. The reading in Sept.ᴼᴸ (see Ziegler) is καὶ θυμιάματα, and Ziegler supposes that the original text was καὶ θύματα of which καὶ θυμιάματα ('and incense') is a corruption and καὶ θυσίαν a doublet. Ziegler (*Beiträge*, pp. 103f.) has turned the argument on its head: if the Greek translator of the book of Jeremiah elsewhere uses θυσία to render זבח, there is reason for urging the originality of καὶ θυσίαν, and Janzen's view (pp. 202f.) that καὶ θυμιάματα is a doublet deriving from a rendering of וזבח as καὶ θύματα is probably correct. Since θυμίαμα/θυμιάματα does not appear in Sept. as a rendering of מנחה, the possibility that καὶ θυμιάματα is an alternative to the transcription καὶ μαναα (so Ziegler) can be dismissed.

In v. 27 Sept. has supposed that לבלתי is also operative with ובא (καὶ μὴ εἰσπορεύεσθαι; also Vulg. *et ne inferatis*; cf. Pesh. *dl' tšqlwn šqwlt' wt'lwn*). There is a difference of sense between MT and Pesh., on the one hand, and Sept. and Vulg. on the other. According to Sept. and Vulg. the intention is to make two separate prohibitions: (*a*) Not to carry loads on the Sabbath (*b*) Not to pass through the gates of Jerusalem on the Sabbath. What is intended (so MT and Pesh.) is rather 'by refraining from carrying loads into Jerusalem through its gates on the Sabbath'.

The identity of שער בני עם (K) or שער בני העם (Q), if a

particular gate is intended, is not known (v. 19). NEB (following
Ehrlich, p. 288) emends to שער בנימין (Brockington, p. 205),
'Benjamin Gate', which is mentioned at 37.13 and 38.7 and
which was presumably a gate on the north side of Jerusalem.
Rudolph notices that the intention of Sept. is to indicate (ἐν ταῖς
πύλαις υἱῶν λαοῦ σου) that no particular gate is identified:
'Stand (in turn) at (all the gates) that the people go in and out.'
The difficulty of this is that καὶ ἐν πάσαις ταῖς πύλαις
Ιερουσαλημ is made redundant (cf. Weiser, p. 150, n. 1, who
suggests that ובכל שערי ירושלם may be later expansion).
Weiser, however, inclines to the view that the further reference
to כל שערי ירושלם is explained by the circumstance that שער
בני העם is a gate of the temple (p. 143, n. 4) and both he and
Rudolph suggest that in this case 'The Lay Gate' is indicated by
the expression שער בני העם. Duhm considers the possibility that
there is a reference to a temple gate which was used by kings and
commoners, but not by priests, but he concludes that שער בני
העם is more probably a gate giving access to the royal residence
from the city. The vagueness of the expression is one of the
evidences of *Schreibtischarbeit* which Volz finds in vv. 19–27,
and the concentration on Sabbath observance has led other
scholars to conclude that the passage is late and probably
post-exilic (Giesebrecht, Duhm, Cornill, Ehrlich, p. 288).

One element in Kimchi's exegesis, that the king had a special
responsibility for Sabbath observance and that it was right
(ראוי) for him to reprove the people, is taken up both by
Rudolph and Weiser. The latter predictably draws the passage
into the context of a Jerusalem temple 'Covenant Festival', and
his view that שער בני העם is a temple gate fits in with this
interpretation. Verse 20 is then a reference to a gathering of king
and people on the occasion of a 'Covenant Festival' and the
hypothesis is supported by the presence of a clause of the
Decalogue (v. 22, וכל מלאכה לא תעשו). Weiser further supposes
that the splendour of a royal, festal entry, with the inhabitants of
Jerusalem and Judah participating in the rites of a festival, is
described in v. 25, and that v. 26 is a further development of this
portrayal, betraying a later point of view (see further below).

How is this passage to be critically assessed and does it have
any connection with the life and times of the prophet Jeremiah?
This question has been answered in literary-critical terms by
Rudolph and Thiel, and in form-critical terms by Weippert and
Nicholson. Rudolph's view is that the style is
Deuteronomic/Deuteronomistic and that the verbose nature of
the prose is shown by the repetition of vv. 21b/22 in v. 24 and
v. 27. Rudolph allocates vv. 19–27 to his Source C and finds
verbal correspondences between it and passages attributed to the

same source. 17.19–27 was seen by the redactor as a good illustration of the allegation in 16.11ff. that Israel did not keep the law. Rudolph supposes that an authentic word of the prophet Jeremiah has been preserved in this passage (so also Weiser and Bright), although it has been supplemented in an unhistorical way. Jeremiah saw in the desecration of the Sabbath a symptom of disobedience and hardness of heart, and this has been developed in the light of the fulfilment of the threat which the prophet attached to disobedience.

Thiel (p. 209) suggests that the connection of vv. 19–27 is rather with the sin which is said to be chiselled on the heart of the people (17.1–4), and he suggests that vv. 5–18 may be a post-Deuteronomistic insertion. His final position is, however, agnostic—the question about the principle of connection envisaged by the redactor must remain undecided. The circumstance that the demand for Sabbath observance is contained in the Decalogue (Exod 20.8–11; Deut 5.12–15), or that a reference in the book of Amos (8.5) shows that Sabbath observance was required in the eighth century B.C. has too general a character to carry an argument in favour of the Jeremianic origin of vv. 19–27. Even Weippert, who on form-critical grounds would argue that proclamation with the structure of 17.19–27 is Jeremianic (p. 103), is not disposed to press the argument in the case of this particular passage (p. 234, n. 31). Her doubts about the Jeremianic origin of the passage derive from its contents and from the manner in which the demand for Sabbath observance is made. Nicholson (*Preaching to the Exiles*, pp. 65f.) is also concerned with the paranetic pattern of vv. 19–27, but he urges (*pace* Weippert) that this pattern is an indication of Deuteronomistic provenance.

Thiel (p. 204) is to be followed in his dissociating of 17.19–27 from the prophet Jeremiah, and little weight attaches to Weiser's argument that the reference to 'kings' is evidence of a pre-exilic background. The circumstance that the author wishes to represent that the words were spoken by the prophet, and is therefore bound to create an appropriate pre-exilic setting, should not be mistaken for an argument in support of the pre-exilic date of the passage. The hypothesis that the passage is exilic (Thiel; also Nicholson) rather than post-exilic is, however, uneconomical. The only piece of first-class evidence bearing on the age of Jer 17.19–27 is Neh 13.15ff., where a similar conflict of Sabbath observance and commercial interests is indicated. Nehemiah protected the Sabbath against the inroads of commerce by closing the gates of Jerusalem and preventing imports from reaching the market in the city. The issue of Sabbath observance comes to a point in the same way in both passages: the demand is made that all commercial activity should cease on the Sabbath day, and the most economical hypothesis is that both passages arise out of what was regarded as a crucial application of the Sabbath commandment in the post-exilic Jewish community.

Thiel holds (pp. 208f.) that the form of 17.19–27 (a sermon incorporating 'alternatives') is characteristic of the Deuteronomistic redactor of the book of Jeremiah (7.1–15 and 22.1–5 are similarly constructed), and asserts that the work of this redactor is to be located in the exilic period. Thiel's exclusion of the possibility of a post-exilic setting turns on his confidence that a clear distinction can be drawn between exilic and post-exilic Deuteronomistic vocabulary. He is therefore driven to postulate that an issue of Sabbath observance which we know to have existed in post-exilic Jerusalem also existed in exilic Jerusalem. There is a double disadvantage in this procedure: there is the substitution of two explanations for a single one, and there is the improbable assertion that Nehemiah's Sabbatarianism does not derive from Babylonian Jewry. From this point of view Nicholson's exilic hypothesis labours under less grievous disadvantages, since he envisages that the Deuteronomistic editors were at work in Babylon and that 17.19–27 reflects the enhanced importance of the Sabbath among the Jews in Babylon rather than in the post-exilic Jerusalem community.

Both Rudolph and Thiel (pp. 205f.) maintain that vv. 25f. contain a promise of restoration: what is envisaged as having been the normal conditions of life in pre-exilic Judah will be restored. The kings will go in and out with a proper ceremonial dignity, and the regular trading operations on which the prosperity of city and countryside depends will be developed without let or hindrance. The future welfare of the community hangs on the observance of the Sabbath. If we allow the exegesis to be dominated by the pre-exilic dress, we necessarily conclude that the passage has a backward-looking character. If, however, we also assert (and this is the position of those who argue for a setting in Jerusalem during the exilic period, or an exilic, Babylonian setting, or a post-exilic Jerusalem setting) that the passage has no historical contact with pre-exilic Jerusalem, it is a reasonable assumption that, in spite of the pre-exilic dress, the portrayal is a way of looking forward rather than looking back; that the promise is not merely that the conditions of life in pre-exilic Judah will be restored, and that the intention is to confront a Jewish community with live alternatives of promise and threat. The promise is not entirely a reversion to the past (Rudolph), and the threat is not to be dissolved into an *aition* of what has already taken place (Thiel). More allowance should be made for the splendour of an eschatological consummation (a Messianic Age) in v. 25, even if it is the protocol of the pre-exilic Judaean court, and the way in which royal processions were organized in that context, which dominates the description.

If the passage is exilic or post-exilic, and is not merely antiquarian in its interest, the point of the composition is the future of the community from which it issues. The conclusion to be drawn is that the passage reflects the importance attached to the Sabbath commandment in the post-exilic Jerusalem community and the belief that its future depended on whether or not it kept the Sabbath. A more splendid realization of the promise of restoration than has yet obtained is looked for. The emphasis which is laid on a proper provision for the Jerusalem cult (v. 26) accords with the thought in Haggai and Malachi that the failure to establish a pure cult and to maintain it in an open-handed way was an obstruction to the great change in the fortunes of the community which had been promised by Deutero-Isaiah. At any rate, in agreement with prophecy from Ezekiel on, hope for the future is centred in Jerusalem. It has a Messianic or Davidic ingredient, and the consummation which is accessible to the people if the Sabbath is kept will be presided over by kings of the House of David. If the Sabbath is not kept and commercial considerations take precedence over what is regarded as the most fundamental of all the commandments (cf. Kimchi, above, p. 416), the community is doomed to destruction.

CHAPTER XVIII

JEREMIAH IN THE POTTER'S HOUSE (18.1–6)

¹This was the message which came to Jeremiah from Yahweh: ²Make your
way to the house of the potter and there I will make my words known to you.
³So I went to the house of the potter and he was working there at his wheel.
⁴When a pot which he was making out of the clay did not turn out right, he
would make another pot, doing what seemed right to him. ⁵Then Yahweh's
word came to me: ⁶Can I not do to you, House of Israel, says Yahweh, what
this potter does to the clay? Like clay in the potter's hands, so are you in my
hands, House of Israel.

The lack of accord between the superscription with its 3rd person
reference (אל ירמיהו) and the indications of a direct address to
Jeremiah (דברי, v. 2; וארד, v. 3; אלי, v. 5) has been noted by
Rudolph and Thiel (pp. 210ff.). For Rudolph the superscription
is an indication of Source C (הדבר אשר היה אל ירמיהו מאת
יהוה לאמר), while Thiel supposes that it is a mark of the
Deuteronomistic redactor of the book of Jeremiah (cf. 7.1; 11.1)
and has replaced an original כה אמר יהוה אלי. The unevenness in
vv. 2, 3, 5 is explained by Rudolph on the assumption that the
Deuteronomic editor, to whom he assigns vv. 1–12, has made use
of an autobiographical piece by Jeremiah. Thiel argues that
vv. 1–6, which are autobiographical and attributable to the
prophet Jeremiah, are to be distinguished from vv. 7–12 which
consist of a Deuteronomistic redaction (see further below).

Janzen (pp. 74, 98f.) supposes that v. 4 (MT) has been
supplemented by בחמר and היוצר from v. 6 and that the original
Hebrew text of v. 4 (בעיניו ; בידו) is indicated by Sept. (pace
Volz). This is partly supported by Vulg. (manibus suis; oculis
eius) which, however, does represent בחמר (e luto).

The nature of the potter's tool, described by MT as 'the two
wheels' (v. 3) is not elucidated by the versions. Sept. apparently
read הָאֲבָנִים (ἐπὶ τῶν λίθων), while επι του οργανου (Aq.,
Symm. and Theod.) and super rotam (Vulg.) are no doubt
simplifications which are indicative of the difficulty caused by
עַל הָאֲבָנִים. The explanation of the dual האבנים given by Bright
('Two stone wheels on a vertical axle, the lower of which was
spun by the feet') appears in Blayney, with an allusion to Ecclus.
38.29f.:

$$\kappa\alpha\grave{\iota}\ \sigma\upsilon\sigma\tau\rho\acute{\epsilon}\phi\omega\nu\ \grave{\epsilon}\nu\ \pi\sigma\acute{o}\nu\ \alpha\grave{\upsilon}\tau\sigma\hat{\upsilon}\ T\rho\sigma\chi\acute{o}\nu$$
$$\grave{\epsilon}\nu\ \beta\rho\alpha\chi\acute{\iota}\sigma\nu\iota\ \alpha\grave{\upsilon}\tau\sigma\hat{\upsilon}\ \tau\upsilon\pi\acute{\omega}\sigma\epsilon\iota\ \pi\eta\lambda\acute{o}\nu$$

One wheel operated by the foot rotates the other wheel on which
the potter works the clay. The view that the verbs in v. 4 are
iterative (Rudolph, Bright) finds expression in NEB. This

understanding of the matter is not shared by the Greek and Latin translators (Sept. διέπεσε and ἐποίησεν; Vulg. *dissipatum est* and *fecit*), but it is perhaps assumed in Kimchi's exegesis, 'The potter makes one vessel after another and the second does not resemble the first; so I am shaping for you evil after evil.'

The exegesis of vv. 1–6 hinges on v. 4 and the adoption of כחמר (Rudolph, Weiser, Bright and Thiel, p. 214, n. 13) is a factor which is particularly influential in the case of Bright who renders כחמר ביד היוצר by 'as clay sometimes will in the potter's hand' and assumes that the interpretation turns on the quality of clay with which the potter is working. His craftsmanship may be frustrated by an inferior piece of clay. This leads to the same kind of exegetical conclusion (the rejection of Judah) as Thiel's assumption (p. 214) that the rejection of the first vessel is a final one and that the clay from which it was made is not re-used for the subsequent, flawless pot. Opposed to this is Calvin's view (adopted by Rudolph) that the clay which constituted the imperfect pot is used again to make a perfect one. Ehrlich (p. 289) has noticed that ב is used to indicate the material out of which a product is made (Exod 38.8; 1 Kgs 15.22), and so בחמר means 'out of clay' (cf. NEB). This explanation should be accepted and בחמר should be regarded as superior to כחמר (some Hebrew manuscripts), the latter betraying the influence of v. 6. The outcome of this discussion is inconclusive: v. 4 could mean that, when a finished pot does not satisfy the potter's standards of craftsmanship, he destroys the form of the object which he has created and reduces it to a formless lump of clay from which he makes another pot. The other meaning, less obvious grammatically, is that the re-use of the clay does not enter into the representation which turns on the replacement of a flawed pot, which is finally rejected, with a flawless pot.

Rudolph's view is that the interpretation of 18.1–4 hinges simply on Yahweh's power of sovereign disposal and that it should not lean either towards renewal or destruction. Verses 7–12 are then a further working-out of this theme of Yahweh's sovereignty, since, on Rudoph's view, vv. 1–12 constitute a unified Deuteronomic composition. Similarly Weiser's understanding of vv. 1–6 is influenced by his persuasion that vv. 1–11 make up a unit which is attributable to the prophet Jeremiah. He takes up Rudolph's thought of Yahweh's sovereignty and unaccountability, but he finds the significance of Jeremiah's encounter with the potter in the prophet's rediscovery of his sense of vocation.

According to Gen 2.7 Yahweh as creator shapes (יצר) man from the dust of the earth, and it is likely that Yahweh's creative activity as described in that verse is envisaged on the model of a potter's command over the clay with which he works. If, however, vv. 1–6 are regarded as a self-contained unit and are not held in connection with vv. 7–12, an examination of the imagery of vv. 1–4 raises other considerations. May's view (*JBL* 61, 1942, p. 144) is that in vv. 1–5 Jeremiah's Deuteronomic biographer is reproducing his source without change, while in vv. 6–12 he is 'paraphrasing or revising in his own unique style and in accordance with his preconceived ideologies'. I assume that May intended the 'original' parable to be vv. 1–4; although he says vv. 1–5, the separation of v. 5 from v. 6 is obviously indefensible. Even so, vv. 5f., whether or not they are an 'original' interpretation of vv. 1–4, are more closely connected with these verses than they are with vv. 7ff.: the sense of a lack of intrinsic connection with what precedes is felt more strongly at v. 7 than at v. 5. The interpretation contained in v. 6 does not, however, supply an interpretation of the imagery in vv. 1–4, but simply establishes a general analogy between the activity of the potter and the activity of Yahweh (cf. Duhm who regards it as trivial and infantile).

The imagery of vv. 1–4 can point either to re-creation or to destruction. Judah is like clay in the hands of the potter: she has not hardened into final apostasy and incorrigibility. The remaking of the defective pot was possible because of the plasticity of the clay, and Judah can be reshaped according to Yahweh's purpose into a community which will command his approval (Cornill, Nicholson). It is not clear that כאשר ישר בעיניו לעשות or כאשר ישר היוצר לעשות lends particular support to this interpretation. This could be claimed if these words were taken as a reference to the perfectionism of the potter or to his aesthetic satisfaction with a perfect pot. What, however, may rather be indicated is the sovereignty of the potter over the clay (cf. Pesh. *'yk dsb'*). Since ישר בעיני can mean both 'approval' and 'choice' in Biblical Hebrew, the first-mentioned nuance cannot be entirely excluded from 18.4, and a passage like Judg 14.3 shows that it may be difficult to decide between 'approval' and 'choice': Delilah was right for Samson or she was the wife of his choice (היא ישרה בעיני). The actual form of the words in 18.4 should be attended to: כאשר ישר בעיני היוצר לעשות suggests the potter's freedom in disposing of the clay as he will, rather than his aesthetic pleasure in the contemplation of a perfect pot.

The second interpretation of vv. 1–6, adopted by Thiel, does not follow the more obvious construction of the grammar, but should, nevertheless, be regarded as probably correct. On this view vv. 1–4 portend the rejection and destruction of Judah (בית ישראל), and the emphasis falls on אחר (v. 4). The meaning of vv. 1–6 is then that Judah has been finally cast off by Yahweh, and the discarding of the defective pot signifies *Vernichtung* (Thiel). Thus vv. 1–6 are to be regarded as a parabolic proclamation of doom (כלה) and at least vv. 1–4 are to be attributed to the prophet Jeremiah. Verses 7–12 are then to be seen as a Deuteronomic/Deuteronomistic development and modification of this message of unqualified doom.

NEITHER WEAL NOR DOOM IS IMMUTABLE (18.7–12)

⁷At one time I might threaten to uproot, smash and destroy a nation or kingdom, ⁸but if that nation should turn from its wickedness,¹ I would recall the disaster which I had planned to bring on it. ⁹At another time I might promise to build or plant a nation or kingdom, ¹⁰but if it did what I regard as evil and disobeyed me, I would recall the good which I had promised to do to it. ¹¹And now, you are to say to the men of Judah and the inhabitants of Jerusalem: These are the words of Yahweh: I am shaping disaster which will fall on you and fashioning plans against you. Turn, every man of you, from his evil way and amend your ways and deeds. ¹²But they answer, It is hopeless! We must pursue our own plans and each of us must follow his own wilful and evil inclinations.

There is little to be said in favour of arguments for the original unity of vv. 1–12. Rudolph supposes that this unity is one which has been created by a Deuteronomic editor, but the form of vv. 2–5 (a dialogue between Yahweh and the prophet Jeremiah) inclines him to the view that an autobiographical piece attributable to the prophet has been incorporated in vv. 1–12. Even on the foundation of his interpretation of v. 4 (p. 125) Bright has not demonstrated convincingly the unity of vv. 1–12. The correlation of quality of clay with right attitude of mind is not obviously appropriate: apostasy has to be equated with bad clay and repentance with good clay, and this is an interpretation which is forced and which is too patently a device for achieving the unity of vv. 1–12.

Weippert (pp. 48–67) notes that vv. 1–12 have been divided into vv. 1–6 and 7–12 by Erbt, May, Hyatt, Thiel, and that vv. 1–12 have been denied to the prophet Jeremiah by Duhm, Hyatt and Rudolph (see, however, above on Rudolph). She holds that vv. 1–12 are Jeremianic and that they form a unity. An important consideration for her is the play in v. 11 on the occurrences of היוצר in vv. 1–6. She also supposes that there is an element of symbolic action in vv. 1–6 and that this contributes to the case for the unity of vv. 1–12. In evaluating אנכי יוצר (v. 11) she takes account of the gap between the imagery (vv. 1–6) and its application in v. 11, but does not think that this

¹ Deleting אשר דברתי עליו (see below, p. 427).

seriously weakens the comparison of יוצר — היוצר with שֶׁקֶר — שֶׁקֶר in 1.11f. (p. 54 n. 1). Her examination of the vocabulary in vv. 7–12 has the aim of proving that it is not Deuteronomic/Deuteronomistic in provenance. She rejects the view that the alternatives which are formulated in vv. 7–10 can be identified as having a Deuteronomic/Deuteronomistic literary and theological stamp. She urges that the posing of alternatives in relation to courses of behaviour and their consequences corresponds to a characteristic mode of human thinking which has deep structural causes.

The appropriateness of invoking symbolic action in order to support the Jeremianic provenance of vv. 1–12 is dubious. To suggest such an affinity to symbolic action and to feel it necessary to say in the next breath that it is the potter who acts and the prophet who observes is an indication of the weakness of the argument which is being conducted. If the prophet does not himself act symbolically, what is the point in introducing the consideration of symbolic action? We have to reckon rather with the same triggering of prophetic sensitivity and insight as is indicated by the almond branch and the cauldron in Jer 1.11–15.

Weippert's account of vv. 7–10 is also laboured and unconvincing. The resemblance between these verses and the Nathan parable is difficult to detect, and the view that they represent a secondary theorizing is hard to resist. She has shown that the vocabulary in vv. 7–10 is not found in Deuteronomic/Deuteronomistic literature, but the great leap which she takes from this position to her final conclusion is well shown by her treatment of רעה and טובה (vv. 8, 10). This is very general vocabulary, but she urges that it is derived from 'prophetic tradition' and that it serves to interpret the metaphorical infinitives: לנתוש ולנתוץ ולהאביד are interpreted by רעה and לבנת ולנטע by טובה. This relatedness of nouns and verbs demonstrates that both the series of infinitives and the nouns רעה and טובה reflect the linguistic habits of the prophet Jeremiah (pp. 203–209; cf. Berridge, pp. 57ff.). This is an unacceptable conclusion. It is one thing to make factual observations about the absence of vocabulary from Deuteronomic/Deuteronomistic literature; it is an entirely different matter to establish a particular connection between this prose and the prophet Jeremiah, and Weippert's arguments are incapable of achieving the latter objective.

Verses 1–12 are not to be regarded as a unity (agreeing with Thiel, pp. 210–218; cf. Nicholson). Thiel's division of the passage into three parts (vv. 1–6; 7–10; 11–12) should be accepted, but v. 12 should be regarded as secondary (so Weiser). Thiel notes that the verses are addressed to different parties:

vv. 1–6 to the prophet Jeremiah, with a message (v. 6) for בית
ישראל; vv. 7–10 to גוי and ממלכה, and vv. 11f. to איש יהודה and
יושבי ירושלם. The centre of exegetical concern should be (so
Thiel) how the parts of vv. 1–12 relate with each other, rather
than whether the passage is Jeremianic or non-Jeremianic. On
this latter matter Thiel is to be followed: vv. 1–6 (or, at least,
vv. 1–4) are Jeremianic and signify doom for Judah (see above,
pp. 422f.), whereas vv. 7–12 are to be understood as a later
qualification and amplification of vv. 1–6 and are not to be
assigned to the prophet Jeremiah. Thiel holds that the
formulation of alternatives in vv. 7–10 is an indication of exilic,
Deuteronomistic provenance (cf. above, p. 424). The possibility
of repentance is envisaged as open to all peoples and Yahweh can
revise his intention to judge and destroy. According to Thiel this
means no less than that every nation can participate in Yahweh's
plan of salvation, and the reference to a nation winning
Yahweh's approval must be interpreted in terms of the keeping
of the Law.

The main misgiving to be expressed in relation to this account
is that Thiel has attempted a too particular exegesis of vv. 7–10
and has not allowed sufficiently for its hypothetical and
theoretical character. It is unlikely that it reflects a deep concern
for the destiny of the Gentile world, or that the possibility of
particular, historical nations keeping the Law and thereby
commending themselves to Yahweh is a serious part of it. It
represents rather the construction of a hypothetical case, but the
only particular application which is envisaged is to the Jews
themselves.

Otherwise, what is surprising in both Weippert and Thiel is
that they have produced an argument for the relatedness of
vv. 1–6 and v. 11, but have not followed it up. If יוצר in v. 11 is a
play on היוצר in vv. 1–6, the distance between v. 11 and the
nearest, preceding occurrence of היוצר (v. 6) is a matter which
should awaken curiosity and raise questions (cf. Kimchi who
glosses יוצר in v. 11 with מחרש and who says, 'He uses this as a
deliberate allusion to the paragraph of the potter', that is,
vv. 1–6). The conclusion which should be drawn is that v. 11 was
originally contiguous with v. 6 and has been separated from the
latter by the later insertion of vv. 7–10.

To the unit vv. 1–6, which is probably to be attributed to the
prophet Jeremiah and which proclaims unconditional doom for
Judah, v. 11 was added as an exegetical modification involving a
play on היוצר. This verse, as Thiel has noticed, explains בית
ישראל (v. 6) as 'men of Judah' and 'inhabitants of Jerusalem',
and it has the form of a word from Yahweh to Jeremiah which
the prophet is instructed to convey to the community. The

message is that Yahweh is fashioning or shaping (יוֹצֵר) doom for
his people, that he is planning their destruction, but that they
may be saved if they repent and amend their way of life. Thus
the 'shaping' activity of the potter is associated with the shaping
of plans by Yahweh, but the significant, theological modification
is the attachment of a saving clause, and the opening up of the
possibility of repentance and escape from doom.

However indecisive may be the indications gathered from the
vocabulary in vv. 7–11, there can be little doubt that they
embody Deuteronomic theology, and that their view of the office
of prophet conforms to the Deuteronomic typology, with its
emphasis on his intercessory function and his concern to call for
repentance and amendment of life (see above, pp. 324, 333).
Thus the theological modification achieved by v. 11 over against
vv. 1–6 has an unmistakeable Deuteronomic/Deuteronomistic
stamp. Nor is there any doubt that the connection between
vv. 1–6 and v. 11 is more apparent than the connection between
vv. 1–6 and vv. 7–10. The conclusion to be drawn is that vv. 7–10
represent a later theorizing and a drawing out of the crucial
function of repentance in the Deuteronomic scheme. It may be
(as Thiel has supposed) that the Deuteronomic exegete intended
vv. 7–10 as an explanation of the potter model in vv. 1–6 and for
this reason made these verses contiguous with vv. 1–6. Bright's
exegesis of vv. 1–6 (the potter's results depends on the quality of
the clay which he uses) accords with what Thiel takes to have
been the Deuteronomistic intention in vv. 7–10. But vv. 7–10 are
not fitted for the function of interpreting a parable: they amount
to a general, theological statement, with a carefully contrived
structure, and they have too abstract an aspect to entitle them to
be considered seriously as an interpretation of the parable of the
potter and his clay. They represent a process of theological
reflection which takes off from the more particular v. 11 which,
although it too is a secondary exegetical modification of vv. 1–6,
connects more credibly with these verses than do vv. 7–10.

Verse 12 is a subsequent and inferior addition to v. 11:
whether it was made before or after v. 11 was separated from
v. 6 by the interposition of vv. 7–10 cannot be determined. נוֹאָשׁ
was a source of difficulty here to the versions as it was at 2.25.
The correct sense of נוֹאָשׁ is indicated by Aq. (απηλπισται),
Symm. (εξεκακησαμεν), Vulg. (desperavimus) and Kimchi,
'When you say this to them, they will reply to you נוֹאָשׁ, that is,
our hearts are too full of despair to follow Yahweh'. Verse 12 is a
patchwork which has the marks of inferior imitation and whose
purpose (cf. Weiser and Thiel) is to establish that the invitation
to repent has been rejected and so to build a bridge to vv. 13–17.
The first part of the verse echoes 2.25 (נוֹאָשׁ לוֹא כִּי אָהַבְתִּי זָרִים)

ואחריהם אלך) and the second part (ואיש שררות לבו הרע נעשה)
utilizes a word-string which is found in several places in the
prose of the book of Jeremiah (3.17; 7.24; 9.13; 11.8; 13.10;
16.12), once in poetry in the same book (23.17) and once in the
book of Deuteronomy (29.18). In all the other Jeremiah passages
except 16.12 (second person), the word-string is used in
connection with third person description, and only here (18.12)
and in Deut 29.18 in connection with words put into the mouth
of the people.

The only textual point of substance which remains to be
discussed is the Hebrew text of v. 8: אשר דברתי עליו is not
represented by Sept. and Pesh. (cf. Janzen, p. 40). There is no
doubt that the text of MT is unsatisfactory; the difficulty is that
רעתו in ושב הגוי ההוא מרעתו can mean only 'its wrong-doing',
whereas the sense of רעה which is required as the antecedent of
אשר in the clause אשר דברתי עליו is 'disaster' or 'doom'. In all
the circumstances the shorter text indicated by Sept. and Pesh. is
the better one. NEB overcomes the difficulty by the dubious
grammatical expedient of treating הגוי rather than רעתו as the
antecedent of אשר: 'But if the nation which I have threatened
turns back from its wicked ways'.

Finally there is the question whether Weiser's literalism
makes any theological contribution to what the word 'hears'
means in such a context as this or to the elucidation of 'word of
God'. Rudolph's urge to explore the moment of revelation and to
interiorize and humanize it is an inescapable theological task. A
commentary is not the right genre for a full treatment of a
theology of prophecy, but something ought to be said at this
point. We cannot simply be content with a pedestrian application
of language in a transaction between man and God. Language
can achieve no more than an analogical account of the mystery:
the verbalization is a 'translation' or 'transmutation' of an
encounter with God. Because we read that Yahweh commanded
the prophet to go to a potter's house in order to hear his word, we
are not to conclude that there is a simple correspondence
between the verbalization of the encounter with God and the
mysterious experience itself (as Weiser supposes). We cannot be
content with an external 'talking' God as the terminus of our
understanding of revelation and 'word of God'. Hence Rudolph's
approach is in principle the right one: the observation in the
potter's shop is an ordinary, everyday one, but it takes on the
aspect of a parable and it is concentrated in a point of light so
brilliant that it is appropriated by the prophet as 'word of God'.
The words which the prophet uses to express this overwhelming
conviction that he has encountered God and truth are human
words, spoken by a man to men, in the language which only men

speak. God does not speak in Hebrew or in any other language. The internalizing and humanizing of the encounter with God is implied in its reduction to language—is an inescapable consequence of its reduction to language. The only alternative to this linguistic and humanizing transmutation is an ineffable, unspeakable encounter with God—a relapse into silence and speechlessness.

THE INEXPLICABLE CHOICE OF DEATH (18.13–17)

[13]Therefore these are the words of Yahweh:
Enquire if you will among the nations!
Who has ever heard the like of this?
The virgin Israel has done a most horrible thing!
[14]Does the snow ever disappear from the rocky slopes of the Lebanon?
Do cool waters flowing from a distant source ever fail?[1]
[15]My people have forgotten me;
they have offered sacrifices to idols—
idols which make them stumble while they tread the old paths;
so they venture on to (new) tracks and unmade roads,
[16]making their own land an object which appals,
a spectacle at which men for ever after whistle in horror,
at which all travellers are appalled,
shaking their heads at its awfulness.
[17]I will scatter them as an east wind would,
dispersing them before their enemies.
I will show them[2] my back not my face
in the day when disaster falls on them.

The inexplicable character of Israel's apostasy is emphasized in 18.13 as in 2.10–13 by introducing a reference to other nations, but the topic is not developed in that direction as it was in the earlier passage. Nothing more is said than that enquiries should be made in other countries to discover whether there are any parallels to Israel's apostasy. The implication of this is that her pattern of behaviour is strange by any human standards and is inexplicable. The theme is illustrated not by comparing Israel's religious habits with those of her neighbours, as in 2.10–13, but by rhetorical questions directed towards certain unchanging aspects of nature (v. 14). These are questions which demand a negative answer (so Duhm), and their function is to underline the unthinkability of any inconstancy or wayward unpredictability in these processes, and by this device to throw into strong relief the chaotic and horrible elements in Israel's behaviour. What she has done is not only irrational and detrimental to her own well-being, but is also behaviour which

---

[1] Reading יִנָּשְׁתוּ (see below, p. 429).
[2] Reading אַרְאֵם (see below, p. 434).

awakens a shudder of horror (שַׁעֲרֻרִת), just as the sight of a
devastated land or of the idolatry of Jerusalem prophets awakens
שַׁעֲרוּרָה (5.30; 23.14). Even Yahweh himself is represented as
feeling this tingle of horror as he contemplates how Israel has
behaved.

In v. 14 Calvin and KJV suppose that there is a reference to
melting snow and waters descending from the heights of
Lebanon (similarly Ehrlich, p. 289, with הִיעָזֹב emended to
היכזב). KJV ('cold flowing waters that come from another
place') is explained by Lowth as a reference to 'waters conveyed
in pipes or conduits for common use'. Duhm deals with v. 14a by
emending שדי to שריון (Cornill) and מצור to כפור: 'Does frost
ever forsake Sirion or snow Lebanon?' Sirion (Hermon), as the
highest peak of the Anti-Lebanon range, is the match for
Lebanon.

The least obscure part of v. 14a is שלג לבנון and it is
surprising that Rudolph and NEB have disturbed this phrase in
the process of emending the line. NEB has transposed לבנון to
make it follow מצור and has pointed שדי as שָׂדַי ('fall'?): 'Will
the snow cease to fall on the rocky slopes of Lebanon?'
(Brockington, p. 206). Rudolph emends הִיעָזֹב to הֲיֵעָבֵר (Volz)
and constructs מצור שריון out of מצור שדי with the help of the ון
ending of לבנון and on the assumption that ר has been corrupted
into ד: 'Does the white snow (שלג לבן) disappear from the rocks
of Sirion?' Another possibility indicated by W. F. Albright
(*HUCA* 23, 1950/1951, pp. 23f.), Bright, M. J. Dahood (*ZAW*
74, 1962, pp. 207–209) and BHS is that צור should be read as
צור and the line translated: 'Will flints forsake the fields or the
snow Lebanon?' Albright and BHS emend מצור to צור, while
Dahood attaches *mem* to הִיעָזֹב as an enclitic. The first part of
the line is then a reference to pieces of flint strewn on the surface
of the fields in the Palestine hill country—as permanent a
feature of the landscape as the snow of Lebanon.

In v. 14b the most obvious difficulty resides in ינתשו, since 'be
uprooted' does not give the sense which is needed, but the
word-string מים זרים קרים has also been viewed with suspicion.
The adoption of ינשתו for ינתשו is generally followed (Duhm,
Ehrlich, Rudolph, Weiser, Bright, NEB, Brockington, p. 206,
Albright, L. A. Snijders, *OTS* 10, 1954, p. 48, n. 54). According
to Duhm the emendation originated with Cocceius, but I have
not been able to find it in the *Lexicon* or the *Opera*. It is not clear
whether Albright has a scribal error in mind or a variant
characterized by a metathesis of שׁ and ת (Duhm allows both
possibilities). Dahood derives ינתשו from נשה 'forget' (a form
with an infixed ת) and argues that there is contextual support for
this sense (עזב and שכח). He explains זרים in terms of זור

'press', 'cause to flow' and קרים with reference to Ugaritic *qr* 'spring: 'Or do men forget flowing waters, running springs?'

Snijders suggests that Targ. מבוע (Jer 18.14) is an indication that זרם has been read for זרים, but this does not stand up to scrutiny. זרם, however, is suggested by Rashi and may be implied by Targ. מי מטר. It has been adopted by the translators of NEB (Brockington, p. 206): 'Will cool rain streaming in torrents ever fail?' מים זרם is grammatically difficult (unless the enclitic ם is to be invoked), and the phrase which is elsewhere attested is זרם מים (Isa 28.2; Hab 3.10). To return to Snijders' point: an examination of Targ. shows that, if an attempt is to be made to correlate MT with Targ., the conclusion which must be reached is that זרים is rendered by מטר 'rain' and קרים by מי מבוע 'spring' (cf. the emendation of קרים to מְקֹרִים, and Dahood's attempt to explain קרים on the basis of Ugaritic *qr*). Snijders considers the possibility that מים קרים, 'strange waters', is a reference to water which is unusually cold as contrasted with that of rivers 'flowing through the warm lowlands'. He supposes that because זרים was taken in this sense it was glossed by קרים, and that the word-order in Pesh. (*my' qryr' nwkry'*) is an indication of the secondary character of קרים. The view which Snijders eventually reaches (p. 48 n. 54) is that זרים is to be derived from זור 'withdraw', 'deviate from', that מים זרים means 'running-away water', and that קרים is an erroneous gloss on זרים. If we consider the exegetical implications of these various ways of dealing with the text of v. 14, we find that the principal lines of interpretation are these:

(*a*) Rudolph: The form of the rhetorical question relates to the snow on the slopes of Hermon and the copious waters (מקרים נוזלים) of the Nile (ממצרים). These are permanent, natural features which are paradigms of constancy.

(*b*) Albright, Bright and Dahood: There are three paradigmatic, natural features in v. 14: the flint which is always present on the surface of the fields, the snow which caps Lebanon and the waters which flow from unfailing springs. Snijders has the second and the third of these.

(*c*) NEB: The snow is ever-present on the rocky slopes of Lebanon, and the cool, torrential rains never fail. Apart from the grammatical difficulty involved in NEB's treatment of v. 14b, which has been noticed, the thought of cool, unfailing torrential rain does not seem to be appropriate to the climatic conditions of Palestine.

It could be that 'breasts' (שדי read as שדי, Sept., Pesh., Symm.) refer to the peaks of a mountain range (cf. 'The Paps of Jura'), in which case two permanent, natural features are identified by Sept. and Pesh. in v. 14a: the configurations of the

mountains (צור = Aramaic טור = Syriac *ṭwr* and in parallelism
with לבנון) and the snows which cap Lebanon. There is little
resemblance between Sept. in v. 14b and the Hebrew text, but
ἀνέμῳ is perhaps an indication that קדים 'east wind' has been
read (cf. Rudolph) rather than קרים. ינתשו is apparently
rendered by ἐκκλινεῖ, זרים by βιαίως and נוזלים by a passive
(φερόμενον): 'Does water which is borne violently by the wind
deviate?'.

Targ. is further removed from MT: 'Just as the snow which
falls on the slopes of Lebanon will never fail, so the rain-water
which falls and the copious waters of the springs will not fail.'
מצור does not appear to be represented in Targ.'s paraphrase,
but otherwise both Vulg. and Targ. (cf. Symm.) show only one
image in v. 14a, where Sept. and Pesh. show two. It is a
temptation to make a connection, as Rashi does, between the
snow on Lebanon and the ample waters which are mentioned in
v. 14b: 'Will a man ever lack who drinks water … which comes
from the snow of Lebanon and is pure? Or will ample, living
water which has been untouched by man (= זרים) ever fail?' The
חיים נובעים (cf. Targ.) element of this exegesis probably
corresponds to קרים נוזלים — cool, fast-flowing spring-water.
The difficulty about this is that the imagery in v. 14a appears to
function not in connection with the spate of water yielded by
melting snow, but rather in relation to mountains which are
permanently capped by snow, and so to snow which does not
melt.

Kimchi like Rashi interprets on the basis of one image in
v. 14a, and like Rashi he neglects the aspect of 'snow' in that
image and concentrates on the aspect of plentiful water. The
second משל in v. 14b is thought by Kimchi (cf. Lowth) to refer
to water which has been piped underground over a long distance,
so that it might be made available to a township. It is cool and
pure and is called זרים because it comes from a strange and
distant place. נוזלים is explained as the flow of water through
pipes rather than as the flowing water of a river or spring. The
interpretation of the second משל is linked to his argument that
נתש is a variant form of נטש, so that עזיבה (v. 14a) and נתישה
(v. 14b) are synonyms, both pointing to the inexplicability of
Judah's desertion of Yahweh.

There is no doubt that the images in v. 14 deal with certain
constant features of landscape and climate, and that they
function in order to throw into high relief the irrational and
incredible character of Judah's apostasy. Thus the connection
between v. 14 and v. 15 is clear, but the details of the imagery in
v. 14 present considerable difficulty. שלג לבנון is the least
obscure part of v. 14a and no emendation which tampers with

this should be allowed (Rudolph and NEB are thus ruled out). If one is thinking of a single image in v. 14a the best that can be done is to render it, 'Does the snow ever disappear from the rocky slopes of the Lebanon?' If one thinks in terms of two images, the choice lies between Albright's proposal and the rendering of Sept. and Pesh. Albright's explanation requires the emendation of מצור to צור (cf., however, Dahood, above, p. 429), and the two permanent features are then the flint which lies on the surface of the fields and the snow on the heights of the Lebanon. The unchanging aspects of nature in v. 14a, according to Pesh. are the contours of the mountains (צור = *twr* 'mountain') and the snow on the heights of the Lebanon (cf. Sept.). The difficulty about this lies in elucidating שדי satisfactorily as 'breasts': the dual of שד 'breast' is שדים and the plural ought to be שדים. Although 'Do the paps of the mountains ever disappear or the snow of the Lebanon?' is an attractive rendering, it founders on the grammar of שדי.

If ינשתו is read in v. 14b, the principal, remaining obstacle to the elucidation of the line is מים זרים, and the only direct help which we have with this phrase is the sense which it has in 2 Kgs 19.24 (Isa 37.25 in 1QIsa[a]). There מים זרים refers to waters of foreign countries and it is on this sense of the phrase that Kimchi and Weiser build (cf. Snijders, p. 48). 'Distant waters' is perhaps the best that can be made of the image, and Rashi has something of this nuance with his thought of 'virgin waters' unspoilt by man. מים זרים are then waters from a distant source whose beginnings are touched with fascination and mystery, which come unbidden out of the unknown into a landscape which is familiar and of which they form an unfailing feature.

But Judah has done the inexplicable thing: the thought which can hardly be entertained, because of the violence which it does to rational expectations and the sense of what is fitting, has been carried into practice. Yahweh has been rejected and worship has been offered to non-gods. The main difficulties in v. 15 are these: (*a*) ויכשלום can be accommodated only if the non-gods (לשוא יקטרו) are taken as the subject and the suffix is referred to the inhabitants of Judah, 'And they made them stumble in their (established) ways, in the old paths'. (*b*) נתיבות is an imperfect parallel to דרך לא סלולה and an element corresponding to לא סלולה is desiderated. According to Vulg. and Pesh., the Israelites or the inhabitants of Judah stumble on the old ways, and both versions make the grammar easier by translating שבילי עולם or שבולי עולם as if it were בשבילי עולם (Vulg. *in semitis saecula*; Pesh. *bšbyl' d'lm*). One could argue that this is the grammar of MT and that ב functions both with דרכיהם and שבילי עולם. Otherwise, שבילי עולם is in apposition to דרכיהם (Duhm

supposes that שבילי עולם is a post-exilic gloss and that it refers
to the bad old ways—Baal worship—of pre-exilic generations).

Targ. renders ויכשלום as if it were וְאַכְשִׁלֵם, and this is adopted
by Volz and Rudolph (שבילי עולם = inveterate apostasy). Targ.
supposes that דרכיהם refers to 'evil ways' and sets up an
antithesis between these and the old paths (שבילי עולם).
According to Kimchi נביאי השקר are the מכשילים and the
grammar of v. 15b has to be filled out by construing שבילי עולם
as לעזוב שבילי עולם: 'And they (the false prophets) made them
stumble in their ways so that they forsook the old paths.'
Similarly Calvin supposes that the people are made to stumble
by false teachers. Vulg. and Pesh. indicate וַיִּכָּשְׁלוּ, and this has
been adopted by Duhm and Ehrlich (p. 289, ויכשלו מדרכיהם).
This makes the people themselves the grammatical subject and
Dahood's pointing וַיִּכְשְׁלוּם (mem enclitic) has the same effect
(ZAW 74, pp. 207–209). Thus, according to MT, it is the idols
who cause the people to stumble; according to Targ., Volz and
Rudolph (ואכשילם) Yahweh is the stumbling-block, and
according to Vulg., Pesh., Duhm, Ehrlich, BHS, the subject is
the people themselves.

MT וַיַּכְשִׁלוּם deserves careful consideration. The שבילי עולם
ought not to present obstacles to the feet or to have an irregular,
treacherous surface which makes the going difficult (cf. Prov
4.11f., 'I will guide you on the road of wisdom, I will lead you
along plain tracks. Your stride will not be cramped when you
walk, and if you run you will not stumble'). Hence it is the
baneful influence of the idols which creates obstacles on what
should be safe roads (so Lowth), and it is because of this that
these well-trodden paths with their even surfaces are forsaken
for paths which have not been made-up (cf. Aq. <οδον>
ανοδευτον 'an impassable road') and which present pot-holes and
other hazards to the traveller. This is imagery which conveys
Israel's apostasy, her 'lostness' on paths which are dangerous and
in travelling along which she is not rightly guided.

Verse 16 deals with the consequences of Judah's behaviour
and Yahweh's final threat is uttered in v. 17. There is weight in
Rudolph's point (also Weiser and Bright) that לשמה (v. 16), in
view of ישם (v. 16b), refers to the shock and horror and inner
desolation of those who see the devastated land rather than to
the devastated land itself. Of the versions only Pesh. which
renders לשמה by ltmh' and ישם by ntmh lends support to this.
There is difficulty in combining שמה meaning 'devastation' and
ישם referring to inward feelings of shock, desolation and horror,
as Rashi and Kimchi do, particularly since the adjacency of שמה
to שרוקת עולם suggests that it too refers to an emotional recoil
from a scene of devastation rather than to the devastation itself.

שרוקת (K) or שריקת (Q) is correctly rendered by Sept. (σύριγμα), Vulg. (*sibilum*) and Pesh. (*mšrwqyt'*) as 'whistling' or 'hissing', and the paraphrase of Targ. (אשתממות עלם) makes a contribution to the exegesis: the ruins will never again be rebuilt, and for ever afterwards they will be viewed by the person who passes them with a sense of shock, or, according to Symm.(?) but less probably, with a contemptuous jeer (καταγελωτα <αιωνιον>). What is envisaged here is the sharp intake of breath, the hissing through the teeth, which is an instinctive response to a spectacle of devastation. It produces a profound, inner disturbance (ישם) and external indications of deep agitation (ויניד בראשו). Rudolph, on the other hand, supposes that the whistling and the shaking of the head constitute an apotropaic ritual.

In v. 17 it is the east wind—a wind which blasts and blights and scatters—which is the figure of the dispersion that will follow Yahweh's judgement, portrayed as a military defeat (רוח קדים) (לפני אויב). is paraphrased by Sept. (καύσωνα), Vulg. (*urens*) and Pesh. (*dšwb'*) as a scorching wind. The destructive properties of the east wind are well attested: corn is blasted by it (Gen 41.6,23,27); it can destroy a fortified city (Isa 27.8); it is a destructive wind (Ezek 17.10; 19.12) which causes shipwreck (Ezek 27.26); it causes the withering of a gourd and is described as חרישית (Jon 4.8). Ephraim is destroyed by an east wind—a blast from Yahweh rising over the desert (Hos 13.15; cf. Jer 4.11; 13.24); the wicked man is lifted up and battered by the east wind (Job 27.21; cf. Jer. 4.12—the destructive power of the wind coming from the desert).

In v. 17b אֶרְאֵם, 'I will see them', has to be pointed as אַרְאֵם, 'I will show them'. This is how it has been read by the versions. Yahweh says of his people in 2.26f. כי פנו אלי ערף לוא פנים and this is indicative of their adamant refusal to respond to his appeal. Yet when disaster strikes them, it is to Yahweh that they appeal for help. Let the idols which they have made come to their help, since they are in deep distress (2.28). Such is Yahweh's rejoinder to their cry for deliverance. Similarly in 18.17 he indicates that he will reciprocate their attitude to him; he will turn his back on them and will have no regard to their cries for help as they flee from their enemies (Rashi) in a moment of defeat and disaster.

REACTION TO A PLOT AGAINST JEREMIAH (18.18–23)

[18]Come, let us lay plans against Jeremiah, they said, for the priest will never fail to instruct, nor the wise man to advise, nor the prophet to speak Yahweh's

word. Let us bring charges against him, and let us not be influenced by anything that he says.

[19]Have regard to me, O Yahweh,
attend to the charges made against me.
[20]Is good to be repaid with evil?[1]
Remember how I stood in your presence
to make a plea on their behalf,
to avert your anger from them.
[21]Therefore, consign their children to famine
and shed their blood with the sword.
May their wives be bereft of children and widowed,
may their men be mortally wounded,
their young men hacked by the sword in battle.
[22]May a cry of distress be heard from their houses,
when you bring raiders against them without warning.
They have dug a pit to trap me[2]
and have hidden snares for my feet.
[23]You know, O Yahweh,
all their plans to take my life;
do not cover over their iniquity,
nor wipe out their sin from your sight.
Let them be cast out from your presence,[3]
when your anger burns act against them.

Rudolph (cf. Duhm) has noted that according to the present, editorial disposition of the verses, the threatening words of vv. 13–17 are represented as the reason for the plot against Jeremiah described in v. 18, but neither he nor Weiser supposes that the connection between vv. 13–17 and v. 18 is original and intrinsic. The general view, shared by Rudolph and Weiser, is that vv. 18–23 constitute a firm unity, and, in particular, that v. 18 is essentially connected with vv. 19–23. Thiel (217f.) notices that v. 18 is prose and vv. 19–23 verse, he observes that the saying about priest, wise man and prophet appears in a variant form in Ezek 7.26, and he enquires whether in the present context D has taken up a stock saying and directed it towards his intention of displaying the *hubris* of Jeremiah's opponents. The resumption of נקשיבה (v. 18) by הקשיבה (v. 19), regarded by Rudolph and Weiser as a deliberate artistic device which demonstrates the integrity of vv. 18–23, is taken by Thiel as evidence of an artificial juncture, and so as a decisive indication that v. 18 was not originally joined with vv. 19–23.

Differing exegetical possibilities for v. 18 have been noted by Rudolph: (*a*) We have at our disposal recognised and authoritative sources of guidance and policy and have more than adequate resources to discredit Jeremiah's prophecies (cf. Duhm). (*b*) The falseness of Jeremiah's prophecies of doom and

---

[1] Deleting כי כרו שוחה לנפשי (see below, pp. 439f.).

[2] See below, pp. 439f.

[3] Reading מֻשְׁלָכִים מִלְּפָנֶיךָ (see below, p. 441).

the emptiness of his words are evident to us from the circumstance that they have not been fulfilled. The recognised guides of the community whom he has traduced are shown to have been right, and we should lay plans to expose and punish the prophet. The conspirators are then (so Rudolph and Weiser) probably to be identified with representatives of the three influential groups mentioned in v. 18.

On the assumption that there is no intrinsic connection between v. 18 and vv. 19–23 Thiel argues (*pace* Rudolph) that v. 18, taken by itself, says nothing about an attempt on Jeremiah's life, and he supposes that the intention of the Deuteronomistic editor is to represent as an opinion of the community that Jeremiah's prophecies of doom have not been fulfilled and that his words can be safely ignored in the future. Verse 18 is a Deuteronomistic construction of Jeremiah's isolation in his community; a portrayal of the powerful organs of authority with which he had collided and of the manner in which the people wrote him off. It is a device which provides the impetus for the bitter complaint of vv. 19–23.

In favour of Thiel's view is the circumstance that a threat to Jeremiah's life in v. 18 is explicit only if the text of Sept. and Pesh. (in separate respects) is preferred to that of MT. Thus Rudolph reads בלשונו (haplography of ו ; Pesh. *blšnh*) and deletes אל (Sept. καὶ ἀκουσόμεθα). In this he is followed by Weiser, and the Greek text is regarded sympathetically by Bright and Nicholson (cf. Ehrlich, pp. 290f., who adopts בלשונו for different reasons). If we take the text adopted by Rudolph and Weiser, with contributions from Pesh. and Sept. (ונכהו בלשונו ונקשיבה את כל דבריו) the meaning of v. 18 is that the conspirators, whoever they may be, are to listen carefully to everything that Jeremiah says in order to compile for future use against him a dossier of incriminating words. This could be construed as a threat on his life, as a gathering of evidence with a view to a future trial for sedition or blasphemy and the exaction of the death penalty. This is how the sense is developed by Weiser. It should, however, be appreciated that the versional evidence for this exegesis is unsatisfactory, since the text on which it depends is not found intact in any one version. The transformation of ודבר מנביא into ואולפן מספר in Targ. may be derived from the indications of friction and conflict between Jeremiah and the סופרים in two passages (2.8 and 8.8f.). The fragment from Qumran Cave 4 (4QJer^a) confirms MT in respect of בלשון and ואל (Janzen, p. 179).

In their interpretation of 18.18 both Rashi and Kimchi are influenced by 11.18–23. Rashi supposes that the conspirators here as at 11.21 are the villagers of Anathoth, and so he

presumably understands v. 18 as a reference to a threat against
Jeremiah's life (Kimchi states this explicitly). The latter treats
18.18–23 as a unity and associates ונחשבה על ירמיהו מחשבות
(18.18) with כי עלי חשבו מחשבות (11.19). Hence when he
explains כי כרו שוחה לנפשי (18.20) as the attempt of Jeremiah's
enemies to make him drink deadly poison, he is reverting to his
exegesis of 11.19 and is indicating that his interpretation of חשב
מחשבה is the same in 18.18 as it was in 11.19. On ונכהו בלשון
he comments, 'We shall inform against him to the king, so that
he will put him to death' (agreeing with Duhm).

The conclusion is that v. 18 is not intrinsically connected with
vv. 19–23, that v. 18 is an editorial contribution (Thiel) and that
the intention is to supply a context and an occasion for
vv. 19–23. The textual judgement of Rudolph and Weiser is
suspect: they have established an explicit threat to kill Jeremiah
by adopting separate pickings from Sept. and Pesh. MT (v. 18)
contains two resolves: (a) Let us build up a case against him, so
that we may indict him effectively—this probably constitutes a
threat to Jeremiah's life. (b) Let us not be weighed down by his
prophecies of doom. Thiel's fundamental argument is better
served by this type of exegesis than by the conclusion that a
threat to Jeremiah's life is entirely absent from v. 18. If the
Deuteronomistic editor was supplying an occasion for vv. 19–23,
he was aware that a threat to Jeremiah's life was present in these
verses (v. 20? and vv. 22f.), and the plot which he describes in
his editorial contribution ought, on Thiel's premisses, to be
interpreted in the light of the information supplied in vv. 19–23.
A closer consideration of the way in which the saying in v. 18
('Guidance will always be supplied by the priest and advice by
the wise man and the revealed word by the prophet') is exploited
suggests that Jeremiah's opponents are saying that the pillars of
the establishment stand firm and that each is secure in his own
speciality. Against Jeremiah they range a powerful coalition of
intellectual and spiritual leadership: the priest is a specialist in
תורה, the wise man in עצה and the prophet in דבר. Jeremiah is a
charlatan and should be treated accordingly. R. N. Whybray's
suggestion (BZAW 135, 1974, p. 30) that the priest, wise man
and prophet are being designated as mere talkers from whose
words no consequences flow should be compared with Ehrlich's
exegesis (p. 290).

If one ignores the 'Covenant Festival' framework of
interpretation which Weiser is always invoking, the particular
autobiographical aspects of vv. 19–23 are more striking than the
connections with cultic vocabulary and imagery which he has
noted. That Jeremiah was burdened with a concern for the
well-being of his community is well-attested, but this does not

show that he was a cultic intercessor in the sense intended by
Reventlow (who does not deal with this passage), nor does עמדי
לפניך (v. 20) necessarily bear this out. The point on which
vv. 19–23 turn is so personal and particular that the passage
cannot be explained as a cultic *Gattung*—a literary exemplar
with a general, representative application. Jeremiah is reacting
to what he regards as an intolerable provocation. He has seen
with an awful clarity the slide towards doom, but his expressions
of concern and anguish have been rewarded with hostility and he
has been contemptuously spurned. He reacts angrily, calling
down Yahweh's judgement on those who have used him so badly.
It is hard to believe that any representative, cultic intercessor
could have prayed in this way, or that there was any cultic model
which conformed to the sentiments of vv. 19–23. Nor is it clear
that the most convincing prototype for the portrayal of famine,
pestilence and sword (on 'pestilence' see further below) is a
cultic one. This mode of description can be naturally
accommodated to particular, historical circumstances associated
with invasion, the rigours of war and siege, political collapse and
military defeat.

The ריב aspect of 18.19 can be compared with 12.1, but
Jeremiah is not here constructing a legal argument with a view
to establishing his innocence (*pace* Rudolph) and winning an
acknowledgement of it from Yahweh. His complaint is not set in
the context of theodicy: it is not Yahweh whom he arraigns but
the malignant hostility of his enemies. His concern is not with
the inequities of divine government as they bear hard on him, but
with the punishment of his enemies which he asks Yahweh to
execute. There is not much at stake exegetically in the choice
between יריבי (MT—preferred by Duhm) and ריבי which is
favoured by Ehrlich (p. 291), Rudolph, Weiser and Bright. ריבי
would seem to be indicated by Sept. τοῦ δικαιώματός μου, and
perhaps by Pesh. *'wlbny* and Targ. עלבני. If the text is ושמע
לקול יריבי, the meaning is, 'And listen to the threats which my
adversaries utter against me' (so Vulg. *adversariorum meorum*);
if it is ושמע לקול ריבי, the meaning is, 'Listen to my case
(against my enemies)'.

תחת טובה רעה (v. 20) describes an unnatural ingratitude or
unrelenting hostility which is unmoved by evidences of his
generous concern for others. As a prophet he has endeavoured to
shield his community from Yahweh's anger, to plead in
mitigation of their offences with all the strength of his soul, to
engage all his sympathy for them in this task of intercession and
to win from Yahweh a continuance of his forbearance. Jeremiah,
fully aware of the enormity of their offences against Yahweh,
has, nevertheless, made out the best possible case for them

(לדבר עליהם טובה), but his magnanimity of spirit and intensity
of prophetic concern have earned only active hostility, even to
the extent of designs against his life.

כי כרה שוחה לנפשי (v. 20) is deleted by Giesebrecht (Duhm,
Rudolph) as an insertion from v. 22 and the relation of the texts
of these two verses is discussed by Janzen (p. 27). At v. 22 there
is a K-Q differentiation (שׁוּחָה — שִׁיחָה), and it may be that the
Greek translator has read שִׁיחָה in both places (v. 20 and v. 22),
although it is perplexing that the rendering of כי כרו שיחה
differs so much in one place from the other. When Janzen argues
(p. 90) against Giesebrecht that ἐνεχείρησαν λόγον does not
represent a periphrastic rendering of כרו שוחה, he does not
explain how כרו comes to be translated as συνελάλησαν in v. 20
and ἐνεχείρησαν in v. 22. It may be, despite what Janzen says
(p. 27), that we should reckon with flat renderings of a
metaphorical expression in both verses, in the interests of a
pedestrian clarity. The metaphors are restored by Aq. at v. 20
and v. 22, where Q שׁוחה is read (ωρυξαν βοθρον), but a mixture
of figure and interpretation is represented by Symm. at v. 20
(ωρυξαν διαφθοραν), while the metaphors are fully transformed
by Symm. at v. 22 into κατεσκευασαν διαφθοραν, 'They have
prepared destruction'. Vulg., Pesh. and Targ. read שׁוחה at v. 22,
and preserve the figure of digging a pit at both v. 20 and v. 22.

In view of MT ופחים טמנו לרגלי (v. 22), rendered by Sept. as
καὶ παγίδας ἔκρυψαν ἐπ᾽ ἐμέ, there can be litle doubt that the
sense which is desiderated for the additional stich in Sept. at
v. 20 is, 'And they have concealed their snares to trap me'. The
mistranslation which produced κόλασιν is explicable on the basis
of the sense elsewhere attached by Greek translators to מכשׁול in
the phrase מכשׁול עון. (Sept., Ezek 14.3,4,7, 18.30, 44.12;
Theod., Ezek 7.19), and the Hebrew text which should be
postulated is ומכשׁול(ם) טמנו לרגלי or the like. Of τὴν κόλασιν
αὐτῶν Janzen says (p. 27), 'The word here probably renders
פחם', but he gives us no inkling of how κόλασις can have
emerged as a rendering of פח.

The final word on this problem is that we have to reckon with
a distich whose text was variable. This is seen in the K-Q
differentiation in v. 22 (שׁוחה; שׁיחה), and in the variants לנפשי
(v. 20): ללכדני (v. 22). This distich, with its variants magnified
by differing paraphrases, is preserved in verses 20 and 22 of
Sept., whereas only one stich is preserved in v. 20 of MT. The
circumstance that there are 5 stichs in v. 20 (MT—6 in Sept.)
and 4 in v. 22 (MT) creates a presumption that v. 22 is the place
where the distich belongs (Giesebrecht, Duhm, Rudolph, NEB,
Brockington, p. 206). It has been inserted in v. 20 perhaps

because it was felt that some explication of הישלם תחת טובה
רעה was needed at this point.

The striking feature of vv. 21–23 is precisely the mixture of a
proclamation of doom (vv. 21–22a), which is central to
Jeremiah's ministry, with an intense, compulsive, emotional
outburst which demands doom and punishment as a personal
vindication for the wrongs which have been done to him
(vv. 22b–23). It is the presence of the latter which persuades
Duhm that vv. 21–23 should not be assigned to the prophet
Jeremiah, but the details on which attention is focused when the
'gruesomeness' of vv. 21–23 is considered (cf. Rudolph and
Weiser) do not necessarily have the significance which has been
attached to them. The particularity of vv. 21–23 is better
brought out by observing that the onset of doom for the
community, which is characteristic of Jeremiah's prophetic
foresight, is here peculiarly motivated in terms of personal
revenge. Kimchi glosses הרגי מות (v. 21) as ימותו בדבר; he is
followed by Blayney, and, in more recent times, by Duhm,
Ehrlich (p. 291), Rudolph and Weiser. On מכי חרב Kimchi
comments that the בחורים are the fighting men who go out to
battle. The situation which is envisaged is apparently the one
which elsewhere is evident in Jeremiah's premonitions of the fate
which would ultimately overtake the Judaean community. Hence
if there is an exceptional vindictiveness and ruthlessness in
vv. 21–23 it does not reside in the details of the final doom and
its extension to women and children (as has been commonly
asserted), since this is explained by the historical situation which
is portrayed: by the impact of invasion (כי תביא עליהם גדוד
פתאם), by the grievous consequences for all members of a
community when there is a political and military collapse and
the sharpness of distress is universal (תשמע זעקה מבתיהם). The
remarkable aspect of vv. 21–23 is, therefore, that this picture of
final doom is not communicated by a 'word of Yahweh', but
appears in a prayer and is oriented towards the satisfaction of
Jeremiah's revenge on his enemies and his imperious demand
that they should be punished.

In this connection it is difficult to believe that the hunting
figures in v. 22b or the statement in v. 23 that men were plotting
to put Jeremiah to death (את כל עצתם עלי למות) can have
applied to all the community. They must refer to a particular
group of virulent opponents who have sworn enmity against the
prophet. The great, coming disaster which is the burden of his
prophecy, which he foresees with awful clarity and can hardly
endure, is here refracted and shrunk by his volcanic emotion into
a matter of private vindication: 'You know how poisonous is their
attitude to me, so act against them before your anger cools'—as

if he cannot wait a moment longer for his revenge and fears the possibility of Yahweh's forbearance and mercy.

The textual difficulties of vv. 21–23 are not considerable: Rashi observes that the *yodh* of תמחי (v. 23) is superfluous and cites ותזני (Ezek 16.17) as another example of a *lamedh he* verb with an otiose *yodh*. GK 75 ii supposes that the correct form is תְּמַח. Targ. connects והגרם (v. 21) with a post-biblical Hebrew, Aramaic and Arabic root (נגר 'saw', 'cut', hence נַגָּר 'carpenter') and renders והגרם על ידי חרב as ותביבינון על ידי קטולי חרבא, 'And cut them by means of those who slay with the sword'. Kimchi explains והגרם על ידי חרב in terms of the blood which flows from wounds inflicted by the sword (הדם הנגר), and this idea is taken up by KJV ('And pour out their *blood* by the force of the sword'), by Blayney ('And drain them by means of the sword') and, not very felicitously, by Bright ('Spill them out to the power of the sword'). BDB 'deliver them over to' is in agreement with Pesh. ('*šlm*) and modern translators follow this trend. The sense 'cut' is attractive here ('Cut them to pieces with the sword') and in two other places (Ezek 35.5; Ps 63.11) where הגיר is connected with על ידי חרב. It is likely, however, that נגר 'cut' has a narrower, more technical sense and relates particularly to the operations carried out by a carpenter. Moreover, the causative form is difficult to explain in connection with it and is not found in post-biblical Hebrew, Aramaic and Arabic. Hence the choice lies between interpreting 'Cause them to flow into the power of the sword' as 'Deliver them up to the power of the sword', and retaining a more particular nuance of shedding blood ('Shed their blood by means of the sword').

The problem of מכשלים (v. 23) is partly caused by the obscurity of the expression of והיו מכשלים לפניך. The sense is much improved by reading מֻשְׁלָכִים with 1 Hebrew manuscript, especially if a haplography of מ is postulated and the text is read as משלכים מלפניך (Ehrlich, p. 291), 'so that they are cast out from your presence'. This should be adopted. BHS supposes that משלכים is supported by Pesh. *rmyn*, but this like Targ. רמן and Vulg. *corruentes* may derive from מכשלים. The curious rendering of Sept. (ἡ ἀσθένεια αὐτῶν) shows that the final *mem* of מכשלים was read as a suffix, and should be compared with Sept.'s rendering of ויכשלום at v. 15. Hence ἡ ἀσθένεια αὐτῶν points to מכשולם (so Rudolph). Rudolph translates מכשול as *Anstoss*: 'Let their offences (what has caused them to stumble) be ever present to you'. The thought of being 'hurled down' in Yahweh's presence or of being brought 'stumbling' into his presence is represented by the renderings of Weiser, Bright and NEB. The picture thus conjured up is apparently that of a prisoner brought unceremoniously into the presence of one who is to determine his punishment and decide his fate.

CHAPTER XIX

JERUSALEM WILL BE SHATTERED LIKE AN EARTHENWARE JUG
(19.1–15)

¹These are the words of Yahweh: Go and buy an earthenware jug, and take with you¹ some of the elders and the priests.² ²Go out to the valley of Ben Hinnom, where the Gate of the Potsherds gives access to it, and proclaim there the words which I shall speak to you. ³Say, Hear the word of Yahweh, kings of Judah and inhabitants of Jerusalem. These are the words of Yahweh Sabaoth, God of Israel: I am about to bring such a disaster on this place that those who hear of it will have tingling ears. ⁴They have forsaken me and have made this place into a foreign temple, and have sacrificed in it to alien gods whom neither they nor their forefathers nor the kings of Judah knew. They have filled this place with the blood of the innocent. ⁵They have built shrines to Baal, to sacrifice their children as burnt-offerings to Baal, which I did not command or require, and which I never contemplated. ⁶Therefore, the days are coming, says Yahweh, when this place will no longer be called Topeth and the valley of Ben Hinnom, but the valley of Slaughter. ⁷I will make null and void the policies of Judah and Jerusalem in this place, and I will cut them down with the sword wielded by their enemies and those who seek their lives. I will give their corpses as food to the vultures and wild beasts. ⁸I will make this city an object which appals, a spectacle at which men whistle in horror, at which all travellers are appalled, whistling in horror at the sight of all her wounds. ⁹I will make them eat the flesh of their sons and their daughters; they will eat one another's flesh in the straits to which their enemies and those who seek their lives reduce them by siege. ¹⁰You are to shatter the jug in the presence of those who accompany you. ¹¹Say to them: These are the words of Yahweh Sabaoth: I will shatter this people and this city as one shatters an earthenware jug, so that it is beyond repair.³ ¹²Thus will I do to this place and to its inhabitants, says Yahweh, making this city like Topheth. ¹³The houses of Jerusalem and those of the kings of Judah will be like the place Topheth, those houses polluted by idolatry, every house on whose roof sacrifices were offered to all the host of heaven and libations were poured to alien gods. ¹⁴Jeremiah returned from Topheth, where Yahweh had sent him to prophesy, and stood in the court of the house of Yahweh and addressed all the people. ¹⁵These are the words of Yahweh Sabaoth, God of Israel: I am about to bring on this city and on all its villages the disaster with which I threatened it; for its people have stiffened their necks, refusing to listen to my words.

It is likely that τότε (Sept.) is a rendering of כה influenced by the intention of establishing a connection between the end of chapter 18 and 19.1. It is possible, however, that אז rather than כה was read by the Greek translator (cf. Ziegler, *Beiträge*, pp. 22; Thiel, p. 220). The support of some Hebrew manuscripts, Sept. (πρὸς με) and Pesh. ('ly) for כה אמר יהוה אלי may mean no more than that a shorter כה אמר יהוה has been spelt out as כה אמר יהוה אלי: it was concluded that the prophet Jeremiah himself rather

---

¹ Reading ולקחת אתך (see below, p. 444).
² Reading ומהכהנים (see below, p. 444).
³ Deleting ובתפת יקברו מאין מקום לקבור (see below, p. 446).

than a third party was giving this account of the words which he had received from Yahweh, and this is a reasonable inference (cf. Thiel, pp. 220f.).

The phrase בקבק יוצר חרש is awkward: בקבק itself is identified by A. M. Honeyman (*PEQ*, 1939, pp. 79f.) and J. L. Kelso (*BASOR* Suppl. 5–6, 1948, p. 17 and plate 20) as a narrow-necked jug. The phrase is explained by Rashi as 'a potter's vessel made of clay', and Kimchi elucidates the grammar by assuming that חרש is short for מחרש. This understanding of the phrase is represented by Vulg. (*lagunculam figuli testeam*), whereas Sept. (πεπλασμένον) apparently read בקבק יצור חרש, 'a vessel fashioned from clay' (adopted by Duhm). Targ. (as Kimchi observes) translates the Hebrew as if it were בקבק חרש יוצר, and Pesh. does not represent חרש.

A verb is needed in MT before ומזקני העם and is supplied by Sept., Pesh. and Targ.: והלכת מזקני העם (Sept., Pesh., Targ.) or ולקחת אתך מזקני העם (Rudolph, Weiser, NEB, Brockington, p. 206) has to be read in order to make sense of the Hebrew. The phrase זקני הכהנים appears in 2 Kgs 19.2 and זקני is represented by Vulg., Pesh. and Targ. at Jer 19.1, but not by Sept. (except Sept.ᴬ and Sept.ᵠ). Janzen (p. 41) supposes that the shorter Greek text is the better one and Sept. καὶ ἀπὸ τῶν ἱέρων = ומהכהנים should be adopted (Rudolph, Weiser), but little is at stake.

On v. 2 Kimchi comments 'from the Gate of the Potsherds they go out into the Valley of Ben Hinnom'. This presupposes the kind of grammar which the versions seek to impose on אשר ויצאת ... פתח שער החרסות. NEB renders, 'on which the Gate of the Potsherds opens', and Weiser's *am Eingang des Scherbentors* is in line with the narrower explanation which he offers of אשר פתח שער החרסות, namely, that the phrase indicates a particular area of the Valley of Ben Hinnom—that adjacent to the Gate of the Potsherds. Rudolph is right to question whether the Hebrew can yield such a sense, but his objection on more general grounds to Weiser's exegesis is not so cogent, since the circumstance that we cannot identify שער החרסות or fix its location with any assurance does not prove that it could not have served the purposes of definition which Weiser attributes to it at the time when the verse was written. Nevertheless, there are good reasons for being suspicious of the present form of v. 2 (cf. Duhm, Thiel, p. 221 n. 8), and (אל) גיא בן הנם אשר can be recognized without too much difficulty as a patch which disturbs the original continuity of the opening of v. 2 (ויצאת(אל)פתח שער החרסות).

Since גיא בן הנם is rendered at 19.6 as πολυανδρεῖον υἱοῦ Εννομ, υἱῶν τῶν τέκνων αὐτῶν is apparently a corruption in the

Greek at 19.2, whether or not it derives from a corrupt Hebrew
text (בני בניהם or בניהם, with υἱῶν a doublet of τέκνων, Ziegler,
Beiträge, p. 22). The interpretation of גיא as πολυανδρεῖον
'graveyard' (cf. 2.23, above p. 45) is connected with the way that
the 'Topheth' theme is used in chapter 7 and here again in
chapter 19, although πολυανδρεῖον is not used to render גיא in
chapter 7. There it is translated more plainly by φάραγξ (vv. 31,
32), and this is the word used by Aq. and Symm. at 19.2 and by
Aq. at 19.6. πολυανδρεῖον is connected with the thought that the
Valley of Ben Hinnom is the cemetery of children offered in
sacrifice, and also with the thought that it will be the graveyard
of the nation—filled with graves until there is no room left
(19.11b, see further below). On the sense of מאין מקום see 7.32
(above, p. 179).

Sept. punctuates v. 4 differently from MT and is followed by
Duhm and Rudolph. This also involves a small change of
MT—the *waw* of ומלאו is not represented by Sept. The issue is
whether the *athnach* should be at יהודה or at אבותיהם: whether
ומלכי יהודה is a part of a parenthetical relative clause which
interrupts the series of actions described in the verse (MT, Vulg.,
Pesh., Targ.) or whether, with a change of ומלאו to מלאו
(Rudolph) or ימלאו (Duhm), ומלכי יהודה is the subject of that
verb (so Sept.). The form of the text in Sept. preserves as a
self-contained entity a phrase (אשר לא ידעום המה ואבותיהם)
which occurs elsewhere in the book of Jeremiah (9.15; cf. 44.3),
but it produces an unusual word-order in the Hebrew text, and it
is not clear that ומלכי יהודה is an emphatic subject which is
placed before its verb for that reason. Is it any more emphatic
than המה ואבותיהם which is placed after לא ידעום? In view of
these counter-considerations the punctuation of MT should be
retained, and in that case 'they' of ומלאו comprehends המה
ואבותיהם ומלכי יהודה.

The versions differ in the sense which they attach to ובקתי
(v. 7). Pesh. and Targ. are nearest to the sense which is now
usually attributed to it, 'nullify' (BDB, KB³, Bright, Weiser).
The sense 'destroy', which is given in Rudolph's translation is
nearer to καὶ σφάξω τὴν βουλὴν Ιουδα (Sept.), where the
intention is clearly to pick up πολυανδρεῖον τῆς σφαγῆς at the
end of v. 6 (cf. Ziegler, *Beiträge*, p. 23): 'The valley of Ben
Hinnom will be called the valley of Slaughter and I will
slaughter' etc. But the figure is too far-fetched—the
'slaughtering' of עצה is an improbable metaphor. There can be
no doubt that ובקתי is a deliberate play on בקבק, and it is this
aspect of the matter which is stressed in the rendering of Symm.
(καὶ ρηξω 'I will shatter'), and which has been revived in the

paraphrase designed by NEB to make the link explicit: 'I will shatter the plans of Judah and Jerusalem as a jar is shattered'.

The most significant of all the deviations of Sept. from MT in chapter 19 occurs at v. 11. The words וכתפת יקברו מאין מקום לקבור are not represented by Sept. Since these words are inconsequential where they appear in the Hebrew text, their absence from Sept. may be regarded as a confirmation that they are what they appear to be—an unskilful interpolation which disturbs a connection established by means of כן אעשה between v. 12 and v. 11 (up to להרפה עוד). Janzen (p. 43) notes that the intrusive character of the final part of v. 11 has been generally recognized and he recalls Volz's view that these words were displaced from the end of 19.6 (cf. 7.31–33). According to Volz, they were first accidentally omitted from the end of 19.6, and a marginal correction was subsequently inserted in the text at the wrong place (at the end of v. 11). This came about because of the presence of כתפת in 19.12, and the desire to associate וכתפת with כתפת. Rudolph's explanation is that וכתפת יקברו מאין מקום לקבור derive from 7.32, were first associated with chapter 19 as a marginal comment on התפת (v. 6), and were subsequently inserted in the text adjacent to כתפת (v. 12) rather than adjacent to התפת (v. 6). Janzen's view is that the words were intended as a gloss on כתפת (v. 12), and that they have been inserted in the text in a way which preserves the intentions of the glossator. A further indication that וכתפת יקברו מאין מקום לקבור have no firm place in the text is the circumstance that they appear in Sept.[l] at the end of v. 13 (Janzen, p. 205 n. 17). It is reasonable to interpret this as a confirmation that these words did indeed constitute a marginal gloss and that there was uncertainty as to the precise reference of the gloss. Its insertion at the end of v. 13 is explicable on the assumption that it was thought to refer to כמקום התפת (v. 13).

Thiel (p. 223) dissents from the opinion of Duhm that these words are an editorial gloss and from Rudolph's explanation of how they come to be inserted at 19.11. He maintains that they can be explained in terms of the structure imposed on the chapter by a Deuteronomistic editor (D). But we should concentrate on the convergence of textual-critical and source-critical considerations as indicated above: there are indications that these words came into the text from the margin and there is the fact that they have a disjointed appearance in the text—whether at the end of v. 11 or the end of v. 13. Hence the shorter text of Sept. should be accepted as evidence that there was a time when the Hebrew ran from להרפה עוד (v. 11) to כה אעשה (v. 12). For the present it will be enough to note that we have now discovered two places in chapter 19 where תפת

references cohere poorly with the text: the patch in v. 2 and the concluding part of v. 11. This in itself is enough to cast serious doubts on Thiel's contention that the 'Topheth' theme is an important element of the pattern imposed on chapter 19 by D.

הטמאים (v. 13) creates a grammatical difficulty which the versions have dealt with in various ways, without achieving a satisfactory solution. If הטמאים is an attributive of בתי ירושלם ובתי מלכי יהודה one would expect it to be positioned after יהודה (pace Kimchi, who comments, 'Referring to the houses of Jerusalem and to the houses of the kings of Judah, and to all the houses'). הטמאים may function in the verse as a limitation ('not all the houses, but only those which are polluted by idolatry'), perhaps, as Duhm suggests, a secondary limitation. This would account for the odd positioning of הטמאים; the limitation would be an attempt to account for the circumstance that not all the houses in Jerusalem had been destroyed, and the concluding part of the verse would be a further explication of the limitation. Thus Rudolph supposes that ל of לכל הבתים has the force of 'namely'.

In v. 15 (Ziegler Beiträge, p. 99; Janzen, p. 26) Sept. has a double rendering of ועל כל עריה: καὶ ἐπὶ πάσας τὰς πόλεις αὐτῆς καὶ ἐπὶ τὰς κώμας αὐτῆς. Ziegler takes καὶ ἐπὶ τὰς κώμας αὐτῆς to be the original and explains the doublet as an attempt to produce an exact rendering for עיר: καὶ ἐπὶ πάσας τὰς πόλεις αὐτῆς has been secondarily inserted as a more precise translation of ועל כל עריה. There is no doubt that καὶ ἐπὶ τὴν πόλιν ταύτην καὶ ἐπὶ τὰς κώμας αὐτῆς (a text supported by the miniscule 106) embodies a better understanding of the Hebrew than πόλεις αὐτῆς, since v. 15 refers to the capital city Jerusalem and its dependent villages, not to the capital city and all the towns of Judah (pace Kimchi). The word used by Pesh. and Targ. for the second occurrence of עיר could well refer to the dependent villages of the capital city (Pesh. qwryh; Targ. קרויתא). The fundamental grammatical point is that the suffix of עריה must refer back to העיר הזאת, that is, to Jerusalem, and that this suggests 'Jerusalem and its dependent settlements' as the correct interpretation.

Giesebrecht appreciated that 19.1-15 was not an original, literary unity, and he divided it into those verses which contain an account of symbolic action (1, 2a*, 10, 11a) and those which contain a sermon on the abomination of Topheth (2a*, 2b-9, 11b-13). The verses containing the account of the symbolic action are resumed in vv. 14-15 and in 20.1-6. Erbt's refinement of this consisted in his assigning to subsequent editorial elaboration v. 2b (וקראת ... אליך), the reference to the valley of Ben Hinnom in v. 2a, and to Topheth in v. 14. This view of the chapter has been developed in terms of a Baruch biography consisting of vv. 1, 2a*, 10, 11a, 14f., 20.1–17, and Rudolph may be singled out as a representative of such a scheme of interpretation.

Rudolph shares the well-established view (Bright, Weiser, Nicholson, Thiel) that the editorial complex which has to be analysed is 19.1–20.1–6, and he supposes that it is composed of the following elements: (a) A nucleus of prophetic, symbolic action contained in vv. 1, 2* (אל) פתח שער החרסות (ויצאת), 10, 11 (without ובתפת יקברו מאין מקום לקבור), 14f. (b) A section which is identifiable in terms of a 'Topheth' theme and which consists of v. 2* (גיא בן הנם אשר) and וקראת . . . אליך), vv. 3–9, 12f. Agreement with the view that (אל) גיא בן הנם אשר (v. 2) is a patch has already been indicated, and there is much to be said in favour of Rudolph's view that the extant form of the chapter has developed from a nucleus containing an account of symbolic action carried out by the prophet Jeremiah. The hiatus between the command to acquire a בקבק (v. 1) and the command to break it (v. 10) is a peculiar and unnatural feature in the chapter as it is now organized which forces itself on the attention. It is a reasonable assumption that a subsequent process of elaboration and expansion has broken an immediate and original connection between vv. 1, 2* and 10.

In so far as he takes issue with Rudolph about the structure of chapter 19 Weiser is wrong in every respect except one. He is wrong in supposing that the extant verse 2 is acceptable Hebrew and that the association between the valley of Ben Hinnom and the breaking of the בקבק is original. His account of the last part of v. 11 is unsatisfactory, and he is very probably mistaken in holding that וקראת . . . אליך (v. 2) is part of the original nucleus of symbolic action. He is wrong in supposing that vv. 12f. are part of the account of Jeremiah's symbolic action, and he takes vv. 14f. too seriously—a failing which he shares with Rudolph. The view that Jeremiah repeats in the temple court what he had said in the valley of Ben Hinnom, so that it might be more widely disseminated among those who had not accompanied him, is as old as Jerome. Rudolph, Weiser and Bright detect the hand of Baruch in v. 14, and so for them it is connected with the first appearance in the book of Jeremiah of a 'biographical' account of the prophet. Weiser and Bright differ from Rudolph in so far as they do not make the Baruch account begin at v. 1, where Rudolph reads ויבא ירמיהו (cf. כה אמר יהוה אל ירמיהו in v. 14). Hence Rudolph's view of the matter is that the strand containing the account of symbolic action is narrated by Baruch (vv. 1, 2*, 10, 11*, 14f.), and that this together with chapter 20.1–6 constitutes the first appearance of the Baruch biography in the book of Jeremiah.

Verses 14f. do not have the sober, historical character attributed to them by Rudolph and Weiser; they do not contain a notice, whether by Baruch or someone else, of an action by the historical prophet Jeremiah, namely, his repeating in the temple-court words which he had first spoken in the valley of Ben Hinnom. The verses are, as Nicholson correctly judges, simply a literary device for linking 19.1–13 to 20.1–6. In order that the confrontation between Jeremiah and Pashhur (20.1–6) may take place there must be a reason for it, and the provocative words spoken by Jeremiah in the temple precincts supply that reason. If vv. 14f. are a linking device, they should be regarded as the last stage in the organization of chapter 19, excepting the addition at the end of v. 11 which has no measure of coherence and has hardly any claim to enter into an account of the growth of chapter 19 to its extant shape. If vv. 14f. represent the last stage in the organization of chapter 19, we have to suppose that at their point of entry the Tophet references are already established in the chapter, so that ויבא ירמיהו מהתפת is what we should expect (*pace* Rudolph and Nicholson; cf. Thiel, p. 226), and the emendation of מהתפת to מהפתח loses its *raison d'être*.

Rudolph's view that וליושביו (v. 12) is an insertion or gloss deriving from the mistaken supposition that למקום הזה refers to Jerusalem should be rejected (so Weiser). It follows from a view of the last part of v. 11, which is generally agreed, that כן אעשה (v. 12) is to be understood as a resumption of the words which explain the symbolic action in v. 11, that is, as following directly from להרפה עוד. Verse 12 is secondary comment or exegetical elaboration generated *particularly* by vv. 10–11* and having a specific relationship to these verses (*pace* Thiel, pp. 219ff.). There is no mention of Topheth or the valley of Ben Hinnom in vv. 10–11*, but a specific threat is developed against the city of Jerusalem and its inhabitants (את העם הזה ואת העיר הזאת). It is, therefore, wrong-headed to argue that מקום in v. 12 does not refer to Jerusalem (Rudolph), or to cast suspicion on וליושביו. The main concern of v. 12 is to elaborate כבה אשבר את העם הזה ואת העיר הזאת (v. 11), and an intention to intertwine 'city and people' with 'Topheth' does not find expression until the appearance of כתפת at the end of v. 12. Verse 13 is still principally occupied with the ruins of the buildings in Jerusalem, but a similar device (כמקום התפת) is again used to link the themes. In both verses תפת is a symbol or similitude of 'ruin', 'desolation', 'death' (cf. Sept.), but the threat is directed against Jerusalem, its people and its buildings.

Rudolph urges that המקום הזה in vv. 3, 4, 7, 12 refers to the valley of Ben Hinnom or Topheth. Disagreement with this view has already been expressed in respect of v. 12 (above, p. 449), and Rudolph is also probably wrong in respect of v. 3, 4 and 7. Thiel (p. 224) similarly supposes that המקום הזה refers to Topheth in vv. 3, 4, 6, 7, 12. He says: 'Given the situation which is presupposed (v. 2a) the reference must be to Topheth in verses 3, 4, 6, 7, 12, 13.' This rests on an account of the growth of chapter 19 which should not be followed. It assumes that vv. 2–9 constitute a Deuteronomistic composition, and that the addition to v. 2a (גיא בן הנם אשר (אל)) and the supplying of v. 2b (וקראת . . . אליך) are integral parts of this composition. We should suppose rather that the growth represented by vv. 2b, 3–9 took place first and that this gave rise to the patch in v. 2a. The difference between the accounts given by Rudolph and Thiel of vv. 3–9 is that whereas Rudolph thinks of the passage as a patchwork or mosaic of verses which occur elsewhere in the book of Jeremiah or other books of the Old Testament, Thiel seeks to explain it as the well-rounded composition of a Deuteronomistic author. Thus Rudolph remarks that the interpolations (vv. 3–9, 12f.) are almost entirely put together from verses which are known to us in other contexts, and that, for the most part, they connect with passages which are recognizably part of the Deuteronomistic editing of the book of Jeremiah, or with Deuteronomic/Deuteronomistic passages outside the book of Jeremiah. Hence Rudolph is inclined to conclude that this material should be assigned to his Source C, although against this he raises the consideration that its author might have been expected to avoid so much repetition. Thiel (p. 221) describes the Deuteronomistic sermon as consisting of an introduction (vv. 2f.), an indictment (vv. 4f.) and a general proclamation of judgement on the sanctuary of Topheth in the valley of Ben Hinnom and on Jerusalem itself (vv. 6–9, 11b–13). The construction, the ordering of the thoughts, and the terminology, indicate that the sermon was formulated by D.

Against Thiel points already made should be raised again: they concern the patch in v. 2a and the final words of v. 11. These are the most poorly integrated and the most suspect items in chapter 19. It is a travesty to represent them as bricks of a Deuteronomistic edifice. Hence when an explanation is offered of how chapter 19 has achieved its present form, the most marginal consideration should be the gloss at the end of v. 11, while the patch in v. 2a should also be regarded as a late accommodation. Weiser's argument (p. 161 n. 2) is that Rudolph's account of vv. 3–9 does not do justice to the literary integrity of the passage, but the answer to this must be an expression of doubt whether the passage possesses the kind of literary integrity which Weiser assigns to it. He says that the judgement of Rudolph and others that vv. 3–9 have been put together from verses which exist in other places is a misunderstanding of the cohesiveness of style which characterizes liturgical language. The only reply which need be made to Weiser is that all indeed would be well if things were as he says they are and thinks that he finds them. For those who do not receive this impression of seamlessness and cohesion from vv. 3–9 there are problems which have to be faced, and they have to set out to understand how this part of the chapter could have arrived at its present shape.

The following account of the structure and growth of chapter 19 is proposed:

(a) The nucleus of the chapter consists of the account of the shattering of the בקבק and the explanation of its symbolism (vv. 1, 2a without גיא בן הנם אשר (אל), 10, 11 without ובתפת יקברו מאין מקום לקבור).

(b) The next stage is constituted by the supplying of a sermon whose aim is to provide a more extensive explication of the symbolic action. This sermon (*pace* Rudolph and Thiel) was not shaped originally by a 'Topheth' theme; in the first place it was triggered by an intention to elucidate further the symbolic breaking of the בקבק and its content is appropriate to this function. At this point the sermon consisted of the latter part of v. 2 (וקראת ... אליך), vv. 3f., 7–9.

(c) So constituted, the sermon is not oriented towards a 'Topheth' theme, and המקום הזה in vv. 3, 4, 7 refers not to Topheth or the valley of Ben Hinnom but to Jerusalem. The sermon should be interpreted in the light of the primary explanation of the symbolic action supplied in v. 11 (ככה אשבר את העם הזה ואת העיר הזאת) and should be regarded as an elaboration of this nuclear explanation. This accords well with the plain indications of v. 3—on the assumption that at this stage v. 2 still reads ויצאת (אל) פתח שער החרסות. Those addressed are the 'kings of Judah' and the 'inhabitants of Jerusalem', and the threat to bring disaster על המקום הזה is most naturally understood as a threat against Jerusalem. The plural 'kings of Judah' is a problem whatever interpretation of v. 3 is adopted, but if anything is to be deduced from the plural form, it is the distance of the author from the age of Judaean monarchy. The plural is a mark of lateness and is indicative of a time when the monarchy had ceased to be, so that it is apprehended as a continuity of kings which has been terminated rather than as the reign of a particular king.

If v. 3 is susceptible of interpretation as a threat against Jerusalem, it is no less true that v. 4 is better understood as referring to apostasy in a Jerusalem context rather than in a

Topheth context. The vocabulary, moreover, might even require
a narrowing down of the reference of המקום הזה, so that וינכרו
את המקום הזה is seen as a particular allusion to the desecration
of the temple by alien cults which is then spelled out further by
what follows, namely, ויקטרו בו לאלהים אחרים. That v. 4 deals
with apostasy in Jerusalem and not in a Topheth context is
confirmed by the closing words ומלאו את המקום הזה דם נקים. It
could be argued that this is an allusion to the sacrificing of
innocent children in the gruesome cult which was practised in
the valley of Ben Hinnom, but the contention is not borne out by
the associations of דם נקי in the prophetic literature and
elsewhere in the Old Testament. In none of the places where it
occurs does it have any connection with the enormities of child
sacrifice in the valley of Ben Hinnom, except, arguably, in
Ps 106.38, where the sacrifice of children to demons (שדים) is
further described as a shedding of innocent blood—the blood of
sons and daughters. In all the other passages which contain a
reference to the shedding of דם נקי what is indicated is lawless
and violent behaviour and the oppression of the innocent (Deut
19.10; 1 Sam 19.5; 2 Kgs 21.16; 24.4; Isa 59.7; Jer 2.34; 7.6;
22.3; 26.15; Joel 4.19; Prov 6.17). Passages which deserve special
mention are 2 Kgs 21.16 and 24.4 where Manasseh is said to
have poured out so much innocent blood that he filled Jerusalem
with it (cf. especially 24.4, וימלא את ירושלם דם נקי with Jer
19.4, ומלאו את המקום הזה דם נקים). The passages which clinch
the matter and against whose testimony it is difficult to argue are
Jer 7.6 and 22.3. In neither of these can במקום הזה refer to the
valley of Ben Hinnom. In 7.6 the reference is either to the
Jerusalem temple, which is the setting of the sermon, or to the
city of Jerusalem, and in 22.3, where the speech is set in the
royal palace (22.1), the allusion is presumably to Jerusalem. If
this is demonstrated for ודם נקי אל תשפכו במקום הזה in 7.6 and
22.3, the conclusion that ומלאו את המקום הזה דם נקים (19.4)
refers to Jerusalem and not to Topheth is irresistible.

If המקום הזה refers to Jerusalem rather than to Topheth in
v. 4, the continuity between v. 4 and v. 7 is evident, for v. 7 is
unmistakably directed towards Judah and Jerusalem. Moreover,
of all the verses in the passage (vv. 3–9), verse 7 is the one whose
connection with the nucleus of symbolic action is indubitable in
view of the play on בקבק in ובקתי. It may be objected that if
במקום הזה in v. 7 refers to Jerusalem, the sense of the Hebrew
leaves something to be desired: 'I shall nullify the policies of
Judah and Jerusalem in Jerusalem.' This, however, is not a
consideration to which great weight should be attached, and the
obstacles to an understanding of v. 7 are much more formidable
on the assumption that במקום הזה is a reference to Topheth.

This is so because the vocabulary with which the verse opens has political connections and must be regarded as directed against the king(s) and statesmen of Judah and their policies: ובקתי את עצת יהודה וירושלם has no appropriateness whatever in connection with idolatry and religious apostasy, and certainly not as a threat intended to establish a likeness between the fate of Topheth and the fate of Judah and Jerusalem. Further, if ובקתי is generated by בקבק, one has to take account of how the symbolic action is elucidated in v. 11, since in view of the link ובקתי : בקבק, one should be guided by this in any consideration of the threat intended by vv. 7–9. There is no doubt (ignoring the gloss at the end of v. 11) that the symbolic action is explained as a threat against Jerusalem and its population (ככה אשבר את העם הזה ואת העיר הזאת), and consequently בקתו in v. 7, which derives from בקבק, should be understood as an elaboration of the same threat. Moreover, the details in vv. 7–9 confirm that this is so: במקום הזה in the sentence ובקתי את עצת יהודה וירושלם במקום הזה is not a severe difficulty, and there is no problem in equating המקום הזה with Jerusalem—the centre where the statesmen of Judah are located and where they fashion their policies for the country. The Hebrew of v. 7 is simply a way of saying: I will make null and void the policies which the statesmen formulate here in Jerusalem for the state of Judah, and so the sequel will be not security for Judah but a devastating military defeat at the hands of her enemies (והפלתים בחרב לפני איביהם).

After the carnage of battle the unburied corpses will be carrion for vultures and wild animals. It should be noted particularly that ונתתי את נבלתם למאכל לעוף השמים ולבהמת הארץ (v. 7) is not introduced here in the context of unburied corpses in the valley of Ben Hinnom, but in the context of carnage on a battlefield (see further below). The resumption of v. 7 in vv. 8f. is entirely in accord with the direction which has been established for the exegesis. Verse 8 threatens Jerusalem with desolation and devastation, and describes the effect which this terrible spectacle will have on those who see it as they pass by (see above, pp. 433f.). The horrific wounds inflicted on Jerusalem will appal those who see them, and a sharp expelling of the breath, indicative of the terror which the sight inspires, will issue as a kind of whistling. It is this which is intended by שרקה and ישרק, and not, as some have supposed, a whistle of derision. The military setting is preserved in v. 9 which describes more particularly the consequence of siege and famine conditions: the degeneration into cannibalism and into the deepest pit of human degradation is also part of Yahweh's judgement (והאכלתים). This is what the population will be reduced to when the enemy tightens its grip on Jerusalem, and when they are driven by desperation to unnatural and unthinkable excesses of cannibalism (on the vocabulary of v. 9 see further below).

The argument under (c) has been that the 'sermon' which expands the message conveyed by the symbolic action in v. 11, and which consists of vv. 2,* 3, 4, 7–9, has nothing to do with the valley of Ben Hinnom or Topheth. It develops and elaborates the threat delivered against Jerusalem and its population in the symbolic action and its spoken accompaniment.

(d) The next stage in the growth of chapter 19 is one which has been already described, namely, the resumption of ככה להרפה עוד ... אשבר (v. 11) by כן אעשה (v. 12), whereby the nuclear explanation of the symbolic action (v. 11*) is expanded in vv. 12f. וליושביו is original in v. 12, and, if this is so, למקום הזה must refer to Jerusalem. The point on which attention must now be focused is that the 'Topheth' theme makes its first entry into the chapter at the end of v. 12, and it is important to note the circumstances in which this takes place. Topheth plays an ancillary rather than a leading role in v. 12, and attention is still concentrated on the fate of Jerusalem. כתפת functions at the end of v. 12 as a paradigm of ruin or devastation. In order to say in the strongest way and the most horrific terms that Jerusalem will be devastated, Yahweh declares that he will make Jerusalem like Topheth. If this is a correct account, the view that the Topheth theme has found its way into chapter 19 because of the physical adjacency of the 'Gate of Potsherds' and the valley of Ben Hinnom is one which should be questioned and even repudiated. We do not know where the 'Gate of Potsherds' was located, but, in any case, the insertion in v. 2a, which seeks to fix its location with reference to the valley of Ben Hinnom, had not (ex hypothesi) yet been inserted at the point in the growth of the chapter which we have now reached.

The patch in v. 2a was necessitated by the earlier entrance of the Topheth theme in chapter 19, and the proximity of the 'Gate of Potsherds' to the valley of Ben Hinnom cannot therefore be the prime cause of the presence of the Topheth theme in chapter 19. Rather, it was as a paradigm of ruin and desolation that תפת made its entry at the end of v. 12 in order to underline the terror of Jerusalem's devastation. The simile in v. 13 (כמקום התפת) functions in a similar way: this verse is principally about houses in Jerusalem which have been made unclean by idolatry – by the astral cults practised on their roofs. The threat against these buildings, including buildings in the palace complex, is expressed by saying that they will be כמקום התפת: they will be reduced to rubble.

(e) The next stage is the insertion of vv. 5 and 6 which was
encouraged by the presence of תפת in vv. 12 and 13, but, more
immediately, by a mistaken exegesis of v. 4. The references to
idolatry in v. 4 were understood as allusions to the sacrifice of
children in the valley of Ben Hinnom, and the two occurrences of
מקום were equated with Topheth or the valley of Ben Hinnom.
In one passage (Ps 106.38; see above, p. 452) דם נקי is associated
with child sacrifice, and such an interpretation of the closing
words of v. 4 (ומלאו את המקום הזה דם נקים) may, in particular,
have encouraged the exegesis of v. 4 which is contained in vv. 5f.
The subject matter of vv. 5f. is, in all probability, derived
directly from 7.31f., and a further impetus to the drawing of the
exegetical conclusions found in 19.5f. is perhaps to be discovered
in   7.33: והיתה נבלת העם הזה למאכל לעוף השמים ולבהמת הארץ
ואין מחריד. The similarity of this to ונתתי את נבלתם למאכל לעוף
השמים ולבהמת הארץ (19.7) may have confirmed the exegete in
his opinion that the latter was another element of the Topheth
theme in chapter 19. In this exegesis of 19.7 and in other
respects he was misguided and mistaken. 19.5f. are an erroneous
exegesis of 19.4, and, in particular, the context of 7.33 is
different from that of 19.7. The Topheth theme is more firmly
embedded in chapter 7 than it is in chapter 19: whereas the
reference to unburied corpses in 19.7 occurs in a battlefield
context *simpliciter*, the reference in 7.33 occurs in a battlefield
and Topheth context. This should be maintained, even if the
close relationship between 19.5f. and 7.31f. were to lead us to
conclude that ונתתי את נבלתם למאכל לעוף השמים ולבהמת הארץ
had been quarried from 7.33 (see further below). 7.33 follows on
immediately from וקברו בתפת מאין מקום and what is envisaged
in that verse is perhaps that Topheth will be the scene of military
defeat and carnage (cf. גיא ההרגה — 7.32). There will be many
unburied corpses with no one to protect them from the
depredations of vultures and wild beasts. Carnage which is the
consequence of battle is linked to Topheth in 7.33 as it is not in
19.7.

(f) The final stages are to be found in v. 2a* and vv. 14f. The
latter have been explained as a device for linking 19.1–13 to
20.1–6 (see above, p. 449) and thereby providing a pretext for
the confrontation between Jeremiah and Pashur. The remaining
task is to comment on מהתפת (v. 14), and it is evident that this
(if it is original; see above, p. 449) presupposes the prior
existence of גיא בן הנם (v. 2). In making the link the editor
represents that Jeremiah returned from Topheth to the court of
the temple, and this shows that he was already reading a text in
v. 2 according to which Jeremiah had gone out to the valley of
Ben Hinnom. These then are the final instalments of the

development of the Topheth theme in chapter 19, apart from the inconsequential ובתפת יקברו מאין מקום לקבור at the close of v. 11. In view of the references to Topheth in vv. 5f. Jeremiah is now represented by means of the patch in v. 2 as having gone to the valley of Ben Hinnom rather than to the 'Gate of Potsherds', and as having returned from Hinnom to the temple court. The insertion at the end of v. 11 is so incoherent that it cannot be meaningfully incorporated into this account of the growth of chapter 19. It can, however, be said that it was probably inserted after the addition of vv. 5f., since whatever impetus there was to insert it is supplied by these verses. We should have expected it to come after גיא ההרגה (v. 6), since the words which appear after גיא ההרגה in 7.32 are very similar to those at the end of 19.11:

ובתפת יקברו מאין מקום לקבור 19.11:

וקברו בתפת מאין מקום 7.32:

We may, therefore, hazard a guess that ובתפת יקברו מאין מקום לקבור were originally located at the end of 19.6, that they fell out of the text and were reinserted in the wrong place for reasons which have already been discussed (see above, p. 446, where the alternative possibility that the words originate as a marginal gloss on 19.6 is considered).

The intention of the foregoing discussion has been to explain the form of MT rather than to make deletions from it, but two deletions have been proposed:

(a) That ומזקני הכהנים should be emended to ומהכהנים (v. 1).

(b) That ובתפת יקברו מאין מקום לקבור should be deleted (v. 11).

According to Rudolph the 'interpolations' in chapter 19 consist of vv. 2b, 3–9, 12–13, and these have been culled from elsewhere in the book of Jeremiah or from other Old Testament books whose prose is Deuteronomic or Deuteronomistic. Thiel (pp. 222f.) sets out in detail his account of the Deuteronomistic connections of the so-called Topheth sermon (vv. 2–9). While Rudolph and Thiel search for the affiliations of the prose in Jeremiah 19 with Deuteronomic/Deuteronomistic prose, Weippert's concern (pp. 184–191, 218–222) is to discover reasons for doubting these connections and for establishing the distinctive character of the prose of the book of Jeremiah, even for positing the dependence of Deuteronomic/Deuteronomistic passages on the prose of the book of Jeremiah. In so far as she shows that the prose of the book of Jeremiah has particularities of vocabulary and nuance her work has value, because it directs our attention to the circumstance that the prose is part of a body of material—a corpus—which has its own special characteristics. It is more important to consider carefully how the prose functions in the context of the book of Jeremiah than to be too preoccupied with the not necessarily profitable pursuit of Deuteronomic or Deuteronomistic affiliations.

Weippert, however, draws false conclusions about the prose of the book of Jeremiah, because she is too committed to the task of establishing that the prophet Jeremiah was the author of the prose. She does not have the right kind of interest in the ways in which the prose functions in the book of Jeremiah: to seek to relate the prose to the concerns of the Jeremianic corpus is an admirable objective, but to attempt further to locate it in the time of the prophet Jeremiah and to suppose that the prose is, for the most part, his prose, is a recipe for a misunderstanding of how it functions in the book. We should assume, rather, that our extant book of Jeremiah is the product of a complicated, literary history, and that the processes by which it arrived at its present shape operated over a long period. The prose of the book of Jeremiah is bound up with these processes. We should think of the extant book as text and commentary and understand the prose as exegesis operating on a nucleus of material which is sometimes poetry, although in chapter 19 it is prose.

Does the nucleus of symbolic action in chapter 19 in fact take us into the historical context of Jeremiah's ministry? Does it give us a historical account of symbolic action carried out by the prophet Jeremiah? The answer should probably be affirmative, but in any case the symbolic action and its primary explication, whether or not it establishes contact with the prophet Jeremiah, is the core of chapter 19. Everything else in the chapter is organized around it and was generated by it. It is with these processes of exegetical elaboration that the prose of the book of Jeremiah is associated, and it is in connection with them that it functions.

Further attention may now be devoted to the nucleus of symbolic action in chapter 19, and an additional argument will be advanced to support the contention that v. 2 has been tampered with, that the Topheth reference is a patch, and that the particular point of the association of בקבק and שער החרסות has been obscured by it. The rendering of Targ. (תרע קלקלתא), which is quoted by Rashi, perhaps indicates that שער החרסות is understood as 'rubbish tip'. Rashi (also Kimchi) himself identifies שער החרסות with the 'Dung Gate' (Neh 2.13; 3.14; 12.31), and a modern commentator (Weiser) supposes that this has much in its favour. It has to be accepted (cf. Rudolph and Nicholson) that there is probably no future in seeking to identify שער החרסות, but another remark of Rashi is more interesting: he observes that potsherds were scattered at שער החרסות. This would seem to indicate a rubbish tip, and the thought is made more explicit by Rudolph who supposes that the gate took its name from the 'city refuse dump' located beside it. Nicholson offers a more specialized explanation, namely, that 'it acquired its name because it was near a dump where potters, whose workshops were possibly in the Hinnom valley, discarded broken or defective pottery'. The appropriateness of the association of the breaking of the בקבק with שער החרסות is simply that the symbolic action is to take place at the dump where broken pottery is heaped—Jerusalem and its population are to be consigned by Yahweh to the rubbish heap. This appropriateness is destroyed by גיא בן הנם אשר (אל), and this is a confirmation that these words were not part of the original form of verse 2. Originally the account stated that Jeremiah and those who accompanied him went to the tip where broken pots were heaped, and there Jeremiah shattered the בקבק and explained the significance of his action (vv. 10 and 11). Just as the בקבק was irreparably smashed, like all the other broken pots in the tip, so would Jerusalem and its inhabitants be irreparably broken by Yahweh's judgement.

The question how Jeremiah construed the power inherent in such symbolic action does not admit of a certain answer. It is now widely maintained that symbolic action is not simply a parable of coming judgement, but a creation or predetermination of that judgement (Rudolph, Weiser, Bright, Nicholson). It is not simply that the prophet intends by the symbolism to convey a message to his audience. More than that, he makes inevitable the eventuation of what is symbolized. That the action has a connection with sympathetic magic is presupposed by Rudolph and Weiser, and the assertion of the latter that 'in view of the command of God it is divested of its magical character' is not obviously cogent. Weiser tends to assume that the introduction of a divine fiat is a solution for all theological problems. If the prophet did indeed act with magical intention, his action is no less magical because it was commanded by Yahweh.

This view of prophetic, symbolic action raises far-reaching issues, and if it is a correct interpretation of how the canonical prophets understood their prophetic endowment, it is not a consideration which can be limited to symbolic action. We are not being invited to form a view of a narrow sector of prophetic activity. We are rather confronted with an understanding of prophetic 'power' which would have to be applied to prophetic words no less than prophetic actions, and which impinges on our overall understanding of the beliefs held by the canonical prophets concerning the nature of their endowment and vocation. It is a matter of the greatest difficulty to attain certainty about how the prophets construed their office and what intentions and beliefs they possessed. We have to beware that we do not attribute to them an intellectual and moral refinement which we would like them to possess, but which they may in fact have lacked. Those who assert that they regarded their words and actions as having a quasi-magical power to create the future events to which these referred may be right; those who assume that the prophets are nearer to our modernity in their appreciation of the functions of language and symbolic action are possibly mistaken. They were then more antique men than we had supposed, wedded to notions of language and symbols from which we are alienated. We are not, however, logically compelled to adopt this view of the canonical prophets. If we cannot assert that it is wrong, we can at least say that it is not necessarily right. It is a view which shifts the centre of significance from the semantic content of prophetic words to an extra-semantic aspect of wonder-working power. The opinion may be ventured that the consequences of this shift are disastrous. It is the quality and profundity of the prophetic utterance, its authentic humanity, its piercing vision of the truth, its exceptional discernment and the anguish with which it is touched (for prophets do not arrive at the truth without suffering for it), which enable it to be a word of God. It is this and not a power of incantation or sympathetic magic which lends it endurance and enables it to live and be meaningful even in our times.

CHAPTER XX

JEREMIAH AND PASHHUR (20.1–6)

[1]When Pashhur, son of Immer, the priest, who was the chief overseer of the house of Yahweh, heard Jeremiah uttering these words of prophecy, [2]he had him flogged and put in the stocks at the Upper Benjamin Gate in the house of Yahweh. [3]Next day Pashhur released him from the stocks, and Jeremiah said to him, Your name is no longer Pashhur; Yahweh has given you the name Magor[1] (Terror). [4]These are the words of Yahweh, I will make you a terror to yourself and to all your friends, and they will fall by the sword of their enemies, while you look on. I will give all Judah into the hands of the king of Babylon, and he will deport them to Babylon and strike them down with the sword. [5]I will give all the riches of this city, the fruit of all its toil, all its treasures and all the wealth of the kings of Judah[2] into the hands of their enemies who will seize them as spoil and bring them to Babylon. [6]You Pashhur and all the members of your household will go into exile and come to Babylon; there you will die and be buried, you and all your friends to whom you uttered false prophecies.

Pesh. probably understands פָּקִיד (v. 1) as a reference to a particular function discharged by a senior priestly official (*whw pqwd' hw' šlyṭ'*), and this is how the matter is represented by those who regard Pashhur as the head of the temple police (Rudolph) or as an official having a special responsibility for the maintenance of public order and decorum in the temple precincts (Duhm, Weiser, Bright). נָגִיד is indicative of Pashhur's rank, and only a high-ranking priestly official would order the flogging and detention of a prophet (cf. Duhm and Ehrlich, pp. 292f.).

There is evidence in the versions of uncertainty about the meaning of מַהְפֶּכֶת (v. 2), whether it is a prison building or an instrument for detention or torture. The sense 'prison' (*ḥdrt'*) is given by Pesh. and by Rashi (מְקוֹם הָאֲסוּרִים). Vulg. *nervum* 'fetters' point to 'custody' as does Targ. כְּפָתָא 'stocks'?. 'Torture' is indicated by Symm. βασανιστηριον 'torture-chamber', or στρεβλωτηριον 'instrument of torture' (attested by Jerome). Kimchi notes that there are some who interpret מַהְפֶּכֶת as 'prison' (= בֵּית הַסֹּהַר, Gen 39.20ff.), and that his father explained it as an instrument made of two pieces of wood in which the necks of prisoners were inserted. The translation 'stocks' may be thought to gather some support from etymological considerations in so far as מַהְפֶּכֶת suggests an instrument in which the body is unnaturally confined or distorted. 'Torture-chamber'? (Symm.) would comprise both custody and torture, but the reference is probably to custody rather than torture: 'torture', perhaps suggested by the

[1] Deleting מִסָּבִיב (see below, pp. 461, 463f.).
[2] Deleting אֶת (see below, p. 465).

etymology, represents a magnification of Pashhur's ill-treatment of Jeremiah. It is not obvious why a temple gate should be called the Upper Benjamin Gate, and since the Benjamin Gate was evidently a city gate (37.13; cf. 38.7), Duhm has concluded that both gates were located in the northern wall of the city.

The main problem in 20.1–6 is constituted by the new name given to Pashhur by Jeremiah. מסביב (v. 3) is explicitly represented (κυκλόθεν) only by Sept.[OL], and μέτοικον (without κυκλόθεν) has been taken as an indication that the Greek translator had before him a Hebrew text from which מסביב was absent, and that מסביב is a secondary insertion from 20.10 (cf. Janzen, p. 173). Against this view both A. M. Honeyman (*VT* 4, 1954, pp. 424–426) and L. Wächter (*ZAW* 74, 1962, pp. 57–62) argue that the apparent absence of anything corresponding to מסביב in Sept. is to be explained in terms of the rendering of מגור as μέτοικον 'exile'. If the original text is thought to be מגור, comparison with Isa 31.9 is invited, whereas if it is מגור מסביב, the other occurrences of this phrase have to be taken into consideration (Jer 6.25; 20.10; 46.5; 49.29; Ps 31.14; Lam 2.22).

Targ. (*pace* Honeyman) does not associate מגור with מגר 'destroy' in Jer 6.25, 20.10, 46.5 and 49.29, but with II גור (BDB and KB[3]) from which the sense of 'assembling with hostile intent' or 'encirclement' is derived. There can be little doubt that Symm. (the Hexaplaric readings are given by Jerome) derives the same sense *congregatum* (20.3) in the same way, and Sept. συναθροιζομένων κυκλόθεν at 20.10. Ibn Janah (A. Neubauer, p. 129) founds the sense 'gather' on Isa 54.15 which he refers to the gathering of Gog and Magog against Israel. This implies the attaching of the sense 'gather with hostile intent' to גור. The assertion that מגר means 'destroy' is itself dubious. There are two biblical occurrences, one a Qal passive participle (Ezek 21.17) and the other a Piel perfect (Ps 89.45), and BDB and KB[3] give the sense as 'cast' or 'cast down' (cf. Ibn Janah, p. 363, who explains the Piel as 'fall', 'cause to fall').

Another aspect of Honeyman's argument (p. 425) is that the contexts in which מגור מסביב appears point to the sense 'destruction' rather than 'terror'. All that can be shown by these contexts is that there is an association between מגור and the 'destruction' wrought by invaders. This, however, can be explained on the assumption that invasion and carnage are the cause of the 'terror', rather than taken as a proof that מגור means 'destruction'. It is not necessary to establish that Pashhur is the 'cause of the terror' in order to justify the translation 'Terror all round' for מגור מסביב. אי כבוד (1 Sam 4.21) is a name which indicates that the glory has departed, but the child bearing the name is not the cause of the glory having departed.

Isaiah's child is called מהר שלל חש בז (Isa 8.3), as a sign of the imminent fall of Damascus and Samaria to Assyria, but the child is not the cause of this impending disaster.

There are three lexicographies of מגור with which we have to reckon: (a) There is the derivation from II גור with the sense 'gather against'. (b) There is the sense 'dread' which is derived from III גור, which is supported by Vulg. (*pavorem*), by Rashi (וראה) and by Kimchi (פחד). (c) There is the derivation from I גור which is indicated by all the Sept. renderings of מגור מסביב, and by Pesh. (*twtb'*), Aq. (*peregrinum*) and Symm. (*ablatum*) at Jer 20.3. There are, perhaps, special reasons why מגור has been understood in terms of migration and exile at Jer 20.1–6 (cf. L. Wächter, op. cit., pp. 59f.). The renderings of Sept. (μέτοικον at v. 3 and μετοικίαν at v. 4) are influenced by the explicit references to exile in Babylon (vv. 4–6). There is another consideration which suggests that vv. 4–6 are to be explained as secondary exegesis of מגור: vv. 4–6 may arise from an understanding of מגור or מגור מסביב similar to that preserved in Sept. מגור (v. 3) is thus assumed, as in Sept., to derive from I גור 'to sojourn', 'to be exiled', is resumed by מגור (v. 4), and in an extended exegesis is explicated as invasion, slaughter and exile. Hence the understanding of מגור (v. 3), attested by Sept., Pesh., Aq. and Symm., was shared by the exegete whose interpretation of v. 3 is preserved in MT vv. 4–6 (*pace* W. L. Holladay, *JBL* 91, 1972, pp. 303–320 and D. L. Christensen, *JBL* 92, 1973, pp. 498–502).

Two aspects of Rashi's treatment of the names have been subsequently influential: (a) The supposition that there is an intention to set up an antithesis similar to that of נעמי and מרה (Ruth 1.20), although Rashi's account turns on a play with the name פשחור and not on an antithesis of פשחור and מגור מסביב. (b) The assumption that the שחור of פשחור is to be associated with Aramaic סחור on which מסביב is a play. The second of these is adopted by J. D. Michaelis and by W. Gesenius (*Thesaurus* ii, 1840, p. 1135). Gesenius explains פשחור as an abbreviated form whose elements are פשח and שחור : he relates פשח to Arabic *fasuḥa* 'be wide' and שחור to Aramaic סחור 'around'. It is not surprising that Aramaic סחור has been steadily postulated as an element of פשחור, when it is borne in mind that the idea is readily put in our minds by Targ.'s rendering of מסביב (מסחור סחור). E. Nestle (*ZDMG* 61, 1907, pp. 196f.) takes the logical step of searching for another Aramaic element in פשחור and he elucidates פש in terms of Aramaic פוש 'remain', 'be settled'. Hence מגור מסביב is related antithetically to פשחור: not *ringsum bleibend* but *rundum wandernd*. To a name indicative of a settled, stable life Jeremiah opposes מגור

מסביב which is indicative of the life of a rootless, homeless wanderer (deriving מגור from גור 'to sojourn').

Duhm's explanation is bound up with his view that the entire passage (vv. 1–6) has a late, midrashic character and is a kind of etymological aetiology. He is not, therefore, enquiring about a scientific etymology of Pashhur (nor is Nestle), but is simply trying to discover the etymology which was imposed on the name and which triggered מגור מסביב as an antithesis, out of which activity the narrative was spun. In dependence on H. Ewald (*Die Propheten des Alten Bundes*, ii, 2nd. ed., 1868, p. 186) he associates פש with Hebrew פוש and makes the dubious supposition that contextual considerations at Jer 50.11 (the proximity of תשמחי and תעלזי) establish the sense 'joy' for the פש of פשחור. The intention of the author, according to Duhm, was to set up an antithesis between 'Joy all around' and 'Terror all around'.

Another view which is founded on a correlation of שחור (סחור) and מסביב is that of W. L. Holladay (op. cit., pp. 313f.). The elements of Holladay's solution are similar to those employed by Nestle, but the sense 'prosperity', 'fruitfulness' for Aramaic פוש is the one on which he fastens. The name 'Fruitful on every side' which embodies the promises made to the patriarchs (cf. Gen 12.1–3) is changed to 'Terror on every side' (invasion and carnage) or 'Deportation on every side' (not a sojourning in Canaan, but a deportation to Babylon). One has the feeling that the patriarchs have been dragged in by the scruff of the neck. By making Pashhur a paradigm of a general disaster Holladay accentuates a difficulty of which Duhm was conscious and which is inherent in מגור מסביב. If the meaning is 'Terror on every side', this is not well suited to the issuing of a personal threat against Pashhur, and it becomes such only in so far as we envisage that he is brought down in the general ruin of Judah.

We have noticed in connection with these elucidations that they do not necessarily assume a point of departure from a sober etymology of פשחור. Thus Nestle attributes vv. 1–6 to the prophet Jeremiah and maintains that the prophet recognized the foreignness of the name פשחור and analyzed it into Aramaic elements. He is, however, willing to concede that the etymology may be mistaken and that פשחור may be an Egyptian name ('Son of Horus'), as W. Spiegelberg (*ZDMG* 53, 1899, p. 635) had maintained. S. Ahiṭuv (*IEJ* 20, 1970, pp. 95f.) has noted that the name Pashhur is known from two Hebrew seals, and a Hebrew ostracon from Arad. He supposes that Sept. does not represent מסביב (see above, p. 461) and that the postulating of שחור as an element of פשחור is misguided. Spiegelberg's etymology of פשחור is correct (so Ahiṭub) and *p šri n ḥr* is an attested theophoric name. The absence of *n* (the mark of the genitive) and the dropping of *r* does not cause difficulty and examples of these orthographies can be cited. If we conclude, as we probably should, that פשחור ('Son of Horus') is an Egyptian name, it does reduce the objectivity of attempts to establish a relationship between פשחור and מגור מסביב founded on another and false etymology of פשחור. We no longer have a reliable point of departure (a true etymology) to which these explanations can be anchored. Instead we have to accept statements which cannot be controlled about the false etymologies of פשחור which were employed in order to bring מגור מסביב into play.

There is a modern tendency (cf. Weiser, p. 166, n. 1; Bright) to give up the attempt to find a word-play on פשחור in מגור מסביב, and this would seem to be the right conclusion. All the more so if מסביב is not original in 20.3 (see above, p. 461), since in that case the connection מסביב — שחור can no longer be sustained. A further indication that מגור rather than מגור מסביב was original in 20.3 may be detected in the circumstance that מגור without מסביב occurs in v. 4. May not this have been a precise resumption of a מגור which originally was the final word of v. 3? This train of thought is accommodating to Janzen's supposition that מסביב has been imported from v. 10, where, in contradistinction to v. 3, it is explicitly represented in Sept. (κυκλόθεν).

Rudolph (following Giesebrecht, Volz and others) urges that v. 4 should be translated, 'I will give you up to the power of terror, you and all your friends' (cf. Bright, p. 132). In order to render v. 4 Rudolph's way (he has the support of Vulg. and Pesh.) we have to suppose that the suffixes of לך and לכל אהביך pick up the suffix of נתנך and are governed by נתן. But in Biblical Hebrew this would be expressed as אתך ואת כל אהביך. The correct translation is therefore, 'I will make you a terror to yourself and to all your friends' (NEB), and v. 4 then indicates that the name (מסביב) מגור given to Pashhur will be indicative not only of his personal fate and that of his family (cf. v. 6), but also of the terror, demoralization and disintegration which will overtake his circle of friends and the entire community.

It is unlikely that כל אהביך in verses 4 and 6 refers to a different group from ישבי ביתך (v. 6). His 'friends' are perhaps the colleagues with whom he is professionally associated and who have identified themselves closely with his oppressive measures against the prophet Jeremiah (Weiser). Already Kimchi was exercised with the apparent discrepancy between verses 4 and 6. Rudolph's mode of reconciling verses 4 and 6 does not differ greatly from Kimchi: he observes that the two

occurrences of כל, one in v. 4a and the other in v. 6a, should not
be thought to create a difficulty—the meaning is simply that
some will die in Judah and some will go into exile, while Pashhur
himself and his family will suffer exile, and will die and be
buried in a foreign land. Rudolph and Weiser also pick up (cf.
Kimchi) the thought of burial in an unclean land (Amos
7.17—ארץ טמאה), and the fate of Pashhur is compared with
that of Amaziah. Burial in an unclean land for a cultic officer
charged with the maintenance of cultic purity is a punishment
which fits the crime.

Verse 5 makes perfectly good sense without the elements
which are missing from Sept. (cf. Janzen, p. 117); this point can
be made more forcefully in so far as the effect of אתן is to give
the syntax of the verse an unexpected twist, and ובזזום ולקחום
may very well be the consequence of a process of piling on the
agony. There is little doubt that v. 5 refers to wealth which has
been accumulated in a city as a result of sustained endeavours
(יגיעה), and, in particular, to the treasures of the kings of Judah.
All these are to be pillaged and brought to Babylon. Again in
v. 6 Sept. has a shorter text than MT, one which is entirely
adequate and may be earlier than MT. Janzen's suggestion
(p. 119) that there may be a haplography in Sept. caused by the
two occurrences of ושם does not work, because (a) It does not
explain why תבוא is not represented by Sept. and (b) It does not
explain why תמות is represented by Sept. In so far as MT is
intelligible, the textual observations which have been made do
not amount to proposals to make deletions from MT, but אתן
should be deleted from v. 5. The insertion may have been
encouraged by the presence of אתן in v. 4.

The view that Baruch's biography of Jeremiah first appears at
chapter 19 (1, 2 *, 10f., 14f.; 20.1–6) has been rejected. In
agreement with Thiel 19.14f. is explained as an editorial bridge
which enables Jeremiah to make his inflammatory speech in the
temple court and so triggers the action of Pashhur who was
responsible for maintaining order and decorum in that area. It
should not, therefore, be supposed that 19.1, 2 *, 10f., 14f.,
20.1–6 constitutes a reliable, historical source on the basis of
which a sequence of events in the ministry of the pre-exilic
prophet Jeremiah can be reconstructed: his symbolic action at
the Gate of the Potsherds (19.1, 2 *, 10f.), his repetition of a
message of doom in the temple court (19.14f.), his arrest or
torture by the chief of the temple police and its sequel (20.1–6).
There is no reason to doubt the attribution of the breaking of the
jug and its explanation to Jeremiah, and his confrontation with
Pashhur is entirely credible, but it should not be supposed that

there was an original, historical connection between the two incidents.

20.1 in its extant form is also part of the bridging device: this must be the case with את הדברים האלה which refers back to 19.15 (so Thiel). But, in all probability, 20.1 is influenced in a more thorough-going way by its bridging function. The report of a confrontation between Jeremiah and Pashhur may be a genuine, historical recollection, but it was separate from the symbolic action of breaking the jug, while the extant form of 20.1 is dictated by the intention of establishing a historical sequence between the symbolic action and the conflict with Pashhur.

It has already been argued that 20.4–6 are to be understood as an exegesis of מגור (מסביב) (above, p. 462), and are consequently a secondary expansion of v. 3. Those scholars who are sceptical about the reference to Pashhur as a prophet have good reasons for their scepticism (cf. Thiel, p. 227, n. 24, Nicholson), but instead of supposing that אשר נבאת להם בשקר is an extraneous element in vv. 4–6, we should understand it as part and parcel of the exegetical intention of vv. 4–6. Rudolph does not find anything incongruous in the idea that Pashhur was a temple prophet, and Weiser remarks that the distinction between prophet and priest cannot be so sharply drawn as is sometimes supposed. Thiel's view that it is unlikely that there would be any wavering in the line of demarcation between prophet and priest in the late pre-exilic period is the opposite of this (p. 227 n. 24). Already Kimchi had portrayed Pashhur as a שלום prophet. If, however, we accept as historically accurate that Pashhur was a priestly official of high rank charged with preserving good order in the temple, can we take seriously the suggestion that he was also a temple prophet? Someone supervising police functions in the temple area was probably far removed from a prophetic function.

I. Meyer (*Jeremia und die falschen Propheten*, 1977) has argued that reports of conflict between Jeremiah and שלום prophets constitute a genuine, historical recollection. Such conflict arose out of the special conditions associated with Jeremiah's ministry, but was developed and systematized in exilic times in furtherance of a tendency to attach all the opposition which had been encountered by the prophet Jeremiah to prophetic opponents. This was part and parcel of the Deuteronomic/Deuteronomistic search for a theological explanation of the fall of Jerusalem and the exile (cf. Thiel, p. 229). It is likely that the operation of some such explanatory principle has produced the representation that the collision between Jeremiah and Pashhur was between a true prophet and a false one (cf. the tendency of the Targum on Jeremiah to specify as 'false prophets' those who are represented as Jeremiah's opponents).

The mention of בבל in vv. 4–6 is probably a pointer that the Babylonian exile was already an accomplished fact. Rudolph takes it as an indication that we should assign the event reported here (the clash with Pashhur) to c. 605 (Bright, pp. 133, 174f., between 609 and 605), when the advances of Nebuchadrezzar showed that Babylon was now the decisive power in the Near East. Rudolph supposes that the clash with Pashhur preceded the interdict on Jeremiah's presence in the temple (36.5), but was later than the events of chapter 26, when Jeremiah was rescued by the politicians from the clutches of the priests and prophets of the Jerusalem temple. The interdict is assumed to have been the consequence of Jeremiah's confrontation with Pashhur (also Bright). The repressive measures of Pashhur are to be seen as a resort to harassment after the failure of the attempt on Jeremiah's life reported in chapter 26. The opinion has already been expressed that scholars have tended to be too sanguine about the possibility of attaching pieces of prophetic literature to a precise historical background, and this caution should be borne in mind in the present case.

A PROPHET BROUGHT INTO CONTEMPT (20.7–9)

[7]You deceived me, O Yahweh, and I was deceived,
you overcame me and prevailed.
I have become a subject of mirth at all times,
everyone jeers at me.
[8]Whenever I speak, I must cry out in anguish,
proclaiming violence and outrage;
the word of Yahweh has become to me
a continual source of insult and derision.
[9]If I say, I will put it out of my mind,
I will not speak another word in his name,
it is like a burning fire within me,
it is imprisoned in my body.
I am worn out containing it
and can do so no longer.

At 20.7, according to Duhm, we reach the oasis of a Jeremianic poem (vv. 7–11) after a trek through a desert. It is clear, therefore that he does not suppose that there is an intrinsic connection between the Pashhur incident (vv. 1–6) and vv. 7ff. Rudolph also discounts this possibility and D. J. A. Clines and D. M. Gunn (*ZAW* 88, 1976, p. 404) say of vv. 1–6 that they are in all probability not the occasion of vv. 7ff. The juncture may be indicative of an editorial view that Jeremiah's inner turmoil and prophetic dilemma arise out of the sense of outrage which he feels after his treatment at the hands of Pashhur (cf. Clines and Gunn, pp. 402ff.).

The transition from assurance of deliverance and praise of God (vv. 11–13) to a cursing of the day of one's birth is harsh (Weiser), and even if we suppose that vv. 12 and 13 are later interpolations, this does not effectively mitigate the impression of discontinuity between verses 11 and 14. Nor is Duhm's observation that vv. 11f. are an afterthought, added by Jeremiah when the agitation expressed in vv. 7–10 had abated, a satisfactory answer. Rudolph asks whether the range of feeling, from joy and assurance to cursing and despair in vv. 7–18, is not explicable as an oscillation caused by a great inner conflict—by the struggles of a prophetic soul. These considerations are not, however, sufficiently compelling to support the conclusion that vv. 7–18 constitute a continuous utterance of the prophet.

Weiser (also Bright) holds that vv. 7–13 constitute a unity. He supposes a liturgical model to satisfy which he argues that the original order of the verses was 7–10, 12, 11, 13. These verses are to be interpreted in a liturgical setting and are a combination of lament and thanksgiving as in Pss 6, 13, 22, 28, and 30. The lament has a narrative form in which there is a description of distress, and prayer for deliverance appears in v. 12. Assurance of deliverance is expressed in v. 11, and the command to praise God (plural imperatives) is addressed by the prophet to the worshipping congregation. There are difficulties in the form of Weiser's argument, and his hypothesis lacks economy: (*a*) Although 20.12 is almost identical with 11.20 and is probably secondary in chapter 20 (so Duhm, Baumgartner, p. 48, Volz and Rudolph), Weiser supposes that it is original in both places and that its repetition is explicable in terms of the stereotyped language of prayer (p. 170 n. 1). (*b*) He has to reverse the order of vv. 11 and 12 to make the passage conform to his liturgical model, and then he appeals to the model to dispose of an objection to v. 12 which is founded on the extant order of the verses in MT. The right conclusion is that vv. 12 and 13 are secondary (so Duhm) in the context of vv. 7–13. The firmest part of the argument of Clines and Gunn (pp. 397f.) that vv. 7–13 encapsulate 'a developed pattern of thought' is the contention that the elements of vocabulary which are common to v. 7 and v. 10 (פתה and יכל) are a demonstration of the structural integrity of vv. 7–10. This has to be weighed with other considerations, and a more probable conclusion than the one reached by Clines and Gunn is that פתה and יכל in v. 10 are catchwords which have promoted the adjacency of vv. 7–9 and

v. 10. The uses of פתה and יכל in v. 7 (v. 9) and v. 10 are not identical: if the image in v. 7 is that of a virgin who has been seduced (see below), it is unlikely that anything of this attaches to יפתה ונוכלה לו (v. 10) which refers to a cunning plot which will take Jeremiah unawares. ותוכל (v. 7) alludes to Yahweh's overcoming of Jeremiah's resistance, and ולא אוכל (v. 9) to Jeremiah's inability to suppress the prophetic word, whereas ולא יכלו (v. 11) refers to the inability of Jeremiah's persecutors to achieve their objectives.

Baumgartner (pp. 63–66) discerns affinities of style and vocabulary between 20.7–9 and laments in the book of Psalms. But it is the aspect of prophetic originality and of the singularity of Jeremiah's experience rather than that of imitation which he finally emphasizes. He describes v. 8 as prophetic in its entire scope. Again, although he compares ואמרתי (v. 9) with its use to introduce thoughts or words in the psalms (30.7; 31.15, 23; 32.5; 38.17; 39.2; 94.18; 116.11; 119.57; 140.7; 142.6), it is clear that his exegetical interest is in the singularity of Jeremiah's experience as this is conveyed by v. 9 (p. 65).

The only grammatical difficulty in v. 7 is constituted by חזקתני which is explained by Rudolph as an equivalence of חזקת לי or חזקת ממני. This is how it is taken by Vulg. (*fortior me fuisti*). The emendation of חזקתני to החזקתני (Ehrlich, p. 293, Baumgartner, Weiser, Berridge) is intended to achieve a transitive sense, 'grasped me' or 'overpowered me', but does not have much support from the uses of the Hiphil of חזק in Biblical Hebrew. One would have expected החזקת בי (see below on Deut 22.25 and 2 Sam 13.11). For Weiser and Berridge (op. cit., pp. 151–155) the emendation has particular exegetical implications, since it combines with their view that a single image of seduction and violation is sustained throughout v. 7a. Support for this interpretation is found in the use of פתה (Exod 22.15) in relation to the seduction of a virgin, and also in the use of the Hiphil of חזק with reference to forcing a woman to have sexual intercourse (Deut 22.25–27; 2 Sam 13.11; following A. Heschel, *Die Prophetie*, 1936, pp. 92f.). Among the versions only Pesh. (*ḥsntny*) can be said to lend direct support to this exegesis, since *ḥsn* is used in Syriac of the forcing of a woman.

Neither Rashi nor Kimchi gives any indication that they are aware of the figure of a deceived and violated virgin in v. 7a, and they relate the language of the verse without any mediating imagery to the circumstances of Jeremiah's call, particularly his unwillingness to respond to it which was brushed aside by Yahweh. Neither Lowth nor Blayney explore the imagery, but both are concerned to soften the charge of deceit levelled against Yahweh. Lowth suggests that פתיתני יהוה ואפת refers to the

pressure exercised by Yahweh and the overcoming of Jeremiah's
unwillingness to assume the prophetic office. Blayney holds that
Jeremiah is not charging Yahweh with deceit, but is confessing
that he was 'dazzled' by the prospect of holding a prophetic
office. The thought of Yahweh exercising undue pressure is also
disposed of by Blayney, since he explains חזקתני ותוכל (חזק,
Piel) in terms of the effective encouragement given by Yahweh
to Jeremiah. Calvin's apologetic in relation to the problem of
Yahweh cheating Jeremiah is a different one. The language is
ironic and is a device adopted by the prophet in the face of
allegations that he is an impostor. By saying that his adversaries
can be right only if Yahweh is the deceiver, he is saying with the
greatest emphasis that they cannot be right.

Both Baumgartner and Rudolph suppose that there are two
independent but complementary images in v. 7a: Yahweh's
deception of Jeremiah is like the seduction of an innocent girl;
Yahweh has arranged a contest with a weak adversary, and has
fought or wrestled with an opponent who was no match for him.
In view, however, of the evidence that פתה is legal vocabulary
for seduction (Exod 22.15) and of the use of חזק (Hiphil) to
indicate the forcing of a woman (Deut 22.25), the right
conclusion is that v. 7a employs the language of seduction and
violation. Jeremiah feels a deep sense of betrayal in view of his
sorrowful experiences as a prophet and the bitterness of the
outcome of his acquiescence. Yahweh overpowered him, crushed
his resistance and compelled him to be a prophet, and he has
found the office a bed of nails. The consequence to which he
gives particular expression in v. 7b is that he has become a figure
of cruel fun and an object of contempt. This goes on all the time
(כל היום) and more or less everyone takes part in it (כלה). There
is no problem in the use of ה to represent the 3rd masc. sing.
suffix, since the earliest extant Hebrew inscriptions attest this
use. Kimchi is right in giving a collective reference to כלה (דרך
כלל), and this is present in the renderings of Vulg. (omnes),
Pesh. (klhwn) and Targ. (כולהון).

It is notable that it is derision rather than any reference to
ill-treatment which appears in v. 7b, and this is one reason why
an intrinsic connection between vv. 1–6 and 7–9 should not be
sought. It is not evident that vv. 7–9 are triggered by Jeremiah's
ill-treatment at the hands of Pashhur. Rudolph concludes that
the catastrophe had not enveloped Jerusalem, that this
circumstance explains the contempt in which the prophet is held,
and that the passage should probably be dated in the time of
Jehoiakim. Nicholson concludes that the lament belongs to the
early years of Jeremiah's ministry 'well before the storm-clouds
which eventually brought disaster to the nation had appeared'.

But a too particular reference should not be sought for v. 7b. It should not be supposed that there is an allusion to unfulfilled prophecies of doom and that chronological conclusions can be drawn from the verse. What Jeremiah cannot bear is that he should be reduced to a huge joke, to a target of general ridicule. That the effect of prophetic obedience should be the sabotaging of his right to be regarded as a serious and reasonable person and that he should be metamorphosed into a weird crank was more than could be borne. This is the thought to which he returns again in v. 8b, where the reference to the prophetic word is explicit: it is obedience to his task as God's spokesman which draws on him insult and ridicule.

The import of v. 8a is less clear and there are various possibilities. It is clear that Targ. refers v. 8a to the utterance of Jeremiah's prophetic message: 'For whenever I raise my voice, weeping and crying out, it is concerning plunderers and looters that I prophesy.' It is likely that the other versions share this understanding of v. 8a. Thus Aq. has κεκραξομαι for אזעק and Pesh. agrees with Targ. in its paraphrase of חמס ושד אקרא, 'It was about plunderers and looters that I was preaching', that is, 'I was uttering prophecies of doom' (also Vulg. vastitatem, Aq. προνομην). This is also the view of v. 8a which appears in Rashi: 'For whenever I speak to them, I am compelled to shout and raise my voice, and I never proclaim good to them but prophecies of חמס and שד.' Kimchi also sides with this exegesis, but he introduces the thought of a quid pro quo in connection with חמס ושד : the prophet threatens the people with what they have inflicted on him.

Baumgartner (p. 64) and Rudolph suppose that v. 8a is a cry for help (אזעק) uttered by the prophet in the face of the persecution to which he is subject. It is not altogether clear what Weiser's view of v. 8a is, but he observes that חמס ושד is a phrase used elsewhere in the prophetic literature (Jer 6.7; Ezek 45.9; Amos 3.10; Hab 1.3) of an oppressive and unjust regime, and that in Jer 20.8 the prophet is represented as suffering persecution in his own person. This suggests that Weiser agrees with Rudolph and Baumgartner, but he also supposes an allusion to prophecies of doom, since he remarks: 'He (Jeremiah) encounters deaf ears and contemptuous rejection with his constant criticism and threats of disaster.' Bright leaves open the alternatives of threats of doom and the criticism of a cruel and arbitrary regime in his exegesis, while in settling for the former Nicholson follows a line of interpretation which is set by Pesh., Targ., Rashi and Kimchi.

Berridge's attempt (p. 154) to represent that the figure of a violated virgin is sustained throughout vv. 7–8 must be regarded as unsuccessful. Even if it is present in both stichs of v. 7a, it is not the key to the understanding of v. 7b. Are we to suppose that in v. 7b the prophet is still likening himself to a virgin who has suffered outrage? Is he saying that he has suffered the contempt and cruel jests which are heaped on a girl who has been seduced or forced? The answer to these questions must be in the negative, and it is then a mistake to suppose that seduction imagery is present in v. 7b or that it is revived in v. 8a. Berridge, however, is probably right to maintain (cf. Bright) that חמס ושד is a kind of expletive, an explosive expression by means of which emotional pressure is lowered, and the view that חמס ושד is indicative of such an explosion of intense personal feeling is compatible with the form of the motive clause in v. 8b. What is it that creates such unbearable inner pressures and contradictions? It is the circumstance that the oracles which Jeremiah has to proclaim have made him into a target for insult and ridicule (so Ehrlich, p. 293).

The view that v. 8a is a reference to prophecies of doom uttered by Jeremiah should be rejected, because it does not account satisfactorily for the Hebrew of v. 8a, or for the nature of the connection between v. 8a and v. 8b. אזעק must mean something like 'I cry out for help', and if this is so, חמס ושד אקרא cannot be an allusion to prophecies of doom. It too like אזעק must refer to an expression of inner desperation and extremity. In v. 8a the prophet describes himself as one who is under constant siege, a beleaguered soul, hard-pressed and continually crying out for help. In v. 8b he explains why he has been reduced to this condition: it is the consequence of his obedience to his prophetic vocation. He has spoken the prophetic word and the result has been that he has suffered a loss of self-esteem and of general reputation. There is no other biblical evidence that חמס ושד is a reference to prophecies of doom. In the passages already noted (above, p. 471) what is indicated is not future doom, but conditions of injustice, lawlessness and oppression already existing in the community. Hence the biblical evidence lends support to the view that חמס ושד אקרא refers to Jeremiah's criticism of the moral condition of the Judaean community (Lowth; cf. 6.7), but this interpretation of v. 8a does not cohere well with אזעק or with v. 8b. The conclusion is that אדבר, אזעק and חמס ושד אקרא do not refer particularly to prophetic utterances of the prophet Jeremiah, whether of doom or reproof. They do not contain any direct reference to ill-treatment or persecution. He is saying that his speech has been reduced to a continuous cry for help (מדי אדבר אזעק), to an explosive verbal expression of inner desperation (חמס ושד אקרא),

and that it is his obedience to his prophetic calling which has
reduced him to this condition.

It appears that Kimchi is influenced by an assumption of
parallelism between the first two stichs of v. 9: because the
second stich clearly indicates Yahweh (בשמו), it is supposed that
the suffix of אזכרנו also refers to Yahweh. This translation
appears in Bright and in NEB ('I will call him to mind no
more'). Rudolph and Weiser opt for 'it', and this is probably
correct. If the parallelism of v. 9a is thought to constitute an
argument for 'him', the counter-considerations are more
powerful. It is precisely דבר יהוה which brings the prophet into
contempt (v. 8), and it is the word of Yahweh which burns like a
fire within him (v. 9). Hence a reference to דבר יהוה precedes
and follows אזכרנו, and the right conclusion is that the suffix of
אזכרנו picks up דבר יהוה and is resumed by והיה בלבי כאש
בערת.

The masculine form of עצר is accounted for by GK132d in
terms of the dislike of the over-use of feminine forms: when two
adjectives follow a feminine noun, the first may be feminine
(בערת) and the second masculine (עצר). The renderings of Sept.
and Pesh., both of which introduce the idea of fire, probably rest
on the same grammar as that of GK: they assume that עצר is to
be connected with אש. This understanding of the matter is also
found in Rashi and Kimchi. It does not, however, appear to be
necessary to construe the line in this way, creating a
grammatical difficulty which requires a special explanation. The
simile is simply that the word of the Lord is like a blazing fire
(כאש בערת), and עצר בעצמתי is a resumption of והיה בלבי (cf.
Vulg., Claususque in ossibus meis) not of כאש בערת. עצר
בעצמתי is just another way of expressing the confinement or
imprisonment of דבר יהוה which is also indicated by והיה בלבי,
and the simile which expresses what it is like to have the word of
Yahweh so locked up within oneself is כאש בערת — it is like
trying to contain a conflagration. The sense of כלכל (v. 9)
indicated by the versions (Aq., Symm., Vulg., Pesh., Targ.) is
'endure'. This finds general favour (cf. Baumgartner, Rudolph
and Weiser, auszuhalten), but it is the thought of containment
rather than the more general one of endurance which has to be
identified (cf. Bright, 'And I struggle to hold it in'; NEB, 'And I
was weary with holding it under'). It is not simply that the
prophet is worn out and can endure no longer, but rather that the
struggle to contain the word of God within him, to deny it
expression and to suppress the utterance which wells up within
him, drains him of all strength and energy.

Jeremiah's effort to remain silent is interpreted by Weiser as
rebellion, and his awareness that he cannot maintain this silence

as the awakening of a sense of guilt. The human being should not be so severed from the prophet who speaks the word of God; it should be appreciated that the prophetic word arises out of the depths of human suffering, and that it is the product of a conflict which is both agonizing and fruitful. The prophetic word is born out of Jeremiah's human anguish, and it is because there is this great tumult of inward conflict and contradiction that he reaches that vision of the truth which stamps him as a prophet. Prophetic conflict is not to be interpreted as rebellion and guilt or reduced to human frailty.

Rudolph argues with reference to Amos 3.8 and 1 Cor 9.16 that a feeling of compulsion is the mark of an authentic prophetic utterance. This thought of compulsion (עַל כָּרְחִי) is present in the exegesis of v. 9 which appears in Rashi and Kimchi. Rudolph comments, 'The prophet cannot do what he would like to do, but speaks because he must, even when he does not will it.' But language of this kind raises the same order of theological difficulties as the language of Weiser. The prophet's sense of being compelled to speak is significant psychologically and, perhaps, theologically, but it is none other than he who speaks. No other voice sounds but his voice, and what he says arises out of his own sorrowful but enriching experience. Then again the statement that the prophet does not will what he speaks is too reckless and dangerous an interpretation of compulsion to win acceptance. If he speaks against his will, his freedom is overwhelmed by a force which he cannot resist, and his utterance is no more his than that of a man whose integrity has been destroyed by violence or torture or drugs.

The contribution which 'compulsion' can make to our understanding of the mystery of prophetic experience and the nature of revelation is exaggerated by Rudolph. There is no all-embracing explanation of these problems waiting to be captured. The most that can be made of 'compulsion' is that what we are loath to utter and can only utter after overcoming inner resistance is not so subject to the dangers of wilfulness, self-assertiveness or self-deception as those utterances which we have a natural inclination to make. The thoughts which are congenial to us and which we are inclined to embrace, or the attitudes which are agreeable with our desire for security are more liable to error than those which force themselves on us because they have a truth which we cannot ultimately evade and to which we must give expression, even if we fear or shrink from the consequences of so speaking.

The compulsion exercised by 'truth' or 'word of God' does not simply overpower or suppress or abrogate the inner conflict: all the elements that contribute to the tumult and sorrow in the prophet's soul are necessary to his vision of the truth. In that case it has to be asserted that 'word of God' does not mean 'non-human words'. Yet, if these words constitute a 'revelation', they must proceed from an encounter between the prophet and God. It is the absolute belief in the reality of this meeting and engagement to which the prophet gives expression when he prefaces his words with 'Thus says Yahweh'. But the relation between this encounter and the prophet's speech is not simple or immediate. The experience of so engaging God is mysterious and even ineffable, and an expression of its significance can be achieved only by a process of 'translating' it into human language and filtering it through human experience. The 'translation' will be inadequate, but in the speech of men and out of a grasp of the truth which it is given to an exceptional person to possess, he endeavours to communicate in a linguistic form the significance of his meeting with God.

There are also particular reasons for Jeremiah's unwillingness to speak what his conviction of truth compels him to speak, for he has told us that it has consequences which he can no longer endure. It has destroyed his credibility as a human being in the eyes of his contemporaries; it has made him into an absurd extremist; it has encouraged so cruel a caricature of him that he feels that his character has been assassinated in the process of fulfilling his prophetic vocation. Because he spoke the truth which impinged on his mind, he has been divested of all credibility and seriousness as a human being and exists to be laughed at.

THREATENED BUT INDOMITABLE (20.10–13)

[10]I hear the whispering of many—Terror on every side!:
Denounce him! Let us denounce him.
All who pass for my friends
are waiting for me to stumble:
Perhaps he will be taken in and we shall have him at our mercy,
then we shall have our revenge on him.
[11]But Yahweh like a ruthless warrior is with me;
therefore my pursuers will stumble and achieve nothing.
They will suffer deep shame at their lack of success,
disgrace which will never be forgotten.
[12]But you, Yahweh Sabaoth, test the righteous,
you see into men's deepest thoughts.
Let me see you wreak vengeance on them,
for I have confided my case to you.
[13]Sing to Yahweh, praise Yahweh,
for he has rescued the poor man from the power of evil-doers.

Baumgartner's observations (pp. 48–51; 63–66) on the differences between vv. 7–9 and 10–11 constitute an argument for the lack of a significant continuity between the two passages (*pace* Rashi, Duhm, Rudolph). In vv. 7–9 the essential feature is that Jeremiah has been reduced to a laughing-stock by the demands of his prophetic vocation, that his self-respect has been violated, and his claims to be taken seriously as a person destroyed. His insistent note of doom has persuaded most people that he is unhinged and that he should be treated as a joke. Yet, when he determines that he will say no more, he is compelled by a conviction that his words of doom have the power of truth. The situation which is outlined in vv. 10f. is quite different. Here he is aware of a general conspiracy, whose agents he cannot certainly identify, and which represents a sharp threat to his life, but he is resilient and is confident that his enemies will be disconcerted and defeated.

There are differences of opinion as to whether or not מגור מסביב is original in 20.10, and Baumgartner (p. 48), following Erbt and others, has supposed that the expression is secondary and is derived from Ps 31.14. The impetus to insert it would be supplied by the preceding words (כי שמעתי דבת רבים) which are identical in both passages. Thiel (p. 228 n. 26) has noted that Duhm and Volz drew the reverse conclusion, namely, that Ps 31.14 was dependent on Jer 20.10, although Volz too maintained that מגור מסביב was an insertion in 20.10. Duhm holds that כי שמעתי דבת רבים מגור מסביב was a marginal comment at Ps 31.14, and includes מגור מסביב in his 'original' text of Jer 20.10. The problem of how to define the relationship between the two passages may not admit of a certain answer, but it should be noted that in Ps 31.14 כי is a more convincing connective than it is at Jer 20.10.

The matter of מגור מסביב in v. 10 is a bigger one: it touches on the nature of the expression and whether it is ever part of the syntax of the passages in which it occurs. This question demands a negative answer, and in that case מגור מסביב has to be regarded, wherever it occurs, as an exclamation or interjection. This is in general agreement with the view of Berridge (pp. 90f.) that מגור מסביב is a kind of shout, but he elaborates this by associating it with Holy War, and he leans on the work of R. Bach (*WMANT* 9, 1962, pp. 51ff.). It is factually correct that three of the passages involving מגור מסביב are related to circumstances of military defeat, rout and pillage (Jer 6.25; 46.5; 49.29), and H. J. Kraus is broadly right in his view that מגור מסביב is a type of proverbial interjection connected with desperate and terror-filled situations (*BK* 15, 1960, p. 250). מגור מסביב should certainly be rendered as an asyndetic interjection at Jer 6.25, 46.5 and 49.29 (Terror all around!; NEB, Terror let loose!), and no attempt should be made to incorporate it into the syntax of these verses.

The only passage where this treatment does not seem appropriate is Lam 2.22, where the modification of מגור מסביב (מגורי מסביב), 'what causes me terror on every side' or 'those who terrify me on every side' (W. Rudolph, (*KAT* 17, 1962, p. 221) is syntactically connected with the rest of the verse. Rudolph's rendering rests on the emendation of מגורי to מגוררי. Even so the yardstick applied to Jer 6.25, 46.5, 49.29 would be appropriate for 20.10. That מגור מסביב in 20.10 has to be understood as an asyndetic parenthesis by means of which Jeremiah expresses his feelings is a correct conclusion, and if the expression is to be justified as original in the verse, the justification has to be achieved on this basis.

This is not a view which has prevailed in either ancient or modern times, and the construing of v. 10 is influenced in important respects by the treatment which is accorded to מגור מסביב. The ancient versions attempted to integrate it syntactically in v. 10: Sept. ὅτι ἤκουσα ψόγον πολλῶν συναθροιζομένων κυκλόθε (κυκλόθεν), 'For I have heard the slander of many who are closing in around me'. Pesh. and Targ. agree with the sense of Sept., and Vulg. incorporates מגור מסביב into the syntax of the verse in a different manner. There are those modern scholars who delete מגור מסביב from 20.10 (Baumgartner; NEB, Brockington, p. 206), while others explain it as an interjection, but suppose that it is spoken by the conspirators. According to this view it is part of the speech of Jeremiah's enemies, and not an exclamatory parenthesis by means of which the prophet gives expression to a feeling of being hemmed in by conspiracy and enmity.

Rudolph and Weiser assume that the conspirators take up an expression used by Jeremiah in connection with his prophecies of doom and deploy it against him as a kind of taunt or mocking gesture (also Ehrlich, p. 293 and Bright). Given the assumption that מגור מסביב is part of the speech of Jeremiah's enemies, the only parenthetical interruption of their words is constituted by כל אנוש שלימי שמרי צלעי which is interposed by the prophet. The speech then resumes with אולי יפתה and continues to the end of the verse. If, however, מגור מסביב is interposed by Jeremiah, there are two interruptions to the speech of the conspirators in v. 10, and a more natural sequence would ensue if הגידי followed immediately after כי שמעתי דבת רבים. This might be taken as a consideration weighing against the originality of מגור מסביב in 20.10. Duhm and Baumgartner have been influenced by Sept. and represent an unbroken sequence for the speech of the conspirators by means of emendations of MT.

Duhm adopts שמרו, שלומו and צלעו; Baumgartner, שמרו, שלומיו and צעדיו: 'Come let us inform on him; all you who are his friends watch his steps'.

דבת רבים is indicative of the whispered intrigues of conspirators rather than of slander (Sept. ψόγον) or invective (Vulg. *contumelias*). Nor does Pesh. *rny'* 'mocking' capture the sense, while Targ. resorts to the general rendering מילי 'words'. Rashi correctly glosses דבה with מתלחשים 'whispering', and aptly cites 2 Sam 12.19 (וירא דוד כי עבדיו מתלחשים). Kimchi ('the evil which they speak against me') inclines to the sense of Sept. and Vulg., and 'slander' is found in Calvin, KJV and Lowth, whereas 'whisper' is adopted by Duhm, Rudolph, Weiser, Bright and NEB. All these shades of meaning can be accommodated by דבה, and while what is indicated is perhaps a design against Jeremiah's life rather than an assassination of his character, the aspects of detraction and invective may also may be included. The prophet is aware of the buzz of a widely spread conspiracy, and perhaps a process of denigration and incitement, and he feels sharply the threat against his person.

הגידו ונגידנו (v. 10) is understood by Sept. in relation to conspiracy (ἐπισύστητε καὶ ἐπισυστῶμεν αὐτῷ), and by Vulg. of persecution (*persequimini et persequamur eum*). Pesh. paraphrases, 'Inform on him to us and we shall rise against him', and Rashi introduces the thought of employing false testimony in a judical context. The thought that Jeremiah was to be denounced to the king is present in both Rashi and Kimchi. This view that the conspirators are seeking an occasion to denounce the prophet is generally accepted (cf. Baumgartner, p. 50), and Weiser, assuming a close relation between 20.10 and chapter 26, supposes that those who plot against Jeremiah are ecclesiastics rather than politicians, and that the outcome of this conspiracy was the attempt on Jeremiah's life by the temple authorities recorded in 26.

When he makes his interjection, Jeremiah says that those who are closely associated with him and who affect friendship are in the employment of his enemies as spies, and are seeking evidence to indict him. How Sept. ἐπίνοια 'intentions', 'designs' is derived from צלע is a puzzle. Vulg. *latus* 'side' offers a rendering of צלע which is present in the other Greek versions (Aq., Symm., Theod.) and is probably indicated by Ibn Janah's remark (Neubauer, p. 611) that צלע in Jer 20.10 has the sense of Arabic *ḍl'*. Both Baumgartner and Rudolph note that there is no attested use of צלע meaning 'side' ('watching at my side') in relation to a person in Biblical Hebrew. The sense 'stumbling' is indicated by Kimchi and is probably also intended by Rashi's gloss on שמרי צלעי, 'keeping a look-out for my downfall'. This is in accord with the lexicography of BDB which associates צלע in Jer 20.10 with II צלע 'limp', 'stumble', and also with that of KB² (I צלע 'limp'). This is probably correct, although 'watching at my side' accords with the force of Jeremiah's parenthetical observation, namely, that those who adopt the posture of friendship and are in the closest contact with him may be spies in the service of his enemies.

Hence the words 'Perchance he may be duped (or 'outwitted')' have to be read along with the kind of situation which is indicated by כל אנוש שלומי שמרי צלעי. That Jeremiah's enemies are on the watch for the first indication of injudicious words or rash actions has added piquancy if we bear in mind that those who present the sharpest threat to him have all the advantages of friends. He cannot certainly identify his friends and his enemies, and those who enjoy his confidence and are well placed to keep him under the closest surveillance may turn out to be the spies who are setting a trap for him.

Kimchi links the affirmation of confidence in v. 11 with the assurance given to the prophet in the call narrative, 'And they will fight against you but will not prevail' (1.19). On a rising tide of confidence Jeremiah hurls defiance at his enemies and predicts the utter failure of their plans and their irretrievable humiliation. They are in hot pursuit of him, but they will stumble and their efforts to catch him will have no success. ולא יכלו is a mocking echo of the expressed intentions of the conspirators – ונוכלה לו. Sept., Vulg. and Pesh. connect כי לא השכילו with lack of perceptiveness rather than lack of success, but the latter is represented by Targ. (לא יצלחון) and Kimchi who aptly cites 1 Sam 18.14 (ויהי דוד לכל דרכיו משכיל, 'And David was successful in all his enterprises'). There is general agreement among modern commentators (Duhm; Ehrlich, p. 294; Bright, Weiser, NEB) that לא השכילו refers to unskilful action and lack of success, but Rudolph represents strongly the other thought of lack of perceptiveness (*Toren die sie sind!*). It is unlikely that there is this nuance in לא השכילו (it is present in Rashi), but if it is assumed, the exegesis of the verse becomes more subtle. There is blindness in the malevolence of the opposition which Jeremiah encounters. It is the hostility of minds filled with darkness and with no capacity for the perception of truth. That is why for all its intensity and diabolical cunning it is doomed to failure and will end in shame and disgrace for its practitioners. At any rate, Jeremiah reasserts his confidence that truth will prevail. His profound and sorrowful grasp of the realities of Judah's condition will be sustained by Yahweh, and those who resist it, however sophisticated their tactics, will be undone. Sept. and Vulg. attach כי לא השכילו to the second stich of v. 11, but this destroys their balance and should be discounted. Targ. has introduced a verb (יחפינון) in order to deal with the grammatical awkwardness of כלמת עולם לא תשכח: 'And everlasting shame which will not pass away will cover them.' כלמת עולם should be regarded as loosely governed by בשו, and this is hinted at by Kimchi's comment, 'And their shame will constitute disgrace (כלמה) which will not be erased, for they will be a curse in the mouths of men for ever'.

There are small differences between the texts of 20.12 and 11.20: instead of בחן צדיק 11.20 has שפט צדק, and instead of ראה כליות ולב 11.20 has בחן כליות ולב. The following table will show that the versions except Vulg., perhaps under the influence of 11.20, have represented צדק at 20.12, and this is found in a few Hebrew manuscrips:

	11.20	20.12
Sept.	δίκαια	δίκαια
Vulg.	iuste	iusti
Pesh.	qwšt'	zdq'
Targ.	קשוט	קשוט

Against the correct view that v. 12 coheres poorly with the context and is probably an insertion from 11.20, Weiser argues for its originality (above, p. 468). Weiser's intention is not to make Jeremiah into a cultic prophet but to establish that he adopted a positive attitude to the liturgy of the 'Covenant Cult', and, at the same time, to maintain the particular and unique aspects of his individual, prophetic experience: in this case to represent a conflict between him and the authorities of the Jerusalem temple. The kind of reconciliation which Weiser seeks to effect with his postulation of a covenant festival and an actual cultic setting for 20.9–13 is not credible. Can we believe that Jeremiah would have taken part in proceedings of the Jerusalem cult and have adopted a positive attitude to its liturgy at a time when (*ex hypothesi*) his life was being threatened by the authorities of the Jerusalem temple who had moved against him because he had predicted the destruction of that temple (26.4–6)?

The merit of Weiser's treatment of v. 13 is that he does recognize that the plural imperatives constitute a problem, for this awareness does not seem to be present in the exegesis of v. 13 offered by Baumgartner (p. 51) and Rudolph, while Duhm, regards the verse as a fragment in the style of a psalm which originated as a marginal comment. Kimchi is aware of the plural imperatives and comments on שירו ליהוה: 'He (Jeremiah) says this with reference to the חסידים who were in Jerusalem'. Jeremiah is presumably the speaker, but to whom does he speak? (cf. Kimchi, above). Baumgartner gives us no help with this question. Nor is the quotation from Köberle, which Rudolph introduces with approval, of any help in this regard. It does, however, lead us into the most important question to be asked about v. 13—whether אביון is to be regarded as a suitable or even credible designation of the prophet Jeremiah. Baumgartner contents himself with an endeavour to establish that the 'righteous poor' are already a class in the time of Amos (2.6; 5.12), and that 'psalms of the poor' were in existence in Jeremiah's time. So he concludes (p. 51), 'Jeremiah could, in view of his procedure of transferring the expressions of the 'Lament' to his own situation, so designate himself'. But he has emphasised Jeremiah's pugnacious attitude to the conspirators and this does not agree well with the situation and disposition of an אביון. Weiser (p. 173 n. 3) observes that in the self-designation of the prophet as אביון the theme 'need of help' is expressed: the distressed petitioner seeks relief from his distress. Weiser has represented that vv. 10–13 have to be related to Jeremiah's clash with the authorities of the Jerusalem temple, in connection with his prediction recorded in chapter 26 that the temple would be destroyed. Is it conceivable that a personality so powerful and disturbing that he constituted a threat to the ecclesiastical establishment, and also, as we know from elsewhere in the book, to the king and the political establishment, could be described as an אביון?

Hence v. 13 must be explained as the response of a pious reader or commentator to Jeremiah's affirmation of confidence, and certainty of victory over his enemies. It is thought to be an appropriate snatch of an invitation to thanksgiving with which to celebrate Jeremiah's victory. Although in the circumstances of vv. 10f. Jeremiah is not an אביון, it is understandable that he should be so viewed by the pious psalmist, for what strikes him is the defencelessness of the prophet in the grip of powerful oppressors (מרעים), and yet his victory over them through Yahweh's power. Whether v. 13 originally followed v. 11 and was subsequently separated from it by the insertion of v. 12, or whether the order of the build-up was rather vv. 11, 12, 13, is impossible to ascertain. Although the conclusion is that v. 12 has been inserted from 11.20, and v. 13 is also secondary and is not explicable as a word of the prophet Jeremiah, this should not be taken as a proposal that vv. 12f. are to be deleted. There is no single, universally applicable criterion which will enable us to decide whether deletion is the best course or whether we should stop short of deletion and simply express a view about the present form of MT and how this has come about. It is inevitable that one will fall into inconsistencies of one kind or another. The degree of incoherence or unintelligibility presented by the material which is deemed to be secondary is an important factor, but so is also its quantity. It is one thing to delete or emend a word, but it is another matter to take away two verses from MT. It is this latter consideration which has prevailed here, in spite of a firm conclusion that neither v. 11 nor v. 12 coheres well in the context vv. 10–13.

A CURSE ON THE DAY I WAS BORN! (20.14–18)

[14]Cursed be the day on which I was born!
The day on which my mother bore me,
may it remain unblessed!
[15]Cursed be the man who brought my father news:
A male child has been born to you,
who showered congratulations on him.
[16]May that man be like the cities
overthrown by Yahweh without compunction;
may he hear cries of distress in the morning
and loud shouts at noonday;
[17]because I was not killed at birth,
that my mother might be my grave
and her womb hold a child never born.
[18]Why then did I emerge from the womb
to see (only) toil and trouble
and to end my days in shame?

Baumgartner (p. 67 n. 3) follows an impressive list of commentators (including Graf, Giesebrecht, Duhm, Erbt) in concluding that Job 3 is dependent on Jer 20.14–18, and Rudolph has judged it to be an imitation of the Jeremiah passage. It is doubtful whether the question of literary dependence on one side or the other is the right one to raise, while the explanation which is content to focus on the general character of such a loathing for life as both passages manifest is hardly adequate (cf. Weiser). The argument would then be that men fall prey to such a dark and utter revulsion for life and that the language which is summoned to depict the colours of such a mood has a general similarity in cases which otherwise have no connection with each other.

But there are resemblances between the patterns of expression in the two passages which are sufficiently particular to suggest that certain conventions are being followed and that literary ingredients thought to be appropriate or necessary to the expression of a curse on the day of one's birth are being used. It should be asked whether the kind of opposition which has been set up between the two passages (Baumgartner, pp. 66f., Weiser) is not overdone. It is alleged that Jer 20.14–18 is an artless, passionate cry of anguish, whereas Job 3 is a more contrived literary expression of disenchantment with life, in which the problem is treated intellectually with a display of rich literary resources and mythological allusions and with a certain detachment or coldness.

It is not evident that Job 3 is sophisticated in a bad sense, that it lacks truth of sentiment or high seriousness. It is a noble poem rather than a literary exercise on a conventional theme, it does not descend to a display of mere cleverness, the sentiments are not artificial nor are they frozen by a too intellectual treatment. The subject is developed by a remarkable succession of appropriate thoughts clothed in elevated language, and the chapter has a claim to be regarded as fine poetry. The passages are disparate in so far as the Jeremiah passage contains a briefer expression of the subject 'A curse on the day of my birth' than the Job passage. To this Duhm has added an antithesis of roughness and literary polish in so far as he is persuaded that Jer 20.14–18 is rough-hewn—a first literary transcription of Jeremiah's tumultuous feelings which never received a final form and polish.

The thought that literary conventions were brought into play in cursing the day of one's birth, and that it is a stylized composition with identifiable stereotypes is not new. It is elegantly expressed by Lowth (followed by Blayney) and has recently been touched on by Clines and Gunn (pp. 405–407). One can detect an apologetic motive in Lowth's treatment of the matter. We should not mistake for spleen or personal vindictiveness Jeremiah's outbursts against the messenger who brought to his father the news of his birth (so Lowth). These are literary techniques for expressing profound sorrow and perplexity, and so Jeremiah is to be exculpated from the charge of outrageous and irreverent behaviour with which Calvin taxed him. The other aspect of Lowth's interpretation is even more interesting. He supposes (as does Duhm) that 'birthday' means not simply the actual day of birth, but the recurring anniversaries of that day and that the composition is the antitype of a birthday greeting—a kind of black birthday greeting: a birthday has become an occasion not for felicitations (אל יהי ברוך — v. 14) but for cursing.

If there is such a model involved—a black birthday greeting—it did not operate in a rigid way. There were different mixes for the ingredients, and the poet could, without too much fettering of his genius, indulge his literary preferences and follow the flight of his imagination. Nevertheless, the degree of correspondence between the treatment of the subject in the two passages is so impressive that it is difficult to resist the conclusion that there was a given literary mould into which a poetic effusion on the subject 'A curse on the day of my birth' was poured. The scaffolding consists of the following items:

(*a*) The opening: A curse on the day when I was born (Jer 20.14; Job 3.3–10)

(*b*) The announcement of the birth (Jer 20.15; Job 3.3).

(*c*) The thought of the mother's womb as a grave, or the idea of being still-born (Jer 20.17; Job 3.11, 16).

(*d*) The question, 'Why did I emerge from the womb to encounter a life of suffering and woe?' (Jer 20.18; Job 3.20–26 — למה in both passages).

The first item is developed at considerable length in Job 3.3–10. The circumstance that there is so much of this in Job 3 has encouraged the supposition that a similar situation obtains in Jer 20.14–18. Thus Duhm argued that האיש ההוא (v. 16) was a gloss, and Rudolph and Weiser propose that האיש ההוא should be emended to היום ההוא, the intention in both cases being to establish that v. 16 resumes v. 14 and that vv. 16f. refer to the day of birth and not to the messenger. Such a precise correspondence between the two passages should not be envisaged, nor is it borne out in other respects. For example, with regard to point (*b*)—leaving the disputed v. 16 out of consideration for the time being—there is a fuller treatment of the human messenger in the Jeremiah passage (v. 15) than there is in Job. In Job there is no human messenger, only a message which is delivered by a personified 'Night'.

Further differences appear in item (*c*) which is strikingly expressed in Jer 20.17 in two variants of the same idea: the womb as a grave and a pregnancy which does not culminate in a birth. These are not exactly paralleled in Job 3.11,16, for emerging dead from the womb is different from the incarceration of a dead foetus in the womb. In any case the development of the 'grave' idea is different in Job 3.13–19: the grave is the symbol of rest and repose and of release from the tempest of life. These are reflections which embrace men whose styles of life are far apart, and who are released by death from widely differing conditions and estates. This is a treatment of the 'grave' theme which has no point of contact with the Jeremiah passage, and it appears to have had a special fascination for the author of Job 3, for he returns to it (vv. 21f.) in connection with his treatment of (*d*). The general expression of (*d*) is that life ushers one into an experience of prolonged and unrelieved misery and trouble (Jer 20.18): life is summed up in suffering and shame at the end, and a question-mark is placed over the whole of it. This is the tenor of Job 3.20–26 also, apart from the special orientation of vv. 21f.

There is a difference between art and artificiality, and the circumstance that there was a literary mode for the cursing of the day of one's birth does not detract from the reality of Jeremiah's desperation or the terror of his pessimism and repudiation of life. It is true that the balance between convention and truth of expression, between tradition and spontaneity or freshness is a general literary problem and that such a balance is always a fine one. The constraints imposed by the discipline of an order in the form of literary conventions may be conducive to a chaste and refined work of art. On the other hand, conventions may take control and a poem may degenerate into an exhibition of linguistic skill without vision or depth of sentiment. But the circumstance that a human being under the impact of tempestuous emotions achieves an ordered expression of his anguish in accord with a recognized literary mode does not destroy his feelings or rob them of their immediacy.

Duhm (Rudolph, Weiser) supposes that the absence from the poem of any cursing of Jeremiah's parents (cf. 15.10) is evidence of a reserve created by his deep respect for them, and that the messenger who announces his birth is then a kind of surrogate or scapegoat. The curse which, for reasons of filial piety, the prophet would not launch against his father and mother falls on the head of the unfortunate messenger who had supposed that he was the bearer of good news, when he brought to the father word of the son's birth. This question about the involvement of the messenger in the curse, is already found in Kimchi, but is the wrong kind of question. The circumstance that there is an announcement of the birth also in Job 3 and that there is no cursing of parents there either makes it probable that the reason why there is no cursing of parents in Jer 20.14–18 is simply that it was not an item in the literary scheme of cursing the day of one's birth. Again, the presence of the cursing of the messenger in the Jeremiah passage has to be related to the particular way in which the poet has developed 'the announcement of the birth' item. The same type of criticism is to be levelled against the speculations of Rudolph and Weiser concerning the reasons for the publication of the curse in vv. 14–18. The prophet (so it is urged) sought to achieve an inner catharsis and to humiliate himself publicly by openly acknowledging what had been a secret descent into despair and apostasy. There was also, so it is urged, the intention to help those who were similarly threatened by an engulfing, black pessimism. But there is no way of testing these proposals, interesting though they may be, and the better course is to refrain from making them.

Similarly Duhm's remark, received sympathetically by Rudolph, that suicide is not seen as a way of escape for the totally disillusioned person in the Old Testament is not entirely borne out by the evidence (cf. 1 Sam 31.4–6; 2 Sam 17.23), but,

486   COMMENTARY ON JEREMIAH

apart from this, the absence of any reference to suicide in Jer 20.14–18 and Job 3 is probably sufficiently explained by the circumstance that it was not part of the literary pattern of cursing the day of one's birth. Moreover, Duhm's remarks may rest on a wrong understanding of Jeremiah's pessimism. Not all despair, not even the deepest despair, is necessarily linked to suicide, and the black mood which finds expression in Jer 20.14–18 needs a more sensitive and positive appraisal. Although Rudolph's remark that exaltation and depression are complementary modes of experience in men of deep and excruciating insight is not to be accepted as an argument for the unity of Jer 20.7–18, it does make a contribution to our understanding of vv. 14–18. The power of a prophetic mind to penetrate beneath the surface of things and to achieve a singular commerce with the truth is not exercised without inner strife and spiritual suffering. Those who see so much and so clearly have a fineness of constitution and a capacity for feeling which make them vulnerable to bewilderment and pessimism.

The textual difficulties in vv. 14–18 are not considerable, but some matters merit special treatment. אל יהי ברוך (v. 14) may be regarded as a *leitotes* or understatement which matches ארור and is part of a chiasmus: the order of יום אשר ילדתני אמי and אל יהי ברוך is reversed as compared with their matching elements in the preceding line. Another reason, however, for the choice of אל יהי ברוך has been suggested above (p. 483), namely that it serves to point the contrast between 'happy birthday greetings' and the antitype which is constituted by cursing the day of one's birth. In v. 15 ילד לך בן זכר has to be compared with הרה גבר (Job 3.3). On the specification of the sex of the child Kimchi comments, 'Men rejoice over a male child, but are sad concerning a female'. The messenger has the joy of bringing good news to the father who is hoping for a son and is fearful lest the announcement of the birth may be a disappointment to him (cf. Baumgartner). In the event his highest hopes are realized, and the messenger has the congenial task of conveying news which will give pleasure in the highest degree (בשר). One can, therefore, see that the entrance of the figure of the messenger into a 'A curse on the day of my birth' is functionally important in connection with the experiences of disillusionment and hopelessness which are being represented and explored. The one who brought the good news now falls under the curse, for the day of birth can no longer be regarded as an occasion of rejoicing and an event full of hope. Where there is no conviction that life is touched with blessing, its value cannot be confidently affirmed, and birth has to be viewed as the beginning of tribulation.

Ehrlich (pp. 294f.) has noticed that שמח (Piel) has the special sense of 'congratulate', 'convey felicitations' in post-biblical Hebrew (לשמח חתן וכלה), and this gives a different nuance to שמח שמחהו: it is not so much the conveying of good news as the offering of congratulations which is indicated by שמח שמחהו. The good news has been communicated and the pleasure given by ילד לך בן זכר, and this is followed by the offering of hearty congratulations. This must be regarded as a serious alternative to 'filling him with joy'.

In v. 16 the versions (Sept., Vulg., Pesh) assumed that והיה and ושמע had the force of jussives and this is a reasonable procedure. It has already been urged (above, p. 484) that a comparison of Jer 20.14–18 with Job 3.3–10 does not, by itself, furnish a decisive indication that היום ההוא is preferable to האיש ההוא. The force of this argument, as it is conducted by Rudolph and Weiser, is weakened by the fact that the correctness of האיש in v. 15 is not questioned. If the cursing of the day of birth were unbroken in vv. 14–16, as it is in Job 3.3–10, the argument for היום in v. 16 would be stronger. Further, it is not obvious that the simile in v. 16, which is cumbersome in any case, is made sharper or more transparent by the adoption of היום ההוא. Duhm and Weiser have urged that the allusion to times of the day within the simile (בעת בבקר; צהרים) creates a presumption in favour of היום over against האיש, but more attention has to be given to the simile itself before the weightiness of this can be fully assessed. The association of כערים אשר הפך יהוה with the overthrow of Sodom and Gomorrah is suggested by the similarity of the language in Gen 19.25 (ויהפך את הערים האל), and this exegesis is found in Jerome and Rashi. There is no reason to doubt the rightness of this, and if it is correct what is represented is a judgement (ולא נחם) of Yahweh enforced by a natural catastrophe. The problem, however, is that there are elements of vocabulary in v. 16b which suggest rather military defeat and the terror of enemy invasion. Thus תרועת מלחמה occurs at 4.19 and צהרים (6.4) is represented as a time of day when an attack might be launched. It may be that we have two separate images (so Weiser) and that the messenger or the day of birth is cursed first with reference to Sodom and Gomorrah and then with reference to a day of military disaster. It would, however, be a more economical hypothesis if v. 16b could be subsumed under the Sodom and Gomorrah representation (the attempt of L. Prijs to do this, *VT* 14, 1964, pp. 104–108, is too contrived).

The martial connections of תרועה in Biblical Hebrew are strong (Num 23.21; Josh 6.5, 20; 1 Sam 4.5, 6; Jer 4.19; 49.2; Ezek 21.27; Amos 1.14; Zeph 1.16; Job 39.25), and BDB supposes that they are also present in Jer 20.16. If we interpret

אשר הפך יהוה ולא נחם as a reference to military disaster, we can then suppose that זעקה is the cry of distress of the victims, and תרועה the war cries of soldiers intoxicated with victory and wreaking havoc among the vanquished. If we try to incorporate v. 16b into the 'Sodom and Gomorrah' interpretation, we have to regard זעקה and תרועה as more or less synonymous, both being cries of distress issuing from those who are caught up in Yahweh's anger on that day of judgement. Kimchi supposes that the cries are those of relations and friends of the victims, so that what is indicated is the wailing of mourners, and this may be compared with an alternative exegesis offered by Lowth, influenced by the thought that the genre is a variation on the funeral dirge.

We should conclude in the interests of economy that v. 16b refers to Sodom and Gomorrah on the day of judgement. Is this representation better served by היום than it is by האיש? If האיש is read the sense is: May the man who brought news of the birth be like Sodom and Gomorrah which were overthrown by Yahweh's judgement on a day when they rang with cries of distress issuing from their citizens. If היום is read, we have to, assume that the simile is imperfectly articulated and that what is intended is something like: May that day be like (the day on) which Yahweh overthrew Sodom and Gomorrah; may it hear cries of distress in the morning, shouts of anguish at noon. In view of the fact that the versions support האיש, that there is no other textual evidence in support of היום, and that האיש is present in v. 15 in any case, an emendation of MT is unjustifiable.

It has been usual to argue (Duhm, Cornill, Baumgartner, Rudolph, Weiser, Bright) that מרחם (v. 17) is an error attributable to the influence of מרחם (v. 18), and that Sept. (ἐν μήτρᾳ) and Pesh. (bmrb") indicate ברחם. Whether in fact these versions read ברחם is doubtful (cf. Vulg. a vulva and Targ. ממעיין). More probably the translations of Sept. and Pesh. were influenced by the persuasion that 'at birth' (cf. מרחם, Job 3.11) did not furnish a sufficiently exact parallel for ותהי לי אמי קברי: the parallelism appeared to require ברחם — not death at birth but death in the womb (cf. M. J. Dahood, Biblica 44, 1963, pp. 204f.: מרחם to be pointed מְרֻחָם, 'enwombed'). The resemblance between מרחם אמות (Job 3.11) and מותתני מרחם is sufficiently close to create a presumption in favour of the rightness of MT at v. 17, and one may suppose, as NEB does, that מותתני מרחם is a sufficiently flexible expression to comprehend death in the womb ('because death did not claim me before birth'), as well as death at birth, the sense at Job 3.11.

If האיש is retained in v. 16 and is regarded as the subject of מותתני (so Baumgartner), vv. 15–17 are directed against the

messenger who announced the birth, and the recrimination in
v. 17 is that he did not destroy the foetus before birth. That אֲשֶׁר
means 'because' (Duhm = יַעַן אֲשֶׁר), as Sept. (ὅτι) and Vulg.
(qui) suppose, is correct, but the verse which is introduced by
אֲשֶׁר (v. 17) does not connect so particularly with v. 16 as is
thought by those who make either הָאִישׁ or הַיּוֹם the subject of
מוֹתְתַנִי. Rather אֲשֶׁר introduces a reason for the entire cursing
process, and it brings this process to a conclusion, for v. 18 is not
a continuation of it. The agonizing Why? is a protest against the
senselessness and cruelty of life and a repudiation of its meaning
and value, but it is not part of a curse.

The correct understanding of v. 17 (cf. L. Prijs, op. cit.,
pp. 107f.) is that it relates to all that has gone before. The fury
of Jeremiah's cursing of the day of his birth is explained by his
repudiation of life and his totally negative estimation of it
(v. 17). It would have been better for him if life had never begun.
Hence the paraphrase of Targ.: 'Alas! that it was not ordained
for me that I should die in the womb.' This is the direction
followed by both Rashi and Kimchi. On אֲשֶׁר לֹא מוֹתְתַנִי Rashi
comments מַלְאַךְ הַמּוֹת מֵרֶחֶם, 'the angel of death at birth' and
this is an equivalence of 'because life was not withdrawn from
me before I had been born'. The conclusion is that אֲשֶׁר לֹא
מוֹתְתַנִי relates to the entire, preceding process of cursing and
that it elucidates the repugnance for life and the repudiation of it
which the cursing implies. לֹא מוֹתְתַנִי is correctly construed as an
impersonal construction to be rendered as a passive: 'Because my
life was not extinguished before I was born, so that my mother's
womb might have become my grave'.

If וְרַחְמָה (without mappiq, cf. GK 91e) means 'and her
womb', there is the problem of explaining the feminine gender of
הָרַת (fem. sing. part. Qal of הָרָה?), since רֶחֶם is masc. gender.
The versions (Sept., Vulg., Pesh.) overcame this difficulty by
assuming that הָרַת was construct state of הָרָה 'conception' or
'pregnancy'. M. Wallenstein (VT 7, 1957, pp. 209–213) has
noted that מְרַחֶמֶת means 'mother' in a Qumran hymn (p. 213),
and, with reference to Judg 5.30, רַחַם רַחֲמָתַיִם, 'a damsel or two'
and Mesha 17, רַחֲמֹת 'damsels', 'female slaves' (cf. J. C. L.
Gibson, Syrian Semitic Inscriptions, i, pp. 75f.), has suggested
that מְרַחֵם (Jer 20.17) should be regarded as a synonym of אִמִּי,
'and she who conceived me for ever pregnant'. The folk-lorist
associations of the thought of a never-ending pregnancy have
been noted by Baumgartner (p. 67 n. 1): a woman carrying
around for a lifetime a child of which she will never be delivered,
whose womb is the sepulchre of a dead mass rather than the
matrix of a child which will be born.

Verse 18 is introduced by Why?, but no answer is expected.

The lines of Jeremiah's existence are too firmly drawn to admit change and his destiny cannot be modified. This passage is not at all to be understood merely as a yielding to despair which was a temporary aberration (so Weiser), a time of weakness and failure which has no contribution to make to Jeremiah's prophetic vision of the truth (the tendency of Baumgartner's remarks, p. 67). Jeremiah understood what was happening to Judah and this foreknowledge wrought havoc within his own life. To suppose that his despair and rebellion are one thing (a private, human matter) and his affirmation that Judah was doomed is another, is to misunderstand the delicate balance between commitment to the truth and openness to despair which characterizes those who suffer for their sensitivity and involvement. In so far as Prijs (op. cit., pp. 106ff.) emphasizes this aspect of vv. 14–18 his exegesis is to be commended. Jeremiah's despair was not a temporary aberration (*pace* Rudolph, pp. 133f.), but was a threat which was always present, an abyss over which the prophet was always suspended. The conviction that he bore in his human frame God's truth about the destiny of his own community was not easily sustained. It was a burden which had to be borne and a truth which had to be affirmed strenuously when tides of despair rose to swamp it. It bore the marks of inner struggle and unrelieved contradictions, and of journeys into despair which would have to be endured to the end.

CHAPTER XXI

YAHWEH IS FIGHTING AGAINST JERUSALEM (21.1–7)

¹Jeremiah received this word from Yahweh, when Zedekiah, the king, sent to him Pashhur, son of Malchiah, and Zephaniah the priest, son of Maaseiah, with this request: ²Ask Yahweh to come to our help, for Nebuchadrezzar, king of Babylon, is besieging us. Perhaps Yahweh will perform a miracle for us as he has done in the past and Nebuchadrezzar will lift the siege. ³Jeremiah said to them: This is what you are to say to Zedekiah: ⁴These are the words of Yahweh, God of Israel: The weapons of war, which are in your hands, with which you are fighting the king of Babylon, I will turn away from the Chaldaeans who are besieging your walls and will concentrate them on the heart of this city. ⁵I in person will fight against you with outstretched hand and a strong arm, with anger and rage and great fury. ⁶I will strike down the inhabitants of this city, both man and beast. They will be victims of a great pestilence. ⁷Afterwards (This is Yahweh's word) I will give Zedekiah, king of Judah, and his officials and the people who are left[1] in this city, who have survived pestilence, sword and famine, into the power of Nebuchadrezzar king of Babylon—into the power of their enemies and those who seek their lives. Nebuchadrezzar will put them to the sword without sparing them, without pity or mercy.

It is a reasonable assumption that the intention of the final editor of 21.1–10 was to represent a sequence of events having a rough correspondence with those indicated by chapter 52.4–16 (cf. 39.1–10; 2 Kgs 25.1–12). On this view vv. 1–6 deal with the siege which was a consequence of Zedekiah's rebellion against Nebuchadrezzar and the tightening of that siege. It began in the tenth month of the ninth year of his reign and continued until the fourth month of the eleventh year, when the defenders were on the point of being starved into submission (52.6). At this point (ואחרי כן, 21.7) Zedekiah and his soldiers broke out of the city, but Zedekiah was overtaken and captured; he was blinded, put in chains, carried off to Babylon and made a prisoner for life (52.6–11). The details of 21.7 cannot be accommodated to this account, but there is a reference to Zedekiah and his professional soldiers (or, perhaps, court officials — עבדיו), and we may suppose that the people who were left in the city (on the text, see further below) are those who remained in Jerusalem after the exit of Zedekiah and his party.

We cannot, however, improve on this imperfect correspondence between 52.4–16 (39.1–10; 2 Kgs 25.1–12) and 21.1–10. What follows in 52.12 is the movement of Nebuchadrezzar's army into Jerusalem, the burning of temple and palace and all the great houses, and the demolishing of the walls. Those who remained in the city were deported to Babylon,

---

[1] Reading ואת העם הנשארים (see below, p. 501).

including those who had deserted or surrendered to the Babylonians, and only a few were left behind to cultivate the land. Thus, if 21.8–10 is located after Zedekiah's break-out (as the editor may have intended), and is understood as a last appeal by Jeremiah to those remaining in the city, the terms of the appeal ('Surrender and save yourselves') cannot be reconciled with what is said to have happened in 52.12–16, where those who had deserted (surrendered) to the Babylonians were not singled out for special treatment, but were deported along with the others. The ground of Jeremiah's appeal in 21.8–10 is that the city is doomed and that those who remain in it will share its fate, while those who surrender to the Babylonians will be safe, but, according to 52.12–16, those who were in the city when the final assault was made and those who had earlier deserted (surrendered) to the Babylonians shared the same fate.

No amount of shuffling of the different accounts of the siege of Jerusalem and of Jeremiah's interviews with Zedekiah will produce a coherent whole. The words contained in 34.1–5 are said to have been spoken by Jeremiah while Nebuchadrezzar was laying siege to Jerusalem and to the towns of Judah (v. 6), and they belong to the same period as 21.1–10. Yet, on any interpretation of 34.1–5, the words spoken to the king are in conflict with the statement of 21.7 that Zedekiah will be put to the sword. Within 34.1–6 itself there would appear to be an incompatibility between what is said in v. 3, which has a threatening aspect ('You shall not escape the clutches of the king of Babylon. You shall be captured and brought into the king's presence in Babylon as a prisoner'), and what is said in vv. 4f., which has a reassuring aspect ('You shall not be slain; you shall die in peace'). The matter hinges on whether 'die in peace' in this context means no more than 'Your life will be spared' or 'You will die a natural death', and is therefore compatible with capture, exile and imprisonment. Weippert's argument (pp. 69f.) that 34.2–7 rather than 21.1–7 has the appearance of *ex eventu* prophecy assumes that the former is reconcilable with the account of these events which is given in 52.4–11 (39.4–7), but the problem constituted by 'die in peace' is then exacerbated. Is the slaying of Zedekiah's sons in his presence, the gouging out of his eyes, his deportation and imprisonment for life in Babylon a credible fulfilment of a prediction that he would die in peace? The correct appraisal is that neither 21.1–7 nor 34.2–7 is compatible with the fate of Zedekiah as described in 52.4–11 (39.4–7).

The passage which has been thought to have a special relationship with 21.1–7 is 37.3–10, but it is not obvious why scholars have supposed that 21.1–7 is derived from 37.3–10, or is a compilation of which 37.3–10 is a major constituent (Duhm, Skinner, Rudolph, Thiel, p. 231, n. 3). An examination of these two passages shows that it is not so much a matter of conflicting testimony as of divergent concerns with which we have to reckon: 37.3–10 does not deal overtly with the fate of Zedekiah, but with the fate of Jerusalem. The circumstances of the interview between Jeremiah and Zedekiah (so we are told) were the raising of the Babylonian siege brought about by a relieving Egyptian army. Jeremiah's word to the king was that the Babylonians would come back and press the siege to a successful conclusion. Jerusalem would not be spared: it would be set on fire and destroyed. The message concentrates on the certain fate of Jerusalem. Simply from the point of view of the coherence of 37.3–10, it is not obvious that the 'embassy' (v. 3) is more convincing in that context than it is in the context of 21.1–7. When the siege had been lifted and the crisis was less acute what impetus was there for the king to send two representatives to Jeremiah with a plea for special prophetic intercession? The verse about the sending of the embassy does not have any *raison d'être* in connection with the circumstances reported in vv. 5–10. In 21.1–7, on the other hand, when Jerusalem is under siege, the function and the appositeness of the 'embassy' in the literary context is more easily discernible. Thiel (p. 232), who holds that 21.1–3 is dependent on 37.3–7, has to make the uneconomical assumption that his postulated Deuteronomistic editor created a new historical situation for the embassy in 21.1–7 in order to confer on his narrative a larger, independent existence.

A certain confusion has resulted from the circumstance that in the judgements which they have passed on these passages scholars have been influenced by a mixture of literary and historiographical considerations. For example, the concern to establish the independence of 21.1–7 over against 37.3–10 (Weiser, Bright; cf. Thiel, p. 231 n. 3) is not simply a statement about the literary independence of 21.1–7, but tends also to be directed towards the vindication of the historicity of 21.1–7. The statement which has been made above is limited to the observation that the 'embassy' fits better into the literary context of 21.1–7 than into that of 37.3–10, and that the subject-matter of 37.3–10 (the certain doom of Jerusalem) is more limited than that of 21.1–7. The case for the literary interdependence of 21.1–7 and 37.3–10 is weak.

Further, the judgement of scholars who suppose that 37.3–10 is the principal source of 21.1–7 (Duhm, Rudolph, Thiel, p. 231) has been influenced by prior source-critical and historiographical assumptions. They assume that 37.3–10 is part of Baruch's 'memoirs', and that as such it is historically more reliable than

the contents of 21.1–10 which are thought by Rudolph
(following Mowinckel) to belong to Source C, and by Thiel to be
a Deuteronomistic composition. The critical assumption of
Duhm, on the other hand, is that 21.1–10 betrays the activity of
the post-exilic *Ergänzer* whom he postulates. But the
assumptions of Rudolph and Thiel create insoluble literary
problems, and Weippert (pp. 69f.) is right to ask Rudolph why
the compiler of 21.1–7 did such a shoddy job, if the passage is, as
Rudolph maintains, an *ex eventu* composition which makes use
of 37.3–10,17, 34.2–7, 38.1–3,14–23 (all, according to Rudolph,
parts of Baruch's memoirs).

In fact, however, 21.1–10 does not have the literary
cohesiveness which Rudolph claims for it, and cannot be credibly
interpreted as a sequence of events contained in vv. 1–7 and
vv. 8–10. That this is so for vv. 8–10 has been acknowledged by
Weiser, Bright and Thiel (p. 235), but v. 7 is no more a
convincing continuation of v. 6 than vv. 8–10 are of v. 7. Nor is
Thiel's attempt (pp. 230–237) to demonstrate that 21.1–10 is the
composition of a Deuteronomistic author beset by fewer
difficulties. It is an elaborate hypothesis concerning the
Deuteronomistic expansion of a core of sayings in v. 4 and v. 9,
attributable to the prophet Jeremiah; it is well argued, but it is
fraught with uncertainties.

It may have been the intention of the final editor of 21.1–10 to
represent that Jeremiah's appeal in vv. 8–10 was made after
Zedekiah and his men had broken out from Jerusalem and when
the final assault was taking place, but the actual contents of
21.1–7 will not permit such a sequence of events. Whatever
textual conclusions are reached in respect of v. 7 (see further
below) its contents do not allow for any survivors to whom the
prophet could have spoken in the terms of vv. 8–10. This leads to
the observation that the choice between life and death which
Jeremiah is said to have held out to the people in these verses fits
better into the context of 38 than it does into the context of
21.1–10, although Rudolph has concluded that 38.2 is derived
from 21.9 and is an addition in chapter 38.

The problem of coherence is, however, already present in
21.1–7: ואחרי כן at the beginning of v. 7 indicates a sequence of
events, but the sequence which is described does not follow from
v. 6, because vv. 5f. describe an all-embracing destruction, and
with them matters come to an end. The conclusion is that the
editor of 21.1–10 has attempted to portray a sequence of events
corresponding imperfectly with the sequence in Jer 52.4–16
(39.1–10; 2 Kgs 25.1–12), but that the contents of vv. 5–6 will
not allow the continuation in v. 7 indicated by ואחרי כן, and the
contents of v. 7 will not allow the continuation in vv. 8–10.

Rudolph has observed that there is a sudden transition from the reign of Jehoiakim to the final period of the monarchy which requires explanation, and Weiser has remarked that there is a gap of ten years between 21.1–10 and the events dealt with in chapter 20. Thiel (p. 231) has also noted that 21.1–10 is chronologically misplaced: a reference to the siege of Jerusalem at this point in the book is not to be expected. What then are the particular reasons for the positioning of 21.1–10. An old answer (J. D. Michaelis; cf. Rudolph) is that 21.1–10 is stitched to chapter 20 by means of 'Pashhur', although the Pashhur of 21.1 is a different person from the Pashhur of 20.1–6. Rudolph's answer is a refinement of this: it utilizes the repetition of the name 'Pashhur', but only in so far as this is regarded as an echo which heightens the contrast between the persecuted prophet of 20.1–6, and the prophet whose advice is sought after by the king and who enjoys prestige and authority. It was in order to point the contrast that 21.1–10 was located where it now stands in the book of Jeremiah (cf. Thiel, p. 231). Thiel supposes that 21.1–10 was composed by his postulated Deuteronomistic editor as an introduction for the verses concerning kings and leaders which follow in the literary complex 21–24 (p. 230). The intention of this editor or author is to emphasize the unrelenting character of Yahweh's judgement, and the relation of 21.1–10 to what follows is that of threat of doom to *Begründung*. Hence the explanation of the position of 21.1–10 is to be found not by looking back to chapter 20, but by looking forward to the chapters with which 21.1–10 is bound up, in the complex 21–24 (p. 237).

YAHWEH IS FIGHTING AGAINST JERUSALEM (21.1–6)

According to Mowinchel and Rudolph the introductory formula (הדבר אשר היה אל ירמיהו מאת יהוה), which occurs in 11 places in the book of Jeremiah (7.1; 11.1; 18.1; 21.1; 25.1 (without מאת יהוה); 30.1; 32.1; 34.1,8; 35.1; 40.1), is a mark of a postulated Source C (*pace* Weiser who assigns 21.1–10, an account in the 3rd person, to Baruch; similarly Weippert, p. 73 n. 207). Weippert (pp. 72f.) argues that the formula is not necessarily a mark of the postulated Source C, and urges that in 18.1–12, 32.1–44 and 35.1–19 there is a lack of intrinsic connection between the formula and what follows it. The grammatical connections of the introductory formula within vv. 1–2 are such that it cannot be regarded as a superscription of chapter 21–24 (*pace* Thiel, p. 230). The argument that it does not lead on to a word of Yahweh (Thiel) is not to be taken too

seriously: this may be an indication that צדקיהו ... כשלח is a
secondary elaboration which defines the historical occasion of
the oracle (vv. 4–6), in a manner akin to psalm titles, but it does
not lead to the conclusion that הדבר אשר היה אל ירמיהו מאת
יהוה, with its present connections in vv. 1–2, is intended as a
superscription for 21–24. In any case the difficulties should not
be exaggerated, for, without straining too hard for sense, vv. 1–3
can be read in such a way that the word of Yahweh to which v. 1
refers is seen to make its entrance at v. 3, and כשלח ... מעלינו is
then construed as a parenthesis.

If it were assumed that the references to the embassy in 21.2
and 37.3 had historical value, we might suppose that the king's
representatives were in fact Jehucal ben Shelemiah and
Zephaniah ben Maaseiah (so 37.3), and that Pashhur has been
substituted for Jehucal ben Shelemiah in 21.2 to secure the
effects described above (p. 495). In this connection it should be
noted that Jehucal (Jucal) and Pashhur are associated in 38.1,
where they are said to have overheard the saying of Jeremiah
which appears at 38.2 and 21.9, and, as statesmen concerned for
the morale of the civilian population, to have reported it to the
king.

There are no textual difficulties in v. 2: Nebuchadrezzar
reflects *Nabū-kudurri-uṣur* more accurately than
Nebuchadnezzar. It always occurs in Ezekiel and is usual in
Jeremiah. Only in chapters 27–29 (except 29.21) and (in some
editions) 34.1 and 39.5 does the form with נ appear. This the
form which prevails elsewhere in the Hebrew Bible. The
meaning of the Babylonian name is either 'Nabu guards the
boundary' or 'Nabu guards the son' (*kudurru* = *aplu*, see
Rudolph). The sense of דרש נא בעדנו את יהוה is 'Ask Yahweh
to intervene and save us from the otherwise inevitable outcome
of Nebuchadrezzar's siege' (so Ehrlich, p. 295), rather than 'Ask
Yahweh to declare his will to us through your prophetic
mediation in this moment of extreme danger'. The king's
deputies are pleading with the prophet to exert his influence in
order to persuade Yahweh to intervene and effect a miraculous
deliverance (ככל נפלאתיו). They can see no hope for the besieged
city, unless an extraordinary turn of events forces
Nebuchadrezzar to lift the siege and withdraw. The king's
representatives are asking Jeremiah for a reassuring oracle of the
kind which Isaiah is said to have uttered (Isa 37.33–35; 2 Kgs
19.32–34) and are looking for a miracle of the kind which saved
Jerusalem on that earlier occasion (Isa 37.36–37; 2 Kgs
19.35–36). Weiser (cf. Rudolph, Bright, Nicholson) doubts the
rightness of this conclusion and supposes that נפלאתיו refers to
saving acts celebrated in the cult.

The degree of similarity between 21.1–3 and 37.3–5 (*pace* Thiel; above, p. 496) is impressive only in two regards: (*a*) The common feature of a deputation. (*b*) The verbal resemblances between the pleas of the deputies:

דרש נא בעדנו את יהוה 21.2

התפלל נא בעדנו אל יהוה אלהינו 37.3

What this signifies for the literary interdependence of the two passages is uncertain, but in all the circumstances the best conclusion is perhaps that בשלח ... צדקיה is a secondary elaboration and represents an attempt to provide a suitable historical occasion for the prophetic words contained in vv. 4–6. If this is so, the text originally ran הדבר אשר היה אל ירמיהו מאת יהוה כה אמר יהוה. There is, however, no textual support from the versions for this, and it is no more than a guess. If vv. 1b–3 are secondary, v. 3 can no longer be regarded as a reliable indication of the original destination of the oracle in vv. 4–6. There is, however, not very much at stake: if vv. 1–4 are an original unity, we would expect the oracle to be addressed to Zedekiah, since it was given as a reply to his enquiry, but, in any case, it is clear that the words are not simply about the fate of Zedekiah, but about his kingdom, capital city and subjects. They are in no sense a private message to Zedekiah, but a public proclamation about the fate of Jerusalem and Judah.

The most interesting feature of the shorter text of Sept. (Janzen, pp. 43, 205 n. 18) is the absence of any representation of ואספתי אותם and Janzen (cf. Duhm) is right to dispute Giesebrecht's opinion that these words are necessary to the syntax of v. 4. In more general respects he is right in his estimate that MT is an expansion of a shorter text (cf. Bright, p. 215 n. 4), rather than, as Rudolph and Weippert (p. 67 n. 178) suppose, that Sept. is an abridgement of MT. Janzen assumes that ואספתי אותם was inserted to ease the grammatical construction of the verse which the secondary relative clause (אשר בידכם) and the expansion (את מלך בבל ו) had made less transparent.

Thiel's 'original' text of v. 4 runs as follows:

הנני מסב את כלי המלחמה מחוץ לחומה

ואספתי אותם אל תוך העיר הזאת

There is a poor correlation between this and the text of Sept., and there are two factors, in particular, which distort Thiel's judgement on v. 4: (*a*) His concern to reconstruct an original saying with parallelism which leads him to retain ואספתי אותם. (*b*) His concern to make the contribution of the Deuteronomistic author begin with the alleged key-word נלחמים. ואספתי אותם does not create unintelligibility and need not be deleted. It should be said, however, that it has not succeeded as an

explanatory gloss, and that the reference of the suffix of את has
been a source of contention. It has been referred to כלי המלחמה
by some and to הכשדים by others. The latter is indicated by
Sept.^OL (cf. Jerome) and by Theodotion (αυτους), and has found
support from Kimchi, Ehrlich, Volz and Nötscher (cf. Duhm: it
is ambiguous, either 'weapons' or 'Chaldaeans'). The other view
is represented by Giesebrecht, Weiser and Rudolph. Weippert
(p. 67 n. 178) is undecided, and Nicholson thinks that the suffix
refers to the Chaldaeans, although he inclines to the view that
ואספתי אותם originated as a marginal comment.

The interpretations which have been offered of v. 4 have been
too general: the siege will be tightened, and the Judaean soldiers
who have been operating outside the city will be forced to retire
within the walls (Rudolph, Weiser). In the case of Bright this
exegesis is supported by the interpretation of כלי המלחמה as a
metonymy for 'Judaean soldiers', so that ואספתי אותם means
that these soldiers will be 'pulled back' into the city. Weippert
(p. 84; ZAW 82, 1970, p. 401) notes this as a traditional but
unsatisfactory interpretation of v. 4. If we are guided by Sept.
and assume that ואספתי אותם is intended to explicate this
shorter text, we must conclude that the suffix of את refers to כלי
המלחמה. Yahweh will fight against the defenders of Jerusalem,
and the weapons which ought to be pointed against the besieging
Babylonians will be directed by Yahweh against the city and its
inhabitants. By attending to the particularity of the
representation in v. 4, we are brought to a conclusion which
contradicts Thiel's view that the idea of Yahweh fighting against
Israel is a contribution of his Deuteronomistic author. On the
contrary, it is embedded in the 'original saying' which he
reconstitutes, for there is no good reason for supposing that the
connection of אשר אתם נלחמים with הנני מסב את כלי המלחמה
בם (which is represented by Sept.) is not original.

The view that v. 4 is a representation of 'Holy War' in reverse
has been developed at length by Weippert (ZAW 82, 1970,
pp. 402–409) who has associated v. 4 with passages in which
Yahweh is depicted as instilling panic in the ranks of Israel's
enemies, so that they turn their arms against their comrades and
engage in an orgy of self-destruction. In order to explain the
transference of panic and self-destructive madness (מהומה) from
Israel's enemies to Israel itself Weippert appeals to curses in
Hittite (c. 1300 B.C.) and Assyrian (672 B.C.) treaties, where
the curse which will operate if the treaty is broken will be a
self-destructive use of arms induced by gods. Hence Weippert
concludes that Jer 21.4 refers either to suicide or to reciprocal
slaughter.

The thought that in vv. 5–6 there is a reversal of the concept

'Yahweh fighting for Israel' has been developed by Rudolph, Weiser, Thiel (p. 233 n. 6 with reference to G. von Rad, *Der heilige Krieg im alten Israel*[4], 1965), and is already to be found in Duhm. This subject is also treated by Berridge (pp. 117f.) with reference to J. Soggin (*VT* 10, 1960, pp. 79–83). It is maintained that the language of v. 5 (ביד נטויה ובזרוע חזקה) has been wrenched out of the context of Yahweh's action to deliver Israel from Egypt, and is now used of a God who fights against his people rather than for them. That there is in Jer 21.5 a unique reversal of adjectives in relation to the other occurrences of ביד חזקה ובזרוע נטויה is noted by Thiel (p. 233) and Berridge (p. 117).

Janzen (p. 43) supposes that the longer texts of MT at 21.5 and 42.18 are probably secondary expansions, whereas Weippert holds that 'triadic' expressions (ובאף ובחמה ובקצף גדול; cf. מן הדבר מן החרב ומן הרעב at 21.7) are a stylistic feature of the prose of the book of Jeremiah (p. 82). Rudolph and Thiel emphasize the Deuteronomic/Deuteronomistic associations of ביד נטויה ובזרוע חזקה (*pace* Weiser; Weippert, *Die Prosareden*, p. 82). ובאף ובחמה ובקצף גדול is paralleled by Deut 29.27. The extent of the Deuteronomic/Deuteronomistic affiliations of the vocabulary of v. 5 does not matter much, unless so much weight is placed on them that vv. 5–6 are regarded as a subsequent Deuteronomic/Deuteronomistic padding of the substance of v. 4. The cohesiveness of vv. 4–6 (apart from בדבר גדול ימתו) is so impressive that such a conjecture need not be hazarded. The theme of Yahweh fighting against Israel is firmly established in v. 4 and is developed in a coherent way in vv. 5–6* (up to את האדם ואת הבהמה), and there is no reason to doubt the unity of these verses. Yahweh turns the weapons which should be used in the defence of Jerusalem against the defenders themselves (v. 4) and he fights against them ובאף ובחמה ובקצף גדול, venting his fury on them. Is this vocabulary and mode of representation capable of being interpreted as a reference to the decimation of the population of Jerusalem by epidemic under siege conditions? Kimchi comments on (v. 5), 'The Chaldaeans will fight against you from the outside, and I shall fight against you with a great pestilence, for I shall smite you and your livestock'. This is how בדבר גדול ימתו is related to what precedes in vv. 4–6 by Rudolph and Weiser. Nevertheless, the correct answer to the question which was asked above is a negative one: הכיתי (v. 6) is not a reference to the striking down of the inhabitants of Jerusalem by plague, but is a continuation of the portrayal of Yahweh as a warrior, employing defensive weapons against Jerusalem and inflicting massive casualties. It is a slaughter carried out with כלי המלחמה and not a decimation effected by plague. If this is so, what is the explanation of the appearance of בדבר גדול ימתו at the end of v. 6?

We may explain it as an exegetical addition which is wrong but not inept, in so far as the Hiphil of נכה is used in Biblical Hebrew of the inflicting of plagues by Yahweh (BDB 646a). We may suppose, as Weiser does, that it is a deliberate allusion to the plague which was said to have decimated Sennacherib's army, when he was investing Jerusalem (2 Kgs 19.35; Isa 37.36). In that case Jeremiah's prediction of what will happen is portrayed as the antitype of that miraculous deliverance: plague was the weapon with which Yahweh winnowed the besieging Assyrian army, and now it is the weapon which he will employ against the inhabitants of Jerusalem.

The intention of בדבר גדול ימתו is rather to establish that the part of Jeremiah's oracle in vv. 4–6 corresponds with 2 Kgs 25.1–3 (Jer 52.4–6). It should be noted that these parallel passages conclude with a reference to severe famine in Jerusalem caused by the siege, and to the threat of starvation facing its inhabitants. Their continuation (2 Kgs 25.4; Jer 52.7) is an allusion to the break-out from Jerusalem effected by the king and his soldiers. It is, therefore, probable that בדבר גדול ימתו seeks to associate Jer 21.4–6 with the description of Jerusalem reduced by famine and decimated by plague in the period of the siege prior to the break-out of Zedekiah and his soldiers. It is connected with an editorial endeavour to provide a three-stage timetable for vv. 1–10, with which, however, the contents of the passage cannot be reconciled and to which they are not amenable. Hence בדבר גדול ימתו does not contribute to the original sense of vv. 4–6.

DOOM FOR ZEDEKIAH AND FOR THE REMNANT (21.7)

Verse 7 is not amenable to the explanation which is given to it by Jerome (first of all the prophecy is about the whole city; now it is predicted of Zedekiah in particular, and of those who remained after pestilence, sword and famine, that they will be captured by Nebuchadrezzar and mercilessly put to the sword). Rudolph and Weiser express similar views. The correct understanding of v. 7 is rather that it is a subsequent expansion founded on a misreading of vv. 1–6 and connected with the addition at the end of v. 6 (בדבר גדול ימתו) which is evidence of that misreading. The narrative is continued in v. 7 (ואחרי כן) on the erroneous assumption that the point in the history of the siege which has been reached is the one at which Zedekiah and his party seek to escape from the city and to avoid Babylonian encirclement.

הַנִּשְׁאָרִים (v. 7) should be adopted (Sept., Pesh., Targ) for MT
וְאֵת הַנִּשְׁאָרִים. Otherwise, it is not obvious that Janzen (p. 41)
gives a correct account of the additions to MT in v. 7. Thiel
(p. 234) has noticed that וְהִכָּם בְּחֶרֶב occurs at 20.4 with
Nebuchadrezzar as subject, and וְהִכָּם should be preferred to
וְהִכָּם in v. 7 (so Vulg. *et percutiet eos*; Pesh. *wnmḥ' 'nwn*; Targ.
וִימְחִינּוּן), although the plural is indicated by Sept. (καὶ
κατακόψουσιν αὐτούς). The 3rd singular verbs at the end of v. 7
are a strong indication that וְהִכָּם should be read as וְהִכָּם, and the
conclusion which should be drawn is that נבוכדראצר is the
subject of these verbs, and that וּבְיַד אֹיְבֵיהֶם וּבְיַד מְבַקְשֵׁי נַפְשָׁם
(which, except for the second occurrence of וּבְיַד, is represented
by Sept.), is a secondary expansion perhaps on the basis of such
passages as 19.7, 34.21 and 44.30. Jerome attests a Greek text in
which בְּיַד אֹיְבֵיהֶם as well as בְּיַד נבוכדראצר מֶלֶךְ בָּבֶל וּ is
unrepresented (εἰς χεῖρας τῶν ζητούντων τὰς ψυχὰς αὐτῶν).

The conclusion is that a Hebrew text earlier than MT read as
follows:

ואחרי כן נאם יהוה אתן את צדקיהו מלך יהודה ואת עבדיו ואת
העם הנשארים בעיר הזאת מן הדבר מן החרב ומן הרעב ביד
נבוכדראצר מלך בבל והכם לפי חרב לא יחום עליהם ולא יחמל ולא
ירחם

This discussion, however, does not declare an intention to make
deletions from MT and restore an 'original text'. Like all the
other textual observations on 21.1–7 it is intended as a
contribution to our understanding of the extant Hebrew text.
What, however, is established, here and elsewhere in vv. 1–7, is
that MT contains secondary expansions of an earlier and shorter
Hebrew text.

21.7 has in view those who have survived the rigours of siege
and have escaped death, whether in battle or as a consequence of
famine and decimation. The effort of the king and his party to
break out of the city will be unsuccessful. They will fall into the
hand of Nebuchadrezzar, and along with those who are left in
the city will be mercilessly put to the sword.

A CHOICE BETWEEN LIFE AND DEATH (21.8–10)

[8]To this people you are to say: These are the words of Yahweh: I am giving
you a choice between a way of life and a way of death. [9]Whoever remains in
this city will die by sword or famine or pestilence; whoever goes out and
surrenders to the Chaldaeans who are besieging you will survive—his life will
be spared. [10]I have set my face against this city; I have decreed evil and not
good for it (this is Yahweh's word). It will be given into the power of the king
of Babylon and he will burn it to the ground.

There are no considerable textual difficulties in this passage:
38.2, which corresponds closely with 21.9, has an additional וחי
at the end of the verse, but is otherwise a shorter text, without
ונפל and הצרים עליכם. According to BDB נפל על means 'deserts
to' (so Vulg. *et transfugerit ad*), while the sense 'surrender' or
'submission' is given by Sept. (προσχωρῆσαι πρὸς), by Targ.
(וישתמע ל) and by NEB. וחי (38.2) no doubt indicates correctly
that והיתה לו נפשו לשלל means escaping with one's life and
nothing more (not saving one's life without a fight, as Ehrlich
p. 296f. maintains). This is how the Hebrew is paraphrased by
Pesh. (*wmšwzb npšh*) and Targ. ותהי ליה נפשיה לשיזבא, 'And
he will possess his life to preserve (it)'. לשלל, which is translated
literally by Sept. at 21.9 (εἰς σκῦλα; cf. Vulg. *quasi spolium*) is
rendered more idiomatically (εἰς εὕρεμα) at 38.2 (Sept. 45.2),
39.18 (46.18) and 45.5 (51.35). These are the only places in the
Hebrew Bible where the expression occurs, and so it is peculiar
to the prose of the book of Jeremiah. εἰς εὕρεμα 'as a windfall'
gives some indication of how the idiom was understood by the
Greek translator. Its function is to emphasize that the person
who escapes with his life in a context of general disaster is
extraordinarily fortunate: in the circumstances bare survival is a
'windfall'. Kimchi, who glosses שלל with ריוח 'profit', is near to
the nuance of εὕρεμα: to escape with his life is 'profit', 'as if he
had taken it in spoil'. Bright (pp. 184f.), followed by Nicholson,
supposes that the idiom originates as wry, military humour:
surviving a defeat is to be regarded as a kind of acquisition of
booty.

Rudolph's exegesis of vv. 8–10 has an apologetic orientation
(like that of Weiser and Nicholson) and he is concerned to
establish that there was nothing unworthy or unpatriotic in the
prophet's stance, that this advice rested on his knowledge of
Yahweh's will and not on political calculations. In Weiser and
Berridge (pp. 204f.) the prophetic and cultic connections of
21.8–10 are emphasized: Weiser says that כי שמתי פני (v. 10) is
an expression indicative of theophany with a view to judgement,
probably derived from Amos 9.4 (ושמתי עיני עליהם לרעה ולא
לטובה; similarly Thiel p. 236; Weippert, p. 207). References to
Jerusalem being burned with fire are frequent in prophetic
predictions (Jer 11.16; 32.29; 34.2, 22; 37.8; 38.18, 23; Amos
1.4,7,10,12,14; 2.2,5). Weiser's conclusion is that the vocabulary
of 21.8–10 is not Deuteronomic/Deuteronomistic (cf. Rudolph)
and that these verses do not have an *ex eventu* character. In this
he is in accord with Berridge who holds that the alternatives of
life and death which are held out have a cultic anchorage and are
fundamental to the 'covenant concept' (he does not mention the

resemblance of v. 8 to Deut 30.15). The formulation of alternatives is not evidence of a late, systematic categorization (*pace* S. Herrmann, *BWANT* 5. 5, 1965, p. 168).

According to Thiel (pp. 235f.) the formulation in general terms of a choice between life and death (v. 8) is derived from Deut 30.15 (cf. Rudolph), and this is related to the particular case of survival after the fall of Jerusalem. Thiel supposes that the core of v. 9 is a saying of the prophet Jeremiah and that this can be recovered by removing the accretions of the Deuteronomistic editor. These are (*a*) בחרב וברעב ובדבר. (*b*) והיתה לו נפשו לשלל (*d*). הצרים עליכם (*c*) ונפל. The original saying of Jeremiah (הישב בעיר הזאת ימות והיוצא אל הכשדים יחיה) serves to illustrate the difference between prophetic proclamation and Deuteronomistic preaching: the first is not formulated conditionally and does not explicitly exhort or persuade; it defines the possibility of decision in a specific situation, while the Deuteronomistic preaching is more concerned to inculcate a permanent style of behaviour. The first part of v. 10 (so Thiel) has vocabulary which with slight alterations appears in 24.6 and 44.11, and the second part has a text which the Deuteronomistic editor derived from 34.2b.

Whether or not Thiel is correct in his supposition that an original saying of the prophet Jeremiah is recoverable from v. 9, the form of the argument by which he seeks to demonstrate this is not altogether cogent. It is not clear that the participles in v. 9 do produce the unevenness or incohesiveness in vv. 8–10 which Thiel alleges, and the integrity or coherence of vv. 8–10 can be satisfactorily described. The passage opens with a statement about the alternatives of life and death which are set before the people, and this in itself (את דרך החיים ואת דרך המות) is capable of a general interpretation in terms of the 'two ways' (cf. *Proverbs*, pp. 306ff.) in which a man can live his life, and so as a reference to a style of life and a steady pursuit of goals rather than a single, crucial decision. It is evident, however, that the intention is to concentrate the antithesis of life and death on the particular choices which are set out in v. 9, and the transition from v. 8 to v. 9 is a perfectly smooth one, without a hint of inconcinnity. The choice between life and death in this particular, historical moment can be reduced to a choice between staying in Jerusalem and perishing, and getting out of Jerusalem, submitting to the Babylonians and surviving, even if it is a bare survival. The transition from v. 9 to v. 10 is equally uncomplicated and convincing. It has the form of a motive clause which explains and comments further on the naked character of the choice set out in v. 9. The city of Jerusalem is doomed; Yahweh has decreed its destruction and has given it into the power of the king of Babylon who will set it ablaze. There is no problem of formal unevenness in the movement from the participles of v. 9 to the 'I' of v. 10 (*pace* Thiel). The speaker throughout vv. 8–10 is Yahweh, and having stated in v. 9 an inescapable choice, he explains in v. 10 why this is so: 'Because I have set my face against this city' etc.

The battle lines of the debate on the linguistic affiliations of 21.8–10 are too firmly drawn and it is doubtful, given its present polarization, whether it can have any fruitful issue. Scholars like Weiser, Berridge (pp. 204f.) and Weippert are concerned to establish that 21.8–10 is an authentic saying of the prophet Jeremiah and they suppose that they can do this if they demonstrate that the language of these verses does not have Deuteronomic/Deuteronomistic affiliations, but their method does not possess this order of logical power. Thus Thiel assumes that 21.10 derives from Amos 9.4, but there is no *logical* inconsistency in his further assumption that it has been quarried by his Deuteronomistic editor from this source. Weippert (p. 207), with reference to Amos 9.4, may assert that there is no reason for denying 21.10 to the prophet Jeremiah, provided it is understood that this is a weak statement and does not say anything decisive. Again the statement that והיתה לו נפשו לשלל occurs only four times in the Hebrew Bible, and that all of these occurrences are in the prose of the book of Jeremiah, is not necessarily so decisive as Berridge supposes, and Thiel's supposition that they are all contributed by a Deuteronomistic editor is not illogical. The narrow arguments of Weippert can be regarded as successful only in so far as they are directed against the proposition that the Deuteronomic/Deuteronomistic character of the prose of the book of Jeremiah is always capable of demonstration by a process of cross-references. Her method does not dispose of the case for important connections between the prose of the book of Jeremiah and Deuteronomic/Deuteronomistic prose.

It is open to those who argue like Thiel to say to Weippert (and this is a reasonable interpretation of the evidence) that she is misled by her concern to claim the prose of the book of Jeremiah for the prophet Jeremiah, and that instead this prose should be regarded as an additional archive of the type of prose which has been described as Deuteronomic/Deuteronomistic. Nevertheless, it would be an advantage to concentrate attention on the prose of the book of Jeremiah as an integral part of that particular *corpus* and as having a relation to the special features of the *corpus*, rather than suffering the distractions of continually moving to and fro between the book of Jeremiah and the Deuteronomic/Deuteronomistic literature.

All the passages which Weippert cites from the book of
Jeremiah in connection with the series חרב, רעב and דבר are
prose, and her method of argument begs the question whether or
not this prose is attributable to the prophet Jeremiah in person
(pp. 149–180). If Jeremiah could have created the compressed,
tripartite formula (21.7,9) on the basis of earlier use (and that is
her hypothesis), there can be no objection in principle to the
proposition that prose writers subsequent to Jeremiah made the
innovation on the basis of earlier use. Further the indication
given by the poetry of 5.12 (cf. 14.13,15 which is prose) is that
the combination of חרב and רעב originates in the proclamation
of the opponents of Jeremiah, that he takes it up in formulating
his rejoinder, and that it is an aspect of the polemic against שלום
prophecy which finds expression in other poetic passages of the
book (6.13; 23.15–24).

Another aspect of the matter which should be noted is that
there are significantly fewer occurrences of the 'triad' in Sept.
than in MT, and that in 21.9, for example, Sept. (ἐν μαχαίρᾳ
καὶ ἐν λιμῷ) does not represent דבר. This has been investigated
by Janzen (pp. 43f., 205 n. 19) and his results may be briefly
stated. Weippert's triad occurs 15 times in the MT of the book of
Jeremiah (14.12; 21.7,9; 24.10; 27.8,13; 29.17,18; 32.24,36;
34.17; 38.2; 42.17,22; 44.13), and a combination of two items
appears 10 times in MT (5.12; 14.13,15 (twice),16; 16.4; 44.12
(twice),18,27). In Sept. one item of the threefold formula (MT)
is missing at 21.9, 27.8 (34.6), 32.24 (39.24), 38.2 (45.2),
42.17,22 (49.17,22), 44.13 (51.13). The order indicated by Sept.
in all these cases is חרב followed by רעב, and דבר is not
represented. A piece of text containing the threefold formula,
present in MT at 37.13 and 29.17,18, is missing from Sept. at
34.12f. and 36.15ff.

A reasonable inference from this is that where the Greek
translator does not represent דבר, he was reading a Hebrew text
which did not have דבר (so Janzen, pp. 118, 149; *pace*
Giesebrecht). A comparison of MT and Sept. suggests that the
preponderance of the threefold formula in MT was due to an
editorial process of systematization and expansion which was
largely incomplete when the Septuagint translation of the book
of Jeremiah was made. The combination of the pair חרב and
רעב occurs in poetry only at 5.12, and there as an expression of
false confidence which the prophet Jeremiah produces *verbatim*
(וחרב ורעב לוא נראה). In all the other prose passages, both
those with two terms and those with three, the formulations are
directed against the expectation of שלום and are constituent
parts of predictions of doom. Another verse of poetry, which is a
prediction of doom, and in which חרב and רעב appear, may have

been the point of departure of all the doom-laden prose passages, and may also have supplied some of the impetus to round off the formula in these passages with the addition of דבר. In 15.2 there are four items (חרב ; רעב; מות; שבי), and it should be noted that 'death' is the regular rendering of דבר in Pesh. (*mwt'*) and Targ. (מותא), so that there are good reasons for equating מות in 15.2 with דבר. The conclusion to be drawn is that the poetry of Jeremiah may have generated the twofold and threefold formulae in the prose passages, but that the processes which eventually produced the dominance of the threefold formula in MT are far removed from the historical Jeremiah, and that Weippert is wide of the mark in supposing that בחרב וברעב ובדבר is his literary creation.

CONCERNING THE ROYAL HOUSE OF JUDAH (21.11–12)

¹¹To the royal house of Judah: Hear the word of Yahweh:
¹²O House of David, these are the words of Yahweh:
Give legal redress without delay,
rescue the one who is wronged from his pursuer.
Otherwise, my hot anger will issue like fire,
it will burn and no one will quench it.¹

The view that the ו of ולבית מלך יהודה should be deleted and that לבית מלך יהודה is a superscription for the sayings collected in 21.11–23.8, which concern the royal house of Judah and individual kings, is represented by Duhm, Weiser and Rudolph among others. The position of these sayings in the book is explained (Rudolph) by the circumstance that they follow a royal oracle in 21.1–7. The ו of ולבית מלך יהודה received attention from Jerome and Kimchi, and both explained it in the same way. The significance of ו, according to Jerome and Kimchi, is that it links vv. 11ff. to the preceding verses. Words spoken to the people (v. 8) are to be followed by words spoken to the royal house of Judah, and the verb is omitted (ולבית מלך יהודה תאמר). Rudolph is right in his view that לבית מלך יהודה refers to the collection of sayings which follow in 21.12–23.8, and that the attachment of ו is a secondary, editorial attempt to connect it also with what precedes by creating the impression that ולבית מלך יהודה follows on from ואל העם הזה תאמר.

Rudolph supposes that v. 13b (מי יחת עלינו ומי יבוא במעונותינו) is a cocky answer to the threat issued in v. 12b (פן תצא כאש חמתי ובערה ואין מכבה) — a type of answer which the description of Jerusalem's strong defensive position in v. 13a already adumbrates. His emendations also have the effect of

¹Deleting מפני רע מעלליהם (see below, p. 510).

cementing vv. 13f. to vv. 11f., since he observes that הָעֹפֶל (instead of הָעֵמֶק ; cf. הַמִּשְׁגָּב for הַמִּישֹׁר) was the site of Solomon's palace (see further below). Similarly Weiser remarks that the refusal of the members of the royal house who are addressed in v. 11f. is contained in v. 13, and that to this the prophet replies with a sharpened threat (v. 14). That a convincing transition cannot be effected from v. 12 to v. 13 has been noticed by Bright and Thiel (p. 238 n. 21). יֹשֶׁבֶת הָעֵמֶק is an address to a site (a city), and so v. 13 cannot be regarded as a resumption of vv. 11f. which are addressed to בֵּית דָּוִד. Further יֹשֶׁבֶת in v. 13a is vocative and the 3rd feminine suffixes in v. 14b are not a natural resumption of it. Rudolph supposes that הָאֹמְרִים (v. 13b) should be translated 'They who say' rather than 'You who say', and so he fixes the transition from second to third person at this point. For him the problem consists not in the 3rd feminine suffixes in v. 14b, but in the 2nd person plural suffixes in v. 14a, and this confirms him in his view that v. 14a is secondary.

Thiel (p. 238 n. 22) reinforces his argument that there is no intrinsic connection between 21.11f. and 21.13f. by his observations on the relation between 21.11f. and 22.1–5. He is right in maintaining against Stade, Giesebrecht, Cornill and Volz that the poetry in 21.11f. is the source of the prose in 22.1–5 rather than a poetic distillation of the prose. His description of 22.1–5 as an expanded prose paraphrase of the 'text' contained in 21.11f. is essentially correct. The circumstance that 22.1–5 is related to 21.11f. in the manner described above does not preclude the possibility that 22.1–5 was always separated from 21.11f. by 21.13f. (cf. Nicholson who supposes that the association of vv. 13f. with vv. 11f. may have been caused by the 'fire' imagery which is common to both). Thiel's view is probably correct, but it is influenced by his conviction that 21.13f. has been concocted from other passages, and that it is a post-Deuteronomistic addition.

The saying in 21.12 is addressed to בֵּית דָּוִד and the nature of the demand with the attached warning indicates that the Davidic king is responsible to ensure that justice is properly administered. He should have a particular care for those who are least able to look after themselves and who might not be safeguarded, even when the legal processes are working correctly and normally. The assumption that the king has an ultimate responsibility for seeing that justice is done, and that he should be readily accessible to listen to complaints about miscarriages of justice is found in several passages in 2 Samuel. Along with this there is an emphasis on the extraordinary legal acumen of the king and the luminosity of his judgements. The latter finds expression particularly in the formulae which appear in the account of the interview of David with the woman of Tekoa (2 Sam 14.17), and in the narrative of Solomon's masterly judgement when confronted with the conflicting claims of two women over the maternity of a child (1 Kgs 3.28).

The other aspect of the matter is the responsibility of the king to use his extraordinary legal endowment rightly in order to ensure justice for all classes and conditions of men in the land. This duty is defined in Ps 72.1–4 (cf. E. Hammershaimb, *Some Aspects of Old Testament Prophecy from Isaiah to Malachi*, 1966, p. 36), with special reference to the poor and the oppressed, and Hammershaimb has noticed (ibid., pp. 68f.) that the widow, the orphan and the oppressed are a special care of the king *qua* judge in the Ugaritic texts (J. C. L. Gibson, op. cit., 16.6.33f., p. 101, *ltdn dn àlmnt lṭṭpṭ ṭpṭ qṣr npš*; 16.6.49f., p. 102, *lpnk ltšlḥm ytm b'd kslk àlmnt*). There is the assumption of this kind of responsibility in the case which is constructed by Nathan (2 Sam 12.1–4) and to which David replies with a vehement assertion of his intention to redress the injustice done to the poor man and to punish the oppressor (2 Sam 12.5f.). The behaviour of Absalom, as it is described in 2 Sam 15, points to the same conclusion. We must suppose that 15.2 refers to individuals who make the journey to Jerusalem in order to secure redress for legal grievances and who labour under a sense of injustice (כל האיש אשר יהיה לו ריב לבוא אל המלך למשפט).

The versions are all agreed that לבקר means 'early in the day' (Sept. τὸ πρωί; Vulg. *mane*; Pesh. *bṣpr'*; Targ. לצפרא). Bright toys with the idea that it may have been the custom to judge cases in morning sessions at the city gate, but he eventually comes down on the side of the meaning 'every morning' (cf. Lowth, 'The Courts of Judicature usually sat in the morning'). 'Every morning' agrees with Weiser's translation and is the effect which Rudolph seeks to secure with his emendation of לבקר to לַבְּקָרִים (haplography of *mem*). His rendering (*jederzeit*) introduces another nuance—that of 'expeditiousness' in the discharge of justice. The king is to make himself available at all times to hear cases and redress legal wrongs, and he must see to it that there is no procrastination in the legal system. Kimchi also introduces the thought that the hearing of cases may be a matter of urgency. This sense 'expeditiously' or 'without delay' is probably the right one for לבקר, and its connection with 'in the morning', 'early', to which all the versions point, is nicely illustrated by NEB's 'betimes' which means 'early' but which has the nuance 'without delay'.

There is no doubt that in some passages גזל and עשק (v. 12) refer to 'robbery' and 'oppression' in a plain sense and to infringements of the content of the law in these particular respects. This would seem to be the case in Deut 28.29, Lev 19.13, Ezek 18.7,12,16,18, and, probably, in Ps 62.11. Certainly in the Deuteronomy and Ezekiel passages גזל and עשק occur in a context of particular transgressions of the law and are themselves most naturally understood as referring to particular offences, 'robbery' and 'oppressiveness'. But the matter has to be judged differently in other passages.

Isa 10.2: לחטות מדין דלים ולגזל משפט עניי עמי
61.8: כי אני יהוה אהב משפט שנא גזל בעולה
Eccles 5.7: אם עשק רש וגזל משפט וצדק תראה

In Isa 10.2 גזל משפט must refer to a miscarriage of justice, or a wresting of the processes of justice, and the figure of violently coercing judicial processes is continued with a reference to the despoiling of widows and orphans (שלל and בזז). In Isa 61.8 it is more reasonable to conclude that גזל בעולה is a general expression, indicative of injustice and a tampering with legal machinery, rather than to suppose that it is connected with a particular kind of transgression of the law. There is a precise, antithetic parallelism of אהב and שנא, and the same should be assumed for משפט and גזל בעולה. That עשק is also capable of a technical, legal sense is shown by Eccles 5.7, since עשק רש must be understood in the light of the more specific phrase which is parallel to it (וגזל משפט וצדק). The latter must refer to a 'plundering of justice'—a violent distortion of legal processes which produces injustice.

Such a sense is indicated by Sept., Vulg. and Pesh. at 21.12. The textual points which arise from a comparison of MT with Sept. are not so important; they have exegetical rather than textual significance and do not indicate that the Greek translator had a Hebrew text different from MT (*pace* Rudolph and Janzen, p. 28). What Sept. indicates by means of καὶ κατευθύνατε διηρπασμένον ἐκ χειρὸς ἀδικοῦντος αὐτόν is a 'rectification' of legal abuses. This is more explicit in Aq. and Symm. whose rendering of עושק is συκοφανοῦντος αὐτόν. והצילו גזול מיד עושק refers to the putting right of perversions of justice caused by perjury. The same line of exegesis is found in Vulg. (*de manu calumniantis*) and Pesh. which uses the same verb to translate both גזול and עושק: *ṭlm* probably has the sense 'calumniate', 'accuse falsely' (*wpṣw lṭlym' mn mn dṭlm lh*). Jerome's exegesis agrees with this: 'And deliver the man who is oppressed by the power of the perjurer, so that you do not display partiality in judgement; but when the rich oppress the poor, let the rule of God weigh more with you than the power of the pursuer' (where 'pursuer' has a legal sense).

Targ. assumes that גזול and עושק have their plain sense and is followed by Rashi and Kimchi. The latter understands גזול as 'rob' and explains עושק as the oppressiveness of a moneylender. This is the direction which has been taken by modern translators and commentators (Rudolph, Weiser, Bright, Freehof; NEB, 'Rescue the victim from his oppressor'). Jer 21.12 should be interpreted in the same way as Isa 61.8, and גזול מיד עושק should be regarded as an antithesis of משפט in the first stich. To the general demand that justice should be expeditiously administered is added a more specific demand that the person who has suffered injustice as a consequence of perjury, or some other judicial malpractice, should have the wrong redressed. The warning attached to the demand is couched in language almost identical with that of 4.4. There is very little to choose in respect of sense between 'issue like fire' and 'kindle like fire', and the one supplies as good parallelism for ובערה as does the other (cf. S. Esh., *VT* 4, 1954, pp. 305–307; *pace* G. R. Driver, VT, 1, 1950, p. 244). Yahweh's anger is envisaged as a fire which once it has begun to burn will defy all efforts to extinguish it. The fire of his judgement will blaze until everything is destroyed.

The circumstance that מפני רע מעלליהם (v. 12) is not represented by Sept. is taken by Janzen (p. 44) as an indication that it has been imported into the Hebrew of 21.12 from 4.4 (so Stade, Rudolph, Weiser, Thiel, p. 238 n. 20). Thiel notes the grammatical incongruence of מעלליהם (Q, Vulg., Pesh., Theod. — מעלליכם) and suggests that the phrase is a late addition to the Hebrew of 21.12. The third person plural suffix (K) makes the phrase suitable as a marginal comment which has been taken into the text, but cannot be reconciled with the assumption that there was an intention to equalize 21.12 and 4.4. This can only be presumed on the basis of Q מעלליכם which should, however be regarded as a subsequent adjustment in the interests of grammatical congruence. Moreover, מפני רע מעלליהם is not represented by Sept. and this is an independent indication of a shorter Hebrew text from which מפני רע מעלליהם was absent. The phrase, as a marginal comment, explained why the threat was being issued and the commentator was no doubt influenced by 4.4.

THREATS AGAINST JERUSALEM (21.13–14)

[13]I have punishment in store for you, says Yahweh,
who are enthroned in the valley,
the rock in the plain;
who say: Who can swoop on us
and attack our homes?
[14]I will punish you as you deserve, says Yahweh,

I will set fire to Jerusalem's woodlands,
and it will devour all her environs.

It should be assumed that Jerusalem is the subject of the saying in 21.13f.; this view is not established in the versions, but it is as early as Jerome and is found in Rashi and Kimchi. Sept. supposes that Tyre is addressed in v. 13a and its interpretation of the saying is influenced by this point of departure. On this view the address is to Tyre (צור), sited in a valley (ישבת העמק = κατοικοῦντα τὴν κοιλάδα) on level ground (המישר is rendered by an adjective, τὴν πεδινήν, which is an attributive of צור). Hence it is the inhabitants of Tyre who boast in v. 13b, and it is on Tyre that judgement is to fall: the feminine suffixes in v. 14b refer to Tyre—its woodlands and environs will be enveloped in flames. Thus for Sept. vv. 13f. is an oracle against a foreign nation (cf. Bright, who cites the expressions used of Moab in 48.8,21,28f., and Thiel, p. 238 n. 21, who says that the style and vocabulary of 21.13f. are reminiscent of passages containing oracles against foreign nations). This interpretation of צור is found only in Sept., and in Aq., according to Jerome. The latter observed that צור can be read as צור 'rock' (so Symm. πετρα), צור 'Tyre', and צור 'straitened' (presumably a postulated Qal passive participle of צור; cf. Theod. συνεχομενη). Rashi comments on ישבת העמק, 'Jerusalem, which is in the middle of a valley', and this is followed by Kimchi who comments on ישבת העמק, 'because it (Jerusalem) is in an elevated position and its surroundings are a valley. Similarly he names it צור המישר, because it is rock (צור) and hill (הר) and its surroundings are a plain (מישר).'

The versions are divided in their understanding of יחת: Sept. τίς πτοήσει ἡμᾶς ('Who can frighten us?') derives it from חתת, and this is probably the derivation indicated by Vulg. (Quis percutiet nos?), except that it is the sense 'shock' or 'shatter' which is being extracted from חתת. This derivation is not queried by Jerome, but the indications are that he prefers 'frighten' to 'shatter' (quis terrere nos poterit?) Both Pesh. (mn n't' 'lyn) and Targ. (מן ייחות עלנא) correctly derive יחת from נחת 'descend', and this is generally followed by modern commentators. The meaning is that Jerusalem has a commanding site and that this confers great advantages in respect of security and defensibility. The awareness of holding such a strong, defensive position is represented (Rudolph and Weiser) as generating such confidence that what amounts to an affirmation of impregnability is made. The מעונות which will never be penetrated are understood by Sept., Vulg. and Pesh. in a quite general way as 'dwellings', although Targ. supposes that there is a more particular reference to fortifications (בירניתנא).

Verse 14a is not represented by Sept. and Janzen (p. 44) concludes that it was imported into the Hebrew text from 23.2 (הנני פקד עליכם את רע מעלליכם נאם יהוה). An implication of Janzen's argument is that מפני רע מעלליהם had been imported into v. 12 (above, p. 510) prior to the attraction of the distich from 23.2 to 21.14. ביערה is rendered as 'in its woodland' by Sept. (ἐν τῷ δρυμῷ αὐτῆς), Vulg. (*in saltu eius*) and in the text of Targ. which Sperber prints (בחרשה). The text of Targ. in Miqraoth Gedoloth has בקרוחא 'in its villages', and this agrees with Pesh. (*bqwryh*). According to Kimchi 'its forest' is to be explained in connection with the figure of 'fire' and 'flames', since the destruction of a forest is associated in the mind with a forest fire. The city and its surrounding villages (Pesh. and Targ.) will be destroyed by fire, that is, they will be destroyed as a forest often is.

Rudolph and Weiser suppose that vv. 11–14 are a unity and conclude that there is a particular reference to the site of the palace buildings and those who occupy them in v. 13 and that the arrogance expressed in v. 13b emanates from these royal quarters (above, pp. 506f.). Rudolph and Weiser make emendations in v. 13a in order to achieve this exegesis, and both read צור המשגב, 'the rock on the height', instead of MT צור המישר. Rudolph also emends ישבת העמק to ישבת העפל, and this is an indication of how his judgement is affected by his persuasion that vv. 11–14 are a unity. The reference is to the south-east hill where the royal buildings were sited (cf. Weiser, p. 182 n. 1) and which rose up sheer from the floor of the valley beneath. This is also Weiser's exegesis, but he achieves it by elucidating ישבת העמק on the analogy of ישב הכרבים (1 Sam 4.4; 2 Sam 6.2), 'enthroned over the valley' (similarly Bright). The influence of these presuppositions is also seen in the conclusion that ביערה is an allusion to the cedar with which the royal palaces were constructed (Rudolph, Bright), or, even more specifically, to the 'House of the Forest of Lebanon', the cedar building (1 Kgs 7.2ff.; Isa 22.8; cf. Jer 22.7) which served as an arsenal (Weiser). In that case בית דוד (v. 12) plays on the ambivalence of בית and v. 14 is directed against the royal complex of buildings and their residents.

There is, however, inconsistency between this kind of exegesis and the emendation of סביביה to סבכה (Rudolph), and Weiser's appreciation that if ביערה means 'against its cedar palaces', it conjoins better with סביביה than with סבכה is correct. The parallelism of יער and סבך ('woodland' and 'thicket') reduces the credibility of Rudolph's exegesis and makes the supposed reference to royal buildings of cedar less probable.

A more general difficulty which has been felt by modern

commentators is that ישבת העמק and צור המישר are
inappropriate descriptions of the site of Jerusalem (cf. Duhm).
Bright (also Thiel, p. 238 n. 21) thinks that 21.13f. is a mosaic of
fragments and that epithets originally descriptive of some other
place (Bright points to the descriptions of Moab in 48.8,21,28f.)
have been applied to Jerusalem, despite their inappropriateness
(cf. Nicholson). The descriptions of the site of Jerusalem in
v. 13a are, however, not manifestly inappropriate, and Weiser's
view that ישבת העמק should be understood on the analogy of
ישב הכרובים deserves serious consideration: Jerusalem's
elevated position, dominating lower ground, is envisaged as an
exalted throne on which the city rests, and if this is acceptable,
'rock in the plain' is a credible complementary description of
Jerusalem's site (cf. Rashi and Kimchi).

The conclusion to be drawn is that MT should be retained in
vv. 13f. and that these verses do not contain a special, royal
reference, either to members of the Davidic dynasty or to the site
of the royal palaces. There is an allusion to the strong, defensive
position of Jerusalem and to the defiant confidence which this
awakens in its inhabitants who feel secure against every threat of
military attack and penetration. The harsh transition from direct
address ('You that are located above the valley, the rock in the
plain') to third person is perhaps not altogether intolerable, but
it means that the saying concludes with a distich in which
Yahweh speaks *about* Jerusalem rather than speaking *to* it.
Alternatively one might suppose that the inhabitants of
Jerusalem are still being addressed in v. 14b and that the 3rd
person suffixes are accounted for by the circumstance that v. 14b
deals specifically with the destruction of the environs of
Jerusalem. In addition there is the obscurity of ביערה which is
reflected in the exegetical expedients which have been adopted to
deal with it. The 'cedar palace' exegesis should be rejected, as
should also the equation of יער with villages (Pesh., Targ.,
Kimchi) which has been suggested by the parallel term סביביה.
In view of the uncertainty the wisest course is not to look beyond
the plainest interpretation of ביערה and to suppose, as NEB does
('I will kindle fire on the heathland around you'), that v. 14
alludes to the woodland around the city which will be destroyed
by enemy action (cf. W. McKane, *VT* 32, 1982, pp. 59–73).

CHAPTER XXII

AN ADDRESS TO THE KING OF JUDAH (22.1–5)

¹These are the words of Yahweh: Go down to the palace of the king of Judah and speak there this word: ²Say, Hear the word of Yahweh, king of Judah, you that sit on David's throne, you, your officials and those in your service who come through these gates. ³These are the words of Yahweh: Do what is just and right, rescue the one who is wronged from his pursuer, do not oppress the alien, the orphan and the widow¹ and do not shed innocent blood in this place. ⁴If you carry out this instruction faithfully, kings who sit on David's throne will come through the gates of this palace in chariots and on horses, with their officials and those in their service. ⁵If you do not obey these words, I swear solemnly, says Yahweh, that this palace shall be reduced to ruins.

There are no difficult textual problems in 22.1–5. Sept., Vulg. and Pesh. ease the syntax of v. 3 by representing ויתום and ואל תחמסו. A comparison of 22.3 with 7.6 (MT) suggests that יתום is more original. The correct explanation of אל תנו אל תחמסו may be that MT at 22.3 is conflate. There is no support from the versions for the view (Duhm, Rudolph, Weiser, Bright) that ועבד(י)ו ועמו (v. 4) is an addition, perhaps derived from v. 2 (אתה ועבדיך ועמך). Rudolph observes that it is grammatically suspect (K. עבדו; Q עבדיו) and that, following מלכים, it ought to have been הם ועבדיהם ועמם. Duhm holds that the phrase is unintelligible in the singular, but it can be defended as having a distributive force, 'each king with his officials and retinue'. Sept. and Vulg. have felt the difficulty and have made the grammar more normal. עשוק (v. 3) as compared with עשק (21.12) is perhaps best explained as a scribal error (so Duhm), but Kimchi supposes that it is a form on the analogy of קרוב, having the same sense as עושק 'oppressor'.

Kimchi's observation that רד בית מלך (v. 1) is an indication that the prophet is located on the temple hill when he receives the word of Yahweh has been repeated by modern commentators (Rudolph, Weiser). Kimchi identifies בשערים האלה (22.2) with the gates of the temple (שערי העזרה) and similarly with ובאו שערי הבית הזה (v. 4). The alternative interpretation which he gives for הבית הזה ('the royal palace') is certainly the correct one, and in this connection he comments, 'For he (the prophet) says "riding on chariots and horses", and one does not enter the temple court riding a horse.' If הבית הזה is the royal palace, בשערים האלה (v. 2) must also refer to the gates of the palace.

A fundamental consideration is whether 22.1–5 is to be understood as an expanded version of 21.12 and derived from it (Duhm, Rudolph, Thiel, p. 238), or whether it is an utterance

¹ Deleting אל תחמסו (see below).

with similarities to 21.12 but having its own separate, historical occasion (Kimchi and Weiser). Weiser observes the affinities of 22.3 with 21.12, but rejects the hypothesis of a secondary prose expansion. He opts rather for the historicity of the notice, and searches for an occasion when the prophet Jeremiah repeated and supplemented the demand which he had made in 21.12. In 22.3b he detects the tailoring of a traditional formulation to a particular occasion: the ceremonial entry of the Davidic king through the palace gates where the people are assembled at the annual Festival of Enthronement. Weiser locates 22.1–5 in the reign of Jehoiakim and aligns it with those sayings in 22.13ff. in which exception is taken to the king's extravagant building projects.

The part of Weiser's argument which attempts to account for the fuller form of 22.3 as compared with 21.12, is not cogent. The wider audience (see further below) does not explain the additions in 22.3: simply because 21.12 and 22.3 are addressed to the king and, irrespective of the composition of the audience in 22.3, a mention of strangers, orphans and widows would be as appropriate in the one as in the other. The postulated larger audience of 22.3 does not explain why this verse refers to strangers, orphans and widows, while 21.12 does not.

Rudolph's view is that 22.1–5 is a parallel passage in prose to the poetry of 21.11–14 and that the vocabularly points unmistakably to his Source C. Rudolph notes that Jeremiah is represented in 22.1 as being in the temple area (רד בית מלך) and he supposes that 22.1–5 may originally have been the continuation in Source C of 7.1–8.3 which was enacted in the temple area. The removal of 22.1–5 to its present position was the consequence of a desire to make it contiguous with other royal sayings.

Thiel holds (pp. 238f). that 22.2–5 is an expansion in prose of the poetic text in 21.12: 22.2–5 is a prose sermon derived from 21.12. There are similarities between Rudolph and Thiel: Rudolph assigns 22.1–5 to his Source C and Thiel to his Deuteronomistic editor of the book of Jeremiah, but the prose passages which they use to determine the linguistic affiliations of 22.1–5 are, for the most part the same: 22.2 is compared with 17.19,20, 7.2; 22.3 with 7.6; 22.4 with 17.25, 13.13; 22.5b (Thiel) with 7.34b and 27.17b. Rudolph, however, intends no more than that all these passages, on grounds of vocabulary and style, must be assigned to a common source, whereas Thiel is urging that D quarried vocabulary from 7.1–15 and 17.19–27 and re-used it to formulate 22.1–5.

The comparison of 22.4 with 27.25 deserves some attention,

because similar vocabulary occurs in both and this suggests that both refer to the same kind of state procession:

22.4: מלכים ישבים לדוד על כסאו רכבים ברכב ובסוסים

17.25: מלכים ושרים ישבים על כסא דוד רכבים ברכב ובסוסים. On the other hand, the gates which are envisaged in connection with these processions in 17.25 are the city gates (ובאו בשערי העיר הזאת) and the alternatives which are set out in 17.25–27 focus on Jerusalem and not the Davidic dynasty as in 22.4f. Moreover, the issue on which the destiny of Jerusalem hinges in chapter 17 is Sabbath observance and this is far removed from the matters of judicial impartiality and social justice on which 21.12 and 22.1–5 hang. From another point of view the appearance of the vocabulary of a state procession in a context different from that of 22.1–5 is damaging to Weiser's attempt to pinpoint a specific ceremonial occasion in his interpretation of that passage. We have no reason to suppose that מלכים ישבים . . . ברכב ובסוסים can be precisely allocated to a ceremonial moment in the palace court on the occasion of the festival of Yahweh's enthronement. On the contrary, it is used in 17.25 of state processions coming into Jerusalem through the city gates, and we cannot say anything more particular about this phraseology than that it is intended as a reference to the pomp and splendour of royal processions which are envisaged as a regular feature of the Judaean monarchy and for which there would be diverse occasions.

There is no doubt that איש יהודה וישבי ירושלם (17.25) means 'the population of Judah and the inhabitants of Jerusalem'. It might be then supposed that the formulation of 22.2,4 has a one to one correspondence with that of 17.25, that שרים 'statesmen' can be equated with עבדים 'officials' and that עם means the populace (Vulg. *populus*). It is not clear that this is a correct reading of 22.2,4 in the context of 22.1–5. Those who come through the palace gates are not the king, his officials and the general population, unless we suppose that what is described is a state procession in which the populace bring up the rear. Otherwise serious consideration should be given to the possibility that עמך and עמו refer to 'people of the king', that is, members of the royal establishment, perhaps of inferior status to those who are classed as עבדים. The possibility that עם might refer to a military contingent should not be entirely overlooked, but is less likely. If עם does not mean 'populace', Thiel's argument (p. 239) that D included the general population with the king, because of a history of apostasy for which the people no less than their leaders were responsible, falls to the ground.

The extension and modification of דינו לבקר משפט והצילו גזול מיד עושק (21.12) in 22.3 involves the addition of references to

specific breaches of social justice. It may be supposed that these
are thought of as particularly crucial areas concerning
underprivileged, weak and defenceless members of the
community who can easily be exploited, and that they are in a
decisive respect test cases by means of which the seriousness and
determination of the king to preside over a just community can
be ascertained. It may be that the author of 22.1–5 assumed that
דינו לבקר משפט והצילו גזול מיד עושק (21.12) referred to specific
breaches of social justice (robbery and oppressive behaviour)
rather than to a defective functioning of judicial processes (see
above, pp. 507–510), and that he consequently attached further
concrete demands connected with especially weak or vulnerable
members of the community who were liable to harsh and
arbitrary treatment. במקום הזה (22.3) must refer to the palace
or to Jerusalem (cf. 7.6, where במקום הזה alludes either to
Jerusalem or to the temple; see above, p. 161), and so the king in
particular is being warned not to use his power in a naked and
arbitrary way without regard for equity, for inalienable human
rights, and for his responsibility to deal faithfully with every
individual member of his community. He is not to stamp out
opposition or silence protest by a ruthless exercise of power; he is
not to preside over a reign of terror. (On דם נקי see above,
pp. 452f).

The alternative formulation of 22.4f. is a device for summing
up the possibilities, similar to 17.24–27 and 21.8–10. The palace
will be the hub of the kingdom and will be alive with the pomp
and ceremony of a royal way of life for so long as the king is the
defender of the just community demanded by Yahweh. If he fails
to maintain justice and to shield those who are weak and easily
exploited and oppressed, his failure will be total, and the palace
instead of being a living centre of kingship and a physical
manifestation of its splendour and majesty will be reduced to a
desolate ruin. There is a place for the Davidic king only if he
defends a community which conforms to Yahweh's standards of
social justice (cf. Nicholson). This is probably a wider view of
royal responsibility than that intended by 21.12, where the point
is perhaps rather that the king is responsible for right legal
decisions and for the proper functioning of the machinery of
justice.

THE PALACE IS TIMBER RIPE FOR FELLING (22.6–7)

[6]These are the words of Yahweh concerning the palace of the king of Judah:
  You are like Gilead to me,
  like the peaks of Lebanon.

I swear that I will make a wilderness of you,
you shall be like towns deserted and derelict.
⁷I will set apart men to destroy you,
each equipped with his tools.
They will cut down your choice cedars
and cast them on the fire.

22.6f., with their complicated imagery, are a description of the
scene of desolation and ruin produced by the destruction of the
king's palace. The view that the comparison in v. 6 implies the
high regard in which Yahweh holds the palace, which is found in
Weiser, Rudolph ('The royal palace with its splendid buildings is
likened to Gilead . . . and the peak of Lebanon, so that Yahweh
himself has joy in them') and NEB ('Though you are as dear to
me as Gilead or as the heights of Lebanon'), is already present in
Targ. and Rashi. Rashi links Gilead and temple in respect of
medical virtues: Gilead is a source of *materia medica*, and
healing influences issue from the temple (cf. Freehof).

One can see in Jerome and Kimchi the tendency to widen the
reference of vv. 6f., to suppose that they envisage not only the
destruction of the palace but a more general destruction
involving palace, temple and the city of Jerusalem. Thus Jerome
comments: 'He threatens the royal residence and the city of
Jerusalem and the temple which he names *caput Libani*. With
all their settlements they will be reduced to desolation, not by the
power of the king of Babylon but by Yahweh himself.' The
reference to settlements is an exegesis of ערים לא נושבה similar
to that of Duhm and Ehrlich (p. 297). It has persuaded both
these scholars that vv. 6f. cannot be regarded as a way of
describing the destruction of the palace, and Duhm holds that
the editor has attached a wrong label (כי כה אמר יהוה על בית
מלך יהודה) to these verses. Neither מדבר nor ערים לא נושבו (Q)
necessitates such a conclusion: both may be regarded as
metaphors which are called up to create an impression of
desolation and devastation in relation to the palace.

The assumption that there is a 'Though you are as dear to me'
type of simile at the beginning of v. 6 should be given up, and so
the supposition that the references to destruction and desolation
are introduced by a 'Nevertheless'. We should postulate rather a
simple comparison of בית המלך with גלעד and ראש הלבנון. 'You
are like Gilead and the peak of Lebanon to me'. This leads on to
the destructive imagery without any unexpected twist or reversal
of the sequence of thought. We must then, as was appreciated by
Targ., Jerome, Rashi and Kimchi, explain the simile with
reference to the timber for which Gilead and Lebanon were
famous (so Bright and Nicholson), and, particularly, with
reference to cedar timbers. An appreciation that such a simile is

a factor in the interpretation of the passage does not necessarily lead to a correct understanding of its significance. Jerome thinks that the figure operates in a manner reminiscent of fable and that the cedars are *potentes* or *principes civitatis*. This resembles BDB which takes מבחר ארזיך as a figure for a human *élite* (cf. the use of trees as human types in the fable of Jotham, Judg 9.8–15). Targ. also supposes that there is a human reference and interprets מבחר ארזיך (cf. *mḥmd àrzh* in Ugaritic; Gibson, 4. vi.21, p. 63) as 'pick of your soldiers'. The figure of 22.7 is explained by Rashi in connection with the appearance of 'Lebanon' in v. 6. He does not offer a detailed elucidation of v. 7, but what he clearly means is that the destruction (which he perhaps regards as more general than the destruction of the palace) is expressed as a felling of choice cedars, in view of the simile 'You are like Lebanon to me' (v. 6). Kimchi cites 22.14 (צפון בארז, 'panelled with cedar'), which occurs as a reference to Jehoiakim's palace, and he therefore establishes a more precise connection between 'cedar' and a king's palace. Kimchi, however, also cites 52.13, which alludes to the burning of temple, palace and all the houses of Jerusalem, and this is what he apparently reads into 22.6f.

The particular association between 'palace' and 'cedar' is the one which has to be pursued in order to achieve a more complete elucidation of the passage. This connection is evident from 2 Sam 7.2,7, where David describes his palace as 'a house of cedar', and Baal's palace (his residence *qua* king) is described as *bt 'rzm* in the Ugaritic texts (Gibson, 4. v 72, p. 61). A building in the Jerusalem palace complex was named 'The House of the Forest of Lebanon' (1 Kgs 7.2–5). Hence 22.6f. should be interpreted precisely as a reference to the destruction of a royal palace. It is the palace site which will be a wasteland (מדבר) after the destruction of the buildings, or which will be like derelict, uninhabited settlements. מדבר is presumably not to be taken literally and no more is ערים לא נושבו; if the one is a symbol of desolation and ruin, so is the other matching element in the parallelism. The figure indicated by וקדשתי עליך משחתים איש וכליו is not immediately a military one, although it is susceptible of a military interpretation (the destructive fury of an invading army). Hence in so far as 'Holy War' interpretations rest on the assumption that the figure itself is a martial one (Weiser, Berridge, p. 84), they are not well founded. The משחתים are neither supernatural 'angels of death' (cf. Exod 12.23; 2 Sam 24.16), as Weiser supposes, nor yet human warriors 'sanctified' (וקדשתי) for Holy War as Yahweh's agents (Berridge). The aspect of 'ritual setting apart' is not stressed by the versions (Sept. ἐπάξω; Pesh. *w'ṭyb*; Targ. ואזמין), except for

Vulg. (*Et sanctificabo*); nor is it stressed by Rashi (זמנתי) and
Kimchi (אזמן). The sense which is taken from וקדשתי (Vulg.
excepted) is 'assign', 'ordain' rather than 'set apart for Holy
War'. The משחתים are 'lumberjacks', and וכליו is a reference to
their tools, as Kimchi held (וכלי מפצו לחפיל הבית), and Rudolph
correctly maintains.

Although an interpretation in terms of invading soldiers is
ultimately correct, it is important to maintain a distinction
between the figure and its interpretation (as Targ. does). The
משחתים cut down the choice cedar timbers of the palace as if
they were felling ripe timber in the forests of Gilead and
Lebanon. It is in view of this that Yahweh says: 'You are like
Gilead and the peak of Lebanon to me'. But the explanation
cannot achieve complete neatness, for ripe timber has a high
value and the felling of cedar trees at the right time envisages
their constructive use in handsome buildings, whereas the
משחתים who fell the cedar timbers of the palace do it as a work
preparatory to an act of final destruction with 'sledgehammers'
(cf. Kimchi) rather than axes; and so they are 'demolition
agents' rather than 'lumberjacks'. The valuable and stately
timbers are to feed a great conflagration and be reduced to
charred remains. Their ashes symbolize the finality of a kind of
death—the death of an institution and a community. These
verses therefore contain a special orientation of Jeremiah's
prophecies of doom against his community and its institutions.

WHY HAS SUCH A FATE OVERTAKEN JERUSALEM? (22.8–9)

[8]Many nations will pass by this city and in conversation the question will be
asked: Why has Yahweh done such a thing to this great city? [9]The answer
will be: Because they abandoned their covenant with Yahweh, their God, and
worshipped alien gods and served them.

The assumption that Jerusalem is introduced here for the first
time (Rudolph, Weiser, Thiel, p. 240) has to be modified if
21.13f. are concerned with Jerusalem (above, pp. 511–513). A
fundamental question is whether we are to explain the
question-answer procedure which is found in the prose of the
book of Jeremiah (5. 19; 9.11–15; 16.10–13; 22.8f.) as a device
for giving expression to the proleptic certainty of the historical
prophet Jeremiah that judgement will fall on Jerusalem *in the
future*, or whether we should rather conclude that the form of
these passages is evidence that they arise after the fall of
Jerusalem and Judah. The latter is certainly the *prima facie*
indication of 5. 19 (עשה) and 9.11 עַל מַה אָבְדָה הָאָרֶץ), whereas

the question of 16.10 relates to threats of judgement (על מה
דבר יהוה עלינו) rather than to judgement fulfilled. It is unlikely,
however, that any of these passages reaches back to the prophet
Jeremiah: they are to be explained as a method for dealing with
problems which became acute after the fall of Jerusalem. An
explanation is offered in terms of apostasy, and the
appropriateness of incorporating this explanation in the book of
Jeremiah consists in the circumstance that it constitutes an
acceptance and vindication of Jeremiah's prophecies of doom.
The Jewish community, whether in the exile or after the exile, is
embracing the words of judgement spoken by the prophet
Jeremiah against his own and preceding generations.

22.8f., however, do not fit so well into a context of Jewish
agonizing and search for explanations after the fall of Jerusalem
as do 5.19, 9.11–15 and 16.10–13, where it is the perplexity of
those who have suffered judgement and dismemberment which
finds expression in the questions, and where the answers are
given in the form of 'word of Yahweh' (prophetic oracles). This
type of enquiry and answer can plausibly be associated with
expressions of perplexity and a clamour for enlightenment which
are an assimilation of prophetic predictions of doom: the
acknowledgement that they were true and their absorption into
the circumstances of loss and disintegration. The question in
22.8 is not, Why did this happen to us?, but Why did this happen
to Judah? It is a question which is asked by outsiders, who
indeed are appalled by a spectacle of desolation, but whose
religious faith is not at stake and who are not threatened by
theological contradiction. Thus Thiel's proposal (p. 240) that all
these question-answer formulations are variant expressions of a
catechetical procedure which was in wide use in Deuteronomistic
circles during the exile lacks cogency. It is intelligible in relation
to Jer 5.19, 9.11–15 and 16.10–13, but it is inappropriate for Jer
22.8f., Deut 29.23–25 and 1 Kgs 9.8f.

Jer 22.8f. is particularly connected with Deut 29.23–25 by the
appearance of גוים and ברית in both; it is particularly connected
with 1 Kgs 9.8f. by the appearance of עבר על in both; it is
partially connected with Jer 19.8 in that both these passages
feature עבר על and both refer specifically to Jerusalem. The
form of the connection of גוים and the question-answer
construction is more credible in Deut 29.23–25 than it is in Jer
22.8f.; and the form of the connection of the עבר על phraseology
and the question-answer construction is more credible in 1 Kgs
9.8f. than it is in Jer 22.8f.

The reasons for this may be stated as follows. In Deut 29.23
the form of words is ואמרו כל הגוים and this is followed by על
מה עשה יהוה. What is represented here is not the presence of

גוים on the soil of the devastated land and their gazing on the spectacle, but rather that the ruin which has overtaken the land has become a topic of conversation and enquiry in the wider world. It is certainly odd that כל הגוים should ask the question in the form in which it appears (Why has *Yahweh* done, etc.), and more odd that there should be among the גוים those who could produce the kind of theological answer which is given (על אשר עזבו את ברית יחוה), but the total representation is not incoherent and does not have the order of improbability of Jer 22.8f., where ועברו גוים רבים על העיר הזאת is hard to credit. The representation of 'many nations' or 'nations' (Sept.; cf. Janzen, p. 44) passing by the devastated Jerusalem and being so appalled by the spectacle as to demand an explanation is an incongruous one. One has the impression that such an unintelligent portrayal could only have arisen through the unskilful use of borrowed material. The appropriate form of the עבר על phraseology is כל עבר על (1 Kgs 9.8f.; Jer 19.8; 49.17; 50.13) and this can be combined neatly enough with the question-answer formulation, as it is in 1 Kgs 9.8f.: individual travellers who pass by the ruins of Jerusalem will be appalled by what they see and will ask why a disaster of such magnitude has overtaken the city. This amounts to an argument that Jer 22.8b results from a poorly constructed conflation of Deut 29.23–25 (the גוים theme) and 1 Kgs 9.8f. (כל עבר על). If these verses arose in this way, Rudolph, Weiser and Thiel attribute too high a degree of purposefulness to them. They have a low order of rationality.

MOURN FOR THE KING GOING INTO EXILE NOT FOR THE DEAD KING (22.10–12)

> [10]Do not weep and grieve for the one who is dead,
> weep your heart out for the one who is about to be banished;
> for he will never come back,
> never see his native land.
> [11]These are the words of Yahweh concerning Shallum, son of Josiah, king of Judah, who succeeded Josiah, his father, on the throne and has gone into exile from this place: He will never come back; [12]he will die in the place to which he has been banished and will never see this land again.

There is general agreement (cf. Thiel, pp. 240f). that vv. 11f. are a prose commentary on the poetic saying in v. 10 and the renderings of the versions have proceeded on this assumption. הלך (v. 10) is explained as אשר יצא מן המקום הזה (v. 11), and so is understood as a going into exile—a forcible removal (במקום אשר הגלו אתו שם, v. 12) from Jerusalem (מן המקום הזה, v. 11).

עוד כי לא ישוב עוד v. 10) is resumed by לא ישוב שם עוד (v. 11) and
its consequences are drawn out in שם ימות (v. 12). וראה את ארץ
מולדתו (v. 10) is picked up by ואת הארץ הזאת לא יראה עוד
(v. 12). That Sept. links הלך (v. 10) with יצא (v. 11) is shown by
the circumstance that it renders the first by τὸν ἐκπορευόμενον
and the second by ὃς ἐξῆλθεν (similarly Vulg. *qui egreditur* and
qui egressus est). This is explicit in Targ. where הלך is rendered
as לדגלו and יצא as דגלא. The versions have therefore assumed
that vv. 11f. represent a correct exegesis of v. 10 and this view
has been generally maintained. It is found in Jerome and in
Rashi and Kimchi, with differences in the details of their
interpretation of הלך, and it prevails among modern
commentators. This confidence in the reliability of vv. 11f. finds
expression in the attribution of these verses to Baruch (Volz,
Rudolph), or even to Jeremiah himself as a later prose
explanation of a poetic saying (Weiser).

The suggestion that Jeremiah may have written a prose
commentary on his own poetry is, as Thiel observes (p. 241
n. 33), an odd one and is unlikely to be correct. A detailed prose
elucidation of a verse of poetry with cryptic features is more
probably due to a commentator who is distinct from the poet and
who perceives a need and an opportunity for exegesis. It is likely
that v. 10 is to be understood as a word of Yahweh which the
prophet is communicating, although there is no explicit
indication that it is an oracle, but (*pace* Weiser) vv. 11f. are not
correctly described as an oracular reformulation of v. 10. They
are not at all concerned with אל תבכו למת ואל תנדו לו and they
connect with v. 10 at the point where they identify the subject of
הלך with שלם.

But is the identification of a reference to Shallum in v. 10
correct? There are no serious textual or linguistic difficulties in
the verse, but there are one or two items which deserve attention.
We have to ascertain that the verse does in fact refer to a
particular individual and is not simply a general, proverbial type
of saying. If v. 10 is considered by itself, and apart from the
interpretation given to it in vv. 11f., the question arises whether
'going into exile' is a correct understanding of הלך. There is only
one other passage in Biblical Hebrew (1 Chr 5.41) which
certainly lends support to the view that הלך can be used with the
sense 'going into exile'. (ויהוצדק הלך בהגלות יהוה את יהודה).
Ezek 37.21 might be regarded as a second passage, but it is
arguable that the sense needed to translate הלכו there is simply
'went'. The possibility that הלך in Jer 22.10a means 'dying'
rather than 'going' and that the sense of v. 10a is 'Do not weep
and lament for the dead, weep rather for the dying' should at
least be investigated. There is a nice correspondence between this

advice and the behaviour which is attributed to David in 2 Sam 12.15ff., when Bathsheba's child is dangerously ill, especially between Jer 22.10 and 2 Sam 12.23: ועתה מת למה זה אני צם האוכל להשיבו עוד אני הלך אליו והוא לא ישוב אלי. There is no difficulty in establishing that הלך (cf. Arabic *halaka*) has the sense 'about to die' in Biblical Hebrew, although it is needful to distinguish between (*a*) passages where הלך itself has this sense, and (*b*) passages where this sense is given not by הלך itself but by a combination of הלך and other words, and where the semantic value of הלך is simply 'go': (*a*) Gen 15.2; Ps 39.74; 2 Chr 21.20; Eccles 1.4. (*b*) Gen 25.32; Josh 23.14 (cf. 1 Kgs 2.2); 2 Sam 12.23 (cf. Eccles 9.10); Eccles 3.20 (cf. 6.6); 12.5; 1 Chr 17.11.

Jer 22.10 has not been included by the dictionaries in the semantic area indicated above (cf. BDB on הלך in Jer 22.10, 'of one going into exile'). It might be supposed that this reflects the preponderant influence exerted by vv. 11f. on the understanding of v. 10, but in fact the appropriateness of the sense 'dying' is already called in question by the character of the motive clause in v. 10b which is almost certainly a reference to exile and permanent banishment. If v. 10a means 'Do not engage in elaborate mourning rites for the dead; rather show sympathy and give succour to the dying', the motive clause in v. 10b is less well connected with v. 10a than we are entitled to require. It does not provide grounds for discriminating between מת and הלך = 'dying': the person who is dead will not return and the person who is dying will not return; neither will again see the land of his birth. So what basis is there (on this hypothesis) for discriminating between מת and הלך? The sense 'going into exile' does not arise only from vv. 11f., but is already present in v. 10b. It does not matter in this regard whether we think that there are two verbs ('He will not come back again, nor see his native land'), or whether ישוב is an auxiliary, as Rudolph supposes ('He will never again see his native land'). The first of these alternatives is preferred by NEB.

Who then is the מת and who is the הלך (the one going into exile)? There is nothing in vv. 11f. corresponding with אל תבכו למת ואל תנדו לו (v. 10) and these verses consequently offer no elucidation of מת. They do, however, identify הלך as שלם who is characterized as המלך תחת יאשיהו. The question which has to be asked is whether this clause indicates that שלם was Josiah's immediate successor and so is to be identified with Jehoahaz, as most scholars suppose (Lowth, Venema, Blayney, Cornill, Rudolph, Weiser, Bright, Freehof, Thiel, pp. 240f.), probably correctly, or whether it refers to one of the three sons of Josiah who became king and not necessarily to Josiah's immediate successor.

Although Jerome does not explicitly identify מֵת, there is no doubt that he supposes a reference to Jehoiakim (*quo mortuo regnavit filius eius Iechonias*), and this is confirmed by his comment on vv. 18f. which refers back to v. 10 (see below, p. 527). The identification of מֵת with Jehoiakim is found in Rashi and Kimchi, 'Jehoiakim who died *en route* when they were deporting him from Jerusalem'. Rashi supposes that הֹלֵךְ refers both to Jehoiachin and Zedekiah and that שַׁלֻּם refers to Zedekiah (agreeing with Jerome). Kimchi, on the other hand, identifies both הֹלֵךְ and שַׁלֻּם with Jehoiachin ('He was a grandson of Josiah, but grandsons are reckoned as sons'), although he notes the interpretation favoured by Rashi and also Abraham ibn Ezra's view that שַׁלֻּם is Jehoahaz.

The modern interpretation of 22.10–12 derives, at least in part, from Ibn Ezra: Do not brood over the death of Josiah and the disaster at Megiddo (מֵת = Josiah), but focus your sympathy and sorrow on Jehoahaz, hardly crowned, but about to suffer an exile in Egypt from which he will never return (2 Kgs 23.34). The action of עַם הָאָרֶץ (2 Kgs 23.30) in making Jehoahaz king is thought to indicate that they favoured him particularly and looked to him to continue the policies of Josiah; that Jehoiakim, who was first in line for the throne, was deliberately passed over. The reaction of Necho is explained on the assumption that he had not been consulted, that he was not prepared to tolerate a king who would continue the independent policies of Josiah, and that he consequently deposed Jehoahaz and installed Jehoiakim as a puppet king (so Rudolph, Weiser, Berridge, pp. 106f., Bright, Nicholson).

A change of name associated with accession to the throne is attested in 2 Kgs 23.34, where Eliakim is given the new name Jehoiakim by Pharaoh Necho, and in 2 Kgs 24.17, where Mattaniah is renamed Zedekiah by Nebuchadrezzar. It may therefore be supposed that Jehoahaz was the regnal name of Shallum (so Blayney; see A. M. Honeyman, *JBL*, 1948, pp. 19f.). But the equation of Shallum with Jehoahaz is not helped by the only other passage in the Hebrew Bible where the name Shallum occurs (1 Chr 3.15). There he is represented as the fourth son of Josiah, coming after Johanan, the first born, Jehoiakim and Zedekiah. The only other scrap of evidence is to be found in Lucianic manuscripts of Sept. (mostly in corrections), where Ιωαχαζ instead of Σελλημα appears for שַׁלֻּ(וּ)ם (22ᶜ, 48ᶜ, 96ᶜ, 231 mg., 763, see Ziegler). These should be regarded as exegetical indications rather than as strict, textual evidence. They do not indicate that a Hebrew text with יהואחז was read by a Greek translator, but only an exegetical opinion that Shallum is to be identified with Jehoahaz.

Hence we are thrown back on the clause in Jer 22.11 and the case for the equation of Shallum with Jehoahaz must rest principally on המלך תחת יאשיהו אביו. There is no doubt, however, that this can bear the weight of the case, since מלך תחת is a regular expression for the accession of a king following the death or deposition of his predecessor (2 Sam 16.8, Saul/David; 1 Kgs 14.20, Jeroboam/Nadab; 1 Kgs 14.31, Rehoboam/Abijah; 2 Kgs 8.15, Ben Hadad/Hazael; 2 Kgs 13.24, Hazael/Ben Hadad). The conclusion is that 22.10 contains a reference to a king who was deceased and to another who was about to be deposed and deported, who would never again see his own land or be restored to his throne. A later prose commentary on the poetic saying identifies הלך with Jehoahaz, but offers no help with the identification of מת. It is therefore uncertain whether we should envisage the original contrast as between Josiah and Jehoahaz (as modern scholars suppose), or between Jehoiakim and Jehoiachin (Kimchi). In the latter case it would be a contrast between a king who was released by death from the consequences of his own folly and irresponsibility ('Do not weep and mourn for him') and a king who would rot in exile simply because he had accepted the responsibility of high office and before he had a chance to prove himself and make his mark ('Weep bitterly for the one who is about to be banished').

JEHOIAKIM: AN IRRESPONSIBLE KING (22.13–19)

[13]Shame on him who builds his palace with injustice
and his upper rooms with inequity,
who makes his countrymen work without payment,
denying them their wages;
[14]who says: I will build a palace for myself,
with spacious upper rooms;
windows[1] will be set in it,
it will be panelled with cedar and painted with vermilion.
[15]Do you become a king
because of the splendour of your cedar?
Your father ate and drank,
but he did what was just and right
and he prospered.
[16]He saw to it that the poor and the oppressed got justice
and his affairs prospered.
Is not this a proof that he knew me?, says Yahweh.
[17]But you have eyes and a mind for nothing but gain,
for shedding innocent blood,
for oppression and the cruel misuse of power.
[18]Therefore these are the words of Yahweh to Jehoiakim, son of Josiah, king of Judah:
There will be no mourning refrain for him:

[1] Reading חלונים (see below, p. 529).

Alas my brother! Alas brother![1]
There will be no mourning refrain for him:
Alas Lord! Alas for his royal dignity!
[19]His burial will be an ass's burial:
he will be dragged away and cast outside the gates of Jerusalem.

Kimchi supposes that vv. 13–19 are an exposition of מת (v. 10; Jehoiakim) and Jerome's comment on vv. 18f. explicitly equates מת with Jehoiakim. Both Rudolph and Weiser note the unevenness of the style of 22.13–19: vv. 13f. concern Jehoiakim but are not addressed to him; direct address begins at v. 15 and runs to the end of v. 17, but the references to the king in vv. 18f., where the transition is made from indictment to proclamation of doom, are again in the 3rd person. The verses are thought (Rudolph and Weiser) to attach to circumstances at the beginning of Jehoiakim's reign, when he might have had the opportunity of engaging in building projects. Jehoiakim was impecunious because of the tribute levied on him by Egypt (2 Kgs 23.35), but his vanity outran his means and excited him to make his palace buildings more magnificent and impressive (Duhm). Duhm has noticed that the contrast between Josiah and Jehoiakim is not the Deuteronomistic one: Jehoiakim is not condemned for his cultic sins (cf. 2 Kgs 23.37) and Josiah is not praised for his Yahwistic piety (cf. 2 Kgs 23.25). Jehoiakim is condemned for a love of ostentation combined with meanness and oppressiveness and Josiah is praised for plain living and just administration of affairs (see further below). Thiel, on the other hand, finds evidence (pp. 241f). of the intervention of a Deuteronomistic editor in vv. 17f., in the further specification of Jehoiakim as בן יאשיהו מלך יהודה (v. 18) and in v. 17b: the juxtaposition of עשק and רצץ occurs in Deut 28.33 and 1 Sam 12.3; the charge levelled against Jehoiakim in v. 17b (ועל דם הנקי לשפוך) goes beyond vv. 13–17a and recalls 2 Kgs 24.4.

Even so, vv. 13–19 hang together reasonably well and there are no serious problems of discontinuity or incoherence (*pace* Duhm). It is likely, as Berridge argues (pp. 194f). that בלא צדק and בלא משפט (v. 13) should be related precisely to the statement in v. 13b that Jehoiakim treated his fellow-countrymen like slaves and did not pay them for their work (Symm. καταδουλουται δωρεαν). Kimchi comments on ברעהו יעבד חנם, 'Referring to those who worked in the building of the houses and were given no wages.' ופעלו לא יתן לו is then synonymous parallelism, with an anomalous pointing (ופעלו) which should perhaps be altered to ופעלו (Brockington, p. 206) which here has the sense 'wages' (= פעלה), as at Job 7.2. This is how it was taken by the versions (Sept. μισθόν; Vulg. *mercedem*;

[1] See below, p. 533.

Targ. אגריה; Pesh. *'grh*). The other nuance of בלא צדק and בלא
משפט should not be entirely neglected, and what is then
indicated is a gross disproportion and a total failure of political
judgement: the absurdity of Jehoiakim's affectation of regal
splendour, his delusions of grandeur and the flight from political
realities on which he has embarked. He is a fool as well as a
knave.

מרוחים is pointed as מְרֻוָּחִים (a noun—Brockington, p. 206,
following Cornill) to overcome the grammatical incongruence of
וְעֲלִיּוֹת מְרֻוָּחִים (cf. Duhm). The uncertainty about the sense of
מרוחים is already reflected in the versions and is commented on
by Kimchi (Sept. 'ριπιστά 'well-aired' (cf. NEB, 'airy
roof-chambers'); Aq., Symm. ευρυχωρα 'spacious'; similarly
Vulg. *spatiosa*). Kimchi favours 'spacious' (רחבה) but remarks,
'It is possible that מרוחים could be connected with רוח, as if to
say that the wind would come into them—they were made for
summer days.' It is likely that מרוחים represents a further
development of the thought of palatial building and generous
dimensions already indicated by בית מדות. This is the view of
BDB and KB², but Duhm and NEB prefer 'well-aired', following
Sept.

The construction of v. 14 is not altogether plain sailing. There
is a question about the extent of the passage which is put into the
mouth of the king, and a decision about this depends on the way
in which v. 14b is construed. If it is construed actively with
Jehoiakim as the subject of the verbs, his own words must be
supposed to end at מרוחים. Only if the verbs are understood
passively can v. 14b be a continuation of the king's speech.
Differences of opinion about this are detectable in the versions,
but Vulg. (probably also Pesh. and Targ). indicates that the
king's words end at מרוחים. Among modern scholars Rudolph,
Weiser, Bright and Freehof all suppose that the king's speech
comes to an end there and that Jehoiakim is the grammatical
subject of קרע and the verbs which follow it in v. 14b. וקרע לו
should rather be taken as 'and one will cut out for it (לו referring
to בית), impersonal 3rd person singular, equivalent to a passive,
the remaining verbs, whether as past participles or infinitive
absolutes (pointing ספון as סָפוּן; Ehrlich, p. 298; Brockington,
p. 206), should be taken in the same way, and the king's words
should be assumed to run to the end of v. 14. However the
difficulty of חלוני is resolved (see below), we should translate,
'And windows? will be cut out for it; it will be clad with cedar
and painted with vermilion'. The passive participle סָפוּן occurs
at 1 Kgs 7.3,7 and Hag 1.4. It could be argued that סָפוּן in 22.14
has arisen because someone was misled by this use into thinking
that it should also hold in 22.14, but the more straightforward

argument is that this evidence indicates the rightness of צָפוֹן in
22.14. In that case the right move would be to repoint מָשׁוֹחַ as
מְשׁוּחַ (Duhm) or מָשׁוּחַ (BDB), and all this would accord with
the passive sense which has been attributed to v. 14b above.

חַלּוֹנָי 'my windows' (MT) cannot be right and it is rendered by
the versions as if it were חַלּוֹנִים. The suggestion that חַלּוֹנָי is an
abbreviated form of חַלּוֹנִים is made by Kimchi, and by Blayney,
with an appeal to the ancient versions and to Kennicott. The
redivision of consonants (חַלּוֹנָיו צָפוֹן), which is adopted by NEB
(Brockington, p. 206), has been attributed to J. D. Michaelis,
but it is known to Blayney who ascribes it to 'Dr. Durell', and
has found it in one Hebrew manuscript. The redivision requires
the assumption that the king's words end at מְרֻוָּחִים and that לוֹ
means 'for himself' (Vulg. and Targ.). NEB, which continues the
speech to the end of v. 14, makes an illegitimate use of it,
concealing the difficulty by its translation of וְקָרַע לוֹ חַלּוֹנָיו, 'Set
windows in it'. חַלּוֹנָי is emended by Rudolph and Weiser to חַלּוֹן
and a reference is detected to a special, ceremonial window at
which the king would show himself to the populace or from
which he might address them (cf. H. Gressmann, *Eucharisterion
für H. Gunkel*, 1923, p. 26 n. 1). In that case לוֹ means 'for
himself' and the king's speech comes to an end at מְרֻוָּחִים, and
this is how the matter appears in Rudolph's translation. The
conclusion is that v. 14 consists throughout of words put into the
mouth of Jehoiakim, that חַלּוֹנָיו is not consistent with this
assumption and that חַלּוֹנָי should be emended to חַלּוֹנִים.

The difference between MT and Sept. in vv. 15f. and the
perplexity occasioned by the latter was already remarked on by
Jerome: *iuxta LXX vero quem sensum habeant intellegere non
possum*. Sept. reads: 'Will competing with Ahaz, your father
make you a king? They do not eat and drink. It would have been
better for you to do justice and righteousness. They had no
knowledge; they did not maintain justice for the afflicted or the
poor. Does not this amount to your not knowing me?' It is
obvious that no appeal should be made to this text for any
emendations of MT; that it is a desperate expedient to appeal to
βέλτιον ἦν for the insertion of וְטוֹב לוֹ (replacing MT אָז טוֹב לוֹ)
after שָׁתָה (Duhm, Cornill, Rudolph, Bright); that it is doubtful
whether the absence of any representation of אָז טוֹב (v. 16) is
highly significant, especially since οὐκ ἔγνωσαν has nothing
corresponding with it in MT. If אָז טוֹב (v. 16) is to be deleted,
Sept. should not be leaned on too heavily for support (*pace*
Brockington, p. 206), and the case should be made out in terms
of a partial dittography of אָז טוֹב לוֹ in v. 15 (so Rudolph).

However the form מִתְחָרֶה is to be explained, whether as a
Tiphel (GK55h) or a denominative from תַּחֲרָה 'strife' (KB³; cf.

J. Blau, *VT* 7, 1957, pp. 387f.), the only other occurrence of it in Biblical Hebrew at Jer 12.5 (ואיך תתחרה את הסוסים) may have suggested that it ought to involve competition with another person and this is how התמלך כי אתה מתחרה בארז has been paraphrased by Targ.: 'Do you think that you are like the first king?' (כמלכא קדמאה, correctly identified by Kimchi with David). The possibility that ארז (v. 15) is a corruption connected with the previous occurrence of ארז (v. 14) should not be entirely neglected. It does not, however, lead anywhere, because אחז (Sept). or אחאב (Sept.^) is not an impressive 'original' text, and if we go beyond this in search of another candidate, we are in a realm of speculation. אחז is consistent with אביך only if אביך means 'your forefather', but there is no way of reconciling אחאב with אביך. Another aspect of the occurrence of אחז in Sept. is its possible connection with the unusual word-order of MT: the alteration of ארז to אחז may have been brought about by the conviction that a proper name to which אביך could be attached was desiderated and the possibility that אביך should be joined to what follows it may not have been considered. At any rate the sense of MT and its proper grammatical connections have been missed by Sept. If it is assumed that מתחרה בארז is a correct text, the meaning of the opening part of v. 15 is, 'Do you suppose that your royal renown will be securely established by going one better than other kings in your lavish use of cedar to adorn your palace?'

The interpretation placed on 'eating and drinking' by Kimchi is still strongly represented by modern scholars (Lowth, Blayney, Cornill, Rudolph, Weiser, Bright, Nicholson). On אביך הלוא אכל ושתה ועשה משפט וצדקה Kimchi comments, 'According to the manner of kings Josiah enjoyed his good life, but since he did justice and righteousness it was well with him and he enjoyed well-being all his days.' Volz's view that a sense of what was socially equitable and the will to maintain it came as easily to Josiah as the natural activities of eating and drinking (cf. Ehrlich, p. 298) contrasts with Procksch's supposition (*Zahn Festschrift*, 1928, pp. 39f). that 'eating and drinking' refers to the scrupulousness of Josiah in the matter of religious observance and his participation in cultic meals (cf. M. Buber, *The Prophetic Faith*, 1949, pp. 162f., who supposes an allusion to the covenant meal of Exod 24.11). Procksch is almost certainly offering a wrong interpretation of the verse (so Rudolph), and it is also unlikely that Duhm is right in his view that 'eating and drinking' is a reference to plain living and high thinking.

The demand for משפט and צדקה is made more specific in v. 16 by the reference to the judicial obligations which rest on the

king. It is his responsibility to ensure that the weaker members
of the community do in fact and not merely in theory enjoy
equality before the law (see above, pp. 507–510, 517). This is a
concern to preserve an effective reciprocity of rights in the
community despite differences of station, power and wealth
among the individuals who constitute it. He must be vigilant that
these rights are not infringed by new departures against which
older forms of safeguards will not avail, and always alive to what
is necessary to preserve them. It is the will to implement
whatever is required to achieve these ends which constitutes
'knowledge of Yahweh' (above, pp. 212f.).

Jeremiah has a realistic appreciation of kingship. He knows
that Judah's king is bound to observe the royal style of life which
obtains for all kings. What offends him is that Jehoiakim makes
a show of kingship which he combines with a neglect of the
fundamentals of good rule. The test whether or not the king of
Judah understands his religious duty is the kind of political and
social order over which he presides. If he has a grasp of his duty,
this will find expression and materialize in the quality of
corporate life which he achieves and this is his knowledge of
Yahweh. But an overriding ethical sense should not be attributed
to טוב, either in v. 15, or in v. 16, if אז טוב is retained there,
although Vulg. and Pesh. incline to this in v. 16, and אז טוב then
becomes a summing up of the king's judicial activity: 'And he
did what was beneficent'. What is indicated by טוב is not so
much the virtue of Josiah as the sound prosperity and personal
fulfilment issuing from a state of affairs where royal style is
combined with social health.

Obsessiveness and a diseased ambition drive Jehoiakim to
oppressive and ruthless behaviour (v. 17b is a Deuteronomistic
elaboration, according to Thiel, see above, p. 527). It is
uncertain whether or not Sept. ἀδίκημα 'injustices' registers an
intention to relate עשק with legal malpractices and so to connect
v. 17 with the previous verses: Jehoiakim failed in the royal
responsibilities which Josiah had fulfilled with such exemplary
diligence. This motive has certainly operated in Vulg., where
there is a rendering which also affects מרוצה and which is close
to that of Aq. and Symm. (Vulg. *Et ad calumniam, et ad
cursum mali operis*; Aq., Symm., και επι την συκοφαντιαν και
επι τον δρομον του ποιειν). עשק is understood as perjury (or
defamation in connection with false legal testimony) and מרוצה
is derived from רוץ 'run'. Vulg. makes sense of this by inserting
mali, so that על המרוצה לעשות is taken to mean 'for a course of
evil action'. Kimchi cites 1 Sam 12.3 (ואת מי עשקתי את מי
רצותי), derives מרוצה from רצץ and glosses it with שבר
'shattering'. Rashi also correctly connects מרוצה with רצץ and

comments, 'He reproves him for oppression (עֹשֶׁק) and crushing
(רִיצוּץ) of the poor'.

Jehoiakim is obsessed by greed (בצע) which restricts his vision
and consumes his energies, and makes him a depraved despot.
This understanding of בצע (v. 17) is represented by Sept., Vulg.,
Targ., Rashi and Kimchi. The threat issued against Jehoiakim in
the oracle of judgement (vv. 18f). is that his death will not be
mourned and his body will not be buried. Targ. makes the
reference to the king explicit by rendering אדון as מלכא and הדה
as מלכותיה (cf. Rashi תפארתו), that is, royal dominion or
kingship. It is unlikely that Pesh. rests on a different Hebrew
text from MT. It is more probable that the deviations from MT
in Pesh. are the result of a perplexity which was felt with אחות
(why 'sister' in the context of mourning for a king?) and הדה.
The Syriac translator (on this view) solved his problems by
rendering the Hebrew as if it read:

הוי אחי והוי אחי

הוי אדון והוי אדון

There is nothing corresponding to Sept. οὐαὶ ἐπὶ τὸν ἄνδρα
τοῦτον in MT and nothing in Sept. corresponding to והוי אחות
and והוי הדה. Rudolph, Weiser and Bright have incorporated הוי
על האיש הזה into their text. The contention that these words
have fallen out of MT through homoioteleuton involves a slack
use of the term—the scribe's eye shifted from the closing letters
of יהודה to הזה and so he accidentally passed over הוי על האיש
הזה. If the assumption is made that οὐαὶ ἐπὶ τον ἄνδρα τοῦτον
rests on a Hebrew text different from MT, the same logic should
be applied to the other deviations from MT in Sept. In other
words if הוי על האיש הזה is to be inserted, והוי אחות and והוי
הדה should be deleted. But, assuming that this is the 'original'
text, what motive can be discovered for creating a difficulty by
the subsequent insertion of והוי אחות, or what explanation can
be given of how it arose if it is an accidental corruption? The
case is different with והוי הדה which can credibly be envisaged
as arising from a secondary elaboration of הוי אדון. הוי אדון ו,
on the other hand, could fall under suspicion in terms of the
principle *lectio difficilior potior*. Moreover, הוי על האיש הזה is
formally suspect, because it involves a use of הוי which is
disengaged from mourning rites. The point of v. 18 is that הוי
will not be uttered in connection with Jehoiakim's death and this
would be obscured by a more general use of הוי if הוי על האיש
הזה were original to the verse.

Duhm's defence of והוי אחות which he emends to והוי אחותי
is similar to that of Kimchi: Jeremiah is repeating a general
formula for burials and the sense is that nothing normally
associated with burial will attend the death of Jehoiakim (also

Rudolph). If an appeal is made to a 'general formula', it has to be supposed that a selective principle was not applied: the omission of אחות if a man were mourned and of אחי if a woman were mourned. This kind of argument is not helped by the reference to the mourners' cry in 1 Kgs 13.30 (ויספדו עליו הוי אחי) which does no more than show that הוי אחי was used in mourning for a dead man. On the other hand, Jer 34.5 (והוי אדון יספדו לך) does confirm that הוי אדון was a proper style of mourning for a dead king. The emendation of אחות to אֲחָוָתוֹ 'his brotherliness' (cf. Zech 11.14; so Giesebrecht, Ehrlich, p. 299) is an attempt to remove the difficulty of אחות 'sister'. It is also removed if we accept the view that אחות is used of a man in קינה (KB³, p. 31a, referring to H. Jahnow, *BZAW* 36, 1923, pp. 66, 86), or G. R. Driver's suggestion (*JTS* 12, 1961, pp. 62f). that the ת of אחות is to be explained on the analogy of Arabic *'abâta* 'O Father' (W. Wright, *A Grammar of the Arabic Language*², 1875, p. 101). Driver similarly explains the ה of הדה, following F. C. Burkitt (*JTS* 28, 1927, p. 408). M. J. Dahood (*CBQ* 23, 1961, 462–464) connects אדון with Ugaritic *'adn* 'father', but W. F. Albright (*JAOS* 74, 1954, p. 228) argues that אדון is unrelated to Ugaritic *'adn* 'father'. The proposal that the king is addressed as 'father' is intelligible in isolation, but a combination of brother and sister, followed by one of father and mother (reading הֹרָה, cf. Hos 2.7; Ct 3.4) compounds the difficulty caused by אחות. 'Alas for the king! (אדין), alas for his majesty!' yields satisfactory sense and should be retained. Driver's morphology of אחות is not altogether convincing, but it is the best solution which is on offer and is adopted by NEB.

That קבורת חמור יקבר (v. 19) means 'unburied' is indicated by the epexegesis of the remainder of v. 19. It is an interpretation which is explicit in Targ. and which appears in Jerome: 'He says finely that he is buried with "the burial of an ass". In other words he signifies unburied, torn to pieces by beasts and birds; for this is the burial of an ass.' The circumstance that the ass is an unclean animal in terms of the dietary definitions of Lev 11.1–8 and Deut 14.3–8 has no bearing on the functioning of the imagery (*pace* Nicholson). Kimchi is evidently relying on 2 Chr 36.6 and is assuming that Jehoiakim was restored to Jerusalem after a captivity in Babylon, and that he died and was left unburied outside Jerusalem when he was being exiled for a second time. This takes no account of 2 Kgs 24.6, but the conflicting character of the two passages is noted by Jerome. There is a further prediction that the corpse of Jehoiakim will lie unburied in Jer 36.30: 'And his corpse shall be cast out (and exposed) to heat by day and frost by night.'

According to 2 Kgs 24.6 and 2 Chr 36.8 (Sept). Jehoiakim

was buried in the family grave and this is questioned by modern scholars principally because it falsifies a doubly attested prediction of the prophet Jeremiah. Hence the supposition that his grave was desecrated and his body disinterred when Nebuchadrezzar captured Jerusalem in 587/6 (Giesebrecht, Cornill, Rudolph, Weiser; cf. Nicholson, 'There is no evidence for the view advanced by some commentators that his body was later disinterred and dishonoured'). Why should the question have been raised at all? Duhm's contention that a lack of agreement between Jeremiah's prediction and the circumstances of Jehoiakim's end is an indication of the earliness of the prediction has more substance to it than Weiser's view that a prediction would not have been preserved if events had not confirmed it. It is not a valid objection to this way of arguing that there is a conflict of testimony between 2 Kgs 24.6 and 2 Chr 36.6, because 2 Chr 36.6 is as incompatible with Jer 22.19 and 36.30 as is 2 Kgs 24.6; for 22.19 does not envisage the unburied Jehoiakim in exile (מהלאה לשערי ירושלם), nor is there any reason to suppose that 36.30 does either. 2 Chr 36.6 can be introduced into the argument only if a further assumption like that of Kimchi is brought into play.

JERUSALEM LAMENTS IN VAIN (22.20–23)

[20]Climb Lebanon and cry out,
lament loudly on Bashan,
shout your distress from Abarim,
for all your friends will be broken.
[21]I warned you when you were prosperous,
but you said, I will not listen.
This has been your way from your youth,
you would never listen to my voice.
[22]A wind will carry away all your leaders,
your friends will go into exile;
then they will suffer shame and disgrace
as a punishment for all their evil-doing.
[23]You that dwell in Lebanon,
lodged high among the cedars.
How you will groan[1] when birth-pangs overtake you,
agonies like those of a woman in labour!

The grammar of עלי הלבנון (v. 20) is probably the same as that of עלה השער (Ruth 4.1), ויעל עליהו בסערה השמים (2 Kgs 2.11) and ואם יעלו השמים (Amos 9.2). This is how the matter is understood by the versions. A solution in terms of 'O Lebanon' = 'O Jerusalem' in v. 20 (cf. v. 23) is ruled out by the presence of Basham and Abarim, for they indicate that we have to reckon

[1] Reading ננחת (see below, p. 536).

with a group of neighbouring mountain ranges (Lebanon, Bashan and Abarim), and they preclude us from attaching to 'Lebanon' a sense different from the one attached to them. The versions found difficulty with מעברים : Targ. identified עברים with a 'crossing-place' in the temple precincts and Vulg. supposes that the lament is to be addressed 'to those who are passing by' (cf. 19.8; 22.8). Sept. and Pesh. have read the Hebrew as מעבר ים (Sept. εἰς τὸ πέραν τῆς θαλάσσης; Pesh. *mn 'bry ym'*), and, according to Jerome, Theod. rendered it by *trans mare*.

Kimchi explains v. 20 as a poetic representation or משל, but he dissociates עברים from לבנון and בשן in so far as he does not identify מעברים as a reference to a mountain range. He explains it as מכל עבר ומכל צד, 'Call in all directions, but it will not profit you'. But in what way does the imagery function? What is the connection between high mountains (Lebanon and Bashan) and the activity of lamentation? Kimchi's answer is that 'from mountains the sounds of those who raise a cry are heard at a great distance'. Hence the sense of v. 20 is: 'Secure the most advantageous places for proclamation and call in all directions for help (if you will), but no help will come to you, for the power of your allies will be broken' (or, 'is broken', see below). מאהביך are identified with foreign allies, and thus Kimchi gives an exegetical lead which is not to be had in the versions either in v. 20 or v. 22 (Sept. ἐρασταί; Vulg. *amatores*; Pesh. *rḥmyky*: Targ. רחמך).

דברתי (v. 21) is elucidated by Targ. as, 'I sent to you all my servants, the prophets', indicating that the reference is to prophetic oracles which have gone unheeded. The singular form שַׁלְוָתֵךְ is represented by a few Hebrew manuscripts, by Aq. and Symm. (εὐθηνία σου), by Vulg. (*abundantia tua*) and Pesh. (*khynwtky*). The sense indicated by these versions and by Targ. (כד הוית יתבא שליוא) is that of affluence and security, whereas Sept. (ἐν τῇ παραπτώσει σου) points to apostasy and has been explained on the basis of Aramaic שלו, 'neglect', 'remissness' (שָׁלוּתֵךְ, cf. Dan 6.5; Ezra 4.22; 6.9). Sept. is perhaps influenced by the circumstance that the theme of the verse is endemic apostasy and an addiction to disobedience: נעוריך, associated with חסד in 2.2, is here connected with apostasy in accord with 2.7 (cf. 3.25). Although it is Lady Jerusalem in particular who is addressed, the history of apostasy attributed to her is Israel's history and it began at an early stage (2.7).

Verse 22 is the one on which the interpretation of vv. 20–23 principally hinges. It is clear that Sept., Vulg. and Pesh. have all read MT רֹעַיִךְ, while Targ.'s paraphrase, 'All your leaders (פרנסך) will be scattered to every wind', also rests on MT. BDB

explains תרעה רוח as a use of רעה similar to Mic 5.5 (ורעו את
ארץ אשור בחרב): the semantic development is from 'grazing' to
'stripping' to 'devastating'. A different explanation takes off from
'shepherding' rather than 'grazing' and Duhm argues that תרעה
רוח is acceptable only because it is preceded by רעיך 'your
shepherds' and that the vocalization of MT is therefore to be
preserved. The meaning is 'A wind will shepherd all your
shepherds', that is, will carry them off to destruction (cf. NEB,
'The wind shall carry away all your friends'—pointing רעיך as
רֵעֶיךָ).

The only divergence from the ancient consensus that רעיך
should be read as רֹעֶיךָ is to be found in Aq. and Symm. (τους
εταιρους σου = רֵעֶיךָ). כל רעיך is also apparently what the Greek
translator (Sept). read at the end of v. 22, since ἀπὸ πάντων τῶν
φιλούντων σε indicates this rather than MT מכל רעתך. The
argument against רֵעֶיךָ for רֹעֶיךָ is that it destroys the word play
between רֹעֶיךָ and תרעה (so Duhm and Rudolph), and so the
poetic conceit embodied in the first stich: 'Your leaders who have
"shepherded" you so disastrously will be in turn "shepherded"
by a destructive wind' (see Duhm, above). Kimchi's exegesis of
Targ. פרנסך ('kings of Assyria and Egypt'), founded on Hebrew
רֹעֶיךָ, must be rejected, because רעים (רעה) is used consistently
of native kings and political leaders, not of foreign allies and
conquerors (2 Sam 5.2, 7.7; Jer 3.15; Ezek 34.2,8,10,23).

ישבתי (v. 23) is explained (GK 90n) as a forma mixta,
consisting of יֹשֶׁבְתְּ and יָשַׁבְתִּי, and it is supposed that מקננתי is a
case of assimilation to a form which immediately precedes it.
Both are taken by the Massoretes (Q ישבת and מְקֻנַּנְתְּ) as
segholate participial forms, 3rd person feminine singular. At
10.17 Q is יֹשֶׁבֶת, whereas here it is ישבת. יָשַׁבְתִּי (2nd feminine
singular) does not give the sense which is needed in either
passage: not 'you dwelt' but 'you that dwell'. BDB (following
Kimchi) derives נחנת from חנן (KJV, 'How gracious wilt thou
be'). Ehrlich (p. 300) seeks to improve the sense by achieving a
contrast of 'raised high' and 'brought low'. He suggests that
נחנת is to be derived from נחת and that there is a dissimilation
of ת to נ: 'You come down (to earth) when birth pangs overtake
you'. The more widely accepted view is that נחנת is a corruption
of נֶאֱנַחַתְּ (נאנחת) 'groan' (Hitzig and others; cf. GK 25f. n. 1).
Rudolph (also KB³) indicates a metathesis: נחנת < ננחת <
נאנחת. The versions (Sept. καταστενάξεις; Vulg. congemuisti;
Pesh. mttnḥ') appear to have associated נחנת with אנח. Again
Sept. (ἐνοσσεύουσα), Vulg. (nidificas) and Pesh. (mqnt) have all
identified מקננת as a denominative of קן 'nest'. Targ. has
apparently linked ארזים with royal buildings panelled in cedar
(22.14). This is in line with the exegesis of Rashi and Kimchi,

and 'Lebanon', as the source of cedar and a component of the
name of one of the royal buildings (see on 22.6f.; 13–18), can
also be drawn into the discussion, as it is by Kimchi and some
modern commentators. There are two different explanations of
Lebanon in Kimchi's exegesis: (a) You dwell in a land adjacent
to Lebanon, but you will not do so much longer, that is, a threat
of exile. (b) Lebanon and cedars are a significant juxtaposition,
because the great houses were clad with cedars from Lebanon.

A thoroughgoing interpretation of vv. 20–23 in terms of
broken allies (v. 20) on whom a false reliance has been placed
can be achieved if רעיך (v. 22) is read as רֵעַיִךְ, and the sense
'foreign allies' is attached to מאהביך. Such a meaning for אהב
can be demonstrated from Hos 8.9 (אפרים התנו אהבים) and
perhaps Jer 30.14 (כל מאהביך שכחוך; cf. Jer 4.30 מאסו בך
אגבים נפשך יבקשו). The exegesis of vv. 20–23 is not greatly
altered if MT רעיך (= Judaean leaders) is read and מאהביך is
explained as foreign allies in vv. 20 and 22 (Weiser, Bright), but
the parallelism in v. 22 is then no longer synonymous. If it is
assumed that the parallelism must be synonymous in v. 22
(Weiser and Bright deny that there is any such compulsion), and
if רעיך are Judaean leaders, מאהביך must also refer to Judaean
leaders in vv. 20 and 22, and this is Rudolph's solution (cf.
Nicholson).

Kimchi's interpretation of v. 20 is the one which, in general
outline, still holds sway: the mountain ranges which are
mentioned are Lebanon in the north, Bashan in the north-east
and Abarim in northern Moab (Num 33.47f.; Kimchi differs in
this detail, see above p. 535). Duhm describes Abarim as 'the
most northerly spurs of the Moabite mountains at the northern
end of the Dead Sea'. Whether the thought that Palestine could
be seen from these mountains, as it was seen by Moses from
Nebo (which is equated with Abarim, cf. Num 27.12, עלה אל הר
העברים הזה with Deut 32.49, עלה אל הר העברים הזה הר נבו),
enters into this verse is dubious. There is, as Kimchi has
indicated, a touch of satire in the command which is addressed
to Lady Jerusalem. That the 2nd singular feminine imperative
does indicate such an address is assured, because it is an
established practice in the poetry of the book of Jeremiah (2.1–3,
23f., 33; 3.1f.; 4.30f.; 6.23–26; 11.15f.; 13.20–22, 26f.; 21.13f.).
The satire consists in the suggestion that Jerusalem should shout
for help from the most effective vantage points, directing her
cries to her foreign allies. Let her ascend the highest mountains
in order to broadcast her appeal, but it will all be in vain, for her
allies are broken (or, will be broken), and they have power
neither to help themselves nor to help her. Verse 21 is then
reminiscence involving recrimination: Jerusalem has had many

warnings and ample opportunities to mend her ways, but she has met them all with a studied recalcitrance, enjoying an untroubled prosperity and unable to discern even the smallest cloud in the sky. In this respect Jerusalem inherited the fatal characteristics of Israel which almost from the beginning (2.2; cf. 2.7) had a *penchant* for apostasy and wrongheadedness.

The divergence in interpretation comes out particularly in v. 22, which on one view is a threat issued against both the leaders of Judah and her foreign allies, on another only against her foreign allies, and on a third only against the leaders of Judah. MT רעיך should be retained and so a reference to Judaean leaders should be retained (see above, p. 536.). The explanation of מאהביך in vv. 20 and 22 as foreign allies (Kimchi) is made difficult by בשבי ילכו in v. 22. This is vocabulary usually associated with a threat directed against Israel or Judah. The difficulty of Rudolph's solution (also Thiel, p. 242) is that there is no evidence that מאהביך can be used of Judaean leaders. However these matters are finally resolved, and leaving them open for the moment, the latter part of v. 22 describes the rude encounter of Jerusalem with reality. Her illusions will be shattered and she will suffer the shock of defeat and disgrace. Suffering as intense as the pangs of a woman giving birth to a child will overtake her (cf. 4.31; 6.24).

Apart from the particularities of interpretation (see further below) it would appear that in general terms Weiser is right and Rudolph wrong in respect of v. 23. That is to say, v. 23 is not moving beyond the point of disaster to which v. 22b refers and threatening a worse disaster in 586 than that of 597. Rather v. 23 is an epexegesis of v. 22b and refers to the same judgement as כי אז תבשי ונכלמת מכל רעתך. The 'nesting' figure which is commented on by Rashi and Kimchi is further developed by Rudolph and Weiser: the Lady Jerusalem enjoying the luxury and refinement of splendid, cedar-clad palaces feels as proud and secure as an eagle nesting in the loftiest cedars of Lebanon. It is generally appreciated that the symbolism of Lebanon in v. 23 is different from that in v. 20; ישבתי בלבנון may have been inspired by ישבת העמק, used of Jerusalem in 21.13, and לבנון and ארזים may have been inspired by 22.6 and 14 respectively. In other words the vocabulary and symbolism of v. 23 perhaps disengage it from vv. 20–22, and a factor in its composition may have been the desire to associate vv. 20–23 more closely with royal sayings (22.6,14), since it is not itself a royal saying (*pace* Duhm; see below).

If the difficulty constituted by בשבי ילכו is discounted, the best conclusion in all the circumstances is that רעיך refers to Judaean leaders, and מאהביך to foreign allies, in both v. 20 and

v. 22. Jerusalem's internal leaders will be swept out of power,
leaving the community like a ship without a rudder, and external
allies on whom hopes have been pinned will prove broken
supports. There is, however, another possibility which should not
be left entirely out of view, namely, that מאהביך in vv. 20 and 22
is a reference to other gods after whom Jerusalem has gone
'whoring', and that רעיך (v. 22) should be read as רֵעַיִךְ. In the
passages featuring Lady Jerusalem already noted this is a
prominent trait of her behaviour (2.23f., 33; 3.1–3; 13.22, 26f.),
and 2.25 (כי אהבתי זרים ואחריהם אלך) and 3.1 (ואת זנית רעים
רבים/) describe Jerusalem's/Israel's infatuation with 'strange
gods'. It is true that the elucidation of the 'harlot' imagery is not
a simple matter, and that it can be used of Judah's addiction to
foreign alliances no less than her infatuation with other gods.
There are some passages where it is difficult to make a decision
one way or the other (Jer 22.20,22; 30.14; Lam 1.19; Ezek
16.33,36,37; 23.5,9,22). But the מאהבים of the book of Hosea
(2.7,9,12,14,15) with whom Israel plays the harlot are certainly
strange gods and not foreign allies. The point of v. 20 is then,
'Lament your plight and plead with these gods "on every high
hill" ': Lebanon, Bashan and Abarim are poetic and concrete
representations of the 'on every high hill' theme (cf. 3.21a,
above, p. 80.; H. Schmökel, *Heilige Hochzeit und Hohes Lied*,
1956, pp. 32f., 75). Nothing will come of your frantic devotion to
these gods (cf. 2.25). Your infatuation with them will bring you
no help, for they are broken supports (cf. 2.28). Jerusalem has
been well warned what the consequences of such 'harlotry' would
be, but from the early period of the nation's life there was a
fascination for other gods which in the end was to prove
irreversible and fatal (cf. 2.25b).

The place of 22.20–23 between a Jehoiakim saying
(vv. 13–19) and Jehoiachin sayings (vv. 24–30) has been taken
as an indication of the historical circumstances out of which the
unit comes, and it has been thought that it reflects a situation
just prior to the capitulation of Jerusalem to Nebuchadrezzar
and the deportation of her leaders in 597 (Weiser, Bright, Thiel,
p. 242, Nicholson), or that it is written in the wake of these
events (Rudolph). The tenses which are used create some
uncertainty in this regard for נשברו (v. 20) contrasts with תרעה
and ילכו (v. 22). כי אז תבשי ונכלמת is surely 'For then you will
be discomfited and disgraced' and not 'For now you will be
discomfited and disgraced' (Rudolph). Even so one has to resort
to the convenient assumption that נשברו (v. 20) is a 'prophetic
perfect' in order to create a consistent representation of an event
which lies in the future.

No doubt we are entitled to conclude that whoever was

responsible for the organization of the material in the chapter intended to convey the impression that vv. 20–23 belong to the end of Jehoiakim's reign, but there is not very impressive internal evidence to enable us to define the saying historically. It exists if כל רעיך תרעה רוח is interpreted as the sweeping of Jerusalem's leaders into exile in 597. It should also be appreciated that vv. 20–23 do not contain a royal saying: they are addressed to Jerusalem and they might be said to interrupt a continuity of theme between vv. 13–19 and vv. 24–30. They may have been inserted because of the references to Lebanon and cedars, since this appears to establish a royal connection in view of the use of this vocabulary in royal sayings (22.6,13). This would mean that the incentive to insert the unit would not have existed until vv. 20–22 were secondarily elaborated by v. 23, if v. 23 is indeed secondary (see above, p. 538).

CONIAH IS DOOMED TO DIE IN EXILE (22.24–27)

[24]By my life, says Yahweh, Coniah, son of Jehoiakim, king of Judah, shall no longer be a signet ring on my right hand. I will pull you off from my finger (O Coniah)! [25]I will give you up to those who seek your life, to those whom you dread, to Nebuchadrezzar, king of Babylon, and to the Chaldaeans. [26] I will cast you out, with the mother who bore you, into a land[1] where you were not born, and there you shall die. [27]But they shall never return to the land to which they cherish false hopes of returning.

There is apparently a primary textual difficulty in v. 24 caused by the 2nd person suffix at the end of the verse. Vulg. (*evellam eum*) has made the adjustment which seems necessary. 'I would remove it' or 'I would remove him' is adopted by Duhm, Rudolph and Weiser, and the corruption is explained by Thiel (p. 243 n. 39), following Duhm, Erbt and Cornill, as a consequence of the form of direct address in vv. 25–26. Since a Deuteronomistic editor (so Thiel) cast vv. 25f. in this style, he altered the 3rd person suffix which was original at the end of v. 24 in order to ease the process of transition. This is a most unsatisfactory explanation of אתקנך (see further below), and it is understandable that Duhm who pursues a similar line of thought has to postulate a tasteless and infantile post-exilic *Ergänzer*.

אתקנך should be approached differently and a solution to the problem should be sought by placing on v. 24 a grammatical construction different from the one which is normally assumed. The understanding of v. 24 which prevails in Sept., Vulg., Pesh., is, 'Even if (כי אם) Coniah were (or, "is") a signet ring in my right hand, nevertheless (כי) I would (or, "will") pull you off'

---

[1] Deleting אחרת (see below, p. 545).

(Vulg., 'it' or 'him'). כי אם is similarly understood in the exegesis of Jerome and of Kimchi: 'Even if Coniah is like a signet ring on the right hand, which is never removed from it, I shall remove you from there and pull you off.' A new departure is necessary and כי אם should be construed as a rare variant of the אם of the oath, coming as it does after חי אני נאם יהוה. This is presumably the grammatical basis of NEB's translation: 'By my life, says the Lord, Coniah, son of Jehoiakim, king of Judah, shall be the signet ring on my right hand no longer.' Such a use of כי אם is attested in two passages, 1 Sam 25.34 and 2 Sam 3.35 (GK 149d). The second כי can be rendered as 'surely' (BDB, p. 472c), as in 1 Kgs 2.23 (כי בנפשו דבר אדניהו את הדבר הזה), or as 'for' (so Targ.). Whether כי is 'surely' or 'for' the transition to the second person is somewhat harsh, but it is not impossible, as it is if כי אם is translated by 'even if'. Hence on this grammatical foundation MT אתקנך should be retained.

The signet ring embodies power of the highest kind and, as Jerome and Kimchi have observed, is jealously guarded by its possessor and never removed from his person. It is set in the context of international statesmanship in the description of Ahikar, the vizier of Esarhaddon, who is 'Bearer of the Seal' (A. E. Cowley, *Aramaic Papyri of the Fifth Century B.C.*, 1923, p. 212; W. McKane, *PWM*, 1965, p. 29). In 1 Kgs 21.8 it is reported that Jezebel wrote letters in the name of Ahab and sealed them with his signet ring (ויתחתם בחתמו), and in Esth 8.8 there is a reference to a document which is to be written concerning the Jews in the name of the king (בשם המלך) and which is to be sealed with the royal signet ring (ונחתום בטבעת המלך). The use of the signet ring in Jer 22.24 as a literary image involves quite an elaborate process of transference: it is not the ring on the vizier's finger conferring a delegated royal authority; it is the ring on a finger of Yahweh's right hand which symbolizes the Davidic king. Weiser may be correct in supposing that the image touches on the particularly close and intense relation which was thought to obtain between Yahweh and the Davidic king in the context of Messianic kingship (Ps 2.7ff.; 89.26ff.; 110). The ring which is inseparable from the person of the statesman is made to symbolize the peculiar closeness of the relation between Yahweh and his anointed king, and the gifts and powers with which he is endowed in virtue of his vocation. It might be thought that such a bond is indissoluble, but events will prove otherwise! The application of the image of the signet ring to Jehoiachin in Jer 22.24 may be an original literary departure—the creation of a new piece of imagery—and Hag 2.23 may be dependent on the Jeremiah passage. If so, it is a deliberate reversal of the function of the image, as compared with 22.24, in its application to Jehoiachin's grandson (1 Chr 3.17; cf. Rudolph).

The way in which the relation of v. 24 to vv. 25–27 is conceived depends in some degree on decisions which are made about the form of v. 24. The view that בן יהויקים מלך יהודה is a secondary specification of כניהו is held by Rudolph, Weiser and Thiel (p. 242 n. 38), following Duhm, Erbt and Cornill, although there is no support for a shorter text from Sept. or the other versions. Rudolph and Weiser set out v. 24 thus emended as poetry. In BHS Rudolph no longer proposes that these words should be deleted, and he has given up the attempt to make poetry out of the verse. The contention that v. 24 was poetry had significance for the structure of vv. 24–27, because it was argued (Rudolph) that this passage was to be understood on the analogy of 22.10–12, where v. 10 is poetry and vv. 11f. prose comment on v. 10. Nevertheless, v. 24 is prose of a different kind from vv. 25–27, with an imaginative texture, conferred by the image of the signet ring, and having an affinity in this respect with poetry. These are features which are not possessed by vv. 25–27. It should be regarded as the kernel of vv. 24–27, the text by which vv. 25–27 are generated.

Verse 25 is plodding and ponderous (cf. Duhm), and vv. 26f. have an ordinary character, partly relieved in v. 27 by the interesting idiom מנשאים את נפשם (see below). Verses 24–27 do not have a literary cohesiveness, whether on Rudolph's terms (in his commentary) or on Thiel's terms (pp. 242–244), or Weippert's terms (pp. 182f.). Not on Rudolph's terms, because there are objections to the statement that vv. 25–27 are a commentary on v. 24, and these are founded on the grammatical form of vv. 25–27. If vv. 25–27 constitute a composition, how are we to explain the circumstance that vv. 25f. are direct address, while v. 27 is formulated in the 3rd person plural? Verse 27 does not cohere with vv. 25f., nor does v. 26 cohere perfectly with v. 25 (see below).

Thiel proceeds on the assumption that vv. 25–27 are a Deuteronomistic composition and that they are part of the general plan of an editor who created a framework for 21.1–23.8. On v. 25 (p. 243) he remarks that the word-string נתן ביד occurs frequently in D (his postulated Deuteronomistic editor), but it is dubious whether such a commonplace combination, which, according to Weippert (p. 182 n. 340), occurs 179 times in Biblical Hebrew, is a stylistic feature which will identify an author or a school. Apart from this, Thiel's argument limps, because the parallels which he cites in order to demonstrate that v. 25 is a product of D are not exact parallels. Thus he argues that ביד מבקשי נפשך וביד אשר אתה יגור מפניהם

is a variant of the more usual ביד איבך וביד מבקשי נפשך, but
neither 19.7 nor 19.9, which he cites, has precisely this form.

16.13 is not an impressive parallel for v. 26: there is nothing in
v. 26 corresponding to מעל הארץ in 16.13, nor is there anything
in 16.13 to match the particularity of the ילד references: ואת
אמך אשר ילדתך which is resumed by אשר לא ילדתם שם. How
does Thiel know that the mention of the king's mother in v. 26 is
suggested to D by 2 Kgs 24.12? There is no close similarity
between these passages: in the Kings passage ואמו is an item in a
list (הוא ואמו ועבדיו . . . ושריסיו). Thiel's answer to the
contention that 16.13 and 22.26 are not closely parallel as they
now stand is a special application of Ehrlich's emendation
(p. 300): D altered אשר לא ידעתם to אשר לא ילדתם שם in view
of the mention of the king's mother in v. 26.

Thiel (p. 243 n. 40) agrees with Duhm that there is a
particularly impressive correspondence between 22.11f. and
22.27 (Duhm describes 22.27 as an imitation of 22.11f.). Close
examination does not confirm such a correspondence; nor does
v. 27a have a precise verbal resemblance to either 44.14 or
22.12b. Why is v. 27 formulated in the 3rd person plural? Thiel's
answer is that this is a deliberate device by D to effect a
transition to v. 28. In that case D creates confusion in v. 24 (by
changing אתקנו to אתקנך) in order to effect a transition to v. 25,
and spoils the (*ex hypothesi*) cohesion of vv. 25–27 in order to
effect a transition to v. 28. There is no future for such a process
of argument.

Weippert (pp. 182f). lays out the facts well, but her
conclusions do not follow from them; the difficulties in the path
of her attempt to show that we are in the presence of stylistic
traits of the prose of the prophet Jeremiah are these:
(*a*) Particular conclusions about a prose style cannot be drawn
from such a commonplace expression as נתן ביד (see p. 182
n. 340—it occurs 179 times in Biblical Hebrew).
(*b*) The continuation of נתן ביד with איב is ordinary, convenient
and predictable. No conclusion about a distinctive prose style of
the prophet Jeremiah should be gathered from it.
(*c*) The only significant expression for Weippert's purpose is then
מבקשי נפשך or the like: the resumption of איב with a
synonymous expression is not surprising, given the tendency of
this prose to spell things out, but the expression מבקשי נפשך is
distinctive.   It   does   not   come   from   a
Deuteronomic/Deuteronomistic source, but it is found once in
the poetry of the book of Jeremiah (4.30, נפשך יבקשו), and in
other passages of prose in the book (11.21; 19.7,9; 21.7; 34.20f.;
44.30; 49.37). This may be taken as an indication that those who
were responsible for the prose expansions of the book of

Jeremiah used vocabulary which they picked up from poetic sections of the book.

So far as 22.24–27 is concerned, the 'nucleus' which is subject to expansion is v. 24. Against Weippert who would claim this supplementary prose for the prophet Jeremiah (also Weiser with reservations), and against Thiel who supposes that it is the outcome of systematic editing, the argument here is that it is *ad hoc* exegetical expansion, that its horizons are not wider than v. 24, and that we cannot be confident it is all of a piece. In this particular case the differences between MT and Sept. in v. 25 deserve attention (see below), and there is much to be said for Duhm's view, which Thiel mentions (p. 243 n. 41) but rejects, that v. 27 is 'an addition to an addition'. Nothing of a firm nature can be said about the relationship between 22.27 and 44.14, but the idiom which occurs in both is an interesting one (מנשאים את נפשם — see below). It is clear that v. 27 does not derive immediately from v. 24, because while v. 24 might have given rise to exegesis in the 3rd person singular in view of יהיה, it could not have generated exegesis in the 3rd person plural. Hence in this respect v. 27 assumes v. 26, because v. 26 is the verse which introduces the king's mother and which makes the plural in v. 27 intelligible. The broken grammatical relationship between v. 26 and v. 27 is repaired in Pesh, where v. 27 is cast in 2nd person plurals.

The Greek translator (Sept). had a Hebrew text of v. 25 which was shorter than MT (cf. Janzen, pp. 41f.), and MT is the consequence of a process of supplementation which produced four occurrences of ביד (וביד) instead of two occurrences of ביד, and which inserted a reference to Nebuchadrezzar (וביד נבוכדראצר מלך בבל) in order to fill out ביד הכשדים which was originally an epexegesis of מבקשי נפשך. This particular verse (v. 25) indicates that it was thought to be a legitimate activity to supplement the text, but, as already remarked, the horizons of this kind of activity are narrow and do not exceed the confines of the verse itself. There is no proposal here to emend MT, but an attempt has been made to explain how the text arrived at its extant form and to indicate what kind of text it is.

In view of v. 26 there is a significant omission in v. 25: there is no reference to the king's mother. If there exists in vv. 25f. a continuous exegetical contribution why is the threat delivered against Coniah alone in v. 25 and the threat against his mother not introduced until v. 26? Might not this indicate that v. 26 is another exegetical comment on v. 24 which is separate from v. 25 and has a different orientation? Verse 24 was the subject of continued exegetical interest and the comment in v. 26 is developed in a different way. It introduces a play on ילד,

formulating the threat by resuming ואת אמך אשר ילדתך with
אשר לא ילדתם שם, and it concentrates on the aspects of exile and
death in exile.

There is, however, one specific textual point to be made about
v. 26: והטלתי אתך ואת אמך אשר ילדתך על הארץ אחרת has to be
compared with 16.13 (על הארץ אשר לא ידעתם) and 22.28 (על
הארץ אשר לא ידעו). על הארץ אחרת constitutes a grammatical
problem, and Vulg. (*in terram alienam*), Pesh. (*l'r'' 'ḥrt'*) and
Targ. (לארע אחרי) have rendered it as if it were ארץ אחרת or
הארץ האחרת. Sept. has εἰς γῆν and this has been supposed to
indicate a Hebrew text without the definite article (so Rudolph,
Weiser and Bright). Bright suggests that MT may be a conflate
text: (*a*) על ארץ אחרת and (*b*) על ארץ אשר לא ילדתם שם. This,
however, does not explain how על הארץ arose in MT. It can be
shown that the Greek translator read על הארץ in v. 26 and not
על ארץ, because he translated על הארץ at 22.28 and 16.13 by εἰς
γῆν. This is a matter of a difference of use as between Hebrew
and Greek, where the translator judged that while the definite
article was appropriate in Hebrew it would not be appropriate in
Greek. Thus it can be shown that the intrusive element in 22.26
is אחרת, that the text of 22.26, like that of 22.28 and 16.13, was
originally על הארץ, and that this is what Sept. represents. Where
then does אחרת come from? Thiel's account (p. 243) that אחרת
is due to the influence of Deut 29.27 (וישלכם אל ארץ אחרת)
should be accepted. אחרת should be deleted; it has been added
secondarily to 22.26 and has created a grammatical difficulty.

The assumption that the idiom מנשאים את נפשם means
'yearning' or 'longing' is represented by Sept. (εὔχονται ταῖς
ψυχαῖς αὐτῶν) and Aq. (επαιρουσι την ψυχην αυτων) and by
modern commentators and translators (Rudolph, Weiser, Bright,
Freehof, NEB). Targ. introduces the sense of false expectations
('deceiving themselves') and this is developed by Kimchi with
special reference to 'false prophets'. This the sense which Ehrlich
is after with his emendation of מנשאים to מנשאים or משיאם
(p. 300) which, however, is unnecessary. The idiom is an
interesting analogue of English 'raising (false) hopes'. What is
indicated is not just a longing to return to Jerusalem, but false
expectations of a return which will be contradicted by events,
and the form of MT (לשוב שם שמה is not represented by Sept).
may be emphatic: 'To the land to which they have raised false
hopes of returning, *thither* (שמה) they will not return.' The
threat of death in exile which is expressed by ושם תמותו in v. 26
is expressed in v. 27 by לא ישבו. Hopes are entertained of a
return home, but they will be contradicted by the historical
realities which will unfold.

DECREE DOOM FOR CONIAH (22.28–30)

[28]Is this man Coniah a despised and broken idol? Is he a useless article of pottery? Why are he and his children cast out and exiled in an alien land? [29]Land! Land! Land! Hear the word of Yahweh. [30]These are the words of Yahweh: Record that this man is stripped of rank, one ill-fated in his lifetime. None of his children will achieve custody of the throne of David, or become a king again in Judah.

In Sept. v. 28 does not have the form of a question and it also appears as a statement in Pesh. and Targ.. Sept. has a shorter text than MT: נפוץ האיש הזה ,העצב and הוא וזרעו are not represented. עצב ='pot' is not an assured meaning; it is a *hapax* which is explained, on the basis of עצב 'fashioned', as 'a thing fashioned' (cf. Ehrlich, p. 301, who supposes that it is a manufactured article), but only Vulg. among the versions gives the sense 'pot' (*vas*). העצב is rendered as 'contemptible' by Pesh. (*bsyr'*) and Targ. (בסירא). This probably arises from עצב 'idol', since we know that בשת 'shame' was a surrogate for בעל. The uncertainty which prevailed about the sense of העצב is conveyed by the Hexaplaric evidence: Aq. rendered it as $\delta\iota\alpha\pi\acute{o}\nu\eta\mu\alpha$, 'what is gained by toil', connecting it with what is shown in BDB as I עצב rather than with II עצב. Symm., according to Jerome, had the same sense from it as Pesh. and Targ.. Rashi comments on העצב נבזה: 'Perchance this man is an idol (image), broken and despised, who is cast off from my presence as if he were useless.' Kimchi observes that the ה of העצב is interrogative and like Rashi connects עצב with עצבים 'images' which he glosses as צלמים. It would appear that NEB has returned to this lexicography ('Is he a mere puppet?'; cf. Freehof, 'a despised, broken image').

Modern scholars have tended to assume the rightness of עצב 'pot' (Rudolph, Weiser, Bright, Thiel, p. 244, Berridge, pp. 179–181). This, however, is not a consequence of further lexicographical or philological elucidation of עצב and depends, perhaps heavily, on an assumption of synonymous parallelism, whereby the sense of עצב is determined by that of כלי. Duhm, on the other hand, had rendered עצב as *Gebild* ('image'), and NEB has disposed entirely of the 'pottery' imagery by assigning to כלי its more general meaning of 'article' or 'utensil' (cf. Ehrlich, p. 301). The implication of the translations and interpretations of עצב in Targ., Pesh., Symm., Rashi and Kimchi is that we have to reckon with two distinct literary images: (*a*) Is Coniah like a contemptible, empty, powerless idol? (*b*) Is he like a useless pot which is thrown on the rubbish heap?

Janzen (p. 119) supposes that האיש הזה (v. 28) is absent from Sept. by haplography: the scribe's eye shifted from הז of נבזה to

זה of הזה. The more widely held view (Duhm, Rudolph, Weiser, Bright) is that האיש הזה has been inserted into v. 28 from v. 30. The suggestion of Rudolph (following Volz) that נפוץ is a corrupt dittography of אין חפץ does not command great confidence: נפוץ is separated from אין חפץ in the *ex hypothesi* original text by כניהו אם כלי and it is difficult to see how in these circumstances the dittography could have taken place. It should be noted, however, that the Syriac translator was apparently rendering a Hebrew text from which נפוץ was absent (*bsyr' wšyṭ' gbr' hn'*). At any rate there is little doubt that נפוץ, whether original or secondary (it is not represented by Sept.), means 'shattered' (from נפץ) and not 'scattered' (from פוץ), although no support for the former sense is to be found in the versions. Aq. derives נפוץ (נָפוּץ) from פוץ 'scatter' (διεσκορπισμενον) and an allusion to exile is probably intended. This is entirely explicit in the extended paraphrase of Targ.: נפוץ is rendered as מטלטלא 'removed', and this is followed by, 'Why are he and his sons removed (הוטלו) and taken into exile (השלכו), into a land which they do not know?' Moreover, Targ. continues the theme of exile in its interpretation of v. 29, 'From his own land they exiled him to another land' (see further below).

Rashi and Kimchi, on the other hand, certainly derive נפוץ from נפץ and this is the sense usually adopted by modern scholars (Rudolph, Weiser, Berridge, pp. 179–181, Freehof, NEB), although Thiel (see below) favours a derivation from פוץ. Berridge (p. 179 n. 354) makes נָפוּץ the foundation of an elaborate interpretation of v. 28, according to which its background is to be sought in Egyptian execration rituals, and so he associates it with Ps 2.9 (cf. H. J. Kraus, *BK* xv/1, p. 20). He holds that the reference to the breaking of a בקבק (19.10) shows that Jeremiah was familiar with such rituals (cf. G. Fohrer, *JBL* 80, p. 311; *ATANT* 25, pp. 29f.). That the verse is to be set in such a framework is very dubious, but, in addition, the foundations are unsure, since עצב probably does not mean 'potter's vessel' and נפוץ may not be original in v. 28.

It is likely that at v. 28 Sept. is representing a Hebrew text which is shorter than MT (so Duhm). It is supposed that the reason for the addition in MT is to be found in the form of v. 30 which deals not only with the fate of Jehoiachin but also with that of his offspring. The argument would be that the insertion of הוא וזרעו and the making plural of the singular verbs represented by Sept. (ידע; השלך; הוטל) gives v. 28 a scope which coincides with that of v. 30 (so Rudolph). It is then tempting to argue that v. 30, in its original form, referred only to Jehoiachin and that כי לא יצלח מזרעו איש ישב על כסא דוד ומשל עוד ביהודה is an addition, and this is the direction which Thiel's argument takes (pp. 244f.). The difficulty is that there is no textual evidence to support it, and that such evidence as there is (the non- representation of גבר לא יצלח בימיו in Sept). would point to these words as the secondary element in v. 30 (see further below).

An interesting point which Duhm raises, and which has been taken up again by Thiel, is whether אשר לא ידעו fits the imagery in the remainder of verse 29. The sense is (so Duhm) that Coniah will be thrown away like a useless pot, and the reference to exile produced by על הארץ אשר לא ידעו is inappropriate. Thiel's text (pp. 244f). is the same as Duhm's, except that he deletes in addition והשלכו:

> העצב נבזה כניחו
> אם כלי אין חפץ בו
> מדוע הוטל על הארץ

Thiel's assumption that נפוץ is to be derived from פוץ is probably mistaken, and his detection of the activity of D rests partly on this assumption. פוץ and שלך were probably inserted by D (so Thiel) to explain the preceding, general verbs (נבזה and הוטל) as a reference to the exile of Jehoiachin (Coniah), and the concluding relative clause is also an insertion by D with this function. It not only leaves behind the image of the discarded pot (p. 245 n. 3—following Duhm and Volz), but contains items of vocabulary probably attributable to D. D, following the linguistic habit of the book of Deuteronomy, often connects this clause with אלהים אחרים (7.9; 19.4; 44.3; cf. Deut 11.28; 13.3,7,14; 28.64; 29.25), once with people among whom Judah will be exiled (9.15; cf. Deut 28.33,36). Verse 28 (cf. v. 24) is a lament over the rejection of Jehoiachin in which he is envisaged as a useless vessel which has been cast out. In all this Thiel makes the doubtful assumption that עצב means 'pot': that we have to reckon with two expressions of a single image in v. 28 and not with two separate images.

One further detail in v. 28 which deserves attention is the sense of חפץ. The versions favour 'utility' (Sept. χρεία; Pesh. ḥshw; Targ. צרוך), but Vulg. (voluptate) indicates 'pleasure', and Jerome notices the alternatives offered by Vulg. and Sept. (voluptate sive utilitate). Modern scholars are divided and BDB renders כלי אין חפץ בו as 'a vessel wherein is no pleasure'. This sense is also indicated by Duhm, Weiser, Bright, Freehof and NEB ('unwanted'), whereas Rudolph (wertloses Gerät) opts for the other sense. The phrase occurs in two other places (Jer 48.38 and Hos 8.8) which support the sense 'useless' rather than 'displeasing', although the distinction between 'useless' and 'unwanted' is a fine one. In Jer 48.38 the image of the broken and useless pot is confirmed by the mode of application (כי שברתי את מואב). The value of arguing whether or not

Jeremiah derived the expression כלי אין חפץ בו from Hosea is
very questionable. It is to be expected that such an expression
would be in wide use and available for anyone with a *penchant*
for a striking phrase, speaking or writing Hebrew. Its
appearance in Hosea and Jeremiah demonstrates no more than
that it was an idiom which both knew, and the circumstance that
it appears only in these books and not elsewhere should be
regarded as accidental and insignificant (*pace*, Berridge, p. 180
n. 358).

Sept. represents only two occurrences of ארץ (v. 29) and
Janzen (p. 117) supposes that the third occurrence is omitted
from Sept. by haplography. The address to the land, according to
Kimchi, is really an address to אנשי ארץ and this is shown by
כתבו (v. 30). Hence he supposes, and this is the generally
accepted view (cf. Thiel, p. 245), that שמעי דבר יהוה connects
with כתבו את האיש הזה. This is consistent with the conclusion
(although it is not Kimchi's conclusion) that כה אמר יהוה
(v. 30), which is not represented by Sept., is an intrusion (so
Janzen, p. 85) which should be deleted (so Rudolph, Weiser and
Bright). J. Herrmann (*ZAW*, 1950, pp. 321f.) has noticed the
presence of threefold expressions in Babylonian incantations,
and in particular the occurrence of *irṣitum irṣitum irṣitum*.

Two questions arise from כתבו את האיש הזה ערירי (v. 30). To
whom are the words addressed? What is the meaning of ערירי?
The reference is so specific that it appears to require the
assumption that an official activity is indicated: that those who
register or record are doing so in an official capacity. Hence it
has been suggested that we have to envisage an official register of
Jerusalem citizens (Rudolph), or a census list (Bright), or a list
of those who were in the line of succession to the throne of David
(Weiser), and that this is what is entailed in the command כתבו
את האיש הזה ערירי. It is argued (Rudolph, Bright and Weiser)
that ערירי does not indicate that Jehoiachin would be childless
in a plain sense, but rather that his offspring, because they were
living in exile, would lose their right of succession to the Davidic
throne.

These opinions presuppose that vv. 28–30 are to be located
after Jehoiachin's deportation in 597, that although Jehoiachin
had wives at the time of his deportation (2 Kgs 24.18) he had no
children, and that the prediction is not contradicted by the
circumstance that sons were born to him in exile (1 Chr 3.17f.).
Rudolph is concerned to assert that the prediction of vv. 28–30
was fulfilled, and he argues more generally that Jeremiah's
predictions in all these royal sayings (with the possible exception
of vv. 13–19) were fulfilled.

It is, however, a serious question whether such an emphasis on

the accuracy of Jeremiah's prediction in vv. 28–30 has not had a
bad effect on the exegesis of the passage, and in this connection
Rudolph's contention that v. 30 clinches the sense of עֲרִירִי which
he favours should be challenged. It is not at all clear that v. 30
functions in such a way as to preclude עֲרִירִי from having the
sense 'doomed to childlessness', although this is not necessarily
the right sense (cf. G. R. Driver, *JQR* 28, p. 115: עֲרִירִי, 'stripped
of honour', 'stripped of rights'). The latter part of v. 30 does not
fix the sense of עֲרִירִי and we are not required to read into it such
a meaning as 'If he has sons they are doomed never to sit on the
throne of David or to exercise kingship in Judah'. צלח in כי לא
יצלח מזרעו should not be pressed into service in support of this
view, and Vulg. has correctly taken this clause to mean no more
than *Nec enim erit de semine eius*. Verse 30 is either simply an
epexegesis of עֲרִירִי or else its intention is to extend the scope of
עֲרִירִי so as to include Jehoiachin's offspring in the proclamation
of doom (so Thiel, p. 245 n. 48; see further below).

There are three further occurrences of עֲרִירִי in Biblical
Hebrew (Gen 15.2; Lev 20.20,21). The fundamental sense of
עָרַר is 'strip' (BDB), and 'stripped of children' is almost
certainly the right sense in Gen 15.2, where Abraham says to his
servant וְאָנֹכִי הוֹלֵךְ עֲרִירִי. The sense of עֲרִירִים in Lev 20.20,21 is
more obscure, but it appears to be rather 'stripped of rights' (cf.
Driver, above). There is a particular contrast in the renderings of
עֲרִירִי (Jer 22.30) in Sept. and Pesh. (Sept. ἐκκήρυκτον ἄνθρωπον,
Pesh. *mkrz' dl' bnyn*). Sept. renders עֲרִירִי as 'banished by public
proclamation', which is a reference to Jehoiachin's exile, whereas
Pesh. understands it as 'proscribed from having children', that is,
doomed to childlessness. This is the sense which appears in Vulg.
(*sterilem*) and in Targ. (דלא ילד); also in Aq. (ανδρα αγονον),
ἀναυξητον in his second edition, according to Jerome. This
Jerome glosses as *non crescentum* and is a reference to
childlessness (cf. Sept. οὐ μὴ αὐξηθῇ ἐκ σπέρματος αὐτοῦ).
Symm. translates עֲרִירִי as κενον 'empty'—απηλλοτριωμενον
looks like a doublet and means 'banished into exile' which agrees
with Sept.

The circumstance that גבר לא יצלח בימיו is not represented by
Sept. is noticed by Jerome and these words have widely been
regarded as an intrusion (Giesebrecht, Cornill, Volz, Rudolph,
Weiser, Bright). Rudolph's view, echoed by Bright, is that גבר
לא יצלח בימיו does not connect well with כתבו nor cohere with
the idea of a register. In other words, כתבו את האיש הזה עֲרִירִי
should lead directly to the thought that Jehoiachin's sons will not
be 'registered' as having a right of succession to the throne.
According to Rudolph, גבר לא יצלח בימיו was added by someone
who knew that Jehoiachin had sons and who wished to

reinterpret ערירי as a reference to the hard fate of Jehoiachin himself. If the latter part of v. 30 establishes the correct sense of ערירי (which is not 'childless', according to Rudolph), what need is there for a reinterpretation of ערירי (גבר לא יצלח בימיו) in order to shift the meaning away from 'childless'? (cf. Thiel, p. 245 n. 48). This objection to Rudolph's view is unanswerable. Thiel's postulated 'original' text for v. 30 is as follows:

כתבו את האיש הזה ערירי

גבר לא יצלח בימיו

He attributes the remaining part of v. 30 to his Deuteronomistic editor. Thiel's 'original' text should be given serious consideration, despite the fact that there is textual evidence to support the view that גבר לא יצלח בימיו is an intrusion in v. 30 (its non-representation in Sept). and no evidence to support the 'original' text which is postulated. This text, nevertheless, is a credible line of poetry with synonymous parallelism, in so far as גבר is a synonym of איש and לא יצלח בימיו is epexegesis of ערירי. In the כי clause it appears as if לא יצלח, originally used of Jehoiachin himself, is re-used in connection with a concern to extend his 'lack of success' to his offspring. If גבר לא יצלח בימיו is correct epexegesis of ערירי, this establishes its sense as 'stripped of rank' or 'deposed', and it is a short step from this to the thought of banishment or exile (Sept.).

Thus vv. 28–30 are concerned originally only with the fate of Jehoiachin, and the extension of their scope to his offspring is secondary, not only in v. 28 (הוא וזרעו) but also in v. 30. The impetus to make this extension is supplied by ערירי, understood as 'childless'. Indeed if ערירי is thought to have this sense, a reference to Jehoiachin's children appears necessary. Verse 30, like v. 28, focuses on the evil fate of the king, and ערירי has nothing to do originally with a right to succeed to the throne or a register of the citizens of Jerusalem. It is simply a summons to write down for posterity the hard destiny of Jehoiachin, to place on permanent record that he was a luckless king, stripped of his kingship, deposed and banished, one whose fortunes would never be reversed, who would never taste success nor have the satisfaction of restoration.

Rudolph supposes that the background to these verses is a residual, popular hope that Jehoiachin will be restored rather than any feelings or reflections of Jeremiah himself about Jehoiachin. Verses 28–30 are then a response to the unwillingness of the people to believe that with Jehoiachin's deposition a chapter had been finally closed. To nurse a hope that Jehoiachin will come back is self-deceit, and all such thoughts should be banished from the mind. Weiser's complicated account is also along these lines, and the passage is seen as *kerygma* rather than as an expression of personal sorrow. On the other hand Thiel (p. 245) describes vv. 28–30 as a lament for Jehoiachin and Berridge (p. 180) suggests that Jeremiah voices a lamentation on his own behalf and on that of the people (cf. M. Sekine, *VT* 9, 1959, p. 49; E. Jenni, *ATANT*, 29, p. 58). Bright similarly detects in vv. 28–30 'a tone of deepest pity'. It is not clear that Weiser is right in holding that Jeremiah puts a question which is not at all a question in his own mind, and that he puts it only to enter a rebuttal of it in v. 30. It may be right not to limit vv. 28–30 to sorrowful reflection by Jeremiah on the fate of Jehoiachin and to include in it the element of *kerygma* for which Rudolph and Weiser have pleaded, but we are not then required to deny that it is informed with Jeremiah's own pity and sadness, and this impression is strengthened if vv. 28–30 are originally concentrated entirely on the figure of Jehoiachin, on the wonder and terror of his destiny.

CHAPTER XXIII

SHEPHERDS AND THEIR FLOCKS (23.1–4)

¹Shame on the shepherds who lead astray and scatter the flock which they
should tend and lead!,¹ says Yahweh. ²Therefore these are the words of
Yahweh, God of Israel, to those who tend and lead my people: You have
scattered and dispersed my flock and have failed to take care of them. I will
not fail to take care of² your evil deeds, says Yahweh. ³I will gather what is
left of my flock from all the lands where I have dispersed them, and I will
restore them to their own pastures, where they will be fruitful and increase. ⁴I
will set over them shepherds who will tend and lead them; they shall no longer
be filled with fear and terror and none of them shall be lost. This is the word
of Yahweh.

That הוי רעים can mean 'Woe to the shepherds' (Vulg). rather
than 'Woe on you shepherds' (Sept). is shown, for example, by
הוי בנה ביתו 'Woe to him who builds his house' (22.13). This
matter is of some importance because Rudolph supposes that v. 1
is a general condemnation of 'shepherds', that is, political
leaders, and does not have a particular reference to the
negligence and irresponsibility of Judah's rulers. There are
others (Weiser, Bright, Freehof, NEB) who tend to agree with
him in so far as they render הוי רעים as 'Woe to the shepherds'
and do not construe רעים as a vocative.

A more important question arises in v. 2, where a decision has
to be made whether the threatening word of Yahweh, introduced
by לכן כה אמר יהוה אלהי ישראל, is spoken *to* the negligent
shepherds or *concerning* or *against* them. There is no doubt
that Sept.'s rendering of על as ἐπὶ in v. 2 is connected with the
vocative construction indicated in v. 1. If the 'shepherds' of
Judah are directly addressed in v. 1, we expect that the
allegations and threats in v. 2 will also be directed to them.
However, Vulg., which does not indicate a vocative in v. 1,
nevertheless, renders על הרעים as *ad pastores*, and this shows
that the problems of v. 1 and v. 2 just discussed are separable:
that either 'Woe to the shepherds' or 'Woe to you shepherds' can
be tolerated in v. 1, but that a choice has to be made in v. 2
between על = אל, indicating direct address, and על 'concerning'
(Rudolph, Weiser, Bright, NEB) or 'against' (Freehof). But if
'concerning the shepherds' or 'against the shepherds' is correct,
v. 2 is not addressed to these shepherds, and we then have to
make an assumption like that of Rudolph and Weiser that vv. 1f.
were addressed to the people of Judah in the reign of Zedekiah.
But if this indeed were the situation presupposed, the verbs and

¹Reading מרעיתם (see below, pp. 554).

²That is, 'punish'.

suffixes in v. 2 referring to the shepherds (אתם ; הפצתם ; ותדחום
; פקדתם ולא ; עליכם ; מעלליכם) would require to be 3rd person
and not 2nd person. In other words the grammatical construction
of v. 2 leaves us no option but to equate על with אל and to
conclude that the shepherds are directly addressed.

Of the verbs employed in vv. 1f. מאבדים is the only one which
might seem not to fit into the picture which is being drawn, but
BDB (cf. Ehrlich, p. 302) concludes correctly that here אבד has
the sense 'lose' 'allow to go astray', and that a similar sense is to
be detected in Eccles 3.6, where אבד (Piel) is in antithetical
parallelism with לבקש 'seek': עת לבקש ועת לאבד, 'A time to seek
and a time to lose' (NEB). This sense is represented by Rudolph,
Bright and NEB (which reverses the order of מאבדים ומפצים,
'scatter and be lost'). BDB proposes the sense 'pasturing' or
'shepherding' for מרעיתי in this verse, and so צון מרעיתי means
'the flock for whose pasturing I am responsible'. In the context of
the allegation of negligence levelled against the shepherds it does
not seem appropriate that Yahweh himself should claim this
responsibility (cf. Duhm, Ehrlich, p. 302). The point of the
accusation is that it is a responsibility which the רעים have failed
to discharge conscientiously and that as a consequence
judgement will fall on them. It is possible that Sept. (τῆς νομῆς
αὐτῶν) is the consequence of a striving after sense by the Greek
translator (a conjectural emendation) rather than an indication
of a Hebrew text different from MT, but מרעיתם is desiderated
(Duhm, Ehrlich, p. 302) and a comparison with 10.21b suggests
itself: the shepherds lack discernment and all their flock is
scattered (וכל מרעיתם נפוצה). But if מרעיתם is adopted, v. 1
should be translated, 'Woe to the shepherds (pace Sept). who
allow the flock which they are charged to shepherd to go astray
and be scattered' (so Rudolph and Weiser).

The allegation is elaborated in v. 2 and is coupled with an
explicit threat of judgement. Sept. may have judged that על
הרעים הרעים could be adequately rendered into Greek by ἐπὶ
τοὺς ποιμαίνοντας (pace Janzen, p. 117). The connection of
'remissness' and 'judgement' is effected with some artistry by a
play on the different senses of פקד, as has been generally noted
(cf. Duhm): you did not take care of them properly (ולא פקדתם
אתם; cf. Rashi, לא נזהרתם לשמרם), and so I will punish you for
your evil deeds (הנני פקד עליכם). There is no doubt that Targ.
interprets the scattering of the sheep as a reference to exile. This
is evident from the rendering of ותדחום as טלטילתונון, 'and
removed them', or 'and caused them to be displaced'. This is the
verb which is used by Targ. at 22.28 to render נפוץ (= נָפוֹץ) and
הוטלו, the synonym of which, השלכו, is rendered by אתגליאו. In

this respect Kimchi's exegesis follows Targ., since he comments on vv. 1f., 'You lost (מאבדים) and scattered them in exile'.

Rudolph, Weiser and Bright suppose that vv. 1f. reflect conditions in Judah in the reign of Zedekiah. The imagery does not refer to deportation (not even to the deportation of 597), but is to be interpreted rather in terms of the misgovernment and mismanagement of the Judaean community by the רעים who had gained the upper hand over the weak king Zedekiah and whose policies were detrimental to the well-being and security of the people (Jer 34–39). It is urged that a reference to Zedekiah and his times is to be expected in order to round off the series of royal sayings and that the lack of an explicit mention of him is perhaps connected with widely felt doubts about his legitimacy (Weiser, p. 197 n. 2).

The view that 23.1f. has such a particular, historical reference should not be lightly accepted. It is doubtful whether רעים in vv. 1f. refers to the שרים rather than to the kings of Judah (the opinion of Rashi and Kimchi) and a more modest and safer estimate is that 23.1f. is a summarizing conclusion of the royal sayings and a way of rounding them off (cf. Jerome—the saying against Jehoiachin (22.29f.) sounds the death knell of the kings of Judah). There is the possibility that 23.1f. represents a re-use of vocabulary and imagery which is to be found in the poetry of the book of Jeremiah (22.22; 10.21). If this were so, it would be improbable that 23.1f. are attributable to the prophet Jeremiah. Behind this statement is the assumption that the prophet would be unlikely to reformulate in prose what he had uttered as poetry (cf. Thiel, p. 247, who assigns vv. 1–4 to his Deuteronomistic editor and who says that 23.1 'explicitly resumes 10.21'). Another consideration is that the theme of negligent shepherds and scattered sheep is developed elaborately and extensively in Ezek 34, and it has to be asked seriously whether this is actual prophetic proclamation or rather a use of the forms of the oracle in order to engage in theological reflection and state conclusions. Hence while 23.1f. might be rightly understood as allegations and threats uttered by the prophet Jeremiah in the reign of Zedekiah, implying that the Davidic monarchy had made shipwreck, the other possibility that they represent words put into the mouth of the prophet by a later generation, which wished to identify itself with him and endorse his attitude to the kings of Judah, should not be neglected (see further below). For the time being all that need be asserted is that 22.22 and 10.21 comprehend the entire theme of 23.1f.—undiscriminating and insubordinate 'shepherds' (kings) and a 'flock' (people) who are scattered.

It will be convenient to deal separately with the matter of the

literary coherence or non-coherence of 23.1–4 and to leave
historical questions in abeyance. It has been held (above,
pp. 553f). that the 2nd person plural verbs and suffixes in v. 2
demonstrate that this verse is addressed directly to הרעים. It
makes sense to address allegations and threats to 'negligent
shepherds', but it makes no sense to address to them, in
particular, a promise concerning new and better 'shepherds'
(v. 4). Moreover, the 3rd person plural verbs and suffixes of v. 4
certainly refer to שארית צאני (v. 3) and not to עמי or צאני
(v. 2). Hence the argument represented here is not simply or
principally that vv. 1, 2, 4, do not constitute a coherent unit
(*pace* Rudolph; cf. Weiser and Thiel, p. 247 n. 54), but also that
vv. 1f. cannot be combined with vv. 3f.: v. 1 coheres with v. 2 and
v. 3 with v. 4, but the two groups do not cohere with each other
(following Cornill). The negative and threatening aspect of
vv. 1f. cannot be combined with the promises of return from exile
and good leadership contained in vv. 3f., because such elements
of promise have no appropriateness in an address to negligent
shepherds. What then is the relation of vv. 3f. to vv. 1f.? The
contents of vv. 3f. (return from exile and the reconstitution of the
community under effective and benevolent leadership) are an
indication that whoever was responsible for the attachment of
these verses assumed, like Targ. and Kimchi, that the imagery of
vv. 1f. referred to exile and dispersion. ואני אקבץ at the
beginning of v. 3 is a response to the conclusion that the
dismemberment and dispersion of the people is indicated in v. 2.

Rudolph's view that v. 3 is secondary is partly founded on a
literary consideration (the imagery of vv. 1f. is absent) and
partly on a historical consideration (the thought of an
ingathering of Israel from all lands would be inappropriate in the
time of Jeremiah). So he ends up with three verses assigned to
Jeremiah and one to a later age. Weiser, who maintains the
literary integrity of vv. 1–4, and who attributes them to the
prophet Jeremiah, is to be contrasted with S. Mowinckel (*Zur
Komposition des Buches Jeremia*, 1914, p. 50) who also
supposes the literary integrity of vv. 1–4, but who explains the
passage as an exilic interpolation based on Ezek 34 (cf. Thiel,
p. 247, n. 52). The argument advanced above, if it is valid, is
effective against all who maintain that vv. 1–4 is a unity, whether
a unity proceeding from the prophet Jeremiah in the reign of
Zedekiah (Weiser; also Bright who adds that its present form
presupposes the exile), or an exilic unity (Mowinckel, Thiel,
Nicholson). Thiel's detailed arguments (pp. 246–248) lose much
of their point once it is shown that vv. 1f. do not cohere with
vv. 3f., because his fundamental contention is that the transition

from judgement to salvation is not to be considered a seam in the
construction of vv. 1–4 (p. 247).

One of Thiel's general arguments (p. 247) for the unity of
vv. 1–4 is that these verses display a structure of parallelism:
You (the negligent shepherds) scattered them (vv. 1f.), and I
(Yahweh) will gather them together again (vv. 3f.). But this is
precisely the parallelism which is destroyed by הדחתי, and the
use of ותדחום (v. 2) to develop a charge of negligence against the
רעים cannot be combined in one context with the use of הדחתי
(v. 3) to express the idea that Yahweh exiled his people as a
punishment for their sins. These are two separate worlds of
ideas: on the one hand the community disintegrated because its
leaders were negligent, and, on the other, the community exiled
by Yahweh as a judgement for its sins. Thus if Thiel (p. 247
n. 55, p. 248) establishes that the idea of Yahweh gathering
together (Jer 29.14; 32.37; cf. Deut 3.3) those whom he has
scattered (Jer 8.3; 27.10) and that the appearance of השיב after
הדיח (Jer 29.14; 32.37) is a characteristic Deuteronomistic train
of thought, he is showing that vv. 3f. are Deuteronomistic, but he
is not showing that vv. 1–4 possess a literary integrity.

That a deliberate attempt has been made by the author of
vv. 3f. to preserve the imagery of negligent shepherds and
scattered sheep is shown not only by והקמתי עליהם רעים ורעום
(v. 4), but also by individual features of the two verses. Of these
צאני (v. 3) is obvious, but the choice of נוחן (v. 3) is also a
deliberate continuation of the imagery, and ולא יפקדו (v. 4)
should be understood in the same way. The latter words are not
represented by Sept., but, whether or not they are a secondary
elaboration, they are correctly understood by Pesh. as continuing
the shepherd-sheep metaphor (wl' nṭ'wn, 'and they will not go
astray'), and are interpreted by Targ, in agreement with its
earlier application of the shepherd-sheep imagery, as a reference
to exile (ולא יזועון, 'and they will not be moved', that is,
displaced from their own land). The Niphal of פקד in v. 4 means
'be missing' (cf. NEB) rather than 'be punished'. Whoever was
responsible for the further play on פקד in v. 4 has not picked up
and reapplied the 'punish' sense of פקד in v. 2 (הנני פקד עליכם),
but has rather developed the word-play further with another
sense of פקד, 'be missing', which could be worked into the
shepherd-sheep metaphor. That ולא יפקדו means 'and none of
them will be missing' is indicated by Rashi and Kimchi (ולא
יחסרו), both of whom cite Num 31.49 (ולא נפקד ממנו איש),
while Rudolph, who takes ולא יפקדו in this way along with
Weiser, Bright and Freehof, cites 1 Sam 25.7 (ולא נפקד להם
מאומה).

To what exile does v. 3 refer and what kind of return does it envisage? Kimchi supposes a reference to a final ingathering in the Messianic Age and connects vv. 3f. with the Messianic promises in vv. 5f. (cf. Freehof). That vv. 3f. refer to a return from the Babylonian exile was asserted by Luzzato (1870; see Freehof) and has recently been repeated by Nicholson who supposes a connection between these verses and passages such as chapters 24 and 40–44. But the description of the return in v. 3 does not fit the circumstances of a return of Jews to Jerusalem from one place of exile. What is described is rather an event of universal significance, a gathering in of Jews from their places of dispersion in all corners of the world. Nor should it be thought that Sept. ἀπὸ πάσης τῆς γῆς for MT מכל הארצות means 'from the whole land of Babylon' and so points to a Hebrew text different from MT (מכל הארץ). Rather than indicating a more limited event Sept. is to be understood as a rendering of מכל הארצות which enhances the universal and final nature of the ingathering, and ἀπὸ πάσης τῆς γῆς is to be translated 'from all the earth' (so Rudolph). In finding a place for a Messianic interpretation of vv. 3f., and in connecting these verses with vv. 5f., Weiser is following Kimchi.

The demonstration that vv. 1f. and vv. 3f. do not cohere is not a demonstration that neither is attributable to the prophet Jeremiah, but if vv. 3f. are generated by vv. 1f. (as I hold), it is improbable that vv. 3f. derive from the same author as vv. 1f. This literary analysis establishes a relative chronology: if vv. 3f. are exilic, vv. 1f. are attributable to the prophet Jeremiah in the reign of Zedekiah or earlier, or to an earlier period of the exile than vv. 3f. However, the view that v. 3 presupposes that the exile and dispersion have already taken place, and is therefore not attributable to the prophet Jeremiah, encounters a contrary assumption that the prophet could have predicted the entire train of events, judgement, exile, dispersion and ingathering. Hence my own assumption has to be admitted, that the probability of vv. 3f. belonging to a later age, exilic or post-exilic, is higher than the probability that they are to be attached to the prophet Jeremiah, because they are then a response to the experience of exile and dispersion and arise from questions which the historical situation poses and which press for an answer.

The portrayal of v. 3 (מכל הארצות) is not connected with the inclusion of the exiles from the former Northern Kingdom (*pace* Weiser), and it cannot be related particularly to the events of 722, 597 and 586. It has an aspect of universality which escapes from such historical restrictions and it contains a promise of total retrieval of all dispersed Jews and of a final consummation (Kimchi). In this connection it ought to be compared with 3.14–16 and there are those who have supposed that 3.15f. and

23.3f. came from the same hand and are more or less identical in content (Duhm; cf. Thiel, p. 248 n. 57). Thiel assigns 23.1–4 to an exilic editor and 3.14–17 to a post-Deuteronomistic and post-exilic corrector (p. 93). Thiel's comment (p. 91) on 3.14b ('The small number of those returning appears to reflect the experiences and disillusionments of the early post-exilic period'). would seem to rest on a misunderstanding, for ולקחתי אתכם אחד מעיר ... והבאתי אתכם ציון does not indicate the paucity of the returning exiles, but is a more picturesque way of expressing the same thought as מכל הארצות (23.3), namely, that not a single, dispersed Jew will be missed, in however small groups they are dispersed; that the retrieval will be total and the return to Zion complete. Hence it is not clear that 3.14–16 can be distinguished from 23.1–4 in the manner attempted by Thiel, or that his conclusion that 3.14–16 is the result of a summarizing of 23.3f. is a just one (p. 248 n. 58). The main features of the portrayal of 23.3f. are present in 3.14–16: the emphasis on return from exile (שובו בנים שובבים, v. 14) and on total retrieval, the promise of discriminating 'shepherds' (רעים כלבי; v. 15) and of an increase of population in the homeland (v. 16).

The conclusion is that 23.3f. is dependent on 23.1f. in the ways which have been indicated (above, pp. 555–557), although vv. 1–4 do not constitute a unity. Hence vv. 3f. are later than vv. 1f.; vv. 1f. may derive from the prophet Jeremiah, but my own view is that they are exilic prose and represent a re-use of language and ideas taken from poetic passages (10.21; 22.22), and that they function as a summing up of the royal sayings. Verses 3–4 are either exilic or post-exilic; they have something of Deutero-Isaiah's wide horizons and of the finality of the vision of the new age, and I am unable to discern any significant distinction between vv. 3f. and 3.14–16. The faith which reaches out to a universal and perfect reintegration of all dispersed Jews on the soil of their own land had been born in the Babylonian exile, and so this aspect of the portrayal does not demand a post-exilic date, although its rise in such a context is intelligible. It could be explained as a response to unfulfilled expectations of a complete and perfect restoration in the post-exilic period.

A FUTURE DAVIDIC KING (23.5–6)

[5]The time is coming, says Yahweh, when I will raise up a righteous branch of David's line, and when he is king he will rule effectively and do what is right and just in the land. [6]In his days Judah will be safe and Israel live securely. This is the name which will be given to him, Yahweh is our righteousness.

If the more widely held view (Rudolph, Weiser, Bright) is accepted, vv. 1–4, which are entirely (Weiser) or mostly (Rudolph) spoken by the prophet Jeremiah in the reign of Zedekiah, are followed by a saying about a future Davidic king uttered at the same period: vv. 5f. resume the subject of v. 4 and envisage the future in terms of good government and security. They are more specific than v. 4, because they affirm that in these future days (הנה ימים באים) leadership will be exercised by a Davidic king. A significant new departure has been made with this setting of the future against the present, and a future king against the Davidic dynasty whose imminent historical eclipse is predicted.

It is possible to escape from this conclusion only by supposing that the prophet Jeremiah is not so dissociating the future from the present; that he is not leaping over the final ruin of the institution of kingship in Judah and projecting a hope of its restoration into a hidden and unspecified future, but that he is rather affirming the durability and revival of the historical Judaean institution. Thus according to J. Klausner (*The Messianic Idea in Israel*, 1955, pp. 103ff). and A. Malamat (*PEQ*, 1951, p. 86) we are to suppose that vv. 5f. were spoken by Jeremiah in the reign of Jehoiakim and that the contrast between present and future which is indicated is a contrast between the misgovernment of Jehoiakim and the quality of leadership which Jeremiah expects from his brother Mattaniah whose accession to the throne he predicts by assigning him a throne name (יהוה צדקנו). Bright partly adopts this view but hesitates over its application.

Most commentators have rightly supposed (cf. Duhm) that הנה ימים באים is indicative of a distant rather than an immediate future and that it does not introduce a prediction which will be effected by replacing one Judaean king with another within the framework of a continuing historical institution of monarchy. It involves rather, as does vv. 1–4, an acceptance of the inevitability of political collapse and disintegration, or else its presupposition is that these have already taken place. There are other difficulties associated with the hypothesis of Klausner and Malamat. A particular problem is created by the assertion that the throne name צדקיהו was adopted by Mattaniah as a consequence of Jeremiah's utterance in 23.6 (וזה שמו אשר יקראו יהיה צדקנו) which gave expression to the prophet's expectation that unlike his brother Jehoiakim he would walk in the ways of his father Josiah. It is clear from 2 Kgs 23.34 and 24.17 that it was the practice of foreign overlords when they installed a king in Judah to designate a

name for him, and that just as Eliakim had his name changed to
Jehoiakim by Pharaoh Necho, so Mattaniah had his name
changed to צדקיהו by Nebuchadrezzar. In the light of this, the
view that Jeremiah gave Mattaniah a cue for his throne name
cannot stand.

הנה ימים באים certainly indicates a decisive break in the
history of the Davidic monarchy and the Judaean state, either
one which is about to take place (if vv. 5f. are assigned to the
reign of Zedekiah), or one which has already taken place (if they
arise out of the experiences of disintegration and exile). It may
still make some sense to insist that this future hope is not,
nevertheless, 'eschatological' (Rudolph and Weiser), because the
portrayal is not that of a Messianic Kingdom beyond the end of
the present age (Rudolph), but it is much more important to
appreciate that the future hope which is here proclaimed accepts
as inevitable the downfall of the historical institution of Davidic
monarchy and does not foresee or indicate any connection in
terms of historical probabilities between the present
circumstances and the future hope.

If one accepts that the imagery is tree imagery, צמח צדיק
(צמח צדק, Ehrlich, p. 302) must be translated 'legitimate shoot'
(Rudolph, Bright) rather than 'righteous shoot' (Weiser,
Freehof, NEB). צמח צדק occurs in a 3rd century B.C.
Phoenician inscription and it was argued by G. A. Cooke (*A
Text Book of North Semitic Inscriptions*, 1903, p. 86), with
reference to Jer 23.5, that it should be rendered 'legitimate
offspring' (cf. A. M. Honeyman, *JEA*, 1940, pp. 57ff., 'rightful
scion'). In another Phoenician inscription dated c.300 B.C. בן
צדק 'legitimate son', 'son and heir', appears (H. Donner—W.
Röllig, *Kanaanäische und Aramäische Inschriften*, ii, 1964,
p. 25). Moreover in Ugaritic literature (14, 12f.; J. C. L. Gibson,
CML, p. 82) *att ṣdqh*, parallel with *mtrḥt yšrh*, must mean
'lawful wife' (cf. G. Widengren, *The King and the Tree of Life*,
1951, pp. 51f.; A. R. Johnson, *Sacral Kingship in Ancient
Israel*[2], 1967, pp. 35f.; J. Swetnam, *Biblica* 46, 1965, pp. 29–40).
It is descent from David which is indicated, but the sense
'righteous' arises from the perception of an association between
צדקה, צמח צדיק (v. 5) and יהוה צדקנו (v. 6).

The 'family tree' figure is an obvious one for a scion of the
House of David and it is a device for expressing a hope in a
future Davidic king which is certainly used in Isa 11.1 (חטר not
צמח) and perhaps at Zech 3.8, if עבדי צמח is indeed a reference
to Zerubbabel. There must be some doubt about this since in
Zech 6.12 Joshua, the high priest, is the one who is crowned and
given the title איש צמח (cf. Duhm). If צמח is in fact used of
Zerubbabel at Zech 3.8, it differs from Jer 23.5 and Isa 11.1

only in so far as the reference is more specific (*pace* Rudolph): Zerubbabel is a contemporary figure and if hope were focused on him as a Davidic Branch, the decisive change which he would bring about was expected in the immediate future. Otherwise it is not evident that צמח functions as a metaphor at Zech 3.8 differently from צמח at Jer 23.5 and חטר at Isa 11.1. Rudolph's concern (also Weiser) is to demonstrate that Jer 23.5f. do not portray 'paradise regained' or a Messianic Age beyond the end of this present age, but simply contain a promise of a future in this present world in which the effective and benevolent rule of a Davidic king will achieve justice within the Israelite community and security from outside dangers. But the futurity of the hope expressed in 23.5f. and its dissociation from the historical circumstances of the present bring it nearer to Isa 11 than he perceives.

Does ומלך מלך (v. 5) mean anything more than 'And a king will rule'? The rendering of Pesh. (*wnmlk bmlkwt'*) suggests that מֶלֶךְ is seen as a device for emphasis ('He will exercise sovereignty'), and Kimchi holds that this is the grammatical function of מֶלֶךְ. It has been supposed (Rudolph, Bright) that as with צדיק and צדקנו here too there is an allusion to Zedekiah, and so ומלך מלך means, 'And he shall exercise real sovereignty'—unlike Zedekiah who was the mere shadow of a king. This is part and parcel of a scheme of interpretation which has been adopted for vv. 5f., but ומלך מלך והשכיל is adequately translated by 'And when he is king, he will rule effectively'. The main thought of והשכיל is perhaps that of implementing policies effectively and successfully, as is indicated by Targ. (ויצלח) and by Rashi and Kimchi (הצליח). Kimchi appositely cites 1 Sam 18.14 which says of David ויהי דוד לכל דרכו משכיל (cf. vv. 5 and 15; also Jer 10.21 and 20.11).

It is the king's responsibility to oversee the processes of justice and to ensure that fair trials take place. Targ.'s interpretation of משפט and צדקה is probably correct (cf. Rashi—they refer to right legal verdicts) and it links up with the demands made on Davidic kings and the criticisms of their performance found in 21.12 (22.3) and 22.13–19. It recalls passages in the books of Samuel where the king's supreme responsibility in these matters is assumed and his incorruptibility expected (2 Sam 12.1–7), where neglect of them is represented as a grave dereliction of duty and a reason for withdrawing loyalty (2 Sam 15.1–6), and where his profound legal acumen is portrayed (2 Sam 14.1–24; cf. 1 Kgs 3.16–28).

There is no doubt that Weiser is right in stressing that the duties which Jeremiah is assigning to the future Davidic king are traditional and belong to the Jerusalem ideology of Davidic kingship. Both he and Rudolph create distortion in two respects: (*a*) They see too much significance in the absence of other traditional traits of the Davidic king from this portrayal and draw substantial conclusions from silence. (*b*) They overestimate (especially Weiser) the significance of the Niphal תושע (v. 6a) and shift the centre of interest from the Davidic king to Yahweh.

We are not to suppose that the prophet Jeremiah is refining and selecting in his description of a future Davidic king, as Rudolph and Weiser suggest; that he is deliberately leaving out of the portrait traditional features which do not appeal to his refined moral tastes, so that nothing is said of the *imperium* of the Davidic king, his military successes and political power, his subjugation of the Gentile world and their acknowledgement of his sovereignty (cf. Ps 2). In the account of the Davidic king and his regime which appears in vv. 5f. he does what historical Davidic kings ought to have done.

Commenting on בימיו תושע . . . ישכן לבטח Rudolph observes that peace and security are created by Yahweh, not by the king, but there is no justification for such an assertion and it ought not to have been introduced into a discussion on vv. 5f. There is nothing in v. 6a to suggest an intention to emphasize the king's dependence on Yahweh; rather Yahweh is declaring what will be achieved by the rule of an able and benevolent king. To suggest that there is a deep theological significance in תושע, as Rudolph does ('But the expression in v. 6a should be attended to very carefully: it is not the king himself who will create, but it will be created in his days, that is, Yahweh is the all-prevailing power'), is wrong, and one has the impression that Yahweh is being dragged into the exegesis by the scruff of the neck. Similarly Weiser introduces the 'covenant concept' and the Davidic king is sunk in an ocean of theocentricity.

The assumption that there should be synonymous parallelism in v. 6a (cf. Rudolph) is not a strong reason for doubting that ישראל is intended as a reference to the former northern kingdom, and ירושלם, which is represented by Sept.[S] at 23.6 and which appears in MT at 33.16, is probably a later revision. The considerations which lead to this conclusion are that 33.15–26 are probably a secondary, prose paraphrase of 23. 5f. and that ירושלם is then indicative of a post-exilic situation, where interest and concern are confined to the Jerusalem community.

יִקְרָאוֹ (v. 6) is explained by GK 60c as a *forma mixta* (יִקְרָא and יִקְרָאוּ). יקראו is rendered as a plural by Vulg., Pesh. and Targ., and this is probably to be accounted for by the circumstance that they have taken the 3rd singular as an impersonal construction with a collective reference, so that it is unlikely that they support the emendation of יִקְרָאוֹ to יִקְרָאוּ, as

Duhm supposes. Kimchi indicates explicitly that it is the king's subjects who will give him his name, whereas Sept. (κύριος) supposes that it is bestowed by Yahweh (cf. Ziegler, *Beiträge*, p. 92; Janzen, pp. 31f.). The interest of Targ.'s paraphrase of צדקנו ('Favourable verdicts will be pronounced for us from the Lord in his days') is that it connects the צדק of צדקנו with משפט וצדקה (v. 5) and gives it a particular legal interpretation (cf. Rashi, above, p. 562). The debate about whether the prophet Jeremiah used צדק or צדקה with the sense 'salvation' (see Rudolph on Volz) is not one to which great weight should be attached, since a distinction between a community, where justice is administered with a particular regard for those who might suffer injustice, and where a sense of well-being and undisturbed security prevails, is hardly to be distinguished from a community which is enjoying a condition of salvation.

The view that there is an allusion to King Zedekiah in יהוה צדקנו is bound up with an exegesis of vv. 5f. which turns on the supposition that a contrast between Zedekiah and the future Davidic king runs through these verses. This, it is alleged, is present in צמח צדיק, in ומלך מלך, in the differing circumstances in which they receive their throne names, and in the throne name יהוה צדקנו which is assigned to the future Davidic king. The view that behind the portrayal of the future king Zedekiah lurks as a kind of antitype or antithesis should be given up (cf. Nicholson), because it is a superfluous hypothesis and it attributes to the portrayal a kind of particularity which it does not possess.

Another dissuasive against the view that יהוה צדקנו is an allusion to Zedekiah is the rich pattern of use displayed by צדק and צדקה in the Hebrew Bible. To leap at a particular and special interpretation of יהוה צדקנו is, in view of this, difficult to justify. The centrality of צדק as a concept of the Jerusalem cult has been explored (A. R. Johnson, *The Labyrinth*, ed. S. H. Hooke, 1935, pp. 73–111; *Sacral Kingship*, pp. 4ff.; 35–37), and it may have been a key idea inherited from the pre-Israelite, Jebusite cult in view of such pieces of evidence as מלכי צדק, a king of Salem (Jerusalem) and a priest of אל עליון (Gen 14.18), אדני צדק, a king of Jerusalem (Josh 10.1,3), and the title of Jerusalem which appears in Isa 1.26 (עיר הצדק) and Jer 31.23 and 50.7 (נוה צדק), whether or not צדק is a theophoric element in all these cases. One has also to take into account the importance of צדק and צדקה for the theology of the Jerusalem cult as indicated by the book of Psalms and the centrality of the demand for צדקה in the prophetic literature. More specifically there is the special association of משפט and צדקה with the Davidic king, present in v. 5 (above, p. 562). Hence a sufficient explanation of the name יהוה צדקנו is that it is a resumption of צמח צדיק and that it is bound up with a description of the future Davidic king which pays particular attention to his legal responsibilities in connection with the machinery of justice, and to his task of creating a community which enjoys a universal well-being and a freedom from all outside threats to its security and integrity.

The historical question is the hardest of all and it cannot be resolved by focusing attention on the language and imagery in 23.5f. The answer depends on whether or not it is supposed that pre-exilic prophets (Amos, Hosea, Micah, Isaiah and Jeremiah) looked beyond the judgement of political dissolution and exile to a reconstruction of the community on the soil of its own land under a Davidic king (cf. W. McKane, *Tradition and Interpretation*, ed. G. W. Anderson, 1979, p. 176 n. 51; pp. 182f.). The other precise consideration (cf. Nicholson) is that there is little evidence of this looking beyond the judgement to a new Davidic king in the book of Jeremiah, and that if we were to conclude that the prophet Jeremiah did have such a glimpse of the future, the entire case would rest on 30.9 and 23.5f. (on 33.15f. see above p. 563). In these circumstances the probability is that 23.5f. belong to a type of exilic or post-exilic hope for the future (see on 23.3f., p. 559) rather than to the closing years of the pre-exilic period.

A NEW OATH IN A NEW AGE (23.7–8)

⁷Therefore the time is coming, says Yahweh, when men will no longer say, 'As Yahweh lives who brought the Israelites out of Egypt'. ⁸Instead they will say, 'As Yahweh lives who brought¹ the descendants of Israel out of a northern land' (and out of all the lands where I dispersed them)², and they will live on their own soil.³

The text of 16.14f. and 23.7f. has already been discussed (above, pp. 373–376). ומכל הארצות אשר הדחתים שם represents a secondary, exegetical widening of the scope of exile and an alternative rubric for the new oath (see above, pp. 375f.): not only those dispersed in Babylon are to be brought back to their own soil, but all the dispersed of Israel, presently scattered across the face of the earth. One of the explanations given for the positioning of 23.7f. (Rudolph, Thiel) is that they represent a further development of the 'regathering' theme of v. 3, and that, in particular, ומכל הארצות אשר הדחתים שם (v. 8) pick up the

¹ Delete ו אשר העלה or ואשר הביא (see above, pp. 374f.).
² See above, pp. 375f.
³ See above, p. 376.

almost identical words in v. 3. This assumes that ומכל הארצות
שם . . . were already part of v. 8 when vv. 7f. were inserted in
their present position in the exilic (Thiel) or the post-exilic
(Rudolph) age.

The view that vv. 7f. are exilic may rest on the kind of
assumptions which have been examined in connection with 23.3
(above, pp. 558–559), namely, that the question of return from
exile and reintegration would not be raised until the exile had
become a fact. This is a reasonable line to take and it may be
these considerations which influence Nicholson when he says
that vv. 7f. presuppose the exile, although he also takes literary
factors into account (the style and vocabulary point to a
Deuteronomic author). Similarly Thiel (pp. 248f.), for a mixture
of theological and literary reasons, urges that a connection
between vv. 7f. and the historical prophet Jeremiah must be
excluded. Conclusions of this kind cannot achieve independence
of theological assumptions, as a comparison with Weiser will
show. For him it is the glory of the prophet Jeremiah and a
testimony to his heroic faith that when his community stood on
the brink of disaster he already descried the time of restoration.

Weiser believes that vv. 7f. fit well into the larger context of
23.1–8, and he and other scholars (Bright, Nicholson, Thiel)
consider that they belong originally to chapter 23 and not to
chapter 16. On the other hand, Duhm, for whom vv. 7f. are
post-exilic expansion, views them as a resumption of vv. 1–4,
particularly of v. 3, and Rudolph's similar opinion that vv. 7f. are
a post-exilic addition allows only a marginal cohesiveness to
these verses in relation to vv. 1–6. This is probably nearer the
truth. There is an affinity of subject matter as between v. 3 and
v. 8 (dispersion and return) and an almost identical series of
words (שם . . . מכל הארצות) common to v. 3 and v. 8, but the
cohesiveness of vv. 7f. with what precedes amounts to no more
than this. If, however, the original text of vv. 7f. is as I have
supposed (see above, pp. 375f.), their point is essentially different
from that of v. 3. The distinctive thought contained in them is
that the new exodus (מארץ צפונה) will replace the old one
(מארץ מצרים) as the decisive saving event, and this does not
have much to do with the ideas of the preceding verses.

The other factor which has to be taken into account is that the
translator of Sept. had before him a Hebrew text in which v. 6
was followed by v. 9. This is clear not only from the appearance
of vv. 7f. (MT) after v. 40 in Sept., but also from the
circumstance that the Greek translator erroneously incorporated
לנבאים (ἐν τοῖς προφήταις) with v. 6. He could not have made
this blunder unless לנבאים had followed immediately after
צדקנו. We therefore have an indication that vv. 7f. did not have

an assured position in the context of chapter 23: in MT they appear after v. 6, and in the Hebrew text translated into Greek they appeared after v. 40.

The view that vv. 7f. are better integrated in chapter 23 than are vv. 14f. in chapter 16 (see above, pp. 373f). is only partially justified. Verses 7f. do not fit into a larger context of vv. 1–8 and they embody ideas which are different from those of v. 3. There are, however, correspondences of vocabulary between v. 3 and v. 8, and between v. 5 and v. 7 (הנה ימים באים) which may have influenced the positioning of vv. 7f. in MT.

CORRUPTION WILL BRING DISASTER (23.9–12)

[9]Concerning the prophets:
> My nerve is broken,
> all my bones are jelly;
> I am like a man dead drunk,
> like one overcome by wine.
> It is Yahweh's dread words that have done it.
[10]"The land is full of adulterers
> and so[1] the soil is parched,
> the rough pastures are bone dry.
> They lead evil lives
> and their power is corrupt.
[11]Prophets and priests are no less tainted,
> even in my house I have found their wickedness at work.
> > This is Yahweh's word.
[12]Therefore they will lose their footing on the road which they take,
> they will stumble in the darkness and come to grief;
> for I will bring disaster on them,
> when their day of reckoning comes.
> > This is Yahweh's word.

The confusion associated with לנבאים (v. 9, MT) and the misunderstandings which have been produced as a consequence are commented on acidly by Jerome. Sept., which erroneously attached לנבאים to 23.6, is specifically mentioned, and other misconstructions which might be regarded as vulnerable to Jerome's criticism are those of Pesh., Targ., Rashi and Kimchi, all of which attempt to incorporate לנבאים in the syntax of v. 9. The general effect of this is to make Jeremiah's inner disintegration and bewilderment a consequence of the activities of other prophets, explicitly false prophets in Targ. Rashi identifies these with the prophets who say שלום יהיה לכם to the people, and this tendency has its greatest exegetical consequences in Kimchi. Jeremiah's predicament, according to Kimchi, is brought about by the circumstances that the false

---

[1]Reading מפני אלה as מפני אלה (see below, p. 570).

prophets claim that their words are דברי קדש and are authorized
by Yahweh, and the prophet's outburst in vv. 9f. is a complaint
to Yahweh for allowing this ambiguity and the resultant
confusion. The people are misled, and were it not for the support
which the false prophets appear to have from Yahweh, the
people would listen to the voice of true prophecy (נביאי האמת)
and repent.

The correct understanding of לנבאים as a general heading is
indicated by Vulg. (*Ad prophetas*) and by Jerome who
appreciated (so Rudolph, Weiser, Berridge, p. 181 and others)
that vv. 9–12 are not particularly occupied with prophets and
that one has to leap over these verses to v. 13 in order to reach
the beginning of a series of sayings about prophets which runs to
the end of the chapter. The collector of 23.9–40 is identified by
Hyatt with Baruch, and the absence of Deuteronomic/
Deuteronomistic marks in the vocabulary and style of this
section is noted by Thiel (p. 249, n. 65). He supposes that the
collection of prophetic sayings is part of the total structure of
chapters 21–24 (words about leaders) created by D, but he finds
little evidence of Deuteronomistic interference in 23.9–40 which
he compares in this respect with the royal sayings. D took over
23.9–40 and fitted these verses into his editorial plan, but he
reserved his own comments on the theme of false prophecy
(apart from 14.13–16) for 27.9f.,14–18 and 28 which is a drama
on that theme. לנבאים is then a general superscription and the
prophet's extreme discomfiture and incapacity cannot be
ascribed to a fatally ambiguous situation created by (false)
prophets (Pesh., Targ., Rashi and Kimchi).

It is not obvious that Baumgartner's comparison (pp. 74f). of
23.9 with 4.19 is altogether apposite, since the imagery of 4.19 is
indicative of anguish, whereas that of v. 9 points rather to
physical and mental collapse. Bright is right to observe that
נשבר לבי בקרבי does not mean that Jeremiah's heart is broken
but rather that his nerve is broken; that he is overtaken by a
pathological lassitude and his mind ceases to function, or else
that he is reduced to great confusion. רחפו כל עצמותי presents
particular difficulties, since רחף occurs only here according to
BDB (I רחף 'be soft', 'relax', distinguished from II רחף 'hover').
This distinction is not maintained by KB, and we now know of an
Ugaritic *rhp* 'hovered', 'soared'. The separation in BDB appeals
to an Arabic cognate *rahafa* 'grow soft', the 'hovering' sense
being reserved for Deut 32.11 (a vulture hovering over its young)
and Gen 1.2 (the רוח אלהים hovering over the face of the
waters). If the 'grow soft', 'relax' sense is adopted for Jer 23.9,
something like the turning of the bones into jelly or the feeling
that the physical frame is dissolving has to be supposed, but the

other sense of 'shaking' or 'quaking' has been postulated as a development of 'hovering' or 'fluttering', and it is this which prevails in the versions (Sept. ἐσαλεύθη; Vulg. *contremuerunt*; Pesh. *z'w*; Targ. זָע) and in Rashi and Kimchi. This experience of loss of physical capacity and mental control is likened to intoxication—to the effects of too much alcohol. The prophet's condition resembles in some respects that of a man who has drunk too much and who is reduced to physical paralysis and mental confusion.

The reason for this unmanning has to be sought in v. 9c (מפני יהוה ומפני דברי קדשו) which, however, are regarded by Duhm as secondary and erroneous explication: the gloss does not conform to Jeremiah's style (cf. Isa 2.10,19,21) and Jeremiah is not shattered by Yahweh's anger but by the sad state of the land. But these words have been explained as a reference forward to vv. 10–12 (Rudolph, Weiser, Berridge, p. 182) which contain 'words of Yahweh'. The reason for Jeremiah's agitation and paralysis is to be found in words which are (or were—Berridge) addressed to him by Yahweh. Here then is a scheme for comprehending vv. 9–12 as a unity: the דברי קדשו which unman the prophet are the words of Yahweh in vv. 10–12. An important factor in this connection is the grammatical evaluation of כי in כי מנאפים מלאה הארץ (v. 10), since Rudolph supposes that כי is simply a marker of the beginning of Yahweh's speech, that v. 10b (containing a second כי) should be deleted (following Duhm), and that the third occurrence of כי (v. 11) is asseverative (GK 159ee). It is likely that כי discharges the same grammatical function in all three places, and it is a weakness in Weiser's scheme, founded on MT, that he treats the first כי as a marker of direct speech, the second as a conjunction (*denn*) and the third as an asseverative (*Ja* = Rudolph). Bright, like Rudolph, is inclined to delete v. 10b (כי . . . מדבר) and supposes that v. 10a ('for the land is full of adulterers') is a further explication of what precedes. Hence the divine speech is confined to vv. 11f. and the status of לכן at the beginning of v. 12 is left obscure ('And so').

The contention that v. 10b does not break the connection between v. 10a and v. 10c is not convincing. Even if the inner connection between guilt and punishment, or evil-doing and curse, is emphasized to the extent of establishing a causal link, it still appears that Rudolph is right to say that a description of corruption which begins at v. 10a and is present in v. 10c is interrupted by v. 10b which therefore has an intrusive aspect. But if v. 10b is secondary, can its intrusion be explained? Giesebrecht and Duhm supposed that v. 10a and v. 10b were textual variants (so Janzen, p. 12) and that v. 10b was a later, corrected form dependent on 12.4. There is no textual evidence to support the deletion of v. 10b, whereas v. 10a is unrepresented in Sept., and this is thought to lend support to the view that MT is conflate. Janzen (*pace* Giesebrecht and Duhm) prefers the variant of Sept., and the implication of this is that v. 10a (כי מנאפים מלאה הארץ) should be deleted. But v. 10a and v. 10b cannot be explained as doublets on the basis of ὅτι ἀπὸ προσώπου τούτων ἐπένθησεν ἡ γῆ, because ἀπὸ προσώπου τούτων hangs in the air in Sept. and is explicable only with reference to מנאפים (v. 10a). This is seen in Pesh. which like Sept. represents כי מפני אלה as כי אפני אלה, but which otherwise more or less reproduces MT, so that *mṭl hlyn* relates to *gyr' whṭwp'* (v. 10a), and also in NEB whose translation rests on אלה (Brockington, p. 207), but which otherwise is founded on MT. Both Duhm and Rudolph maintain that a longer text is required in v. 10 for metrical reasons: Duhm (cf. 9.1) adds וכלם בגדים and Rudolph emends כי מנאפים to כי מרעים ומנאפים. Neither refers to Pesh. which has a longer text than MT (*mṭl dgyr' whṭwp'* = כי מנאפים וחטאים).

The conclusions about the text of v. 10 which are to be drawn from this discussion are these: (*a*) In all the circumstances the advantages to be gained from departing from the text of MT and deleting v. 10b are not sufficiently decisive to justify the operation. In particular, v. 10c is an obscure line (see further below), and even with v. 10b deleted the connection between v. 10a and v. 10c is not transparent. (*b*) MT should be followed except that מפני אלה (Sept. and Pesh). should be read instead of מפני אלה (MT), which is taken by Targ. as a reference to false oaths. This agrees with Jerome's exegesis of ἀπὸ προσώπου ὅρκου (Sept.[o]) and with Rashi and Kimchi. (*c*) The three occurrences of כי (vv. 10 and 11) should all be taken as asseveratives and the 'word of Yahweh' then runs from v. 10 to v. 12.

There is no indication from the versions (Vulg., Pesh. and Targ). that the sense intended by מנאפים (v. 10) is other than the plain one of 'adultery', and the coupling of *gyr' whṭwp'* in Pesh. strengthens this impression. A review of the occurrences of the Qal and Piel of נאף shows that it is used in connection with apostasy or idolatry, certainly in Ezek 23.37 (ואת גלוליהן נאפו) and possibly in Jer 23.14 (נאוף והלך בשקר). In Jer 5.7, 9.2 and 23.10 it is impossible to determine whether we have to reckon with adultery or apostasy. Passages involving Israel, envisaged as a harlot, whether or not נאף appears in them, are a separate category (Jer 2.20ff.; 3.1–5,8f.,20). Rudolph suggests that it is the institution of marriage which is threatened, while Weiser leaves open the two possibilities of sexual immorality and idolatry or apostasy. Sept. (ἐπένθησεν), Vulg. (*luxit*) and Pesh.

('*t'blt*) understand אבל as 'mourn', while Targ. (חרובת) renders it as 'withered' or 'desiccated'. The semantic connections of 'mourn' and 'wither' in association with natural fertility, and the possibility of a mythological background have been discussed at 14.2 (see above, pp. 315–317). Whether it is adultery or apostasy, its consequence is a drought which destroys the fertility of the land and burns up the rough pastures (נאות מדבר).

ותהי מרוצתם רעה (v. 10) means something like 'the race of life which they run is evil' (cf. Sept. ὁ δρομὸς αὐτῶν; Vulg. *cursus eorum*). Targ. emphasizes the capriciousness of their behaviour—they follow their own whims—and supposes that רעה means 'disaster', 'Because they proceed in a wilful way, disaster will overtake them'. Kimchi's gloss on מרוצה (זריזות, 'mobility') probably has the nuance of 'bent' or 'motivation' ('Their bent is towards evil'). לא כן makes poor sense if it is understood as 'not so' (Sept. οὐχ οὕτως; Vulg. *dissimilis*). It should be taken as a synonym of רעה, 'lacking in rectitude', and is correctly glossed by Rashi (לא בדין) and Kimchi (אמת) who compares it with כן in Num 27.7. If, however, the meaning of v. 10c is 'Their way of life and tendency are evil and their power is misused', this does not link very particularly with either adultery or apostasy and a consequent failure of fertility, so that the coherence of v. 10 has not altogether been elucidated. גם (v. 11) marks a movement from the description of the behaviour of the community as a whole to a description of the behaviour of religious leaders in particular. It also produces an intensification of the impression of demoralization: those whose office and vocation identify them as guardians of truth and morality are busy perpetrating evil in the House of God. What precisely is indicated by the רעה which Yahweh finds in them cannot be determined. Rashi and Kimchi conclude that it is idolatry, and this is followed by Nicholson who supposes a reference to pagan cults in the Jerusalem temple which were actively encouraged by prophets and priests. Kimchi associates חנפו with lack of legal impartiality (משוא פנים); Duhm is content to say that חנפו (emended to חנוף חנפו for metrical reasons) refers to a corruption of intentions and action, and he has in mind the grasping greed and lack of integrity mentioned in 6.13f. Ehrlich (p. 303) supposes that חנף has its post-biblical sense of 'flatter': the prophets and priests tell the people what they want to hear. Rudolph, on the other hand, connects חנפו and רעה with his interpretation of מנאפים (v. 9). There is widespread moral decay, especially evident in the breakdown of sexual morality and the disintegration of the institution of marriage. The prophets and priests of the Jerusalem temple, who by their

example and the force of their moral authority should have
rolled back the tide of demoralization, are exposed as morally
bankrupt, and aid and abet the processes of moral decay. Weiser,
who thinks in terms of the rapacity, gluttony and sexual
immorality of prophets and priests, offers a similar interpretation.

לכן (v. 12) introduces a threat which embraces all those whose
behaviour has been condemned in the preceding verses (vv. 10f.).
The figurative language in v. 12ab suggests that they have
embarked on a self-destructive course, whereas the more prosaic
intimation of judgement in v. 12c emphasizes rather that it is
Yahweh who will bring destruction on them. The Masoretic
punctuation joins באפלה to כחלקלקות, and while this makes good
enough sense, it breaks the coincidence of punctuation and
poetic form. Pesh., on the other hand, assumes correctly that
באפלה connects with the words which follow it in v. 12b
(wlhšwk' ntdhwn wnplwn) and this agrees with Duhm, Rudolph,
Weiser and NEB ('They shall be dispersed in the dark and shall
fall there'). NEB ('dispersed') apparently derives ידחו from נדח;
its derivation from דחח or דחה (יִדָּחוּ) yields the sense 'thrown
down' (so Duhm). The versions (also Kimchi) indicate 'tripped'
or 'pushed' (Sept. ὑποσκελισθήσονται; Vulg. impellentur; Pesh.
ntdhwn; Targ. יתקלון 'stumble').

What is the picture which is being constructed in v. 12ab?
Duhm and Rudolph think in terms of wanderers on dangerous
mountain paths who are overtaken by darkness and fall to their
death. The interpretation of v. 12ab should be founded on some
such translation as, 'Therefore the footing will be treacherous in
the road which they take. They will stumble (Sept. and Targ). in
the darkness and come to grief' ('will fall on it'—'it' refers to
דרך). It is the darkness which seals their doom (cf. Kimchi). In
daylight they might have negotiated safely the treacherous
surface of their track, but their destruction is assured by the
darkness which overtakes them and a fatal stumble becomes
inevitable. It can be seen as self-destructive conduct or as a
punishment which Yahweh executes at the appointed time.

Verse 12c (כי אביא עליהם . . . נאם יהוה), which Duhm
deletes as an addition composed from 11.23 and 6.15, is thought
by Rudolph and Weiser (שנת פקדתם) to indicate that judgement
is not envisaged as imminent. This fits in with their supposition
that vv. 9–12 are to be located at the beginning of Jeremiah's
ministry, and they found this on the condition of shock described
in v. 9. The prophet experiences a kind of inward
fragmentation—the shock of a first appreciation of how matters
actually stand—and he is devastated. Hence there is the thought
that up to this point Jeremiah was something of an innocent,
unaware of the true state of affairs in his own community. This

picture of the naïvete of Jeremiah, which is taken by Rudolph from Volz, is present in Weiser in a modified form and is doubted by Berridge (p. 183).

None of the criteria offered for the exact dating of this passage should be regarded as decisive, neither the contention that only a prophet at the outset of his ministry would have been so badly affected by a revelation of existing evil and its consequences (Rudolph, Weiser), nor the argument that שׁנת פקדתם is indicative of a judgement which is still some way off; nor should a different indication of dating be sought in so general a reference as גם בביתי מצאתי רעתם (Nicholson, 609 B.C., when the effects of the Josianic reformation had worn off). Finally it is doubtful whether רעה has the significance as a link which has been attributed to it: a word which produces cohesion and which unifies vv. 10–12 (Rudolph, Weiser). The most that can be said is that the semantic range of רעה has been exploited, so that it is used of evil (vv. 10f). and also its consequences—the 'disaster' of judgement (v. 12).

PROPHETS OF SAMARIA AND JERUSALEM (23.13–15)

[13]In the prophets of Samaria I have seen what is senseless:
they have prophesied by Baal
and have led astray my people Israel.
[14]In the prophets of Jerusalem I have seen what horrifies me:
they commit adultery and practise falsehood,
they encourage evil-doers to persist in evil-doing,
so that no one turns back[1] from his wickedness.
In my sight they are all like Sodom,
those who live in Jerusalem are like Gomorrah.
[15]Therefore these are the words of Yahweh Sabaoth concerning the prophets:
I will give them a poisonous herb to eat
and a poisonous potion to drink,
for from the prophets of Jerusalem
pollution has spread throughout the land.

The fundamental sense of 'lacking salt' is given for תפלה (v. 13) by Aq. ($\alpha\nu\alpha\lambda\sigma\nu$), whereas developed meanings deriving from 'tastelessness' appear elsewhere in the versions. 'Tastelessness' may be understood as 'morally or religiously offensive' (Sept. $\dot{\alpha}\nu o\mu\dot{\eta}\mu\alpha\tau\alpha$ 'impious deeds'; Pesh. *dglwt* 'faithlessness'; Targ. רשׁע 'wickedness'; cf. BDB 'unseemliness', and similarly Duhm, Rudolph, Weiser, Bright, Freehof). But just as 'taste' develops in the direction of 'intellectual discrimination' rather than 'good (aesthetic) taste', so we might suppose that the sense of תפלה in v. 13 is 'lack of intellectual discrimination' and this is

---

[1]Reading לבלתי ישׁבו (see below, p. 576).

represented by Vulg. (*fatuitatem*), Jerome (*stultitiam*) and Symm. (αφροσυνην). The meaning of טחו להם תפל (Ezek 22.28) is that the prophets cover falsehood with a veneer of prophetic authority, and the meaning of תפלה (Jer 23.13), if Kimchi's derivation is accepted, is that the prophets of the northern kingdom camouflaged ('whitewashed') falsehood by laying claim to prophetic authority. תפלה and שערורה (v. 14) are not to be related in terms of differing degrees of severity: the intention is not to represent that the prophets of Samaria are less culpable than the Jerusalem prophets (*pace* Duhm, Rudolph, Weiser, Bright). Gesenius *ineptum* (*Thesaurus* iii, p. 1516a) and NEB, 'men of no sense', should be followed. The prophets of the northern kingdom are charged with leading their community astray, that is, of actively encouraging an apostasy which led to exile and disintegration. The 'seeing' of v. 13 does not have the directness and immediacy of the 'seeing' of v. 14, if we assume (as Volz, Rudolph and Weiser do) that the passage (vv. 13–15) is to be located in the period of Zedekiah and is attributable to the prophet Jeremiah. 'Saw' is not indicative of direct observation in v. 13, whereas we may suppose that 'saw' in v. 14 does have this significance. NEB marks the difference by rendering ראיתי as 'I saw' in v. 13 and 'I see' in v. 14.

תפלה is indicative of astonishment and unbelief in the presence of irrational and stupid behaviour (Symm.; Vulg.; Jerome), whereas שערורה represents a sense of shock and moral revulsion (cf. Sept. φρικτά 'causing shudders'; Targ. שנו, 'something strange or uncanny'). The aspect of moral revulsion appears in Kimchi's gloss on שערורה — 'evil and defiled'. The circumstance that the prophet registers a different kind of reaction in v. 14 does not necessarily indicate that the behaviour which he observes in the Jerusalem prophets is different from that of the prophets of the northern kingdom, although the history of interpretation reveals an impressive unanimity that this is indeed the case. Berridge (p. 13 n. 52) supposes that in 23.10 and 14 'adultery' is probably a metaphor for 'apostasy', but this is not indicated by the versions at v. 10 (above, p. 570) and is not the view of Kimchi, Duhm, Rudolph, Weiser, Bright, Freehof and NEB at v. 14. In the latter verse Sept., Aq., Pesh. and Targ. indicate adulterous behaviour combined with a way of life which is false through and through and which gives comfort to evil-doers (cf. Duhm). That Kimchi takes נאוף literally is clear from his allusion to Jer 29.23 which says of Zedekiah and Ahab, 'And they committed adultery with the wives of their friends'.

The question which has to be raised is whether נבא בשקר is ever a variant of נבא בבעל (which occurs in v. 13), and whether

נאוף והלוך בשקר could mean 'They practise apostasy and idolatry'. In that case the charge laid against the prophets of Jerusalem would be the same as the one alleged against the prophets of the northern kingdom. Rudolph in fact supposes that הנביאים נבאו בשקר (5.31) is equivalent to והנביאים נבאו בבעל (2.8), but a review of the occurrences of נבא בשקר in the book of Jeremiah shows that נבא בשקר more probably refers to the שלום utterances of Yahweh prophets, characterized as falsehood, than to overt apostasy, and there are some occurrences of נבא בשקר or נבא בשמי שקר which are incompatible with the conclusion that נבא בשקר is an equivalence of נבא בבעל (20.6; 23.25; 27.15; 29.9,21).

What is indicated in v. 14 rather than apostasy is the failure of these prophets, either by rebuke or example, to condemn breaches of morality. In particular, the references to Sodom and Gomorrah suggest that נאוף in v. 14 indeed refers to sexual immorality (cf. Duhm, who urges that the simile has its point in the life-style of the inhabitants of Jerusalem rather than as an allusion to the devastating judgement which will fall on them). Does then והלוך בשקר mean that the Jerusalem prophets are hypocrites (so NEB) whose lives are a sham, or is there a more particular reference to the assurances of שלום (Rashi and Kimchi) which they give to the people? There are two possible interpretations of והלוך בשקר: (a) The prophets, themselves adulterers and hypocrites, encourage evil rather than combatting it. (b) The prophets are self-deceived when they suppose that their שלום prophecies are authorized by Yahweh.

A different interpretation of וחזקו ידי מרעים appears in Pesh.: wmḥmsnyn 'ydyhwn mn rḥmyhwn, 'And they support the hands of their friends' (מרעים plural of מרע 'companion'). Instead of the thought of lending encouragement to evil-doers (Rashi) this introduces a reference to lack of impartiality and even-handedness in the exercise of prophetic leadership, but it is not particularly appropriate and מרעים should certainly be taken as 'evil-doers' rather than 'friends'.

The prophets and their constituency, the inhabitants of Jerusalem, are reduced to the same dismal level of moral degradation and the paradigms of such degradation, Sodom and Gomorrah, serve for them. Rudolph urges that וישביה cannot stand and he gives two reasons: (a) It is the Jerusalem prophets who are indicted and not all the inhabitants of Jerusalem. (b) The suffix must refer to Jerusalem, but it is at too great a distance from ירושלם in v. 14a (following Duhm). Hence Duhm would emend וישבי עמרה כעמרה to וישביה כעמרה and Rudolph would emend וישביה to ויחד(ו), 'and one and all'. Rudolph's assertion that the passage (vv. 14f.) is solely about the prophets of

Jerusalem is not borne out by לבלתי שבו איש מרעתו. The sense of this is not in doubt, but the grammatical propriety of combining לבלתי with שבו is doubtful. Duhm proposed שוב for שבו and Ehrlich (p. 303) יָשְׁבוּ — haplography of *yodh* (cf. Rudolph). It is arguable that a reference to the immorality of the inhabitants of Jerusalem comes in well after לבלתי ישבו איש מרעתו. The prophets fail to exercise a moral authority and there is a consequent, widespread decline in moral standards. The distance of וישביה from ירושלם is awkward, but it should be tolerated. Further, the shorter text of Sept., in which על הנבאים is not represented at v. 15, accords better with the presence of וישביה than does MT (cf. Janzen, p. 44, who supposes that על הנבאים is secondary in MT).

The judgement which is threatened is envisaged as at 9.14 (cf. 8.14) as a kind of poison, and 9.14 (above, p. 207) is a prose elaboration of the poetry of 23.15. Yahweh will provide a meal of poisonous herbs to be washed down with a poisonous draught. Judgement is a poison for which there is no antidote and from which there is no recovery (see above, pp. 190f., 192f., 207; see also W. McKane, *VT*, 30, 1980, 474–492, for a 'trial by ordeal' interpretation of 8.14, 9.14 and 23.15). The prophets have spread a miasma throughout the land and Yahweh will hold them responsible for an epidemic of immorality, and will inflict on them death by poisoning, a trial by ordeal whose outcome will demonstrate their guilt. This is an exegesis which rests on the retention of על הנבאים, despite the considerations which favour its deletion (see above). Such a retention of על הנבאים (v. 15) is not incompatible with וישביה (v. 14), because it is the guilt of the prophets for the state of general corruption which is the particular point of v. 15. It is they who have spread a blanket of moral corruption which covers the entire land. חנפה is perhaps this—a pestilence of turpitude—rather than godlessness or apostasy (Weiser, Bright, NEB, Freehof). Hence the rendering 'pollution' (Sept. μολυσμός; Vulg. *pollutio*) is probably the right one.

FALSE PROPHETS AND THEIR CHARACTERISTICS (23.16–22)

[16]These are the words of Yahweh Sabaoth:
  Do not listen to what the prophets say[1]
  who address you with empty words;
  their visions are from within themselves,
  it is not Yahweh's word that they speak.
  [17]They keep saying to those who despise me:[2]

[1] Deleting הנבאים לכם (see below, p. 578).

[2] Reading לְמְנַאֲצַי and deleting דבר יהוה (see below, p. 577).

You will be safe and prosperous;
and to everyone who follows[1] his own wilful inclinations:
Disaster will not overtake you.
[18]Who has had access to Yahweh's secrets that he might see[2] his word? Who has listened for his word[3] and heard it?
[19]A storm[4] has issued from Yahweh,
a whirling tempest;
it circles over the heads of the wicked.
[20]Yahweh's anger will not subside,
until he has finally carried out his aims;
when that time comes you will be fully enlightened.
[21]I did not send the prophets
but they were swift to do my tasks;
I did not speak to them
but they uttered prophecies.
[22]If they had had access to my secrets,
they would have proclaimed[5] my words to my people,
turning them from their wicked ways and evil deeds.

If a unit is to be made out of vv. 16–22, it must be on the assumption that these verses are addressed to the people of Judah. This direct address in the 2nd person plural is evident in v. 16 (אתכם ; לכם ; אל תשמעו) and in v. 20 (תתבוננו בה בינה). Verse 21 is compatible with this view and v. 22 can be fitted into it, although the 'you' of direct address is replaced in this verse by statements about the people (את עמי and the 3rd person suffixes). If v. 17 is to be accommodated to the assumption that vv. 16–22 are direct address, למנאצי, 'to those who despise me', is more appropriate than למנאצי דבר יהוה (Sept.; Pesh.), 'to those who despise the word of Yahweh', though it is not out of the question that Yahweh should so refer to himself in the 3rd person. This observation runs counter to the general view (Duhm, Ehrlich, p. 303, Rudolph, Weiser, Bright, NEB—Brockington, p. 207) that the understanding of למנאצי דבר יהוה found in Sept. and Pesh. should be adopted. Sept. (καὶ πᾶσι τοῖς πορευομένοις) and Vulg. (Et omni qui ambulat) have solved the grammatical problem constituted by וכל הלך (v. 17), but it is unlikely that they had a Hebrew text with ולכל הלך, although this is an emendation which is grammatically necessary (Duhm). There is no textual evidence for the deletion of דבר יהוה, but the question should be raised whether this is a secondary element in the first stich of v. 17. The reason for the insertion of דבר יהוה will have been to make explicit that שלום יהיה לכם was spoken in the name of Yahweh—that there was a

[1] Reading ולכל הלך (see below, p. 577).
[2] Deleting וישמע (see below, p. 581).
[3] Reading דברו (Q).
[4] Deleting חמה (see below, p. 582).
[5] Reading וישמעו (see below, p. 583).

claim to possess authority from Yahweh for such an utterance. In that case the pointing of MT will correctly preserve the intention of the insertion (דְּבַר יהוה) and the pointing of למנאצי found in MT (לְמַנְאֲצַי) will preserve the original text.

Both Duhm and Thiel (p. 251 n. 74) argue that vv. 19f. do not cohere with the preceding verses. Duhm holds that these verses are better integrated with the context where they appear in chapter 30 (vv. 23f). than they are in this chapter. Thiel, on the other hand, maintains that the verses are not integrated in either of the contexts in which they appear (23.19f.; 30.23f.). Rudolph and Bright, for their part, suppose that the verses are original at 23.19f., that 23.16–22 supplies a context for them, and that they are secondary at 30.23f. (following H. Schmidt, *Die Schriften des AT*, II 2, p. 245). Verses 19f. negate the assurances of שלום contained in v. 17 (לא תבוא עליכם רעה ; שלום יהיה לכם) and are connected with vv. 16f. in terms of a contrast between illusion and reality. The link between vv. 19f. and vv. 21f. is less precise, since vv. 21f. are a resumption of vv. 16f.

Verse 18 disturbs the negation of the assurance of שלום (v. 17) which appears in vv. 19f., and suspicion is awakened that it is intrusive (*pace* Nicholson). There is a doubt whether it has poetic form, and if it is prose, this is a further reason for doubting its originality in a poetic passage. It should be explained as a secondary prose insertion (see further below), and vv. 16f., 19f. and 21f. interpreted as a unity. The difficulty of representing the whole as an address by Yahweh to his people cannot be entirely overcome, because he speaks about them rather than to them in v. 22.

הנבאים לכם (v. 16) is not represented by Sept.; it is unnecessary to the sense, it disturbs the metre (3 + 3) and should be deleted (Rudolph, Weiser and Bright). Janzen (p. 44) supposes that it is an insertion from 27.15,16, and Thiel (p. 250) attributes it either to his Deuteronomistic editor or to some other later hand. NEB, 'Who buoy you up with false hopes', captures the sense of מהבלים המה אתכם. It is the vacuous character of the assurances of the prophets (explicitly false prophets in Pesh., *nby' dgl'* and Targ., נביי שקרא) which is stressed: they are as insubstantial as a dream or any other product of the imagination. They exist in the minds of those prophets who proclaim them (חזון לבם ידברו), but otherwise they have no existence and can exert no influence on the historical events with which Judah's fate is bound up.

It is then not deliberate deceit or fraud which is the hallmark of these prophets, for they are convinced that they do indeed speak for Yahweh (so Rudolph and Weiser). They are not guilty of a calculated deceit, but they are deluded, for they equate the

vividness and strength of their own insights and visions with the
word of Yahweh. The problem of prophetic authority is posed in
an urgent way (so Rudolph), for these prophets no less than
Jeremiah preface their words with כה אמר יהוה (see above,
pp. 93–95). The style of prophecy and the public framework of
proclamation are the same whether the content is שלום or רעה
('disaster'). The שלום prophet and the prophet who issues threats
of impending judgement both lay claim to the same office. How
then can it be determined who speaks for Yahweh and who does
not? Verse 17 is addressed to this question.

Sept. has a double rendering of וכל הלך בשררות לבו (v. 17):
(a) πᾶσι τοῖς πορευομένοις τοῖς θελήμασιν αὐτῶν (b) παντὶ τῷ
πορευομένῳ πλάνῃ καρδίας αὐτοῦ. Janzen (p. 28) urges that (a)
is 'old Greek', but (pace Ziegler, Beiträge, p. 96) holds that it
cannot be explained as a translation of MT. He conjectures וכל
הלכים במעצותיהם as a Hebrew Vorlage. Both the variants
derive from MT and the significance of πλάνη is exegetical
rather than textual: it brings out the sense 'going astray' as Pesh.
and Targ. did with מהבלים (v. 16).

In v. 16 it is asserted that there are prophets who have no
public or objective significance, whatever psychological certainty
they may express. Verse 17 supplies information about these
prophetic utterances and provides some justification for the
assertion that they are false. The bubble-like prophecies
mentioned in v. 16 are שלום prophecies (שלום יהיה לכם). Those
who bring comfortable news to Jerusalem and Judah—easy
assurances that they will emerge unscathed from the dangerous
times through which they are living—are not messengers of
Yahweh, but servants of a lie which will destroy the nation.
What is it that establishes שלום prophecies as a lie in these
particular circumstances? It is the unconditional character of the
guarantee of safety and its independence of all ethical definition.
To say to those who despise religious faith and practice שלום
יהיה לכם is to provide evidence that one does not speak the word
of Yahweh. To say to those who are stubborn in their rejection of
Yahweh לא תבוא עליכם רעה is a degeneration of the prophetic
word into nonsense. They perhaps confuse (cf. Nicholson)
patriotism or nationalism with Yahwism. They interpret aspects
of Jerusalem theology (the election of Zion and the everlasting
covenant with the House of David) as an unconditional
guarantee that their ecclesiastical and political institutions are
immune from historical accident or disturbance, and that their
territorial integrity will always be maintained.

The circumstance that v. 17 is poetry gives a special character
to Thiel's claim that it is Deuteronomistic and might be thought
to reduce its probability. It is perhaps to meet this that Thiel

(p. 251) describes the metrical structure of v. 17 as 'not unambiguous'. It is not obvious why Thiel should be so confident that Deut 29.18 is the ultimate source of שררות לב, and the presence of שלום יהיה לי in that verse is not so significant as might at first sight appear. The individual who is persuaded that no evil consequences will flow from his not taking the oath seriously says שלום יהיה לי כי בשררות לבי אלך. It is likely from the context that the reference is to a continuation of idolatrous practices, and this association of שררות לב and idolatry is evident in three of the occurrences of שררות לב in the prose of the book of Jeremiah (9.13; 13.10; 16.12). It is improbable that שררות לב is a reference to idolatry in 23.17, and it is not explicitly so in the remaining three prose passages (3.17; 7.24; 18.12). It is probable that all the occurrences in prose in Jeremiah represent an appropriation of שררות לב from 23.17 (poetry) and a free redeployment of it, in some cases perhaps influenced by Deut 29.18.

The view that the sentiments of v. 18 are those of Job 15.8 (Duhm and Condamin) is favoured by Rudolph and Thiel (p. 251). In that case it is a secondary insertion, it has nothing to do with שלום prophets (unlike v. 22 which it somewhat resembles) and its sense is that Yahweh is hidden from human enquiry; that no one should claim to have an intimate knowledge of him, or to be in a position to transmit that knowledge to others (if וישמע is read). The view that v. 18 is a reference to the prophets declared to be false in v. 17 is found in Jerome who interprets v. 18 as a rhetorical question with a limited application, as compared with the universal application accorded to it by Duhm. It refers specifically to the שלום prophets and is a device for denying that they are in Yahweh's סוד. The same interpretation is found in Kimchi who explains כי כי מי עמד as כי מי מהם עמד, and it appears also in NEB (without any indication of an emendation of MT—see Brockington, p. 207), 'But which of them has stood in the council of the Lord?' 'But' for כי in NEB's rendering (also in Bright) is unacceptable; the sense is 'for' and כי is so understood by Duhm, Rudolph, Weiser and Freehof. Rudolph, who says that v. 18 might do 'at a pinch' on this interpretation, supposes that it can be taken in this way only if מהם is inserted between מי and עמד. Bright (cf. Berridge, pp. 37f). holds that v. 18 is a general question about the credentials of the genuine prophet which is answered by vv. 19f.: not the שלום but the doom prophets speak Yahweh's word.

Janzen (p. 12) identifies doublets in MT of v. 18 through a comparison with Sept. The common element of the two texts is מי עמד בסוד יהוה וירא and the doublets are:

דברו מי הקשיב וישמע   (Sept. *Vorlage*)

מי הקשיב דברו וישמע
Janzen does not account for MT וישמע¹ which does not feature in his reconstruction. The deviation between MT and Sept. should perhaps be elucidated in another way. The expression 'seeing Yahweh's word', which also occurs at 2.31 (הדור אתם ראו דבר יהוה), was felt to be so difficult that וירא was glossed by וישמע. The non-representation of דברו (Q) in Sept. is probably a translational rather than a textual point: it was thought to be unnecessary to represent דברו a second time, since it had already occurred with וירא. Hence the text of Sept. would lead one to conclude that the original Hebrew text may have been:
כי מי עמד בסוד יהוה וירא את דברו מי הקשיב דברו וישמע
The attaching of a suffix to וירא (ויראהו) so as to indicate 'and sees him (Yahweh)' rests on a misunderstanding of the text. It goes back to Pesh. (whzyhy) and is adopted by Rudolph and NEB, 'seen him and heard his word' (no emendation is indicated, Brockington, p. 207). If the view that וישמע¹ is a gloss is not accepted, דברו will have to be regarded as the object of both וירא and וישמע (Duhm, Bright, Freehof). The versions give no support to the view that וישמע² should be vocalized וְיַשְׁמִע (Pesh. wšm'h—the suffix refers to דברו (Q)), but this vocalization is adopted by Graf, Giesebrecht, Rudolph and Weiser. The sense of v. 18, according to Giesebrecht, is that whoever is privy to Yahweh's counsel and is apprised of Yahweh's word has a responsibility to make it public. מי הקשיב דברו וישמע is perhaps rather 'Who has listened carefully to his word and heard it?' (וַיִּשְׁמָע; so Pesh., Bright and NEB).

An examination of the occurrences of סוד (vv. 18,22) in Biblical Hebrew does not enable us to decide between the meanings 'confidence' or the like and 'divine council', since the pattern of use is compatible with either one or the other. 'Intimacy' or 'close converse' does not imply that the prophet is a member of a divine council, and BDB does not include Amos 3.7, Jer 23.18, 22, with those passages where סוד has the sense 'council'. There is no doubt that it does have this sense in passages where it is in parallelism with עדה (Ps 111.1) and קהל (Gen 49.6), or in phrases like סוד עמי (Ezek 13.9) and סוד קדשים (Ps 89.8).

There is nothing in the history of interpretation gathered from the versions (Vulg. 'counsel'; Symm. 'converse' Aq., Pesh., Targ. 'secret'), from Jerome and from Rashi and Kimchi, which connects סוד particularly with the prophet's membership of a divine assembly, although this is how vv. 18 and 22 are understood by Bright and NEB ('council'). The representation is then of the same type as Ps 82 and appeal is made to the plural in Isa 6.8 (לנו ; cf. נחמו נחמו עמי, Isa 40.1) and to Amos 3.7 to support the view that the prophet is envisaged here as a member of a heavenly cabinet and as listening to its deliberations. It is true that עמד לפני can mean entering into someone's service: it is used of David entering the service of Saul (1 Sam 16.22), of Elijah in the service of Yahweh (1 Kgs 17.1; 18.15), of Jeremiah similarly (Jer 15.19), and of priests 'standing before Yahweh' to serve him (Deut 10.8; Judg 20.28; Ezek 44.15; Num 16.9). עמד ב, which occurs only at Jer 23.18 and 22, may not have this technical sense, and a one-to-one closeness of the prophet to Yahweh is more appropriate here than simply his membership of a heavenly cabinet. In virtue of his prophetic office he is in Yahweh's confidence and has a special access to his word. Verse 18 is secondary in the context of vv. 16–22 (above, p. 578). We may suppose that it was generated by a wrong exegesis of v. 22, namely, that the intention of this latter verse was to indicate that there is no one who is privy to Yahweh's secrets.

Verses 19f. oppose the realities of the present to the illusory security which the prophets of vv. 16f. proclaim (above, p. 578). Far from being safe Judah is on the brink of disaster. A storm is brewing up and she will be engulfed by it. The whirlwind of Yahweh's judgement (the Babylonian invasion, according to Jerome) will alight on her and his anger will not abate until retribution has run its full course. The רשעים on whose heads the storm will break are the arrogant Judaeans mentioned in v. 17 who affect a vast superiority over against Yahweh's claims and who are immovable in their stubbornness. Duhm supposes that רשעים is a mark of lateness, of a community which can be classified as רשעים and צדיקים over against the criterion of the Law, and that the eschatological reference at the end of v. 20 (באחרית הימים) is another indication that vv. 19f. are not to be attributed to the prophet Jeremiah (see above, p. 578).

The versions employ various devices to incorporate חמה into the grammar of v. 19 (cf. Pesh. brwgz'; Targ. ברגז). There is little doubt that חמה is a gloss, showing the same interpretation of סערה, in terms of the anger of Yahweh's judgement, as is present in Pesh. and Targ.—an interpretation readily suggested by אף יהוה in v. 20 (so Rudolph, Weiser, Bright). NEB retains חמה, vocalized as חֻמָּה (Brockington, p. 207), 'See what a scorching wind has gone out from the Lord' (G. R. Driver, JQR 28, p. 115). This introduces the idea that it is the hotness of the wind which makes it a wind of judgement (cf. Pesh., 'a judgement which is being kindled'), but the terror of the wind in v. 19 is its tempestuous fury rather than its heat, although 'hotness' is appropriate to its interpretation as the heat of Yahweh's anger in v. 20. But according to v. 19 the wicked are in the eye of the hurricane (cf. NEB, 'It whirls round the heads of the wicked').

Those who despise Yahweh, and to whom assurances of safety have been given, are unrelenting in their wilfulness (הלך בשררות לבו) and Yahweh too is unrelenting in his resolve to implement his designs of judgement (v. 20). His anger will not subside or be withdrawn until he has implemented his resolves (for the technical use of קום and הקים as antitheses of הפיר, in connection with the successful execution of plans which have been drawn up, see W. McKane, *PWM*, pp. 79–85). The view of modern scholars (Rudolph, Weiser, Bright; *pace* Duhm, above, p. 582) is that באחרית הימים is not an eschatological phrase and that it requires some such rendering as 'in the future' or 'afterwards'. This was not the view of Kimchi who explained באחרית הימים as 'in the days of the Messiah'. Probably, what is indicated by באחרית הימים is the aftermath of the judgement. Unteachable by the word of Yahweh they will be taught by the undeniable logic of events. They will have no answer to give to history once it has been made; there will be no gainsaying the public record of Judah's tribulation. A hard lesson will open the eyes of the understanding. Those addressed in v. 20 (תתבוננו בה בינה) are not the שלום prophets (as Weiser appears to say), but the people of Judah who could not distinguish between prophets who uttered שלום and prophets who uttered the word of Yahweh. The discrimination which they eventually acquire will make this distinction clear to them.

Targ. makes explicit that the prophets mentioned in v. 21 are false prophets (נביי שקרא): they are the שלום prophets of vv. 16f. Despite their assumption of prophetic authority they have not been despatched by Yahweh as his messengers and they do not have a word from him to proclaim (cf. 1.7). They are not in Yahweh's confidence (on עמד בסודי see above, p. 582) and are not privy to his disclosures (v. 22). There is the question whether וישמעו (pointed וְיַשְׁמִעוּ, as in MT) is to be regarded as a jussive, or whether (perhaps pointed וַיַשְׁמִעוּ) it is expressive of a possibility which is no longer open (Rudolph, *im irrealen Bedingungssatz*). If it is the latter, וַיַשְׁמִעוּ (Pesh. w'šm'w; Targ. ואשמעו) is the better vocalization. The jussive introduces a different nuance (cf. NEB, 'If they have stood in my council, let them proclaim my words to my people'; similarly Freehof). This is the issuing of a challenge to these prophets to prove their authenticity, but the sense of v. 22 is rather, 'If they had been in my confidence, they would have impressed my words on my people'. The test has already been applied and the matter is closed.

Thiel asks whether the vocabulary of v. 22b (מדרכם הרע

(ומרע מעלליהם) may not point to Deuteronomistic influence: שוב
מדרכם הרע occurs in Deuteronomistic texts (1 Kgs 13.33; 2 Kgs
17.13) and in prose passages in the book of Jeremiah which
Thiel attributes to D (18.11; 25.5; 26.3; 35.15; 36.3,7). He notes,
however, that רע מעלליהם/מעלליכם appears in 'old texts' (Hos
9.15; Isa 1.16; Ps 28.4) and that where it occurs in
Deuteronomistic prose it is associated typically with מפני (Deut
28.20; Jer 4.4; 21.12; 26.3; 44.22). Thiel's conclusion is that v. 22
is not to be attributed to D, even if the portrayal of prophets as
preachers   of   repentance   is   characteristic   of   the
Deuteronomic/Deuteronomistic understanding of the prophetic
office. The call to repentance is a genuine function of the
canonical prophets (cf. Jer 3.12; 4.1; 23.14), and the exercise of
such a moral pressure on the community is advanced here as a
criterion of the true prophet of Yahweh.

Prophets who proclaim easy שלום in the presence of arrogant
unbelief, self-assertive stubbornness, and a way of life which has
settled down to wickedness, are not spokesmen for Yahweh.
Response to the word of Yahweh is a strenuous exercise and is
profoundly disturbing; it shakes the foundations of settled ideas
and modes of behaviour. It calls for the greatest spiritual effort
to amend what is wrong in ideas and attitudes and to make a new
beginning. R. P. Carroll (*St. Th.* 30, 1976, pp. 43–51) finds a
particular illogicality in 23.18–22: Jeremiah demands from the
prophets whom he condemns a degree of success (וישבום) which
he has not himself achieved. To understand v. 22b ('turning
them from their wicked ways and evil deeds') as 'exerting
themselves to turn them from their wicked ways and evil deeds'
is not straining after sense to a greater degree than is often
demanded in the interpretation of the Hebrew Bible. To build 'a
non-cogent argument' on this single verse is less reasonable than
to assume that Jeremiah is no more or less cogent here than he is
elsewhere when he equates threats of doom with Yahweh's word
and שלום prophecy with falsehood. That he is imposing a test of
'success' on שלום prophets—success in inducing a change of
heart in the people—is improbable.

A GOD WHO IS BOTH NEAR AND DISTANT (23.23–24)

> [23]Am I a God close at hand, says Yahweh,
> and not a God set at a distance?
> [24]Can a man take cover and hide from me,
> so that I do not see him?, says Yahweh
> Do I not fill heaven and earth?, says Yahweh.

The main issue of interpretation in v. 23 is raised by the

renderings of Sept. and Pesh. which do not indicate the
interrogative particle ה at the beginning of the verse. Jerome
takes MT, Aquila (μη θεος απο εγγυθεν) and Symmachus to
mean that God is not only near but that he knows those things
which are distant. But the antithesis of near (מקרב) and far
(מרחק) is given a temporal as well as a spatial reference by
Jerome: God knows the future as well as the present. Targ., on
the other hand, equates 'distant' with 'ancient' and develops this
in connection with God's creative activity at the beginning.
According to Kimchi מקרב is a reference to אלהים אחרים who
are חדשים and who have only recently come on the scene
(מקרוב באו; Deut 32.17; cf. Judg 5.8). Kimchi introduces the
אלהים אחרים into his exegesis in connection with מקרב, but he
regards them as 'new gods' not as 'near gods' and he does not
detect a spatial reference in v. 23. In this respect he differs from
Jerome, from Rashi and from subsequent exegetes who associate
אלהי מקרב with אלהים אחרים but who do it on the foundation of
a spatial not a temporal interpretation. The temporal
explanation of v. 23 is found in Hitzig with a reference to Deut
32.17, but his emphasis falls on the connection between
'antiquity' and 'wisdom': 'wisdom' is of high antiquity and is
possessed by אלהי מרחק, but 'new gods' (אלהי מקרב) do not have
it. There are thus three different ways in which the temporal
interpretation has been deployed: Yahweh has knowledge not
only of the present but also of the future (אלהי מרחק) — so
Jerome; Yahweh as אלהי מרחק created the world at the
beginning (Targ., Jerome, Kimchi); Yahweh as אלהי מרחק
possesses ancient wisdom of which אלהי מקרב are ignorant
(Hitzig).

In view of v. 24a מקרב and מרחק must be spatial and not
temporal, and the exegesis of MT has, for the most part,
proceeded on this assumption. It is clear, however, that most
interpreters (Duhm, Volz, Rudolph, Weiser—for example) do
not assign to v. 23 the sense supposed by Jerome and Rashi: Am
I *only* a God who is near at hand and not a God who is distant?
The question (according to Hitzig) is tantamount to a denial
that Yahweh is מקרב and is an assertion that he is מרחק, and
this is how it has been generally taken. Hence v. 23 is converted
into a statement: I am not a God who is מקרב, but a God who is
מרחק. It is not that Yahweh is all-seeing *despite* his distance
(Graf), but that he is all-seeing *because* of his distance
(Naegelsbach, H. Schmidt, Rudolph, Bright).

Both Duhm and Volz (cf. Kimchi) draw Deut 32.17 into the
discussion of v. 23. Duhm sees in אלהי מקרב a reference to local
gods who have their limited sphere of jurisdiction and are
effective only within narrow limits. Volz identifies אלהי מקרב as

the God of the שלום prophets: a *Volkgott* who is wrapped up in his own community and is always ready to jump to its assistance. Volz (Weiser and Nicholson) transforms the anthropomorphic imagery into an opposition of transcendence and immanence. God is not a Being with whom men have much in common; he is the Almighty who keeps his distance and is true to himself; who asserts his sovereign holiness in judging men. The prophets have brought God so near (Weiser; Rudolph, p. 153 n. 3) that they have identified their own aspirations and pictures of the future with God's purpose and will. Verses 23f. (on this view) are connected with the theme of calling the false prophets to account, and against the reduced God of the שלום prophets is set the objective validity of the word of God which invades the psyche of the true prophet. It is this encounter with a God who is מרחק which is the mark of a prophet. One obvious defect of this kind of elaboration is that the connection between v. 23 and v. 24a is obscured. Verse 24a links naturally with v. 23 only if they both contribute to the meaning that Yahweh's scrutiny of men and human affairs is complete and infallible.

G. Quell's contention (*Wahre und falsche Propheten*, p. 215) that the thought that distance enhances the power of scrutiny is illogical, is rebutted by Rudolph for the reason that what is envisaged is an 'aerial view' with perfect coverage. If, however, it were thought that this explanation is too involved, Sept. (Pesh). would come into contention as an alternative text to MT. What are the implications of emending the Hebrew to read אלהי מקרב אני נאם יהוה ולא אלהי מרחק? What considerations could have brought about the (*ex hypothesi*) modification represented by MT? The sense of v. 23, according to Sept. and Pesh., is that God is effectively near and that he is not distant, inaccessible and unreal. The antithesis of מקרב and מרחק is then of the same order as the one applied to Yahweh's commandment in Deut 30.11–14. What kind of theological concern is it that has put a premium on the distance of God by prefixing ה to אלהי מקרב? A major impediment to Giesebrecht's hypothesis that the original form of v. 23 was a threat to later orthodoxy to which it was accommodated by the addition of ה is the אם of v. 24a (so Rudolph, Weiser, Bright), and Rudolph has argued that the structure of vv. 23–24 is governed by a ה . . . אם alternation: if ה is not original in v. 23, אם in v. 24 loses its function and is not susceptible of a grammatical explanation. The presence of אם in v. 24 demonstrates the originality of ה in v. 23, and vv. 23f. can be construed only on the basis of MT in v. 23. This is a powerful argument in relation to which Giesebrecht's explanation that אם is a simple mark of interrogation here as at 1 Kgs 1.27, Isa 29.16, Job 6.12 and 39.13 is weak (cf. GK 150).

If v. 23 means that God is both מקרב and מרחק, there is no difficulty in reconciling v. 23 with v. 24b. If it is a denial that God is מרחק (Sept.), the relationship of v. 23 with v. 24b becomes problematical. Kimchi defines its connection with v. 23 in terms of God's 'superintendence': the meaning is that his 'superintendence' (השגחתן) is effective everywhere in the heavens and the earth. Verse 24 is then a parable of omnipresence rather than a naïve anthropomorphism and this view is also found in Jerome and Giesebrecht (cf. Ehrlich, p. 304) who takes the filling of heaven and earth by Yahweh to mean that he is not enthroned in heaven or any particular place but is a pure Spirit. Duhm, on the other hand, resists the temptation to distil a more refined theology out of vv. 23f.: the ancient world did not have such a concept of omnipresence; the filling of heaven and earth is a corporeal representation indicative of the ubiquity of God rather than of his spiritual omnipresence.

The supposition that v. 23 means 'I am not a God who is מקרב but a God who is מרחק' is a foundation of the argument that vv. 23f. are part of a unit comprising vv. 23–32. Thus against Quell (pp. 214f.) who urges (correctly in my view) that vv. 23f. connect with nothing in chapter 23, Rudolph (also Weiser and Bright) maintains that vv. 23–32 constitute a unit, and that the contribution of vv. 23f. is to establish that Yahweh 'sees through' the שלום prophets who claim authority on the ground of inner experiences, especially dreams. Verses 25–32 are a prose expansion of vv. 16–22. In particular, they take off from descriptions of the שלום prophets in v. 16 (מהבלים המה אתכם) and v. 17 (וילכל הלך בשררות לבו). If vv. 25–32 are explicable as a prose commentary on the preceding poetry, there is a presumption that they were originally contiguous with vv. 16–22 and that this connection has been broken by the subsequent insertion of vv. 23f. which contain an affirmation that God is all-seeing and misses nothing. It may have been thought that this had some appositeness as a theological comment: God was not deceived by the activities of prophets who falsely laid claim to his authority for what they said; there was no way of throwing dust in his eyes or making him suppose that a spurious prophetic activity was a genuine one. There is a need to work very hard in order to establish the relevance of the insertion and the person responsible for it may not have been so greatly exercised about its relevance. At any rate vv. 23f. are not concerned with transcendence and immanence in relation to God (*pace* Duhm, Volz, Rudolph, Weiser, Nicholson) and these verses have no intrinsic connection with any context in chapter 23.

PROPHECY AND DREAMS (23.25–32)

[25]I have heard the falsehoods uttered by the prophets who prophesy in my name: I have had a dream, I have had a dream! [26]How much longer will prophets be minded to utter falsehoods and to make out that their own illusions are prophecy? [27]Will they go on with their plans to make my people defect from me with the dreams which they narrate to each other, just as their forefathers defected from me and worshipped Baal instead? [28]Let the prophet who has a dream narrate it as a dream, and let the prophet who has my word declare it as the truth. What has chaff to do with grain?, says Yahweh. [29]Is not[1] my word like fire, says Yahweh, and like a hammer which splits rock? [30]So I am against the prophets, says Yahweh, who steal my words from each other. [31]I am against the prophets, says Yahweh, who wag their own tongues and claim to speak as my prophets. [32]I am against those who give out as prophecy dreams which are false, says Yahweh; who narrate them and lead my people astray with their falsehoods and wild words, when I have not sent them nor authorized them. They do this people nothing but harm. This is the word of Yahweh.

This is the only passage in the book of Jeremiah which deals at some length with the relation between prophecy and dreams, but the same pejorative estimate of dreams and dreamers is indicated at 27.9 and 29.8. This is true whatever particular modifications of MT חֲלֹמֹתֵיכֶם are adopted at 27.9 and 29.8 (חֹלְמֹתֵיכֶם, 'your female dreamers', according to NEB, in both passages; Brockington, p. 208). The words associated with חלמתיכם make the pejorative reference clear (קסמיכם; ענניכם; כשפיכם). No special relation is to be discerned between 23.25–32 and the passages in Deuteronomy which deal with the criteria of true and false prophecy (13.2–6; 18.14–22). At Deut 13.2–6 חלם חלום appears simply as a particular type of false prophet and the passage is quite differently orientated from Jer 23.25–32. Its point is that an accurate prediction does not establish the authenticity of a prophet, if the prediction is made in the name of a god other than Yahweh. The dream is alluded to as no more than one medium of such a type of false prophecy. In the second Deuteronomic passage there is no mention of dreams and there are no impressive correspondences of vocabulary with Jer 23.25–32, although there is a general convergence in point of view, in so far as 23.25–32 is affirming that a true prophecy is recognizable by its effects.

In Jer 23.25 attention is focused on the claim that dreams are revelatory. These dreamers preface the words which they heard in the context of their dream experience with כה אמר יהוה when they make them public (הנבאים בשמי). Thus Targ. paraphrases, 'The word of prophecy was declared to me in a dream'. Duhm's proposal that a three-fold חלמתי should be read (followed by Rudolph), on the analogy of 7.4 (היכל) and 22.29 (ארץ), is

---

[1] Deleting כה (see below, p. 591).

offered as an instalment of a solution to the difficulties of v. 26., and עד מתי is presumed to be a corruption of the third חלמתי. The two-fold occurrence of חלמתי is explained by J. Meyer (*Jeremia und die falschen Propheten*, 1977, p. 133) as the imitation of a preface to a cultic oracle. The view that עד מתי is an independent sense unit is found in Rashi, Bright, Freehof and Weiser; the last mentioned supposes improbably (p. 207 n. 1) that עד מתי connects with what precedes as part of the utterance of the false prophets: 'What a long time I have had to wait for my dream?' The versions, which do not represent the ה of היש, nevertheless, have difficulty with the grammar of v. 26: 'How long will it be in the minds of the prophets who prophesy falsehood and whose prophecies are intended to deceive?' is not very convincing, although the sense is not seriously obscure. The redivision of היש בלב into הֲיֵשׁב לב, adopted by NEB (Brockington, p. 207), was proposed by Duhm. The new factor in NEB is the attempt to combine this with עד מתי, but it is doubtful whether the resultant Hebrew can bear the interpretation which is put on it: 'How long will it be till they change their tune, these prophets who prophesy lies and give voice to their own inventions?' Another possibility which Rudolph considers but rejects is that the ה of היש is matched by another interrogative ה (החשבים) at the beginning of v. 27. We could then translate: 'Is this what is in the mind of the prophets who prophesy falsehood and whose prophecies are intended to deceive? Are they planning to make my people forget' etc. The conclusion is that the textual and grammatical difficulties of v. 26 are not completely solved, but that the sense is sufficiently well-established. The verse defines the lack of status of those who make a claim to communicate Yahweh's word: their prophecies consist entirely of subjective material. In view of the manner of the continuation of v. 26 in v. 27 (החשבים), it is likely that תרמת לבם refers to an intent to deceive others rather than to a condition of self-deceit (so Sept., Vulg., Pesh., Targ., Rashi and Kimchi).

Janzen (p. 21) discerns textual variants in the differences between MT and Sept. in v. 27 (following Ziegler, *Beiträge*, p. 45): (a) להשכיח את עמי and (b) לשכח את שמי (Sept.). On this view MT is a partial conflation of the variants (it has incorporated שמי from the second variant). The dreams of these prophets are a kind of falsehood (Targ. renders בחלומתם as בשקרהון), and they plan to engender apostasy in the people. That is why the consequences of their activity are compared precisely with apostasy to Baal. The effect is the same as that produced in earlier generations when the forefathers withdrew their allegiance from Yahweh and gave it instead to Baal (so

Kimchi; כ *pretii*). There is also a factor of obstruction, in that so long as these false prophets are vocal, the true prophets will not be heard. Their public utterance will be nullified, just as if it were a broadcast which is 'jammed'. Rudolph and Weiser discern in v. 27 a reference to a process of talking shop about prophetic prowess and endowment: the genuine prophet does not make his vocation into an occasion for egotism. One who is called to proclaim the word of God will not chatter about his calling or the oracles he has received.

It could be argued that חלומו (v. 28 Sept.; cf. Rudolph) is a better match for דברי than חלום, but there is little at stake. The view that v. 28 makes a clear distinction between חלום and דבר is the right one. There must be no blurring of this distinction. Provided dreams are not passed off as word of God, provided that the difference in status is unambiguously maintained, there is no harm in the narration of dreams. Whether or not the verse has a satirical intention (Rudolph, Weiser and Bright), there is certainly an intention to denigrate dream experience. In texts earlier than Jer 23, according to Rudolph, namely, Gen 28.12 and Num 12.6, and in those which he regards as later (Joel 3.1; Job 4.12ff.), dreams are considered to be vehicles of revelation. BDB in its entry for חלום gathers together a number of passages under the rubric, 'Dreams with prophetic meaning, the lowest grade of prophecy!' It is clear from this entry that only in Jer 23.25–32, 27.9, 29.8, Deut 13.2,4,6 and Zech 10.2 are dreams associated specifically with false prophets.

According to Kimchi (cf. Freehof) the intention of 23.25–32 is not to empty dream experience of revelatory significance. The distinction which is being made is not between word of God and dream, but between empty or subjective dreams spun out of the imagination and dreams which are bearers of the word of God. יספר is attached to חלום and ידבר to נבואה (v. 28), because the narration of a dream is the narration of words in which the understanding does not participate, but which are spoken by the power of the imagination. But the words of a prophetic dream, to which ידבר is attached, are significant. The sense of v. 28 is then, 'Understanding of me cannot be achieved by the power of the imagination'. According to Kimchi the two categories in our passage are not 'dream' and 'word of Yahweh', but 'ordinary dream' and 'revelatory dream'. This exegesis of v. 28 is untenable.

The proverb ('What has chaff to do with grain?'), rendered by Pesh. as 'Why do you mix chaff with grain?', is thought by Targ. to refer to the separation of the righteous and the wicked. More appositely Rashi paraphrases it as 'What has שקר to do with אמת?' The proverb is an equation of dreams (all dreams) with chaff and of the word of Yahweh with grain. It is a dissociation of all dream experience from the revealed word of Yahweh. The passage establishes a negative, but it says nothing about the psychological states which are associated with the reception of the word of God. Verse 29, on the other hand, does describe some of the properties of the authentic word of God.

It is urged by F. L. Hossfeld and I. Meyer (*Prophet gegen Prophet*, 1973, p. 83) that v. 28, which establishes the outright incompatibility of dream and word of God, is secondary in the context vv. 25–32, and that if it is disregarded what emerges from the remaining verses is something short of the assertion that dreams are never revelatory. The intention of the remaining verses, according to this view, is to contrast lying and corrupt dreams with the powerful word of God. In that case it is not denied that the word of God may be communicated through dreams, and the polemic is directed against the misrepresentation that dreams which have no revelatory content are revelatory (cf. T. W. Overholt, *The Threat of Falsehood*, pp. 63–68). This is an unnatural construction to put on the passage, even if v. 28 is abstracted; moreover v. 28 fits into vv. 25–32 perfectly well and the suspicion that it is secondary is unfounded. It gives definitive expression to the general tenor of the passage on the relation of dreams and the word of God.

Janzen (pp. 12, 28), following Ziegler (*Beiträge*, p. 100), detects a conflation in v. 29 and identifies the variants as (*a*) הלא דברי כאש and (*b*) כה דברי כאש. This conflation is fully represented in the main witnesses of Sept. and is partially present in MT (כה/הלא) and in Sept.^{OL} (οὐχ οὕτως οἱ λόγοι μου). This is a sounder approach to the problem of כה than the conjecture of Volz (כוה for כה) which is followed by Rudolph, Weiser, Bright (see, however, the note on p. 150) and NEB (Brockington, p. 207): 'Do not my words scorch like fire?' Hence כה, which is not represented by Vulg. and Pesh., should be deleted from MT. נאם יהוה, which is not represented by Sept. at vv. 23, 24, 28, 31, 32, 32, should be regarded as a secondary element in MT at these verses, but this is not a proposal to delete it (cf. Janzen, p. 201 n. 76).

Psychic material patterned by the imagination may be given the semblance of word of God, but purely subjective phenomena make no impact on the public world and have reality only for the dreamer. The word of God has the refined and mysterious energy of fire and yet has an impact like that of a sledgehammer on rock. Or, if regard is had to Sept. (καὶ ὡς πέλυξ κόπτων πέτραν) and Pesh. (*w'yk przl' dgzr k'p'*), פטיש is a tool for cutting stone and the exegetical point is then the sharpness or incisiveness of the word of God. In any case what is principally set forth is the destructive capacity of the word of God which is portrayed as a causal agent of judgement and doom.

There is another interpretation of v. 29 according to which the effects indicated by the similes should be located within the true prophet: the reference then is not to the causal efficacy and destructive potential of prophecies of doom, but rather to the disturbance and anguish which are associated with the reception of the word of Yahweh by a prophet. This view is represented by Rashi who cites Jer 20.9 (והיה בלבי כאש בערת) and Ezek 3.14 (ויד יהוה עלי חזקה), and Weiser, and Rudolph contain both interpretations in their exegesis: v. 29 describes the effect on Jeremiah of the reception of Yahweh's word (20.9) and also the effects of fire and hammer which it has on the world.

Revelation from Yahweh (so Weiser and I. P. Seierstad, *Die Offenbarungserlebnisse der Propheten Amos, Jesaja und Jeremia*, pp. 233ff.) is an invasion from without, overwhelming the prophet's own thoughts and feelings and possessing a paradoxical foreignness to himself. By these characteristics Jeremiah recognizes the reality and authenticity of the divine word. Weiser's exegesis of v. 29 is principally concerned about the effects within the prophet himself of the reception of the word of God, and he supposes that consequences can be drawn about the nature of revelation. It must be objected that 'thoughts' are either intrinsic to the person who thinks or else they do not exist. It is meaningless to say that a prophet makes a distinction between his own 'thoughts' and 'thoughts' of a different order which do not arise from his cerebral processes and which have such a clarity and power that he gives unquestioning assent to them. This is no better than a thinly veiled variant of verbal inspiration which achieves a correlation between human and divine, consciousness and revelation, by making the prophet into a schizophrenic or by dehumanizing him. The doctrine does not become more intellectually respectable by situating the 'divine invasion' deeper in the prophetic personality rather than asserting that God makes a sporadic use of the prophet's machinery of voice production and feeds his voice through the appropriate human organs in order to achieve the utterance of the divine word.

There is a serious point, however, to the assertion that the prophets are possessed of an exceptional conviction and assurance, that they have penetrated to the deepest truth about the significance of the situations in which they are involved, and that when they give expression to this certainty, they do it out of a sense of crushing responsibility. The 'truths' which they speak are time-bound; they possess profound historical insights piercing far below the superficialities of more shallow appraisals, breaking the shell of a more mundane understanding of affairs and arriving at the deepest significance of the historical hour. Hence their 'truths' do not have the form of logical universality and they are not reached by processes of sustained argument.

The לכן of v. 30 introduces a series of threats against prophets who are impostors, all of which (vv. 30–32) are introduced by הנני על. This view of v. 30 has been opposed by H. J. Stoebe (*Th.Z.* 20, p. 402) and A. R. Johnson (*The Cultic Prophet in Ancient Israel²*, 1962, pp. 47ff.). Johnson concludes from דברי that the 'stolen' oracles are genuine words of Yahweh and that the stealing refers to the re-use of earlier oracles or to participation in a traffic in oracles. Hence Johnson urges that v. 30 does not deal with non-prophets who misrepresent themselves as prophets, but rather with prophets who abuse their office. This should be compared with the view of Berridge (pp. 32f.) that the verse 'possibly contains an indication that these prophets accommodated earlier, genuine prophetic words to a situation where they were no longer valid'. But v. 30 has to be considered in the context of vv. 25–32 and the נבאים of v. 30 are not to be disengaged from those who are mentioned in vv. 25–28. The passage is about the absolute distinction between chaff and grain, between dreams and word of God, between prophets and non-prophets, and this scheme of interpretation must apply in vv. 30–32. It should, however, be noted that Jeremiah has no other word for these impostors but נבאים. Hence in respect of title or office, as publicly or externally viewed, there is no way of drawing a distinction between prophets and non-prophets.

The versions (Sept. τοὺς κλέπτοντας; Vulg. *qui furantur*) have taken גנב (v. 30) in its plain sense and have indicated a stealing of oracles: a kind of espionage, with one prophet acquiring access to the 'prophetic intelligence' of another. Rashi and especially Kimchi are dependent on the Babylonian Talmud (*Sanhedrin* 89a), and Kimchi gives a detailed account of the circumstances in which the process of spying and overhearing took place. Duhm supposes that there is an allusion to a kind of plagiarism (similarly Rudolph), and Volz observes that these prophets narrated their 'revelations' first within their own professional circles and that these might on occasions be misappropriated by their colleagues. A more idiomatic interpretation of the charge of stealing is that it amounts to an ironical debunking of a claim to speak for Yahweh (so R. Hentschke, *BZAW* 75, 1957, p. 164 n. 3). The 'stealing' functions as a decisive demonstration that what they speak—sometimes stolen property—is certainly not Yahweh's word. The point of R. J. Zwi Werblowsky's attempt to show that גנב can have the technical sense of 'receiving oracles

594 COMMENTARY ON JEREMIAH

in night visions' is not altogether clear (*VT* 6, 1956, pp. 105f.), since it cannot have this sense in the phrase מגנבי דברי איש מאת רעהו.

The sense of Sept. (v. 31 is not represented by Sept.ᴮ) is something like, 'I am against the prophets who dream while they sleep and utter their dreams as prophecies'. The Sept. version of v. 31 binds that verse to the dream/word antithesis of vv. 25–28. הלקחים לשונם is explained by Targ. as דמתנבן כרעות לבהון, 'who prophesy as their fancy takes them'. Words which derive from human invention and which are produced by those who have linguistic fluency (הלקחים לשונם) are being given out as word of God. They are being uttered in the oracular style and are represented as revelation (וינאמו נאם). With this interpretation Rashi and Kimchi agree: 'Who instruct (המלמדים) their tongue, saying that their words are an oracle of Yahweh, after the manner of true prophets' (Rashi). On וינאמו נאם BDB remarks, 'They uttered their own words in the prophetic manner—gave them out as an utterance of Yahweh' (also Weiser and Bright). Duhm (also Rudolph and Hossfeld/Meyer, p. 81) understands וינאמו נאם differently: הלקחים לשונם וינאמו נאם indicates wild and ill-considered utterance. According to this view וינאמו נאם means 'And they make empty noises' rather than 'And they represent their words as נאם יהוה'.

The versions have exercised some freedom in their renderings of v. 32, but they are translating MT (*pace* Janzen, p. 119). Thus Sept. and Pesh. have supplied a subject for נבאי ('The prophets who prophesy') and Pesh. has introduced a more particular word for נבאי in order to convey the idea of dream-visions (*dḥzyn ḥlm' dgl'*). The only other particular issue in v. 32 is the sense of ובפחזותם which Sept. associates closely with ויתעו and renders ἐν τοῖς πλάνοις αὐτῶν—the people are led astray by the falsehoods and errors of those whose empty dreams are published as word of God. This view is represented by Rudolph who renders פחזות as *Schwindel* 'fraud' or 'deceit', and is not far removed from Kimchi's gloss (ובקלותם) which is further explained as 'with the slightness of their knowledge' and is illustrated by Judg 9.4 (אנשים ריקים ופחזים). Duhm supposes that פחזות is a raucous bragging and shouting associated with drunkenness and carousals, whereas there is an early line of exegesis which takes פחזות to denote thaumaturgy: it is related to the claims of these dreamers to work wonders. This is perhaps what is indicated by Aq. and Symm. (ἐν θαμβήσεσιν αυτων) and certainly by Vulg. (*in miraculis suis*). ἐν θαμβήσεσιν αυτων might mean rather 'in their confusion', an alternative sense for פחזות noted by Jerome (*in stuporibus suis*) and represented by

Rashi (תמהון). The sense of 'recklessness' or 'wantonness' (Pesh. *phzwt'*), which appears in the modern dictionaries (cf. Weiser and NEB, 'misleading my people with wild and reckless falsehoods'), is probably the right one, and in a description of Jerusalem's prophets in Zeph. 3.4 פחזים is a parallel expression to אנשי בגדות.

Thiel (pp. 252f.) has noticed that v. 32 sums up the contents of vv. 25–31 and contains a comprehensive indictment of the would-be prophets: they are not authorized by Yahweh but they spin oracles out of their empty and insubstantial dreams, and by making them public they contaminate the people with their own lies and lead them astray. They engage in this activity with an air of *braggadocio* and are careless of the consequences of their activities. The concluding part of the verse employs the device of *leitotes* or understatement in a form which is elsewhere applied to idols (2.8,11; 16.19). To say that these prophets do nothing useful or helpful for the people is tantamount to saying that their effect is altogether damaging and corrupting.

Thiel's conclusion is that his Deuteronomistic editor contributed only vv. 17 and 32 to the collection of sayings about the prophets which he appropriated (23.9–32; cf. Hossfeld/Meyer, p. 85—vv. 9–32 were in existence before D). This contrasts with Nicholson's supposition (*Preaching to the Exiles*, pp. 102f.; *Jeremiah*, pp. 199f.) that 23.25–32 took shape in the exilic period and reflect the concern of the Deuteronomistic movement with the problem of false prophecy. It is not obvious why he is so assured on general grounds that the present form of 23.25–32 reflects conditions and concerns of the exilic period rather than those of Jeremiah's own time, and Rudolph, for example, has allocated the verses to his A source (p. xv). Nor is there any trace in 23.25–32 of a disillusionment with the prophetic office (*pace* Nicholson, *Jeremiah*, pp. 199f.). Not a grain of doubt is expressed that the prophetic word of Yahweh has the energy of fire and the power of a hammer. It is the intensity with which this conviction is held which sets the tone of the passage. It is the circumstance that there *certainly* is a true prophetic word of God which makes the ambiguity of true and false and the lack of hard, external, discriminating criteria so piquant and so potentially tragic. Duhm's argument for the lateness of the passage, that prophecy is viewed as guidance or instruction derived from the Law, regarded as the complete form of revelation, is not anchored in the text.

It could, however, be urged that 23.25–32 arose out of reflections among exiles about the meaning of disintegration and dispersion and how these experiences were theologically explicable in relation to the different kinds of prophetic activity which characterized the final period of the history of the pre-exilic Judaean state. The ambiguity created by the שלום prophets would be a factor, and a complementary aspect of this type of theological concern would be the vindication of the doom prophets who now emerged clearly, in the wake of the exile, as those who had spoken the truth. In fact, however, it is not possible by this type of general argument to show that the exilic period fits the problems which are thrown up in 23.25–32 better than the actual historical ministry of the prophet Jeremiah, and Meyer (*Jeremia und die falschen Propheten*, p. 140) has argued that the 'authenticity' controversy comes to a head in the period of the prophet Jeremiah. Meyer does not suppose that we have words of Jeremiah in 23.25–32: he conjectures that we have here evidence of a 'pamphlet' which circulated in Jerusalem when the controversy was at its height, which was founded on the preaching of Jeremiah and which was intended to make a popular impact.

Weippert's statistics (pp. 110ff.; 118ff.) do not show, as she supposes they do, that we are encountering in 23.25–32 a distinctive prose style of the prophet Jeremiah. The circumstance that there is one piece of poetry featuring הנביאים נבאו בשקר (5.31) and that it may be attributed to the prophet Jeremiah, does not necessarily indicate that prose passages with this vocabulary are also to be attributed to Jeremiah. An alternative account is that the prose is a kind of subsequent commentary in which themes touched on in poetry are given an extended treatment in the course of which poetic vocabulary is re-used. Hence the disengagement of prose in the book of Jeremiah from precise Deuteronomic/Deuteronomistic affiliations, which she achieves, is not a proof that a prose style of the prophet Jeremiah has been discovered, nor is the presence of common elements of vocabulary in the poetry and the prose such a proof.

It is tempting to suggest that the arrangement of vocabulary in 23.32 is founded on the poetry of 23.21, but the correspondence would have been more impressive if דבר rather than צוה had appeared at v. 32. The verbs in v. 32 correspond to those of 1.7 and only in 14.14 have all three verbs been used. There is no doubt that 'sending' and 'commanding to speak' function as an affirmation of a prophetic call (1.7), just as the negatives constitute a denial that there is such a call, and since it has been argued that the call narrative in chapter 1, whose poetic form is questionable, reflects the final shape of the book of the prophet Jeremiah rather than the historical ministry of Jeremiah, 23.21 becomes a crucial passage: it is poetry and it displays this type of concern.

The conclusion is that, in all probability, 23.25–32 does not derive from the prophet Jeremiah (cf. Meyer, above, p. 596), but that, on the other hand, there are no decisive indications that it is more appropriate to concerns about true and false prophecy in the exilic period than it is to the life and times of the prophet Jeremiah. On the contrary, the passage reflects a fateful, lingering ambiguity between true and false prophecy which no external criteria could clarify, on which Jeremiah saw his witness founder, and because of which he charged Yahweh with deceit (4.10).

AGAINST A SATIRICAL USE OF משא (23.33–40)

[33]When you are asked by this people[1] what burdensome word you have from Yahweh, you will say to them, You are the burden[2] and I will throw you down. This is Yahweh's word. [34]I will punish prophets, priests and people who speak of 'Yahweh's burden', both the man who does it and his household. [35]When you converse with one another, your question should be phrased, What is Yahweh's answer?, or, What did Yahweh say? [36]You shall make no further mention[3] of 'Yahweh's burden', for that 'burden' is what he entrusts to the man who bears his word. You twist the words of the living God, Yahweh Sabaoth, our God. [37]This is how you are to address a prophet, What answer has Yahweh given to you?, or, What word has Yahweh spoken? [38]Therefore[4] these are the words of Yahweh: Because you speak of 'Yahweh's burden', although I sent a message warning you not to do so, [39]I will carry you off[5] and throw you down, far from my presence. I will abandon the city which I gave to you and to your forefathers. [40]I will lay on you an everlasting reproach, a shame which will never pass away or be forgotten.

Jerome refers to Aq. $\ἅρμα$ which he elucidates as *onus* (= Vulg.), *pondus*. He supposes that משא at the beginning of a prophetic oracle is a technical term for a prophecy of doom: hence it is 'heavy', 'burdensome'. Thus it was clear from the title of the prophecy what kind of prediction would follow. Jerome explains v. 33 as a play on משא, so that when Jeremiah is asked מה משא יהוה, the intention of those who put the question is to poke fun at his unfulfilled prophecies of doom. The same interpretation of v. 33 is present in Kimchi who observes that Jeremiah's questioners were playing on the ambivalence of משא and were enquiring in a derisory way what new burdens he proposed to heap on them in the name of Yahweh. On this view he is being chaffed as one who sees disaster round every corner and who confuses his own jaundiced condition with Yahweh's word.

Another opinion is that the question מה משא יהוה has no

[1] Deleting או הנביא או כהן (see below, p. 603).
[2] Reading אתם המשא (see below, p. 599).
[3] Reading תזכרו (see below, p. 600).
[4] Deleting ואם משא יהוה תאמרו (see below, p. 601).
[5] See below, pp. 601f.

aspect of taunt or derision. It is doubtful whether the versions can be cited in support of the view that the ambivalence of מַשָּׂא is being exploited in v. 33. Thus *onus* (Vulg.) is the usual rendering of 'oracle', and the same state of affairs is indicated by Pesh. (*ptgm'* 'word') and Targ. (נבואה 'prophecy'). Hence there is the contention (Volz, Rudolph, Weiser) that מה משא יהוה is a genuine request for the 'word of Yahweh', addressed to a prophet whose stock had risen because his earlier predictions of doom had been fulfilled or partially fulfilled. Verse 33 is then located in the reign of Zedekiah (21.1–10), when Jerusalem was under seige and Jeremiah's help was sought. The satirical intention enters only with the brusque and hard nature of Jeremiah's reply: it is he who imports the sarcastic nuance into the context by using the oracle/burden ambivalence. The harshness of the answer is explained by the circumstances in which it was uttered: Yahweh's patience is at an end; he has 'carried' his people long enough, but now he is about to disburden himself of them (Ehrlich, p. 304, Weiser).

According to H. Torczyner (*MGWJ* 76, 1932, pp. 273–84) and H. M. Weil (*RHR* 118, 1938, pp. 201–208) מַשָּׂא is to be read as מַשָּׁא 'loan' or 'pledge' (Neh 5.7,10; 10.32; cf. מַשָּׁאָה, Deut 24.10 and Prov 22.26, and מַשֶּׁה, Deut 15.2). The reason (so Weil) why Jeremiah replies so sharply (v. 33) is that the question (מה משא יהוה) is insulting and contains an inuendo that he is Yahweh's pawn. The present form of MT is the consequence of dogmatic alterations: the representation that Yahweh was a lender was felt to be objectionable, but the thought of 'lending' was allowed to stand in v. 39, because there is no mention of Yahweh.

Like Weil Torczyner urges that נטש in v. 33 and v. 39 is a synonym of עזב and cannot denote the throwing down of a burden. עזב and נטש are synonyms in Neh 5.10 and 10.32, and in association with מַשָּׂא they refer to the renouncing of a claim. But Rashi and Kimchi gloss ונטשתי (v. 33) with ועזבתי, and yet suppose that Jeremiah's reply indicates that Yahweh will unburden himself of his people. The argument that 'forsake' cannot be stretched to include the laying down of a burden was not therefore accepted by them. The association of מַשָּׂא and עזב (Neh 5.10), and מַשָּׂא and נטש (Neh 10.32), noted by Torczyner, is an interesting observation, but it is not a decisive indication that מַשָּׂא in Jer 23.33–40 was originally 'loan' or 'pledge' rather than 'oracle', 'burden'.

Verses 33–40, according to Torczyner, represent the popular view that Israel is Yahweh's possession or property. He may temporarily allow her to fall into alien hands ('lend her out'), but she will always be redeemed. The people are being lulled into a false sense of security by the שלום prophets and it is this which makes Jeremiah angry: Israel will be given as a pledge or loaned out and will be abandoned. The loan will not be temporary and there will be no redemption (vv. 33, 39). But is the representation that Israel is loaned out by Yahweh (even if the loan is only temporary), an appropriate or even credible symbol for a sense of security or unshakable expectations of שלום?

If מְשָא means 'loan' or 'pledge', what is intended by the question which is addressed to the prophet? Weil makes a shot at answering this, because he assumes that מְשָא is being applied in a derisory way to Jeremiah. Even so, 'How is Yahweh's pledge?' is an improbable sense for מה משא יהוה (v. 33). Torczyner is in a worse case, because if מְשָא is being used as a symbol of שלום prophecy to which the questioners are attached, what can they possibly mean by asking Jeremiah מה מְשָא יהוה?

Sept. and Vulg. have read את מה (MT אֶת מָה) as אַתֶּם and P. Wernberg-Møller proposes אַתֶּמָה (VT 6, 1956, pp. 315f.). Either אתם (so Houbigant) or אתמה should be read, and Jerome's interpretation of מה משא יהוה discussed above (p. 597) should be adopted. The verse turns on the ambivalence of משא ('oracle' and 'burden') and מה משא יהוה is a satirical reference to the gloomy prophet Jeremiah whose utterances are always 'heavy' with doom: What is your latest doom-laden word from Yahweh? We should not, however, suppose that this word-play rests on anything more than the existence of the homonyms משא 'burden' and משא 'utterance' or 'oracle'. We should not conclude that a nuance of 'burden' attaching to 'oracle' ('doom-laden oracle') supplies the connection between the two senses which are in play. (For a fuller treatment see W. McKane, BZAW, 150, 1980, pp. 35–40.) The weakness of the second interpretation (above, pp. 597f.) is that it does not adequately account for the sharpness of Jeremiah's reply. If he had been approached with a genuine and honest request for a 'word of God', there would have been no occasion to round on his interlocutors as he does in the final part of v. 33. To the extent that Torczyner discerns the key to the understanding of vv. 33–40 in a conflict between שלום and doom prophecy, he is in accord with the interpretation of v. 33 which is favoured here.

An implication of this explanation of v. 33 is dissent from the reasons given by Rudolph and Weiser why v. 34 cannot be reconciled with v. 33. Verse 34 (cf. Torczyner) is not just terminological fussiness (Rudolph, Weiser) about what is the right word to describe a communication received by a prophet from Yahweh. It is rather a proscription which is related to a substantial theological matter: the conflict between שלום and doom prophecy. Those who deride the prophet of doom by asking tongue in cheek מה משא יהוה will suffer for it. If there is a lack of coherence between v. 33 and v. 34, it does not consist in the circumstance that an interdict on the use of משא has no foundation in v. 33, but rather in the change from a national (v. 33) to an individual context (על האיש ההוא ועל ביתו, v. 34).

תזכרו (v. 36—MT תִזְכְּרוּ) should be read as תִּזְכְּרוּ in accordance with Sept. (μὴ ὀνομάζετε ἔτι). This sense of not mentioning or using the term משא any more has been secured by the use of the passive in Vulg. (ultra non memorabitur) and Pesh. (l' ttdkwrn twb). משא because of its satirical associations and debunking intent is to be avoided (vv. 35, 37). In conversation one should say מה ענה יהוה ומה דבר יהוה and in addressing a prophet מה ענך יהוה ומה דבר יהוה.

The difficult part of v. 36 consists of כי המשא יהיה לאיש דברו. Both Sept. and Vulg. suppose that דברו is the grammatical subject, and the sense of Vulg. is certainly, 'For his own word will be (or "is") המשא to each man'. Pesh., which probably rests on the same Hebrew syntax, has understood דברו differently from Vulg.: 'Because his prophecy (that is, the word which he receives from Yahweh) will be המשא to a man'. This is not altogether transparent, but perhaps משא is being defined as a term which should be reserved for 'word of God' and not used with satirical intent. The Hebrew grammar presupposed by Targ. is different, since לאיש דברו is construed as a construct relationship, 'to the man of his word', and the suffix refers to Yahweh. Two distinct interpretations of כי המשא יהיה לאיש דברו are encountered in the versions, and Rashi and Kimchi, the first of which has variants:

1. (a) A משא is a word of God revealed only to a true prophet who is a bearer of his word. Hence Rashi supposes that vv. 33–40 are an elaboration of the accusation that false prophets steal oracles from true prophets which he finds in v. 30. This interpretation is founded on the grammar 'man of his word' (Targ.)

(b) This is founded on a different grammar—דברו is taken as the subject. משא means נבואה 'prophecy' and this comes to expression as a 'word of Yahweh' (Pesh.?, Kimchi).

2. משא (Yahweh's word) is being confused with the private opinions of individual men which they give out as if they were 'word of Yahweh' (Vulg.).

When we look at modern opinions, we find that NEB ('You shall never again mention "the burden of the Lord"; that is reserved for the man to whom he entrusts his message') corresponds with 1. (a), and that Freehof's translation ('for every man's own word shall be his burden') corresponds with 2. The first of these should be adopted. The modern view which commands most support (Ehrlich, p. 305, Rudolph, Bright) requires a repointing of הַמַּשָׂא (MT) to הַמַּשָׂא and כִּי הַמַּשָׂא לָאִישׁ דברו is then rendered, 'For is his word a burden to anyone?' The weakness of this is that it does not explain adequately the subsequent mention of the 'twisting' of God's word (in v. 36). It provides too weak a reason for the interdict on the use of משׂא and it obscures the polemical employment of משׂא out of which the interdict arises. 'True prophecy (or 'God's word') is not burdensome to anyone' is not entirely appropriate in the circumstances. Rather 'Doom prophecy is a mark of true prophecy' is what is desiderated. The prophet of doom is the one who speaks Yahweh's word. The twisting of Yahweh's word then consists in the utterance of שׁלום prophets (Kimchi) and if so, it reflects the same polemical situation as that uncovered in v. 33.

The shorter Greek text is grammatically easier than MT at v. 38, since ואם משׂא יהוה תאמרו does not entirely cohere with יען אמרכם (cf. Janzen, p. 223 n. 35). The view that נטשׁ cannot refer to the casting down of a burden (Weil and Torczyner) has already been discussed (above, p. 598). A similar point is introduced by Janzen (p. 44, p. 206 n. 22) in connection with v. 39 and is the foundation of his argument that מעל פני (not represented by Sept.) is not original. He contends that ונטשׁתי אתכם means 'And I shall abandon you' and that it is inappropriately associated with מעל פני. However, it should be noted that נטשׁ is understood as 'cast out' by Sept. and Vulg. in v. 33 and as 'uproot' by Pesh. In v. 39 Sept. uses the same word to render ונטשׁתי (καὶ ῥάσσω), Pesh., with another word, indicates 'cast out' (wʾšdykwn), while Vulg. (derelinquam) indicates 'abandon' (as opposed to proiiciam 'cast out' in v. 33). Targ.'s וארחיק for ונטשׁתי in v. 39 points not to 'abandonment' but rather to 'removal' (into exile). Hence the versions (except Vulg.) represent 'casting out into exile' for נטשׁ at v. 39 rather than simply 'abandonment'.

What has emerged is that the problem in v. 39 is bigger than מעל פני : one sense of נטשׁ ('cast out', 'exile') suits אתכם and another ('abandon') suits ואת העיר אשׁר נתתי לכם ולאבותיכם. Even if it is urged that the sense 'cast out' or the like is a development from 'abandon' or 'desert', two different senses of 'abandon' are involved. The first is either 'abandoning (a burden)' or 'abandoning (to exile)', and this (ונטשׁתי אתכם) has been reinforced by מעל פני. The second sense of 'abandon' involves not the removal of Israel, but Yahweh's desertion of Jerusalem (ונטשׁתי את העיר). Since Sept. does not represent מעל פני, the conclusion should be drawn that this was the final addition made to v. 39 in the process of forming MT. It is appropriate in relation to ונטשׁתי אתכם ('And I will cast you out

from my sight'), and inappropriate in relation to וגשתי את
העיר which requires the sense 'abandon' or 'desert'. But the
latter is a further disturbing factor in the verse and should be
regarded as a secondary elaboration, introducing the new idea
that Yahweh would 'abandon' Jerusalem. The original sense of
v. 39 was the same as that of v. 33, and it terminated like v. 33
with וגשתי אתכם.

אתכם גשא (v. 39) is not represented by Sept. and Janzen
(pp. 99f.) supposes that it is a corruption of what was originally
a 'marginal variant to וגשיתי'. Over against MT וגשיתי and גשא
there is some support from Hebrew manuscripts for וגשיתי and
גשא. Kimchi derives וגשיתי and גשא from גשה 'forget' (so NEB
footnote; cf. Bright, p. 151) in which case there is a substitution
of א for ה in the spelling of the infinitive absolute. וגשיתי = גשאתי
is indicated by Sept., Aq., Symm., Vulg. and Pesh. It assumes a
further play on משא and is an explanation of v. 39 which is
widely followed (Jerome, Calvin, Lowth, Duhm, Rudolph,
Weiser and others; see W. McKane, *BZAW* 150, p. 51). Those
who use משא satirically, as a measure of their refusal to take
prophecies of judgement seriously, will themselves be carried off
into exile.

The view that v. 33 is a kernel attributable to Jeremiah which
has been elaborately expanded and that vv. 34–40 is one of the
latest passages in the Hebrew Bible is found in Duhm and is
further represented by Volz, Rudolph, Bright, Thiel (p. 253).
According to Duhm, v. 36b (כי המשא יהיה . . . אלחינו) is a
gloss and v. 37 is a doublet of v. 35; vv. 34–36a have more
credibility than vv. 38–40, because the author of the former
addressed himself to the circumstances of his own time, whereas
the latter contains the absurd proposition that the downfall of
Judah was the consequence of the misuse of משא. משא (so Volz)
was still an acceptable term for 'word of God' at the period when
the book of Malachi was written (1.1), and so vv. 34–40 must be
very late. The passage betrays Talmudic niceties and illumines
the piety of certain circles in the time of Jesus.

If those responsible for vv. 34–40 were so pedantic and fussy
about terminological niceties as is claimed, it is strange that they
did not feel uncomfortable about the firmly established position
of משא 'word of God' in the prophetic literature. Volz builds his
argument for the lateness of vv. 34–40 on the presence of משא in
these other prophetic contexts, and the implication is that a
sufficient time must have elapsed after the latest of these
occurrences to permit the development whereby משא became a
suspect word. The argument is unsatisfactory; it introduces too
elaborate assumptions. All those mentioned above who separate
v. 33 from vv. 34–40 do so on the assumption that there is no

satirical intent in the question מה משא יהוה and that the point of
v. 33 is taken wrongly in v. 34. I have dissented from these
reasons for disengaging v. 34 from v. 33 (above, pp. 599f.), but
there are two other considerations which make it probable that
the separation of v. 33 from the remainder of the passage is a
correct move:

(*a*) The suggestion that או הנביא או כהן has been imported into
v. 33 from v. 34 (Rudolph, Weiser) should be supplemented by
the observation that the word-order of the three terms (עם ; נביא
; כהן) differs in the two verses: in v. 33 it is עם, נביא and כהן; in
v. 34 נביא, כהן and עם. It is not merely that או הנביא או כהן has
been tagged on to העם הזה in v. 33. A more significant factor is
that העם הזה (v. 33) has a different sense from העם (v. 34): העם
הזה means the Judaean community in an all-inclusive sense, and
so או הנביא או כהן is an unconvincing and superfluous
supplementation, whereas העם means the 'laymen' in the
community—those who are neither prophets nor priests.

(*b*) ופקדתי על האיש ההוא ועל ביתו (v. 34) does not cohere with
v. 33, if, as I have argued, that verse reflects a conflict of שלום
and doom prophecy, for in that case the matter at stake is not the
fate of individuals or households, but the fate of the nation.
Hence it is likely that vv. 34ff. represent the attempts of later
generations, living in historical circumstances greatly different
from those of the late pre-exilic period, to elucidate the conflict
between Jeremiah and the שלום prophets, in the course of which
they seek to identify themselves with the pre-exilic prophet of
doom. על האיש ההוא ועל ביתו (v. 34) reveals a situation where
individuals and households are seen as severally and separately
determining their own destinies by whether or not they accept
the witness of a pre-exilic prophet of doom. This is not a decision
on which the fate of the nation hangs, but rather a type of
decision made by individuals which creates distinctions within
the community and divides it into different categories, into those
who decide for Yahweh and those who expose themselves to
judgement by deciding against him. The exile is viewed as
inflicting a humiliation on God's people which will never be
effaced (v. 40; cf. 20.11); it is a chapter of shame which will
always testify against them.

The supposition that there is nothing in vv. 34–40 but
terminological fussiness or tedious word-chopping or incredible
representation is mistaken. There is an attempt to recapture the
significance of the conflict between שלום and doom prophecy in
the time of Jeremiah, and so the contention (Rudolph, Weiser,
Thiel, p. 253) that vv. 33–40 do not cohere well with a section
(vv. 9–32) which deals with true and false prophecy is not
altogether correct. What is intended by vv. 33–40 is an

acknowledgement that Jeremiah was vindicated by events: the post-exilic(?) Jewish community must confess that this prophet of doom spoke the word of God and identify themselves with him over against the prophets whose assurances of שלום were proved false by destruction, defeat and exile.

CHAPTER XXIV

GOOD AND BAD FIGS (24.1–10)

[1]Yahweh showed me two baskets of figs placed[1] before the temple of Yahweh, after Nebuchadrezzar, king of Babylon, had deported from Jerusalem Jeconiah, son of Jehoiakim, king of Judah, with the statesmen of Judah, the craftsmen and the tradesmen(?),[2] and had taken them to Babylon. [2]The first basket contained very good figs, like figs which are the first of the harvest; the other basket very bad figs, so bad as to be inedible. [3]Yahweh said to me, What do you see, Jeremiah? I said, Figs, the good ones very good and the bad ones very bad, so bad as to be inedible. [4]Yahweh's word came to me,[3] [5]I will acknowledge the Judaeans whom I exiled from this place to the land of the Chaldaeans to be like these good figs. [6]I will mark them out for favour and bring them back to this land. I will build them up and not demolish, plant them and not uproot. [7]I will give them a mind to know me, for I am Yahweh; they will be my people and I will be their God, for they will return to me with all their heart. [8]I will make Zedekiah, king of Judah, his statesmen, the inhabitants of Jerusalem who are left in this land and those who reside in Egypt, like the bad figs which are inedible.[4] [9]I will make them an object of horror[5] to all the kingdoms of the world, a reproach, a proverb, a taunt and a curse.[6] [10]I will despatch against them sword, famine and pestilence, until no trace is left of them in the land which I gave to them and their forefathers.

The chronological reference in v. 1 is regarded as secondary by Ehrlich (p. 306), Rudolph, Weiser and Bright (derived from 2 Kgs 24.14–16), and, on the assumption that the verse is modelled on Amos 7.1,4,7, 8.1, it is urged (Duhm, Rudolph, Berridge, p. 65) that כה has been omitted by haplography (cf. תשכח at the end of 23.40). With the chronological notice deleted תראני . . . יהוה connects directly with הדוד אחד (v. 2). דודאי (v. 1) appears elsewhere as the plural of דודי 'mandrake', and Duhm (Ehrlich, p. 305) emends דודאי to דודי, the usual construct plural of דוד. The versions and Kimchi give 'basket' as the sense of דוד in Jer 24. Rashi glosses דודאי with קדרות 'pots', and Ibn Janâḥ (p. 154) notes that דוד has this sense at 2 Chr 35.13, but that 'basket' is appropriate at Jer 24.1,2. Similarly Gesenius (*Thesaurus* i, p. 324), and Honeyman (*PEQ*, 1939, p. 80) who observes that דוד belongs to a class of words which only secondarily denote a ceramic article, and that in 2 Kgs 10.7, Jer 24.1f. and Ps 81.7 it signifies a basket.

The opinion that מועדים, which one would expect to have the

---

[1] Reading מודעים (see below, pp. 605f.).

[2] See below, pp. 607f.

[3] Deleting כה אמר יהוה אלהי ישראל (see below, p. 608).

[4] Deleting כי כה אמר יהוה (see below, p. 609).

[5] Deleting לרעה (see below, p. 617).

[6] Deleting בכל המקמות אשר אדיחם שם (see below, p. 611).

sense 'summoned' or the like, cannot mean 'set' or 'placed' (as
BDB supposes, p. 417a; cf. KB³, p. 401a) at Jer 24.1 and Ezek
21.21 (מְעֻדוֹת) is found in Giesebrecht (עוֹמְדִים), Duhm
(מָעֳמָדִים) and Rudolph (עוֹמְדִים or מֶעֳמָדִים). G. R. Driver's
opinion that the meaning assigned to מוּעָדִים in BDB makes it
'bear a sense alien to its whole usage' (*JBL*, 1934, p. 288) is
echoed by D. W. Thomas (*JTS*, 1952, p. 55). Rudolph considers
that Driver's philology, which connects מוּעָדִים with Arabic
ma'du(n) 'tender, fresh fruit', is improbable. The sense,
according to Driver, is 'two baskets of ripe figs'. Rudolph views
with more favour Winton Thomas's postulation of a homonym of
ידע 'know' on the basis of Arabic *wada'a* 'place'. This involves
the metathesis of ע and ד (מוּדָעִים), and produces the same sense
as Duhm's emendation. It has been accepted by NEB
(Brockington, p. 207), and the support of Sept. is claimed for it
('set out in front of the sanctuary of the Lord'). It is unlikely that
the Greek translator read a Hebrew text different from MT.
Rather it was assumed by Sept. (κειμένους), Vulg. (*positi*), Pesh.
(*symn*) and Targ. (מַחְתִּין) that מוּעָדִים, derived from יָעַד, could
bear the sense 'placed'. Similarly Rashi and Kimchi gloss מוּעָדִים
with מוּכָנִים. A defence of מוּעָדִים is found in Ehrlich (p. 305)
who supposes that the meaning is 'labelled': a description of the
contents of the two baskets of figs is attached to them. Ehrlich
assumes that מוּעָדִים is a Hophal participle of עוּד.

The type of explanation of 'set before the House of Yahweh'
(reading מוּדָעִים) which is attempted will depend on whether the
vision is regarded as an experience of the prophet Jeremiah
(Rudolph, Weiser, Bright), or rather as a literary device in a
passage stemming from a later date and modelled on
representations of prophetic visions which appear in the book of
Amos and, perhaps, in Jer 1.11–14. Ehrlich (p. 306) explains
לפני היכל יהוה as a gloss whose function is to create a reference
to the offering of first fruits and to explain the two baskets of
fruit in this context. A somewhat similar conclusion was also
reached by Cornill, but he considered that מוּעָדִים was part of
the gloss and deleted it too. Volz, Weiser and Rudolph agree in
rejecting the proposal that מוּעָדִים לפני היכל יהוה is a reference
to the offering of first fruits (as Duhm supposed). Rudolph
follows Volz, for the most part, in developing the thought that we
have to reckon with 'residues' of sense data which reappear in
dreams, sometimes in confused and inexplicable combinations.
Hence the most that can be said is that at some time or other
during a fig harvest Jeremiah must have seen figs disposed in
baskets in front of houses (Volz—in gardens), the good ones for
human consumption and the bad ones for animal food. It is this

observation which is metamorphosed into two baskets of figs
before the temple in his vision.

The list of those who accompanied Jeconiah (Jehoiachin) into
exile (v. 1) is shorter than the list in 29.2 (+ הגבירה and
הסריסים). It is to be regarded as a summary of a longer and
more informative list and as assuming a knowledge of 2 Kgs
24.14–16 (Duhm). In that case it is taken as evidence of the
distance of the compiler from the historical events which he
describes. He is unconcerned that his incomplete list cannot be
equated with the גולה, an equation which is assumed in the
interpretation which appears in v. 5. He is not exercised with
historical detail but with a theory that the bearers of normative
Judaism stem from Jehoiachin and those deported with him in
597 (cf. Duhm).

The members of Jehoiachin's party are his statesmen or
officials, skilled artisans and המסגר which is a puzzle. Sept.
δεσμώτας 'prisoners' shows that המסגר has been associated with
סגר 'shut', and this is also evident at 2 Kgs 24.16, where,
however, τὸν συνκλείοντα presumably indicates someone
guarding prisoners (cf. Duhm) rather than prisoners. This is how
המסגר is taken by Pesh. (dḥš') and probably Targ., although
תרעיא might indicate 'locksmiths', an identification which has
found favour with modern scholars. The sense 'locksmith' is
found in Gesenius (ii, p. 938): claustrarius (opifex) qui claustra
et pessulos facit. The sense 'goldsmith' (Vulg.) is favoured by A.
Bea (Biblica 23, 1942, p. 82 n. 1) on the foundation of זהב סגור
(1 Kgs 6.20). It is mentioned as a possibility by Rudolph along
with 'joiner', but he has 'locksmith' in his translation. G. R.
Driver (JQR 28, pp. 116–118) connects מסגר with Akkadian
sigrīte (sigirtu); this loan word has been 'assimilated to or
confused with' (p. 118) מסגר 'prison' 'by some process of popular
etymology'. What Driver supposes the original form of the loan
word to have been is not clear. Did it have a prefixed מ, and if so,
why, since the postulated Akkadian model is sigirtu or sikirtu
(W. von Soden, Akkadisches Handwörterbuch, sekretu(m),
p. 1036), 'a woman in a harem'? Are we to suppose that the
prefixing of the מ was part of the process by means of which the
assimilation to or the confusion with מסגר 'prison' was achieved?
When Rudolph says that המסגר 'harem' does not fit into the
context of the list, his point is presumably that its appearance
after החרש 'craftsmen' is inapposite: one would have expected
the palace women to appear in association with the king and his
officials as a palace group and not after a transition had been
made to craftsmen. In other words, the presumption is (so Bea)
that we have to reckon with a class of specialist workmen
(Giesebrecht: possibly skilled engineers engaged in the

construction of weapons of war and siege machines; Duhm: belonging with החרש to a corps of engineers, according to 2 Kgs 24.16). Even so, the form מסגר remains a problem, since we might have expected a formation of the same type as חָרָשׁ (סַגָּר), if 'joiner', or 'locksmith' or 'enchaser' (Vulg. *inclusorem*) were the right type of solution. המסגר should perhaps be read as הַמַּסְגֵּר, and this is presumably what the Greek translator did at 2 Kgs 24.16 (τὸν συνκλείοντα) in order to achieve the sense 'prison-warder' (cf. Duhm).

The point of the simile in v. 2 is not to identify the figs in one basket as the first of the harvest (see above, p. 606), but rather to make a statement about their quality by comparing them with the high quality, first figs of the harvest (so Volz and Rudolph). The contrast is not between early and late figs (*pace* Kimchi), but between figs which are a delicacy and figs in another basket which are unfit for human consumption. There is an element of repetition in vv. 2 and 3 to which Thiel (p. 259) has drawn attention and which is thought to constitute a departure from the supposed models, or else a conflation of them. In 1.11–14 the prophet's scrutiny of the object of the vision is triggered by Yahweh's question: these visions take off with a divine question and are a concatenation of what is found in Amos 7.7–9 and 8.1–3, where the question is preceded by an account of a vision experienced by the prophet, introduced by כה הראני יהוה. Amos 7.1–3 and 4–6, on the other hand, do not feature the divine question and incorporate more detail in what is immediately connected with כה הראני יהוה. The closest similarity is between Jer 24.1–3 and Amos 7.7–9, 8.1–3: in the Amos passages the prophet repeats what he has already observed in response to Yahweh's question and this is the case in Jer 24.1–3.

The argument against the originality of כה אמר יהוה אלהי ישראל (v. 5), which is represented by all the versions, is that it does not suit the context of auditory elements within a visionary experience (Rudolph and Weiser). Yahweh is disclosing his will to the prophet (הראני יהוה) through the medium of a vision, and the prophet is giving an account of this experience. The emphasis falls on this disclosure, achieved by dialogue, and not on a responsibility laid on the prophet to communicate Yahweh's word to the people. But it is the latter which is indicated by the so-called messenger formula. This is inapposite, because what follows in v. 5 is an explication of the vision for the benefit of the prophet and not a message which he is charged to communicate.

Otherwise, the most significant aspect of v. 5 is that Jehoiachin (Jeconiah) and those who went into exile with him in 597 are defined as את גלות יהודה. The remarkable character of this equation should not be overlooked, for what would appear to be intended is that the Jehoiachin group constituted the entire, Babylonian, exilic community. (אשר שלחתי מן המקום הזה ארץ כשדים), and that the deportees of 586 do not come into the reckoning as part of the גלות יהודה. A concern to emphasize the aspect of 'grace' (Rudolph and Weiser) is not beside the point, but it should not be carried so far as to deny that the likening of Jehoiachin and his group to good figs is a statement about their worth (cf. Jerome), and the likening of Zedekiah and his group to bad figs is a statement about their worthlessness. The assigning of different destinies has a relation to desert and is not an exercise of bare sovereignty. This sovereign bestowal is emphasized in vv. 6f. and attention is drawn to it by the parenthetical כי אני יהוה (v. 7). It is Yahweh who builds and plants; it is he who performs a work of inner renewal (Duhm discerns here the influence of Ezek 36.26), bestowing on his people a spiritual vitality and a heightened moral sensitivity, all of which constitutes a 'knowledge' of him. In these ways he cements a new relation between himself and them, effectively becoming their God and enabling them to become his people. 'Enabling' is used deliberately, because the ancient versions understood כי as 'for' or 'because' and not as 'when' or 'if' (Sept. ὅτι; Vulg. *quia*; Pesh. *kd*; Targ. ארי), and modern scholars are right to maintain this interpretation (Rudolph, Weiser, Bright, Freehof, NEB). The meaning of כי ישבו אלי בכל לבם (v. 7) is not that Yahweh's work of rehabilitation is conditional on the wholehearted repentance of his people, but rather that this wholehearted repentance is part and parcel of his work of restoration.

It has been argued that the messenger formula at the beginning of v. 5 should be deleted and this argument should be extended to embrace כי כה אמר יהוה (v. 8). The formulae are located in corresponding places in both verses and they are probably related phenomena. The deletion of כי כה אמר יהוה in v. 8 produces an unbroken development of the כ . . . כן sequence. The similitude which is appropriate for Zedekiah and his party, for those who survive in 586 and live on in Jerusalem, is the basket of inedible figs. The view, extracted from v. 5, that Jehoiachin, and those exiled with him in 597, comprise the entire Babylonian, exilic community is reinforced by this account (v. 8) of what is to happen (has happened) to the inhabitants of Judah in the wake of the disastrous events of 586. According to Jer 52.9–11 (2 Kgs 25.6f.) Zedekiah's sons were slain before his own eyes at Riblah, as were his שרים, and the blinded king was taken away to rot in prison in Babylon. The interpretation which appears in 24.8 is that there was no enhancement of the Babylonian גולה in 586, that Zedekiah, his sons and leading officials, met their deserts and that those who survived either continued their lives in Judah or emigrated to Egypt.

Those who believe that chapter 24 derives, for the most part, from the historical prophet Jeremiah locate the passage between the years 597 and 586, and the emigration to Egypt which is alluded to is thought to have taken place during that period or earlier (Giesebrecht, Cornill, Rudolph, Weiser, Bright). Those who hold that it took place betwen 597 and 586 (Rudolph, Weiser, Bright) connect it with the polarization of political opinion in Judah into pro-Babylonian and pro-Egyptian camps. The latter group, or some among them, realized that they had lost out after the events of 597, which demonstrated Babylonian strength, and so they withdrew and achieved safety in the land for which they had declared their political allegiance. Moreover, a historical framework is provided for the elucidation of the antithesis between Jehoiachin and Zedekiah: those who were left in the city learned nothing from the demonstration of Nebuchadrezzar's power in 597 and interpreted their escape as a mark of Yahweh's favour. Jehoiachin and those who went with him were the cream of the population; Jeremiah could make no impression on those who were left, gave them up for lost, and reposed the future in the גולה of 597.

The impression which we gather elsewhere of Jeremiah's attitude to Zedekiah and those left in Jerusalem is quite different (cf. H. G. May, *JBL* 61, 1942, pp. 148f.). Chapters 27ff. may not be an irreproachable historical source, but they represent a stance of the prophet Jeremiah which has more inherent, historical probability than what has been attributed to him on the foundation of chapter 24. May has noticed that, according to 27.1ff. Jeremiah offered hope to those who remained in Jerusalem after 597, provided they submitted to Nebuchadrezzar, and that, according to chapter 40, he threw in his lot with those who survived after 586. The conclusion presses that chapter 24 is a later schematizing of history under the influence of a theory or a dogma, rather than a reliable account of the attitude of Jeremiah to Zedekiah and the inhabitants of Jerusalem in the years between 597 and 586.

Those who argue (Thiel, pp. 257, 261; Nicholson) that והישבים בארץ מצרים has to be understood in connection with chapters 42ff., and is a reference to events after the fall of Jerusalem in 586, are following an interpretation which is as old as Kimchi. There can be little doubt that this is the correct identification of the historical allusion in 24.8, and, according to 43.5–7, the emigration to Egypt at that time was a considerable one. The author of chapter 24 builds on this and represents that only two groups need be distinguished in the aftermath of 586:

those who remained in Jerusalem and those who went to Egypt. Hence he ignores the testimony of 39.9f. (2 Kgs 25.11f.) that after Jerusalem had been reduced its inhabitants were deported to Babylon, and only the poorest and least influential citizens were left behind.

In view of עד תמם מעל האדמה אשר נתתי להם ולאבותיהם (v. 10) it would appear that vv. 9–10 are concerned only with those who are left in Jerusalem and not with those who are resident in Egypt. This suggests that והישבים בארץ מצרים (v. 8) is a secondary insertion (cf. Volz.; Thiel, p. 256 n. 86) and that vv. 9–10 were continuous with בארץ הזאת. At any rate בכל המקמות אשר אדיחם שם (v. 9) is inappropriate and should be deleted (an addition derived from Deut 28.37, according to Rudolph). לרעה, which is not represented by Sept., is regarded by Janzen (p. 32) as a doublet of לזועה (Q. לזעוה). Sept., Vulg., Pesh. and Targ. are all building on the sense 'shake' in their rendering of לזועה, but 'dispersion' (Sept. and Vulg.) perhaps betrays the influence of the adjoining והישבים בארץ מצרים (v. 8). 'Shaking' is interpreted by BDB and KB[3] as 'trembling', and the meaning of ונתתים לזועה is taken to be, 'And I will make them an object which evokes terror'—a terrible spectacle. This is probably correct and לחרפה would similarly mean 'an offensive spectacle'. The aspect of 'cutting speech' for שנינה is seized on by BDB and KB[2] and is reflected in Sept. εἰς μῖσος which, however, is a one-sided rendering (= שנאה, according to H. Weippert, p. 189, n. 365). Those left in the land will be 'proverbial' in the sense that they will be a paradigm (משל) of ruin and disgrace, and as such will be suitable subjects for cruel jests—for baiting and taunting (שנינה).

For the idea that those left in Jerusalem are a community on whom a curse has fallen, and whose accursedness is plain to the world, NEB substitutes the thought that קללה is a further development of the trend indicated by משל and שנינה. Since קלל has the sense 'to be held in light esteem', 'to be contemned', קללה is translated as 'object of ridicule'. But the form קללה is not attested with such a meaning. Those who are so reduced and accursed (קללה) will not survive on the soil of their own land, for Yahweh will pursue them with sword, famine and pestilence until he makes an end of them.

The opinion that chapter 24 is, for the most part, to be attributed to the prophet Jeremiah and that it is to be elucidated against the background of the years 597–586 has been rejected. Other possibilities which require further examination are: (*a*) That there is a Jeremianic nucleus with considerable secondary editing and elaboration. (*b*) That we should think in terms of an exilic composition whose interests and tendency are to be elucidated in connection with the exilic situation. (*c*) That the nature of the antithesis between Jehoiachin and Zedekiah, between those who were exiled in 597 and those who survived in 586, whether in Jerusalem or Egypt, is most adequately interpreted in relation to the post-exilic Jerusalem community.

(*a*) Nicholson's account falls principally into division (*b*), but he does assert that chapter 24 has a Jeremianic nucleus, relating to a historical situation which developed between 597 and 586, as well as incorporating an exilic interpretation. The chapter is an example of how a saying originally spoken by Jeremiah was taken up by Deuteronomistic editors. The striking imagery is evidence of a foundation in an authentic saying of the prophet himself, but an interpretation solely in terms of Jeremiah's teaching is inadequate (*Preaching to the Exiles*, p. 110).

Thiel (pp. 258ff.) has made an attempt to elucidate 24 on this basis, and an earlier enterprise similar in character, is that of W. Erbt (*Jeremia und seine Zeit*, 1902, 122ff.). The Jeremianic kernel is said to consist of vv. 3, 4, 5*, 8*, and its point is to set up an antithesis between the Babylonian גולה and those who emigrated to Egypt. It is to be dated in final period of Jeremiah's activity after the fall of Jerusalem in 586, and אתן (v. 8) should be emended to אגיר 'pour out', 'deliver up', in order to effect a word-play between אכיר (v. 5) and אגיר. So much for Erbt. Thiel, for his part, experiments with a similar reconstruction and finally departs from it. The conclusion which he reaches is that chapter 24 like 29.10–19, proclaims salvation for the exiles and judgement for those who are left behind, and the passage is best explained as a Deuteronomistic composition through and through. The effort to construct an original Jeremianic unit should be given up: the chapter is a unity created by the Deuteronomistic editor of the book of Jeremiah with the help of Amos 7.1–8, 8.1ff., Jer 1.11–14 and other Deuteronomistic stereotypes.

(*b*) The conclusion that a Jeremianic kernel should not be sought is correct, and the insight that chapter 24 is a compilation in which other parts of the Hebrew Bible are used should also be accepted. The statement that the antithesis which is formulated is between the Babylon גולה and those who remained in Jerusalem after 586 is defective, and this affects the attempts of Nicholson and Thiel to show that chapter 24 is best understood in the framework of an exilic situation. The chapter is not obviously explicable as an exilic composition on Nicholson's terms (op. cit., p. 110; *Jeremiah 1–25*, p. 206), because it in effect denies that any Jews were deported to Babylonia in 586. It has a theory that the Babylonian גולה was composed entirely of those who went into exile with Jehoiachin. A development of this, which is probably secondary (so Volz; see above p. 611), is that the Jews who left Judah after 586 went to Egypt and not to Babylon (24.8). This is a theory whose appropriateness and relevance are not obvious in connection with an exilic community in Babylon which in fact was made up of those who had been deported there in 586 as well as those who had preceded them in 597. It is this theory which is entailed by the antithesis of Jehoiachin and Zedekiah, not an opposition of those who went into exile in Babylon and those who remained in Judah or emigrated to Egypt. Hence the exilic setting in Babylon is not a credible historical background for chapter 24.

Thiel (pp. 260f.) supposes that 21.1–10 and 24 are used by the Deuteronomistic editor to enclose the predictions of doom concerning Zedekiah which are contained in the collection of royal sayings. 21.1–10 points forward to and 24 refers back to indictments of kings and prophets. Beyond the judgement which is predicted in these the editor (D) descries salvation and a new relationship with God, appropriating promises which already appear at the end of the royal texts (23.3f., 7f.) These expectations are more fully portrayed in later passages (29.10–14; 31.31–34; 32.36–44). The apportioning of salvation to the Babylonian exiles and judgement to those who remain in Jerusalem is explicable against the background of the events of 586. The rejection of those left behind in Jerusalem and of the Egyptian diaspora is a reaction by the Jews in Babylon to the failure of these groups to face up to the implications of a shattering judgement and to display a sober and chastened mood. The objections lodged against Nicholson's account of the relevance of chapter 24 to an exilic setting apply equally to what Thiel has said. The opposition of Jehoiachin and Zedekiah is an opposition of 597 and 586, and it equates the Babylonian גולה with those who were deported to Babylon with Jehoiachin in 597.

(c) The post-exilic interpretation of chapter 24 is present in Duhm and H. G. May (*JBL*, 1942, pp. 148f.). The truncated list (v. 1) is an indication (so Duhm) that knowledge of a fuller list (2 Kgs 24.14–16) is assumed. The author could have expressed himself with such a lack of completeness only if he were at a distance from the period of Jehoiachin, and his assertion that the Jews of his time derived from those who went into exile in 597 was no more than a theory or, better, a play of phantasy with no genealogical foundation. The object of the chapter is to make a distinction between Jehoiachin and Zedekiah, and so between the two groups whose destinies were joined to these two kings. The author probably assumed (cf. 2 Kgs 14.14) that only a rabble remained in the land after 597 and was concerned to trace the ancestry of the Jews of his day from the more distinguished sections of the community who had been deported with Jehoiachin in 597.

Duhm proposes that it is the stringent separatism of the נבדלים in the context of the post-exilic Jerusalem community which is reflected in the chapter (Ezra 6.19ff.; 9.1; 10.11; Neh 9.2; cf. May, 148f.). These נבדלים were probably Jews who had returned from Babylon, or, at least, had identified themselves with the Judaism of the returning exiles, and they would appear to have gained the ascendancy in the post-exilic Jerusalem community in the time of our author. His theory is that not many Jews were deported to Babylon in 586, and that those who did go there were put to death or were assimilated to the native population.

Duhm, however, is aware that he does not have a final answer to the problems of chapter 24, whether in terms of a cleavage in the time of Ezra and Nehemiah, or its widening after the foundation of the Samaritan community, or internecine religious conflicts during the Greek period. He observes in connection with והישבים בארץ מצרים (v. 8) that a certain rivalry had always existed between Babylonian and Egyptian Jews, but that this may have been fanned into enmity by a fresh emigration of Jew to Egypt, some as prisoners, some voluntarily, in the reign of Ptolemy Soter (321–283). He sums up his theory in these terms: 'It offers only a general elucidation of this notable chapter and does not give sufficient support for a firm dating.' A solution in terms of a post-exilic setting, like the exilic solution, is difficult to reconcile with the nature of the account given in chapter 24. All that is needed to make the point which is attributed by Duhm to the author of chapter 24 is a simple antithesis between those who went into exile, whether in 597 or 586, and those who did not go into exile. What interest could he possibly have had in the middle of the fifth century or later in asserting that the only bearers of Judaism were those who had been deported with Jehoiachin in 597? Hence the particular nature of the antithesis between Jehoiachin and Zedekiah does not appear to fit the post-exilic hypothesis particularly well, although it is less vulnerable than other accounts of the chapter. The verdict must be that the puzzle has not been solved.

Thiel (pp. 253ff.) holds that 24.6ff. is permeated with Deuteronomistic vocabulary, and he concludes, as we have seen, that the chapter as a whole is the product of a Deuteronomistic editor. This editor has used the book of Amos as a model at the beginning of the chapter, has taken a chronological notice from 2 Kgs 24.14–16, and has quarried the beginning of v. 6 from Amos 9.4. These words (ושמתי עיני עליהם לטובה) differ only slightly from vocabulary which appears at 21.10 and 44.11, and

these passages are also to be attributed to D. Thiel considers that
בכל המקמות אשר אדיחם שם (v. 9) is an integral part of the D
composition, although he acknowledges that there is an
inconcinnity between it and v. 10 (see above, p. 611).

Thiel has some success in showing that chapter 24 is a
compilation in which vocabulary and word-strings have been
appropriated from other parts of the Hebrew Bible, but his
defence of בכל המקמות אשר אדיחם שם is unconvincing, and he
might have noted that the so-called 'covenant formula', which
occurs four times in Jeremiah (24.7; 31.1,33; 32.38), and once in
Zech 8.8, appears to have a special affinity with the book of
Ezekiel (11.20; 36.28; 37.23,27), as was noticed by Duhm.
Thiel's contention that (a) לזועה . . . לחרפה ולמשל לשנינה
ובניתם ולא (b), ולקללה את החרב את הרעב ואת הדבר and (c)
אהרס ונטעתים ולא אתוש are Deuteronomic or Deuteronomistic
word-strings has been subjected to a close scrutiny by H.
Weippert.

On (a) Weippert (pp. 187–189) observes that שמה occurs ten
times in Jeremiah out of the fourteen occurrences of the series
(15.4; 19.8; 24.9; 25.9,11,18; 29.18; 34.17; 42.18; 44.8,12,22;
49.13; 51.37) and only at Deut 28.37 in the
Deuteronomic/Deuteronomistic literature; שרקה occurs five
times in Jeremiah and otherwise only at Mic 6.16 and 2 Chr
29.8; חרפה occurs six times in Jeremiah and only at Josh 5.9 in
the Deuteronomic/Deuteronomistic literature. Hence three of
the terms which are regular constituents of the series in the prose
of the book of Jeremiah cannot be derived from the
Deuteronomic/Deuteronomistic tradition, and the connections
of אלה and קללה in that tradition are functionally different from
those which obtain in Jeremiah: in the former אלה is juxtaposed
with ברית and קללה with ברכה.

It is not necessary to conclude (as Weippert does) that there is
a direct literary relationship between Deut 28.25 and the
Jeremiah passages with זועה (15.4; 24.9; 29.18; 34.17). If,
however, such a relation is entertained, it should be noticed that
the resemblance between the passages is particularly marked
where לזועה (לזעוה) is not an item in a series (cf. Deut 28.25
ונתתים לזועה לכל with Jer 15.4, וחיית לזעוה לכל ממלכות הארץ
(ונתתי אתכם לזועה לכל ממלכות הארץ and 34.17, ממלכות הארץ).
Moreover, the construction of the series was probably a work of
compilation, and it is arguable (pace Weippert) that זועה has
been quarried from Deut 28.25 in order to furnish an item for
the series. Hence little weight should be attached to Weippert's
contention that the priority of זועה in the Jeremiah passages
over זעוה in Deut 28.25 is assured by the circumstance that זועה
is an item in a series at Jer 24.9 and 29.18.

On (*b*) the form of Weippert's argument (pp. 149–180; see above pp. 326–327) may dissuade us from too readily attributing prose in the book of Jeremiah to Deuteronomic or Deuteronomistic models. It cannot achieve the end at which she aims, namely, that of positively identifying a prose style of the prophet Jeremiah. On (*c*) Weippert observes (p. 202) that there is nothing comparable to this type of word-string in the book of Deuteronomy or in the Deuteronomistic parts of the Hebrew Bible. The view that its characteristic use is to describe the consummation of a *Heilsgeschichte* is not borne out by the facts. Only in 24.6 and 42.10 does it have this function; salvation and doom are interwoven in 31.28; 1.10 and 18.7–10 are concerned equally with salvation and doom, and 45.4 only with doom. What Weippert has demonstrated is that this stereotype cannot be particularly connected with Deuteronomic or Deuteronomistic parts of the Hebrew Bible, neither in respect of material constituents nor theological tendency.

The chapter, as Duhm has said, is a historical riddle which cannot be completely solved. It can, however, be asserted with some confidence that historical matters are represented in such a way as to make it improbable that we have a record of the activity of the prophet Jeremiah between the years 597 and 586. The representation itself is almost certainly that no Jews were deported to Babylon after the fall of Jerusalem in 586; that those who remained in the city and those who emigrated to Egypt (perhaps a secondary development) were doomed to extinction. Hence chapter 24 does not formulate an antithesis between those who were deported to Babylon and those who remained in Jerusalem during the exilic period.

If a post-exilic solution is pursued, chapter 24 is the expression of a theory, issuing from Jews who returned to Jerusalem from Babylon, that the inhabitants of Judah and Jerusalem whom they encountered were not Jews. But what would have been the point of maintaining at this date the antithesis of Jehoiachin and Zedekiah, or the representation that the Babylonian גולה consisted only of those who were deported to Babylon in 597? This assertion, contradicting the facts about the composition of the Jewish community in Babylon, had no function to serve in the time of Ezra and Nehemiah or later.

Evidences of secondary insertions in the text of 24.1–10 have been noticed, and there is the question whether this amounts to a proposal that these should be deleted. This ought to depend on the effect of the insertions: whether they destroy or obscure intelligibility, or whether a significant exegetical development can be detected in them which ought to be preserved, even if it is secondary. Judged by these criteria והישבים בארץ מצרים (v. 8)

should be retained and כה אמר יהוה אלהי ישראל (v. 5), כי כה
אמר יהוה (v. 8) and בכל המקמות אשר אדיחם שם (v. 9) deleted.
לרעה (v. 9), which is not represented by Sept., may be a variant
of לזועה. It disturbs the word-string לזועה לכל ממלכות הארץ and
should be deleted.

CHAPTER XXV

JUDAH AND JERUSALEM CONDEMNED (25.1–7)

¹The word which came to Jeremiah concerning all the people of Judah in the fourth year of Jehoiakim, son of Josiah, king of Judah (the first year of Nebuchadrezzar, king of Babylon). ²Jeremiah, the prophet, spoke in these terms to all the people of Judah and all the inhabitants of Jerusalem: ³From the thirteenth year of Josiah, son of Amon, king of Judah, and up to the present time, twenty-three years in all, I have been receiving the word of Yahweh and have addressed you urgently and ceaselessly, but you have not listened. ⁴Yahweh has been sending all his servants, the prophets, to you, urgently and ceaselessly, but you did not listen and had no inclination to hear. ⁵Their message was, Let every one return from his wicked way and evil deeds, and so you will dwell in the land which Yahweh gave to you and your forefathers from ancient days and for all time coming. ⁶Do not go after alien gods to serve them and bow down to them, and do not enrage me with the idols which you make; then I will do you no harm. ⁷You did not listen to me, says Yahweh, but enraged me¹ with the idols which you made, to your own hurt.

The versions vary in the indications which they give for עַל in vv. 1 and 2: it is clear that the first occurrence of עַל in v. 1 must be taken as equivalent to אֶל (so Kimchi; cf. Ehrlich, p. 307), but the second occurence could mean either (*a*) 'concerning' or (*b*) 'to be addressed to' = אֶל. In v. 2 it is unlikely that עַל has a different sense from the אֶל which follows it, and this is how the matter is understood by Sept. (πρός) and Vulg. (*ad*; also Kimchi). The form רֵאשִׁית (v. 1) has aroused suspicion and Giesebrecht and Duhm replace it with רֵאשָׁנָה. אַשְׁכֵּים (v. 3) was explained by Duhm as an Aramaism deriving from a copyist and an equivalent of Hebrew הַשְׁכֵּם (agreeing with Kimchi) which appears in a Geniza fragment and some manuscripts (cf. Ehrlich, p. 307). Rudolph supposes rather that אַשְׁכֵּים is a scribal error caused by the circumstance that the three words which precede it all begin with א. It is evident that Pesh. read אשכים (MT אַשְׁכֵּים) as אַשְׁכֵּים, and hence rendered אשכים ודבר as *qdmt blywm w'mrt* ('I rose early and said').

Apart from such small variations as the non-representation in Sept. of כֹּל (כל ישבי ירושלם, v. 2, and כל עבדיו, v. 4; cf. Janzen, p. 66) and לשמע (v. 4), and the representation of בשלש instead of MT מִן שְׁלֹשׁ (v. 3), the main differences between Sept. and MT are as follows:

(*a*) The note which synchronizes the fourth year of Jehoiakim with the first year of Nebuchadrezzar (v. 1) is absent from Sept.

(*b*) ירמיהו הנביא (v. 2) is not represented by Sept.

(*c*) היה דבר יהוה אלי (v. 3) is not represented by Sept.

¹ Reading either תַּכְעִסֵנִי or תַּכְעִסוּנִי (see below, p. 620).

(d) ולא שמעתם (v. 3) is not represented by Sept.

(e) Instead of ושלח יהוה אליכם את כל עבדיו הנבאים (v. 4, MT), Sept. represents ואשלח אליכם את עבדי הנבאים.

(f) Instead of נתן יהוה (MT, v. 5) Sept. represents נתתי.

(g) Instead of ולא ארע לכם (MT, v. 6) Sept. represents לרע לכם (cf. v. 7, MT; Ehrlich, p. 307) or, perhaps (so Rudolph), להרע לכם (τοῦ κακῶσαι ὑμᾶς).

(h) Only ולא שמעתם אלי of v. 7 (MT) is represented by Sept.

If the Hebrew text indicated by Sept. is compared with the 'original' text favoured by Rudolph and Weiser (cf. Bright, p. 156), we find that Sept. is followed in v. 3 (ולא שמעתם is deleted) and in v. 7, where only ולא שמעתם אלי is retained. The differences are that Rudolph retains the reference to Nebuchadrezzar (v. 1) and היה דבר יהוה אלי (v. 3), while he deletes vv. 4 and 6. He supposes that the notice which synchronizes the fourth year of Jehoiakim with the first year of Nebuchadrezzar has been omitted by the Greek translator because of an animus which he had against Babylon, but this is an explanation which Janzen (p. 100) doubts. It is more likely that the presence of this note in MT is to be elucidated as a learned gloss which synchronized Judaean and Babylonian chronologies (so Giesebrecht, Duhm, Bright, p. 160). The possible inexactness of the synchronism would not be a decisive consideration in determining the relative merits of MT and Sept. The problem is that Nebuchadrezzar's first regnal year does not overlap with the fourth year of Jehoiakim (April 605–April 604), since it begins in April 604. To overcome this J. Lewy (*Forschungen zur alten Geschichte Vorderasiens*, 1925, p. 27) and E. Vogt (*SVT* 4, 1957, pp. 84f.) have suggested that השנה הראשנית refers to the period between Nebuchadrezzar's accession and the beginning of his first regnal year (September 605–April 604).

Janzen's general view is that the differences between MT and Sept. are the consequence of secondary expansions of MT, and the implication of this is that Sept. depends on a Hebrew text which was shorter than the extant text of the Hebrew Bible. Thus, following Giesebrecht, Duhm, Volz and Rudolph, he supposes (p. 44) that ולא שמעתם (v. 3) is an insertion from 7.13 (25.4; 35.14). In connection with היה דבר יהוה אלי (v. 3) he argues (p. 100) against the conclusion (Volz) that Sept. is here the consequence of an abridgement of MT. Sept. has the form 'word of the Lord' throughout, whereas if היה דבר יהוה אלי is present in v. 3, the 'I' of ואדבר must be identified with the 'I' of אלי, and so Jeremiah is the speaker. While MT is consistent with a view that in vv. 2f. Jeremiah is reminiscing autobiographically *about* his prophetic vocation, the Greek text represents that he is proclaiming the word of Yahweh. Hence v. 4 is represented in Sept. as ואשלח אליכם את עבדי הנבאים, and v. 5 as אשר נתתי לכם, where the 'I' is Yahweh. It is clear that what is happening here is not connected with the dislike of the translator for the too full style of Baruch (Volz), but is bound up with the form of the text as word of Yahweh in Sept.

Janzen (p. 13) holds that the part of v. 7 which is not represented by Sept. is a doublet of v. 6b (so Duhm, 'a variant or correction of v. 6b', and Rudolph). His further contention that ὅπως μὴ παροργίζητέ με does not render ולא תכעיסו אותי and that the *Vorlage* of Sept. was למען לא הכעסוני (p. 194 n. 11) should be rejected. Either Q (למען הכעסני) or a modification of K (למען תכעסוני; cf. Pesh. w'rgztwnny) makes sense in v. 7. In any case Janzen's postulated *Vorlage* does not explain the text of Sept., since הכעסוני is not a rendering of παροργίζητέ με.

Thiel (p. 265) has noted that whereas Sept. has a consistent form (word of Yahweh), it is impossible to achieve any kind of consistency with MT: v. 3 cannot be construed as word of Yahweh, while vv. 6f. can be nothing but word of Yahweh. Moreover, there are contrary indications within v. 3 (cf. Janzen, p. 100), since the word-string ואדבר אליכם אשכים (השכם) ודבר and variants of it are always used in the book of Jeremiah with Yahweh as the grammatical subject (7.13,25; 11.7; 26.5; 29.19; 32.33; 35.14,15; 44.4). Rudolph's text is shaped by the assumption that the passage consisted originally of recollection by Jeremiah. All, however, is not plain sailing for him, even with his reconstructed text, and Bright (p. 156) is too sanguine when he says, 'If one omits the last sentence of v. 3, together with vv. 4,6 and 7b, ... a consistent address by Jeremiah remains' (that is, indications of word of God or oracle disappear from the passage). Thiel (p. 265) is aware that הדבר אשר היה (אל) ירמיהו על (v. 1) is a preparation for the proclamation of the word of Yahweh and not for a recollection of Jeremiah's experiences as a prophet, and since these words remain in Rudolph's text, they tell against his general view of the form of the passage. Moreover, it is Yahweh and not Jeremiah *qua* Jeremiah who is represented as saying ולא שמעתם אלי (v. 7). This point was made by Duhm, and that this is how MT understands v. 7 is evident from the presence of נאם יהוה. It is an understanding which is shared by Targ., since only Yahweh could have said ולא קבילתון למימרי.

In the form in which it is preserved in MT v. 4 could only have been spoken by the prophet Jeremiah concerning Yahweh (וישלח יהוה) and it may justly be seized on as a clue to the intentions of MT. Despite the impediments already mentioned, it would appear that the intention of the extant text of MT

(contradicted only by הדבר אשר היה על (אל) ירמיהו in v. 1 and
נאם יהוה in v. 7) is to make a distinction between the 'I' of
Jeremiah and the 'I' of Yahweh, and to present the passage as
reminiscence rather than proclamation. If there is proclamation
in it (vv. 5–7), this has to be set within the frame of the prophet's
recollection: it is not *present* delivery of the word of Yahweh, but
a recalling of forms of prophetic proclamation from *past*
prophetic experience. The reason why Rudolph deletes v. 4 (also
Weiser) is that he finds it a disturbing feature in a passage which
(*ex hypothesi*) is purely occupied with personal reminiscences of
the prophet Jeremiah, not with the witness of prophets in
general. We have reached a point where a decision has to be
made about the relative merits of MT and Sept. What do the
differences between MT and Sept. tell us about the history of the
Hebrew text? Is Sept. a witness to a different and shorter text
than MT? Or is there only one Hebrew text from which Sept.
has been derived by a process of abridgement and correction?

The first of these two views is the one held by Janzen and the
second is advanced by Thiel (pp. 264f.). Thiel maintains that the
abridgements and modifications in Sept. are designed to convert
the passage into word of Yahweh throughout. Thiel reads too
much into the absence of any representation of ירמיהו הנביא
(v. 2) in Sept. On the other hand, a Greek translator concerned
to represent vv. 1–7 as word of Yahweh would have had a motive
to delete היה דבר יהוה אלי (above, p. 619). But the theory does
not work with ולא שמעתם (v. 3) which is not represented by
Sept. In Sept. לאמר (v. 5) connects with καὶ ἀπέστελλον (v. 4).
Thus if the Greek translator were correcting MT in order to
make 25.1–7 word of Yahweh, he had no need to delete ולא
שמעתם. Thiel's critical position is curious (pp. 266f.): his
'original' text (the composition of D) is word of Yahweh
(vv. 3b–7), and he agrees that Sept. has the form of word of
Yahweh, but he, nevertheless, argues that Sept. is the
consequence of an abridgement and correction of MT. The
text-critical argument for the superiority of the shorter text
(Sept.) in vv. 6f. is difficult to resist, and Thiel's procedures in
respect of vv. 3b–7 are an illustration of his tendency to exalt his
speculative literary criticism over the more solid indications
given by texts which actually exist. His argument has an odd
appearance. On the one hand, he holds that D's text (the original
form of the text in vv. 3b–7) is the same as the text of Sept. in
vv. 4–5; on the other hand, that Sept. is a product of an
abridgement of MT which is a post-Deuteronomistic
modification of D.

We return to a comparison of MT and Sept., and the case
which is being made is that the shorter Greek text is the more

original and that the Hebrew text which underlies it has been expanded and modified in MT. The aim of this process is to represent that 25.1–7 is prophetic reminiscence rather than prophetic proclamation, and the insertion of היה דבר יהוה אלי (v. 3), along with the change to a reference to Yahweh in the third person (v. 4), is connected with it. The insertion of ירמיהו הנביא (v. 2) may be intended to reinforce the same interpretation, but this is less clear. On this view even vv. 5–7 are a recollection by Jeremiah of the content of prophetic preaching (connecting with v. 4) and not a proclamation which is *now* being made in Yahweh's name. Further additions in MT are of a different kind: the chronological notice in v. 1 is a learned gloss and v. 7b is constituted by a textual variant of v. 6b.

The difficulty which is felt with the view that v. 3a is a word of Yahweh is genuine and this is a problem not capable of final elucidation. What seems to be a personal reminiscence ('From the thirteenth year of Josiah, son of Amon, king of Judah, and up to the present time, these twenty-three years, I have addressed you urgently and ceaselessly') mingles with the 'I' of Yahweh in אדבר. This is the verse which influences Thiel's attitude to Sept. and it may have triggered the process by which vv. 1–7 are reshaped as prophetic reminiscence throughout and which produced MT. However, it does not move me from the history of the text which I have given or from my persuasion that Sept. rests on a shorter Hebrew text than MT. The difficulty is bound up with the character of 25.1–7. This is presented as a proclamation of the word of Yahweh which sums up and reviews the prophetic activity of Jeremiah over a period of twenty-three years. It is this which produces the awkward coalescence of personal, human recollection (v. 3a) and word of Yahweh (v. 3b). But the difficulty is perhaps generated by our drawing a distinction between 'I' = Jeremiah and 'I' = Yahweh which was not felt so clearly by whoever was responsible for the original form of the passage. A review of Jeremiah's activity is a review of Yahweh's activity, in so far as Jeremiah has faithfully represented the word of Yahweh, and in these terms no inappropriateness was felt in the juxtaposing of v. 3a and 3b.

The logical outcome of this discussion would seem to be the adoption of the text of Sept., but there are reasons why this course should not be followed. The general rule which has been adopted is not to emend MT or to subtract from it for as long as it maintains a tolerable level of intelligibility. To emend it or take away from it would be to suppress part of the history of the Hebrew text, that part which lies between the Hebrew text underlying Sept. and the extant shape of MT. Hence along with the assertion that the Hebrew *Vorlage* of Sept. represents an earlier and more cohesive text than MT there goes the counter-assertion that it is the duty of a commentator on the Hebrew text to maintain the final form of that text in MT.

JUDGEMENT ON JUDAH AND THEN ON ITS ENEMIES (25.8–14)

⁸Therefore these are the words of Yahweh Sabaoth: Because you have disregarded my words ⁹I will send for all the tribes of the north, says Yahweh, and for Nebuchadrezzar, king of Babylon, my servant, and I will bring them against this land and its inhabitants and all those nations which border on it. I will annihilate them and make their countries a spectacle at which men will be appalled and whistle in horror, a reproach[1] for ever afterwards. ¹⁰I will silence sounds of joy and gladness, the voice of the bridegroom and the bride; I will silence the noise of the handmill and put out the light of the lamp. ¹¹All this land will be reduced to a ruin and a waste, and these nations will be subject to the king of Babylon for seventy years. ¹²When seventy years have passed, I will punish the sin of the king of Babylon and his nation, says Yahweh, and I will make the land of the Chaldaeans a waste for ever afterwards. ¹³I will bring on that land all the threats which I uttered against it, everything written in this book which Jeremiah prophesied against all the nations. ¹⁴Mighty nations and great kings will reduce them to slavery,[2] and so I will repay them according to their deeds and actions.

והחרמתים (v. 9) is taken by KB³ (Duhm, Rudolph, Weiser, Bright) as a reference to the 'ban' (ḥerem) and so (Weiser) as an indication of 'holy war' in reverse, where Judah is dedicated to destruction. BDB, on the other hand, assumes that this is a case of a more generalized use of החרים, so that all that is intended is 'destroy', 'exterminate', without any more particular or technical nuance. The ancient versions, for the most part, did not detect any reference to the 'ban' so far as we can judge from the renderings which they offer. Only in Aq. and Symm. (καὶ αναθεματι(σ)ω αυτους) can support be found for a more technical interpretation of והחרמתים. It is not therefore clear that החרמתים means anything more than 'destroy' in v. 9. עבד ב (v. 14) is correctly understood by BDB (cf. Duhm) 'to work by means of others' (pace Ehrlich, p. 308), that is, to enslave. That the third person plural suffix (בם) refers to Babylon is noted by Rashi (כבני בבל = בם). גם המה ('even them') refers backward to בם and the grammatical subject is 'Mighty Nations and great kings' (so Pesh.; cf. GK 135g). Both Rashi and Kimchi observe that עבדו is being used for the more normal יעבדו, while Ehrlich (p. 308) restores יעבדו on the assumption of a haplography of י (followed by NEB—Brockington, p. 207).

καὶ θήσομαι αὐτοὺς (v. 12) is perhaps a rendering of MT ושמתי אתו rather than an indication that the Greek translator

---

[1] Reading ולהחרפת (see below, p. 624).

[2] Reading יעבדו (see above, p. 623).

read ושמתים. In that case the masculine אתו (emended to אתה by Ehrlich, p. 308, and Rudolph) has been taken as a resumption of הגוי ההוא and so as a collective singular. The more important differences between MT and Sept. are these:

(a)   נאם יהוה ואל נבכדראצר מלך בבל עבדי   (v. 9)   is   not represented by Sept.

(b) For ולחרבות עולם (v. 9) Sept. represents לחרפת עולם. The only other passages with the word-string שמה, שרקה, and חרפה are Jer 29.18 and Mic 6.16, and the first of these is missing from Sept. The difficulty about ולחרבות is that this type of word-string (see on 18.16, above p. 433, and 19.8) is connected with feelings which are aroused by a scene of desolation rather than with the physical ruins themselves. This is presumably why Driver (*JQR* 28, pp. 118f.) explains חרבות as cognate with Syriac *ḥrb'* 'idle gossip' or the like. It is unlikely that ולחרבות עולם (v. 9) or לחרבה (v. 18) rests on such philology: the other versions (Aq., Symm., Vulg., Pesh., Targ.) have understood חרבות עולם as ruined places which will never be rebuilt, and this is how Sept. has taken לחרבה (εἰς ἐρήμωσιν) at 25.18 (32.4). It is difficult to believe that the Greek translator made a change at 25.9 or that there was a subsequent alteration, when the representation of לחרבה survives without change in a similar word-string at 25.18. This suggests that the Hebrew text read by the Greek translator at 25.9 was ולחרפת עולם.

(c) For MT קול רחים (v. 10) Sept. (ὀσμὴν μύρου) represents ריח מור (see Ziegler, *Beiträge*, p. 45). Only Sept.[L] (φωνὴν μύλου) represents MT. Ziegler urges that קול רחים is a misfit in the series, because 'the sound of the handmill' does not evoke a joy which will no longer be heard in captivity. Rather it is the work which prisoners do (Isa 47.2; Lam 5.13). The perfume of myrrh like the joy of wedding festivities and the gleam of the lamp is a mark of social rejoicing (so Ziegler, adopting ריח מור).

(d) Sept. does not represent האלה את מלך בבל (v. 11) and instead of הגוים represents בגוים (ἐν τοῖς ἔθνεσιν; cf. Ehrlich, p. 308, who favours MT).

(e) Sept. does not represent על מלך בבל ו (v. 12).

(f) Sept. does not represent נאם יהוה את עונם ועל ארץ כשדים (v. 12)

(g)   אשר נבא ירמיהו על כל הגוים   (v. 13) appears in Sept. ('Ἀ ἐπροφήτευσεν Ιερεμίας ἐπὶ τὰ ἔθνη τὰ Αιλαμ) as a superscription to 25.15ff. (= MT 49.34ff.).

(h) Sept. does not represent v. 14.

The expansions in MT are explanatory glosses or exegesis whose aim is to identify Judah's enemy with Babylon, and, more particularly, with Nebuchadrezzar. Kimchi remarked that אל (v. 9), connects not with לקח but with שלח, and once this is

appreciated the grammatical peculiarity of the verse is apparent
(cf. Duhm) and ואל נבוכדראצר מלך בבל עבדי stands out as an
addition. This comment is attached (cf. Janzen, p. 44) in order to
identify the enemy from the north with Nebuchadrezzar and to
affirm that the work of destruction which he carries out is
Yahweh's work (cf. W. E. Lemke, *CBQ*, 28, 1966, pp. 45–50—a
later identification of Nebuchadrezzar with the enemy from the
north). Similarly in v. 12 הגוי ההוא, which is to be identified
(following Sept.) with the enemy from the north (v. 9), is
equated by means of explanatory comment with מלך בבל and
ארץ כשדים. Retribution will fall on Judah's destroyer and
Babylon will be a waste for all time coming. This interpretation
is spelled out further by v. 14 which elaborates the theme of
retribution. Babylon, once an imperial power, will be reduced to
servitude by mighty nations and great kings, and this will be a
kind of poetic justice.

The view expressed by Duhm and Thiel (p. 271) is that ועל כל
ועבדו הגוים האלה את מלך בבל   (v. 9)   and   הגוים האלה סביב
(v. 11) are additions whose purpose is to connect vv. 1–13 with
oracles against the nations adjoining Judah in 26.2ff. (Sept.)
= 46.2ff. (MT). Rudolph (Weiser) holds a similar opinion, but he
supposes that the addition in v. 11b is limited to הגוים האלה and
that the "original" form of the verse is ועבדו את מלך בבל שבעים
שנה. These proposals are not supported by a shorter Greek text
in v. 9, and although Sept. does not represent האלה את מלך בבל
in v. 11, the Greek translator apparently read ועבדו בגוים (καὶ
δουλεύσουσιν ἐν τοῖς 'ἔθνεσιν). In these circumstances it is not
clear that the appearance of הגוים האלה in vv. 9 and 11 has the
significance which Duhm and others attach to it. It is possible,
however, that this is a case where the Hebrew text underlying
Sept. already had a secondary expansion which is also in MT,
whose function is to link 25.1–13* with the oracles against the
nations adjoining Judah which appear in 46.2ff. (MT) and
26.2ff. (Sept.).

There is no doubt that הארץ הזאת (v. 11) refers to Judah and
that the verse, whether in MT or Sept., or as emended by
Rudolph, refers to the devastation of Judah and the subjection of
her inhabitants for seventy years. Rudolph's text is unlikely to be
right, because we have established as a characteristic of the
expansions in MT over against Sept. the identification of Judah's
enemies with Babylon, and את מלך בבל, which is not represented
by Sept., is an elaboration of this kind. Thus Rudolph's view that
ἐν τοῖς 'ἔθνεσιν is not related to הגוים האלה (MT) but is a
circumlocution of את מלך בבל is mistaken. Rather ἐν τοῖς 'ἔθνεσιν
should be taken seriously as an indication that the Greek
translator read a Hebrew text with בגוים. The meaning of Sept.

is that the Judaeans will be in exile (in servitude among the nations) for seventy years. The change from בגוים to הגוים האלה in MT is perhaps connected with the accommodating of the gloss את מלך בבל, and its effect is to connect v. 11 with כל הגוים האלה סביב (v. 9) who, according to MT, are to be laid waste by Nebuchadrezzar along with Judah. Hence it should be concluded that Sept. gives us access to a shorter Hebrew text than MT in v. 11 (so F. Schwally, *ZAW* 8, 1888, p. 181, and others).

The crux is unquestionably הארץ ההיא (v. 13) and the arguments about the interpretation of vv. 8–14 turn on it. According to Rudolph and Thiel the whole of v. 12 is an addition, since the passage (vv. 8–13*) is concerned only with Judah's punishment and not with the retribution which will eventually fall on Judah's destroyer (Babylon). Thus Rudolph holds that v. 12a derives from 29.10 and that v. 12b derives from 51.26,62. Verse 12, according to Thiel (p. 271), was part of a post-Deuteronomistic redaction which connected vv. 8–13 with the oracles against foreign nations and which was responsible for the transitional piece or superscription which appears in v. 13 (אשר נבא ירמיהו על כל הגוים). Duhm, on the other hand, holds that the connection between v. 12 and v. 14 is broken by an intrusive v. 13, and since he discounts v. 11b and follows Sept. in v. 12, הגוי ההוא is a reference to the enemy from the north (v. 9). The meaning of v. 12 is then that after seventy years Yahweh will exact retribution on the enemy from the north (a deliberately cryptic term), and will so decimate it that it will never recover.

In order to sustain the view that vv. 8–13* refer only to a catastrophe which will overtake Judah, Rudolph and Thiel (p. 271 n. 21) argue that an original הארץ הזאת (v. 13), connecting with הארץ הזאת = Judah (v. 11) has been altered to הארץ ההיא, referring to Babylon (cf. v. 12, MT), to which בם and גם המה in v. 14 also refer. But Sept. which represents הגוי ההוא as τὸ ἔθνος ἐκεῖνο in v. 12 also represents הארץ ההיא at v. 13 (τὴν γῆν ἐκείνην). If then Sept. is followed (a text with a substantial existence), it is clear that the passage has a different meaning from what Rudolph and Thiel, with their respective 'original' texts, would attach to it. It is not entirely taken up with the threat of judgement against Judah. It predicts that retribution will fall on הגוי ההוא (v. 12) and on הארץ ההיא (v. 13), and in the text of Sept. this can only be a reference to the enemy from the north (v. 9—πατριὰν ἀπὸ βορρᾶ).

The prime characteristic of the longer MT is that it identifies the enemy from the north with Nebuchadrezzar and the Babylonians. Thus its additions have the character of exegesis or

commentary. In Sept., on the other hand, there is no further
elucidation of the enemy from the north. According to Sept.,
Judah, because of its lack of trust in Yahweh and disobedience
(v. 8), is about to be vanquished by an enemy from the north
who will devastate both Judah and the countries surrounding
her, and leave behind a scene of desolation which will evoke
astonishment and terror (v. 9). In a land emptied of its
inhabitants who have been dispersed among the nations (v. 11),
the sounds of human occupation will disappear (v. 10). What
were once homes will become abandoned and will be reduced to
ruinous buildings in which no light will shine when darkness
approaches. The day will not open with the sound of grinding
(Kimchi) as women set about their domestic tasks and prepare
grain or spices for the needs of their households. The joyful
sounds associated with wedding festivities will no longer be
heard. Places of human settlement in Judah will become
crumbling ruins and the inhabitants of the land will go into exile
(v. 11). After an interval of seventy years Yahweh will exact
retribution on the nation which ravaged and destroyed Judah
and will reduce it to a waste (v. 12). It follows from this
exposition of Sept. that את כל הכתוב בספר הזה (v. 13) can only
refer to the oracles against foreign nations contained in 25.14ff.
(MT 46 ff.). This is so because the threats in v. 13 are uttered
against the enemy from the north and it is they who are said to
be written in הספר הזה. Consistent with this אשר נבא ירמיהו על
כל הגוים (v. 13) appears in Sept. as a superscription to the
oracles against the nations. It should, however, be noticed that
MT in v. 13 requires an interpretation which virtually coincides
with that of Sept. In view of what has preceded in MT, הארץ
ההיא (v. 13) refers to Babylon, and the book containing
Yahweh's threats is identified wth the oracles against foreign
nations (אשר נבא ירמיהו על כל הגוים). This exegesis is
developed further in v. 14, where it is said that Babylon will be
overtaken by the fate which she deserves: she exercised an
imperial sway, but she will be reduced to servitude by powerful
nations and great kings.

The modern attempts to deal with the figure of seventy years
are influenced by historical assumptions associated with 25.11f.
Rudolph and Weiser are inclined to conclude that the seventy
years of v. 11 is a prediction made by the prophet Jeremiah and
to treat the seventy as a round number. It represents a lifetime
(Ps 90.10; Job 42.16) and the intention is to establish that no one
living at the time when the disaster fell will see the day of
liberation. C. F. Whitley's concern (*VT* 4, 1954, pp. 60–72; *VT*
7, 1957, pp. 416–418) is to establish that the seventy-year period
runs from 586 to the completion of the temple in the second year

of Darius Hystaspes (516). He holds that the number seventy in
25.11f. represents a post-exilic computation which was probably
dependent on 29.10. This ground had been well covered by
Duhm who had considered a number of possibilities. He
favoured the view that the author of 25.11f. was dependent on
Zech 1.12 whose computation assumed the dates 586–516. Like
Whitley he considered that the figure seventy in 25.11f. was of
late origin, but he differed from Whitley in asserting that it was
not derived from 29.10.

O. Plöger's inclination (*Erlanger Forschungen*, 10, 1959,
pp. 125–130) is to accept Rudolph's view that in the Jeremiah
passages seventy is a round number (p. 128). On Zech 1.12
(pp. 125f., 128f.) he agrees with Duhm that the period 586–516
is indicated, but he argues that in 2 Chr 36.20f. the lower limit is
given by the year in which, as a consequence of the activity of
Ezra and Nehemiah, the theocracy was fully realized. Hence the
seventy year period runs from 515 (the completion of the
temple) to 445. With this anti-eschatological scheme which
encapsulates the fulfilment in an institutional perfection he
contrasts the eschatological tendency in Dan 9.2, where he
detects a polemical note against the Jerusalem establishment. In
these circles there was a concern to interpret the scheme of
seventy years in such a way as to leave it open to a future,
eschatological fulfilment.

A quest after the *ipsissima verba* of the prophet Jeremiah in
the study of 25.1–14, is hardly at all evident, except in the case
of H. Weippert whose attempts to dissociate the prose of the
book of Jeremiah from Deuteronomic and Deuteronomistic
connections are related to a conviction that it represents a
distinctive prose vocabulary and style of the prophet Jeremiah.
She is concerned to show that the correspondences between the
prose in vv. 1–14 and Deuteronomic/Deuteronomistic patterns
are not so exact as to support the conclusion that these verses are
dependent on Deuteronomic/Deuteronomistic models (pp. 126f.,
147f., 187–191, 212–216).

The issues which are raised by Weippert's method have
already been discussed (see above, p. 596), but they may be
taken up again in connection with the sentence with which she
concludes her treatment of מַעְלָל + דרך (25.5): *Es bleibt somit
nur der Schluss dass die Zusammenstellung beider Nomina und
deren Beziehung auf die Verben שׁוב und יטב (H) eine
jeremianische Spracheigentümlichkeit darstellen* (p. 148). The
answer to this must be that her method can show only that the
correspondence between prose patterns in the book of Jeremiah
and Deuteronomic/Deuteronomistic prose is non-existent or less
exact than has been represented, and that the effort to

demonstrate the literary dependence of this prose on
Deuteronomic/Deuteronomistic models cannot be carried
through successfully. What she cannot establish by her method,
although this is what she intends by *eine jeremianische
Spracheigentümlichkeit*, is that she has alighted on the prose
style of the prophet Jeremiah. It should be obvious that it is a
much simpler task to disengage the prose of the book of
Jeremiah from Deuteronomic/Deuteronomistic prose than it is
to demonstrate that this prose is none other than the *ipsissima
verba* of the prophet Jeremiah. In demonstrating that the
correspondences between patterns of prose in the book of
Jeremiah and those of Deuteronomic/Deuteronomistic prose are
sometimes looser than has been represented Weippert has
performed a valuable service, but the correct deduction from her
findings is that the prose of Jeremiah should be studied as an
integral part of the body of material assembled in that book, and
that scholarship should not go to and fro so much between the
book of Jeremiah and the Deuteronomic/Deuteronomistic
literature. Since the prose of the book of Jeremiah is the product
of the ongoing growth and development of a prophetic book, we
should expect it to have its own character and themes.

Two points concerning 25.1–14 and relating to the connections
between poetry and prose in the book of Jeremiah may be
touched on. The combination of מעלל + דרך + שוב (v. 5) is
already given by the poetry of 23.22 (וישבום מדרכם הרע ומרע
מעלליהם), and the right conclusion is probably that the prose is
generated by the poetry: the vocabulary of the poetry is used
again in order to enlarge the *corpus* which is represented as the
'book of Jeremiah'. Similarly the occurrences of לשמה ולשרקה in
prose sequences in the book of Jeremiah (19.8; 25.9,18; 29.18)
should be related to לשמה שרוקת עולם (K) or לשמה שְׁרִיקוֹת
עוֹלָם (Q) at 18.16. Hence vocabulary which is common to poetry
and prose is not necessarily a proof that Jeremiah is the author
of the prose.

The principal distinction which has to be drawn in respect of
25.1–14 is between those who take the date 605 (v. 1) seriously
(Rudolph, Weiser, Bright, E. Vogt, *SVT* 4, 1957, pp. 84f.), and
those who explain the passage against the background of the
exile or the post-exilic period (Duhm, Nicholson, Thiel).
According to the first view, the victory of Nebuchadrezzar at
Carchemish is seen as ushering in a new historical era in which
Jeremiah identifies the enemy from the north with Babylon. The
summary of his prophetic activity over a period of twenty-three
years is occasioned by the conviction that a critical juncture has
been reached and that his prophetic threats are about to be taken
up in a defeat which Nebuchadrezzar will inflict on Judah. The

passage is attributed by Rudolph to his Source C, so that although he attaches value to it as a historical source, he holds that it comes to us in Deuteronomic dress. Weiser distinguishes between the form in which the contents of 25.1–14 were orally delivered by the prophet Jeremiah and the extant literary form which he regards as longer than the oral message and attributable to Baruch. According to Nicholson (*Jeremiah*, p. 209; cf. *Preaching to the Exiles*, pp. 34, 56f.) 25.1–14 is a Deuteronomic summation of the first half of the book of Jeremiah, with an exact chronological notice, a typical Deuteronomic feature. It betrays an understanding of the prophet and his functions which conforms to Deut 18.9–22. Thus possession of the land is made conditional on a change of heart and submission to Yahweh's will as revealed in his Law, and the point is reinforced by word-play (v. 5, שובו — ושבו).

The opinion that 25.1–14 give no access to the historical prophet Jeremiah is not new and Thiel (p. 262 n. 3) observes that it is found in F. Schwally (*ZAW* 8, 1888, p. 184). The passage derives from a redactor of the book of Jeremiah who inserted the summary of Jeremiah's prophetic activity after that part of the book which he supposed to contain the oracles uttered by Jeremiah between the thirteenth year of Josiah and the fourth year of Jehoiakim (cf. H. Birkeland, *Zum hebräischen Traditionswesen*, 1938, pp. 44–46; J. P. Hyatt. *IB* 5, pp. 789, 998–1001). Duhm supposes that the passage is post-exilic in date, later than Zech 1.12 (see above, p. 628), but earlier than 2 Chr 36.21 and Dan 9. No passage in the book of Jeremiah is more of a patchwork than it is. Its author either did not know of chapters 21.1ff. and 24, or else he paid no attention to them, and in an unhistorical way he represented all the pre-exilic generations as idolators.

In Thiel's view (pp. 267f.) 25.1–14 is partly exilic and partly post-exilic: on a composition attributable to D there has been imposed a post-Deuteronomistic redaction (PD). The composition of D with its reconstituted introduction (see above, p. 621) had the form of word of Yahweh. The various echoes of chapter 7 (which Thiel also attributes to D) in 25.1–13 (v. 3b and 7.13; v. 4 and 7.25b, 26a; v. 5 and 7.7; v. 6 and 7.6, 18f.; vv. 10, 11a and 7.34) persuade him that we have to reckon with the literary habits of the same author in both passages rather than with secondary insertions into 25.1–13 from chapter 7. Since (*ex hypothesi*) the original D composition regarded Yahweh as the speaker, everything in vv. 1–3 which is inconsistent with this is attached to the PD redaction. The PD redaction (pp. 269f.) also supplies the synchronizing reference to the first year of Nebuchadrezzar, and this chronological

reference like the insertions in vv. 8–13 prepares the ground for
the sayings against the nations. The PD dates are derived from
1.2 (thirteenth year of Josiah) and 36.1 (fourth year of
Jehoiakim), and the interval (twenty-three years) agrees with
36.2. The references to 1.2 and 36.1 make it certain that PD
intended to connect the contents of chapters 1–25.13 with the
scroll referred to in chapter 36, but the intention was even more
precise. What precedes 25.1–13 is identified by PD with that
part of the scroll which contains the words על ישראל ועל יהודה
(36.2), and 25.1–13 is conceived as a bridge between sayings
against Israel and Judah, and sayings against the nations.

If the date 605/4 is taken seriously in 25.1 and 36.1, as it is by
Rudolph and Vogt, it is natural that the next step should be to
enquire about the relation between the scroll and 25.1–13, and
that the Babylonian Chronicle (D. J. Wiseman, *Chronicles of
Chaldaean Kings in the British Museum*, 1956, pp. 68f.) should
be drawn into the discussion. Rudolph urges that the *Urrolle* was
written at a later point in the year 605/4 than 25.1–13 in order
to reinforce Jeremiah's message of doom, since false hopes had
been raised by Nebuchadrezzar's return home in August 605
and February 604. According to Vogt (op. cit., pp. 84f.)
Jeremiah began to dictate his scroll to Baruch in March 604 at
the latest, whereas the speech (25.1–14), of which the scroll is a
developed and longer version, was made at an earlier point in the
year, perhaps shortly after Nebuchadrezzar's accession in
September 605.

Another factor, apart from the date, is the reference to הספר
הזה (v. 13), and Weiser supposes that הספר הזה is to be
identified with the scroll and that 25.1–13 is the conclusion of
the scroll. This connects with a line of interpretation noted by
Rudolph according to which 25.1–13 is either the preface to the
scroll (H. Schmidt, Rothstein, Volz and others) or its conclusion
(Skinner, p. 240, Birkeland, op. cit., pp. 44f., Hyatt and others).
But הספר הזה can be identified with the scroll only if הארץ ההיא
(v. 13) has been emended to הארץ הזאת, and I have argued
(above, pp. 626f.) that this emendation should not be adopted.
Hence all the theories about the relation of 25.1–13 or 25.1–14
to the scroll should be discounted. This statement applies to
Bright (p. 163) who like Weiser interprets 25.1–13 against the
historical background of 605/4 and who urges that הספר הזה is
to be equated with the scroll of Jeremiah's prophecies, whether
in its original form or as supplemented. This dissuasive also
applies to those who dissociate 25.1–13 from the age of the
prophet Jeremiah, but who, nevertheless, founding on בספר הזה,
assume a connection between it and the scroll. According to
Rudolph, 'All that is written in this book' refers either to the

Source C collection of Jeremiah's words, or to chapters 1–20 which are principally concerned with events from the reigns of Josiah and Jehoiakim. Chapters 21–24 disturb the chronological scheme and are a later insertion. A modification of this position is adopted by Thiel (p. 273) in respect of the original composition of D: בספר הזה refers to D's composition of Jeremiah's words in 1.1–25.13.

The second part of this discussion deals with the relation of 25.1–14(13) to the oracles against foreign nations in the book of Jeremiah. Duhm argues that if the foreign oracles had originally come immediately after אשר נבא ירמיהו על כל הגוים, the oracle against Babylon would have come first, whereas this does not happen either in MT or Sept. This is not an argument whose cogency is obvious, since Duhm himself has urged that explicit identifications of הגוי ההוא (v. 12), and הארץ ההיא (v. 13) with Babylon, which are not present in Sept., derive from secondary processes of explication in MT. Even if it were held that הגוי ההוא or הארץ ההיא would naturally be identified with Babylon (the enemy from the north = Babylon), the subsequent reference to the entire collection of foreign oracles, in which the words against Babylon are contained, is not difficult or inappropriate.

Duhm does not attend sufficiently to the order of the text in Sept., where the oracles against foreign nations follow 25.13 (25.15–30.11). On the other hand, I am not so sure that Sept.'s representation of אשר נבא ירמיהו על כל הגוים as a superscription to 25.15ff., which is thought by Rudolph, Weiser, Nicholson and Bright to preserve the original function of this clause, is correct. Without this clause, and given the retention of הארץ ההיא, בספר הזה hangs in the air, unless one adopts the somewhat lame conclusion that it is to be equated with the entire book of Jeremiah. The original function of אשר נבא ירמיהו על כל הגוים is more probably preserved by MT: it identifies הספר הזה as the oracles against foreign nations which form the continuation of the book of Jeremiah at this point, according to Sept.

C. Rietzschel's view (*Das Problem der Urrolle. Ein Beitrag zur Redaktionsgeschichte des Jeremiabuches*, 1966, pp. 25–90) has a point of contact with Duhm's treatment in so far as Rietzschel supposes that the oracle against Babylon must originally have followed after בספר הזה. His assumption that even without epexegetical glosses הגוי ההוא (v. 12) and הארץ ההיא (v. 13) should be identified with Babylon is reasonable, but it is not sufficient to bear the weight of his conclusion that the oracle against Babylon (MT, 50–51; Sept., 27–28) must originally have followed after בספר הזה, and that the insertion of אשר נבא ירמיהו על כל הגוים was a consequence of the interposition of oracles against other nations between בספר הזה and the oracle against Babylon.

We have a text (MT) in which אשר נבא ירמיהו על כל הגוים ought to lead on to oracles against foreign nations, and another (Sept.) in which these words are a superscription to oracles against foreign nations. It is unprofitable to try to get behind these hard textual indications in order to set up alternative dispositions of the material, but there is enough in the textual evidence to indicate that in the Hebrew text of the book of Jeremiah the oracles against foreign nations originally made their entry at this point.

THE WINE OF YAHWEH'S WRATH (25.15–29)

[15]These were the words of Yahweh, the God of Israel, to me: Take this cup of wine (a cup of wrath)[1] from my hand and make all the nations to whom I send you drink from it. [16]When they drink, they will vomit and go mad, because of the sword which I am sending among them. [17]I took the cup from Yahweh's hand and I made all the nations to whom Yahweh sent me drink from it: [18]Jerusalem and the towns of Judah, its kings and statesmen, reducing it to a waste and making them a spectacle at which men are appalled and whistle in horror.[2] [19]Pharaoh, king of Egypt, his officials and statesmen, all his own people [20]and all the foreigners in Egypt.[3] All the kings of Philistine territory, Ashkelon, Gaza, Ekron, and what remained of Ashdod. [21]Edom, Moab and the Ammonites, [22]all the kings of Tyre, all the kings of Sidon and the kings of the islands which are over the sea. [23]Dedan, Tema and Buz and all who crop the hair on their temples, [24]dwellers in the desert, (all the kings of the Arabs).[4] [25]All the kings of Elam[5] and all the kings of the Medes; [26]all the kings of the north, those who are neighbours and those far removed from each other; all the kingdoms[6] on the face of the earth, (and after them the king of Sheshak will drink).[7] [27]Say to them: These are the words of Yahweh Sabaoth, the God of Israel: Drink and be drunk and vomit and fall down never to rise again, because of the sword which I am sending among you. [28]If they should refuse to take the cup from your hand to drink, say to them: These are the words of Yahweh Sabaoth: You have no choice, you must drink. [29]On the city which is called by my name I am beginning my work of destruction and do you suppose that you will go unpunished? You will not go unpunished, for I am summoning a sword against all the inhabitants of the earth, says Yahweh Sabaoth.

Sept. (32.1–15) again has a shorter text than MT and the principal differences feature prominently in the discussion which follows. כי, which is certainly secondary (cf. Rudolph) is not

[1] See below, pp. 634, 641.
[2] Deleting ולקללה כיום הזה (see below, pp. 637, 641).
[3] Deleting ואת כל מלכי ארץ העוץ (see below, pp. 637, 641).
[4] Deleting ואת כל מלכי ערב (see below, pp. 638f., 641).
[5] Deleting ואת כל מלכי זמרי (see below, pp. 639, 641).
[6] Deleting הארץ (see below, pp. 640, 641).
[7] See below, pp. 640, 641.

represented in Sept. (MT, v. 15; Sept., v. 1), and החמה which
presents a grammatical difficulty, would seem to have been read
by Sept. as an adjective ('undiluted'; החמה?). Driver (*JQR* 28,
p. 119) appeals to Sept. and Saadya in adopting this vocalization
of החמה, and cites Arabic *ḥumayyan* 'strength of wine' (cf.
Jerome, who glosses ἀκράτου as *non mixti*). Rudolph supposes
that החמה is secondary but apposite exegesis of כוס היין הזאת —
identifying the cup as that of Yahweh's wrath.

Rudolph's grammatical point (contested by Weiser) that the
relative clause in v. 15 places a limitation on את כל הגוים, and
already anticipates the list which follows in vv. 18ff., is perhaps
but not certainly correct. Rudolph and Weiser are influenced by
the divergent views which they hold of the list of nations in
vv. 18–26: for Rudolph vv. 15–26* is a literary unit, whereas for
Weiser the list is an intrusion which breaks an original
connection between vv. 15f. and vv. 27–29 (see further below).

In v. 16 Sept. is not representing MT ושתו and is
understanding והתגעשו as a synonym of וקיו (= וקיאו) in v. 27
(ἐξεμοῦνται in v. 16 and ἐξεμέσατε in v. 27). Aq., Vulg., Pesh.
and Targ. indicate 'confusion' and 'derangement' for והתגעשו, a
loss of physical and mental control caused by drunkenness.
Hence Jerome glosses התגעשו as *inebriabuntur*. Kimchi takes
געש and רעש as synonyms, but the question is whether
'convulsion' is to be understood as 'reeling' or whether it is the
convulsion of sickness and vomiting (So Sept., and Symm.
σπαραχθήσονται 'retching'). 'Reeling' is given by BDB and
'vomiting' or 'retching' by G. R. Driver (*Welt des Orients*, 1960,
p. 406) and KB³. Rashi and Kimchi, in their comments on v. 27,
suppose that no more is indicated by vomiting than the
consequence of over-indulgence in alcohol. But is the madness of
v. 16 (והתהללו) simply the wildness caused by drink, a process of
going berserk which happens to some who are crazed by alcohol,
or is it something more extraordinary?

There are then two possibilities: (*a*) The figure turns simply on
the cup which intoxicates and produces physical and mental
disorders. (*b*) The contents of the cup have a poisonous aspect,
the poison induces sickness and a madness which does not wear
off (cf. v. 27, ונפלו ולא תקומו) like the effects of drunkenness.
Passages like 13.12–14 and 23.9 are explicable in terms of a
figure of drunkenness and do not appear to rest on more
extraordinary imagery. The prophet likens his loss of capacity to
the effects of drink on a man (23.9), and destructive, internecine
strife is regarded as ˙exemplifying irrational and suicidal
attitudes which are associated with drunkenness (13.12–14).
There are, however, three passages (8.14; 9.14; 23.15) which
certainly refer to the administering of poison, and it appears that

Targ. has associated 25.16 with these passages. In all of them מי ראש is rendered as 'A cup of curse, as poisonous as a serpent's venom', and at 25.15 Targ. translates כוס היין החמה הזאת as כסא דחמר לוטא הדין, 'This cup of the wine of curse'. H. Ringgren (*SEÅ* 17, 1952, pp. 19–30) concentrates on intoxication rather than poison and describes intoxication as a 'Chaos motif' which is embedded in the rites of the New Year festival. He finds a reference to the intoxication of a 'god-king' in Ps 78.65, and a connection between intoxication and the judgement or fate of enemies in the 'cup of wrath' passages (pp. 27ff.). It is perhaps his intention to relate the 'cup of wrath' passages to the ritual of a New Year Festival, but it is not clear that he achieves this. H. A. Brongers (*OTS* 15, 1969, pp. 177–192) is right in insisting that the 'cup of wrath' passages are not adequately explained in terms of strong wine and an advanced state of intoxication, but he is wrong in supposing that because the wine is simply 'poison', there is no possibility of relating these passages to the thought of test or ordeal, to a method of discriminating between guilt and innocence, of arriving at a verdict and consummating a judgement. Of Jer 25.15ff. it can be said categorically that it is a representation of the judgement of Jerusalem and of the other nations which are listed.

The ritual of ordeal described in Num 5.11ff. is a promising *point d'appui* (cf. Rudolph): the cup which features in this ritual becomes a cup of curse, if the woman who drinks it is indeed guilty of unfaithfulness to her husband, and it causes her to abort. If, on the other hand, she is innocent, the cup has no evil effects on her. There can be little doubt that Targ.'s כס דלוט is indicating a connection between מי ראש and the ritual of ordeal in the passages mentioned above (8.14; 9.14; 23.15), and that the translation adopted by Targ. at 25.15 brings this verse also into the same field of interpretation. That the wine turns to poison in the mouths of those who drink it and brings on madness is a demonstration that the nations are guilty, and only because they are guilty does the cup have so evil consequences. In that case the figure does not turn on the intoxicating effects of the wine or the paralysis of drunkenness, but rather on the guilt which is proved by the cup which turns to poison. It is not then a question of the allocation or determination of fate (Brongers): the guilt of these nations is established, their sins are catalogued and their ripeness for judgement demonstrated.

That the contents of the cup should be wine is, however, highly paradoxical: not מי ראש nor לענה but wine. Hence there is in the cup of wine the suggestion of a banquet of death, and we have to employ the anti-banquet theme (H. Gressmann, *ZNW* 20, 1921, pp. 227–229), the gruesome reversal of the benevolent host and wholesome hospitality, in order to elucidate the 'cup of wrath' metaphor. The nations are gathered for a banquet, but the wine which is supplied will not gladden their hearts; instead of reaching a climax of good cheer it will end in sickness, madness and destruction (for a fuller account see W. McKane, *VT* 30, 1980, pp. 474–492). All this suggests that 'vomiting' rather than 'reeling' is the correct understanding of והתגעשו and that it is a synonym of וקיו (v. 27).

The incongruousness of מפני החרב אשר אנכי שלח בינתם (v. 16) in relation to the imagery of the cup was noted by Duhm, H. Bardtke (*ZAW* 12, 1935, pp. 221ff.) and others. The observation that החרב is incongruous at v. 16 is not modified by the suggestion that it has been inserted into v. 16 from v. 27, because it is just as discordant at v. 27 as it is at v. 16, and the punctuation of MT at v. 27 correctly indicates that the inability to rise (ולא תקומו) is the effect of drinking from the cup and not of a sword blow. Apart from this the power and mysteriousness of the figure of the doom-laden cup is destroyed or, at least, impaired by the matter of factness of the reference to military carnage, as Duhm perceived. It is not enough to say (Weiser) that the sword is an interpretation of the cup of doom, because if the intention was to predict judgement by war and slaughter, it would have been better to do this plainly rather than to begin with a figure whose lack of plainness and explicitness creates an atmosphere of doom and terror which is then to be let down unceremoniously with a bathetic jolt.

There is no evidence from Sept. that a shorter Hebrew text ever existed. The author may have been more concerned to provide a clear indication of the historical outworking of his imagery than he was with the incongruity of combining a figure of trial by ordeal with an interpretation in terms of military carnage. The discord is, however, jarring, and it is reasonable to ask whether such a combination of imagery and interpretation would ever have been designed. The 'sword' references may be the consequence of an assumption about the unity of 25.1–29 and a supposition that in vv. 15ff. Babylon is still to be envisaged as the nation which executes Yahweh's judgement. There are other indications (see below on vv. 18 and 26) that this assumption, which is erroneous, has produced modifications in vv. 15–26. If מפני החרב אשר אנכי שלח בינתם (v. 16) falls into this category, it should no longer be argued that the clause is primary in v. 27 and secondary in v. 16. The right explanation would be rather (cf. Bardtke, p. 221) that it is secondary interpretation in v. 16, showing the influence of vv. 1–13 and arising out of a desire to make an integrated unity out of chapter

25. In that case it was already part of the text of v. 16 when vv. 27–29 were composed (see further below) and was imitated in v. 27.

Janzen (p. 45) is correct in concluding that ולקללה in v. 18 (not represented by Sept. and Pesh.) is a secondary supplementation on the model of 24.9 and other passages. כיום הזה (absent from Sept.) is a different kind of addition which places the judgement and devastation of Jerusalem and Judah in the past and so changes the portrayal of an imminent train of judgement beginning with Jerusalem and then involving the nations. It is a modification of the text which accommodates the passage to an unevenness of fulfilment by noting that Jerusalem and Judah have been devastated, while the judgement of the nations still lies in the future. It is probable that v. 18 as a whole is secondary, since we are not prepared for a mention of Jerusalem and Judah by either v. 15 or v. 17 (כל הגוים). It would appear that v. 18 derives from the assumption that vv. 1–14 and vv. 15ff. are an integrated account, and that the portrayal in vv. 15ff. must therefore have regard to the preceding verses of the chapter. In vv. 1–13 (especially vv. 9–11) the judgement of Judah and Jerusalem is the first and principal matter and so they are placed first in the list of those who are to drink Yahweh's cup of judgement (vv. 18–26). A more precise reason for the placing of Jerusalem and Judah at the head of the list may be the allusion in v. 29 to Yahweh's judgements beginning with his own people (מחל להרע). The difficulty here is in deciding whether v. 29 has triggered v. 18 or *vice versa* (see further on v. 29).

The list of nations to whom Jeremiah is to offer Yahweh's cup of wrath begins with Egypt as do the oracles on foreign nations (MT 46.1ff.; Sept. 26.1ff.—ignoring 25.15–19 on Elam). ואת כל הערב (v. 20) refers back to Egypt and not forward to the Philistines and this is clearer in Sept. where v. 20 begins with καὶ πάντα τὸν λαὸν αὐτοῦ and not with ואת כל הערב (καὶ πάντας τοὺς συμμείκτους) as in MT. According to Sept. ואת כל הערב is a reference to a mixed population (cf. Kimchi ערבוביא 'mixed elements', and Jerome, commenting on Sept. συμμείκτος, 'People of the region who were not Egyptian, but strangers and aliens'). Targ. renders ואת כל הערב as וית כל סמכותא, 'all the auxiliaries' (or, 'allies'), and this is how the phrase is interpreted by both Rashi and Kimchi. All this is in accord with the modern view that we have to reckon with foreign communities resident in Egypt, with 'colonists, mercenaries and traders' (Weiser, p. 224 n. 2). There is nothing in Sept. corresponding to ואת כל מלכי ארץ העוץ and Duhm is correct in concluding that this is an expansion connected with the erroneous supposition that ואת כל הערב is a reference to 'Arabs' which was then associated with the Hauran or the Edomite region. We should assume an appositional relationship between ואת כל מלכי ארץ פלשתים and the cities which are subsequently listed: 'all the kings of Philistia' are to be identified with the kings of the city states specified. The absence of Gath from the list is explained by Jerome as the consequence of the nearness of that city to Ashdod and by Kimchi because it had been annexed by Israel after its capture by David. Kimchi also offers an explanation of שארית אשדוד : when Nebuchadrezzar captured it, it had already been partly destroyed by the king of Egypt or by someone else. This is in accord with the modern view that an earlier siege by Psammetichus I (Herodotus ii, 157) is indicated by the phrase. Duhm entertains the possibility of a later historical reference: a sacking by Judas Maccabaeus (1 Macc 5.68) or by Jonathan (1 Macc 10.84). According to Josh 19.43, Ekron was part of Israel, and this is correlated by Rudolph with its annexation by Josiah towards the end of his reign. He suggests that the boundaries may have again been redrawn or that it remained a place foreign to the Judaean consciousness, but he is more inclined to conclude, in view of its absence in 47.5, that Ekron is an addition at 25.20.

In v. 22 there is nothing in Sept. corresponding to האי which the other versions render as 'island' (Aq., Theod.) or 'islands' (Vulg., Pesh.). According to Victor Antiochensis (see Ziegler), this island was commonly identified by interpreters with Cyprus, and Jerome comments: *Transit Cyprum et Rhodum et insulas quae appellantur* κυκλάδες; *et hae enim a Babyloniis occupatae sunt* (κυκλάδες = islands in the Aegean around Delos). This may be compared with Rashi's comment: 'All those whom he has enumerated up to this point were dwellers in the land of Israel.' The transition from the soil of Palestine to overseas territories which were captured by Nebuchadrezzar is not so much the point as is the association of Phoenician cities and their overseas colonies, and this must be the sense of Sept. which conjoins καὶ βασιλεῖς Τύρου καὶ βασιλεῖς Σιδῶνος with καὶ βασιλεῖς τοὺς ἐν τῷ πέραν τῆς θαλάσσης (the two occurrences of כל in MT are not represented by Sept.).

Verses 23f. contain references to a group of desert communities: Dedan has been identified by W. F. Albright with the oasis of el-'Ulā in the northern Hijaz (*BHTh* 16, pp. 7f.; cf. KB³), and תימא is the modern Teima in North-West Arabia. The location of בוז is not so well established, but it is located in East Arabia by Albright (op. cit., p. 8 n. 2; cf. KB³). Since the phrase כל קצוצי פאה הישבים במדבר occurs at 9.25 (השכנים is substituted for הישבים at 25.24), there is a suspicion that the words ואת כל מכלי ערב ואת כל מלכי הערב, which break the connection between כל קצוצי פאה and השכנים במדבר, are an intrusion. Moreover, the intrusive element itself is clearly made up of doublets, and the translator of Sept. was reading a Hebrew text which had only one of them and which he mistranslated (Sept., 32.10) under the influence of ואת כל העוב (v. 20). The doublet in v. 24 is an exegetical gloss on כל קצוצי פאה השכנים במדבר which identifies these as Arabian kings, and it has no connection with ואת כל העוב in v. 20, with which it has been erroneously harmonized by Sept. (*pace* Janzen, p. 13).

Jerome (Vulg. *qui attonsi sunt in comam*) and the other versions find a reference in קצוצי פאה to a particular kind of hair-cut, and the rendering of Targ. here and at 9.25 and 49.32 (וית כל מקפי פתא) establishes a connection between קצוצי פאה in these passages and Lev 19.27 (לא תקפו פאת ראשכם), where this way of cutting the hair is forbidden (so also W. R. Smith, *Religion of the Semites*[3], 1927, p. 325 n. 2). This interpretation of כל קצוצי פאה is not followed by Rashi and Kimchi who suppose that קצוצי פאה are those who live in the deep desert, at the furthest edges of civilization (קצה = קצץ). Thus Kimchi comments השכנים בקצה העולם באתו. The phrase *pàt mdbr* (*mlbr*) occurs in Ugaritic with the sense 'fringe of the desert' (J. C. L. Gibson, *CML*, 12.i, 35, p. 134; 14, 193, p. 87; 23, 68, p. 127; = A. Herdner, *Corpus des Tablettes en Cunéiformes Alphabétiques*, pp. 54, 65, 100).

The interpretation of Rashi and Kimchi, reinforced by the Ugaritic *pàt mdbr*, deserves serious consideration. It is adopted by NEB in the three Jeremiah passages ('who haunt (roam) the fringes of the desert'). Its weakness in 9.25 and 25.23 consists in the circumstance that כל קצוצי פאה הישבים במדבר is made into a tautology. If the order were reversed, we could say that קצוצי פאה is a more precise designation (those in the deep desert) than השכנים במדבר, but as it is we have *ex hypothesi* a precise term followed by a weaker and more general one. 'Those in the deepest desert who live in the desert' is unlikely to be right.

The absence of anything corresponding to ואת כל מלכי זמרי (v. 25) in Sept. is almost certainly an indication that these words were not in the Hebrew text which was translated. Kimchi concludes that זמרי is a desert locality and connects it with Gen 25.2: זמרן was a son of Keturah and זמרי is a Keturite region. The suggestion that זמרי is a cipher for רומאי 'Romans' (gematria—both add up to 257) is noted by Duhm and ruled out by Volz (cf. KB[3]). ואת כל מלכי זמרי should be explained as a gloss on ואת כל מלכי עילם, featuring Athbash, with זמרי emended to זמכי (so F. Perles, *Analekten zur Textkritik des Alten Testaments*, 1922, pp. 39, 100; cf. Janzen, pp. 13f.). The case for such an assumption is strengthened by the circumstance that ששך (v. 26) is certainly Athbash for בבל and is so understood by Targ. (ומלכא דבבל).

The points to be noted in v. 26 are the representation of מלכי הצפון in Sept. as βασιλεῖς ἀπὸ ἀπηλιώτου, 'kings of the east', and the non-representation of הארץ (also in Pesh.). The combination of vagueness and universality in the verse after the specific listing of nations which precedes it is striking. What can כל מלכי הצפון הקרבים והרחקים איש אל אחיו mean? Ehrlich (p. 309) urges that the sense is 'Kings of the north who are related to each other (הקרבים) and those who are not' (הרחקים). NEB makes a brave effort with 'neighbours or far apart', but there is an impression of woolliness and a suspicion that words are being run together without anything particular being communicated. It is unlikely that כל מלכי הצפון should be identified with כל משפחות צפון (v. 9), for v. 26 apparently has the function of including by means of a general reference any nation not listed (cf. Weiser who regards it as a bridge between the preceding verses and the reference to the world judgement in vv. 27–29). The deletion of הארץ relieves the anomalous grammar which was noted by Kimchi, and if כל ממלכות הארץ were to be read, it would add nothing to the sense of the verse. The intention cannot be to designate 'worldly kingdoms' as opposed to 'non-worldly kingdoms' (cf. Duhm).

ומלך ששך ישתה אחריהם (v. 26) is not indicated by Sept. and is certainly secondary. Pesh (mlk' 'ršky') meaning 'the principal king' rests on a recognition of the Athbash. This is clear from the use of the same term at 51.41, where the parallelism (בבל in the Hebrew text) makes the Athbash palpable. At 25.26 the Athbash was recognized by Targ., Jerome, Rashi and Kimchi, and it is evident that we have an almost painfully deliberate tagging on of Babylon in order to make this the last act in the judgement of the nations. This can be explained both with reference to 25.1–13 and to the order of the oracles against the foreign nations in chapters 46–51 in which the oracle against Babylon is the climax. But the addition is generated more particularly by the idea that vv. 15–26 have to be harmonized with vv. 1–13, and that the seventy years of Babylon's hegemony is the period of Yahweh's judgements (cf. v. 11). When the seventy-year period is up, Babylon itself will be ripe for judgement (v. 12) and will then drink Yahweh's cup of wrath. If the addition in v. 26 depends on such a use of vv. 11f., we have an indication of its lateness, because it presupposes a text of vv. 11f. which includes the secondary additions to these verses (see above, p. 624). Without these additions there is no indication in vv. 11f. that Babylon, having been Yahweh's instrument, would finally succumb to his judgement.

In virtue of the indication that Yahweh begins his work of judgement in Jerusalem (אנכי מחל להרע, v. 29), there is evidently a relation between v. 18 and v. 29, but where the priority lies cannot be ascertained. It could be supposed that v. 29 has taken its cue from an order of judgement which was already fully set out and which began with Jerusalem and Judah (v. 18). If vv. 27–29 cannot be integrated intelligibly with the preceding verses and are later than them (see further below), a possible line of argument is that v. 18 had already been inserted (see above, p. 637) before vv. 27–29 were added and that it produced the אכני מחל להרע of v. 29 (so Rudolph). But there are no textual indications to help us, since Sept. has both v. 18 and v. 29, and it would be equally reasonable to argue that v. 18 is a subsequent and more deliberate attempt to set out an order of judgement in accord with the indications supplied by v. 29.

It is appropriate at this point to sum up the complicated discussion of the text and exegesis of vv. 15–29 by indicating the places where MT lacks intelligibility, or where it has no exegetical contribution to make, and where it is proposed to depart from it

(a) החמה (v. 15) is probably a gloss (see above, p. 634), but it is exegetically apposite and it is shown in the translation as (a cup of wrath).

(b) מפני החרב ... בינתם (vv. 16, 27) is unskilful, but there is no textual evidence to support its deletion and it is retained in the translation (above, p. 636).

(c) ולקללה כיום הזה (v. 18) is deleted in agreement with Sept. (p. 637).

(d) ואת כל מלכי ארץ העוץ (v. 20) should be deleted, because it is out of place in a list of Philistine cities and it is not represented by Sept. (p. 637).

(e) ואת כל מלכי ערב ואת כל מלכי הערב (v. 24) is a conflation of a gloss (pp. 638f.). It is shown in the translation as (all the kings of the Arabs).

(f) ואת כל מלכי זמרי (v. 25) is emended to ואת כל מלכי זמכי and deleted as an equivalence of ואת כל מלכי עילם with Athbash (p. 639). It is not represented by Sept.

(g) הארץ (v. 26), which is not represented by Sept., is deleted (p. 640).

(h) ומלך ששך ישתה אחריהם (v. 26) is an addition with ששך an Athbash for בבל, and it is not represented by Sept. Its function is to portray the judgement of Babylon as the last act in the judgement of the nations and it is shown in the translation as (and after them the king of Sheshak will drink) (p. 640.)

The view of Weiser (following Volz, p. 390. n. 2 and C. Kuhl, ZAW 65, 1953, pp. 5ff.) that vv. 15f., 27–38 constitute a literary

unity which has been interrupted by the list of nations in
vv. 17–26 can be maintained only if it is argued that v. 17 is part
of the intrusive section, but it is not evident that this is so. On the
contrary, there is no reason why v. 17 should not be regarded as
a continuation of v. 16, since vv. 15–17 cohere perfectly well
(agreeing with H. Bardtke, op. cit., p. 221.) The portrayal
contained in vv. 15–17 is brought to a conclusion by v. 17—the
prophet takes the cup from Yahweh's hand and gives it to the
nations to drink (so Duhm and Rudolph.) If this is so, vv. 27–29
cannot be regarded as continuous with vv. 15–17. There is no
question of choice or of the possibility of refusal, and vv. 28f.
introduce ideas which are incompatible with the preceding
representation. Rudolph's assumption that specified nations are
already envisaged in v. 15 (את כל הגוים אשר אנכי שלח אותך
אליהם) is probably correct, and if so the list (vv. 17–26) is not
intrusive, but is rather an essential continuation of the preceding
verses. On the other hand, vv. 27–29 are a new and later
development in which the imagery of the cup is appropriated and
applied in a manner which is incompatible with vv. 15–17. The
possibility that the nations will refuse to drink is countenanced
and the assertion that such a refusal will not be tolerated is
connected with a prior judgement inflicted on Jerusalem. It is
clear that the judgement of Jerusalem and Judah has no place in
vv. 15–26 and that its appearance in v. 18 and v. 29 is indicative
of the influence of vv. 1–14(13) on vv. 15ff. and of an attempt to
make an integrated unity out of the chapter.

On the other hand, the interpenetration of the two parts of the
chapter (vv. 1–14(13) and vv. 15ff.) is not so complete as
Rudolph indicates, and it is doubtful whether he is justified in
assuming that Nebuchadrezzar's function as Yahweh's
instrument in bringing the nations to judgement is involved in
the imagery of the cup of wrath. There is no mention of
Nebuchadrezzar in vv. 15ff., and it is unlikely that the nations
who drink the cup of wrath are to be equated with those who are
mentioned in v. 9 and v. 11. The nations of v. 9 are those around
Judah, perhaps in league with her against Nebuchadrezzar, and
who share her fate. The reference to גוים in v. 11 is probably the
same, but if Sept. is followed (above, pp. 625f.), the reference is
to Judah's servitude in exile among the nations. It is perhaps the
assumption that the imagery of the intoxicating or poisonous cup
is to be explained in terms of bloody victories achieved by
Nebuchadrezzar which has produced an interpretation in terms
of the 'sword'. The imagery of the cup of wrath (above,
pp. 634–636) is not so nearly related to the notion of
Nebuchadrezzar, Yahweh's avenger, as Rudolph supposes.

This has a bearing on the reformation of the list as proposed by Rudolph, since he prunes it in such a way that it consists only of nations who are part of Judah's world in the time of Jeremiah, and who would have been threatened by Nebuchadrezzar at the same time as she was. Hence his view that the list consisted originally of Egypt, the Philistine cities (v. 20), Edom, Moab and Ammon (v. 21) and communities in North Arabia (vv. 23–24*.) A more important consideration for Rudolph is the achieving of a correspondence between the list and the nations who are the subjects of individual oracles in chapters 46–51. This cannot be done perfectly, because Damascus, which is threatened in 49.23ff., does not appear in the list (Weiser suggests that it was therefore a later insertion in the oracles against foreign nations.) Moreover, the Arabian communities mentioned in v. 23 are not identical with those in 49.20 and 28 (Teman, Kedar and Hazer.) If we go along with this line of thought, we may suppose that there is some relation between 25.15–26* and the oracles against foreign nations. According to Rudolph (also Nicholson) 25.15–26* constituted an introduction to these oracles, and, according to Weiser, they constituted a conclusion to them. If the original order was the present order of Sept., and 26–31 (Sept.) were removed to the end of the book in the Hebrew Bible (46–51), why were 25.15–26 not also removed? Had they been recognized as the introduction to the oracles against foreign nations, their continuity with these oracles would not have been so broken (Weiser.) This part of Weiser's argument is not entirely conclusive, but it does show that if the oracles against foreign nations were moved from one position to another in the Hebrew Bible, 25.15–26 were not identified as the introduction to these oracles at that time.

The other part of Weiser's argument, relating to the structure of vv. 15–38, is that the list intervening between v. 16 and v. 27 originates as a consequence of the severance of vv. 15f., 27–38 from the oracles against foreign nations. If this is so, the alleged secondary and intrusive list ought not to be a feature of the Greek text (32.1–24.) It is *ex hypothesi* caused by the displacement of the foreign oracles in MT, but there is *ex hypothesi* no such displacement in Sept., and the reasons alleged for the intrusion of the list do not obtain in Sept. If Weiser's argument were cogent, there should be no 'secondary' list in Sept. Nevertheless, if the positioning of the foreign oracles in Sept. is the original positioning, the place of 25.15–38 (Sept. 32.1–24) at the end of these oracles suggests that they are a conclusion rather than an introduction. In that case we have to suppose that the foreign oracles originally immediately preceded 25.15–38 in the Hebrew Bible, following on from 25.13 (whether or not אשר נבא ירמיהו על כל הגוים was originally their superscription as in Sept.; cf. 46.1) and that when they were moved to the end of the book vv. 15–38* were left in their original place. What M. de Roche has to say (*JSOT* 10, 1978, p. 67) in connection with his reconstruction of 25.15–29 rests on a misunderstanding There is no question of vv. 15–29 having been transported from one place to another. The question is rather whether the foreign oracles originally appeared after 25.13(14) as they do in Sept. and have been relocated in MT (46–51.) If it was Sept. that relocated the text, this did not involve any alteration in the position of 25.15–29. It involved (*ex hypothesi*) the insertion of the foreign oracles between 25.13 and 25.15–38 (Sept. 32.1–24.)

It may be said, however, on more general grounds, that vv. 15–26* answer better to a preliminary table of contents than they do to a summary conclusion of the foreign oracles. What is the point of recapitulation in a list after the nations have been dealt with in detail, unless we think of it as a kind of index? A preliminary table of contents, associated with a memorable figure related to the administration of judgement, is perhaps the more attractive idea, but it all hangs in the air and no certainty is to be had.

Like Kimchi (מראה הנבואה) and Weiser, Rudolph thinks that we have to reckon with a visionary experience of the prophet Jeremiah in 25.15–26* and that the visual, auditory and executive aspects of the portrayal are contained within such an experience. Hence, although Rudolph holds that מפני חחרב אשר אנכי שלח בינתם is secondary in v. 16, he, nevertheless, maintains that the figure of the nations drinking the fatal cup, which is proffered to them by the prophet, has to be converted into the actual, concrete historical disasters which overtook them as a consequence of Nebuchadrezzar's conquests, so that we have a specific, historical background, related to Jeremiah's time, against which the passage is to be interpreted (similarly Bright.) Weiser also relates the passage to the historical prophet Jeremiah, but since his account of its literary structure is different, he effects the connection with the prophet's times in a different manner. The units on which he focuses attention are vv. 15f., 27–29, and his concern is to establish that there is no reason why Jeremiah should not have been occupied with the concept of a world judgement. But Weiser's argument has plausibility only if his account of the literary structure of vv. 15–38 is adopted (see above, pp. 641f.) and reasons have been given why this should not be done.

When we come to Nicholson we find that vv. 15f. are regarded as probably a Jeremianic nucleus and that the remainder of vv. 15–29 is described as a Deuteronomic composition. The implication of this is that the historical background of vv. 17–29 is exilic: Babylon is the dominant power and the passage derives from a period before the conquest of Babylon by Cyrus. This part of Nicholson's exposition is to be compared with Bright's statement that the passage is not later than 550, that Babylon is the ruling power and that Persia is not mentioned. The remark about the lack of any mention of Persia should be considered in connection with the reference to עילם and מדי in v. 25. How are we to interpret this reference? If we try to relate it to the oracles against the foreign nations, we find that there is a mention of עילם (MT 49.34ff.; Sept. 25.14ff.) but not of מדי. We also discover (cf. Bright's remark that there is no mention of Persia in the passage) that Sept. renders ואת כל מלכי מדי as καὶ πάντας βασιλεῖς Περσῶν. It would appear that the Greek translator understood MT as a reference to the components of imperial Persia rather than to the earlier history of Elamites and Medes before the period of the Persian empire. The assumption of 49.34 ('at the beginning of the reign of Zedekiah, the king'), on the other hand, is that the oracle is directed against Elam at an earlier historical phase, but the reason why Rudolph and Weiser delete 25.25 in their reformed list is their disinclination to believe that Elamites and Medes were within the historical horizons of Judah at that period. Duhm assumes that עילם and מדי in v. 25 constitute a reference to the Persians, and he observes that the Jews came into close contact with the Medes only after the latter had been united with Elam under one sceptre. He supposes that the preserving of a distinction between עילם and מדי is either a pedantic display of learning (a demonstration that the author knew that they had independent histories before they became components of Persia), or an indication of the ignorance of one who wrote a long time after the disappearance of the Persian empire.

The exilic date (Nicholson) is feasible in relation to עילם and מדי only if it is assumed that we have here a pre-Persian reference to these peoples, but it is unlikely that they would have attracted the attention of the Jews in the exilic period or that any attention would have been paid to them prior to the time when the Persian empire became the arbiter of Jewish fortunes. The other assumption which Nicholson makes is that the use of Athbash in v. 26 can be explained only as a code employed at a time when it would have been politically inexpedient to make an open reference to Babylon, and so as indicative of the period of Babylonian suzerainty (also Freehof.) This should be repudiated. Janzen (p. 122) argues in the opposite way to Nicholson, and supposes that Athbash is a mark of lateness. That no confidence should be reposed in the contention that Athbash must be a code used in the period of Babylonian power is seen from its use at 51.41, where both שׁשׁך and בבל appear, and also from the juxtaposition of עילם and זמכי in 25.25, if the emendation of זמרי to זמכי is accepted. The other arguments which must be employed against the assertion that the reference to Babylon locates the passage in the period of Babylonian suzerainty are textual and literary in character. ומלך ששך ישתה אחריהם (v. 26) is not represented by Sept. and is peripheral in relation to the literary structure of vv. 15–26. It has been characterized (Duhm, Rudolph, Weiser) as a palpably obvious addition designed to make good what appeared to be a deficiency: the lack of any mention of Babylon. The references at 25.11f. encouraged the thought that Babylon would be the last to suffer judgement and Babylon has the final position in the oracles against foreign nations. It is in these terms that the addition and its phrasing are to be understood, but it has no contribution to make to the determination of the historical background of vv. 15–29.

It does not avail to appeal to 1.5 and 10 in order to support the contention that Jeremiah was indeed a prophet to the nations, unless one believes with Bardtke (op. cit., pp. 212–220) that these references give reliable historical information about the earliest phase of Jeremiah's ministry. It is possible that the description of the nature and scope of Jeremiah's prophetic activity in the call narrative is no more than a recognition of the fact that oracles against foreign nations are part of the contents of the book which bears his name. In that case the references do no more than register an existing state of affairs and are not an independent historical testimony: they depend on the presence in the book of Jeremiah of oracles against foreign nations, but they do not demonstrate that the historical Jeremiah indeed delivered oracles against foreign nations (see above, p. 14.) This agrees in essence with Thiel (p. 69) and Duhm.

There are some modifications which should be made to vv. 15–26, principally on the foundation of the text of Sept., but there are no grounds for deleting עילם and מדי. Nor does it appear that vv. 15f. or vv. 15–17 are separable from vv. 18–26 and can be regarded as a Jeremianic nucleus. Verses 15–26* have to be regarded as a unity, and if עילם and מדי are taken as an allusion to the Persian empire, as they almost certainly should, we are brought down to the Persian period. This is perhaps the most that can be said, but a more determined effort might be made to claim the imagery of the cup of wrath for the prophet Jeremiah, if there was a conviction that he was indeed a prophet to the nations. The most fundamental opposition of premisses is contained in the assertion that he was a prophet to the nations and the counter-assertion that he was not a prophet

to the nations. One way or the other a far-reaching assumption
has to be made, an assumption rather than a demonstration, and
any subsequent process of reasoning, however close and cogent,
cannot be disengaged from the initial assumption. That
Jeremiah was not a prophet to the nations is the assumption to
which I have inclined.

YAHWEH JUDGES THE NATIONS (25.30–38)

[30]You are to prophesy all these words to them and say:
   Yahweh roars from on high,
   from his holy dwelling he raises his voice.
   He roars threats against his own land,
   he sings out Hedad! like those who tread grapes
   to all the inhabitants of the earth.
[31]The din reaches to the ends of the earth,
   for Yahweh is laying a charge against the nations,
   he is entering into judgement with all mankind,
   he is giving up the wicked to the sword.
      This is Yahweh's word.
[32]These are the words of Yahweh Sabaoth:
   Evil is spreading from nation to nation,
   a great storm is brewing at the far corners of the earth.
[33]Those slain by Yahweh on that day will stretch from one end of the earth to
the other. They will not be mourned or collected for burial; they will become
dung on the surface of the ground.
   [34]Wail you shepherds and cry out in distress,
   sprinkle yourselves (with ashes) you flockmasters;
   the time for your slaughter has come[1]
   and you will fall like choice rams.[2]
[35]The shepherds will find no safe retreat,
   none of the flockmasters will survive.
[36]A cry of distress rises from the shepherds,
   wailing from the flockmasters,
   for Yahweh has ravaged their pastures
[37]and their lush meadows are ruined.
      This is what Yahweh's hot anger has done.
[38]The enemy has advanced like a young lion leaving its lair;
   their land has been devastated
   by the sword of the oppressor[3]
   and the heat of Yahweh's anger.

Verse 30 is attached to v. 29 by representing that it and the
following verses contain a further message which the prophet has
received from Yahweh. But vv. 30f., in which Yahweh is referred
to in the third person, are not obviously 'word of Yahweh'. Vulg.
(*Impios tradidi gladio, dicit Dominus*) has overcome this by
employing the first person (MT נתנם) in the stich immediately

---

[1] Deleting ותפוצותיכם (see below, pp. 652f..)
[2] Reading כאילי חמדה (see below, pp. 651–653.)
[3] Reading חרב היונה (see below, pp. 654–656.)

preceding נאם יהוה (v. 31.) Otherwise, the verses have to be understood as a description of Yahweh's advent to judge Jerusalem (?) and the nations and its terrible manifestations, rather than a declaration of intent by Yahweh himself.

Where is Yahweh thought to dwell? וממעון קדשו like מרום could be identified either with heaven or the Jerusalem temple (v. 30.) It may be inferred from the rendering of על נוהו in Sept. that the Greek translator did not intend the Jerusalem temple by either ἀφ᾽ ὑψηλοῦ or ἀπὸ τοῦ ἁγίου αὐτοῦ : ἐπὶ τοῦ τόπου αὐτοῦ indicates an equivalence with על מקומו and מקום is either the Jerusalem temple or Jerusalem. If it is the Jerusalem temple or Jerusalem which is being threatened, it is evident that the place from which Yahweh issues his threat is not envisaged as Jerusalem: he has removed his presence from the Jerusalem temple. Vulg. has associated נוה (נאה) with the sense 'beauty' (*super decorem suum*; also Aq. and Theod. επι της ευπρεπειας αυτου), and if *super decorem suum* alludes to the temple, as Jerome supposed (*hoc est super templum*), Yahweh's dwelling-place in v. 30 (Vulg. *de excelso*; *de habitaculo sancto suo*) is not the Jerusalem temple. The same indications for על נוהו are given by Pesh. and Targ. (cf. Kimchi בית המקרש.) We may conclude that the versions probably regarded ממרום and ממעון קדשו as references to heaven and this is an exegesis which is followed by modern scholars (Duhm, Rudolph, Bright.)

The argument for an identification with Zion has been conducted by Weiser who urges that the same concept is in play here as in Amos 1.2 and Joel 4.16 and that the change of vocabulary from מציון to ממרום does not imply a removal of Yahweh's dwelling-place from the Jerusalem temple to heaven. The view that Jer 25.30f. is dependent on Amos 1.2 and Joel 4.16 and is a deliberate modification of these passages (Duhm, Rudolph) is denied by Weiser. He associates Yahweh's epiphany above the ark (ממרום) with his appearance in the clouds and assumes that Yahweh's 'shouts' are claps of thunder which herald his presence. Related to this is his ingenious but unconvincing interpretation of היךד: 'a thunderous shout', alluding to the thundering of Hadad, the Syrian-Palestinian storm god. But v. 30 contains Yahweh's threatening speech as a judge rather than a description of natural phenomena which herald his advent, and יתן קולו has to be taken in conjunction with שאג ישאג על נוהו. The latter cannot be explained as a thunderclap and must be understood as a word of threatening judgement. If this is so, יתן קולו should be explained as the utterance of threats rather than as the thunder which accompanies a theophany (cf. Kimchi—a משל, 'As if he shouted and raised his voice and the nations came when they heard'.)

There remains the problem of הידד כדרכים יענה whose appropriateness to Yahweh's judgements against his own land and all the earth is not obvious. The הידד of those who tread grapes is not a lament and may not be regarded as a response to an intimation of imminent doom. Hence ענה does not mean 'reply' and the grammatical subjects of יענה and דרכים are not identical (pace Sept., Aq., Targ..) The conclusion that Yahweh is the grammatical subject of יענה is the right one, and יענה should be explained as ענה 'sing out' rather than ענה 'reply', in agreement with BDB (cf. Vulg. concinetur). What is indicated by Vulg. (Celeuma quasi calcantium concinetur) is perhaps a working-song, designed to maintain a rhythm of activity (cf. Rashi, 'Those who do heavy manual work call out loudly to spur on and encourage each other'; similarly Kimchi). Jerome, on the other hand, supposes that the shout of those who tread the grapes is a sad one (carmen lugubre), and he discerns a connection between the red juice of the grape and the blood which will be spilt when Yahweh executes his judgements.

The connection between the treading out of the juice of the grape and the flowing of blood, established by Jerome, is doubtless the key. That הידד is the glad cry of those who tread the grapes, whose cessation is an indication that joy has departed, is clear from Jer 48.33, and in other passages (Isa 16.9f.; Jer 51.14; cf. Joel 4.13; Lam 1.15) הידד is used to form an association between victorious enemies on the rampage and harvesters treading grapes. הידד is still a cry of exultation, but it is now heard in a different context and it is blood which flows rather than the juice of the grapes. In v. 30 Yahweh is represented as exulting in judgement, singing out his הידד like those who tread the grapes, as he deals doom to his people. This is in accord with the more fully developed imagery of Isa 63.1ff. (see W. McKane, VT 30, 1980, p. 488).

Whether אל כל ישבי הארץ is to be attached to the preceding part of v. 30 (so MT, Vulg., Pesh., Targ.) or connected with what follows (Sept.) is not a matter of great importance. Metrical considerations are influential and the adjustment of MT produces an even number of stichs in both v. 30 and v. 31. The first two stichs of v. 31 then exhibit a 4 + 2 pattern (so Rudolph), and the penalty which has to be paid is that the second stich is very weak (עד קצה הארץ). Metrical considerations do not have the degree of certainty which entitles them to prevail, and אל כל ישבי הארץ should be connected with what precedes as in MT. The representation that Yahweh's judgement will first be carried out against his own land and then against the nations of the world is in accord with 25.8–11 and 18.

Yahweh stentorian summons reaches to the ends of the earth:

he has allegations to make against the nations and he summons them to court in order that he may bring forward evidence which will establish their guilt—a guilt which is universally shared (לכל בשר). The rendering of Targ. gives an exegetical indication: the assumption is not that there is a universal wickedness among the nations, but that a separation of righteous and wicked has to be effected (cf. Duhm). It does not appear, however, that vv. 30f. are portraying a judgement of this kind. The emphasis is on retribution, and this is to fall on Yahweh's own people (על נוחו) as well as on the Gentile world, but there is no indication that a bifurcation of retribution and reward, punishment and vindication, is intended. The condemnation is universal and the judgement inescapable: only evil awaiting punishment is in view. The reference to the sword as the instrument of retribution is possibly connected with the representation in the preceding part of the chapter: the sword is introduced along with the cup of wrath (see above, pp. 636f.), and in MT Nebuchadrezzar appears as Yahweh's avenging instrument. It is, therefore, a possibility that the mention of חרב in v. 31, like its mention at v. 16 (cf. v. 27) derives from the prominent place which has been secondarily accorded to Nebuchadrezzar in vv. 8ff. (see above, pp. 623ff.). In that case v. 31 assumes the text of MT in the earlier parts of the chapter and is later than the developments of the Hebrew text which have been postulated.

The disastrous judgement (רעה) spreads from one nation to another (v. 32). Duhm thinks that a self-destructive intoxication or madness is indicated ('one nation will attack the other'). This would suggest a connection with the disintegration brought about through internecine feuding portrayed by 13.12–14 and so with the cup of Yahweh's wrath (see above, pp. 292–298; W. McKane, *Terrien Festschrift*, pp. 107–120). The cup of wrath features in Rudolph's exegesis, since he regards v. 32 as an elucidation given by Yahweh of the vision of the cup of wrath (vv. 15ff.): that the prophet proffered the cup to a succession of nations signifies that doom will fall on one nation after another. The great storm which arises at the extremities of the earth is connected by Rudolph with the enemy from the north who comes מארץ צפון מירכתי ארץ (6.22), and who is the instrument of Yahweh's judgement against Judah in the earlier form of the Hebrew text in 25.8ff. Similarly Duhm supposes that the judgement is triggered by the enemy from the north, as in Ezek chapters 38 and 39 (Gog), and is consummated in an orgy of self-destruction: the world tears itself apart in conflict; it becomes a battlefield and then a cemetery (v. 33). The equation of סער גדול with the enemy from the north is given by the combined evidence of 6.22 and 10.22. Hence סער גדול refers to the storm of war and military assault, the march of empire and the carnage of conquest. It is in this way that Yahweh will inflict punishment on the nations, and it is possible that the verse hangs together with the extant form of the text in 25.8ff. (MT) according to which the enemy from the north is to be identified with Nebuchadrezzar (so Rudolph).

Verse 33 is an isolated verse of prose in a context of poetry and should be regarded as a secondary insertion (Duhm, Rudolph, Bright, Janzen, p. 133). It is constituted by exegetical comment on vv. 31f. (הרשעים נתנם לחרב), and the comment has been made by conflating word-strings which appear elsewhere in the book of Jeremiah: לא יספדו ולא יקברו לא יאספו ולא at 8.2, and יקברו at 16.4. Whether derived from 12.12 (so Rudolph) or the verses immediately preceding it (v. 31, עד קצה הארץ; cf. v. 32, מירכתי ארץ), מקצה הארץ ועד קצה הארץ confirms the view that in v. 33 vocabulary from other parts of the book of Jeremiah has been used again in order to elaborate on vv. 31f. חללי יהוה, at the beginning of v. 33, is in accord with the mention of חרב (v. 31), for the enemy from the north (v. 32) will be Yahweh's instrument. There will be a carnage on a world-wide scale; there will be no respite for mourning and no possibility of retrieval and burial (cf. 8.2 and 16.4).

Because it portrays universal judgement v. 31 is disengaged by Rudolph from the prophet Jeremiah, and v. 33, which has a similar portrayal, is explained as a comment on v. 31. But is it possible to make a clean distinction between v. 31 and v. 32 on these terms? Does הנה רעה יצאת מגוי אל גוי not point to a judgement as wide-ranging as that of v. 31 and v. 33? Hence, while there may be other reasons for arguing that vv. 30f. are a separate unit, these are not reasons which would lead us to conclude that v. 33 is a comment on v. 31 and not on v. 32, and that vv. 32, 34–37 are an original unit, as Rudolph maintains (see further below).

אדירי הצאן (v. 34) are the flockmasters who, like the shepherds (רעים), are figures for political leaders (so Targ. and Kimchi; the latter explains מרעיתם (v. 36) as 'nations'). Sept. (οἱ κριοὶ τῶν προβάτων) follows this interpretation, but constructs a different image and supposes that these leaders are envisaged as 'rams of the flock'. (On the use of animals to symbolize grandees see G. R. Driver, *CML*, p. 136 n. 4, *èl* 'ram', 'duke'; p. 150, *zb* 'gazelle', 'baron', 'lord'. In Ps 35.17 the כפירים 'young lions' are powerful oppressors.) The circumstance that κριοί is used to render אדירי at vv. 34, 35 and 36 has an important bearing on the evaluation of ὥσπερ οἱ κριοὶ οἱ ἐκλεκτοί (MT ככלי חמדה), and makes one hesitate to assume that the Greek translator had before him a Hebrew text which read כאילי חמדה (Rudolph, Bright, p. 159, Janzen, p. 14).

ותפוצותיכם (v. 34) is not represented by Sept.; it appears in Pesh. as *wttbrwn*, 'and you will be shattered', and is rendered by Targ. as ותתבדרון, 'and you will be scattered'. Hence both versions assume a verb, and only a verb will fit into the syntax of the verse. Pesh. apparently connects the Hebrew form with נפץ 'shatter' (ונפצתים or the like), and Targ. with פוץ 'scatter' (ותפוצו or the like). GK 911 suggests that ותפוצותיכם is a mixed form whose components are תפוצו, 'you will be scattered' and הפיצותיכם, 'I shall scatter you'. 'Shatter' (so Rudolph) is the sense which is needed in conjunction with כלי חמדה, and the corrupt text in MT is then most easily explained on the assumption that a form of פוץ is being used with the sense 'shatter', perhaps הפיצותיכם. Janzen's view (pp. 14, 194 n. 17), following Bright (p. 159) is that traces of a conflate text are present in MT: that one variant is ונפצתיכם ככלי חמדה (cf. Weiser, p. 222 n. 1) and the other ונפלתם כאילי חמדה. He regards 'And I shall shatter you like a prized vase' as the secondary variant. Rudolph follows Sept. as does NEB ('And you shall fall like fine rams'). It could be urged that because the Greek translator encountered כאילי חמדה at the end of v. 34 he arrived at the idea of rendering אדירי as κριοί (see above, pp. 651f., for the counter-consideration). Support for the doublet theory is gathered from the fact that if ותפוצותיכם is emended to 'I shall shatter you' or 'you will be shattered', the order of ideas ('shatter' followed by 'fall' rather than 'fall' followed by 'shatter') is odd.

The leaders of the nations have reached a fateful 'fulness of time' and they are compared (so Sept.) to splendid, unblemished sacrificial victims—rams which are 'felled' in order to provide sacrificial offerings. It is surprising that A. Bentzen (*OTS* 8, 1950, pp. 85–99), who supposes that Amos 1.2–2.16 and Jer 25.20ff. are judgement scenes whose structure is influenced by execration rituals, does not make anything of this reference to the smashing of a pot (assuming the text ונפצתים ככלי חמדה or the like). The leaders of the nations are splendid but fragile, and are vulnerable to a sudden fall and consequent disintegration like a valuable and much treasured piece of pottery (cf. Kimchi). It may be thought that the assumed change of figure is a fatal disadvantage: your time has come to be slaughtered like animals followed by the quite different figure of a precious but fragile vase. It is difficult to reach a firm conclusion, and the foregoing discussion itself reveals an oscillation of opinion and judgement. The sequence of 'shatter' followed by 'fall' is an unsatisfactory feature of MT (emended), but, on the other hand, כלי חמדה

seems to me more convincing than כאילי חמדה. Would חמדה be used of a fine or unblemished animal? The latter of these two evils is perhaps the lesser, and I propose to represent a single image in the manner of Sept. by deleting ותפוצותיכם and reading ונפלתם כאילי חמדה.

There will be no possibility of escape from this devastating judgement; it is an assignment with slaughter and there is no asylum which אדירי הצאן can reach, no devices by which they can secure their survival (v. 35). They have no outlet but to lament their impending fate and the ravages suffered by their 'pastures' (v. 36) at Yahweh's hand. מרעיתם would more naturally be taken to refer to the destruction of lands (Vulg., Aq., Symm.) rather than their populations (Sept., Targ., Kimchi). It was argued by Duhm (also Bright and Janzen, p. 14) that מפני חרון אף יהוה (v. 37) is a misplaced variant of ומפני חרון אפו (v. 38) and should be deleted. In that case v. 37 (MT) should disappear and ונדמו נאות השלום become the fourth stich of v. 36. ונדמו נאות השלום refers to the destruction of prosperous, fertile fields (cf. Kimchi—נאות השלום, a משל for towns and cities), and the parallelism would then suggest that מרעיתם does indeed signify 'pastures'. No support is to be had from the versions for the deletion of מפני חרון אף יהוה (v. 37). The conclusion that ומפני חרון אפו (v. 38) is original flies in the face of the only significant textual evidence which we have—that supplied by Sept. which does not represent ומפני חרון אפו at the end of v. 38 (cf. Janzen, p. 14, for another view). The weightiest reason for deleting מפני חרון אף יהוה at the end of v. 37 is the strong impression that ונדמו נאות השלום balances the preceding stich and that מפני חרון אף יהוה hangs in the air. But perhaps it is deliberately isolated, so that it functions as a final flourish or reiteration, as it does at 4.8, 26 and 12.13.

Rudolph holds that the positioning of v. 38 is connected with a misinterpretation of vv. 34–37: the רעים and אדירי הצאן have been identified with Judaean political leaders and it has been thought that these verses had this limited reference (cf. ארצם, v. 38) as opposed to the wider context of vv. 31–33. In fact there is nothing in vv. 34–37 which is incompatible with this narrower interpretation of them (see further below), and if it were adopted, it could be argued that vv. 34–38 are a unit dealing with Judah, the state of despair to which its leaders are reduced and the devastation which it suffers. There is evidently a relation between v. 38 and 4.7, where the figure of the lion (אריה not כפיר) appears in connection with the threat presented to Judah by the enemy from the north (4.6). The intention of v. 38 may then be (so Rudolph) to announce that the destruction of Judah threatened in 4.6f. has now been accomplished. The lion is then

Nebuchadrezzar who has ravaged Judah. One may conjecture that the references to the enemy from the north in 25.8–14 (cf. Weiser) have suggested the re-employment of 4.7 at this point.

Targ. seeks to preserve the continuity of v. 38 with the preceding verses by representing that the כפיר is one of the kings (מלכיא = אדירי הצאן and רעים) exposed to judgement: 'A king is exiled from his (capital) city'. Rashi follows Targ.: 'A king goes into exile from his (capital) city, like a lion leaving its lair.' Jerome takes Yahweh as the grammatical subject and connects v. 38 with *rugiens rugiet super decorem suum* (v. 30): Yahweh leaves his sanctuary as a lion its den and the devastation of the land follows from Yahweh's desertion of his dwelling-place (similarly Kimchi). In more modern times this exegesis of v. 38a is represented by Ehrlich (pp. 309f.) and Weiser, with different nuances. It is improbable that Yahweh is the grammatical subject of עזב and 4.7 is perhaps the best clue to the interpretation of 25.38. The difficulty is created by the circumstance that the reference to the enemy or the enemy king makes an abrupt entrance at v. 38, and the preceding verses might lead us to expect that v. 38 contains a reference to the evacuation of a devastated Judah by its demoralized leaders (v. 35, רעים and אדירי הצאן). This is the interpretation favoured by NEB: 'They flee like a young lion abandoning his lair, for their land has become a waste.' One would then, however, expect or even demand עזבו instead of עזב in grammatical agreement with רעים and אדירי הצאן.

The major problem of v. 38 is constituted by מפני חרון היונה. If the Greek translator had read the consonants as מפני חרב היונה, we would have expected the translation ἀπὸ προσώπου μαχαίρας τοῦ μεγάλου, 'because of the sword of the powerful (oppressor)'. τῆς μεγάλης suggests that a relative function is being attached to the definite article (cp. GK 126w, 'the sword which oppresses' for מפני חרב היונה, MT 46.16, 50.16). If היונה is regarded as an attributive adjective at v. 38, MT is ungrammatical on two counts, the definite article is needed with חרון and חרון, being masculine in gender, does not agree with היונה (cf. Duhm who emends to החרב היונה and Rudolph, חרבו היונה). Ehrlich (pp. 309f.) argues that the Qal participle of ינה cannot have the sense 'oppressive' or 'cruel', and if this were given weight, it would rule out the emendations of Duhm and Rudolph and also BDB's explanation of היונה as a feminine collective: מפני חרון היונה means 'because of the hot anger of the oppressors'. Both Pesh. (*rwgzh dmry'*) and Vulg. (*furoris Domini* for אפו) are expressing the view that it is Yahweh's anger to which reference is made in v. 38b. Pesh. identifies היונה (so read) with Yahweh, and the rendering of יונה by 'dove'

(Vulg.) is also found in Aq. and Theod. (τῆς περιστερας). It can hardly be right (see A. Condamin, *Biblica* 12, 1931, pp. 242f.), but it is taken seriously by L. Saint-Paul Girard (*RB* 10, 1931, pp. 92f.) who supposes that there is a reference to Ishtar *qua* goddess of war whose symbol is the dove.

46.16 and 50.16 have to be brought to bear on the discussion concerning מפני חרון היונה or מפני חרב היונה in 25.38. The more so since the rendering of Targ. at 25.38 has been equalized with the renderings of מפני חרב היונה at 46.16 and 50.16. An interesting feature of the Targumic paraphrase in all these passages is the introduction of a reference to intoxicating wine (כחמר מרויא) in association with the 'hostile sword', and this must be explained as an allusion to Yahweh's cup of wrath in 25.15ff., where there is a similar conjoining (v. 16) of wine and sword. Since Targ. at 25.38 does not derive from a Hebrew text different from MT, the wider question which is raised is whether חרב in 20 Hebrew manuscripts or μαχαίρας in Sept. is not to be explained as the consequence of a harmonization of 25.38 with 46.16 and 50.16. מפני חרון הינה, 'because of the hot anger of the oppressor' makes good enough sense, but if the first stich of v. 38b is so read, the second is reduced to a tautology, unless it is supposed that the first refers to the חרון of the enemy (Nebuchadrezzar) and the second to the אף of Yahweh—a method of affirming that the fury is ultimately his.

It will be seen that v. 38 is exegetically complex: Vulg. and Pesh. are concerned to establish that v. 38b contains a reference to Yahweh's anger, and this is also the view of Weiser. If Yahweh is assumed to be the grammatical subject of עזב (Jerome, Kimchi, Weiser), the reference in both stichs of v. 38b must then be to Yahweh's anger. Rudolph, on the other hand, concludes that the lethal sword and the blazing anger are allusions to the destruction of the land by the Babylonians: ומפני חרון אפו refers to the lion's anger and the lion is Nebuchadrezzar. But Rudolph retains מפני חרון אף יהוה at v. 37 and we then have to assume that two almost identical phrases have different references in adjoining verses. A more probable conclusion is that v. 38a is picking up 4.7 and refers to Judah's enemy, but that the final stich of v. 38b is tracing the devastation wrought by the Babylonians to its ultimate source in Yahweh. In that case היונה refers to the Babylonians and ומפני חרון אפו to Yahweh. This kind of division in v. 38b would also seem to be indicated by NEB's rendering, founded on a different interpretation of v. 38a (the demoralized leaders of Judah are the grammatical subject of עזב), 'wasted by the cruel sword and by his anger'. It is difficult to reach an assured conclusion on the text of vv. 37f., but the best decision that can be made is to retain

מפני חרון אף יהוה at v. 37, while regarding ונדמו נאות השלום as in parallelism with כי שדד יהוה את מרעיתם, and to read מפני חרב היונה at v. 38b (despite the reservations expressed above, p. 655).

Rudolph's view of the literary structure of vv. 30–38 follows the lines of his criticism of vv. 16–29. Because they portray a world-wide judgement vv. 30f., 33 are separable from vv. 32, 34–37 which constitute a unit, interrupted by a secondary verse in prose (v. 33) which is a comment on v. 31. Verse 38 is not continuous with v. 37 and owes its positioning to a misinterpretation of vv. 34–37. Judah and its leaders are erroneously thought to be the subject matter of these verses, and v. 38 itself concentrates on the fate of Judah. The view that vv. 30f. constitute a literary unit is found in Duhm, Weiser and Bright, but while Duhm and Bright regard v. 33 as an intrusion, Weiser holds that it is an integral part of a unit consisting of vv. 32f. (p. 227 n. 4). Bright's second unit is vv. 32–38 (minus v. 33) and Weiser's third is vv. 34–38. Neither Bright nor Weiser is troubled by the lack of coherence between v. 37 and v. 38 which was felt by Rudolph.

The most important matter in all of this is the relation of v. 38 to the preceding verses. There is no doubt that עד קצה הארץ (v. 31) means 'to the ends of the earth' and that מגוי אל גוי (v. 32) is indicative of a universal judgement. On the other hand, על נוהו (v. 30) appears to single out Jerusalem or Judah in particular (see above, p. 648), and so the question whether vv. 34–37 refer to the leaders of all the nations caught up in Yahweh's judgement (Rudolph) or to the political leaders (רעים; אדירי הצאן) of Judah is not an idle one. We may have to reckon with an oscillation between universal judgement and a special judgement focusing on Judah in vv. 30–38*, and in that case v. 38 is not discontinuous with what precedes in the manner that Rudolph supposes. We may agree with Rudolph, however, that if v. 38 is a secondary addition, it rests on a particular exegesis of vv. 34–37, namely, that רעים and אדירי הצאן are the political leaders of Judah.

The critical separation which Rudolph makes is connected with his view that vv. 32, 34–37 envisage the judgement of which Nebuchadrezzar was the instrument and which was visited on a limited number of nations—those retained in his sifted list (vv. 16–26*). Hence vv. 32, 34–37 refer to events in the time of the prophet Jeremiah and may be attributed to him. The tendency of Weiser (cf. Bright) is to attach the entire passage to the historical Jeremiah (vv. 30–38), and at the other pole is Duhm who proposes a date in the latter decades of the second century B.C. Duhm is influenced by his conviction that vv. 30–38

are a *pastische*, and particularly by his assumption that these
verses are an imitation of Zech 11.3–7. There is evidence of
resemblances between verses in our passage and those found
elsewhere, inside and outside the book of Jeremiah, and these
have been noted in the course of the exegesis. Even if we were to
suppose that the literary dependence is always on the side of
25.30–38, this would not inevitably lead to the conclusion that
they are no more than a patchwork, although it would supply
reasons for taking such a possibility seriously. Thus it may be
that יהוה ממרום ישאג וממעון קדשו יתן קולו (v. 30) is a
modification of Amos 1.2 and Joel 4.16 and that וסער גדול יעור
מירכתי ארץ (v. 32) is derived from Jer 6.22 and 10.22. Verse 33
is probably composed by conflating word-strings which appear
elsewhere in the book of Jeremiah (8.2; 16.4; 12.12; 25.31), and
v. 35 is perhaps an echo of the first stich of Amos 2.14 (ואבד
מנום מקל). Verse 38a would appear to have been generated by
4.7. The statement that Zech 11.3–7 has served as a model for
vv. 34–38 (Duhm) is of a much more dubious kind. One cannot
find a progression of ideas in one passage corresponding to a
similar progression in the other, or an ordering of images in one
matched by a similar ordering in the other. Duhm's own account
of the matter does not establish that Zech 11.3–7 served as a
model: only three verses are brought into play. The thought of
ripeness for slaughter is found in Zech 11.4,7, but the verse
which has to bear the brunt of the hypothesis is Zech 11.3 (קול
שאגת כפירים כי שדד גאון הירדן) which is presented as the kernel
of Jer 25.36–38. The difficulties are even greater than this: there
is nothing in the Zechariah passage comparable to the first two
stichs of v. 36, and the resemblance of the third and fourth stichs
to Zech 11.3 is remote. The connection between v. 38 and Zech
11.3 depends on an emendation of v. 38 and the supposition that
the 'lion' reference in v. 38 is of the same kind as the one in Zech
11.3. This is almost certainly a wrong exegesis of v. 38. Hence
the claim for a very late date which Duhm founds on the
Zechariah passage must be denied to him, and his argument
then consists of his impression that vv. 30–38 have an
apocalyptic flavour: proud earthly kingdoms will be destroyed
and their lands laid waste; we are transported to the period when
Isa 26.20–27.1 was written—to the last decades of the second
century B.C. My own inclination is not to raise historical
questions, unless I am satisfied that it is possible to answer them
in a reasonably firm way from the text (see above, pp. 646f.).
Even then what I have to say is of a very tentative nature. There
may be indications for a relative dating of vv. 30–38, if we were
to suppose that v. 31 assumes the text of MT in the earlier part
of the chapter (see above, p. 650), and if we were to draw a

similar conclusion in respect of v. 32 (see above, pp. 650f.). If in vv. 15–29 we are brought down to the Persian period (see above, p. 646), the implication of this line of argument is that vv. 30–38 are later than vv. 15–29. I am aware, however, of the extreme fragility of this statement and that it may represent a process of building on sand. The final word must be that here as elsewhere in the book of Jeremiah the attaching of pieces of text to a particular set of historical circumstances is more dubious than has been generally allowed.